Henry L. Roediger, III
RICE UNIVERSITY

Elizabeth Deutsch Capaldi
UNIVERSITY OF FLORIDA

Scott G. Paris
UNIVERSITY OF MICHIGAN

Janet Polivy
UNIVERSITY OF TORONTO

C. Peter Herman
UNIVERSITY OF TORONTO

Psychology

FOURTH EDITION

West
Publishing
Company

MINNEAPOLIS/ST. PAUL

NEW YORK

LOS ANGELES

SAN FRANCISCO

COVER AND CHAPTER OPENING ILLUSTRATIONS   MALCOLM TARLOFSKY
COMPOSITION   PARKWOOD COMPOSITION
COPYEDITING   JANET GREENBLATT
INDEXING   TERRY CASEY

PHOTO CREDITS AND
ACKKNOWLEDGEMENTS APPEAR
FOLLOWING SUBJECT INDEX

WEST'S COMMITMENT TO THE ENVIRONMENT

In 1906, West Publishing Company began recycling materials left over from the production of books. This began a tradition of efficient and responsible use of resources. Today, 100% of our legal bound volumes are printed acid free, recycled paper consisting of 50% new paper pulp and 50% paper that has undergone a de-inking process. We also use vegetable-based inks to print all of our books. West recycles nearly 22,650,000 pounds of scrap paper annually—the equivalent of 187,500 trees. Since the 1960s, West has devised ways to capture and recycle waste inks, solvents, oils, and vapors created in the printing process. We also recycle plastics of all kinds, wood, glass, corrugated cardboard, and batteries, and have eliminated the use of polystyrene book packaging. We at West are proud of the longevity and the scope of our commitment to the environment.

West pocket parts and advance sheets are printed on recyclable paper and can be collected and recycled with newspapers. Staples do not have to be removed. Bound volumes can be recycled after removing the cover.

PRODUCTION, PREPRESS, PRINTING AND BINDING BY WEST PUBLISHING COMPANY.

Printed with **Printwise**
Environmentally Advanced Water Washable Ink

British Library Cataloguing-in-Publication Data. A catalogue record for this book is available from the British Library.

COPYRIGHT © 1996   BY WEST PUBLISHING COMPANY
610 Opperman Drive
P.O. Box 64526
St. Paul, MN 55164–0526

Library of Congress Cataloging-in-Publication Data

Psychology / Henry L. Roediger III ... [et al.]. — 4th ed.
     p.   cm.
   Includes bibliographical references and indexes.
   ISBN 0–314–06160–6 (hard : alk. paper)
   1. Psychology.   I. Roediger, Henry L.
BF121.P7915   1996
150—dc20

95–43775
CIP

CONTENTS IN BRIEF

CONTENTS

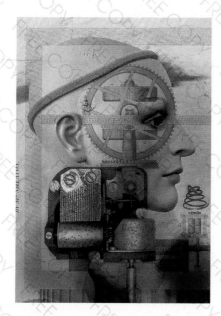

Chapter 2
BIOLOGICAL BASES OF BEHAVIOR 43

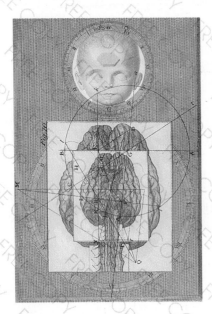

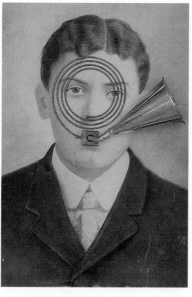

Chapter 3
SENSATION 87

Chapter 4
PERCEPTION 133

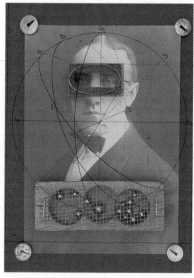

Chapter 5
CONSCIOUSNESS AND ATTENTION 173

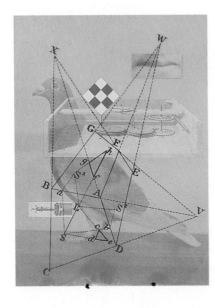

Chapter 6
CONDITIONING AND LEARNING 223

Chapter 7
REMEMBERING AND FORGETTING 259

CONCEPT SUMMARY
Types of Memory 262

CONTROVERSY
Does Photographic Memory Exist? 274

Chapter 8
THOUGHT AND LANGUAGE 307

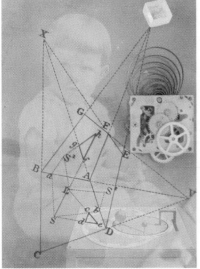

Chapter 9
INFANCY AND CHILDHOOD 351

CASE STUDY
Social and Hormonal Effects on Gender Identity 396

Chapter 10
ADOLESCENCE AND ADULTHOOD 407

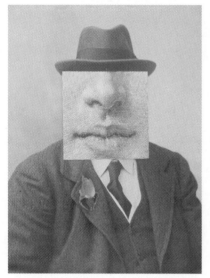

CONTROVERSY
Why Do Males Excel in Math 416

CONCEPT SUMMARY
Puberty 422

PSYCHOLOGY IN OUR TIMES
Gender Differences in the Workforce 434

CASE STUDY
Old and Proud 444

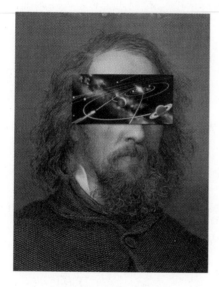

CASE STUDY
Harriet, The Musical Savant 456

CONCEPT SUMMARY
Characteristics of Tests 464

Chapter 11
INTELLIGENCE AND
MENTAL ABILITIES 451

Chapter 12
MOTIVATION AND EMOTION 493

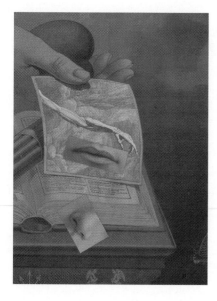

Chapter 13
STRESS AND HEALTH 533

CONTENTS

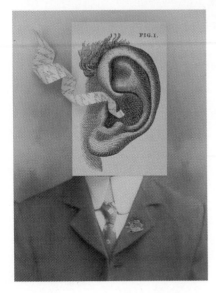

Chapter 14
PERSONALITY 565

Concept Summary
Defense Mechanisms 575

CONTROVERSY
Subliminal Psychodynamics 576

CONTROVERSY
Does Personality Theory Include Women? 583

PSYCHOLOGY IN OUR TIMES
Personality and Health 596

CASE STUDY
B.F. Skinner 602

Chapter 15
PSYCHOPATHOLOGY 611

CONTENTS

Chapter 16
THERAPIES 659

Chapter 17
SOCIAL PSYCHOLOGY 709

Chapter 18
FIELDS OF APPLIED PSYCHOLOGY 757

Appendix A
AN INTRODUCTION TO STATISTICS A1

Appendix B
BECOMING A CRITICAL READER A21

PREFACE

The field of psychology can be described by many adjectives: *fascinating*, *diverse*, and *relevant* are ones that come readily to mind. The rapid advance in knowledge continues to startle us. Even since our previous ediition of ***Psychology***, just a few years ago, many new discoveries have been made about human behavior, which are represented in these pages.

Presenting the field of psychology in a text for the first course represents an enormous challenge, both for teachers and for textbook writers. Our goal in writing this text is straightforward: to provide the best possible introduction to psychology for beginning students. We present an up-to-date picture of modern psychology, including important discoveries, both classic and new. We aim for our coverage to be comprehensive without being overpowering or too detailed; we wanted our writing to be clear and lively; we hoped our presentation of the field would be engaging, yet intellectually responsible. We present the classic achievements in the first hundred and thirty years of psychology as a science, but we also explore the discipline's frontier areas that are just emerging and relate the controversies that confront the field.

The first three editions of ***Psychology*** enjoyed considerable success in the marketplace, and we have received valuable information from many users that has greatly shaped and improved this revision. We have carefully considered the comments of students, instructors, and specialists in relevant fields in crafting the book you now hold. The Fourth Edition contains many new features and instructors who used past editions will discover changes on almost every page.

Plan of the Book

We describe here the key features of the textbook, many of which are new to this edition.

Themes of Psychology

One difficulty in presenting psychology to the beginning student is its great diversity. Students can become bewildered at the wide variety of topics in the course and fail to see common threads running through the field. To overcome this problem, we have oriented our text around five themes, or sets of concerns, prominent in contemporary psychology. These themes concern different sets of factors that affect behavior: a biological theme, a learning theme, a cognitive theme, a developmental theme, and a sociocultural theme. Each theme suggests a particular approach to the subject matter under discussion, whether it be perception, intelligence, or abnormal behavior. The themes are introduced to the students in the first chapter, but briefly, we consider (a) biological underpinnings of particular phenomena; (b) how a particular topic under consideration is affected by learning and experience; (c) how cognitive processes operate in understanding the topic; (d) how the topic under consideration develops and changes over the lifespan; and (e) how the topic is affected by the social or cultural context of the larger society. For instance, in Chapter 4 we consider how visual perception and visual illusions are affected by biological, learning, cognitive, developmental, and sociocultural factors.

These five themes are carried throughout the text, in every chapter. Of course, not all themes fit every chapter equally well. (Sociocultural factors do not play a role in how the retina receives light energy and converts it into the bioelectrical energy of the nervous system.) Therefore, the five themes will be represented to a greater or lesser extent in the various chapters, depending on their appropriateness. Some themes are so important that entire chapters are devoted to them. Chapter 2 represents the biological theme, Chapter 6 the learning theme, Chapters 4, 5, 7, and 8 the cognitive theme, Chapters 9 and 10 the developmental theme, and Chapter 17 (and to a great extent, 18) the sociocultural theme. However, in almost all of the chapters, each of the five themes is represented at some level.

The five themes serve to organize the material of our text across chapters so that students can appreciate unifying aspects of psychology.

Chapter Organization

The material in the text is organized into eighteen chapters, shown in the Table of Contents, as well as in two Appendices. We have followed the organization that has become standard in the introductory psychology course of proceeding from processes operating largely within the individual (biological bases of behavior, sensation and perception, learning and remembering); to higher mental processes, such as thinking and intelligence; then to development across the lifespan to topics that embrace the whole individual, such as personality, and finally to behavior in larger contexts as represented by social psychology, organizational psychology, and other topics.

Organization Within Chapters

The chapers follow a consistent format, to familiarize students with the structure of the book. After Chapter 1, each chapter begins with an outline and a set of thematic questions, to orient the student to the themes represented in that chapter. The chapter begins with a high-interest opening example and the greater part of the chapter is represented in four or five main topics, noted by main (centered) headings. These headings note the four or five new topics covered in the chapter and form the basis of the Table of Contents. Several features appear in every chapter, which we discuss in turn.

• *Psychology in Our Times* explores an interesting topical problem in contemporary society relevant to the topic of the chapter. For example, in Chapter 3 we ask if loud rock music can cause hearing loss; in Chapter 9 we consider why kids turn off to school; and in Chapter 17 we consider examples of contagious behavior.
• *Controversy.* This popular feature appeared in our earlier editions. In each chapter we consider a controversial topic, covering both sides of the debate and coming to some reasoned conclusion (if one is warranted). In Chaper 3 we consider the issue of extrasensory perception; in Chapter 10 we ask why males often exceed females in mathematical tests; and in Chapter 11 we consider the debate swirling around **The Bell Curve,** a book on I.Q. and how it matters to our society.

- *Concept Summaries* appear in most chapters, where needed, to summarize previous text material. These features appear where the authors and reviewers thought they were most needed to reiterate an important concept or to review a critical point.
- *Case Studies.* Each chapter includes at least one case study to provide a vivid illustration of a particular phenomenon. The case studies help bring the material alive by providing a concrete example.
- *Themes in Review.* This section appears at the end of each chapter and briefly reviews how the five themes of the text are represented in the chapter.
- *Key Terms* appear boldfaced in the text and are also listed at the end of the chapter. Each of these terms is also defined in the Glossary at the end of the book.
- *Summary.* A numbered summary of the main points in a chapter also appears at the end of the chapter.
- *For Critical Analysis* is a feature that provides thought-provoking questions that can be discussed on the basis of material in the chapter. These questions are designed to foster critical thinking about the material in the chapter and appear at the very end. They are appropriate for classroom discussion.
- *Suggested Readings* are also provided near the end of each chapter. They give appropriate places for the interested student to find out more about the topics in the chapters.
- *Psychology on the Internet* tells where more information about particular topics can be obtained on the World Wide Web. For example, many visual and auditory phenomena described in Chapters 3 and 4 can be accessed at various sites on the Web. These sites usually provide color displays or sound.

Critical Thinking

The Fourth Edition of **Psychology** places a greater emphasis than ever on critical thinking. Throughout the text we have tried to emphasize the logic by which psychologists evaluate evidence and come to conclusions. The *Controversy* feature in each chapter shows both sides of a current controversy and concludes with a question to spur students to think further about the issue. In addition, at the end of each chapter *For Critical Analysis* provides thought-provoking questions that would lead students to think critically about the material in the chapter. Appendix A, *Introduction to Statistics,* has a section on misuses of statistics and how to recognize them. Appendix B, *Becoming a Critical Reader,* is useful in developing critical skills in reading articles.

Emphasis on Diversity

This text has increased emphasis on diversity, in terms of ethnicity, race, culture, gender, and age. We consider selected examples here:

Chapter 1 has a box on female pioneers in psychology. Chapter 2 has a considerable amount of information on gender differences such as how sex hormones create differences in the brain, in physical appearance, in degree of lateralization of the brain, and in spatial reasoning. We also consider gender differences in mate selection, in monogamy, and in parental involvement in child rearing. In Chapter 3 we have a section on gender differences in colorblindness, material on race and colorblindness, and a section on gender differences in identifying odors. Chapter 4 contains information on cultural differences in perceiving pictures and in certain visual illusions.

Chapter 5 has material on cultural differences in alcohol use and a segment on use of alcohol among the Tirikis, where alcohol is routinely used but there is no alcoholism. We also have material on Jewish/Irish differences in the use of alcohol.

Chapter 6 explores observational learning and socialization in different cultures. We discuss diversity in approaches to school settings and to cultural adjustments to the school setting. The issue of individualistic versus collectivist approaches in various cultures is also discussed, as well as the stress that different cultures place on the value of schooling.

Chapter 7 contains a discussion of infantile amnesia and Chapter 8 contains a lengthy discussion about the influence of culture on language and thought, including discussion of people who speak the language Dyirbal and how it affects their thought.

Chapters 9 and 10 are devoted to development across the lifespan and include cross-cultural examples of (and class differences in) nutrition and mental and physical development. In addition, there is a discussion of how parental styles differ in various cultures and how this difference produces changes in development. Chapter 10 includes material on differences in the sexes in secondary sexual characteristics and in general development, as well as a discussion of differences in sexual intimacy and different stereotypic academic expectations for males and females. The *Controversy* feature in 10 is devoted to why boys excel in math. We also discuss gender identity in Chapter 10, as well as providing further information on gender differences in patterns of social interaction, on suicide rates, and in the workforce. Material about race and ethnicity also appears in this chapter, such as discussion of race differences in pregnancy and birthrates, in the risk of being a victim of violent crime, and in attitudes toward retirement.

Chapter 11 considers the controversial issue of I.Q. differences among races and of cultural bias in labeling people of different races as mentally retarded. We also consider why a disproportionate number of ethnic minorities and non-English speakers appear in special education classes and have a section on "science, politics, and racism in intelligence testing." There is also a section on gender differences in susceptibility to different types of mental retardation.

Chapter 12 includes material and ethnic differences in food preferences, on cross-cultural differences in the frequency of sexual intercourse, on cultural preferences for sexually desirable behavior, and on cross-cultural equivalence of matching faces to particular emotions. We discuss race and gender differences in premarital sexuality and the *Controversy* box asks, "Are men or women more emotional?"

Chapter 13 has a section on gender differences and the effects of stress on marriage, on sex differences in aggression and the role of testosterone in aggression, and on sex differences and the effect of social relationships on mortality rates. We include material about how diets differ across cultures and how the type of food that people eat may affect rates of heart disease.

Chapter 14 contains material on the cross-cultural appearance of the "big five" personality traits, whereas Chapter 15 considers again alcohol use and abuse among different ethnic groups. Material is also included in Chapter 15 on gender differences in eating disorders and depression, and in some personality disorders and phobias.

Chapter 16 includes a section on how people of different races and ethnicity benefit (or do not) from psychotherapy. There is also material on gender differences in therapy.

Chapter 17 includes considerable new material on ethnicity and culture. There is a cross-cultural comparison of views on individualism, as well as a considerable amount of material about prejudice, both with regard to ethnic and to racial differences. (We also include material on how to reduce prejudice.) Another section is devoted to examining self-esteem in various stigmatized groups and includes a discussion of the effects of affirmative action on self-esteem. Finally, there is a discussion on Chapter 17 of authoritarian versus nonauthoritarian cultures.

Chapter 18 contains material on gender discrimination in the workplace and on racial differences and biases in eyewitness identification.

The above listing is not exhaustive, but gives some of the more prominent examples of how issues of diversity are treated in greater detail in the Fourth Edition than in our previous editions.

Supporting Materials

The Fourth Edition of *Psychology* comes with a complete and expanded package of learning and teaching aids, for both students and teachers. We list and discuss each here.

SUPPLEMENTS FOR THE STUDENT

We include many interesting and helpful features that should aid students in their first course in psychology.

• **The Study Guide,** prepared by Barbara and David Basden of Fresno State University, includes page referenced learning objectives, vocabulary checks, matching test analogies, sample essay questions, activities, and an interesting feature called *Psychology in Everyday Life*.

• **Readings in Psychology,** edited by Kathleen B. McDermott and Henry L. Roediger, III, of Rice University, includes a selection of interesting, relevant articles prepared with introductions. This reader should provide a useful adjunct for professors who want students to be exposed to other material.

• **How Psychology Works,** by Mary Susan Weldon and David R. Smith of the University of California, Santa Cruz, considers how psychologists critically view various events and occurrences in their lives. The book emphasizes critical thinking about psychological topics.

• **College Survival Guide: Hints and References to Aid College Students, Third Edition,** by Bruce M. Rowe of Los Angeles Pierce College, provides students with constructive and informative tips such as how to manage their time effectively and how to study for and to take examinations.

• **Mind Scope Software,** by Robert Hendersen of Grand Valley State University, includes applied psychological exercises to run on IBM computers. This unique program consists of laboratory experiments which students perform on themselves. Students generate real, not simulated results from their own performance.

• **Psychware Software,** by Robert S. Slotnik of the New York Institute of Technology, includes classic psychological experiments to run on Apple II computers. It lets students apply principles of operant conditioning, test their memory, explore social behavior, and much more. Each exercise is highly interactive and features engaging graphics.

• **Cross-cultural Perspectives in Introductory Psychology, Second Edition,** is by William Price of North Country Community College and Rich Crapo of Utah State University. This 150-page paperback contains articles on American ethnic groups, as well as other cultures around the world. It is designed to raise students' awareness, understanding, and tolerance of other cultures.

SUPPLEMENTS FOR INSTRUCTORS

A full line of materials is available for instructors of the introductory psychology course.

- **The Instructor's Manual,** prepared by Denny LeCompte of Louisiana State University, contains learning objectives, chapter outlines, ideas for exercises and demonstrations, alternate lecture outlines, supplementary lectures, suggestions for films and further readings, as well as references for teaching psychology and a list of resource materials.
- **The Test Bank,** prepared by Carolyn Meyer of Lake Sumter Community College, includes 125 multiple choice questions and two to three essay questions per chapter.
- **Transparency Acetates** include full-color illustrations of major concepts presented in the text for classroom display for qualifying instructors.
- **WESTEST™ 3.1** is the computeriized testing system of West Publishing Company for DOS, Windows, or Macintosh computers. It allows instructors to create, edit, store, and print exams. Instructors may randomly generate or selectively choose questions and add new or existing questions. WESTEST™ is accompanied by West Classroom Management software, a program that allows the instructor to store, record, and work with student data. Call-in testing is also available. (This feature is available for instructors meeting certain qualifications).
- **Images of Psychology: West's Video Disk Library of Human Behavior** (1994). This two-disk set contains almost two hours of video material. Focused video clips range from two to six minutes in length and cover a wide range of introductory psychology topics. The clips feature original research footage, classic experiments, interviews with prominent psychologists, and investigations of psychological phenomena.
- **West's Lecture Builder Software** gives instructors the power to select and store a series of video disk images for specific lectures and then play them back in class.
- **Grade Improvement: Taking Charge of Your Learning** is a videotape designed for first-year college students or students re-entering college. The 30-minute video teaches, through an upbeat and entertaining delivery, a variety of strategies students can employ to enjoy success in school.
- The **Discovering Psychology** video series contains 26 half-hour programs designed to encourage personal development and to stimulate curiosity and creative thinking. This series integrates both historical and a cutting-edge perspective of the field. New developments are measured against historical breakthroughs and theories are tested by the recent findings of leading researchers.
- **Astound** by Gold Disk Inc., is a start of the art presentation graphics program that provides professors with visual support in the classroom. Using Astound, adopters can create exciting presentations with animated text, graphics, and sound. Qualifying adopters will receive customized presentations along with the Astound package, thus allowing them to display and edit lecture material provided by West and/or to create their own material.

Acknowledgments

Writing a textbook is a cooperative enterprise. Many of our colleagues have been instrumental in helping us develop this book through four editions. People who were instrumental in reviewing chapters for the first three editions are listed on the following two pages:

Paul R. Abramson	University of California, Los Angeles
Bem P. Allen	Western Illinois University
Eileen Astor-Steton	Bloomburg University of Pennsylvania
Ruth L. Ault	Davidson College
Frank Bagrash	California State University, Fullerton
Michael Bailey	Northwestern University
Bruce L. Baker	University of California, Los Angeles
Linda Baker	University of Maryland
Barbara H. Basden	California State University, Fresno
William Beckwith	University of North Dakota
Horace O. Black	Golden West College
Brian H. Bland	The University of Calgary
Pam Blewitt	Villanova University
Thomas J. Bouchard, Jr.	University of Minnesota
Richard Bowen	Loyola University, Chicago
Nyla Branscombe	University of Kansas
J. Jay Braun	Arizona State University
Celia Bronell	University of Pittsburgh
Thomas Brothen	University of Minnesota
Mary Kay Stevenson Busemeyer	Purdue University
James Byrnes	University of Maryland
James F. Calhoun	University of Georgia
David E. Campbell	Humboldt State University
John P. Capitanio	University of Massachusetts, Boston
Thomas H. Carr	Michigan State University
Robert C. Carson	Duke University
Bruce Carter	Syracuse University
Garvin Chastain	Boise State University
David Chiszar	University of Colorado
Margaret S. Clark	Carnegie-Mellon University
Betty D. Clayton	Hinds Community College
Helen J. Crawford	The University of Wyoming
Frank Curcio	Boston University
Robert Dale	Southeast Louisiana University
Helen B. Daly	State University of New York College at Oswego
Robert DaPrato	Solano Community College
Stephen F. Davis	Emporia State University
Joseph F. DeBold	Tufts University
Anthony J. DeCasper	The University of North Carolina at Greensboro
Douglas R. Denney	University of Kansas
David H. Dodd	University of Utah
Michael Domjan	University of Texas
John W. Donahoe	University of Massachusetts, Amherst
James L. Dupree	Humboldt State University
William O. Dwyer	Memphis State University
James Dykes, Jr.	University of Texas, San Antonio
David R. Evans	The University of Western Ontario
Rand B. Evans	Texas A & M University
Russell H. Fazio	Indiana University
Barry Fish	Eastern Michigan University
Arthur D. Fisk	Georgia Institute of Technology
Sandy Rappaport Fiske	Onondoga Community College
Hiram E. Fitzgerald	Michigan State University
Donald J. Foss	The University of Texas at Austin
Paul W. Fox	University of Minnesota
Robert A. Frank	University of Cincinnati
Philip E. Freedman	The University of Illinois at Chicago
Grace Gallian	Kennesaw State College
James Geiwitz	Carnegie Mellon University
David Gilden	Vanderbilt University
M. M. Gittis	Youngstown State University
Michael J. Goldstein	University of California, Los Angeles
Sherryl Goodman	Emory University
Richard L. Gottwald	Indiana University at South Bend
Carol Grams	Orange Coast College
Robert Green	Case Western University
Richard A. Griggs	University of Florida
Ronald Growney	The University of Connecticut
Judith Harackiewicz	Columbia University
Reid Hastie	University of Colorado
Todd Heatherton	Case Western Reserve University
Peter C. Holland	Duke University
Karen L. Hollis	Mt. Holyoke College
I. M. Hulicka	State University of New York College at Buffalo
Carrol E. Izard	University of Delaware
John Jonides	The University of Michigan
Lynn R. Kahle	University of Oregon
Gary Kannenberg	Webseter University
Robert A. Karlin	Rutgers University
Wesley Kaspro	Northern Illinois University
Saul M. Kassin	Williams College
Paul Kelly	Toronto General Hospital
Katherine W. Klein	North Carolina State University
Stephen B. Klein	Fort Hays State University

Terry Knapp	University of Nevada, Las Vegas	David Schneider	Rice University
Lynn T. Koslowski	University of Toronto	E. Eugene Schultz	The University of North Carolina at Ashville
Barry J. Krikstone	University of Waterloo	Richard Schweickert	Purdue University
Mark Kunkel	Texas Tech University	Mary Anne Sedney	Providence College
Randy Larsen	University of Michigan	Beth A. Shapiro	Emory University
Kenneth Laughery	Rice University	Jack Sherman	University of California, Los Angeles
Michael Levine	Kenyon Unviersity		
Kenneth R. Livingston	Vassar College	Eliot Smith	Purdue University
Jerry Long	University of Houston	Steven M. Smith	Texas A & M University
Katherine Loveland	Rice University	Richard M. Sorrentino	The University of Western Ontario
G. William Lucker	University of Texas, El Paso		
Duane R. Martin	The University of Texas at Arlington	John A. Stern	Washington University
		Judith M. Stern	Rutgers University
Randi Martin	Rice University	Robert J. Sternberg	Yale University
Terry Maul	San Bernardino Valley College	Joseph P. Stokes	The University of Illinois at Chicago
Richard Mayer	University of California, Santa Barbara		
		Michael Tanenhaus	Wayne State University
Laura McCloskey	University of Arizona	Shelley E. Taylor	University of California, Los Angeles
Susan McFadden	University of Wisconsin, Oshkosh		
		W. Scott Terry	University of North Carolina at Charlotte
Robert Meisel	Purdue University		
Eleanor Midkiff	Eastern Illinois University	Philip E. Tetlock	University of California, Berkeley
Denis Mitchell	University of Southern California		
		Joseph B. Thompson	Washington and Lee University
Neil M. Montgomery	Keene State University	Ross Thompson	University of Nebraska
Douglas Mook	University of Virginia	Gordon Timothy	Ricks College
James C. Morrison	Youngston State University	Dennis C. Turk	Yale University
James S. Nairne	Purdue University	Peter Urcuioli	Purdue University
Steve Noble	North Georgia College	Gerald S. Wasserman	Purdue University
Antonio A. Nuñez	Michigan State University	Michael J. Watkins	Rice University
Gayle Olson	University of New Orleans	Robert C. Webb	Suffolk University
Matthew Olson	Hamline University	Roger Wells	Carleton University, Canada
Patricia Owen	St. Mary's University	W. Beryl West	Middle Tennessee State University
Kay Pasley	Colorado State University		
Steven Penrod	University of Minnesota	Catherine C. Whitehouse	Western Maryland College
David W. Perkins	Ball State University	Paul Whitney	Washington State University
Ronald H. Peters	Iowa State University	Arthur Wingfield	Brandeis University
James R. Pomerantz	Brown University	Kathleen M. White	Boston University
Michael Posner	University of Oregon	Randolph H. Whitworth	The University of Texas at El Paso
Michael E. Rashotte	The Florida State University		
George V. Rebec	Indiana University	Paul T. P. Wong	Trent University
Freda Rebelsky	Boston University	D. Louis Wood	University of Arkansas at Little Rock
Joseph de Rivera	Clark University		
Betty Rider	Elizabethtown College	Diane S. Woodruff	Temple University
Richard J. Sanders	The University of North Carolina at Wilmington	Robert S. Wyer, Jr.	The University of Illinois
		Paul Young	Houghton College
Connie Schick	Bloomsburg University of Pennsylvania	Betty Zimmerberg	Williams College

To those instructors and specialists in various fields who provided invaluable advice on drafts of chapters, or on the whole manuscript before the Fourth Edition, we extend our deepest appreciation:

Louis E. Banderet
Northeastern University

William Calhoun
The University of Tennessee at Knoxville

Ronald Gandelman
Rutgers University

Harvey J. Ginsburg
Southwest Texas State University

Keven W. Greve
University of New Orleans

Christine L. Hanswick
Pacific Lutheran University

Roger Harnish
Rochester Institute of Technology

Judith Hunt
Sonoma State University

Philip M. Merikle
University of Waterloo

Carolyn J. Meyer
Lake Sumter Community College

Laurence Miller
Western Washington University

James L. Mosley
University of Calgary

Robert G. Pellegrini
San Jose State University

Gary Poole
Simon Frazier University

Albert L. Porterfield
Oberlin College

Philip L. Rice
Moorhead State University

Ernest Roberts
University of Alabama

D. Kim Sawry
The University of North Carolina at Wilmington

Betsy Schoenfelt
Western Kentucky University

Anthony Thompson
Lakehead University

Harry A. Tiemann
Mesa State University

Douglas Wardell
The University of Alberta

Valerie Willman
Purdue University-North Central

Deborah Winters
New Mexico State University

Many other people have helped us develop our text over the years. We especially thank our Sponsoring editor, Clyde Perlee, for his many brilliant suggestions for improving the Fourth Edition. We could not have written the book without his inspiration. Jan Lamar, our Developmental Editor, has provided us with key assistance at every step along the way. We greatly appreciate her patience and unflagging good humor. Bill Stryker, our Production Editor, has been a joy throughout the production process. We greatly appreciate his innovative design and his many artistic touches, as well as his outstanding judgment, which have greatly improved the text. Janet Greenblatt, our copyeditor, provided a deft touch to our prose and added many felicitous phrases. Beth Kennedy has greatly aided in photo selection and attending to many other important details. We also greatly appreciate Erin Ryan's and Stephanie Buss's efforts on our behalf in marketing our textbook.

We also owe a debt to a number of other people. Mary Schiller initially interested us in embarking on this project years ago. More recently, many students have helped in creation of the Fourth Edition. We would like to thank especially Ryan Brown, Jody Hughes, Lyn Goff, Ron Haas, Bettina Johnson, Denny LeCompte, Kathleen McDermott, Jennifer Mireles, Keith Rozendal, and Cynthia Willis for their contributions.

As this lengthy listing shows, writing a textbook is truly a cooperative venture. The authors receive critical advice and help from many people—students, professors, colleagues, specialists in the various content areas, and professionals at the publishing company. To the instructors reading this Preface, we hope you will like our text and will consider it for adoption in your courses. If you have comments on any aspects of the text, or suggestions for improvements in the future, we would be pleased to receive them.

Henry L. Roediger, III
Elizabeth D. Capaldi
Scott G. Paris
Janet Polivy
C. Peter Herman

SOME ADVICE TO STUDENTS

Our goal in writing ths book is to provide you with a broad, informative look at contemporary psychology. We are eager for you to use the book successfully, so we would like to give you some advice you might find useful.

- **Become familiar with the organization of the text.** Being aware of the overall organization of the book will help guide you through it. After an introductory chapter describing the nature of psychology, the next seven chapters describe fundamental processes that occur within the person—biological bases of behavior, sensation, perception, consciousness of the world, learning, memory, and thinking. The next ten chapters of the book describe people in more complete terms—their development, their intelligence and intellectual capacity, their motivations and emotional states, and their personalities. We also include chapters on abnormal behavior and therapy. In the last two chapters, we describe social forces that affect individual behavior and then turn to the fields of applied psychology. Thus, in rough terms, the organization of the book moves from within a person, to a consideration of the person as a whole, and finally to a discussion of outside social forces that act upon the individual.

- **Become familiar with the features of the text.** Each chapter has similar organization with features designed to highlight different aspects of the material. There are usually five or six main topic headings. In addition, each chapter contains three special features entitled *Controversy*, *Psychology in Our Times*, and a *Case Study*. In *Controversy* you will encounter issues that require further research and debate among psychologists. Although past research has provided a foundation of knowledge, many issues are actively investigated and many ideas hotly contested. In *Psychology in Our Times* we write about a contemporary topic that you may recently have seen or read about in the media. The aim is to describe how psychologists approach this topic. The *Case Study* in each chapter provides a concrete instance of a phenomenon described in the chapter.

- **Look for the common themes of psychology.** The topics in which psychologists are interested include a wide diversity of issues. In fact, the topics are so different that the introductory psychology course may seem disjointed. However, there are common threads (or themes) that run through almost all topics. To provide coherence to our text we orient all chapters after the first around five common themes: biological, learning, cognitive, developmental and sociocultural. These themes are explained in Chapter 1 and serve as a useful guide to orient you to the subject matter in each chapter.

- **Look over each chapter before you begin reading.** Start by studying the chapter outline on the opening page of each chapter. Read the Thematic

Questions to see what you will be learning about. Then skim through the chapter, looking at each heading and reading a bit here and there. You might also read the chapter summary, which lists the chapter's main points.

• **Force yourself to think as your read.** Many students try to read too quickly. It is much more effective to read slowly and to think constructively as you read. When you come to a heading, ask yourself what topics are likely to follow. Note the logical connection between what you have just read and what you are about to read. At the end of the section look away from the book and try to summarize in your own words the central points. (If you cannot recall them at this point you will have difficulty later on.) Reread sections when your self-test shows that you did not comprehend the material the first time around. Further advice on becoming a critical reader appears in Appendix B.

• **Make an outline of the material.** One way to read constructively is to outline the material in your own words, or at least to take notes on the important points. Another way is to underline critical passages with a marker for further study later.

• **Reread and relearn material.** Read a chapter once and then read other chapters or material from other courses before reading the chapter again. Reward yourself for studying, too. Set a reasonable goal for studying for a day, so that once you meet that goal, you can go to the movies, or whatever.

• **Begin studying for exams well in advance.** Feeling prepared will help relieve the test anxiety so many students experience. To prepare for exams you should test yourself by using the Study Guide available with the text.

Finally, if you have comments on the book, please write to us. We would enjoy hearing from you.

Henry L. Roediger, III
Elizabeth D. Capaldi
Scott G. Paris
Janet Polivy
C. Peter Herman

ABOUT THE AUTHORS

Henry L. Roediger, III, is Lynette S. Autrey Professor of Psychology at Rice University, where he has taught since 1988. He received a B.A. in psychology from Washington and Lee University in 1969 and a Ph.D. in cognitive psychology from Yale University in 1973. He has previously taught at Purdue University (1973–1988) and also spent three years as a visiting professor at the University of Toronto. His research interests lie in cognitive psychology, particularly in human learning and memory. He has published over 80 articles and chapters on these topics. In addition, he has published two other textbooks, *Experimental Psychology: Understanding Psychological Research* and *Research Methods in Psychology* (both with B. H. Kantowitz and D. G. Elmes). He also edited (with F. I. M. Craik), *Varieties of Memory and Consciousness: Essays in Honour of Endel Tulving.*

Roediger is founding editor of *Psychonomic Bulletin & Review* and is Consulting Editor for the *Journal of Memory and Language* and for *Memory.* He previously served as the Editor of the *Journal of Experimental Psychology: Learning, Memory, & Cognition* from 1985 through 1989 and was its Associate Editor from 1981 to 1984.

Roediger was elected to the Governing Board of the Psychonomic Society (1986–1991) and served as its Chair (1989–1990). He also chaired the Publications Committee of the Psychonomic Society and has been Chair of the American Psychological Association Council of Editors (1988–1989). In addition, he has served as Secretary-Treasurer and President (1992–1993) of the Midwestern Psychological Association. He has been elected to Fellow status in the American Psychological Association, the American Psychological Society, the Canadian Psychological Association, and the American Association for the Advancement of Science. He is a member of the Society of Experimental Psychologists. Roediger received a Guggenheim Fellowship for the 1994–1995 academic year to begin writing a book on Memory Illusions.

Elizabeth Deutsch Capaldi is Professor of Psychology at the University of Florida where she has taught since 1988. She received her B.A. from the University of Rochester in 1965 and her Ph.D. in experimental psychology from the University of Texas in 1969. She was previously on the faculty at Purdue University (1969–1988) and was head of the Department of Psychological Sciences there (1983–1988) and Assistant Dean of the Graduate School (1982–1986). Professor Capaldi's research has focused on animal learning and motivation. She has contributed over 60 chapters, articles, and reviews and edited (with T. L. Powley) *Taste, Experience, and Feeding.* She is Associate Editor of *Psychonomic Bulletin & Review* and a Consulting Editor for the *Journal of Experimental Psychology: Animal Behavior Processes.* She currently serves on the Governing Board of the Psychonomic Society and on the Board of Directors of the American Psychological Society, of which she is also Secretary. Professor Capaldi has been elected to Fellow Status in the American Psychological Association, American Psychological Society, and the American Association for the Advancement of Science and served as President of the Midwestern Psychological Association.

Scott Paris is a Professor of Psychology and Education at the University of Michigan where he graduated with a B.A. in 1986. Since receiving his Ph.D. from Indiana University in 1972, he has been on the faculty at Purdue University and been a Visiting Professor at Stanford, UCLA, The University of Hawaii, the University of Auckland, New Zealand, the Flinders University, the University of Newcastle, and the University of Queensland in Australia. His research has examined how children's motivation and metacognition contribute to the development of self-regulated learning. He has created educational materials to help children acquire reading and learning strategies and has worked extensively with teachers to design instruction and assessment that promote literacy learning. He has also studied how students, teachers, and parents regard and respond to standardized achievement tests and how authentic classroom assessments and students' portfolios can enhance motivation and learning in school. Professor Paris is on the editorial boards of six journals and has published seven books and written more that 100 book chapters and research articles. He is a co-author of *Developmental Psychology* (6th ed, 1994, McGraw-Hill) and *Becoming Reflective Students and Teachers* (1994, APA). He teaches developmental and educational psychology courses at Michigan. In 1993 Professor Paris received the Dean's Award for Undergraduate teaching and in 1995 he received the University of Michigan AMOCO Faculty award for Distinguished Teaching.

Janet Polivy is Professor of Psychology and Psychiatry at the University of Toronto. She received her B.Sc. from Tufts University in 1971, and her Ph.D. from Northwestern University in 1975. Before moving to Canada to the University of Toronto, she taught at Loyola University of Chicago. Professor Polivy's research interests have focused on aspects of personality and motivation, in particular on eating behavior, eating disorders, and the effects of dieting, as well as on aspects of emotion. She has written more than 75 scholarly articles and book chapters, as well as a book (with C.P. Herman) which was runner-up for the American Psychological Association's media communication award in 1984. She was associate editor of the *Journal of Personality* from 1981–1986, and is on the editorial boards of the *Journal of Abnormal Psychology* and the *International Journal of Eating Disorders*. She is a member of the American Psychological Society, the Canadian Psychological Association, and the Association for the Advancement of Behavior Therapy, and has served as a consultant on government panels and task forces (on obesity) for both the United States and Canadian governments. She was elected to the Council of the Ontario College of Psychologists for a three year term in April 1994, where she is responsible for helping to interpret and apply the laws governing the practice of psychology in Ontario, Canada.

C. Peter Herman is Professor of Psychology at the University of Toronto. He received his B.A. *cum laude* with honors in psychology from Yale University in 1968 and his Ph.D. in social psychology from Columbia University in 1972. He taught personality and abnormal psychology at Northwestern University from 1972 to 1976, before returning to Toronto, his hometown. He was associate Editor (1977–1981) and Editor-in-Chief (1981–1986) of the *Journal of Personality*, and he as also served as an Advisory Editor for *Contemporary Psychology*. He has published over 80 research articles and book chapters and more than 50 book reviews, has co-edited five books and is co-author (with Janet Polivy) of *Breaking the Diet Habit*. He has served as a peer reviewer for 40 different journals and granting agencies. His research interests center on eating and other appetitive behaviors, cognitive effects of deprivation, and social influences on behavior. He is a member of the Society for the Study of Ingestive Behavior. He currently teaches courses in personality psychology and research methods. In 1993, he won the Dean's Excellence Award in Research and Teaching from the faculty of Arts and Science at the University of Toronto.

Psychology

Fourth Edition

THE NATURE of PSYCHOLOGY

Chapter 1

1

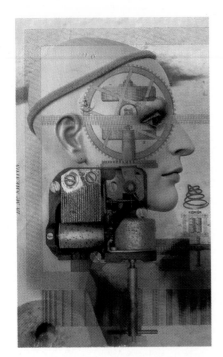

What is psychology about? Mind (or mental processes) and behavior. In some ways, you already know about psychology because you have spent a good part of your life thinking about these topics, in trying to explain your own thoughts and feelings and the behavior of your friends and family. The aim of psychology is to explain behavior, both our overt actions and the great variety of private unseen behaviors such as perceiving, remembering, imagining, and dreaming. We are all, in a sense, amateur psychologists, because all of us wonder why people act as they do. Consider just a few of the interesting and perplexing cases we will meet in this text:

• A young man is wandering at dawn, talking rapidly to his friends about great plans for making a movie that will change the world. A derelict wanders over and admires his boots; the young man immediately takes them off and gives them away. He also takes off his shirt and gives it to the man, insisting that these things are really his. At this point, his friends lead the young man away. What is happening here? We consider this man's case in Chapter 15.

• Early in this century, German society was captivated by Clever Hans, the calculating horse. When given simple arithmetic problems by his owner, the horse tapped the correct answer with his forefoot. Hans could perform the same feat when tested by other people, and he could also answer questions about spelling, reading, and music! Many were convinced by Hans's performance, but a psychologist eventually proved that Hans was not endowed with special mental powers. Nevertheless, in some ways he was a very clever horse. We learn Clever Hans's secret in Chapter 6.

• A woman suffers brain damage that leaves her with a special problem: She cannot recognize familiar faces, including those of relatives and other loved ones. However, she recognizes other objects, talks, and remembers events. Furthermore, she has not forgotten the people she fails to recognize, because she has no problem identifying her relatives by their voices. How can this woman fail to recognize faces but perceive other objects normally? Even more perplexing, when connected to special equipment that measures her responses, the woman shows signs that she does recognize her relatives in pictures. Yet, she insists that she cannot, and the researchers are convinced that she isn't lying. Can the mind recognize people at one level but not another? We consider such cases and what they mean in Chapter 5.

• In the United States in the mid-1960s, a rash of crimes occurred in which the perepetrators all used the same scam: They called an airline, claiming to have placed an altitude-sensitive bomb on board a plane. They said that unless they were given money for instructions on how to deactivate the bomb, the bomb would explode as the plane landed. A wave of similar crimes occurred in Canada and Australia shortly thereafter. What caused them? We learn the answer in this chapter.

All of these cases interest psychologists. Yet, they are so different. Clearly, the field of psychology encompasses a wide variety of topics. Spend a few minutes leafing through this book, and you will quickly discover that psychologists ask questions about every aspect of human behavior. Your survey may turn up some of the following questions:

• *Do some people have photographic memories?* Although most people create mental images (e.g., they can walk through their house "in their mind"), some claim to store exact replicas of their experiences in their "mind's eye" and to be able to report these images as faithfully as if looking at a picture. Chapter 7 explores this phenomenon more fully.

• *Do people inherit some aspects of their mental abilities and personalities from their parents, just as they inherit eye color, hair color, and height?* Research indicates that the answer is yes. Although learning plays a large role in the development of intelligence and personality, there is a genetic component, too. Chapters 2, 11, and 14 consider this topic.

• *How and why do we sometimes perceive the world inaccurately?* Look at the two blue rectangles in Figure 1.1. The top of object A appears long and narrow, while the top of object B seems thicker and shorter; yet the two colored surfaces are actually the same size. If you don't believe this, trace the outline of A on a sheet of paper, turn the paper sideways, and place it over B. Were you fooled by this visual illusion? As the saying goes, don't believe everything you see. Chapter 4 discusses visual illusions.

• *What causes mental disorders?* For example, what causes the severe hallucinations that make some people believe they are controlled and persecuted by others? And why are millions of people depressed and thousands driven to suicide every year? These perplexing questions are discussed in Chapters 15 and 16.

• *How do people change as they get older?* How do various abilities, such as perceiving and remembering, develop? How do people adjust to new social relationships, new jobs, family changes, and old age? Chapters 9 and 10 focus on these issues.

• *Does watching violence on television and in the movies make people more aggressive?* We consider this issue later in this chapter when we discuss the research methods that psychologists use.

Defining Psychology

If psychologists in 1910 had been asked for a definition of psychology, they might have defined it as the study of mind and mental processes. That is because early psychologists concentrated on studying mental life (conscious experience) by having people describe their perceptions and feelings. A couple of decades later, psychologists called *behaviorists* were rejecting this approach and studying only actual behavior, because it alone could be directly observed and measured. Thus, between 1930 and 1950, most psychologists would have defined psychology as the study of behavior. Since the 1950s and 1960s, psychologists have studied the problems of mental experience that the behaviorists rejected—topics such as imagining, remembering, and dreaming—but they have adopted objective methods to study these inherently private events.

Psychology is defined today as the scientific study of mind (mental processes) and behavior. Psychologists observe behavior and then draw inferences about the mental processes that may have produced the behavior. However, you should know that not all psychologists agree with the exact definition given here. The scope of psychology is so broad that there is disagreement even about the definition of the field. (Recall the different types of questions that psychologists investigate and the diverse cases they consider.)

We now turn to a brief survey of the history of psychology.

Early Influences on Psychology

Hermann Ebbinghaus (1850–1909), one of psychology's pioneers, prefaced his greatest work *Memory* (1885) with these words: "From the most ancient subject we shall produce the newest science." Psychology is indeed an ancient subject: people have always been interested in how the mind works and what determines behavior. As

FIGURE 1.1
A Shape Illusion

Seeing can be deceiving. The colored surface of object A appears to be longer and narrower than the top of object B, yet the two shaded portions are actually the same size. To check this, trace the outline of the top of A on a sheet of paper, turn it sideways, and place it over the top of B.

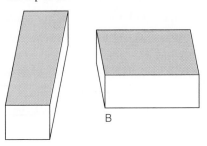

far back as the fourth and fifth centuries B.C., Socrates, Plato, and Aristotle addressed various aspects of psychology, and many other great thinkers have written on these subjects throughout the ages. Some questions have been addressed repeatedly: How do humans perceive, remember, and know the world around them? Does a person's knowledge come entirely from experience, or is it partly innate? How much of human behavior reflects inherited factors, and how much has been shaped by experience?

COPERNICUS: RETHINKING OUR PLACE IN THE UNIVERSE

Despite a long history of interest in psychological topics, *scientific* psychology was slow to develop, and today is just a little more than 100 years old. Scientific psychology denotes the application of scientific analysis—observing events, testing theories, and conducting experiments—to understand psychological phenomena. One reason psychology as a science developed so slowly was the age-old belief that human beings exist at the center of a universe made just for us. Moreover, humankind was viewed as something special and apart from the rest of the world—so unique, in fact, as to defy the kind of scientific analysis usually applied to inanimate objects and animals. Until this belief was challenged, there was no room for the scientific study of human behavior or mental processes. The revolutionary ideas of Nicolaus Copernicus (1473–1543) in the sixteenth century represented one such challenge. He argued that the earth was not at the center of the universe; quite the contrary, the earth (and the other planets) revolved around the sun. Because these ideas directly challenged the accepted view that the earth (and its people) held a supreme position in the universe, Copernicus delayed publication of his theories until the year of his death. He rightly suspected that his ideas would create a firestorm of controversy. This new view suggested that human beings, like all other creatures, just might be subject to natural laws and could therefore be studied systematically.

DESCARTES: FROM DUALISM TO INTERACTIONISM

Changes in some basic theological and philosophical beliefs also paved the way to a scientific psychology. For centuries, theologians insisted that the human mind (also called the spirit or soul) had free will and was not governed by natural laws; hence, it was beyond the realm of study. Philosophers similarly argued that while most natural phenomena could be explained by mechanical and mathematical principles, the human mind, with its free will, could not be understood that way. This view, known as *dualism*, maintains that humans are composed of two elements: a body and a mind (or soul). The human body was believed to be a shell that housed the soul, and while the mind, or soul, could act upon the body, the body could not act upon the soul.

René Descartes proposed interaction between mind and body.

René Descartes (1596–1650), a French philosopher and mathematician, revised the position of dualism by proposing mind-body *interactionism* (Lowry, 1982). Descartes suggested that the body was not slave to the mind and that the mind and body affected each other. This idea was important to the development of psychology because it challenged the absolute supremacy of the soul. Descartes also promoted the idea that the human body had a machinelike quality of its own, making humans seem more like other animals and therefore subject to certain "laws of nature." Thus, the human *body*, at least, could be studied scientifically. Descartes went on to propose various mechanisms by which perception and body movement might be explained.

THE EMPIRICISTS

Before psychology could really develop, the idea had to arise that the *mind*, not just the body, could be studied scientifically. One step in this direction occurred in England, where Thomas Hobbes (1588–1679) established the school of thought known as **empiricism,** maintaining that the contents of the mind originated from sensory experience. Thus, empiricists believe that sensory experience is the primary source of knowledge. Another British empiricist, John Locke (1632–1704), argued that the association of ideas was a guiding principle of the mind; if two things are experienced at approximately the same time, then they are likely to be mentally associated. This principle of *associationism* remains an important psychological concept even now (Raaijmakers, 1993). With the approaches of empiricism and associationism, mental events were seen to operate according to the laws of nature. And by the end of the seventeenth century, the idea that mental phenomena could be understood by lawful, mechanistic principles was gaining support.

EARLY EXPERIMENTS IN PSYCHOLOGY

More than 100 years later, empiricism got a futher boost when a German physicist named Hermann von Helmholtz (1821–1894) became one of the first scientists to conduct psychology experiments. According to legend, he and three other radical young physicists signed a blood oath in the 1840s, declaring that all forces in the human organism were physical and chemical (instead of spiritual). Helmholtz pioneered experiments in a number of important fields, including measuring the speed of impulse transmission in the nervous system.

Another German physicist, Gustav Fechner (1801–1887), was also an early contributor to psychology. Fechner was interested in the way physical stimulation, such as different intensities of light, translated into psychological experience. In his major work, *Elements of Psychophysics,* published in 1860, he explored these questions: How does increasing the intensity of a light heighten its perceived brightness? And how much brighter must a light of a certain intensity become before people notice the difference? In addressing these and similar problems, Fechner helped found the field called psychophysics, discussed in Chapter 3.

DARWIN AND THE THEORY OF EVOLUTION

Another powerful influence on the development of scientific psychology was Charles Darwin's *theory of evolution*—the gradual development of species from earlier forms—as announced in *The Origin of Species* in 1859. Although evolutionary theory had many precursors, Darwin (1809–1882) heavily documented the process of "descent through modification" through his careful observations, collected over a long period.

Darwin proposed a specific mechanism for evolution, known today as *natural selection* (discussed in Chapter 2). In brief, as environments change, certain traits became more beneficial than others, causing some animals to reproduce successfully and others to become extinct (because their qualities no longer permit survival in the changed environment). Thus, "survival of the fittest" describes how animals adapt over long periods to changes in the local environment. Darwin's theory had important implications for psychology: Because humans were now thought to have evolved from other animals, animal behavior could be studied for insights into human behavior. By the

Gustav Fechner initiated the field of psychophysics.

Charles Darwin's theory of evolution by natural selection had a great impact on the developing science of psychology, especially for those in the functional school.

turn of the century, these ideas had opened the door to comparative psychology—the comparison of behavior across species.

In sum, before a scientific psychology could develop, astronomers, philosophers, physicists, and biologists had to challenge the theories in their respective fields that were precluding humans from scientific examination.

Early Schools of Psychology

The field of psychology did not develop by an even flow of events. From the very beginning of scientific psychology in the late 1800s, psychologists had fundamental disagreements over the field's appropriate subject matter and proper methods of study. As a result, various schools of thought developed from 1880 to 1930. They are of more than just historical interest because each school still influences modern psychology.

STRUCTURALISM: THE ELEMENTS OF CONSCIOUSNESS

Modern psychology is often formally dated from 1879. In that year, the first psychology laboratory was established in Leipzig, Germany, by Wilhelm Wundt (1832–1920). Wundt was probably the first person to call himself a psychologist, and his influence on the field was tremendous, partly as a result of his prolific writing. (It is estimated that he published 50,000 pages.) Wundt's original laboratory consisted of one classroom, which he soon filled with equipment largely made by his own hands (Hilgard, 1987). During its first year in existence, two students attended the school: G. Stanley Hall, an American, and Max Friedrich, a German. Hall, who already held a Ph.D. from Harvard, would later found the first psychological laboratory in America in 1883 at Johns Hopkins University.

Wundt developed the first systematic approach to psychology, now called **structuralism.** This theory explored the structure of conscious experience—that is, what a person was aware of during an experience. Proponents of structuralism believed that psychology should concern itself with the elementary processes of conscious experience. They considered three primary questions: (1) What are the elements of experience? (2) How are they combined? and (3) What causes the elements to combine?

Structuralists identified three major components of conscious experience: sensations, images, and affections. *Sensations* include sights, sounds, smells, tastes, and feelings; *images* represent experiences not actually present, such as memories; and *affections* pertain to emotional reactions, such as love, joy, and jealousy. These elements were believed to be combined into normal conscious experience by the process of association.

The structural psychologists broke down complex experiences into their elementary components (sensations, images, and affections) by a technique known as *analytic introspection*. Instead of viewing conscious experience as a continuous flow, introspectionists recorded the discrete, conscious contents of an experience. Typical instructions were to "be as attentive as possible to the object or process which gives rise to the sensation, and, when the object is removed or the process completed, recall the sensation by an act of memory as vividly and completely as you can" (Leahey, 1991, p. 63). Therefore, subjects would not report seeing a beautiful flower but instead would describe the sensations of experiencing that flower—size, shape, texture, color, brightness, and so on—as well as the images and affections that the flower evoked.

Structuralism became an important influence on North American psychology when one of Wundt's students, an Englishman named Edward Bradford Titchener (1867–1927), set up a laboratory at Cornell University. Although Titchener disagreed

Wilhelm Wundt is credited with founding the first psychology laboratory in 1879 and founding the school of structuralism.

Edward Bradford Titchener brought Wundt's program to America and named it structuralism.

John Dewey, the father of functionalism, also made great contributions to education and philosophy.

William James, the first famous American psychologist, taught at Harvard.

with Wundt on some issues (Hilgard, 1987), these differences seem minor today. Titchener was an extremely important figure in American and Canadian psychology because he trained a generation of students in the structuralist tradition. In fact, although Wundt developed the field we now call structuralism, Titchener actually gave the approach its name.

The proponents of this first school of psychology soon found themselves under attack. Many outside the structuralist camp found analytic introspection sterile and boring. What's more, introspection proved unreliable, because different introspectionists could not agree on elementary parts of the same experience. Nevertheless, Titchener and his students believed that the structuralist program described how psychology should be studied and argued against newer trends. By 1920, however, the structuralists had been pushed from the forefront of the field.

FUNCTIONALISM: THE USES OF THE MIND

Unlike structuralism, which developed in Germany and was transported to the United States, functionalism grew up in the United States. **Functionalism** is so named because it emphasizes the functions of conscious experience and behavior. Why did particular behaviors and experiences (such as emotions) evolve? What purpose do they serve?

Functionalism was strongly influenced by Darwin's theory of evolution, which swept through intellectual circles in both Europe and North America in the late 1800s. Darwin's theory fundamentally changed humankind's place in the order of nature. For psychologists, Darwin's theory raised fascinating questions: Do human mental processes have an evolutionary history? Are our capabilities, such as learning from experience, similar to those of other animals? Did most human characteristics develop as adaptations, permitting successful reproduction? These questions helped give rise to functionalism between 1890 and 1910. According to Boring (1950), functionalist psychology is concerned with "success in living, with the adaptation of the organism to its environment, and with the organism's adaptation of its environment to itself" (p. 551).

Whereas structuralists asked questions about the contents of the mind, functionalists were interested in the uses (functions) of mental processes. In other words, functionalists favored problems of practical significance which meant studying mental activity and behavior in their natural contexts. Functionalists argued that because psychological processes were continuous, ongoing events, they could not be frozen and dissected, as the structuralists proposed.

Functionalism is usually associated with John Dewey (1859–1952) and the two universities where he taught, the University of Chicago and Columbia University. Another great American psychologist, sometimes considered a functionalist although not strictly part of the school, was William James (1842–1910). His landmark two-volume work, *The Principles of Psychology* (1890), is still widely read today. Like the functionalists, he conceived of mental processes as active and continuous, like a stream that flowed in a continuous yet changing fashion—essentially, a *stream of consciousness*. The ideas of Dewey and James led to several trends previously discouraged by structuralists. For example, psychology broadened to include a variety of people (children, the mentally ill) and species (chimpanzees, dogs) that could not be studied through analytic introspection. In addition, research was applied to practical problems. In fact, the functionalists were the first American psychologists to develop intelligence tests to classify children (a topic discussed in Chapter 11).

John B. Watson, the father of behaviorism, eventually left academics to pursue a successful career in advertising.

BEHAVIORISM: EXCLUDING THE MIND FROM PSYCHOLOGY

Another school of psychology that developed in North America was behaviorism, probably the most debated approach to studying human behavior.

John Watson: The First Behaviorist. Behaviorism can be dated from 1913, when John B. Watson (1878–1958) published a paper entitled "Psychology as the Behaviorist Views It," in which he firmly stated that psychology should be "the science of behavior." Although trained in the functionalist tradition at the University of Chicago, Watson rejected the tenets of functionalism when he announced that psychologists should focus on behavior instead of mind, mental processes, and conscious experience. Watson also attacked structuralism's emphasis on introspection, consciousness, and mental content as inappropriate for scientific explanation. In addition, he insisted that psychology abandon introspective methods that created inconsistent results from one laboratory to the next. Instead, Watson argued, psychologists should limit their study to what all reasonable people could agree on—overt behavior. Watson wrote:

> I believe we can write a psychology, define it as 'the science of behavior,' and never go back on our definition: never use the terms consciousness, mental states, introspectively verifiable, imagery, and the like. It can be done in terms of habit formation, habit integration, and the like. Furthermore, I believe it is really worthwhile to make the attempt now. (1913, pp. 166–167)

Behaviorism attracted many psychologists who wanted to avoid complicated arguments about the nature of consciousness and images or the number of sensations in an experience. They were intent on establishing psychology as a natural science. Its subject was observable behavior of people and animals. It should be noted that most behaviorists did not deny the *existence* of mind and consciousness; they merely argued that these concepts were not useful in a scientific context.

The Impact of Logical Positivism. Behaviorism was part of a philosophical movement known as *logical positivism,* which influenced physics and linguistics, in addition to psychology, during the 1920s and 1930s. Logical positivism promoted the idea that all knowledge should be expressed in statements that can be verified by empirical means, or direct observation (Ayer, 1936). The positivists introduced a critical concept into psychology: the operational definition. An *operational definition* of a scientific concept describes the measurement processes (or operations) used to define it. For example, while the dictionary definition of hunger—sensations that arise when a person or animal has not eaten—would satisfy most people, it would not satisfy a behaviorist, because no procedure for measuring hunger is specified. A behaviorist might operationally define hunger as the number of hours an animal has been deprived of food. And that same behaviorist might also assume that we could increase the level of hunger in the animal by increasing the hours of food deprivation from, say, 8 to 16 to 24. The operational definition, unlike the dictionary one, permits a precise statement about how the defined concept is measured. Indeed, behaviorists would avoid the concept of hunger altogether and substitute "hours of food deprivation." Operational definitions encourage precise measurement and communication among researchers.

Behaviorists argued that the proper goal of psychology was to describe, explain, predict, and control behavior. Their emphasis was on the way experience molded behavior, so they had a natural interest in the learning process. They tended to study learning in animals other than humans, because greater control could be maintained over their environments.

B.F. Skinner is the most famous modern champion of behaviorism. His novel, *Walden Two* (1948), portrayed a society built on behaviorist ideas and principles.

Max Wertheimer created clever perceptual demonstrations that supported the Gestalt view of perception.

B. F. Skinner. Behaviorism attracted a large number of critics, both from the field of psychology and from other disciplines. Today, most critics debate the ideas of B. F. Skinner (1904–1990), who has been called a radical behaviorist for his insistence that psychologists never try to explain behavior by reference to internal causes (biological or psycological ones). And today, many behaviorists themselves disagree with some of Skinner's ideas. Indeed, several behaviorist positions currently exist. Moreover, some basic ideas of the behaviorist movement, such as operational definitions, have permeated contemporary psychology. However, while almost all psychologists would agree that the study of behavior is central to psychology, only a few would reject all use of mental or biological constructs as explanations for behavior. Early behaviorists excluded many topics from psychology—such as perception, emotion, and cognition—that are of primary concern today.

GESTALT PSYCHOLOGY: PERCEPTION OF THE WHOLE

Functionalism and behaviorism developed in the United States partly in reaction to structuralism. About the same time, another protest against structuralism arose on its home ground in Germany. **Gestalt psychology,** a reaction against the structural idea of perception as the sum of many independent sensations, argued that people perceived the world in unitary wholes, or gestalts (from the German *gestalten*, which translates roughly as "whole," "pattern," or "organization"). The three most notable founders of the Gestalt movement were Max Wertheimer (1880–1943), Wolfgang Köhler (1887–1967), and Kurt Koffka (1886–1941).

Max Wertheimer and the other Gestalt psychologists produced many demonstrations of the unity of perceptual processes, beginning with *apparent motion*. Wertheimer discovered that when two lights were spaced a slight distance apart in the dark and then lit successively at short intervals, a curious perceptual phenomenon occurred. Rather than seeing two lights being lit alternately, the observer saw only one light that appeared to move back and forth. Because the light appeared to move through empty space, a region producing no actual sensations, the phenomenon could not be explained by the structuralist approach. How could there be perception without sensation? Gestalt psychologists answered that we perceive by organizing sensations into patterns or shapes. Thus, the perception we construct may not reflect precisely the sensations that caused it. A more familiar example of apparent motion is the illusion of movement produced by the movies, created by a rapid succession of still pictures. Human perceptual systems integrate these scenes into continuous motion. We will consider more examples of the Gestalt approach to perception in Chapter 4.

Although Gestalt psychology originally began as a protest against structuralism, soon its proponents were arguing with behaviorists. The Gestaltists objected to the behaviorists' analysis of complex phenomena in terms of elementary behaviors, just as they had objected to the structuralists' theory of elementary sensations. Behaviorists, for their part, found the concepts of Gestalt psychology every bit as vague as the concepts of structuralism and functionalism, and were further alienated by the way Gestalt psychologists relied on reports of conscious experience for their data. Even worse, the Gestaltists were often content merely to demonstrate a phenomenon rather than to study it carefully through behavioral methods. The Gestalt influence remains strong in some areas of psychology, particularly in the study of perception, memory, and thinking. In addition, the Gestalt viewpoint greatly influenced the development of social psychology through proponents such as Kurt Lewin and Fritz Heider, who were trained in this school.

PSYCHOANALYSIS: SIGMUND FREUD AND THE UNCONSCIOUS MIND

Sigmund Freud, the father of psychoanalysis.

Sigmund Freud (1856–1939) is best known as the founder of **psychoanalysis,** an approach that emphasizes the importance of unconscious forces in the development of personality and mental disorders. Trained as a physician, Freud practiced medicine in Vienna, where his early observations led him to conclude that some physical symptoms might have psychological causes. Freud developed the idea that most mental problems were caused by conflicts and emotions the patient wasn't aware of. He believed that psychological problems in adults could be traced to traumatic episodes in early childhood. Memories of those events would cause anxiety if allowed into consciousness, so these memories were blocked from consciousness, or repressed, although they remained in the unconscious part of the mind. In Freud's view, many of the bizarre symptoms of mental illness were outlets for these repressed memories. The task of the psychoanalyst, therefore, was to help bring these memories into consciousness. This was achieved through free association and the interpretation of dreams. Dreams, Freud argued, were the "royal road to the unconscious." Once these repressed memories were brought to consciousness, the patient would then be able to deal with them rationally and relieve the psychological disturbance. (A more detailed description of Freud's theory is given in Chapter 14.)

Freud's theory is creative, complicated, and controversial. His analysis helped initiate the systematic study of personality development, motivation, abnormal behavior, and therapies for mental problems. It has also been roundly criticized by many psychologists (particularly behaviorists) as vague and generally untestable. Freud did, however, call attention to a number of interesting phenomena, such as dreams, slips of the tongue, and memory lapses, which have received careful scientific study more recently. In general, the psychoanalytic tradition forces psychologists to confront the

CONCEPT SUMMARY

FIVE SCHOOLS OF PSYCHOLOGY

SCHOOL	SUBJECT MATTER	RESEARCH GOALS	RESEARCH METHODS
Structuralism	Conscious experience	To break down conscious experience into its basic components: sensations, images, affections	Analytic introspection
Functionalism	The function of mental processes and how they help people adapt	To study mental processes in their natural contexts; to discover what effects they have	Both objective measures and informal observation and introspection
Behaviorism	Behavior: how it is changed under different conditions, with an emphasis on learning	Description, explanation, prediction, and control of behavior	Objective measures of behavior; formal experiments
Gestalt Psychology	Subjective experience, with an emphasis on perception, memory, and thinking	To understand the phenomena of conscious experience in holistic terms (not to analyze experience into arbitrary categories)	Subjective reports; some behavioral measures; demonstrations
Psychoanalysis	Abnormal human behavior	To understand normal and abnormal personality through study of abnormal cases	Lengthy dialogues with patients to uncover unconscious fears and memories; free association; dream interpretation

issue of what motivates behavior—whether normal or abnormal. Today, other types of psychoanalytic theory have emerged from the traditional Freudian ideas.

Women Pioneers in Psychology

If you flip through the preceding pages and look at the names and pictures of the people involved in founding psychology, you will notice one thing: They are all men. Indeed, when psychology was being established as a discipline about a century ago, women (and minorities) were generally excluded from graduate education in all fields of study. While many colleges were created specifically for women, it was difficult for women to advance beyond the undergraduate level because universities maintained policies to exclude them from graduate education and teaching posts. Things are quite different today. In fact, more than half of all graduate students in psychology are women. Although prejudice has not been erased entirely, certainly this century has seen a dramatic reduction in discrimination within academia in America and other Western nations, both for women and for members of minority groups.

Although the early history of psychology is dominated by males, there are a few shining exceptions. Against the odds, some women persevered in the study of psychology and made important contributions to the field. Consider the careers of two of these women: Mary Whiton Calkins and Christine Ladd-Franklin.

Mary Whiton Calkins (1863–1930) graduated from Smith College with a bachelor's degree in 1885. Wellesley College hired her as an instructor in Greek, but because she was also interested in philosophy, a colleague recommended her for a new appointment in psychology. Calkins took a leave of absence to study philosophy and psychology at Radcliffe College (1890–1891) and then continued as a "guest" graduate student at Harvard from 1891 to 1895. At Harvard she had the good fortune of enrolling in William James's seminar just after his publication of *Principles of Psychology*. Because she was the only student enrolled, the meetings took place around the fireplace of his home. Although Calkins completed all the requirements for her Ph.D. and received letters of support from James and other psychologists, Harvard refused to grant a doctorate to a woman. Officials at Radcliffe College later offered her a doctorate for her work at Harvard, but she refused the offer on principle.

In 1891, Calkins set up a laboratory at Wellesley (Furumoto, 1990). She conducted research in several different areas. She was interested in the factors affecting the formation of associations, and she studied these in a series of experiments published in 1894 and 1896. Although she was not primarily interested in memory, her work produced many important insights about such phenomena, some of which were lost to psychology at the time and only rediscovered much later (Madigan & O'Hara, 1992). For example, it was Calkins who invented the method of paired-associate learning. In this technique, subjects study pairs of random items (e.g. spoon–airplane) and later are tested for their knowledge of the association by being given one item (spoon) and asked to recall the other item (airplane).

Calkins eventually turned to the psychology of the self, where she favored an introspective approach and argued that the awareness of self could be felt in every introspective act. However, Titchener, the great American introspectionist, disagreed with her, and the two maintained a running debate over this issue (Furumoto, 1991).

Calkins was elected the first female president of the American Psychological Association in 1905. Her presidential address, later published under the title "A Reconciliation Between Structural and Functional Psychology" (1906), argued for

Mary Calkins, a student of William James, was interested in the factors affecting the formation of associations and invented the method of paired-associate learning.

Christine Ladd-Franklin made startling discoveries about vision and how people perceive color.

consensus between the two schools and a recognition of the strengths of each approach. Calkins was also interested in philosophical issues and was elected president of the American Philosophical Association in 1918, again the first woman to hold the office. She continued to teach at Wellesley until the end of her remarkable career.

Christine Ladd (1847–1930) graduated from Vassar College in 1869. A few years later, she wanted to do graduate work in mathematics at Johns Hopkins University but women were not admitted. Fortunately, a mathematician pursued her case with the administration and won support for her. Ladd completed all the work for a doctorate degree between the years 1878 and 1882, but, just as with Mary Calkins at Harvard, the university refused to grant the degree. Johns Hopkins rectified this error by granting her the degree 45 years late, in 1926, only 4 years before she died.

In 1882, Ladd married Fabian Franklin, a mathematics instructor at Johns Hopkins, and published as Ladd-Franklin thereafter. Her husband was supportive of her career, and when she became interested in vision and psychology during a sabbatical in Germany, he encouraged her aspirations. Women were not admitted for study in German universities, but once again she managed to find support, this time at the University of Göttingen, where she made some startling discoveries about vision. Foremost among these was a new theory of how people perceive color, which was presented at the International Congress of Experimental Psychology in London in 1892. Upon returning to North America, she occasionally taught logic and psychology at Johns Hopkins University. And when her husband decided to leave academia for a career in writing and journalism, she went with him to New York. There she received a part-time appointment at Columbia University, where she taught from 1910 until her death in 1930 (Furumoto, 1992). Throughout her long career, Ladd-Franklin championed her theory of color vision, although it has since been replaced.

Mary Whiton Calkins and Christine Ladd-Franklin are only two of the early women in psychology who were able to overcome long odds and gender discrimination to complete their life's work.

Themes in Contemporary Psychology

If you examine the chapter titles in this text, you may be surprised by the wide variety of topics represented. These range from the operation of a single neuron, to learning, thinking, and personality, to the actions of whole groups of people, to the even broader field of organizational psychology. Despite the apparent diversity, certain organizing principles, or themes, underlie all aspects of psychology.

We have organized the chapters in this text according to five basic themes. Try to keep these themes in mind as you read. At the beginning of each chapter, a series of questions will orient you as to how the themes apply to the particular chapter. Then, at the end of the chapter, a section called "Themes in Review" will summarize the main points. Here, then, are our five organizing themes for psychology:

• **The Biological Theme.** The biological bases of behavior are obvious when an accident causes brain damage and produces abnormal behavior. However, there are biological underpinnings to all behavior, making this an important theme in the book. For example, we will see that certain behavior disorders (or "mental" illnesses) can be directly traced to chemical imbalances in the brain. Biological factors include those related to the nervous system, as well as other internal factors, such as production of hormones.

- **The Learning Theme.** Despite the importance of biological factors, most important human behaviors are shaped through learning and experience. We learn our native language, our food preferences and aversions, how to ride a bicycle, and how to do long division. In fact, practically every important human behavior is shaped by learning. Therefore, how behavior may change as a function of experience is a second major theme of the book.

- **The Cognitive Theme.** Modern psychology is heavily influenced by the cognitive approach. Psychologists study how people and other animals perceive the world and represent it. How is information from the outside world transformed by perceptual processes and then later retrieved? We can ask this question about simple events, such as reading a newspaper, or about something as complex as how we perceive other people. Cognitive psychologists study perceiving, remembering, reading, writing, reasoning, thinking, and other mental activities. Those who study cognitive development are interested in how children's minds develop. Those who study social cognition are interested in how people perceive, remember, and think about each other. Thus, a third major theme in this book is the cognitive theme.

- **The Developmental Theme.** All creatures change greatly over their life span. The human infant is radically different from the 3-year-old; the 3-year-old is nothing like the teenager; and still other important changes occur as a person passes from adulthood into old age. Psychologists increasingly recognize that they must study behavior over the entire life span of the individual. Every important human behavior changes with age. Thus, the developmental theme is a fourth important theme.

- **The Sociocultural Theme.** Human (and nonhuman) behavior does not occur in isolation. Psychologists tend to concentrate on the behavior of individuals, but this behavior is shaped and molded by the social and cultural context in which a person lives. People often act differently in groups than they do by themselves. In addition, people living in different societies and cultures may learn very different rules for interacting with other people. A fifth important theme, therefore, is the sociocultural theme.

Each of these five themes will be represented to a greater or lesser extent in each chapter. For example, in the study of sensation and perception, the biological, learning, cognitive, and developmental themes play a greater role than the sociocultural theme, even though sociocultural factors are at work in perception (as we see on pages 167–168). By considering these five themes in each chapter, you will come to appreciate the coherent set of issues that psychologists face in every topic they examine.

Research Methods in Psychology

Psychologists are curious about many different phenomena; they want to know how the human mind works and why people behave the way they do. But how do psychologists study these topics? What methods produce reliable information?

A distinction is often made between two basic types of psychological research: descriptive (nonexperimental) research and experimental research (Kantowitz, Roediger, & Elmes, 1994). **Descriptive research** makes use of various techniques, such as psychological tests and case studies, to describe phenomena of interest to researchers. In one important type of descriptive research—*correlational research*—different measures of behavior are related to one another (or co-related) to see if they change in predictable ways. Descriptive research techniques are tremendously impor-

LEVELS OF EXPLANATION: WHAT IS THE APPROPRIATE WAY TO EXPLAIN HUMAN BEHAVIOR?

Some scientists argue that the only appropriate way to explain human behavior is to reduce the higher factors to their biological underpinnings, as represented in the biological theme. This molecular approach to explaining psychological phenomena is called **reductionism.** Its proponents argue that biological factors are the real causes of human behavior, so all learning, cognitive, social, and developmental changes must ultimately be reduced to biological changes. However, most psychologists reject reductionism in favor of multiple levels of explanation.

Because psychologists take varying approaches to their subject matter, they often try to explain the same phenomenon in different ways. The different types of explanations can be arranged in a hierarchy, as shown in Figure 1.2. The elements of the hierarchy range from social and cultural forces, which might be emphasized by anthropologists and sociologists, to the cognitive processes of the individual, to the various biochemical and genetic determinants of behavior. The cultural and social factors correspond to the sociocultural theme of the book. The learning and cognitive themes are represented as factors working at the level of the individual. Also working at the

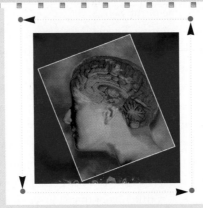

individual level are the systematic differences between individuals, such as their personalities. For example, some peole are outgoing and friendly, while others are shy and more socially withdrawn. Although these personality differences are not represented as a theme in the book, they are very important in explaining some differences in behavior. At the bottom of the hierarchy are the biological factors determining behavior.

Reductionists argue that all the upper-level factors should be reduced to those at the bottom of the hierarchy in Figure 1.2. The counterargument is that the whole range of factors in the figure, those at each level, must be considered to explain most complex behaviors. Let's see how this applies to

the problem of obesity. Why are many people in Western nations overweight? Do we all overeat? What causes the problem?

First, consider *genetic* factors: Weight is determined in part by inheritance. Identical twins adopted shortly after birth tend to weigh about the same when adults, despite growing up in different families. Second, consider *physiology:* If parts of the brain that regulate eating function improperly, then the impulses signaling satiety ("I've had enough") are shut off; or perhaps metabolic factors that control fat deposits may have gone awry. Third, *learning* may play a role in obesity: Many children are taught to eat everything on their plates, regardless of whether they are hungry. This leads, fourth, to *cognitive* factors: Some psychologists propose that overweight people are more sensitive to external cues about food than they are to internal, physiological cues (Schachter, 1971); they tend to eat when food is visible and attractive (external cues) and ignore the physiological cues telling them that they have had enough. Fifth, some researchers propose that *personality* variables are important: People may eat to relieve stress or may deliberately gain weight to avoid the stress of interpersonal

tant in psychology, but because they only describe behavior, they cannot pinpoint the factors causing the behavior, although they may provide important clues. Many psychologists prefer **experimental research,** in which researchers manipulate, or vary, one factor in a controlled situation (experiment) to see how it influences the behavior of interest. The differences in research methods will become clearer as we describe them in more detail.

Almost all research methods share certain features. A researcher identifies a phenomenon of interest, either from personal observation or from prior research, and becomes familiar with the scientific literature on that topic. The researcher usually develops or adapts a **theory,** an interrelated set of ideas used to explain a phenomenon, and from that theory develops a **hypothesis,** a specific, testable proposition about some specific situation or phenomenon. The researcher then develops a specific **prediction,** or forecast, of what will happen if the hypothesis is correct. Next, the researcher collects evidence, or **data,** pertaining to the prediction. (Remember, one observation is a *datum*; many observations are *data*.) After the data are collected, the

FIGURE 1.2
Hierarchy of How to Explain Behavior

Researchers consider various levels in explaining many psychological phenomena. This hierarchy can be applied to the range of factors causing obesity, described in the text. Higher-level, or molar, factors are at the top, with lower-level, or molecular factors at the bottom. The arrows indicate that factors at the different levels interact.

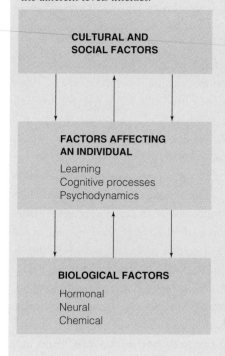

CULTURAL AND SOCIAL FACTORS

FACTORS AFFECTING AN INDIVIDUAL
Learning
Cognitive processes
Psychodynamics

BIOLOGICAL FACTORS
Hormonal
Neural
Chemical

relations, especially sexual situations. Sixth, *social and cultural* factors encourage people to become overweight: In nations where food is plentiful, advertisers have turned eating into a national pastime.

Thus, researchers explain obesity in many ways. Genetic, biochemical, and other physiological factors are important, as are learning, cognitive, and personality factors. Social and cultural factors, too, must be taken into account. So which factor "correctly" explains the problem? Most psychologists would argue that no single level of explanation is sufficient. Instead, most complicated psychological phenomena can be understood only when we consider various factors operating at different levels. When explanations are arranged in a hierarchy, as in Figure 1.2, biological and chemical factors are on the lowest level, called the *molecular level;* cognitive, learning, and personality factors enter just above; and social and cultural factors occupy the highest level, called the *molar* level. The different levels are not independent and usually affect one another, which is indicated in Figure 1.2 by the arrows between levels. If food is plentiful, for example, it may be

eaten to relieve stress, with biochemical consequences.

Another example helps illustrate this point. Cognitive psychologists, who attempt to describe the structure and processes of the mind, defend an abstract level of explanation by employing a computer analogy. Suppose a Martian landed on earth and wanted to know how a computer worked. (Computers, of course, require complicated electronic circuitry and programs that control their operation.) Should the Martian first study electronic circuitry or computer programming to understand the computer? The answer depends on the type of knowledge desired, whether at a molecular level (circuitry) or at a molar level (programming). Cognitive psychologists defend their molar explanations of behavior in terms of abstract cognitive processes by saying that they are interested in the "program" that governs human behavior. By this analogy, psychobiologists deal with the internal circuitry of the mind. Ideally, the approaches complement one another. Discoveries about aspects of the "program" aid the study of neural function, and vice versa.

researcher analyzes them and compares the results with the prediction. If the prediction is verified, then the hypothesis and theory have been upheld. If the prediction is not verified, then the researcher must find out why. Was the research a fair test? Does the theory need to be modified?

To further understand the steps in the research process, let's see how different research methods can be used to address the following question: Does watching violence on TV lead to aggressiveness in viewers?

DESCRIPTIVE RESEARCH TECHNIQUES

Investigating any phenomenon first requires a precise description of its features. Only after this preliminary stage can scientists develop theories to explain the phenomenon. Psychologists use several techniques to describe behavior, including naturalistic observation, case studies, interviews, surveys, psychological tests, and correlational analyses that may include information from the other descriptive techniques.

Naturalistic Observation.   Simple observation can spark interest in many phenomena. Perhaps a psychologist's two children are watching a Three Stooges movie on television. Larry smacks Curly, Curly swats Moe, and Moe knocks the others' heads together. After the movie, the psychologist discovers his children smacking, swatting, and pinching each other, in apparent imitation of the Three Stooges. A fight ensues, and both children are punished.

Not surprisingly, the psychologist wonders if his children should watch such programs. This question leads to the more general question about the relationship between watching violence on TV and aggressive behavior. Actually, the Three Stooges are relatively tame by today's standards. Many television shows depict murders, rapes, torture, and maiming dozens of times over the course of a season. How many murders do you think the average adolescent has witnessed on TV? The answer is 18,000 (Hoffman et al., 1994). Although the number of violent acts on television has actually remained fairly steady over the years, the violence is portrayed more graphically. Moreover, children, adolescents, and adults are exposed to much more violence in movie theaters and elsewhere.

Casual observations of interesting phenomena often lead to research questions, but observation of one or two suggestive cases does not permit a general conclusion. After all, any one case might represent the exception to the rule. More rigorous research methods are needed.

As the name implies, **naturalistic observation** is a research technique in which behavior is studied in its natural context, outside the laboratory. The case of the psychologist who observed his children fighting does not qualify as naturalistic observation because naturalistic observation is much more systematic. Typically, researchers note how often, when, and in what context the behavior occurs. Such careful procedures characterize the work of **ethologists,** who study the behavior of animals in the wild. Ethologists sample the animals' behavior at certain times and record the details as completely as possible.

One drawback of this technique is that the subjects being observed may behave differently if they know that they are being watched. This tendency seems especially true of humans. If a psychologist is interested in whether watching violence on TV increases aggressiveness, and if the participants in the study know this, the participants may not respond naturally. They may act less aggressively than they normally would because they know that aggressiveness is considered undesirable; or they might act more aggressively than usual to "help" the researcher. When a researcher's presence affects the behavior being observed, the observations are said to be **reactive,** because they are partly a reaction to the observer. Researchers engaged in naturalistic observation (or any other research) strive for **nonreactive,** or **unobtrusive, techniques** to study behavior. For example, when studying animals in the wild, researchers may build blinds to hide themselves from the animals, or they may let the novelty of their presence wear off before they begin recording data.

Naturalistic observation is often useful in the first stage of research and helps provide clues to understanding a phenomenon. In studies of humans, such research is often supplemental to case studies, interviews, surveys, and psychological tests.

Case Studies.   A **case study** is the intensive investigation of one person or one particular instance of some phenomenon. By examining one case in detail, a researcher hopes to discover general principles concerning the phenomenon. (For example, Freud based his psychoanalytic theory on intensive case studies of his

THE DOOMSDAY FLIGHT

In December 1966, *Doomsday Flight*, a made-for-television movie, was shown despite the protests of the Airline Pilots Association. The plot contained a blueprint for extortion in which the extortionist ran little risk of detection. In the movie, a caller telephoned an airline saying that one of its planes, already in flight, contained an altitude-sensitive bomb that would detonate as the plane descended. The extortionist demanded a large sum of money in return for information about the location of the bomb and how it could be disarmed. The Airline Pilots Association feared that the film's plot could be a model of how to threaten airlines.

A case study of events following the appearance of this movie on television proved that the pilots' fears were well founded (Stanley & Riera, 1976). The week after *Doomsday Flight* was shown in the United States, numerous airlines received demands for money in exchange for information that would save the airplanes in flight. Many callers mentioned altitude-sensitive bombs. Furthermore, this phenomenon occurred again when *Doomsday Flight* was shown in Canada, France, and Australia. (In Australia, someone successfully extorted $500,000 from Qantas Airlines.)

patients.) Throughout this text, we include case studies to illustrate some point. Each will be preceded by the logo that appears in the margin above. We now apply this research method to our example, in the box above.

This case study focuses on a crime that seems to have been copied from a television program. If the criminals are caught, they can be closely questioned about the events leading up to the crime. If their description of the crime closely follows a similar one portrayed on TV, it might be plausible to suppose that the real crime was modeled after the televised one.

The *Doomsday Flight* case and other similar case studies (Stanley & Riera, 1976) document dramatic instances of the influence of television on aggressive behavior. Critics of the case study method, however, point to its limitations. For example, one difficulty with case studies is the question of generalizability: Does the effect of viewing violent crimes on television apply to all viewers and programs? Does TV violence provoke aggressive behavior in the general population, or are these isolated responses in a few abnormal personalities? Further, *Doomsday Flight* and certain other shows portray powerful, distinctive crimes. But do the more mundane, repetitive crimes viewed on television have similar effects? Similarly, many critics have questioned whether the principles that Freud derived from the case histories of a few Viennese patients apply to all personalities.

Psychologists generally do not view the case study method as a source of conclusive evidence because it does not permit a researcher to alter conditions and see how different circumstances affect behavior. This method, however, can produce interesting, even vital, information when conducted appropriately (Yin, 1989). Indeed, it may be the only research tool available to study the effects of unique events, such as hijackings, accidents, and natural disasters. Much of neuropsychology, to pick but one field, is based on information deduced from clever case studies of brain-damaged people, although usually other techniques (such as experiments on the patients) are employed, too (Caramazza, 1986; McCloskey, 1993).

Interviews.   Researchers can gather information about people's behaviors, attitudes, and circumstances by asking direct questions. In an **interview,** a person responds to a series of questions that usually require brief objective responses. An interview can be conducted by a specially trained interviewer who provides the questions in as neutral a manner as possible, or it can be administered as a questionnaire. Of course, an interview can also be conducted as part of the case study approach.

In a large-scale British study, Belson (1978) interviewed 1,500 adolescent boys in London, England. The interview was extensive, and Belson was able to obtain much information about the boys' patterns of watching television and their aggressiveness. The data were analyzed by separating the boys into two groups—those who viewed a lot of violence on television and those who watched relatively little. Belson then examined how aggressive the two groups were and found an association between the two measures: The boys who watched more violence on television were more aggressive. In addition, their violent behavior tended to be more serious than that of the group that watched less violent television.

Does this pattern indicate that watching violence on television causes boys to be more aggressive? Belson (1978) concluded from his own analysis and other data that the answer is yes. However, this conclusion can be questioned. For one thing, the sheer amount of television watching is also positively linked to aggressiveness, which means that the amount of violence on TV may not have been the critical factor in determining aggression (Freedman, 1984). Another possibility is that the causal relation is actually the reverse: Children who are more aggressive (because of parental influence or other factors) may enjoy watching more violence on TV.

Although interviews, like case studies, help to describe behavior, they rarely allow researchers to pinpoint causes for the behavior. Also, they can be distorted by the types of questions asked, especially about undesirable behaviors (such as committing crimes) or about personal matters (such as sexual behavior).

Surveys.   A **survey** is a sampling of opinions of a small proportion of a population from which a researcher then draws conclusions about the entire population. A survey can be used to measure opinions about politicians, television shows, confidence in the economy, and many other issues. The critical factor in survey research is to obtain an unbiased sample to ensure accurate generalizations about the population. A famous blunder in survey research was the prediction of the 1936 presidential election from a poll taken by *Literary Digest* magazine. The *Literary Digest* polled its readers and concluded that Alf Landon would beat Franklin D. Roosevelt in a landslide. But the magazine's readership numbered more Republicans than Democrats, so the sample in the survey was not representative of the general population. Roosevelt won handily. The same situation arose 12 years later when virtually all public-opinion polls predicted that Thomas Dewey would beat Harry Truman in the 1948 elec-

Biased polls predicted that Dewey would defeat Truman in the 1948 presidential election. When the vote was still close late on the election night, some newspapers even went to press proclaiming Dewey's victory. Here Truman holds up one paper's blooper headline the day after the victory.

tion. These polls were based on random samples, but the samples were taken from telephone directories and the survey done by telephone. In 1948, household telephones were not as common as they are today, so the pollsters tapped opinions of only the more affluent part of the electorate. The voting was quite close, and some newspapers even went to press with headlines proclaiming Dewey's victory. However, when the final vote was tallied, Truman won, to the surprise of the pollsters.

Today, survey researchers employ sophisticated techniques to make sure that the chosen samples are representative of the population at large. Any time researchers make generalizations about a population from a sample, however, there is some chance of error. Fortunately, the chances of error in a survey can be estimated and often are reported. You have probably heard statements such as, "In our survey of candidates, we show Sebatian Weisdorf leading Larry Jacoby with 50 percent of voters favoring Weisdorf, 40 percent favoring Jacoby, and 10 percent undecided. However, there is a 6 percent margin of error with these numbers." This means that the percentage of people favoring Weisdorf may vary from 44 percent to 56 percent, and 34 percent to 46 percent for Jacoby. These numbers indicate the small chance that more voters actually prefer Jacoby to Weisdorf. However, this outcome is statistically unlikely.

Surveys can help describe various psychological phenomena by obtaining the answers to pertinent questions: What percentage of young adults visit a psychologist or other mental health worker? What percentage of new mothers breast-feed their babies? What percentage of college students have engaged in premarital sex? What percentage of people over age 65 have been victims of crime in the last 12 months? As with interviews, one potential drawback in survey research is the potential lack of honesty and forthrightness on the part of the respondents. For instance, people may refuse to answer questions about sensitive behaviors such as sex and crime or they may provide answers that are socially acceptable but not necessarily true.

Although no large-scale survey of the American population has assessed the relation between watching violence on television and aggressive behavior, Belson's (1978) interview study leads to the confident prediction that the two factors are related. Even so, survey research does not tell researchers whether watching violent TV *causes* aggression.

Psychological Tests. Psychologists have developed numerous paper-and-pencil **psychological tests** to measure and describe people's capabilities, characteristics, and interests. Chief among these are tests that measure mental abilities (intelligence tests) and personality characteristics. (These are reviewed in Chapters 11 and 14.) Other tests are designed to measure mental disorders, vocational interests, and creativity. You are no doubt familiar with the Scholastic Assessment Test (SAT), which many colleges and universities require for admittance.

Psychological tests provide useful information for describing and classifying people and for predicting behavior. And because they measure individual differences among people, they frequently reveal a dimension that other research tools cannot provide. For example, if researchers had measured intelligence in Belson's interview study, then they could have considered the question of whether intelligence affects the relation between watching violent TV and aggression. Perhaps watching violence on TV is not associated with aggressiveness in more intelligent individuals. Or maybe watching violence on TV makes intelligent people *less* aggressive.

A researcher's choice of naturalistic observation, case studies, psychological tests, interviews, or survey research depends on the circumstances and goals of the research.

Although such techniques provide useful information, descriptive research is usually considered only a first step. Rarely does detailed description permit a researcher to predict the behavior or explain why it occurs. The correlational technique, described in the next section, is still descriptive but permits researchers to relate variables and make predictions.

Correlational Research.   One way to investigate a phenomenon is to study a number of cases, note the characteristics of each case, and determine whether the characteristics are related. For example, height and weight tend to go together. Moreover, height and weight generally go together in the same direction. That is, taller people usually weigh more than shorter people. This type of observation is said to be correlational, and the relationship between the two sets of measures is a **correlation.** In a correlational analysis, a researcher wants to determine if two measures, or variables, are related. A **variable** is any characteristic that can change and that can be measured or manipulated. Height and weight are variables. The correlational approach is a descriptive technique in that two variables existing in nature are related to each other. (The researcher doesn't attempt to manipulate one of the variables to see its effect on the other, as in experimental research.)

A *correlation coefficient*—a term we use many times in this book— is a statistical measure of the relation between two variables. It can range from +1.00 through 0 to −1.00. A *positive correlation* occurs when two variables change together in the same direction. For example, height and weight tend to be positively correlated (taller people are heavier), so the correlation coefficient for height and weight will be greater than 0. A correlation near 0 indicates that the two variables are not related. For example, weight and intelligence are not correlated. If measures of weight and intelligence were taken from a large group of people, there would be no systematic relation between the two measures, and the correlation coefficient would be near 0. A *negative correlation* means that as one variable increases, the other decreases. For example, there is a negative correlation between frequency of smoking and life span. The more a person smokes, the shorter the life expectancy. (Correlations are discussed more fully in Appendix A, which serves as an introduction to the use of statistics in psychology.)

Children watch great amounts of violence on television. The average adolescent has seen about 18,000 murders on TV.

Let's consider two additional correlations to illustrate both their usefulness and their drawbacks. First, some studies show that cigarette smoking is positively correlated with developing lung cancer. That is, the more cigarettes you smoke, the more likely you are to develop lung cancer. Another positive correlation exists between watching violent television programs and measures of aggression (such as the tendency for schoolchildren to fight or for adults to commit crimes). The correlation is far from perfect in both cases. Some people smoke heavily and never develop lung cancer, and some people view much violence on television and never fight or commit crimes. Still, the correlation permits us to make predictions. Therefore, all else being equal, we can predict that a heavy smoker will be more likely to develop lung cancer than a non-smoker. Similarly, a child who sees much violence on television is more likely to fight with peers. Correlations are most useful for making predictions about behaviors and the stronger the correlation (the nearer to +1.00 or −1.00), the better the prediction.

It is tempting to conclude from correlational studies that smoking causes lung cancer and watching television violence causes aggression. However, both of these conclusions are unwarranted. Always remember that *correlation does not indicate causation*. For example, children who are already aggressive may prefer to watch violence on television. Thus, some other factor may cause both the children's aggressiveness and the desire to watch violent television programs. As for smoking, perhaps physiological factors that make smoking pleasant for some people are also related to the still-mysterious causes of lung cancer. The danger of correlational research is that we can arrive at misleading conclusions by ignoring other factors. Further research is necessary to pin down a cause-and-effect relationship. (For the two examples used here, however, other research does support the causal link between smoking and lung cancer and between watching violence on TV and aggression.)

To summarize, correlational analyses provide information about the relation between two variables but cannot reveal conclusively the reasons for the relation. This problem, called **confounding,** develops when a researcher cannot be sure which of two factors caused some result because they varied together. The factors are said to be *confounded*. In the case of the simple correlation between a preference for watching violence on TV and aggressiveness, it could be that: (a) watching violence on TV tends to increase aggressiveness, (b) aggressive people like to watch violent TV programs, or (c) a third factor (such as type of parental upbringing) causes both. The potential for confounding is always present in correlational research. Sometimes it can be overcome by statistical procedures that take other factors into account; in other cases, researchers can obtain a pattern of correlations over time that permits better causal statements. However, correlational research rarely can rule out the possible causal role of other factors. Experimental research is generally preferred to correlational research, because the potential for confounding is greatly reduced.

EXPERIMENTAL RESEARCH

In correlational research a researcher observes relations between variables that occur naturally. In experimental research, an investigator creates a situation that allows for controlled observation. The essence of the *experimental method* is to vary some aspect of a situation, control all others, and then observe the effects of the variation on the behavior of interest. For example, to determine the effects of watching violent TV on aggression, a researcher would show equivalent groups of children

Are children more prone to violent behavior after viewing violence?

either violent or neutral TV programs and then measure how aggressively they behave later.

The simplest case of experimental research involves an *experimental condition* and a *control condition*. The experimental condition contains the variable of interest (watching violent TV); the control condition does not, but is included for comparison. The two conditions are arranged as similarly as possible except for the one critical factor of interest. For example, imagine that a researcher has identified two important characteristics of people in the control condition of a study on the effects of violent TV. One factor might be the gender of the subjects and the other factor their age (fifth or sixth graders). If the researcher is interested in the effects of a critical variable, such as watching violent TV, the experimental and control groups would be arranged to have equal numbers of boys and girls and fifth- and sixth-graders; but in the experimental condition three important factors exist, (age, gender, and watching violent TV), whereas in the control condition, there are only two (age and gender). In comparing the effects of the experimental and control conditions, the researcher can see what effect the critical factor (watching violent TV) has on behavior. The two other factors have been held constant in the two conditions, so the conditions differ only in the factor of interest. This is the logic of the experimental method.

An important component of experimental logic is the random assignment of research participants to the experimental and control conditions to avoid confounded variables. In random assignment, subjects are equally likely to be placed in each condition, thus eliminating bias. For example, suppose boys were assigned to the experimental condition and girls to the control. If a difference was found between the two conditions, the researcher would not know whether the difference was due to the variable of interest or the subjects' gender or both. The gender variable would be confounded with the experimental variable.

Now let's consider a frequently cited experiment by Robert Liebert and Robert Baron (1972) designed to determine the effects of television violence on children's behavior. This experiment serves to illustrate many points about experimental research. An overview of the stages of research (both descriptive and experimental) is presented in Figure 1.3.

The First Steps.   Research is often sparked by casual observations. It may also be stimulated by prior research, conversations with friends or colleagues, or some other source. The trick to formulating a research problem from a casual observation is to take commonplace examples and see what general principle or causal factor is at work.

For most problems in psychology, casual observation is not enough to prompt an original investigation, because other researchers may have already investigated the problem of interest. Thus, a researcher must become familiar with prior research on the problem. But it is important to become familiar with the literature without becoming biased or limited by it.

When Liebert and Baron conducted their experiment, previous research indicated that violent TV programs might cause aggressive behavior later. However, most prior work was marked by three features that Liebert and Baron believed needed correction. First, most prior work was with adults, and the authors wanted to know if children would show similar effects because they watch so much television. Second, most prior work utilized children's films specially created for the experiments, and the authors wanted to observe the influence of actual television programming. Third, the children in prior studies were all too often directed to watch the film; Liebert and Baron wanted a more natural setting, where the children would be exposed to a TV show without necessarily having to watch it.

Generating a Hypothesis.   From the initial observations that spark research, a researcher generates a theory or hypothesis that can be translated into an experiment. Theories and hypotheses were mentioned earlier in the chapter but need to be explained in more detail here. A **theory** is a set of statements proposing concepts and relationships to explain a phenomenon. The statements of a theory are explicit and fairly formal. Famous scientific theories include Einstein's theory of relativity and Darwin's theory of evolution by natural selection.

A *hypothesis* is a less formal conjecture put forward to explain some facts and predict others. The hypothesis may be developed from a more formal theory or may simply be a hunch. Experiments are created to test hypotheses. A scientific hypothesis is useful only if it can be tested to produce observable results that bear on its truth or falsity.

FIGURE 1.3
Stages in the Research Process

Research often proceeds from some initial observations that arouse curiosity to more systematic experimental inquiry.

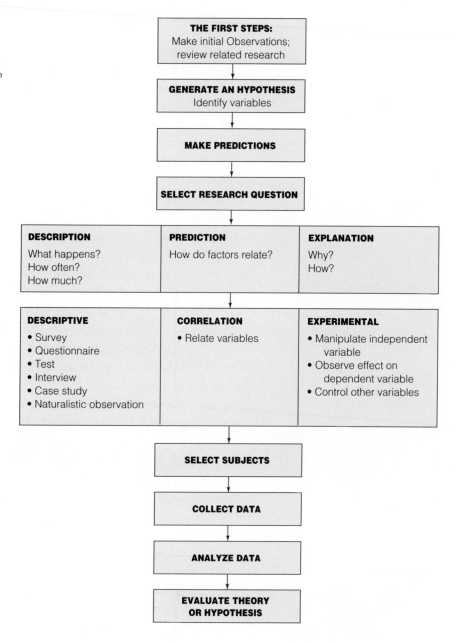

Most research about the effects of television on behavior has been conducted within the general framework of *social learning theory*, which maintains that people learn from and imitate the behavior of others (Bandura, 1965, 1977). The specific hypothesis that Liebert and Baron tested is straightforward: If children watch violent television shows, then they should be more aggressive.

Making Predictions. The next stage in the scientific process is to predict the results of the experiment. This step may be difficult if the theory is complex and the forecast not obvious. Furthermore, specific predictions may require further assumptions and a chain of reasoning. However, in the case of the effects of violent television on behavior, the prediction is straightforward: Liebert and Baron predicted that if children viewed violent behavior on television, they later would be more aggressive than an equivalent group of children who did not view violent television.

Creating an Experiment. Recall that the simplest type of experiment involves two conditions, an experimental condition and a control condition, that are similar in all respects except for the variable of interest. However, the actual creation of any experiment involves many choices that may affect its outcome. Consider some of the questions that must be answered before conducting an experiment like Liebert and Baron's. How old should the children be? Should they all be the same age or different ages? What kind of violent TV show should be used, and should more than one be used? How long should the show last? What should children in the control condition do—watch no TV or watch a different type of show? How should aggressive behavior be measured? This list can go on indefinitely, but the critical point is that the creation of any experiment involves many choices that may affect its outcome.

Liebert and Baron chose to have as their subjects children ranging in age from 5 to 9. All the children were from either Yellow Springs or Xenia, Ohio, near the Fels Research Institute, where the experiment was conducted. A total of 136 children were tested (with the permission of their parents)—68 boys and 68 girls. Half the subjects served in an experimental condition (viewing a segment from a violent TV show) and half served in a control condition (viewing a segment from a nonviolent show).

When each child and parent appeared at the laboratory, they were greeted by one of the researchers. After an initial phase in which the experiment was explained to the parent and permission was requested, the child was escorted to a waiting room. The experimenter suggested that the child watch TV for a few minutes until the experimenter was ready. If the child was in the experimental group, he or she saw a taped segment beginning with two commercials and a 3½-minute segment from "The Untouchables" that had a simple story line. It included two fist-fighting scenes, a chase, a knifing, and two shootings. If the child was in the control group, then he or she saw the commercials followed by an interesting and active sports scene (involving hurdle races and a high jump) for the critical 3½-minute period. Both tapes ended with a commercial for automobile tires.

When the tape ended, the experimenter returned and took the child to another room. The child sat in front of a gray metallic box that had a white light in the center and two buttons below it. A green button was labeled *help* and a red button *hurt*. The child was told that the box was hooked up to a game played in the next room by another child. (Wires led through the wall from the box.) The experimenter explained

Bungee jumping is exciting, but dangerous. Why do you think people do it? What research methods might be useful in studying this behavior and in testing your idea about why people jump?

that when the white light appeared, the other child was starting to play the game. The child seated before the box was told that he or she could make the game easier for the other child by pushing the green button. On the other hand, he or she could make the game more difficult by pushing the red button. The child also was told that the longer the button was pushed, the more it would help or hurt the other child. The purpose of this phase of the experiment was to measure aggression. If the child held the *hurt* button down, this would reflect aggression. Notice, however, that the child did have an alternative response (he or she could help).

In the final phase of the experiment, the child was taken to a play room that contained some toys, including two "aggressive" toys (a gun and a knife). The child was observed through a one-way mirror and scored for aggressive responses (playing with the gun or knife or hitting a doll). The experiment ended after the play session.

Collecting and Analyzing the Data.   The next step in the research process is to test the subjects, collect the data, and analyze the data using statistics. In the Liebert and Baron experiment, each session lasted about an hour, and additional time was required to set up the experiment, contact the children's parents, and collect the data. (Keep in mind that the 136 children tested in the experimental and control conditions were treated identically except for the content of the 3½-minute segment.)

The primary measure of aggression was the total amount of time each child pushed the red *hurt* button when the white light appeared. (The light came on 20 times for each child tested, so each child had 20 opportunities to hurt or help another child.) The mean (average) total duration of the hurt response is displayed in Figure 1.4 for the boys and girls in the two conditions. The results reveal that both boys and girls who viewed the violent film pushed the *hurt* button longer than those who saw the nonviolent sports show. (Statistical analyses showed that it was highly unlikely that differences this large would occur by chance.)

Evaluating the Hypothesis and Theory.   After the data have been collected and evaluated statistically (see Appendix A for more on this phase of research), researchers relate the findings to their initial predictions. Obviously, researchers are pleased when their experimental results support their hypotheses and theories; but if experimental results do not support the theories, researchers should not despair. If a theory's prediction is consistently disconfirmed by results from several experiments, then an important discovery has been made. The theory is wrong, at least in certain ways, and needs to be replaced by a more satisfactory theory. Finding unexpected (unpredicted) results advances the field by making researchers modify or surrender incorrect theories and develop new ones. These features of generating hypotheses, testing them empirically, and replacing disconfirmed ideas by better ones distinguish science from other inquiries.

In the case of Liebert and Baron's research, the results were consistent with the hypothesis that children who watch violent programs will be more aggressive, when given the appropriate opportunity, than children who do not watch violent TV programs. When the results from the "free play" period were analyzed, they tended to lead to the same conclusion. Children (especially young boys) who had seen the violent segment tended to play more aggressively. Thus, the data from the experiment supported social learning theory: children seemed to learn from observing the behavior of others on TV and changed their behavior accordingly.

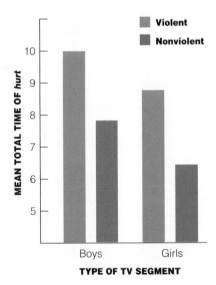

FIGURE 1.4
Results of Liebert & Baron (1972)

Both boys and girls pushed the *hurt* button longer after watching a violent TV scene than after watching a nonviolent (sports) scene.

SOURCE: Liebert & Bacon, 1972. Table 1, p. 472.

Types of Variables. It is time to become familiar with three important variables found in most experiments: *independent, dependent,* and *control variables*. Variables, you will recall, are characteristics of a situation that can be manipulated or measured.

Independent variables are those that a researcher manipulates during an experiment to discover their effects on behavior. In the experiment just described, the independent variable was the type of TV segment that the children watched (violent or nonviolent).

Dependent variables are those that an experimenter measures as part of the experiment. They are so named because what they show typically *depends* on the level of the independent variable. The dependent variables in the Liebert and Bacon experiment were the total time the children pushed the *hurt* button when the white light appeared and the amount of aggressive behavior they displayed in the free-play situation.

Control variables are aspects of an experiment held constant by the experimenter. Liebert and Baron controlled the amount of TV the children saw and the particular experimenter testing the children (the same woman in all cases). In addition, they randomly assigned subjects to the experimental and control conditions so that, on average, each condition would have roughly the same kind of subjects. By controlling or randomly assigning all variables except the independent variable, an experimenter can be reasonably certain that the observed effect is due to the independent variable rather than some confounded variable. Once again, this control is the primary reason that experiments are the preferred method of psychological research. Other factors are held constant and do not vary with the independent variables to confound the outcome of the research. In naturalistic observation or correlational research, such confoundings cannot be ruled out.

Independent variables, then, are those that are manipulated; dependent variables are those that are measured; and control variables are those that are held constant. The Liebert and Baron experiment involved one independent variable (type of TV segment, violent or nonviolent) and two dependent variables (total time the *hurt* button was pushed and amount of aggressive play). Because manipulation of the independent variable had an effect on the dependent variables (with other variables controlled), we conclude that the independent variable led to, or caused, the change in the dependent variables. Therefore, we also conclude that in this experiment, watching violent TV programming heightened aggression. Keep in mind, however, that there are some limitations on this claim. Outside the lab, other causes of aggression exist, and these may be more powerful than watching violence on TV. Therefore, the Liebert and Baron experiment shows only that watching violent TV can increase aggressiveness; it does not show that watching TV is the sole, or even the most important, cause of aggressiveness or even that watching violent TV will cause aggression in all situations.

The Liebert and Baron experiment involved another type of variable called a subject variable. **Subject variables** denote individual differences among people (such as height, intelligence, age, and personality). Subject variables are like independent variables, in that their effect on the dependent variable is examined. However, unlike independent variables, they cannot be manipulated. Obviously, Liebert and Bacon could not randomly assign the children in their experiment to be male or female. Instead, they assigned an equal number of boys and girls to each group. In general, the experimenter tries to match the subjects in the two groups on relevant subject variables (such as age and education).

Subject variables are often of great interest to psychologists, especially those who study individual differences. Important subject variables for humans include gender, age, race, and personality type (e.g., introverted versus extroverted). Because these characteristics cannot be randomly assigned as with true independent variables, the possibility of confounded factors is more likely than with true independent variables. For example, if males were found to be more aggressive than females, we might erroneously conclude that gender played a crucial role in aggression. However, gender is also confounded with body size. It may be that larger people of either sex are more aggressive.

The technical name for Liebert and Baron's experimental design is a *multifactor experiment* because it includes both experimental treatment (violent or nonviolent TV segments) and gender as variables (or factors). Many experiments can be extended to include several variables. Such multifactor experiments are useful because they may provide more information than single-factor experiments. For example, they can show whether the effect of one variable (watching violent or nonviolent TV) generalizes over another factor (whether the effect is the same for boys and girls). Liebert and Baron showed roughly equal effects of watching violent TV for children of both sexes, although boys were slightly more aggressive overall.

Two Common Criticisms of Experimental Research.   The Liebert and Baron experiment is often cited as a good example of experimental research on the effects of violent TV on behavior, but it and similar experiments have been criticized, too. Consider two common criticisms often directed at experimental research.

1.   *This experiment simply confirms common sense. After all, everyone knows that watching violence on TV is bad.* Although many people believe that watching violence on TV is bad, scientific research like Liebert and Baron's confirms the belief. Indeed, casual observation about the world often produces faulty answers. For example, the earth is not flat even though it appears that way, and the sun does not revolve about the earth as does the moon. People believed both of these ideas for centuries, however, because of direct observation. In contrast to direct observation, systematic research can uncover erroneous beliefs and modify them: Seeing should not always lead to believing (recall Figure 1.1). Indeed, not everyone believes that the link between violent TV and aggressive behavior is obvious. As we shall soon see, one researcher (Freedman 1984, 1986) argues that the case made for the link by current research is not convincing.

2.   *Laboratory research like the study by Liebert and Baron (1972) is artificial. After all, in real life children are not asked to push a button to 'hurt' another child playing a game.* While this is certainly true, the conclusion that such laboratory research should not be conducted, or cannot be informative, is not. "Real life" involves complex situations, and the purpose of studying behavior in a laboratory is to distill the behavior of interest to its essential characteristics. Irrelevant factors are stripped away or controlled so that the critical factors can be manipulated and their effects on behavior observed. Of course, what an experimenter regards as irrelevant and strips away may later turn out to be critical. Here again we see that any experiment involves a set of choices. For example, perhaps Liebert and Baron would not have found that watching violent TV increased aggressiveness if they had used a different TV program or a different response besides pushing a *hurt* button. A single experiment rarely settles

The *Power Rangers* show has been criticized as encouraging violent behavior in the children who watch it.

any issue; rather, many studies with varying methods are needed to provide a more complete understanding of the phenomenon.

CONVERGING EVIDENCE AND SCIENTIFIC PROGRESS

Students new to psychology may become dismayed by the slow pace of scientific work. Each of the research methods that we reviewed has advantages and drawbacks. Case studies, interviews, surveys, and naturalistic observation are descriptive; they tell what happened with some accuracy, but rarely how or why. Correlational research informs about relations between variables and permits predictions of one variable based on knowing the level of another variable. Usually, however, correlational research cannot answer questions about cause and effect because of the potential of confounded factors. Laboratory experiments permit assessments of causation but run the risk of omitting important variables from an experiment. Field experiments overcome the problem of artificiality, but are difficult, raise ethical questions, and may lead to a loss of control over the situation, thus jeopardizing internal validity. How, you may wonder, is any progress ever possible? Well, don't despair. The outlook for a science of psychology is not really bleak at all.

No single research method or piece of research can give all the answers, and researchers must consider the possible limitations and alternative interpretations to any research finding. However, when many different studies using different methods and procedures point to the same conclusion, we can be fairly confident in making causal conclusions.

On any important question, such as whether watching violent TV causes an increase in aggressiveness, dozens and possibly hundreds of studies are conducted. Although any study taken by itself will have flaws and limitations, when results from numerous studies are combined, a relatively consistent picture will emerge (Rosenthal, 1984). In the case of the effects of violent television on behavior, most experts agree that watching violent TV programming increases aggressiveness (e.g., Friedrich-Cofer & Huston, 1986; Wood, Wong, & Chachere, 1991). Critics of this conclusion still exist (e.g., Freedman, 1986), and most researchers agree that the effect of watching violent TV is not overpowering. Still, results from case studies, interviews, correlational studies, laboratory experiments, and field experiments all point in the same direction: watching violent TV leads to more aggressive behavior.

The popular view of science is that it progresses by great leaps, as in the cases of Copernicus, Newton, Darwin, and Einstein. Although such leaps do occur, progress in most fields is better characterized as a shuffle (two steps forward, one step back) than a leap. The so-called critical experiment that changes the direction of a whole scientific field is rare—and usually only apparent long after the fact. But we feel confident that psychology and other scientific fields are making progress.

If you doubt this claim about progress, try the following experiment: Go to your library and find the section where the general psychology texts are kept. Choose a few books, each from a different era, (say, 1920, 1950, and 1970). Next, select a topic (e.g., hunger and eating, remembering, or intelligence) and see what each text says about the chosen topic. Then compare these treatments with the one in this text. We confidently predict that you will find greater knowledge and understanding about each topic over the years. Sometimes, ideas that seemed so plausible and well supported in 1920 are viewed as hopelessly wrong now, thanks to an additional 75 years of evidence. True, in another 75 years (or, if we are lucky, in much less time), the ideas and views in this text may also be replaced. But that very fact illustrates the slow but steady progress we make in psychology. Evidence gradually converges from many pieces of research, all probing the unknown in slightly different ways, to replace incomplete hypotheses and theories with more accurate ones.

Research Issues in Psychology

Several important topics in psychological research cut across the various research methods. We consider the issues of validity of research, laboratory and field research.

INTERNAL AND EXTERNAL VALIDITY

Research is said to have **internal validity** if the conclusion drawn about the cause-and-effect relation between variables is sound. Is the researcher justified to conclude that the independent variable affected the dependent variable? The main reason for doubting the internal validity of research is that some other variable might have been confounded with the independent variable of interest.

In general, case studies and correlational studies lack internal validity because of the potential for confounded variables. Experimental methods foster greater internal validity because they hold constant these other variables (which then become control variables) to make the effects of the independent variable clearer.

External validity refers to the generalizability of findings beyond the research setting, which we touched on in our discussion of the effects of TV violence. Over what range of conditions does a conclusion remain valid? Does it generalize to other populations? (Rats to humans? Males to females? Caucasians to Asians?) Does it apply to different measures of behavior? Does it apply to different ways of varying the independent variable? A researcher can deprive an animal of food for different numbers of hours or reduce its weight to various percentages of its normal body weight (first to 95 percent, then to 90 percent, and so on). Will these two ways of varying hunger—hours of deprivation and percentage of body weight—affect behavior identically? Will findings of one study generalize to the other method? These are all questions of external validity. And what about the Liebert and Baron experiment? Do their findings hold in more natural situations?

There is only one way to determine the external validity of research findings: to perform more research to see if the conclusions generalize (Yuille, 1993). This takes us to the issue of laboratory and field research.

LABORATORY AND FIELD RESEARCH

Much experimental research in psychology is done in the laboratory, where researchers can control certain aspects of a given natural behavior. In the Liebert and Baron experiment, researchers tried to create, in a laboratory situation, the "real-world" conditions of watching a violent TV program. If the conclusion about watching violence on television had not been confirmed in the laboratory, would this mean that the phenomenon did not exist or simply that the artificial laboratory conditions failed to capture the critical variables? Some psychologists (and probably many students) believe that psychological research too often has been artificial (Neisser, 1976). The contention is that psychologists often overemphasize experimental control and waste time and effort studying artificial laboratory situations. In other words, laboratory situations may lack external validity.

One way to try to maximize both internal and external validity is to conduct controlled research in the *field*—that is, in natural settings. In field research, investigators attempt to add some control to the natural situation and then vary certain factors to see how they affect behavior. While interesting findings may be obtained, there are also pitfalls to this method. Ethical problems arise when we experiment with people who have not given their permission to be studied. Moreover, the degree of control in natural situations is usually limited; thus, there is always the possibility of confounding from uncontrolled variables, which in turn reduces internal validity.

Freedman (1984) has criticized laboratory research on the effects of TV violence on aggression as lacking in external validity. For instance, he regards measures of aggression such as pushing buttons or hitting dolls as mere analogues of actual aggression. Furthermore, the violent films were often not actual TV shows, but ones created for the experiment. Finally, aggression may have been seen as an acceptable response in these experiments (by instructing the subjects to "Push the red button if you want to hurt the child in the next room").

Several investigators have conducted field experiments on the effects of viewing media violence. For example, Parke and his colleagues (1977) carried out field experiments with male juvenile delinquents living in small-group cottages in minimum-security institutions in Belgium and the United States. The boys' normal rate of aggressive behavior was measured in three categories: physical threats (such as fist waving), verbal aggression (taunting and cursing), and assault (hitting, choking, or kicking). In one study, a three-week baseline rate of aggression was established for each boy: How aggressive was he for this period? Then the boys in one cottage were exposed over a one-week period to a diet of five violent movies (the experimental condition). The boys in a second cottage saw five nonviolent films (the control condition). Those who had viewed the violent movies showed significant increases in aggressive behavior over their original rate in most categories of aggression. Those in the control group showed no similar tendencies.

Because it maximizes external validity, more researchers are turning to field research. Yet, in so doing, they must often sacrifice the very reason for conducting experiments in the first place—control over conditions and hence internal validity.

Developmental psychologists study infants perceptual abilities, as well as other aspects of cognitive development such as memory and language.

Laboratory research, which permits this control, is critically important (Banaji & Crowder, 1989; Mook, 1983). It has served other sciences well, and there seems little reason the same cannot be true in psychology. For example, physicists have discovered interesting properties of matter from studying its behavior in a vacuum, yet no natural vacuums exist on our planet. When a laboratory analogue of some phenomenon is created, it is usually desirable to mimic aspects of the naturally occurring situation as closely as possible. But the main reason for laboratory research is to test causal hypotheses about the relationship between variables (what effect does the independent variable have on the control variable?) rather than establish the generality (external validity) of this relationship (does it occur in the same way in natural settings?) (Berkowitz & Donnerstein, 1982).

BASIC AND APPLIED RESEARCH

A distinction is often made between applied and basic research. **Applied research** aims at solving a practical problem; **basic research** is done to discover basic facts about a phenomenon. The distinction may be somewhat arbitrary, and different research projects may have varying degrees of both basic and applied research.

It is easy to understand why people want to solve practical problems, and scientists often have trouble convincing people that basic research deserves just as much attention and support. Why do scientists spend their time working on problems whose solutions seem unlikely to provide immediate practical benefit? The obvious answer, of course, is the desire to satisfy intellectual curiosity, to know how and why a phenomenon occurs. But the more subtle reason to favor basic research is that it often leads to more practical benefits in the long run. Basic research is concerned with understanding the general principles that govern some phenomenon; a great number of practical applications may flow from this knowledge. While applied research may answer some specific question, it may not provide the general knowledge to solve other problems. However, even applied research opens up new areas and provides basic understanding of phenomena (Garner, 1972). For example, interest in the problems that air-traffic controllers face in simultaneously monitoring information from different sources led psychologists to basic research on divided attention, a topic discussed in Chapter 5.

Psychologists who study attention may discover basic principles that will help in design of environments where people must monitor many sources of information like these air traffic controlers.

Psychologists who work in areas such as psychobiology and cognitive psychology tend to concentrate on basic research, whereas clinical, industrial, and school psychologists usually do applied research. Probably too much has been made of the distinction between basic and applied research. Good basic research often pays dividends in application. Conversely, good applied research may serve to highlight basic principles of behavior.

ETHICS IN RESEARCH

Psychologists often encounter thorny ethical issues. The American Psychological Association (1981) has published a manual providing guidance on issues of research ethics and other matters. The APA's *Ethical Principles of Psychologists and Code of Conduct* was revised in 1992. It covers ethics both of research and of clinical practice; we consider research ethics here.

Use of Humans in Research. The ethical principles of the APA encourage researchers to treat human participants in a considerate manner. The *informed consent* of participants is required, meaning that the potential subjects must agree to participate after being told the general conditions of the experiment. Extremely stressful research procedures are forbidden, and people are given the right to leave the situation if they feel uncomfortable. Any stress must be brief and mild, and it must be offset by gains in knowledge that should come from the research.

Most psychologists take elaborate safeguards to ensure that their research is conducted within accepted ethical standards. After an experiment, there is usually a debriefing session during which participants are told the purpose of the research and what has been learned.

In most colleges and universities, committees ensure that research conforms with ethical standards. Because many students reading this book will be asked to participate in research as part of a course requirement or for extra credit, you should be assured that any such research will have been approved by an ethical standards committee.

Consider once more the Liebert and Baron experiment. Because the children were potentially exposed to harm, Liebert and Baron followed careful procedures to mini-

A psychologist can unobtrusively observe this child through a one-way mirror.

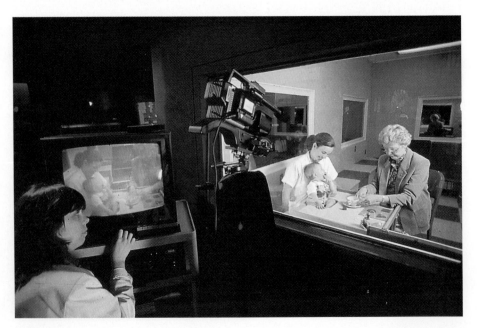

mize that possibility. When the parents and children arrived, one of the researchers explained the purpose and procedures of the experiment to the parents before the experiment began. Parents signed an "informed consent" statement if they agreed to permit their children to participate in the experiment. (All parents agreed.) The experimenter also watched the children carefully and excused any who became upset during the procedure. (Nine of the younger children were excused because they cried or did not want to be separated from their mothers.)

Use of Nonhuman Animals in Research. Much of the research in psychology is conducted with animals other than humans. Students sometimes find this surprising and disheartening. Isn't the goal of psychology to understand the behavior of humans? While most psychologists might answer yes, others are interested in the psychology of animals in its own right, hoping to answer some of the fascinating questions of animal behavior. How do homing pigeons find their way home? Why is it so hard to poison rats? How do wolves and other animals establish social hierarchies? Other psychologists study the behavior of so-called lower animals with the hope of finding principles that will generalize to the behavior of humans. Many types of research, such as those requiring brain surgery, cannot be done with humans for ethical or practical reasons.

The difficulty in applying research done with one species to another species, including humans, is that of *generality of results*. How do investigators know that findings derived from one species will generalize to another? Researchers usually assume that animal research can provide clues for human behavior, and they abandon this assumption only when forced to by contrary evidence. The problem of whether results from animal research should apply to humans is not, of course, unique to psychology. For example, if some substance (e.g., saccharin) is shown to cause cancer in laboratory mice, should the government ban the item from supermarket shelves? Clearly, these are difficult questions to answer. However, as you will see later in this text, many findings from research on animals do indeed apply directly to humans.

Just as there are ethical guidelines for research with humans, so, too, have ethical standards been established for research with animals, with university and government committees approving and overseeing animal experiments. In general, animals must be housed in clean environments and suffer no unnecessary pain or discomfort during experiments. Of course, many experiments being carried out with animals would not be possible with humans, and this is true in both psychological research and biological (veterinary or medical) research. In recent years, animal rights groups have protested many types of animal research and uncovered some apparent abuses. However, most research is conducted within the ethical standards established for the care and maintenance of laboratory animals.

Work with animals carries great benefits both for humans and for the treatment of animals in veterinary settings. Neal Miller (1985) has described many of the benefits to humans that have grown out of basic research with animals. These include rehabilitation of neuromuscular disorders; discovery and testing of drugs for the treatment of anxiety, psychoses, and Parkinson's disease; knowledge about drug addiction; and many aspects of psychotherapy and behavioral medicine. The ethical issues of experimenting on animals are difficult ones, but most psychologists believe that such research is permissible for its potential benefits, so long as it is conducted within the established ethical guidelines.

"For crying out loud, gentlemen! That's us! Someone's installed the one-way mirror in backward!"

THE FAR SIDE, by Gary Larson. Copyright Universal Press Syndicate. Reprinted with permission. All rights reserved.

Professional Roles in Psychology

We have briefly described the history of psychology and some types of research psychologists conduct, but what do psychologists actually do? You are probably most familiar with the image of psychologists as professionals who help people solve their problems—certainly a major focus of clinical and counseling psychologists. But the range of activities in psychology is much greater. Psychologists teach and conduct research in colleges and universities. They also work in industry to conduct research and tackle practical problems. The American Psychological Association (APA) counts some 132,000 members (as of 1995). To get a feel for the wide variety of issues that interest psychologists, review the 51 divisions of the APA shown in Table 1.1.

TABLE 1.1
American Psychological Association Divisions. (There are no Divisions 4 and 11.)

Division 1: General Psychology	Division 27: Community Psychology
Division 2: Teaching of Psychology	Division 28: Psychopharmacology
Division 3: Experimental Psychology	Division 29: Psychotherapy
Division 5: Evaluation, Measurement & Statistics	Division 30: Psychological Hypnosis
Division 6: Behavioral Neuroscience & Comparative Psychology	Division 31: State Psychological Association Affairs
Division 7: Developmental Psychology	Division 32: Humanistic Psychology
Division 8: Society for Personality & Social Psychology	Division 33: Mental Retardation & Developmental Disabilities
Division 9: The Society for the Psychological Study of Social Issues (SPSSI)	Division 34: Population & Environmental Psychology
Division 10: Psychology & the Arts	Division 35: Psychology of Women
Division 12: Clinical Psychology	Division 36: Psychology of Religion
Division 13: Consulting Psychology	Division 37: Child, Youth & Family Services
Division 14: The Society for Industrial & Organizational Psychology	Division 38: Health Psychology
Division 15: Educational Psychology	Division 39: Psychoanalysis
Division 16: School Psychology	Division 40: Clinical Neuropsychology
Division 17: Counseling Psychology	Division 41: American Psychology—Law Society
Division 18: Psychologists in Public Service	Division 42: Psychologists in Independent Practice
Division 19: Military Psychology	Division 43: Family Psychology
Division 20: Adult Development & Aging	Division 44: Society for the Psychological Study of Lesbian & Gay Issues
Division 21: Applied Experimental & Engineering Psychologists	Division 45: Society for the Psychological Study of Ethnic Minority Issues
Division 22: Rehabilitation Psychology	Division 46: Media Psychology
Division 23: Society for Consumer Psychology	Division 47: Exercise & Sport Psychology
Division 24: Theoretical & Philosophical Psychology	Division 48: Peace Psychology
Division 25: Experimental Analysis of Behavior	Division 49: Group Psychology & Group Psychotherapy
Division 26: History of Psychology	Division 50: Addictions
	Division 51: Society for the Psychological Study of Men & Masculity

Now let's consider some important specialties within psychology.

1. *Experimental psychologists*, as the name implies, rely almost exclusively on experiments to study behavior and mental life. They study biological bases of behavior (psychobiology), animal learning and behavior, and cognitive processes (perception, memory, language, thought). The topics covered in experimental psychology are sometimes referred to as the basic areas in psychology (e.g., perception, learning), although many psychologists dispute this claim. Historically, the label experimental psychologist has been applied to researchers studying psychobiology, learning, and cognitive processes. However, psychologists interested in other topics have also adopted experimental methods.

2. *Social psychologists* are interested in the way social factors affect cognition and behavior and in the various ways an individual's behavior is affected by others. For example, when do people offer help in a crisis situation? Social psychologists are also concerned with group processes, such as the ways leaders emerge. They study how people perceive, judge, and remember others, why they conform to rules and obey orders, and how relationships develop between people. These topics are discussed in Chapter 17.

3. *Personality psychologists* are concerned with individual differences among people, and they have developed a number of tests to measure such differences, as we will see in Chapter 14. Why do different people (e.g., extroverts and introverts) often behave differently in the same situation? Personality psychologists ask such questions and try to classify people to predict their behavior.

4. *Developmental psychologists* study the physical and psychological changes that accompany growth and aging. They are concerned with the effects of maturation and experience across the life span from birth through adolescence to adulthood to old age. These psychologists may study people at particular ages, such as infancy or adolescence, or they may be interested in how specific skills, such as memory, change with age (see Chapters 9 and 10).

5. *Clinical and counseling psychologists* are practitioners who perform therapy to relieve psychological distress. In fact, just over half the members of the American Psychological Association engage in therapy. Clinical psychologists hold Ph.D. or Psy.D. (doctor of psychology) degrees and receive four to six years of training in research and clinical skills, as well as a one-year internship for further training. They diagnose and treat mental and behavior problems that range from ordinary anxiety to more debilitating disorders. Clinical psychologists work in mental hospitals, mental health clinics, universities, other institutions, and private practice. Counseling psychologists usually hold Ph.D. or Ed.D. (doctor of education) degrees. They are trained to counsel marital, vocational, and/or other personal problems not associated with a particular mental illness. They work in hospitals, schools, corporations, and private practice. These issues are discussed in Chapters 15 and 16.

People often confuse clinical psychologists with psychiatrists. Typically, psychologists hold a Ph.D. or a Psy.D., while psychiatrists are doctors of medicine (M.D.s) who specialize in psychiatry. Psychiatrists can prescribe drugs, whereas clinical psychologists cannot (although this soon may change). Clinical psychologists often work in conjunction with psychiatrists. Students interested in pursuing a career in clinical psychology should be aware that at least four to six years of postgraduate training are required.

THE MEDIA IMAGE OF PSYCHOLOGY

People have some pretty strange ideas about psychology. Professional psychologists are accustomed to reactions of alarm or suspicion when they state their profession. People remark, "Uh oh, I'd better be careful around you," or "Oh! I'd better watch what I say!" Many people believe that psychologists have unusual powers to penetrate other people's minds, even in casual meetings.

How do people get such misguided ideas about psychologists and what they do? The answer is not hard to find: The media provide all sorts of images about psychologists and their activities. Walk into any bookstore and you are likely to find a bizarre collection of titles. Here are some recent titles uncovered by one of the authors on a trip to a local bookstore: *Use Both Sides of Your Brain; Why Women Worry and How to Stop; The Feeling Good Handbook; Your Past Lives: A Reincarnation Handbook; and Wrestling with Love: How Men Struggle With Intimacy.*

Some of these books are written by professional psychologists, but others are written by people hoping to cash in on the self-help movement in the United States. There is a long publishing history in the United States of very popular and profitable books designed to improve the human condition. Some of these books are excellent, but dozens more are written by pseudopsychologists who promise to make our lives happier or more meaningful if only we will follow the simple prescriptions they provide. As a result, psychologists sometimes seem like quacks, if not frauds. An entertaining book analyzing the success of self-help books is *I'm Dysfunctional, You're Dysfunctional,* by Wendy Kaminer.

Another source of exposure to psychology is through television. The image of the clinical psychologist (one who practices therapy) may be of a kind person who talks to people about their problems. Other therapists are portrayed as somber, bearded, and out of touch, speaking an arcane language while patients lie on a couch and recount their dreams (a caricature of Freudian therapy).

Psychologists also appear on TV and radio talk shows. Indeed, some promise to provide answers to questions

6. *Organizational and industrial psychologists* are concerned with psychological factors in large organizations and industry. They may develop or analyze organizational hierarchies, create tests to match people with appropriate jobs, or improve morale and working conditions. They study topics such as leadership, personnel selection, and prediction of employee behavior. Organizational and industrial psychology is considered in Chapter 18.

7. *Human factors psychologists* consider the human factor to make equipment (e.g. computers) more "user friendly." An increasing number of industries are hiring psychologists to devise more efficient interactions between people and machines and to promote motivation and job satisfaction. Human factors psychologists also work in advertising, consumer behavior, and marketing research. Human factors psychology is discussed in Chapter 18.

8. *Health psychologists* study the relation between psychological factors (such as depression or stress) and physical health. They study why people engage in behaviors that, in the long run, damage their health (smoking, tanning, overeating, taking drugs). They also ask how these behaviors can be changed. Other questions of concern to health psychologists are why certain people are more prone to heart disease or cancer and how patients can be encouraged to follow the regimen of medicine and

called in from listeners about psychological problems. One radio program is called "The Two-Minute Shrink," and the speaker aims to provide a 2-minute answer to questions that the caller asks. Needless to say, most professional psychologists disapprove of such "fast-food" therapy.

The popular daytime TV talk shows, such as "Oprah!," "Geraldo," and "Sally Jessie Raphael" often focus upon psychological issues. However, when psychologists appear on these shows, the format rarely allows them time to develop their points thoroughly. As a result, they communicate in

Many people receive their image of psychology by wathing TV shows that portray psychologists.

sound bites and often state conclusions that sound odd to the audience.

Another role in which the public sees psychologists and psychiatrists (medical doctors with a specialization in mental illness and its treatment) is as expert witnesses at trials. In celebrated cases in which someone pleads not guilty by reason of insanity, psychologists and psychiatrists testify their opinion of the mental state of the defendant at the time he or she committed the crime. Often, the testimonies will conflict, because even the most well-intentioned and knowledgeable people can examine the same evidence and come to different conclusions. While this happens in any field, it seems more noticeable in a highly publicized trial.

Many professional psychologists cringe at the portrayal of psychology and psychologists in the media. However, it would be wrong to blame the media entirely for misrepresentation because a grain of truth often exists in the portrayal. After all, a number of licensed professional psychologists engage in instant radio analysis, write embarrassing books, and advocate questionable therapies. While other psychologists may look askance at these practices, it is not the media that created the mischief but the publicity-seeking psychologists themselves.

therapy recommended by their doctors. These questions and others will be taken up in Chapters 13 and 14.

9. *Educational psychologists* study factors related to learning and teaching. Some work directly with students and teachers in school settings; others conduct research or provide training in universities and colleges. Many educational psychologists have practical goals of improving effective teaching practices and student achievement.

10. *School psychologists* are usually employed in elementary and secondary schools. They administer diagnostic tests such as aptitude, intelligence, and personality tests. They use the tests to guide instructors and to place and advise students. They are also trained to evaluate learning and emotional problems and to counsel students (see Chapter 18).

As is evident from Table 1.1, we have touched on only some of the specialties within psychology. As psychology branches out into other fields, it spawns additional subdisciplines. For example, some people now call themselves environmental psychologists because they study how noise pollution, air pollution, and crowding affect people's behavior (see Chapter 18). In addition, some psychologists belong to more than one division of the APA and may take on more than one role (such as conducting research and having a clinical practice).

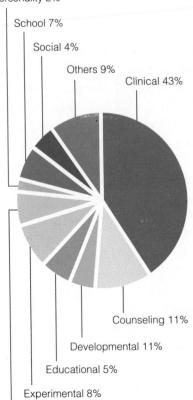

FIGURE 1.5
How Psychologists Divide Their Field

The chart shows the percentages of members of the American Psychological Association specializing in different areas of psychology.

SOURCE: Based on data from Stapp & Fulcher, 1981, Table 2.

The American Psychological Association, headquartered in Washington, D.C., began as a scholarly society of academic psychologists, but in the 1940s began to admit psychologists who focused on the private practice of clinical psychology. Since then, the APA has gradually shifted from a scholarly body with academic interests to a more diverse professional society concerned with issues of interest to practicing clinicians (e.g., having their services included under various health insurance plans, as are the services of psychiatrists). Figure 1.5 shows the breakdown of specialties among the 132,000 members of the American Psychological Association.

The academic/scientist and practitioner/clinician groups coexisted uneasily within the APA for many years, with the latter gradually gaining ascendancy. In 1988, a group of academic/scientist psychologists formed a new organization called the American Psychological Society (APS), which has about 15,000 members as of 1995. Some psychologists have left the APA for the APS, whereas others have elected to maintain membership in both organizations.

Psychology will no doubt continue to develop as a professional field, grappling with complicated issues of scientific research, providing mental health services, and improving people's lives. In all likelihood, both the American Psychological Association and the American Psychological Society (as well as other, smaller organizations) will play critical leadership roles.

SUMMARY

1 Psychology is the study of mental processes and behavior. Psychologists study mental processes indirectly by studying behavior.

2 Scientific psychology began in the mid-1800s. The structuralist school of psychology was concerned with the study of conscious experience through analytic introspection; the functionalist school was concerned with the adaptive significance of mental processes; behaviorists believed that psychology should be the science of behavior; Gestaltists argued for the study of the phenomena of conscious experience, mostly through verbal reports—and opposed the division of perceptual events into independent sensations; the psychoanalytic approach was concerned with unconscious motivations.

3 Five themes of modern psychology are represented in this text: biology, learning, cognition, development, and sociocultural environment. These five themes can be applied to most topics in psychology and show that behavior is caused by many variables operating simultaneously.

4 Explanations for psychological phenomena are offered on various levels, ranging from biochemical to social factors. Most complex phenomena must be analyzed in terms of factors operating at different levels, from molecular (neural or hormonal factors) to molar (social or cultural factors).

5 Methods of psychological research differ and include descriptive techniques (naturalistic observation, case studies, surveys, interviews, psychological tests, and correlational analyses) and laboratory experimentation.

6 Naturalistic observation involves the study of a behavior under naturally occurring conditions. A case study is the intensive investigation of a single incident or event. Surveys and interviews usually involve less information from each person than a case study, but many more people are observed. The conclusions drawn from these types of research are usually limited, but the methods can identify ideas for more systematic research.

7 Correlational research involves measuring two variables to see if the variables are related. Even if the two measures are related, researchers cannot conclude a causal relationship exists because there is always the possibility that a third variable produced the observed results. This situation is called a confounding of variables.

8 Experimental research generally is preferred to other types of research because confounding can be minimized and firmer conclusions drawn. In experiments, the manipulated variable is the independent variable; the variable that is observed and measured is the dependent variable; and the variables held constant are the control variables. Subject variables are characteristics such as gender and they are examined for differences on the dependent variable, with the other variables held constant.

9 Internal validity is the soundness of research conclusions: Is the researcher correct in attributing the change in the dependent variable to the independent variable? External validity is the generalizability of research findings: Do they apply to other subjects, other settings, and other manipulations and measures? Laboratory research typically has high internal validity, whereas field research has high external validity.

10 Numerous subfields or areas of special interest have developed within psychology. Most important are experimental, social, personality, developmental, clinical, counseling, organizational, industrial, human factors, health, educational, and school psychology.

11 Basic research aims to uncover general principles that govern some phenomenon, whereas applied research aims at solving practical problems. Sometimes findings from basic research can be applied to solve pressing technological, medical, or social problems.

KEY TERMS

psychology (p. 3)

structuralism (p. 6)

functionalism (p. 7)

behaviorism (p. 8)

Gestalt psychology (p. 9)

psychoanalysis (p. 10)

reductionism (p. 14)

descriptive research (p. 13)

experimental research (p. 14)

theory (p. 14)

hypothesis (p. 14)

predictions (p. 14)

data (p. 14)

naturalistic observation (p. 16)

ethologists (p. 16)

reactive observations (p. 16)

nonreactive (unobtrusive) techniques (p. 16)

case study (p. 16)

interview (p. 18)

survey (p.18)

psychological tests (p. 19)

correlation (p. 20)

variable (p. 20)

confounding (p. 21)

independent variables (p. 26)

dependent variables (p. 26)

control variables (p. 26)

subject variables (p. 26)

internal validity (p. 29)

external validity (p. 29)

applied research (p. 31)

basic research (p. 31)

FOR CRITICAL ANALYSIS

1 Psychology developed as a science much later than many other fields. Why do you think this was? Discuss four reasons why psychology developed relatively late compared to other scientific fields.

2 The various schools of psychology make different assumptions about how to study mental processes and behavior. If you had been a psychologist in 1935, during the heyday of the various schools, which one would you have advocated? Describe what attracts you to that position.

3 What are the advantages and disadvantages of experimental research as compared to correlational research?

4 Find a recent report on psychological research in a newspaper or magazine. What research techniques were used? Were the conclusions drawn appropriate? (See Appendix B on how to critically read an article about psychology).

5 Think of three ways you have seen psychologists portrayed in the media. Do you think that the portraits were accurately drawn?

6 In this chapter we reviewed ten specializations of psychology. Which one appeals most to you? Why?

SUGGESTED READINGS

AMERICAN PSYCHOLOGICAL ASSOCIATION. (1978). *A career in psychology*. Washington, DC: American Psychological Association. Information is provided on the different fields and careers within psychology. There is also discussion of what types of training are necessary to become a psychologist. You may obtain a free copy by writing to the American Psychological Association, 750 First Street, N.E., Washington, DC 20002-4242.

ELMES, D. G., KANTOWITZ, B. H., & ROEDIGER, H. L. (1995). *Research methods in psychology* (5th ed.). St. Paul: West. An introduction to research methods in psychology.

HEIDBREDER, E. (1933). *Seven psychologies*. New York: Appleton-Century-Crofts. A lucid account of seven schools of psychology, including structuralism, functionalism, behaviorism, Gestalt psychology, and psychoanalysis.

HILGARD, E. R. (1987). *Psychology in America: A historical survey*. San Diego: Harcourt Brace Jovanovich. A comprehensive survey of the first 100 years of psychology in America by a leading scholar who has been in the forefront of the field for over 60 years.

LEAHEY, T. H. (1991). *A history of modern psychology*. Englewood Cliffs, NJ: Prentice Hall. An excellent history of psychology, with a chapter devoted to cognitive science.

PSYCHOLOGY ON THE INTERNET

At the end of each chapter in this book, you will find a section called Psychology on the Internet. This section provides you with extra sources of information relevant to the topics covered in the chapter and introduces you to the Internet as a resource for education and research.

INTRODUCTION TO THE INTERNET

The Internet is a global computer network made up of smaller computer networks. Just as the computers and related equipment (e.g., printers, scanners, and storage devices) on your campus are connected and able to "talk" to one another via network connections, the computer network on your campus is connected to networks at other schools, organizations, and corporations. As a result of this complex web of connections, the way we exchange information has changed dramatically. For example, written correspondence that once traveled through the mail in paper form can now reach destinations across the street or around the world in a matter of seconds via electronic mail (E-mail). Similarly, people interested in a particular topic can participate in discussion groups (Listservs and Usenet groups) in which people from all over the world express their opinions.

Both services (E-mail and discussion group access) should be relatively easy to obtain through your school's computer center. Usually, this involves applying for a mainframe or UNIX account. When your account is created, you will be given a UserID and password that allow you to access the programs (including E-mail and, at most schools, a Usenet reader) on your school's computer system. You will then be able to send and receive E-mail, subscribe to Listservs, and read and post information on Usenet groups. In later chapters, Psychology on the Internet will provide specific instructions for subscribing to various listservs.

INTERNET RESOURCES

In addition to the communication services already mentioned, the Internet allows access to a variety of educational and research resources. These resources range from text-based information from academic institutions, professional organizations, and private corporations to searchable databases of phone listings and library holdings and software archives containing computer programs that can be obtained free of charge (freeware) or for a fee.

There are two main systems by which these resources are made available–Gophers and World Wide Web (WWW). Both systems allow the user to "navigate" easily between resource sites on the Internet, but the two systems differ in the structure they impose on that navigation and the types of information that can be accessed. Information available through Gophers is generally arranged hierarchically, with information becoming more specific as one navigates deeper into the hierarchy. In WWW, "links" maintained by the information provider allow the user to jump directly to related information of varying degrees of specificity or to information on unrelated topics. Although this structure can, at times, be a bit confusing, it allows a greater degree of flexibility in searching for information. In addition to greater flexibility, WWW also provides direct access to graphics and sound as well as text-based information. More importantly, WWW can be used to access information on Gophers and Usenet groups.

Therefore, owing to the greater power and flexibility of WWW browsing tools, most of the sites in Psychology on the Internet will be listed by their WWW location (or URL–Uniform Resource Locator). You should not need a special UserID and password to use Gopher or World Wide Web the way you do with E-mail. Simply ask your computer center support personnel about availability of Netscape or Mosaic–the two most popular World Wide Web browsing tools. If you have not used these tools before, do not worry; they are very easy to learn, and most computer lab attendants will be happy to show you how they work. In addition, many schools offer short tutorials on using Internet tools such as E-mail, Gopher, and WWW browsing tools.

THE NATURE OF PSYCHOLOGY

You can find a great deal of information about psychology on the Internet. Using WWW browsing tools such as Netscape and Mosaic, you can find additional information related to the nature of psychology by visiting the following sites:

American Psychological Association
(http://www.apa.org/)

American Psychological Society
(http://www.hanover.edu/psych/APS/aps.html)

These home pages provide information on a wide range of topics of interest to psychology students, including information on membership in these professional organizations, press releases outlining the organizations' views on topics of public interest, and links to Internet resources for psychologists.

PsyScope
(http://poppy.psy.cmu.edu/psyscope/)

From this home page, you can download PsyScope, a Macintosh application that allows you to design and run your own psychology experiments. Full documentation for the program and a sample experiment are also available for free downloading.

Compsych
(gopher://baryon.hawk.plattsburgh.edu:70/11/.ftp/pub/compsych)

This site provides descriptions of and distribution information for several PC applications related to psychology. These applications range from programs for running specific experiments to teaching tools and tutorials on specific issues.

MacPsych Archive
(gopher://gopher.stolaf.edu/11/Internet%20Resources/S\st.%olaf%20Sponsored%20Mailing%20Lists/MacPsych)

The MacPsych Archive provides in-depth information on the use of computers in psychology. In addition to making freeware and shareware applications available, this site serves as a forum for discussing technical issues regarding software and hardware solutions to problems faced by experimental and survey researchers.

On Being a Scientist: Responsible Conduct in Research
(http://xerxes.nas.edu/nap/online/obas)

The National Academy of Sciences provides this booklet on-line as a formal introduction to research ethics.

Human Subjects
(http://www.psych.bangor.ac.uk/deptpsych/Ethics/HumanResearch.html)

This site focuses on guidelines for the ethical treatment of human subjects in a variety of research settings. In addition to general information regarding the ethical treatment of human subjects, this site provides links to guidelines established by specific organizations around the world.

Psych Web
(http://www.gasou.edu/psychweb/psychweb.htm)

If you are currently a psychology major or are thinking about becoming one, this home page is for you. It contains information on career opportunities in psychology, tips on writing a psychology research paper, and a comprehensive list of psychology resources available on the Internet.

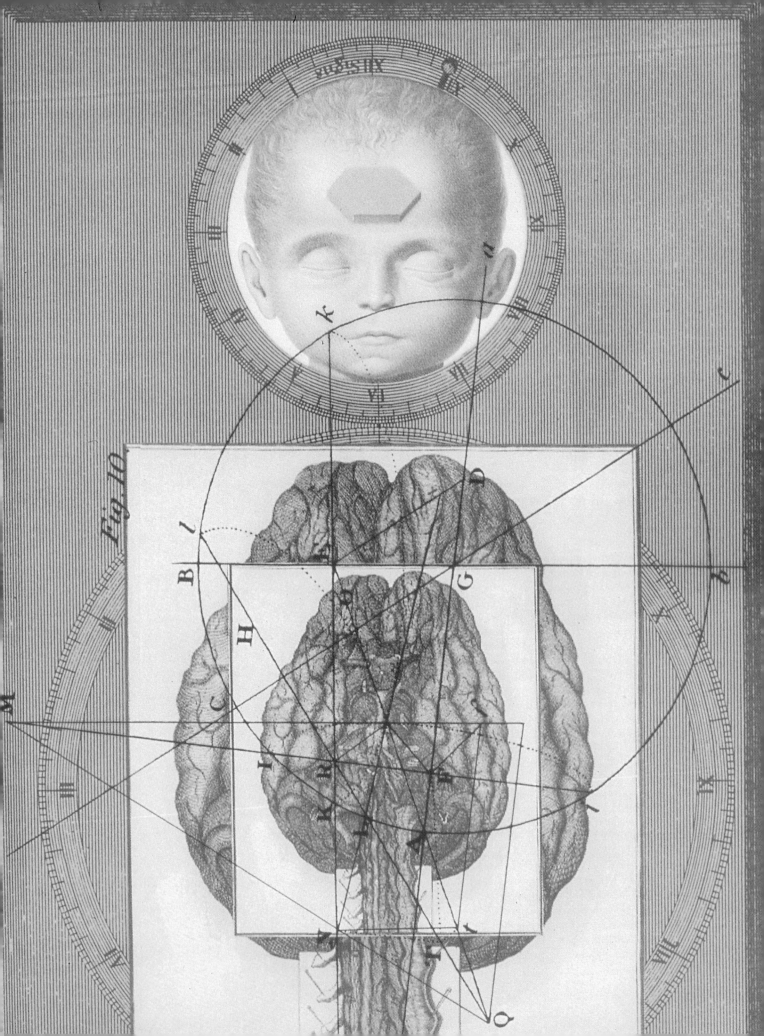

BIOLOGICAL BASES OF BEHAVIOR

Chapter 2

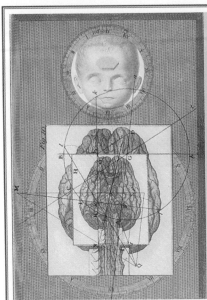

BIOLOGICAL THEME
What is the basic structure of the nervous system? How does it function? How can we determine the influence of heredity on behavior? Are the brains of men and women different?

LEARNING THEME
Where is information stored in the brain?

COGNITIVE THEME
In what part of the brain does thinking occur? How can this be measured?

DEVELOPMENTAL THEME
How do nerve cells develop their structured form?

SOCIOCULTURAL THEME
Does human social behavior have a biological basis?

As your eyes scan this printed page, a small miracle is taking place within your skull. The cells within your brain, which make up a dazzling, complex network of electrical currents, are relaying information at speeds of up to 200 miles per hour. Somehow these electrical transmissions guide your eyes across the page, help you to perceive the size and shapes of letters, and let you translate these patterns of ink into a meaningful message. Meanwhile, a similar network of cells is performing another complicated task: regulating your heart, your lungs, and all the muscles in your body. Your brain is a product of millions of years of evolution and a joint product of your heredity and your experiences. All your thoughts originate in your brain; everything you learn is stored there; and all your conscious experience is produced there, as well as many unconscious processes.

How does the brain manage to do all this? Answering this question is one of the tasks of biopsychologists (also called psychobiologists). Every day these scientists make new discoveries about brain function, discoveries with important implications for psychology. But it is when the brain malfunctions that we sometimes learn the most. In this chapter, you will meet Mr. P, a brain-damaged man who would shave only the right side of his face. And you will see how schizophrenia and depression, two of the most common mental disorders, are also related to brain malfunction. In centuries past, these illnesses were seen first as disorders of the spirit and then as disorders of the humors and organs of the body. Understanding how these disorders are related to brain malfunction has led to successful treatments for schizophrenia and depression, as you will see in this chapter and later in Chapter 16.

Neurons and Transmission of Information

The basic element of the brain is the **neuron,** or nerve cell, and its function is to communicate with other neurons. To perform any function—to breathe, sing, or write the great American novel—we must rely on the information going from neuron to neuron. Moreover, many aspects of behavior are directly related to the properties of the neuron. In fact, depression and schizophrenia—two devastating psychological dis-

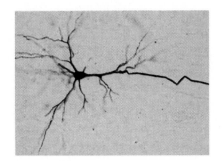

FIGURE 2.1
Photograph of Neuron

orders—may be produced by neuronal malfunction. To understand such disorders, as well as normal psychological functioning we must understand the structure of neurons and how they communicate.

THE STRUCTURE OF NEURONS

Neurons come in many different shapes and sizes, but most have the same major components: a cell body, dendrites, and an axon. The neuron's cell body contains structures also found in other cells such as the nucleus, which contains the organism's genetic information, and components that perform the metabolic work of the cell. The *dendrites* are a network of tiny fibers, like the branches of a tree, that reach out from the cell body (*dendron* is Greek for tree). The *axon* is a long, slender fiber that also extends from the cell body (see Figure 2.1). What we refer to as nerves are actually closely packed bundles of axons.

There are three basic types of neurons (see Figure 2.2) *Sensory* neurons receive information from the body's tissues and sensory organs and convey this information *to* the brain and spinal cord. *Motor* neurons carry signals *from* the brain and spinal cord

FIGURE 2.2
Neurons

A. The dendrites of *sensory neurons* receive information about the outside environment, and the axons of these cells pass this information on to other neurons. B. The dendrites of *motor neurons* receive signals from neurons in the brain and spinal cord, and the axons of these cells activate the muscles, organs, and glands of the body. Also shown is the myelin sheath covering the axon. C. This is a highly simplified drawing of the network of neurons in the brain. Most *interneurons* connect with many other neurons. The dendrites of interneurons receive information from other neurons, and the axons of these neurons send information to other neurons.

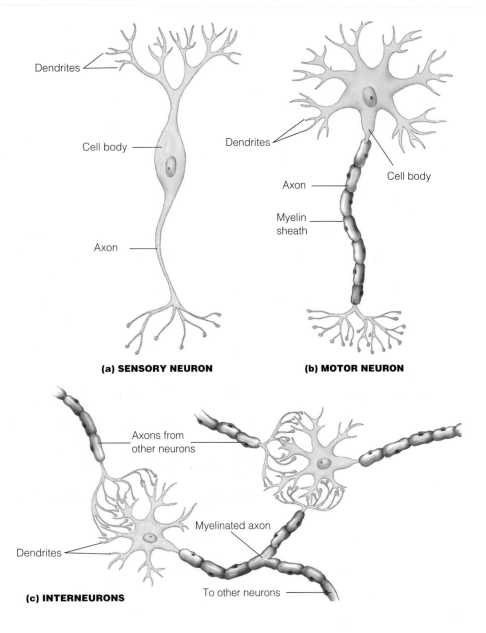

to the muscles, organs, and glands of the body. *Interneurons* carry information between neurons. The myelin sheath which covers some axons speeds up signals as we will discuss later. In the simplest case, a sensory neuron receives information about the environment and passes it to an interneuron, which then sends a signal to a motor neuron, which then signals a response.

Estimates of the number of neurons in the human body vary widely; but the brain alone contains perhaps 100 billion neurons. In fact, just 1 gram of brain tissue can contain 200 million neurons, and most of these neurons come into contact with many others (the average brain weighs approximately 1,400 grams, or about 3 pounds).

As you can imagine, if 1 gram of brain tissue can contain 200 million neurons, human neurons must be very small indeed, making them difficult to study. Luckily, neurons in other animals look and act much like human neurons. Scientists have learned about neurons primarily by studying the axon of the giant squid. A squid axon can be up to 1 millimeter in diameter, making it relatively easy to manipulate and study. Research on this giant neuron has taught us how neurons communicate information.

CONDUCTION OF INFORMATION WITHIN A NEURON

Conduction of information within a neuron is an electrochemical process. You are probably already familiar with the electrical component. By placing electrodes on exposed area of the scalp, we can record a person's brain waves in a graph of the electrical activity over relatively large areas of the brain. But what happens at the level of the individual neuron?

The Resting Potential.   Each neuron has a resting, or noncommunicating state. This resting state is actually fairly active, however, being maintained by active processes in the neuron. The key to both the resting state and the communicating state is the neuron's cell membrane, which surrounds the entire neuron, including the axon. There are gates, or pores, in the membrane and electrically charged atoms called *ions* pass through these gates to travel from one side of the membrane to the other. But these gates can open and close, allowing only certain ions to pass through. The most important ions in this process are sodium (Na+) and potassium (K+).

When the neuron is at rest, sodium (Na+) is more abundant in the fluid outside of the cell, while potassium (K+) and various large, negatively charged protein molecules are more abundant within the cell. This difference in distribution of charged ions produces a slight negative potential inside the cell membrane relative to the outside, just like the positive and negative poles of a battery. This electrical potential is called the *resting potential*. Figure 2.3 shows the concentration of some of the most important ions inside and outside a neuron when the neuron is at rest.

The Action Potential.   When a resting neuron is stimulated by a signal from another neuron or by some experimental electrical pulse, the potential difference across the cell membrane is changed. In general, an excitatory signal from another neuron reduces the voltage difference across the cell membrane, and an inhibitory signal increases the voltage difference. When an excitatory signal is received, the sodium gates begin to open and sodium flows into the cell. With a small increase in the membrane potential this inflow of sodium is matched by an outflow of potassium. But if the membrane potential reaches a certain point (about -45mV), the sodium gates open

FIGURE 2.3
Ion Concentration of a Neuron at Rest

The drawing shows the relative concentration of some of the most important ions inside and outside the axon of a resting (nonconducting) neuron. Fluid inside the axon has a relatively high concentration of positively charged potassium ions (K^+) and negatively charged proteins and a relatively low concentration of sodium ions (Na^+) and chloride ions (Cl^-). Because of the unequal distribution of ions, the inside of the axon is negatively charged compared to the outside.

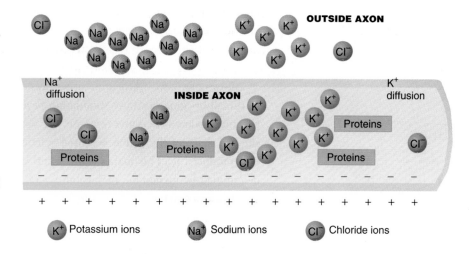

widely, and there is a dramatic rush of sodium ions into the cell, faster than can be compensated for by the outflow of potassium. The membrane potential at which the sodium gates open wide enough to trigger the massive inrush of sodium is called the **threshold.** This massive inrush of sodium changes the membrane potential even more, letting in even more sodium. Finally, enough sodium enters the cell to totally reverse the polarity of the membrane, initiating the **action potential,** the signal that communicates information in the nervous system, (see Figure 2.4).

What would happen if sodium ions could not enter the cell? Action potentials would be prevented from occurring, and no signals would be sent. The local anesthetic Novocain, given by most dentists, prevents sodium ions from entering the membrane in the area injected, thereby preventing communication of pain from that area. (See Kalat, 1992 for more information on action potentials).

Immediately after conduction of the action potential (called *firing*), the membrane's potential is still large enough to produce an action potential, and yet the cell does not

FIGURE 2.4
Action Potential

Electrical stimulation of the membrane causes it to become more permeable to sodiums ions (Na^+). As a result, the membrane's potential increases. At about −45 millivolts, the membrane becomes completely permeable to sodium, and its charge momentarily reverses from negative to positive. A massive flow of sodium into the cell occurs, causing the membrane potential to shoot up to +50 millivolts. This sudden reversal in potential is called the *action potential.*

SOURCE: Kolb & Whishaw, 1985.

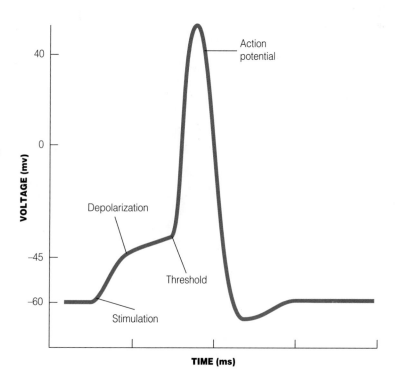

fire again in response. There is a brief period following an action potential when the neuron is resistant to firing; this is called the **refractory period.** The refractory period lasts for 1 or 2 milliseconds after an action potential.

All-or-none law. A neuron either fires or doesn't fire, just like a gun. According to the **all-or-none law,** any stimulation beyond the threshold, regardless of how far beyond, produces the same response, the action potential shown in Figure 2.4. The size and shape of the action potential is independent of the intensity of the stimulus that produced it. This makes sense when you consider that an action potential is determined by membrane permeability, i.e., the extent to which ions can cross the membrane. Therefore, the intensity of an action potential is a property of the cell, not of the stimulus. Once elicited, an action potential continues down the length of the axon to its end, like a spark igniting a fuse. A spark travels a fuse without diminishing.

If the action potential is all or none, then how do we distinguish intense stimuli, such as bright lights, from less intense stimuli (dim lights)? Intensity affects the *number* of neurons that fire, with more neurons firing for intense stimuli. Also, more intense stimuli trigger an increase in the *rate* of firing.

Myelinated Axons. Have you ever seen your hand touch something hot and real-ized that you were going to feel pain before you actually felt the pain? In this case pain signals take longer to reach your brain, be processed and produce a response than the visual signals. Some axons are more than a meter long, and normal transmission of nerve impulses is fairly slow. However, nature has developed a way of speeding up the flow of information along axons, the myelin sheath. The **myelin sheath** is a thin fatty tissue that insulates some axons in short segments separated by gaps called *nodes of*

FIGURE 2.5
The Myelin Sheath

This axon is surrounded by a layer of thin fatty tissue called the myelin sheath. It is broken at intervals of about 1 millimeter by short, unmyelinated sec-tions. The myelin insulates the axon by blocking the movement of ions, so action potentials jump electrically from one unmyelinated section to the next. This type of conduction occurs at a much faster rate than conduction on axons without a myelin sheath.

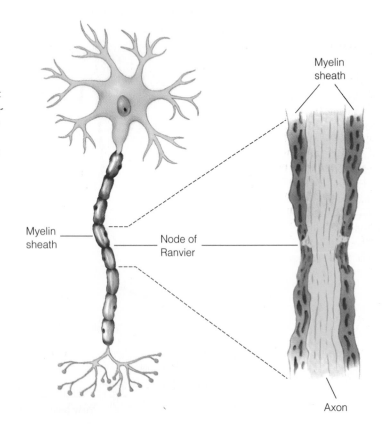

Ranvier (see Figure 2.5). The action potential does not travel along the segments covered with myelin, but jumps from gap to gap, greatly increasing the speed of the signal.

Some diseases, such as multiple sclerosis, destroy the myelin sheath, resulting in slower nerve conduction. Moreover, gross malnutrition during the early period of myelination of the brain can disrupt development of the myelin sheath, sometimes causing mental retardation (Davison & Dobbing, 1966).

SYNAPTIC TRANSMISSION

Almost a century ago, Charles Scott Sherrington (1906) studied reflexes in dogs. A **reflex** is a response that occurs automatically to a stimulus, such as the jerking of your leg to a firm tap on your knee. When a dog's foot is pinched, the dog raises the pinched leg. But Sherrington noted a delay between the pinch and the response. Sherrington measured the total time it took from stimulation to response and found that it was significantly longer than the known time for an impulse to travel along the axons involved in this reflex. He concluded that conduction must be slower at the junction of one neuron and another than it is along the axon. Although some of his colleagues believed neurons were physically connected, Sherrington inferred that there must be spaces between neurons. Later research proved Sherrington to be right.

The gap between the terminals of the axon of one neuron and the dendrites, cell body, or axon of another neuron is called the **synapse** (see Figure 2.6). But if there is a gap between neurons, how does the signal cross the gap? The answer lies in the chemical component of neural transmission. The arrival of an action potential at the axon terminal causes the cell to release a small amount of chemical into the synapse. This chemical, called **neurotransmitter,** communicates a signal from one neuron to another, and the process of communication by neurotransmitters is called *neurotransmission*. The neurotransmitter diffuses across the synapse to the receiving membrane, where it temporarily attaches to that membrane. The distance the neurotransmitter must travel is only 0.02 to 0.05 micrometer (a micrometer is one-millionth of a meter), and the neurotransmitter gets across in less than 10 microseconds.

The receiving neuron contains specialized receptor sites that can interact with arriving neurotransmitters and initiate the receiving cell's response. The surface of the receiving cell contains many different kinds of receptor sites, enabling the cell to receive many different neurotransmitters. The neurotransmitter acts on the specialized receptor sites to change the permeability of the receiving cell's membrane. Depending on the neurotransmitter and the type of receptor site involved, this alteration in membrane permeability can either excite (+) or inhibit (−) the action potential in the receiving cell. A neuron in the brain can share synapses with thousands of other neurons. A neuron may receive excitatory signals from some neurons at the same time as it receives inhibitory signals from other neurons. The intensity of stimulation is determined by the number of molecules of neurotransmitter. Whether the receiving neuron will fire or not depends on whether or not the excitatory signals combined are greater than the inhibitory signals combined.

After entering the synapse, the neurotransmitter is either deactivated or reabsorbed into the sending neuron. If the neurotransmitter were to remain in the synapse, continued communication among cells would be impossible. In fact, many drugs affect these processes. For example, amphetamine blocks reabsorption and also blocks an enzyme that deactivates two neurotransmitters, norepinephrine and dopamine. Now let's take a look at some specific neurotransmitters and their effects.

FIGURE 2.6
Synaptic Transmission

When an action potential arrives at the terminal of an axon, neurotransmitter is released. The activation of the receptor site by the neurotransmitter excites or inhibits the receiving neuron.

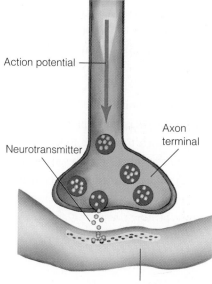

Action potential

Neurotransmitter

Axon terminal

Receiving neuron's dendrites or cell body containing receptor sites

NEUROTRANSMITTERS

There are over 50 different neurotransmitters, each producing its own specific effects on particular parts of the brain. Even the same neurotransmitter can have different effects, depending on the specific section of the brain involved.

Dopamine.   A patient with Parkinson's disease can have such severe hand tremors that holding a glass of water is impossible. In some patients, the hand repeatedly moves up and down out of the patient's control. Other patients have still other movement problems. This disease is caused by the death of neurons containing the neurotransmitter dopamine. An overrelease of dopamine in a different set of neurons may be responsible for schizophrenia, a severe mental disorder characterized by emotional turmoil, hallucinations, and delusions (see page 647). We have not yet identified which of many possible causes of excess dopamine is related to the occurrence of schizophrenic symptoms (Taubes, 1994). No relation seems to exist between Parkinson's disease, caused by too little dopamine, and schizophrenia, perhaps related to too much dopamine, because two different sets of neurons are responsible for the disorders.

Chemicals can often treat disorders produced by neurotransmitter malfunction which makes sense, since neurotransmitters are chemicals. Drugs that block dopamine activity have been successfully used to alleviate the symptoms of schizophrenia. But dopamine itself cannot be administered to Parkinson's patients because it cannot enter the brain from the bloodstream. However, L-dopa, the substance in the brain from which dopamine is made, can enter the brain from the bloodstream. L-dopa has been used successfully to treat Parkinson's disease.

Can you see the potential problem with increasing or decreasing dopamine levels in the whole brain? Because L-dopa increases dopamine levels in all dopamine circuits, a side effect may sometimes be hallucinations and delusions, symptoms occurring in schizophrenia. Likewise, drugs used to treat schizophrenia, which decrease dopamine levels, can result in symptoms like those of Parkinson's disease. Dopamine also appears to affect mood, as do norepinephrine and serotonin, two other neurotransmitters.

Norepinephrine and Serotonin.   Antidepressant drugs were discovered almost by accident. Doctors treating tuberculosis with a drug called iproniazid noticed that their patients experienced a curious side effect, a rather dramatic elevation of mood. The drug appeared to increase the availability of three neurotransmitters: norepinephrine, dopamine and serotonin. The connection between these transmitters and mood was further established when imipramine, a drug used successfully to treat depression, also proved to increase the availability of norepinephrine and serotonin in the brain. Sleep deprivation and other stressors, in contrast, seem to decrease norepinephrine levels (Block et al., 1994). And amphetamine, a drug well known to elevate mood, also releases norepinephrine and dopamine in the brain. On the other hand, reserpine, a drug formerly used to treat high blood pressure, has the opposite effect. In fact, it caused serious depression in as many as 15 percent of the patients taking it. Reserpine, researchers have discovered, depletes the brain's store of norepinephrine and serotonin. This research suggests that a decrease in norepinephrine, dopamine, or serotonin may precipitate depressive attacks. This work has led to the development of even more effective antidepressant drugs.

Acetylcholine.   This neurotransmitter works primarily on motor nerves and causes skeletal muscles to contract. In general acetylcholine is an excitatory neurotransmitter; that is, it causes the receiving cell to fire. Botulism toxin, which can be present in improperly prepared food, prevents release of acetylcholine, resulting in paralysis and often death. Venom of the black widow spider, on the other hand, causes a large release of acetylcholine, creating muscle spasms. The drug curare, used by South American Indians in poison darts, blocks certain receptors for acetylcholine, including those that control the muscles for breathing. A person unable to breathe because of curare may remain fully conscious up to the point of death. Myasthenia gravis, a disorder characterized by muscular weakness, is a result of too few receptor sites for acetylcholine in the muscle membrane and insensitivity of those that exist.

Acetylcholine also is involved in memory (Pertrillo, Ritter, & Powers, 1994) and may have a role in Alzheimer's disease.

Endorphins.   In the brain there are certain locations called receptor sites, that are sensitive to particular neurotransmitters. Some of these receptor sites were shown to be sensitive to morphine and other opiates. But why would the brain have receptors for opiates? Researchers believed that there must be an opiate-like substance produced in the body that stimulates these receptors. Indeed there is, and these substances were named endorphins—"the morphine within." Endorphins are neurotransmitters that stimulate the same receptors as morphine and other opiate drugs. Endorphins have powerful pain-reducing effects, just like morphine, and endorphin release is the body's own mechanism for dealing with pain. Endorphins may cause the so-called runner's high, the euphoria some joggers experience. Presumably, the pain from running causes endorphins to be released. Endorphin release may also be stimulated by acupuncture, the Chinese art of placing sharp needles under the skin as a cure for many ailments, a topic considered in the next chapter.

DEVELOPMENT OF NEURONS

There are four major stages that are distinguished in the development of neurons: proliferation, migration, differentiation, and myelination. *Proliferation* is the production of new cells. In humans most proliferation of neurons occurs before birth. Although there are neurons throughout the body, they are particularly clustered together in the brain and spinal cord. Pasko Rakic (1988) has shown that, except for sensory neurons in the olfactory (smell) system, all of the neurons in the brains of primates are formed before birth. Some of the neurons remain in the part of the brain where they begin, while others *migrate* towards their eventual locations in the brain.

At first, neurons look like any other cell, but then they *differentiate*, forming dendrites and an axon. Finally some axons *myelinate* (develop a myelin sheath). As neural development proceeds, distinct groups of neurons appears, and bands of axons emerge that connect neuron groups. The eventual result is the highly organized network of connections that we refer to as the nervous system.

Many environmental factors can influence neuron development. Malnutrition can greatly hinder proper myelination and in rats, consumption of alcohol by the mother has been shown to affect proliferation and migration of neurons in the fetus (Miller, 1986). In humans, this may be responsible for the low IQs associated with fetal alcohol syndrome, a disorder caused by alcohol passing from the bloodstream of the mother to the bloodstream of the fetus. Fetal alcohol syndrome is characterized by various degrees of mental retardation, hyperactivity, decreased alertness, and motor problems. In children with fetal alcohol syndrome, dendrites tend to have less branching and to be shorter than in normal children.

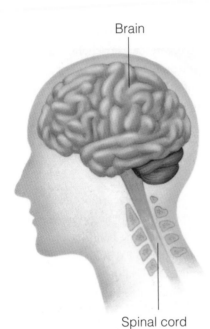

FIGURE 2.7
Relationship of the Spinal Cord and Brain to the Head and Neck

The brain and spinal cord together are called the central nervous system.

The roots entering the spinal cord as seen in this rear view are mostly incoming fibers from sense organs in the skin and muscles.

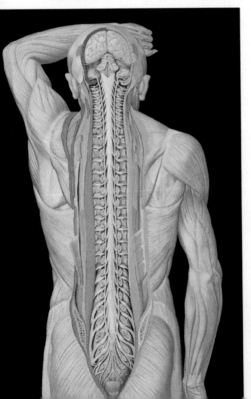

Overview of the Nervous System

The body's entire collection of neurons is called the **nervous system.** Beginning with only a small number of neurons early in the fetus, the human nervous system grows to contain billions of neurons that take on different sizes, shapes, and physiological characteristics.

The two main divisions of the nervous system are the central nervous system and the peripheral nervous system. Let's consider each in turn.

THE CENTRAL NERVOUS SYSTEM

The brain and spinal cord together make up the **central nervous system.** The **spinal cord** is a narrow tube that extends the length of the back, from the hips to the base of the skull, where it joins the brain. The human brain is a very soft and fairly heavy mass, typically weighing about 1400 grams, or a bit over three pounds. It floats in cerebrospinal fluid, a liquid which protects it from shock. The fluid also surrounds the spinal cord, and both the spinal cord and the brain are encased by bone—the vertebral column and skull, respectively (see Figure 2.7).

Traditionally, the spinal cord has been thought to control simple reflexes, while more complicated functions have been attributed to the brain. Your spinal cord conducts pain impulses allowing you to remove your hand from a hot stove before you are aware of pain. Beyond simple reflexes the brain is necessary for response. Humans can neither stand nor walk without the integration of information above the spinal cord.

THE PERIPHERAL NERVOUS SYSTEM

All of the nervous system that is outside the brain and spinal cord is called the **peripheral nervous system.** This system consists largely of sensory neurons (nerve cells that carry information from sensory receptors to the central nervous system) and motor neurons (nerve cells that carry information from the central nervous system to the organs, glands, and muscles).

The peripheral nervous system has two divisions: the somatic nervous system and the autonomic nervous system (see Figure 2.8). The **somatic nervous system** controls the body's interactions with the outside world. Sensory neurons carry messages from the eyes, ears and other major receptor organs, while motor neurons activate skeletal muscles, such as those that move your arms and legs. In contrast the **autonomic nervous system** controls the body's internal environment. Sensory neurons carry information from the internal organs back to the central nervous system, while motor neurons activate the muscles of the internal organs and regulate the glands. Thus, it is the autonomic nervous system that controls the stomach, heart, lungs, blood vessels, gut, and gallbladder influencing such processes such as respiration and digestion.

The autonomic nervous system itself has two divisions: sympathetic and parasympathetic. In general, these two divisions work in opposition: the **sympathetic nervous system** regulates reactions that expend energy, being most active during times of physical or emotional stress and excitement. The **parasympathetic nervous system,** in contrast, regulates reactions that restore energy, being most dominant during times of peace and quiet. With some exceptions, the parasympathetic and sympathetic nervous systems influence the same organs—the heart, blood vessels, and intestines—but they control opposite reactions, as shown in Figure 2.9.

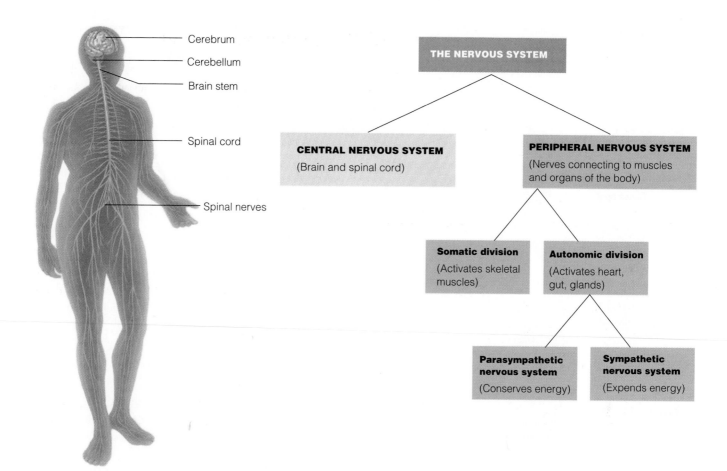

FIGURE 2.8
The Nervous System

This diagram outlines the relationship between the major parts of the nervous system.

Here are some reactions reported by people experiencing arousal of the sympathetic nervous system (these were reported by combat fliers right before a mission): pounding heart and rapid pulse, irritability, dryness in throat or mouth, nervous perspiration or "cold sweat", butterflies in stomach, need to urinate often, and trembling. Some of these reactions are produced directly by the sympathetic nervous system (e.g., pounding heart and rapid pulse), others are a result of the inhibition of the parasympathetic reactions when the sympathetic nervous system is active (e.g., dryness in the throat or mouth). With parasympathetic activity reactions such as digestion, of which salivation is a part, are active. Thus inhibiting parasympathetic activity produces a dry mouth.

Certain drugs can also block parasympathetic activity or increase sympathetic activity. Common cold remedies block sinus fluids (the desired effect), but also inhibit salivation and digestion and increase heart rate, annoying side effects.

The autonomic nervous system is of great importance in emotion and stress and will be discussed in more detail in Chapter 13.

The Brain

The brain is the organ that thinks and controls all of the body's responses except for spinal reflexes. The importance of the brain is shown by the fact that 20% of the blood from the heart flows to the brain. A six-second interruption of that flow causes unconsciousness, and irreversible brain damage occurs within a few minutes. A major goal in the study of the brain has been to determine whether and how the various parts of the brain relate to behavior and experience. To unravel these relations, scientists use a number of different methods.

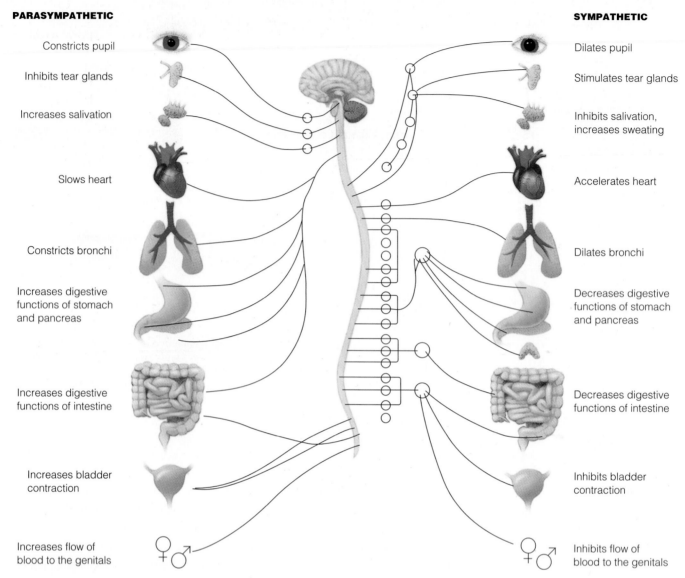

Constricts pupil — Dilates pupil

Inhibits tear glands — Stimulates tear glands

Increases salivation — Inhibits salivation, increases sweating

Slows heart — Accelerates heart

Constricts bronchi — Dilates bronchi

Increases digestive functions of stomach and pancreas — Decreases digestive functions of stomach and pancreas

Increases digestive functions of intestine — Decreases digestive functions of intestine

Increases bladder contraction — Inhibits bladder contraction

Increases flow of blood to the genitals — Inhibits flow of blood to the genitals

FIGURE 2.9
The Autonomic Nervous System

The peripheral autonomic nervous system consists of the parasympathetic (left) and sympathetic (right) nervous systems. Parasympathetic nerves travel from the brain stem and bottom of the spinal cord directly to the organs; sympathetic nerves travel from the remainder of the spinal cord to sympathetic ganglia and then to the organs. Both sets of nerves control the same organs, but have opposite effects on those organs.

TECHNIQUES FOR STUDYING THE BRAIN

One early idea was that brain bumps could be felt on the skull, and these would reflect particular talents located in different areas of the brain. Actually, though, the brain's general shape does not vary from person to person. Other methods must be used to relate the brain to behavior (Thompson, 1993).

Lesion Experiments. Since the earliest time, people have observed the effects of brain injury on behavior, and this is still one of the primary methods of relating brain to behavior. It has long been known that damage to the left side of the head is more likely to produce language difficulties than damage to the right side. In animals, surgical *lesions* can be made in the brain (destruction of specific tissue) to determine the effect on behavior. The basic idea is to remove part of the brain and see what behavior is missing. One finding of lesion experiments is that damage to one area of the brain causes rats to overeat, whereas damage to another area causes them to cease eating as we mentioned in Chapter 1.

Electrical Activity. Because the neuronal signal is in part electrical, brain activity can be measured by measuring its electrical activity. The *electroencephalograph*

(EEG) records electrical activity by way of electrodes attached to the scalp. Although the EEG can measure only gross electrical activity of the brain, the technique can be quite sensitive and has been used to study neural correlates of many types of behavior. In Chapter 5, for example, we will see how EEG activity can discriminate between awake and sleeping people, and among the various stages of sleep.

The EEG apparatus can be used to record the brain's activity in response to specific stimuli. Electrical responses of the brain in response to specific sensory stimuli are called *event-related potentials*. Any sensory stimulus elicits electrical activity in some area of the brain; if the individual pays attention to the stimulus, a different electrical response appears. These responses are used, then, to measure sensation, perception, attention and other cognitive processes.

Electrical Stimulation. It is also possible to insert electrodes into the brain and briefly stimulate certain areas to see how increased activity in those areas affects experience and behavior. Surprisingly, *electrical stimulation* of the brain is not a new procedure. In fact, the first such experiments were carried out in 1874 by a Cincinnati surgeon named Robert Bartholow (Penfield & Rasmussen, 1968). He used as his unwitting subject his own house servant! In an account of this amazing procedure, Bartholow observed that his "patient" apparently felt no pain from the crude procedure. Indeed, electrical stimulation of the brain is painless. We have learned much about the brain from reports of patients undergoing brain surgery whose brains have been stimulated electrically as a natural consequence of the surgical procedure.

Brain Scans. *Positron emission tomography (PET)* is a visual technique in which the subject is given radioactively labeled glucose, which is then metabolized by the brain. The most active area of the brain uses the most glucose, so by measuring the radioactivity of different brain areas, researchers can see which area is most metabolically active during a particular activity and thus which brain area is specialized for which task. We will show you some results of this procedure in Figure 2.18.

Another recent procedure is *magnetic resonance imaging (MRI)* which basically measures the energy released by hydrogen atoms. Because the density of hydrogen atoms varies with the density of different regions of tissue an image of the different densities of tissue can be obtained. Figure 2.10 shows an MRI of a human brain.

Until recently, MRI techniques could provide only structural information. However, functional MRI techniques have now been developed that measure changes in brain activity while people perform a task (Cohen, Noll, & Schneider, 1993). These techniques measure oxygen-related changes in the brain. The MRI signal increases in areas with increased blood flow, reflecting increased brain activity. This technique is capable of detecting very small differences in location of activity, smaller than those detectable by PET.

It is reassuring that a number of different techniques give a consistent picture of how the various brain parts relate to behavior, the topic to which we now turn. We will begin with the part of the brain closest to the spinal cord and move through the layers of the brain until we reach the surface.

THE BRAIN STEM

Figure 2.11 (bottom drawing) shows the structures in the *brain stem*. We share these structures with all vertebrate animals. The lowest part of the brain stem is the **medulla,**

FIGURE 2.10
MRI of a Living Brain

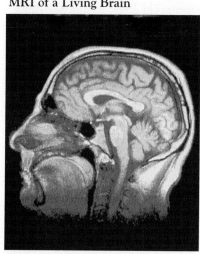

FIGURE 2.11
The Brain Stem, Thalamus, and Hippocampus

Shown in the lower drawing are the medulla, pons, midbrain, and the thalamus. The upper drawing shows the cerebellum, thalamus, and hippocampus.

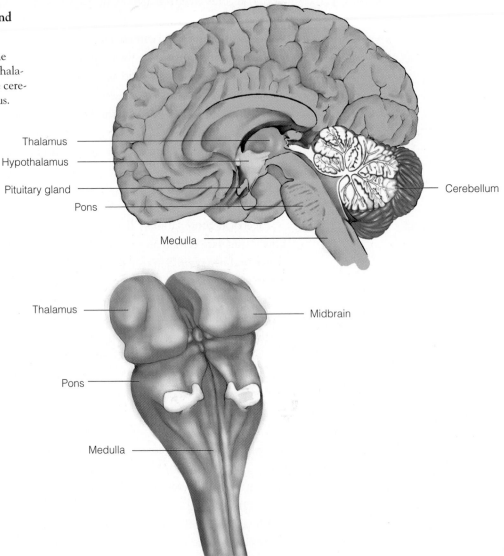

Thalamus
Hypothalamus
Pituitary gland
Pons
Medulla
Cerebellum

Thalamus
Midbrain
Pons
Medulla

the continuation of the spinal cord into the brain. The medulla controls our heartbeat and breathing, basic functions for survival and it does so without input from other parts of the brain. Thus we do not have to "think about" breathing or making our heart beat, the medulla does it for us. As you might suspect given its function, injury to the medulla can result in death.

In front of the medulla is the *pons* (the Latin word for "bridge"). This area consists of fibers connecting the body and the brain. The fibers cross from right to left and vice versa, linking the left side of the body to the right side of the brain and the right side of the body to the left side of the brain. These fibers form the "bridge" through which information from the body passes as it goes to the brain.

The upper portion of the brain stem contains an area referred to as the *midbrain*. This area coordinates whole-body and eye movements with visual and auditory stimuli, and contributes to the control of movement. Parkinson's disease is associated with degeneration of neurons in one part of the midbrain.

In the center of the brain stem (in the medulla and pons) is a complex region with many groups of neuron cell bodies and short and long nerve fibers. This network of cells is called the **reticular formation,** also known as the **reticular activating system** because of its involvement in the activation or arousal of other parts of the brain. It controls sleeping and waking. Electrical stimulation of a certain part of the reticular activating system can waken a sleeping animal. While you might think that electrical stimulation of any part of the body would waken a sleeping animal, remember that electrical stimulation of the brain is not sensed as an electrical shock. Rather, electrical stimulation of the brain produces action potentials mimicking normal brain response. Electrical stimulation of another part of the reticular activating system can produce coma in an animal.

THE CEREBELLUM

Off to the back of the brain above the medulla is another structure we share with other vertebrates—the **cerebellum,** or "little brain" (see Figure 2.11, top). The cerebellum coordinates information from the spinal cord and other parts of the brain to make movements smooth and precise. Damage to the cerebellum produces jerky patterns of movement and can also cause problems in maintaining equilibrium and posture. A test for damage to the cerebellum is the finger-to-nose test. The patient is instructed to hold one arm straight out and then to touch his or her nose as quickly as possible when instructed to do so. A person with cerebellar damage will have trouble with the initial movement. By the way, this is also a test of alcohol intoxication because the cerebellum is one of the first areas of the brain to be affected by alcohol. Recent data also show the cerebellum is important in learning and memory (Daum et al., 1993).

THE THALAMUS AND THE HYPOTHALAMUS

The **thalamus** forms a bulge at the top of the brain stem and is completely covered by other parts of the brain (see Figure 2.11). The thalamus can be thought of as the brain's relay station, directing information from sensory receptors on the periphery of the body to higher layers of the brain. Sensory information from the eyes goes to one region of the brain, information from the ears to another region, and information from the skin to still another. The thalamus also integrates information coming from other parts of the brain and sends it to the cerebellum and medulla.

The **hypothalamus,** a tiny structure lying beneath the thalamus (hypo is Greek for "under") (see Figure 2.11, top), plays a role in regulating the internal state of the body, especially hunger, thirst, sex and temperature regulation. Lesions in one part of the hypothalamus cause rats to overeat; if a different part is lesioned the rats stop eating and become very thin. Still other lesions affect mating behavior (Yahr & Jacobsen, 1994). These effects are discussed more fully in Chapter 12.

One part of the hypothalamus that has stirred great interest is an area loosely termed the "pleasure center." It was discovered by James Olds while he was trying to stimulate the reticular formation in rats (see Olds, 1973). In Olds's experiments a rat with an electrode implanted in its brain was free to move around a square enclosure. Every time the rat entered a particular corner Olds sent low-level electrical stimulation to its brain. Olds thought that the rat would avoid the corner, but the rat kept returning to it. In fact, it would go to any corner where Olds chose to deliver current upon the rat's arrival (see Figure 2.12). In a series of experiments, Olds established that the current proved to be rewarding, or pleasurable, when it was sent to a certain part of the hypothalamus.

FIGURE 2.12
Rewarding Effects of Brain Stimulation

This is a reenactment of the discovery of self-stimulation done a few months after the actual discovery. Jim Olds is holding the rat. The rat would approach any location in the box that produced brain stimulation in a particular location in the hypothalamus.

SOURCE: Milner, P. M. (1989). The discovery of self-stimulation and other stories. Neuroscience & Biobehavioral Reviews 13, 61–67.

In a related experiment, Olds put a rat in a box with a lever the rat could press. This box had been invented earlier by Harvard psychologist B. F. Skinner, and is called the Skinner box; Skinner's contributions are discussed further in Chapter 6. In other experiments, it had been shown that hungry rats would learn to push the lever for food. Whether and how often a rat will push the lever are objective measures of how rewarding food is. In Olds's experiments every time the rat pressed the lever, current was directed to the spot in the brain that Olds had found earlier. The results were amazing. The rat pressed the lever constantly. In the initial study (Olds & Milner, 1954), individual rats pushed the lever more than 700 times an hour. In subsequent studies some rats pressed up to 5,000 times an hour for 24 consecutive hours, rested, then returned for more. They would even tolerate shock, walking across an electrified grid floor, to get to the lever.

Why is stimulation to certain areas of the hypothalamus so rewarding? One theory is that the stimulation provides both motivation and reward. Normally a reward such as food will satiate and thus reduce hunger. But if, as seems the case in brain stimulation, the stimulus provides both reward and motivation, then satiation will never occur. Moreover, there is some speculation that this region of the hypothalamus may produce sexual motivation and reward. Stimulation of this location in brain surgery patients can cause the patients to become amorous toward the nurse or surgeon, and one patient reported that the sensation was like "almost having an orgasm."

THE LIMBIC SYSTEM

Some groups of similar cell bodies in the thalamus, hypothalamus, and part of the brain above these structures form a kind of border around the brain stem. These structures are referred to as the **limbic system** (*limbic* is from the Latin meaning "border"). Figure 2.13 shows three important structures of the limbic system. Two of these structures seem to be involved in aggressive behavior. The *amygdala* appears to facilitate aggressive instincts and lesions (destruction of cells) in the amygdala tend to suppress attack in wild animals (Carlson, 1986). The *septum* apparently restrains aggression but the effects seem to vary by species. While septal lesions in rats induce highly aggres-

FIGURE 2.13
The Limbic System

The majority of the hippocampus is located out of view, in the interior of each hemisphere. The septum is also located out of view in the interior of the area indicated. The amygdala and septum appear to be involved in aggressive behavior, while the hippocampus is involved in memory.

SOURCES: Kalat, J. W. (1981). *Biological Psychology* (2nd ed.). Belmont, California: Wadsworth Publishing, p. 299. Thompson, 1985, p. 307.

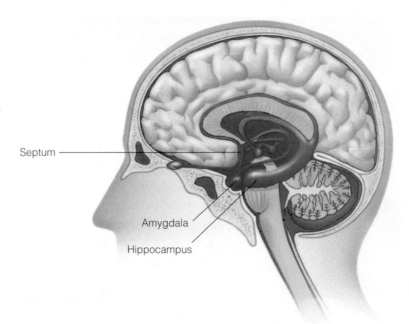

Septum

Amygdala

Hippocampus

sive behavior (Brady & Nauta, 1953), mice flee rather than fight (Slotnick, McMullen, & Fleischer, 1974), and cats sometimes become more affectionate rather than more aggressive (Glendenning, 1972). In violent humans, portions of the limbic system have sometimes been removed in an attempt to control their aggression, a controversial procedure to say the least.

The third important structure of the limbic system, the **hippocampus,** has been associated with memory. The hippocampus's role in memory is dramatized by H.M., a man who underwent surgery to correct a serious epileptic condition. The surgeon removed all of H.M.'s hippocampus and amygdala. The surgery successfully treated the epilepsy but resulted in serious side effects. H.M.'s memory of life before his surgery was fine, but he could not store certain kinds of new memories. If you met H.M. and talked to him for a while and then left and returned a few minutes later, he would have no memory of you. The following comments by H.M. reveal just how disturbing a situation this was: "Right now, I'm wondering, have I done or said anything amiss? You see, at this moment everything looks clear to me, but what happened just before? That's what worries me. It's like waking from a dream. Just don't remember." H.M. and the role of the hippocampus in memory are discussed further in Chapter 7.

THE CEREBRAL CORTEX

The **cerebral hemispheres** are the two large structures forming the top of the brain, one on the left, the other on the right. The thin covering of the cerebral hemispheres is the **cerebral cortex,** which forms the surface of the brain like the bark on a tree (*cortex* is from the Lain, meaning "bark"). The cerebral cortex appears gray and so is said to consist of gray matter, mostly cell bodies and short, unmyelinated axons. This is why Agatha Christie's famous detective, Hercule Poirot, refers to his "little gray cells" when talking about his brain. The white matter, which consists of myelinated axons of the cell bodies, is on the inside of the brain; white matter plus various subcortical structures make up the *cerebrum*. The human cerebral cortex is about 1/4 inch thick. Its deep folds give it a big surface, allowing our brain to contain a large number of neurons but still fit inside our skull. A smooth brain that fit into our skull would have considerably less surface area.

In the course of evolution, the addition of the cerebellum to the back of the brain stem allowed coordination of movement; the development of the cerebellum plus the development of the cerebral hemispheres completes the brain of mammals. The human brain evolved from the brain of other mammals with no basic change in design. However, the cerebral hemispheres and the cerebellum of humans are relatively larger than in other mammals (see Figure 2.14). Humans have the largest cerebral cortex relative to total brain size. Many other mammals have smaller, relatively smooth cortexes; reptiles and amphibians have smaller yet; and fish have none. In essence the cerebral cortex makes us distinctively human. It constitutes a large percentage of the human brain and is the source of reasoning, imagining, consciousness, and language.

The surface of each hemisphere is divided into four sections, or **lobes: *frontal, temporal, parietal,*** and ***occipital*** (see Figure 2.15). The surface of the cortex is separated by natural grooves called sulci (singular is sulcus) and fissures. The *central sulcus* separates the frontal lobe from the parietal lobe; the *lateral fissure* constitutes the boundary of the temporal lobe; and the *longitudinal fissure* separates the right and left halves.

(a) View of the brain from above, with the front of the brain at the top of the photograph. (b) A cross-section of the cerebellum.

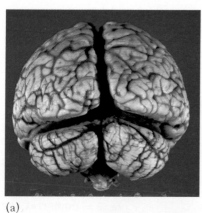

(a)

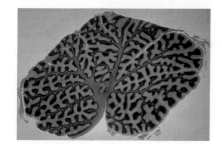

(b)

FIGURE 2.14
Comparison of Brain Sizes

This photograph shows some brains of different animals. Notice how large the human brain is compared to those of other animals.

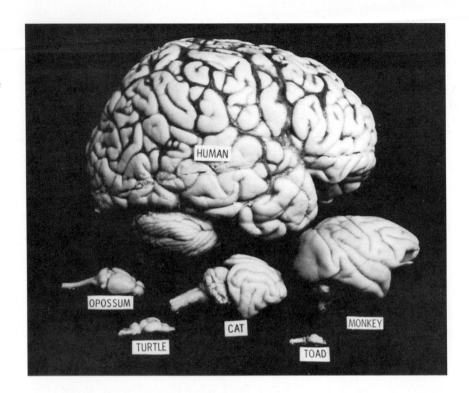

Scientists have found that some areas of the cortex, mostly toward the back of the brain, seem to be sensory in function; that is, they receive information from other parts of the body or the environment. Other areas, mostly toward the middle front of the brain, appear to have a motor function and are involved in controlling bodily movements (see Figure 2.15). Still other areas, termed association areas, are involved in language, thinking, and memory. We will describe each of these areas individually, but bear in mind that all of them work together in a normal human being. Our divisions are therefore somewhat arbitrary.

FIGURE 2.15
Map of the Left Side of the Cerebral Cortex

This drawing depicts the major sections of the brain—the frontal, temporal, parietal, and occipital lobes—and indicates some of the major functions of each area.

SOURCE: Netter, 1983.

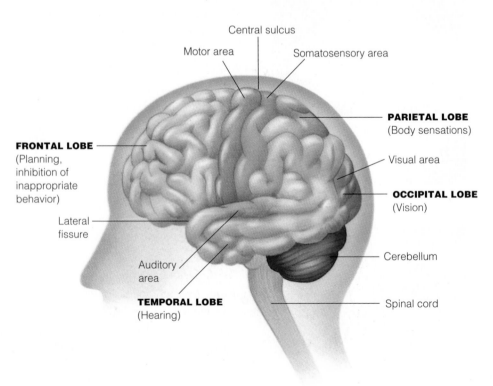

FIGURE 2.16

Functions of the Sensory Cortex

This cross section of the human brain shows the localization of function within the sensory cortex. Only one side of the figure is labeled; the other side is a mirror image of the one shown. The right side of the cortex receives sensations from the left side of the body; the left side of the cortex receives sensations from the right side of the body. The amount of cortex devoted to a part of the body is related to how sensitive that area is. For example, a large amount of area is devoted to the lips and hands.

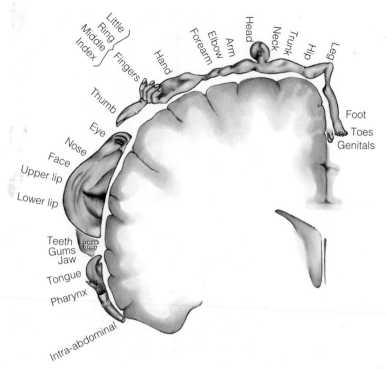

The Sensory Cortex. Three different regions of the cortex have been identified as **primary sensory areas:** the *somatosensory*, the visual, and the auditory. The somatosensory area receives sensations of touch, pain, temperature, and positioning of the body. It runs across the middle of the cerebral cortex in the front of the parietal lobe, as shown in Figure 2.15. This area of the cortex has been mapped through a process of first electrically stimulating areas of the cortex and then seeing where a patient feels sensation. Also, scientists have observed how damage to particular areas causes a loss in sensation in particular body parts. These two methods combined have produced the map of the somatosensory cortex shown in Figure 2.16.

The size of the area devoted to receiving sensations from a particular body part reflects the sensitivity of that body part and not the size of that body part. Look at Figure 2.16 and notice how much area is devoted to the mouth and hands. Compare that with the amount of area devoted to the leg. Also notice that only one side of the somatosensory cortex is shown in Figure 2.16; the other side is its mirror image. Remember, the right hemisphere receives sensations from the left side of the body, and the left hemisphere receives sensations from the right side. So damage to your right somatosensory cortex would interfere with sensation from the left side of your body, and vice versa.

The sensory areas of the brain receive raw, uninterpreted information. For example, consider the *visual area* in the occipital lobe (see Figure 2.15). When this area is stimulated electrically, subjects report seeing flashes of light. This area does not "see objects," but rather receives raw visual information. Interpretation of visual information is done in a different part of the brain, as we will discuss in Chapter 3. The *auditory area* is positioned in the temporal lobe. When stimulated in this area, subjects report hearing sounds.

The Motor Cortex. The **primary motor area** of the cortex is located along a narrow strip at the back of the frontal lobes. In the motor cortex the amount of area devoted to a particular body part reflects the precision of movement possible with that body part. In Figure 2.17 look at the amount of motor cortex devoted to the fingers and mouth compared to the amount devoted to the hip.

The left side of the motor cortex controls movement on the right side of the body, and the right side of the motor cortex controls movement on the left side of the body. You wouldn't necessarily be paralyzed by damage to your motor cortex. If only part of the motor area were damaged, you would be unable to perform precise movements with the body part associated with that area. If, however, large parts of your motor area were damaged, you would be paralyzed on the side of the body opposite to the motor area damaged.

Association Areas. Only a relatively small part of the cortex is devoted to the sensory and motor areas. The remaining parts of the cortex are called **association areas** because early researchers hypothesized that associations between sensory input and motor output were made in these areas. How the association areas function is still unclear, but generally they seem to store and process information.

Humans have the greatest amount of association cortex. The increase in association cortex is largely responsible for the increase in brain size when the human brain is compared with the brains of other primates. Damage to association areas causes disturbances in behavior that are fascinating, because they show how complex both brain and behavior are.

In Ken Kesey's *One Flew Over the Cuckoo's Nest* (1962) the main character is subjected to a frontal lobotomy, a procedure that severs connections between the frontal lobe and the rest of the brain, cutting through association areas. The aim of this procedure is to reduce hostility. Although a frontal lobotomy usually does reduce emotionality, it also impairs the ability to keep track of the order of events and may interfere with memory and abstract reasoning. Many complex behaviors and our ability to plan and think ahead are controlled by the frontal lobes. A frontal lobotomy thus interferes with more than just emotionality. Modern use of psychosurgery will be discussed in Chapter 16, but frontal lobotomies are rarely performed today.

FIGURE 2.17
Functions of the Motor Cortex

This cross section of the human brain indicates the localization of function within the motor cortex. Only one side of the figure is labeled; the other side is a mirror image of the one shown. The right side of the cortex governs movement on the left side of the body; the left side of the cortex governs movement in on the right side of the body. The amount of area in the cortex devoted to a particular part of the body is related to the complexity of movement in that part of the body. Notice the amount of cortex devoted to the lips, jaw, and tongue, used in the complex activity of speech.

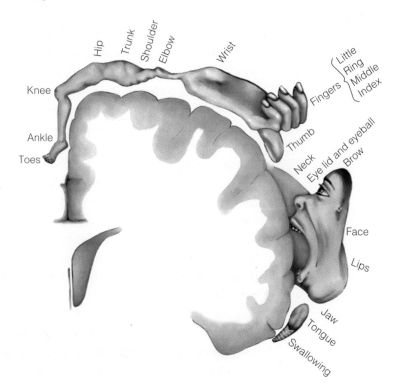

Some brain-damaged patients cannot name or recognize the fingers on either hand (a condition called finger agnosia). This bizarre symptom can result from damage to the *left* parietal cortex. Such damage more typically causes difficulty in writing, performing mathematical operations and distinguishing right from left. Damage to the *right* parietal cortex can produce a phenomenon called "sensory neglect," where the patient does not notice the left side of objects. The patient may dress or wash only the right side of the body and eat only the right half of the pancake at breakfast. Consider the case of Mr. P, who suffered damage to his right parietal cortex.

CASE STUDY

THE RIGHT-SIDED WORLD OF MR. P.

"Mr. P., 67-year-old man, had suffered a right parietal stroke. At the time of our first seeing him (24 hours after admission) he had no visual field defect. He did, however, have a variety of other symptoms. (1) Mr. P neglected the left side of his body and of the world. When asked to lift up his arms, he failed to lift his left arm but could do so if one took his arm and asked him to lift it. When asked to draw a clock face, he crowded all the numbers onto the right side of the clock. When asked to read compound words such as ice cream or football, he read "cream" and "ball." When he dressed, he did not attempt to put on the left side of his clothing (a form of dressing apraxia), and when he shaved, he shaved only the right side of his face. He ignored tactile sensation on the left side of his body. Finally, he appeared unaware that anything was wrong with him and was uncertain as to what all the fuss was about. . . In spite of all these disturbances Mr. P knew where he was and what day it was, and he could recognize his family's faces. He also had good language functions: he could talk, read, and write normally."

Because patients with damage to the right parietal association cortex often have difficulty orienting themselves, distinguishing right from left, or using maps the right parietal cortex can be said to be responsible for one form of self-awareness: the perception of space and our location in it.

SOURCE: Kolb & Whishaw, 1985, pp. 388–389.

Damage to the association areas in the temporal-occipital region can result in problems in visually identifying complex forms, although visual input still reaches the primary visual sensory cortex. For example, some patients may have difficulty picking out which one of four complex patterns differs from the others. Other patients are unable to recognize stimuli. Some rare patients cannot recognize faces, although they are able to recognize objects, forms and colors. And some individuals may not even recognize their own face when they see it in a mirror.

Some of the localization of function we have been discussing is revealed in the PET scans in Figure 2.18.

Brain Plasticity. Although we have discussed the brain as though its structure is fixed, it is important to realize that brain organization and function can change, a characteristic called **plasticity.** The brain has considerable plasticity throughout life (Greenough, 1986). Although the development of entire new neurons has not been demonstrated in the adult brain of any primate, the dendrites of rats can and do grow

FIGURE 2.18
Cerebral Cortex Functions as
Shown by PET

Greater brain activity is indicated by
red. PET scans 1 and 2 were taken,
respectively, when a visual stimulus was
presented, producing a response in the
visual cortex, and when an auditory
stimulus was presented, producing a
response in the auditory cortex. A cognitive task (scan 3) produced frontal
cortex activity, while a memory task
(scan 4) caused activity in the hippocampus. Finally, a motor task (scan 5)
involving the right hand caused
increased activity in the left motor
cortex.

SOURCE: Phelps, M. E. & Mazziotta, J. C. (1985).

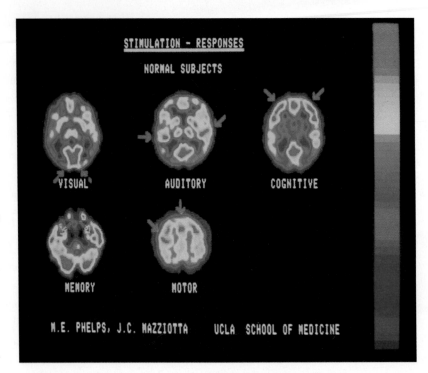

and retract. For example, rats reared in complex environments (e.g., groups of 10 or 12
with constantly changing objects to investigate) have substantially thicker and heavier cortexes than littermates housed individually.

Brain researchers do not know exactly how information is stored and processed in
the cortex. Sometimes, loss of brain cells produces loss of memory and a disturbance in
mental function. However, people suffering from hydrocephalus (literally, "water-
heads") can exhibit severe loss of brain tissue with little decline of function. In this
disease, a disturbance of cerebrospinal fluid leads to great swelling of the channels, or
ventricles, within the brain. When the ventricle walls expand, the overlying brain tissue is damaged.

One interpretation of such cases of brain damage with little loss of function is that
the cortex has considerable spare capacity. If damage to the brain occurs slowly, this
spare capacity can take over brain functions. Also, brain structures unaffected by the
hydrocephalus may be capable of carrying out many of the functions ascribed to the
cortex. Another factor is that brain damage in the young often has less severe effects
than similar damage in adults, and hydrocephalus is a disease of the young. However,
some hydrocephalics do show significant deficits. Clearly, we have much to learn in
this area.

Until recently, researchers believed that all the plasticity in the brain was in the
higher cortical areas, with the primary sensory and motor cortexes fixed in the adult
brain. This idea of a "hard-wired" brain stemmed from the Nobel-Prize winning experiments of David Hubel and Torsten Wiesel to be described in Chapter 3. Briefly, these
researchers found that certain neurons in the cat respond preferentially to either the
right or left eye. If one of the kitten's eyes is sewn shut during development, the portion of the brain that normally would respond to that eye never did.

More recent experiments show that even in the adult brain, "re-mapping" can
occur. Some of the most surprising results come from the famous Silver Spring monkeys. These monkeys served as subjects in experiments by Edward Taub, a researcher
interested in how rehabilitation occurs following brain damage. He destroyed the

point where the sensory nerves from one arm entered the monkeys' spinal cord, but never finished his work because his laboratory was raided by animal rights activists in 1981. His monkeys were confiscated and kept alive. In 1987 Tim Pons at the National Institute of Mental Health tested the brains of the monkeys for changes in their sensory maps. He found that the region of the cortex that would have responded to the arm now responded to touches to the face. This finding is absolutely astounding to brain researchers because of the magnitude of the reorganization it implies. Approximately one-third of the entire sensory map in these monkeys had changed. Similar results have been obtained in humans who have lost an arm. Studies such as these are forcing us to revise some of our previous view of the brain and the degree to which it can change.

HEMISPHERIC LATERALIZATION

Your brain on the surface looks fairly symmetrical. The right hemisphere seems much the same as the left. Yet, research over the past hundred years has indicated that the two halves of the brain are specialized to perform different functions.

Locating the Speech and Language Centers of The Brain. In 1869, a French physician named Paul Broca reviewed evidence from a number of cases of brain damage. He concluded that injury to a certain part of the left cerebral hemisphere caused a person's speech to become slow and labored but did not much affect the person's ability to understand speech (Boring, 1950). Broca discovered that when the same place was damaged in the right side of the brain, no speech impairment occurred. Because of the importance of his discovery, the area of the left brain that seems to control speech production was named **Broca's area,** and the difficulty in speaking was called *Broca's aphasia*.

About 15 years later, Carl Wernicke reported a language disorder in which the person experienced difficulty transferring into oral speech the sounds he or she heard. This language disorder, called *Wernicke's aphasia*, was associated with a different area of the left hemisphere, **Wernicke's area.** Because patients with Wernicke's aphasia speak rapidly but have little language comprehension, they do not make much sense. Examples of these speech disorders are presented in the following case studies.

CASE STUDY

BROCA'S APHASIA AND WERNICKE'S APHASIA

The following examples of aphasic speech were collected by Howard Gardner and are reported in his book *The Shattered Mind: The Person After Brain Damage* (1975).

BROCA'S APHASIA

David Ford was a 39-year-old Coast Guard radio operator who suffered a stroke. Afterward he had lost the ability to use language, was confused, and had a weakness in his right arm and leg. The following interview occurred about three months after the stroke, when Ford was less confused, was alert, and scored in the normal range on nonverbal measures of intelligence.

I asked Mr. Ford about his work before he entered the hospital.

"I'm a sig . . . no . . . man . . . uh, well, . . . again." These words were emitted slowly, and with great effort. The sounds were not clearly articulated; each syllable was uttered harshly, explosively, in a throaty voice. With practice, it was possible to understand him, but at first I encountered considerable difficulty in this.

"Let me help you," I interjected. "You were a signal . . ."

"A sig-nal man . . . right," Ford completed my phrase triumphantly.

"Were you in the Coast Guard?"

"No, er, yes, yes . . . ship . . . Massachu . . . chusetts . . . Coast-[??]guard . . . years." He raised his hands twice, indicating the number "nineteen."

"Oh, you were in the Coast Guard for nineteen years."

"Oh . . . boy . . . right . . . right," he replied.

"Why are you in the hospital, Mr. Ford?"

Ford looked at me a bit strangely, as if to say, Isn't it patently obvious? He pointed to his paralyzed arm and said, "Arm no good," then to his mouth and said

"Speech . . . can't say . . . talk, you see."

"What happened to make you lose your speech?"

"Head, fall, Jesus Christ, me no good, str, str . . . oh Jesus . . . stroke."

"I see. Could you tell me, Mr. Ford, what you've been doing in the hospital?"

"Yes, sure. Me go, er, uh, P.T. nine o'cot, speech . . . two times . . . read . . . wr . . . ripe, er, rike, er write . . . practice . . . get-ting better."

"And have you been going home on weekends?"

"Why, yes . . . Thursday, er, er, er, no, er, Friday . . . Bar-ba-ra . . . wife . . . and, oh, car . . . drive . . . purnpike . . . you know . . . rest and . . . tee-vee."

"Are you able to understand everything on television?"

"Oh, yes, yes . . . well . . . al-most." Ford grinned a bit.

As can be seen, Mr. Ford's output in this brief exchange was extremely slow and effortful. Nearly every sound required a "fresh start," and many were

imperfectly pronounced. However, his comprehension of the questions seemed good. (pp. 60–61)

WERNICKE'S APHASIA

A second patient, Philip Gorgan, was quite weak for a few days immediately after his admission to the hospital, but after that he had no difficulty carrying on a conversation with perfect grammar. However, his speech rarely made sense to his listeners.

"What brings you to the hospital?" I asked the seventy-two-year-old retired butcher four weeks after his admission to the hospital.

"Boy, I'm sweating, I'm awful nervous, you know, once in a while I get caught up, I can't mention the tarripoi, a month ago, quite a little, I've done a lot well, I impose a lot, while, on the other hand, you know what I mean, I have to run around, look it over, trebbin and all that sort of stuff."

I attempted several times to break in, but was unable to do so against this relentlessly steady and rapid outflow. Finally, I put up my hand, rested it on Gorgan's shoulder, and was able to gain a moment's reprieve.

"Thank you, Mr. Gorgan, I want to ask you a few—"

"Oh, sure, go ahead, any old thing you want. If I could I would. Oh, I'm taking the word the wrong way to say, all of the barbers here whenever they stop you it's going around and around, if you know what I mean, that is tying and tying for repucer, repuceration, well, we were trying the best that we could while another time it was with the beds over there the same thing. . . ." (p. 68)

SOURCE: Gardner, 1975. Reprinted by permission of Alfred A. Knopf, Inc.

A third speech disorder, *conduction aphasia,* is associated with damage to the neural connection between Broca's area and Wernicke's area. Because Wernicke's area is not damaged and is connected to other areas besides Broca's, language comprehension is nearly normal; and because Broca's area is intact, pronunciation is normal. What the person says, however, has little connection to what the person hears, so it is extremely difficult for the patient to carry on a normal conversation. A person with conduction aphasia can carry out commands (because comprehension is not impaired) but cannot repeat them, because the connection between Wernicke's area and Broca's area is impaired (Geschwind, 1972). Figure 2.19 illustrates the areas in the brain that are related to speech production.

Left-Handers vs. Right-Handers. Are the brains of right-handed people different from those of left-handers? The answer seems to be yes. About 95 percent of all right-handed people have speech abilities localized in the left hemisphere (Halpern, 1992). Thus, damage to the left hemisphere produces speech disorders, whereas right hemisphere damage does not. This situation is not as clear-cut for left-handers. One estimate is that 70 percent of left-handers have speech and language control in their left hemisphere, 15 percent have control in their right hemisphere, and 15 percent divide control of speech and language abilities between the two hemispheres (Springer & Deutsch, 1993). Thus, brain damage to the right hemisphere, rather than the left, can produce language disorders in some people. And it should be noted here that more males are left-handed than female. The Psychology in Our Times feature on page 26 discusses whether the brains of men and women are fundamentally different.

The Split-Brain Experiments. Until the middle of the twentieth century, the primary neurological generalization regarding higher mental processes was that speech was localized in the left cerebral hemisphere in right-handers. In fact, most researchers believed that the left side of the brain was dominant not only for speech, but for all other information processing (Levy, 1980). Therefore, the left hemisphere was called the dominant, or major, hemisphere, and the right hemisphere was called the non-dominant or minor hemisphere.

FIGURE 2.19
Major Areas in the Brain Related to Speech

Damage to *Broca's area* causes slow, labored speech with no effect on speech understanding. Damage to *Wernicke's area* causes loss of understanding of speech and quick, articulate speech with no meaningful content. Damage to the *conduction area* between Broca's area and Wernicke's area produces a lack of relationship between speech comprehension and speech production. These language disorders are produced in most people by damage to the left hemisphere.

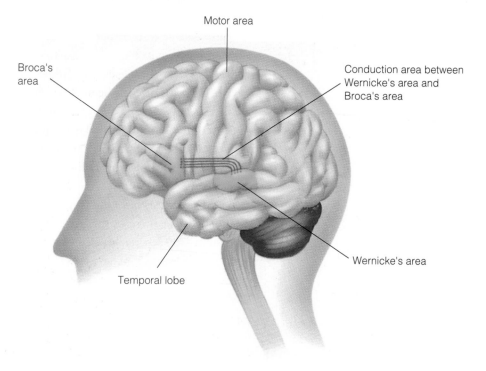

Motor area

Broca's area

Conduction area between Wernicke's area and Broca's area

Wernicke's area

Temporal lobe

More recent studies have shown, however, that the right side of the brain is not as inferior as it once seemed. Interest in the right hemisphere was provoked in large part by the work of Roger Sperry and his colleagues (Sperry, 1970, 1974; Sperry, Gazzaniga, & Bogen, 1969), who performed experiments on **split-brain patients.** (For his contributions to this research, Sperry was awarded a Nobel Prize in medicine in 1981.) The biggest connection between the hemispheres consists of a massive fiber bundle called the **corpus callosum.** In certain cases of epilepsy, a seizure can travel by means of the corpus callosum from one side of the brain to the other. When the fibers are severed, the disorder may be controlled; the patient gets relief and can perform quite normally.

Patients who have had their corpus callosum severed are referred to as split-brain patients because the corpus callosum no longer connects the hemispheres, thereby isolating information in one hemisphere or the other.

Split-brain patients offered researchers like Sperry a unique opportunity to study the brain, but the researchers had to resolve several thorny problems before proceeding. Because verbal abilities are customarily controlled by one hemisphere, usually the left, when you are talking to a split-brain person, you are talking to the left hemisphere. The right hemisphere is "mute." In the laboratory, however, sensory information can be presented to the right hemisphere alone or to the left hemisphere alone. For example, a blindfolded split-brain patient can name a simple object felt by the right hand because sensory information from the right hand goes to the left hemisphere, where language production is controlled. If the object is placed in the left hand, however, the patient cannot name the object because the right hemisphere is mute. If the blindfold is removed, the patient can point to the recently touched object with the left hand. The patient might even say "I don't know what it is," at the same time pointing with the left hand to the correct choice. Of course researchers must prevent the split-brain person from watching the left hand pick up the object in the center or right visual field, because then the left hemisphere will know what is going on. Such an experiment shows that the right hemisphere is capable of perceiving, remembering, and demonstrating its knowledge by initiating movement, although it is incapable of verbalizing these experiences.

Studying the visual operations of each hemisphere is a little trickier. Because of the distribution of fibers in the optic system, information presented to each eye is projected almost equally to both hemispheres. Thus, information received by the right eye does not simply go to the left hemisphere, and information from the left eye does not simply go to the right hemisphere. Instead, information in the right half of each eye's visual field goes to the left hemisphere, and information in the left half of each eye's visual field goes to the right hemisphere (see Figure 3.10). To ensure that information is presented to only one hemisphere, researchers instruct the split-brain patient to fixate on (look at) a point. Then information projected to the right half of the visual field goes only to the left hemisphere, and the right hemisphere "sees" objects on the left half of the visual field.

Such experiments have shown that the right hemisphere has functions of its own that complement those of the left hemisphere. The right hemisphere, for example, seems superior in accurately perceiving and remembering stimuli too complex to specify in words. Patients who have suffered damage to certain portions of the right hemisphere have great difficulty remembering familiar faces seen in snapshots (Yin, 1970). Work with split-brain patients has confirmed and extended these findings. In one experiment (Levy, Trevarthen, & Sperry, 1972) split-brain patients were presented with a photograph that was a combination of two different faces, the right half of one

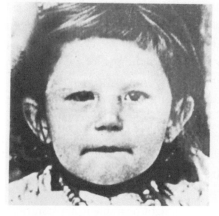

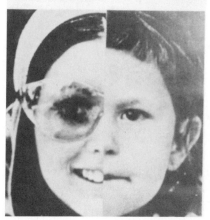

FIGURE 2.20
Photos Used to Test Split-Brain Patients

The composite photo is presented to split-brain patients. When asked which of the photos they have seen, the patients will pick the child if asked to respond verbally. This is the face presented to the right visual field and thus "seen" by the verbal left hemisphere. The respondents do not report anything unusual about the face; rather, they report seeing a whole face.

face and the left half of another (see Figure 2.20). This composite was shown to the patients quickly so that the two halves met at the point of fixation. When only half pictures were shown to one-half the visual field, the split-brain patients saw whole pictures, their brains completed them (Nebes, 1974). So with a composite, presumably each hemisphere would "see" a different whole picture. This appeared to be the case. When asked what they had seen, the patients always described the right-field face, that is, the one seen by the left hemisphere. They did not report anything unusual about it, but said they had seen a complete face. When asked to point with their left hand to the picture they saw, they pointed to the left-field face, seen by the right hemisphere. This result seems to indicate that the right hemisphere is dominant for the perception of complex visual stimuli (Levy, 1980; Nebes, 1974).

The right hemisphere also appears to have a highly developed spatial and pattern sense. If each side of the brain in a split-brain patient receives a simple line drawing and the patient is asked to copy it, the left hand (controlled by the right hemisphere) will do a better job than the right hand (controlled by the left hemisphere), even in right-handed patients. As you can see in Figure 2.21, a split-brain patient did a much better job of copying the cross and the rectangle with his left hand (controlled by his right hemisphere) than with his right hand, despite being right-handed.

Aside from visual and spatial abilities, the right hemisphere has some limited language abilities; studies have shown that it can understand simple spoken or written language (Levy, 1983). For example, subjects using their right hemispheres could correctly indicate whether they "saw" an object described by the experimenter, but they could not indicate whether the object had a name (Levy & Trevarthen, 1974). A split-brain person who hears a verbal description of an object can feel objects with the

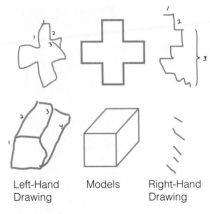

FIGURE 2.21
Drawings by a Split-Brain Patient

Left-Hand   Models   Right-Hand
Drawing   Drawing

Drawings of the models were done by a split-brain patient with his right hand and with his left hand. He did a much better job with his left hand (controlled by the right hemisphere) than with his right hand, despite being right-handed.

SOURCE: Bogen, 1969.

left hand (right hemisphere) and pick up the correct object, so the right hemisphere must understand the name of the object.

Finally, some studies suggest that the right hemisphere can be important in the accurate interpretation of emotional stimuli and in communication of emotion (Tucker, 1981). In one study, photos of faces displaying emotion were divided, and the right and left halves were combined with their mirror images (see Figure 2.22). Researchers presented the combined photos to a panel of judges, who indicated that the left side of the face in right-handers expressed emotion more intensely than the right side of the face (Sackheim, Gur, & Saucy, 1978). Damage to the right hemisphere interferes with production of facial expressions of emotion and with understanding other people's facial expressions of emotion (Borod, Koff, Lorch, & Nicholas, 1986). The right hemisphere also contributes to the emotional content of speech; people who have suffered damage to the right hemisphere speak with less emotion than normal (Shapiro & Danly, 1985).

Traditionally, psychologists have viewed the brain and consciousness as a unit: the "I" used in speech referred to one's consciousness. But split-brain research seems to indicate there is more than one "I." In a split-brain patient the speaking left hemisphere is totally unaware of the nonspeaking right hemisphere. We explore implications of split-brain patients for the study of consciousness in Chapter 5. The part of the brain of which we are aware may be only one part of the brain, a part whose function is to interpret the operation of the many other nonconscious parts (Gazzaniga, 1985). However, the conclusion that there are two types of consciousness may be hard for us to accept, especially if it is based on research with only a small number of split brain patients. Does it also hold true for normal adults? As the next section will demonstrate, the answer seems to be yes.

CONCEPT SUMMARY

SPLINT BRAIN PATIENTS

	RIGHT HEMISPHERE	LEFT HEMISPHERE
Cognitive Functions	Limited language	Full language abilities
Vision	Receives stimuli from left visual field, superior in complex visual stimuli such as faces	Receives stimuli from right visual field
Motor Function	Left side of body	Right side of body
Spatial Ability	Superior	—

Other Evidence of Lateralization. Fortunately, the main findings about cerebral organization obtained with split-brain patients and people who have suffered brain damage have been confirmed by other experiments on normal (non-brain-damaged) people. For example, Doreen Kimura (1961, 1964) presented different information simultaneously to the two ears of normal people and asked the subjects to report what they heard. When presented with words, the subjects tended to recall the ones sent to the right ear slightly better than the words ones sent to the left ear. When presented

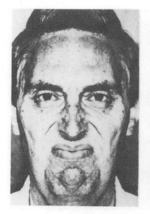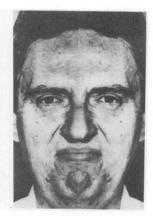

FIGURE 2.22
Three Faces of Emotion

The original photograph is shown in the middle. It was divided in half, and the left half with its mirror image is shown on the left. The right half and its mirror image is shown on the right. The expression of disgust is much more evident in the photograph on the left. This suggests that emotions are expressed more intensely by the left side of the face, controlled by the right hemisphere.

with competing melodies, however, the subjects could identify those played to the left ear slightly better than those played to the right. In general, Kimura and other researchers found that there was a left-ear advantage for music and other noises. These findings are consistent with other research on cerebral organization that shows that neural connections are stronger from each ear to the cerebral hemisphere on the opposite side of the head. Thus, information from the right ear is analyzed primarily by the left hemisphere, resulting in the right-ear advantage for speech. Information from the left ear is analyzed by the right hemisphere, leading to the left-ear advantage for nonspeech sounds. Results using positron emission tomography substantiate these findings (Phelps & Mazziotta, 1985). Figure 2.23 shows the results of a PET scan: Consistent with conclusions reached on the basis of studying the behavior of split-brain patients and normal subjects, verbal stimuli primarily activate the left hemisphere, while music primarily activates the right hemisphere.

In another study, R. C. Gur and colleagues. (1982) gave people verbal or visual tasks to perform and measured blood flow in the two hemispheres during task performance and during rest periods. Blood flow in both hemispheres was greater when people performed the tasks than when they rested, but the flow was greater in the left

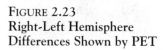
FIGURE 2.23
Right-Left Hemisphere Differences Shown by PET

As the bottom part of this photograph shows, verbal auditory stimuli primarily activate the left hemisphere, while music primarily activates the right hemisphere. (The top of each brain is the front, so the left side is the left hemisphere, and the right side is the right hemisphere.) Simultaneous music and language activate both hemispheres, as shown in the upper right half of the photograph.

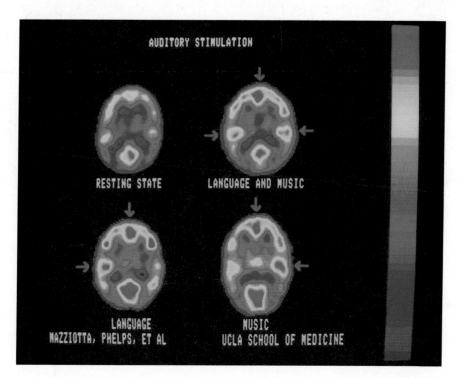

ARE THE BRAINS OF MEN AND WOMEN DIFFERENT?

In the nineteenth century physicians claimed that women had "smaller brains with less capacity" (cited in Halpern, 1992, p. 140). Actually, men's brains do tend to be larger than those of women, but then, men generally are larger than women. But the difference in brain size between men and women cannot be accounted for just in terms of body size. Men's brains are on average 15% larger than those of women, about twice the difference in average body size between men and women (Gibbons, 1991).

There are also structural differences between the brains of men and women, although these are not visible to the naked eye. These differences are primarily in the hypothalamus, which is responsible for reproductive behavior. There is a small structure termed the sexually dimorphic nucleus (SDN). The SDN is 2 1/2 times larger in men than in women. The function of the SDN is unknown, although there is speculation that it is involved in sexual identity. And the corpus callosum, the bundle of nerve fibers that connects the right and left hemispheres, starts out larger in men, but then decreases in size with age. In women, its size remains stable over time. It is hypothesized that these sex differences in the corpus callosum are related to supposed differences in the degree to which female and male brains are lateralized, or the degree to which right and left hemisphere function differs.

It appears that the male brain is more likely to have visual-spatial abilities, such as those needed to put together a jigsaw puzzle, localized in the right hemisphere, and verbal abilities in the left hemisphere; the female brain is more likely to be bilateral, so that verbal and visual-spatial abilities are represented in both hemispheres. Consistent with this idea, Bryden (1988) found 74 percent of females but 81 percent of males responded more quickly to letters or words presented to their right ear than to those presented to their left ear. This indicates that men have a somewhat greater left hemisphere dominance for responding to verbal stimuli. Most researchers find that when stimuli are presented briefly to specific visual fields, males show greater right visual field superiority for verbal materials (e.g., Voyer & Bryden, 1990) and greater left visual field advantage for spatial stimuli (e.g., Kimura & Durnford, 1974). Comparable studies with females produce contradictory results. The most common conclusion from this literature is that women's hemispheres are more symmetrical than men's (Halpern, 1992). This conclusion is not universally supported because results of experiments are not always consistent. But as pointed out by Halpern (1992), the most com-

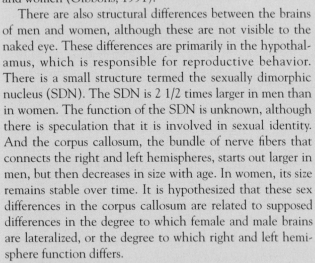

pelling point is that when differences in hemispheric specialization are found, lateralization is always greater in males than in females.

If this difference in lateralization is real, what does it mean for behavior? If females are more likely to use both hemispheres for processing verbal information, this could explain why they are less likely than males to have reading disabilities, dyslexia, stuttering, and speech disorders. If verbal abilities are represented in both hemispheres, females would be less susceptible to local brain injury or trauma interfering with speech and language. Levy (1976) suggested that because verbal abilities seem to be represented in both hemispheres in females, there may be no location for possible dominance by spatial abilities. Thus females would be less likely to have strong spatial abilities. Some researchers have suggested that male left-handers are most likely to have spatial abilities localized in the right hemisphere and to have this the "dominant" hemisphere. This would explain why left-handed males are over-represented among architects, engineers, mathematicians, artists, and chess masters.

Males and females differ reliably in spatial reasoning, with males being superior. This difference has persisted over time and also holds across cultures (Holden, 1991), making biologically oriented researchers conclude that biology must have a role in this cognitive difference between men and women. Others believe that sex differences are produced by sociocultural factors. Cognitive differences between males and females in verbal and math ability have decreased in recent years, coinciding with a trend to treat males and females more alike (Holden, 1991). Perhaps the only brain differences between males and females relate only to those parts of the brain that control reproductive function; perhaps cognition is determined primarily by psychosocial factors rather than by biology. This issue remains unsettled. Figure 2.24 shows some of the differences between men and women on various tasks as reported by Kimura (1992).

hemisphere when they performed verbal tasks and greater in the right hemisphere when they performed spatial tasks. Studies such as these indicate a firm basis for the belief that the hemispheres of the brain are differentially involved in processing different sorts of information.

Some investigators have suggested that the asymmetry of function is greater in males than in females (Springer & Deutsch, 1993). That is, right-handed males seem to have verbal operations more isolated in the left hemisphere, while right-handed females are more likely to show some language functioning in the right hemisphere as well as the left. This possibility is discussed in Psychology in Our Times.

FIGURE 2.24
Differences between Men and Women on Various Tasks

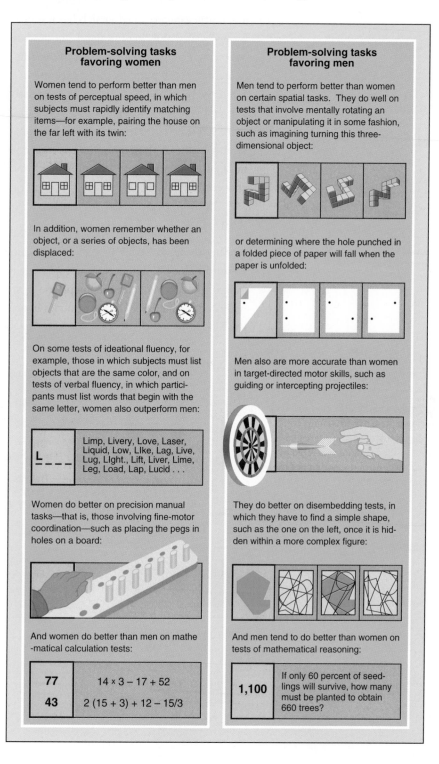

Problem-solving tasks favoring women

Women tend to perform better than men on tests of perceptual speed, in which subjects must rapidly identify matching items—for example, pairing the house on the far left with its twin:

In addition, women remember whether an object, or a series of objects, has been displaced:

On some tests of ideational fluency, for example, those in which subjects must list objects that are the same color, and on tests of verbal fluency, in which participants must list words that begin with the same letter, women also outperform men:

L _ _ _   Limp, Livery, Love, Laser, Liquid, Low, LIke, Lag, Live, Lug, LIght., Lift, Liver, Lime, Leg, Load, Lap, Lucid . . .

Women do better on precision manual tasks—that is, those involving fine-motor coordination—such as placing the pegs in holes on a board:

And women do better than men on mathe-matical calculation tests:

77   14 × 3 – 17 + 52
43   2 (15 + 3) + 12 – 15/3

Problem-solving tasks favoring men

Men tend to perform better than women on certain spatial tasks. They do well on tests that involve mentally rotating an object or manipulating it in some fashion, such as imagining turning this three-dimensional object:

or determining where the hole punched in a folded piece of paper will fall when the paper is unfolded:

Men also are more accurate than women in target-directed motor skills, such as guiding or intercepting projectiles:

They do better on disembedding tests, in which they have to find a simple shape, such as the one on the left, once it is hidden within a more complex figure:

And men tend to do better than women on tests of mathematical reasoning:

1,100   If only 60 percent of seedlings will survive, how many must be planted to obtain 660 trees?

The Endocrine System

The **endocrine system** consists of a set of glands secreting **hormones,** chemical messengers carried by the bloodstream to other body organs (*endocrine* means "inside secreting"). The endocrine system is under the control of the nervous system.

The major endocrine glands are shown in Figure 2.25.

THE PITUITARY GLAND

The endocrine system is linked to the nervous system by effects of the hypothalamus on the *pituitary gland,* which lies just below the hypothalamus. The pituitary gland is often called the "master gland," because its secretions control the activity of other endocrine glands. This may be a misleading name, however, because the hypothalamus controls the pituitary gland's secretion; the pituitary gland itself does not initiate activity. The hypothalamus controls the activity of the pituitary gland by the production and release of hormones that travel to the pituitary gland. These hormones may then be released into the general circulation, or they may in turn stimulate the synthesis and release of pituitary hormones. Some pituitary hormones have direct effects, but most of them stimulate the production and release of other hormones by other endocrine glands.

THE ADRENAL GLANDS

The *adrenal glands* lie just above the kidneys (adrenal is from the Latin, meaning "toward kidney"). Their central core, called the adrenal medulla, secretes the hormones epinephrine and norepinephrine in stressful situations (epinephrine is another name for adrenaline). These hormones increase the liver's sugar output and accelerate the heart rate and the surge of blood to the skeletal muscles, reinforcing the action of

FIGURE 2.25
Location of the Major Endocrine Glands

Thee glands secrete hormones into the bloodstream. The hypothalamus controls the activity of the pituitary gland, and most of the hormones secreted by the pituitary control the activity of the other endocrine glands.

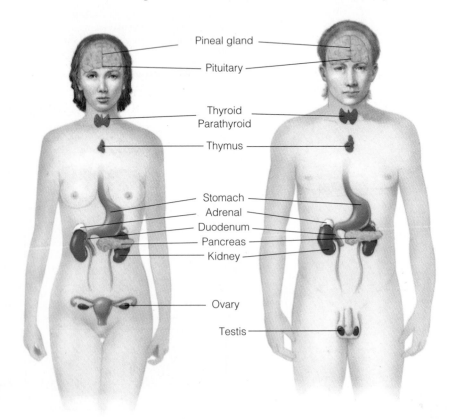

Pineal gland

Pituitary

Thyroid
Parathyroid

Thymus

Stomach
Adrenal
Duodenum
Pancreas
Kidney

Ovary

Testis

the sympathetic nervous system. People often say that their "adrenaline is flowing" to indicate excitement. Norepinephrine is also an excitatory neurotransmitter for organs controlled by the sympathetic nervous system (see pages 52–53). When the body must react to stress, the sympathetic nervous system and the endocrine system work together. (The long-term effects of continued stress are considered in Chapter 13.)

The outer portion of the adrenal glands is called the adrenal cortex. It generates a large number of chemicals, including *androgens*, the male sex hormones. Androgens are secreted by the adrenal glands of both men and women. When the adrenal cortex overproduces male hormones in a woman, a malelike appearance may result.

THE SEX GLANDS

The sex glands, or gonads, synthesize reproductive hormones under influence of the hypothalamus by way of the pituitary gland. These hormones cause tissues to have male or female characteristics. In women the ovaries release the female sex hormones *estrogen* and *progesterone*. These hormones regulate the female cycle of ovulation and menstruation. The effects of the sex hormones in producing sex differences in the brain, as well as in physical appearance and behavior are discussed in Chapter 10.

Geschwind and Galaburda (1985) suggest sex hormones may be involved in the differences between males and females in asymmetry of brain function discussed in Psychology and Our Times. High levels of the male sex hormone testosterone may delay the maturation of the left hemisphere and may also retard the growth of various structures in the immune system. This could produce a tendency toward left-handedness, well-developed right hemisphere functions but weaker left hemisphere functions, and immune system disorders. Indeed, the combination of left-handedness and immune system disorders is also linked to abnormalities such as dyslexia and stuttering, as well as to artistic, musical, and mathematical talent. Because males are more likely to be exposed to testosterone prenatally, they should be more affected. Indeed, boys are more likely than girls to be left-handed, to be gifted mathematically, to stutter, and to have dyslexia (Kolata, 1983). However, the variations from one individual to another are much larger than the average differences between males and females (Byne, Bleier, & Houston, 1988).

Social and environmental factors can affect hormones. In many animals behavior of the male can stimulate sex hormones in the female and vice versa. In ring doves (pigeons), for example, the male struts around, coos, and displays before a female. This behavior leads to increased estrogen production in the female. The male, in turn, seems to be excited by observing the female and his androgen production increases. Moreover, sitting on eggs for 14 days increases production of the hormone prolactin in either male or female doves, stimulating the production of crop milk and predisposing them to take care of their babies (Davidson, 1972).

THE PINEAL GLAND

The lack of melatonin, a hormone released by the pineal gland, is thought by some psychologists to be the basis of a problem called "seasonal affective disorder" where the long fall and winter produces depression in some people. This disorder is accompanied by greater sleepiness, increased appetite, weight gain, fatigue, daytime drowsiness, and a craving for carbohydrates. Sunlight causes melatonin to be released, so the long winter months lead to its decreased production. Successful treatment can be achieved by using bright artificial light at least 12 times brighter than ordinary indoor light.

Exposure to bright light in the morning (but not the evening) leads to earlier night-time secretion of melatonin and reduction in depression (Lewy et al., 1987). Bright light treatment has also been shown to shift human daily biological rhythm, making it easier to adjust to "jet lag" and other situations of drastic time change (Czeizler et al., 1989). After a long plane trip across time zones, it's a good idea to spend a lot of time in bright sunlight to adjust easily to the new time.

You can think of the endocrine system as a second communication system in the body in addition to, and under the control of, the nervous system. The nervous system sends signals electrically and chemically; the endocrine system sends signals chemically, by release of hormones into the bloodstream.

Evolution, Genetics, and Behavior

The theory of evolution is central to the biological sciences. It assumes that all existing species have evolved over millions of years. Our understanding of the way evolution may have occurred is largely due to the work of Charles Darwin (1809-1882) and Gregor Mendel (1822-1884). Darwin developed the theory of natural selection, and Mendel provided the foundation for the science of genetics. Evolutionary theory and genetics were brought together in the 1930s with the development of the "modern synthetic theory of evolution" or the modern synthesis, as it is more commonly known.

Darwin published his theory in 1859 under the title *On the Origin of the Species by Means of Natural Selection, or the Preservation of Favoured Races in the Struggle for Life*. In every species, Darwin wrote, individuals differ, and these differences derive in part from heredity. If one individual proves more fertile or survives longer than another, its chances of leaving descendants become greater. This had been recognized for centuries. Darwin's **theory of natural selection** suggested that such selective survival could be a mechanism for changes in organisms. If an inherited trait influenced the likelihood of surviving to maturity and reproducing, then there would be more individuals possessing this trait in successive generations. Thus, gradually, the characteristics of a population could change, and over a sufficiently long period, the changes could become so great that they would amount to a new species. The phrase "survival of the fittest" came to encapsulate Darwin's theory. For Darwin the concept of fitness simply referred to the production of offspring that would themselves successfully reproduce. Organisms that produced more viable offspring were fitter.

GENETICS: FROM PEA PLANTS TO PEOPLE

The study of genetics began with the work of Gregor Mendel, an Augustinian monk who conducted research on peas. By crossing plants and observing their characteristics over many generations, Mendel concluded that some traits of the plants passed from parent to offspring and that the traits were not always visible in the offspring when they were visible in the parents, or vice versa. Some attributes could be transmitted from "grandparent" to "grandchild" without being manifest in the physical appearance of the intervening generation. In 1909, the name **gene** was proposed for the fixed element, or fundamental unit, of heredity. Today, we know that information in genes is coded as a sequence of complex molecular bases forming part of the large molecule deoxyribonucleic acid (DNA). The term **genotype** stands for the genetic composition of an individual, while **phenotype** refers to the visible, measurable characteristics, or traits of an individual, including behavior. Although phenotype is related to genotype, the two are not the same; unlike the genotype the phenotype may be influenced by environmental factors.

Now let's see how some basic principles of genetics apply to people. Each person receives half of his/her genes from each parent. Genes come in pairs (one from each parent), and they are contained within **chromosomes** in each cell of the body. Except for the sex cells, every human cell contains 46 chromosomes, 23 from the mother and 23 from the father. Each sex cell (sperm or ovum) contains 23 of a possible 46 chromosomes (or one member of each pair of chromosomes found in the cells). The cell always contains 23 chromosomes out of the 46, but which particular 23 chromosomes varies from cell to cell. At the time of conception the sperm from the father and the ovum from the mother unite to produce a new cell, called a *zygote*, which will develop into a new human being.

Because each ovum has 23 of a possible 46 chromosomes from the mother and each sperm has 23 of a possible 46 chromosomes from the father, the same parents can produce many different zygotes having different combinations of chromosomes. The odds are overwhelmingly against any two humans being genetic duplicates, except in the case of identical twins. In general, however, there is genetic variation among children of the same parents. If you are not an identical twin, you are a unique genetic individual. Note, however, that children of the same parents are more genetically similar than are children of different parents. On the average, siblings share half of their genes. But also note that **fraternal twins** (dizygotic twins) develop from two different zygotes and so are no more similar in heredity than other brothers and sisters. **Identical twins** (monozygotic twins) develop from a single zygote and therefore have identical genes.

Clearly, there is a great deal of genetic variation within species; that is, individuals differ in what genes they possess. And according to the theory of natural selection, the genetic make-up of an organism influences fitness or its likelihood of having viable offspring. As a result, the sum of all genes, called the *gene pool*, changes over generations. Obviously, organisms that do not reproduce do not add their genes to the gene pool of the next generation, whereas individuals who bear more viable offspring contribute more of their genes. Changes in the gene pool are not mere fluctuations but are cumulative, accounting for "descent with modification" over time or evolution. The idea that genes are the fundamental unit of evolution has been proposed by sociobiologists, who believe that many social behaviors are actually inherited traits. (See Controversy, p. 78.)

BEHAVIOR GENETICS

As we have seen, individual variation occurs within every species, and some of that variation reflects differences in the genes among individuals. However, a portion of the variation is also due to the environments in which individuals live or the experiences that they have. The field of **behavior genetics** analyzes the contributions of genotype and environment to behavior.

All the characteristics possessed by you or any animal are affected by genes and environment. Behavior geneticists ask how the environment and genes operate together to produce a particular characteristic. For example, drinking milk is harmless for many people because they have the enzyme necessary to digest milk. If this enzyme is lacking, as it is in some populations, milk acts like a mild poison: its lactose (milk

SOCIOBIOLOGY: SHOULD WE LOOK TO THE GENES?

In his highly influential book *Sociobiology: The New Synthesis*, E. O. Wilson defines **sociobiology** as "the systematic study of the biological basis of all social behavior" (Wilson, 1975, p. 4). Its practitioners aim to understand all types of social behavior, including such complex behaviors as aggression, altruism, dominance, and sexual attraction, in evolutionary terms, by emphasizing how each behavior is consistent with the principle of natural selection. We can discuss the sociobiological approach by considering the problem of altruism.

Altruism is defined as any action that benefits other species members but does not benefit the individual who performs the action. For example, an animal can risk its life to save its offspring or its mate. But if a particular individual dies to save another prior to reproducing, its genes will not be passed on to the next generation. This implies that over generations, genes for this variety of altruism will be selected out. Yet, animals, including humans, continue to show altruistic behaviors. How can this fact be reconciled with evolutionary theory?

This paradox can be resolved if the idea of individual fitness is replaced by the concept of inclusive fitness. Fitness is the ability to produce offspring that subsequently reproduce. Whereas **individual fitness** refers to the individual's chance of reproducing, **inclusive fitness** is the sum of an individual's own fitness plus the fitness of relatives who share a high percentage of the same genes. Individuals may actually make a greater contribution of their own genes to the next generation's gene pool by sacrificing themselves to save their relatives. Because an individual shares an average of 50 percent of his or her genes with brothers and sisters, 50 percent with children, and 25 percent with uncles, aunts, nephews, and nieces, more of the individual's genes can survive if enough relatives are saved by self-sacrifice. For example, if a man dies for the sake of three brothers, about 1 1/2 times his genes will survive and potentially be passed on to the next generation. By

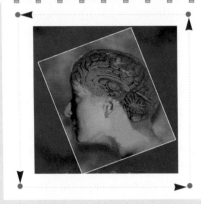

focusing on genes as the fundamental unit of evolution sociobiologists provide an answer to the riddle of altruism in animals.

Now let's consider the application of sociobiology to some aspects of mate selection. In choosing mates, males and females of most mammalian species (including humans) often employ different strategies. A female who must bear and care for the young is most likely to be successful in passing on her genes if she mates with the best male available, best in the sense of producing more offspring that will survive or being able to care for offspring once they have arrived. A male, on the other hand, has enough sperm to impregnate incredibly large numbers of females, and he is more likely to pass on his genes by impregnating as many females as possible. In many species, females mate with the winner of fights, that is, the stronger male. Do you think human behavior fits this model? Some do, pointing out that males often compete for a female, and males tend to be less monogamous than females. As you can imagine, the idea that a male's biology goes against monogamy is very controversial.

David Buss (1994) distinguishes between short-term and long-term mating strategies. Short-term mating is more important to men, Buss suggests, while women are more interested in long-term commitment. Buss finds that the average man is willing to have intercourse with a woman after knowing her only one week, while most women are highly unlikely to be willing to have intercourse after such a short

period of time. These data come from a sample of 148 college students. Buss relates this difference in mating strategy to the difference in parental investment. The minimum parental investment by a female is the 9-month gestation period, usually also followed by a nursing period. In males, the minimum parental investment is a few minutes, the time necessary to contribute sperm. This difference in minimum parental investment may account for women being choosier regarding mating partners (Buss, 1994). In a study by Clark and Hatfield (cited in Buss, 1994), college students were approached by an attractive member of the opposite sex, who asked, "Would you go out on a date with me tonight?" "Would you go back to my apartment with me tonight?" or "Would you have sex with me tonight?" Half the women said yes to a date, 6 percent agreed to go to the apartment and none agreed to have sex. Half the men also agreed to the date, but 69 percent agreed to go to the apartment and 75 percent agreed to have sex. The men found the sexual request flattering; the women found it strange and insulting.

The desire to seek long-term mates who can protect children also explains the tendency for women to look for mates with high social status and good financial prospects, a tendency reported across many cultures (Buss, 1994).

Attempts to explain behavior in sociobiological terms usually involve indirect arguments and analogies that may indeed be plausible, but contrary arguments are also plausible. And many of the behaviors studied by sociobiologists are heavily influenced by sociocultural factors. Thus, many people question whether sociobiological ideas provide an accurate account of human behavior.

sugar) produces a gastrointestinal disorder. Because the ability or inability to digest milk is seen as hereditary, it is appropriate to say that the difference among people in the ability to digest milk is produced by differences in their genes.

In general, the strategy to determine if differences in genes relate to differences in behavior is simple: Locate organisms of different genotypes, hold the environment constant, and see if behaviors differ. Since genes are not directly observable, determining genotypes may prove difficult. An observer cannot infer that organisms that look alike (have similar phenotypes) also have similar genotypes. With subjects other than humans, behavior geneticists employ two methods: strain comparison and selective breeding.

Strain Comparison.   The strain comparison method employs **inbred strains** of mice and other animals. These are produced by mating brothers and sisters, then mating brothers and sisters among the offspring, and so on. After at least 20 generations, virtual identity of genes results; that is, members of a particular strain of mice have the same genes. Many different inbred strains of mice have been developed. When two different strains are reared in the same environment, disparities in their behavior are related to variations in their genes. Inbred strains differ, for example, in the reinforcing effects of alcohol (Elmer, Meisch, & George, 1987), taste perception (Tobach, Bellin, & Das, 1974), seizure susceptibility (Deckard et al. 1976), and performance in many learning situations (e.g., Anisman, 1975). Indeed, it is much easier to find strains of animals that differ on a particular task than to find strains that do not (Plomin, DeFries, & McClearn, 1990).

Selective Breeding.   In **selective breeding,** phenotype rather than genotype determines the choice of animals. Recall that a phenotype is any observable trait. Behavior geneticists usually measure a behavioral trait and select animals for breeding on the basis of it. For example, an experimenter might record the activity of animals in an open field. (In the laboratory, an open field is a large, walled-in area with sections marked on the floor.) Highly emotional animals are less active in the open field than less emotional ones. Males that score high in activity are mated with high-scoring females; low-scoring males are mated with low-scoring females. Activity of the offspring is measured, and again, mating is based on comparable levels of activity. If activity has a genetic component, over generations the activity scores of the high and low lines should diverge. Results of a study in which investigators selected mating pairs on the basis of activity scores in the open field are shown in Figure 2.26 (DeFries, Hegmann, & Halcomb, 1974). Two high-scoring and two low-scoring lines were bred. To control possible environmental changes over generations, researchers bred two randomly bred lines as well. Figure 2.26 shows the scores of one of each type of line. As you can see, the scores of the high and low lines diverged over the 20 generations: Those of the high line increased, while those of the low line decreased. The control line's scores did not change appreciably. These data indicate that differences in genes play a role in producing disparities in open-field activity.

Often whether a difference in genes is expressed in behavior depends on environmental variation. For example, in one well-known study, rats were selectively bred for speed in learning a maze, producing a group of rapid learners (maze-bright rats) and a group of slow learners (maze-dull rats) (Cooper & Zubek, 1958). The two groups differed significantly in performance, however, only if they were reared in a normal environment. When the environment was restricted (plain gray cages), they did about the

FIGURE 2.26
Open-Field Activity Scores for
Three Lines of Mice Bred over 20
Generations

The top line shows the scores of animals
bred for high activity; the middle line
shows the control animals, which were
randomly bred; and the bottom line
shows the scores for mice bred for low
activity. The divergence on the activity
scores over generations suggests that
there is a genetic component to open-
field activity.

SOURCE: DeFries, Hegmann, & Halcomb, 1974.

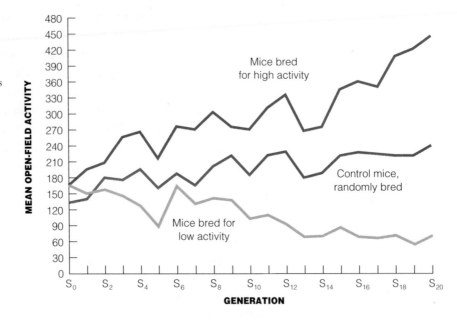

same, poorly; the superiority of the rapid learners was not evident. When the environment was enriched by many movable toys in the cages, the rapid learners did only a
little better than the slow learners and the slow learners' performance was much
improved. The difference between the maze-bright and maze-dull rats was large only
in the normal environment. This evidence further supports the idea that environmental and genetic influences combine to produce behavior.

Although most of our knowledge of animal behavior genetics comes from studies of
inbred or selectively bred strains, this field is being revolutionized by advances in molecular genetics. With modern molecular genetic technology, we can study DNA variation of any species directly (Plomin et al., 1990).

In some ways, studying the relationship between genes and behavior in humans is
similar to such studies with nonhuman animals. Researchers need to find people
whose genotype and environments are known and then compare the behavior of people whose genotypes are different but whose environments are the same. Any difference in behavior would then be related to the difference in genotype. In human
beings, however, inbreeding and selective breeding obviously cannot be used for ethical reasons, so geneticists have developed other methods. Comparing identical and
fraternal twins, in twin studies, is one way to measure genetic influences on human
behavior. Another way is to study people in the same family and trace the appearance
of a trait over generations.

Twin Studies. If genes strongly influence a trait, identical twins should be more
similar in that trait than fraternal twins; identical twins share identical genes, while
fraternal twins do not. To determine if there is a genetic basis for schizophrenia, for
example, one strategy is to find schizophrenics who are members of twin pairs and
then to measure the percentage of co-twins who also have schizophrenia. The percentage is called the **concordance rate.** In 1982 Gottesman and Shields presented the
results of five twin studies of schizophrenia since 1966, all of which obtained a higher
concordance rate among identical twins than among fraternal twins (average concordance was .46 for identical twins and .14 for fraternal twins). Kendler and Robinette
(1983) studied all male twins who were U.S. veterans of World War II. They found

Identical twins are genetically identical and so are always the same gender and always look alike (right photograph). Fraternal twins are no more alike genetically than other brothers and sisters and so can be the same or different genders and may or may not look alike (left photograph). The fraternal twins shown are Betty and David Deutsch visiting Santa Claus. Even though they are twins, Betty is taller than David because girls mature at a faster rate. However, David grew to 6'1", seven inches taller than his sister and played professional basketball for the New York Knickerbockers. (Betty is now Betty Capaldi, one of the authors of your book.)

concordances for schizophrenia of .31 for 164 pairs of identical twins and .065 for 268 pairs of fraternal twins. These results suggest a genetic basis for schizophrenia. Of course, you should also realize that a concordance rate of less than 1 between identical twins means that environmental factors must also play a role in schizophrenia. Actually, the study of differences within pairs of identical twins is an important method of identifying environmental influences.

Although these results suggest a genetic basis for schizophrenia, a higher concordance rate for identical twins than for fraternal twins could also be due to a greater similarity of environment. Identical twins are more likely to dress alike and be treated alike. This argument can be made even when twins reared apart are studied, because identical twins are more likely to be placed in similar environments when adopted than are fraternal twins. However, identical twins reared apart are rare. While there is one ongoing study in the United States of such twins (Bouchard, 1984, see Chapter 14), and two studies in Scandinavia, one estimate is that all the world's literature adds up to fewer than 100 pairs (Plomin et al., 1990). Twin studies will be considered further in Chapters 11 and 14. Studies of adopted children are more common in family studies, considered next.

Family Studies.   Another method used to measure a genetic influence on behavior is to study families. Family members have similar genes. You share half your genes with your mother and half with your father. On average, you also share half your genes with your brothers and sisters. However, most families also live together, so if families share a common trait, it could be related to common environment or common genes, or both.

Nearsightedness, or myopia, clearly runs in families, but is it determined by hereditary factors or environmental factors? Zadnik (reported in Iarovici, 1994) studied 716 schoolchildren in a town near Berkeley, California. Nearsightedness usually develops between the ages of 8 and 14, so she studied this age-group and measured the number of hours spent reading, playing videogames, and watching television. When she controlled for differences in these behaviors, she found that if both parents were myopic, 12.2 percent of the children were myopic, while 8.2 percent were myopic when only one parent was myopic and 2.7 percent if neither parent was myopic. This suggests a strong hereditary factor in myopia. There was also a small effect of the amount of "near work." A large amount of near work seems to cause a defect in development of the normal self-correcting mechanism that adjusts the length of the eye to focus correctly. Thus, both environmental and hereditary factors influence myopia.

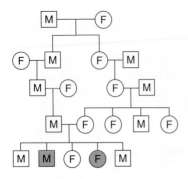

FIGURE 2.27
A Family History of the Occurrence of Epilepsy

Shown at the top are the great-great-grandparents, and below the following generations. A blue symbol indicates epilepsy, an open symbol indicates an unaffected individual. Females are represented by circles, males by squares. Parents are joined by a horizontal marriage line, with offspring listed below. Brothers and sisters are connected to a horizontal line that is joined by a perpendicular line to their parent's marriage line. As you can see, the disease occurred in two of five children from a marriage between people descended from the same ancestor. This suggests a recessive mode of inheritance.

One way to separate environmental and hereditary factors is to study adopted children. Heston (1966) found people born to schizophrenic mothers who were permanently separated from them before they were 1 month old and reared in foster or adoptive homes. Another group of children who also had been separated from their biological mothers before reaching 1 month of age and reared in foster homes were used as controls. The biological mothers of the control children had no record of psychiatric problems. As adults, the children of schizophrenic mothers showed significantly greater incidence of schizophrenia than did the control subjects. These data, consistent with those from the twin studies, point to a possible genetic factor in schizophrenia. Rosenthal and his colleagues (e.g., 1972) replicated these findings.

In another type of family study, investigators measure a trait within a family over generations. The pattern of appearance in family members over generations can suggest specific hypotheses about the way genes are related to the trait. Not all genes are directly reflected in observable traits (phenotype is not the same as genotype). Recessive genes, genes that lie dormant in some people, will not be expressed in a phenotype unless both members of a pair of genes are recessive. Blue eyes, for example, are determined by recessive genes. If a trait is carried by a recessive gene, the pattern of the trait's appearance needs to follow the pattern expected for a recessive trait. For example, look at the diagram in Figure 2.27 that illustrates the occurrence of epilepsy in a specific family. Notice that the parents of the two afflicted children are normal, but they have the same great-great-grandparents. This is a strong indicator of recessive inheritance in which a trait appears in one generation after having lain dormant in previous generations.

In later chapters, we will present many more studies based on the methods we have outlined here. Human behavior genetics has been especially important in research on cognitive, social, and physical development (Chapter 9), intelligence (Chapter 11), and personality (Chapter 14) and psychopathology (Chapter 15). In both Chapters 12 and 13, we will discuss the evolution of specific behaviors and behavior patterns. As you will see, the interactions of biological and environmental factors are central concerns of psychology.

THEMES IN REVIEW

This chapter has explored the *biological* basis of behavior and mental processes. Somehow, in a way we do not completely understand, the brain processes and stores information. While our conscious experience and most *cognition* is produced in the cerebral cortex, the cerebellum and hippocampus both influence *learning* and memory, and the hypothalamus and limbic system are important in motivation and emotion. The brain is not a static organ. Neurons organize themselves in a normal *developmental* process beginning before birth, and achieve a normal adult pattern. However, this pattern can be modified by experience and injury in the adult animal. Finally, we have seen that biological processes also may influence *social* behavior, as stressed by the field of sociobiology. *Learning, sociocultural* and *cognitive* factors are often considered to be independent of *biological* factors. Yet, the influence of all these factors must somehow be reflected in the brain. Ultimately, we hope to understand how the brain stores and processes all of its experiences.

SUMMARY

1 The basic unit of the nervous system is the neuron, which consists of a cell body, dendrites, and an axon. Neural conduction is an electrochemical process. Changes in the permeability of the cell membrane produce electrical changes that, if strong enough, create an action potential. An action potential travels down an axon causing terminal buttons to release neurotransmitters. These neurotransmitters cross the synaptic cleft to the dendrites and cell body of the next neuron.

2 The central nervous system consists of the brain and spinal cord. All neurons in the body outside the central nervous system are part of the peripheral nervous system, which includes the somatic and autonomic nervous systems. The autonomic nervous system consists of the parasympathetic system, important in reactions maintaining and restoring the body, and the sympathetic nervous system, important in emotional reactions.

3 The brain stem contains the medulla, pons, and midbrain, which are vital to the basic biological functions of sensing and moving. Also part of the brain stem, the cerebellum coordinates movements, and the reticular activating system is important in sleep and arousal.

4 The thalamus transmits information from the body to the brain and within the brain. The hypothalamus plays an important role in motivation (hunger, thirst, sex, temperature regulation) and regulates the endocrine system, a chemical communication system within the body. In general, the hypothalamus stimulates the pituitary gland to secrete hormones, some of which have direct effects and some of which stimulate the production and release of hormones by other endocrine glands.

5 The limbic system is important in emotion (amygdala, septum), and in memory (hippocampus).

6 The cerebral cortex is divided into four areas, or lobes: frontal, temporal, parietal, and occipital. Sensory areas of the cortex are located in the parietal, occipital, and temporal lobes; a motor area occupies the frontal lobes; and association areas are present in all lobes.

7 Studies of split-brain patients have indicated that, to some extent, humans have two brains, with each hemisphere of the brain being dominant for various functions (for example, the left hemisphere is dominant for speech for most people).

8 According to the modern synthetic theory of evolution, individuals vary in their genes; this variation influences the likelihood of having viable offspring (fitness). As a result, the gene pool changes over generations, and with the passage of enough time, these changes become so great that they produce distinct species, thereby accounting for evolution of different species.

9 In behavior genetics, organisms with different genes are compared to see if their behavior also differs. In animals this is done by using inbred strains of animals or by selective breeding. In humans, behavior genetic methods include comparing identical and fraternal twins, and examining family histories of behavior patterns.

KEY TERMS

neuron (p. 46)

threshold (p. 47)

action potential (p. 47)

refractory period (p. 48)

all-or-none law (p. 48)

myelin sheath (p. 48)

reflex (p. 49)

synapse (p. 49)

neurotransmitter (p. 49)

nervous system (p. 52)

central nervous system (p. 52)

spinal cord (p. 52)

peripheral nervous system (p. 52)

somatic nervous system (p. 52)

autonomic nervous system (p. 52)

sympathetic nervous system (p. 52)

parasympathetic nervous system (p. 52)

medulla (p. 55–56)

reticular formation (p. 56)

reticular activating system (p. 56)

cerebellum (p. 57)

thalamus (p. 57)

hypothalamus (p. 57)

limbic system (p. 58)

hippocampus (p. 59)

cerebral hemispheres (p. 59)

cerebral cortex (p. 59)

lobes (p. 59)

frontal lobe (p. 59)

temporal lobe (p. 59)

parietal lobe (p. 59)

occipital lobe (p. 59)

primary sensory areas (p. 61)

primary motor areas (p. 61)

association areas (p. 62)

plasticity (p. 63)

Broca's area (p. 65)

Wernicke's area (p. 65)

split-brain patient (p. 68)

corpus callosum (p. 68)

endocrine system (p. 74)

hormones (p. 74)

theory of natural selection (p. 76)

gene (p. 76)

genotype (p. 76)

phenotype (p. 76)

chromosomes (p. 77)

fraternal or dizygotic twins (p. 77)

identical or monozygotic twins (p. 77)

sociobiology (p. 78)

altruism (p. 78)

individual fitness (p. 78)

inclusive fitness (p. 78)

behavior genetics (p. 77)

inbred strains (p. 79)

selective breeding (p. 79)

concordance rate (p. 80)

FOR CRITICAL ANALYSIS

1 Would you advise someone under a lot of stress to take a cold medicine? Explain how your answer illustrates the basic properties of the autonomic nervous system.

2 Explain how tapping of the fingers of someone's right or left hand can measure the degree of brain lateralization.

3 Multiple sclerosis destroys the myelin sheaths of axons. What symptoms would you expect to find in this disease?

4 One way to understand brain function is to destroy or disrupt part of the brain by lesions and then measure the effect on behavior. Explain why you cannot be sure that the part of the brain you destroyed is responsible for the behavioral effect.

SUGGESTED READINGS

CARLSON, N. R. (1991). *Physiology of behavior* (4th edition). Boston: Allyn & Bacon. An excellent overview of methods and current knowledge in physiological psychology.

GARDNER, H. (1975). *The shattered mind: The person after brain damage*. New York: Vintage Books/Random House. This account details what happens to people whose brains are injured by disease or accidents and the lessons provided for the normal functioning of the brain.

GAZZANIGA, M. (Ed.) (1995). *The cognitive neurosciences*. Cambridge, MA: The MIT Press. A major source book about the neural basis of mind and behavior. Articles are by leading experts in the field.

KALAT, J. W. (1992). *Biological psychology* (4th edition) Belmont, California: Wadsworth Publishing Co. An excellent overview of biological psychology that makes the relevance of biological psychology to behavior particularly clear.

KOLB, B. & WHISHAW, I. Q. (1994). *Fundamentals of human neuropsychology* (4th. Ed.) New York: Freeman. An excellent coverage of human brain function, including many descriptions of results of specific types of brain damage.

LEGER, D. W. (1992). *Biological foundations of behavior: An integrative approach*. New York: HarperCollins. A text that integrates the physiological, genetic, and evolutionary aspects of biological psychology.

PLOMIN, R., DEFRIES, J. C., & McCLEARN, G. E. (1990). *Behavioral genetics: A primer*. Second Edition. New York: W. H. Freeman and Company. An overview of behavior genetics including new methods based on advances in molecular genetics, and presenting up-to-date information on genetic basis of traits and behaviors in humans.

THOMPSEN, R. F. (1993). *The brain: A neuroscience primer*. Second Edition. New York: W. H. Freeman and Company. An excellent introduction to neuroscience, from the neuron to higher cognition.

PSYCHOLOGY ON THE INTERNET

Neurosciences Internet Resource Guide
(http://http2.sils.umich.edu:80/Public/nirg/nirg1.htmI#alpha)

This site contains links to introductory materials and interactive tutorials concerning biological psychology and neuroanatomy. Free software such as Neuroanatomy Foundations and Brainstack provide users with "tours" of the nervous system. Color digital images highlighting the different functional areas of the brain and reviews of educational and research tools are also provided.

Psych Web's List of Psychology Resources
(http://www.gasou.edu/psychweb/resource/bytopic.html)

In addition to providing links to other neuroscience sites on the Internet, this site provides access to a number of archives containing MRI and PET images of the brain.

Basic Neural Processes Tutorial
(http://psych.hanover.edu/Krantz/neurotut.html)

This tutorial provides the user with an interactive learning experience. Activities include an on-line quiz on neural anatomy, pictorial tours of the brain, and a glossary of terms related to biological psychology.

Neurosciences on the Internet
(http://www.lm.com:80/~nab/

This is a good starting place for information on a wide range of topics in neuroscience. The extensive table of contents lists links to professional organizations, image and software archives, electronic journals, and neuroscience research centers.

SENSATION

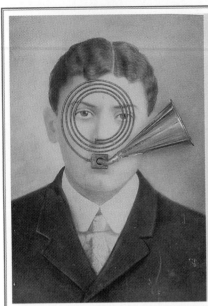

BIOLOGICAL THEME
How do our senses collect information from the environment and how does the brain process this information?

DEVELOPMENTAL THEME
How do our senses change with age?

LEARNING THEME
Do we learn to sense things differently? How do we learn to like foods that initially taste bad to us?

COGNITIVE THEME
Do we sense information automatically, or do cognitive processes affect even our basic sensations?

Consider the case of a 33-year-old mathematician who had an amazing ability to taste food and then name all of the ingredients it contained. This skill depended not so much on his sense of taste as on his acute sense of smell. Then, while taking a walk one evening, he stepped into the street and was struck by a car, causing him to fall backward and hit his head on the pavement. It wasn't until he got out of the hospital that he realized the most startling result of his accident: He had lost his sense of smell.

His taste buds still worked, so he could identify whether foods tasted salty, bitter, sour, or sweet. He had, however, lost his ability to identify the ingredients of his meals. Without his sense of smell, food was essentially tasteless. Of course, he missed out on all the rich smells that surround us: freshly cut grass, clean laundry, the beach—even the dentist's office. Some might argue that such a loss, although unfortunate, is not truly debilitating. But consider this: He was nearly killed by a fire in his apartment building because he could not smell the smoke, and he was struck with food poisoning because he could not smell that his food was spoiled. Moreover, he was vulnerable to gas leaks. Seven years after his accident, the man sued the driver of the vehicle that had struck him, because many of his misfortunes, as well as his depression, seemed to be related to his loss of smell. The courts decided in his favor (Ackerman, 1990).

This case illustrates the serious consequences of losing any of our senses, even the "lowly" sense of smell. Our sensory systems usually work well to keep us in touch with the world, so we hardly think about what marvelous devices they are. We know the world only through our sensory receptors—our eyes, ears, nose, and other sensory organs. But, if any of those receptors cease to function, a part of the world becomes unavailable to us. Imagine becoming blind, or deaf, or losing the capacity to smell, to taste, or sense pleasure and pain through your skin.

In this chapter, we will see how the sensory receptors produce the raw information that the brain can then interpret into the full-blown experience called perception. In Chapter 4, we will examine how the mind perceives the world; and in Chapter 5, we will examine the next step—conscious awareness of the world.

Our sensory processes—seeing, hearing, tasting, smelling, touching and feeling—all work to keep us informed about our environment, especially those aspects necessary for our survival. However, it is only when our sensory systems break down that we truly realize their importance.

From Sensation to Perception

The human sensory systems are remarkably sensitive and powerful. Like the heart, they work at their jobs constantly. As you read this page, more than 250 million light receptors in your eyes are relaying information about the lines and squiggles to your brain, which sorts and interprets the information. **Sensation** is the reception of stimulation from the environment; **perception** is the organization, interpretation, and understanding of that stimulation. Although sensation and perception are treated in separate chapters in this book, it is best to think of them as two points along a continuum rather than as two different processes. From the instant a stimulus strikes one of the sensory receptors, the difficult but surprisingly rapid job of interpretation begins; there really isn't a sharp boundary between sensation and perception, although sometimes it is useful to distinguish between them. For instance, detecting the sound of a note plucked on a guitar is an example of sensation. Identifying a sequence of notes as a familiar song is an example of perception. As you will see in Chapter 4, the processes of perception concern the various ways that people construct organized, meaningful percepts of the world from the often fragmentary information provided by their senses.

The different roles of sensation and perception are dramatically illustrated in Figure 3.1. At first glance, this photograph probably makes little sense. Can you figure out what it represents? Stare at it for a few moments before reading the next paragraph.

If you guessed that the photograph shows a Dalmatian walking with its nose to the ground toward an object in the upper left corner, you're right. What is the point of this demonstration? When you first looked at the photo, your sensory processes were presumably working as well as ever. Your eyes were faithfully relaying information to your brain about which parts of the picture were black and which were white.

FIGURE 3.1
A Hidden Object

The difficulty most people have interpreting this photo illustrates the distinction between sensation and perception. Their senses pick up the information in the photo, but the quality is so poor that perception of the object is quite laborious.

Nevertheless, this information was incoherent because your perceptual processes were initially unable to organize the chaos of ink blotches. Perception usually operates so quickly that you are not aware of the brief delay between seeing and understanding. But in this case, the wait was noticeable. During the delay, your perceptual processes were interpreting the patterns of light and dark so that you could understand the scene.

Now try another example, one that is even more difficult. Look at the patterns in Figure 3.2. What do you see? Give yourself at least 15 seconds before turning to Figure 3.3 on page 91. Again, you can see that perceptions are not always achieved automatically, especially when the stimulus information is of poor quality. Perception takes effort, with clues from the senses being fit together to produce a complete picture.

Classifying the Senses

Most people learn quite early about the five basic senses: vision, audition, taste, smell, and touch. Few know that this five-way classification dates back to the Greek philosopher Aristotle. In fact, we now know that Aristotle's classification was rather arbitrary and that there are more than five senses. For example, touch (or the **skin senses** as they are more properly called) tells much more than an object's texture; it also registers temperature, vibration, and pain. And, you can sense the position of your limbs (the *kinesthetic sense*) and state of balance with respect to gravity (the *equilibratory sense*) without drawing on the five classical senses. In addition, much perceptual experience results from the senses working in close coordination. Locating an object often depends on eyes, ears, and skin senses working simultaneously. For example, you will find it harder to pinpoint the origin of a sound with your eyes closed.

Vision

Each sense has a characteristic sequence of internal neural events leading from the registration of a stimulus in the external world to the brain's eventual interpretation of that stimulus. In vision, light is reflected from an object into the eye and is converted to an electrochemical signal carried by the nervous system to the various brain centers. From there, the information is interpreted, giving rise to the conscious experience of seeing.

In this chapter, we will follow the same general path: from physical processes in the external world, to sensory processes, to the processing of the sensory information in the brain. Because more information is known about vision than about any of the other senses, we will consider it in greater detail. But first we need to understand the

FIGURE 3.2

Another Hidden Animal

Examine this illustration for 15 seconds. Can you see an animal? If you cannot, turn to Figure 3.3 on page 91.

SOURCE: Sekuler & Blake, 1994, p. 15.

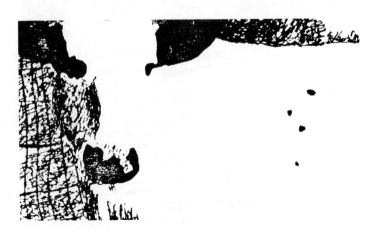

physics of light. Only then can we consider how the eye operates and how visual stimulation gets from the eyes to the brain. Each of these processes is necessary to understand both sensation and perception. The processes of visual perception—of organizing and interpreting the meaning of visual sensations—are considered further in Chapter 4.

THE PHYSICS OF LIGHT

Light is part of a class of energy known as electromagnetic radiation. This energy can be thought of as traveling in waves, and different kinds of electromagnetic radiation have different wavelengths. This is illustrated in Figure 3.4, where it is evident that light is only a small part of the total range of electromagnetic radiation. Because the human eye is sensitive only to this particular region of the electromagnetic spectrum, we call this region the **visible spectrum.** Thus, humans are blind to the infrared, ultraviolet, radio, TV, X-ray, and microwave portions of the spectrum. Other animals are not. Certain insects may look at a flower that appears solidly colored to us and discern patterns on the petals that are visible only in the ultraviolet range. We generally believe that our senses put us in direct contact with the physical world, but actually we see only a limited portion of what is around us.

The **intensity** of light, a physical property, affects the psychological experience of **brightness.** In general, the more intense a light source, the brighter a light will appear. When light illuminates an object, part of the light is absorbed and part is reflected from the object's surface. The brightness of an object depends on the intensity of the light that is reflected into our eyes. The proportion of light that an object reflects (its *reflectance*) determines its **lightness.** A surface that reflects a high proportion of the light striking it (about 80 to 90 percent) is seen as white, like the blank spaces on this page. A surface that reflects between 0 and 10 percent of the light is seen as black, like the type on this page. A surface that reflects an intermediate percentage of light is seen as gray. Thus, when a light illuminates an object, the intensity of that light will determine the object's *brightness*, but the proportion of light that is reflected will determine its *lightness*.

Lightness is independent of brightness because the perception of lightness depends on reflectance. Reflectance is a property of an object's surface, and it does not change when the brightness of the light shining on it changes. The borders of this page will look white whether the page is in bright sunlight or in dark shadow. And a blacktop road will appear black whether it is seen at dusk or in broad daylight. In fact, a blacktop road in the noonday sun reflects more light to the eye than does a white shirt worn

FIGURE 3.3

The Animal Revealed

The picture of a cow is more readily seen in this figure than in Figure 3.2 What features make the perception of this picture much easier?

SOURCE: Sekuler & Blake, 1994, p. 16.

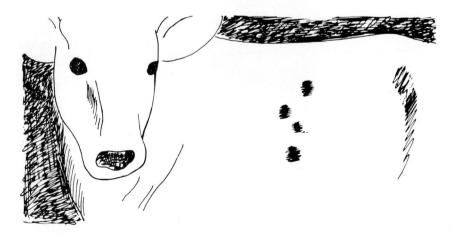

indoors in the evening. (You can verify that with any light meter, such as the kind built into many cameras.) Yet the road looks black and the shirt looks white because the lightness is determined by comparing the amount of light in the environment with the amount reflected from the surface. The fact that humans can accurately perceive the lightness (reflectance) of an object despite great variations in brightness (intensity of the light) is referred to as *lightness constancy*.

A second important property of light is wavelength, which affects the light's color, or **hue**. **Wavelength** is the distance between adjacent crests of the light waves; it is measured in *nanometers*, or billionths of a meter. As the wavelength of light increases through the visible spectrum, which ranges roughly from 400 to 750 nanometers, humans see the color of light changing from violet through blue, green, yellow, and orange to red (see Figure 3.4). Color perception, however, involves factors other than the registration of wavelength. For example, many colors, such as brown, pink, and even white, are not in the spectrum. (Have you ever seen brown in a rainbow?) Such colors embody several different wavelengths that the human visual system mixes, in

FIGURE 3.4

The Visible Spectrum

The range of the electromagnetic spectrum is portrayed at the bottom, from cosmic rays and gamma rays, with very small wavelengths, to long waves of radio and AC circuits. Human eyes are sensitive only to the visible spectrum. The different wavelengths in the visible spectrum create the perception of various colors.

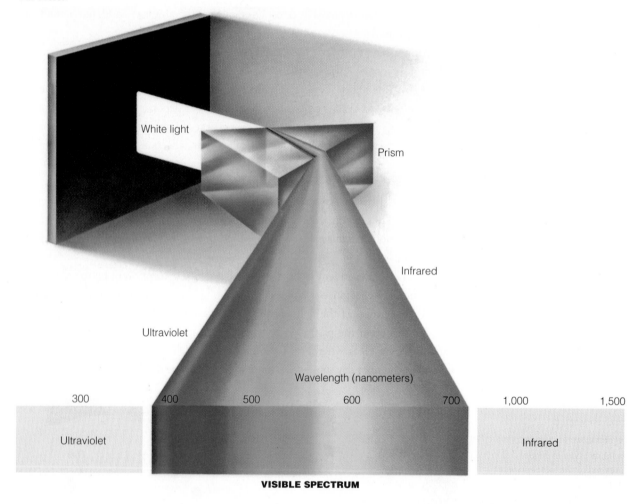

effect, to produce the experience of such nonspectral colors. The numerous combinations possible give an almost infinite variety of available colors.

Ordinarily, light is the stimulus for visual sensations, but these sensations may come about in other ways. Pressure applied to the eye or a sharp blow to the head can make you "see stars." Similarly, electrical stimulation of the brain or eye disease can produce visual sensations (Dobelle, 1977; Schultz & Melzack, 1991). Also, a flickering white light appears to take on a variety of colors at different flicker rates; these hues are called *subjective colors* (see Figure 3.5). However, before dealing with such unusual forms of vision, let us examine the normal functioning of the visual system.

THE EYE

The human eye is a fascinating device with intricate parts. The function of the eye is to focus a pattern of light entering the eye onto the light-sensitive surface on the back of the eye, called the **retina,** much as a camera lens focuses an image on film. The image focused on the retina is inverted (see Figure 3.6). Like the camera, the eye must bend, or refract, rays of light to achieve this focusing. The **cornea**, the transparent part of the eye's outer surface where light first contacts the eye, performs most of this bending. Unlike the mechanical camera, the eye is composed of flexible living tissues under precise muscular control, so we must be careful not to assume too much from our analogy. Figure 3.7 compares the sturcture of the eye with that of a camera.

Let's follow a beam of light through the eye. After traversing the cornea and a body of fluid known as the aqueous humor, the light passes through the **pupil**, an opening in the iris. The **iris** is the pigmented structure that gives eyes their brown, blue, or green color. Its muscles control the size of the pupil. The pupil typically opens wider in the dark, allowing more light into the eye, and narrows in bright light. Thus, the pupil is analogous to the aperture, or f-stop, on an adjustable camera lens.

After shooting through the pupil and fluid called the aqueous humor, light enters the **lens,** which focuses the light through further bending of rays, or refraction. Unlike the camera's glass lens, the eye's lens is flexible. Its thickness is controlled by a set of muscles, called *ciliary muscles*, that stretch and release the lens in a process called **accommodation.** In this way, the eye can be finely tuned to focus on objects at different distances. The light then continues through the fluid of the vitreous humor to the retina lining the back of the eye.

The aqueous and vitreous humors, shown in Figure 3.7, are thick, clear fluids that supply nutrients to the interior parts of the eye, eliminating the need for many blood vessels that would interfere with vision. (There are some blood vessels inside the eye, however, which you can inspect by shining a flashlight into your eye at an angle, while looking at a plain white surface.) The fluids of the eye sometimes contain dark blobs called *floaters*, which, as the name suggests, seem to float in front of your line of vision. Floaters are a result of dead cells and other debris in the eye fluids that cast shadows on the retina (Wade & Swanston, 1991). People sometimes mistake floaters for objects in the outside world.

The Retina. The *retina*, a thin sheet of tissue lining the back of the eyeball, contains about 127 million light-sensitive receptor cells that convert light energy into the electrochemical language of the nervous system. These receptor cells contain photopigments that react chemically when exposed to light. Their reactions ultimately cause neural signals to be sent to the brain. This general process is called *transduction*

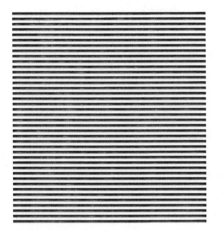

FIGURE 3.5

Subjective Colors

After staring at the pattern for several moments, you should be able to see faint colors in the spaces between the black lines. You may need to jiggle the page slightly to get the effect. Such subjective colors appear in much "op art."

FIGURE 3.6

Picture of an Image on the Retina

By using a specially constructed camera the photographer was actually able to capture the retina of a person's eye as the person viewed a woman talking on a telephone. Notice that the image is inverted. The yellow region at the right of the photo indicates the blind spot, where the optic nerve exits the eye.

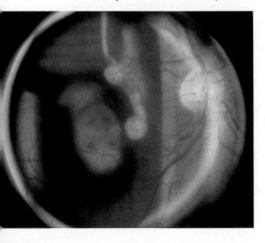

FIGURE 3.7

An Eye and a Camera

Although it is incorrect to think of human visual perception as operating in exactly the same way as a camera, there are some similarities between the two. In both cases, an adjustable lens focuses sharp images on a photosensitive surface, the retina in the eye and film in the camera.

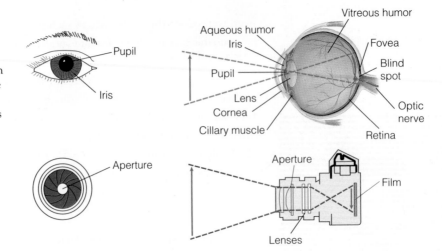

because the light energy is changed, or transduced, into the electrochemical signals of the nervous system.

Approximately 7 million of the 127 million receptor cells in each eye are called cones. **Cones** are the receptor cells that are largely responsible for the detection of color. However, they are poor at detecting light of low intensity, so they require a large amount of light to become activated. This is why colors are so hard to see in the dark, as when you try to match socks early in the morning. Cones are most numerous in the central region of the retina called the **fovea**, the area of sharpest vision for color and detail. When you want to look at an object closely, you move your eyes until the image of that object is centered on the fovea.

The remaining 120 million receptors in the eye are called rods. **Rods** are the receptor cells that are largely responsible for peripheral vision, or vision away from the fovea. Accordingly, rods are absent from the fovea, but they increase in density with distance from it. Rods appear to play a relatively minor role in color vision, but they are very good at detecting low light intensities, so they are responsible for night vision. Early astronomers and mariners used this property of the rods in trying to detect dim stars. They discovered that it is easier to see a faint star in the night sky if you look slightly away from it, rather than directly at it. When you look away from it, you move the image of the star from the cone-filled fovea into the rod-filled portion of the retina. Thus, the star can be seen more easily, because rods are more sensitive to light than cones.

Relaying the Visual Message to the Brain. The retina contains other cells besides rods and cones (see Figure 3.8). Neural signals from the receptors are passed along to other specialized neural cells, first to the *bipolar cells* and then to the *ganglion cells*. These cells collect information from the receptors and compress it by eliminating unimportant or repetitive signals. The **optic nerve**, a part of the eye composed of the axons of the ganglion cells, is about as thick as a pencil and contains about 1 million nerve fibers. The 127 million receptors communicate with the brain through these 1 million nerve fibers, so information at the retinal level must be recoded or repackaged before it is relayed to the brain. Thus, the retina is actually a complex signal-processing network that tells the brain only about important, changing features of the visual field, such as the edges of surfaces, movement, or sudden changes in light levels. After all the cells of the retina have analyzed the visual field, the essential signals are dispatched to the brain along the optic nerve.

FIGURE 3.8

Cross Section of the Human Retina

The retina is a complex network of cells for processing the information in light. At the bottom of the figure are the basic receptor cells, the rods and cones. Information from the rods and cones is transmitted to other levels of organization in the retina. During this higher-level collection of signals, information is compressed: Signals from 127 million receptor cells in each retina must be recoded to be transmitted over the 1 million optic nerve fibers leading to the brain. Notice that before light is received by the rods and cones, it must pass through the cell bodies making up the higher levels of organization. This arrangement, which may have resulted from the eye evolving as an outgrowth of the brain, in fact causes little problem.

SOURCE: Cornsweet, 1970.

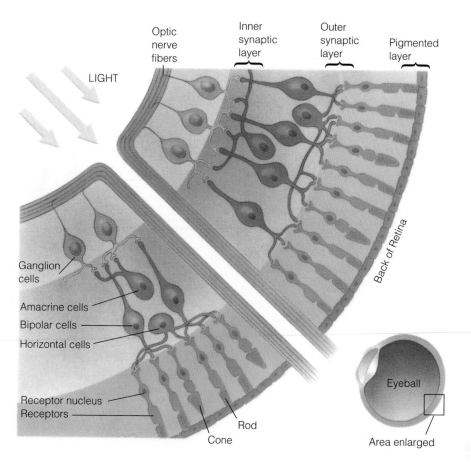

FIGURE 3.9

How to Find Your Blind Spot

Hold the book close to you. Close your left eye and fixate on the dog with your right eye. If the book is close enough, you will still be able to see the cat on the right. Move the book away from you slowly. The cat will disappear from view when it crosses the blind spot of your right retina at a distance of about 10 inches. It may be necessary to move the book back and forth a bit to find your blind spot.

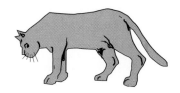

Because the rods and cones are in the interior portion of the eye, and because the bipolar and ganglion cells come before the rods and cones, it is necessary for the neural signals to exit the eye on their journey to the brain. All signals leave on neurons that exit the eye in one place, creating a whole in the back of each eye (see Figure 3.8). There are no rods and cones where this hole exists. This results in a single **blind spot,** a hole in the field of vision in each eye (see Figure 3.9). Fortunately, the brain constructs an image that "fills in" this hole, so we are not usually aware of our blind spot (Ramachandran & Gregory, 1991).

After the neural signals have left the retina by way of the optic nerve, they proceed to the brain for further analysis (see Figure 3.10). The *optic chiasma* is where information from the two eyes comes together. (The name comes from the Greek letter chi, or χ, which the structure resembles). The next stopping point for visual signals in the brain is the *lateral geniculate nucleus.* There are two such nuclei, one on each side of the brain, and each receives signals from both eyes. It is believed that the way in which color information is signaled to the brain may be dramatically altered at the lateral geniculate nucleus into a type of temporal (time-based) code (Kaufman, 1974). Different colors may be signaled by different rhythms of neural firing (Tritsch, 1991).

95

FIGURE 3.10

Neural Pathways for Visual Information

Light from the left visual field (to the left of where you fixate) strikes the right side of the retina, while light from the right visual field is received by the left side. The neural signals are carried to the optic chiasma, to the lateral geniculate nucleus, and then to the visual cortex. Notice that information from the right visual field goes to the left hemisphere of the brain, while that from the left visual field goes to the right hemisphere. Although information from the two eyes appears to meet at the optic chiasma, the neural tracts actually remain separated until they reach the lateral geniculate nucleus.

FIGURE 3.11

Nearsighted and Farsighted Eyes

For the nearsighted eye, distant objects are focused in front of the retina. Concave lenses correct this problem by causing light rays to diverge. For the farsighted eye, the point of focus is behind the retina. Convex lenses correct this problem by causing light rays to converge.

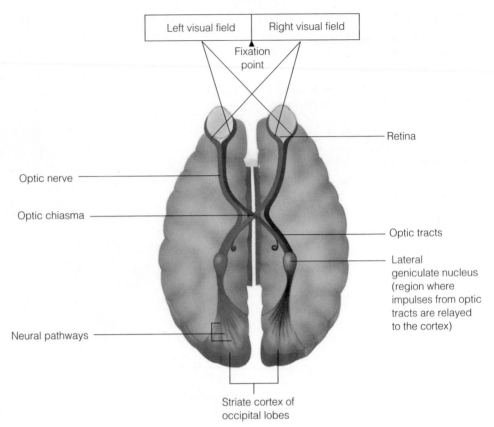

NEARSIGHTED EYE

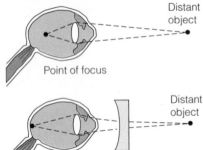

Distant object

Point of focus

Distant object

Concave lens

FARSIGHTED EYE

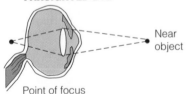

Near object

Point of focus

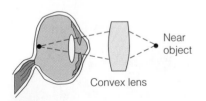

Near object

Convex lens

This may explain why flickering white lights, or moving black and white patterns, may generate subjective colors: The flickering of the stimulus may be mimicking the neural time code for color (see Figure 3.5 again).

After leaving the lateral geniculate nucleus, most of the neural signals travel to the *striate (visual) cortex* in the occipital lobe at the rear of the brain, where, it is believed, basic information about the visual scene is extracted from the neural signals. The striate cortex has been the topic of much research over the past three decades, beginning with the work of David H. Hubel and Torsten N. Wiesel (1968, 1979). Their investigations, for which they won a Nobel Prize in 1981, have been aided enormously by single-cell recording techniques that permit a probe to monitor the electrical activity of individual neurons in the cortex. Hubel and Wiesel focused visual patterns on the retina of a test animal and observed the neuronal response. Many cortical cells have proved quite selective, responding only to very particular stimuli, such as lines slanted at a specific angle. Some visual scientists believe that these cells, which have been dubbed *feature detectors*, find the critical features of visual stimuli. These features help in the recognition of shapes (such as letters) and perhaps more complex forms.

Now that we have traced the visual image through the eyeball and retina and into the brain, let's examine some common defects of the eye that can be corrected with glasses.

Nearsightedness, Farsightedness, and Astigmatism. For us to perceive the world properly, visual images must be focused sharply on the retina. However, certain structural problems of the eye can prevent proper focusing. The result: Many people need glasses. Frequently, the problem is the shape of the eyeball itself (see Figure 3.11). The cornea and lens bring the image to a focus at a specific location in the eye.

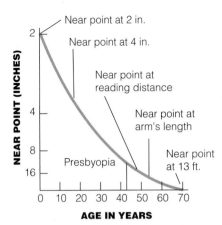

FIGURE 3.12

The Near Point

The graph shows how the near point (the closest distance at which an object can be seen clearly) changes with age. For newborns, the near point is 2 inches and for college students it increases to 4 inches. With the onset of presbyopia in the fourth and fifth decades of life, the near point greatly increases. Most older people need some form of lenses to see nearby objects and to read. Note that the vertical axis on the graph plots inches from few (at the top) to many (at the bottom) on a logarithmic scale.

SOURCE: Sekuler & Blake, 1994, p. 52.

FIGURE 3.13

Test for Astigmatism

Fixate on the center dot. Without moving your eyes, notice whether some of the black lines look noticeably lighter than others. If so, you may have astigmatism. If you wear corrective lenses (either eyeglasses or contact lenses), test yourself both with and without the lenses. (Most lenses correct for astigmatism if it is slight.) Astigmatism results when the cornea is not shaped in a perfect sphere. Most people have a small degree of astigmatism, but if the cornea is greatly misshapen vision will be blurred unless corrective lenses are worn.

SOURCE: Sekuler & Blake, 1994, p. 52.

If the shape of the eye is distorted, so that the retina is not located at this point of focus, the image on the retina will be blurred. If the retina is behind the point of focus, a person suffers from nearsightedness, or **myopia**, and has difficulty seeing objects at a distance. If the retina is ahead of the point of focus, the diagnosis is farsightedness, or **hyperopia**, and the person finds it hard to see objects that are close. **Presbyopia** is a type of farsightedness that results from aging of the lens. With time, the interior portions of the lens stiffen, and the lens is less able to change shape to bring objects into focus. For this reason, as people age, the nearest distance at which they can see an object without blur—their *near point*—becomes more distant, as shown in Figure 3.12.

Another common problem is **astigmatism**, in which visual images are not focused to the same degree on different parts of the retina. Astigmatism results from abnormalities in the shape of the cornea, which should be spherical. These abnormalities distort the retinal images so that lines of cetain orientations are in sharper focus than others. For example, the horizontal and vertical bars of a cross may not appear equally sharp. (See Figure 3.13 to test yourself for astigmatism.)

Fortunately, all these problems are easy to correct with eyeglasses or contact lenses. But certain optical defects, such as presbyopia, do worsen with age. Have you ever noticed an older person holding a newspaper at arm's length to read it? People with normal vision early in life often require glasses in their 40s or 50s to correct for presbyopia (see Figure 3.12).

HOW CONTEXT AFFECTS VISION

The properties perceived in an object are determined not only by the object itself but by its context in space and time. For example, an object's apparent lightness and color are affected by the nature of the objects around it (*spatial context*) and by the lightness and color that a person has seen just before looking at the object (*temporal contrast*).

Spatial Context. In the phenomenon known as **simultaneous contrast**, a patch of gray will look darker if surrounded by a light border and lighter if surrounded by a dark border (see Figure 3.14). This effect results in part from the interaction of cells in the retina that tend to suppress one another's activity. In this process of **lateral inhibition,** when one cell responds vigorously to bright light, it reduces the level of activity of adjacent cells (Cornsweet, 1970; Wade & Swanston, 1991). Since apparent brightness is determined by the level of neural activity, the brain interprets the reduced activity of the adjacent cells as indicating that these inhibited cells are not being exposed to bright light. For this reason, the gray patch in Figure 3.14 appears darker

FIGURE 3.14
Simultaneous Contrast

The apparent lightness of objects depends on the lightness of surrounding objects. The center squares of the drawing are all the same shade of gray, but they appear to be different because of their contexts.

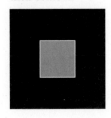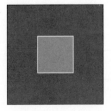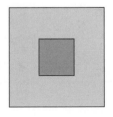

when surrounded by a bright border. The bright border inhibits firing of the cells that relay light from the center square, making it look darker than it really is. Simultaneous contrast also occurs with color (see Figure 3.15).

Temporal Contrast. What we perceive at any moment is affected by what has come before. A familiar example is **dark adaptation,** the time it takes our eyes to adjust to a a dimly lit room after leaving an area with bright light. When we first come in, the room may seem quite dark; but half an hour later, the room appears much lighter. The change, however, is in our eyes and not in the actual light in the room. By the same token, when we leave a darkened room and enter a brightly lit area, we may be temporarily blinded before **light adaptation** is complete. Both dark and light adaptation result in part from changes in the chemical composition of the rods and cones caused by the presence and absence of light. The cones adapt to darkness much more rapidly than do the rods. However, even when fully adapted, the cones are not nearly as sensitive to light as the rods. As Figure 3.16 shows, adaptation is pretty much complete after about 30 minutes.

FIGURE 3.15

Color Contrast

The two X's in artist Joseph Albers's work are printed with exactly the same ink. They reflect exactly the same wavelength of light, but are perceived as differing in color. The top X looks yellow-green, whereas the bottom X looks gray or violet. If you examine the place where the two X's intersect, on the left side of the figure, you will see that they are indeed the same color. (It helps if you cover the surrounding colors and see only the lines.)

SOURCE: Reprinted by permission of Yale University Press.

FIGURE 3.16

Dark Adaptation Curve

The curve shows the intensity of the dimmest light that a person can perceive after being placed in the dark. At first, only intense lights can be seen, but as time passes, progressively dimmer lights become perceptible. The curve contains a clear break after about the 8-minute point. The first 8 minutes indicate the rapid adaptation of the cones; the following 30 minutes show the slower (but more complete) adaptation of the rods.

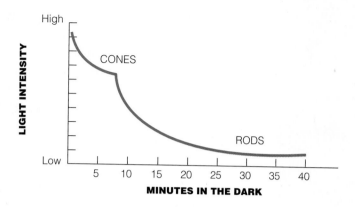

COLOR VISION

Colors vary along three basic dimensions: hue, brightness, and saturation (see Figure 3.17). *Hue*, which is nearly synonymous with the everyday meaning of color, is determined by the wavelength of light entering the eye (remember Figure 3.4). A light with a wavelength of approximately 475 nanometers will appear to be pure blue and will show no traces of green or violet. Wavelengths of 515 and 580 nanometers will be seen as pure green and pure yellow, respectively; those of 700 nanometers or more will look reddish. The *brightness* dimension corresponds to the intensity of the light, as already discussed. **Saturation** is defined as the proportion of chromatic (colored) light to achromatic (black/white/gray) light. The more noncolored light in the color mixture, the less saturated it is. Colors low in saturation look "washed out," as do brightly colored clothes after many washings. Saturation is a measure of the purity of the light's hue: The purer it is (i.e., the less achromatic light present), the greater the color's saturation. This can be a difficult concept to grasp, but the following example may help.

Suppose you have two cans of paint, one red and one white. If you begin mixing the white into the red, the hue of the mixture remains red, but its saturation declines as the percentage of white increases. The mixture is no longer a true (saturated) red but a desaturated red, or pink. As more and more white is added, the saturation declines further, and the red component becomes barely perceptible. The same process of desaturation would apply if black paint were added to the red paint.

The Spectrum Revisited.   Besides discovering the laws of motion, Sir Isaac Newton was also the first person (in 1704) to demonstrate that shining white light

FIGURE 3.17

The Three Dimensions of Color

In popular usage, the word *color* is used to refer to hue, which is only one of the three independent dimensions that make up any color. Hue is the dimension represented horizontally across the top of this figure, ranging from red to violet. Brightness is depicted on the vertical axis, and it decreases as you move downward. The third dimension, saturation, appears on the diagonal, and it decreases as you move toward the lower right corner.

SOURCE: Color Plate 1 from Sekuler, R., & Blake, R. (1994). *Perception.* (3rd ed.). New York: McGraw-Hill, Inc. (between pages 204–205).

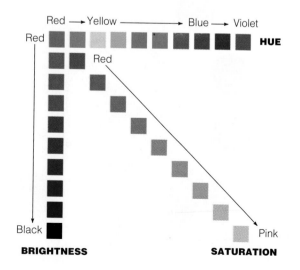

By passing white light through a prism, Isaac Newton discovered that white light contains all the colors of the spectrum. Above is a picture showing white light shining through a prism.

FIGURE 3.18

The Color Circle

Complementary colors are placed on opposite sides of the color circle. That is, if colors from opposite sides are mixed in proper proportions, they yield a neutral gray. Notice that blue and yellow are not precisely complementary. Rather, the true complement to blue is orange-yellow and the true complement to yellow if violet-blue.

(e.g., sunlight) through a prism separates it into all the hues of the visible spectrum, creating a rainbow. Thus, he showed that white light is really a mixture of all the wavelengths in the visible spectrum.

Why is white light seen as white rather than as a dazzling array of all spectral hues? To answer this question, let's consider Figure 3.18. This representation of the **color circle** is constructed by placing similar hues at adjacent locations. The order of these colors parallels the order of hues in the spectrum, but the circle has some additional interesting properties. First, the four unique hues of vision—red, yellow, green, and blue—are equally spaced. (The other hues can be described as combinations of unique hues; for example, violet is reddish blue.) A second interesting property of the color circle is that two colors that stand on exact opposite sides of the circle are **complementary colors**. If, for example, yellow and blue spotlights are projected on the same area of a screen, they will cancel each other to form a neutral (achromatic) gray. Similarly, the combination of red and green lights (or any other pair of lights from opposite sides of the wheel) produces a neutral gray.

These facts of color mixture may seem to contradict what you already know. After all, don't yellow and blue paints combine to form green? Certainly. Yellow and blue *paints* mix to form green, but yellow and blue *lights* mix to form gray. The explanation for this apparent paradox involves the difference between *additive* and *subtractive* color mixture. The color circle describes additive color mixture. An additive color mixture occurs when different wavelengths of light stimulate the same part of the retina simultaneously. For example, if blue and yellow lights were to shine in your eyes at the same time, you would see a neutral gray (see the left side of Figure 3.19).

Subtractive color mixture results from the reflective properties of the surfaces of objects. When light falls on a colored object, some wavelengths are absorbed and others are reflected. White surfaces reflect all of the wavelengths, so light is reflected unchanged off of these surfaces. For a blue object, all wavelengths *except* those corresponding to blue are absorbed, and only the blue is reflected. If the surface absorbs all of the light wavelengths, then we see it as black. Mixing different pigments, such as paints or crayons, causes different wavelengths to be absorbed, or subtracted, from the light. The remaining wavelengths in the reflected light determine the hue we see (see

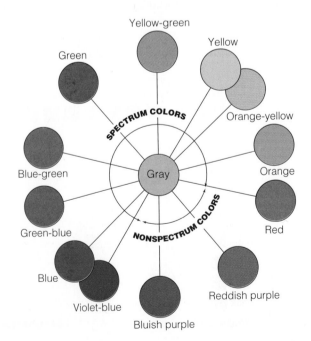

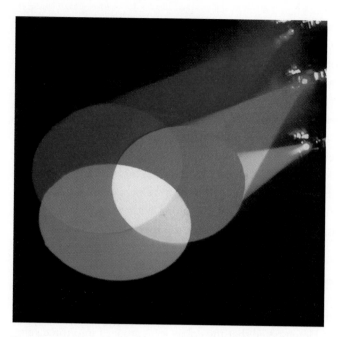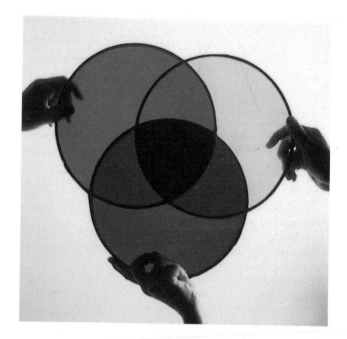

FIGURE 3.19

Additive and Subtractive Color Mixture

Additive color mixture (left) involves mixing of lights. Red and green lights combine to yield yellow, for example, and all three lights combine to form white. Mixing any two lights produces the complement of the third light, as shown. When the three lights are mixed in the proper proportion, any color of the spectrum an be produced by additive color mixture. Subtractive color mixture (right) takes place when pigments are mixed or (as here) when light is perceived through colored filters placed over one another. A yellow paint absorbs (subtracts) nonyellow wavelengths and reflects the yellow wavelength. Similarly, a blue paint absorbs nonblue wavelengths. When yellow and blue paints are mixed, the result is a pigment that reflects wavelengths between yellow and blue, which are green. In subtractive color mixture, complementary colors mix to produce black.

Figure 3.19). Therefore, an object's color is not inherent in the object but results from the interpretation that our visual system draws from the light reflected from the object.

The Trichromatic Theory. We explained earlier that the cones are responsible for color vision. But the exact mechanism producing color has been much debated. The longest-standing theory is known as the **Young-Helmholtz trichromatic theory**. It was first proposed by Thomas Young in 1802, before the existence of cones was even known, and was modified 50 years later by Hermann von Helmholtz. The theory emerges from the observation that all the colors of the spectrum can be derived from mixing only three wavelengths of light—hence the name *trichromatic*. These three wavelengths correspond to red, green, and blue, which are called the three **primary colors**. (Note that yellow, according to this theory, is *not* a primary color.)

The modern version of this theory relates the primary colors to three distinct types of cones in the retina. Each type of cone is most sensitive to a different wavelength of light (435, 535, or 565 nanometers) because of the specific light-sensitive substance, or photopigment, contained in the cone. Loosely referred to as short-, medium-, and long-wavelength cones, each type responds to a broad band of wavelengths, as Figure 3.20 shows. For example, a medium-wavelength cone responds most vigorously to light in the green region of the spectrum, but it also responds to wavelengths on either side of green, with diminishing intensity. According to the Young-Helmholtz trichromatic theory, the perception of color is determined by the relative level of activity in the three cone systems, the only information available to the brain after the light is transduced by the receptors in the retina. Any particular color produces some level of activity in all three cone systems, but the particular combination or ratio of activity levels uniquely pinpoints the color of light entering the eye.

The evidence supporting this theory is fairly strong because researchers have had some success in isolating the three separate cone systems. Also, trichromatic theory can provide a good explanation for color blindness. In people with normal color vision, all three cone systems are working well. However, in people with the usual forms of color

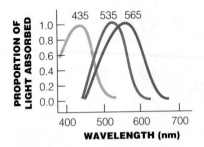

FIGURE 3.20

Responses of the Three Cone Systems

The graph shows the responses of the three cone systems to lights of varying wavelengths. One cone system is maximally sensitive to short-wavelength (435-nanometer) light, one to medium-wavelength (535-nanometer) light, and one to long-wavelength (565 nanometer) light. According to the trichromatic theory of color vision first articulated by Young and Helmholtz, the perception of all colors depends on the relative level of activity in the three cone systems.

deficiency, one cone system (typically affecting red or green) is malfunctioning or missing. And if all three cone systems are missing, a person is unable to perceive any color whatsoever. However, total color blindness is quite rare, except among albinos. In albinism, virtually all pigments are absent from the body. This means that albinos lack all color vision, since the light-sensitive pigments in their cones are missing. Furthermore, their foveas (which contain only cones) do not function. Albinos learn to compensate somewhat by making jerky eye movements to keep images off the fovea.

Despite considerable evidence for the trichromatic theory of color vision, certain phenomena pose difficulties for it. For example, why should complementary colors mix to form gray? And why do subjects pick out yellow as a "pure" color (defined as not showing any trace of being a mixture of colors), along with blue, red, and green (Coren, Ward, and Enns, 1994)? There is another theory of color vision that can address these problems.

The Opponent-Process Theory. The **opponent-process theory** of color vision was originally proposed by Ewald Hering in 1878. Hering believed that there were six primary color systems (red, green, blue, yellow, black, and white) rather than the three of the trichromatic theory. He proposed that the colors were grouped into three pairs: a red-green system, a blue-yellow system, and a black-white system. (As you know, when the two members of any of these pairs are mixed, they produce gray. This observation led Hering to group his six primary systems into these three opponent pairs.)

According to opponent-process theory, championed in modern times by Leo Hurvich and Dorothea Jameson (1957, 1974), the two members of each pair work in opposition to each other by means of neural inhibition (thus the name *opponent-process*). Thus, only one member of each opponent pair can be signaled at a time. This is why you will never see shades such as bluish yellow or reddish green. Seeing red inhibits seeing green, because the signal indicating the presence of red simultaneously prevents the transmission of a signal indicating green (and vice versa). The blue and yellow systems are linked in a similar manner. The black-white system operates similarly, but it only reacts to achromatic light. Therefore, the black-white system can only contribute to the perception of brightness and saturation. We rely on the red-green and blue-yellow systems for information about hue.

The opponent-process theory explains why we see white light as achromatic (colorless) rather than seeing all the separate hues that it contains. Opponent-process theory proposes that if a stimulus activates both members of an opponent pair equally, the two will mutually inhibit each other, and the net contribution will be zero. Thus, when we look at white light (which contains all the wavelengths of the spectrum), all the color systems are equally stimulated, and both the red-green and blue-yellow systems are balanced, because of mutual inhibition within the opponent pairs. Thus, no hue information is passed on, and we see an achromatic (colorless) light.

Opponent-process theory accounts for a number of other phenomena of color vision, including color blindness. Color-blind individuals are rarely blind to all colors; usually, the deficiency affects pairs of colors, with the red-green pair the most frequently absent. Yellow-blue color blindness is much more rare.

The opponent-process theory also explains negative-color *afterimages* quite well. If you stare for a minute or so at a bright green patch and then turn your gaze to a blank white wall, a red patch will appear to float before your eyes. Try this experiment using Figure 3.21. When you stare at the green stripes for 60 seconds or more, you fatigue the green component of the red-green system. The red component is not being stimulated, however, so it does not tire. When you turn your eyes to the white surface, the

FIGURE 3.21

Color Afterimages

Stare at the dot in the center of the flag for 1 minute. Afterward, fixate quickly at a white sheet of paper. You should see a faint image of the traditional red, white, and blue U.S. flag. Notice that the colors in the original are the complements of red, white, and blue, namely, green, black, and yellow.

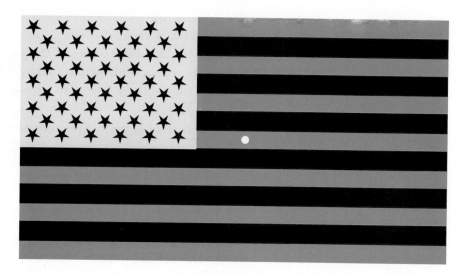

light it reflects stimulates the red and green systems equally, but since the green system is fatigued, it cannot respond as vigorously as the fresh red system. The balance in the opponent pair has been disturbed, and the lopsided response in favor of the red system produces the red afterimage.

Most contemporary psychologists hold that color vision reflects contributions of both the trichromatic and the opponent-process theories. Figure 3.22 shows how a trichromatic system operating at the level of the cone receptors can combine with an opponent-process system working at later stages within the visual system (Hurvich, 1978).

CONCEPT SUMMARY

THEORIES OF COLOR VISION

In the trichromatic theory, each type of cone sends a signal to the brain, which interprets the signals as three different colors. In the opponent-process theory, each type of cone sends either an excitatory or an inhibitory message to the brain, which interprets the excitation as one color and the inhibition as another color. In the combined theory, three types of cones send messages to cells in the thalamus that either excite or inhibit the opponent-process cells.

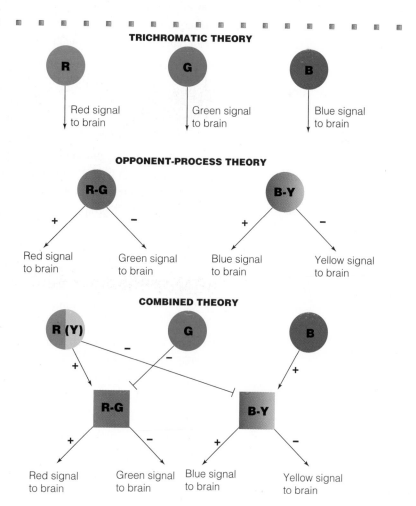

Gender and Age Differences in Color Blindness. People can differ widely in their perception of color. Of course, in most people, the differences are relatively small. However, in a sizable portion of the population, color perception is noticeably impaired. The popular name for this difficulty is *color blindness,* but the more appropriate name is *color deficiency.* The most common form of color deficiency is to confuse red and green.

Color deficiency is much more prevalent in males than in females. Among Caucasians, for example, it is estimated that about 8 percent of males have some form of color deficiency, compared to only 1 or 2 percent of females. The male tendency for color blindness generalizes across racial groups, but some groups seem to be more vulnerable than others. The best current evidence is that 8 percent of Caucasian males, 5 percent of Asiatic males, and only 3 percent of African American and Native American males are color deficient (Sekuler & Blake, 1994). These differences —and especially the difference between males and females—suggest that color deficiencies are caused by genetic defects in the same chromosomes that determine gender. In particular, the most common forms of color deficiency reside on the X chromosome (Nathans, 1989).

Many white males reading this book may be color deficient and not even know it. (One of the authors didn't find out until he was in high school.) This is an interesting fact in its own right, but can easily be explained. First, most types of color deficiency are not dramatic; few people are totally "color-blind." Most color-deficient people do see colors, but see them differently. Second, people who are color deficient have learned the commonly accepted names for the colors they perceive. Therefore, the way a color deficient person sees green may not be exactly the way a person with normal color vision sees green, but the color-deficient person has learned the appropriate color name (say, for grass). Finally, color-deficient people can learn color names on the basis of light reflected by the object. Lightness and color are typically correlated, so by using lightness information, the color-deficient person can compensate for lack of color perception.

How can you tell if you are color deficient? Specially constructed tests can easily reveal the impairment. One of the most popular is the Ishihara test, in which there are 16 patterns of dots. Four of these patterns are reproduced in Figure 3.23. To take the test, examine each pattern carefully and compare your answers with those given in the caption. (This test may not be entirely accurate, because only four patterns are included here, and color reproduction in books is never completely faithful.)

The Ishihara test has been designed to make it difficult to fake color blindness. For example, in pattern 3, people with normal color vision see a number, but those with a deficiency see a random pattern. In pattern 4, people with normal color vision see only a random pattern, but those with the most common type of red-green deficiency usually see a number. This last example works because color-deficient people are more sensitive to differences in lightness than are people with normal color vision. Thus, they can pick out numbers (such as in pattern 4) through subtle lightness cues, which most people with normal color vision cannot see.

So far, we have considered color deficiencies that have a genetic basis. However, other color vision problems are acquired during life. For example, people with diabetes often develop damage to the structure of the eye, which can change color vision and create a host of other problems (including blindness). In addition, alcoholics frequently show a reduced sensitivity to colors in the long-wavelength (red/orange) range, making these colors appear darker and desaturated. Because color deficiency in alco-

FIGURE 3.23

Four Patterns from the Ishihara Color Blindness Test

When viewing pattern 1, people with normal color vision will see 29, and those with a red-green deficiency will see 70. Similarly, in pattern 2, normals will see 74; those with a red-green deficiency will see 21. Color-deficient people have a very hard time reading pattern 3, whereas people with normal color vision will see a 2. The case is reversed in pattern 4, where most normals only see a jumble of dots, but red-green-deficient individuals usually see a 2.

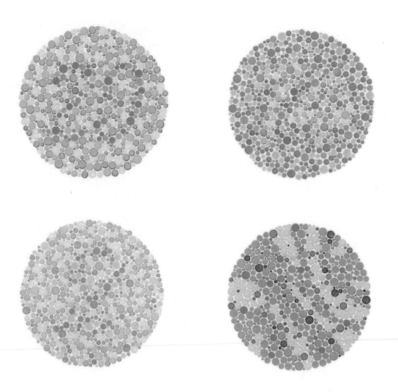

holics is caused by a vitamin B12 deficiency, B12 supplements, can return color vision to normal.

There is one other type of color deficiency that affects all people as they grow older. After about the age of 50, the lens of the eye gradually begins to turn yellow. Therefore, blue light tends to be absorbed by the lens, while the rest of the light is transmitted. This makes colors appear different; blues in particular can appear darker and may be confused with greens (Weale, 1982). This difference can create problems, such as trying to distinguish between green and blue pills that have been prescribed.

In sum, people differ in how they perceive color. And although males are more likely than females to be color deficient, eventually we all develop at least a mild form of color deficiency because of the aging lens.

Audition

Audition, like vision, tells us about the objects around us so that we can decide to approach or avoid them. More importantly, hearing allows us to enjoy a rich form of communication—spoken language, as well as the pleasure of music. Before we explore how the ear and the brain deal with sound stimuli, let's consider the physical basis of sound.

THE PHYSICS OF SOUND

Sound ultimately arises from vibrations. When an object vibrates, it sets air particles in motion. In particular, this vibration compresses the air into traveling waves of high and low pressure. Sound does not travel in a vacuum; there is no sound in outer space or on the moon, because there is no air. A simple type of sound wave, a sine wave (see Figure 3.24), has two important properties: amplitude and frequency. **Amplitude** refers to the height and depth of the wave, which physically correspond to the maximum and minimum pressure levels in the wave. Roughly speaking, the amplitude, or intensity, of a sound wave affects the **loudness** of the sound, just as the intensity of a light partly determines its brightness. Sound intensities are measured in *decibels* (see Figure 3.25). The greater the decibel level of the sound, the louder the sound. Exposure to extremely loud sounds can lead to a condition known as *tinnitus*, often described as a "ringing in the ears." Tinnitus can be severely debilitating in extreme cases, preventing its victims from concentrating long enough to complete even simple tasks (Goldstein, 1989).

A sound wave's second important property is its **frequency,** the number of complete cycles (e.g., high pressure to low pressure and back to high) that the wave undergoes in a given time. The frequency of a sound is determined by its wavelength. Just as a light's wavelength determines its hue, the frequency of a sound determines its **pitch,** or how "high" or "low" a sound is. Sound frequency is usually measured in *hertz,* or cycles per second. The lowest-pitched note on a piano has a frequency of 27.5 hertz; the highest stands at 4,180 hertz. (Every doubling of frequency corresponds to one octave.) The frequency range of human hearing under ideal conditions runs from about 20 to 20,000 Hz, although the upper limit of hearing may fall below 10,000 hertz as we age. Vibrations below 20 hertz may be felt, but they are not heard. Figure 3.26 gives the range of sound frequencies that can be heard by various species.

THE EAR

The starting point for hearing is, of course, the ear. Traditionally, the ear is divided into three main parts: the outer, middle, and inner ears (see Figure 3.27). The **outer ear** contains the **pinna,** the odd-shaped flap that protrudes from the side of the head,

FIGURE 3.24

The Physical Properties of Sound

The tuning fork vibrates, and this movement sets up a wave of varying pressure within the air molecules surround it. The pressure in the area of greatest compression of air molecules determines the amplitude of the wave, and the number of these peaks passing a point per second defines the wave's frequency. The sinusoidal representation of a sound wave can thus be thought of as a plot of pressure (on the vertical axis) versus time (on the horizontal axis), measured at a single point in space.

SOURCE: Adapted from Klinke, R. (1986). The physiology of hearing. In R. F. Schmidt (Ed.), *Fundamentals of sensory physiology.* New York: Springer-Verlag.

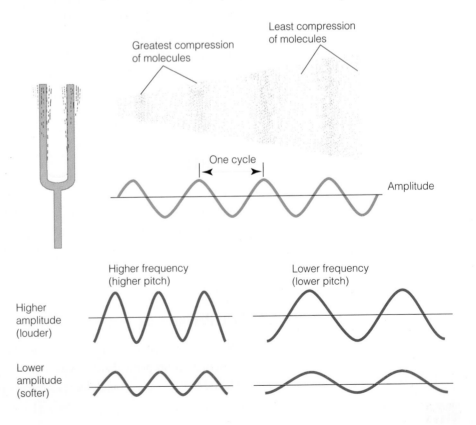

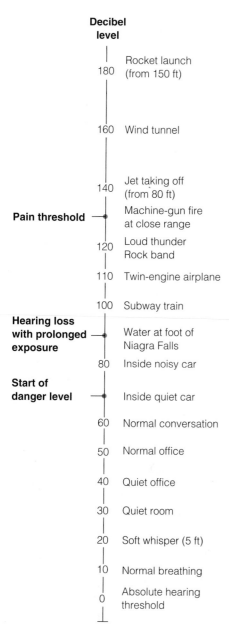

180	Rocket launch (from 150 ft)
160	Wind tunnel
140	Jet taking off (from 80 ft)
	Machine-gun fire at close range
120	Loud thunder / Rock band
110	Twin-engine airplane
100	Subway train
	Water at foot of Niagra Falls
80	Inside noisy car
	Inside quiet car
60	Normal conversation
50	Normal office
40	Quiet office
30	Quiet room
20	Soft whisper (5 ft)
10	Normal breathing
0	Absolute hearing threshold

Pain threshold →

Hearing loss with prolonged exposure →

Start of danger level →

FIGURE 3.25

The Decibel Scale

The decibel scale measures the loudness of a sound in relation to a standard that is at the threshold of hearing (the softest sound that can be heard).

and the **auditory canal.** The pinna collects and funnels sound waves into the auditory canal, where the waves strike the **tympanic membrane** (eardrum) and set it vibrating.

The eardrum serves as the entrance to the **middle ear.** The back side of the eardrum is connected to a set of three interlinked bones called **ossicles** that are named, in order, the *malleus* (or hammer), *incus* (or anvil), and *stapes* (or stirrup). (Remember the sequence M-I-S and you can't miss.) When the eardrum is nudged into motion by sound waves, the ossicles act like a system of levers that amplify the intensity of the sound signal. If the ossicles become rigid, as often occurs with age, then they cannot carry sound forward as well. This problem is known as **conduction deafness** and can be helped by hearing aids, which amplify the sound.

When the ossicles vibrate in response to sound, the foot of the last bone, the stapes, moves against the final major structure of the ear, the **cochlea** (see Figure 3.28). The cochlea, which resides in the **inner ear,** is a snail-shaped structure of bone that is hollow and filled with a salty fluid. The stapes actually strikes on an opening called the **oval window** in the otherwise rigid cochlea, setting up pressure waves in the fluid.

The inside of the cochlea is completely lined with soft membranes, the most important of which is known as the **basilar membrane** (see Figure 3.28). When pressure waves move through the fluid in the cochlea, they create bulges against the basilar membrane. The basilar membrane is lined with *hair cells,* and when a bulge travels down the membrane, the hairs are pressed against a neighboring membrane. The hair cells in turn convert this mechanical bending into neural impulses that are sent to the brain along the *auditory nerve* (Zwislocki, 1981; Corey & Roper, 1992).

FIGURE 3.26

Differences in Hearing Among Species

Animals of different species are sensitive to sound waves of very different frequencies. For example, humans, dogs, and elephants are all sensitive to relatively low frequencies, but none of these species can hear sounds in the very high frequencies to which bats and moths are sensitive. Notice, however, that dogs and cats are sensitive to much higher pitched sounds than are humans.

SOURCE: Redrawn from the data of Hefner & Hefner, 1985, and Fullerd & Barclay, 1980.

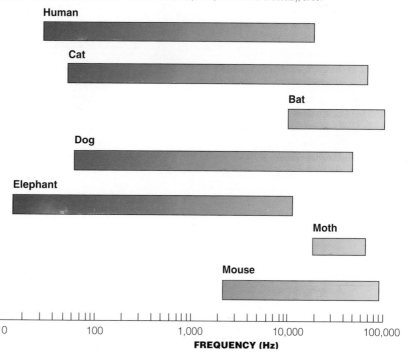

FIGURE 3.27

Main Parts of the Human Ear

The pinna funnels sound through the auditory canal to the tympanic membrane (eardrum), which vibrates. The vibrations are carried and amplified by the three small bones of the middle ear to the cochlea of the inner ear. The pattern of vibration sets fluid in the cochlea in motion, and this motion activates hair cells that send nerve impulses to the brain via the auditory nerve. The semicircular canals of the inner ear are not involved in hearing, but they play a large role in the equilibratory system, which is responsible for balance.

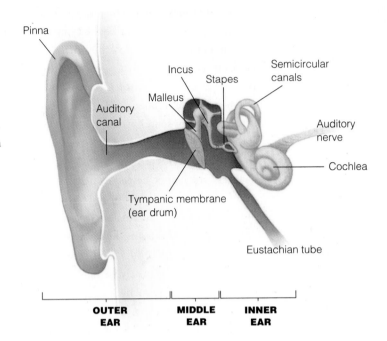

In some people, the hair cells of the cochlea are absent or not functional, causing **sensorineural deafness,** or nerve deafness. Because no signals are sent to the auditory nerve, conventional hearing aids are of no help. However, a prosthesis has been developed that can provide a kind of artificial hearing (Loeb, 1985). The **cochlear implant,** as it is called, is surgically inserted into the patient's ear. After the operation, the implant receives sound waves from a microphone on the outer ear that are then converted into electrical signals. These signals, which roughly correspond to the original

FIGURE 3.28

A Look into the Ear

This is a simplified view of the middle ear and inner ear. Sound from the eardrum causes the ossicles (malleus, incus and stapes) to move. Then pressure at the stapes causes the oval window to pulsate, which in turn causes waves in the fluid in the cochlea that surround the basilar membrane. The waves in the fluid are registered by the basiliar membrane. The loudness and pitch of the sound are relayed to the brain by the frequency and pattern of hair cells firing on the basilar membrane.

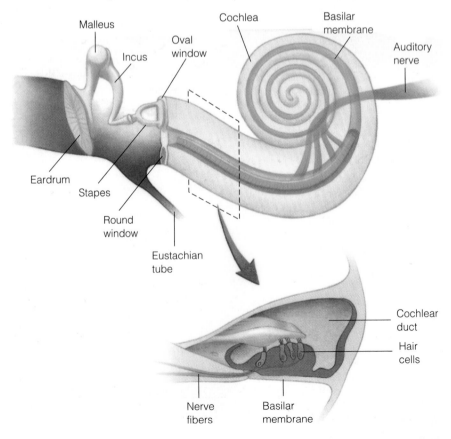

sound, are transmitted to the auditory nerve by an electrode that coils through the cochlea. Even with the implant, patients do not "hear" in the same sense that people with normal hearing do. But the implant allows them to detect the onset and offset of sounds and sense such things as the rhythm and cadence of speech, thereby aiding in lipreading. For the profoundly deaf, even this modest hearing can greatly improve the quality of life. Research on cochlear implants continues and promises to deliver even richer auditory experience to the deaf (Fryauf-Bertschy, Tyler, Kelsay, & Gantz, 1992).

DETECTING LOUDNESS AND PITCH

How do the amplitudes and frequencies of sound waves become registered in the ear so that they can be signaled to the brain? When a sound enters the ear, it eventually leads to a neural response, or firing, in the hair cells. The greater the amplitude of the sound wave, the greater the number of hair cells that respond. Thus, the brain records the loudness of a sound partially by determining how many different cells are sending it signals. In addition, the rate at which neural firing occurs affects the loudness of a sound. So loudness is registered in two ways: by the number of hair cells responding to the sound and by their rate of firing.

Place Theory.   The registration of frequency in the ear is more complex than that of amplitude. Our ideas about pitch perception derive largely from the early research of Helmholtz and, more recently, Georg von Békésy, who won the Nobel Prize for his work in 1961. Békésy discovered that the bulge traveling down the basilar membrane in response to a sound reaches maximum size at some point and then quickly collapses. Moreover, the place on the basilar membrane where this maximum bulge occurs is different for different frequencies. Thus, **place theory** postulates that the brain gets clues about the frequency of the sound entering the ear by determining where the hair cells along the basiliar membrane are firing most vigorously.

Frequency Theory.   A second theory of pitch perception is based on the observation that when a hair cell fires, its rhythm of firing is synchronized with the frequency of the sound entering the ear. For a tone of intermediate frequency (say, 262 hertz, or middle C on a piano), a given hair cell responds at the same steady rate of 262 firings per second! Thus, **frequency theory** states that the rhythm of signals received by the brain provides a clue about the frequency of the sound entering the ear.

Of course, as the frequency of the sound increases, a single hair cell is hard pressed to keep firing with the same frequency as the sound wave. Most nerve cells in the body cannot fire more than 1,000 times a second, which implies that an individual hair cell cannot match a sound with a frequency exceeding 1,000 hertz. Groups of hair cells can, however. Each cell fires in response to a cycle of the sound wave—but not to every cycle. Instead, as Figure 3.29 shows, the cells stagger their firing so that there is always at least one cell firing for each cycle of the sound wave. Thus, the hair cells operate according to the **volley principle** (Wever & Bray, 1937), an analogy based on the method of firing muskets popular during the Revolutionary War. Because of the time it took to reload their muskets, two ranks of soldiers would fire alternately. While one rank fired, the other would reload, and vice versa, resulting in volleys of continuous firing. The principle is the same with the firing of hair cells. When one is recovering from its last firing, a neighboring cell fires. Together, groups of cells can fire at extremely high frequencies of sound, even if no single cell can respond fast enough.

FIGURE 3.29

The Volley Principle

No single nerve cell of the ear can respond to every cycle of a high-pitched sound. However, several cells can stagger their firing to do so. In this case, each cell responds to every third cycle. Consequently, there is always at least one cell firing for each cycle. In this way, frequency of firing still covers the pitch of sounds occurring at frequencies greater than 1,000 cycles per second.

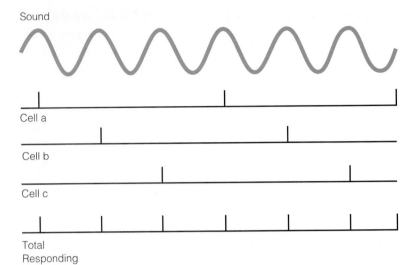

Which view of pitch perception is correct: place theory or frequency theory? Current views hold that both are correct, but that they operate over different ranges. (Recall the similar coexistence of the trichromatic and opponent-process theories of color vision.) For low-frequency sounds, frequency theory appears to be correct; for high-frequency sounds, place theory prevails. For sounds of intermediate frequency (400 to 4,000 hertz), the ear may use both the frequency and the place mechanisms to signal pitch (Green, 1976; Coren et al., 1994).

AUDITORY LOCALIZATION

Besides knowing the pitch and loudness of sounds entering our ears, it is useful to recognize where the sound originates, a process known as **auditory localization.** Most people can localize sounds fairly well, even with their eyes closed. The British physicist Lord John Rayleigh was the first to measure this ability in the 1800s. He drew a large circle on a lawn and marked it off in degrees. While his assistants moved around the circle, stopping at different spots and making noises, he tried to point to the source of each sound while standing blindfolded in the center of the circle. Rayleigh was accurate to within a few degrees.

Why are we so adept at localizing sounds in space, even with our eyes closed? Basically, it is because we have two ears, not one, and the sounds reaching them differ slightly. One difference is in the intensity of the sounds. If a sound occurs on our right side, the sound wave reaching the right ear will be slightly more intense than that reaching the left because the latter will have to circle the head to reach the far ear. A second difference involves time of arrival. Sound travels through air at the relatively slow rate of about 1,100 feet per second. Thus, a sound on our left will strike the left ear fractions of a second before it reaches the right ear. The human auditory system is remarkably good at detecting these minuscule time differences and using them to localize sound. Of course, these processes occur so quickly that we not conscious of them.

What happens when a sound comes from a source directly in front of us? Since its source is the same distance from each ear, there will be no difference in the amplitude or time of arrival at the two ears. Thus, we will hear the sound coming from neither the left nor the right. The sounds reaching our two ears will be identical when a sound comes from directly behind us as well, so how can we tell if the sound is coming from the front or from behind (or, for that matter, from below or above)? We can simply

CAN LOUD MUSIC CAUSE PERMANENT HEARING LOSS?

Hearing loss is one of the most common physical affliction affecting modern society. It is estimated that in the United States alone, some 18 million people suffer some loss of hearing (Travis, 1992). Fortunately, relatively few people suffer total loss of sensitivity to sound, or complete deafness. Rather, the hearing loss is usually only for selective frequency ranges.

Hearing loss may be caused by many things—head injuries, measles or mumps, allergies, or simply aging. However, continual exposure to loud noise is also a major cause. We are bombarded with loud noise from traffic, movies, construction work, and music. The music at many bars and clubs seems quite loud to those with normal hearing, perhaps because it is often controlled by employees who have permanent hearing loss. In recent years, people have increasingly subjected themselves to loud music over earphones from portable radios, tape players, and other devices. In fact, some manufacturers now provide warnings in their brochures and on the volume control stating that high volume may damage normal hearing.

Two types of hearing loss can result from exposure to loud sounds; one short-lived and one permanent. The short-lived phenomenon is called a *temporary threshold shift* (Miller, 1978; Laroche, Hétu, & Poirier, 1989). After listening to loud sounds, a person is temporarily unable to notice soft sounds that previously would have been easily perceptible. Not surprisingly, the louder the noise and the longer a person has listened to it, the greater the hearing loss and the longer it lasts. You may have noticed when leaving a particularly loud concert that there is a faint ringing in your ears, and sounds that were normally perceptible, such as a companion's voice, seem much harder to understand. Recovery from such temporary threshold shifts may take from a few hours in mild cases to a few days in more severe cases.

Exposure to very loud noise may also cause damage to the hair cells in the inner ear, which most experts believe do not regenerate. Thus, the resulting hearing loss is essentially permanent. Even a single very loud sound, such as a gunshot at close range, may cause such permanent loss; thus, soldiers, hunters, and others who are exposed to continual close-range gunfire are particularly at risk. And individuals work-

ing at airports and construction sites are also at risk because of their continual exposure to extreme noise levels. Indeed, one study showed that farmers' repeated exposure to the squealing of pigs caused hearing loss (Kristensen & Gimseng, 1988). Many companies now recognize the danger of constant exposure to loud noise and provide their workers with protective devices, such as earplugs. Of course, wearing earplugs in the work place can also increase the accident rate.

Not surprisingly, studies have shown that loud music has harmful and permanent effects on hearing. This is true both for professional musicians, who are repeatedly exposed to amplified music (Axelsson & Lindgren, 1978), and for those who regularly attend concerts. In one study, college students who regularly attended concerts were compared with a control group that did not. The regular concertgoers showed mild hearing loss relative to the control group, even though they were unaware that their hearing had been impaired (Hanson & Fearn, 1975).

We have been assuming that long-term hearing loss is *permanent*, which is the opinion of most experts at the moment. However, exciting new evidence from studies of fish and birds indicates that damaged hair cells *can* regenerate, at least in some species (Travis, 1992). This surprising finding offers hope that the same may be true in mammals, including humans. If it can be shown that hair cells will regenerate in humans, then we may be able to develop ways to encourage the regeneration of noise-damaged hair cells. However, this idea remains speculative, and so far there is no cure for the type of hearing loss induced by loud noise.

turn our head, thereby placing one ear nearer to the sound source. Have you ever noticed a dog tilting its head from side to side in response to an unknown sound? It is not trying to look at the problem from a different angle; it is getting a fix on the sound's origin.

Although we gather most of the information about our environment from our eyes and ears, life would be perilous without our other senses. If we did not smell and taste, we could not recognize poisonous foods or gases. And if we lost our skin senses, we might ignore wounds or freezing temperatures.

Smell

For many animals, the sense of smell appears to be more important than seeing or hearing for warning of predators and recognizing prey, mates, and offspring. The sense of smell is far keener in dogs, for example, than in humans. If a human can barely detect an odor of a certain concentration, a dog will probably be able to detect the same odor when it is weakened to one-hundredth that strength! The reason is not that human olfactory receptors (smell receptors) are weak, but that dogs have about a billion receptors compared to the relatively paltry 10 million in our olfactory system (Moulton, 1977; Goldstein, 1989). In addition, dogs have a much greater proportion of their sensory cortex devoted to olfaction than do humans.

Smell and taste are called *chemical senses*, because receptors in the nose and tongue register chemical substances that come in contact with them. Smells arise when molecules in the air dissolve in the nose's internal lining high in the nasal passages. The dominant theory about the sense of smell is the **stereochemical theory of odors,**

FIGURE 3.30
The Sense of Smell

Receptors in the nose are designed to match the shape of a wide variety of molecules in the air. Neural signals are relayed to the olfactory area and then to the olfactory bulb in the brain.

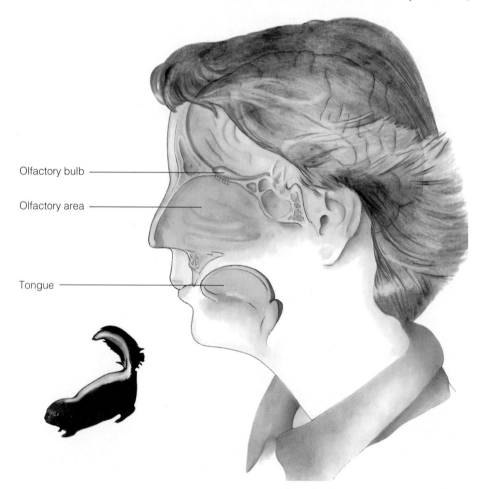

Olfactory bulb

Olfactory area

Tongue

which holds that the receptors in the nose are configured to match the wide variety of shapes of molecules suspended in the air (Amoore, 1970; Farbman, 1992). Molecules entering the nose fit their appropriate receptors the way a key fits the lock it is designed to open (Schiff, 1980). When activated, these receptors send messages directly to the **olfactory bulb,** located below and to the front of the brain; the higher cortical centers of the bran interpret these neural signals as smells.

As is true with vision, the olfactory system adapts quickly to unchanging stimulation. That is, we stop noticing odors after being exposed to them for even a short time. The adaptation of smell is more complete than the adaptation of vision, and people are often unaware of even powerful odors after becoming adapted to them. Smell adaptation can be a blessing for people living near a malfunctioning sewage plant, but people can also adapt to gradual exposure to a poisonous gas, such as automobile exhaust fumes, before recognizing the danger.

DETECTING AND IDENTIFYING ODORS

Although the human nose is not as sensitive as that of other animals, it is quite adept at detecting odors. For example, people can detect ethyl mercaptan, which smells quite bad, even when it occurs in concentrations as weak as 1 part per 50 billion parts of air. For this reason, mercaptan is put into odorless natural gas to warn users of gas leaks (Engen, 1982). However, the sensitivity of the nose to smells varies tremendously from odor to odor, and smell sensitivity shows considerable individual variation. Some people are in effect "blind" to some odors and cannot detect them at any concentration (Amoore, Pelosi, & Forrester, 1977).

The olfactory system may be quite sensitive in detecting smells, but people are much poorer at actually identifying smells (Sekuler & Blake, 1994). Of course, this ability varies widely for different odors and people's familiarity with them. William Cain (1982) tested college students on their ability to identify 80 relatively common odors. The results are presented in Figure 3.31. The 80 odors that he tested are ranked from those accurately identified by the largest percentage of subjects (at the left) to those identified by the fewest subjects (at the right). More than 90 percent of the subjects were able to identify correctly the odors of coffee, peanut butter, Vicks, and chocolate, but fewer than 40 percent were able to identify lighter fluid, cleaning fluid, and cough syrup.

The bars in the figure represent gender differences in identifying particular odors, white bars indicating female superiority and black bars indicating male superiority. The length of the bar represents the difference between the sexes in the percentage

FIGURE 3.31

Naming of Odors

The figure shows the relative abilities of male and female college students to identify 80 common odors. The graph ranges from easily identified odors at the left to odors that were harder to name at the right. The bars show the differences between the sexes in naming odors, with white bars representing female superiority and black bars showing male superiority. In general, females identified odors more accurately than did males.

SOURCE: Sekuler & Blake, 1994, p. 429. Data adapted from Cain, 1982.

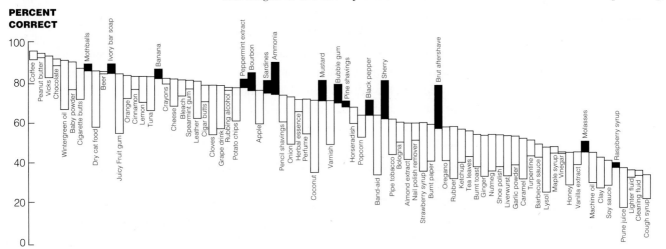

identifying the odor. Thus, for example, women are much better than men at identifying the smell of coconut, but only slightly better at identifying the smell of crayons. No difference exists between the sexes in identifying the smell of beer. The large number of white bars in the graph indicates that women are generally much better at identifying odors than men, a result also obtained in other studies (Cain, 1988).

Are blind people more sensitive to smell than sighted people? If so, this outcome would confirm the common belief that the loss of one sense makes the others more acute. Murphy and Cain (1986) investigated this question. They found that their blind subjects were actually somewhat *less* sensitive at detecting odors (is an odor there?) than were sighted subjects tested blindfolded. However, they identified (recognized) the odors better than the controls. This identification advantage is probably due to the greater attention blind people pay to odors in their environments and their greater practice in naming them (e.g., when making requests for food). Still, the ability to detect odors did not improve in the blind subjects, so some general "olfactory ability" does not seem to be enhanced in the blind. This outcome agrees with other evidence that basic capacities of blind people in their remaining senses are not better than those of their sighted counterparts.

THE NATURE OF PHEROMONES

In many animal species, smell is used to identify mates, parents, and offspring. For example, mother birds may feed their young only if they have a familiar scent. If the mother's young have been marked by strange odors, the mother may reject them as impostors. This is why you should not handle a baby bird if it falls from the nest.

Females of many species, including some mammals, produce scents called **pheromones** from specialized glands. The pheromones attract potential mates and control mate selection in many cases. Males also produce distinctive scents. You have probably noticed that male dogs sniff one another when they meet and that they mark their territories by urinating at various locations. Should an intruding dog urinate within another dog's territory, the dog with original claim to the territory will rush over and spray the spot to reclaim it. Dogs can often be seen spraying and counter-spraying repeatedly, each trying to leave his own scent last to claim the territory as his.

Do pheromones play a role in human behavior? Their role, if any, in human sexual attraction is unclear, but humans do seem able to detect differences among people's smells. Russell (1976) had college students bathe in clear water and wear plain T-shirts and no deodorant for 24 hours. The shirts were then collected and placed in containers, and the subjects were asked to choose their own shirt from among three, two of which were selected randomly from other participants. One shirt had been worn by a member of the same sex as the subject and the other by a member of the opposite sex. Seventy-six percent of the subjects tested were able to select their shirts from among the three presented, which is considerably better than the chance rate of 33 percent. In addition, the subjects were able to choose which of the other shirts had been worn by males and which by females with a better than chance percentage. Similar studies have shown that subjects can determine the sex of a person by smelling the person's hands (Wallace, 1977) or breath (Doty et al., 1982). As in the smell identification study, women generally perform better on these tasks than do men.

These studies show that humans are at least sensitive to sex-related scents and that smell can potentially play some role in attraction and mate selection. Smell seems likely to play a minor role, however, alongside such powerful cues as physical appearance and social influence (see Chapter 17).

Taste

Compared to vision and hearing, the sense of taste is relatively poorly developed in humans. The tongue is actually sensitive to a mere handful of properties: salty, sweet, sour, and bitter. These properties are detected by the 10,000 or so taste buds that line the tongue, as well as some that lie on the roof of the mouth. Taste buds live only a few days and are then replaced by new ones. Most individual taste buds respond to more than one taste, so a substance's taste probably arises from the pattern of neural activity across many taste buds (Pfaffman, 1955; Di Lorenzo, 1989). Of course, the sensations of texture, temperature, and pain (for those who spice their meals with chili peppers) also add considerably to the enjoyment of eating (Bartoshuk, 1991).

People often attribute the pleasure of eating good food to the sense of taste, but more often it is the smell that induces enjoyment. (You have doubtless noticed that food tastes like cardboard when you have a head cold and your nasal passages are congested.) In fact, people are often unable to identify tastes of common substances when prevented from smelling them (see Figure 3.32). If you would like to see how much smell influences tastes, try eating something while holding your nostrils tightly shut with one hand. You will probably discover that the food tastes much more bland than when you remove your hand. When you release your nostrils, you experience the

FIGURE 3.32

How Smell Influences Taste

People were asked to identify certain substances when they could both smell and taste the substance and also when they could only taste the substance but were prevented from smelling it. Of the 21 common substances shown on the left, all were identified better in the smell plus taste condition (black bars) than in the taste alone condition (white bars). We rarely realize how much what we call "taste" is really a combination of taste and smell.

(Data adapted from Mozel, Smith, Smith, Sullivan, & Sewender, 1969.)

SOURCE: Figure reprinted from R. Sekuler and R. Blake (1994). *Perception* (3rd edition). New York: McGraw Hill Publishing Company, page 451.

An orange will taste bitter after brushing your teeth. Your sweet receptors have adapted, so you taste the sour in the orange and not the sweet.

change as one of taste, yet obviously it is a change in smell. It is as though we fuse the two senses in responding to food and call the fusion "taste." Controlled experiments show the same thing (Murphy, Cain, and Bartoshuk 1977). Great chefs know the importance of smell in taste and often refuse to prepare their fine meals when they have a cold and therefore cannot "taste" the food.

TASTE AFTEREFFECTS

Just as the nose adapts rapidly to odor, the tongue adapts quickly to flavors. The first salted peanut tastes much saltier than the second. Similarly, orange juice usually tastes more sour if we drink it immediately after brushing our teeth (Schiff, 1980). This occurs because the tongue adapts to the toothpaste's sweetness and registers only the sourness of the juice, which has both sweet and sour components.

The fact that taste, like the other senses, shows strong adaptation paves the way for some curious aftereffects and illusions, which you can demonstrate yourself. We typically think of water as being "tasteless," but water can be tasted under certain conditions. Fill four glasses with distilled water and then strongly flavor three of them by mixing a teaspoonful of salt in one, lemon juice in a second, and sugar in a third. Sip the plain water to note what it tastes like, and then choose one of the other glasses. Drink a mouthful of the salt solution and swish it around for 30 or 40 seconds before spitting it out. Taste the plain water again, and you will notice that it tastes somewhat bitter and sour. After this effect wears off, try the experiment with the other solutions. If you adapt your taste buds to the sour lemon solution, the water will taste sweet, and after you hold the sweet water in your mouth, the plain water will taste sour.

These taste aftereffects, or illusions, may remind you of the color aftereffects in vision that we discussed earlier. However, the color afterimages are reciprocal (due to the operation of complementary opponent pairs), whereas the taste aftereffects do not always show this complementary pairing. Fatiguing the red system in vision produces a faint green afterimage, and vice versa; but the same reciprocity does not always hold in taste. Adapting the mouth to a salty taste makes plain water taste sour or bitter, but adapting it to a sour taste makes plain water taste sweet, not salty. This implies that unlike vision, taste does not involve opponent-process mechanisms. A practical point to remember is that the way our food tastes during a meal can depend dramatically on the other foods being eaten with it. Thus, context plays a role in taste, as in vision, even if the mechanisms differ.

TASTE PREFERENCES

People show reliable taste preferences, which seem to change in consistent ways with age (Cowart, 1981). Almost all species, including humans, prefer sweet tastes to bitter ones. This is an important adaptation, because sweet foods usually are high in energy value (calories) and bitter substances are often poisonous. Natural aversions to bitter tastes can be overcome, however. For instance, people typically react negatively to their first tastes of beer, coffee, and club soda, but on repeated exposure may grow to like all three. Several studies have shown that children prefer stronger concentrations of sweet than do adults and that the "sweet tooth" of childhood does not usually survive into adulthood (Desor, Greene, & Maller, 1975). Changes in taste preference with age may reflect organic maturation or simply changing preferences with experience.

At about the age of 2, children become *neophobic*; that is, they don't like the taste of anything new (*neo* means new, *phobic* means fearful). But research has shown that if such children are fed a new food ten or more times, they grow to like it more and more (Birch & Marlin, 1982; Birch, 1990). This finding suggests that urging a child to try a new food "just once" is unlikely to change the child's mind about its taste.; but if parents can get the child to take a bite of peas (or whatever) ten different times, the child will probably learn to like it. In fact, many food preferences are learned in just this way as part of a person's cultural experience. Children of one culture may grow up enjoying many foods that children in another culture would find quite strange.

Touch: The Skin Senses

At least three types of sensation are usually lumped together as the sense of touch: pressure, temperature, and pain. The skin contains various receptors that act together in ways that are still a bit mysterious, and it is not uniformly sensitive to all of three properties across its entire surface. When a small patch of skin is touched with tiny needles that have been heated or chilled, some areas in the patch sense only heat, some only cold, and some neither. Likewise, the skin is not uniformly sensitive to pressure. If you close your eyes while two pointed objects are pressed against your skin simultaneously, often it will feel as if only one object is touching you. The distance by which the objects must be separated to be experienced as two objects rather than one is called the *two-point threshold*. In fact, this measurement has shown that sensitivity of the skin varies from one region of the body to another; for example, it is much greater on the fingertips than on the back.

Aristotle first noticed a curious illusion of touch that you can easily demonstrate for yourself (Coren et al., 1994). Hold your index and middle fingers together as shown in Figure 3.33a and touch the spot between them with a pencil. You should feel the pencil as a single object, producing a single sensation (although two fingers are stimulated, it seems like one touch). Now cross your fingers as shown in Figure 3.33b and touch the intersection again. You will register the same experience as two different touches. (The illusion may be stronger if you close your eyes and have someone else touch your fingers with the pencil.) The likely explanation for this phenomenon is that when the pencil touches the inside of the two fingers as in (a), the information is processed by the same (or overlapping) areas of the sensory cortex (see Figure 2.16, on page 61).

FIGURE 3.33

Aristotle's Illusion of Touch

If you hold your hands as shown in (a) and touch them with a pencil, you will feel one sensation. However, if you cross your fingers as in (b) and touch them with the pencil, you feel two separate sensations; if your eyes are closed, it may even feel like two different objects are hitting your fingers.

SOURCE: Coren, Ward & Enns, 1984

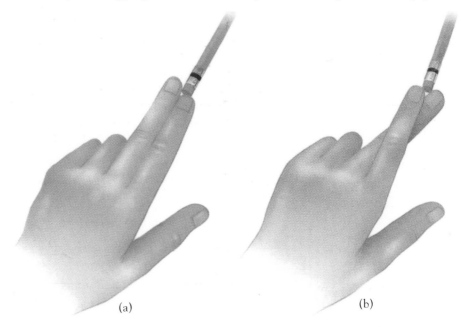

(a)   (b)

Coney Island Polar Bears. These men belong to a club in New York that makes an annual practice of taking a winter dip in the ocean. Our bodies will tolerate extreme cold for brief periods. Fortunately, most of these men are well padded.

This results in the sensation of one touch. But when the outside of the two fingers are stimulated, as in (b), the information is probably registered in different areas of the sensory cortex and interpreted as two different experiences.

The skin is more adept at sensing changes in stimulation than at registering unchanging stimuli. A new watch or ring feels odd at first, but you hardly notice it after a day or two. A change will lead you to notice it again. (Try wearing your watch on the opposite wrist.) The skin is particularly sensitive to the *rate* at which stimulation changes. For instance, because metal conducts heat rapidly and extracts warmth from the skin faster than wood, a piece of cold metal will feel much colder than an equally cold block of wood (Schiff, 1980).

To anyone who has plunged into the chilly water of an ocean beach or a mountain lake, adaptation to temperature is a familiar experience. After a minute or two, the goose bumps vanish. You may want to try a temperature adaptation experiment originally suggested by John Locke in the seventeenth century. Fill three bowls with water of different temperatures: hot, cold, and lukewarm. Dip your left hand into the bowl with hot water and your right hand into the one with cold water. Keep them there for about a minute. Then thrust both hands into the bowl of lukewarm water. The lukewarm water will seem cool to your left hand and warm to your right! This illusion of touch seems strange, since you are aware that both hands are in the same bowl. This aftereffect is similar to the ones described for color and taste.

PAIN

Perception of pain is not well understood. Some people feel no pain; that is, they lack sensitivity to it. While this might seem advantageous, they are in constant danger of serious, yet undetected, injury or disease (Melzack & Wall, 1989). They may burn or cut themselves and not even realize it. Moreover, pain does not always occur from damage to bodily tissues; up to 60 percent of amputees experience "phantom limb" pain in arms or legs long since removed. This experience of pain is as real to these people as the pain caused by tissue damage (Melzack, 1989). Also, psychiatric patients sometimes report severe pain for which no organic cause can be found (Veilleux & Melzack, 1976).

Gate-Control Theory. One explanation of pain has been proposed by Ronald Melzack and Patrick Wall (1965). According to the **gate-control theory,** sensations of pain result from activation of certain nerve fibers that lead to specific centers of the brain responsible for pain perception. When these fibers are activated—say, by an injury—the neural "gate" to the brain is opened for pain sensations. The theory also postulates another set of neural fibers that, when activated, reduce the effects of the pain fibers and "close the gate" on the pain sensations. The theory proposes that neural activity arising from other stimuli (e.g., stimuli producing general excitement) may close the gate to pain signals. The important idea is that signals from the brain can be sent to other parts of the body to modify the incoming pain signals (Warga, 1987).

Gate-control theory may help explain some common phenomena of pain. For example, it has been reported that patients feel less pain when dentists working on them play music; the music may help close the gate for pain. Similarly, Melzack (1970) reported that amputees feel less phantom limb pain when the residual limb is massaged. The massaging may activate fibers that close the gate to pain.

The Chinese have long used *acupuncture,* a method of pain control in which the acupuncturist inserts needles into various parts of the body, depending on the pain's source. One theory of acupuncture's effectiveness is that the needles stimulate the fibers that block activation of the pain. Another theory accounting for this phenomenon is that the needles cause the brain to release substances to block the pain.

The puzzle of pain involves many curious phenomena besides the pain relief from acupuncture. For example pain often seems unrelated to the amount of tissue damage suffered by an individual (Wall, 1979). This fact disputes the simple idea that pain is just a specific sensation caused by increasing tissue damage, which is the way the medical profession has viewed it until the past 20 years or so.

There are dramatic differences in how people perceive pain. Beecher (1956) compared injuries suffered by soldiers in battle with similar injuries received by civilians during surgery. The civilians required narcotics more often than did the soldiers, probably indicating that the civilians' pain was greater. Sometimes psychological procedures can block pain, as when chronic pain sufferers are hypnotized and given the suggestion that their pain has diminished. Finally, another mystery is why people who have taken ineffective and harmless substances (*placebos)* often report pain relief if the placebos are given with the understanding that they will relieve pain.

Endorphins.   While gate-control theory explains some of these phenomena, recent research poses another interesting interpretation. It has long been known that some drugs, such as morphine and heroin, block pain (Melzack, 1990). As discussed in Chapter 2, researchers in the mid-1970s discovered that these drugs relieve pain by clogging the synapses between neurons, so that the transmission of the pain signals along the neurons cannot occur. But why should the brain have receptors in the synapse that can be affected by drugs like morphine?

One answer to this question is that the brain itself controls pain by manufacturing a substance similar to morphine. In other words, the brain produces its own pain-relieving drugs. This startling idea proved true when researchers discovered a class of substances known as *enkephalins* (from the Greek, meaning "in the head") (Terenius & Wahlstrom, 1975; Coren et al., 1994). The morphinelike factor was found in high concentrations in patients suffering from a disease causing severe facial pain.

Currently, the term **endorphins** is used to refer to a whole class of substances that are produced by the body to reduce pain (*endorphin* means "the morphine within"). Imagine an animal that has been attacked by another animal. The attacked animal will likely be afraid and in pain. Robert Bolles and Michael Fanselow (1980, 1984) have theorized that endorphins function to reduce the immediate pain so that the animal can escape from the fear-arousing situation. Experimental research supports this idea. For example, if an animal is placed into a situation in which it has previously

The pain relief arising from acupuncture seems to involve release of endorphins.

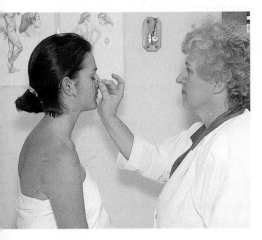

been shocked, the animal experiences less pain when shocked again. (The animal's reaction to the pain can be measured by how quickly it moves to avoid the painful stimulus.) The assumption is that the animal's brain began producing endorphins when it was placed in the same context where it had previously been shocked. The endorphins are assumed to have caused the pain relief, or *analgesia*, from the shocks (Fanselow, 1984; Watkins & Mayer, 1982). Similarly, people's expectations may cause release of endorphins, and this may account for the pain relief from placebos, acupuncture, and hypnosis.

The role of endorphins in pain control is still something of a mystery, but the discoveries mentioned in this section are clearly breakthroughs. Pain signals call attention to tissue damage, but sometimes pain persists long after it serves any useful biological function (as in the throbbing pain of a toothache or the terrible pain experienced by terminal cancer patients). The discovery of endorphins and the recent developments in gate-control theory give rise to the hope that better ways of overcoming pain will soon be found.

Kinesthesis and Equilibration

Aristotle's classical categorization of the five senses omitted two important sources of sense information. **Kinesthesis** tells us the position of our limbs through sense organs in muscles, tendons, and joints, and it allows us to react when we stumble or slip. As with our other sensory systems, we hardly even know that kinesthesis is functioning until it fails. When your foot "falls asleep" and you try to walk, the strange feeling signals the lack of kinesthetic feedback.

Equilibration is the technical term for keeping our balance; it involves information from the *equilibratory senses* in the inner ear meshing with kinesthetic feedback. One equilibratory sense organ consists of three semicircular canals filled with a fluid that moves as the head turns (see Figure 3.27). When the fluid shifts in a certain way, it signals motion. When the motion is extreme (as in the rear of a swaying bus), a person can feel dizzy and nauseated. This is especially noticeable when visual information mismatches information registered by the equilibratory senses. On a large ship, your equilibratory senses indicate that you are in motion because the boat is rocking with the waves, but your sense of vision tells you that you are stationary relative to the deck. This conflicting sensory information often leads to "seasickness." One helpful hint to avoid this malady is to focus on the horizon instead of the boat so that your visual input matches your equilibratory input. (The horizon will be rocking and tilting in the same manner that your equilibratory senses indicate your body is moving.)

The *vestibular sacs* are other organs used for equilibration, and they are located at the base of the semicircular canals. Movement of fluid in these sacs signals motion and the tilt of the head. The equilibratory and kinesthetic senses usually work in tandem, unnoticed by us until they malfunction. Motion sickness is one type of malfunction. A potentially more serious example is the illusion experienced by pilots when the airplane changes speed and banks during turns. In cases of poor visibility, pilots guide their flights by instrument readings rather than trusting the information they get from their equilibratory senses.

Psychophysics

We have now discussed how the sensory systems operate. But how do psychologists measure sensory capabilities? For example, what is the intensity of the faintest tone that the human ear can detect, and how is it gauged? This area of study is called **psychophysics** because it is concerned with how changes in physical stimulation from the environment become translated into psychological experience.

Psychophysics is one of the oldest disciplines in scientific psychology. In fact, true laboratory experiments in psychology began with psychophysical research. Psychophysics addresses an old philosophical question: How is stimulation from the external world translated into conscious experience? If the intensity of a light is doubled, for example, does its perceived brightness also double? As we will see, the answer is no.

THRESHOLDS

A central issue of psychophysics is the appropriate way to measure sensory capacities. The earliest form of psychophysical measurement was a determination of sensory thresholds.

Absolute Threshold. An **absolute threshold** is the lowest level of stimulus energy that a person can perceive. Here is how it is measured. Subjects are presented with a number of weak stimuli, such as tones, in several test trials and are asked each time whether they can detect the stimulus. Because the energy levels of these test stimuli are at the limit of our sensory abilities, the same stimulus energy may not be noticed on different trials. For this reason, the absolute threshold has been defined as the energy value where the stimulus is correctly detected 50 percent of the time (an arbitrary, but useful, cutoff point). To determine if a person is arbitrarily guessing or simply answering yes for every test trial, *catch trials* are inserted in which no stimulus is presented at all.

If we wanted to measure the absolute threshold for a sound of a particular pitch, we would begin by giving trials in which the amplitude, or loudness, of the signal is so low that it cannot be detected by anyone. We would then gradually increase the loudness on successive trials, randomly mixed with silent catch trials, until the subject could hear the sound. This procedure would be repeated many times to ensure a reliable response.

By measuring thresholds in this way and then plotting the number of positive responses at every level of intensity, experimenters can create a psychophysical function (see Figure 3.34). The psychophysical function relates the changes in physical stimulation to their psychological correlates. In our example, the psychophysical function would relate the tone's amplitude (physical stimulation) to the detection of the signal (psychological event).

Table 3.1 lists some common values for the absolute thresholds of the different senses. Bear in mind that values differ from person to person and even for the same person at different times, depending on context, motivation, and alertness.

Just-Noticeable Difference. A second type of threshold is the *relative threshold*, or **difference threshold**, the amount of stimulation necessary to detect a difference between two stimuli 50 percent of the time. A procedure often used to determine difference thresholds is to compare a series of comparison stimuli against a standard stimulus. Some of the comparison stimuli are almost the same as the standard; others differ by quite a bit. The smallest change from the standard stimulus that an observer can notice is called the **just-noticeable difference (jnd).**

FIGURE 3.34

Psychophysical Function

A psychophysical function relates changes in units of physical energy to an observer's responses. In this case, the observer's responses are the percentage of times he or she said yes to indicate that he or she detected a signal. The absolute threshold is defined as the amount of stimulation that produces a positive response 50 percent of the time.

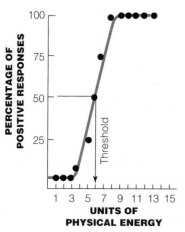

TABLE 3.1
Absolute Thresholds

SENSE	THRESHOLD
Vision	A candle flame seen at 30 miles on a dark, clear night
Audition	The tick of a watch under quiet conditions at 20 feet
Taste	One teaspoon of sugar in 2 gallons of water
Smell	One drop of perfume diffused into the entire volume of a 6-room apartment
Touch	The wing of a fly falling on one's cheek from a distance of 1 centimeter

This table shows how powerful the senses are, under ideal conditions, in detecting weak stimulation. Of course, the absolute threshold varies from person to person.

SOURCE: Brown et al., 1962.

TABLE 3.2
Common Constant Values for the Weber Fractions

SENSE	WEBER FRACTION ($\Delta I/I$)
Vision (brightness, white light)	1/60
Kinesthesis (lifted weights)	1/50
Pain (thermally aroused on skin)	1/30
Audition (tone of middle pitch and moderate loudness)	1/10
Pressure (cutaneous pressure)	1/7
Smell (odor of India rubber)	1/4
Taste (table salt)	1/3

The Weber fraction is the proportional amount of increase in intensity needed to produce a just noticeable difference (jnd). The smaller the fraction, the less change is necessary to produce a jnd. Thus, less than a 2 percent change in white light is needed to be detectable, while a 25 percent difference is needed in the smell of India rubber for it to be noticed.

SOURCE: Schiffman, 1976

Psychophysicists have long known that the jnd is not a constant for most sensory properties; instead, it depends on the magnitude of the standard stimulus. For example, people can tell the difference between a 1-pound standard weight and a 2-pound comparison weight much more easily than between a 31-pound standard and a 32-pound comparison weight, even though the difference is 1 pound in both cases. In general, the greater the magnitude of a standard stimulus, the greater the difference between the standard and comparison stimuli must be before a difference can be noticed. Stated another way, the greater the standard stimulus, the greater the difference threshold, or jnd.

In 1834, a German scientist named Ernst Weber proposed that the jnd is a constant proportion, or fraction, of the magnitude of a stimulus. That is, if 1 gram must be added to a 10-gram standard weight for a jnd, then 10 grams would have to be added to a 100-gram standard weight to produce a jnd. This idea, known as **Weber's law,** may be summarized as $\Delta I/I$ = Constant, where I is the intensity of the standard stimulus and ΔI is the difference in intensity that is just noticeable. For such sensory properties as brightness, loudness, and pitch, Weber's law is accurate at intermediate levels of stimulation; however, it breaks down when the standard stimulus is very strong or weak. Table 3.2 shows the values of the Weber fraction for a variety of common sensory properties.

PSYCHOPHYSICAL SCALING

Recall once more that the intensity of a light and its perceived brightness are not the same. As the intensity of a light increases, at what rate does its brightness grow? Imagine the effect that lighting a single candle in a dark room achieves, compared to lighting one in a well-lit room. If brightness is plotted as a function of intensity, as in Figure 3.35, the graph shows that brightness does not increase linearly with increasing intensity (e.g., doubling the intensity does not double the reported brightness). Most sensory systems, in fact, are highly nonlinear, which may help explain the high cost of stereo equipment. A 60-watt amplifier offers twice the intensity of a 30-watt amplifier, yet your ears will hardly notice the difference. To double the loudness of your stereo, you may need to invest in an extremely powerful amplifier.

Measuring the relationship between the physical intensity of a stimulus and its perceived intensity is called **psychophysical scaling.** One famous technique, devised by

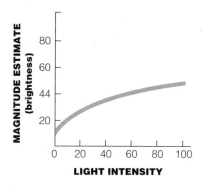

FIGURE 3.35

Stevens's Magnitude Estimation Method

The function for brightness was obtained using Stevens's magnitude estimation method. Notice that the function is curved, indicating that as light intensity is doubled, say, from 40 to 80, brightness increases much more slowly, from roughly 35 to 43.

SOURCE: Stevens, 1962.

Gustav Fechner in 1860, assumes that each extra jnd added to the intensity of a stimulus increases its apparent intensity by a constant amount. An example makes this clear.

To construct this type of scale for loudness, use any device that produces tones of known physical intensity, such as a stereo receiver. Set the tuner between stations so that you have a constant noise. Adjust the volume control to the absolute threshold of hearing, so that you can just barely hear the sound. Mark a 0 at the relevant place on the dial. Next, have a friend turn the control until you can just detect an increase in volume. Do this carefully, and repeat the measurement several times to ensure accuracy. When you have located this setting on the volume control, place a second mark on the dial to indicate its location, and label it 1. Repeat the process a number of times until the volume becomes unpleasantly loud, trying to make each jump a constant increase in loudness. When you have finished, the dial will be covered with marks, which will constitute Fechner's scale for loudness. If you were now to go back and record the physical intensity of the sound at each of your marks, your psychophysical scale would be complete.

An alternative way to construct a psychophysical scale for loudness is a procedure devised in 1956 by S. S. Stevens. **Magnitude estimation** involves playing tones of varying intensity levels and asking listeners to supply a number indicating how loud each sounds. Suppose you begin with a tone of intermediate loudness and your subject responds with a magnitude estimate of 100. At this point, you instruct your subject that a tone twice as loud should be designated 200, a tone only half as loud should be rated 50, and so on. You would then present a long series of tones and record your subject's loudness estimates of each. When you were finished, you would compare the physical intensities of the tones you had presented with the magnitude estimates that your subject made. The result would be Stevens's psychophysical scale of loudness.

The scales of both Fechner and Stevens may be shown in a graph that plots the reported intensity of the stimulus against its physical intensity. The results are usually smooth and orderly and can be described quite well by mathematical equations. An example of the psychophysical function for brightness determined by Stevens's method of magnitude estimation appears in Figure 3.35. Note again how it is curved, not linear: Our sensory systems do not track changes in stimuli in direct proportion to the magnitude of the change.

SIGNAL DETECTION THEORY

One final theory, imported to psychology from communication science, has redefined our understanding of thresholds. Recall that the absolute threshold is the weakest detectable intensity of a stimulus. The basic idea behind the threshold is that it constitutes a boundary between perceptibility and imperceptibility. Stimuli below the threshold evoke no response in the sensory system; those above the threshold result in conscious experience. This implies that sensation is an "all-or-none" matter and that a stimulus is either detectable or not.

There are two basic problems with this notion. First, sensory experience is not always all-or-none; instead, we are often unsure whether we are perceiving a weak stimulus (such as seeing a faint star in the night sky or hearing the telephone ringing while we are in the shower). The second problem involves the methods used to measure thresholds. In a hearing test, for example, how do researchers know for sure that the subject really perceives a tone whenever the subject *claims* to hear something? A

IS THERE A "SIXTH SENSE"?

Aristotle identified the classic five senses (vision, audition, smell, taste and touch), but his list is incomplete. Touch can be broken down into other qualities, and kinesthesis and equilibration also provide information. Are there still other ways in which some people can gather information?

We have all heard of people who seem to possess a "sixth sense," or extrasensory perception (ESP). The field devoted to the study of such extraordinary powers is called **parapsychology**, and parapsychologists frequently examine claims of psychokinesis and ESP. *Psychokinesis* refers to the ability of the mind to move or otherwise control objects. *Extrasensory perception* includes *clairvoyance*, the awareness of objects or events that cannot be observed directly; *telepathy* (mind reading), the transmission of thoughts from one person's mind to another; and *precognition*, the ability to see into the future. Psychologists, philosophers, physicists, and magicians have long debated whether the ideas of parapsychology should be regarded as fact or

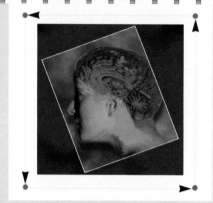

fantasy.

The inspiration for much work in parapsychology in the United States came from J. B. Rhine. Rhine became interested in spiritual mediums, people who claim to make contact with the dead and convey messages from the dead to the living. Rhine's investigations led him to conclude that the mediums were in fact using telepathy to read the minds of the people who were trying to communicate with deceased relatives. Thus, they would obtain information that seemed to come from a ghostly netherworld. Whether they were using telepathy or

simply picking up normal sensory cues from the deceased person's relative is a matter of debate.

Parapsychologists recognize that little useful scientific knowledge can be obtained from isolated cases, especially since the chance of fakery is so high. They therefore undertake laboratory experiments. In a telepathy experiment known as the Ganzfeld procedure, one person sits in a room and attempts to transmit messages to another person in another room. The sender looks at a randomly chosen drawing, photograph, or short film clip. Meanwhile, the receiver tries to determine what is being transmitted at that time. Then the receiver is asked to identify which of four test images match the image "transmitted" during the sending period. Since there are four images at test, a receiver who is merely guessing should be correct 25 percent of the time, on average. Therefore, the existence of parapsychological powers depends on whether there are people who can consistently perform the task better than predicted by chance, as

subject who wants to appear especially sensitive may simply keep his or her hand raised. Since sensation is so inherently private, how could anyone tell if the subject was lying?

As mentioned earlier, psychophysicists have tackled these problems by including catch trials in tests, where no stimulus is presented. If the subject reports perceiving a stimulus in any of these catch trials, it is clear that the subject is not responding accurately, deliberately or otherwise. Or is it? Virtually all subjects make such errors, which are called *false alarms*. Subjects are often unsure whether they detect a stimulus or not, so they guess, sometimes incorrectly. Responses to a stimulus is not matter of certainty; it involves a *judgment* on the part of the subject. That is, subjects must decide if they truly have perceived a very weak stimulus or if they have merely imagined it.

Signal detection theory provides a formal, mathematical model of the decision process that subjects use when their thresholds are being measured (Green & Swets, 1966; MacMillan & Creelman, 1991). This theory holds that the basic all-or-none idea behind thresholds is wrong. In its place, the theory's adherents propose that sen-

If so, and if it can be proved that the people achieved the feat without using any cues from their senses, such a result would constitute evidence for ESP and Bem and Honorton (1994) concluded that such evidence exists.

Over the years, believers have found evidence for telepathy, clairvoyance, and precognition. Yet, most psychologists remain skeptical for several reasons. First, the experiments cited by believers often do not produce the same results when repeated in other laboratories. Second, some of the tasks used in ESP research are quite complex, and determining what level of performance to expect by chance alone becomes difficult (Diaconis, 1978). Third, there have been some outright cases of fraud in parapsychological investigations (Kurtz, 1985; Gardner, 1989). (However, parapsychology is not unique in this respect; charges of fraud have occured in other areas of science as well.) Fourth, claims of paranormal ability conflict so sharply with our knowledge about the other senses. Where, for example, are telepathic waves received (or, for that matter, transmitted) in the body? Through what physical medium do they pass?

Fifth, if some people do possess powers of precognition, why aren't they busy warning of impending disasters like earthquakes? Why don't they get rich in Las Vegas or on Wall Street?

Many people still believe in parapsychological phenomena, and the debate continues. As in many academic fields, parapsychology has its own devoted band of researchers, and its journals and research institutes. It also has its critics. For example, the Committee for the Scientific Investigation of Claims of the Paranormal, a group of professionals from a wide variety of fields, is devoted to the scientific study of parapsychology as well as to other areas on the far fringes of science, including UFOs, the Bermuda Triangle, astrology, the Loch Ness monster, and "things that go bump in the night." They have also investigated the feats of such self-proclaimed psychics as Uri Geller, who bent metal keys and spoons to demon-

strate his supposed psychokinetic powers. The committee members concluded that Geller was a fraud after one member, magician James Randi, used stage magic to repeat the demonstrations (Hyman, 1989).

Along the same lines, a team of psychologists was recently commissioned by the U.S. Army and the National Research Council to evaluate a variety of techniques that may enhance human performance, including some parapsychological phenomena. The committee concluded that there was no scientific basis for belief in the existence of paranormal phenomena (Swets & Bjork, 1990).

Parapsychology is fascinating and deserves further investigation, but it must be approached scientifically and with full consideration of all possible explanations. Two interesting books about the scientific study of parapsychology are *Silver Threads: Twenty-Five Years of Parapsychology Research* (1993) and *Pseudoscience and the Paranormal: A Critical Examination of the Evidence* (1992). The first presents psychic research in a positive light; the second is critical.

sation is a graded, or continuous, experience. As the intensity of a stimulus increases from zero, it gradually becomes more perceptible; it does not spring full blown into consciousness at a specific level of stimulus intensity.

Sensation is a graded experience because all sensory systems contain a steady background of randomly varying signals, called **noise.** This internal noise may be compared to the static heard on radio or the snow seen on television when the set is not tuned. Noise comes from many sources, one of them the sensory system itself. To demonstrate this phenomenon, place yourself in a lightproof environment, such as a closed closet at night. After you have adapted to the dark, look around. Of course, you won't be able to see anything, but is your sensory experience one of total blackness? No. It will be an intermediate level of gray. Why? Because the neurons in your visual system are firing spontaneously and randomly, even in the absence of physical stimulation. In other words, you are experiencing the noise in your own visual system. Likewise, if you enter a soundproof chamber, you hear auditory noise instead of silence. The sounds of your breathing and of the blood rushing through your ears also add to the noise.

		Yes	No
SIGNAL OCCURS	Yes	Hit	Miss
	No	False alarm	Correct rejection

FIGURE 3.36
Responses in Signal Detection Theory

If a signal actually occurs on a trial and the subject says yes (it occurred), then the trial is a hit. If a signal occurs and the subject says no, then the trial is a miss. If no signal occurs and the subject says yes, then the trial is a false alarm. If the subject says no when the signal did not occur, then the trial is a correct rejection.

According to signal detection theory, when you are presented with a physical stimulus, your sensory response to it simply adds to this ever-present background noise. It is the sum of the signal plus the noise that reaches your conscious awareness. When you are asked whether you detect a stimulus in a threshold test, your problem is to judge whether you detect a genuine stimulus or only the noise. Often there is no way to tell, so you make your best guess. The theory says that you make this guess by setting a *criterion*, or cutoff point, for yourself. This criterion is the sensation intensity level you are willing to accept as indicating that a signal is present. If you detect a sensation level above your criterion, you will say, "Yes, I perceive a stimulus"; otherwise, you will say "No, I don't." Sometimes on catch trials, where no stimulus is presented, the noise alone in your sensory channels will be sufficiently intense to exceed your criterion, and you will commit a false alarm. Similarly, if a weak stimulus has been presented to you, but your personal noise level at the moment happens to be quite low, the sum of signal plus noise still might not be great enough to exceed your established criterion. You will therefore say no, even though a stimulus is present. This second type of error is simply called a miss (see Figure 3.36).

By measuring the frequencies of hits and false alarms, researchers can measure a subject's actual sensitivity to the stimulus using the mathematics of the theory. In addition, they can compute a second measure that indicates where the subject has set the criterion level. These two measures are relatively independent of each other, and the measures can easily separate sensitive observers from subjects who simply like to say, "Yes, I detected it." Furthermore, these calculations have been used to show that nonsensory factors can influence where subjects set their criterion. For example, increasing the motivation to do well on the detection task (by rewarding a high number of hits combined with a low number of false alarms) can cause subjects to raise their criterion level.

Although we have been discussing signal detection theory as it applies to sensation, its use extends far beyond that. In general, signal detection theory is a useful conceptual tool for any situation in which yes/no decisions are made in an imperfect ("noisy") environment. Signal detection theory has also proved useful in several other areas of psychology, such as in the study of memory and decision making (Gescheider, 1985; Macmillan & Creelman, 1991), as well as in the identification of suspects in police lineups (Wells, 1993).

THEMES IN REVIEW

The primary theme of this chapter has been biological. Our sensory receptors are highly developed biological constructions that receive external stimulation and begin the chain of events that provides full blown perceptions. The transmission of information from the senses to the brain operates through different neural channels, depending on the sensory system, but the same basic sequence occurs from receptors to brain. Therefore, most of the phenomena we have considered in this chapter have strong biological origins. Even such phenomena as colored afterimages and contrast effects have their basis in the operation of the sensory systems. Color deficiency is also biological in origin, since it is genetic,

predominantly occurring in males.

Another important theme in this chapter has been that of development, because sensory abilities change over the life span. In general, our senses are less sharp in infancy, develop rapidly through early childhood, and then become less acute as we age. One graphic illustration is shown in Figure 3.12, which shows the near point for people of different ages. We also saw that there are systematic changes in taste and hearing, with children preferring sweeter foods than their elders, and older people gradually losing their ability to hear at higher frequencies.

Cognitive contributions to sensory performance are apparent when we attempt to measure sensory thresh-

olds. Even this simple judgment has cognitive components, because a person trying to detect weak tones will say, "Yes, I hear one" more frequently if the payoffs for doing so are high. The approach of signal detection theory attempts to take this judgment process into account and argues that sensory thresholds reflect more than just the abilities of our sensory systems. The other two themes of our text—the learning and sociocultural themes—have not been prominent in this chapter, although we did discuss the roles of learning and culture in some food preferences. However, as we consider higher aspects of perception in Chapter 4, we will see that learning and cultural concerns become quite significant.

SUMMARY

1 Sensation refers to the reception of stimulation from the environment through the senses; perception refers to the interpretation and understanding of that stimulation.

2 Scientists have identified at least two other sources of sense information beyond the original five listed by Aristotle: kinesthesis (feedback about the position of the limbs) and equilibratory information (balance). In addition, the sense of touch can be broken down into more specific categories of pressure, pain, and temperature

3 The eyes are sensitive to a small band of the entire electromagnetic spectrum, the visible spectrum. The wavelength of light determines the hue that we see, while the intensity of light determines its brightness. Light is bent, or refracted, by the cornea and lens of the eye to be focused on the light-sensitive retina. The fovea is the area of the retina that can see the sharpest detail; it contains only the photoreceptors known as cones, which are responsible for color vision. The rods are the other type of photoreceptor, and they are concentrated outside the fovea. The rods are responsible for detecting black and white, for peripheral vision, and for night vision.

4 How an object is perceived depends on the context in which it is placed. Simultaneous contrast is partly due to lateral inhibition, or the inhibiting effect that the firing of one neuron has on the firing of its neighbors.

5 The two main theories of color vision are the trichromatic and opponent-process theories. According to trichromatic theory, color perception is determined by the differing responses of three types of cones in the retina. According to opponent-process theory, three types of systems work in opposing pairs (red-green, blue-yellow, and black-white). The first two systems are responsible for detecting color. A modern synthesis of these theories suggests that each may be partly correct; trichromatic theory may operate at the level of receptors in the retina, whereas opponent-process theory may operate at later stages in the visual system.

6 Sound waves vary in frequency and amplitude. Frequency determines the pitch of the sound, and amplitude partly determines the loudness of the sound. The outer ear funnels sound waves to the eardrum and the small bones of the middle ear, which amplify and conduct the vibrations to the inner ear. The cochlea of the inner ear is filled with fluid that activates particular hair cells and initiates neural firing. The auditory nerve carries the impulses to the brain.

7 The basilar membrane in the cochlea contains hair cells. The intensity, or loudness, of sound is coded by the number of hair cells that are activated. Pitch is coded by both the place of stimulation on the basilar membrane and the frequency of activation.

8 The stereochemical theory of smell holds that receptors in the nose are designed specifically to match the shape of the wide variety of molecules in the air. These receptors then signal the olfactory bulb in the brain for the detection of smell.

9 The many taste buds that cover certain areas of the tongue are our receptors for taste. We taste combinations of sweet, salty, sour, and bitter. Taste preferences change with age. Children like sweets more than adults do.

10 Gate-control theory maintains that pain can be modified by factors that open and close neural "gates" controlling incoming pain signals. Endorphins are substances produced by the brain that block pain sensations by blocking certain neural transmissions.

11 Psychophysics is the study of how changes in physical stimulation are translated into psychological experience. Two basic psychophysical measures are the absolute threshold and the difference threshold. The absolute threshold is the smallest amount of stimulation that can be detected by a sense receptor. The difference threshold is the smallest change in stimulation that can be detected.

12 Psychophysical scales relate physical energy, such as light intensity, to its psychological experience, such as brightness. Graphs of such scales are generally curved, indicating that sensation does not change in a linear fashion with changes in stimulation.

13 Signal detection theory claims that sensation is not an all-or-nothing event. It emphasizes the judgments that subjects must make in detecting a stimulus, as well as their individual sensory sensitivity. The theory has shown that our sensory sensitivity is subject to motivational factors such as rewards.

14 Some researchers have argued for a mysterious "sixth sense," that of extrasensory perception. Parapsychology is the study of telepathy (mind reading), clairvoyance (awareness of objects and events not directly observed), precognition (awareness of future events), and psychokinesis (the ability to move objects mentally). Although some research has supported the notion of extrasensory perception, most psychologists remain skeptical.

KEY TERMS

sensation (p. 89)

perception (p. 89)

skin senses (p. 90)

visible spectrum (p. 91)

intensity (p. 91)

brightness (p. 91)

lightness (p. 91)

hue (p. 92)

wavelength (p. 92)

retina (p. 93)

cornea (p. 93)

pupil (p. 93)

iris (p. 93)

lens (p. 93)

accommodation (p. 93)

cones (p. 94)

fovea (p. 94)

rods (p. 94)

optic nerve (p. 94)

blind spot (p. 95)

myopia (p. 97)

hyperopia (p. 97)

presbyopia (p. 97)

astigmatism (p. 97)

simultaneous contrast (p. 97)

lateral inhibition (p. 97)

dark adaptation (p. 98)

light adaptation (p. 98)

saturation (p. 99)

color circle (p. 100)

complementary colors (p. 100)

Young-Helmholtz trichromatic theory
   (p. 100)

primary colors (p. 101)

opponent-process theory (p. 102)

amplitude (p. 106)

loudness (p. 106)

frequency (p. 106)

pitch (p. 106)

outer ear (p. 106)

pinna (p. 106)

auditory canal (p. 107)

tympanic membrane (p. 107)

middle ear (p. 107)

ossicles (p. 107)

conduction deafness (p. 107)

cochlea (p. 107)

inner ear (p. 107)

oval window (p. 107)

basilar membrane (p. 107)

sensorineural deafness (p. 108)

cochlear implant (p. 108)

place theory (p. 109)

frequency theory (p. 109)

volley principle (p. 109–110)

auditory localization (p. 110)

stereochemical theory of odors
   (p. 112–113)

olfactory bulb (p. 113)

pheromones (p. 114)

gate-control theory (p. 118)

endorphins (p. 119)

kinesthesis (p. 120)

equilibration (p. 120)

psychophysics (p. 121)

absolute threshold (p. 121)

difference threshold (p. 121)

just noticeable difference (jnd) (p. 121)

Weber's law (p. 122)

psychophysical scaling (p. 122)

magnitude estimation (p. 123)

signal detection theory (p. 123–124)

parapsychology (p. 124)

noise (p. 125)

FOR CRITICAL ANALYSIS

❶ Each of our senses is limited in the stimulation to which it is sensitive. For example, our eyes perceive only light in the visible spectrum, but the visible spectrum is only a fraction of the entire electromagnetic spectrum. Why do you suppose we cannot directly sense the TV, radio, and gamma waves that surround us all the time?

❷ During World War II and the Korean War, color-deficient men were sought to fly reconnaissance missions because they could "see through" camouflage better than men with normal color vision. Why do you think they could do this?

❸ Several curious illusions of taste and touch were discussed in this chapter. Most people have their own peculiar sensations to relate. Describe a curious phenomenon of taste or touch that you have noticed, and try to explain it using the principles we have discussed.

❹ Do you believe in extrasensory perception or other abnormal phenomena? If so, how could you convince a skeptic (such as your psychology professor) that you are right?

❺ From the standpoint of signal detection theory, defend the following statement: "There is no such thing as an absolute sensory threshold."

❻ When something happens that affects our sense of smell, such as having a cold, we complain that it affects how things taste. Why do you think people confuse taste and smell?

SUGGESTED READINGS

GESCHEIDER, G. A. (1985). *Psychophysics: Method, theory, and application* (2nd ed.). Hillsdale, NJ: Erlbaum. An excellent introduction to the field of psychophysics, this work includes discussions of thresholds, psychophysical scaling, and the theory of signal detection.

HINES T. (1992). *Pseudoscience and the paranormal.* Buffalo, NY: Prometheus Books. A comprehensive look at the claims of parapsychology that provides scientific explanations of each issue and discusses why people persist in their beliefs even when presented with contradictory evidence.

COREN, S., WARD, L. M., & ENNS, J. T. (1994). *Sensation and perception* (4th ed.). Fort Worth, TX: Harcourt Brace. This is an up-to-date text that provides a survey of information about all the senses, with vision and hearing treated in the greatest detail.

LINDSAY, P. H., & NORMAN, D. A. (1977). *Human information processing* (2nd ed.). New York: Academic Press. The first few chapters contain helpful information about vision and audition. Psychophysics is also included, and the appendix provides an extensive introduction to signal detection theory.

MELZACK, R., & WALL, P. D. (1989). *The challenge of pain.* New York: Penguin USA. A fascinating book about the puzzles of pain and how they can be interpreted in terms of gate-control theory.

SEKULER, R., & BLAKE, R. (1994). *Perception.* (3rd ed.). New York: McGraw-Hill. An outstanding textbook on sensation and perception written by two leading researchers. As in most texts, vision is treated most thoroughly, but two excellent chapters are devoted to hearing and one chapter to smell and taste.

PSYCHOLOGY ON THE INTERNET

Sensation and Perception Tutorial

(http://psych.hanover.edu/Krantz/sen_tut.html)

This tutorial, by the author of the Basic Neural Processes Tutorial (see Psychology on the Internet, Chapter 2) covers some basic concepts in sensation and perception and includes an introduction to how neurons in the visual cortex process incoming spatial information.

Audition Tutorial

(http://lecaine.music.mcgill.ca/~welch/auditory/Auditory.html)

This site provides an excellent introduction to the concepts related to audition. It provides information on the history of experimentation in acoustics, a primer of acoustics and auditory perception, and demonstrations of acoustic concepts.

Vision and Color Vision Phenomena

(http://www.exploratorium.edu/imagery/exhibits.html)

Several impressive demonstrations of visual phenomena can be found here. In addition to allowing the users to participate in the demonsatrations on-line, this home page provides brief explanations of the phenomena. One of the demonstrations that works particularly well is that of color after images.

PERCEPTION

Chapter 4

BIOLOGICAL THEME
How are some visual illusions caused by the nervous system?

LEARNING THEME
Do we need to learn to see, or does perceiving happen automatically, as we develop?

COGNITIVE THEME
Does what we expect to see shape what we do see?

DEVELOPMENTAL THEME
Do babies perceive the world in a very different way from adults? How can psychologists find out what babies perceive?

SOCIOCULTURAL THEME
Do people from different cultures perceive basic properties in the same way? For example, do people from preliterate societies perceive pictures in the same way people in Western cultures do?

Consider the plight of Mr. S. After recovering from a case of carbon monoxide poisoning, Mr. S. seemed normal in many ways. His memory seemed fine, his speech was good, and he remained quite intelligent. However, something was wrong: Mr. S. could not identify the objects in his environment. In fact, when he looked at objects, pictures of objects, faces, body parts, letters, or geometric figures, he could not recognize or name what he saw (Benson & Greenberg, 1969). And yet, his sense of vision was, in many ways, not impaired. He was able to manipulate his wheelchair around the hospital ward without bumping into things, distinguish between two lights that were only slightly different in brightness, correctly identify colors, and detect small objects when they moved. Thus, many of Mr. S.'s visual abilities were intact, but the critical ability to recognize objects was severely damaged.

Mr. S.'s problem, called *visual form agnosia* (Farah, 1990), was specific to his visual perception (*agnosia* means "not knowing, or recognizing"). For example, if Mr. S. touched an orange, he could identify it; if asked to describe an orange, he could do so quite accurately; but if he looked at an orange he could not say its name. When asked to identify objects, his responses seemed to be guesses based on color and size. He said that a safety pin was silver and shiny "like a watch or a nail clipper," and he guessed that a rubber eraser was "a small ball" (Farah, 1990, p. 8).

Visual form agnosia illustrates the distinction between sensation, discussed in Chapter 3, and perception, our topic of this chapter. Mr. S. had no trouble *sensing* the visual stimuli in his environment; but he failed to *perceive* (interpret) them accurately. His ability to organize and interpret the sensory information relayed to his brain from his receptor organs (perception) was impaired.

Of course, even those of us with normal perceptual abilities do not perceive ever stimulus with complete accuracy every time. Just think of all the times you've mistakenly heard the phone ringing while you were taking a shower. And if you've ever driven through the desert, then you know how real a mirage can seem. Such errors of perception can be astonishing, but researchers who study perception are more surprised by how *veridical* (accurate) perception normally is than by its occasional confusions. Scientists and engineers may soon be able to build robots that can mimic human behavior by sensing and manipulating objects in their environment, such as machine parts moving down a conveyor belt. In the process, these researchers are rapidly gaining an understanding of the problems perception entails and an appreciation of the perceptual abilities that we often take for granted.

In this chapter, we will focus primarily on visual perception, although most of the principles to be discussed apply just as well to other perceptual systems. We begin the chapter with a discussion of perceptual organization as we ask the question, Why does the world look the way it does? You may recall that in Chapter 3 we asked why particular wavelengths of light produce the colors we experience; in this chapter, we ask why the particular sensory stimuli our receptors detect lead to an effortless perception of a coherent and well-organized three-dimensional scene. We will then consider the question of pattern recognition, or how we identify the various shapes and patterns in the world from the raw sensations that our senses collect. How, for example, do we recognize a lion as a lion? The visual sensory system (that is, the retinas and the brain structures that connect to them) detects simple features in the visual field, such as line segments, corners, and angles. In a like manner, the ear and auditory centers of the brain detect the frequencies and amplitudes of sound waves entering the ears. From this seemingly random collection of sensory details, our perceptual systems must construct an ordered and meaningful picture of the world, complete with barking dogs and talking people. No robots yet exist that are capable of identifying a dog in a photograph. Yet humans do so effortlessly. How?

Next we will discuss the perception of depth, size, and shape and our amazing ability to judge these qualities so accurately even in a rapidly changing environment. We well then turn our attention to perceptual illusions; often entertaining, these interesting phenomena offer clues for understanding how veridical perception is achieved. We will see that some illusions have their origins in biological factors, whereas others seem to be learned through experience with the world. The role of experience is explored further in the final section, where we consider such questions as how we adjust to new perceptual conditions, how we respond to perceptual deprivation, how infants learn to perceive for the first time (a topic that is continued in Chapter 9), and how our culture influences our perception of the world. As these questions indicate, all the themes of the book (biological, developmental, cognitive, learning, and socio-cultural) are needed to understand perception.

Perceptual Organization

The millions of rods and cones in each retina respond with electrical signals when we examine the world around us. But we are only aware of the objects we are viewing—not what our individual rods and cones are doing. If we were conscious of our rods and cones, we might see the world as a vast array of points varying in color and brightness rather than as a layout of natural objects in our environment. The structuring of elementary sensations such as points, lines, and edges into the objects we perceive is called **perceptual organization.** During the first half of the twentieth century, the Gestalt psychologists studied this process of constructing perceptions from raw sensory data. They argued that perception was more than, or at least different from, the sum of our sensations. Just as the nature of a molecule depends on both its component atoms and their arrangement, the nature of a perceptual experience depends on both the sensations produced at the receptors and the way those sensations are arranged into whole patterns, or gestalts.

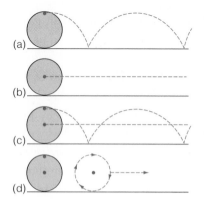

FIGURE 4.1

A Gestalt Demonstration

In (a), a single light is placed on the rim of a wheel as it rolls in the dark. A viewer sees the cycloid motion traced by the dashed lines. In (b), the light is placed on the hub, and an observer sees horizontal motion. In (c), both lights are turned on, but the dashed lines shown are not what an observer sees. In this case, a + b ≠ c. Instead (d) shows how people actually see the stimuli: one light circling around another as the whole configuration rolls. Thus, the simultaneous perception of both lights is not simply the sum of the parts.

SOURCE: Krech & Crutchfield, 1958.

FIGURE 4.2

Perceptual Grouping Principles

Parts (a) and (b) show groupings by similarity: Rows or columns of stimuli similar in brightness group together. Part (c) shows grouping by proximity: nearby stimuli tend to group in units. The dots group together as columns rather than rows. Part (d) demonstrates good continuation: Stimuli that flow smoothly into one another are seen as forming a single group, so we see two intersecting lines *ab* and *cd*, not the other possible pairs (*ad* and *cb*; *ac* and *bd*).

A GESTALT DEMONSTRATION

The experiment shown in Figure 4.1 illustrates one Gestalt concept. Suppose a light is attached to the rim of a bicycle wheel, and the wheel is rolled across a dark room. What does an observer see? Not the wheel, because the room is dark. Only the light, moving in a *cycloid* path, is perceived (see Figure 4.1a). If the light is moved to the wheel's center, an observer sees only a point of light moving horizontally across the room (b). In neither case is anything resembling a rolling wheel perceived. Now, imagine that two lights are attached to the wheel, one on the rim and one at the center. If the two perceptual experiences simply were added together, the observer would see one light following a cycloid path and one following a straight line (c). But that is not what happens. In fact, the two lights are perceived as forming a unified, rolling wheel (d), and even the most persistent viewer cannot see the cycloid path of the light on the rim (Duncker, 1929; Johansson, 1975).

This demonstration supports the Gestalt claim that the perception of a whole pattern, or configuration of stimuli, differs from the simple sum of its perceived parts. An observer perceives the pattern or relationships among the parts instead of an unorganized collection of parts.

GROUPING AND FIGURE-GROUND PRINCIPLES

The Gestalt psychologists provided two sets of principles to describe how visual perceptions are organized into meaningful wholes (Kubovy & Pomerantz, 1981). The first set deals with perceptual grouping, the second with figure-ground segregation.

Perceptual Grouping.   *Perceptual grouping*, illustrated in Figure 4.2, is the way that spatial patterns are organized into larger units. Part (a) shows a square grid with alternate rows of dots in different colors. Because of the way the dots are colored, you are more likely to see these dots as being organized in rows (across the page) than in columns (down the page). In part (b), you are more likely to see the dots organized in columns. Parts (a) and (b) demonstrate grouping by *similarity*; similar stimuli tend to be grouped into the same unit more readily than dissimilar stimuli. Part (c) demonstrates the comparable principle of grouping by *proximity*; stimuli that are close together are generally put in the same unit more frequently than stimuli that are farther apart. Thus, the dots are organized in columns rather than rows. Part (d) shows how

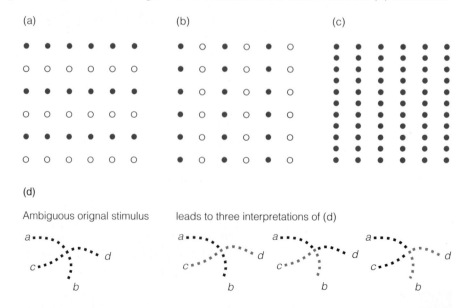

FIGURE 4.3

The Urge to Organize

Examine the figure, and notice the many different patterns that your perceptual system organizes the elements into. These organized patterns will seem to shift as you notice the other ordered arrangements that are possible.

SOURCE: Coren, S., Ward, L. M., & Enns, J. T. (1994). *Sensation and Perception* (4th ed.). Fort Worth, TX: Harcourt Brace College Publishers. p. 380.

Perceiving a car moving behind a picket fence is easy for the human visual system, but quite different for artificial systems. You could see the car more easily from a videotape than from these four pictures. Which Gestalt principle would account for this difference?

stimuli are grouped by the principle of *good continuation*; stimuli that flow smoothly into one another are more likely to be seen as a single group than those that do not.

These Gestalt principles help provide a scientific understanding for our everyday visual perceptions of the world. Imagine watching a moving car passing on the other side of a picket fence. Although its image on the retina is cut into thin slices by the fence, you still perceive the car as a unitary object. This occurs, in part, because of similarity and good continuation: The slices of the car are similar in color and texture, and they flow smoothly into one another. So your perceptual system constructs a percept of a whole car, even though you see only isolated slices. Robots and other computerized perceptual devices have previously been baffled by such images, and most would have failed to see the car through the fence. Recently, however, computer simulations based on the organization of neurons in the visual system and programmed to utilize Gestalt grouping principles have had some success in interpreting such scenes accurately (Finkel & Sajda, 1994).

Our perceptual system seems to have a built-in tendency to organize visual elements into coherent patterns, and this urge seems to be involuntary, as Figure 4.3 demonstrates. Notice how each of the small elements fits into several different patterns of larger organization. Does your perception seem to shift from one possibility to another as you try to make sense out of the display?

Grouping also occurs in auditory perception. When we listen to someone speak, we may have the impression that brief pauses clearly separate the speaker's words. However, when the sound waves of a speaker's voice are recorded and examined, we find that the words aren't separated. Although the sound stream in speech does contain silent intervals, they occur no more frequently between words than they do within words, so they are of little help in picking out the individual words of a sentence (Lively, Pisoni, & Goldinger, 1994). Similarly, when we listen to people speaking foreign languages, we often get the impression that they are talking too fast and running words together. In fact, they *are* running their words together, but the same is true of those who speak our own language. When we listen to English, our perceptual system separates the smeared sound elements so that we perceive distinct words.

CONCEPT SUMMARY

GESTALT PRINCIPLES OF PERCEPTUAL GROUPING

- **SIMILARITY**—stimuli or events that are similar tend to be grouped in the same unit more readily than dissimilar stimuli.

- **PROXIMITY**—stimuli or events that are close together are generally placed in the same unit, relative to stimuli further apart.

- **GOOD CONTINUATION**—stimuli or events that flow smoothly into one another are more likely to be placed in a single group than those that do not.

FIGURE 4.4

Figure-Ground Reversal

This figure may be seen as a single vase or as two faces in silhouette looking directly at one another. (If you look closely at the faces, you will see that the one on the right is Queen Elizabeth II and the one on the left is her husband, Prince Philip.) If you have trouble seeing the faces, note that the deepest indentations in the vase represent noses.

Figure Ground Segregation. The second set of Gestalt principles for perceptual organization involves **figure-ground segregation**, the way our perceptual system separates an object (figure) from its background context (ground). A demonstration of the concept is shown in Figure 4.4. If you stare at the figure long enough, you will perceive it either as a single vase or as two faces looking at one another. It is difficult to detect both images simultaneously. When you see the vase, the areas that look like faces become the background rather than objects.

Many animals have evolved so that their color, shape, and size let them blend into their surroundings. Such camouflage defies the object recognition systems of predators, confounding the predators' methods of separating figure and ground. Figure 4.5 shows two examples of this natural camouflage. What principles of perceptual organization are exploited to make the animals hard to see?

Although psychologists do not completely understand how the perceptual system solves grouping and figure-ground problems, the visual system can sometimes provide a remarkably sensible interpretation of confusing scenes. Recent evidence has suggested that mechanisms sensitive to *spatial frequency* (the size and sharpness of details in a given area, or the graininess of its texture) may be involved in separating foreground and background. Areas of high spatial frequency (high detail, very grainy texture) are more often perceived as being in the foreground (Coren et al., 1994; Klymenko & Weisstein, 1986). Also, the Gestalt principle of good continuation seems to be especially important in separating figure and ground (Finkel & Sajda, 1994).

Most people have little trouble seeing the horses in Figure 4.6, even though the patterns on the horses are similar to those of the background. (What Gestalt principles might account for our ease in perceiving the horses?) Figure-ground segregation is important in recognizing objects like the horses, but sometimes the process is reversed; that is, in some cases recognizing shapes (such as the horses in Figure 4.6) helps identify the figure and its background (Peterson & Gibson, 1993). Although Gestalt principles may help explain why we perceive the horses in the scene, the precise mechanisms still elude us. And even if this perceptual process were completely understood,

FIGURE 4.5

Natural Camouflage

Many animals have evolved specialized coloration or body shape that help them blend in with their surroundings. Natural camouflage utilizes many of the Gestalt principles of grouping, making it difficult for predators to separate the animals from the background of its habitat.

As with other animals, humans try to disguise their presence through camouflage.

would it explain why we recognize the figures as horses rather than as cows? What is it about the segregated set of blobs that makes them appear horselike? For that matter, what characteristics must any stimulus possess to be a horse or a dog?

Pattern Recognition

We recognize dogs immediately and without error every day, but exactly how do we do this? We've already discussed the first steps in this process, perceptual grouping and figure-ground separation, identifying what elements of the visual scene "belong together," composing discrete objects. Now the task for our perceptual system is to decide what exactly these objects are. This feat of identification is called **pattern recognition**, the process of classifying stimuli into meaningful object categories.

An early theory of pattern recognition was **template matching theory**. According to this theory, when you encounter a visual stimulus, your perceptual system attempts to fit it to one of the many *templates*, or molds, that exist in your memory and represent all of the objects that you know. If and when a template is found to match the stimulus, you recognize the object. The problem with template matching theory is that an object can vary in appearance considerably without disrupting perception. For instance, as Figure 4.7 shows, you can easily recognize the letters of the alphabet, regardless of whether they are uppercase, lowercase, handwritten, or typewritten. Furthermore, you can instantly recognize an A written in a font you have never seen before. If perception were dependent on matching a stimulus to a particular template,

FIGURE 4.6

Pintos

Most people can readily perceive the horses (the figures) despite the similarity between figure and ground. Gestalt principles, such as good continuation, can help account for this ability, but machine vision systems probably would be unable to determine the nature of the figures, which humans can do relatively easily.

SOURCE: *Pintos*, Bev Doolittle, 1979. The Greenwich Workshop, Trumbul, CT.

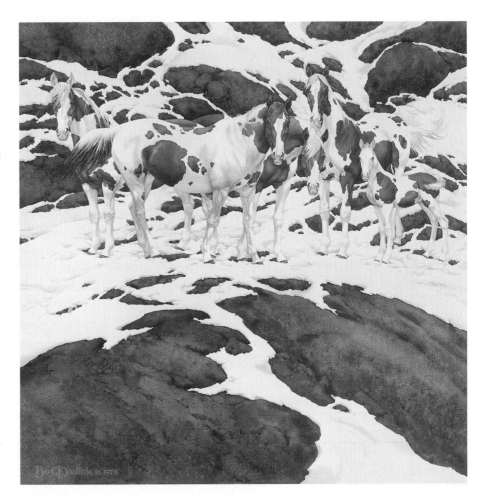

FIGURE 4.7

Pattern Recognition

A set of features can be defined for upper- and lowercase letters (A or a). People probably recognize letters by noting the critical features that distinguish one letter from another. Most people can easily recognize all of these patterns as the letter A, even though they vary greatly in shape, size, and orientation.

unfamiliar stimuli would be unrecognizable, because you would not possess the appropriate template. Because of these problems, template theory has been largely discredited. Instead of an entire template of an object, most theories now assume that it is the component *features* of an object that are important in pattern recognition.

We can identify almost any object or event as a *pattern* or bundle of features. To define a dog, for example, we begin with a set of features: four legs, a hairy coat, a tail. Of course, so far this list describes a cat as well as a dog. We can add further features like round pupils (cats have vertical slits) and smooth tongues (cats' tongues feel like sandpaper), leaving out features such as antlers and flippers. Finally, we should allow some leeway for features that might be *missing* in a particular dog, such as a tail that has been bobbed. Most theories of human pattern recognition hold that our visual system uses these types of features in recognizing objects. When we think about it this way, we see that the category *dog* is a complex, abstract concept.

Theories of pattern recognition can be grouped into two classes: bottom-up and top-down. In general, **bottom-up theories** assume that perception starts with raw sensory information collected from the environment and then combines it into meaningful, recognizable units. **Top-down theories**, on the other hand, assume that perception starts with prior knowledge of the environment, which then guides the search for sensory information to confirm this knowledge. The names bottom-up and top-down reflect the belief that sensory receptors (eyes, ears, etc.) are at the bottom of the perceptual systems, while the perceptual areas of the brain are at the top.

Both bottom-up and top-down approaches assume that the perceptual system detects the kinds of features previously mentioned. Thus, while template matching theory depicts letters as whole objects, feature theories depict letters as being composed of separate elements (such as horizontal, vertical, and diagonal line segments and simple curves). For example, if you know that a letter contains just one vertical and one horizontal line, it must be either a *T* or an *L*. Letter recognition can be complicated, because letters can be printed in so many different ways (again, see Figure 4.7). But feature theories can cope with these variations by concentrating on each letter's distinct features.

BOTTOM-UP THEORIES

According to bottom-up theories, pattern recognition begins with the rods and cones, at the very bottom of the visual system (in the retina). In Chapter 3, we described cells called *feature detectors* in the visual cortex that respond to simple features like lines and angles in different positions. These feature detectors are located very near the bottom of the visual system, not far above the rods and cones from which they receive signals. In bottom-up theories, the features extracted by these specialized cells are compared to the various features that define abstract categories, such as dog and chair, at the top of the visual system (in the cortex). The visual system recognizes an object when it finds a match for the extracted features within the categories stored in memory.

Proponents of the bottom-up approach believe that we recognize letters by recording which feature detectors are activated when we look at the pattern. The line and angle detector cells feed into another set of cells, which may be called *letter detectors*. For example, a letter detector for *L* would be excited by feature detectors responding to horizontal and vertical lines, but it would be inhibited by detectors signaling diagonal lines, which are not contained in an *L*. Although bottom-up models of pattern recognition can become complicated, they do a good job of explaining certain errors of perception. For example, they predict that letters with similar features, such as *E* and *F*, will be confused more often than those with dissimilar features, such as *E* and *O*, a prediction that has been confirmed (Ivry & Prinzmetal, 1991; Townsend, 1971).

Pandemonium.   An early and somewhat fanciful model of bottom-up pattern recognition was **Pandemonium** (Selfridge, 1959), in which a hierarchy of "demons" detect features and transform them into perceptions in the manner we have just described (see Figure 4.8). Although Pandemonium was simply an abstract model describing pattern recognition, later physiological evidence has suggested that the process may in fact resemble Selfridge's imaginative theory: At the bottom of the visual system, image demons (similar to the rods in the retina) pass on information about the patterns of light in the stimulus to feature demons (similar to the feature detector neurons), which respond to the presence of a particular feature in the information reported by the image demons.

Marr's Model: The Primal Sketch.   More currently, the bottom-up approach has been the basis of attempts to construct machines that can see. One line of research that appears promising stems from the work of David Marr (1982). Marr's model works automatically from the visual image, without the system knowing in advance what to expect. (For this reason, we mention it under bottom-up models.)

Figure 4.9a shows a plant in front of a chain-link fence. Figure 4.9b illustrates the first step in Marr's approach in analyzing the image. Marr's system assumes that any sudden change in brightness indicates the presence of an edge, and these edges are denoted by lines in the *primal* (first) *sketch*. The second and third stages in Marr's representation add depth and other details to the primal sketch. The final stage of Marr's scheme is the construction of a three-dimensional model of the objects in the scene.

FIGURE 4.8

Pandemonium

In this model of pattern recognition, processing is entirely from the bottom up. Image demons yell when they detect patches of light reflected from a stimulus; feature demons yell in response to particular image demons; cognitive demons yell in response to particular feature demons; and finally, the decision demon resolves the whole issue by responding to a particular cognitive demon, thereby recognizing the stimulus.

SOURCE: (from p. 256 of Levin, M. W., & Shefner, J. M. (1991). *Fundamentals of sensation and perception* (2nd ed.). Pacifica Grove, Calif.: Brooks/Cole.)

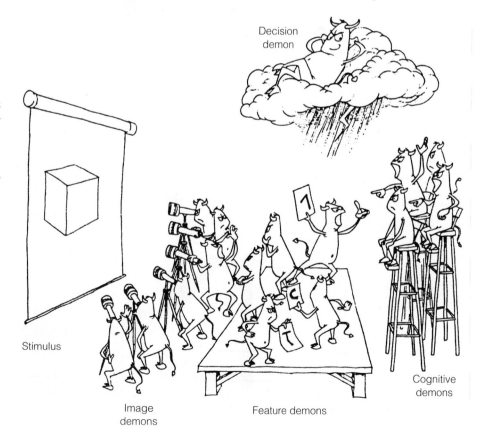

Decision demon

Stimulus

Image demons

Feature demons

Cognitive demons

FIGURE 4.9

The Construction of a Primal Sketch

(a) A photograph of a plant in front of a chain-link fence. (b) The first step, according to Marr's bottom-up theory of object recognition, in converting the image to a form in which lines reveal where sudden intensity changes exist in the original image.

SOURCE: Marr, 1982, pp. 58, 72.

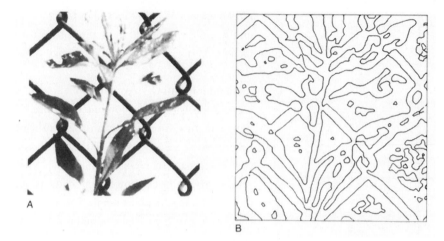

Constructing the three-dimensional model is rather like constructing an animal from blocks or cylinders (see Figure 4.10). The essential information that allows us to distinguish one animal from another is provided through the cylinders.

Marr's model is a bold attempt to answer the basic question of object recognition: How are distinguishing features represented (Humphrey & Jolicoeur, 1993)? Marr tried to answer this question in a form that could be used by scientists to construct mechanical visual systems. However, no entirely successful system has been developed

FIGURE 4.10

Three-Dimensional Sketches

Notice how well these simple sketches for limbs, quadrupeds, bipeds, and birds capture differences both across and within the four categories.

SOURCE: Marr, 1982, p. 319.

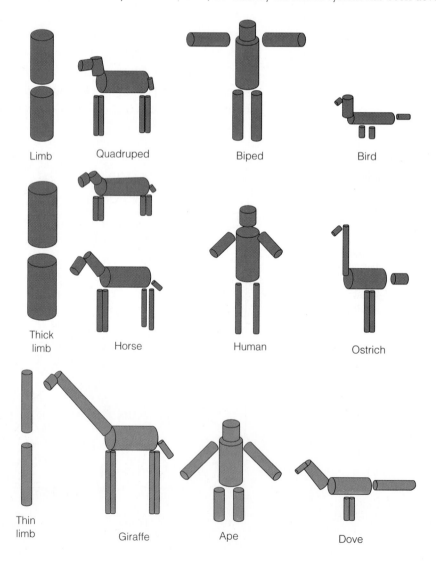

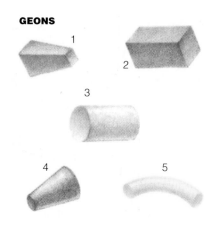

GEONS

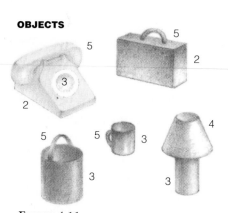

OBJECTS

FIGURE 4.11

Geons and Objects

The shapes on the top illustrate 5 of the 36 or so geons postulated to underlie our ability to recognize objects. According to Biderman's recognition-by-components theory, we recognize objects, such as those on the bottom, by recovering their geons from their visual images.

FIGURE 4.12

What Is It?

The object shown is actually quite common, but you are seeing it from a perspective that obscures the critical components (geons) used to recognize it. See Figure 4.13 if you are stumped.

to date, despite the great efforts of psychologists, engineers, and computer scientists.

Recognition by Components. Irving Biederman (1987) has proposed a theory that applies Marr's model to human perception and object recognition. Biederman's theory, called **recognition by components**, proposes that people recognize complex objects by decomposing them into their basic component parts. To consider a crude analogy, all English words are composed of letters arranged in various combinations; the letters are the basic elements that permit us to recognize whole words. In Biederman's theory, a fairly small number of primitive elements—called **geons**—can represent thousands of objects in the environment when arranged in various combinations (Biederman & Cooper, 1991; Humphrey & Khan, 1992).

Biederman (1987) has proposed that about 36 geons are needed to account for recognition of objects. (Five of the 36 are pictured in Figure 4.11.) Evidence supports Biederman's idea that the ease with which we reconize objects varies directly with the number of geons that we perceive. For example, try to recognize the object shown in Figure 4.12. Can you do it? If not, turn the page. The blender is easy to recognize in Figure 4.13 because all the component geons are visible.

These bottom-up theories are quite powerful. At the same time, however, most researchers acknowledge that other sources of information—the perceiver's past experience, expectations, and knowledge—also influence pattern recognition. This leads to top-down models, which assume that perception involves an active process that uses past knowledge to help determine what objects are in the environment.

TOP-DOWN THEORIES

In bottom-up theories, pattern recognition begins down at the receptor organs and works up to the perceptual centers of the brain. In the top-down approach, the perceptual system uses prior expectations (from higher up in the brain) to guide the search for sensory information in the environment. As sensory information is collected, it is combined with general knowledge about the world to actively construct what we perceive. The top-down, or *constructive*, approach to perception maintains that sensory information alone is generally inadequate to explain the richness of our perceptual experience. Instead, what people expect to see helps determine what they do see. *Perceptual set* refers to our predisposition, based on past experience, that influences our perception of objects.

According to top-down theorists, the brain uses prior knowledge to form hypotheses about what pattern is present and then actively selects the features required to test the hypotheses. Consider again the recognition of letters. When we encounter the letter *q* in English, we can almost be certain that the next letter will be a *u*. Therefore, it would be most efficient to search only for those few features that define a *u*. If the first three letters of a four-letter word are *bow*, what is the last letter likely to be? If it is an English word, the word is probably *bowl* or *bows*. To decide which, we need only check whether the last letter contains any curved lines. It would be a waste of time for the brain to bother analyzing all the features in the letter when one or two features will suffice.

The Effect of Context. Top-down models let perceivers skip unnecessary steps, and this may explain how pattern recognition works so rapidly. Unlike their bottom-up counterparts, top-down models also explain certain context effects in perception, as depicted in Figure 4.14. The same arrangement of lines can be recognized as the letter

FIGURE 4.13

A Blender with Its Geons Exposed

Viewed from its customary perspective, the blender is easy to recognize. According to Biederman's theory, we recognize complex objects by recovering their critical parts, the geons. We usually recognize objects easily because recovery of the geons provides overlapping information that converges on a single object.

H or the letter A, depending on its context. The context—the words of the sentence that have been read up to that point, or the adjacent letters—gives the perceptual system a hypothesis to test (e.g., R - T can only be completed with a limited number of letters to form an English word). If the stimulus fits the hypothesis well enough, the hypothesis is accepted and recognition is complete.

Top-down models help explain other powerful effects of context in perception. For instance, a whole triangle can be recognized faster than any of its features (i.e., faster than any of the three line segments that make up the triangle) (Pomerantz, 1981); a word can be recognized more accurately in a flash than any of its letters individually (Healy, 1994; Reicher, 1969); and an object can be recognized better in an appropriate setting than in isolation (Biederman, 1981). In all of these cases, a bottom-up model would lead us to expect the opposite results.

The Word Superiority Effect. Let's take a closer look at our tendency to reconize words faster than letters. Gerald Reicher (1969) tested people's perceptions of single letters versus the same letters appearing in words. For example, words (such as *cash* or *cast*) and letters (*h* or *t*) were shown to subjects at a very fast rate, too fast to be perceived accurately. After the stimulus had vanished, the subjects were asked to identify the letters (*h* or *t*) that had appeared. Reicher demonstrated that a letter could be perceived more readily when it occurred in the context of a word than when it appeared singly; this finding is quite surprising when you realize that more information is contained in a word than in a single letter.

Recent research has shown that embedding a letter within a word can boost its recognition even with much longer presentation times than the brief glimpses used by Reicher. Specifically, Prinzmetal (1992) showed that when words were presented on a computer screen in small type (like reading at a distance), subjects were more likely to recognize a letter when it was embedded in a word than when it was surrounded by symbols such as #. This effect occurred even with long presentation times of the stimuli.

The **word superiority effect**—the superior perception of a letter when it appears in a word rather than by itself—implies that we do not read in a letter-by-letter manner in which one letter is processed, then the next, and so on until the whole word is grasped. If reading occurred in a letter-by-letter fashion, then four letters making up a word could not possibly be read as efficiently as a single letter. Clearly, the context of the whole word (acting in a top-down fashion) makes the perception of the letters more efficient.

The Inverted Face Phenomenon. Let's consider a final example of the powerful effects of context on perception: the *inverted face phenomenon*, first noted by Thompson (1980). Look at the two upside-down faces shown in Figure 4.15. They look a bit odd, because you don't usually see faces upside down, but neither really stands out. Now turn the book upside down (so that the faces are right-side up). Now one face is easily recognizable as Vanna White, but the other face looks grotesque.

FIGURE 4.14

A Context Effect

The context of an object or pattern helps determine a viewer's recognition of it. In this example, the same pattern can be recognized as an *A* or an *H*.

THE RAT SAT ON THE CHAIR

Figure 4.15

The Inverted Face Phenomenon

The context in which features appear can greatly change our own interpretation of those features. When viewed upside down, these faces look rather similar, but when you look at them right-side up, one looks dreadful.

ʎƃoloɥɔʎsd
ʎƃoloɥɔʎsd

FIGURE 4.16

Another Inverted Figure Phenomenon

This figure shows that the inverted "face" phenomenon applies to other figures as well. These words appear similar when viewed upside down, but not when seen right-side up.

If you examine the two pictures, you will discover that the horrific photo was created simply by inverting the eyes and mouth in the face. Why do the faces look fairly similar when they are inverted but so different when viewed right-side up? Rock (1988) argues that the orientation of figures affects their perceived shape because in mentally rotating an inverted object, some of the information about the relationships between its parts is lost. Thus, when Vanna-from-hell is viewed upside down, the mouth and eyes look fine and the whole scene seems more or less like any other inverted face. But when viewed in the context of an upright face, as we usually perceive faces, the upside-down eyes and mouth seem grotesque.

Bartlett and Searcy (1993) also claim that inverting a face (or other scene) impairs processing of the whole scene, especially the arrangement of its elements. Thus, the upside-down faces in Figure 4.15 generally seem okay because the process of inverting them makes it harder to group elements in the appropriate way. But when we view these stimuli right-side up, the deviations jump out at us because our normal grouping processes are working.

According to Rock (1988) the phenomenon occurs with objects other than faces, as demonstrated in Figure 4.16, although the effect is not as dramatic (Tanaka & Farah, 1991). At a quick glance, the two upside-down words look identical. But turn the words right-side up, and it becomes clear that one is a normal word and the other just a little bit unusual. As with the faces, the words appear quite different when viewed in their normal, right-side up orientation.

INTERACTIVE THEORIES

Which theory is correct—top-down or bottom-up? Actually, both viewpoints are correct. In most situations, our senses provide enough information for bottom-up processing to permit us to see the world accurately, although top-down processes may sharpen our perception. When information from our senses is poor (as when we try to make things out in the dark) or ambiguous, then top-down processes operate strongly. For example, you might mistake a shadow on your bedroom wall for an intruder, especially after watching a scary movie.

Recognizing that both top-down and bottom-up processes play a role in perception, many researchers have proposed **interactive theories,** claiming there is an interplay between sensory and higher-level cognitive factors. For example, most researchers view reading as an interplay between top-down expectations and bottom-up processes (Jacoby, 1983; Levy & Kirsner, 1989).

A Connectionist Model. An interactive model of reading is portrayed in Figure 4.17. It is called a **connectionist model** because of the connections (represented by lines) between elements in the model. Don't worry about the details of the figure; simply note the three levels of representation: lines, letters, and words (McClelland & Rumelhart, 1981). The arrows in Figure 4.17 indicate activation, and the dots signal inhibition.

The model includes bottom-up processing features, more or less like Pandemonium in Figure 4.8. When line detectors are activated, they partially activate letters that contain that line and at the same time inhibit letters that do not. For example, the horizontal line detector partially activates the detector for *T* but inhibits the detector for *N*. Similarly, activation of a letter detector for *T* will in turn tend to activate detectors for words containing a *T* (*trap, trip*) and inhibit detectors for words that do not contain a *T* (*able*).

The model also shows top-down influences from words to letters. In its top-down operation, each word inhibits detectors for letters not contained in the words, which effectively switches off detectors for features that are unlikely to appear. Thus, if you were reading a passage that started out, "My car wouldn't start so I didn't make it to my class on _____," the detector for the word *time* would be activated by the sentence context. This would then cause detectors for letters not contained in the word *time* to be inhibited. When letter detectors are inhibited, the detectors for the features that make up those letters will also be inhibited, thereby allowing activation at the word level to affect detection at the feature level. By working simultaneously from the top down and the bottom up, word recognition takes place extremely quickly, because readers can predict upcoming words and letters from context. Of course, when a word appears that is totally unpredictable, top-down processes actually interfere with perception, and we have to do a double-take to read what is actually printed on the page.

FIGURE 4.17

A Model of Reading

This diagram shows McClelland and Rummelhart's (1981) connectionist model for the recognition of printed words. The model incorporates both bottom-up signals, sent from the feature detectors at the bottom to the word detectors at the top, and top-down signals going in the opposite direction. These signals are both excitatory (connections ending in arrows) and inhibitory (ending in dots). Because it has both sorts of processes, the model represents an interactive approach to perception.

SOURCE: McClelland & Rumelhart, 1981, p. 380.

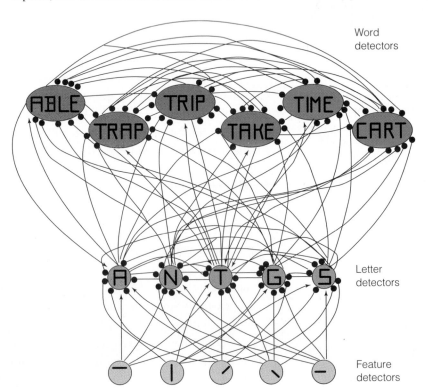

LETTER-BY-LETTER READERS

We have seen evidence that reading does not occur in a letter-by-letter fashion. If we read that way, the process would be much slower than it actually is. Also, the word superiority effect—the fact that we can apprehend a letter in a word more readily than when the letter is presented by itself—argues that top-down processes influence reading. However, some people who have suffered brain damage do read in a letter-by-letter fashion. Patterson and Kay (1982) analyzed four patients whose brain damage had made them unable to read words in a normal way. When presented with a word such as *shepard,* these patients could not read it aloud quickly and fluently as people normally do. But if they were permitted to read each letter, either aloud or to themselves, in a left to right order, then they could name the whole word! So the patient would say S, H, E, P, A, R, D, pause, and then say "SHEPARD." They would also know the meaning of the word once they said it, but apparently not before that point. Letter-by-letter readers are very slow, of course, and it took the fastest of Patterson and Kay's (1982) four patients an average of 7.6 seconds to read three letter words and 19.5 seconds for words that were nine to ten letters.

Some letter-by-letter readers are almost perfectly accurate, never missing a word (Warrington & Shallice, 1980). However, others will misidentify letters fairly frequently. For example, a patient given the word *spade* but then sounding out the letters S, H, A, D, E then says the word "shade," not spade. So the letter-by-letter reader's ability to name words is determined by the letters that are pronounced, not the letters on the page (Ellis & Young, 1988).

What are the implications of cases of letter-by-letter readers for normal reading?

First, their performance adds further evidence that normal readers do not operate in a strictly letter-by-letter fashion to read words. The process would be much too slow, as we see from these people who can only read in a letter-by-letter fashion. Second, Warrington and Shallice (1980) proposed that normal readers use what they called a *visual word form system* for reading. That is, all of us have thousands of representations of the forms of words stored in our brains and we can read rapidly by activating those word forms all at once, rather than piecing together words letter by letter. Warrington and Shallice (1980) argued that letter-by-letter readers have lost the ability to use the visual word form system for reading, which accounts for their disability. Instead, the way they seem to read words is by reversing the operations of spelling. In normal spelling, a person hears a word and then says or writes the letters. In the letter-by-letter reader, the process is reversed: imagine that you had to identify words when someone reads them out loud to you, letter by letter. So you hear "S,Q,U,A,S,H" and you have to say "squash." This task is possible, but not easy, for most of us. However, for letter-by-letter readers, it is their only way of gaining information from printed words, by sounding out each letter through this slow, effortful process and then grasping it all at once when they have finished. The evidence that letter-by-letter readers do use this process is that their reading ability is generally related to their ability to spell words when they hear them (Ellis & Young, 1988). So cases of letter-by-letter readers inform researchers both about how reading normally occurs, as well as how these brain-damaged people cope with the loss of visual word forms that we normally use to read.

Ambiguous and Reversible Figures. Of course, top-down and bottom-up theories of perception apply to perceptual tasks other than letter and word recognition. Psychologists and artists have created a number of visual patterns that illustrate the interaction of bottom-up and top-down processes. Some of these are illustrated in Figure 4.18. Before reading the caption, look at the patterns. Does each seem to "flip" spontaneously into some new pattern after you examine it for several seconds? Because they can be perceived in more than one way, many researchers believe that bottom-up processing alone is not at work here. After all, the same visual features on the printed page produce both versions of each figure. Thus, these ambiguous figures also show the operation of top-down processes, actively assembling visual features into different organizations (Long, Toppino, & Mondin, 1992).

Subjective Contours. Other phenomena that call for an interactive explanation are **subjective contours**, outlines of shapes that are seen even though no physical edges or lines are present. Figure 4.19 shows a pair of triangles whose edges seem real until you scrutinize them. Edge detectors (which signal edges by noting where the brightness of a surface changes), working in the cortex strictly from the bottom up, should not detect the apparent lines because there are in fact no physical (brightness) edges. However, Lesher (1995) summarizes evidence that neural mechanisms in the visual cortex help generate illusory contours. But the lines must be filled in partly by top-down processes that expect edges to exist because of the context cues in the dis-

FIGURE 4.18

Ambiguous or Reversible Figures

In each case, at least two interpretations can arise from the same sensory pattern. (a) You can see either a beautiful young woman or an unattractive old one. (b) Is it a rabbit or a duck? (c) Stare at an interior corner of the cube (known as the *Necker cube*) that you think is nearest to you. You will suddenly discover that it has become the farthest corner because the cube spontaneously reverses in depth. (The "vase" in Figure 4.4 is another reversible figure.) (d) Viewed up close, this picture reveals a woman examining herself in the mirror; at a distance, the same scene reveals a skull.

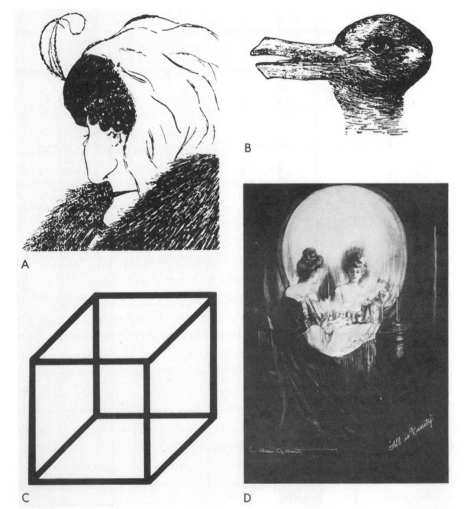

A

B

C

D

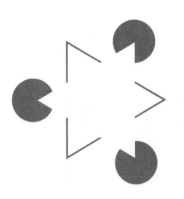

FIGURE 4.19

Subjective Contours

In the figure on the left, the viewer has a strong impression of a white triangle that is not really present in the figure. The triangle seems whiter than the background, although it is not. On the right, the same illusory triangle appears in black.

SOURCE: Kanizsa, 1976.

FIGURE 4.20

The Subjective Necker Cube

The Necker cube can be seen either as floating on top of the red disks or, if figure and ground are reversed, as floating behind a light surface with holes in it. In the first case, subjective contours are seen; in the second case, they are not.

SOURCE: Bradley, Dumais, & Petry, 1976.

play. Figure 4.20 demonstrates subjective contours with the help of the reversible Necker cube of Figure 4.18. The display can be seen as a Necker cube either floating above some red disks or floating in a red space behind a white surface with holes in it (as though you were seeing the cube through a slice of Swiss cheese). Seeing these two possibilities takes some effort, but it's worth it.

Subjective contours have been studied for nearly 100 years (Lesher, 1995; Purghe & Coren, 1992). Despite the considerable effort that has been devoted to understanding them, there is still no generally accepted explanation (Lesher, 1995). Some researchers believe that lateral inhibition at early stages in the nervous system (a bottom-up influence) contributes to the perception of subjective contours (Coren, 1991). Other investigators claim that certain cues about the distance of the figure within the subjective contour stimuli lead us to perceive lines where none exist (a top-down influence). We expect to see them there, defining the edges of an object that is lying in front of the other elements of the stimulus, which we perceive to be the background (Gordon & Earle, 1992; Peterhans & von der Heydt, 1991).

Subjective contours are visual images that do not necessarily correspond with the information from our sensory receptors. But they are not alone in that respect. When we dream, most of us "see" things that can be quite lifelike; likewise, drugs and biochemical imbalances can lead to intense hallucinations in people who are wide awake. On a less extreme scale, people often experience visual images that they find pleasant and useful in planning and solving problems (see Chapter 8). However, some scientists are troubled by the idea of studying something so subjective and unobservable as a person's private mental images. A disagreement about the scientific status of visual imagery is outlined in "Controversy: Are Mental Images Like Perceptions?"

Depth, Size, and Shape Perception

When you look at a dog, you not only recognize it, but also gain information about its depth (or distance from you), its size, and its shape. However, identifying depth, size, and shape is more difficult than you might think. For example, the size of the image that an object projects onto the retina (see Figure 3.7 on page 94) depends on both the physical size of the object and its distance from the viewer. And, the perception of depth requires that we extract an enormous amount of information from a visual scene, perform numerous calculations based on these data, and then organize the results into a unified three-dimensional view.

Answer the following question before reading further: How many windows are there in the room where you sleep? Most people can answer this question with little difficulty, and many report that they arrive at the answer by forming a mental image of their bedroom and then scanning the image, just as they would scan the room if they were standing in it. Do we really think in images? If we do, how similar is imagining to actually perceiving?

A debate about **mental imagery** has persisted for almost 100 years. As described in Chapter 1, the early psychologists asked observers to rate the vividness of their mental images. The behaviorists, however, rejected the study of mental imagery, arguing that if it could not be directly observed in behavior then it could not be studied scientifically. In fact, the behaviorists succeeded in excluding the study of imagery from experimental psychology for nearly 50 years, until its reappearance in the 1960s. The debate resurfaced as well (Paivio, 1975; Pylyshyn, 1973).

Contemporary psychologists are not content to rely solely on introspection to study imagery. If images cannot be studied directly, psychologists can do the next best thing: study them *indi-*

rectly by observing their effect on behavior. Imagery researchers say, in essence, "If images are real, what effects on behavior can we predict?" Interestingly, many predictions have been confirmed by careful experiments (Kosslyn, 1994; Paivio, 1986).

One prediction is that if images are like perceptions, they may depend on the same brain mechanisms (Farah, 1988). Ruggieri (1991) confirmed this prediction by having his subjects imagine a scene while focusing on a blank white screen and then abruptly covering up one of their eyes. He found that in the majority of the subjects, the interruption of the light falling on the retina strongly modified the images that his subjects had been

generating. Also, if images and perceptions must share the same brain structures, then it should be difficult to experience images and perceptions at the same time because the same neural circuitry could not be used for two different purposes at once. (Try imagining your mother's face with your eyes closed and then with them open while you watch TV.)

Some studies (Craver-Lemley & Reeves, 1992; Segal, 1971) have shown that when people are instructed to generate visual images (such as a flock of birds in flight), their ability to detect weak visual stimuli drops, but perception of auditory stimuli is relatively unaffected. Similarly, if asked to imagine an auditory event (such as an orchestra playing loudly), their perceptual sensitivity drops much more for auditory stimuli than for visual stimuli. When we imagine sights or sounds, the ability to perceive actual stimuli in the same sense modality is diminished. These findings indicate that imagining and perceiving seem to rely on the same structures in the brain.

Another prediction is that if mental images are similar to perceptions, then both should be scanned in a similar fashion. In one experiment, Stephen Kosslyn (1980; Kosslyn, Ball, & Reiser,

PERCEPTION OF DEPTH

Recall from Chapter 3 that the retina of each eye is a tissue layer lining the back of the eye's interior. It is essentially a two-dimensional surface, having only height and width. But if the retina has only two dimensions, how do we see the world in three dimensions? What **depth cues**—information indicating the distance of an object from an observer—do we use to perceive depth?

Binocular Disparity. One reason that we are capable of depth perception is that our eyes are several inches apart, enabling us to see the world from two slightly different perspectives. Therefore, each retina receives a slightly different view of the same object. This difference, called **binocular disparity,** can be demonstrated by looking at this page while alternately blinking one eye at a time; the page will appear to shift its position. Normally, the brain combines the two images into a single three-dimensional, or stereoscopic, image. The stereoscope, or 3-D viewer, works by presenting photographs of a scene taken from two slightly different points, projecting one image into the right eye and the other image into the left, just as if our eyes had seen

1978) asked college students to memorize a map of an imaginary island, like the one shown in Figure 4.21. After removing the map from their sight, he asked students to form a mental image of the map and to focus their attention on a particular landmark, such as the well in the lower left-hand corner. The test began when the subjects were asked to scan their mental images from that landmark to another landmark he named and to press a button when their scan was complete. Kosslyn measured how quickly these scans were made. He found that his subjects were fastest in scanning to nearby locations; the more distant the feature, the longer the scan took. We would expect such results if subjects

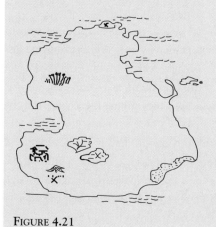

FIGURE 4.21

Image Scanning

SOURCE: Kosslyn Ball, & Reiser, 1978, p. 51.

were actually scanning an imaginary scene with spatial properties like those of a real scene. Again, this result suggests that perception of mental images is similar to actual visual perception.

These illustrations are only a small sample of the experiments supporting the claim that images are like perceptions. We must note, however, that this evidence is largely circumstantial and in no way proves that mental images are comparable to perceptions. Some psychologists remain skeptical about images, pointing out that people who claim to experience them often cannot use them effectively. For example, it is common for students struggling with an exam question to report that they can see the page of their textbook where the answer lies, but they cannot quite make out the words well enough to read them! For a demonstration, look now at the geometric figure shown in Figure 4.22 and memorize it before reading any further. Without looking back at the figure, decide from your mental image whether it contains any parallelograms. If you cannot remember, look back at the figure. You will find that it contains three.

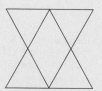

FIGURE 4.22

Image in the Mind's Eye

Most people find this question easy to answer when they examine the figure but hard when they examine their mental images. If mental images are as vivid and detailed as some people claim, why is this image so hard to scan for hidden parallelograms?

Despite doubts by some psychologists, the study of visual imagery has returned to psychology. Some researchers study imagery associated with dreaming (Chapter 5). Others have shown that imagery often greatly improves the ability to remember information (Chapter 7). Still others study the ways in which images can be manipulated and transformed as people think creatively (Chapter 8). Imagery is also used in some types of psychological therapies (Chapter 16). Although some doubts linger, research on mental imagery has shown that imagination can be studied objectively and used for many purposes.

two different views. This is analogous to the stereophonic sounds on records, tapes, and compact discs, which were recorded "in stereo" by placing two microphones at different locations to simulate the separation between the ears.

Basically, the visual system must shift the neural representation of images from each eye until they line up with each other, which helps us to perceive an object's depth. The closer the object is to the observer, the more shifting needed for alignment. To convince yourself of this point, blink your eyes one at a time while staring at a finger held only a few inches from your face and then as far as your arm can reach. Your finger will appear to jump around more when it is close to your eyes. Thus, to produce the single image in normal viewing, the brain must do more shifting for near than for far objects.

In a recent study, Miller (1991) found that alcohol affects our ability to merge binocular images. As blood alcohol level increases, so does the time it takes to fuse images, especially for objects at very near or at far distances. Also, the maximum distance at which subjects could successfully fuse images decreased as alcohol consump-

FIGURE 4.23

Monocular Depth Cues

Which face seems closest to you? The faces are really all the same distance from you, but you interpret the increasingly smaller images as receding in depth, or distance, from you.

SOURCE: Miller, 1962.

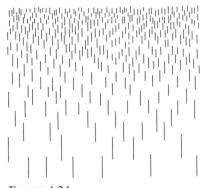

FIGURE 4.24

Texture Gradients

The texture gradients in this "landscape" are vertical lines that grow shorter and become more densely packed, giving an impression of depth.

SOURCE: Neisser, 1968.

FIGURE 4.25

A Texture Gradient Size Illusion

Which of these cylinders is the largest? All three are actually the same size, but the texture gradient and linear perspective make them appear different.

SOURCE: Gibson, 1950.

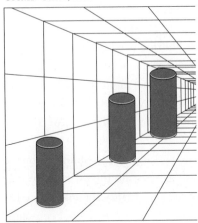

tion increased. A surprising result of this study was that these visual deficits occurred at alcohol levels far below the legal driving limit in most states. So, in addition to motor skills, learning, memory, and judgment, alcohol affects what we see.

Monocular Depth Cues. Even with one eye closed, people can still see reasonably good depth because of **monocular cues,** factors used by only one eye to judge distance. *Size of the retinal image* is one such cue, because as the distance to the object increases, the image it projects on the retina shrinks. Looking at Figure 4.23, we perceive the shrinking faces as receding in depth because they mimic the changes in the retinal image for a receding object.

Another monocular cue involves *texture gradients*, or the density of the texture of the environment. Examples are shown in Figures 4.24 and 4.25. As the texture of the image becomes more finely grained, the observer sees the image receding. Although the distant image actually contains less detail, all the details are bunched together to give the fine-grained appearance and to make the object appear further away.

Sketch artists usually draw scenes in depth by first sketching lines that approach a vanishing point on the horizon. Figure 4.25 shows an illusion of size that is based on changing the apparent distance of three cylinders through the use of texture gradients and *linear perspective*, the convergence of lines toward a vanishing point.

Interposition, or overlap, provides another monocular depth cue, as illustrated in Figure 4.26. When one object blocks out the view of another, the first one appears to be closer than the second.

Motion parallax, a depth cue that operates only with moving stimuli, occurs when the images of nearby objects sweep across a moving person's field of vision faster than the images of faraway objects. This effect is easy to observe from a moving car (see Figure 4.27). The pavement seems to fly by at great speed while trees on the horizon appear to move more slowly. Objects at still greater distances (e.g., the moon) appear not to move at all relative to the car, or they appear to drift in the same direction.

Artists use various monocular cues to give their work a sense of depth. Can you identify the cues used by Georges Seurat in his postimpressionist masterpiece shown in Figure 4.28? Notice how Seurat uses less saturated colors to portray extremely distant objects in the scene. This illustrates the role of contrast and saturation as monocular depth cues (known collectively as *aerial perspective*). The atmosphere scatters the light reflected from extremely distant objects, causing them to appear less sharp and the colors less saturated (Troscianko, Montagnon, Le Clerc, Malbert, & Chanteau, 1991).

FIGURE 4.26

An Interposition Cue

This figure is seen as one square partly blocking another. It is difficult to see this figure without perceiving this depth relationship.

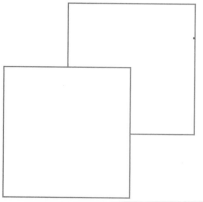

FIGURE 4.27

Motion Parallax

When a person moves in a car or train, nearby objects seem to rush by in the opposite direction. Faraway objects, beyond the fixation point, seem to move very slowly in the same direction. These differences can serve as cues for the relative distance of objects.

Direction of passenger's motion

FIGURE 4.28

The artist Georges Seurat, in his late nineteenth-century masterpiece *La Grande Jatte*, projects strong images of depth by using monocular cues.

PERCEPTUAL CONSTANCY: SIZE, SHAPE, AND LIGHTNESS

The perception of size might appear to be simple, but it is not. In general, the larger an object, the larger the image projected onto the retina (see Figures 3.7 and 3.11, on pages 94 and 96). But as we stated before, the retinal size of an object depends on the object's distance from the viewer as well as the object's size.

A similar problem arises in the perception of shape. The shape of the retinal image of an object depends partly on the angle from which the object is viewed. This is demonstrated in Figure 4.29, where the figure appears to be either an ellipse or a circle, depending on the viewing angle.

Why don't people appear to shrink as they walk away? When we follow a moving object with our eyes, the size and shape of its retinal image change continuously; nevertheless, we normally see the object as remaining constant in both shape and size. This phenomenon whereby objects appear to have constant properties despite changes in their retinal images is known as **perceptual constancy.** *Size* and *shape constancy* are only two of a large number of constancies in perception. Another example is *lightness constancy*. Recall from Chapter 3 that a black road looks black whether it is viewed in broad daylight or in twilight. (Thus, we accurately perceive its lightness, despite the wide variations in the light reflected from the surface.) Such constancies are enormously valuable because they correct our perceptions and allow us to see the true shapes, sizes, and colors in the world, rather than the shifting retinal images. However, there are limits to the amount of correction the constancies can provide. When we look down from the top of a very tall building, the people below look ant-size, even though we know they are not. Fortunately, this breakdown of the constancies occurs only in extreme situations.

Psychologists have long puzzled over the way the perceptual systems achieve constancy. We can better understand the constancies by first examining the distinction between proximal and distal stimuli. A **proximal stimulus** is a pattern of physical energy, such as a series of sound waves or a pattern of light waves, that strikes a sensory receptor. Proximal stimuli are what actually contact our senses. The light striking the retina is a proximal stimulus, as is the sound pattern that strikes our eardrums. A **distal stimulus** is the actual object that produces the pattern of physical energy that becomes the proximal stimulus. For example, a painting is a distal stimulus that reflects light. Once reflected, some of the light enters our eyes and strikes the retina. The reflected light is a proximal stimulus.

The existence of the perceptual constancies demonstrates that perceptual experience is tied more closely to distal stimuli than to proximal stimuli. Thus, if you pick up this book and move it closer to you and then farther away, you will perceive the book's size and shape as remaining the same; the distal stimulus (the book itself) retains its size and shape, although the proximal stimulus (the retinal image of the book) fluctuates over a large range.

A powerful illusion based on shape constancy is illustrated in Figure 4.30, which we originally introduced in Chapter 1. The two dark surfaces representing the tops of the objects in (a) and (b) appear to be quite different in shape. The top of the object in (a) appears long and narrow, while the top of the object in (b) appears thicker and shorter. Yet the two darkened surfaces in (a) and (b) are actually congruent! That is, if you trace the outline of the top of (a) on a sheet of paper, it will fit exactly over the top of (b) when properly rotated. You will probably want to trace this to see for yourself; the illusion is so compelling that most people don't believe that the two dark sur-

FIGURE 4.29

Shape Perception at a Slant

This shape is an ellipse as it is drawn on paper. You can see it either as an ellipse or as a circle hat is viewed from an angle.

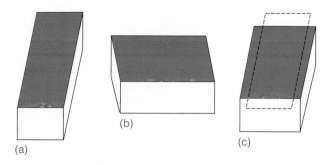

FIGURE 4.30

A Shape Constancy Illusion

The shaded parallelogram in part (b) is congruent with the one in (a) and with the dashed outline in (c). That is, if you cut out the shaded area in (a), it would fit exactly on the shaded area in (b). If you are skeptical, try tracing the outlines of these parallelograms on thin paper and placing them on top of one another.

SOURCE: Shepard, 1981.

(a) (b) (c)

faces can possibly be the same size and shape. Most people falsely assume that the surfaces would actually fit as shown in (c).

This illusion demonstrates the essential idea of how constancies are achieved. The shapes seem three-dimensional even though they are shown on the page in only two dimensions. The visual system takes the available cues in the retinal image (proximal stimuli) and uses these cues to construct the probable shape of the distal stimuli. In Figure 4.30, you see the lines as rectangular blocks. Thus, you tend to perceive all the surfaces as rectangular and as meeting at 90-degree angles. If you look carefully, however, you will discover that the dark surfaces are not rectangular at all; they do *not* contain 90-degree angles. Thus, the proximal stimuli are not rectangular either. Your perceptual system has constructed the most plausible scene from the proximal stimuli, thus creating the illusion. If your perceptions depended solely on the information in the proximal stimuli, the illusion would not occur, because the proximal stimuli have the same shape. However, since our perceptual system normally does its best to construct a mental model of the distal stimuli from the proximal stimuli, you perceive the two dark surfaces as varying in shape. Similar principles operate in other visual illusions.

Visual Illusions

Perceptual illusions arise whenever there is a disagreement between distal stimuli—objects in the real world—and our perceptions of these objects. Sometimes these disagreements originate in the environment, sometimes in our organs of perception, and sometimes in the brain as it constructs our percepts. Although illusions can occur for all of our perceptual systems, we will limit our discussion to those affecting the visual perceptual system.

Stage magicians often incorporate visual illusions into their act to surprise and perplex their audience. To perceptual psychologists, however, illusions are more than mere amusements; they are the key to understanding how normal perception operates (Coren & Girgus, 1978; Gordon & Earle, 1992). The senses usually operate so quickly and accurately that they are sometimes taken for granted. When illusions occur, we become aware of the normally unnoticed processes of sensation and perception. By examining illusions closely, we may learn how we perceive the world as accurately as we do.

ILLUSIONS THAT ORIGINATE IN THE RECEPTORS

A number of visual illusions can be traced to processes occurring in the eye long before neural signals reach the brain. One retina-based illusion, called **Hermann's grid,** is shown in Figure 4.31. The faint gray spots you see at the intersections of the white bars are purely illusory; if you stare at one of them, it disappears. The illusion created by the grid is due to lateral inhibition in the retina (which was also responsible

FIGURE 4.31

Hermann's Grid

(a) Illusory gray spots appear at each intersection except the one you are looking at. This illusion is caused by lateral inhibition, a form of interaction among neural cells in the retina.
(b) Lateral inhibition makes regions surrounded by lighter areas appear darker. Because the white regions at the intersections are surrounded by white on four sides, whereas the white regions away from the intersections are surrounded by white on only two sides, the regions in the intersections are more inhibited and therefore appear darker.

SOURCE: Sekuler & Blake, 1994, p. 77.

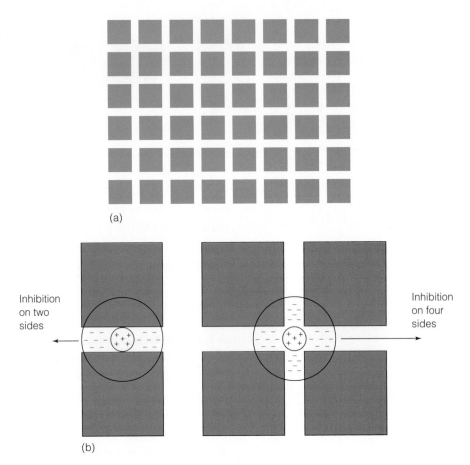

(a)

Inhibition on two sides

Inhibition on four sides

(b)

for the simultaneous contrast effect shown in Figure 3.14, on page 97). The intersections are surrounded by more white space than surrounds the other white regions of the figure, as shown in Figure 4.31. Because white regions inhibit neighboring neural cells from firing, the intersections are more inhibited than the other white regions and so appear darker. The spots disappear when you look at them because lateral inhibition is much weaker in the fovea than in the eye's periphery. Lateral inhibition normally increases the perception of contrast and sharpens fuzzy or blurred edges. Thus, the illusory spots actually result from a system that normally improves our vision.

ILLUSIONS THAT ORIGINATE IN THE BRAIN

Although some illusions originate in our sensory organs, an even greater number arise only after signals arrive in the brain for further processing. Because the brain is so complex, we do not know exactly where in the brain these illusions originate; but this does not prevent us from learning how they operate.

McCollough Effect. One striking example of such illusions is called the **McCollough effect** (McCollough, 1965), demonstrated in Figure 4.32. First look at part (c) and confirm that it is entirely black and white. Now spend the next 5 minutes (it's worth the effort!) shifting your gaze back and forth between the colored parts (a) and (b), spending about 10 seconds on each before shifting to the other. Keep your gaze near the middle of each square, and don't alter your viewing distance or the tilt of your head during the 5-minute period. When the time is up, look again at part (c) and you will now see faint but unmistakable colors where before you saw only black and white. Notice that you see green (the color of the horizontal stripes during the 5-

minute adaptation) in the sections of part (c) where the stripes are vertical. Where the stripes are horizontal in part (c), you perceive red, the color of the vertical stripes in part (b). If you tilt your head (or the book) 45 degrees as you look at part (c), these illusory colors will disappear; a 90-degree tilt will make the colors reverse! Although you need to spend a little time and effort on this illusion, the effect is dramatic. (If you have a red-green color deficiency, however, you probably won't see the colors).

What is the meaning of this dramatic illusion? On the surface, it resembles the conventional colored afterimages discussed in Chapter 3. For example, adaptation to green produces an afterimage of red or pink, and vice versa. There are important differences between colored afterimages and the McCollough effect, however. First, the colors seen here depend completely on the orientation of the black and white stripes presented during the adaptation period. Orientation does not matter for standard afterimages. Second, this effect does not wear away in a matter of seconds like most colored afterimages. If you are like most people, this effect will last for hours, or even days, if you completed the full 5-minute adaptation.

What causes the McCollough effect? Conventional colored afterimages were accounted for in Chapter 3 by separate components of the visual system that respond to red, green, yellow, blue, black, and white. The McCollough effect can also be explained in terms of separate components, but the components are feature detectors located higher in the brain. These feature detectors are sensitive not just to color but to combinations of color and orientation. In other words, the McCollough effect suggests the existence of "red-vertical edge detectors," "green-horizontal edge detectors," and so forth, a possibility that agrees well with findings of brain physiologists (Harris,

FIGURE 4.32

The McCollough Effect

Following the instructions in the text, stare alternatively at (a) and (b) for about 5 minutes. Then look at part (c) and you will notice faint colors that change as you rotate the book clockwise and counterclockwise.

SOURCE: Frisby, 1980, p. 70.

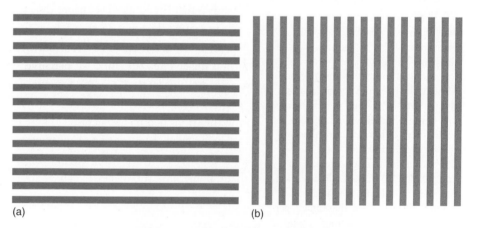

(a) (b)

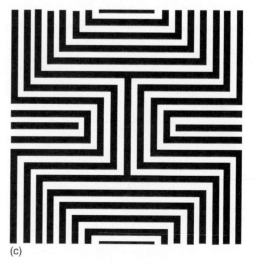

(c)

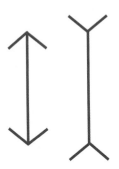

FIGURE 4.33

The Müller-Lyer, or Arrow, Illusion

The line with the outgoing fins appears to be longer, but is it? See Figure 4.35.

FIGURE 4.34

Four Well-Known Spatial Illusions

The illusions are named after their dicoverers. (a) In the Ponzo illusion, the upper horizontal line appears longer, but is not. (b) In the Poggendorf illusion, the two lines do not look as though they would meet behind the figure, but in fact they are in line with each other. (c) In the Hering illusion, the middle vertical lines appear to be bowed, but they are actually straight and parallel. (d) In the Zöllner illusion, too, the vertical lines are straight and parallel. Illusions show that human perception is fallible and not just a copy of the image on the retina.

1987). However, the lengthy persistence of the McCollough effect remains a puzzle. Conventional colored afterimages are explained by the fatiguing of cones during the adaptation period. These afterimages dissipate as quickly as the cones recover from fatigue. The fact that the McCollough effect lasts for days virtually eliminates fatigue as an explanation, but no generally accepted alternative explanation has yet been offered (Dodwell & Humphrey, 1990).

Spatial Illusions. Other striking illusions that originate in the brain are **spatial illusions,** which involve distortion of geometric shapes, such as the length or straightness of line segments. In the **Müller-Lyer illusion,** shown in Figure 4.33, the two vertical lines appear to be unequal in length even though they are identical. (Measure them if you are doubtful.) Some other well-known spatial illusions are shown in Figure 4.34.

Researchers have been able to show that the Müller-Lyer illusion does not arise in the retina. When the different elements of the figure are presented separately to the two eyes—that is, the lines presented to one eye and the fins to the other—the illusion still occurs. This means that the illusion must arise at some later point in the visual system where the signals from the two eyes are combined in the brain, probably in the visual cortex (Julesz, 1971).

Earlier in the chapter, we presented an illusion that results from the operation of the perceptual constancies, which normally help keep perception stable (see Figure 4.30). What about spatial illusions such as the Müller-Lyer? Do they also result from a normally useful process gone wrong? British psychologist R. L. Gregory (1978) has answered yes: Such illusions are due to the mechanisms that maintain size constancy. He argues that the Müller-Lyer figure is seen in depth, since its fins provide cues to linear perspective. Figure 4.35 shows how the fins of the Müller-Lyer illusion may be interpreted as depth cues. The two center vertical lines in (a) and (b) are the same retinal image size, but since we perceive the one in (a) as receding in depth, we assume that it is larger. Gregory's account of the Müller-Lyer illusion is not universally accepted, because the illusion has been produced with figures specially designed to omit the strong depth cues mentioned here (Gordon & Earle, 1992).

These explanations of spatial illusions complement the idea that observers determine the size of objects from inferences or intelligent guesses about their distance from them. Sometimes those guesses can be misguided. In Figure 4.36, the person on the

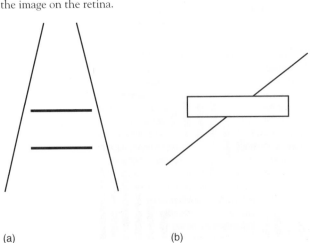

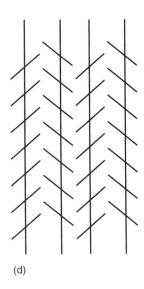

(a) (b) (c) (d)

FIGURE 4.35

R. L. Gregory's Explanation for the Müller-Lyer Illusion

The lines of the Müller-Lyer illusion are visible in these two scenes. The scene in (a) seems to recede from the observer into the paper, so the center vertical line appears father away than the corresponding line in (b), which seems to jut out from the page toward the observer. These differences in perceived distances lead to the variations in size "seen" by the observer.

SOURCE: Gregory, 1978.

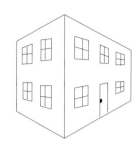

right looks much larger than the person standing in the left corner, but they are actually the same size. The illusion occurs because your visual system has made an intelligent, but mistaken, guess that the room is rectangular. This is reasonable because the angles in the room look like right angles and because most rooms are rectangular. But this room is trapezoidal, not rectangular; its geometry is shown in Figure 4.37. The person who appears smaller is actually much farther away than the person who looks larger. By failing to notice this depth difference, the viewer sees an illusory size difference. This, of course, is a demonstration specially constructed to mislead you. (If you were actually standing inside this room, would you still be fooled?) Nevertheless, it clearly shows how perception may be built on wrong guesses or assumptions.

FIGURE 4.36
Illusory Size Differences

The person on the right looks much larger than the person on the left. Impossible? No. The person on the left is farther away from the viewing point.

FIGURE 4.37

Actual Shape of the Room in Figure 4.36

In this diagram, the back wall slopes away from the viewer, to the left, but the walls are arranged to provide the same retinal image as a normal rectangular room. Thus, the viewer is misled into accepting the incorrect perceptual hypothesis that the room is rectangular and that the person on the right is larger than the person on the left.

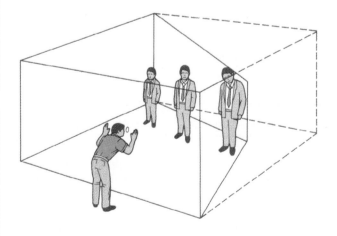

UNIDENTIFIED FLYING OBJECTS AND OTHER ILLUSIONS IN THE REAL WORLD

Many of the illusions presented in this chapter appear only under laboratory or staged conditions. Do we also experience illusions outside the laboratory? Yes, although we don't always recognize them as illusions.

UFOs: Real or Illusion?

From time to time, newspapers carry reports of people sighting unidentified flying objects (UFOs). One common scenario is that a driver late at night will see an unexplainable object outside the car window. Similar reports have been made by airplane pilots. In other cases, hunters or hikers out in the deep woods will see unexplained objects. These UFOs create ripples of excitement when reported in the newspapers. Indeed, UFO sightings usually come in waves, with one report quickly leading to a host of others. This might mean that UFOs descend on earth in waves or (perhaps more likely) that the publicity about one sighting causes others to have similar perceptions. Despite the lack of convincing physical evidence for their existence, UFOs ae widely discussed on television and in the newpapers (Shaeffer, 1992).

How can we explain UFO sightings? Some scientists believe that at least some UFO sightings are the result of perceptual illusions (Klass, 1974). If UFOs were really descending upon the earth, they might occasionally turn up in the middle of the Super Bowl or in other places where there were thousands of viewers, television cameras, and well-lit conditions. But this has never happened. The sightings are usually off in the dim woods or occurring at night, when there is poor visibility and conditions are ripe for perceptual illusions.

During periodic surges in UFO reports, many people look to the sky in the hope of seeing curious objects; in so doing, they often mistake weather balloons for spaceships. Consider a case reported by Klass (1974):

During the nationwide UFO flap in the fall of 1973 . . ., Mr. and Mrs. James Thulke of Chicago were returning home from an auto trip to the East. They had stopped near Jackson, Michigan, for food, and when they emerged from the restaurant, they noticed several groups of people staring at something in the sky to the north. The sun was just setting, Thulke told me, but the sky was still light. Looking to the north, Thulke said, he and his wife saw a curious object which was "too bright to be a star." It seemed to be stationary, about 50 degrees above the horizon, and it was glowing too brightly for

him to determine the object's shape with the naked eye.

Fortunately, Thulke had very powerful binoculars in his car, with a zoom-type lens that could provide variable magnification, from 7 to 14 power. Viewing the object with the binoculars set at minimum magnification (7 power), he said the UFO seemed to be tear-drop shaped and *internally illuminated*. But when he shifted to 14 power, he quickly identified the UFO as a weather balloon whose bright illumination came from the setting rays of the sun. When Thulke informed the other puzzled UFO watchers that it was only a weather balloon, some accepted his word and departed. But others wanted to see for themselves, and Thulke obliged. Still some lingered on, not wanting to believe the UFO was only a weather balloon. When the Thulkes departed and headed west, he told me, they saw cars, campers, and trucks stopped along the expressway for many miles, with their passengers gazing at the mysterious UFO in the sky. For these people, that weather balloon will always be an Unidentified Flying Object.

Probably many UFO sightings involve this kind of mistaken identification, and others involve perceptual misjudgments. In fact, many UFO sightings occur under conditions similar to those that perceptual psychologists deliberately set up in their labs to make it easier to cause illusions: darkened conditions, stimuli of poor quality, and short exposure times.

Other Illusions Demystified

Most of the illusions we encounter are natural, everyday occurrences. And most can be explained with the help of a little scientific thinking. To use an example from auditory perception, have you ever noticed how the pitch of an ambulance siren appears to drop as the vehicle passes you and races off? This is known as the *Doppler effect*. The illusion has more to do with the physical properties of sound waves than with any error in your auditory system. When the vehicle is approaching you, the sound waves or air pressure differences created by the siren are compressed by the vehicle's speed, so the frequency of the waves increases. As the vehicle moves away from you, the opposite situation prevails: The frequency of the waves diminishes, and the apparent pitch of the siren drops.

Then we have the *bent pencil illusion*. A pencil appears to bend where it enters a glass of water, as shown in Figure

4.38. Again, this illusion is due to physical causes—in this case the properties of light—and not to an error in your visual system. Light rays bend when they pass from air to water. The water serves as a prism and shifts the optical image. You can see this illusion whenever an oar, stick, or some other object is partly in the water.

In contrast to the Doppler effect and the bent pencil illusion, which are caused by physical phenomena, many illusions originate entirely within the perceiver. One common example (although rarely studied by psychologists) is the *rubber pencil illusion* (Pomerantz, 1983). If you hold a pencil between your thumb and index finger and wiggle it rapidly, the pencil does not maintain its rigid appearance, but seems to bend as if it were rubber. The illusion is probably caused by visual persistence: Objects may appear to persist after stimulation has been shut off or has changed. The pencil appears rubbery because the brain attempts to interpret a smeared image being relayed through the visual system. Another common example of visual persistence is the enduring image left when a bright light (such as a flashbulb) suddenly explodes in the visual field. These common illusions originate in the receptors.

Other real-world illusions derive from neural processes occurring higher up in the perceptual system. One of the most common and controversial is the *moon illusion*. You may have noticed that the moon looks much larger when it is near the horizon than when it is at its highest point in the sky (its zenith). The effect is shown in Figure 4.39. The moon's projected image on the retina is the same size in both cases; if you photographed the moon at the horizon and at its zenith and measured its size on the developed pictures, it would be the same size in both pictures. Note that a similar illusion occurs for the stellar constellations (Reed & Krupinski, 1992).

The cause of the moon illusion has been hotly debated for centuries. C. F. Reed (1984) has offered an interesting explanation of the moon illusion. He points out that as objects move in the sky from the horizon to cross over our heads, their retinal image size usually grows steadily. For example, a bird or an approaching airplane may be only a speck on the

FIGURE 4.38

The Bent Pencil Illusion

horizon, but its retinal size will become quite large if it flies at a low altitude directly over us. Because the moon is so far away from us (239,000 miles), it does not produce an enlarged retinal image as it crosses the sky. But because we are accustomed to seeing such enlargement for moving objects, we mistakenly interpret the moon as shrinking as it passes overhead.

Another illusion involving the moon is called **induced motion.** If we look at the moon through fast-moving clouds on a windy night, it may appear to be racing in the opposite direction from the clouds. This illusion may occur because the moving clouds tend to produce involuntary tracking eye movements. The effort to suppress these eye movements may give the illusion of motion in the stationary object (Humber & Sherrick, 1993). Similarly, if you are sitting in a parked car and a car beside you moves forward or backward, you may perceive your own car to be moving. However, you can immediately tell which one is moving if you look at the road between the cars or at some other stationary frame of reference. This illusion demonstrates that the visual system is much better at perceiving the motion of objects relative to one another than at perceiving the true motion of any one object.

Motion also plays a role in what is called the *waterfall illusion*. If you stare directly for a minute or so at the plunging water of a waterfall and then shift your gaze to a stationary cliff, the rocks of the cliff will seem briefly to drift upward. (The waterfall needs to be relatively narrow so that it does not fill the field of vision.) The same mechanisms causing the waterfall illusion may also explain the illusion that occurs when a car abruptly stops after traveling at high speeds. For a few moments after the car stops moving, the passengers may feel as though the car were going backward. These illusions seem to result from the

FIGURE 4.39

The Moon Illusion

fatiguing of feature detectors for motion in the visual system (similar to the effect of colored afterimages, explained in Chapter 3).

We again misperceive motion in this next illusion. When two lights are flashed on and off, one just after the other, we tend to perceive that a single light moves from the first light's position to that of the second. This effect, known as **apparent motion,** accounts for the movement in electronic advertising signs and the casino lights of Las Vegas. In fact, it is also responsible for the illusion of motion seen in motion pictures and television, which actually present to the screen only a rapid succession of still snapshots. The movement we perceive in movies is an illusion.

You may be unaware of the existence of our final example, but it is worth arranging conditions to see it. Imagine looking down a long corridor that has a fairly small window at the end, through which you see a large sign in the distance. Your perspective in viewing the sign is called a *vista*. Now suppose you walk rapidly toward the window, keeping your eye on the sign. You might expect the sign to appear to get larger and to appear to get closer to you, because its visual image on your retina is getting larger as you approach the window. Exactly the opposite happens; the sign appears to grow smaller and become farther away! This phenomenon, called the *vista paradox,* has been recently investigated by James Walker, Reta Rupich, and Jack Powell (1989). Its explanation is not entirely clear at this point, but under certain conditions, an object enclosed in a frame looks larger than the same object having no frame (Weintraub & Schneck, 1986). As you move quite close to the window, the frame becomes less apparent, and so the object may appear to decrease in size. Other factors, including induced motion arising from the expansion of the frame's image, are probably at work as well (Reinhardt-Rutland, 1990; Walker et al., 1989).

None of the illusions we have considered here can really explain the sightings of UFOs. But they all show that illusions do occur outside the laboratory and can affect our daily lives.

The Role of Learning in Perception

Although we are all subject to visual illusions, perception is usually accurate, or veridical. Veridical perception is not achieved solely by passive, bottom-up processing of sensory data. It needs help from top-down processes to take context into account and make educated hypotheses about the stimuli present in the physical world beyond the information available to the senses. Does this need for intelligent guesswork mean that people need to *learn* to see?

This question is at the root of a controversy over **nativism** and **empiricism.** Nativism is the position that some knowledge is innate; the empiricist position maintains that knowledge comes through perceptual experience. Nativists believe that human beings are born with the ability to perceive stimuli and that learning plays only a small role in perceptual development. The empiricists claim that all knowledge comes from experience, and this applies to the knowledge required for perception. Without sensory experiences, say the empiricists, people would know nothing about the world, and this lack of knowledge would prevent top-down processes from operating. Thus, the empiricists would claim that perception would be difficult or even impossible for such people until they acquired the necessary sensory knowledge.

This argument is often referred to as the **nature versus nurture** debate. Is human behavior determined by the genetically inherited characteristics provided by nature? Do our experiences shape and nurture our behavior? It is not necessary that one position be completely correct and the other all wrong. Some types of perception may be greatly influenced by learning, while other types of perception may be built-in from birth, remaining unchanged by experience. Current evidence favors this compromise position. One classical method of studying the role of learning in perception is to examine people who have regained their sight.

RESTORED VISION: MAKING THE BLIND SEE

The seventeenth-century British philosopher John Locke received a letter from his colleague William Molyneaux that posed this question:

> Suppose a man born blind, now adult, and taught by his touch to distinguish between a cube and a sphere of the same metal, nighly and of the same bigness, so as to tell, when he felt one and the other, which is the cube, which is the sphere. Suppose then the cube and the sphere placed on a table and the blind man made to see . . . could [he] by his sight, before he touched them . . . now distinguish and tell which is the globe, which the cube? (Locke, 1690/1950)

Molyneaux answered his own question by saying no. Locke, the good empiricist, agreed. Without the knowledge obtained through visual experience, Molyneaux's hypothetical man would be stumped.

The experiment that Molyneaux and Locke imagined has actually been performed many times. Psychologists have examined people born blind who have acquired sight by surgery. A good number see little detail at first and fail to distinguish between even simple shapes (Von Senden, 1960). They are able to detect objects, fixate on them, and scan and follow them if the objects move, so perhaps these abilities are innate. Usually, these patients cannot recognize objects by sight, even those that they can identify by touch, such as keys, fruit, and the faces of loved ones. They might be able to identify triangles, but only by counting corners. Sometimes, after long training, they develop useful vision and become able to recognize objects on sight. Others are unable to acquire visual perception and give up; in effect, they revert to their earlier, sightless way of life, usually after a period of emotional disturbance (Heil, 1987). These facts seem to implicate the role of experience in perception

The evidence from people with restored vision may not be as significant as it might seem. Although these cases appear to be critical experiments showing the role of experience in perception, several problems arise with their interpretation (Gregory, 1978). Until recently, many people had their vision restored by having the lenses in their eyes removed. First, this surgery may not have been successful in removing all of the causes of the person's blindness. Second, it may take some time for patients to fully recover from such operations, so some of the immediate difficulties in perception may be due to a slow healing process. Finally, a few fortunate patients seem to see quite well very soon after surgery. Thus, the outcomes of cases of restored vision are so variable and can be due to so many factors other than lack of visual experience that it is probably best not to rely too heavily on them (Gregory, 1987; Heil, 1987). However, several other lines of evidence are important in trying to determine the roles of nature and nurture in perception. We will examine four: the effects of visual deprivation, the effects of temporary sensory distortions, the extent of perceptual capabilities in infants, and the cultural influences on perception.

VISUAL DEPRIVATION

Another way to approach Molyneaux's question is to test the perceptual abilities of animals that were deprived of perceptual experiences while they were young (Mitchell, 1989). A typical experiment involves raising cats, monkeys, or chimpanzees with translucent goggles that allow light to pass through but destroy images. Such studies have shown that visual deprivation has little effect on simple perceptual tasks such as distinguishing differences in color, size, or brightness. However, more complex abilities that require the recognition of patterns or the tracking of moving objects become seriously damaged after lengthy deprivation (Riesen, 1960, 1965). This evidence supports the empiricist claim that experience is essential in perceptual development, although the inherited structure of the visual system is present before learning can occur.

The importance of experience is further demonstrated by neurophysiological recordings taken from animals raised in environments that contained only very specific stimuli. Kittens raised in pens that contained only horizontal and vertical stripes were tested to determine if they were sensitive to diagonal stripes, which they had never seen. The kittens acted as though they were blind to diagonal lines. In fact, it appeared that they lacked the neurons normally present in the visual cortex that are sensitive to diagonal lines (Mitchell, 1980). These feature-detecting cells atrophied, just as muscles do when they are not exercised.

A more subtle type of visual deprivation prevents an animal's active involvement with its environment. The animals have visual experiences, but of a passive kind. Held and Hein (1963) placed two kittens in baskets attached to opposite ends of a rod that could rotate around a central point, as shown in Figure 4.40. One basket contained holes for the kitten's legs so that the animal could walk around the test chamber in a circle; the other basket had no leg holes. When the first kitten walked about, the second was carried along passively. Both kittens were thus exposed to essentially identical visual stimulation. When they were tested later, only the kittens that had been allowed to walk showed normal perceptual capabilities. The kittens that had been passively carried seemed functionally blind in many ways. They did not blink at objects thrust toward them, nor did they raise their paws defensively. Clearly, visual stimulation alone was not sufficient for normal perceptual development. The passive kittens lacked *proprioceptive feedback* (the sensing of the limbs' positions from active movement), which is apparently essential for perceptual development. That kind of feedback is also important for adaptation to visual distortions, which we consider next.

EFFECTS OF VISUAL DISTORTION ON PERCEPTION

Another way to determine how experience shapes perception is to study how people adapt to lenses that produce visual distortion. The first experiment of this type was by George M. Stratton (1897). He blindfolded one eye and wore a lens system over the other that inverted the visual image on the retina and reversed it from left to right. (Recall from Chapter 3 that the retinal image is normally inverted and reversed because of the lens of the eye; Stratton's lenses actually flipped the retinal image upright.)

In one experiment, Stratton wore the lenses continuously for eight days. At first, he was totally disoriented and unable to walk without bumping into things. Imagine having to look up to see the floor or to reach to the left to grasp an object that appears to be on your right! Stratton eventually learned to walk and even to ride a bicycle and play sports while wearing the lens system. He concluded that if he were to wear the lenses indefinitely, he would adapt completely, a conclusion confirmed by more recent research (Welch, 1978). A subject who wore a similar lens system for 30 days eventually learned to drive a car while wearing the lens (Snyder & Pronko, 1952).

How does the world appear to these subjects? Is their visual system eventually altered so that nothing appears disoriented, or do they simply learn to reach up for objects that appear to be below them? Earlier in this century, the first view was widely accepted—that with prolonged experience the world would appear right-side up again.

FIGURE 4.40

Apparatus Used in Held and Hein's Deprivation Experiment

Both kittens were exposed to the same visual stimulation, but only one was actively moving about. The other kitten was carried passively. When visual stimulation was limited to this situation, only the active kitten was later able to perform visual tasks. The passive kitten seemed effectively blind.

SOURCE: Held & Hein, 1963.

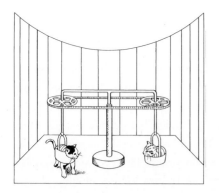

(a)   (b)

Visual Distortion (a) This man is wearing goggles that transform the visual world by inverting and reversing the visual field with prisms. (b) How the world would look through such an apparatus. Research with such lenses helps psychologists understand how people adapt to severe distortion in sensory information.

However, more recent research has proved this belief to be incorrect (Harris, 1980). The second view, which holds that the proprioceptive sense is changed, has been shown to be more accurate; the sense of touch is "educated" by experience with the distorted visual environment (Redding & Wallace, 1988).

PERCEPTION IN INFANTS

Another way to examine the role of learning in perception is to test the perceptual capabilities of human infants. This touches on the developmental theme of our text and can shed some light on the nature versus nurture debate. If a newborn can perceive a stimulus in much the same way as an adult, that would be evidence for the innateness of perceptual ability. If not, it would indicate either that the perceptual task has to be learned or that the infant's perceptual system hasn't matured physiologically to the level the task requires. It takes considerable patience and ingenuity to determine what the world looks like to an infant. After all, infants can't tell researchers what they see, and researchers can't tell infants what to do. Even worse, infants often pay no attention to the stimuli poked at them; instead, they fall asleep or cry or look at their toes and fingers instead of the stimuli.

In the nineteenth century, William James asserted that the infant's world must be a "blooming, buzzing confusion" (James, 1890). James would have been quite surprised to learn of the remarkable perceptual abilities that psychologists now know infants possess. To be sure, they do not see the world as clearly as adults do, but this is largely a result of physiological immaturity rather than lack of experience. For example, an infant's eyes do not focus well on objects that are more than about a foot away, so infants are quite nearsighted (Hainline & Abramov, 1992; Maurer, 1975). It probably takes about six months for an infant's vision to approach adult levels (Banks & Dannemiller, 1987; Marg et al., 1976), and other evidence shows that the eye movements of 4- to 5-year-old children differ systematically from those of adults (Aslin, 1987; Kowler & Martins, 1982). Nonetheless, infants have greater perceptual abilities than researchers had expected prior to the experiments of the past 20 years.

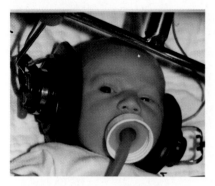

One way to determine what babies perceive is to measure how their rate of sucking varies in response to changes in their environment. The device shown here measures sucking as the baby listens to different voices.

Babies prefer their mother's voices to those of other women even when tested a few days after birth.

Although more will be reported in Chapter 9, one example of research with infants will be cited in this chapter. This example was chosen because it points up the difficulty in conclusively answering the nature/nurture question about perceptual abilities.

Anthony DeCasper and his associates (DeCasper & Fifer, 1980; DeCasper & Prescott, 1984) have asked the interesting question, Can newborns perceive their mothers' voices as different from that of other women? But how can we know what an infant perceives? How can the infant respond to indicate perception?

DeCasper and Fifer (1980) adapted a technique known as *high-amplitude sucking*, which has proved useful in much research with infants (Juscyzk, 1985). The general idea is that if babies modify their sucking patterns in response to external events, then they must be able to tell the events apart. DeCasper and Fifer tested infants that were only 2 or 3 days old by giving them artificial nipples on which they could suck to produce sounds. One pattern of sucking let each baby hear its own mother's voice, whereas a different pattern of sucking produced another woman's voice. The critical question was whether a newborn could learn the pattern that produced its own mother's voice. The exciting answer was yes, a finding that has been confirmed in later studies (Burnham, 1993).

How can newborns already recognize their mother's voice? One possibility is that infants come into the world biologically prepared to distinguish their own parents from other people. In other words, something in their genetic code permits their remarkable ability to distinguish their own mother's voices from that of other women only two to three days after birth. The logic outlined previously for separating nature from nurture would support this interpretation because abilities that are shown soon after birth are assumed to have a genetically determined component. DeCasper, however, rejects the notion that this ability is inherited in favor of the idea that it arises from prenatal experience, or learning in the womb (DeCasper & Fifer, 1980).

Several facts support the conclusion that the infant's ability is due to such prenatal nurturing (Gottlieb, 1985). First, sounds of low frequency, such as those of human speech, have been shown to penetrate the uterus and amniotic sac, where the fetus resides for nine months prior to birth. Second, the fetus has been shown to respond differentially to sounds in the external environment (Read & Miller, 1977). Thus, in all likelihood, the newborn's preference for its mother's voices is caused by the continuous presence of that voice throughout prenatal development.

Although newborns can distinguish among male voices, they will not suck differentially to hear their father's voice (DeCasper & Prescott, 1984). At first glance, this evidence seems to support the nurture (learning) position, because there is certainly greater prenatal exposure to the mother's voice than to the father's voice. Proponents of the nature view could argue, however, that infants are genetically predisposed to hone in on a single female voice. An experiment by DeCasper and Spence (1986) settled this question: They had women read a particular passage aloud every day for the last six weeks of their pregnancy. After birth, the infants preferred (i.e., they sucked more) to hear a recording of their mothers reading the old passage rather than a new passage. Infants whose mothers had not read the passage during pregnancy showed no preference. The usual assumption that abilities occurring very early in life are genetically determined seems unlikely in this case.

The ability of infants to distinguish and prefer their mother's voice illustrates the complexity of distinguishing contributions of genetics from those of experience on behavior. Even the perceptual abilities of infants are probably due to a combination of hereditary and environmental influences.

FIGURE 4.41

The Circular Culture of the Zulus

Zulus live in a culture in which there are few straight lines and corners. Since they are not accustomed to judging depth from these cues, they are not affected by certain spatial illusions (such as the Müller-Lyer illusion) as much as people who are raised in Western cultures with rectangular architecture.

FIGURE 4.42

An Ambiguous Figure?

Rural Kenyans sometimes called this picture a snake, an elephant, or a crocodile. Apparently, they focused on parts (e.g., the neck looks like a snake) to interpret the entire picture.

THE INFLUENCE OF CULTURE ON PERCEPTION

If learning plays a large role in perception, then we might expect that culture would also influence perception, since people raised in different cultures have different perceptual experiences. Surprisingly, there is relatively little research on this important sociocultural issue that represents a major theme in this text. Nevertheless, we will explore two different lines of research (another related line will be discussed in Chapter 8). In particular, we will consider if some visual illusions are universal, or if they are only experienced by people raised in certain cultures. Then, we will consider cross-cultural differences in the perception of pictures.

An interesting set of experiments by Segall, Campbell, and Herskovits (1966) suggests that the Müller-Lyer illusion (see Figure 4.33) may be absent, or greatly reduced, in people raised in some environments. They tested some Zulu people of South Africa who had little experience with typical Western structures (rectangular buildings with straight lines). If Gregory's (1978) theory of the Müller-Lyer illusion is correct (see Figure 4.35), then it would make sense that the Zulus and others who had little experience with rectilinear architecture would accurately perceive the two shafts as being equal in length (see Figure 4.41.). Indeed, the Zulus appeared immune to the illusion. Of course, illusions that originate in the receptors, such as Hermann's grid in Figure 4.31, are shared by all people. However, some cognitive illusions that depend on experience may occur differentially in people who live in different cultures.

Deregowski (1989) has argued that there may be fundamental differences in the way people in certain cultures perceive pictures. Some people who have never seen pictures often fail to grasp the scene, especially if it is a bit unusual. Sometimes people unfamiliar with pictures seem to use only part of the picture to guess what it represents. For example, Shaw (1969) showed the picture in Figure 4.42 to people in rural Kenya. Some people identified the animal as a snake, others said it was a crocodile, and still others guessed it was an elephant. According to Shaw, these responses were perfectly understandable if the observers were focusing on only one detail. The feet in the picture look like an elephant's; the head and neck resemble a snake's; and the markings on the shell are similar to those of a Kenyan crocodile.

A picture is a two-dimensional representation of a real, three-dimensional scene. Although it seems natural to people in Western cultures to interpret pictures as three-dimensional scenes, this may be a learned ability. Deregowski (1989) argues that the principles of perception, which have been largely derived from experiments with Western subjects, may be too limited and in need of modification. This position has attracted critics (Biederman, 1989; Coren, 1989), who maintain that the quality of the research thus far does not reveal any general differences in perception as a function of culture.

Research with children in Western cultures bolsters the conclusion that perception of pictures is not automatic. When Sigel (1978) asked children to sort pictures into categories, he found that they had great difficulty with the task. When he later gave them actual objects to sort, the children had little trouble. Apparently, the children had difficulty in recognizing the objects in the pictures. You may have experienced a similar difficulty when looking at X rays. Novices have great difficulty in perceiving and remembering abnormalities in X rays, a job that experienced radiologists can accomplish easily (Myles-Worsley, Johnston, & Simons, 1988). Learning probably plays a large role in perceiving meaningful patterns from complex displays. Psychologists are just beginning to explore these more complicated aspects of the effects of experience on perception by studying how perception varies among diverse populations with differing experiences.

THEMES IN REVIEW

The five prominent themes in psychology are all strongly represented in this chapter. We have seen that there are biological constraints to perception. Without input from the receptor organs (the eyes, the ears, etc.) perception of the external world would not be possible. In addition, some of the visual illusions (such as Hermann's grid) arise from biological properties of the visual system (lateral inhibition).

Cognitive factors are clearly at work, too, in the top-down (or constructive) processes of perception. Phenomena such as reversible figures, subjective contours, and spatial illusions show the constructive role of expectancies and hypotheses in shaping perception. In some cases, we bend the sensory input to see what we expect to see.

We also see developmental trends in perception. Apparently, children do not perceive pictures in the same way that adults do, but must develop the ability to perceive objects in pictures. Nonetheless, many perceptual abilities are present in infants, and one of the frontiers of current research is discovering what infants perceive and know. Even 2- or 3-day-old babies can recognize their mother's voice and prefer it over that of other women.

Learning, too, seems to be an essential aspect of the perceptual process. Animal research has shown that deprivation of visual stimulation greatly inhibits perceptual growth, and if an animal doesn't have experience with certain stimuli, then it may not be able to perceive those stimuli later on. Similar results have been found in

studies of blind people who have had their sight surgically restored. And researchers who utilized prism glasses in their studies found that people can learn to adapt to the distorted view of the world through learning and experience.

Finally, sociocultural factors are also at work in perception. Although the evidence is still preliminary, it appears that people from some cultures are not subject to certain spatial illusions, such as the Müller-Lyer. In addition, people from some non-Western cultures do not perceive pictures the same way as people from Western cultures, who learned how to perceive them at an early age. In short, our complex perception of the world is shaped by biological, cognitive, developmental, learning, and cultural factors.

SUMMARY

1 Perception is the process of interpreting sensory information from the receptor organs to produce an organized image of the environment.

2 Occasionally our perceptual system deceives us with illusions, but a major challenge to psychologists lies in explaining how perception works as veridically, or accurately, as it does.

3 The Gestalt psychologists argued that the perception of a stimulus is more than the sum of the sensations it produces. They developed principles of grouping and figure-ground segregation to describe perceptual organization. Grouping links stimulus elements into units by the principles of proximity, similarity, and good continuation, among others. Figure-ground segregation means that any region of a stimulus is perceived either as figure or ground, but not both.

4 Pattern recognition refers to the ability to classify the stimuli we perceive into familiar categories. Bottom-up models of pattern recognition work passively to categorize a stimulus from the features it possesses. Top-down models include an active component that guides recognition through the use of context and expectations. Today's theorists prefer interactive models that combine the top-down and bottom-up processes, as in the connectionist model of reading.

5 Depth perception is possible through the use of a large variety of depth cues, some of which depend on using both eyes (binocular cues). Other cues only require input from one eye to give a sense of depth (monocular cues). Depth, size, and shape perception all show the operation of the perceptual constancies, which tie perceptions closer to distal than to proximal stimuli.

6 Some illusions occur in the brain and may be due to inappropriate operation of the perceptual constancies. Other illusions occur in the receptor organs. Still other illusions are caused by physical effects in the environment and do not reflect any error in the sensory or perceptual system. Although certain illusions are apparent only under laboratory conditions, many occur in everyday situations outside the lab. Most illusions provide useful clues about the way normal perception operates, and many illusions are caused by processes that ordinarily improve perception.

7 Learning plays a definite role in perception, supplementing innate abilities. People who acquire vision after a lifetime of blindness often encounter difficulty perceiving for some time. Animals deprived of perceptual experience have similar problems.

8 People can adjust to drastic distortions in their sensory input, such as those created by glasses that invert or shift the retinal image. This adjustment takes time, however, and appears to involve more change in the proprioceptive system than in the visual system, although both may be affected.

9 It is too simplistic to consider the nature versus nurture argument as an either-or matter. For most types of perception, both nature and nurture can account for human abilities. For depth and color perception, innate factors appear to play a role, but learning plays an important role for many other perceptual tasks. This is true for recognition of objects, adaptation to distorted vision, and various other complex forms of perception. Even though infants can recognize their mother's voice, the ability probably arises through prenatal learning rather than through innate ability. And people from different cultures may learn to perceive in different ways.

KEY TERMS

perceptual organization (p. 135)

figure-ground segregation (p. 138)

pattern recognition (p. 139)

template matching theory (p. 139)

bottom-up theories (p. 140)

top-down theories (p. 140)

Pandemonium (p. 141)

recognition by components (p. 143)

geons (p. 143)

word superiority effect (p. 144)

interactive theories (p. 145)

connectionist model (p. 146)

subjective contours (p. 148)

mental imagery (p. 150)

depth cues (p. 150)

binocular disparity (p. 150)

monocular cues (p. 152)

perceptual constancy (p. 154)

proximal stimulus (p. 154)

distal stimulus (p. 154)

illusions (p. 155)

Hermann's grid (p. 156)

McCollough effect (p. 156–157)

spatial illusions (p. 158–159)

Müller-Lyer illusion (p. 158)

induced motion (p. 161)

apparent motion (p. 162)

nativism (p. 162)

empiricism (p. 162)

nature versus nurture (p. 162)

FOR CRITICAL ANALYSIS

1 The following statement is often used to summarize the Gestalt approach to perception: The whole is greater than the sum of its parts. Cite three perceptual phenomena that seem to support this claim.

2 There is another statement often employed by those who support the constructive view of perception: A perceiver does not see the retinal image, but sees with the aid of the retinal image. Defend this claim by citing several cases in which the perceptual experience that a person constructs differs from the image on the retina.

3 Some psychologists believe that imagining involves some of the same neural mechanisms as perceiving. Imagining would involve the constructive processes of perceiving without the bottom-up, or data-driven, processes. What are some other common experiences that seem to involve constructive aspects of cognition without relying on sensory input?

4 Many visual illusions were described in the chapter. Can you think of others that were omitted? Are there perceptual experiences that you have had that seem to be illusions? (*Hint:* One often occurs when you are driving along a straight road in intense heat.)

5 Some of the material in the chapter supported the claim that what we perceive is partly influenced by learning. What are some examples of this in everyday life? For example, are there people whose training and experience on the job make their perception of certain displays or situations sharper than those of other people who do not have those particular jobs or training?

SUGGESTED READINGS

ALOIMONOS, Y., & ROSENFELD, A. (1991). Computer vision. *Science, 253,* 1249–1254. A brief overview of 20 years of research efforts to achieve computers and robots with humanlike vision.

GREGORY, R. L. (1990). *Eye and brain: The psychology of seeing* (4th ed.). Princeton, NJ: Princeton University Press. This popular introduction to the psychology of visual perception is a good starting point for supplementary information.

HERSHENSON, M., Ed. (1989). *The moon illusion: An anomaly of visual space perception?* Hillsdale, NJ: Erlbaum. A collection of essays by leading perceptual psychologists on one of the oldest perceptual puzzles and how its study informs perceptual processes.

SEKULER, R., & BLAKE, R. (1994). *Perception* (3rd ed.). New York: McGraw-Hill. An excellent text that explores more deeply many of the topics introduced in this chapter.

SHEPARD, R. N. (1990). *Mind Sights.* New York: Freeman. An interesting book that showcases many visual illusions and discusses the principles of perception that underlie them.

PSYCHOLOGY ON THE INTERNET

Sensation and Perception Tutorial
(http://psych.hanover.edu/Krantz/sen_tut.html)

This tutorial, by the author of the Basic Neural Processes tutorial (see Psychology on the Internet, Chapter 2) covers some basic concepts in sensation and perception and includes an in-depth explanation of the concept of "Receptive Fields."

Sound Perception
(http://sln.fi.edu/~helfrich/music/psychaco.html)

In addition to providing a written introduction to acoustics and sound perception, this site teaches visitors about sound perception using examples of auditory illusions and demonstrations of central concepts such as frequency, amplitude, and timbre.

Selected Projects in Cognitive Science
(http://www.socsci.uci.edu/cogsci/projects/projects.html)

At this site you can look at the results of several experiments dealing with visual and auditory perception and experience the stimuli used in these experiments. These experiments cover topics such as the factors affecting recognition of novel objects and the use of color in visual search. Background information about the problems being studied and explanations of the results are provided.

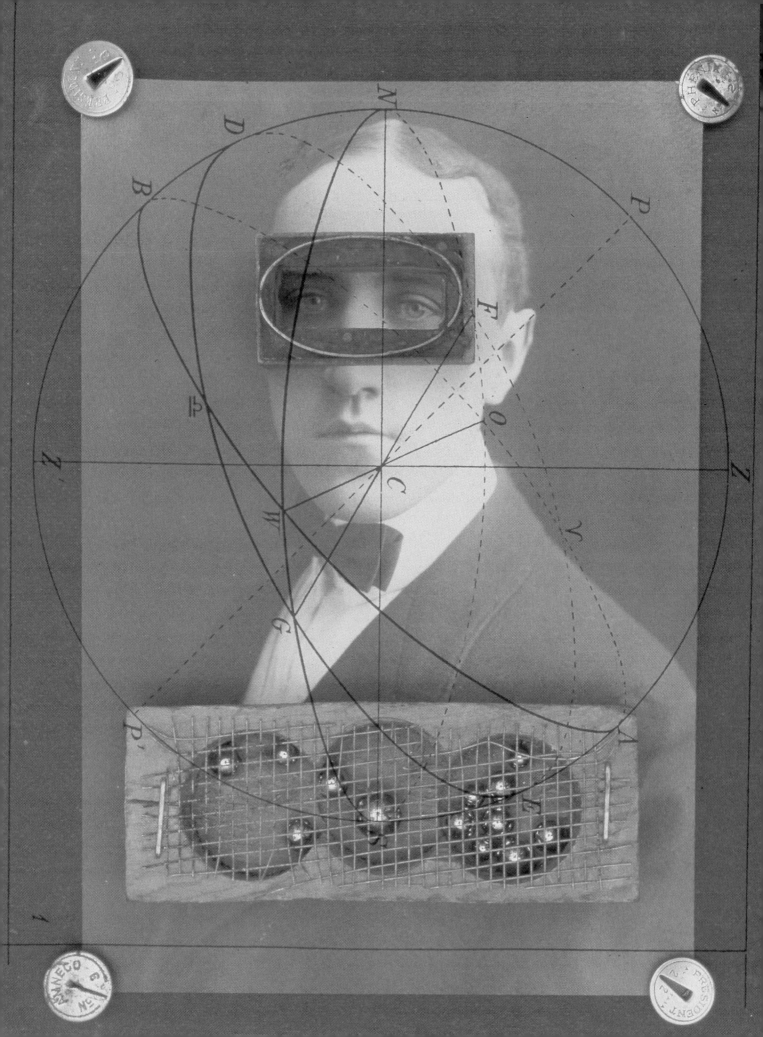

CONSCIOUSNESS and ATTENTION

Chapter 5

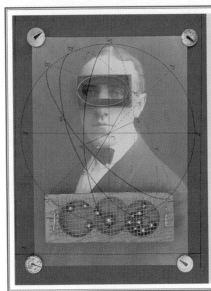

Is it possible to know something without being aware that you know it? Consider the case of two women who have the disorder known as *prosopagnosia*. They are unable to recognize faces, even of well-known people, because of damage in the occipital lobe of the brain (see Figure 2.15, on page 60). They cannot recognize the faces of close friends or relatives, and one of them cannot even recognize her own face in the mirror! Unexpectedly, many of their other cognitive functions, such as language ability and perception of objects other than faces, are perfectly normal.

The usual way of testing for prosopagnosia is simply to show patients a series of photographs and ask them to name the person in each. The faces include those of friends, relatives, celebrities, and strangers. Patients with the disorder perform dismally, unable to name people they have known for years. The difficulty is not in having forgotten the people, for the people can be immediately identified when a recording of the person's voice is presented with the photograph. The deficit is specific to the visual identification of faces (Farah, 1990).

Daniel Tranel and Antonio Damasio (1985) tested the two women for their ability to name faces from pictures. At the same time, the researchers recorded changes in the electrical conductivity of their skin, a procedure similar to that used in lie detector tests. They discovered that although the patients were unable to name close friends and relatives from their pictures, there was a distinct change in the women's electrodermal response when these pictures were shown—but not when photos of strangers were shown. Thus, the physiological processes that signal recognition seemed to be intact, but the results of these processes could not be translated into conscious experience. Put another way, the changes in physiology imply that the women "knew" the faces, but were not consciously aware of the recognition (Bauer & Verfaellie, 1988).

The fact that we can know something at one level but not be conscious of this knowledge will be a recurring theme in this chapter. We will first describe normal waking consciousness and factors that control what people attend to in their environment. Next, we will examine how "unconscious" factors sometimes influence attention and the processing of information. We will then return to a topic from Chapter 2—hemispheric specialization—to explore the implications for two types of conscious experience. Finally, we will consider some altered states of consciousness: sleep and

Brain-damaged patients with prosopagnosia cannot identify these well-known faces—or those of their family, for that matter—but physiological measures show that (at some cognitive level) the person is judged to be familiar to the patients.

hypnosis, and drug-induced changes in consciousness. But before we launch into any of these fascinating topics, we need to discuss a concept that is fundamental to this chapter: consciousness.

What Is Consciousness?

An accurate definition of consciousness has eluded philosophers for centuries and stumped psychologists for the past 100 years, and no general agreement is in sight (Baars, 1988; Natsoulas, 1983). The term is used in many different ways; and as the eminent psychologist George Miller (1962) put it, "Consciousness is a word worn smooth by a million tongues." The behaviorists even tried to remove the term entirely from the language of psychology, partly because of its vagueness. Nevertheless, the term cannot be ignored, because it refers to a state that is immediately familiar to everyone. The following definition will serve our purpose here: **Consciousness** is the current awareness of external or internal stimuli—that is, of objects in the environment (external stimuli) and of bodily sensations, memories, feelings, and thoughts (internal stimuli). Now that we have defined consciousness, how do we describe it?

In Western civilization, a spatial metaphor has typically been used to characterize the conscious mind (Jaynes, 1976). People usually describe the mind as a *container* or *space* in which ideas and memories are stored (Lakoff & Johnson, 1980; Roediger, 1980). They *hold* ideas in mind, or they have ideas in the *front* or *back* or at the top of their minds. Some people are said to have *broad, deep,* or *open* minds, while other minds are described as *narrow, shallow,* or *closed*. Consciousness, accordingly, can be thought of as an awareness of events occuring in this mental space.

William James, using a rather different metaphor, described consciousness as a "stream" of awareness. He wrote, "Our normal waking consciousness, rational consciousness as we call it, is but one special type of consciousness, whilst all about it, parted from it by the filmiest of screens, there lie potential forms of consciousness entirely different" (1902/1963, p. 388).

Psychologists have found it useful to distinguish four mental states: the conscious, preconscious, unconscious, and nonconscious. External and internal events of which we are aware are said to be in consciousness. Only a few memories and thoughts can be held in consciousness at any one time; most remain in a preconscious or unconscious state.

If memories can be called into consciousness fairly easily, they are said to be in a **preconscious** state. For example, as you read this paragraph, you may not be thinking of the name of your psychology instructor or the names of your best friends or brothers and sisters. But if you are asked for those names, they are available in memory and immediately accessible to conscious experience (Kihlstrom, 1987; Tulving & Pearlstone, 1966).

Unconscious ideas and memories are those that cannot be brought to mind easily. Sigmund Freud popularized the idea that many important memories and thoughts reside in an unconscious state. Through his study of patients with various disorders, Freud came to believe that the major factor in emotional problems was childhood trauma (see Chapter 14). Memories of painful childhood experiences were repressed, or converted into an unconscious mental state. Although these memories could not easily be made conscious, Freud felt that they could nevertheless affect thoughts and behavior.

The concept of the unconscious remains controversial in modern psychology. Psychologists often try to study the unobservable inner world of the mind indirectly by observing overt behavior, just as astrophysicists strive to detect black holes in space by noting their effects on light and neighboring bodies. But if unconscious mental processes cannot be observed directly, how can psychologists measure repressed memories? If repression simply refers to any memories that are not easily called into consciousness, then repression undoubtedly occurs (Davis, 1987; Erdelyi & Goldberg, 1979). If repression is taken to mean the unconscious suppression of a painful past, however, it becomes harder to study.

It is important to distinguish between unconscious and nonconscious processes (Lewicki, Hill, & Czyzewska, 1992). We categorize a process as **nonconscious** when it cannot possibly be hauled into consciousness; it is unconscious if it *can* be brought into consciousness, albeit with great difficulty. We are not aware of many of our bodily processes. For example, we are not directly conscious of the workings of the rods and cones in our eyes (described in Chapter 3), or of the functioning of the kidneys, lungs, and heart. We can become conscious of the *effects* of nonconscious processes (e.g., heavy breathing, a pounding heart), but we normally cannot become conscious of the processes themselves.

Now that we have briefly summarized the terms used to describe the states of consciousness, we will look at the various ways psychologists investigate this slippery topic. Most of this chapter will illustrate the cognitive and biological themes of the text, but the learning, developmental, and sociocultural themes will also be represented.

CONCEPT SUMMARY

CONSCIOUS EVENTS:	External or internal stimuli of which a person is aware.
PRECONSCIOUS EVENTS:	Processes, thoughts, or memories that can easily be called to mind.
UNCONSCIOUS EVENTS:	Processes, thoughts, or memories that cannot easily be called to mind.
NONCONSCIOUS EVENTS:	Processes that, by their nature, cannot ever be called to mind.

Attention

There is a limit to what we can keep "in mind." We can focus on only a few things (sensations, memories, thoughts) at one time. When we are overloaded with too much information (i.e., when voices, sights, and thoughts overwhelm us), we need to concentrate on one source of information and exclude the others.

Attention is the process by which we focus our perception on a limited number of stimuli, excluding other sources of information present. This leads to a greater awareness of the selected stimuli, essentially putting a "spotlight" of consciousness on the stimuli. How do we decide where to direct the spotlight of consciousness? As you stare at this page, you could be paying attention to the voice of a radio disc jockey, to a tingling in your feet, to the rumbling of a hungry stomach, or to other noise in the background. You could be daydreaming, having sexual fantasies, remembering what happened to you last night, or planning what you will do tomorrow. You probably already know that paying attention to what you are reading is often difficult. Many different stimuli compete for your attention, making it hard to concentrate on one type of information to the exclusion of others; the more stimuli present, the harder it is to attend to any one of them.

Research on newborns indicates that from birth, we possess the ability to actively focus our attention to prevent information from overloading our attentional capacities. "Even from the neonatal period, patterns of attention demonstrate active selection and filtering of features of the environment. Infants are not simply passive recipients of experience, but appear to be searching and selective perceivers" (Bornstein, 1990, p. 4). This ability to sort information through focused attention appears to persist throughout life, without any age-related decline. However, the elderly do show deficits in the amount of information they are able to hold in attention at any one time (Madden, 1990).

SELECTIVE ATTENTION

In the 1950s, psychologists became interested in **selective attention**—the process of selecting one message from the environment and ignoring others. They were asked to determine how air-traffic controllers attended to one important message while listening to many messages at one time. To coordinate departures and arrivals as well as prevent midair collisions, the controllers had to direct the pilots while receiving reports from many different planes almost simultaneously. Because the pilots' voices and messages often sounded alike, the controllers occasionally made mistakes, with regrettable results.

Some people work in an environment that involves continual information overload. In these cases, people must switch attention rapidly among several sources of information.

In order to effectively do their jobs, air traffic controllers must concentrate only on specific stimuli and exclude all others.

To study the problem, the psychologists devised a test called *speech shadowing* to track the way people attend to messages (Cherry, 1953). As shown in Figure 5.1, the subjects wore headphones through which two different messages were played, one to each ear. The listener was instructed to repeat back all the words that reached one ear and to try to ignore the words that entered the other ear. You can get some idea of this task by placing yourself between two radios tuned to different stations. Try to repeat back everything you hear from one source and ignore the other. The result of your experiment should confirm what psychologists found in the original experiment. Even when the accepted message (the one on which the listener was to focus) was delivered much faster than normal speech, the subject could repeat it back with few errors and remember it fairly well on the test giver later. The rejected (ignored) message was remembered poorly. One experimenter reported that subjects could not recognize the rejected message above a chance level, even when it was quite simple and repeated 35 times (Moray, 1959).

Beacause the two messages were usually equally loud and otherwise physically similar, poor memory for the rejected message was purely psychological, reflecting a lack of attention to the material. The psychologists helped solve the air controllers' problem by discovering the characteristics that made messages easily distinguishable. They found that almost any physical difference between messages, such as loudness or pitch, helped the subjects attend to the competing messages better (Cherry, 1953).

A far less crucial but much more common example of selective attention involves how we screen all the stimuli we're exposed to at noisy parties. Picture yourself in the middle of a room trying to listen to someone speaking softly while loud conversations and music are going on around you. Surprisingly, you can usually follow the conversation without too much difficulty, which shows the power of selective attention. (This ability to select a message and to ignore the competing ones is sometimes called the *cocktail party phenomenon*.) To help keep your attention focused on your partner, you use both visual and auditory cues. For example, looking at your partner's face and lip movements helps you to select the relevant message.

You have probably also experienced another curious phenomenon in the cocktail party situation. Even though you intently follow one conversation and seem unaware of others, you may suddenly hear your name mentioned in another conversation,

FIGURE 5.1

Speech Shadowing

In this experiment, the subject is presented with two messages simultaneously, one to each ear. The task is to repeat back one message and ignore the other one. This task is frequently used to study selective attention.

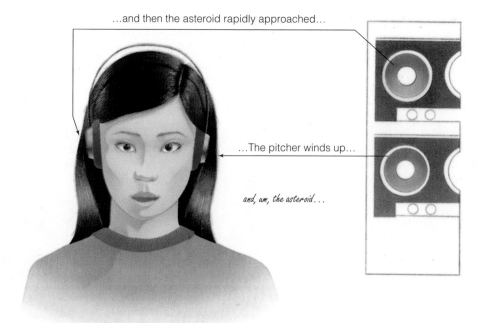

...and then the asteroid rapidly approached...

...The pitcher winds up...

and, um, the asteroid...

immediately drawing your attention to that conversation. How can we explain this overriding of the processes involved in selective attention? This question leads us to the various theories, or models, of selective attention.

MODELS OF SELECTIVE ATTENTION

Since the mid-1950s, psychologists have developed several different models to explain selective attention. Let's explain the most prominent of these theories.

Filter Theory. The first important theory about selective attention was developed by Donald Broadbent (1957, 1958). Broadbent proposed that psychologists can chart the passage of information through the mind in the same way that engineers can map the flow of electricity through a wiring system. He postulated the existence of two separate systems: the sensory system and the perceptual system. The sensory system retains information briefly after it reaches the sense organs. Because it can hold more than one sort of information at the same time from multiple sources, it is said to have *parallel transmission*. The perceptual system is roughly equivalent to conscious attention. It decides what to pay attention to and then selects one of the signals in the sensory system, according to the individual's current need for information. Broadbent (1958) held that processing in the perceptual system is *serial* (i.e., the individual can process only one thing at a time). He also assumed that if the perceptual system did not process information soon after it reached the sensory system, then the information would be lost. Thus, his theory assumed that there was a *filter* between the sensory and perceptual systems that screened out data not selected by the perceptual system (see Figure 5.2). Broadbent's model is called **filter theory** after this crucial active component (Duncan, 1993).

Early-Selection Versus Late-Selection Models. Studies of selective attention aim to discover how it is possible to attend to one message in the face of other equally distinct messages. Broadbent's filter theory proposed that the competing messages are filtered out at the level of the senses, *before* the information is processed. Since the attended signal is selected for further attention early in processing, filter theory is called an **early-selection theory** of attention.

Remember the example of listening to a conversation at a cocktail party when you suddenly hear your name mentioned nearby? You hear your name and quickly switch your attention. If you were filtering out the other conversations before they were processed for meaning (i.e., before they could reach the perceptual system), then how could you catch your name in a competing conversation?

Broadbent suggested that you could do so by occasionally switching the setting of the filter to other perceptual channels to sample the information there, just as a bored TV viewer might "surf" the various channels to check out the other programs. Then again, the words from another conversation might not be filtered out at a sensory level at all, but unconsciously perceived, contrary to Broadbent's filter theory. Important signals, such as your name, would break through into consciousness after their unconscious identification. If signals from the environment are identified without benefit of conscious attention, then perhaps the focusing effect of attention does not occur at a sensory level (as Broadbent theorized), but later in the sequence of perceptual processes. This possibility is realized in late-selection theories of attention.

Broadbent's filter theory was important because it was the first model of attention

FIGURE 5.2

Broadbent's Filter Theory of Attention

All signals from the outside world are briefly held in a peripheral sensory system. Signals can be held in parallel in the sensory system; in other words, many signals can be registered simultaneously. One signal is selected for further processing by the perceptual system. Signals can be fully perceived only one at a time, or serially. How do people select one signal and ignore others? According to filter theory, ignored signals are "filtered out" at the level of the senses so that they do not interfere with selected signals. Because the selection occurs early in the sensory-perceptual process, filter theory is called an early-selection theory of attention.

SOURCE: Broadbent, 1958.

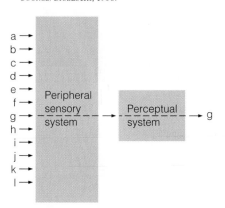

and because it demonstrated that mental processes could be conceived as a flow of information. However, a number of studies have shown that some of the information in the rejected message is not screened out at the level of the senses, and this weakens the validity of the filtering concept. The evidence points to some "leakage" in the attentional filter, since the mind seems to process some signals automatically without conscious awareness (Näätänen, 1992).

In one experiment, Neville Moray (1959) utilized the method of speech shadowing to demonstrate this leakage. He occasionally instructed his subjects, through the headphones, to switch their attention from one message to the other. When Moray embedded the instruction in the accepted message, the subjects usually switched without trouble, but when the instruction was put in the rejected message, they missed it every time. This part of the experiment supported filter theory. If the rejected message were being filtered out before being processed beyond the sensory level, the listener would not notice the instruction to switch and so could not act on it. However, Moray found that when the instruction to switch ears was placed in the rejected message and was preceded by the subject's name ("Mary, switch ears"), the instruction was followed 30 percent of the time. Thus, he concluded that ignored information was not completely shut out at the level of the senses; some of it apparently seeped through, to be processed for meaning. A person's name is a particularly sensitive cue that seems to be perceived almost automatically.

Two different theories have been proposed to account for a subject's response to seemingly ignored information. **Attenuation theory,** like filter theory, proposes that attention plays an "early" role in perceptual processing; but the attenuating filter only weakens signals as they pass between the sensory and perceptual systems instead of blocking them entirely (Treisman & Geffen, 1967).

The second approach, called **late-selection theory,** proposes that all signals coming from the outside world receive considerable perceptual processing (they are processed for their meaning), but only at an unconscious level. Some control process selects the most relevant or important signal for conscious, attentional processing (Näätänen, 1992; Norman, 1968). (Figure 5.3 compares late-selection theory with filter theory.)

The basic difference between early-selection theories of attention (like filter theory) and the newer late-selection theories is the level at which attention is believed to have its effects. According to early-selection theories, unattended information is screened out at the level of the senses—before it is perceived. According to late-selection theories, all information is processed through the early stages of perception. Attention to a single source occurs much later, with conscious awareness. If late-selection theories are true, we face the exciting possibility that unattended signals

© 1976 Ziggy and Friends, Inc. Distributed by Universal Press Syndicate. Reprinted with permission.

FIGURE 5.3

Two Models of Selective Attention

(a) According to filter theory, a person selectively attends to information by filtering at a sensory level. The signal that receives perceptual analysis guides a person's response. (b) According to late-selection theories, all stimuli receive some perceptual processing, but only one is attended to and used to make responses.

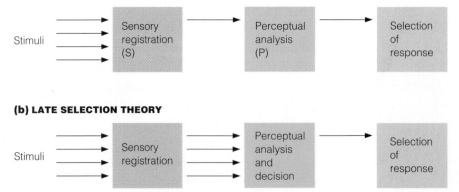

from the environment can register in our minds and affect our behavior without our conscious awareness of them. Can we be influenced by stimuli of which we are unaware? (See "Psychology in Our Times: Effects of Subliminal Stimulation" on pages 182–183)

ATTENTION AND SEARCH

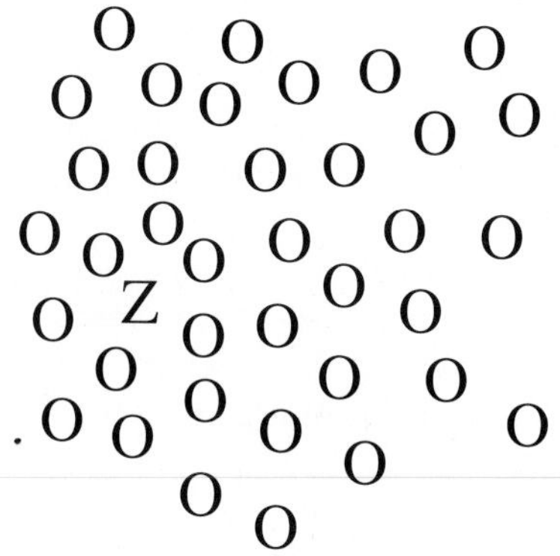

Imagine that you are meeting a friend who is about to go on leave from the navy. You're meeting his ship as it docks, so you expect to see him in uniform. When you arrive at the dock, you see many sailors disembarking wearing the same uniform, so you must search carefully for your friend. How do you do this? If we think of our attentional capacity as a spotlight, then you will need to focus your attentional spotlight on the individuals as they come off the ship. When the people are similar, your search must be careful and focused. But suppose that your friend is 7 feet 2 inches tall. Now your search is easy; you are looking for just one distinctive feature, because the other sailors will probably be shorter.

Ulric Neisser (1967) developed a laboratory analogue of these sorts of search processes by asking students to scan for a particular letter in a page of letters arranged in 50 lines of 6 letters each. Subjects pressed a key when they found the single target letter they were searching for in a field of other distractor letters. Students became quite fast at the task with practice, but the nature of the task affected their speed. For example, if the target letter had many angles (such as a *K*) and the distractor letters were all rounded (such as *C*, *O*, and *Q*), then the search was very fast. This is called a **feature search,** because the target (*K*) can be distinguished from the distractors by a single feature—like looking for your tall friend among people of normal size. More difficult is the **conjunction search,** which involves looking for a stimulus that has similar features to other stimuli. This is like trying to find a *K* among many other angular letters such as *Z*, *W*, *X*, *F*, and *Y*—or like looking for your friend of normal height among all the other sailors.

How do you recognize your friend when you see him? For that matter, how do we recognize the letter *Z* or the word *zebra*? Anne Treisman (1986, 1989) has proposed that two different processes are used in the kinds of search we have described. First, try to find the *Z* in Figure 5.4. The *Z* seems to pop out of the background of *O*'s. You do not have to pay attention to each letter to find the *Z*, so the pop-out effect represents a **preattentive process** (occurring before attentional processes are brought into play).

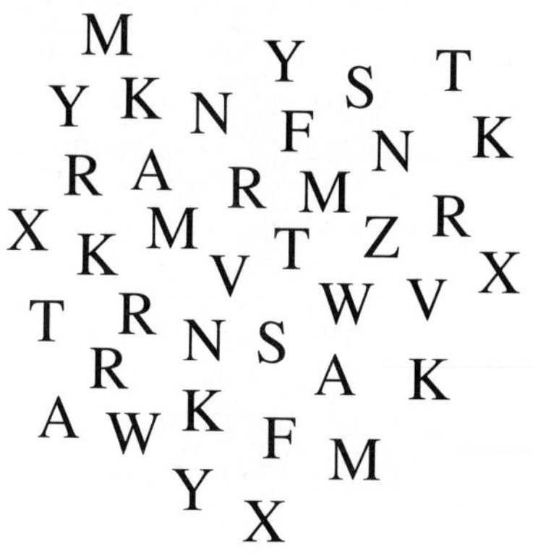

Now try to find the *Z* in Figure 5.5. Unless your eye happens to fall right on it, the process will take longer. Because the distractors share features in common with the target, they force you to look for the unique combination of features that specifies *Z*. This requires a second processing stage, one where focused attention is necessary to combine the features (Treisman, 1993).

Treisman (1989) maintained that primitive features of perception can be discovered through experiments in which subjects' speed to find objects in displays like Figures 5.4 and 5.5 is measured. She has identified the following primitive features from reviewing the research in this field: curvature, tilt, color, line ends, contrast, closed areas, brightness, and movement. These features are extracted from a stimulus during the early, preattentional phase of processing in a series of proposed mental "maps" of the visual field, one for each primitive feature. Thus, in the preattentive stage of attention, we would hold a map telling us where all of the movement was occurring in the visual field, as well as separate maps for diagonal lines, various colors,

FIGURE 5.4

Search for the Z

Even though the Z is surrounded by many other letters, it "pops out" at you. This "pop out" effect is a hallmark of preattentive feature searches.

FIGURE 5.5
Search for the Z

When the Z is placed among other angular letters, you are forced to use a focused search for a conjunction of features.

EFFECTS OF SUBLIMINAL STIMULATION

You may have read or heard about the effects of subliminal stimuli. *Subliminal* means "below the threshold of awareness," and subliminal stimuli are messages that we don't notice but that might still affect our behavior. Can subliminal advertising make us buy things we don't want? Can hidden messages in rock music cause antisocial behavior? On the positive side, can subliminal messages help us improve our memory or help us learn a foreign language? Audiotapes purported to help the listener via subliminal information come with impressive claims from their manufacturers. The alleged influence of subliminal messages has been a topic of debate for years.

Consider a much-publicized study reported to the press by James Vicary in 1957. Vicary claimed to have flashed messages, such as "Eat popcorn," very quickly during the showing of a movie (Naylor & Lawshe, 1958). These messages were displayed during the movie at such rapid rates that the viewers were not aware of seeing them. Nevertheless, Vicary reported that popcorn sales increased 58 percent during intermission. This study seemed to show that stimuli presented too fast to be consciously perceived could be registered below the level of awareness and affect a person's behavior; **subliminal perception** seemed real.

The popcorn study received wide publicity and generated concern (if not hysteria) among many people who felt threatened by the possibility of subliminal bombardment by advertisers and others. What has received much less publicity is the fact that in 1962, James Vicary admitted that the popcorn study never occurred: He fabricated it to promote his failing marketing business (Pratkanis, 1992).

Despite Vicary's admission, most Americans have heard of subliminal advertising and believe that such ads are effective (Zanot, Pincus, & Lamp, 1983). Are they justified in their belief?

If subliminal ads are to have any persuasive effect, they must first be perceived at some level. Psychologists have studied the problem of subliminal perception for years, with mixed results (Coren, 1984; Dixon, 1981). Demonstrating perception without awareness is extremely difficult. If a person sees a stimulus, it can be consciously identified very rapidly, probably in less than half a second. Given that conscious perception is so quick, how can researchers determine whether the perception of a brief stimulus was conscious or unconscious? And even if a person's ignorance of the stimulus can be ensured, how can researchers measure the effects of a subliminal stimulus? Obviously, researchers cannot ask people to report the experience directly because the subjects cannot do so by

definition if it is truly subliminal. The effects of the subliminal stimulus must be measured through its effects on the processing of some other stimulus or on some other behavior. For example, some researchers have found that subliminally presented stimuli often reappear in the subject's subsequent dreams, an experience known as the Poetzel phenomenon (Kihlstrom, 1987).

Anthony Marcel (1983) reported a fascinating study that seems to support the hypothesis of subliminal perception. He capitalized on a phenomenon known as **semantic priming,** whereby a subject can identify a second word more quickly after having been exposed to (primed by) a semantically related word. For example, if someone has just read the word *doctor,* identifying a related word, such as *nurse,* will be speeded up. In Marcel's version of the task, subjects were only asked to decide whether or not the second stimulus was a word. Thus, they would say yes to *nurse* and no to *narse.* When the first and second words were related in terms of meaning (*doctor-nurse*), subjects could decide that the second was a word more quickly than when the two words were unrelated (*banker-nurse*).

Marcel wondered if he could produce semantic priming if the first word in the related pair was presented so quickly that the subjects could not see it. That is, if *doctor* were presented in such a way that the subjects would not consciously detect it, would it still speed the processing of *nurse?* Four conditions occurred in Marcel's experiment: Either the two words were related or they were not related, and either the first word was visible or it was invisible to the viewers. When the first word was invisible, it was presented so quickly that the viewers could not even detect that a word had been shown, much less name it. In short, it was a subliminal stimulus.

Marcel's experiment provided evidence of subliminal perception. The response to the second word (*nurse*) was accelerated even when the related first word (*doctor*) was invisible to the viewers. Figure 5.4 shows that semantic priming was almost as effective when the first word was invisible as when it was visible! Even though the viewers could not detect the first word consciously, the information must have been unconsciously registered in the cognitive system because they processed the second word faster.

Marcel's work has created much excitement and controversy among cognitive psychologists. The basic phenomena have been replicated and extended (e.g., Balota, 1983; Dagenbach, Carr, & Wilhelmsen, 1989). However, further

experiments show that subjects can discriminate, at well-above chance levels, between trials with a prime and trials with no prime, even when they claim they are guessing and are never able to see a prime (Holender, 1986; Merikle, 1992). In other words, even when people claim they see nothing, objective measures show that they *do* see something. Consequently, subliminal perception has come to be defined by psychologists in a more "subjective" fashion: When observers are affected by a stimulus that they claim not to have experienced, that stimulus is said to have been perceived subliminally (Moore, 1992). Defined in this way, many researchers agree that subliminal perception exists.

Given that subliminal perception occurs, does it pose a great threat to the public, as some have claimed (Key, 1973, 1990)? Can advertisers and others present messages to make people favor one product over another or buy things they really don't need? As with most aspects of science, no absolute answer is possible. However, recent research on a currently popular form of subliminal persuasion suggests that it has no effect whatsoever (Merikle, 1992). Specifically, psychologists have evaluated the efficacy of the self-help audiotapes that are widely sold in bookstores and through the mail. When these audiotapes are played, the listener hears soothing sounds such as waves crashing on a beach or crickets chirping, but the distributors claim that "subliminal messages" are embedded in the tapes. These subliminal messages allegedly help the listener to lose weight, improve memory, stop smoking, or even improve psychic abilities.

In one study, people listened for several weeks to audiotapes designed to improve either self-esteem or memory (Greenwald, Spangenberg, Pratkanis, & Eskenazi, 1991). Although they were unaware of it at the time, half of the subjects who listened to tapes labeled "self-esteem" really heard the alleged memory tapes, and half of the subjects who listened to tapes labeled "memory" really heard self-esteem tapes. All of the self-esteem subjects showed an improvement in self-esteem, even those who actually listened to memory tapes; likewise, all of the memory subjects showed an improvement in memory, even those who actually listened to self-esteem tapes. Obviously, the subliminal message had no specific effect on the subjects; rather, the slight improvements were probably due to a placebo effect. (A placebo effect is one caused by subjects' expectancy that an effect will occur, rather than the variable in the condition). However, similar studies have failed to produce even a placebo effects with such audiotapes (Merikle & Skanes, 1992; Russell, Rowe, & Smouse, 1991). Indeed, these studies found no effect at all on behavior! Thus, the general conclusion from these studies is that these audiotapes have no effect whatsoever on behavior. By the same token, there is no convincing evidence that subliminal ads cause us to buy things or that hidden messages in rock music cause antisocial behavior (Vokey & Read, 1991).

The bulk of the evidence suggests that subliminal advertising poses little or no threat.

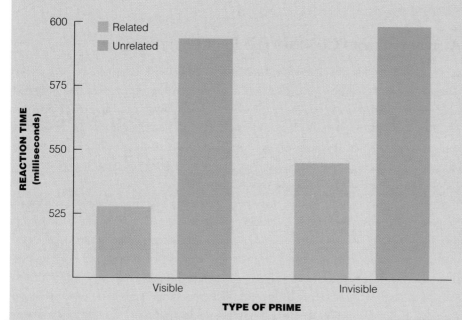

FIGURE 5.6

Marcel's Results Showing Subliminal Perception

The graph shows the time taken by subjects to report whether stimuli flashed before them were words, after first being exposed to priming words. The priming words could either be easily reported (visible condition) or could not be seen (invisible condition). Subjects identified words faster when the words had been preceded by related words. For example, they identified *nurse* as a word more quickly when it was preceded by the prime word *doctor* than when it was preceded by *lawyer*. This semantic priming effect was almost as great when the priming stimulus was invisible as when it was visible. Apparently, information about the first stimulus was registered in the invisible prime condition, even though the subjects could not report the prime.

Display: **L M W**

See: **M**

Report: "I saw a blue M and some other things. Maybe one was red."

FIGURE 5.7

Study of Illusory Conjunctions

When subjects are presented with rapidly displayed visual forms, such as letters, composed of various features (color, angles, line ends), they often report seeing objects based on illusory conjunctions from combining two features from different objects. This seems to indicate that the features are extracted independently during early-stages of processing and combined later. Under conditions of speeded presentation, the features may be combined incorrectly, leading to the perception of illusory conjunctions.

and brightness. According to Treisman (1993), these maps are not overlaid and combined until the second, focused attention stage.

Evidence for these assumptions comes from the study of **illusory conjunctions** of features: When stimuli are flashed briefly, we combine features from two stimuli and "see" a combination that was never presented. The experimental technique is relatively straightforward. Subjects are presented with several stimuli at once, very rapidly. For example, they may be exposed to the three letters of different colors shown in Figure 5.7: a blue *L*, a green *M*, and a red *W*. When asked to report what they see, subjects often report seeing a blue *M* or a green *W*, instead of the green M and red W. According to Treisman, such illusory conjunctions indicate that the features of objects (such as the color blue and the pattern of angles forming an M) are maintained separately during the preattentive phase. The features are "free floating," so they may be incorrectly combined during the focused attention stage to form illusory figures (the blue is combined with the letter pattern M).

Treisman's attentional theory explains how objects attract attention and how features are grouped through attentional processes. The preattentive system directs the attentive system to relevant or changing information, so that the attentive system can focus on these important locations, combine the features, and extract additional details (Ball, Roenker, & Bruni, 1990). How do these ideas relate to those about perception in the previous chapter? You may think of Treisman's proposed processes—preattention and focused attention—operating relatively early in the perceptual process. After the basic features of objects are grouped, recognition may take place through processes suggested by Biederman's (1987) recognition-by-components theory. That is, the basic components of objects are identified and composed into meaningful wholes (see Figure 4.10, on page 142). Although attention and recognition are not yet well understood, the ideas of Treisman, Biederman, and others help develop a better understanding of these complex processes. The complexity of these processes leads to the next important question: If they are so difficult, how can they become so easy with practice?

AUTOMATIC AND CONTROLLED PROCESSING

Many tasks that you do every day become easy and effortless, usually because of the reorganization of cognitive processes into more efficient operation. Reading is a good example. In the first grade, reading each word took significant time and effort, and you could be easily distracted and lose your place. If you now picked up the book that seemed so hard when you were in the first grade, your reading would be quick and effortless. The thousands of hours you have practiced reading since the first grade have changed the nature of this cognitive task (Kolers, 1985).

Cognitive psychologists make a distinction between controlled and automatic mental processes (Posner & Snyder, 1975; Schneider & Shiffrin, 1977). The basic idea is that some mental processes are under our conscious control, while others occur automatically—without our awareness or attention. **Controlled processing** is a function that takes mental effort, can be easily interrupted, and is relatively slow. The confused state of the beginning reader reveals controlled processing. **Automatic processing,** on the other hand, occurs effortlessly (without conscious attention), rapidly, and in a way that makes it hard to interrupt. If the words *the boy* were flashed on a screen in front of you, your processing would likely be automatic (at least relative to a first-grader) because your comprehension of the words would occur quickly, effortlessly, and proba-

The children use great mental effort, or controlled processing, whereas the professional skaters are able to skate beautifully with less mental effort after thousands of hours of practice.

bly unavoidably. (Try looking at a familiar word without thinking of its meaning.) As the example of reading makes clear, automatic and controlled processing can be seen as endpoints on a continuum; a mental process that is under conscious control at first will probably become automatic when it has been practiced thousands of times (Logan, 1985; Venturino, 1991).

The Stroop Task. An experimental situation that has been used for years to study mental processing is the **Stroop color-naming task** (Stroop, 1935). In this experimental situation, the subjects identify colors as fast as they can by saying the name of the color. In one control condition, they identify patches of color; in a second control condition they identify the color of the ink of various written words. In a third condition, the one of greatest interest, the subjects again identify the ink colors of words, but this time the words themselves are the names of other colors. So, for example, a person may see the word *red* written in blue ink, and the task is to say "blue." An example of the Stroop color-naming task is presented in Figure 5.8. Before reading any further, time yourself as you identify the ink colors in each of the three columns.

FIGURE 5.8

The Stroop Task

Time yourself as you identify the ink colors for the items in each of the three columns. Column A contains color patches, B contains words, and C contains words that name colors. Subjects take much longer to name the colors in C.

(a) COLOR PATCHES	(b) WORDS	(c) COLOR NAMES
	habit	green
	sleep	yellow
	person	black
	meal	red
	life	green
	brain	yellow
	dog	blue
	case	black
	fear	red
	normal	blue

As you have probably just discovered, most people are much slower at identifying the colors when the words represent the names of other colors (column C). Although people are somewhat slower at identifying the ink colors of unrelated words (column B) than at identifying color patches (column A), this difference is quite small when compared to the case in which the words are other color names. Most people find identifying colors in the condition requiring competing responses a difficult and frustrating task.

The trouble that subjects have in performing the Stroop task is usually taken to indicate that people process words automatically for their meaning. When subjects respond with the name of the color of the ink (e.g., "blue" for the word *black*), the word *black* is automatically activated anyway, and the two activated responses make it difficult for the subjects to respond correctly or quickly. Even people who have been given extended practice at the Stroop task and have been told to try to suppress or ignore the printed word are still slower to name the colors in the third condition (MacLeod, 1991).

One theory explaining the Stroop effect is that there is a mental "horse race" between the processes involved in identifying colors and in reading words. Because most of us have much more practice reading words than naming colors, the reading response wins the race and slows color naming. That is, when we see the word *red* written in blue ink, we think of red before blue, and thinking of red delays our saying "blue" as the correct response. Thus, the difficulty in performing the Stroop task is attributed to the automatic process of reading the word, which occurs without our intentions (and even contrary to them) and which cannot be brought under conscious control.

However, even when our ability to identify the words is greatly slowed down (as when the words are printed upside down), the Stroop effect persists (Dunbar & MacLeod, 1984). That is, most people are equally slow in calling the ink color of both red and pɘɹ "black." The word should be read much faster in the first case, and so, according to the horse-race theory, the interference should be greater there. The fact that the Stroop effect is just as strong with both types of words seems to signal that the standard horse-race theory may not be accurate. Although there is currently no well-accepted theory explaining the Stroop effect, it remains the focus of research because it represents a blatant failure of selective attention. Even when people try hard to ignore the word and attend only to the ink color, they cannot do so.

The Effects of Practice. Many tasks in life begin under slow, effortful, controlled processing but then become automatic after extensive practice. This is true of walking, driving a car, and even tying your shoelaces. The hallmark of a skilled athlete is the ability to dribble a basketball or perform a complex gymnastics program quickly, smoothly, and without being distracted (i.e., automatically). Of course, such abilities take thousands of hours of practice to achieve. The same experience occurred for most of us when we learned to drive. At first it was a challenging task, consuming our total concentration. Our minds were completely occupied with a multitude of thoughts and worries: Are my hands in the right position on the wheel? What's in the rearview mirror? Am I speeding? But after years of practice, driving has become fairly automatic, and now we can listen to the radio or carry on a conversation without distraction from such worries. We know that we'll be able to handle all of these worries fairly easily, so we don't pay as much attention to them now. However, no complex cognitive task ever becomes fully automatic. Rather, it is a matter of degree.

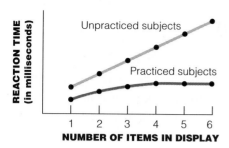

FIGURE 5.9

Controlled and Automatic Search

Subjects were asked to search for one of several letters that appeared in a display containing distractors (digits). Inexperienced subjects took longer to search with increasing numbers of distractors (the top line), which indicates that they were probably searching the items one at a time, in a controlled manner. After much practice, subjects became much faster, their time to search decreased and was unaffected by the number of distractors. The massive practice led to an automatic search of the display.

How can the performance of a task be converted from an effortful, controlled process to an automatic process? This issue has been studied in visual-search tasks similar to those discussed earlier. Richard Shiffrin and Walter Schneider (1977) had subjects search for a set of target letters (e.g., *j*, *d*, and *t*) among a set of distractors (e.g., the digits 1 to 9). The subjects' task was to find one of the target letters in a display, and their reaction time was measured. Sometimes the display contained only distractors, so subjects could not respond without searching for the letter.

Shiffrin and Schneider found that at first, the distractor items greatly slowed the search for the target letters; the more distractors present in the display, the slower the search (see the top line in Figure 5.9). Apparently, the subjects in the experiment were employing a careful, controlled search through the letters to find the target. After a great deal of practice at the task, however (14 days and over 4,000 search trials!), the pattern changed. Now the number of distractors had only a slight influence on the search time, as seen in the lower line in Figure 5.9. Generally speaking, search time for a letter was as fast when there were six distractors as when there were only one or two. Apparently, the tremendous amount of practice enabled the subjects to go from a controlled, deliberate form of processing to one in which the search could be made automatically, at a single glance. For such automatic searching to develop, however, subjects must look for the same items on each trial against a background of different items. In other words, automatic processing will not develop if subjects look for letters against a background of digits on some trials and for digits against a background of letters on other trials. Such search paradigms have been popular ways of studying the development of automatic processing in laboratory experiments (Shiffrin, 1988).

Although most theories assume that extensive practice is necessary for automatic processing to develop, recent experiments by Logan and Klapp (1991) show that such processing can sometimes develop over a short period of time. The task involved "alphabet arithmetic"—for instance, A + 3 = D or B + 1 = C, where A = 1; B = 2; Z = 26. The subjects saw an arithmetic statement flashed briefly and had to quickly decide whether it was true or false. At first, smaller digit values (1 to 5) were related to faster decision times, but Logan and Klapp showed that if subjects memorized the letter-digit relations (A = 1, B = 2, etc.) beforehand, automatic processing developed with less than an hour's practice. Logan and Klapp argue that the essential factor in achieving automatic processing is fast memory retrieval, rather than more efficient cognitive information processing. In most experiments, fast memory retrieval develops over the course of extended practice.

The development of automatic processing in well-practiced tasks is useful in that mental resources can be directed to other matters while the tasks are being performed. Experienced drivers can hold conversations, listen to the radio, or plan for future activities while driving. However, driving this way can sometimes be dangerous, because people may become distracted from the task at hand. In fact, people driving on interstate highways often report that they will suddenly snap alert from some daydream or fantasy to realize that they have not been paying conscious attention to the road for some time. They seem to have been driving on "automatic pilot."

Our discussion of attention and consciousness implies that different types of processes can be brought into play when we perform various tasks. The next section explores whether different parts of the brain play a role in coding different sorts of information, referring back to an issue discussed in Chapter 2, that of hemispheric specialization of the brain.

Hemispheric Specialization and Consciousness

In Chapter 2, we discussed the different functions of the two hemispheres of the brain. In most people, the left hemisphere is primarily responsible for comprehending and producing language, and the right hemisphere controls many nonverbal abilities such as drawing, listening to music, and finding one's way with a map (Iaccino, 1993; Witelson, 1988). Roger Sperry, who pioneered research on hemispheric specialization with split-brain patients (see page 68), maintains that different types of consciousness are also associated with the two hemispheres of these patients:

> Each hemisphere . . . has its own . . . private sensations, perceptions, thoughts, and ideas, all of which are cut off from the corresponding experiences in the opposite hemisphere. Each left and right hemisphere has its own private chain of memories and learning experiences that are inaccessible to recall by the other hemisphere. In many respects each disconnected hemisphere appears to have a "mind of its own" (Sperry, 1974)

Research on split-brain patients has yielded some of the most convincing evidence for different forms of consciousness. Consider the experiment portrayed in Figure 5.10, where information was flashed either to the right or to the left of a fixation point that was straight ahead. Information off to the right (i.e., in the right visual field) went to the left hemisphere, and information shown to the left visual field was transmitted to the right hemisphere (refer back to Figure 3.10, on page 96). In normal people with intact corpus callosums, the information also passed quickly from one hemisphere to the other. But in split-brain patients, the information became "trapped" in either the left or right hemisphere, thereby permitting scientists to discover how it was processed. Michael Gazzaniga, a pioneer in this field, directed written words to one or the other hemisphere and then asked the subjects to identify the words (Gazzaniga, 1970). If the word *pencil* was shown off to the right (transmitted to the left hemisphere), the split-brain patients could name it easily. But if the word was shown off to the left, the subjects could not name it because the right hemisphere could not produce speech. In some trials, instead of asking the subjects to name the presented word, Gazzaniga asked them to pick out the object with their left hand from behind a screen. The patients could do so accurately, since the right hemisphere controlled the left hand. Apparently, then, the right hemisphere has some capacity for comprehending language, but it cannot produce it or translate it into conscious verbal experience.

FIGURE 5.10

Testing a Split-Brain Patient

The patient fixates on a point straight ahead while words are flashed either to the left or to the right. A word flashed to the right is interpreted by the left hemisphere and can easily be named. (The left hemisphere has the capacity to produce speech.) A word flashed to the left, as in the picture, cannot be identified by the right hemisphere, which cannot produce speech. In this case, the person can pick out the object with the left hand (controlled by the right hemisphere), thus showing that the right hemisphere has some capacity to comprehend words.

SOURCE: Gazzaniga, 1967, p. 27.

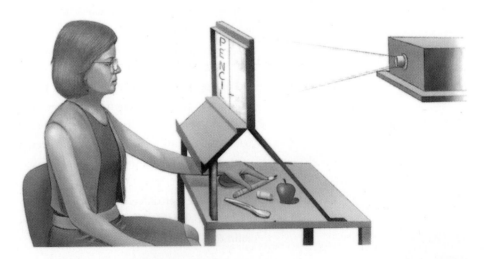

In a similar experiment by Gazzaniga, a split-brain patient was shown a picture of a nude to the right hemisphere. She giggled with embarrassment, but when questioned, she did not know why she was laughing. She remarked, "I don't know . . . nothing. . . . Oh—that funny machine." In that case, the picture produced an unusual reaction that the verbal centers of the left hemisphere could not interpret. In another experiment, Gazzaniga (1989) showed different pictures to the two hemispheres. For example, a picture of a chicken claw was shown to the right visual field (processed by the left hemisphere), and a snow scene was shown in the left visual field (handled by the right hemisphere). The subject's task was to examine a group of pictures and pick the ones associated with the pictures just seen. With his right hand the patient chose a picture of a chicken, and with his left hand a picture of a shovel. Both choices were correct, but when asked about his choices, the split-brain patient provided this explanation: "Oh, that's simple. The chicken claw goes with the chicken, and you need a shovel to clean out the chicken shed" (Gazzaniga, 1989, p. 951). The left hemisphere, whose job it is to interpret experience verbally, had seen the picture of the chicken, but had no knowledge of the snow scene. Thus, it made up a reasonable explanation for the left hand's choice of the shovel.

In other studies, Gazzaniga (1970) observed split-brain patients putting together simple jigsaw puzzles. If allowed to put the puzzles together with their left hand (controlled by the right hemisphere), the subjects had no trouble because the right hemisphere is specialized for such visual and spatial tasks. But when the patients were asked to solve the puzzles with their right hand and to keep their left hand under the table, their performance on the puzzles was dismal because the left hemisphere is poor at such tasks. The patients often appeared frustrated, trying to bring their left hand out from under the table to solve the puzzle, as though the two halves of the brain were struggling to control behavior. The right brain observed the pathetic attempts of the right hand (and left hemisphere) to solve the puzzle. The right brain knew the solution and tried to order the left hand up from under the table to solve it.

A problem sometimes faced by split-brain patients is that the two sides of their bodies engage in conflicting behaviors. For example, one patient reported that when she went to her bedroom closet to choose something to wear, she would reach for what she wanted with her right hand, but her left hand would reach out and choose something else. Similarly, a young split-brain patient who worked in his father's grocery store had difficulty shelving goods because as soon as one hand would place an item where it belonged, the other hand would remove it (Springer & Deutsch, 1993). In most split-brain patients, these extreme behavioral conflicts disappear within a few months of the operation, but for a few patients, these problems persist for years.

The metaphorical war between the two halves of the brain can be observed only in split-brain subjects. In normal people, there is a smooth exchange of information and control between the two hemispheres, because the hemispheres communicate via the corpus callosum. Sperry (1968) has shown that when the pathway is cut, the dual nature of consciousness is revealed. As with other topics in this chapter, there is evidence of an unconscious cognitive system processing information that cannot be brought into conscious awareness and verbalized (Springer & Deutsch, 1993). Gazzaniga (1983, 1989) argues for a modular mind, claiming that cognitive systems within the brain may operate as relatively independent modules controlling different aspects of behavior:

> The emerging picture is that our cognitive system is not a unified network with a single purpose and train of thought. A more accurate metaphor is that our sense of subjective

awareness arises out of our dominant left hemisphere's unrelenting need to explain the actions taken by any one of a multitude of mental systems that dwell within us...These systems, which coexist with the language system, are not necessarily in touch with the language processor prior to a behavior. (1989, p. 536)

The work with split-brain patients shows aspects of mental life normally hidden from view. It also demonstrates the important connection between physiology and consciousness, with split-brain patients exhibiting drastic alterations in consciousness and cognitions as a result of their brain surgery.

The next section adds to our understanding of consciousness by exploring what happens when we lose consciousness by sleeping.

Sleep and Dreams

So far, we have been concerned with ordinary consciousness. In the remaining sections, we will consider states in which consciousness is "lost" or altered. Every night you lose consciousness when you fall asleep, and later you enter an altered state when you dream. Sleeping and dreaming have been studied scientifically for only the last 50 or 60 years, which is surprising, since most of us spend almost a third of our lives sleeping.

The amount of sleep a person needs changes greatly over the course of a lifetime, and there are often enormous differences between individuals of the same age (see Figure 5.11). Newborn babies may snooze 16 hours or more a day, but after their first four weeks, they stay awake for longer and longer periods. Most adults average 7 to 9 hours of sleep nightly. Amount of sleep generally remains stable during adulthood, but it may decrease slightly in old age. However, the amount of sleep the elderly need, or can get, varies; some people sleep more, but many sleep less.

CIRCADIAN RHYTHMS

Sleep is one of many bodily functions that occur in a regular pattern every 24 hours or so. Such patterns are called *circadian rhythms*. (*Circadian* is from the Latin, meaning "about a day.") Almost every physiological response exhibits circadian rhythms, as the

FIGURE 5.11

The Average Duration of Sleep

The data in the figure were obtained in a survey of nearly 1 million adults. The vast majority report sleeping between 7 and 9 hours a night. Only a very small percentage reported sleeping fewer than 5 or more than 10 hours.

The figure appears in A. Borbely (1986). *Secrets of sleep*. New York: Basic Books, p. 43. The data were obtained from D. F. Kripke et al. (1979). Short and long sleep and sleeping pills: Is increased mortality associated? *Archives of General Psychiatry, 36,* 103–116.

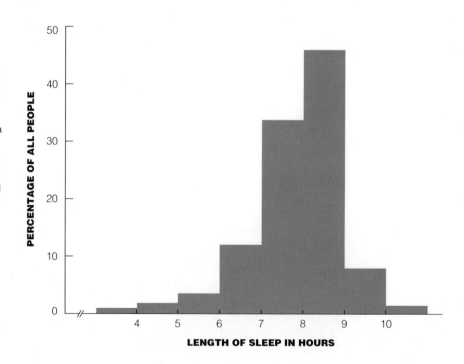

A night of sleep involves continual change, both in physical movement and in the electrical activity of the brain.

FIGURE 5.12
An Electroencephalogram (EEG) Being Recorded

Electrodes are attached to certain points on the skull, and the combined electrical potentials are plotted against time to produce the EEG, a graph showing the pattern of brain waves (see Figure 5.13). The EEG has proved to be a useful measure, but it is still only a crude one, since electrical potentials from many places in the brain are averaged together.

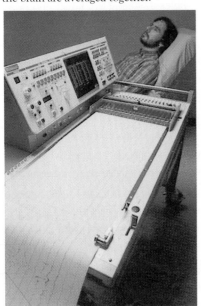

body's internal clock regulates its functioning by complex sets of stimuli, some internal and some external. Even when animals (including people) are placed in controlled environments where all external cues about light and darkness are removed, their bodies continue to show circadian rhythms, although they may gradually drift away from the normal day-and-night cycle. Most humans exhibit a 25-hour cycle rather than a 24-hour cycle in such controlled situations (Hobson, 1989).

Circadian rhythms affect people's energy levels during the day, regardless of how much sleep they have had. Most people feel a surge of energy in the morning hours that is responsible for the "second wind" often experienced after a sleepless night. Likewise, even when people are very tired, they find it very difficult to go to sleep between 7 P.M. and about 9 or 10 P.M., prompting some to refer to this period as a "forbidden zone" for sleep. Finally, there is the well-known afternoon drowsiness that affects so many people. Although we often blame large mid-day meals for this sleepiness, research shows that food intake is not important to this phenomenon; rather, circadian rhythms dictate this sleepiness. Although some societies try to fight this natural low point in the day with coffee or other caffeinated beverages, other societies have a workday that more closely conforms to their circadian rhythms. People in these societies take an afternoon nap, or siesta, often lasting a few hours, and then resume work for several more hours. Overall, however, people in these cultures do not sleep more; they sleep fewer hours at night than people in cultures without the siesta tradition (Dotta, 1990).

Circadian rhythms are *biological* rhythms. They should not be confused with the popular concept of *biorhythms*. Circadian, or biological, rhythms are a well-established phenomenon. Biorhythms, on the other hand, have no scientific basis. Biorhythm "theory" states that at birth, three biorhythm cycles begin: a 33-day intellectual cycle, a 28-day emotional cycle, and a 23-day physical cycle. The cycles have peaks and valleys, and by knowing the date of your birth, you can compute whether you are supposed to be at a high point or low point intellectually, emotionally, or physically. Like the pseudoscience of astrology, biorhythms purport to forecast your behavior throughout your life based solely on your date of birth. Scientific studies of biorhythms show no relation whatsoever between biorhythm predictions and actual intellectual, emotional, and physical functioning (Coleman, 1986; O' Connor & Molly, 1991).

The circadian rhythms seem to have evolved to maximize the effectiveness of our biological systems, with natural lulls and peaks in performance occurring at various points in the day. Sleep is certainly the most drastic change in the daily pattern of activity, leading to intense interest in its nature and purpose.

THE SCIENTIFIC STUDY OF SLEEP

The scientific study of sleep was given a dramatic boost with the development of the *electroencephalograph*, a device that measures changes in the electrical potentials of the brain (see Figure 5.12). Electrodes attached to the scalp measure the combined electrical output of many neurons in the cortex below the scalp. The result is an *electroencephalogram (EEG)*, a record of the brain's electrical activity. Before the electroencephalogram, sleep had been regarded as a single state. This notion had to be changed when EEG recordings revealed several distinct stages of sleep (Arkin, 1991).

The brain waves that characterize the stages of sleep are pictured in Figure 5.13. At the top are the brain waves obtained when a person is awake but resting. The brain waves are of high frequency and low amplitude and are quite irregular. Drowsiness is

FIGURE 5.13

Brain Wave During Sleep

The figure shows how brain waves change systematically from when a person is awake (top) through drowsiness and the stages of sleep (stage 3 is not shown). Brain waves are measured in cycles per second (cps), which generally decrease with deeper sleep. Notice that the brain waves of REM (dreaming) sleep at the bottom resemble those of the waking state at the top.

SOURCE: Hauri, 1977.

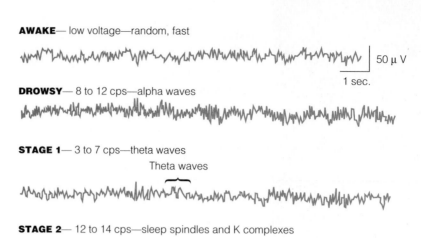

AWAKE— low voltage—random, fast

50 μ V

1 sec.

DROWSY— 8 to 12 cps—alpha waves

STAGE 1— 3 to 7 cps—theta waves

Theta waves

STAGE 2— 12 to 14 cps—sleep spindles and K complexes

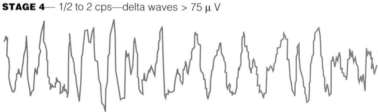

Sleep spindle

K complex —

STAGE 4— 1/2 to 2 cps—delta waves > 75 μ V

REM SLEEP— Low voltage—random, fast with sawtooth waves

Sawtooth waves

marked by alpha waves, and when such waves are present, people usually report a pleasant, relaxed feeling. As a person drifts into stage 1, the brain waves remain fast, but they become more irregular. Theta waves appear. A person awakened in stage 1 will probably deny having been asleep. The brain waves in stage 2 are larger and slower, with occasional K-complexes. Stage 2 sleep is also marked by occasional spindles, or short runs of rhythmic, low-frequency waves. It is more difficult to awaken a person from stage 2 sleep than from stage 1 sleep. Stage 3 is a deeper sleep. The brain waves are still irregular and have spindles, but the amplitude is greater and occasionally, large, slow waves, called delta waves are interspersed. In the deepest stage of sleep, stage 4, the delta waves predominate.

An additional stage of sleep, not numbered, is in some ways the most interesting. Researchers noticed that several times a night, sleepers would enter a stage where their brain waves accelerated almost to the rate of the waking state. The sleepers seemed to enter stage 1, but their eyes moved rapidly underneath the eyelids, and other curious changes occurred. In this stage, the sexual organs almost always became aroused, and breathing and heartbeat became irregular. Because people awakened from this stage usually reported that they had been dreaming (Dement & Kleitman, 1957b), the stage has been called dream sleep. It is also called **REM sleep** (for **R**apid **E**ye **M**ovement). In this stage, sleepers' brain waves suggest that they are close to waking but other signs indicate that they are in the depths of slumber. It is usually more difficult to awaken a

Research participants often wear a cap to hold electrodes in place on the scalp during EEG measurements.

person from REM sleep than from any other stage, perhaps because the sleeper's attention is focused on the dream of the moment rather than on external stimuli.

A NIGHT OF SLEEP

Sleep is a complicated pattern of movement from stage to stage. In Figure 5.14 you can see the sleep stages of one person on three successive nights. The stages are on the vertical axis of each graph and the amount of time since they fell asleep is on the horizontal axis. The time spent in REM sleep is shown by dark bars. This person exhibited the normal pattern of cycling through the various stages of sleep.

Although individual sleep patterns differ widely, a typical night of sleep can be constructed from averages. Sleepers usually progress quickly through stage 1 to stages 2 and 3 and often reach stage 4 within 30 minutes of having fallen asleep (Webb, 1975). In stage 4, sleepers are very relaxed and breathe slowly and evenly. Brain waves during stage 4 show a large response to external stimuli, even though the stimuli do not awaken the sleepers. The stimuli are making their way to central parts of the brain, but they are not being translated into conscious experience. In one study, experimenters spoke to sleeping subjects and recorded their EEG responses to certain words. Among the words were the subjects' own name; the name evoked greater cortical arousal, as shown in the brain waves, than did other words, even though the subjects did not awaken (McDonald et al., 1975; Oswald, Taylor, & Treisman, 1960). Apparently, these people processed information automatically while in the unconscious state of deep sleep.

After sleepers have experienced stage 4 for a while, they start cycling to the other stages. Their first period of REM sleep begins after about an hour and a half of sleep, when they reenter stage 1. This is believed to coincide with their first dream; it is often marked by body movement, such as turning over. The first REM period is the shortest of the night, with a return to other stages in a matter of minutes. The sleepers continue to pass between stages throughout the night in a cyclical pattern.

People average five distinct periods of REM sleep nightly, each usually longer than the previous one and the time between them shorter. If REM sleep is indeed associated with dreaming, as it seems to be, then everyone dreams about five times a night, with each successive dream period longer than the last. However, not all people react in exactly this way every night, as can be seen in Figures 5.14 and 5.15. During the long REM periods in the early morning, body temperature reaches its lowest point, and the

FIGURE 5.14

Three Nights of Sleep

This diagram shows the amount of time one person spent in each stage of sleep over three successive nights. The sleep stage is shown on the vertical axis; the amount of time in each stage is on the horizontal axis. Notice how the person cycled among the different sleep stages and how periods of REM sleep (indicated by the dark bars) generally lasted longer toward morning.

SOURCE: Webb & Agnew, 1968.

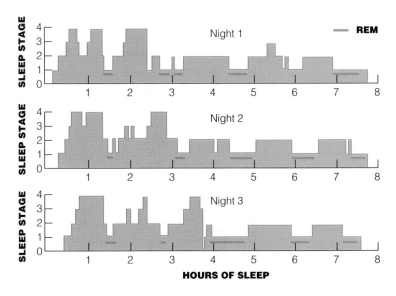

WHAT IS CONSCIOUSNESS?

193

FIGURE 5.15

Typical Sleep Habits

The graph shows the average amount of time a group of young males spent in the different stages of sleep as well as individual variability in time spent in each stage. They spent most of the night in stage 2.

SOURCE: Webb & Agnew, 1973.

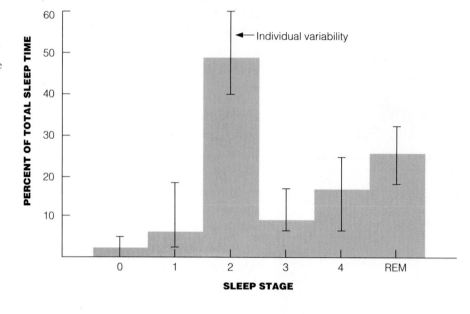

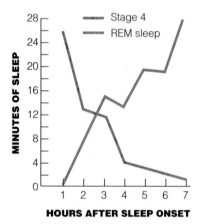

FIGURE 5.16

Stage 4 and REM Sleep

The graph depicts the changes in the amount of stage 4 and REM sleep during the course of a night. At first people spend much more time in stage 4 sleep than in REM sleep, but early in the morning, REM sleep predominates.

SOURCE: Webb & Agnew, 1973.

autonomic nervous system produces the greatest changes in breathing and heart rate. Sleepers usually awaken after a dream period, but they remember only the last dream.

Just as REM periods grow longer during the night, the time spent in stage 4 becomes shorter (see Figure 5.16). Together the two stages account for less than half the time spent sleeping. As Figure 5.15 shows, a great deal of the night is passed in stage 2.

WHY DO WE SLEEP?

Most people assume that sleep has a restorative effect, replenishing something that is used up while we are awake. While awake, for example, we might use up neurochemicals essential to the functioning of the brain, and sleep might replenish their supply. Curiously, there are no firm answers regarding why people sleep, or how much they need to sleep, or whether they even need to sleep at all. According to Richard Thompson (1993),

> There is no obvious reason why humans should have to sleep. Sleep certainly does not provide the body with rest; as far as metabolism goes, sleep is little better than quietly reading a book. Nor does the brain rest during sleep. In [REM] sleep it is more active than when a person is awake but sitting quietly. (p. 204)

Wilse Webb (1975) has proposed the novel theory that sleep evolved simply to keep people quiet at night. Night was a dangerous time for our ancestors because predators were everywhere; creatures that stayed home at night and slept had a better chance of surviving than nonsleeping wanderers.

J. Allan Hobson (1989), a noted sleep researcher, argues that sleep serves at least two general functions. The first function is biological. To begin with, the body's metabolic rate is lowered (although, as already noted, it is no lower than when the individual is resting while awake). Animals with lower metabolic rates are able to conserve energy; they are less likely to venture out at night, the coldest time. In addition, there is, as we have said, a common assumption that sleep (especially REM sleep) has a restorative function involving regeneration of important brain chemicals; as of yet, however, no specific neurotransmitters have been identified (Thompson, 1993). So, the first function of sleep is to help maintain homeostasis, or the body's equilibrium.

The second main function of sleep proposed by Hobson is more speculative: a reorganization in the brain of information learned during the day. One idea is that an automatic consolidation of important information occurs during sleep, especially during dream sleep. "We seem to be rememorizing our memory every night of our lives" (Hobson, 1989, p. 199). However, there is no direct evidence in support of this theory, and other researchers have proposed the opposite idea: that certain types of sleep help us forget nonessential information (Crick & Mitchison, 1983)!

Effects of Sleep Deprivation.   Although the reasons that people sleep have not been completely determined, researchers have tried to discover the importance of sleep by studying what happens to humans and other animals when they are deprived of it. When rats are totally deprived of sleep, their mechanisms for regulating energy break down. Their food intake goes up, but they nonetheless lose weight and eventually die (Rechtshaffen et al., 1983). Although prolonged experiments have never been performed with humans, people have kept themselves awake or participated in experiments in which sleep is reduced, thereby adding to our knowledge about the effects of sleep deprivation. We consider two instances of prolonged sleep deprivation in the Case Study section.

CASE STUDY

PROLONGED SLEEP LOSS

Some people have kept themselves awake for lengthy periods for various reasons. However, the results of these attempts are inconsistent. To illustrate these variable effects of extreme sleep loss, we will consider two celebrated cases of sleep deprivation. The first is that of Peter Tripp, a thirty-two-year-old New York disc jockey, who undertook to stay awake for 200 hours (about 8 days) in a glass booth in Times Square in January 1959. The stunt was undertaken for the benefit of the March of Dimes and was supervised by doctors and scientists. The following fascinating description of Tripp's experience comes from a government report concerned with sleep:

Almost from the first, the desire to sleep was so strong that Tripp was fighting to keep himself awake. After little more than 2 days and 2 nights he began to have visual illusions; for example, he reported finding cobwebs in his shoes. By about 100 hours the simple daily tests that required only minimal mental agility and attention were torture to him. He was having trouble remembering things, and his visual illusions were perturbing: he saw the tweed suit of one of the scientists as a suit of fuzzy worms. After 120 hours he went across the street to a room in the Hotel Astor, where

he periodically washed and changed clothes. He opened a bureau drawer and dashed out into the hall for help. The drawer, as he had seen it, was ablaze. Perhaps in an effort to explain this and other visions to himself he decided that the doctors had set the illusory fire, deliberately, to test him and frighten him. About this time he developed a habit of staring at the wall clock in the Times Square booth. As he later explained, the face of the clock bore the face of an actor friend, and he had begun to wonder whether he were Peter Tripp, or the friend whose face he saw in the clock. The daily tests were almost unendurable for Tripp and those who were studying him. "He looked like a blind animal trying to feel his way through a maze." A simple algebraic formula that he had earlier solved with ease now required such superhuman effort that Tripp broke down, frightened at his inability to solve the problem, fighting to perform. Scientists saw the spectacle of a suave New York radio entertainer trying vainly to find his way through the alphabet.

By 170 hours the agony had become almost unbearable to watch. At times Tripp was no longer sure he was himself, and frequently tried to gain proof of his identity. Although he behaved as if he were awake, his brain wave patterns resembled those of sleep. In his psychotic delusions he was convinced that the doctors were in a conspiracy against him to send him to jail. On the last morning of his wakathon, Tripp was examined by Dr. Harold Wolff of Cornell. The late Dr. Wolff had a somewhat archaic manner of dress, and to Tripp he must have appeared funebrial. Tripp undressed as requested, and lay down on the table for medical examination, but as he gazed up at the doctor he came to the gruesome decision that the man was actually an undertaker, about to bury him alive. With this grim insight, Tripp leapt for the door, and tore into the Astor hall with several doctors in pursuit. At the end of the 200 sleepless hours, nightmare hallucination and reality merged, and he felt he was the victim of a sadistic conspiracy among the doctors. (Luce, 1966)

Some researchers have inferred from Tripp's and similar cases that sleep is critical to mental functioning, and that if people are deprived of it for long periods, they tend to exhibit symptoms associated with mental illness. But other cases have shown much less strain. In 1965 Randy Gardner, a San Diego high school student, decided to stay awake for 264 hours, or 11 days, as part of a high school science project. He also wanted to break the world record for sleeplessness. Gardner was watched at home by his parents, a doctor, and two sleep

researchers. He whiled away the time by talking to friends and family and playing pinball, among other activities. He became very tired, sometimes seemed a bit confused, and occasionally experienced the *hatband illusion* (a feeling of pressure around the head). But at the end of 11 days he appeared before TV cameras and comported himself perfectly naturally, manifesting none of the symptoms that had plagued Peter Tripp. The conclusion here would seem to be that sleep loss has little affect.

Why the discrepancy between the Tripp and Gardner cases? There is no certain answer, but one reason may have to do with their environments. Tripp was in a highly charged, emotional atmosphere, and he was tested and checked regularly with many people watching. Gardner was at home with family and friends and insulated from hoopla. Another possible reason is that Gardner was younger than Tripp and probably in better physical condition.

One noted researcher, William Dement (1976), has suggested that anyone who is young, highly motivated, and in good physical condition may be able to go without sleep more or less indefinitely. This conclusion is complicated, however, by the discovery that no-sleep marathons may be flawed by catnaps (called *microsleeps* by researchers) that have gone undetected because the napper's eyes remained open. Furthermore, many studies show that sleep deprivation does affect performance on physical and cognitive tasks (Dinges & Kribbs, 1991).

Participants in no-sleep marathons as described in the case study section seem to bounce back rapidly. After Randy Gardner stayed awake for 264 hours and 12 minutes, he fell asleep and woke up a little under 15 hours later. The second night he slept 8 hours and his sleep cycle was nearly back to normal. More recent, well-controlled studies also lead to the conclusion that people can recover relatively rapidly from sleep deprivation (Rosa, Bonnet, & Warm, 1983).

Although we have discussed some of the effects of sleep deprivation over a single, extended period of time, a more common situation is a restriction on the number of hours a person can sleep each night (e.g., if there is a baby in the house). Many studies have been conducted on the effects of sleep restriction. If people are permitted to sleep only 2 to 5 hours nightly and not at all during the day, their performance deteriorates over time on many tasks (Carskadon & Roth, 1991; Webb, 1975). Because REM sleep occurs in the latter part of the sleep cycle, such subjects at first lose a good deal of their REM sleep. Later in the experiment, however, they experience more REM sleep than

In the movie "They Shoot Horses, Don't They?" participants in a dance contest kept going for days without sleep.

normal in the first hours of sleep, but this compensation takes a week to develop in some cases.

How does sleep restriction affect normal people? The most common effects are extreme weariness, lapses in attention, hand tremors, irritability, and the hatband illusion (a feeling of pressure around the head). People also report being more depressed, less energetic, and less friendly; very rarely will a person report hallucinations and disordered thought. Performance can also be affected. It is often assumed that complex tasks will suffer the most during loss of sleep, but most studies have demonstrated that simple tasks calling for sustained attention are impaired the earliest and most profoundly. Indeed, many researchers conclude that attentional deficits lead to most of the problems on performance. And since most cognitive or perceptual tasks require attention to some extent, they may all eventually show impairment under sleep deprivation (Dinges & Kribbs, 1991).

How Much Sleep Do We Need? As mentioned at the outset, the average amount of daily sleep varies over a person's life span from over 16 hours a day for newborns to about 6 hours for older people. Most college students sleep 7 to 8 hours. Moreover, sleep requirements vary considerably among individuals. Although surveys show that 90 percent of Americans sleep between 6 and 9 hours each night, there are some people who require less than 6 and others who require more than 9. Sleep researchers have documented several cases in which people required as little as 3 hours of sleep to maintain normal functioning (Borbely, 1986; Thorpy & Yager, 1991). The reasons for these large differences are not known.

To determine your own sleep requirements, try sleeping on an 8-hour schedule for one week. If you do not feel alert and well rested, increase the time you sleep by half an hour each week until you do. If eight hours of sleep leave you alert and well rested, reduce your sleeping time by half an hour each week until you reach a point at which you no longer feel rested and alert after a night's sleep. This method should give you a reasonable idea as to what your personal sleep requirements are at this point in your life (Coleman, 1986).

SLEEP DISORDERS

Several disorders of sleep have been identified. Some involve the inability to sleep, another is suddenly falling asleep at inapproiate times, and yet others involve talking or walking during sleep.

Insomnia. Most people cherish their hours of slumber, but a sizable segment of the population dreads the night because of sleeplessness. When asked, "Do you often have trouble falling asleep and staying asleep?" some 14 percent of those questioned answer yes. Another 30 percent say sometimes. Sales of over-the-counter and prescription drugs for people who experience sleeplessness total millions of dollars yearly and indicate the prevalence of the most common sleep disorder: **insomnia.**

Insomnia actually includes many types of sleep disturbances. The most frequent difficulty is in falling asleep, but some people go to sleep quickly and wake a number of times during the night. Others complain of sleeping lightly, which usually means they do a lot of stage 1 sleep and less than normal stage 4 sleep.

Situational insomnia has a sudden onset and seems to be due to emotional stress, such as a death in the family, divorce, or job loss. The crisis will pass, and with it the insomnia. Physicians often prescribe sedatives during such emergencies.

In *benign insomnia,* people complain of poor sleep or lack of sleep when in fact they sleep within the normal range. This occurs most often when people try to match their sleep to some imagined standard. Some people believe that they sleep too little, others too much. The best therapy is reassurance that they are sleeping normally. Some therapists recommend that patients keep a "sleep diary" to record the amount of sleep they get each night, and this in itself can often provide reassurance.

Arrhythmic insomnia results from a disruption in the normal cycle of daily life. It may be caused by an altered work schedule, such as the "graveyard shift" (midnight to 8 A.M.) in factories and other round-the-clock operations, or by jet travel and the resulting jet lag. The environmental cues that signal sleep are disrupted, so sufferers do not feel sleepy when it is "time to go to sleep." On a short-term basis, the only palliative lies in sedatives. For long-term situations, where the individual takes a job demanding night work, the best solution is to establish a regular routine and time for sleep; the body may eventually fall into a new sleep rhythm, although the adjustment may never be complete (Thorpy & Yager, 1991).

A final type of insomnia is *drug-related insomnia.* The regular use of most *psychoactive drugs* (chemicals that affect the central nervous system and produce changes in mood) results in sleep disorders. While sedatives and barbiturates may make it easier to sleep, they probably lower the quality of sleep because they suppress REM sleep. Many people who use barbiturates to induce sleep become addicted to them, and tolerance to the drug may develop, forcing them to take increasing amounts for the same sleep-inducing effects.

Sleep Apnea. Less common than insomnia is the disorder known as *sleep apnea* (Guilleminault & Dement, 1978; Thorpy & Yager, 1991), characterized by difficulty breathing or an actual inability to breathe while asleep (apnea means "cessation of breathing"). Most sufferers complain of sleeping too much and of being tired all day. They are typically unaware that they may wake themselves some 500 times during the night to breathe or that they are unable to breathe and sleep at the same time. Some researchers believe that apnea may be related to the mysterious crib death syndrome among infants. In adults, apnea is associated with being overweight and with snoring. Therapies may include such simple steps as having patients change their sleep positions (one taped a tennis ball to his back to force himself to sleep on his side), but in other cases, drug therapies or even surgery (to remove obstructions in the throat that hinder breathing) may be necessary (Ridgway, 1989).

Narcolepsy. Another serious sleep disorder is *narcolepsy,* which involves irresistible attacks of sleepiness during the day at inappropriate times; the narcoleptic may doze off when driving a car or even while making love. EEG recordings show that narcoleptics go directly from being wide awake to REM sleep, skipping the other sleep stages. This explains the terrifying hallucinations that sometimes occur at the onset of narcoleptic attacks; they are probably the dreams associated with the beginning of REM sleep.

The cause of narcolepsy is unknown, but it may be genetic in origin; it tends to run in families, and researchers have identified a specific genetic marker that is common to over 90 percent of narcoleptics. The disorder usually occurs between 10 and 20 years of age. Some drugs reduce the frequency of attacks, but there is no known cure (Dement, 1976; Neylan & Reynolds, 1991).

Sleeptalking, Sleepwalking, and Night Terrors.   Three other sleep disorders—*sleeptalking, sleepwalking,* and *night terrors*—are poorly understood (Murray, 1991). You might think that they are associated with vivid dreams, but this is not the case. All three disorders occur when people are in stage 4 sleep, and all occur more frequently in children than in adults. In sleepwalking and sleeptalking, a person is vaguely conscious of the outside world. A sleepwalker can sometimes navigate through a room crowded with furniture, and sleeptalkers sometimes respond to questions and commands. Neither condition seems harmful, although one should try to arrange the house of a sleepwalker so that the person avoids injury. Awakening sleepwalkers is not harmful, contrary to legend, but they will usually be quite confused when wakened. Night terrors occur in children, who awaken with terrified screams. They usually do not report that they are dreaming at the onset of the terrors, nor do the terrors occur during REM sleep, although regular nightmares or "bad dreams" do occur during REM sleep. Night terrors seem to do no permanent harm and may not even be remembered in the morning.

WHY DO WE DREAM?

Dreams have fascinated humans since the dawn of recorded history and probably long before. They have been used to foretell the future and to help make decisions. At the turn of the century, dreams were used in Freudian psychoanalysis to chart the hidden workings of the unconscious mind. Dreams may even have led to the belief in life after death. Primitive people, dreaming of their dead relatives and friends, may have believed that their loved ones still existed in this strange netherworld. Of the roughly 24 years that the average person will have slept by age 72, 5 or 6 years will have been devoted to dreaming.

Dreams have always puzzled people and have been a common theme in art and literature.

Freud's Interpretation of Dreams.   Modern dream analysis dates from the publication of Sigmund Freud's monumental work *The Interpretation of Dreams* (1900/1938). For most people, dreams seem bizarre, nonsensical, or meaningless. Freud, however, believed that "the interpretation of dreams is the royal road to a knowledge of the unconscious activities of the mind" (p. 540). In his view, dreams are an expression of the repressed wishes of the individual, symbolizing ideas that provoke extreme anxiety in conscious thought. Because they cause so much distress, even in dreams these ideas must be disguised. When someone reports a dream, its true meaning is not immediately apparent but requires interpretation. Freud called a person's report of a dream its *manifest content;* it is what a person consciously remembers about the dream and it is subject to distortion. The true meaning of the dream is expressed in its *latent content,* which can be determined only by careful analysis of the symbolism that disguises the true meaning. The latent content includes the individual's repressed wishes, which the dream both expresses and disguises in its symbols.

Freud's interpretation of the latent content of dreams revolved around two topics: sex and aggression. He believed that certain symbols were regularly used in dreams to stand for threatening thoughts and that the appropriate interpretation of dreams depends on the recognition of these symbols and their meaning. Freud was quite creative in his interpretation of symbols, and some of his interpretations might be called far-fetched. Here are a few excerpts from his discussion on symbols in dreams:

> The number of things which are represented symbolically in dreams is not great. . . .
> Parents appear in dreams as emperor and empress, king and queen, or other exalted per-

sonages. . . . Children and brothers and sisters are less tenderly treated, being symbolized as little animals or vermin. Birth is almost invariably represented by some reference to water. . . . An overwhelming majority of symbols in dreams are sexual symbols. . . . The male genital organ is symbolically represented in dreams in many different ways, . . . primarily by objects that resemble it in form, being long and upstanding, such as sticks, umbrellas, poles, trees and the like; also by objects which, like the thing symbolized, have the property of penetrating, and consequently of injuring the body,—that is to say, pointed weapons of all sorts: knives, daggers, lances, sabres. . . .

The female genitalia are symbolically represented by all such objects as share with them the property of enclosing a space or are capable of acting as receptacles: such as pits, hollows and caves, and also jars and bottles, and boxes of all sorts and sizes. . . . From the animal world, snails and mussels at any rate must be cited as unmistakable female symbols; . . . amongst buildings, churches and chapels are symbols of a woman. You see that all these symbols are not equally easy to understand. . . .

Gratification derived from a person's own genitals is indicated by any kind of play, including playing the piano. The symbolic representation of onanism [masturbation] by sliding or gliding and also by pulling of a branch is very typical…Special representations of sexual intercourse are less frequent in dreams than we should expect after all this, but we may mention in this connection rhythmical activities such as dancing, riding and climbing, and also experiencing some violence, e.g. being run over. (Freud, 1924/1952, pp. 161–164)

It is difficult to know what to make of Freud's theory of dream interpretation. His is a rich and creative system, but Freud did not state the theory in a way that allows for scientific scrutiny. After reading Freud, William James wrote to a friend in 1909, "I can make nothing in my own case with his dream theories and obviously 'symbolism' is a most dangerous method." Many others agreed then and today. Consequently, Freud's treatment of dreams is primarily of historical interest to many psychologists. Modern researchers have turned to other means to find out about dreams, mostly through studying the physiology and psychology of REM sleep.

Modern Theories of Dreaming. One basic question to be answered about dreams is whether there is a physiological need for REM sleep, the dream state. Is REM sleep necessary? One way to find out is to deprive people of REM sleep. William Dement (1960) performed one of the earliest such experiments. For five nights, he allowed experimental subjects 6 hours of sleep while monitoring their EEGs and rapid eye movements to determine when the subjects were dreaming; he woke them at the first signs of REM sleep. On recovery nights at the end of the treatment, subjects were allowed normal sleep. These same subjects were also tested in a control condition in which they were awakened an equal number of times over five nights, but always during non-REM sleep.

The findings from the experiment were dramatic. People deprived of REM sleep attempted to enter the REM state with increasing frequency over the five-night period. It was necessary to waken them about twice as many times on the fifth night as on the first. The same was not true in the control condition. Apparently, the REM-deprived subjects were trying to catch up on REM sleep to satisfy a need. In addition, they complained of more psychological discomfort when deprived of REM sleep. As a group they seemed more anxious, and one even quit the experiment. On recovery nights, when allowed to sleep through, subjects deprived of REM sleep spent about 50 percent more time in REM sleep than is normal. This increased REM sleep on recovery nights is called **REM rebound.**

The possibility that REM sleep is necessary for a person's physical and psychological well-being is interesting. Such a finding might support Freud's idea that dreams serve as a safety valve for repressed desires, but this interesting speculation seems to be contradicted by further research. A review of some 40 studies on REM deprivation revealed no systematic ill effects in the deprived subjects (Webb, 1975). These studies do confirm the increasing tendency for people who are REM-deprived to enter REM sleep as well as to experience the REM rebound phenomenon on later nights. There is no clear-cut evidence, however, of psychological disturbance produced by REM deprivation. Some studies have even shown that REM deprivation actually helps relieve depression in some people (Horne, 1991; Vogel, 1975).

Another theory of dreaming, put forward by J. Allan Hobson and Robert W. McCarley (1977), has attracted considerable attention and generated some controversy. Their hypothesis is basically a physiological explanation of REM sleep in which dreaming itself is considered of little importance. The Hobson and McCarley **activation-synthesis hypothesis** argues that all the physiological changes observed in REM sleep (e.g., temporary paralysis as motor control of the muscles is shut off; increased heart rate and respiration; erections in males and an increase in vaginal blood flow in females) result from activation of brain cells in a part of the brain stem called the pons, which is important in the control of sleep and wakefulness. Support for this idea comes from studies in which the pons of a cat is supplied with the chemical neurotransmitter believed to initiate REM sleep. With its brain thus activated, all the symptoms of REM sleep appear, even though the cat is wide awake. This shows that the symptoms of REM sleep are simply a consequence of physiological activation from the brain stem.

What do dreams represent? According to Hobson and McCarley, dreams are the attempts of the higher centers in the brain to interpret or synthesize the random and conflicting signals that are passed along from the lower brain centers. Dreams are often bizarre because the signals from which they are constructed are basically random. This would also explain why dream sequences shift rapidly from one scene to another in disjointed ways. Edwin Kiester (1984) writes that Hobson and McCarley believe that "dreams are nothing more than the thinking brain's valiant efforts to weave a coherent plot out of disparate and contradictory signals from the lower brain centers during sleep" (p. 77). Although Hobson and McCarley do not deny that dreams are related to daily experiences and concerns, everyday matters are probably used only to structure the random signals and are not the prime reason for dreaming (Hobson, 1988).

Why do we dream or enter the REM state? Certainly some important function of REM sleep seems likely, since all mammals sleep and show REM sleep. It has been estimated from babies born prematurely that fetuses about 26 weeks after conception experience almost constant REM sleep. Newborn humans spend about 8 hours a day in REM sleep, with the amount needed dropping off with age, as shown in Figure 5.17. Because of the great amount of REM sleep needed early in life, it has been suggested that this type of sleep may be needed for the brain to develop.

A phenomenon that promises to tell us more about REM sleep and dreaming is **lucid dreaming**—the experience of dreaming and being fully aware that you are dreaming. This kind of dreaming is relatively rare, but most people report at least one episode during their lives (LaBerge, 1990). In a typical study, the experimenters monitor a person's EEG reading during sleep to verify that the subject is in REM sleep. During a period of REM sleep, if the person is experiencing a lucid dream, he or she will give a prearranged signal to the experimenters (a clenched fist or a particular movement of the eyes). Thus, there is physiological evidence that the subject is in REM sleep, and the subject simultaneously signals awareness of the dream.

FIGURE 5.17
Changes in REM Sleep Over the Life Span

The average number of hours spent awake, in REM sleep, and in non–REM sleep are shown over the course of a lifetime. The relative proportion of REM to non-REM sleep changes dramatically across the lifespan. The estimates of sleep prior to birth are educated guesses from babies born prematurely. However, the best guess is that 26 weeks after conception, life is completely devoted to REM sleep. After this period, the proportion of time a person spends in REM (or dreaming) sleep drops steadily until death.

SOURCE: Scientific American Library, a division of HPHLP, distributed by W. H. Freeman & Co.; 41 Madison Avenue; New York, NY 10010 From A. J. Hobson (1989) *Sleep.* New York: Scientific American Library. Figure appears on page 72.

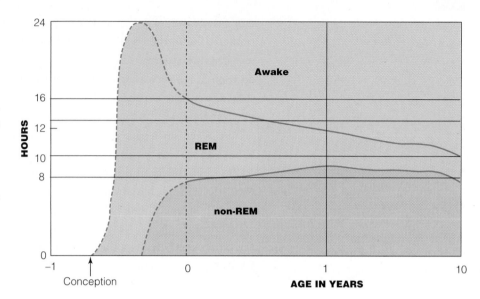

Researchers of lucid dreams take considerable precautions to ensure that their subjects are not "faking" the experience (LaBerge, 1990). The lucid dreamer is aware only of the dream world and is unable to perceive any sensory information from the real world (such as a clock ticking or the feeling of the bedsheets) even when great effort is made. Another aspect of lucid dreaming is that the content of the dreams can often be consciously controlled. For instance, the dreamer can often remember to perform certain actions during a dream. Lucid dreaming challenges the traditional idea that sleep and dreaming necessarily require a loss of normal consciousness. It has only just begun to be studied, however, and more research must be conducted before we make any radical changes in the way we think about sleep and dreaming.

Hypnosis

About 200 years ago, a Frenchman named Anton Mesmer investigated a curious state of consciousness in which people were highly susceptible to suggestion. When Mesmer gave instructions to subjects in this state, they did many things they ordinarily did not do. Mesmer attributed this phenomenon to "animal magnetism," which he considered a mysterious force similar to magnetism in inanimate objects. The technique was originally named *mesmerism*; today it is called *hypnosis*, a term derived from the Greek word for "sleep".

DEFINING HYPNOSIS

Hypnosis has been described as a temporary state of heightened suggestibility in which people will often follow instructions given to them. It is claimed that hypnotized people seem to enter a trancelike state. This definition of hypnosis has been widely accepted in both professional psychology and popular culture, but many psychologists have challenged these claims as well as the very existence of a state called hypnosis. Most of these critics argue that hypnosis is more like a very effective form of communication between the subject and the hypnotist, with the hypnotist using his or her position as an authority figure to exert a strong influence on the behavior of the person being hypnotized (Baker, 1990).

Long controversial within the field of psychology, hypnosis is being intensively investigated today. Some experimental evidence shows that many claims concerning

Mesmer believed that the state of heightened suggestibility now called hypnosis was due to animal magnetism, a force operating between people as magnetism does between some metal objects.

In this painting, Anton Mesmer stands at the back of the group of people. Mesmer was a scientist who believed that illness was caused by an imbalance of magnetic fluids. He is holding a wand, perhaps signifying the skepticism aroused in the scientific community by his early methods of hypnosis.

hypnosis over the years are true. For example, in the years before anesthetic drugs, hypnosis was used to block pain for surgical procedures. Although skeptics criticized the notion that pain from major surgery could be blunted by such means, recent studies show that hypnosis can indeed affect the perception (or reporting) of pain. On the other hand, some claims for hypnosis have not been supported in controlled studies. For example, it is often claimed that people can recollect seemingly forgotten experiences and provide detailed information about them under hypnosis. (See "Controversy: Does Hypnosis Improve Memory Retrieval?")

What exactly is hypnosis? The state is difficult to define precisely, and the means of inducing hypnosis are varied. Typically a hypnotist induces the hypnotic state by asking the subject to fix his or her attention on some object or mental image and suggesting that the subject is feeling relaxed and sleepy. However, hypnotists try to prevent subjects from actually falling asleep, since the full attention of the subject needs to be focused on the suggestions and directions given by the hypnotist. Although most subjects respond to the hypnotist's direction, people cannot be hypnotized against their will and cannot be made to perform antisocial or self-destructive acts while hypnotized. There are few regulations in most states about who may call themselves hypnotists or hypnotic therapists. Before submitting to hypnosis, you should inspect the hypnotist's credentials. Under guidance of an inexperienced hypnotist, the procedure may inadvertently provoke anxiety or stress.

WHO CAN BE HYPNOTIZED?

Hypnosis does not work on everyone. Some 5 to 10 percent of the population are unresponsive to its effects, while about 15 percent are very hypnotizable. Hypnotizability is often measured on a scale consisting of various suggestions, and subjects are rated according to the number of suggestions to which they respond. For example, a subject may be told to hold out an arm for a long time, followed by the suggestion that the arm is growing heavy. If the arm drops noticeably after the suggestion, the subject will have passed that item on the hypnotizability scale. People who follow many of the suggestions on the scale are considered very hypnotizable. They readily respond to hypnotic induction, and their behavior is easily influenced while they are under hypnosis. In fact, Hilgard (1975) has suggested that the response obtained under hypnosis depends more on a person's hypnotizability than on the specific techniques used by the hypnotist.

CONTROVERSY
DOES HYPNOSIS IMPROVE MEMORY RETRIEVAL?

Hypnosis is being used in some police departments (particularly in Los Angeles) as an aid in improving the memory of eyewitnesses to crimes. Sometimes a witness who has been repeatedly questioned may, when interrogated again under hypnosis, remember a critical fact that helps solve the crime (Reiser & Nielson, 1980)

One of the most dramatic instances of the use of hypnosis to refresh the memory of a witness occurred in a kidnapping case in Chowchilla, California (Kroger & Douce, 1979). Near this small town, 26 schoolchildren and their bus driver were ordered from their bus at gunpoint, crowded into vans, and taken to a remote rock quarry, where they were barricaded inside a large cavern. The bus driver and two of the older boys were able to dig their way out and contact police to be rescued. The bus driver's memory was rather hazy when he was questioned later for details that might aid in the capture of the kidnappers. He had tried to memorize the license plate numbers of the kidnappers' vans but could not recall them. He was hypnotized and given the suggestion that he should imagine himself sitting in his favorite chair, watching the events unfold as if on television. Suddenly he recalled two numbers, one of which proved to be close to the license plate of one of the vans (only a single digit was missing). The kidnappers were caught and convicted of the crime.

The usual explanation for such dramatic recoveries is that the brain con-

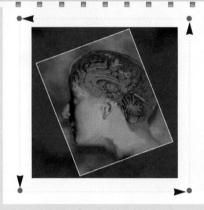

tains faithful records of experience that can be "replayed" with accuracy under the right conditions. However, although this is an appealing notion, it is contra-

dicted by considerable evidence (described in Chapter 7). Often, memory can be quite poor and prone to error, even when people are confident that their recall is accurate. In addition, many researchers have failed to find experimental evidence that hypnosis can be used to improve memory under laboratory conditions (Erdelyi, 1994). Such studies typically find that hypnotized people produce many inaccurate memories that they judge to be authentic. Anecdotal reports like the Chowchilla case are often not convincing, because it is not usually possible (as it was in this case) to verify the remembered details. Orne (1979) reported that many license plate num-

Sometimes police hypnotize witnesses to crimes to try to help them remember more details, but most experts do not believe that hypnosis is effective in aiding memory.

The measuring scales for hypnotizability are quite reliable; when subjects are retested, the scores are usually in good agreement with earlier tests (Bowers, 1983). According to recent evidence, susceptibility to hypnosis remains a relatively stable trait over a 25-year period (Piccione, Hilgard, & Zimbardo, 1989). Surprisingly, hypnotizability is not highly correlated with other personality traits, although people who score high show an ability to control bodily functions, such as sleeping and napping, better than others (Evans, 1977).

Most people who are easily hypnotized are susceptible to *posthypnotic suggestion*, a direction given by the hypnotist that impels the subject to certain behavior after a return to consciousness. Under hypnosis, subjects may be told to tap their feet three times after emerging from their trance. When they do, they are likely to explain, "My

bers that have been recalled under hypnosis belong to cars that couldn't possibly have been involved in the crime. In addition, these anecdotal studies do not use an unhypnotized control group. It may that the same feat could be displayed by nonhypnotized subjects who are strongly motivated by task instructions similar to those given under hypnosis.

Marilyn C. Smith (1983) reviewed the experimental evidence concerning effects of hypnosis on remembering and concluded that there is little or no positive effect when hypnotized subjects are compared to proper controls. Some of the studies that Smith reviewed were conducted under artificial, laboratory conditions, but the same results occurred even in studies using a more natural situation (Malpass & Devine, 1980). Although some experiments have shown hypnosis to be effective in increasing recall, often the improvement is accompanied by a large number of errors (Dywan & Bowers, 1983; Orne, Soskis, Dinges, & Orne, 1984). Thus hypnosis may not have truly improved memory but simply made people more willing to report whatever came to mind or to guess more wildly.

Other studies have shown that people under hypnosis are more confident in their judgments that what they recall is accurate, even when they are wrong (Nogrady, McConkey, & Perry, 1985; Sheehan, 1988). This is especially true for highly hypnotizable people. In addition, information about a prior event suggested to people while they are under hypnosis will sometimes later be recalled as a true fact (Baker, 1990; Laurence & Perry 1983). Because of these problems, many states and

CONTROVERSY

Canadian provinces have passed laws stating that witnesses to crimes who have undergone hypnosis cannot testify in courts of law.

An ingenious study by Ralph E. Geiselman, Ronald P. Fisher, and their colleagues (1985) combined the controlled procedures of the laboratory with important facets of police interrogation. The subjects were undergraduate students who viewed films of violent crimes and were interviewed about the crimes two days later by police officers who had training in interrogation. The police interviewed students under one of three conditions to which they were randomly assigned. In the standard interview, the police questioned the subjects about the crime as detectives are taught to do, by first asking the "witnesses" to report as much as possible about the crime and then following up with specific questions. In the hypnosis interview, the police asked subjects to recall as much as possible and then provided a hypnotic induction. Then the "witnesses" were again asked to report the crime in their own words before the police officer followed up with specific techniques for improving memory. A third condition was called the *cognitive interview* and was based on the researchers' expert knowledge derived from their study of memory (to be discussed in Chapter 7). The police in this condition asked the subjects to describe the crime in

their own words and then tried various techniques to produce additional memories. The recall strategies included having the subjects recall both the external (environmental) context and the internal (mental) context (their thoughts and reactions) as an aid in jogging their memory. The subjects were also asked to recall the events in both forward and backward order, to try to perceive and remember the scene from others' (e.g., the bank robbers') perspectives, and to recall everything possible, even though it might seem irrelevant.

The researchers found that witnesses in the hypnotic interview condition recalled more correct facts than did those in the standard police interview condition, without increasing the number of errors. However, witnesses in the cognitive interview condition recalled the same amount of information and just as accurately as those under hypnosis. After analyzing transcripts of the interviews, the researchers concluded that the police officers in the hypnotic interviews had in fact often used memory-enhancing techniques resembling those used in the cognitive interview. Thus, the improved performance in the hypnotic interview may not have been caused by hypnosis itself, but rather by effective memory retrieval techniques (Geiselman, 1988). Because hypnosis has been shown to produce ill effects on later memory (overconfidence and introduction of false information), the cognitive interview may be a preferable strategy for questioning witnesses to a crime. It produces similar levels of recall, it is easier to teach to investigators, and the testimony is admissible in court.

foot went to sleep." They do not recall the instruction. Although it is a popular theme of television programs, there is no evidence that posthypnotic suggestion can be used to make people commit crimes (Coe, 1977).

Another interesting phenomenon is that of *posthypnotic amnesia*, in which the suggestion is made to the hypnotized subject that he or she will not remember the events of the hypnosis session until given a signal later. In a test given after the hypnosis is lifted, people do show poor recall for the material. On a second test following the signal, however, recall improves. This phenomenon has occurred in many experiments, but the interpretation is still unclear (Kihlstrom, 1984; Spanos & Radtke, 1982). Some researchers feel that the initial difficulty in recall is due to a temporary disrup-

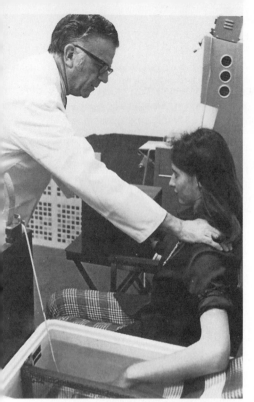

Ernest Hilgard is shown here measuring a hypnotized subject's pain reaction to having her hand placed in ice water. Hilgard discovered that often people will not report pain when asked directly but will indicate pain by other means such as automatic writing. Hilgard argues that there are different levels or types of awareness that can be separated, or dissociated, from one another. Pain reduction in hypnosis may operate by such a dissociation of a conscious level of awareness from others. The pain is felt but not consciously reported, according to Hilgard.

tion of the normal memory retrieval processes, especially since the "forgotten" information has been shown to influence performance on recognition tests and other cognitive tasks (Evans, 1988).

USE OF HYPNOSIS IN PAIN RELIEF

As mentioned previously, one of the most fascinating facets of hypnotic suggestion is in suppressing the experience of pain (Evans, 1990). In one remarkable study by Stern and his colleagues (1977), hypnosis was shown to be more effective than aspirin, Valium, acupuncture, or even morphine in relieving pain. The pain was caused by the administration of intense cold, a standard laboratory technique used in hypnosis studies. In Stern's study, highly hypnotizable subjects showed greater pain relief than others. Similarly, Hilgard and LeBaron (1984) found that hypnosis relieved the pain of highly hypnotizable children who were undergoing treatment for bone marrow cancer.

Other researchers have confirmed the finding that hypnosis can produce greater pain reduction in highly hypnotizable people, than in control subjects who are given the same suggestions while in a normal waking state (Spanos, Perlini, & Robertson, 1989). The exact mechanism by which hypnosis reduces pain is unknown. Some have suggested that the relaxation component of hypnosis is essential to its pain-relieving abilities. To test this hypothesis, Miller, Barabasz, and Barabasz (1991) compared pain reduction in two types of hypnosis, one involving substantial relaxation and the other not. They found substantial pain reduction with both kinds of hypnosis, but no difference between the two, implying that relaxation is not essential to hypnotic pain reduction.

Some researchers have suggested that hypnotic pain reduction reflects a *dissociation*, in which the pain is actually registered in one cognitive system but is blocked from conscious awareness. Hilgard (1977) has developed a procedure that allows relatively direct observation of dissociation using automatic writing. In this procedure, hypnotized people write without apparent knowledge of what they are writing. For example, if hypnotized subjects are instructed to place one hand into a bucket of ice water, they will say that they feel a little pain, but their automatic writing will describe great pain. It is as though their consciousness has been split (or dissociated) under hypnosis. In other words, subjects report feeling little pain, but when another level of consciousness is tapped through automatic writing, the "hidden observer" (to use Hilgard's term) reports pain. At some level the pain may be registered, but it seems blocked from conscious experience (Hilgard, 1986). These results have been replicated by others, but the interpretation in terms of a hidden observer divorced from conscious awareness is not universally accepted (Baker, 1990; Spanos, 1983).

The effects of hypnosis will continue to be investigated for such pain-relieving effects, as well as for other possible uses. In fact, hypnosis is showing some promise as a tool to facilitate psychotherapy. It is most often used by clinical psychologists for the relief of stress, anxiety, phobias, insomnia, and sexual impotence, and it can help in the treatment of alcoholism, smoking, and drug abuse. Finally, although its effectiveness has been disputed, hypnosis has also been widely used as a method to improve memory, a technique that we considered in the preceding Controversy section.

Psychoactive Drugs

Drugs have been used for thousands of years to produce altered states of consciousness, and there is no indication that their popularity is declining (Jarvik, 1990). Drugs that are taken to affect a person's psychological state are called *psychoactive drugs*. In Chapter 15 we consider drugs prescribed for illnesses, such as depression. In this section we describe briefly ones people choose to take, legally or illegally. The most common drugs in North America are caffeine (found in tea, coffee, and some soft drinks), nicotine (found in cigarettes and chewing tobacco), and alcohol, all of which can be purchased legally. Illegal drugs include hallucinogens (such as LSD and mescaline), the opiate narcotics (heroin, opium, and morphine), certain stimulants of the central nervous system (such as amphetamines and cocaine), and barbiturates (such as Librium and quaaludes).

We will now describe the action of these drugs briefly, with reference to their effects on conscious experience. Table 5.1 contains basic information about many controlled drugs.

TABLE 5.1
Commonly Abused Substances and Their Effects

| CLASSIFICATION | DRUGS | PSYCHOLOGICAL EFFECTS | DURATION OF EFFECTS (IN HOURS) | DEPENDENCE POTENTIAL | | TOLERANCE |
				PHYSICAL	PSYCHOLOGICAL	
Depressants (Sedatives)	Alcohol (ethanol)	Relaxation, reduced inhibitions	3 to 6	High	High	Yes
	Barbiturates (e.g. Amytal, Seconal)	Relaxation, disorientation, sleep	1 to 16	High	High	Yes
	Mild tranquilizers (e.g. Librium, Valium)	Reduced anxiety, relaxation, sedation	4 to 8	Moderate	Moderate	Yes
Opiates (Narcotics)	Codeine	Lack of feeling in the body, euphoria, drowsiness, nausea	3 to 6	Moderate	Moderate	Yes
	Heroin			High	High	Yes
	Opium			High	High	Yes
	Morphine			High	High	Yes
Stimulants	Amphetamines (e.g., Benzedrine, Dexedrine)	Increased alertness, excitation, decreased fatigue	2 to 4	Possible	High	Yes
	Caffeine (coffee, cola, tea)	Increased alertness, excitation, decreased fatigue	2 to 4	Possible	Moderate	Yes
	Cocaine	Euphoria, excitation, alertness, decreased fatigue	2 to 3	Possible	High	Yes
	Nicotine	Increased alertness	1 to 2	Possible	High	Yes
Hallucinogens	Lysergic acid diethylamide (LSD) Mescaline, Psilocybin MDA	Distortions, illusions, hallucinations, time disorientation	1 to 8	None	Unknown	Yes
Cannabis	Marijuana, Hashish	Euphoria, relaxed inhibitions, increased appetite, increased sensory sensitivity, disorientation	2 to 4	Unknown	Moderate	Yes

DEPRESSANTS

Several drugs, legal and illegal, depress activity in the central nervous system. We consider alcohol, opiates, and narcoties.

Alcohol. Alcohol is the most popular of the **depressants,** drugs that generally reduce activity in the central nervous system. In small amounts, depressants can act as stimulants by producing relaxation and loosening inhibitions, but in larger quantities they severely impair sensory functions and coordination. Concentrations of 0.10 to 0.15 percent of alcohol in the blood, which can result from drinking as few as three 12-ounce beers, can cause such impairment. At 0.20 percent, a person is severely impaired, and at levels of 0.40 percent, death can occur (see Table 5.2). Many students do not realize how dangerous alcohol is. In 1987, a Yale sophomore by the name of Ted McGuire went to a party with his friends, and apparently drank too much alcohol. He was found dead in his room the next morning (see the Case Study on page 209). Ted McGuire was not an alcoholic—normally not even a heavy drinker—and he had not mixed alcohol with any other drugs. He had simply consumed enough alcohol to induce alcohol poisoning. Therefore, although alcohol is a legal drug, it is still dangerous.

Small amounts of alcohol often produce a pleasurable, relaxed state of consciousness, but larger amounts may cause many people to become belligerent and angry as well as disoriented and confused (Bushman & Cooper, 1990). Alcohol also interferes

TABLE 5.2
Blood Alcohol Levels and Behavior

The concentration of alcohol in the blood depends on a person's sex and weight. Large people have more bodily fluid than small people, and men have more fluid than women of the same weight (because women have a greater amount of fat). Thus, four cans of beer or four glasses of wine consumed during a one-hour period will produce a blood alcohol concentration of .18 in a 100-pound female, .15 in a 100-pound male, .12 in a 150-pound woman, and .10 in a 150-pound man (Ray,1978). These concentrations would produce legal intoxication in most states, so people would be subject to arrest for driving a car. Even small amounts of alcohol can produce relatively grave impairments in judgement and reactions. Great amounts can kill a person.

BLOOD ALCOHOL CONCENTRATION (PERCENTAGE)	BEHAVIORAL EFFECTS
0.05	Reduced alertness, often pleasurable feeling, release of inhibitions, impaired judgment
0.10	Slowed reaction times, impaired motor function, less caution; legal intoxication in many states
0.15	Large increases in reaction times
0.20	Marked depression in sensory and motor capability; decidedly intoxicated
0.25	Severe motor problems, such as staggering; sensory perceptions greatly impaired
0.30	Stuporous but conscious; no comprehension of the world around them
0.35	Surgical anesthesia (passed out); possible death at this point and beyond

SOURCE: Ray, 1983

with memory functions, slows the speed of mental processing, and impairs performance on any complex task (such as driving). Thousands of people are killed every year as a result of drunk drivers. Severe abuse of alcohol may induce hallucinations, which are thought to occur by the action of drugs (and their withdrawal) on the central nervous system (Siegel, 1977). Addicts who are withdrawn from alcohol often suffer *delirium tremens,* popularly known as the D.T.'s. Its most noticeable effect is hand tremors, but the addict also suffers hallucinations, usually visions of terrifying animals such as snakes or nightmarish monsters. The D.T.'s may even be fatal.

CASE STUDY

WHEN ALCOHOL KILLS

Every college student knows that alcohol is bad for performance. We all know that it can slur speech, slow movements, make people unsteady (tipsy) and impair judgment. That is why there are stern admonitions against driving cars or operating other equipment while under the influence of alcohol. But few people realize that alcohol can often have another direct effect: It can kill you.

Ted McGuire was a sophomore at Yale University and an excellent student. One Saturday night he drank too much alcohol with some friends and passed out. His roommates decided to let him sleep it off. But Sunday morning he did not wake up. Ted Mcguire died during the night of alcohol poisoning. His death stunned the Yale community and left his parents and friends grief stricken. How could this happen?

Ted McGuire was not someone who abused alcohol. In fact, he was only a social drinker with a low tolerance for alcohol. He was a model student, having finished in the top two percent of his high school class while being its president. He was a varsity tennis player and co-captain of the basketball team. At Yale he was a pre-medical student, worked in a hospital, and though his studies did not permit him to play varsity athletics, he worked out every day and was in good shape.

So the question remains: How could this happen? How could a bit too much to drink kill a hale and healthy college student? There is no simple answer. Ted made a mistake by drinking too much. His roommates made a mistake by not seeking help. The larger society made a mistake by not drumming home the fact that alcohol is potentially a lethal drug. But you now know this secret and you should use this knowledge to guide your behavior. Don't drink too much. If you see a friend who has drunk too much, to the point of falling down and passing out, seek medical help immediately. Don't wait. Sure, the person might sleep it off—but he or she might die too. After Ted McGuire died at Yale a young woman told the dean of the college, "gee, last Saturday night I passed out, too. But I did not know *that* could happen" (quoted in Gibson, 1987).

Shortly after Ted McGuire's tragic death. Yale sponsored talks to educate the university community on the dangers of alcohol. One speaker was Dr. G. Douglas Talbott, who is a medical doctor and a consultant to the Atlanta Falcons and Atlanta Braves. We end this Case Study by quoting from his remarks to the audience.

"One of the things that bother me tremendously, as I travel throughout the campuses, is that I will ask somebody, 'Are you on drugs?' and they answer 'No. All I do is to use grass and drink beer. I'm not on drugs.'

"My concern is that when we talk about alcohol, we are not looking at the issue that alcohol is a drug...If you take a

Ted McGuire

bottle of wine, or a can of beer, or a bottle of bourbon, and just take off the color and the taste and drip off the water, what do you have? Ether. C_2H_5OH minus water is ether.

"Your brain has no more idea than a pussycat whether you're taking a six-pack of beer, or a glass of vodka...or if you have a mask over your face and you are inhaling ether. Alcohol is a drug.

"Would you fantasize with me? Suppose I told you I had just discovered a new drug C_2H_5OH, ethyl alcohol; that this new drug is a liquid, and it can be used medicinally as an anesthetic agent, as a tranquilizer, as an anticeptic, as a sedative, as a hypnotic; and that it works almost every time on everybody, which it does! Why the discovery of insulin, and of cortisone, and of polio vaccine, all of those things would be dwarfed by the greatest medical discovery of all time—the drug Alcohol.

"And isn't it fascinating, that if this fantasy were true...that if I had just discovered alcohol...this new drug...would be a Class 2 narcotic, by every pharmacological and by every scientific and legal structure we have today, and would require a BNDD number and a triplicate form for prescription."

Dr. Talbott's message is clear: **Alcohol is a dangerous drug.** If you choose to take it, do so in moderation and under safe circumstances. Keep in mind every time that this powerful drug can kill you.

Opiate Narcotics. The *opiate narcotics* constitute another type of depressant. Opium comes from certain types of poppy flowers, and its active ingredients are codeine and morphine (both of which are prescribed by physicians for pain control). Morphine is stronger than codeine, and heroin (which is derived from morphine) is the strongest narcotic of all. Addicts usually sniff or inject heroin, but it can also be eaten or smoked. Using heroin produces intense pleasure, similar to that of an orgasm. Its users develop *drug tolerance* after repeated exposures, and they must take ever-increasing amounts of the drug to achieve the same effect, so addiction often results. Unlike alcoholics, people addicted to opiate narcotics do not lose their sensory and motor functions, but they eventually destroy neural tissue and reduce production of the body's own opiates (the endorphins).

Barbiturates. *Barbiturates* are also depressants and are sometimes prescribed as relaxants for people under stress; they are also prescribed as sleeping pills. Typical effects include lightheadedness, loss of motor coordination, and mild euphoria. Barbiturates depress the central nervous system, and if they are taken with alcohol, the combined effects can cause coma or death. People can develop tolerence to barbiturates within just two weeks of continuous use, and some may become dependent on these drugs. Withdrawal from barbiturates is as severe as with alcohol. Aware of these problems, many physicians today are reluctant to prescribe barbiturates (Thorpy & Yager, 1991).

STIMULANTS

Caffeine and nicotine are the most popular **stimulants,** drugs that generally increase activity in the central nervous system. Stronger stimulants include amphetamines and the very addictive cocaine.

Caffeine. Caffeinated coffee and tea have long been enjoyed for their psychological lift, although they have been banned in some cultures. Carbonated cola drinks contain caffeine, but only about one-third as much as in coffee or tea. Caffeine stimulates all levels of the nervous system; its action on the brain results in a more rapid and clearer flow of thought, relief from drowsiness or fatigue, and greater sustained intellectual effort and association of ideas. Unfortunately, caffeine may also cause adverse effects, including insomnia, restlessness, nervousness, and impaired performance on tasks requiring fine-motor coordination and timing (Millichap, 1993).

Nicotine. The nicotine in tobacco is physiologically addictive, and cigarette smoking is one of the leading causes of disease and death in the United States. Nicotine may have a relaxing or stimulating effect, depending on the circumstances in which it is used and the expectations of the user. Most studies have shown that nicotine increases concentration (attention), mental efficiency (information processing), and the general level of physiological arousal, resulting in a heightened state of awareness that is pleasurable for the nicotine user. The desire to smoke may thus be related to the desire to maintain this heightened state of alertness, and such a motive may override the grave concerns for health that smoking poses (Wesnes & Parrott, 1992).

Amphetamines. *Amphetamines* are stronger stimulants, usually taken in the form of pills with brand names such as Dexedrine and Benzedrine. Popularly, they are known as "speed" or "uppers" because they heighten activity in the central nervous system, increase alertness, reduce boredom and fatigue, and suppress appetite. They were at one time widely prescribed for weight reduction. Used in moderation and only occasionally, these stimulants are not harmful. However, when taken in larger doses or for long periods of time, amphetamines can induce feelings of paranoia. Withdrawal can produce a "crash", a long period of severe depression and fatigue. A dangerous pattern may be established if a person uses sedatives to overcome the effects of the amphetamines and then needs amphetamines to counter the use of the sedatives, as this cycle can be difficult to break.

Crack cocaine is highly addictive and creates severe physical and mental problems.

Cocaine. Cocaine and its derivative, crack, have effects that are quite similar to those of amphetamines, only much more intense. In occasional small doses, these drugs produce alertness, an increased capacity to work or think without fatigue, and an elevation of mood. Users often report feelings of exhilaration, well-being, and self-confidence. In larger doses, brain cells can become overstimulated by the drug, and this may cause them to shut down, sometimes leading to heart or respiratory failure. Novocaine is a synthetic form of cocaine often used as a dental anesthetic because it can shut down neural impulses of pain in this manner, but without cocaine's stimulant effects on the central nervous system. Cocaine is very addictive, and in large doses it can induce paranoid reactions of hostility and suspicion. With prolonged use, hallucinations become common, especially flashing or moving lights ("snow lights") or the feeling that bugs are crawling under the skin ("cocaine bugs") (Flynn, 1991).

HALLUCINOGENS

Hallucinogens take their name from the hallucinations, or alterations of perceptual experience, that they produce. One of the mildest hallucinogenics—and certainly the most common—is marijuana. Other more potent varieties include the psychedelic drugs, which strongly affect visual perception and the experience of time, and some drugs that produce hallucinations but are not classed with the psychedelics. Among these nonpsychedelic hallucinogens is phencyclidine, or "angel dust," which may have dangerous side effects manifested in fits of wild rage.

Marijuana. Marijuana is derived from the leaves and flowers of the hemp plant, *Cannabis sativa*, which has been grown for thousands of years both for its pharmacological value and for the strong fiber of its stem. Smoking is the usual method of ingestion, but it is also often cooked into foods. The resin of the cannabis plant can be concentrated into a potent paste known as hashish, but even in this purified form, it does not seem to have any toxic effects, regardless of dosage. Cannabis smoke is carcinogenic, however, and its tar is more dangerous than that of tobacco smoke. Many people report that the marijuana "high" is similar to fluctuating between a dreaming state and a waking state. Marijuana taken in small quantities produces a mixture of euphoria and sedation in many people and may make listening to music and eating more pleasurable through the subjective intensification of perceptual stimuli. Nevertheless, large doses can lead to severe and frightening hallucinations or acute panic attacks, and even small doses interfere with performance on complex tasks (Golding, 1992).

LSD. The recreational use of psychedelic drugs such as LSD (lysergic acid diethylamide) to alter and "expand" consciousness seems to experience cycles of popularity and disinterest (Lyman & Potter, 1991). Currently, LSD and many of the other psychedelics are experiencing a dramatic increase in popularity. LSD was discovered by Albert Hoffman, who reported his experience on first taking the drug:

> After 40 minutes, I noted the following symptoms in my laboratory journal: slight giddiness, restlessness, difficulty in concentration, visual disturbances, laughing. . . . Later: I lost all count of time, I noticed with dismay that my environment was undergoing progressive changes. My visual field wavered and everything appeared deformed as in a faulty mirror. Space and time became more and more disorganized , and I was overcome by a fear that I was going out of my mind. The worst part of it being that I was clearly aware of my condition. My power of observation was unimpaired. . . . Occasionally, I felt as if I were out of my body. I thought I had died. My ego seemed suspended somewhere in space, from where I saw my dead body lying on the sofa. . . . It was particularly striking how acoustic perceptions, such as the noise of water gushing from a tap or the spoken word, were transformed into optical illusions. I then fell asleep and awakened the next morning somewhat tired but otherwise feeling perfectly well. (As quoted in Ornstein, 1983 p. 167).

Under the influence of LSD, people sometimes experience a dreamy, detached state of consciousness, often described as semireligious, that comes and goes in waves. Attention and cognitive functioning are reduced, which results in a reduction in intellectual and motor tasks (Barber, 1970). Many people also report an altered sense of touch or feelings of heaviness, lightness, or detachment in the body. A few users report hardly any effect, while still fewer experience intense anxiety or panic as the changes in sensation and awareness occur. A small percentage also have unpredictable flashbacks—recurrences of the altered sensations or hallucinations experienced during use that may erupt days, weeks, or even months later.

The drugs described here are often quite harmful, as can be seen from the general effects described in Figure 5.18 and Table 5.1. However, the effects of most drugs are highly variable and seem to depend on the expectations of those who take them. Thus, cognitive factors greatly affect the way a drug acts on us. People often report relief from stress soon after taking a barbiturate, even before the drug itself could possibly work, and it is estimated that up to 50 percent of the subjective "high" from mari-

FIGURE 5.18

Classification of Drugs

All drugs can be classified by the action on the central nervous system: stimulating or depressing. The effects of different drug groups are shown in this chart.

SOURCE: Robert W. Earle.

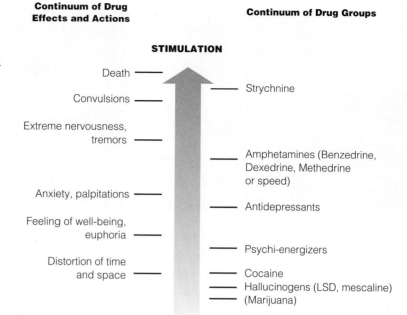

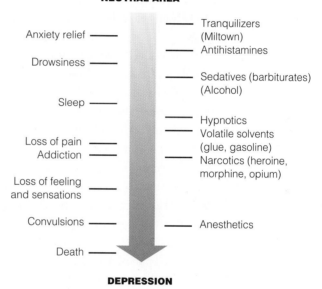

Continuum of Drug Effects and Actions

Continuum of Drug Groups

STIMULATION

| Death |
| Convulsions |
| Extreme nervousness, tremors |
| Anxiety, palpitations |
| Feeling of well-being, euphoria |
| Distortion of time and space |

- Strychnine
- Amphetamines (Benzedrine, Dexedrine, Methedrine or speed)
- Antidepressants
- Psychi-energizers
- Cocaine
- Hallucinogens (LSD, mescaline) (Marijuana)

NEUTRAL AREA

| Anxiety relief |
| Drowsiness |
| Sleep |
| Loss of pain |
| Addiction |
| Loss of feeling and sensations |
| Convulsions |
| Death |

- Tranquilizers (Miltown)
- Antihistamines
- Sedatives (barbiturates) (Alcohol)
- Hypnotics
- Volatile solvents (glue, gasoline)
- Narcotics (heroine, morphine, opium)
- Anesthetics

DEPRESSION

juana results from placebo effects (Golding, 1992). Clearly, drugs affect different people differently. Nevertheless, most of the drugs described here should be regarded as extremely dangerous.

CULTURAL DIFFERENCES IN ALCOHOL USE

The use of drugs that alter mental experience has been prevalent in almost every human culture and society. Various societies have also taken almost every possible attitude toward drugs. Even mild drugs such as caffeine have been banned at times in the past. Today, alcohol is widely available in many cultures, and is even used in religious services. But it is completely prohibited in Arab cultures, where it conflicts with Muslim religious teachings.

Sociologists and anthropologists have studied the use of alcohol in many different societies. For example, W. H. Sangree (1962) studied beer drinking among the Tiriki people of Kenya. Beer plays an integral role in their culture and is used in many cere-

In some countries, even relatively young children are permitted to drink alcohol. In other societies, alcohol is confined to bars and is not a part of daily family life.

monies. When Sangree studied the Tiriki society, he noticed that the women were primarily the workers and "the men were the drones." In the mornings, he observed the women working everywhere, whereas the men rarely appeared until noon. Even when they did appear, their movements were purposeless, and they spent most of the day sitting around beer pots drinking. The elders would resolve local disputes during the day, and the younger males would gather to listen and to drink. Beer drinking was used in virtually all celebrations and festivals including funerals, rituals of initiation, and weddings.

With all the drinking in Tiriki society, perhaps you are conjuring up some image of "drunken primitives." However, this is far from the true picture. Despite the prevalence of beer drinking, alcohol abuse was not a problem in Tiriki society. For one thing, the beer had a very low alcohol content and could not intoxicate a person unless drunk very rapidly in large quantities. In addition, women were rarely permitted to drink at all, and most of the male children were also banned from drinking. Most of the heavy drinking was by the Tiriki elders, who often seemed a bit wobbly to Sangree as he watched them stumble home in the evenings from one of their "community beer drinks." However, Sangree never saw an elder lose control of his actions, reporting that "the web of social attitudes and expectancies around beer drinking evidently are such as to preclude their drinking enough to lose control or express their euphoria in a disruptive or abusive manner" (1962, p. 16). The expectation for drinking among the Tiriki was that a person would be happy, not abusive. Indeed, the local beer was held in an almost religious reverence and was believed to be a way of effectively ridding oneself of the company of witches (believed to plague the tribe).

The tale of beer drinking in Tiriki society demonstrates one of alcohol's remarkable qualities: The effects of the alcohol seem to be as much determined by the expectations of the people using it as by the chemical properties of the substance itself. People who expect to become violent and destructive under alcohol will do so; those who expect to be sexually aroused will also not be disappointed; and those who expect to feel warm euphoria, like the Tiriki, will also have their expectations fulfilled. Moreover, even daily alcohol use need not lead to abuse. As part of the custom and ritual of society, alcohol may be consumed in moderation.

Cross-cultural studies of alcohol demonstrate a great diversity of behavioral outcomes (Marshall, 1979), and we can observe this diversity within American society, too. For example, alcoholism among Jews is extraordinarily rare, but studies in years past have shown that virtually all adult Jewish Americans drink some alcohol each week. On the other hand, Irish American women and children tend to abstain from alcohol completely, and yet alcoholism is a great problem among Irish men. One hypothesis to explain the difference between these groups, living in the same larger society, is the social context of drinking. Because Jewish Americans learn to drink in the home environment, often in the context of religious rituals, they tend to be moderate drinkers. Irish men, on the other hand, typically learn to drink in an atmosphere of barroom conviviality that makes heavy drinking acceptable and the family is not present to provide some check on the amount of alcohol consumed (Heath, 1987).

In many societies, including the United States, the use of alcohol is regarded with "social ambivalence" (Myerson, 1940). On the positive side, alcohol is associated with good times (as portrayed in beer commercials); it is consumed at sporting events, at various ceremonies, and on a great many festive occasions. On the negative side, alcohol causes thousands of deaths per year, numerous health problems, and addiction, and it may lead to the abuse of women and children. Because of these problems, the Eighteenth Amendment—which prohibited the use of alcohol in the United States—was added to the U.S. Constitution in January, 1919. However, Prohibition was deemed a failure. Alcohol use did not stop, but merely went underground and supported a thriving illegal economy. The Twenty-first Amendment repealed prohibition in December, 1935, ending the nation's 15-year experiment prohibiting the use of alcohol.

Cross-cultural studies of alcohol use seem to indicate that when people learn to use alcohol in the context of the family and significant social events, there seems little danger of its abuse. But, when alcohol is relegated to an environment completely separate from the context of family (such as bars), the likelihood of abuse significantly increases.

Reprise: Conscious Awareness and Behavior

The past three chapters, dealing with sensation, perception, and consciousness, have all been broadly concerned with the way information from the outside world is interpreted and used. Humans are usually described as rational beings who collect information from the outside world through their senses and sort it using their higher brain centers to arrive at a plan of action for dealing with their environment. In short, the view is one of bottom-up processing, to return to a distinction made in Chapter 3. Information is continuously processed by lower levels of the nervous system and passed along to higher cognitive centers. Many phenomena and theories discussed in these three chapters reveal that this view, while it seems to fit some cases, is probably wrong. Instead, many factors that people cannot describe exert strong effects on behavior. Because these factors escape conscious description, they are referred to as unconscious. As a review, consider the following phenomena drawn from the previous three chapters:

• In Chapter 3, we described how information from the senses traverses many neural pathways before arriving at the higher cortical centers, where it is translated into conscious experience. In phenomena such as visual agnosia, described at the beginning of Chapter 4, brain damage prevents the relay of information into conscious experience. Also, in the cases of prosopagnosia that began this chapter, the two women could not identify faces verbally but showed a heightened physiological response to them nonetheless.

• In Chapter 4, illusions were described in which the perceiver automatically constructs a percept that does not correspond to the actual scene. The top-down, constructive processes in perception modify the information supplied by the senses in ways of which the perceiver is unaware.

- In the cases of automatic information processing described in this chapter, people respond quickly and unavoidably to information, regardless of their expectations, strategies, or conscious intentions. In some cases, they may even respond to information that is below the threshold of awareness (unconscious or subliminal perception).

- Split-brain patients may be presented with information transmitted to their non-verbal right hemisphere that directs their behavior, but when asked about it, their verbal left hemisphere either cannot explain their actions or constructs a plausible story about them. Again, behavior is guided by a cognitive system divorced from linguistic consciousness.

- Highly hypnotizable subjects, when under hypnosis and guided by appropriate instructions, verbally report that they do not feel pain from a normally unpleasant stimulus. Other responses indicate that the pain is registered at some level. The pain is dissociated from conscious awareness and verbal expression.

- During sleep, we are "unconscious," yet evidence exists that the brain continues to respond differentially to external stimuli. During stage 4 sleep, people still respond on covert measures such as brain waves to the sound of their own name.

As discussed earlier, many metaphors have been used to describe conscious experience—as a place in the mind, for example, or as a stream that runs through the mind. Perhaps it is more appropriate to compare consciousness to a sense organ (Kolers & Roediger, 1984). Not all light or sound energy is detected by the eyes or ears. For example, infrared light cannot be perceived by humans, nor can we hear very high-pitched sounds. Consciousness may be similarly selective. People may be consciously aware of many factors that affect their behavior and thus would be perfectly capable of verbalizing them. Other factors may escape conscious verbal awareness altogether. The influence of unconscious forces does not mean that humans are irrational, as some would argue. Rather, just as the eye is incapable of detecting all electromagnetic radiation, conscious awareness does not extend to all factors that might influence behavior. Consciousness is obviously useful, but like other sensory and cognitive systems, conscious awareness is a system that is selective and fallible.

THEMES IN REVIEW

The study of consciousness is multifaceted, including such diverse topics as attention, hemispheric specialization, sleep and dreams, hypnosis, and the effects of drugs. Four themes of the text are critical for understanding these important topics.

Biological factors come into play in the study of hemispheric specialization. One view is that our conscious experience and memories are the result of our language centers in the left hemisphere essentially "telling a story" about what is happening to us. By this account, factors that may influence our behavior will not become "conscious" if they are not accessible to the left hemisphere processes responsible for producing language. Biological factors are similarly important in sleep and in determining our energy levels during the day. Circadian rhythms determine when we feel tired, but the brain stem also plays a critical role in sleep, and the nightly occurrence of dreaming reveals still other processes that activate the brain, even during sleep.

Cognitive factors are also important in the study of consciousness and attention. By practicing a task, eventually we can devote less conscious attention to it. Our performance becomes much more automatic. Similarly, when we search a visual field for an object, we can use either a controlled search or a much more automatic search in which the desired target pops out from its background. Cognitive factors, such as a person's expectations, have also been shown to play a significant role in determining the effects of a wide variety of drugs.

The ability to select information from the environment through focused attention does not appear to change with development, but is present almost from birth. However, people do show a gradual decline in the information-processing capacity of their attentional systems as they age. Also, development seems to affect the amount of sleep and dreaming that we require. In early life, we spend the majority of our days asleep and dreaming, but both the total hours spent asleep and the amount of time spent dreaming decline with age.

We have also considered sociocultural factors in conscious experience. As noted, alcohol and other drugs have a wide variety of effects, both on different cultures and on the individuals within a culture. Even the pattern of sleep is culturally determined; societies that have a tradition of siestas (such as Spain and Italy) permit people to sleep during the afternoon and, consequently, less at night.

SUMMARY

❶ Consciousness is the current awareness of internal and external stimuli. Its capacity is limited; there is a limit to the number of stimuli of which individuals can be conscious at one time. Preconscious ideas can easily be called into consciousness, while unconscious thoughts cannot be easily retrieved. Nonconscious processes are those of which, in principle, people *cannot* be aware.

❷ People must deal with information overload when more things happen to them than they can attend to. The purpose of selective attention is to find a way to concentrate on one stimulus and ignore others. Broadbent's filter theory maintains that people filter out ignored signals at the level of the senses. Filter theory is an early-selection theory. Experimental evidence has caused others to reject this view; they argue that attention does not affect sensory processes and that information is selected for attention only after it has been processed by the senses. These are called late-selection theories.

❸ Subliminal, or unconscious, perception refers to the behavioral effects of signals too weak to be noticed. Although demonstrations of the phenomenon exist under laboratory conditions, the practical implications (e.g., in advertising) are probably slight.

❹ Search processes involve the ability to distribute attentional resources to locate a desired object. Treisman proposes that a preattentional process can be used in feature searches, where the target differs from distracting objects on only one pronounced feature (looking for a very tall person in a crowd of normal people). When people must search for a complex target involving a conjunction of simple features, a controlled search process is used.

5 Two kinds of information processing can be distinguished: automatic and controlled. Automatic processing occurs rapidly, does not depend on a person's expectations or strategies, and does not require conscious attention or cognitive resources. Controlled processing is the opposite: It is slower, depends on a person's strategy, and uses cognitive resources. As a person practices a new skill, controlled processing gradually gives way to automatic processing, so these processes lie on a continuum.

6 When information is flashed to the right hemisphere and provokes behavior, the split-brain patient may be unable to explain the behavior. This difficulty arises because the verbal centers in the left hemisphere are denied access to the stimulus that caused the behavior. The mind may be composed of various systems that direct behavior but are cut off from centers responsible for verbal consciousness.

7 An altered state of consciousness is experienced daily when people sleep and dream. Researchers study sleep by analyzing patterns of brain waves. There are five stages of sleep. The stage that has attracted the most attention is REM (rapid eye movement) sleep. In this stage, the brain emits electrical signals similar to those emitted when people are awake. When awakened from this stage, people usually report that a dream was in progress.

8 When deprived of sleep, people respond in widely different ways, so no firm conclusions currently can be drawn about the effects of sleep deprivation or the functions and purpose of sleep. The effects of sleep deprivation seem to be overcome relatively rapidly, after only a night or two of uninterrupted sleep.

9 Insomnia embraces a variety of sleep disorders. Almost everyone occasionally suffers from situational insomnia, brought on by stress. Arrhythmic insomnia may occur after jet travel or be caused by working an overnight shift. In sleep apnea, people stop breathing when asleep; in narcolepsy, they fall asleep uncontrollably no matter what they are doing.

10 The function of dreams is not clear. If people are kept from dreaming, they dream more than normal on later nights. This phenomenon is called REM rebound. The Hobson-McCarley activation-synthesis hypothesis maintains that REM sleep is caused by activation in the brain stem that spreads throughout neighboring systems and causes the physiological effects of REM sleep. According to this view, dreaming is the result of the attempts of higher brain centers to interpret the blizzard of random signals generated by neural activity. The bizarre and disjointed nature of dreams is thus expected.

11 The hypnotic trance may be a special state of consciousness in which people are quite responsive to others' suggestions. Often, hypnotized people can do things that they could not do—or would not try to do—when not hypnotized. People cannot be hypnotized against their will, and they will not perform antisocial acts under hypnosis. People differ greatly in their susceptibility to hypnotic suggestion. Highly hypnotizable people show considerably increased ability to tolerate pain under hypnosis. Effects of hypnosis on memory retrieval are more controversial. Many studies show no positive effect of hypnosis on memory. When they are obtained, positive effects may be due to increased guessing under hypnosis or to good memory strategies suggested by the hypnotist, not to the hypnosis itself.

12 Drugs are frequently used to alter consciousness. Stimulants are used to perk people up, but strong ones may lead to addiction. Depressants are used as relaxants, and they may affect coordination. When depressants, such as sleeping pills and alcohol are combined, the result can be deadly. Hallucinogens produce vivid hallucinations, and some people claim these drugs can "expand" consciousness. Many powerful drugs have negative effects on physiology and are addictive. Their use outside the field of medicine is usually illegal.

KEY TERMS

consciousness (p. 175)

preconscious (p. 176)

unconscious (p. 176)

nonconscious (p. 176)

attention (p. 177)

selective attention (p. 177)

filter theory (p. 179)

early-selection theory (p. 179)

attenuation theory (p. 180)

late-selection theory (p. 180)

feature search (p. 181)

preattentive process (p. 181)

conjunction search (p. 181)

subliminal perception (p. 182)

semantic priming (p. 182)

illusory conjunctions (p. 184)

controlled processing (p. 184)

automatic processing (p. 184)

Stroop task (p. 185)

REM sleep (p. 192)

insomnia (p. 197)

REM rebound (p. 200)

activation-synthesis hypothesis (p. 201)

lucid dreaming (p. 201)

hypnosis (p. 202)

depressants (p.208)

stimulants (p. 210)

hallucinogens (p. 211)

FOR CRITICAL ANALYSIS

1 The term *consciousness* is used in many different ways. Try to generate a list of five different ways in which the term is used. Are all the ways that you generated referred to in the chapter? Are there types of conscious experience that were not covered in this chapter?

2 *Attention* is another term that has many meanings. Try to generate five different meanings for the term *attention*. Were they all used in the chapter, or were some important uses of the term omitted?

3 Evidence from studies of split-brain and other brain-damaged patients indicate that there are different "channels" in the mind. That is, a person can know something at one level without being consciously aware of this fact and able to verbalize it. Do you think that this is true only of brain-damaged people, or is it the case for all of us? Try to cite evidence to support your belief.

4 Many people are frightened by the prospect of mental control by subliminal stimulation. Try to develop an argument claiming that subliminal stimulation could be effective. Then, playing devil's advocate, take an opposite view and argue against the effectiveness of subliminal stimulation. Why do you think it is perceived as such a threat?

5 Try to recollect the most recent dream you have had, or at least a memorable one from your recent past. Now try to interpret your dream in light of the symbols noted by Freud in the long passage quoted on pages 199–200. Do you think Freud's account of dreams helps you to understand your own dream?

6 Have you ever been hypnotized or known anyone who was? Describe your experiences and relate them to material in the book: Did you think you had extraordinary mental powers during your experience with hypnosis? Did your friend?

7 What do you think accounts for the prevalence of illegal drugs in our society? Why are they so often used? What needs are they satisfying?

SUGGESTED READINGS

BOWERS, K. S. (1983). *Hypnosis for the seriously curious* (2nd ed.). New York: Norton. This interesting book is written for people who have had little previous experience with hypnotic phenomena.

HOBSON, J. A. (1988). *The dreaming brain.* New York: Basic Books. This book surveys the history of scientific thought about dreaming, but brings matters to the present time. A major section is devoted to the activation-synthesis hypothesis of dreaming that was developed by the author in collaboration with Robert McCarley.

HOBSON, J. A. (1989). *Sleep.* New York: Scientific American Library. An excellent overview of the topics of sleep and dreaming.

JULIEN, R. M. (1995). *A primer of drug action,* 7th ed. New York: Freeman. This book describes the major classes of psychoactive drugs and their effects.

SHIFFRIN, R. M. (1988). Attention. In R. C. Atkinson, R. J. Hernnstein, G. Lindzey, & R. D. Luce (Eds.), *Stevens' Handbook of Experimental Psychology* (3rd ed.). (pp. 739–812). New York: Wiley. The best summary of current work on attention, although written at a higher level than most sources listed in Suggested Readings.

SIEGEL, R. K. (1989). *Intoxication.* New York: Dutton. Consideration of why people seek to become intoxicated.

SPRINGER, S. P., & DEUTSCH, G. (1993). *Left brain, right brain* (4th ed.). New York: Freeman. A recent overview of what is known about hemispheric specialization. The last two chapters are concerned with implications for conscious experience. One chapter is devoted to left-handers.

PSYCHOLOGY ON THE INTERNET

Psycholoquy—Consciousness

(http://cogsci.ecs.soton.ac.uk/~lac/topics.html#consciousness)

"Psycholoquy is a refereed electronic journal sponsored by the American Psychological Association. It publishes articles and peer commentary in all areas of psychology as well as cognitive science, neuroscience, behavioral biology, artificial intelligence, robotics/vision, linguistics and philosophy." This particular collection of Psycholoquy articles debates the nature of consciousness and the value of studying consciousness as a means to understanding psychological processes.

PSYCHE: An Interdisciplinary Journal of Research on Consciousness

(http://psyche.cs.monash.edu.au/)

"PSYCHE…is a refereed electronic journal dedicated to supporting the interdisciplinary exploration of the nature of consciousness and its relation to the brain. PSY-

CHE publishes material relevant to that exploration from the perspectives afforded by the disciplines of cognitive science, philosophy, psychology, physics, neuroscience, artificial intelligence and anthropology. Interdisciplinary discussions are particulary encouraged."

Attention Reading Lists

(http://www.york.ac.uk/depts/psych/web/ug/course/core/rlcognuh.html#L3)
(http://www.york.ac.uk/depts/psych/web/ug/course/core/rlcognuh.html#L4)
(http://www.york.ac.uk/depts/psych/web/ug/course/core/rlcognuh.html#S17)

These sites contain reading lists and reviews of original research, books, and book chapters dealing with models of attention, automaticity, attentional control, and skill acquisition. There are no links to on-line versions of the works referenced, but the reading lists are a valuable asset. Most of the items listed are available in your school's library.

Psycholoquy—Split-Brain Patients

(http://cogsci.ecs.soton.ac.uk/~lac/topics.html#split-brain)

This group of Psycholoquy articles focuses on whether the hemispheric specialization—revealed largely through Sperry's (1970, 1974) work with split brain patients—is indicative of separate types of consciousness.

BISleep

(http://bisleep.medsch.ucla.edu/)

This site, maintained by the Brain Information Service (BIS), is a rich source of information on sleep-related topics. It provides links to: Information on sleep disorders (e.g., apnea, narcolepsy, and insomnia), home pages of sleep labs and clinics around the world, and regional and national societies of researchers and medical practitioners involved in sleep research and clinical practice. BISleep also facilitates the exchange of information about sleep through its on-line bibliography of sleep literature (BiblioSleep) and on-line discussion forums.

Another good source of information on sleep-related topics is the Sleep Medicine Home Page (http://www.cloud9.net:80/~thorpy/). This site provides some of the same information as the BISleep home page, but focuses more on education and treatment of sleep disorders.

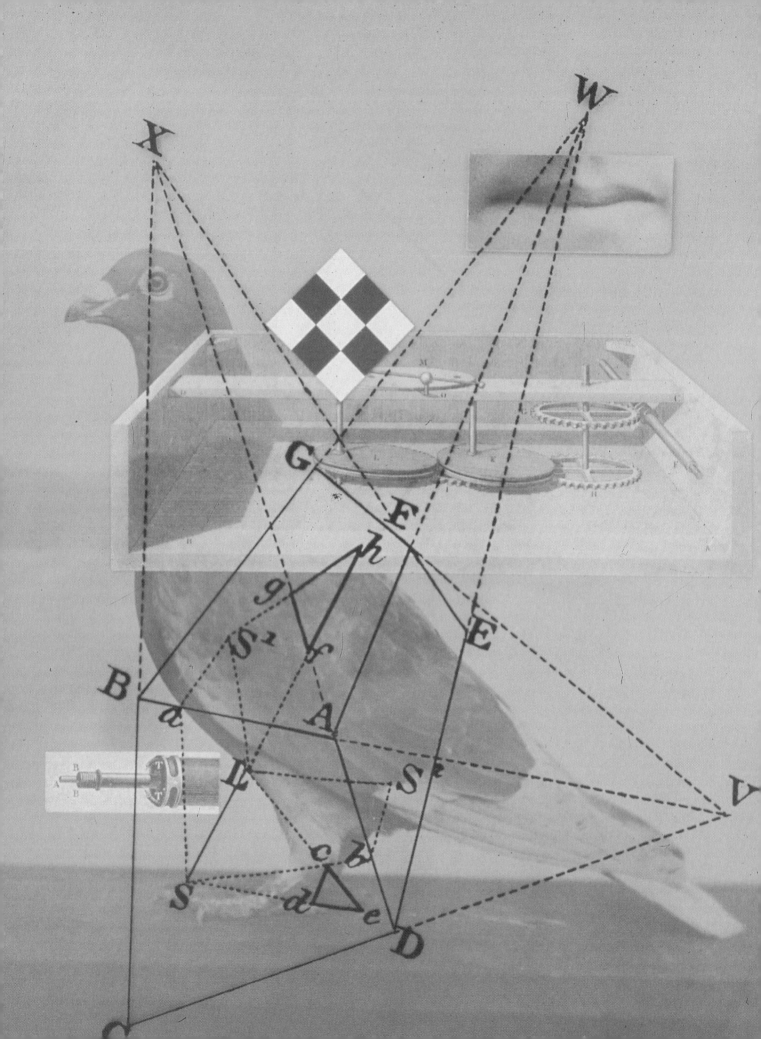

CONDITIONING and LEARNING

Chapter 6

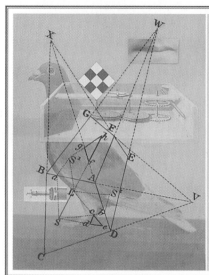

BIOLOGICAL THEME
Is what you learn limited by your genes?

LEARNING THEME
How do we learn about the environment? How do we learn to behave?

COGNITIVE THEME
Do animals think?

DEVELOPMENTAL THEME
How do children learn from their parents' behavior?

SOCIOCULTURAL THEME
Do children's different sociocultural backgrounds affect their performance in school?

In the early 1900s, a remarkable horse named Clever Hans became an instant celebrity in Germany. The horse's owner, Herr von Osten, would read arithmetic problems to Clever Hans, and the horse would tap out the correct answers with a forefoot. When asked to add 8 plus 3, Hans would tap his foot 11 times. The horse was equally adept at addition, subtraction, multiplication, and division; he was also able to answer simple questions about spelling, reading, and musical harmony.

Needless to say, many Germans found Clever Hans's talents hard to believe, and yet von Osten seemed honest. He did not try to profit from his horse's fame. To satisfy the skeptics, the horse was tested in von Osten's absence. Surprisingly, Hans performed just as well when his owner wasn't there.

Could Hans really understand language and do arithmetic? A psychologist performed a series of experiments that finally convinced everyone that while Hans was a very clever horse indeed, his talents did not extend to mathematics. Pfungst (1911) reported that Hans actually accomplished his feats by detecting subtle nonverbal signals provided by his questioners. The researchers noted that when Hans tapped, he would tap quickly at first, then slow down, and then stop at the right place (or sometimes miss by a number or two). They discovered that the questioners tended to incline their heads as they gave Hans a problem, then to straighten up as he neared the correct answer. Hans also seemed to be sensitive to each questioner's eyebrow movements, nostril dilation, and tone of voice. When prevented from seeing or hearing his questioners while he tapped, Hans no longer was able to perform. The horse had simply learned subtle signals from von Osten that indicated when to stop tapping.

The process by which Hans learned the trick that outwitted his human observers is as interesting as the trick itself. He learned to perform a response that was rewarded with attention and food. This type of learning is used by animal trainers today to teach elephants to stand on their front feet, killer whales to "kiss" their trainers, and dolphins to perform long, complex tricks. People also learn to repeat acts that produce favorable results. We learn to say please and thank you, to stop at red lights, and to study hard to do well on a test. All are examples of operant conditioning, a topic covered in this chapter. We will also consider how we learn to form associations between events in our environment (classical conditioning) and how we learn by watching others (observational learning).

Animal trainers use methods of operant conditioning to get their animals to perform amazing feats.

When you learn to drive a car or speak a foreign language, you have changed; you have a new ability. And once you have that new ability, you do not have to learn it again, because learning is a relatively permanent change. We say *relatively* permanent because you may forget some of what you learn (as you will see in Chapter 7) or even unlearn what you have learned. Thus, a general definition of **learning** is a relatively permanent change in behavior or knowledge occurring as a result of experience.

Most principles of learning have come from research with nonhuman subjects. (Variables such as previous experience, genetic background, and motivation can be controlled far better in nonhuman animals than in human beings.) Luckily, the findings from animal laboratories are relevant for human behavior. That is; nonhuman animals learn about their environment and how to behave in it the same way people do. For this reason, many of the principles described in this chapter have been successfully applied to therapies aimed at changing human behavior (see chapter 16).

Classical Conditioning

The fear that many people experience when they hear the sound of a dentist's drill demonstrates the basic idea of classical conditioning. Some patients literally shake when they sit in the dentist's chair, even though modern anesthetics usually prevent them from feeling any pain. These patients associate the chair with past occurrences of pain, and merely sitting in the chair can produce intense fear. Learning to associate one event with another, such as a dentist's chair with pain, is called **classical conditioning.** Because the first person to study this type of learning was Ivan Pavlov, it is sometimes called *Pavlovian conditioning*.

Ivan P. Pavlov (1849–1936) is one of psychology's most esteemed scientists, and yet he did no work in psychology until late in life. In 1904, he was awarded the Nobel Prize in physiology and medicine for his work on digestive secretions. Working with dogs, Pavlov discovered that meat greatly increased stomach secretions and that the mouth also secreted varying amounts of saliva in response to certain foods. A drop of an acidic substance (lemon juice), for instance, produced a large quantity of watery saliva that diluted the acid.

While studying salivary and gastric responses, Pavlov discovered a curious phenomenon. In one experiment, he cut the esophagus of a dog and directed it outside the animal's neck. The dog chewed and swallowed, but food never reached its stomach. Yet, despite the absence of food in the stomach, stomach secretions still occurred. Moreover, even the sight of an empty food dish would trigger stomach secretions and salivation in some dogs. Apparently, the stomach was secreting in anticipation of food. Pavlov realized that he had stumbled on an important finding—a fundamentally new kind of response. Whereas all dogs produced stomach secretions when food was placed in their stomachs and salivated when food was placed in their mouths, only a dog that had certain experiences would do so at the mere sight of a food dish. These responses resulted from learning, a relatively permanent change in behavior produced by experience.

Classical conditioning reveals the interplay among the important themes of the book, especially biology and learning. Stimuli in the environment, such as food, produce automatic biological reactions, such as salivation. The same physiological response, however, can be conditioned to a neutral stimulus as a result of learning. Furthermore, cognitive factors, such as what an individual expects, can also affect classical conditioning.

PAVLOV'S EXPERIMENTS

Pavlov concentrated his experiments on salivary responses because they were easier to measure than stomach secretions. To study how responses are learned, Pavlov first sounded a tone in the presence of a harnessed dog and measured the dog's salivation in response to the tone. To exclude all other stimulation, Pavlov isolated the dog in a soundproof room and conducted the whole experiment by remote control. Immediately after the tone sounded, meat powder was automatically released into a dish in front of the hungry dog. The dog ate the powder, and the amount of saliva that the dog secreted was again measured (see Figures 6.1 and 6.2).

In a typical experiment, Pavlov consistently sounded the tone before releasing food into the dish. He discovered that after a number of tone-food pairings, the tone came to produce salivation by itself. This outcome provided an impressive demonstration of the way some neutral event in the environment, such as a tone, can gain control over behavior. (To experience what Pavlov's dog experienced, think very hard about a slice of pizza, and see if you can feel yourself begin to salivate.)

Pavlov called the event that produced a response without prior learning the **unconditioned stimulus (US).** Meat powder was the US in his experiment with the dog, since meat powder automatically made the dog salivate when placed in the dog's mouth. The **unconditioned response (UR)** was the reaction (salivation) to the unconditioned stimulus. It was a response that occurred automatically, without previous training.

In Pavlov's experiment, the tone began as a neutral stimulus, producing only alertness at the start of the experiment and not the response to be conditioned (salivation). However, after being paired with food on several occasions, the tone by itself became a **conditioned stimulus (CS)** because it then led to the salivation response. Thus, the conditioned stimulus did not bring out the specific response prior to training, but did so after training. The reaction produced by the conditioned stimulus was called the **conditioned response (CR).** In Pavlov's experiment, the conditioned response was the salivation produced by the tone alone once the tone had been paired with the food. Thus, classical conditioning (or Pavlovian conditioning) is the procedure whereby a stimulus (CS) that does not initially produce a reaction is paired with a stimulus (US) that automatically produces a reaction. As a consequence of such CS-US pairings, the CS itself comes to produce the response (CR). The diagram in Figure 6.3 summarizes this procedure.

FIGURE 6.1

Pavlov's Experiment in Classical Conditioning

Ivan Pavlov shown with his research team demonstrating his classical conditioning experiment.

FIGURE 6.2

Pavlov with His Laboratory Apparatus

In this photo Pavlov observes saliva flow in a dog subjected to a classical conditioning procedure in his labratory.

EXAMPLES OF CLASSICAL CONDITIONING IN HUMANS

Classical conditioning is not limited to relatively minor physiological responses such as salivation. Virtually all of the body's reactions to environmental events can be conditioned—including emotional reactions. In a well-known experiment, behaviorists John B. Watson and Rosalie Rayner (1920) taught an infant named Albert to fear a white rat, even though Albert showed no previous fear of rats. They paired the rat (CS) with a loud, unpleasant noise (US). After a few such pairings, little Albert would cry at the sight of a white rat. Albert's new reactions demonstrate that fear is basically the learned anticipation of pain or other undesirable events.

Classical conditioning also plays a role in disease. A worker whose disagreeable supervisor (US) makes the worker tense (UR) can be conditioned to be tense in any situation (CS) associated with that supervisor. If the supervisor raises the worker's blood pressure on the job, ultimately the job itself will induce high blood pressure, even if the supervisor has been fired.

Positive emotions can also be produced by classical conditioning, a fact exploited by advertisers (see "Psychology in Our Times: How Advertisers Take Advantage of Classical Conditioning"). Advertisements pair stimuli that produce positive emotions (beautiful women, breathtaking landscapes, cuddly babies) with the product to be sold. The positive emotions transfer to the product, increasing the probability that it will be selected. By the same token, neutral stimuli that are paired with sexual pleasure (US) will come to elicit sexual arousal. Domjan et al. (1988) showed that male quail were more likely to copulate with a female who had features associated with previous copulations. In humans, male sexual arousal to a picture of boots can be produced by pairing a picture of the boots with pictures of nude women (Rachman & Hodgson, 1968).

FEATURES OF CLASSICAL CONDITIONING

Much of our information about conditioned responses was provided by Pavlov (1927), and his studies still constitute the fundamental basis of our knowledge. The phenomena discovered and named by Pavlov include acquisition, extinction, spontaneous recovery, stimulus generalization, and discrimination.

Acquisition. We acquire responses, so the process by which a conditioned stimulus comes to produce a conditioned response is called **acquisition.** In most classical condi-

FIGURE 6.3

Classical Conditioning Procedure

Before classical conditioning trials, food in the mouth (the unconditioned stimulus, US) elicits salivation (the unconditioned response, UR). The tone (the conditioned stimulus, CS) does not induce salivation before conditioning. After the tone has preceded food a number of times (CS-US pairings), the tone by itself causes salivation (the conditioned response, CR).

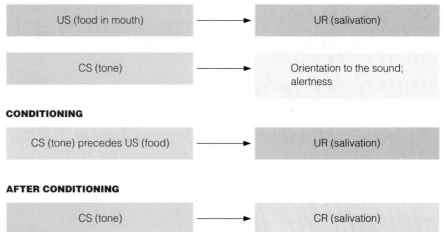

PSYCHOLOGY IN OUR TIMES
HOW ADVERTISERS TAKE ADVANTAGE OF CLASSICAL CONDITIONING

We like to believe that we make rational decisions and are conscious of the things that influence those decisions. Advertisers spend billions of dollars a year on the opposite assumption—that consumer choices are affected by unconscious processes. Does placing a beautiful woman next to a car improve car sales? Or do consumers select cars on the basis of price, performance and other practical considerations? Sales figures and experimental research suggest that the beautiful woman increases car sales. In one experiment, Smith and Engel (1968, cited in Lieberman, 1990) showed adult males a picture of a car with or without a sexually arousing woman dressed in a sleeveless sweater and black lace underwear. Those who viewed the car with the woman rated the car as better designed, more expensive, faster, and more dangerous. It is interesting to note that only 1 out of 23 subjects believed he had been influenced by the presence of a beautiful model.

But is the process described here irrational? On the contrary, it is simply another example of classical conditioning. Because the car (CS) is paired with the beautiful woman (US), an expectation is formed that the two events go together. In fact, using an anonymous toothpaste as the CS and pleasant pictures as the US, Stuart, Shimp and Engle

(1987) showed that many such classical conditioning phenomena occur in advertising.

Associating products with sexually appealing people or other desirable characteristics is a common advertising technique. Controversy arises, however, when the product being promoted is hazardous to one's health, as in the case of tobacco. Television used to be deluged with ads showing attractive people smoking cigarettes: The Marlboro man was the embodiment of the rugged West, while elsewhere, happy couples were shown blissfully smoking together. These ads were removed from television when the evidence linking smoking to cancer could no longer be ignored. The decision to remove the ads was also based on the overwhelming evidence that cigarette ads increase smoking. Nevertheless, ads in print continue to utilize the very same associative techniques, linking Marlboro cigarettes with manly men and Virginia Slims with slim, modern women.

When you look at advertisements, keep classical conditioning in mind. Ask yourself what US the advertiser is associating with the product. Sometimes it is apparent, as in the case of the sexually arousing woman; but other times the unconditioned stimulus is not so obvious.

tioning experiments, several pairings of the CS and US are necessary before the CR is completely acquired. On the first few trials, there may be no response to the CS. As the number of pairings increases, the strength of the CR increases. Figure 6.4 shows

FIGURE 6.4

Acquisition of the Eyeblink CR in Human Subjects

Subjects in group A received 130 trials with a strong air puff as the US. Subjects in group B received 90 trials with a strong air puff followed by 40 trials with a weaker air puff. (After Trapold & Spence, 1960)

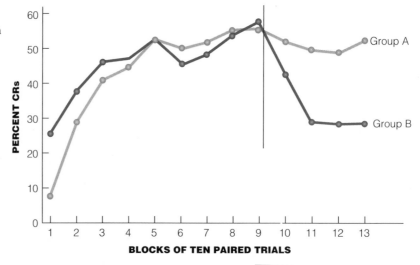

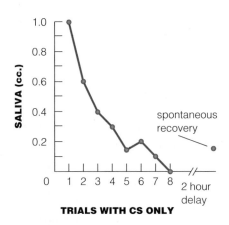

FIGURE 6.5

Extinction and Spontaneous Recovery

Shown is the decrease in salivation over trials when the CS was presented by itself (extinction). Following a rest of 2 hours, the CR recovered.

SOURCE: Data from Pavlov, 1927.

FIGURE 6.6

Stimulus Generalization

The graph shows the size of the galvanic skin response (GSR) for human subjects given tone and shock pairings. Subjects were first trained to give the response to a tone (trainins CS) when it was paired with an electric shock (US). Following training, the subjects were tested with three tones varying in pitch from the training CS. CS1 was most similar to the traing CS, CS2 less similar, and CS3 least similar. The GSR occurred with all three test stimuli (stimulus generalization), but the size of the GSR decreased as the stimuli became less similar to the training CS.

SOURCE: Howard, 1937.

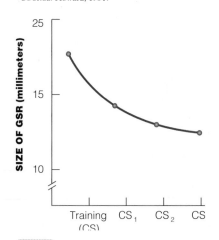

the acquisition phase of an experiment measuring eyeblink conditioning in humans. A puff of air to the eye was used as the US, and the measure of conditioning was the percentage of trials on which a conditioned eyeblink response occurred when the CS was given alone, without the puff of air. As you can see, the likelihood of a CR increased over the first 50 or so trials, although it never exceeded about 55 percent. Some responses are learned much faster. You would need only one painful bite from a dog to learn to fear the dog. And the traumatic experience of being mugged—even once—can produce very long–lasting fear of becoming a victim again.

Extinction and Spontaneous Recovery. After a dog learns to salivate in response to a tone, will it do so forever? The answer is no. If food no longer follows the tone, the dog will eventually stop salivating because it will have learned that no food will come. This process is called extinction of the conditioned response. **Extinction** is the weakening of the CR that occurs when the CS is presented repeatedly without the US.

To extinguish a response, the subject must be given the CS without the US. One way to eliminate a fear of snakes is to expose yourself repeatedly to harmless snakes. However, extinction is often difficult to implement when the stimuli are feared. Because people often avoid feared stimuli, their fear response never extinguishes, and they never discover that some feared stimuli are actually safe. Phobias, or strong irrational fears, can be particularly difficult to eliminate except through deliberate means (discussed later in this chapter and in Chapter 16).

Extinction is not necessarily permanent, particularly if only one extinction session has taken place. A person may believe that she has overcome her fear of flying after successfully completing one or two flights without negative consequences, but the fear may reappear after a period of time. In general, although extinction has supposedly eliminated a CR, the CR may not be gone forever. Often following a rest, the next presentation of the CS produces the CR. This increase in strength of the CR after extinction and a period of rest is called **spontaneous recovery.** After Pavlov's dog had ceased salivating during a series of extinction trials, a rest of 2 hours was given. When the CS was then reintroduced, the dog salivated again (see Figure 6.5). Pavlov interpreted this to mean that the CR was merely suppressed by extinction and not eliminated and that the suppression itself eroded with the passage of time. If repeated extinction sessions take place, however, responses decrease in strength; in time, the conditioned response can be completely eliminated, and spontaneous recovery will no longer occur.

Stimulus Generalization. Researchers observed that Little Albert feared a furry white rabbit in addition to the white rat that originally conditioned his fear (Watson & Rayner, 1920). By a process called **stimulus generalization,** a response conditioned to one stimulus will occur in the presence of other similar stimuli. That is, the CR generalizes to other stimuli.

In one study of this phenomenon, human subjects were given tone (CS) and shock (US) pairings. The shock caused pain and hence fear (UR). The measure of conditioned fear (CR) was a *galvanic skin response (GSR),* a change in skin resistance that reflects emotion. In the test, experimenters sounded various tones and measured the strength of the GSR to each tone. As shown in Figure 6.6, the GSR decreased as the difference between the test stimulus and the original CS increased. Subjects responded strongly to tones that were similar to the tone paired earlier with the shocks.

Stimulus generalization is clearly important for an organism's survival. If there were no generalization, the legitimate fear of a large dog that bit you would not extend to similar dogs. On the other hand, overgeneralization can produce fear of a toy poodle after being bitten by a Doberman pinscher. A third phenomenon discovered by Pavlov—termed discrimination—can correct such overgeneralization.

Discrimination. A **discrimination** is formed when a different reaction occurs to two CSs. If you are bitten by a Doberman, you will fear it and similar dogs because of stimulus generalization. If a large poodle is consistently friendly, however, you won't be afraid of it. The poodle does not bite, so your initial fear of the poodle will weaken because of extinction (presenting the CS without the US leads to weakening of the CR).

The best way to teach a subject to refrain from responding to a cue is by discrimination training. **Discrimination training** consists of randomly intermixing trials with two different CSs and following one CS by the US, but omitting the US after the other CS. If the subject can tell the two CSs apart, then the CR will eventually occur only for the CS that precedes the US. The animal or person has learned to discriminate between the two stimuli and respond appropriately to each.

CONCEPT SUMMARY

BASIC PHENOMENA OF CLASSICAL CONDITIONING

NAME	PROCEDURE	RESULT
Acquisition	CS paired with US	CS produces CR
Extinction	After acquisition, CS is presented without US	CR weakens and ultimately disappears
Spontaneous recovery	Rest is given following extinction	CR, previously weakened by extinction, can reappear
Stimulus generalization	After acquisition, testing is given with stimuli of varying similarity	CR occurs with stimuli that are similar to CS used in training; the greater the similarity between test CS and training CS, the stronger the CR
Discrimination	CS_1 is paired with US, CS_2 is not	CS_1 elicits CR, CS_2 does not, even if CS_1 and CS_2 are similar (as long as subject can tell them apart)

IS CONTIGUITY NECESSARY FOR CONDITIONING?

What determines which two stimuli will be associated? One idea is that stimuli occurring closely in time (*contiguous* stimuli) will become associated. Pavlov's tone closely preceded food, and Little Albert heard the loud noise only when near the rat.

Indeed, most studies have found that the most effective way to produce a classically conditioned response is to give the CS shortly before the US, although the exact length of the interval depends on which CR is being conditioned. For example, the optimum interval seems to be half a second for conditioning an eye blink response using an air puff US in humans (Ross & Ross, 1971); 1 to 4 seconds for conditioning a jaw movement response in rabbits (Gormezano, 1972); and 6 seconds for heart rate conditioning in rats (Fitzgerald & Martin, 1971). As these intervals are all very short, Pavlov believed that a CS and US must occur closely in time to be associated. In other words, **contiguity** of CS and US was the determining factor for which associations would be made.

A major exception to the principle of contiguity occurs in **taste aversion learning,** where people or other animals learn to avoid foods that make them sick. In taste aversion learning, the CS and US can be separated by hours, so contiguity is not necessary for an association to be formed (Logue, 1991). In taste aversion experiments, animals are given a flavored solution (CS) to drink and are then made ill by injection of a drug or by exposure to radiation (US). As a result of feeling sick (UR), the animals acquire an aversion (CR) for the taste of the drink, often after only one trial.

In one of the most influential papers ever published on taste aversion learning, Garcia and Koelling (1966) found that not all stimuli are equally conditionable. Animals seem biologically predisposed to associate some stimuli and not others. That is, they possess **biological constraints** on learning. Garcia and Koelling gave rats saccharin-flavored water from a tube that produced a flash of light and a brief noise when they drank. The rats were then made sick after drinking this bright-noisy-sweet water. Because all three stimuli (light, noise, taste) preceded sickness, the rats should have avoided all three later. Strangely, they did not. While they would not drink sweetened water, they had no problem drinking from a tube that was bright and noisy. Moreover, when a second group of rats were shocked after drinking bright-noisy-sweet water, they later avoided the water from the light and noisy tube, but drank sweet water from a regular tube (see Figure 6.7). Thus, when the UR was illness, animals learned to avoid a certain taste; when the UR was pain and fear, they learned to avoid certain sights and sounds.

What is going on? Try this thought experiment: Imagine that you go to a new restaurant and eat a food you've never had before while hearing some music you've never heard before. The next day, you become nauseated. Would you blame the new food or the new music? This seems obvious, because food is more likely to make you ill than music. The rats appear to have the same expectation. It seems that there is a biological predisposition to learn some associations more easily than others. Food is a more likely source of nausea than noises or lights, so associations between tastes and sickness are learned more easily. Likewise, noise and light are more likely sources of pain than is the taste of food, so the rats more readily associate the noise and light with the painful electric shock.

The study of taste aversions has helped in the treatment of cancer patients, who tend to lose considerable weight during their illness. Because chemotherapy normally produces severe nausea and vomiting, foods eaten before this treatment are prime candidates for learned aversions. Ilene Bernstein (1985) showed that chemotherapy can produce a dislike for a novel flavor of ice cream eaten before the treatment. Giving a novel food as a "scapegoat" flavor right before chemotherapy can reduce aversions to the normal diet, thereby reducing the severe weight loss associated with chemotherapy.

Taste aversion therapy has also been successful in treating alcoholics. In this proce-

FIGURE 6.7

Intake of Water Before and After Conditioning in the Garcia and Koelling (1966) Experiment

(a) Data for the rats that were made ill after drinking saccharin-flavored bright-noisy water. As you can see, their conditioning produced suppression of drinking saccharin-flavored water but no suppression of drinking bright-noisy water. (b) Data for rats shocked when drinking saccharin-flavored bright-noisy water. They avoided the bright-noisy water, but not the saccharin-flavored water.

SOURCE: Lieberman who adapted from Garcia & Koelling.

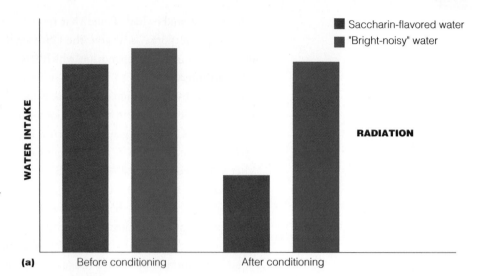

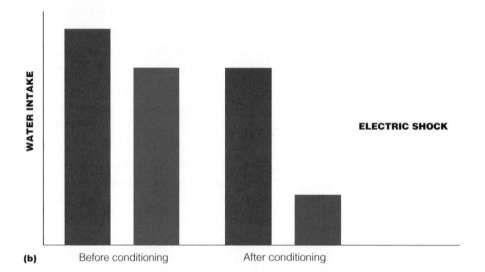

dure, an alcoholic imbibes liquor followed by a substance that induces nausea, eventually acquiring an aversion to alcohol. As you would expect, this method is more successful than punishing drinking with shock because of the biological predisposition to associate illness with consumed substances. Indeed, a number of studies have verified that sickness following alcohol consumption reduces drinking more effectively than does shock (Cannon & Baker, 1981; Cannon et al., 1981).

Biological predispositions have now been discovered in other forms of classical conditioning as well. Some psychologists attempted to reproduce the Watson-Rayner experiment that taught Little Albert to fear white rats. They found that ease of conditioning depends on the stimulus used. For example, it is easier to teach children to fear rats than toy ducks (Kalish, 1981). As we will see later in the chapter, it is also easier to teach animals to fear snakes than flowers. These facts may have an evolutionary basis, because snakes and rats are more dangerous than toy ducks and flowers.

IS CONTIGUITY SUFFICIENT FOR CONDITIONING?

Taste aversion learning showed that contiguity between stimuli is not sufficient for conditioning to occur. A second finding, reported in the 1960s, confirmed this conclusion by showing that the CS must also be a good predictor of the US.

Try to imagine flashing lights that supposedly warn of an approaching train. Imagine that whenever the lights flash, the train may or may not follow, but sometimes the train comes even when the lights do not flash. Because the lights are an unreliable warning signal, you would ignore them and find some other indicator of the approaching train. As this example indicates, the pairing of a CS and a US may not be the crucial factor in producing a CR. Instead, the determinant may be whether the CS can reliably predict the US. Pavlov's early experiments did not distinguish between these alternatives, because the US was always preceded by the CS; it never occurred by itself. More recent experiments have evaluated the effect of sometimes giving the US without the CS having occurred.

In one experiment (Rescorla, 1968), several groups of rats were given the same number of pairings of tone (CS) and shock (US), but the groups were given different numbers of shocks *without* tones. The CR to the tone was weaker in the groups that had received shocks without tones. Even though the groups were given the same number of pairings of the CS and US, the strength of the CR differed among the groups. If the CS can be used to predict the US, there will be a CR, and the CR will be strong if the predictive relationship between the CS and US is strong. These findings show that animals do not mechanically associate any two stimuli just because they happen to be paired. Instead, they seem to make associations only when one stimulus can predict the other.

Further evidence that animals do not blindly, automatically associate contiguous stimuli comes from a phenomenon called blocking. In **blocking,** the presence of a stimulus that already predicts the US prevents (blocks) conditioning to other stimuli. For example, imagine you have already (correctly) learned that a flashing light warns of an approaching train. Imagine now that a new signal (a beeping noise) is consistently added to the flashing light to also warn of the train's approach. Surprisingly, research suggests that you will *not* learn about the relationship between the beeping noise and the train. This is because once a reliable signal is found (the flashing light), learning about additional signals (a beeping noise) appears to be "blocked" (Kamin, 1969).

In one of Leon Kamin's experiments, a "blocking" group of rats received training in which a noise was paired with a shock (noise became the CS). This group then received shock following noise and light presented together. A later test showed that this blocking group did not learn to fear the light, but continued to fear the noise A control group, however, that had been shocked only following a combination of noise and light, learned to fear both the noise and light(see Figure 6.8). Thus, a conditioned response does not occur to a new stimulus if a good predictor of the US has already been found. However, if the noise begins to fail as a predictor, the animals will then learn about the light. For example, if a surprising second shock is given after the first, the rats will learn about the light.

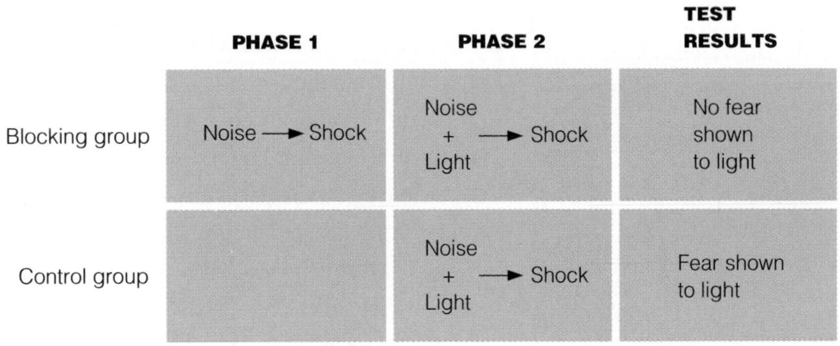

FIGURE 6.8

Blocking

The blocking group and control group in Kamin's (1969) experiment both received the noise-light stimulus before shock in phase 2 and then were tested for fear of the noise and light when each stimulus was presented alone. The control group showed fear of the light. The blocking group, which had previously received pairings of the noise with shock in phase one, showed no fear of the light. Prior learning that the noise predicted shock "blocked" learning that the light also predicted shock.

	PHASE 1	PHASE 2	TEST RESULTS
Blocking group	Noise ➝ Shock	Noise + Light ➝ Shock	No fear shown to light
Control group		Noise + Light ➝ Shock	Fear shown to light

Obviously, classical conditioning is a more active process than Pavlov thought and not merely a mechanical process of associating one stimulus with another. Pavlov would have been pleased; he had hoped that classical conditioning would be a model of all learning. Initially, this did not seem possible, and classical conditioning seemed a rather simplistic type of learning, limited to uninteresting responses such as salivation. Now we understand that classical conditioning involves learning to predict and expect events, a fundamental process that affects many of our responses—including what we feel, what we like to eat, who we love, and how we handle stress. Thus, classical conditioning, although more complex than Pavlov discovered, is indeed a model of much of our learning.

Operant (Instrumental) Conditioning

Classical conditioning involves learning about the environment. A second major form of learning, called **operant conditioning** or **instrumental conditioning,** involves the way responses are modified by their consequences. In studies of classical conditioning, the events (CS and US) are presented to the subject regardless of the subject's behavior; the subject is not required to respond to receive the CS or US (e.g., the tone or the food). In studies of operant conditioning, however, the subject must respond to receive a consequence (e.g., a reward delivered by the experimenter). In this way, we can study how behavior is affected by different consequences. Whereas classical conditioning usually involves conditioning the involuntary responses of the autonomic nervous system (see Chapter 2), operant conditioning involves conditioning skeletal responses, or voluntary responses.

CONCEPT SUMMARY

COMPARISON OF CLASSICAL CONDITIONING AND OPERANT CONDITIONING

	PROCEDURE	WHAT IS LEARNED	TYPE OF RESPONSE
Classical conditioning	Stimuli are presented so that one predicts another	Relationship among stimuli	Involuntary
Operant conditioning	Stimuli are contingent on behavior	How to behave	Voluntary

THORNDIKE'S PUZZLE BOX

Edward L. Thorndike (1874–1949) was the first person to systematically study operant, or instrumental, conditioning. In fact, the prototype for all subsequent instrumental conditioning research was his famous puzzle box experiment. Thorndike put a hungry cat in a box that had a door with a latch on the inside, and he placed food outside the cage (see Figure 6.9). The hungry cat meowed and scratched at the walls trying to escape until it accidentally hit a treadle (a pedal) that operated the latch. The cat escaped and got the food, thus solving the "puzzle." Thorndike repeated this procedure a number of times and discovered that the length of time it took the cat to work the treadle decreased steadily. Thorndike suggested the Law of Effect: responses that pro-

FIGURE 6.9

A Puzzle Box

This puzzle box is similar to the one used by Thorndike. To get out of the box, the animal must step on the treadle, which is attached to a rope that will open the latch on the door.

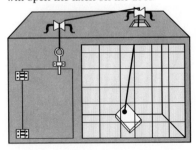

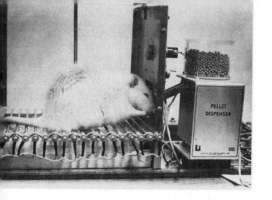

FIGURE 6.10

A Rat in a Skinner Box

The most commonly used apparatus for studying operant conditioning is the Skinner box, invented by B. F. Skinner. When a rat presses a lever, a pellet of food is delivered and the rate of response measured.

FIGURE 6.11

A Pigeon in an Operant Conditioning Chamber

The pigeon pecks a small illuminated disk on the wall of the box. The pecking response is reinforced by delivery of a food pellet.

duced satisfying consequences will be repeated, responses that produce unsatisfying consequences will not be repeated. Moreover, cats that had just been fed stayed in the box, making no effort to solve the puzzle. Thus, the hungry cat had learned to make a response *instrumental* to obtaining food.

THE SKINNER BOX AND OPERANT BEHAVIOR

Today, the most widely used apparatus for studying operant conditioning and performance is the Skinner box, or operant conditioning chamber, invented by B. F. Skinner (1904–1990). As shown in Figure 6.10, the apparatus contains a small lever on one wall that a hungry rat can press to receive a reward, usually a small pellet of food that drops into the small cup near the lever. The box can be adapted for different animals; for example, pigeons can peck a small illuminated disk on the wall to receive a reward (see Figure 6.11).

In the early experiments, the rate of an animal's response (e.g., the repeated occurrences of pressing the lever) was measured with a *cumulative recorder*, the device shown in Figure 6.12. Every time the animal pressed the lever, the recorder moved a pen one step up on a roll of paper moving at a constant speed. When the rat or pigeon did not respond at all, the pen remained where it last stopped and made a horizontal line as the paper came out of the machine. In the modern laboratory of today, data are often collected and analyzed by a computer.

To analyze behavior experimentally, Skinner proposed the concept of an **operant**, a specific unit of behavior. An operant response is a behavior that results in, or is followed by, a particular effect on the environment. For instance, if a rat's pressing a lever results in food, then the lever press is, by definition, an operant response, regardless of whether the rat presses the lever with its nose or its paw. According to Skinner, behavior is defined in terms of its effects on the environment.

THE EFFECTS OF REINFORCEMENT

Skinner suggested that behavior resulting in **reinforcement**—defined as a positive, or satisfying, outcome—is more likely to occur again, a principle clearly related to Thorndike's Law of Effect. Reinforcers are similar to rewards, but they do not have to

FIGURE 6.12

A Cumulative Recorder

A cumulative recorder consists of a roll of paper revolving at a constant speed on which a pen moves up a bit when the subject responds. If the subject does not respond at all, the pen will not move up, and the line (cumulative record) will be horizontal. The more frequently the subject responds, the more frequently the pen will go up, and the steeper will be the incline of the cumulative record.

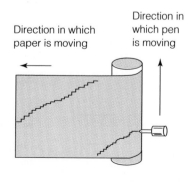

Direction in which paper is moving

Direction in which pen is moving

© 1991 Ziggy and Friends, Inc. Distributed by
Universal Press Syndicate. Reprinted with permission.

be delivered by other people. Many reinforcers are inherent parts of the environment. For example, speeding in a car is reinforced by reaching your destination sooner. Solving puzzles seems to be inherently reinforcing, as is going to movies or watching TV. Of course, reinforcers often come from other people. For example, a baby cries and his mother enters the room; the mother's attention in effect reinforces the behavior of crying. In turn, the child stops crying when the mother enters the room, reinforcing the mother's attentive behavior.

There are two varieties of reinforcement in Skinner's model: positive reinforcement and negative reinforcement. A **positive reinforcer** increases the strength of the response that precedes its delivery. In the Thorndike experiment, the food outside the cage acted as a positive reinforcer for the hungry cat, because when the cat escaped, it could eat the food. A **negative reinforcer** increases the likelihood of the preceding response by its removal. In the previous example, the mother's coming to the baby was negatively reinforced when the infant ceased to cry. Both types of reinforcement increase the strength of the preceding behavior. The difference is that negative reinforcement involves *removing* an *unpleasant* stimulus, while positive reinforcement involves *presenting* a stimulus.

Reinforcers such as food or the removal of shock are referred to as **primary** or **unconditioned reinforcers** because they exert their effect without prior association or experience. Feeding a hungry animal or discontinuing shock have obvious reinforcing properties. Not all stimuli, of course, are as intrinsically reinforcing as these. Money, for instance, serves as a reinforcer because it is associated with primary reinforcers such as food and shelter. Reinforcers, such as money and praise that reinforce by means of association with primary reinforcers are called **secondary** or **conditioned reinforcers.**

Remember that reinforcement, positive or negative, always produces an increase in the rate of response that precedes the reinforcement. A reinforcer, either positive or negative, is defined in terms of its effects. If ice cream fails to strengthen some response in a child, then ice cream is not a reinforcer. Either the child has already eaten too much of it, or perhaps the child is sick and not interested in ice cream at all.

CONCEPT SUMMARY

REINFORCEMENT

	POSITIVE: Presentation increases strength of preceding response.	**NEGATIVE:** Removal increases strength of preceding response.
PRIMARY: unlearned	Food, water	Removal of pain
CONDITIONED: learned	Money, praise	Removal of feared stimulus

SCHEDULES OF REINFORCEMENT

What happens if reinforcement does not follow every response? In everyday life, it is rare for every response to be reinforced. A baby may cry for a long time before anyone picks him up. An actor does not land a part after every audition. When reinforcement occurs for less than 100 percent of responses, it is said to be **partial,** or **intermittent reinforcement,** as opposed to continuous reinforcement, which occurs after every

IS THERE A SINGLE LIST OF REINFORCERS?

A reinforcer is any stimulus or event that increases the rate of the response that produced the stimulus. Some theorists have attempted to describe what makes a reinforcer reinforcing. Hull (1943), for example, suggested that reinforcers satisfy primary, unlearned needs (e.g., food when you are hungry). More recent theorists suggest that there is no one list of reinforcers. Instead, reinforcers vary with the situation and the person (or animal).

David Premack (1962, 1965) suggested that the priorities placed on different activities could be inferred by observing the amount of time a person spent on each activity when all were freely available. He further suggested that more probable behaviors could serve as reinforcers for less probable behaviors, regardless of the behaviors involved. For a particular child, riding a bike might be more probable than reading a book, which is more probable than cleaning a room. Premack's rule states that the opportunity to ride a bike will reinforce reading, and the opportunity to read a book will reinforce room cleaning. The opportunity to read a book, however, would not reinforce bike riding because bike riding is more probable than reading. Therefore, a reinforcer will not strengthen just any response— only those that are less probable. Premack's rule also suggests that any activity can be reinforcing so long as its current probability is greater than that of the response on which it is contingent.

Premack conducted the following

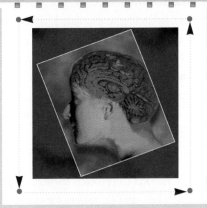

experiment to demonstrate the rule. In one condition, a rat had free access to a water bottle, but its exercise wheel was only available for 1 hour per day. During that hour, the rat's rate of running was higher than its rate of licking. If the rat then had to drink in order to unlock the activity wheel, its rate of drinking increased, showing that the opportunity to run was a reinforcer that increased drinking water. If Premack reversed the relation so that the activity wheel was available for 24 hours and the drinking tube was available for only 1 hour, drinking occurred at a higher rate than running during that hour. If the rat then had to run in order to drink, the rate of running increased. Thus, the relation between running and drinking was reversible: Running could reinforce drinking, and drinking could reinforce running.

One problem with Premack's theory is that a low-probability behavior can reinforce a high-probability behavior if the subject has not been able to per-

form the low-probability behavior for some time. Timberlake and Allison (1974; Timberlake, 1980) proposed response-deprivation theory to account for this contradictory evidence. They proposed that if an organism were deprived of making its normal baseline rate of some response (the dependent response), it would increase any response that allowed it to make the dependent response. For example, if you are accustomed to watching TV 2 hours per day and allowed only to watch for 1/2 hour, the opportunity to watch TV will be reinforcing. Or, if we deprive a rat of food, thereby making its eating less frequent than the normal baseline, the rat will increase any response that produces food. From this point of view, it does not matter what response was more probable initially; what matters is whether the person or animal has been deprived of responding relative to the usual level.

Response deprivation theory does not regard reinforcers as any kind of special stimuli. Instead, reinforcement is the result of an interaction between the most optimal distribution of behavior (measured by an individual's free choice) and restrictions on that distribution imposed by a schedule of reinforcement. Operant conditioning creates a new distribution of responses. Reinforcement effects are just one example of the way an animal adapts to its environment—by distributing responses to make the best of its opportunities (Staddon, 1983).

response. Surprisingly, partial reinforcement can produce a stronger rate of response than continuous reinforcement. To understand how this can happen, you need to know the ways in which intermittent reinforcement can be given. We will discuss four simple reinforcement schedules: fixed ratio, variable ratio, fixed interval, and variable interval (Schwartz & Reisberg, 1993).

Fixed–Ratio Schedules.   On **ratio schedules,** reinforcement is given only after a certain number of responses. On a **fixed-ratio (FR) schedule,** the reinforcer is delivered after every *n* responses. On a FR 10 schedule, for example, every tenth response is followed by a reinforcer. "Piecework" in a factory is a good example of a fixed-ratio schedule. If a worker is paid $1 for every 10 widgets made, the worker is on an FR 10 schedule of reinforcement. Reading 20 pages to study for a test and doing 20 sit-ups to keep fit are other examples of behaviors on fixed-ratio schedules (the reinforcer here is self-reinforcement for completing 20). If an animal begins with an FR 1 schedule (continuous reinforcement), the number of responses required to produce reinforcement can gradually be increased. After an animal has operated on a fixed-ratio schedule for some time, a distinctive pattern of responding develops. After each reinforcer is delivered, there is a brief pause in responding, called the *postreinforcement pause*. After the pause, the subject typically responds at a rapid rate until the next reinforcer is delivered. The high rates of response under fixed-ratio schedules of reinforcement can be seen in Figure 6.13a. The postreinforcement pause is evident in the FR 200 schedule.

Variable Ratio Schedules. On a **variable ratio (VR) schedule,** the number of responses needed to produce reinforcement is not constant. On a VR 10 schedule, the subject receives one reinforcer for every 10 responses *on average*, but the exact number of responses required can vary widely. Typically, the particular number of responses required for the next reinforcer is selected at random. The number of responses necessary on a VR 10 schedule might be 1, 2, 4, 5, 6, 10, 20, and 38. This schedule produces a high rate of response without the pauses seen in the fixed-ratio schedule (see the top line of Figure 6.14). A good example of this schedule is playing a slot machine: it pays off after some number of responses, but the number varies. If you have ever played a slot machine or watched other people playing them, you know that variable ratio-schedules produce a high rate of response.

Fixed-Interval Schedules. On **interval schedules,** the delivery of reinforcement depends on the subject's behavior and the passage of time. On a **fixed-interval (FI) schedule,** the first response after a certain length of time is reinforced. On an FI 1-minute schedule, for example, the first response to occur after 1 minute has passed is reinforced. In the laboratory, a rat may be reinforced with a food pellet for the first response after 1 minute. Then the next pellet will be presented following the first response that occurs after 1 additional minute. And so on. It doesn't matter how many responses the rat makes during the 1 minute interval, because none of them will produce reinforcement. As soon as the 1 minute has passed, however, the next response produces reinforcement. If the rat could tell time perfectly, it would not respond until 1 minute had passed in order to perform most efficiently. But the rat has no clock (and couldn't use one if it did have one), so it typically produces many more responses than necessary to obtain reinforcement. These responses follow a certain pattern: The rat will ultimately pause following each reinforcement and then gradually increase its response rate as the time of reinforcement approaches. This pattern of response is

FIGURE 6.13

A Pigeon's Performance on Fixed Schedules of Reinforcement

(a) Representations of performance on two fixed-ratio schedules. On the fixed-ratio 50 (FR 50) schedule, the rate of responding is uniformly high; on a fixed-ratio 200 (FR 200) schedule, there is a pause following reinforcement. (b) The wavy line shows performance on a 1-minute fixed-interval schedule. Slash marks indicate when reinforcement was delivered. The response rate is low immediately following the reinforcer (the cumulative record is flat), and the rate of responding increases as the time of reinforcement approaches. This produces a cumulative record with a scallop shape; hence the name *fixed-interval scallop*.

SOURCE: Reynolds, 1968.

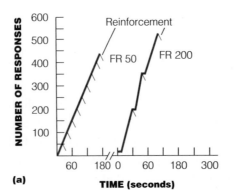

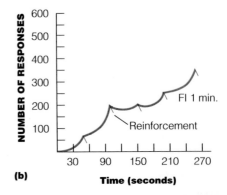

FIGURE 6.14

Performance on Variable Schedules

This graph shows the cumulative records of two pigeons responding. The first pigeon was reinforced on a variable-ratio schedule; the second pigeon was reinforced whenever the first pigeon was, regardless of its number of pecks. This means that the second pigeon was reinforced on a variable-interval schedule; its reinforcement depended not on its number of pecks, but on how long it took the first bird to complete the number of responses necessary to receive reinforcement. The bird on the variable-ratio schedule responded nearly five times as fast as the bird on the variable-interval schedule. (Slashes indicate when reinforcement was delivered.)

SOURCE: Reynolds, 1968.

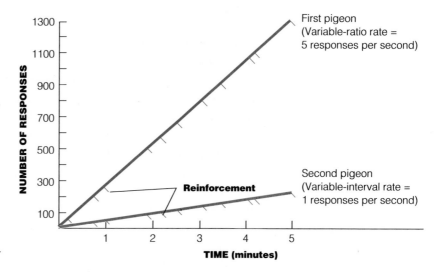

called a *fixed-interval scallop* because the graph it produces has a scalloped shape (see Figure 6.13b). There are many ways the animal may keep track of time in fixed-interval schedules (Zeiler & Powell, 1994).

Few reinforcers in life occur on a regular time schedule. Examples of those that do are the regularly scheduled arrivals of trains and buses. One behavior that is reinforced by these events is looking behavior. The next time you are waiting for a bus or train, observe the rate of looking for the oncoming vehicle. Few people will look for the next train or bus if one has just arrived, because they know that trains and buses arrive at scheduled intervals. As the scheduled arrival of the next train or bus draws near, people will gradually increase the number of times they look down the tracks or street. When the next train or bus arrives, the entire process repeats itself.

Variable-Interval Schedules. On a **variable-interval (VI) schedule,** the time that elapses before a reinforcer will be delivered varies from reinforcer to reinforcer. On a VI 1-minute schedule, the average of the intervals is 1 minute, but the time between one reinforcer and the next might be 7 seconds, then 200 seconds, then 45 seconds, and so on, with the value varying randomly. On variable-interval schedules, a steady, low rate of response typically occurs (see Figure 6.14).

An example of a behavior on a variable-interval schedule is dialing a busy phone number. If the line is engaged, the number of times you dial does not affect getting through. The amount of time before the person hangs up is unpredictable, but the first response after the person does hang up gets reinforced with an answer.

FEATURES OF OPERANT CONDITIONING

Shaping by Successive Approximations. Suppose that you are trying to train a rat to press a lever in a Skinner box. Because the rat is unlikely to press the lever when you put it in the box, it will be impossible to reinforce pushing the lever. The method to produce bar pressing in the first place is called **shaping by successive approximations.** In this technique, the first response the animal makes in the direction of the desired response is reinforced. For example, when the rat moves around the box, it will eventually move in the direction of the lever. As soon as it approaches the lever, release a food pellet. Because a response followed by reinforcement increases in strength, the rat should soon move toward the lever again. But now the requirement for a reinforcement is altered to approximate the desired response more closely: Make sure that the rat touches the lever before the pellet is released. Continue this process until the rat is pressing the lever to obtain more pellets. This technique is called shaping because the animal's behavior is gradually shaped by reinforcing successive approximations of the behavior. Animal trainers use this technique to gradually train whales to jump 15 feet in the air. In humans, shaping has recently been used to restore motor function after strokes. Some disability is due to learned nonuse of limbs, so learning techniques can be used to restore some of these lost functions (Taub et al., 1994).

Often people shape behavior without even realizing it. A parent who yields to a nagging child reinforces the nagging. If the parent decides not to concede the next time it happens, the child may cry. If the parent gives the child what she wants again, the child's crying is reinforced. If the parent then decides to ignore the crying, the child may throw a tantrum, which in turn may cause the parent to yield to the child's request, thereby reinforcing the tantrums. Thus, parents may unwittingly shape problem behavior in their children.

Extinction.   After an operant response is learned, it will weaken and ultimately disappear if the reinforcer is no longer delivered—as in classical conditioning. The procedure of stopping delivery of the reinforcer after conditioning is called **extinction.** An effective means of suppressing behavior is the nonreinforcement (extinction) of that behavior combined with the reinforcement of another behavior. Called **differential reinforcement of other behavior,** or **DRO,** this technique was used successfully to help a 9 year-old boy who scratched and rubbed his body to the point of injury. Let us consider the case of Jerry, described in Cowdery, Iwata, & Pace (1990).

CASE STUDY

JERRY'S SELF-INJURIOUS BEHAVIOR

Jerry was a 9-year-old who exhibited self-injurious behavior (SIB) for at least six years in the form of scratching and rubbing. When he entered the study, he had bandages all over his body (head, neck, arms, legs, and feet). Jerry underwent medical tests to determine if his scratching was the result of an allergic or dermatological condition. All of these tests were negative.

Why do people do such things? Using experimental analysis, Brian Iwata of the University of Florida found that SIB can occur in different individuals for different reasons. Some people resort to SIB to gain attention, others to escape demands, and others to receive a form of self-stimulation. Iwata and other psychologists know that the removal of the source of reinforcement through extinction will reduce such behavior.

A preliminary study showed that scratching was almost continuous when Jerry was left completely alone. In contrast, SIB did not increase when the experimenter paid attention to Jerry when he injured himself. These results suggested that Jerry's SIB was a form of self-stimulation.

One possible way to treat Jerry's SIB would be to cover parts of his body with a shield of some kind so that Jerry couldn't feel his SIB. This was impossible in Jerry's case. His body was covered with wounds, some of which were quite large. There was no way to eliminate stimulation from all these locations. Even if this method were tried, Jerry's tendency to rub two heavily bandaged parts of his body against each other would have caused it to fail.

An alternative approach was tried involving differential reinforcement of other behavior (DRO). The idea was to achieve nonreinforcement (extinction) of Jerry' SIB together with reinforcement of another behavior. A baseline session was first conducted to measure the incidence of Jerry's SIB before treatment. This was necessary to measure what effect (if any) treatment would have on the occurrence of SIB. During this phase, the experimenter told Jerry that she had to leave the room and asked him not to scratch while she was gone. The experimenter then left the room and returned at the end of the session. A one-way mirror allowed researchers outside the room to observe Jerry during this time.

At the beginning of the first treatment session, the experimenter gave the same instructions she had during baseline. She also told Jerry that she would give him a penny upon returning if he did not scratch. The experimenter then left the room and watched him through the observation window. She returned at the end of the interval, briefly examined Jerry to "see if he had scratched," praised him, and gave him a penny if no SIB had occurred. This procedure reinforces all behavior except SIB. If SIB had occurred, the experimenter indicated in a neutral tone that Jerry had scratched while she was gone, regretted that he had not earned the penny, and asked him to try again. This sequence was repeated two more times. At the completion of each session, Jerry was allowed to exchange earned pennies for access to

TV, snacks, video games, and other toys. The interval that Jerry was alone was initially 2 minutes. (Two minutes was the longest amount of time Jerry had refrained from scratching when alone prior to treatment, indicating how severe his problem was.) Gradually, this interval was expanded to 4 minutes. During this first treatment session, SIB immediately decreased to zero from a baseline average of 78 percent (see Figure 6.15). Over many treatment sessions, the interval was gradually extended to 4, 15, and 30 minutes and then to an entire morning. If no SIB occurred, Jerry earned money according to the length of his restraint from SIB. By the end of training, Jerry often refrained from scratching through an entire treatment session, which could last as long as 5 hours.

Jerry's treatment was highly successful. His SIB decreased dramatically, and the procedure successfully extended this reduction for a long period. However, it took a long time to produce these effects (4 months of extensive training), and Jerry's SIB was never completely eliminated. Nonetheless, his SIB was reduced to a point where it was no longer considered a threat to his health. He was released from treatment and allowed to go home.

FIGURE 6.15

The Effects of Differential Reinforcement of Other Behavior (DRO) on Self-Injurious Behavior (SIB)

Jerry's SIB occurred mainly when he was alone. When DRO was introduced, the incidence of SIB dropped immediately.

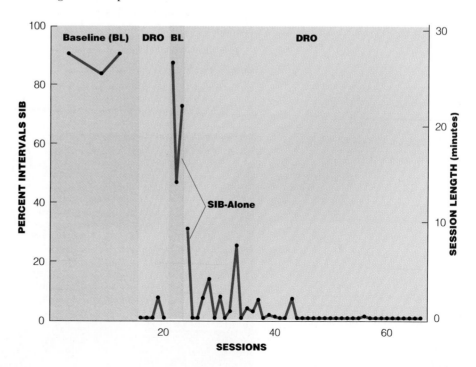

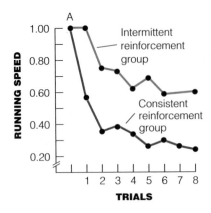

Resistance to Extinction

Intermittent reinforcement produces greater resistance to extinction than continuous reinforcement. This graph shows running speed in a straight-alley runway for two groups of hungry rats. One group was reinforced with food on all of its 60 previous runs down the alley (consistent reinforcement); the other group was reinforced on only half of those 60 runs. Point A shows the running speed for each group at the end of 60 runs. On trials 1 to 8, no reinforcement was given. The group previously given intermittent reinforcement continued to run fast. The group previously given consistent reinforcement stopped running fast very quickly.

SOURCE: Wagner, 1961.

Teachers often use praise to reinforce desired behaviors.

Resistance to Extinction. How long a response will continue when reinforcement is discontinued, or the **resistance to extinction,** depends on the schedule of reinforcement that was initially used to condition the response. If the response was conditioned by continuous reinforcement, then the response decreases rapidly. Imagine a defunct vending machine. Since a vending machine is supposed to pay off on a continuous reinforcement schedule, you are unlikely to try again after losing your money even once. The response will be extinguished in one trial. In contrast, responding will continue much longer if reinforcement for the response has been intermittent. Imagine a broken slot machine that no longer pays off. Since slot machines pay off on a variable-ratio schedule, you might insert many coins into a broken slot machine before you finally gave up. In general, variable-ratio schedules produce greater resistance to extinction; many responses occur even when reinforcement is no longer forthcoming.

Almost any schedule of intermittent or partial reinforcement will produce greater resistance to extinction than continuous reinforcement, a result called the **partial reinforcement extinction effect.** This phenomenon was surprising when first discovered, since researchers had assumed that the more reinforcements an animal received, the greater the resistance to extinction. To examine this phenomenon, imagine that you feed one of your pets at the table only sometimes, and the other always. Then you decide not to feed either pet at the table ever again. Which pet do you think will keep coming to the table longer? The answer is the one you fed there only sometimes. Figure 6.16 shows the results of a study like this using two groups of rats. The group that was rewarded only 50 percent of the time persisted without more reinforcement much longer than subjects whose every response initially was reinforced.

One reason this happens is that a subject trained with intermittent reinforcement has learned that reinforcement follows nonreinforcement. Your pet learns that although it did not get fed at the table last time, it *might* get fed there this time. So when extinction begins, the subject trained with intermittent reinforcement continues to expect reinforcement in the face of nonreinforcement (Capaldi, 1967, 1994). A subject trained with intermittent reinforcement has learned to persist in the face of the frustration produced by the absence of reinforcement, but a subject accustomed to consistent reinforcement has not (Amsel, 1958). Persistence, then, is a learnable trait (Amsel, 1994).

Imagine two children of the same age and intellect, both of whom come from homes where their parents care about them. The teacher notices that Mary works industriously on an assignment, even a difficult one, usually completing all the work given her. John, in contrast, gives up almost immediately, and if asked to continue, he

pouts and whines. Is there a genetic difference between boys and girls? Possibly, but the two children may have different learning histories. Mary may have been praised for working puzzles; her parents may have gradually increased the difficulty of the puzzles and praised her attempts even when if she was not completely successful. So Mary received reinforcement after failure. John's parents, by contrast, may have been happy when he solved problems but may have neglected to praise his unsuccessful attempts. Consequently, John learned to try a task for a few minutes and then, if he could not solve it, give up. The two children respond differently because perseverance has been shaped differently in each. The lesson to be learned from this example is that a parent who always helps a child whenever there is difficulty and provides reinforcement for quitting denies the child the opportunity to learn persistence in tackling difficult problems.

Stimulus Generalization. When parents teach their children to be polite, they want them to be polite everywhere and not just in one particular situation. Research shows that to ensure that behavior will occur in many contexts, it is best to teach the desired response in a variety of contexts. However, learned behavior will occur in contexts similar to the training context without explicit training.

This phenomenon is called **stimulus generalization,** the same phenomenon that occurs in classical conditioning. In the laboratory, a bird trained to peck a yellowish orange key for grain will peck other keys of similar hues. However, the less similar the color is to yellowish orange, the less the bird will peck on those keys, as seen in Figure 6.17 (Guttman & Kalish, 1956).

Discrimination. Sometimes particular behaviors need to be confined only to certain situations. Behavior appropriate in one situation is often inappropriate in another. Singing in a choir is expected, while singing in class is frowned upon (except in music class, of course). Sitting quietly and taking notes in class is proper, but sitting quietly and taking notes at a party is considered weird. Responses are associated with reinforcement only under certain conditions. In **discrimination learning,** responding in the presence of one stimulus is associated with reinforcement, while responding in the presence of a second stimulus is associated with no reinforcement. The subject ultimately responds to a greater extent in the presence of the first stimulus than in the presence of the second, as in classical conditioning.

When a behavior occurs in the presence of one stimulus, but not in the presence of another, control over the behavior by the stimulus, or **stimulus control,** occurs. Behavioral problems are sometimes caused by a lack of appropriate stimulus control. Fortunately, behavioral techniques can be used to correct most problems. For example, some cases of insomnia are due to inappropriate stimulus control. An insomniac may fall asleep easily on a sofa but have difficulty falling asleep once in bed. One reason for this is that the bed may be associated with behaviors other than sleeping, such as watching TV, reading, or eating. One treatment for insomnia is having the patient go into another room if sleep does not occur within a few minutes after getting in bed. This weakens the association between the bed and other activities and strengthens the association between the bed and sleeping. Many insomniacs are helped by this treatment (Morin & Azrin, 1987).

Similarly, you can improve your study habits by studying in a particular place at a particular time and doing nothing else in that place at that time. If you are studying in your chosen place and your mind begins to wander, leave that place and return a short while later. Aim to increase your time spent studying there to further increase the association with studying.

FIGURE 6.17

Stimulus Generalization in Operant Conditioning

A pigeon was reinforced for pecking a yellowish orange key (wavelength 580 nonometers). Responding was greatest to the training color and decreased as the test color became more dissimilar from that used in training.

SOURCE: Adopted from Guttman & Kalish, 1956.

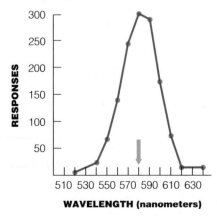

Isolation removes social reinforcement and can be used as a punisher.

PUNISHMENT

In everyday life, a punishment is something that causes pain or discomfort. In behavior theory, punishment is not a type of event, but an effect on behavior. **Punishment** is procedure that weakens behavior. Customarily, punishment consists of the delivery of a unpleasant or aversive stimulus following a response. Common punishments that parents use with children are words of disapproval, yelling, and slapping. However, if these events do not reduce the probability of the preceding response, the procedure is not punishment. Delivery of such events is better termed abuse (Starin, 1991).

Another way to punish is to remove a positive reinforcer. This procedure is called *negative punishment,* which seems redundant but is technically correct. A common example of negative punishment is isolation ("Go to your room"); it involves removal of social reinforcers. Children are given "time-outs" to decrease the preceding problematic behavior.

The important point to remember in learning the terminology is that reinforcers and punishers are defined by their effects on behavior. Reinforcers, both positive and negative, strengthen the preceding behavior. Punishers, both positive and negative, weaken the preceding behavior. *Positive* in these designations refers to delivery of events, and *negative* to removal of events.

The threat of punishment is sometimes used instead of, or in addition to, actual punishment. "Wait until your mother gets home and sees what you did" can be more aversive than what mother actually does when she gets home. In the laboratory, this process is studied by presenting cues that have been paired with aversive events. These conditioned punishers suppress the preceding behavior, just as unconditioned punishers such as shock do.

What constitutes justified punishment in child rearing, schools, and the criminal justice system is a matter of great concern in contemporary society. Certainly, punishment has successfully reduced some forms of criminal behavior. As described by Chance (1994), fines for selling cigarettes to minors in the Chicago area reduced the number of stores conducting such sales from 70 percent to 40 percent. Increasing the fine and adding a one-day suspension of license completely eliminated such sales.

Because punishment suppresses responding, its effects can be studied only if the response is likely to occur without punishment. In the laboratory, the punished response is reinforced first with a positive reinforcer such as food. The basic punishment procedure is to then present an aversive stimulus, such as brief shock, after the specified response. The intensity and immediacy of punishment determine how effectively the preceding response will be suppressed.

CONCEPT SUMMARY

POSITIVE AND NEGATIVE REINFORCEMENT AND PUNISHMENT

	POSITIVE: EVENT ONSET	NEGATIVE: EVENT OFFSET
Reinforcement: Strengthens preceding behavior	Food	Removal of shock
Punishment: Weakens preceding behavior	Shock	Removal of food

Punishment Intensity.   The most commonly used punishment in the laboratory is electric shock. The higher the intensity of shock, the more the response is suppressed (Azrin & Holz, 1966). If shock is weak, a response is only mildly suppressed and may recover completely with repeated use of the weak shock punisher. With a high-intensity shock, a response can be completely suppressed for a very long time. If punishment begins with a weak shock that gradually become more intense, there will be much less suppression of behavior than if the intense shock had been used initially (Azrin, Holz, & Hake, 1963). One interpretation of this finding is that subjects learn to persist in the face of the low-intensity punishment, and by so doing, are less susceptible to the higher intensity. The response conditioned to the low-intensity punishment generalizes to the high-intensity punishment. Moreover, if an animal has learned a response, either by positive or negative reinforcement, sometimes giving brief shock for that behavior maintains the behavior rather than suppressing it—a phenomenon that is still not understood (Lawrence, Hineline & Bersh, 1994). The logical conclusion, however, is that if punishment is to be used, a high-intensity punisher should be used from the beginning.

Delayed Punishment.   Have you ever tried to house-train a dog? If you cannot stay home with the dog, you will not be able to take the dog out or punish it immediately when it has an "accident" on the living room carpet. There are solutions to this house-training problem, but punishing the dog when you come home is not one of them. Delayed punishment is not effective, and the longer the delay between misbehavior and punishment, the less effective the punishment. One criticism of our legal system is that such long delays between crime and punishment make the punishment ineffective. Parents also may have trouble delivering punishment immediately following misconduct, since they cannot continuously monitor their children's behavior. Also, they may not punish every occurrence of the undesired behavior. To be maximally effective, punishment should be used consistently, or else the response will strengthen from the reinforcement received on nonpunished occurrences.

Punishment can also be ineffective if associated with reinforcement, which can even result in an increase in response. Parents are often guilty of associating punishment with reinforcement; after punishing a child, they may hug him or give her a cookie to reassure the child of love. This process becomes complicated because associating punishment directly with expressions of love can reduce the effectiveness of the punishment.

In one laboratory experiment (Azrin & Holz, 1966), pigeons received both food and a mild shock for pecking keys. After key pecking had stabilized, the researchers stopped delivering both the food reinforcement and the shock punishment, and responding declined. Later, they began the shock punishment again, but eliminated the food reinforcement. Surprisingly, key pecking *increased*. At first glance, this finding was highly paradoxical. Why would punishing the response increase its strength? Let us examine the setup once again. In the first phase (when both shock punishment and food were given), the punishment apparently became a signal for positive reinforcement. Accordingly, the punishment increased the rate of response in the final phase, because the pigeons had learned that it was a cue for food.

In everyday life, a punishment can also function as a cue for reinforcement. If parents ignore their children except when they misbehave, the reprimand may be ineffective because it is a form of attention. Misbehavior, then, becomes a means of obtaining wanted attention. This may lead the parents to believe that punishment is ineffective, but actually they made it a signal for care and attention. Therefore, punishment is only ineffective in this case because it serves as a cue for reinforcement in the form of attention.

Use of Punishment Outside the Laboratory. There has always been considerable controversy about the use of punishment outside the laboratory. Books on child rearing often disagree. Some advise no punishment, while others strongly recommend it. There is equal disagreement among social scientists, judges, and the public about punishment's effectiveness in preventing criminal behavior. As we previously described, when punishment (fines) was introduced for selling cigarettes to minors in the Chicago area, sales decreased dramatically (Chance, 1994). However, fines alone did not work for all vendors. Some vendors stopped selling cigarettes only when their licenses were suspended briefly as an additional punishment.

In the laboratory, punishment effectively suppresses responses when three conditions are met: (1) It is relatively intense; (2) it is delivered immediately and consistently after a response; and (3) if not associated with any form of positive reinforcement. Unfortunately, these conditions are often difficult to meet outside the laboratory. Therefore, the effect of punishment varies greatly from situation to situation and from person to person. This variability has led some to claim that punishment simply does not work.

Punishment also may produce undesirable side effects, such as escape, aggression, and apathy (Sidman, 1989). Laboratory studies have verified that shock punishers can produce aggression (Ulrich, Hutchinson, & Azrin, 1965) and motivate escape (Azrin et al., 1965). Motivating children to become aggressive or to run away from home could therefore be an unfortunate effect of using punishment in child rearing. Moreover, few parents can deliver punishment in a detached manner. Punishment is usually associated with anger or agitation and may be an aggressive response to the child's behavior. In extreme cases, child abuse results when a parent's aggressive responses get out of control.

Punishment can be effective if used appropriately. However, the conditions necessary for punishment to be effective (severe, immediate, and consistent punishment not associated with reinforcement) are rarely met. And even when they are, there is still the danger of side effects. Accordingly, punishment should be used sparingly—and only when the conditions are proper for its effective use.

ESCAPE AND AVOIDANCE LEARNING

So far, we have discussed in detail only positive reinforcers (events whose onset increases the strength of the preceding response) and punishers (events whose onset decreases the strength of the preceding response). Remember that there are also negative reinforcers—events whose *removal* is reinforcing. Many people confuse negative reinforcement with punishment. This is because the same event can often be used in both negative reinforcement and punishment. For example, removal of shock is a negative reinforcer, while delivery of shock is a punisher. (See Concept Summary on page 244 to refresh your memory.)

Escape Conditioning. The simplest situation in which to study the effects of negative reinforcement is escape conditioning. In **escape conditioning,** some response terminates an aversive stimulus. For example, removing a pebble from your shoe or turning off your alarm in the morning stops undesirable stimuli. In the laboratory, a rat will learn to escape shock by running away from the shock site. Outside the lab, some children display tantrums, self-injury, and other bizarre behaviors to escape situations they dislike (Carr, Taylor & Robinson, 1991). A more complex behavior motivated by dislike is avoidance learning.

Active Avoidance Learning. In active **avoidance learning,** some active response *prevents* an aversive stimulus. Often, escape learning precedes avoidance learning. If class is boring, you may leave (your escape response terminates an aversive stimulus). Following a number of such experiences, you may no longer attend class at all (your avoidance response prevents the aversive stimulus).

In the laboratory, avoidance learning is often studied in a device called a *shuttle box* that has a movable door or barrier in the middle (see Figure 6.18). The animal subject is placed on one side of the door. When a signal comes on, the experimenter opens the door and an electric shock is sent through the floor grid on the animal's side of the box a moment later. By jumping the barrier to the other side of the box, the animal can escape the shock. After some period of safety, the signal comes on again, indicating that a shock will be sent to the animal through its current floor grid. Once again, the animal can escape the shock, this time by jumping back to the original side. Trials repeat in this manner. Eventually, the animal learns to jump when the signal comes on. Rather than wait until shock occurs and leap away from the shock, the animal has learned to avoid shock by jumping to the other side when the signal comes on.

The most prominent theory of avoidance learning is *two-factor theory* originally proposed by Mowrer in 1947. The first factor is learning to fear the signal: The animal learns the association between the signal and the shock by classical conditioning (the signal is the CS, and the shock is the US). This produces a conditioned response (fear) to the signal. The second factor is learning to escape fear by jumping to the other side. A recent model of this theory has verified that it provides a good explanation for most of the data available on avoidance learning (Zhuikov, Couvillon, & Bitterman, 1994).

Note that even if the shock is turned off, the animal will continue to jump from side to side to avoid it, sometimes for hundreds of trials. Why does the animal jump even when there is no more shock? Then again, how is the animal to know that there

FIGURE 6.18

A Shuttle Box

Overhead lights in the shuttle box are used as the signal for a shock. A dog is put on one side of the box, the light comes on, and later—for example, in 8 seconds—shock is delivered to the grid floor. The barrier is dropped when the light comes on. If the dog jumps when the light comes on, it can avoid the shock. Once the dog goes to the other side, the barrier is closed and another trial begins. The light comes on again after a few seconds, signaling that shock will be delivered again in 8 seconds. Ultimately, the dog learns to avoid shock by shuttling back and forth over the barrier when the light comes on.

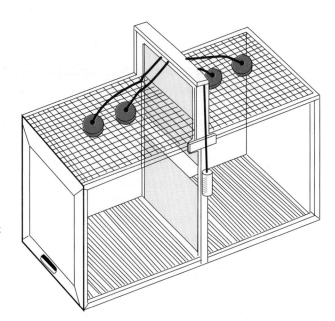

is no more shock? The animal has learned that it will not be shocked if it jumps and that it will be shocked if it fails to jump. In well-learned avoidance, the expectancy of not being shocked for jumping continues to be confirmed, so the animal continues to jump (Seligman & Johnston, 1973). But as long as the animal continues to jump, it cannot learn that it would be completely safe even without jumping. The persistence of some behavior disorders based on avoidance learning can be viewed similarly. For example, consider a man who compulsively washes his hands to prevent illness. Unless the behavior ceases for some other reason, the man cannot learn that hand washing has little effect on his risk of disease.

BIOLOGICAL CONSTRAINTS IN OPERANT CONDITIONING

Some responses cannot be easily trained as avoidance responses because of the subject's biological predisposition (another example of the biological basis of behavior). For example, although rats learn to jump out of a box to avoid shock in only one or two trials (Bolles, 1970), it is very difficult to train them to press bars to avoid shocks. Since rats *are* capable of pressing bars—and have done so for food in hundreds of experiments—why do they find it difficult to avoid shock by bar pressing? One suggestion is that the shocked animals tend to make *species-specific defense responses* (Bolles, 1970). Fleeing and freezing seem to be dominant responses for rats in defensive situations. Thus, it is easy to train rats to jump out of boxes to avoid shock, but difficult to train them to stay there and press bars. The environment determines which of the rats' species-specific responses will occur: They fight if there is something to fight, flee if possible, or freeze if no other response can be made (Fanselow, 1994).

An animal's natural behavior can also interfere with learning when conditioning involves positive reinforcement. Two students of Skinner's formed a business training animals for store displays. In 1961, they summarized some interesting problems they encountered (Breland & Breland, 1961). Trying to reinforce a raccoon for placing coins in a box, they found that the animal would rub the coins together but would not put them in the box. This "misbehavior," as they termed it, occurred even though it was not required for reinforcement. In fact, the misbehavior postponed and sometimes prevented delivery of the reinforcer. Pairing a stimulus (coins) with food elicited the species-normal food-related behavior of rubbing, even though this behavior was not reinforced. Thus, the raccoons rubbed the coins together (their normal response to food), rather than putting them in the box. Similarly, pigeons have been shown to peck a key illuminated just prior to food delivery, even if food is delivered independently of their behavior (Brown & Jenkins, 1968). In fact, the pigeons will peck even if pecking delays the delivery of food (Williams & Williams, 1969). It is not necessary to reinforce a pigeon specifically for pecking a key; they peck the key as long as the light on the key precedes food. This process is called *autoshaping* because the pigeon does not need to be shaped to peck the key; the pigeon, in essence, shapes itself.

Initially, some of these findings were seen as inconsistent with the idea that there are general learning processes applicable to all situations and responses. Today, however, distinctions between general processes and specific biological adaptations are seen as artificial (Shettleworth, 1993). Instead, recent learning research has applied the methods of experimental psychology to phenomena and species outside the traditional learning laboratory to discover general processes. These studies integrate traditional learning studies with biological approaches. Learning theory is now applied to sexual behavior (Domjan, 1994) and developmental phenomena (Hogan, 1994). Also, comparative studies of spatial cognition (Gallistel, 1990) and perceptual processes (Reid & Shettleworth, 1992) are currently in progress.

COGNITIVE FACTORS IN INSTRUMENTAL LEARNING

Another recent trend is to expand the study of animal learning to include animal cognition.

Learned Helplessness.   In 1967, an important phenomenon was discovered almost by accident. A series of studies by Martin Seligman, Bruce Overmier, and Steven Maier (Overmier & Seligman, 1967; Seligman & Maier, 1967) investigated the effects of exposure to uncontrollable shock on subsequent active avoidance learning. They found that this experience had an amazing effect: Animals just sat and whimpered and no longer tried to learn to avoid shock. The researchers called this effect **learned helplessness**—an impairment in learning how to avoid or escape an aversive stimulus following exposure to an inescapable, unavoidable stimulus.

Why did this occur? According to Maier and Seligman (1976), animals exposed to uncontrollable events form a general expectation that shocks are independent of their behavior—that avoidance is impossible. Such an expectation has extremely powerful effects. First, it reduces the animal's motivation to escape. (Since responding has no effect on the pain, what incentive is there to respond?) Second, it reduces the animal's ability to learn later that behavior can be effective. In other words, the inescapable shock produces certain cognitive limitations (yet another way cognitions control behavior).

Learned helplessness has also been studied in humans, with loud tones substituted for shocks. People in the control group simply sit and listen to the tones. Two other groups are told that they can control the tones, but only one of the groups (the experimental group) actually is able to do so. The behavior of the last group (the yoked group) has no effect on the tones; the tones they receive occur in the same manner as for people in the experimental group. Sometimes people in the yoked group (whose behavior has no effect on the noise) act superstitiously. That is, they repeat some behavior that was accidentally paired with tone termination. If subjects are told that their behavior fails to affect the noise, they are more likely to develop learned helplessness (Matute, 1994). The concept of learned helplessness has been extended to many areas of human concern, including depression, susceptibility to heart attacks, and lack of intellectual achievement (Garber & Seligman, 1980). We consider this topic further in Chapter 15.

Learning versus Performance.   The distinction between learning (what we know) and performance (what we do) was first identified in experimental research by Edward C. Tolman. Tolman's work in the 1920s and 1930s clearly showed that learning was not always immediately reflected in performance. In one experiment, a group of recently fed rats was allowed to explore a complex maze with food located at one point inside. The rats wandered aimlessly because they were not hungry. However, when the rats were made hungry at a later time, they ran directly to the food. This shows that the rats had learned where the food was located during their aimless exploration, but at that time had no reason to demonstrate that knowledge. Tolman believed that the rats had formed a **cognitive map,** or internal representation, of the maze during their exploration.

More recent work continues to support Tolman's conclusion about cognitive maps. Much of this work utilizes a radial maze, in which a number of arms extend from a central platform (see Figure 6.19). In this maze, food is placed in every arm. Olton and Samuelson (1976) showed that rats run down each arm once, not wasting any effort reentering arms. When the arms are rebaited, they again enter each only once, but in a different order than the first time. Apparently, they are not merely searching the arms in a fixed order. If food is replaced in an arm before they have ventured into all arms, they still search all the unexplored arms before reentering any, showing that they do not simply use their sense of smell to locate the food. It appears that the rats actually remember which arms they have already entered and avoid those in their search (Roberts, 1984).

An animal in a radial maze does not merely repeat a reinforced response. On the contrary, the data strongly suggest that the rat has a cognitive representation of the maze and the memory capacity to store this information. Thus, the rat makes a new response based on its knowledge of the maze and its memory of what it experienced there. Memory plays a role even in simple learning situations, and some researchers suggest that learning, remembering, and forgetting are intertwined in all conditioning experiments (Bouton, 1994). However, recent data also suggest that there may be common laws underlying behavior in the radial maze and behavior on simple schedules of reinforcement. Behavior on simple reinforcement schedules is not usually explained by the cognitive concepts of thought and memory (Elsmore & McBride, 1994), but these cognitive practices may indeed be involved.

Expectancies. Whereas a cognitive map represents an animal's knowledge of the relationships between events in space, an **expectancy** represents the animal's knowledge of the relationships between events in time. Thus, an expectancy is a mental representation that one event will follow another.

FIGURE 6.19

Eight-Arm Radial Maze

Food is put in each arm, and a rat is placed on the center platform. Optimal performance is to enter each arm only once.

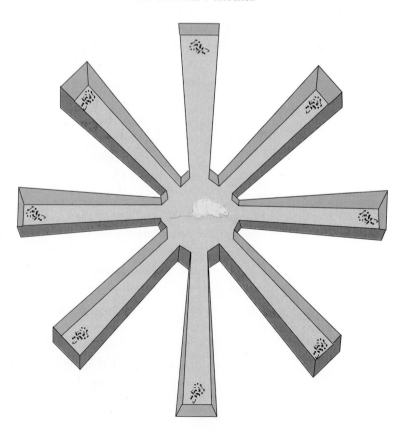

Colwill and Rescorla (1985) showed that rats come to expect the reinforcer received in operant conditioning. In one experiment, they trained rats with two different responses and two different reinforcers: Pressing a lever earned food pellets, while pulling a chain earned a few drops of sugar water. Later, taste aversion was implemented, and each rat was made ill after consuming either sugar water or food pellets. In a subsequent test, the researchers found that rats poisoned for eating food pellets made fewer lever presses, while rats poisoned for drinking sugar water made fewer chain pulls. This outcome shows that the rats expected to receive food pellets for lever pressing. Why else would associating the food pellets with illness affect lever pressing? Likewise, the rats expected to receive sugar water for the chain pulls. Notice that the rats did not require direct punishment for lever pressing or chain pulls. Devaluing the reward associated with either response (by associating the reward with illness) was sufficient to lower responding. In some cases, inhibition results when the expectation of receiving the reinforcer has changed (Bonardi & Hall, 1994).

In general, current theories of learning assume that animals form internal representations of events in their environment and make associations between those representations. Thus, their behavior is based on these cognitive representations or expectancies.

Observational Learning

Will you drink more liquor if your friends drink a lot? Laboratory studies suggest that you will. In one study of drinking in college students (Garlington & Dericco, 1977), subjects were asked to drink in pairs at a simulated bar. One subject was the accomplice of the experimenter and initially matched his drinking to that of the true subject. Subsequently, he either increased or decreased his own rate of drinking. The subject usually increased or decreased his or her drinking in line with the accomplice.

Clearly, people do not imitate all the behavior they see. What determines whether behavior will be imitated? One important factor is the consequences that the person being observed—the **model**—receives for the behavior. You may learn to say "please" by seeing your brother praised for doing so, or you may learn not to talk in class after seeing another student punished for doing so. You can learn persistence by seeing another rewarded for persisting, and you can learn fear by seeing another suffer. In general, observed behavior that is reinforced will be imitated, while that which is punished or not reinforced will not inspire imitation. In some of the earliest studies of such **observational learning,** researchers concentrated on fear reduction.

OBSERVATIONAL LEARNING OF FEAR AND AGGRESSION

Fear. As long ago as 1924, Mary Cover Jones taught children afraid of rabbits to diminish their fear by watching other children play with rabbits. Observational learning is a useful therapeutic technique, and it can also explain how such fears are acquired.

Fears and phobias are not random. For instance, people do not often fear stove tops, even though some danger is associated with them. However, they *do* fear snakes, spiders, and heights. Why do humans associate certain events with aversive consequences? Perhaps we are biologically predisposed to certain fears because of the evolutionary advantage of developing such fears.

To determine whether some stimuli are more likely to become feared through learning than others, Susan Mineka and her colleagues (1987) showed monkeys films

We may be biologically predisposed to fear snakes.

of other monkeys acting fearfully to either snakes or flowers (the tapes were specially edited to combine images of a fearful monkey with images of a flower). After observing the tape, the group that saw a fearful reaction to snakes later showed fear of snakes. The group that saw a fearful reaction to flowers, however, did not develop a fear of flowers. This study shows that there are constraints on the kinds of stimuli monkeys will learn to fear. Fear of snakes is acquired easily, but fear of flowers is not. Observational learning is affected by the same biological constraints that affect classical and operant conditioning.

Aggression. Albert Bandura and his associates have conducted many experiments that demonstate the imitation of aggressive behaviors. In one experiment (Bandura, 1965), 4-year old children individually watched a short film in which an adult acted aggressively toward a large doll. Some of the children subsequently saw the aggressor being reinforced by another adult. The aggressor was given candy and soda and called a "strong champion." Other children saw the aggressor punished for aggression; the model was scolded and warned not to act that way again. The third group of children saw no consequences for aggression on the part of the model. Immediately after viewing the film, the children had the opportunity to play with the doll themselves, along with other toys. The children who saw the model rewarded for aggressive behavior were more likely to imitate the aggressive behavior against the doll than those who saw the model punished. Thus, watching a model get reinforced or punished has effects similar to those of actually receiving reinforcement or punishment (Bandura, 1965).

Note that the observed model in these experiments does not have to be acting in person but can be taped. These experiments therefore have obvious implications for the effects of watching violence on television. As we discussed in Chapter 1, hostility can be learned by watching aggressive people succeed on TV, in video games, or in films.

CHARACTERISTICS OF THE MODEL

A major factor in observational learning is the model. The more power people have, the more we like or admire them, or the greater their prestige, the more likely we are to imitate them (Rosenthal & Bandura, 1978). Children learn from observing their parents—people of great power and prestige in their lives. Therefore, if you do not want your child to smoke, you should not smoke; if you wish to encourage reading, you should read. Whether you intend it or not, your behavior probably influences your child more than your direct reinforcement and punishment of the child's behavior.

CULTURE AND OBSERVATIONAL LEARNING

As soon as they enter the world, children begin learning the requirements of their family, cultural group, and society. Children learn behavior appropriate to their culture by observing their parents, peers, siblings, teachers, other adult models, and the media. Once cultural values are acquired, they in turn can influence future learning. This interaction of sociocultural factors with learning is very important, and it may be the foundation on which sociocultural factors come to influence many other areas of human behavior.

In the United States, children from different cultures unite in a common school setting. Statistics estimate that by the year 2000, 30 to 40 percent of the students in schools across the nation will be those traditionally considered cultural or ethnic minorities. By contrast, the teaching force is 88 percent Anglo and Caucasian. Most teachers have little experience with other cultures, and the culture of the school sometimes conflicts with the culture many children experience at home.

In American universities, international students compose an increasing portion of the student body. Among all nations receiving international students in the 1987–88 academic year, the United States hosted the largest number, 33 percent of the world's total (Zikopoulos, 1987).

Cultural adjustment is one of the major problems facing international students (Thomas & Althen, 1989). Desire to conform to the new environment conflicts with the students' desire to maintain their cultural identity. Students worry about becoming partly Americanized—not fitting in either at home or at school. As one Chinese student put it, "Inevitably, I am going to be influenced by this culture, perhaps in ways that are not now clear to me. But the ways in which I have changed will be obvious to my professional associates, friends, and family" (Paige, 1990, p. 168).

One important characteristic of American culture is the emphasis on individualism as opposed to the collectivism of other cultures (Triandis, 1990). In collectivist cultures, the needs of some identifiable group (the family, a work group, the entire society) supersede those of the individual members. People from collectivist societies would probably agree with these statements: "Children should live at home with their parents until they get married" and "I like to live close to my good friends." A strong individualist, on the other hand, would probably agree with statements like these: "If the group is slowing me down, it is better to leave the group and work alone," and "The most important goal in life is my own happiness." In individualist cultures, a person's likes and dislikes and whether the costs and benefits of an action balance out in favor of the individual are most important. Furthermore, in individualistic cultures, child rearing emphasizes self-reliance, independence, and autonomy. In collectivist cultures, by contrast, children are trained to be obedient, and duty and sacrifice for the group are emphasized.

A collectivist background can interfere with performance in U.S. mainland schools, where methods are based on an individualistic culture. For example, the Hawaiian family emphasizes interdependence and group identity. Thus, Hawaiian children are not motivated by individual awards (gold stars or grades) to the extent that mainland U.S. children are. And because the Hawaiian family attaches greater values to peer interaction and the mutual care of siblings, Hawaiian children are not accustomed to paying attention to one adult for a long period of time. Consequently, cooperative work and learning groups among children in the classroom are more effective in producing learning in children with this background than a lecture style of instruction.

Cultures also differ in the importance placed on formal education. A high value on formal education is characteristic of Japanese culture. Japanese parents make sure that their children do their homework, deny privileges to children who earn poor grades, and point out people who have succeeded as a result of their education. Japanese children spend more time in school than U.S. children and are also exposed to very ambitious expectations set by their families. Diligence, hard work, and persistence are the norm. As a result, Japanese children outscore American children on many standardized tests, as we discuss in Chapter 11.

THEMES IN REVIEW

Biological factors are critical to many aspects of learning. For example, an animal's biology makes some environmental relations easy to learn and others difficult. Biological factors also have an influence in operant conditioning. Conditioning is easier if the taught response is compatible with the animal's natural repertoire of responses to the reinforcer.

Cognitive factors have also proved important to learning. In operant conditioning, animals' cognitive representations of the situation and of the relationship between their response and the reinforcer can either facilitate per-

formance (as in the development of cognitive maps) or interfere with performance (as in learned helplessness). Also, stimuli paired in a classical conditioning situation do not necessarily become associated as automatically as Pavlov assumed. Rather, only the stimulus that is the best predictor becomes associated with a following unconditioned stimulus. Humans and other animals can also learn from observing the behavior and environment of others. Children learn by observing their parents and making associations based on what they witness as much as they do from the reinforcers their parents

give directly for their behavior.

Finally, all the learning processes we have discussed in this chapter operate to instill sociocultural factors. As soon as children enter the world, they begin to recieve reinforcement for behavior in accord with cultural values, recieving punishment for behavior that violates cultural norms. Culture is also learned by observing the behavior of other members of the culture. Sociocultural factors can themselves help or interfere with subsequent learning.

SUMMARY

1 Learning is a relatively permanent change in behavior or knowledge that occurs as a result of experience.

2 There are four basic elements in classical conditioning: an unconditioned stimulus (US) that elicits an unconditioned response (UR) without any previous training; a neutral stimulus that becomes the conditioned stimulus (CS) after it is paired with the US; and the conditioned response (CR), the reaction that the CS comes to elicit after pairing. Numerous responses can be acquired by classical conditioning, including many physiological reactions.

3 After pairing the CS and US in classical conditioning, presenting the CS alone produces weakening of the CR (extinction), although the response will recover with rest following extinction (spontaneous recovery). A CR will occur to other similar CSs, as well as to the original CS (stimulus generalization). If one CS is paired with a US and a different CS is paired with absence of the US, a CR will occur to the first CS, but not to the second (discrimination).

4 Contiguity between a CS and US is neither necessary nor sufficient for conditioning to occur. Conditioning can occur with long delays between the CS and US (as in taste aversion learning). Also, a CS can occur contiguously with the US and fail to become associated with the US if another more biologically relevant CS is present or if a better predictor of the US is present.

5 In instrumental or operant conditioning, a reinforcer is given only if a subject makes the appropriate response. Reinforcers increase the strength of behavior that precedes them; punishers decrease the strength of behavior that precedes them. A positive reinforcer is one whose presentation increases the strength of the preceding response. A negative reinforcer is one whose removal strengthens the preceding response. Reinforcers can be unlearned (primary) or learned (conditioned).

6 Schedules of intermittent reinforcement (when fewer than 100 percent of the responses are reinforced) include interval schedules and ratio schedules. On a ratio schedule, a certain number of responses produces reinforcement. On an interval schedule, the first response after a certain interval has passed is reinforced. Intermittent reinforcement produces greater resistance to extinction than continuous reinforcement.

7 Effective punishment is intense, is delivered immediately and consistently, and is not associated with positive reinforcement.

8 Negative reinforcement includes escape learning, in which a response terminates an aversive stimulus, and active avoidance learning, in which an active response prevents an aversive stimulus.

9 Operant conditioning is easier if conditioning is compatible with the animals' natural, biological responses to reinforcers.

10 Animals are capable of forming cognitive maps. They also form expectancies, the cognitive representation of how two events relate in time.

11 Animals (including people) can learn by observing others without showing their acquired knowledge overtly. This demonstrates that learning (what we know) is not always immediately reflected in performance (what we do).

12 Cultural norms and values have been shown to affect learning in humans. If your cultural background is different from the cultural environment in which you learn, then your performance may be affected by the differences between the two.

KEY TERMS

learning (p. 225)

classical conditioning (p. 225)

unconditioned stimulus (US) (p. 226)

unconditioned response (UR) (p. 226)

conditioned stimulus (CS) (p. 226)

conditioned response (CR) (p. 226)

acquisition (p. 227)

extinction (p. 228, p. 240)

spontaneous recovery (p.229)

stimulus generalization (p. 229, p. 240)

discrimination (p. 230, p.243)

discrimination training (p. 230)

contiguity (p. 231)

taste aversion learning (p. 231)

biological constraints (p. 231)

blocking (p.233)

operant (instrumental) conditioning (p.234)

operant (p.235)

reinforcement (p. 235)

positive reinforcement (p. 236)

negative reinforcement (p. 236)

primary (unconditioned) reinforcer (p. 236)

secondary (conditioned) reinforcer (p. 236)

partial (intermittent) reinforcement (p. 236)

response deprivation theory (p. 237)

ratio schedules (p.237)

fixed-ratio (FR) schedules (p. 237)

variable-ratio (VR) schedules (p. 237)

interval schedules (p. 238)

fixed-interval (FI) schedule (p. 238)

variable-interval (VI) schedules (p. 238)

shaping by successive approximations (p. 239)

FOR CRITICAL ANALYSIS

1 Researchers train two groups of rats to fear a light by pairing the light with shock. One group experiences repeated shocks in the box to be used for training prior to light-shock pairing. The other group does not. The first group shows less fear to the light. One explanation of this postulates that the context (the box) became associated with the shock in phase 1 for the group preexposed to shock. Explain how this could be a form of blocking. (**Hint:** The box itself may become feared.)

2 What would be a good treatment for self-injurious behavior (SIB) that was reinforced by attention? For SIB that was reinforced by escape from demands?

3 Can you explain why the great resistance to extinction of active avoidance learning may be a problem for Mowrer's two-factor theory of avoidance learning?

4 Explain how you would train a dog to heel (i.e., to follow closely near the trainer's left heel when walking) by operant conditioning. Describe two different methods, one using positive reinforcement and one using negative reinforcement.

5 Some theorists have suggested that classical conditioning is an inevitable part of any operant conditioning experiment. Explain why this may be so.

SUGGESTED READINGS

BOWER, G. H., & HILGARD, E. R. (1981). *Theories of learning* (5th ed.). Englewood Cliffs, NJ: Prentice Hall. The latest edition of a classic in the field, this book offers excellent coverage of the theories of learning, including both historical background and recent developments.

CHANCE , P. (1994). *Learning and behavior* (3rd ed.). Pacific Grove, CA.: Brooks/Cole. An excellent undergraduate text covering most of the topics in this chapter.

KALISH, H. I. (1981). *From behavioral science to behavior modification*. New York: McGraw-Hill. An excellent coverage of behavior modification techniques, this book also describes the laboratory work that provided the basis for their development. It makes the connection between basic experimental work and application of this work very clear.

MILLER, L. K. (1980). *Principles of everyday behavior analysis*. Pacific Grove, CA.: Brooks/Cole. Describes how to apply principles used in research in the animal laboratory to your everyday life.

ROITBLAT, H. L. (1987). *Introduction to comparative cognition*. New York: Freeman. An overview of work on cognitive capacities of animals, including language learning in animals.

PSYCHOLOGY ON THE INTERNET

Psycholoquy—Pavlov-Bell

(http://cogsci.ecs.soton.ac.uk/~lac/topics.html#pavlov-bell)

These Psycholoquy articles discuss one detail of the methodology employed by Pavlov in his classical conditioning experiments—whether Pavlov actually used a bell as a conditioned stimulus in any of his experiments. Whereas the outcome of this debate does not have an impact on the validity of Pavlov's conclusions, the articles are interesting in that they provide an historical view of Pavlov's work and the work of other early behaviorists. Several of the articles contain substantial excerpts from Pavlov's original publications.

Journal of the Experimental Analysis of Behavior (JEAB)

(http://www.envmed.rochester.edu/wwwrap/behavior/jaba/jabahome.htm)

Journal of Applied Behavior Analysis (JABA)

(http://www.envmed.rochester.edu/wwwrap/behavior/jeab/jeabhome.htm)

These journals are published by the Society for the Experimental Analysis of Behavior (http://www.envmed.rochester.edu/wwwvgl/seab/seab.htm). JEAB was founded "primarily for the original publication of erxperiments relevant to the behavior of individual organisms," whereas JABA was founded for "the original publication of reports of experimental research involving applications of the experimental analysis of behavior to problems of social importance."

Although these journals are not "true electronic journals" (you cannot view all articles on-line), both journals do provide some on-line services. Users are allowed to access the table of contents from each issue as well as the abstract from each paper. In addition, users are allowed to search a database of abstracts for papers related to specific topics, and both journals allow on-line access to one feature article from each issue.

Behavior analysis—Technical Terms

(gopher://alpha1.csd.uwm.edu/0ftp%3aalpha1.csd.uwm.edu%40/pub/Psychology/BehaviorAnalysis/educational/course/eab-tech-terms-dermer)

This is a list (compiled by Marshall Lev Dermer at the University of Wisconsin—Milwaukee) of technical terms used in behavior analysis. In addition to providing simple definitions of terms such as negative/positive reinforcer, operant conditioning, and extinction, this list provides more detailed information on such topics as the necessary conditions for a stimulus being a reinforcer and Skinner's theory of avoidance behavior.

The Behavior Analysis Home Page at the University of South Florida

(http://www.coedu.usf.edu/behavior/behavior.html)

Experimental Analysis of Behavior at Auburn

(http://www.duc.auburn.edu/~newlamc/)

These sites provide links to professional societies, university research groups and Listserv groups related to behavior analysis.

REMEMBERING and FORGETING

Chapter 7

BIOLOGICAL THEME
What parts of the brain underlie remembering?

LEARNING THEME
Can we remember everything we have learned? If not, why not?

COGNITIVE THEME
What are the best strategies for remembering textbook material?

DEVELOPMENTAL THEME
Why can't we remember what happened to us before we were three years old?

SOCIOCULTURAL THEME
Can what other people say about past events affect memories for the events?

In an article entitled "what college did to me," humorist Robert Benchley facetiously tried to recall all of the things he had learned from his university education. In four productive years, Benchley felt that he had mastered some thirty-nine items, decreasing from twelve in his freshman year to eight in his senior year. Obviously, Benchley had a fairly typical college education, picking up the esoteric knowledge of both academics and everyday experience, as the following selection reveals:

Things I Learned—Freshman Year*

1. Charlemagne either died or was born or did something with the Holy Roman Empire in 800.

2. There is a double ll in the middle of "parallel."

3. French nouns ending in "aison" are feminine.

4. Almost everything you need to know about a subject is in the encyclopedia.

5. A tasty sandwich can be made by spreading peanut butter on raisin bread.

6. The chances are against filling an inside straight

7. There is a law in economics called The Law of Diminishing Returns, which means after a certain margin is reached returns begin to diminish. This may not be correctly stated, but there is a law by that name.

Sophomore Year

1. A good imitation of measles rash can be effected by stabbing the forearm with a stiff whiskbroom.

2. You can sleep undetected in a lecture course by resting the head on the hand as if shading the eyes.

3. The ancient Phoenicians were really Jews, and got as far north as England where they operated tin mines.

4. You can get dressed much quicker in the morning if the night before when you are going to bed you take off your trousers and underdrawers at once, leaving the latter inside the former.

**Source:* Abridged from "What College Did to Me" in *Inside Benchley* by Robert Benchley.© 1921, 1922, 1925, 1927, 1928, 1942 by Harper & Row, Publishers, Inc. Reprinted by permission of the publisher.

Junior Year

1. Pushing your arms back as far as they will go fifty times each day increases your chest measurement.
2. Marcus Aurelius had a son who turned out to be a bad boy.
3. Eight hours of sleep are not necessary.
4. Heraclitus believed fire was the basis of all life.
5. The chances are you will never fill an inside straight.

Senior Year

1. There is as yet no law determining what constitutes trespass in an airplane.
2. Six hours of sleep are not necessary.
3. Bicarbonate of soda taken before retiring makes you feel better the next day.
4. May is the shortest month of the year.

Is this all Benchley really retains from his years in college? What does this say about his memory?

Memory refers to the effect of past experience as stored in the brain and expressed in later behavior. Although only one word is used to describe this marvelous ability, we shall see that many different kinds of performance all reflect memory.

Types of Memory

Memory is not a unitary process, ability, or system. Psychologists have been able to discern a number of different memory abilities that people display. Here we will distinguish between episodic, semantic, and procedural memory, as well as primary and secondary memory; later in the chapter we will encounter a few other categories.

Episodic memory is the type of memory invoked when recollecting personal events (or episodes) from the past (Tulving, 1993). For example, remembering what shirt you wore yesterday, what you ate for breakfast this morning, and what you did last Saturday night are all instances of episodic memory. Episodic memory is usually accompanied by a recollection of the time and place of the event's occurrence. Episodic memory can be contrasted with **semantic memory,** which is memory for facts or knowledge about the world. For example, knowing that zebras have stripes, that Michael Jordan is a famous basketball player, and that a carrot is a type of vegetable are all examples of semantic memory. Note that this type of memory is not as personal as episodic memory; knowledge of this type is widely shared among people within a culture. Also, semantic memories are not usually associated with any specific event or time and place. (Can you remember exactly when you first learned who won World War II?)

In addition to memory for personal experiences and memory for facts, we have a third type of memory: procedural memory. **Procedural memory** is memory for how to do things. For example, we remember how to ride a bicycle, how to play the guitar, and how to walk. These are complicated skills that take a great deal of effort and attention to learn, but once they are learned, they often can be performed almost automatically. Note that whereas episodic and semantic memory may involve only thought, procedural memory also involves overt behavior and motor skills. Certain mental operations, like simple arithmetic, may also be represented by procedural memories.

In his famous book *Principles of Psychology* (1890), William James distinguished between primary and secondary memory. He defined **primary memory** as the stream of thought, or stream of consciousness. Primary memory holds for a very short time the events and stimuli that we have recently experienced. These events are sometimes stored more permanently into **secondary memory,** our memory for the past. Events in secondary memory have to be *retrieved* with more effort than those in primary memory. James regarded secondary memory as true memory. Episodic, semantic, and procedural memory may all be considered types of secondary memory. This distinction between primary and secondary memory is still made, although most researchers now use the terms *short-term memory* and *long-term memory.* More will be said about these later, but briefly, **short-term memory** is largely equivalent to primary memory, whereas **long-term memory** is equivalent to secondary memory.

CONCEPT SUMMARY

TYPES OF MEMORY

Episodic memory:	recollection of personal experiences, or episodes; the episode's time and place of occurrence are usually involved.
Semantic memory:	general knowledge of facts about language and the world; when and where the information was learned is unimportant.
Procedural memory:	knowledge of how to accomplish tasks, usually involving motor skills (e.g., how to ride a bike).
Primary (short-term) memory:	recent events that can be held in mind at one time.
Secondary (long-term) memory:	memory for past events; retrieval takes more effort than for primary memory.

Stages of Memory

Have you ever wondered why some things seem so easy to recall, while other things seem to be immediately and completely forgotten? Why can't we bring back memories of all that has happened to us?

In answering such questions, it is useful to distinguish among three stages in the learning/memory process: *encoding, storage,* and *retrieval* (Melton, 1963). To illustrate these processes, try to recall the capital of Ecuador. If you cannot, do you know at what stage in the memory process that the breakdown occurred? Perhaps you have never heard of Ecuador's capital. In that case, you never acquired the information. **Encoding** (or acquisition) constitutes the first stage in the memory process, and it refers to initial learning. When a person attends to information, it is likely to be stored at least temporarily and sometimes permanently. Thus, **storage** refers to the changes in the nervous system that allow information to be maintained, however briefly. When this happens, we say that a **memory trace** has been created. If you once knew the capital of Ecuador, but cannot recall it now, it may be that the memory trace has faded or decayed. Thus, forgetting can occur because of losses of stored information from memory. Another possibility is that you may have had the fact stored, but were unable to retrieve it. **Retrieval** is the process of getting at and using information in memory. If all three stages in the memory process—encoding, storage, and retrieval—were completed, then you would correctly answer "Quito."

Psychologists typically discuss memory as though it were a container, which is where the idea of storing information in memory comes from (Roediger, 1980b). Theorists have compared the workings of memory to human record keeping, in which the records (memories) are held in various depositories (memory traces). A record player, tape recorder, video recorder, dictionary, library, and computer are all metaphors that have been used. For example, the terms *acquisition, storage,* and *retrieval* can be illustrated by analogy to similar processes in a library. If you go to search for a very old title, you may not find the book because the library never bought it (an acquisition problem), because it was so old that it decayed and fell apart (a storage problem), or because it has been misshelved and cannot be located (a retrieval problem). Of course, no one believes that human memory is exactly like a library, but the analogy is helpful. It is interesting to note that as the technology of record keeping has improved, psychologists have likewise updated the analogy; many theorists now liken memory functions to the operation of computers (Gentner & Grudin, 1985).

The First Experimental Studies of Memory

Psychologists have been studying memory experimentally for over 100 years, employing two general approaches: psychological and physiological. In the psychological approach, theorists abstractly describe the workings of memory with metaphors similar to those used to describe consciousness in Chapter 5. (This approach exemplifies the cognitive theme of the text). Psychologists design experiments to collect evidence about their theories. In the physiological approach to memory, scientists seek to discover the neural bases of memory, either through experimental work with animals or by studying people who have suffered brain damage. (This approach exemplifies the biological theme of the text).

From the beginning, psychologists have asked two primary questions: If a person can no longer recall something, does that mean it is not stored? And if information is stored, how can scientists measure the traces of memories that cannot be recalled?

Ebbinghaus's First Experiments. Hermann Ebbinghaus answered these questions by performing numerous experiments, with himself as the only subject. These pioneering studies were first published in 1885 in a book titled *Memory: A Contribution to Experimental Psychology* (1913), and Ebbinghaus's experimental results have stood the test of time (Roediger, 1985; Slamecka, 1985). The experimental tools he developed, called *nonsense syllables,* were usually syllables in which a vowel was sandwiched between two consonants (e.g., *zok, kep*). Ebbinghaus hoped to minimize the influence of prior knowledge that would have been present had he relied on words, sentences, or (as he sometimes did) passages of poetry. The meaningfulness and familiarity of such everyday items would have made some of them easier to recall than others. Thus, Ebbinghaus used the novel syllables to ensure that the items were equally memorable and to get a measure of memory that he hoped was more "pure."

Ebbinghaus selected items from a pool of 2,300 such syllables and read them aloud at a fixed pace. Then he covered up the list and tried to recite it in order from memory. Of course, with a long list this proved impossible on the first attempt, but he could count the number of syllables he recalled correctly. Then he reread the list and repeated the procedure until he got the entire list right. One way Ebbinghaus measured the difficulty of a list was to count the number of these study/test trials (or the amount of time) needed to achieve one perfect recitation. This is called a *trials to criterion* mea-

Hermann Ebbinhaus originated the scientific study of human memory.

sure of memory. For example, it takes more trials for long lists than for short lists to get to the criterion of one perfectly correct performance.

Ebbinghaus also tested his memory of a list at various times after he had learned it, often by providing himself with the initial syllable as a cue. Sometimes he was unable to recall any of the others from the list. Did this mean that the series he had studied perhaps a month earlier had left no trace in memory? Ebbinghaus developed a method to answer this question. He attempted to relearn the list with study/test trials, just as he had originally. He then discovered that even when he could not recall any items on a list, he often needed fewer trials to relearn the list and could measure the resultant savings. This indicated that the original traces of the experience had not vanished from memory. This *savings method* is still used in memory experiments (e.g., MacLeod, 1988).

Ebbinghaus found that the longer the time between learning and relearning a list, the less savings occurred (the more trials it took to relearn the list). The graph of this relation, known as a *forgetting curve*, is shown in Figure 7.1. Notice that forgetting is quite fast at first, but then it becomes more gradual, a phenomenon confirmed with other testing methods. In fact, modern techniques have shown that forgetting can occur even more rapidly than shown in Figure 7.1. As we shall see, forgetting can be measured in seconds rather than hours. (Have you ever looked up a telephone number, read it out loud correctly, and then forgotten it on the way to the telephone?) The different rates of forgetting that occur when memory is measured in different ways gives rise to the idea that more than one type of memory system may exist, each having a different rate of forgetting. We now turn to this idea that there are different types of systems underlying memory.

Memory Stores and Codes

An influential theory formulated by Richard C. Atkinson and Richard M. Shiffrin (1968, 1971) proposes three different memory storage systems: sensory stores, a short-term store, and a long-term store. **Sensory stores** (one for each of our sensory systems) hold information very briefly after it has reached the sense organs. The **short-term store** holds the information that people are conscious of at any one moment, such as

FIGURE 7.1
A Forgetting Curve

Ebbinghaus measured the savings in relearning a list of nonsense syllables after various periods of time had elapsed since original learning. Notice that forgetting is rapid at first and then levels off.

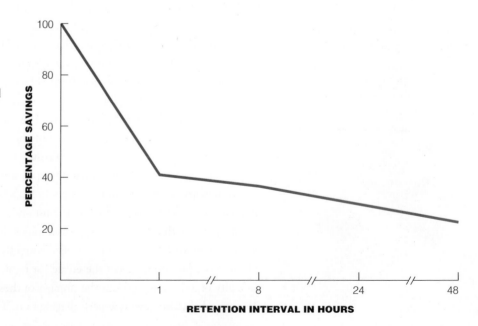

the last few words in this sentence. The **long-term store** holds memories over lengthy periods. (For an overview of Atkinson and Shiffrin's theory, see Figure 7.2.)

In the next few pages, we will discuss the properties of these systems in more detail. But before we start, make sure that you do not take literally the idea of separate stores located in different parts of the brain. The stores are three types of systems with different properties, but probably many areas of the brain participate in the operation of all three.

THE SENSORY STORES

After information has reached the sense organs, it travels through the nervous system to the brain, which interprets it. The information must linger in the nervous system briefly for the brain to have time to interpret it. This "lingering," or persistence, is referred to as sensory storage. Atkinson and Shiffrin assumed that a separate storage system existed for each sense, but only the visual and auditory systems have been studied in any detail. The concept of sensory stores is similar to the sensory system that Broadbent (1958) postulated in his theory of attention, discussed in Chapter 5.

Iconic Storage. When someone takes your picture and uses a flashbulb, you usually see an afterimage (or "icon") of the flash for a few seconds. This afterimage is an example of **iconic storage,** the name of the sensory storage associated with vision (Neisser, 1967).

George Sperling (1960) developed a way to study iconic storage. He flashed a display of letters at a person through a *tachistoscope,* a device that accurately controls the length of time the stimuli are displayed. The letters were presented very briefly (e.g., 30 milliseconds, or 0.03 second). Sperling purposely used too many letters in his displays to permit accurate reporting of all the letters when viewed in a single flash. However, if a tone sounded just after the flash, telling subjects which row of letters to report, the subjects could do so quite well. Sperling also varied the length of time between the flash and the cuing tone, and he found that his subjects could recall fewer letters as the delay of the tone was increased. Because of this decay in performance, Sperling supposed that the letters were held in a rapidly fading iconic storage system, a sensory store.

FIGURE 7.2
Atkinson and Shiffrin's Model of Memory Storage

The relations among the sensory stores, the short-term store, and the long-term store are depicted in this flow chart. There is probably a sensory store for each sense. The short-term store may be thought of as a stage of conscious activity. It controls transfer of information to the long-term store as well as retrieval from the long-term store. It is also responsible for deciding which response should be made. The long-term store is the permanent memory store.

SOURCE: Atkinson & Shiffrin, 1971.

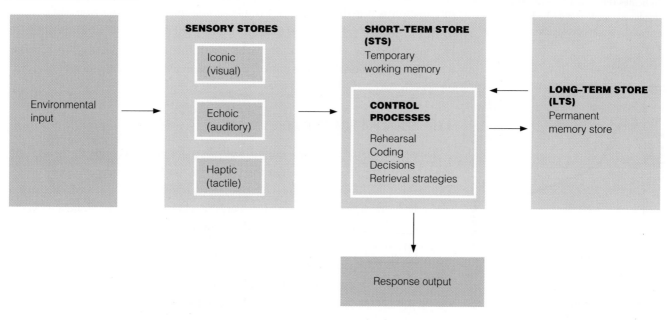

A tachistoscope is a device for presenting visual information for brief periods of time. The person being tested stares down the tube and, in this experiment, pushes a button as quickly as possible when a stimulus is perceived. In Sperling's experiment the subjects reported as many letters as possible from a brief display.

The results from Sperling's (1960) experiment are shown in Figure 7.3. As you can see, the estimated number of letters the subjects could report decreased rapidly with the delay of the tone. From this and other evidence, it appears that an iconic image fades within a second if it is not disturbed by other information shown to the eyes during this period (Crowder, 1992b).

Echoic Storage. The sensory storage system associated with hearing is called **echoic storage,** and it appears to last longer than iconic storage. For example, Darwin, Turvey, and Crowder (1972) used Sperling's technique in a situation where people heard (rather than saw) information. They estimated that the "echo" of the information lasted from 2 to 4 seconds, which contrasts sharply with the fraction of a second the icon seems to last. Logically, we might expect auditory information to persist longer than visual information. Visual information is typically spread out in space; if you scan the environment and miss something, you can look back at it. Auditory information is usually spread out in time; if you miss something, you can't "listen back." It is not surprising, then, that the auditory afterimage (the echo) should last a bit longer than the visual afterimage (the icon); this is more adaptive, since sounds have a greater chance of being missed. Echoic memory is especially useful in perceiving speech.

THE SHORT-TERM STORE

Sensory storage is activated automatically by information coming in through the senses. How long that information stays in the system is beyond conscious control. The case is quite different for the short-term store, which holds the information we are currently aware of, such as the last few words in a conversation. For unrelated verbal material, such as words in a list, it has been estimated that the short-term store may hold from two to five items at a time (Watkins, 1975), permitting very efficient search processes (MacGregor, 1987).

The display in Figure 7.2 illustrates Atkinson and Shiffrin's view of the relations among the various memory stores. Information passes through the sensory stores (or

FIGURE 7.3
The Results of Sperling's Experiment

The graph shows that the number of recalled letters decreases with the delay of the signal. This outcome indicates the rate at which the image faded from the iconic store under the conditions of Sperling's experiment. After 1 second, no further deceases occurred. The bar indicates the time when the letters were displayed, while the dashed line shows when the letters disappeared from the display.

SOURCE: Sperling. 1960.

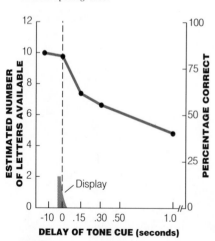

registers) to the short-term store (STS). We can retain this information in the STS as long as we continue to rehearse, or repeat the information. Various **control processes** can be used to transfer information from the short-term store to the long-term store. Rehearsal is one such process, but as you will see, other mental activities aid long-term memory much more than simple repetition. In addition to its function as a link between the sensory stores and the long-term store, the short-term store also serves other functions, such as holding information that has been retrieved from the long-term store.

The Recency and Primacy Effect. A tool often used to study the short-term store is the serial position curve. A **serial position curve** is simply a graph that shows how well pieces of information can be remembered depending on where they are presented in a series (first, second, etc.). For example, Bennet Murdock (1962) presented subjects with lists of 30 or 40 words. After hearing each list, the subjects were asked to recall the words as well as possible in any order. (This task is called free recall because no cues or hints are given, and subjects are free to recall the words in any order.) The results are plotted in Figure 7.4. The most striking aspect is the very good recall of the last few words that were presented. This good recall of the last few things heard or seen is called the **recency effect,** a result caused by recall from the short-term store. Just after they had heard the list, the subjects could recall the last four or five words that were still in short-term memory, regardless of the length of the list. However, if recall was delayed even a few seconds by some distractor task (Glanzer & Cunitz, 1966), the strong recency effect vanished. This suggests that the short-term store, like the sensory stores, can hold information for only a short period of time, before it decays away.

Another point of interest in Figure 7.4 is the elevated recall of the first item or two in the list, a result called the **primacy effect**. The effect was rather small in the free-recall task that Murdock used, but the primacy effect can be quite large and even greater than the recency effect in memory tasks in which people are told to recall events in the order that they were presented. The primacy effect (and recall of items in the middle positions) comes from the long-term memory store, which we will consider shortly.

Working Memory. As mentioned previously, the short-term store includes not only information that has recently passed through the sensory stores, but also information that has been retrieved from the long-term store. Thus, the short-term store is often equated with primary memory, or consciousness. Alan Baddeley has addressed the question of whether the short-term store is equivalent to the **working memory** that we use to accomplish everyday cognitive tasks, such as reasoning and compre-

FIGURE 7.4
The Serial Position Curve in Free Recall

After hearing word lists, subjects recalled the words in each list in any order. Recall was best for the last few items (the recency effect), which reflected recall from the short-term store. There was better recall for the first few words than for words in the middle of the list (the primacy effect).

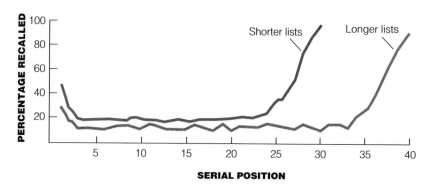

hending (Baddeley, 1986). The method he has used to examine this question is called the *dual task method*, in which people are required to perform two tasks at the same time. If one task causes a great deal of interference with the other task, then it can be assumed that the two tasks require the same mental processes. (If two tasks rely on the same mental processes, it should be hard to do both simultaneously.) Baddeley had his subjects remember a series of digits (a task that requires short-term memory) while they simultaneously performed a reasoning task requiring working memory. When researchers compared the performance of subjects doing both the reasoning task and the digit task to the performance of control subjects doing only the reasoning task, they found that difference in performance was not as large as would be expected if the two tasks were using the same system (i.e., if working memory and short-term memory were equivalent). This finding led Baddeley to postulate that the working memory system consists of several components.

The underlying message here is that tasks such as remembering series of digits do not require exactly the same processes required by more complex tasks, such as reasoning, learning, and comprehending, although both types of tasks require conscious attention and therefore tax the working memory system. Thus, working memory is not a single, unitary system as was once thought; working memory can be broken down into separate components.

THE LONG-TERM STORE

Unlike the short-term store, the long-term store is assumed to have almost unlimited capacity, and forgetting is believed to be quite slow (measured in hours and days, at least—not seconds, as in short-term forgetting). Three types of cognitive representation, referred to as **memory codes**, may be used to store information in long-term memory. We can think of our experiences as represented in memory codes that must be decoded when we remember the information, just as music is stored optically on a compact disc that must be deciphered to be heard. Three types of codes that represent information in the long-term store are the verbal (linguistic), imaginal, and motor codes.

Verbal Codes.   One of the most important codes is the **verbal** (*or linguistic*) **code.** We are freed from dealing only with concrete objects by being able to recode them in terms of relatively arbitrary symbols—words. There is usually no correspondence between a word, such as *iguana,* and what it stands for, except by the convention of language. If we decided to call iguanas *cows* and cows *iguanas,* there would be no problem. Children would simply grow up learning one word instead of the other. Although several forms of verbal coding occur, the most common coding of experience in terms of language is by meaning, or semantics. Such coding can be seen even in simple memory experiments. For example, suppose people are asked to study a list of words containing the word *chair.* Later, they take a test on which they must pick out the studied words from among distractor words that were not on the original list. If *table* (a word that is semantically related to the word chair, since they are both pieces of furniture) is a distractor, people will be more likely to pick it erroneously if the original list had contained *chair* than if it had not (Underwood, 1965). Such false recognitions indicate that people code even isolated words in terms of their meaning.

Imaginal Codes.   **Imaginal codes,** unlike verbal codes, are thought to bear some resemblance to the perception of the experience they represent. Try to count from

Procedural (or motor) memory is responsible for learning and retention of complex motor skills like playing basketball.

memory the number of windows in your house or apartment. You will probably form an image of each room and then mentally walk through each one. A good deal of evidence suggests that such an imaginal mode of thought has properties that differ from those of linguistic representation (Kosslyn, 1980; Paivio, 1986). Shepard (1978) has collected the accounts of many famous scientists and artists who have claimed that imagery was an important part of their work. For example, the chemist August Kekulé dreamt of a snake that bit its own tail; he then woke up with the concept of the benzene ring, which revolutionized organic chemistry. Telling people to form mental images of verbal material can greatly enhance their memory of it, as will be discussed later.

Motor Codes.   A third type of code is the **motor code,** the means of retaining physical skills, such as swimming or bike riding. Motor codes underlie procedural memory. Can an Olympic swimmer give a nonswimmer a verbal description that will allow the nonswimmer to jump in the water and swim? Probably not. The knowledge needed to swim is not stored in a verbal code. Similarly, being able to form a mental picture of swimming probably has little to do with performing the skill; you can likely imagine or remember a breathtaking exhibition of ice skating even if you have never skated. Squire (1987) argues that procedural memory represents a fundamentally different type of memory from that used to remember other sorts of information because it includes motor skills. For example, most motor activities must be learned by doing them, and once learned, are particularly resistant to forgetting (Fitts & Posner, 1967). Even if you have not been swimming or ridden a bicycle in years, with a little practice, your skill will return to its old level. Later we will consider evidence that procedural memory may constitute a separate memory system with different properties than other kinds of memories.

Encoding and Recoding

What is the best way to encode information for a later test? Surprisingly, one answer is to convert the information to a different form, rather than trying to remember the information as it is given to you. Let us explain with an example. In a moment you will be given 15 numbers to remember. Read them once fairly slowly—aloud, if you prefer—and then close your eyes and try to recall the entire series in order. Here are the numbers: 1 4 9 1 6 2 5 3 6 4 9 6 4 8 1. Now repeat them. How did you do? Most people get only seven or eight after reading the series once. You will be able to recall the series perfectly, however, even by the end of the chapter, when you realize that the numbers are the squares of 1 through 9. If we had written them like this—1 4 9 16 25 36 49 64 81—you might have discovered the hidden cognitive strategy of remembering the series more easily.

It is often more efficient not to try to remember information just as it is given, but to change it (or recode it) to a form that will make it easier to recall, a process called **recoding.** (Encoding is the more general term used to describe acquisition of information.) A difficult memorization task can become easy with an appropriate recoding strategy (such as squares of 1 to 9). We can think of these cognitive strategies within the model pictured in Figure 7.2 as control processes that allow information to be transferred from the short-term store (consciousness) to the long-term store.

The concept of recoding and its importance were introduced by George Miller (1956a), who noted that memory is sometimes about as good for material that conveys a lot of information as for material that conveys little. He examined many experiments and discovered that in most cases, people could recall about five to nine things. (The title of his paper even referred to "the magical number 7 ± 2" because the number of items people recalled so often fell within that range.) Surprisingly, the type of material made little difference. For example, people could remember roughly as many words as they could isolated letters. If a group of people were given the letters *g r b s n y f t k w*, they would probably recall about seven of them in order. Similarly, they would remember about seven words from the list *green, rub, bat, snow, noise, yak, father, tree, kind,* and *will.*

Obviously, much more information is contained in the words than in the letters, and yet both types of material can be retained equally well. (Each letter begins the corresponding word in the list.) If people can remember about seven things in order, and if the amount of information conveyed does not really matter, then it is better to try to recode items having little information into items with more information. As Miller (1956b) put it, "To draw a rather farfetched analogy, it is as if we had to carry all our money in a purse that could contain only seven coins. It doesn't matter to the purse, however, whether these coins are pennies or silver dollars." Miller argued that the best way to remember information was to "chunk" as much as possible into the seven or so memory "packets" that could be easily retained. This method of recoding information into a small number of blocks that are more easily remembered is thus referred to as **chunking.**

Recoding is an important tool in overcoming forgetting, since it can be used to package information more economically. This should call to mind the cognitive theme that we have been developing throughout the text. Simply by making a few associations between the items to be remembered, thus recoding them into a more compact representation, the amount of information we can store in our short-term memory can be greatly expanded. We now consider some specific types of recoding.

ORGANIZATION AND VERBAL RECODING

A great deal of research has been done to examine how people organize information when faced with memorization tasks. Much evidence indicates that memorization is an active process, with the rememberer taking the information and converting it to a form that can be more easily recalled. Endel Tulving (1962) asked students to study and recall a list of unrelated words a number of times. Although the words were not associated in any obvious way and their presentation order was scrambled from trial to trial, Tulving discovered that the subjects were building their own organization into the list. They tended to recall the words in the same order from one recall trial to the next. Since this ordering was not built into the list by the researcher, the subjects must have been building it in themselves. Tulving referred to this type of recoding as **subjective organization,** the tendency to impose organization on random events to remember them better.

Another way to study the effects of organization on memory is to give people material either with or without a good organizational scheme for recoding and remembering it. In one study (Bower, Clark, Lesgold, & Winzenz, 1969), subjects were asked to remember 112 words in one of four common categories. The words were presented either in organized fashion (similar to the presentation in Figure 7.5) or at random (in which the same 112 words appeared in any order within the structure). Recall was much greater when the information was organized. After seeing the items once, people who had the organized presentations averaged recall of 73 words, while those who received the random presentation averaged 21. The results indicate that verbal recod-

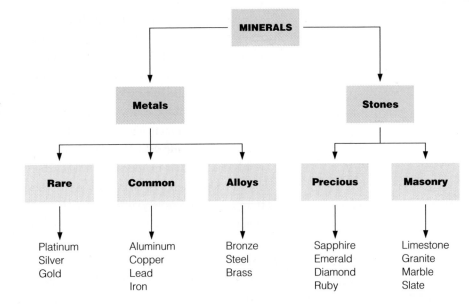

ing—organizing information in terms of what is already known—is an effective way to remember.

Another organizational strategy to remember information is to construct stories about that information. The graph in Figure 7.6 shows the effectiveness of this method. Simply by constructing a story from the words to be remembered, subjects were able to recall up to seven times as many words as subjects who studied the same words in an unorganized fashion.

Experts in particular fields, such as chess or computer programming, can remember huge amounts of new information about their fields. For example, Chase and Simon (1973) showed that a chess master could recall the location of many more pieces after a single brief look at the board at the halfway point in a game than could ordinary players. Presumably, the master had the ability to very quickly recode information about the game into long-term memory. When the experiment was repeated with pieces randomly arranged on the board (thus destroying the organization that playing a game imposes on the pieces), the experts did no better than the nonexperts. Waiters who show remarkable facility in remembering orders without writing notes have also been found to be very adept at recoding (Ericsson & Polson, 1988).

The capacity that experts have for remembering great amounts of information in their domains of expertise does not indicate that they have generally superior memories. Instead, it shows that they have developed efficient cognitive means of recoding information about their specialty into long-term memory so that it can be easily retrieved when needed. Verbal recoding techniques can be quite powerful, but so can other forms of recoding, to which we now turn.

IMAGINAL RECODING

As we have discussed, long-term memory includes imaginal codes as well as verbal codes. Allan Paivio (1969) has proposed that if information is represented in both codes rather than only one, it will be easier to remember, an idea called the **dual coding theory.** Paivio assumes that if we store two different sorts of information about some experience, the chances improve that one code or the other will aid memory later. There is much evidence to support this theory (Paivio, 1986). In one study, subjects were presented with a variety of nouns and asked to rate how easily they could form images of what the words referred to (Paivio, Yuille, & Madigan, 1968). Subjects

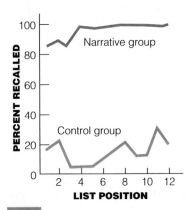

rated words such as *blood* or *hyena* high because these words stood for concrete objects. They ranked words like *democracy* and *truth* low because they represented abstract ideas. In a number of studies, Paivio (1969) compared the memorability of high-imagery words and low-imagery words and found that people were usually able to remember high-imagery words better than low-imagery words in many tasks.

Why does this happen? According to the dual coding hypothesis, when people read either high- or low-imagery words, they automatically activate a verbal code. High-imagery words will tend to activate both verbal and imaginal codes because they are words *and* symbols of concrete things, whereas low-imagery words activate only the verbal code. Therefore, high-imagery words tend to be represented in two codes rather than one, perhaps explaining why they are remembered better than low-imagery words. Moreover, pictures of objects are better remembered than words naming the objects for the same reason (Rajaram, 1993). In one type of experiment, people see either a long series of pictures or a long series of words representing the same objects and are asked to try to remember the pictures or words. Even though the ensuing memory test requires the use of words, those who studied the pictures actually do better than the people who saw only the words. According to dual code theory, presentation of pictures produces a strong trace in the imagery system but also arouses a verbal code because people label the pictures to recall them later.

In another test of the dual code theory, Bower (1972) gave subjects pairs of words (e.g., *thumbtack-pickle*) to remember. When tested, they received the left-hand member of each pair (*thumbtack*) and were asked to recall each right-hand member (*pickle*). The subjects learned five lists with 20 pairs in each list. One group was told to imagine the two objects in interaction (e.g., a giant thumbtack being punched into a large pickle). The control group was instructed simply to learn the pairs. Each subject was tested immediately after each list was presented. The results in Figure 7.7 illustrate the powerful effect of forming interacting images. The subjects told to form images recalled almost twice as many words as did the control subjects, who were not given any special instructions.

Imaginal recoding is used in many of the memory improvement techniques that are discussed later in the chapter. Many popular books suggesting the use of imagery to improve memory say that the technique works better if bizarre images are created (Lorayne & Lucas, 1974). For example, if you needed to remember bananas on a shopping list, the advice is to create an unusual image of them (say, a huge bunch on the hood of your car) rather than a common image (such as a bunch growing on a tree). Evidence on this issue is mixed, with some researchers finding no difference in later recall between material encoded with bizarre images and material encoded with common images (Kroll, Schepeler, & Angin, 1986). Other research indicates that bizarre images may be more effective in aiding memory as long as they are used only occasionally in the context of more common images (McDaniel & Einstein, 1986). Memory is probably best served by using bizarre images to recode the most difficult material, with common images used to remember the rest. One reason is that bizarre images suffer less interference from other material than do common images; because they are so distinctive, bizarre images won't be easily confused with other material (Einstein, McDaniel, & Lackey, 1989).

LEVELS OF PROCESSING

So far, we have presented verbal and imaginal recoding processes separately. Fergus Craik and Robert Lockhart (1972) have advanced an alternative to the notion of sep-

FIGURE 7.7
Effects of Imagery on Memory

In the imagery condition, subjects were told to form interactive images of the objects the words referred to; in the control condition, subjects were not given any special instruction. People given the imagery instructions recalled the words much better than did the people in the control condition

SOURCE: Bower, 1972.

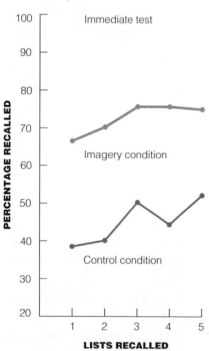

arate memory stores that unifies these coding processes. The **levels-of-processing approach** to memory states that memory is a by-product of perception, and perception can be considered to progress through stages (as discussed in Chapter 4). For example, when we read or hear a word, various mental operations are performed as the word is comprehended. First are relatively superficial sensory analyses of the features that make up the word: acoustic features for spoken language and letter features for written language. Then comes analysis of the word's sound, or its phonological features. Finally, the word must be analyzed for its meaning. Thus, the processing of information can be carried out to different depths, or levels, depending on the stages in the perceptual sequence that are completed, and memory is merely a by-product of this processing—the greater the depth, the better the memory for the material.

A number of experimental results are consistent with this general proposition. Consider the findings from an experiment by Craik and Tulving (1975), who presented undergraduates with 60 words and then asked them questions about each. The questions were designed to control the level of processing of the words. For example, subjects might see the word *BEAR* on a screen and be asked one of the following three questions: Is it in uppercase letters? Does it rhyme with *chair*? Is it an animal? In each case, the answer is yes but the mental operations required to answer the questions cause the words to be processed to different levels. In the first case, only superficial characteristics of the letters need be checked; in the second case, the sound of the word must be processed; in the third case, the meaning must be determined. The experimenters predicted that when memory of the words was tested, it would be better for words that were processed to deeper levels. (The subjects did not expect a memory test when they answered the questions about the words.)

Craik and Tulving's (1975) results confirmed this prediction impressively. They prepared a recognition test on which their subjects were given the 60 words about which they had answered questions, along with 120 new words. The subjects were told to try to recognize and circle exactly 60 words that they thought they had seen and answered questions about before. Chance performance would have been 33 percent (60 out of 180). The results, given in Figure 7.8, show that recognition increased from just above chance for words that received only superficial processing (a question about its appearance) to nearly perfect for words that received deep, semantic-level processing (a question about the word's meaning). The only difference between conditions was the very brief cognitive process that occurred when the subject answered the question. This experiment shows the powerful effect of even rapid encoding (or recoding) operations on memory.

The levels-of-processing ideas were originally considered an alternative to the multistore view of memory (Craik & Lockhart, 1972). However, the levels-of-processing ideas have attracted critics of their own (Baddeley, 1978), and some results are inconsistent with the ideas of a fixed level of processing and of memory improving only with depth of processing (Cermak & Craik, 1979). For example, under some testing conditions, information that is given "shallow" processing is better remembered than that receiving "deep" processing, as will be discussed later in the chapter (page 282).

The results of research produced by the levels-of-processing approach drive home the importance of coding processes for memory. Other research has also shown that people recall information better when they have been actively involved in generating or constructing it at the time it is presented, rather than simply passively reading the information (Clark, 1995; Slamecka & Graf, 1978). This memory phenomenon has been called the *generation effect*, and you can use it to increase your retention when

FIGURE 7.8
Effects of Levels of Processing

Subjects saw a word (e.g., BEAR) and answered one of three types of questions about it. "Is it in uppercase letters"? required people to process only superficial (graphemic) features of the word. "Does it rhyme with *chair*?" caused people to use a phonemic, or sound-based, code to answer the question. "Is it an animal?" forced deep, semantic processing to provide the correct answer. In line with the levels-of-processing ideas, the deeper the level of original processing, the more accurate was recognition on the later test.

SOURCE: Craik & Tulving, 1975.

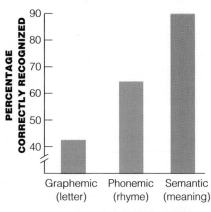

LEVELS OF PROCESSING

DOES PHOTOGRAPHIC MEMORY EXIST?

To some degree, everyone can form images of material when asked to do so. You can easily imagine a dalmation, a football, or your friend's face. Are there people whose capacities for imagery are much greater? Do some people have a photographic memory? The term *photographic memory* implies remembering a scene in photographic detail. How can we tell if someone has a true photographic memory or just very good imagery?

The technical term for photographic memory is **eidetic imagery.** Psychologists have long debated its existence (Crowder, 1992a). The term sometimes refers to a constellation of abilities that does not necessarily imply the existence of a literal "mental photograph." German investigators in the 1930s reported that 30 percent of schoolchildren possessed eidetic imagery, but later researchers criticized the rather loose criteria used to identify these eidetic children (Haber & Haber, 1964). Subsequent research reduced the estimate to about 5 percent of those tested (Leask, Haber, & Haber, 1969), but even the more stringent criteria rely on subjective accounts of what those being tested said they saw. For example, researchers who have reported cases of eidetic imagery—almost always in children—have depended on the chil-

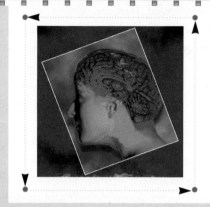

dren's reports that they still "see" a picture after it has been taken away. More conclusive evidence comes from the fact that the children's descriptions of objects from the picture state the right color and the proper locations (Haber, 1979a).

The real difficulty in confirming eidetic memory lies in finding a more objective test. If someone has an image something like a photograph, then he or she should be able to perform tasks that would be easy with a picture but difficult or impossible to do from memory. For example, suppose you have a friend who claims to have a photographic memory for textbooks. Show your friend a textbook page to be studied and "mentally photographed." Then take away the book and say, "Count up eight lines from the

bottom of the page and read the letters from the right to the left side of the page." This would be easy with a photograph, but difficult without one.

As the criteria for proving eidetic imagery have become stricter, fewer people have passed the tests. People may say they still have images before their eyes, but when their memories are tested for the imagined scenes, they prove no more accurate than those of control subjects (Haber, 1979a). This leads to the question of whether anyone possesses a true photographic memory. Charles Stromeyer and Joseph Psotka (1970) reported the case of a woman with seemingly incredible powers of imagery. Describing her as a 23-year-old teacher at Harvard and an artist, they said:

Her eidetic ability is remarkable for she can hallucinate at will a beard on a beardless man, leaves on a barren tree, or a page of poetry in a known foreign language which she can copy from bottom line to the top line as fast as she can write. These visions often obscure a real object. Thus the chin on a beardless man may disappear beneath the hallucinated beard.

In a test given to this woman, a complicated and meaningless random pattern of dots was shown to one eye and, sometime later, a slightly different random pattern to the other eye. If the

you study. For example, try formulating questions about the material you are studying so that you are prompted to generate the correct answer in your own words. And outlining or paraphrasing the material in a chapter will also increase retention owing to the generation effect.

Several practical points can be drawn from this and other research on recoding:

1. When learning new material, don't just read it; try to recode it by relating it to your current knowledge.

2. Seek a good organization—for example, by outlining new information.

3. Create mental images if appropriate.

4. Paraphrase information in your own words.

5. When you come to the end of a section of a text, look away and try to summarize the main points.

patterns were presented separately, a person would see only two meaningless patterns. If presented simultaneously, with one shown to one eye and one to the other, they would fuse, and the person would see a figure floating above the pattern. The only way the woman could detect the figure when the two patterns were separated in time was to store an almost exact image of the first pattern and superimpose it on the second pattern when it was presented later. Stromeyer and Psotka (1970) reported that she could do that even when 24 hours separated the two presentations. Stromeyer and Psotka appear to have designed a foolproof test of a very strong form of eidetic imagery.

The preceding report may not convince the skeptics. Can other people pass the test? The Stromeyer and Psotka study received widespread notice in newspapers and magazines some years ago, and many publications included a simpler test for their readers. The test involved the two dot patterns presented in Figure 7.9, so you can test yourself. Dr. John Merritt (1979) reported that about 30 people of the millions who probably saw the test wrote in with the correct answer, and 15 were then tested under laboratory conditions. None passed. Merritt concluded that eidetic ability, as indicated by the superimposition of one image on another, seems to be a "none-in-a-million phenomenon."

More recently, Helen Crawford, Benjamin Wallace, and their associates

CONTROVERSY

(1986) reported that some people who rated high on hypnotizability scales (see Chapter 5) could pass the fusion test designed by Stromeyer and Psotka (1970). Only a few highly hypnotizable subjects did so, and even then they could only do so when hypnotized. Also, they could not successfully fuse all stimuli presented to them. These findings do give hope, however, that some other people besides the Harvard artist may be able to pass this stringent test.

If eidetic imagery, or photographic memory, does exist (the debate about that is far from over), then it is clear that the ability is very rare. Probably many people who claim to have a photographic memory possess only vivid imagery, just like we all have to one degree or another. Some psychologists have suggested that further study of eidetic imagery is a waste of time (Holding, 1979; Lieblich, 1979), but the positive results of Crawford and associates (1986) seem likely to keep the debate going a while longer, at least.

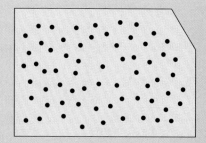

(a)

(b)

FIGURE 7.9
Eidetic Imagery Test

Carefully examine the dot pattern in (a) for several minutes. Move your gaze about to inspect all details. Do not stare at one point. Shut your eyes and try to recall an image of the pattern. If you can build up a good image, look at the dot pattern in (b), and superimpose your image on that dot pattern. Make the rectangular borders coincide exactly. Do you see any numbers or letters? Each pattern alone is a random array of dots, but when one is superimposed on the other, very clear figures will appear. The answer appears on page 276.

Source: Merritt, 1979.

These forms of active recoding will aid your memory. In a later section, we will elaborate on this advice by discussing memory aids, or mnemonic devices, which often incorporate some of the suggestions given here.

Why We Forget

Let us briefly review the major points made thus far: We have three separate memory stores—the sensory, short-term, and long-term stores—and various recoding techniques, or control processes, that transfer information from short-term to long-term memory. Now that we have a coherent model of memory to work with, we are in a better position to answer the two central questions of this chapter: How do we remember? Why do we forget? As we proceed with these questions, we will see how closely related they are.

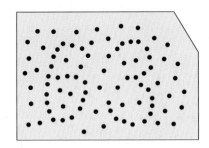

Solution To Figure 7.9

Fusion of the two dot patterns on page 275.

Since Ebbinghaus derived his forgetting curve, a great deal of research has gone into explaining how experiences fade from memory. Two primary explanations for forgetting are decay and interference.

DECAY THEORY

Forgetting from the sensory memories occurs in just a few seconds, or even fractions of a second (depending on the sense modality stimulated), through decay of information. **Decay** usually refers to physiological changes in the neural trace of the experience (i.e., biological changes affect our memories). Forgetting from short-term memory takes place over seconds, while any forgetting from long-term memory occurs over much longer periods—hours, days, weeks. What causes forgetting in these systems? The earliest and simplest answer was that decay of memory traces can explain forgetting from short- and long-term memory, too. The idea that decay causes forgetting from short term memory is still current (Cowan, 1995), but it does not work for long term memory.

Decay of information from the long-term store is not a satisfying explanation (McGeoch, 1932). For one thing, it does not tell us much unless it specifies some mechanism that causes forgetting. What actually decays? Also, decay theory predicts that the longer the interval between learning information and testing, the worse memory should be. In many cases this is true, but when people are given two successive tests, they almost always remember some material on the second test that they had forgotten on the first, a phenomenon known as **reminiscence** (Tulving, 1967). Reminiscence is difficult to account for by decay. By the second test, the memory traces should have decayed even more, yet the total number of items recalled is sometimes actually greater on the second test than on the first test (Erdelyi & Becker, 1974; Payne, 1986). Another important observation—interference—also contradicts a simple decay theory.

INTERFERENCE THEORY

Interference refers to the obstruction of recall that memories sometimes cause for one another. According to decay theory, the most important determinant of forgetting is the time between learning and being tested on material. But a number of experiments have shown that factors other than time help determine forgetting.

In a classic experiment of this kind, Jenkins and Dallenbach (1924) taught a list of nonsense syllables, either late at night or early in the morning, to people who had to learn the list until they could repeat it once perfectly. Then they tested the subjects either 1, 2, 4, or 8 hours later. In one condition, the people slept during the retention interval; in the other condition, they were awake. The researchers found greater forgetting for the people who had been awake (see Figure 7.10). Even following the same period of time (e.g., 4 hours) people recalled less in the awake condition than in the asleep condition. A simple decay theory would predict equal forgetting for the two conditions. This finding suggests that interference from other activities produced additional forgetting in the awake condition.

Findings such as these have led many psychologists to postulate that the primary factor producing forgetting is interference rather than decay. The two general classes of interference are proactive and retroactive interference. **Proactive interference** refers to activities occurring *before* some event that make it difficult to recall the event later. **Retroactive interference** refers to activities occurring *after* some event that obstruct recall of that event. Try to think back to your most recent psychology lecture.

FIGURE 7.10
Forgetting After Sleeping or Staying Awake

Time is not the only important factor in forgetting; activities occurring between learning and testing also influence memory. Notice that the percentage of nonsense syllables subjects remembered decrease faster when they were awake than when they were asleep.

SOURCE: Jenkins & Dallenbach, 1924.

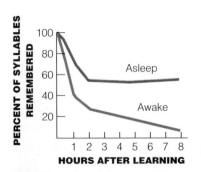

276

You can probably remember the topic and the main points the instructor made. If you were asked to recall the same lecture at the end of the term, you would probably find that you had forgotten it because the information from so many other lectures had interfered. Interference from lectures before that particular lecture was proactive; interference from lectures after that particular lecture was retroactive. These types of interference have been found for many different kinds of events.

The research designs in Figure 7.11 shows how the two types of interference are studied in experiments. At the top of the figure is the simplest arrangement for studying retroactive interference. In an experimental condition, subjects learn some material (called A) and later some other material (called B). The material in both A and B can be words, pictures, sentences, or stories. In the control condition, subjects learn only the A material, and not the B material, but are otherwise treated the same. (During the time the experimental group receives the B material, the controls are given some simple task to prevent them from rehearsing the A material.) After a certain retention interval, all the subjects are tested on A. Typically, the experimental group performs worse than the control group on the test of the A material. The learning of the B material is said to interfere retroactively with the memory of the A material. For example, imagine that you and a friend had to learn the French equivalents for 100 English words, and then only you had to learn the German translations for the same words. Later, if both you and your friend were tested on the French words, you would probably do worse because of retroactive interference from having learned the German words.

For many years, psychologists believed that retroactive interference was the primary source of forgetting (McGeoch, 1932); however, in 1957, Benton J. Underwood showed that proactive interference was also important in determining forgetting and that its influence had gone undetected in previous investigations. The experimental design to study proactive interference is shown at the bottom of Figure 7.11. The interest centers on the effect of prior learning on memory for material learned later. By analysis of numerous studies, Underwood showed that 15 to 75 percent of material that a subject had learned perfectly might be forgotten over 24 hours, depending on the amount of proactive interference. The results of his analysis are shown in Figure 7.12 and confirm that proactive interference can be quite powerful in causing forgetting.

How Much Do We Forget?

How much forgetting occurs for everyday material? This is a difficult question to answer because it is impossible to control how well material has been learned and

---

FIGURE 7.11
Experimental Designs for Studying Interference

In the retroactive interference design, subjects learn some material (A) and then are tested on it. For the experimental group, the test occurs after learning other material (B), which the control group does not learn. The amount of retroactive interference produced by learning B is shown by how much worse the experimental group does on the test of A relative to the control group. In the proactive interference design, subjects are tested on a set of material (B). In the control condition, B is the only material learned. In the experimental condition, subjects learn other material (A) before they learn B. The amount of proactive interference is shown by how much worse the experimental group recalls the B material relative to the control group.

RETROACTIVE INTERFERENCE

	Time ▸			
Experimental group	Learn A	Learn B	Retention interval	Test A
Control group	Learn A	_____	Retention interval	Test A

PROACTIVE INTERFERENCE

Experimental group	Learn A	Learn B	Retention interval	Test B
Control group	_____	Learn B	Retention interval	Test B

The Amount of Forgetting in a 24-Hour Period

In all the studies listed that involved proactive interference, people learned a list perfectly and then were tested on it 24 hours later. What varied was the number of previous lists people had learned before they learned the last, critical list that was tested the next day. There was very little forgetting with few previous lists, and very much with 15 to 20 previous lists. Each point represents a different experiment.

SOURCE: Underwood, 1957.

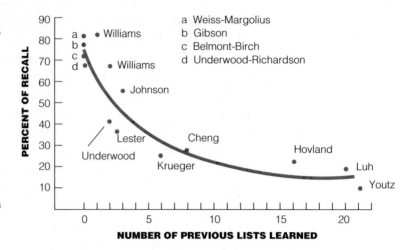

FIGURE 7.13
Long-term Forgetting of Television Programs

The titles of programs that aired for one season are forgotten relatively rapidly over the first few years, but more slowly thereafter. Squire's technique, unlike others, is capable of measuring forgetting over long periods of time for material learned outside a laboratory setting.

SOURCE: Squire, 1989, p. 243.

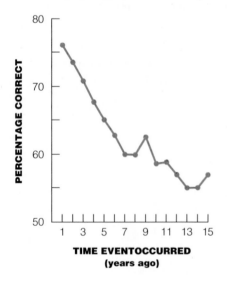

whether it has been rehearsed. Researchers have attempted to answer the question to see if laboratory estimates of forgetting, such as those shown in Figures 7.1 and 7.12, generalize to other material. Larry Squire (1989) has employed an ingenious technique to measure long-term forgetting. He administered multiple-choice tests to people over a 9-year period (from 1978 to 1986), testing their memories of television programs that had aired for only a single season from 1 to 15 years previously. For example, a sample item, from 1974, is the following: "Which of the following is a TV show? (a) Mandrake, (b) Shipmates, (c) Private Nelson, (d) Lucas Tanner." (The correct answer was d.)

Squire's results, presented in Figure 7.13, show that his technique was quite sensitive in measuring forgetting. In general, forgetting occurred steadily over the 15-year period, although little bumps in the forgetting curve occur at 9 and 15 years. Forgetting appears somewhat more rapid in the early years and slows later, agreeing with Ebbinghaus's results in Figure 7.1. The surprise is that forgetting can be measured even over long periods, such as 10 to 15 years.

Other studies using such material as the names and faces of classmates and Spanish vocabulary learned in college have also shown rapid forgetting at first, with the forgetting curve reaching a plateau after a few years and no further forgetting observed (Bahrick, 1984; Bahrick et al., 1975). The causes of these differences in long-term forgetting are poorly understood, but virtually all studies show rapid forgetting at first and little, if any, forgetting over longer time periods.

Is forgetting of general information due to decay or due to interference? This question is impossible to answer because in natural situations, the passage of time and the interference occurring during that time cannot be untangled. Interference is quite likely involved, but its presence does not completely explain the forgetting.

The terms *proactive interference* and *retroactive interfe*rence merely describe situations that produce forgetting; they do not explain why the forgetting occurs. Is interference due to loss of information from storage or from inability to retrieve information? That question is difficult to answer with certainty, but some studies have shown that under appropriate retrieval conditions (e.g., if people are given strong cues or hints when tested), materials forgotten because of interference can be recovered (Tulving & Psotka, 1971). Thus, at least some of the forgetting produced by interference is probably caused by retrieval factors, not permanent loss of information. We now turn to a more in-depth consideration of the way retrieval cues revive "forgotten" memories.

Retrieval

Try to recall all that you can about your year in the fifth grade: the names of your classmates, your teacher, the school layout, things you learned, daily occurrences. Although you probably cannot remember very much, the experiences may not be totally forgotten. Suppose you were to return to the school with its familiar sights: the classroom, the small desks, the water fountains 3 feet off the floor, the auditorium. Seeing these cues, you would probably be reminded of things you had not thought of in years. The memories were obviously not lost, because with appropriate stimuli, or cues, you retrieved them.

Remembering depends not only on having information coded or stored in memory, but also on having an appropriate situation or cue to bring it back into consciousness. This point has been emphasized most forcefully by Endel Tulving (1976, 1991), who argues that "recollection of an event is a joint function of the information stored in memory about the event (the trace) and the information available to the rememberer at the time of attempted retrieval (the cue)." Up to this point in the chapter, we have been primarily concerned with the way information is coded or stored. We will now consider how information is retrieved.

RETRIEVAL CUES

In experiments designed to study retrieval processes, subjects are often tested either with or without external cues. In one experiment, the subjects were asked to remember studied words from common categories such as professions, weapons, and articles of furniture (Tulving & Pearlstone, 1966). Subjects heard both the category names and the words in the categories in long lists such as "Professions—engineer, lawyer; weapons—bomb, cannon; furniture—bed, dresser." They were told they would have to recall only the items in a category, not the category names.

All subjects heard 48 words from 24 different categories (2 words from each category) and were tested in two conditions. In the free-recall condition, subjects were simply asked to recall the words in any order. They averaged 19 words, which means that they forgot about 29. Were the memory traces for these forgotten words lost from the store? The results from the second condition helped to answer this question. In that condition, subjects were given the category names to serve as retrieval cues for the list words. In this cued-recall condition, the subjects averaged 36 words, or almost twice as many as in free recall. Thus, we can conclude that the forgetting in the free-recall condition was due largely to retrieval difficulties rather than to loss of information from storage.

The logic in this experiment essentially parallels your experience in trying to remember your fifth-grade year. If you had forgotten occurrences from that time, but recovered the memories when you got better retrieval cues, then the difficulty was in retrieval and not in the storage phase. In experiments, the way to separate retrieval from storage factors is to vary retrieval conditions while holding storage conditions constant. To the extent that recall changes, retrieval factors are probably involved (Roediger & Guynn, 1996).

Even if retrieval processes are important in reversing forgetting, we can hardly ever rule out the possibility that some forgetting is due to information being lost from memory (Loftus & Loftus, 1980). Consider the experiment just described. People recollected about 19 words in a free-recall condition and about 36 words when they were given retrieval cues. Thus, some of the forgetting under free recall was due to retrieval factors. Yet, even with strong retrieval cues, the subjects still missed about 12 out of the 48 words. Was information about these words lost from memory, or could these words have also been remembered if the subjects had been given even stronger cues? There is no way to answer this question without actually finding the stronger cues.

Wilder Penfield (1958) produced striking, but controversial, evidence that seemed to point to the conclusion that memories are permanent. A neurosurgeon, Penfield used only local anesthetics while operating on his epileptic patients, so that the patients were conscious during their brain surgery. Penfield discovered that when he touched electrodes to parts of the cerebral cortex, the patients sometimes responded with what seemed to be intense memories. One woman seemed to relive giving birth; another heard an old song so vividly that she thought someone was playing it in the room.

These reports convinced Penfield that the brain permanently recorded all experiences and that if he could reactivate the right place, the memory of any occurrence would rush into consciousness. If this were the case, then all forgetting would obviously be due to retrieval failures. This would certainly be strong evidence supporting the notion that our memories are the results of biological changes in our brains and that all of our experiences are recorded in these neural structures. However, most scientists today regard Penfield's evidence with skepticism. For one thing, only a small percentage of his probes during surgery triggered vivid memories (Loftus & Loftus, 1980). More important, some have argued that many of the "memories" were fantasies or hallucinations, like dreams, resulting from the stimulation (Neisser, 1967). It was, of course, difficult to check the accuracy of patients' memories so many years later. Thus, Penfield's experiments do not answer the question of whether memories are permanent.

Another situation in which people sometimes show dramatic recovery of memories is when they are questioned under hypnosis (see Chapter 5, page 204). As with Penfield's evidence, some researchers have used these cases to argue that all experiences leave permanent records and that all forgetting is due to an inability to gain access to this information buried deep in the mind. However, careful examination of the memories produced under hypnosis raises problems similar to those uncovered in Penfield's experiments. As discussed in Chapter 5, highly hypnotizable people will often produce erroneous information when questioned under hypnosis, and they are often unable to distinguish the true facts from the jumble of invented "facts" (Smith, 1983). Thus, the evidence from hypnosis also does not permit the conclusion that all memories are permanent.

Whether or not all memories are permanent, we can be sure that we usually have much more information about our experiences than we can call into consciousness in a free-recall situation, where no cues are given as aids. We turn now to the way retrieval cues cause people to remember things.

THE ENCODING SPECIFICITY HYPOTHESIS

Appropriate retrieval cues can often bring back memories that seem completely forgotten. Why is this? What determines whether a retrieval cue will be effective? One answer is that effectiveness depends greatly on a cue's relation to the way information is coded or stored. Memory of an event will be aided to the extent that the information from the cue matches what is in the memory trace. Endel Tulving and Donald Thomson (1973) called this idea the **encoding specificity hypothesis**. When people experience something, they encode (learn and store) specific aspects of it. They may remember the time it happened, the context, and other things. The encoding specificity hypothesis states that a retrieval cue will prove effective to the extent that it draws upon this encoding. For example, you may remember many more experiences when you return to your grade school because the familiar sights and sounds help to re-create the context in which you encoded the memories. The encoding specificity hypothesis is similar to the concept of stimulus generalization discussed in Chapter 6; the more similar a stimulus is to the original conditioned stimulus, the greater the response will be to it.

In general, people should be able to remember information better if they acquire it and are tested on it in the same context. In an experimental test of this idea, subjects were given 80 words and were asked to recall them the next day in the same or a different context (Smith, Glenberg, & Bjork, 1978). In one context, subjects occupied a large equipment storeroom in the second floor of a building; the experimenter wore jeans and a T-shirt, and the learning and test took place in the morning. The other context was a tastefully decorated and perfumed basement; the experimenter wore a shirt and tie, and the learning and test occurred in the afternoon. Subjects either learned and were tested on the material in the same context or in different contexts on the two days. Those who learned and were tested in the same context recalled an average of 49 of the 80 words; those tested in a different context averaged only 35 words. This represents a startling difference, suggesting that environmental context plays a powerful role in determining retrieval. These initial results may have overstated the case, however. Later researchers have had difficulty replicating these findings (Fernandez & Glenberg, 1985), and even when the effect is obtained, it only occurs on tests of recall and not on recognition (multiple-choice) tests.

To test the educational implications, William Saufley and his associates (1985) examined the performance of several thousand students who took introductory psychology at the University of California at Berkeley over several years. All the students heard lectures in a large hall, but when they were tested, some were randomly assigned to take their tests in the lecture hall (the same context) while others were tested in smaller classrooms (the different context). The researchers never found any difference between the two conditions in test performance over several semesters. (Thus, if you are currently taking introductory psychology under varying conditions, there's no need to panic. The only thing you might need to worry about are essay tests; the Berkeley study used only multiple-choice tests.)

Environmental context seems to play a potent role as a retrieval cue under some circumstances, but not others. The reasons for this variability have not been fully resolved (Bjork & Richardson-Klavehn, 1989). In the case of multiple-choice tests, however, the powerful cues provided by the test itself may overwhelm the more subtle changes in room context and other features of the environment (Eich, 1989).

Changing the nature of the cues themselves can also affect performance. The benefits of keeping study and test cues compatible is also demonstrated by an experiment involving levels of processing (Morris, Bransford, & Franks, 1977). Subjects in this experiment studied words under conditions designed to produce either phonemic (rhyme) or semantic (meaningful) coding. For example, the word *eagle* might be given with either of these two questions: Is it an animal? or Does it rhyme with *legal*? People responded yes or no to each statement. According to the levels-of-processing view, the first question provides for a deeper encoding of the word and therefore should produce a better memory for *eagle* than the second question. This prediction was supported in a standard recognition test in which people had to pick out studied words among others that had not been studied: People recognized rhyme items 63 percent of the time and semantic items 84 percent of the time, confirming past research (see Figure 7.14).

This experiment also contained a rhyme recognition test, in which the experimenters asked the subjects to recognize words that rhymed with the original study words. None of the actual studied words appeared on the test; only words rhyming with them appeared. (For example, *eagle* did not appear on the test, but *beagle* did.) People performed better on this rhyme test if they had studied words in the rhyme condition (49 percent correct) than in the semantic condition (33 percent). To account for this reversal of the normal levels-of-processing effect, Morris, Bransford, and Franks (1977) proposed the concept of **transfer-appropriate processing** whereby different types of processing of the studied materials will be useful depending on how well this processing transfers to the test situation. Thus, the kind of processing an event receives is not inherently good or bad, but depends on the knowledge required by the memory test. The results of the rhyme recognition test also make sense in terms of the encoding specificity hypothesis. Retrieval cues in the rhyme test match the rhyme encoding better than the semantic encoding, so performance is better in the rhyme encoding condition.

The lesson that psychologists have learned from these examples is that the remembrance of some event depends on at least two factors: how the event was encoded and how well the cues at the time of retrieval match the way the information was coded. Even something well represented in memory will not be remembered unless there is appropriate information (or cues) in the retrieval environment to bring the event back to mind.

DISTINCTIVENESS AS AN AID TO RETRIEVAL

Unexpected or unusual events are often easily recalled. If you were asked to remember a three-digit number such as 237, it would prove difficult if the number were placed in a list of 99 other three-digit numbers; but if 237 were placed in a list of 99 words, you would remember it well. This phenomenon, called the **isolation effect** (Hunt, 1995), shows that events that are distinctive in relation to others occurring at about the same time are well remembered. The isolation effect is probably due to the

FIGURE 7.14
Transfer-Appropriate Processing

Subjects answered questions about words (e.g., *eagle*) under conditions that were designed to make them think about the word's meaning (Is it an animal?) or its sound (does it rhyme with *legal?*) Later they were given either a standard recognition test, in which they had to choose the studied words from a long list of words, or a rhyme recognition test, in which they had to identify words that rhymed with the studied words (e.g., *beagle*). The usual levels-of-processing effect was found on the standard recognition test, with semantic processing producing better recognition than rhyme processing. However, on the rhyme recognition test, the case was reversed: Rhyme encoding produced better performance than semantic encoding. Thus, "deep" (or semantic) processing is not inherently better than "shallow" (or phonemic) processing; it all depends on the way the information must be used. Poor processing for one type of test or activity may be good processing for another test.

SOURCE: Morris, Bransford & Franks, 1977.

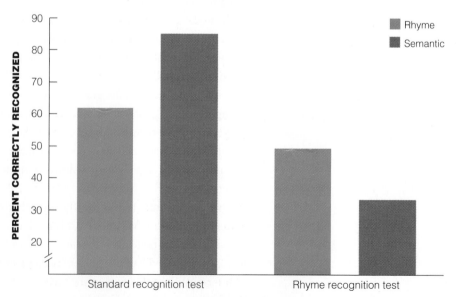

Most people remember with vivid clarity the explosion of the space shuttle *Challenger* in 1986. You may also have the flashbulb memory of where you were, with whom you were talking, and other personal circumstances surrounding the event. Distinctive events that have high impact are well remembered.

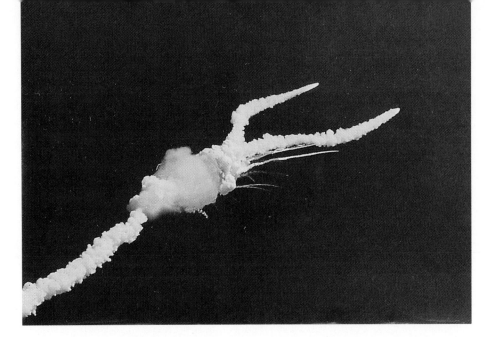

More facts of nature: All forest animals, to this very day, remember exactly where they were and what they were doing when they heard that Bambi's mother had been shot.

role of retrieval factors. The retrieval cue "number" does not help summon 237 from among 99 other numbers; but if there is only one number, then the retrieval of "number" proves effective. Michael Watkins (1979) has proposed that a factor limiting the usefulness of retrieval cues is how overloaded they become. That is, the more memories that are associated with a specific cue, the poorer will be the recall of any one of those memories, a condition called *cue overload*. Distinctive events may be more memorable because they avoid this cue overload. In fact, this may be why the creation of a bizarre mental image aids memory when the other images formed are more common.

That distinctiveness aids memory can also be seen in personal experiences. People frequently remember ordinary occurrences that coincide with an important event. Such vivid recollections of the details surrounding a person's discovery of shocking and upsetting news have been termed **flashbulb memories** (Brown & Kulik, 1977). Many studies have been carried out that test people's recollections of their location and actions during some national tragedy, such as an assassination or natural disaster. For example, Bohannon (1988) studied memories of details surrounding the explosion of the space shuttle *Challenger*. Before reading on, try recalling what you can of your own experience, if you are old enough to remember it. Did you hear about it from the media or from another person? Do you remember what you were doing? How confident are you in your responses? Bohannon constructed a questionnaire containing such items, and distributed it to one large group about two weeks after the explosion and another group eight months later. People seemed to have vivid memories of their reaction to the event, but only if they had a strong emotional reaction to the event or if they rehearsed it over and over with friends and relatives. We have already seen how rehearsal enhances memory; it seems that emotion, too, can sometimes benefit memory (Burke, Heuer, and Reisberg, 1992).

There is some controversy over whether flashbulb memories should be considered a unique phenomenon or simply distinctive memories (McCloskey et al., 1988; Schmidt & Bohannon, 1988; Weaver, 1993). There is little doubt, however, that people do have a good memory for the distinctive events in their lives, whether or not they are accompanied by strong emotional reactions. If you try to remember where you were last New Year's Day, you will probably have an easier job than if you were asked to remember the events of the preceding December 1 or the following February 1. The same is true of other distinctive occasions, such as your birthday or Christmas Day.

Mnemonic Devices

Mnemonic (nee-mon-ik) **devices** are special techniques to improve memory. We have already described a number of factors that aid memory, and the specific techniques that we will now consider combine several of these elements. Some mnemonic techniques date back thousands of years, but the principles underlying their success have been uncovered only recently (Bellezza, 1992). Generally, all mnemonic devices employ two key features. First, they involve a good recoding technique, so that a strong memory trace is constructed. Second, they provide effective retrieval cues. Mnemonics can be developed for virtually any memory task (Higbee, 1988). For example, to remember names, try to associate a prominent feature of the face with the name. Here we consider a few more formal techniques that are fairly easy to learn. You might even want to apply them to your academic studies or to some other area of your life that would benefit from increased memory performance.

THE METHOD OF LOCI

Simonides, an early Greek, was called away from a large banquet to receive a message. In his absence, the roof of the hall collapsed, crushing all who were inside. The dead were mutilated beyond recognition, but Simonides identified their bodies by where they had been sitting. He later used this observation that locations can serve as effective memory cues when he developed his technique, called the *method of loci*, or *location method*, for more general use.

To use the method of loci, you first need to identify a set of familiar places that occur in some natural order (e.g., 20 different locations in your house or apartment or on a familiar path around your school's campus). Any number will do, depending on the number of items you want to be able to remember. To use the locations in remembering a series of items, convert each item to an image, and mentally place it in one of the locations. So, for a grocery list, you would form an image of a loaf of bread and put it in the first location, put an image of eggs in the second, and so on. The locations serve as excellent retrieval cues, since you already know them perfectly. The task then becomes one of "looking" in each place to "see" what is stored there (Bower, 1972). Figure 7.15 illustrates this method.

FIGURE 7.15
The Method of Loci

In using the location technique, people form mental pictures of items in familiar locations. Since the locations form a natural sequence, the order of events can be easily remembered.

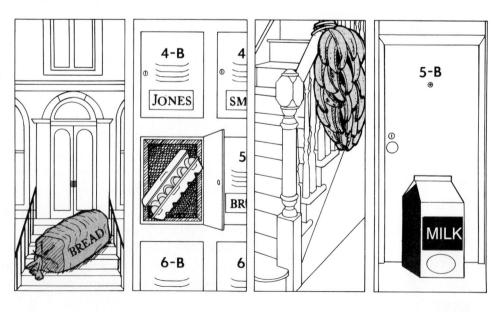

THE PEG METHOD

The *peg method* is based on the same principle as the method of loci, except that the retrieval cues are not locations, but a set of memorized "pegs." There are many peg systems, but in one of the easiest and most popular, shown in the list below, you learn a set of objects that rhyme (more or less) with the numbers 1 to 20. Once these pegs have been learned, each item to be remembered is converted to an image and then imagined to be interacting with the peg word. So to remember the grocery list, you would imagine a gun (the first peg) shooting a loaf of bread, a shoe smashing an egg, and a big bunch of bananas hanging off a tree. Since the pegs have been learned perfectly, they can function as effective retrieval cues. The peg method allows you to recall particular items directly (e.g., what is number 13?) without going through the entire series, as you would probably have to do with the location method.

THE RHYME SYSTEM OF PEGS

One is a gun
Two is a shoe
Three is a tree
Four is a door
Five is knives
Six is sticks
Seven is an oven
Eight is a plate
Nine is wine
Ten is a hen
Eleven is "penny-one," hotdog bun
Twelve is "penny-two," airplane glue
Thirteen is "penny-three," bumble bee
Fourteen is "penny-four," grocery store
Fifteen is "penny-five," big bee hive
Sixteen is "penny-six," magic tricks
Seventeen is "penny-seven," go to heaven
Eighteen is "penny-eight," golden gate
Nineteen is "penny-nine," ball of twine
Twenty is "penny-ten," ballpoint pen

These rhymes associate an object, or peg word, with the numbers from 1 to 20. Once you have learned the rhymes, you can remember a series of items (or points in a speech) by converting each item into an image and imagining it in interaction with each peg word. Thus, each peg allows you to "hang" a memory on it, providing an effective way of remembering things in order.

THE PQ4R METHOD

The two mnemonic devices just described are most useful for remembering names, lists, appointments, or points of a speech. To improve your memory for textbook material, the most suitable strategy is the *PQ4R method*, where PQ4R stands for preview, question, read, reflect, recite, and review (Thomas & Robinson, 1972). Research shows that these steps provide a useful program for improving reading comprehension and for learning course material (Anderson, 1994). The following steps will show you the most effective way to read a chapter in this book.

1. *Preview.* In this important first step, you should survey the chapter. Study the chapter outline and the thematic questions beginning each chapter. Also, look

through the chapter at the headings and identify the sections to be read as units. For example, in this text, each chapter has about five or six main sections. Apply the next four steps to each section as you read it.

2. *Question.* Make up questions about each section, which you can often do just by changing the heading into a question. For example, for this section, ask yourself, "What are mnemonic devices? What is the peg method? What is PQ4R?" and so forth. If you have questions in mind, then you can read with better purpose. If you take a moment to write out the questions before reading, you will remember the material even better.

3. *Read.* Next, read the section carefully, trying to answer your list of questions. The question-generating and question-answering aspects of PQ4R probably provide most of its effectiveness, because they force you to ponder the meaning of the material and to encode it deeply as you read. Recall that generating your own study material enhances your memory for it because of the generation effect.

4. Reflect. As you read the material, think deeply about it in addition to answering the questions. For example, try to think up your own examples, adding to the ones the authors have provided in illustrating some abstract point. Also, try to relate the material to things you already know. One of the surest ways of incorporating new knowledge into memory is to relate it to something you already know well.

5. *Recite.* After you have completed reading the section, look away and try to answer your questions again. If you cannot, then reread each part with which you had difficulty. (If you cannot remember the material just after reading it, what chance do you have later, on the test?)

6. *Review.* After you have read the entire chapter, go through it again, trying to recall its main points. In this text, the Themes in Review and Summary sections at the end of each chapter are designed to help you do this, but you should also try it yourself. Also, try again to answer the questions you constructed.

Tests of the PQ4R method have shown its value (Frase, 1975). Similar techniques have been shown to promote better reading in children (e.g., Paris, Cross, & Lipson, 1984). Although the PQ4R method has been shown to be quite effective, students are sometimes reluctant to use it because it slows them down. But what good is reading rapidly if you don't understand or remember the material you read? The PQ4R method slows reading, but enhances comprehension and memory.

REMEMBERING AS RECONSTRUCTION

Throughout this chapter, we have reported on numerous laboratory experiments where subjects were given a series of pictures, words, or sentences to remember and then were scored on the accuracy of their later recall or recognition. Accurate memories are also crucial to everyday experiences, particularly education, but we also often rely on approximate, slightly inaccurate memories. For example, if a friend says, "Tell me what Gail said when you talked to her yesterday," the request is not for a verbatim record of Gail's remarks. The friend wants the gist, the main points of what Gail had to say.

Often our memories can play surprising tricks on us when we try to reconstruct past events. We may have a definite memory of events, only to find out later that our scenario could not possibly be correct (Roediger & McDermott, 1995). This happened to the famous child psychologist Jean Piaget:

One of my first memories would date, if it were true, from my second year. I can still see, most clearly, the following scene, in which I believed until I was about fifteen. I was sitting in my pram . . . when a man tried to kidnap me. I was held in by the strap fastened round me while my nurse bravely tried to stand between me and the thief. She received various scratches, and I can still see vaguely those on her face. . . . When I was about fifteen, my parents received a letter from my former nurse saying that she had been converted to the Salvation Army. She wanted to confess her past faults, and in particular to return the watch she had been given as a reward on this occasion. She had made up the whole story, faking the scratches. I therefore must have heard, as a child, the account of this story, which my parents believed, and projected it into the past in the form of a visual memory. . . . Many real memories are doubtless of the same order. (Piaget, 1962, pp. 187–188)

As a test of your own memory, try to draw the front side of a U.S. penny from memory. Give yourself 1 minute. Now look at Figure 7.16 and see if you can pick out the correct penny from among the representations there. Despite the fact that you have seen hundreds, and probably thousands, of pennies, the task is not easy. In one study, many students picked the drawings labeled G and M. Neither is correct. Altogether, fewer than half the respondents were able to choose the correct penny, which is A (Nickerson & Adams, 1979). How close is your drawing to it?

How are we to understand such errors of memory? Ideas presented earlier in the chapter can help. Recall that recoding processes are important in remembering; we translate experience into a form that can be more easily remembered, and we try to organize information according to our own knowledge. Information can be erroneously encoded or stored during this process. In addition, when we retrieve information, we may apply general knowledge of events or wishful thinking, so that the story we tell may bear little resemblance to the actual facts, as in Piaget's tale. Both encoding and retrieval are constructive processes. In Chapter 4, when we discussed the constructive nature of perception, we explained many perceptual illusions as arising through constructive activity that normally aids our perception of the world. Similarly, illusions of memory may arise through constructive processes. In fact, remembering past events is similar to the process of *reconstruction* (Hebb, 1949; Neisser, 1967). Just as a paleontologist may take a few bits of fossilized bone from a dinosaur and construct

FIGURE 7.16
Pick the Real Penny

Although you have seen hundreds of pennies, the task of recognizing the correct one is not easy.

SOURCE: Nickerson & Adams, 1979.

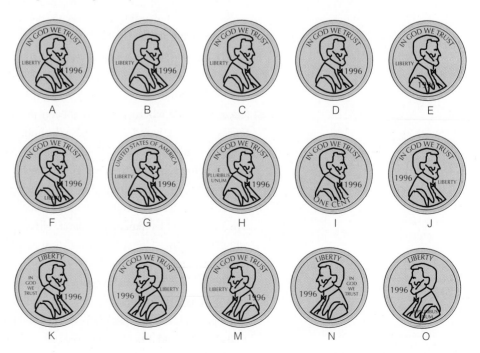

an impressive model of what the beast might have looked like, so, too, a person remembering an event may take a few pieces of fact and weave them together into a coherent, plausible story. However, in the process of reconstruction, errors easily creep in.

SCHEMAS FOR ORGANIZING

The idea that remembering is a constructive process was first advanced by a British psychologist, Sir Frederic Bartlett, in his classic book *Remembering* (1932). Bartlett argued that people tended to remember experiences in terms of **schemas**, general themes that do not contain many specific details. In his experiments, he gave English college students a Native American folktale called "The War of the Ghosts" to remember. The story involved two Indians who were invited by some ghost warriors to raid a neighboring village. The tale contained many implausible, supernatural elements. Bartlett discovered that his English students remembered the story differently from the way it was presented, especially after some time had passed. The students shortened and simplified the story and removed the supernatural elements. They tended to make it resemble a fairytale, a form with which they were more familiar, since they had been raised in a culture that utilized this narrative structure more often than the supernatural structure preferred in Native American cultures. However, Bartlett noted that the main themes (the schemas) of the story were usually preserved.

Schemas can operate during encoding and storage of information to cause people to elaborate on the information provided and store "facts" that are never actually presented. Schemas can also operate at retrieval to guide the reconstruction of the events. For example, if you tell a story about the way a group entered a restaurant and ordered, you may fabricate details when recalling the story because behavior in restaurants usually occurs in a relatively fixed and orderly sequence of events (entering, being seated, ordering, etc.).

In an experiment designed to investigate these issues, Sulin and Dooling (1974) asked students to read and remember the following paragraph:

CAROL HARRIS'S NEED FOR PROFESSIONAL HELP

Carol Harris was a problem child from birth. She was wild, stubborn, and violent. By the time Carol turned eight, she was still unmanageable. Her parents were very concerned about her mental health. There was no good institution for her problem in her state. Her parents finally decided to take some action. They hired a private teacher for Carol.

A second group of students received the same passage, except that Helen Keller's name was substituted for Carol Harris's throughout the passage. A week later, both groups of students were given a recognition test. They were shown sentences and asked to decide whether they had been in the original story. One of the critical sentences was "She was deaf, dumb, and blind." Only 5 percent of the students who had read the Carol Harris version of the story said that this sentence had appeared in it, but 50 percent of the students given the Helen Keller version checked off the sentence as having appeared in the story. Their mistake seems natural. The name Helen Keller probably activated relevant schemas both when students read the story and when they tried to remember it later. However, if they had never learned the relevant schema (i.e., that Helen Keller was deaf and blind), the name change would not have affected their memories for the passage.

Do such errors arise through encoding and storage processes or during retrieval? This issue is usually difficult to decide, and probably processes operating at both times are important. In this case, however, retrieval processes were likely more important. In a later study, students read the passages without a specific name and then were told a week later that the story had been about either Carol Harris or Helen Keller. In this experiment, students tended to make the same pattern of errors. Since the critical information about the person was introduced just before testing, it must have affected retrieval processes (Dooling & Christiaansen, 1977).

In general, the tendency toward reconstruction probably increases over time (Kintsch, 1977). If you were asked to recount what you did on New Year's Day last year, you would probably accurately reproduce more facts than if you were asked to recall New Year's Day in 1985. In the latter case, your "memories" would more likely be reconstructions.

BOUNDARY EXTENSION

Helene Intraub has investigated an interesting reconstructive memory phenomenon known as *boundary extension*, whereby people who are trying to remember a picture tend to recall objects that were not present in the picture but probably existed just outside the boundaries of the picture. For example, if subjects are shown the picture of the garbage can seen in Figure 7.17a and are later asked to draw the picture that they saw, their drawings often include more of the fence than was actually present (see Figure 7.17b). In one experiment, subjects extended boundaries 95 percent of the time (Intraub & Richardson, 1989).

This boundary extension phenomenon occurs for recognition tests as well. In these experiments, subjects study scenes like the one in Figure 7.17a. When they are subsequently shown scenes like the one in Figure 7.17c, subjects frequently say that it is the same picture they viewed earlier. Intraub and her colleagues also invoke the concept of schemas to explain their findings: When people view the picture, it activates a schema of a larger scene that is only partly depicted within the boundaries of the picture. Such a larger scene would in fact be visible if it were being viewed in reality and not just from a picture. Seeing the photograph may bring to mind the schema (and all of the expectations that come along with it) for viewing such a scene in reality. If people remember the activated schema, then the boundaries will tend to move out, to encompass the

FIGURE 7.17
Boundary Extension

After viewing a scene like that in (a) people usually recall it with extended boundaries, as in the drawing in (b). If they are asked if (c) was the original picture they saw, many say yes. Boundary extension shows the constructive nature of nonverbal memory.

SOURCE: Intraub & Richardson, 1989.

(a)   (b)

(c)

scene that the photograph suggests (Intraub, 1992; Intraub, Gottesman, Willey & Zuk, 1996).

EYEWITNESS TESTIMONY

If remembering is constructive, then sometimes even our most cherished memories may consist of more fiction than fact, as in the case of Piaget's memory of the attempted kidnapping. It may even be that the more often we recall something, the more opportunities we have to make errors, with possible practical consequences. Suppose you witness an automobile accident, and the police later question you to determine the person at fault. Will the type of questions you are asked, as well as your responses, change your recollection of the incident? If you appear on the witness stand some time later, will you "remember" facts that never occurred?

Studies by Elizabeth Loftus (1979) suggest that the answer to these questions is yes. Eyewitness evidence is among the most convincing for jurors, but how reliable is it? Loftus and Palmer (1974) asked this question in a study in which people watched a film of a two-car accident and then were asked to fill out questionnaires. There was one critical question. Some people were asked, "How fast were the two cars going when they hit each other?" For others, *hit* was changed to *smashed, collided, bumped,* or *contacted.* Loftus and Palmer found that the verb used in the question determined, to a great extent, people's reports of the cars' speeds. The average speed estimate was 32 mph when the verb was *contacted,* 34 mph when it was *hit,* 38 mph when it was *bumped,* 39 mph when it was *collided,* and 41 mph when it was *smashed.* The conclusion is that leading questions can greatly affect testimony.

About how fast were the cars going when they *smashed* into each other?

People remembered seeing broken glass when "smashed" had been the verb in the earlier question.

In another experiment, Loftus and Palmer (1974) showed 150 people a film of an automobile accident. On a questionnaire, they asked 50 people, "About how fast were the cars going when they *smashed* into each other?" Fifty others were asked the same question, but with *hit* as the verb. The remaining 50, a control group, were not asked about speed. Once again, the speed estimate was higher when *smashed* rather than *hit* was the verb. A week later, all 150 people were again questioned about the accident. One critical question was "Did you see any broken glass?" No broken glass was shown in the film, so yes answers were errors. Only 12 percent of the control group erred, compared to 14 percent of those whose questionnaires used the verb *hit.* But 32 percent of those who read the word *smashed* in the questionnaire answered yes a week later to the question about seeing glass. The leading question apparently caused people to recode the accident so that their memories of it changed. When asked about the event with *smashed,* they may have recoded the accident as more serious. They altered their original memory by integrating it with the information presented in the question.

Other researchers have argued that memory for the event has not been altered in the eyewitness testimony experiment, but rather that the retrieval conditions typically used in such experiments do not promote accurate memory (Zaragoza & Koshmider, 1989). Nonetheless, it is clear that distortions often will arise in reconstructing events from memory, especially when interfering activities occur between the events and their recall (Chandler, 1989; Chandler & Gargano, 1995).

Think of what may happen to the eyewitness of a crime who is trying to be objective and truthful. First comes questioning by police, then by the prosecution and defense attorneys. And the witness will also probably answer the repeated questions of family and friends and may even see accounts of the event in the media. When the witness finally appears before a judge and jury months or even years later, how accurate do you think the testimony will be, especially for small details?

Repressed Memories of Childhood Abuse?

In 1990, a dramatic courtroom trial occurred in Redwood City, California. The defendant was a man named George Franklin, who was 51 years old and was being charged in the death of an 8-year-old girl, Susan K. Nason, who had been murdered more than 20 years earlier, on September 22, 1969. Franklin had been a suspect at the time of the murder, but there was not sufficient evidence to charge him, much less to convict him.

Why was Franklin tried for the murder more than 20 years later? Franklin's daughter, Eileen, came forward and claimed that she had suddenly had a dramatic flashback of a memory that had been repressed for 20 years. She suddenly remembered her father murdering her friend, Susan Nason. Elizabeth Loftus recounts the way Eileen's memory returned:

> Eileen's memory did not come back all at once. She claimed that her first flashback came one afternoon in January, 1989, when she was playing with her two-year-old son, Aaron, and her five-year-old daughter, Jessica. At one moment, Jessica looked up and asked her mother a question like "Isn't that right, Mommy?" A memory of Susan Nason suddenly came back. Eileen recalled the look of betrayal in Susie's eyes just before the murder. Later, more fragments would return, until Eileen had a rich and detailed memory of the scene. She remembered her father sexually assaulting Susie in the back of the van. She remembered that Susie was struggling as she said "No, don't" and "Stop." She remembered her father saying "Now Susie," and she even mimicked his precise intonation. Next, her memory took the three of them outside the van, where she saw her father with his hands raised above his head with a rock in them. She remembered screaming. She remembered walking back to where Susie lay, covered with blood, the silver ring on her finger smashed. (Loftus, 1993, p. 518)

Armed with this new evidence, the prosecutor charged George Franklin with the murder. During the trial, experts debated whether a 20-year-old memory rearoused in this fashion could be believed. In the end, however, the jury accepted the new evidence. They deliberated less than one day. Because of Eileen's confidence and the amount of detail in her memory, George Franklin was convicted of murder in the first degree and is now serving a long prison sentence. However, in 1995 a higher court overturned his original conviction; he will likely be tried again.

This case is not unique. Indeed, it seems to have been among the first of a wave of similar cases happening all over the United States. Hundreds of people, including celebrities like Roseanne, have come forward to accuse their parents of childhood sexual abuse. Usually, the mem-

ories of such abuse are uncovered during the course of psychological therapy.

The problem of childhood sexual abuse is horrifying and recent evidence indicates that it may be more prevalent than previously believed. Most people who are abused probably remember the events very well, as with other emotional memories. Therapists work hard to relieve the pain of people who suffered from abuse. The remarks below pertain to only one phenomenon: claims of recovering memories of once forgotten childhood sexual abuse. No one condones sexual abuse, but no one should condone potentially false accusations of abuse, either. Such accusations can ruin the lives of individuals and whole families, just as sexual abuse itself can.

Some therapists, treating their clients for depression or other problems, try to discover what factors are causing the depression. Some therapists may suggest to their clients that childhood sexual abuse could be part of the problem. Are the therapists helping clients to retrieve repressed memories of abuse, or is the notion of abuse being planted in the client's mind during the course of therapy and then later believed to be true? Are "memories" of abuse actually being produced, or constructed, during the course of therapy, when they never occurred at all? This is essentially the argument of many of the accused parents, who claim that the accusations are completely false and that their children never mentioned being abused until they underwent extensive therapy. These are very difficult issues to decide, because the events under question typically happened long ago, and there is usually no independent evidence to confirm or disprove the memories of abuse.

George Franklin

Eileen Franklin-Lisker

Therapists and police officers are often quite impressed with the amount of detail in the accuser's account. Surely, they reason, if this person expresses the memory so confidently and includes so much detail, then it is probably accurate. But is this really so? Recall how details about an event that a person has witnessed can be inserted at a later point in time and then confidently remembered, even if they are false. Perhaps some therapists are inadvertently planting details by recounting other cases to the client, and then the client creates his or her own story from this jumble of details. For example, Loftus (1993) points out that many of the details in Eileen Franklin's "memory" of her father's murder of Susan Nason were actually contained in media reports of the time, which Franklin had gone back and read. Loftus also points out that some details changed across the repeated retellings of Eileen's story. For example, she originally told police that her father was driving her and her sister Janice to school when they saw Susie and that Mr. Franklin made Janice get out of the van when Susie got in. However, in recounting the story months later, Eileen did not report Janice being in the van. Also, in the original statements, Eileen said that the trip occurred either going to school in the morning or going back to school from lunch. Yet, during the preliminary hearing, after she had probably been reminded that Susie had not been reported missing until after school was out, Eileen now recalled that it was in the late afternoon because the sun was low. Because Eileen's report changed with repeated retellings, possibly in response to learning more details from police or from reading old newspaper accounts, at least some portions of these distant memories are wrong. Of course, other details of the memories could be accurate.

If the memories are not authentic, where may they originate? As already noted, one possibility is during the therapeutic process itself (Lindsay & Reed, 1994). Many people entering therapy are, almost by definition, unhappy and confused about themselves. Perhaps when therapists suggest that part of the cause could be childhood sexual abuse, they lead the patient down a road that eventually confirms this diagnosis. Some therapeutic techniques may encourage creation of false memories. For example, therapists may hypnotize their clients in an attempt to have them recover memories of abuse. But as discussed in Chapter 5, little or no evidence exists showing that hypnosis aids memory retrieval. However, highly hypnotizable people often do later accept "memories" they produce under hypnosis as accurate, even when they are not. Another technique frequently used is guided imagery or visualization, whereby a therapist suggests that the client imagine that abuse occurred and visualize specific people as the potential perpetrators (a father, an uncle, or a teacher). This technique may aid recovery of memories if the events actually occurred, but may help create false memories of the events that did not happen, with imagined happenings being confused with real events (as has been demonstrated in many experiments; Lindsay & Read, 1994). Not all therapists use techniques such as hypnosis and guided imagery, but a recent survey of British and American therapists shows that many do (Poole, Lindsay, Memon, & Bull, 1995).

Therapy for sexual abuse may include reading books about the problem. One of the most popular books used by therapists for survivors of incest is *The Courage to Heal* (Bass & Davis, 1988). The book is intended to serve as a

Amnesia

The term **amnesia** covers a whole range of problems, but all involve cases of dramatic forgetting.

TYPES OF AMNESIA

People who are involved in automobile collisions or other accidents in which the head receives a sharp blow often receive a concussion (swelling of the tissues surrounding the brain) and may lapse into unconsciousness. Upon recovery, they may suffer memory losses for events either before or after the accident. **Retrograde amnesia** refers to loss of memory for events prior to the accident; **anterograde amnesia** refers to memory lapses for experiences after the accident. If the concussion is relatively mild, often the amnesia will lift and the patient's memory for some of the events will return. In the case of severe concussions, the events may be permanently forgotten. Psychologists study amnesias caused by brain damage in the hope of gaining a better understanding of the normal workings of memory and the way in which biological factors constrain its operation.

guide or handbook for women who have experienced sexual abuse as children. In one place, readers are told, "If you are unable to remember any specific instances like the ones mentioned above, but still have a feeling something abusive happened to you, it probably did" (p. 21). On the next page, the reader is told:

You may think you don't have memories, but often as you begin to talk about what you do remember, there emerges a constellation of feelings, reactions, and recollections that add up to substantial information. To say, "I was abused" you don't need the kind of recall that would stand up in a court of law. Often the knowledge that you were abused starts from a tiny feeling and intuition . . . . Assume your feelings are valid. So far, no one we've talked to thought she might have been abused, and then later discovered that she hadn't been. The progression always goes the other way, from suspicion to confirmation. If you think you were abused and your life shows the symptoms, then you were. (p. 22)

What are the symptoms that might be used as evidence? The authors list low self-esteem, thoughts of suicide or depression, and sexual dysfunction. Surely, people could experience any or all of these symptoms without necessarily having been sexually abused as a child.

Of course, it is impossible to know if the recovered memories of childhood sexual abuse are accurate. Some probably are; some probably are not. The proportion of accurate memories is anyone's guess. However, it is true that something can be confidently remembered and yet be completely inaccurate. The story of Piaget's kidnapping illustrates this point. And in an experimental setting, Loftus (1993) has created such inaccurate memories in students. In collaboration with parents and siblings, she gives students several scenarios that might have happened to them as children. Some of the scenarios are true happenings that actually occurred during childhood, and others are false. One involves an occasion on which the child was lost in a shopping mall, an episode that was false in all cases as far as the parents and siblings could recollect. Nevertheless, after reading the scenario of being lost, some students said that they could remember it. At first the memory was fragmentary, but it usually grew stronger, and the number of details being recovered increased with repeated testing. This type of experiment shows that at least in some cases, memories of traumatic events can spring full blown from suggestions, when in fact the under question never happened. Other researchers have reported similar results (Ceci, Huffman, Smith & Loftus, 1994; Hyman, Husband & Billings, 1995).

Clearly this new experimental evidence does not mean that any particular recovered memory of child abuse is not a true recollection. There is no way to know in individual cases, short of corroborating evidence. The research about constructive processes in memory simply points out the need to be very cautious in accepting uncritically the reports of patients who have been in extensive therapy, where events of abuse may have been suggested by the therapist or by reading about similar cases (Lindsay & Reed, 1994).

Several different conditions are referred to as amnesia. One condition, **transient global amnesia,** is marked by a relatively brief amnesic period in which the person becomes extremely forgetful (Kritchevsky, 1992). Transient global amnesia lasts at least several hours and maybe a bit longer. The person's memory gradually reappears over the course of several hours to a day. This type of amnesia is doubtless due to some brief and passing pathology in the brain (perhaps a minor stroke or some other obstruction that deprives parts of the brain of blood). Typically, all of the person's other perceptual and language functions remain intact. A patient with transient global amnesia will often repeat the same question many times, but be unable to remember the answer just given. Such patients do not lose their sense of identity, and yet they can't understand what is wrong. Happily, such episodes clear up relatively quickly without medical treatment.

More dramatic cases are seen in **functional amnesias** (Kihlstrom & Schacter, 1992), memory disorders in which an individual's sense of personal identity is altered. (*Functional* means that no known brain disorder causes the amnesia). Functional amnesia may come in the form of multiple personality disorder, characterized by the spontaneous change from one personal identity to another. Often these patients are

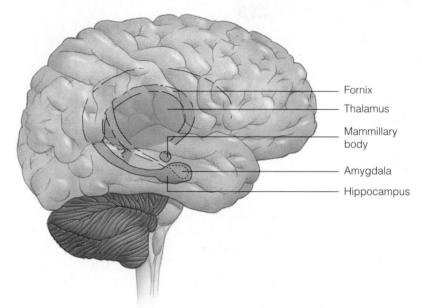

FIGURE 7.18
Structures Critical for Explicit Memory

This schematic drawing shows structures in the temporal lobe responsible for remembering, especially the hippocampus and amygdala. The frontal lobes are also probably important for remembering. Brain damage to these areas impairs remembering.

Labels: Fornix, Thalamus, Mammillary body, Amygdala, Hippocampus

unable to recall what transpired while the other "personality" was controlling their behavior. (These sorts of experiences are described more fully in Chapter 15.) Another type of amnesia, **infantile (childhood) amnesia,** is actually the natural inability of most people to remember any events that occurred before age 3 or 4. (This phenomenon is discussed shortly.) And finally there is **organic amnesia,** a loss of memory due to specific damage to the brain.

Neuropsychologists—those interested in discovering the neural foundations of cognition and behavior—have spent years searching for clues about the way the brain stores memories. The task is not a simple one. In 1915, Karl Lashley began a search for the locus of the engram (or memory trace) in animals. He removed various parts of the brain and then tested animals to see if they had forgotten responses learned before the operation or if their abilities to learn new responses were damaged. Summarizing decades of work in 1950, he wrote: "It is not possible to demonstrate the isolated localization of a memory trace anywhere in the nervous system. Limited regions may be essential for learning or retention of a particular activity, but . . . the engram is represented throughout the region" (p. 478). This animal research should caution against the simple notion that any one structure in the human brain is likely to be the seat of memory. However, damage to the temporal lobes, the frontal lobes, and the hippocampus (see Figure 7.18) often produce amnesias in humans (Shimamura, 1992).

We will consider two cases here. One represents the most famous patient/subject studied by neuropsychological researchers, known by his initials—H. M. and the other is a striking recent case known as Greg F.

CASE STUDIES

AMNESIC PATIENTS: PEOPLE WHO CANNOT REMEMBER

THE CASE OF H. M.

In 1953, just three years after Lashley had pronounced that the location of the engram could not be found, neurosurgeon William Scoville inadvertently made a discovery that set researchers off on the trail once again. His patient, H. M., had epilepsy that was growing worse despite heavy medication. Scoville operated and removed large parts of H. M.'s temporal lobes in an attempt to cure the epilepsy. When H. M. recovered, he experienced severe anterograde amnesia. He seemed incapable of learning new material, although his intelligence was above normal, his vocabulary was good, his speech and language comprehension were normal, and he was able to remember events that had happened before his operation. After more than 40 years, he remains incapable of performing virtually any sort of memory task in which he is given information and then asked to recall it after a delay. Like other amnesic patients, however, he can recall the last few words from a list if he is tested immediately. This has led some researchers to explain amnesia by distinguishing between short-term and long-term memory. According to this view, the brain mechanisms damaged in amnesic patients prevent information from being transferred from a short-term state to a more permanent memory system (the long-term store).

Laboratory memory tasks aren't the only things that H. M. has difficulty performing. For example, he went to work at a rehabilitation center after his father's death, where he performed monotonous tasks usually given to severely retarded people. Even after he had worked at the job every day (except weekends) for six months, he was still incapable of describing the place he worked, what he did there, or the route by which he was driven to and from work each day. On the other hand, H. M. did show some limited ability to learn the floor plan of the house in which he lived, and he had some idea of the two surrounding blocks in his neighborhood. Beyond that, he was lost (Milner, Corkin, & Teuber, 1968).

THE CASE OF GREG F.

Greg F. grew up in New York in a middle class home in the 1950s. He was bright and seemed destined for college and a successful career. However, in the late 1960s, like many other young Americans, Greg became disaffected with "the system," his parents, and school. He dropped out, lost touch with his family, and eventually joined the Krishna Consciousness Movement, moving to their New Orleans temple in 1971. There, Greg began having problems seeing, but was told that he was lit by an inner light that would help him see.

Greg's family became worried about him. When they went to investigate, "they were filled with horror: their lean, hairy son had become fat and hairless; he wore a continual 'stupid' smile on his face (this was at least his father's word for it); he kept bursting into bits of song and verse" (Sacks, 1992, p. 53). In addition, he showed little emotion, was not interested in his current surroundings or events, and was totally blind!

Greg was removed from the temple and hospitalized. Brain imaging showed a large benign tumor of the pituitary gland that had destroyed neural pathways involved with vision and memory. Neurosurgeons could remove the tumor, but could not repair the damage already done to neighboring neural systems. Greg, at 25, had to be hospitalized for life. Since 1977, Greg has been studied by Dr. Oliver Sacks, and it is from Sacks (1992) that this account comes.

The damage to Greg's brain caused by the tumor resulted in profound abnormalities in his memory. He was able to follow a current conversation reasonably well, replying appropriately to questions. However, he usually gave the wrong answer if he was asked to remember an event that had occurred since 1970. He also failed even the simplest memory tests. When given a short list of words and then distracted for a minute, he was unable to recall them. He had similar problems in remembering stories and the names of people he had met. In other words, Greg showed the classic symptoms of organic amnesia.

Greg F. participated actively in a Grateful Dead concert, talked excitedly about it all the way home, but had totally forgotten it the next morning.

The following incident will illustrate just how severe this memory dysfunction can be. Greg could remember things from the time prior to his tumor, and one of his favorite memories was of the rock group The Grateful Dead. He listened to their music constantly and had attended their concerts in New York in the late 1960s. He could easily recall the names of the band members, events about them, and their songs, but only up to the period where his tumor began to affect his memory. In August 1991, Dr. Sacks arranged for Greg to attend a Grateful Dead concert in New York's Madison Square Garden. Greg became very excited when told he was going to the concert, and he loved the first part of the concert, when the old songs were played. He clapped and sang constantly, and he did not want to leave between sets.

When they finally left, Greg said, "That was fantastic. I will always remember it. I had the time of my life." Greg and Dr. Sacks talked about the concert all the way back to the hospital, with Greg following and contributing to the conversation.

The next morning, Dr. Sacks arrived at the hospital early and spoke to Greg in the dining room. He asked him about The Grateful Dead. "Great group," Greg said "I love them. I heard them in Central Park and at the Fillmore East." When Dr. Sacks asked "Didn't you just hear them at Madison Square Garden?" Greg replied, "No, I've never been to the Garden." (Sacks, 1992, p. 62).

Greg had no conscious recollection of the concert that he had enthusiastically attended less than 12 hours before.

KORSAKOFF'S SYNDROME

Amnesia can be produced by various maladies other than direct injuries to the brain from surgery, tumors or accidents. For example, *Korsakoff's syndrome* is a condition that afflicts chronic alcoholics who have also been malnourished and have suffered irreversible brain damage owing to a lack of vitamin B_1. In the late 1800s, the syndrome was first identified by a Russian physician, S. S. Korsakoff. Patients with the syndrome often seem perfectly normal on a first meeting: They can speak fluently and intelligently, and their knowledge of events that occurred before their bouts with alcohol is normal. They also reason accurately and can even play cards and chess. But these patients will often ask the same questions repeatedly, even after hearing the answers, and they often tell the same stories over and over. Consider the following description of a person with Korsakoff's syndrome:

> Only after a long conversation with the patient, one may note that at times he utterly confuses events and that he remembers absolutely nothing of what goes on around him: he does not remember whether he had his dinner. . . . On occasion the patient forgets what happened to him just an instant ago: you came in, conversed with him, and stepped out for one minute, then you come in again and the patient has absolutely no recollection that you had already been with him. Patients of this type read the same page over and over again, sometimes for hours, because they are absolutely unable to remember what they had read. (Oscar-Berman, 1980, p. 410)

INFANTILE AMNESIA

A remarkable fact, but one you have probably noted, is that people are generally unable to remember experiences that occurred in their first few years of life. However, many theories of child development suggest that early experiences in life are tremendously influential, and we know that even very young babies have the capability of profiting from experience they learn and remember (Rovee-Collier, 1993).

Infantile, or childhood, amnesia is a mysterious phenomenon, but psychologists are gradually learning more about it. If people are asked to date their earliest memories, the average age is 3 1/2 years, with a range from 2 to 7 or 8 years of age (Neisser, 1992). When it is possible to check these early memories against parents' recollections, they generally prove accurate. However, the early memories are often quite fragmentary, with people remembering only single episodes of some event. Some people claim to have memories from as early as 1 or 2, but usually the memories are of repetitive acts that might have occurred many different times over the years (e.g., an annual vacation at a particular spot). Therefore, these memories may not be trustworthy.

Why does childhood amnesia occur? Several possible reasons have been advanced (Howe & Courage, 1993). First, the human brain is not fully developed at birth and continues to mature in the early years of life, as is true in all mammals. It might be that the neural structures critical for episodic memory, generally those in the frontal lobes and in the critical structure called the hippocampus (see Figure 7.18), continue to develop after birth. By this hypothesis, the learning and retention that does occur in infants and very young children would be due to the operation of other memory systems, such as those responsible for procedural memory (Nadel & Zola-Morgan, 1984). Interestingly, other mammals also seem to show infantile amnesia. For example, when 12-day-old rats learn a response to the same criterion as do adult rats and are then tested later, the response is lost much more rapidly in the younger rats. So, one factor explaining infantile amnesia is that the structures in the nervous system responsible for conscious recollection, or episodic memory—also called **explicit memory**—do not develop sufficiently until after the first few years of life.

The best guess is that the neural structures supporting performance on explicit memory tests develop between ages 2 and 3. At least, studies show that 2 1/2 year old children can recall events such as trips or holidays that took place 6 months earlier. One study showed that events occurring to children around age 2 1/2 could still be recollected 18 months later, when the children were 4 (Fivush & Hammond, 1990). Indeed, the 4-year-old children sometimes accurately remembered details that they had not recalled originally many months before.

Neisser (1992) notes that another idea, the concept of schema, may also help to explain childhood amnesia. From research discussed earlier in the chapter, we know that organizing events helps us recall them. As adults, we think of our lives as having a story or narrative. We traverse "a definite course marked by certain milestones and periods: Progression through school, a succession of friends, a number of developmental phases, special events that occurred at certain dates and times" (Neisser, 1992, p. 29). Young children may not yet have this kind of schema of their lives, and they may not be able to fit in events and remember them well because they lack this narrative. Early memories may seem fragmentary and disjointed because they are; they have not yet been fitted into a schema or narrative of one's life (Howe & Courage, 1993).

IMPLICIT MEMORY

Although patients suffering from organic amnesia often seem incapable of learning and remembering after the onset of their disease (i.e., they suffer anterograde amnesia), some studies indicate that amnesics may actually learn much more than anecdotal reports and previous research suggest. In fact, amnesics perform perfectly normally on some tests. Their difficulty may be traced to an inability to translate their knowledge into a consciously accessible form. They may know something, but not be aware that they do. **Implicit memory** refers to retention in the absence of attempts at conscious recollection, or explicit memory (Schacter, 1987).

One of the first such studies illustrating these "hidden" memories in amnesics involved motor skills. Milner and her colleagues (1968) asked H. M. to trace an outline on a sheet of paper in front of him while looking at the actual scene in a mirror. Because mirror drawing involves a left-to-right reversal, the task is very difficult even for normal people. H. M. was tested on three successive days. He performed better on the task every day, showing that he was capable of learning. When he was brought back into the situation each day, he was asked if he had ever done the task before. He always declared that he had not, but he nonetheless showed strong improvements over the three days. Thus, H. M. could obviously learn to perform the motor task, but was unaware of his competence. Such a situation is referred to as a *dissociation*—the separation of a person's conscious knowledge from other aspects of his or her behavior.

Amnesics have traditionally been assumed to have virtually no memory for verbal material. They often fail to learn their doctors' names even after hundreds of introductions, and they repeat the same comments and stories after very short delays. Surprisingly, more recent research shows that amnesics perform just as well as normal people on some measures of verbal retention. For example, Peter Graf, Larry Squire, and George Mandler (1984) tested 17 patients classified as amnesic. Seven suffered from Korsakoff's syndrome, and eight others were severely depressed patients who were receiving electroconvulsive therapy (ECT). This procedure, which is discussed more fully in Chapter 16, involves passing electric current briefly through electrodes attached to the scalp; it usually produces temporary amnesia. Two other subjects were called "anoxic" amnesics because they had become amnesic after the oxygen supply to the brain was cut off for a time. Appropriate control groups were found for these amnesic patients. For example, the controls for the Korsakoff patients were other chronic alcoholics who were hospitalized but who had not developed Korsakoff's syndrome.

All subjects were given several 10 word lists to memorize, and after each list, their memories were tested in one of two ways. First, the subjects were asked to recall as many words as they could in any order they wanted. This free-recall test required the subjects to consciously recall the words. The second test, a word completion test, was not presented as a test of memory at all. The subjects were given 20 sets of three-letter cues, such as *inf* or *per*, and were instructed to say the first word that came to mind beginning with those three letters (e.g., *infant* or *personal*). Half the three-letter cues represented words that had appeared in the study list, while the other half represented words that had not been studied. Subjects were told nothing about the relation of the cues to the words in the list, but were simply instructed to say the first word that popped into mind beginning with those letters. The researchers assumed that if patients completed the word stems with words from the list more often than for non-studied control words, then the word completion test measures retention for the words.

The results are shown in Figure 7.19. The amnesic patients performed much worse than their controls on free recall. This is no surprise, of course, because, by definition, amnesics are poor at recalling information. The interesting finding comes from the word completion task. Both groups performed much better than chance, and amnesics performed just as well as normal subjects—in fact, slightly better. Apparently, the amnesic patients registered presentation of the words (they learned about them), but

CHAPTER SEVEN
REMEMBERING AND FORGETTING

298

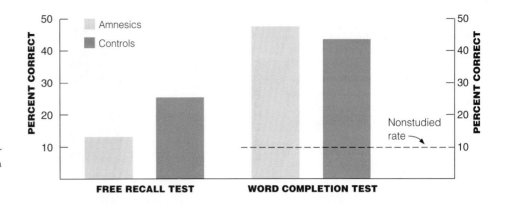

FIGURE 7.19
Verbal Memory in Amnesics

Amnesic patients and controls both received lists of words and then were given two tests after each list—free recall and word completion. In free recall, which requires conscious recollection of the words from the list, the amnesics did much worse than the controls. In the word completion test, both groups were told to produce the first word to come to mind when given three-letter cues (e.g., *per* for *permanent*). In this test, the amnesics and normals did not differ significantly. The word completion test reflects learning because both groups did much better than if they had not studied the words (as indicated by the dashed line). Amnesics often show normal levels of retention, even for verbal materials, if the memory test does not require that they be consciously aware of the previous learning episode.

SOURCE: Graf, Squire & Mandler, 1984.

were unable to express this knowledge on a test measuring conscious recollection.

The word completion test represents another measure of implicit memory The test does not require people to recall recent events; rather, it measures their learning indirectly. When amnesics' memories are measured on tests that do not require conscious awareness (implicit memory tests), they show normal learning and retention. Put another way, the brain-damaged patients may be "amnesic" only on certain tests of retention; on other tests, they are perfectly normal.

How can we explain the fact that amnesics are so impaired on tests involving conscious recollection, but unimpaired on tests reflecting implicit knowledge? The most popular proposal is that different memory systems in the brain are responsible for retention on different tests (Squire, 1987; Tulving, 1993). For example, Squire distinguishes between declarative and procedural memory. *Declarative memory* involves knowledge that can be verbalized (about which people can make declarations). Episodic memory (memory for personal episodes or experiences) is part of declarative memory. According to Squire, this system is damaged in most common forms of amnesia. The parts of the brain involved include areas surrounding the hippocampus, the amygdala, the diencephalon, and possibly the frontal lobes (see Figure 7.18). Damage to these structures causes people to lose their ability to retrieve personal experiences. Squire and colleagues (1992) also argue that the semantic memory system is damaged in most amnesic patients because they have great difficulty learning new facts about the world around them. However, the *procedural memory system*, which is responsible for learning motor skills, for classical and operant conditioning, and for the priming of prior knowledge that is tapped by implicit memory tests, remains intact.

The defining characteristic of implicit memory tests is that they are not presented to subjects as tests of memory. Remembering is not mentioned; instead, the subjects are asked to do some new task (such as completing fragmented words or naming pictures with parts missing). The measure of interest is the effect that previous exposure to words or pictures has on the subjects' abilities to later complete the fragmented forms.

Implicit memory tests also reveal many surprising phenomena when they are used to test memory in normal people. For example, earlier in the chapter, we stated that people can more easily recall items from a list if the items are presented as pictures instead of as words (Madigan, 1983). This superiority occurs on many different kinds of explicit memory tests However, Weldon and Roediger (1987) showed that on one common implicit memory test (completing fragmented words; e.g., changing e_ _ ph _ _ t to <u>elephant</u>), prior study of words produced better performance than did prior study of pictures (see Figure 7.20). So some "laws" of memory, such as pictures

FIGURE 7.20
Results of the Weldon and Roediger Experiment (1987)

After studying words and pictures, normal subjects took either a free recall test (an explicit test) or a word completion test (an implicit test). In the word completion test, subjects completed, to the best of their abilities, words with missing letters. Some word fragments represented previously studied words, some represented concepts exposed as pictures, and some other fragments corresponded to items that had not been studied (for a measure of baseline performance). The results on the left show that in free recall, pictures were better remembered than words, a result that replicates the usual finding on explicit tests. However, prior study of words produced much better performance on the implicit, word completion, test than did earlier study of pictures.

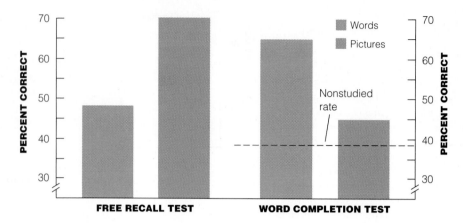

being better retained than words, apparently do not apply to implicit memory tests (Roediger & McDermott, 1993).

We end this chapter by turning to a central question posed by work on amnesics: What is it like to function without a memory for personal experiences? H. M. once described his mental state as "like waking from a dream." Another amnesic, K. C., was incapable of remembering personal experiences after a traffic accident, but his general intelligence was unimpaired. Although most research has centered on what amnesics can remember from their past, Endel Tulving (1985) tested K. C. on his concept of the future. When asked what he would be doing when he left "here" (the interview) or would be doing tomorrow, K. C. replied that he did not know. Here is part of an interview between Tulving and K. C.:

> Tulving: Let's try the question again about the future. What will you be doing tomorrow?
> (There is a 15-second pause.)
> K. C.: smiles faintly, then says: I don't know.
> Tulving: Do you remember the question?
> K. C.: About what I'll be doing tomorrow?
> Tulving: Yes, would you describe your state of mind when you try to think about it?
> (A 5-second pause.)
> K. C.: Blank, I guess.

Later, when questioned further, K. C. produced two analogies for his state of mind when he tried to think about the future. Once he said, "It's like being in a room with nothing there and having a guy tell you to find a chair, and there's nothing there." On a different occasion, he said, "It's like swimming in the middle of a lake. There's nothing there to hold you up or do anything with" (Tulving, 1985). A person with no memories of personal experiences loses the concept of both past and future, which points up the critical importance of conscious remembering for life as we know it.

THEMES IN REVIEW

The biological theme has been illustrated in this chapter with our description of the neural foundations of memory. The cases of amnesia resulting from brain damage help pinpoint the structures of the brain (especially the hippocampus and its surrounding structures as well as the frontal lobes) that are largely responsible for the experience of conscious recollection. Infantile amnesia can also be attributed to immaturities in the structure of the brain, which implies that memory and the biological structures of the brain are linked.

Developmental aspects of memory are also critical. People have few memories from the first three or four years of their life (the phenomenon of infantile, or childhood, amnesia), and the ability to remember increases dramatically over the childhood years. In addition, although it was not discussed here, we will see in Chapter 10 that the ability to remember declines in old age.

Obviously, many cognitive factors are at work in memory, and almost the entire chapter has been concerned with these. The type of encoding activity or mental process applied to material greatly affects its memorability, as does the amount of organization inherent in or imposed on the knowledge and how much we already know about the subject. In addition, the interpretation of cues in the environment when we attempt to retrieve help determine whether recollection will be successful.

We have also seen that learning can play a role in memory. We can greatly enhance our memory by learning how to apply mnemonic techniques to more effectively encode the material we wish to learn. Also, amnesics appear to have no memory, but they can often show improvements in acquiring procedural memories, such as learning how to draw figures while looking in a mirror.

Finally, we have seen sociocultural factors at work in remembering. In cases of both eyewitness testimony and memories of childhood abuse, it seems likely that other people can greatly influence our memory. Recall Piaget's recollections of a kidnapping that never occurred. Also, the English college students who recalled the American Indian folktale tended to change their memories of the story to fit the format of a fairytale, a familiar narrative structure in their culture.

SUMMARY

1 Memory is not a unitary phenomenon. Psychologists distinguish between episodic memory (for personal experiences) and semantic memory (for general knowledge). Procedural memory refers to knowledge of skills and habits.

2 Failures of memory may be due to inadequate acquisition, storage, or retrieval of information. Acquisition refers to initial learning, storage to retention of a memory over time, and retrieval to use of stored information.

3 Hermann Ebbinghaus was the first to study memory objectively. He measured the difficulty of learning lists of nonsense syllables by recording the number of trials taken to recite a series perfectly. He later measured retention by relearning the lists after some interval of time had passed and observing savings in the number of trials taken.

4 Some researchers believe that different types of memory are held in different stores. Sensory stores hold information briefly while it is analyzed; the short-term store holds information for some seconds after it has been analyzed; and the long-term store holds information for longer periods, perhaps permanently.

5 The iconic store is the sensory register for vision, while the echoic store is the sensory register for hearing, or audition. It is generally assumed that the echoic store holds information longer than the iconic store.

6 Recoding of information is a key to remembering. People can usually remember material better if they recode it into a form that matches their past knowledge.

guage and imagery. Few, if any, people have the ability to remember an image of photographic quality. However, people do generally remember verbal information better if they try to recode it in mental images.

7 The levels-of-processing approach to memory conceives of events as being perceptually processed to different depths, or levels, depending on the degree of meaningful analysis they are given. Memory is thought to be related to the depth of processing, with deeper processing leading to better retention. Whether a certain type of processing leads to good memory performance depends on the type of test used, so the concept of transfer-appropriate processing may be preferable to the levels-of-processing idea. The type of memory trace produced by a recoding process may lead to good or poor performance on a test, depending on how appropriately the acquired knowledge transfers to the test.

8 One explanation for forgetting information is interference from events that occur before or after the information is processed. Events that occur before the critical event provide proactive interference; those that occur later provide retroactive interference. The idea of trace decay has been discredited as a complete theory of forgetting.

9 When information is forgotten, it can sometimes be recalled when people are given appropriate retrieval cues. Retrieval cues seem to be effective when they recreate the original learning context. This idea is referred to as the encoding specificity hypothesis: Retrieval cues are effective to the extent that their information matches the information stored in the memory trace.

10 Research does not allow us to conclude that all memories are retained permanently, but we can show that many cases of forgetting can be reversed with appropriate cues or hints. Thus, forgetting is often due to failures in the retrieval process. Information may be permanently lost from memory, too.

11 Mnemonic devices are memory aids. Two effective devices involve placing images in imaginal locations (the method of loci) or "hanging" images on mental pegs (the peg method). Both these techniques are effective in allowing recall of items in order. The PQ4R method (preview, question, read, reflect, recite, review) is an effective method of studying text material.

12 Remembering can be viewed as a constructive activity, especially for distant events. People may remember some facts accurately but may weave them together and elaborate them with details that never actually occurred. Our recollections may represent some combination of fact and fantasy, especially when they have been repeated to others on different occasions. Constructive aspects of memory may be seen in research on eyewitness testimony, boundary extension in remembering pictures, and schematic processing of prose passages.

13 Amnesia refers to loss of memory, usually as a result of some injury to the brain. Retrograde amnesia is loss of memories before the damage; anterograde amnesia is the name for memory problems occurring after the brain trauma. Transient global amnesia refers to brief episodes of forgetting that are presumably due to unknown stoppages of blood flow in the brain, but the condition clears up in a matter of hours or (at most) days. Functional amnesia refers to more dramatic cases of forgetting over several days or a week, where even personal identity may be lost. The cases are called functional because no known brain damage is involved. Organic amnesia is the name given to a variety of disorders that result from brain damage.

14 The most studied case of organic amnesia is that of H. M., who seemed incapable of learning new verbal material after the surgery that left him amnesic. H. M. and other amnesics can learn motor skills in a relatively normal manner, although they may deny ever having done a task more than once. Recent research shows that amnesics can even retain verbal materials if their memories are probed by tests that do not require them to be consciously aware of the prior experiences (implicit memory tests).

15 Implicit memory tests are those that measure retention indirectly, with prior experiences revealed in ongoing behavior without intentional recollection. Explicit memory tests are those involving conscious recollection; during the test, people are asked to recall or to recognize their prior experiences. The contrast between explicit and implicit forms of test is of interest because many factors affect the two types of test differently.

16 Infantile (childhood) amnesia refers to the fact that people generally cannot remember events that happened in the first few years of life. This amnesia may be due to (a) the brain continuing to mature after birth, especially structures critical to explicit memory and/or (b) children not having yet developed a sense of personal identity in a "life narrative" or schema in which to place events.

KEY TERMS

episodic memory (p. 261)

semantic memory (p. 261)

procedural memory (p. 261)

primary memory (p. 261–262)

secondary memory (p. 262)

short-term memory (p. 262)

long-term memory (p. 262)

encoding (p. 262)

storage (p. 262)

memory trace (p. 262)

retrieval (p. 262)

sensory stores (p. 264)

short-term store (p. 264)

long-term store (p. 265)

iconic storage (p. 265)

echoic storage (p. 266)

control processes (p. 267)

serial position curve (p. 267)

recency effect (p. 267)

primacy effect (p. 267)

working memory (p. 267)

memory codes (p. 268)

verbal code (p. 268)

imaginal codes (p. 268)

motor code (p. 269)

recoding (p. 269)

subjective organization (p. 270)

dual coding theory (p. 271)

levels-of-processing approach (p. 273)

eidetic imagery (p. 274)

reminiscence (p. 276)

interference (p. 276)

proactive interference (p. 276)

retroactive interference (p. 276)

encoding specificity hypothesis (p. 280)

transfer-appropriate processing (p. 282)

isolation effect (p. 282)

flashbulb memories (p. 283)

mnemonic devices (p. 284)

schemas (p. 288)

amnesia (p. 292)

retrograde amnesia (p. 292)

anterograde amnesia (p. 292)

transient global amnesia (p. 293)

functional amnesias (p. 293)

infantile (childhood) amnesia (p. 294)

organic amnesia (p. 294)

explicit memory (p. 297)

implicit memory (p. 298)

FOR CRITICAL ANALYSIS

1 Psychologists interested in learning and memory would ideally like to have a measure of memory that can tell us the availability of what is stored in the brain. However, all the measures that we have so far tell us what information is accessible or retrievable only on a particular test. Do you see any hope that psychologists can develop a test that would be a more perfect indicator of a person's knowledge?

2 After reading this chapter, make suggestions for enhancing the learning/memory process for educational purposes. What study strategies would you suggest? What kinds of tests do you think teachers should give? Are certain types of tests more appropriate in elementary school, high school, or college?

3 The great philosopher Friedrich Nietzsche wrote "The existence of forgetting has never been proved: We only know that some things do not come to our mind when we want them to." What do you think of this statement? What evidence do you think would convince Nietzsche that forgetting truly does occur? Or is there no good evidence of true forgetting?

4 Most people have vivid memories of the first occasion that something happened—the first day in college, the first love affair, and so on. Why do you think this happens? Try to explain this phenomenon in terms of the concepts discussed in the chapter.

5 Can you think of any effective methods that psychologists could use to try to gain evidence of the reality of repressed memories that seem to be recovered? (Remember, the experiments must be ethically acceptable.) If you cannot think of experiments or research that would be ethically defensible to conduct, does this mean that the topic of repressed memories is simply out of bounds for scientific investigation?

6 Defend the idea that remembering is a constructive process, like perceiving. What analogies are there in the two domains?

SUGGESTED READINGS

BENNE, B. (1988). *WASPLEG and other mnemonics*. Dallas, TX: Taylor. A fascinating reference book of mnemonics collected from many fields. WASPLEG employs the first-letter mnemonic for the seven deadly sins: wrath, avarice, sloth, pride, lust, envy, and gluttony.

GREENE, R. L. (1992). *Human memory: Paradigms and paradoxes*. Erlbaum. Organized according to nine important paradigms in memory research, this book includes sections on iconic memory, the recency effect, encoding, eyewitness memory, and implicit memory.

HIGBEE, K. L. (1988). *Your memory: How it works and how to improve it* (2nd ed.). Englewood Cliffs, NJ: Prentice Hall. This memory improvement book draws heavily on academic research. A number of mnemonic devices are discussed, as well as the practical problems of remembering more from textbooks, remembering names and faces, and remembering cards that have been played.

LURIA, A. R. (1987). *The mind of a mnemonist*. Cambridge MA: Harvard University Press. A fascinating account of a man with a phenomenally good memory, who seemed unable to forget. Besides trying to explain his unusual memory, the author discusses the personal problems created by the mnemonist's unusual capacity for imagery.

Pendergrast, M. (1995). *Victims of memory: Incest accusations and shattered lives.* Hinesburg, VT: Upper Access Press. A readable book on the repressed memory/recovered memory controversy, but touching on many other controversial issues, too.

SCHWARTZ, B. & REISBERG, D. (1991). *Learning and memory.* New York: Norton. This textbook provides an excellent treatment of both animal learning and human learning and memory.

SQUIRE, L. R. (1992). *Encyclopedia of Learning and Memory.* New York: MacMillan. This volume provides entries on virtually all topics of learning and memory, written by leading experts for a broad audience.

SEARLEMAN, A. & HERRMAN, D. (1994). *Memory from a broader perspective.* New York: McGraw-Hill. A wide-ranging text that examines many facets of learning and memory.

PSYCHOLOGY ON THE INTERNET

Mind Tools

(http://www.demon.co.uk/mindtool/memory.html)

This site provides an introduction to mnemonic techniques and information on how to use these techniques effectively. Also provided are explanations of several mnemonic devices and their use in everyday life.

Memory Reading Lists

(http://www.york.ac.uk/depts/psych/web/ug/course/core/rlcogch.html)
(http://www.york.ac.uk/depts/psych/web/ug/course/core/cognvh/rlcognh.html)

These sites contain reading lists of original research, books, and book chapters dealing with the structure of memory and working memory. There are no links to on-line versions of the works referenced, but the reading lists are a valuable asset. Most of the items listed are available in your school's library.

Journal of Experimental Psychology: Learning, Memory, and Cognition

(http://www.apa.org/journals/jeplmc.html)

For information on recent research concerning memory, visit the home page for the American Psychological Association's Journal of Experimental Psychology: Learning, Memory, and Cognition.

Amnesia Research Lab

(http://hermes.cns.uiuc.edu/ARLHomePage.html)

The Amnesia Research Lab (ARL) at the University of Illinois conducts research on "the organization of human memory and the neural systems underlying memory." Included at this site are descriptions of the ARL's current projects (including introductions to the research questions being addressed, results of the studies, and interpretations of those results) as well as links to other sites related to psychology and cognitive neuroscience.

False Memory Syndrome Foundation

(http://iquest.com/~fitz/fmsf)

This site provides a definition of False Memory Syndrome (FMS) and outlines the purpose of the foundation. It also contains a bibliography of scholarly works and popular press articles related to FMS and provides access information for the FMS Listserv group.

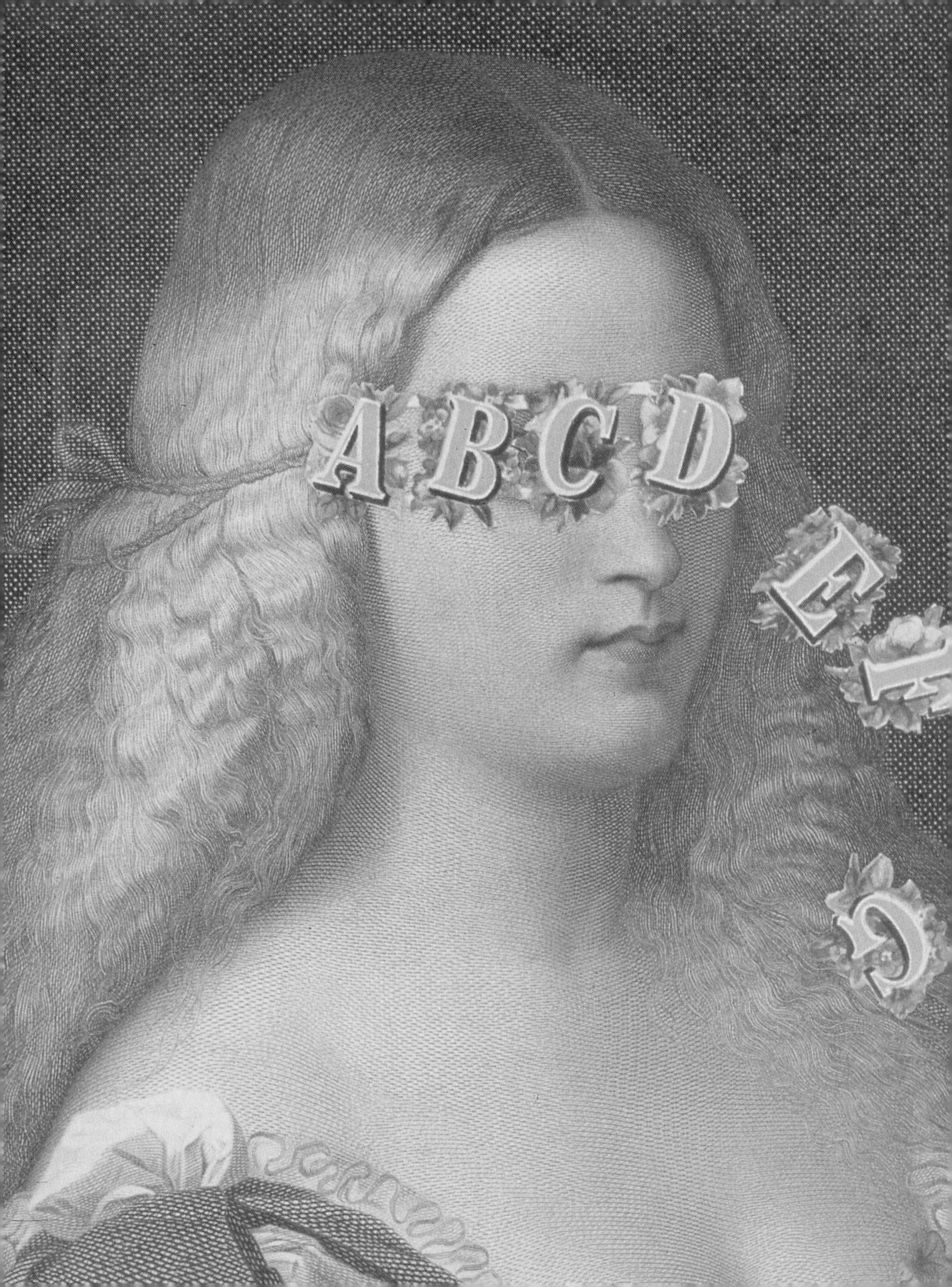
A B C D

THOUGHT and LANGUAGE

Chapter 8

Consider the following problem: Inside each of three separate, equal-sized boxes are two separate small boxes. Inside each small box there are four smaller boxes. How many boxes are there altogether?

How did you solve the problem? Did you, like some students, calculate $3 \times 2 \times 4$ and say that there are 24 boxes? If you think that the solution was too simple, you're right. First, try to imagine the boxes; then count them. The larger boxes must also be included in the total. (Did you get 33 boxes without drawing a picture?)

Thinking is a cognitive process that is directed to comprehension of the world and to solving problems. It is a complicated ingredient of much of what we say and do and it can involve imagery, language, and symbols and can be used to solve problems, make decisions, and communicate (Moyer, 1992). However, like the notion of consciousness, it is hard to isolate and define.

Thinking has three basic characteristics. First, it is *abstract*; we can reason about objects that are intangible, hypothetical, or simply not present. Second, thinking is *symbolic*; we often use words, numbers, and images to represent things. And third, thinking is *relational*; we often try to link, or associate, different aspects of people, events, and objects. Thinking is sometimes biased and sometimes illogical. Psychologists are interested in explaining the creative insights we humans achieve through thinking—as well as the errors in thought that we sometimes make.

In this chapter, we consider how the abstract, symbolic, and relational characteristics of thinking are evident as we solve problems, make decisions, identify concepts, and communicate. We begin with a topic familiar to any student who has wrestled with a midterm exam—problem solving.

Problem Solving

According to John Anderson (1985), **problem solving** is behavior directed toward achieving a goal. It usually includes consideration of the conditions surrounding the problem, called *searching the problem space*, and consideration of alternative means to solving the problem, often referred to as *problem-solving strategies*. Experts use a variety of sophisticated strategies to diagnose and solve problems, but there are some steps that can promote successful problem solving no matter what the problem and what the strategy.

FIVE STEPS OF PROBLEM SOLVING

John Bransford and Barry Stein (1993) advocate a five-step system of thinking, known as IDEAL, to promote effective problem solving:

I = Identify the problem.

D = Define and represent the problem.

E = Explore possible strategies.

A = Act on the strategies.

L = Look back and evaluate the effects of your activities.

The importance of these steps may become clearer if you apply them to specific problems.

Identifying the Problem. Suppose you have to give an important presentation to your new boss at 8 A.M. You pack your briefcase and get in your car, but the car won't start. Do you (a) lift the hood and get your toolbox, (b) ask your neighbor for help, or (c) phone for a taxi? Your dilemma identifies your problem. The initial definition or interpretation of a problem is the most important step to a successful solution. Since the goal is to reach work on time without getting grease on your clothes, (c) may be the best choice.

Defining and Representing the Problem. Identifying a problem shades into the next stage, defining and representing it. You may become sidetracked in your thinking if you do not identify and define the primary problem or if you complicate simple problems unnecessarily. Figure 8.1 shows a circle with a radius of 5 inches. Can you determine the length of line *c*? To solve this problem, you may have started recalling the formula for the length of a right triangle's hypotenuse; but this approach unnecessarily complicates the problem. Visualize an imaginary line from the middle of the circle to the right angle of the triangle. This other diagonal in the rectangle forms a radius to the circle, so it is is equal to 5 inches. Line *c* is therefore also 5 inches long.

Now look at the books shown in Figure 8.2 and solve this problem:

> A set of 10 books is arranged in orderly fashion on a shelf. Each book has 100 pages (i.e., sheets of paper with printing on both sides), making 1,000 pages in all. A worm, starting on the first page of the first book, eats through to the last page of the last book. How many pages does it eat?

The answer is 802. Look again at the picture and you will see why 99 pages in each of the first and last books were untouched. (The worm had to eat only one page in the first and last books because the leftmost page on the shelf is actually the *last* page of volume I, not the first. Also, the worm reaches the last page of volume X immediately after eating through volume IX.) This example illustrates why it is important to represent the problem accurately before trying to generate a solution. An inaccurate representation can often lead to a simple, yet incorrect, solution (Kahney, 1993).

Exploring Possible Strategies. Failure to generate a wide variety of possible strategies can often hinder problem solving. The problems shown in Figure 8.3 are difficult because most people do not consider unconventional solutions. They tend to think about two-dimensional objects when trying to solve problem A, lines only within the square of dots in solving problem B, and equal-sized squares when thinking about problem C. The solutions (on page 312) seem simple as soon as these constraints are ignored.

FIGURE 8.1
What Is the Length of Line c?

Many times we make problem solving difficult by overlooking the obvious. In this case, the length of line *c* does not need to be calculated since it is the same length as a second (imaginary) diagonal, drawn from the middle of the circle to the right angle of the triangle. This line is a radius of the circle and the same length as line *c*.

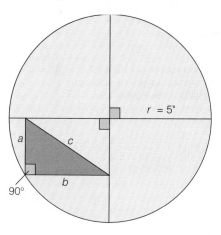

FIGURE 8.2
The Worm Problem

Each volume on the shelf contains 100 pages of paper. If a worm eats through the volumes beginning at the first page of volume I and ending at the last page of volume X, how many pages does it eat?

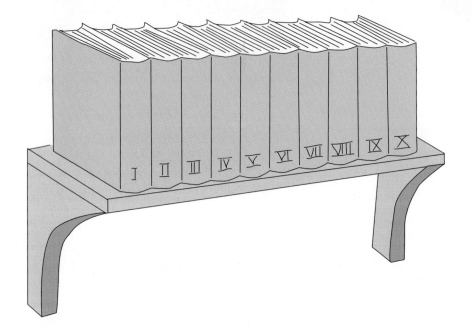

Bransford and Stein (1993) posed this problem to a group of students:

Generate as many reasons as you can to explain why, when he comes to visit me, at my apartment, my cousin always gets off the elevator five floors below my floor and walks the rest of the way.

Typical responses included "he needs the exercise," "he wants to surprise you," "he visits somebody else along the way," and "the elevator is broken." A seldom-mentioned possibility was" he is so short that he can only reach the button for the floor five floors below your apartment."

The tendency for people to limit their solutions to conventional ways of solving problems is referred to as **functional fixedness**. We often perceive objects according to their traditional functions and fail to explore novel uses. Thus, when confronted with new problems, we cannot move beyond the solutions we know to find new ways of using familiar objects. For example, subjects often have difficulty in finding a way to hang a coat in a bare room when supplied with only two long, thin pieces of wood and a clamp. (They are not allowed to use the walls in their solution.) One good, but uncommon, solution is to clamp the boards together, wedge them tightly between the floor and ceiling, and hang the coat on the clamp. Functional fixedness usually pre-

FIGURE 8.3
Mind Teasers

Solutions are on page 312.

PROBLEM A   Assemble the six equal matchsticks into four equilateral triangles so that each side is equal in length to one match.

PROBLEM B   Without lifting your pencil from the page or retracing anywhere, connect all nine dots by drawing four four straight, continuous lines.

PROBLEM C   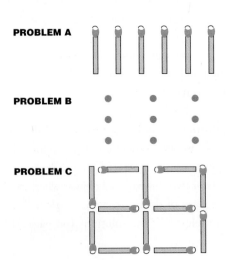 Arrange a dozen matchsticks in four squares as shown. By moving only two matches, make seven squares.

How can a candle be attached in an upright position so that no wax drips on the floor?

FIGURE 8.4
The Tower of Hanoi Problem

The object of this puzzle is to move the disks one at a time from peg 1 to peg 3 in the fewest moves possible (seven moves). A larger disk can never be placed on top of a smaller one. (The solution is on page 312.)

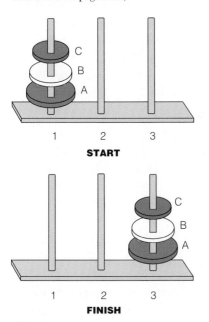

vents subjects from envisioning such novel functions for these objects (Duncker, 1945).

In Karl Duncker's (1945) study of creative problem solving, subjects were given a candle, some tacks, and a box of matches, and were asked to attach the candle upright to the wall so that the wax would not drip on the floor. Glucksberg and Weisberg (1966) modified Duncker's problem by telling one group of subjects to label the objects—box, tacks, candle, and matches—but giving no such instructions to another group. The group that used labels solved the problem in 30 to 40 seconds. The group that did not use labels averaged nearly 9 minutes; its members did not recognize that they could tack the box to the wall to hold the candle. Evidently, labeling the box helped the first group to understand that the box was more than a container for the matches.

Acting on the Strategies and Looking Back to Evaluate their Effectiveness. After you generate various strategies, you must try them out and evaluate their effectiveness. As experienced chess players know, systematically checking the consequences of various options helps to avoid impulsive actions or false solutions. Consider the Tower of Hanoi problem shown in Figure 8.4. The object of this game is to move three disks, one at a time, from the first peg to the third peg. A larger disk can never cover a smaller disk. Can you find a way to move the disks in only seven moves? The seven-step solution requires planning, checking, and revising. For example, many people imagine moving the small disk C to peg 2 and disk B to peg 3, but it is quickly apparent that this is a dead end. Disk C must be moved to 3, B to 2, and then C to 2 so that A can be at the bottom of 3. Then C is moved back to 1, B to 3, and finally C to 3.

Although some problems are solved by trial and error, expert problem solvers often anticipate possible outcomes without actually trying out the strategies. They imagine the consequences and evaluate the effectiveness of various options as they mentally solve the problem in several different ways. Both age and experience contribute to effective planning and checking as part of problem solving.

PROBLEM-SOLVING STRATEGIES

Some strategies used in problem solving are **algorithms,** procedures guaranteed to lead to solutions. For example, the seven-step process involved in solving the Tower of Hanoi problem is an algorithm; so is the mathematical formula $A = \pi r^2$ for finding the area of a circle. When properly used, algorithms always lead to correct solutions, but they have two potential shortcomings. First, people often blindly follow the rules, not bothering to check whether the algorithm applies to the problem at hand or if the answer produced is correct. Second, it is not always practical to follow the logical steps of an algorithm. If you were working a crossword puzzle with an entry _ a _ d _ _ a _ for "state bird of Illinois," you would not combine all possible letter combinations in algorithmic fashion. Instead you would probably use a **heuristic,** or rule-of-thumb strategy, and try only the consonants in the first and last blanks. An even more efficient method would be to test some likely names of birds until you discovered *cardinal*.

Heuristics are mental shortcuts. Unlike algorithmic rules that always work, heuristics are strategies that we learn to apply to particular situations. They do not always lead to correct answers, but they provide general guidelines about possible solutions. They save a lot of time and effort by limiting the solutions attempted to only those that are most likely to work. Every task has specific heuristics associated with it, and "troubleshooting" is based on experience with the problem and knowing which heuris-

The solution to Duncker's functional fixedness problem demonstrating creative problem solving.

SOLUTIONS TO FIGURE 8.3

PROBLEM A

Six matches form a pyramid.

PROBLEM B

PROBLEM C

SOLUTION TO FIGURE 8.4
Sequence of moves is C3, B2, C2, A3, C1, B3, C3.

tics apply. That is partly why "experts" like plumbers isolate the most likely causes of such annoyances as stopped-up drains and leaky pipes so quickly. Knowing heuristics is part of what makes a good cook, golfer, plumber, or auto mechanic. There are also heuristics that you can use to help make you a good problem solver, including the IDEAL steps given earlier and the scientific method discussed in Chapter 1.

Another good heuristic is **subgoal analysis,** the process of reducing a complex problem to a series of smaller, more easily solved problems. For example, if your task is to paint a room and the table and chairs in it, you may identify the following subgoals: paint the ceiling first by standing on the chairs; next paint the walls; and finally paint the furniture. Subgoal analysis may also involve working backward from a solution. Heuristics like these can lead to faster solutions than algorithms, but they don't always work. They are really hunches based on experience that work in a variety of situations.

Still another effective heuristic is an **analogy,** in which information about one problem is applied to another problem with a similar structure. Consider the following:

> Suppose you are a doctor faced with a patient who has a malignant tumor in his stomach. It is impossible to operate on the patient, but unless the tumor is destroyed the patient will die. There is a kind of ray that can be used to destroy the tumor. If the rays reach the tumor all at once at a sufficiently high intensity, the tumor will be destroyed. Unfortunately, at this intensity the healthy tissue that the rays pass through on the way to the tumor will also be destroyed. At lower intensities the rays are harmless to healthy tissue, but they will not affect the tumor either. What type of procedure might be used to destroy the tumor with the rays, and at the same time avoid destroying the healthy tissue? (Gick & Holyoak, 1980, pp. 307–308)

This problem was devised by Karl Duncker (1945), who asked adults to think aloud as they tried to solve it. Several possible solutions are illustrated in Figure 8.5. Many of Duncker's subjects (40 percent) misinterpreted the problem and suggested an operation to expose the tumor (i.e., their representations of the problem and its constraints were incorrect). An additional 29 percent suggested impractical solutions, such as directing the rays to the stomach through an open route such as the esophagus or intestines. Only 5 percent thought of the best solution: to disperse the intensity of the rays by aiming several weak rays at the tumor from different points. Thus, rays would be weak when passing through healthy tissue, but strong at the affected organ where they intersected.

Would subjects be more likely to solve the radiation problem if they had just learned the solution to a similar problem? Mary Gick and Keith Holyoak (1980) investigated how adults transfer general solutions from one problem to another. In one study, they read the following passage to 10 subjects before giving them the radiation problem:

> A fortress was located in the center of the country. Many roads radiated out from the fortress. A general wanted to capture the fortress with his army. The general wanted to prevent mines on the roads from destroying his army and neighboring villages. As a result the entire army could not attack the fortress along one road. However, the entire army was needed to capture the fortress. So an attack by one small group would not succeed. The general therefore divided his army into several small groups. He positioned the small groups at the heads of different roads. The small groups simultaneously converged on the fortress. In this way the army captured the fortress. (p. 311)

This story is analogous to the radiation problem and provides a solution based on dispersion of the army (or rays). All 10 subjects who heard this story suggested similar dispersion solutions to the radiation problem, while no subjects in the control condi-

PROBLEM

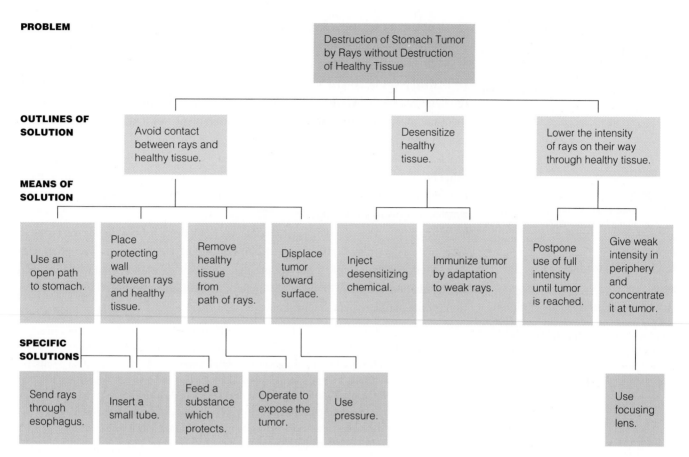

FIGURE 8.5
Possible Solutions to Duncker's (1945) Tumor Problem

Notice how different ideas are contained in each branch, with the solutions becoming progressively more specific. The method of talking through a problem has often been used to reveal sequences of attempts to solve problems.

SOURCE: Wortman & Loftus, 1981.

tion (those who did not hear the story of the army) thought of these options.

Imagery may play a key role in creative thinking with analogies. Seeing an image of one set of relations can make us think of a similar set of relations applicable to another situation. It is said that Gutenberg's invention of the printing press was developed partly by analogy from the presses used to make wine and coins. And the personal reflections of August Kekulé, 25 years after he proposed the ring structure of the benzene molecule, shows the vividness of analogical visual thinking:

> I turned my chair to the fire and dozed. Again the atoms were gamboling before my eyes. This time the smaller groups kept modestly in the background. My mental eye, rendered more acute by repeated visions of this kind, could now distinguish larger structures, of manifold conformation; long rows, sometimes more closely fitted together; all twining and twisting in snakelike motion. But look! What was that? One of the snakes had seized hold of its own tail, and the form whirled mockingly before my eyes. (Cited in Koestler, 1964)

MENTAL SET AND INCUBATION EFFECTS

Heuristics are powerful tactics for problem solving, but they do not always work. Repeated use of heuristics to solve similar problems can eventually create certain expectations and biases—essentially, a **mental set**—that can actually interfere with problem solving. For example, if 3 cats can kill 3 rats in 3 minutes, how long will it take 100 cats to kill 100 rats? Did you say 100 minutes or 1 minute? Think again why a good answer is actually 3 minutes. (It takes a cat 3 minutes to kill a rat, so as long as there is an equal number of cats and rats, it will take 3 minutes for the cats to kill the rats.)

The tendency to depend on heuristics even when they are no longer appropriate was illustrated by Abraham Luchins (1946). He presented subjects with three water

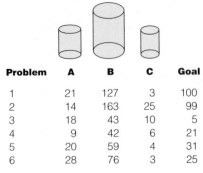

Problem	A	B	C	Goal
1	21	127	3	100
2	14	163	25	99
3	18	43	10	5
4	9	42	6	21
5	20	59	4	31
6	28	76	3	25

Imagine that each jar has the capacity listed. How would you measure out the amount in the last column?

FIGURE 8.6
Luchins's Water Jars

Try to solve each problem by using the jars A, B and C to obtain the goal. You will see a general rule emerging in your solutions. After solving the first five problems, most of Luchins's subjects could not solve the sixth. Why not?

SOURCE: Luchins, 1946.

jars of different sizes and a series of problems (see Figure 8.6). The goal was to measure out the amount of water shown in the chart using the listed capacities of each jar. For example, in the first problem you can see that 100 quarts can be obtained by filling up jar B, then pouring 21 quarts into jar A and 3 quarts into C twice. Each of the first five problems can be solved with the formula $B - A - 2C$, but this apparent rule yields an incorrect answer for problem 6. This last measurement task requires only two of the jars (A and C), and that may be why two-thirds of Luchins's subjects could not solve problem 6 after solving the first five. Subjects in a control condition who received five other problems (not requiring the $B - A - 2C$ solution) had no trouble with problem 6. Clearly, creative problem solving requires flexibility to generate alternative solutions and to overcome mental set.

What can be done to counteract mental set? Sometimes it helps to put the problem aside after a determined effort, rather than continuing to work on it. The phenomenon of suddenly being able to solve a problem after setting it aside for a while is called the **incubation effect.** A dramatic example of incubation is provided by the recollections of the mathematician Henri Poincaré (1913):

> For fifteen days I strove to prove there could not be any functions like those I have since called Fuchsian functions. I was then very ignorant; every day I seated myself at my work table, stayed an hour or two, tried a great number of combinations and reached no results. One evening, contrary to my custom, I drank black coffee and could not sleep. Ideas rose in crowds; I felt them collide until pairs interlocked, so to speak, making a stable combination. By the next morning I had established the existence of a class of Fuchsian functions, those which come from the hypergeometric series; I had only to write out the results, which took but a few hours. (p. 58)

Incubation is a precursor to **insight,** or the sudden comprehension of a new idea. There is some controversy about whether and how incubation occurs. Some researchers claim that intuitive judgments are often misguided (Kahneman, Slovic, & Tversky, 1982); some claim that insight is sudden and unpredictable (Metcalf, 1986); and still others suggest that intuition and insight are gradual accumulations of knowledge that become more coherent, organized, and correct with incubation. For example, Kenneth Bowers and his colleagues (1990) found that adults can synthesize information about problems that they cannot solve initially and get sudden hunches or intuitions about correct answers. The researchers presented two kinds of sketches to adult subjects (see Figure 8.7) These sketches showed either random lines or schematic outlines of familiar objects that the subjects had to identify. Only a third of the pictures were identified correctly, but most adults could tell which pictures showed real objects, even if they could not tell what the objects were. The probability that the subjects could identify the pictures using only hunches was well above chance. The researchers concluded that the subjects gradually identified clues and built associations about the identities of the objects. The same guiding effect of intuition was observed in other tasks and suggests that Poincaré's experience of insight might have been a consequence of recombining old ideas in novel ways following an incubation period.

COGNITIVE EXPERTISE

Some people are expert problem solvers. Students who take hundreds of exams, mechanics who repair a variety of disabled automobiles, and doctors who make diverse medical diagnoses all have a wealth of practical experience that may qualify them as experts. Expertise, however, involves more than practice and knowledge of lots of facts. Research has shown that experts differ from inexperienced, or novice, problem

FIGURE 8.7
Which Drawings Show Real Objects?

Adults who were not able to identify the camel or the whistle were still able to tell which picture of each pair showed an object. Their intuitions show that various clues are used to identify objects and that incubation can lead to sudden understanding.

SOURCE: Bowers, Regehr, Balthazard, & Parker, 1990.

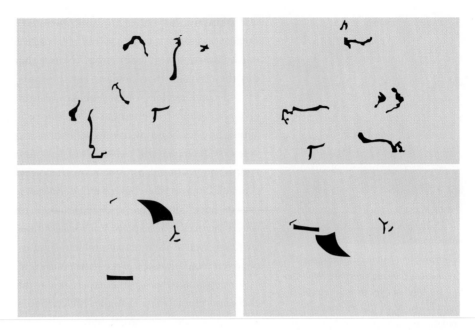

solvers in two fundamental ways: They recognize patterns in the problem space, and they are more likely to use principles and concepts to guide their attempts to solve problems.

Cognitive scientists have studied the differences between experts and novices in several fields, one of the first being chess. As discussed in Chapter 7, William Chase and Herbert Simon (1973) gave subjects 5 to 10 seconds to view a chess board containing about 25 pieces arranged in a game situation. They found that chess experts could reconstruct the positions of 20 or more pieces, while unskilled players did well to replace 5 or 6 pieces correctly. A thorough understanding of the game allowed the experts to group together more chess pieces and spatial arrangements in memory. Chase and Simon hypothesized that the experts were perceiving and remembering the relations between the pieces on the board, while the novices were merely storing the positions in an unorganized fashion, which is harder to recall (see Chapter 7). In fact, if the pieces were randomly arranged on the chess board, experts could remember their positions no better than novices.

Cognitive expertise in the field of physics has also been studied. Michelene Chi, Paul Feltovich, and Robert Glaser (1981) asked subjects to sort 24 physics problems (taken from a college textbook) into categories based on the similarities of solutions. The problems included questions about forces on pulleys and the velocity of an object sliding down an inclined plane. The experts were eight advanced Ph.D. students in physics, and the novices were eight undergraduates who had just completed a semester course on mechanics. The researchers collected data on the groups into which problems were sorted, response times, and subjects' reasons for the grouping arrangements.

Surprisingly, the experts took longer to sort the problems. They spent an average of 45 seconds on each problem, while novices required only an average of 30 seconds to categorize each one. Both novices and experts sorted the problems into about eight groups, but the category criteria differed significantly. Novices categorized the problems on the basis of superficial features—whether the problems were based on inclined planes, friction, or revolving objects. Experts were not fooled by superficial features; instead, they categorized problems according to underlying physical principles such as the conservation of momentum or energy. Some even said explicitly, "These can all be solved by Newton's second law" or "$F = ma$" or the "work-energy theorem."

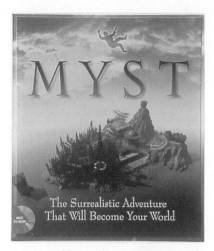

Expert problem solvers use patterns and principles as the test alternate hypotheses. This kind of expertise is helpful when playing *Myst*, the enormously popular computer game, that presents tantilizing problems for the user as they navigate a mysterious and puzzling multimedia environment.

Larkin and her colleagues (1980) noted four fundamental differences between novices and experts as they solved physics problems. First, experts solved the problems much faster and with fewer errors. (Notice that experts may take longer to analyze and sort the problems than novices, but the actual time required to solve the problems is less.) Second, novices solved problems by working backward from the unknown to the given situation, while experts worked forward (except for very difficult problems). Third, novices often mentioned equations explicitly and then substituted given values; experts apparently did much of this automatically and simply stated the result. Fourth, novices tended to focus on the verbal statements of problems, while experts generated images, sketches, or representations of the problems. The results reveal that experts have conceptual knowledge about physical principles that is different from that of novices. The experts' knowledge influences their perceptions of problem similarities as well as their actual problem-solving behavior. Novices, lacking such a complete representation of the problems, must rely on less sophisticated analyses.

Understanding cognitive expertise can be extended to many specialties besides chess and physics. For example, McKeithen and colleagues (1981) compared novice and expert computer programmers. They found that expert programmers organize knowledge according to programming principles and can use the principles to chunk and recall more information than novices. Lesgold (1988) has investigated how expert radiologists differ from novices. The experts in his study were staff physicians with at least 10 years of experience who had viewed about half a million X rays; the novices were medical students who had little experience viewing X rays. Lesgold presented the subjects with X rays that were difficult to diagnose and asked them to analyze the problems and to explain their diagnosis. Lesgold (1988) and his colleagues observed that the expert radiologists (1) spent more time analyzing the problem and described it with more conceptual terms than the novices; (2) began to execute relevant general plans more quickly than the novices; (3) exhibited flexibility and revision of their diagnoses; (4) could analyze several objects that overlapped in a film; (5) derived new diagnoses based on new evidence; and (6) often considered additional but irrelevant diagnoses.

Additionally, Kundel & Nodine (1975) demonstrated that experienced radiologists could detect and name more than 70 percent of the abnormalities in X rays presented to them for only one-fifth of a second. This is just enough time for the eyes to fixate on the X ray, but not long enough to allow for a scan of the film. Therefore, not only do experts have a great deal of factual and organized knowledge available, but they can also access it extremely quickly.

These studies clearly indicate that cognitive expertise improves one's ability to see the underlying characteristics of problems. Experts search for and encode information differently from novices and subsequently solve problems better than novices. But novice-expert differences are not all-or-nothing classifications. Consistent with our developmental theme, there is a time-dependent continuum of expertise that we shall examine in Chapters 9 and 10, where we learn how children and adults become experts in many areas.

Reasoning

Psychologists study many different kinds of thinking. In this section, we focus on two important kinds of thinking: logical thinking and decision making. Research has shown that children and adults, as well as novices and experts, differ greatly in the way they reason about logical problems and decisions.

Logical Thinking

Problem solving, as we have seen, is a broad topic that includes many cognitive processes. Logical thinking is a special kind of problem solving for evaluating the truth or likelihood of different statements. Psychologists study how people use logical rules to guide their thinking. We will examine two kinds of logical thinking here: deductive reasoning and inductive reasoning. As you will see, people seldom follow straightforward logical rules as they reason.

Deductive Reasoning. Deductive reasoning involves making inferences from general cases to particular events. It is an all-or-none kind of reasoning, because if the premises (general cases) are true, then the conclusion (the particular event) must also be true. One kind of deduction is called *conditional reasoning*. It can be represented in a three-sentence statement called a *syllogism* that states, "If such and such is true, then so and so is true. Such and such is true. Therefore, so and so must be true." This is abbreviated symbolically by "If p, then q; p, therefore q." Consider an example of reasoning from a syllogism provided by Mayer (1992, p.138):

1. If there is a solar eclipse, then the streets will be dark.
2. There is a solar eclipse.
3. Therefore, the streets are dark.

Is this a valid syllogism? The answer is yes. Most people have little difficulty with this syllogism as it is stated here. But what if we change premise (2) to "The streets are dark." Does this imply logically that (3) "There is a solar eclipse"? No. This is the *fallacy of affirming the consequent* of the premise of the syllogism. (The consequence is the second part of the "if-then" relation in the premise.) Many studies have shown that adults and children alike do not usually interpret conditional arguments in the way that formal logic requires (Paris, 1975; Wason & Johnson-Laird, 1972). Instead, most people seem to think that a syllogism is true if they know both p and q to be true from their general knowledge of the world; otherwise, they think it is false (Rips, 1988). That is, people use their experiences and expectations to evaluate the truth of statements in the form "if p, then q."

It is obvious that the premise "The streets are dark" does not necessarily imply that an eclipse is occurring; after all, the streets become dark every night. But suppose that the syllogism had been stated differently:

1. If it is night, then the streets will be dark.
2. The streets are dark.
3. Therefore, it is night.

Is this true? Many people would answer yes in this instance, because the example fits our general knowledge of the world and we do not think of a counterexample (e.g., that there might be a solar eclipse). However, even if plausible, the conclusion that it is night still involves the logical fallacy of affirming the consequent.

A second kind of deductive reasoning is *categorical reasoning*. Categorical statements take four forms:

- All A are B.
- No A are B.
- Some A are B.
- Some A are not B.

Here is syllogism requiring categorical reasoning:

- All fraternity men are handsome.
- All handsome men are conceited.
- Therefore, all fraternity men are conceited.

It is easy to determine that this syllogism is logically true. But notice how your own biases and beliefs will make you either agree or disagree with the conclusion. Moreover, the information can be complicated by switching terms A and B (e.g., All handsome men are fraternity men; All fraternity men are conceited; Therefore, all handsome men are conceited) or by switching the order of the premises. In addition, negative terms can be used (e.g., All handsome men are not conceited), and any of the four conclusions can be reached about the A:B or B:A relations. In fact, there are hundreds of ways to state categorical syllogisms, but only a few are logically valid (Johnson-Laird & Steedman, 1978; Mayer, 1992).

This may explain why categorical reasoning is so difficult for most people. Instead of following logical rules, adults often judge statements according to their personal beliefs. For example, Markovits and Nantel (1989) asked college students to judge if the given conclusions followed logically from the given premises in syllogisms such as these:

- All things that are smoked are good for the health.
- Cigarettes are smoked.
- Cigarettes are good for the health.

or

- All animals love water.
- Cats do not like water.
- Cats are not animals.

The researchers compared students' reasoning on these syllogisms to identical syllogisms that substituted nonsense words like *ramadions* for *cigarettes* and *selacians* for *cats*. Reasoning was more logical when unfamiliar terms were used because beliefs about cigarettes and cats interfered with the subjects' categorical reasoning. Thus, we can see that expectations and beliefs introduce bias into logical thinking (Pratkanis & Greenwald, 1989).

A third type of deduction, called *linear reasoning*, involves thinking about how the elements in a series relate to each other. If John is taller than Fred, and Fred is taller than Max, who is the tallest? You can deduce that the answer is John because of the unambiguous relationship between the men's heights. But once again, the problem can be complicated by adding more elements to the series, changing terms (e.g., from taller to shorter), and adding negative statements: "If John is taller than Fred, and Fred is not as short as Max, then who is the shortest?" (Max.)

How do people reason about linear syllogisms? One view is that people construct spatial representations, or mental images, of the entire series by fitting each pair into one image (Potts, 1978; Scholz & Potts, 1974). Thus, a series of statements asserting that A is more than B, D is less than C, and C is less than B can be converted to an ordered mental image of A B C D. When subjects are then asked, "Is A more than C?" or "Is C less than A?" all they have to do is "read off" the right answer from the image. This example illustrates how logical thinking, language comprehension, and mental imagery can all influence reasoning.

Inductive Reasoning. **Inductive reasoning** is a process of reasoning from specific instances to general conclusions; the conclusions are only *likely* to be true if the premises are true. Thus, inductive reasoning is probabilistic. Induction refers to the discovery or construction of a rule that links together elements in a relation. For example, to solve a problem "*x* is to *y* as *p* is to *t*," you would need to induce a relation that is similar for both pairs. Both problem solving and concept learning can involve induction.

Three common types of problems used to study inductive reasoning are based on classification, series completion, and analogies. Examples are illustrated in Figure 8.8. The classification problems involve identifying attributes that are shared by the words and figures. The series completion tasks require people to discover the rules that were used to produce the series. For example, the series 2, 3, 5, 9, 17 is produced by multiplying the previous number by 2 and then subtracting 1. Analogies have been studied extensively by researchers because they may reflect both intellectual and creative ability. For this reason, analogy problems are often included on intelligence tests. Robert Sternberg (1985) has outlined three critical processes for solving analogy problems:

1. *Encode* the critical features of the left relation—for example, taste in "sugar is to sweet" in Figure 8.8.
2. *Combine* the two words that occupy the same position in each relational pair to discover the conceptual relation between them (in terms of the critical feature you determined in step 1). For example, sugar and lemon are opposites in regard to taste.
3. *Compare* the first pair of items to the second pair of items to generate the missing term: "Lemon is to _____ ."

Mapping the relation between the pairs of items yields sour as the answer. Poor problem-solving procedures or the inability to detect shared attributes or underlying relations can hinder analogical reasoning.

MAKING DECISIONS

Imagine that you visit a carnival booth where you can buy a chance to pop a balloon with money in it. Suppose there are 10 red balloons, one of which has a $5 bill in

FIGURE 8.8
Inductive Reasoning Problems

Three kinds of problems are often used to test the ways that people induce relations among items. The problems can be presented verbally or visually, and they vary widely in difficulty.

SOURCE: Pellegrino, 1985, p. 50.

CLASSIFICATION PROBLEMS

Verbal

mouse   wolf   bear   —   A. rose   B. lion   C. run   D. hungry   E. brown

Figural

SERIES COMPLETION PROBLEMS

Letter Series

j   k   q   r   k   l   r   s   l   m   s   —   —   —   —

Number Series

32   11   33   15   34   19   35   —   —   —   —

ANALOGY PROBLEMS

Verbal (A:B :: C:D)   **Numerical (A:B :: C:D :: E:F)**

Sugar:Sweet :: Lemon:—   7:21 :: 5:15 :: 4:—
Yellow Sour Fruit Squeeze Tea   15:19 :: 8:12 :: 5:—

Classification problems: Verbal, B;
Figure C, Letter series, t, m, n, t;
Number Series, 23, 36, 27, 37. Solutions
to analogy problems: Verbal, Sour,
Numerical, 12, 9.

it. Suppose there are also 100 yellow balloons, one of which has a $100 bill in it. If it costs $1 to pop any balloon and you are going to pop just one balloon, which color would you choose?

If you made your choice based on a rational algorithm, you would pop a yellow balloon, because the *subjective expected utility*, or *SEU*, is higher. To calculate SEU, we multiply the value of an outcome by its probability. The outcome value of a red balloon is $5 dollars, and the probability is one chance out of 10, or 0.10. Thus, the SEU for choosing a red balloon is 0.50, and the SEU for choosing a yellow balloon is 1.00, or twice as high. Although people sometimes calculate the odds and payoffs for choices in this rational manner, everyday decisions are usually made under conditions of uncertainty that invite several kinds of irrational biases.

Emotional Biases. You make decisions every day. Should you study or should you go to the party? Should you buy new clothes now or wait for a sale? Should you major in psychology? A good decision maker might analyze the problem, list the alternatives, and weigh each option for its advantages and disadvantages. If you were to follow these logical and systematic steps for making decisions, you would operate like a good statistician to calculate the odds of different gains and losses of your various options. Mann and Janis (1982) have labeled this kind of behavior "vigilant decision making." However, they also suggest that emotional conflicts often lead us astray. Decision makers who are worried about their material gains and losses or their social esteem often make less than optimal decisions owing to these outside pressures. According to Mann and Janis, people often adopt the following coping patterns when faced with stress about making a decision:

1. They continue the previous behavior, ignoring or dismissing information about potential gains and losses.
2. They accept uncritically a recommended course of action, usually to comply with the decisions of others or to gain their approval.
3. They avoid decision making by procrastinating, shifting responsibility to someone else, or rationalizing the choice of the least objectionable alternative. Statements such as "I really didn't want that anyway" or "Nobody will find out" reflect this type of defensive coping.
4. They impulsively seize on a solution that promises immediate relief.

Obviously, these four responses to a stressful decision should be avoided in making a choice among alternatives.

When Heuristics Fail. Recall that heuristics are mental shortcuts in the problem-solving process. Some of these heuristics can facilitate problem solving; others illustrate how previous experiences can make our decision making appear irrational. Suppose that there are two hospitals that each have occasional days on which 60 percent or more of their births are males. Hospital A is in a small city and averages only 15 births per day, while hospital B is in a large city and averages 45 births per day. At which hospital will you expect to have more days on which 60 percent or more of the births are male? Or do you think they will be equal? Kahneman and Tversky (1973) found that most adults responded that the hospitals would be equal, apparently because both hospitals were judged to have about average birth rates (about 50 percent males, as predicted by chance). Applying the *representativeness heuristic*, most people judged hospitals A and B to be representative of the average. This rule of thumb is sometimes valid and useful because separate members of the same population often do resemble each other (Gilovich, 1991). Unfortunately, this heuristic often leads to errors, because it ignores the *law of large numbers*, which holds that atypical events (such as birth rates of 60 percent or more males) are more likely to occur among small samples. Thus, the correct conclusion is that hospital A will have more days of high birth rates for males.

Another heuristic that leads to biased decisions is based on the *availability* of information (Tversky & Kahneman, 1982)—whether objects and events can easily be brought to mind in the course of thinking about a problem. Availability depends on experience and memory and is thus colored by salience, imagination, and personal bias, as well as all the other elements that affect the memorability of information (see Chapter 7). For example, if you had recently been bitten by a dog, then your subsequent decisions about whether to approach dogs would be strongly affected by this one negative, easily recalled, and highly salient experience. Thus, you might decide not to trust new dogs on the basis of your memory of being bitten, although it is likely that you have had hundreds of other, positive experiences with dogs that weren't as easily brought to mind for whatever reasons. The differential availability of information has often been used to explain why peoples' estimates of risks are so often inaccurate. (See "Psychology in Our Times: The Availability Heuristic and Misperceptions of Risk.")

Some judgmental heuristics are based on notions of honesty and fairness. Consider the following scenario from Thaler (1985, p. 206):

> You are lying on the beach on a hot day. All you have to drink is ice water. For the last hour you have been thinking about how much you would enjoy a nice cold bottle of your favorite brand of beer. A companion gets up to go make a phone call and offers to bring back a beer from the only nearby place where beer is sold, a fancy resort hotel. He says that the beer might be expensive and so asks how much you would be willing to pay for the beer. He says that he will buy the beer if it costs as much or less than the price you state. But if it costs more than the price you state he will not buy it. You trust your friend and there is no chance of bargaining with the bartender. What price do you state?

The median price stated by adults in Thaler's study was $2.65. Then Thaler (1985) presented the problem to another group of subjects with one small change. Instead of a fancy hotel, subjects were told that the beer would be purchased from a small, run-down grocery store from the store's owner. According to SEU theory, the value of the outcome and its probability would not change by changing the place of purchase, so this should not make any difference. However, adults stated that they would only be willing to pay an average of $1.50 if the beer was to come from the run-down store! Their expectations about overhead expenses, relative prices, and fair play made them willing to pay more at the fancy hotel.

Statistical Misconceptions. Most people either have a poor understanding of statistical principles or simply ignore them when making decisions. Tversky and Kahneman (1982) interviewed former Philadelphia 76ers coach Billy Cunningham and his players about basketball shooting and found that the players believed in the reality of a "hot hand." Because they believed that they were more likely to make a shot after they had just made one or two others, players might easily decide to shoot again immediately after having just made a shot. Examination of shooting records in games revealed little evidence to support the idea of a "hot hand." Indeed, the 76ers were slightly more likely to score baskets after *missed* shots than after previous baskets. Why the false belief in a "hot hand"?

Tversky says it is because most people forget that random sequences of numbers can contain streaks. If you were to flip a coin 20 times, there is about a 50-50 chance of

THE AVAILABILITY HEURISTIC AND MISPERCEPTIONS OF RISK

Would you like to live next to a nuclear power plant? How would you feel about living near a prison? These may sound like dangerous prospects, and probably you would be motivated to move elsewhere if given the chance. However, if you smoke cigarettes, commute to school or work, or eat fatty foods, the relative risks to you are far greater than living in either of these locales. There are many factors affecting the way people weigh one risk against another, but one determining variable is the availability of information regarding the risk of each prospect in the decision maker's mind.

A particular risk may become salient when the negative effects of the risk are reported in the news media or it becomes a popular topic of conversation. Indeed, the mass media are the primary source of risk beliefs and information about the consequences of risks (Tonn et al., 1990). However, the amount of coverage that a certain risk receives has more to do with the practical requirements of news reporting and external pressures on news organizations than on the relative importance of the risk as a danger (Klaidman, 1991; Singer & Endreny, 1993). For example, studies show that people consistently overestimate the likelihood of certain causes of death (e.g., airplane accidents, botulism, fires, and homicide) while other causes are systematically underestimated (e.g., diabetes, heart disease, stomach cancer, and stroke) (Combs & Slovic, 1984; Slovic, Fischhoff, & Lichtenstein, 1976). One reason for these misperceptions is media coverage. Each year, cancer

and heart disease claim about 16 times more lives than do accidents, yet the researchers found that newspapers offered more than 6 times as many articles about accidental deaths as about deaths caused by illness. This kind of unequal reporting results in different amounts of information available to people making decisions about risks, and the more heavily covered risks may seem disproportionately dangerous.

In another study, Slovic and his colleagues (1976) asked four groups of people—college students, members of the League of Women Voters in Oregon, business professionals, and experts at risk assessment—to rate 30 technologies and activities in terms of "the risk to society of dying." The items included handguns, pesticides, food coloring, and nuclear power. Many of the risk estimates were similar among groups; however, some were dramatically different. Students and members of the League of Women Voters rated nuclear power as number one in riskiness; businesspeople ranked it eighth, and risk experts ranked it twentieth, below electrical power, railroads, and even bicycling. When the researchers looked at the actual risk statistics, they found that the experts were relying on actual data more than were other groups, who were probably influenced by media reports and their personal beliefs.

More recently, Heath, Acklin, and Wiley (1991) have found that cognitive heuristics such as availability affect the way doctors think about their own exposure to the HIV virus. The researchers measured the amount of time the

getting four heads in a row. There is a 25 percent chance that five heads in a row will come up, and there is a 10 percent chance of a streak of six. Most people assume that random sequences should alternate between outcomes more than they actually do. That is, random sequences sometimes seem to contain too many streaks of identical or consecutively ordered results than we expect to see in a random sample; this assumption is known as the *clustering illusion*, because people tend to see events as occurring in clusters even when they really do not (Gilovich, 1991). Tversky reasons that basketball players are more sensitive to the streaks of four, five, or six shots that they may make in a game than to the fact that it is just a chance occurrence.

doctors talked with their colleagues and family members about AIDS and the amount they read about AIDS in professional journals. The study showed that the more the doctors read about AIDS, the more they worried about being exposed to the HIV virus. One important factor affecting the doctors' perceived risk was whether or not they had imagined themselves being infected, presumably an important and easily recalled scenario owing to its personal relevance and frightening implications. Further, the study demonstrated that availability and imagining were related to the perceived risk of HIV exposure, regardless of the actual exposure to HIV-positive patients.

Taking all of this evidence together, public perceptions of risk seem to be irrational and almost unrelated to the true danger posed by such risks. But this may not be the whole story. The disproportionate fear of certain environmental pollutants is often cited as an example of risk perception outweighing the actual danger. However, such worry may be a perfectly rational view, since the public often believes that technical regulators cannot be trusted, that the experts aren't trained as well as they should be, and that accidents can easily be caused by human error (Wandersman & Hallman, 1993). Furthermore, the process of quantitative risk assessment, which is often used to determine the accuracy of people's risks, is at best an inexact science. It often requires the assessors to make large assumptions given the frequent absence of reliable empirical data on environmental hazards. In addition, quantitative risk assessment depends on the assessors' personal judgments as well as the estimation of costs and benefits for things that society values but which aren't readily converted into quantitative terms (Singer & Endreny, 1993; Wandersman & Hallman, 1993).

Regardless of the actual risk from environmental hazards, it seems clear that risk perception is influenced by both the

nature of the hazard and the ease of bringing the relevant information to mind. Because the availability of knowledge can be influenced by numerous factors (such as the personal relevance of the information), it makes sense that the nature of the risk being judged is an important factor in risk perception. In fact, even for two risks that have equal magnitudes, most people feel that the one they are forced to take or that is unfairly distributed, unusual, or undetectable is worse than the risk that falls under individual control, is evenly distributed, or seems natural, familiar, or detectable (Wandersman & Hallman, 1993). And because risk perception is influenced by the way we interpret our situation, social and cultural factors also affect how we use heuristics in risk assessment (Trimpop, 1994).

If the availability heuristic biases our judgments, decision making, and perceptions and interpretations of the world, then it follows that availability may contribute to a wide range of psychological topics. Stereotypes might be formed through biased media coverage of negative (or positive) events associated with a particular group, and stereotypes already present might be reinforced if stereotypers only choose to hear information that supports their views. If stereotypers limit their contact with the stereotyped group (thus reducing the chance of obtaining information that contradicts their stereotype), then the knowledge available to them will remain biased. Also, availability may be at work in political decision making. Foreign countries (especially the less developed nations) only receive news coverage in America during times of war or other crises, so U.S. foreign policy debate may be affected by a skewed view of those societies. Domestically, the public discussion of crime is often out of proportion to the actual level of crime, sometimes creating unjustified public distress and political backlash. Can you think of other areas where availability may affect your own judgments and decisions?

A second common example of how people misuse statistical principles involves the *gambler's fallacy* (also discussed in Appendix A under "Misuses of Statistics"). Gamblers often believe that if they have been on a losing streak, their luck is bound to change and they will win on the next round of the game. Sometimes they use the same reasoning in reverse, believing that if they have been winning consistently, they should quit because they are bound to lose soon. Let's say, for example, that a gambler won three times in a row by betting heads on a coin toss. The gambler might change to tails on the next toss, reasoning as follows: "The coin is fair, so the probability of heads is only 0.50. Because heads has come up three times in a row, a tails toss is due

People often have inaccurate assessments of the laws of probability, which helps explain why they lose money at gambling. The odds always favor "the house," or the casino,

to even things up. Therefore, I should now bet tails." But this reasoning ignores the fact that coin tosses are independent events, and the next toss will not be influenced by the previous tosses. The coin has no "memory" of prior tosses, as the gambler seems to assume. The gambler's fallacy and the basketball player's notion of a "hot hand" are exactly opposite: One believes that the streak will continue and the other believes that the streak must change. In both cases, however, the players are neglecting the principles of statistical probability.

A third example of poor statistical reasoning is the neglect of *base-rate* information (Nisbett & Ross, 1980), where people fail to consider the frequency of occurrence of different events. Consider this example:

> A taxicab is involved in a hit-and-run accident. Two cab companies serve the city: Green operates 85 percent of the cabs, and Blue operates the remaining 15 percent. A witness identifies the hit-and-run cab as blue. When the court tests the reliability of the witness under circumstances similar to those of the night of the accident, he correctly identifies the color of the cab 80 percent of the time and misidentifies it 20 percent. What is the probability that the cab involved in the accident was blue as the witness stated?

Most people conclude that if the witness was 80 percent accurate, then the odds are 80 percent that the taxicab was blue. In fact, it is more likely that the cab was green. To understand this problem, imagine that the witness sees 100 accidents instead of just one. The laws of probability say that about 85 of those accidents will involve green cabs and 15 will involve blue cabs (because that is the ratio of cabs). If the person mistakenly identifies 20 percent of the green cabs as blue, he is misidentifing 17 cabs. Conversely, if he correctly identifies 80 percent of the blue cabs, he is spotting only 12 of the 15 blue cabs. Thus, of the 29 times (17 errors + 12 correct identifications) the witness says he saw a blue cab, he is wrong on 17 occasions, an error rate of almost 60 percent. In other words, the odds are 60-40 that the witness has misidentified a green cab rather than correctly identifying a blue one.

Children often neglect base-rate information. Jacobs and Potenza (1991) presented children in grades 1, 3, and 6, as well as college students, scenarios like the following:

> Mike's dresser drawer contains three pairs of white socks and six pairs of colored socks. One morning Mike is late for school and grabs a pair of socks without looking. Which socks do you think he chose?

Because two-thirds of the pairs of socks are colored, someone properly taking this information into account would guess that Mike pulled out a pair of colored socks. Yet, fewer than 25 percent of the explanations given by first graders mentioned the base-rate information (i.e., the different numbers of white and colored socks). Most of the children stated their preferred sock color or made up stories to explain their choices. Older children and adults, in contrast, used the base-rate information to explain the scenarios. Jacobs and Potenza (1991) also observed improvements with age in the use of representativeness heuristics. Thus, increased use of mental heuristics may depend on both experience and the development of other cognitive abilities, which of course should remind you again of the developmental theme of the text.

Is there any way to counteract the statistical biases so evident in the way people make decisions? Apparently, certain college courses may help improve logical thinking and statistical reasoning. Lehman and Nisbett (1990) found that social science majors improved their statistical reasoning more than students in natural sciences or humanities, while students in the latter two groups improved their conditional reasoning (i.e., "if x, then y") more than social science majors. However, even providing proof that a certain statistical inference is invalid often does little to change people's belief in its truth. For example, when Thomas Gilovich (1991) presented believers in "hot hand" basketball shooting with clear-cut data proving that the phenomenon does not exist, their initial reaction was to insist that the belief is valid and that the data are not! In fact, this kind of reaction has been shown to apply to a surprisingly wide range of beliefs (Lord, Ross, and Lepper, 1979).

The Framing Effect.   Research on decision making has shown that people reason differently about anticipated gains and losses. Suppose that you are the surgeon general of the United States and are faced with the following situation:

The United States is preparing for the outbreak of an unusual disease that is expected to kill 600 people. Two alternative programs to combat the disease have been proposed. Assume that the exact scientific estimates of the consequences of the programs are as follows:

- If program A is adopted, 200 people will be saved.
- If program B is adopted, there is a one-third probability that 600 people will be saved and a two-thirds probability that no one will be saved.

Which of the two programs would you favor?

When the outcomes were stated in terms of lives saved in an experiment by Tversky and Kahneman (1981), 72 percent of the people surveyed chose program A, apparently to avoid the risks. They then presented the same scenario to other subjects and asked them to choose either C or D.

- If program C is adopted, 400 people will die.
- If program D is adopted, there is a one-third probability that no one will die and a two-thirds probability that 600 people will die.

Because most people regard as unacceptable the certain loss of life in program C, 78 percent chose program D. But notice that program C is exactly the same as program A, and program D is the same as program B. In fact, all of the programs actually lead to the same outcome if the probabilities in B and D are 1.00: 200 people live and 400 die. Yet, when given the choice between A and B, people chose A, and when given the choice between C and D, people made the opposite decision and chose D. The difference is in how the problems are framed. The researchers concluded that when problems were framed in terms of losses, people were risk takers. They apparently reasoned with a "no guts, no glory" attitude. But when decisions were framed in terms of possible gains, people avoided risks and used reasoning more like "a bird in the hand is worth two in the bush." The anticipated lives saved or lost clearly influenced the decision-making process. Moreover, this framing effect influenced the decisions of statistically knowledgeable subjects as much as it affected subjects who knew little about statistics (Kahneman & Tversky, 1984).

Rational models of decision making, such as SEU theory, cannot explain this paradoxical attitude toward risks, but *prospect theory* proposed by Kahneman and Tversky (1979) does. The main feature of prospect theory is that people tend to avoid losses. They are not afraid to take risks; rather, they are afraid to lose. To many people, the prospect of a gain often isn't worth the pain of a loss. Prospect theory calls attention to the way problems are framed in terms of relative gains and losses, even though the probabilities of the choices remain equal. One implication of prospect theory is that people will continue an endeavor once they have invested time, money, or effort. This is what economists call the *sunk cost effect,* and Arkes and Blumer (1985) present evidence that people often act contrary to rational economic considerations:

Assume that you have spent $100 on a ticket for a weekend ski trip to Michigan. Several weeks later you buy a $50 ticket for a weekend ski trip to Wisconsin. You think you will enjoy the Wisconsin trip more and are looking forward to it. But you discover that both trips are for the same weekend. You can't return the tickets, and it is too late to sell them. You must use one ticket and not the other. Which trip do you go on? (p. 126)

Only 46 percent of the subjects chose the Wisconsin trip even though the total loss of money was the same (they've already spent the $150) and the Wisconsin weekend was expected to be more enjoyable. Apparently, subjects chose the option of greater investment to minimize perceived losses and to avoid appearing wasteful. This same type of reasoning underlies continued spending on projects that presently look as though they may lead to potential losses. So aversive is the thought of the loss that people will "throw good money after bad." Prospect theory and the sunk cost effect have obvious relevance for decision makers in business, medicine, the military, and any other field in which choices must be made about gains and losses.

Identifying Concepts

We organize much of our knowledge about the world according to **concepts**, mental representations for categorizing information. Concepts can influence perception, memory, and language. They are a fundamental aspect of cognition, and as you will see in Chapter 9, much of children's development involves learning new concepts about objects and people. Furthermore, most of the words in any language can be considered category labels, and most human communication involves the exchange of categorical information (Mechelen & Michalski, 1993).

Some concepts can be identified without any difficulty—for example, the people included in the category "presidents of the United States." This kind of concept is well defined, because each member of the category shares some critical attributes that define the concept. Many concepts are difficult to pin down, however. For example, can you say exactly what the differences are between the two members of each of these pairs: chair-bench, cup-glass, and jacket-coat? How can we define them as distinctive, nonoverlapping concepts? It is not easy to separate related objects; many concepts have uncertain, or "fuzzy," boundaries (Murphy, 1993).

THE CLASSICAL VIEW

To study how people form concepts, psychologists create situations in which subjects must devise rules about the way objects are related to one another. These studies are sometimes referred to as *concept identification studies*. Imagine, for example, that you are given a deck of playing cards and asked to discover the rule for putting cards into two groups, the winners and the losers. You pick up a four of hearts and put it in the winner pile, and you are told "wrong." Then you place a nine of clubs in the winner pile and are told "right." Do you know the rule? Probably not, but as you learn about the placement of successive cards, you may discover a rule (e.g., any card that is in a black suit or is an odd number is a winner).

More complicated versions of such tasks were used by Bruner, Goodnow, and Austin (1956) in a classic study of concept learning. The researchers showed people a variety of rectangular boxes on white cards. The cards varied in four ways: the number of objects in the boxes (one, two, or three), the number of borders around the boxes (one, two, or three), the shapes within the boxes (cross, circle, or square), and the color of the shapes (green, black, or red). The experimenters presented various cards to the subjects who made and tested hypotheses about what the concept might be. The relations among the attributes on the cards could reflect a wide range of rules. For example, "any red shape but not more than one border" might define a particular concept tested by the experimenter. The researchers found that some concepts—for example, the conjunction "red *and* square"—could be identified more quickly and with fewer errors than other concepts—for example, the disjunction "red *or* square." Bruner and his colleagues also analyzed how people devised strategies to test their hypotheses about each concept. With so many features to consider, the subjects often focused on a single feature at a time and tested hypotheses by a rule of "win-stay, lose-shift," meaning stick with your hypothesis about each feature until it is disconfirmed, and then try another.

Other psychologists criticized this task for being too difficult and peculiar; the concepts that were used seem to be defined by arbitrary relationships. They also pointed out that many concepts cannot be defined simply by listing their attributes, and those concepts may be harder to identify than everyday concepts about objects in the world. Instead of focussing on arbitrary categories, other psychologists have examined how people reason about natural concepts, considered next.

PROTOTYPES AND NATURAL CATEGORIES

The philosopher Ludwig Wittgenstein (1953) proposed that the members of a category do not necessarily have one thing in common or even a set of common attributes. Instead, they may share a *family resemblance*. Wittgenstein considered *games* a good example of a concept in which items share a family resemblance but differ on many specific features. *Games* refers to a vast category of different things that have many similarities, but not all games share all of them. Thus, the individual instances of the category *games*, such as checkers, ping pong, baseball, bridge, and water polo, may look considerably different yet still share sufficient similarities to make them like other games.

Prototypes. Eleanor Rosch (1975) introduced the notion of prototype to capture the variety of similarities that members of a category might display. A **prototype** is a representative sample of a class of things; it is the best example of most of the family resemblances. Whether we used colors, pets, or fruits as our category, you would be able to choose a prototype for each one, perhaps a particular shade of red, an average-looking dog, and an ordinary apple. It is easy to see that prototypes are abstractions of many features, some perceptual and some not readily apparent. Prototypes may even be ideal representatives of many features; thus, an exact match to the prototype may not actually exist in reality.

Labov (1973) illustrated how difficult it is to draw the boundaries between concepts. Examine the 19 objects in Figure 8.9. As you move from object 1 to object 4, do you label some objects "cups" and some "bowls"? As you move from object 5 to object 9, when is the object more like a pitcher than a cup? Subjects who were asked to make similar judgments showed no clear or consistent pattern of labeling the objects, even though some objects are more typical of one category or another.

When we form concepts, we often imagine a prototype and then compare objects to the prototype. Cantor, Mischel, and Schwartz (1982) have shown, for example, that people perceive social situations such as parties, work, job interviews, and family dinners according to relatively orderly and easily recalled sets of prototypical features. But are concepts really defined by sets of prototypical features? Douglas Medin and his

FIGURE 8.9
"Fuzzy" Concept Boundaries

Look at these 19 objects and try to decide which of them belong in the category *cups*. Are there some that seem to be better examples of cups than others? On what basis are you making your judgments?

SOURCE: Labov, W. (1973). The boundaries of words and their meanings. In C. J. N. Bailey & R. W. Shuy (Eds.), *New ways of analyzing variations in English.* Washington, D.C.: Georgetown University Press. p. 354.

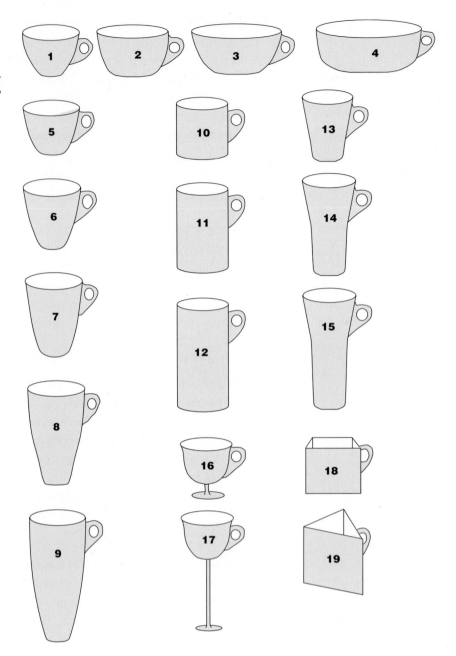

colleagues propose that people do use such constructed prototypical examples to compare objects for classification in a process that shares many features with decision making (Medin et al., 1995). Other psychologists argue that concepts cannot be defined adequately by lists of features, by typical characteristics, or by prototypes (Smith & Osherson, 1984).

Natural Concepts. One line of recent research suggests that some conceptual categories are "natural." By this we mean that such concepts are simple, familiar to us, often encountered, and easily characterized by prototypes (Sternberg, 1982). Frank Keil (1981) has suggested that some basic categories, such as *living things* or *intelligent beings*, help establish the boundaries of natural concepts. (Thus, *thinking fish* or *talking refrigerators* are unnatural concepts.) Concepts based on natural events are learned more easily and more quickly than arbitrary relations (like the attributes of cards or categories of human artifacts, such as furniture or games). Some psychologists argue

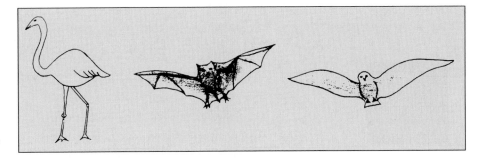

FIGURE 8.10
Children's Categorical Reasoning

These pictures were used in a study of children's categorical reasoning conducted by Gelman and Markman (1986). Four-year-old children were shown the pictures and were asked whether the blackbird feeds its young like the bat (which closely resembles the blackbird, but does not belong to the same category, birds) or if it feeds its young like the flamingo (a bird, despite the differences in appearance). The children reasoned accurately in this situation, and were not taken in by the surface similarities between the bat and blackbird.

SOURCE: Gelman, S. A., & Markman, E. M. (1986). Categories and induction in young children. *Cognition*, 23, 183–209.

that natural events have deep, underlying similarities that make them more coherent concepts, easier to abstract, and more available as everyday sources of information.

Children apparently learn natural concepts more easily than other concepts because natural concepts provide coherent frameworks for organizing their world (Carey, 1982; Markman & Callanan, 1984). Wellman and Gelman (1988) argue that children as young as 3 to 4 years of age can understand natural categories and are not limited to concepts based on perceptual features and concrete properties. For example, Gelman and Markman (1986) showed 4-year-olds a picture of a flamingo and told them that it feeds mashed-up food to its young (see Figure 8.10). The children also saw a picture of a bat and were told that it feeds milk to its young. Then the children were shown a picture of a blackbird that looked similar to the bat and were asked whether it feeds its young mashed-up food or milk. The 4-year-olds said mashed-up food, which indicates that they made correct inferences based on the similar category membership of the flamingo and the blackbird rather than the similar appearance of the bat and the blackbird. Thus, young children display inductive reasoning as well as concepts of natural kinds.

MENTAL MODELS

Some researchers suggest that the way we identify concepts and reason about categories depends on the theories that we hold about the objects and events (Keil, 1989). These theories include intuitions, knowledge, and beliefs about how objects are related to each other, and the theory is similar to the notions of family resemblance and prototypes because our hypotheses reflect the common arrangement of properties in the world. Some of the humor of Far Side cartoons may be due to the improbability of some of the concepts and instances.

Children's theories of how the world should be divided are different in various cultures and also change over time with increased experience. Consequently, we see that developmental and sociocultural factors can come to affect people's concepts, as they do so many other aspects of human thought and behavior. For example, Farrar, Raney, and Boyer (1992) have shown that as children acquire greater knowledge about animals and objects, they use the categorical information to make more sophisticated inferences. This also points out the importance of learning in concept formation and how the development of expertise in an area may be reflected in richer, more differentiated categories as we learn more about the subject.

Solving problems, making decisions, and identifying concepts are important aspects of thinking. These cognitive processes can be enhanced or impaired by different strategies, algorithms, and heuristics. It is also evident that language and thinking skills are intertwined. In the remainder of this chapter we explore the nature of language and its relation to thinking.

THE FAR SIDE   By GARY LARSON

Luposlipaphobia: The fear of being pursued by timber wolves around a kitchen table while wearing socks on a newly waxed floor.

THE FAR SIDE, by Gary Larson. Copyright, 1985, UniversalPress Syndicate. Reprinted with permission. All rights reserved.

WOMEN, FIRE, AND DANGEROUS THINGS

The language we speak provides us with prepackaged mental models of how the world works, of what things belong to the same category. Consider how the language of Dyirbal, spoken by native people in Australia, places women, fire, and dangerous things in the same category. This categorization implies that these three things have something in common. In fact, they do. All possible events in Dyirbal are categorized by four words: *bayi*, *balan*, *balam*, and *bala*. One of these four words must precede every spoken noun. Women, fire, and dangerous things all share the same modifying category. Here are some further examples of items classified in each category:

bayi: men, most snakes, most fishes, some birds, most insects, the moon, and some spears

balan: women, some snakes, some fishes, most birds, water, sun, fire, fighting, and dangerous things

balam: all edible fruit and the plants that bear them, ferns, honey, cigarettes, wine, and cake

bala: parts of the body, meat, most trees, and language

(Benjafield, 1992, p. 78).

In his book *Women, Fire, and Dangerous Things* (1987), George Lakoff reviewed R. W. Dixon's (1963) observations of the Dyirbal people and their language to investigate possible causes for such categorization. In interviews with Dyirbali, Dixon asked why nouns were classified into four categories. Dixon found that the general reason for grouping these events together was that they share a common "domain of experience" among the Dyirbal. Thus, if men do most of the hunting in a culture, then men, animals, and weapons may be in the same category. However, there was still no direct explanation for the grouping of women, fire, and dangerous things.

Lakoff further analyzed the culture of the Dyirbal and its effects on their con-

ceptual system, which could help explain these connections. Myths are a fundamental part of the Dyirbal society, and things connected by myth or belief are placed in the same category. Lakoff found that one especially important myth of the Dyirbal described the moon as the husband of the sun. Therefore, the female sun was placed in the *balan* category with other female objects. Since the sun is associated with fire (a dangerous thing), fire also is considered part of the *balan* category. Thus, the connection between women and dangerous things was established through a series of associations known as *chaining* (one item is associated to another, then to another, like links in a chain).

By studying the evolution of the Dyirbal language as English-speaking Australians introduced the English language and technology, Lakoff observed that the peripheral associations of dangerous things broke from the *balan* category and "female" remained the central organizing theme of the category. This breakdown implies that the connection between women and dangerous things was not central to the category and was easily modified.

Lakoff's analysis of the conceptual system of the Dyirbal reveals a systematic organization of events, objects, and words that undergoes refinement according to their cognitive models of their world. Because cultures often identify such concepts in their world according to underlying principles, any changes in the culture can be examined to uncover changes in the concepts people use. Therefore, psychologists find it useful to study cultural influences because they can reveal fundamental aspects of thinking. Later in the chapter, we consider additional evidence about the influence of language on thinking.

The Nature of Language

As you read this chapter, you are comprehending written language and reasoning about the information, two complex cognitive processes. **Language** is a means of symbolic communication based on sounds, written symbols, and gestures. All languages have a **grammar,** a set of explicit or implicit rules that specify how sound, structure, and meaning are connected. **Linguistics** is the study of language and its rules; **psycholinguistics** is the study of the way language and its rules influence the ways in which people speak, write, read, and think.

BASIC UNITS OF SOUND AND MEANING

The basic units of any language are its sounds, called **phonemes.** Phonemes include vowels, consonants, and blends. Each language has a certain number of phonemes; English, for example, has 46. Other languages have many more, and some have considerably fewer. Each language also has rules for acceptable combinations of sounds. In English you are unlikely to hear the consonant sequence *pm,* but you will often hear *mp.* Thus, *thump* is consistent with English sounds, but *pmet* is not. These rules of acceptability, called **phonological rules,** tell us how to combine the sounds of our language. They form part of our **linguistic competence,** our implicit knowledge about language.

In speaking, we produce each phoneme in a distinctive manner. In English, vowel sounds are created by a continuous airflow through the vocal tract; consonants are produced by stopping the airflow. Movements of the tongue, lips, and teeth modify the flow of air in the vocal tract to create the various sounds we hear (see Figure 8.11). The lips are pressed together to form the sounds *p* and *b,* for example, whereas *d* and *t* emerge when the tongue presses against the roof of the mouth or against the teeth.

FIGURE 8.11
The Vocal Apparatus and Positions of Articulation

Phonemes are produced by stopping or regulating the airflow in the mouth. Say the sounds *b, t, m,* and *l* aloud and you will notice how the lips, teeth, and tongue are used to form different sounds.

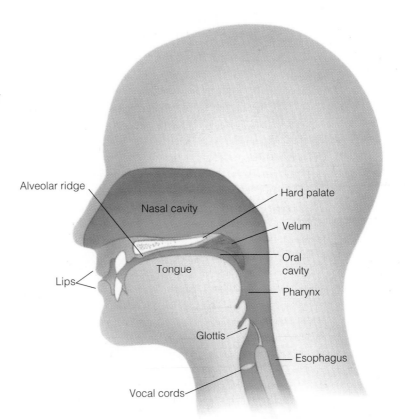

Phonemes are the basic sounds of language, and morphemes are meaningful combinations of phonemes. A **morpheme** is the smallest unit of meaningful language. Some morphemes are words, but some words consist of more than one morpheme. Consider the word *sport*. It has one morpheme. Add *s* to form *sports*, and the result is two morphemes. Now add the morphemes *un*, *man*, and *like* to generate *unsportsmanlike*. Many complex and compound words include several morphemes in combinations of stems, prefixes, and suffixes. Morphemes are combined in regular ways to modify the meanings of words. *Inflection*, for example, is the addition of linguistic markers to denote the case, plurality, or possession of a word. Here are the rules for a few basic English inflections:

- Plural nouns: apples = apple + s
- Third-person singular verbs: jumps = jump + s
- Past-tense verbs: kissed = kiss + ed
- Progressive verbs: eating = eat + ing
- Comparative adjectives: longer = long + er
- Superlative adjectives: fastest = fast + est
- Possessive nouns: Max's = Max + 's

As you are well aware, English rules often have exceptions, or *irregular* forms that must be learned. "He bringed me the can" is wrong, even if it follows the rule of adding *ed* to the verb to form the past tense. In fact, English is far less regular (or bound by firm, exceptionless rules) than many other languages.

THE STRUCTURE OF LANGUAGE

Language includes more than just formulas for combining speech sounds and morphemes. It also depends on **syntax,** a classification system of words as well as the rules for their combination. In English, words are classified as nouns, verbs, and adjectives (to identify just a few), and numerous rules govern their combination in sentences. For example, adjectives usually precede nouns in English sentences.

One way to understand the relations among words in a sentence is to diagram the sentence. Consider the sentence "The wicked vampire bites the girl." In this simple declarative sentence, articles precede nouns, the adjective precedes and modifies a noun, and the subject of the sentence comes before the verb. The tree diagram in Figure 8.12 shows the hierarchical relations among the parts of speech for this sen-

FIGURE 8.12
A Tree Diagram of a Simple Sentence

The diagram specifies grammatical relationships among sentence parts.

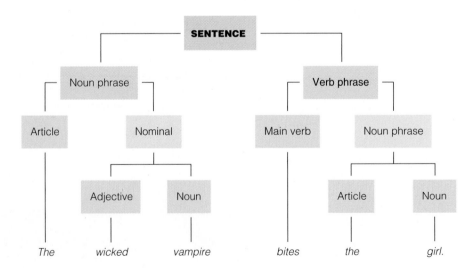

tence. Notice that the sentence has two main components—a noun phrase and a verb phrase. Each of these phrases has specific parts (articles, adjective, verb, and nouns). Such tree diagrams can help us understand the structural relations among words. For example, consider the sentence "Visiting relatives can be a nuisance." It is ambiguous because *visiting* can be a noun (perhaps with you doing the visiting), or *visiting* can be an adjective modifying *relatives* who are visiting you. These different syntactic relations are evident in Figure 8.13.

We usually remain unaware of the rules of grammar, but they are part of our linguistic competence. This means that even though we cannot easily state all the rules of syntax, we can recognize well-formed sentences. Consider these two sentences:

1. Colorless green ideas sleep furiously.
2. Green furiously sleep ideas colorless.

Both sentences are nonsense, yet we can recognize sentence 1 as acceptable syntax and sentence 2 as unacceptable.

Does syntax influence language processing? Yes. Both speed and accuracy of understanding are affected. For example, the effects of linguistic structure may be measured by giving people sentences to memorize and then determining which words they are likely to forget. Neal Johnson (1965) presented adults with such sentences as "The tall boy saved the dying woman." After several such sentences were presented, each word

FIGURE 8.13
Ambiguous Sentences

Diagramming the syntactic relations among words in sentences can help to untangle the meanings. In *a*, *relatives* is the subject of the sentence; in *b*, *visiting* is the subject of the sentence. Thus, the ambiguity is whether to treat the word *visiting* as a modifier or as a noun.

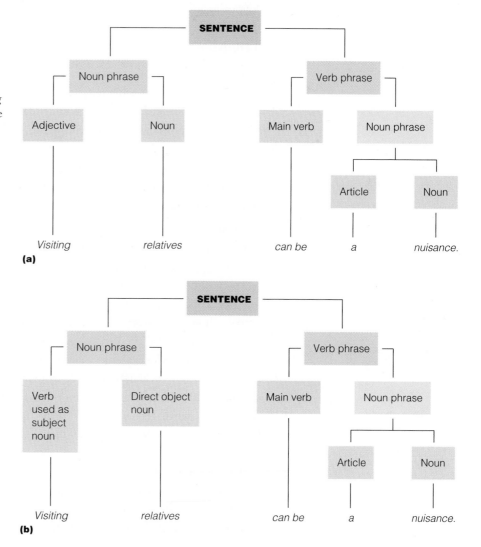

was then repeated for the subjects as a cue to remembering the next word. If remembering sentences were like learning a list of unrelated words, errors would occur with roughly equal frequency between all words; but errors turned up most often between syntactic boundaries, or grammatical units (e.g., between the subject "the tall boy" and the predicate "saved the dying woman"), and less often within phrases.

Perhaps the effect of syntax on our linguistic competence is more vivid when we consider the humor of *linguistic ambiguity*. A sign in a restaurant said, "Shoes are required to eat in the cafeteria." Underneath it, someone wrote, "But socks can eat wherever they like."

Sometimes a speaker or writer intends language to have multiple meanings, as in metaphors, analogies, and puns. But slips of the tongue and "bloopers" are, by definition, accidental; and in written language, newspaper headlines are a frequent source of unintended linguistic ambiguity. Just consider the following examples that the **Columbia Journalism Review** found:

Prostitutes Appeal to Pope
Police Help Murder Victims
Suicide More Common Than Thought
Teenage Prostitution Problem Is Mounting
American Sentenced to Life in Scotland

Thus, ambiguity can be an obstacle to clear communication, a clever tool used by politicians and advertisers, and even a source of amusement.

THE MEANING OF LANGUAGE

The grammatical rules presented so far describe the **surface structure** of sentences, a linguistic term that roughly refers to the actual words expressed in a sentence. Such structure can vary in expressing the same idea. For example, the following sentences all differ in form yet have the same meaning:

The old professor dropped his notes.
The notes were dropped by the old professor.
The professor, who was old, dropped his notes.

Linguist Noam Chomsky (1965), who revolutionized thinking about the structure of language, devised a theory to explain how meaning in the deep structure of language could result in different expressions of the same idea. **Deep structure** refers to the speaker's intended message and to the linguistic relations that constrain a sentence's meaning. In the preceding examples, each sentence has the same deep structure of ideas and grammatical relations, but the surface structure, the actual wording, varies. Chomsky's theory of **transformational grammar** postulated that particular "transformation rules" are used to generate appropriate surface structures from deep structures. These rules enable us to insert words, change word order, or turn statements into questions or exclamations while systematically preserving the deep structure of meaning. Although some controversy exists over the best way to characterize the deep structure of a language, most psychologists and linguists agree that a distinction should be made between deep and surface structures when considering grammatical structure in general.

The meaning expressed in language is called **semantics.** A sentence can be formed from acceptable phonemes and morphemes and put together in proper syntactic order and yet still be meaningless. "Colorless green ideas sleep furiously" defies semantic interpretation, but "My brother is an only child" is interpretable; in fact, it is amusing.

There are many levels of understanding for language and various criteria that we can apply to comprehension. The richness of semantics allows endless creative language expressions. We should also note that semantics applies to many levels of language, from morphemes to sentences to lengthy discourse.

Language communicates meaning, but meaning is not inherent in the symbol systems known as words and sentences. Meaning is constructed in the mind; therefore, it is a cognitive product. Meaning is also influenced by the sociocultural factors that surround us all. Declarations, questions, orders, and threats have meaning for both speaker and listener because each understands the generally agreed upon meanings of the words as well as the social context that further shapes that meaning. Language thus directs social exchanges by expressing the thoughts and intentions of the participants.

In conversation or written text, a social interchange of information occurs between listeners and speakers, between readers and authors. This exchange is termed a *speech act*, a social and linguistic unit of analysis that includes a message, the intent of the speaker, and the effect of the message on the listener. Each of the following sentences can be part of different kinds of speech acts:

> What was Zorro's real name?
> I know who is buried in Grant's tomb.
> Please don't hit me with that!
> I now pronounce you husband and wife.
> Give me all of your money—or else!

Because language is a shared medium, it demands a consensus between users about the way words are employed to convey meaning. This is the *pragmatic* aspect of language, because the listener and speaker must adjust communication so that both are speaking with terms whose meanings they know and agree upon. Without consensus, people would speak idiosyncratically like Humpty Dumpty in Lewis Carroll's *Through the Looking Glass*:

> "When I use a word," Humpty Dumpty said, in a rather scornful tone, "it means just what I choose it to mean—neither more nor less." "The question is," said Alice, "whether you can make words mean so many different things." "The question is," said Humpty Dumpty, "which is to be master—that's all."

Humpty Dumpty might want words to mean what he chooses them to mean, but no one would understand him. In fact, this is exactly what happens when we enter a work group whose members have developed a jargon for talking about events important to their work. We cannot understand them until we learn the consensual meaning of the terms. Does learning certain words for concepts affect the way we think about those concepts? We consider the relation between language and thought in the section beginning on page 339.

Cognitive Processes in Language Comprehension

There are many cues to the meaning of language: gestures, facial expressions, the situation, the topic, and previous comments of the participants. We do not comprehend language in a vacuum, nor do we only interpret and retain individual sentences. Language comprehension requires generating, inferring, and consolidating meaning from speech or writing, guided by knowledge of the world and the context of language. For example, if a stranger tapped you on the shoulder and said, "There's no quiz this week," your comprehension would require more than linguistic analysis of the sentence. You might ask, "Who's he? Is he in my class? What quiz? You mean we've had quizzes the past weeks? Why is he telling me?" If the tip came from a classmate and your class usually has weekly quizzes, you would readily understand the message.

We will briefly discuss some research findings that support a series of propositions about language comprehension:

1. People usually remember the meaning of sentences but may forget the surface structure or form in which the information was presented.
2. An appropriate context and previous information about the topic of conversation facilitate comprehension and memory.
3. Language comprehension is a constructive process dependent on other knowledge.

Note that the items in this list correspond well with our understanding of the way memory works, as we discussed in Chapter 7.

REMEMBERING THE MEANING

Consider the first proposition. People seldom recall complex material word for word; instead, they remember the gist of the message. In other words, the ideas of the linguistic deep structure may be retained, but the wording of the sentence is usually forgotten. To examine this notion, Jacquelyne Sachs (1967) tested the memories of adults for specific sentences immediately after they had read passages she had given them and 30 to 45 seconds later, after the subjects had continued reading. One sentence was "He sent a letter about it to Galileo, the great Italian scientist." When Sachs stopped her subjects, she gave them a recognition test that included either the original sentence, a sentence that meant the same thing but had the word order changed (e.g., "He sent Galileo, the great Italian scientist, a letter about it"), or a sentence that changed the meaning (e.g., "Galileo, the great Italian scientist, sent him a letter about it"). When tested immediately after reading the sentence, subjects accurately identified both new sentences as new. After delays, they rejected the sentence with the different meaning, but frequently said that the new word order in the other choice was identical to what they had read previously. Thus, Sachs confirmed that people forget the surface structure of sentences while recalling the gist of the information.

THE ROLE OF CONTEXT

The second proposition says that the context in which we hear or read something greatly affects how we understand language. The sentence "The haystack was important because the cloth ripped" is confusing until an additional cue is provided: a torn parachute. Now you can create a context, or mental image, that makes the sentence easy to understand. Context can include prior knowledge, words, text, pictures, places, people—anything that can help us understand language. To demonstrate this point to yourself, read the following paragraph:

If the balloons popped, the sound would not be able to carry since everything would be too far away from the correct floor. A closed window would also prevent the sound from carrying since most buildings tend to be well insulated. Since the whole operation depends on a steady flow of electricity, a break in the middle of the wire would also cause problems. Of course the fellow could shout, but the human voice is not loud enough to carry that far. An additional problem is that a string could break on the instrument. Then there would be no accompaniment to the message. It is clear that the best situation would involve less distance. Then there would be fewer potential problems. With face-to-face contact, the least number of things could go wrong. (Bransford & Johnson, 1972, p. 11)

You probably rate this passage low on comprehensibility and would recall only a few ideas presented in it. However, if you had looked at the drawing in Figure 8.14 before reading, the passage probably would have made more sense.

Bransford and Johnson (1972) read this passage to three groups of adults: those who had no picture, those who had seen a picture with the same objects but in inappropriate positions, and ones who had the correct picture displayed to them before or after they heard the passage. The only condition that improved understanding of the passage was when the picture was given beforehand. Memory for the passage also improved. Bransford and his colleagues have shown in many studies that context is a prerequisite for understanding pictures, sentences, and stories.

Context aids language comprehension because people base conversations on shared topics and understanding of a listener's point of view (although children sometimes have difficulty doing so). Thus, new information is related to previous statements and comprehended according to relationships among sentences. Conversations and comprehension sometimes break down when participants do not share the same "given" information. Haviland and Clark (1974) used the term *given-new contract* to describe how a speaker and listener specify the common topic (or "given" information) and add comments. For example, Haviland and Clark presented the following sentences to adult subjects:

1. We got some beer out of the trunk. The beer was warm.
2. We checked the picnic supplies. The beer was warm.

They wanted to determine if the subjects could comprehend the test sentence "The beer was warm" more quickly in case 1 than in case 2. Subjects listened to each sentence and pushed a button as soon as they understood the test sentence. They were significantly faster at understanding when presented with the sentences in case 1 because the test sentence followed the "given" information. The phrase "some beer" provided an explicit context, or shared knowledge, that facilitated comprehension.

UNDERSTANDING AS A CONSTRUCTIVE PROCESS

According to the third proposition, expectations and knowledge guide the interpretation of language. In Chapter 7, we showed how experience affects memory by describing Elizabeth Loftus's experiments on eyewitness testimony. The same processes operate for linguistic comprehension. Many studies have shown that people process

FIGURE 8.14
Context Aid for Language Comprehension

In the study by Bransford and Johnson (1972), adults could not recall or comprehend much of a story unless they were provided with the picture on the left before they heard the passage. Showing the left-hand picture after hearing the story or seeing the picture on the right before hearing the story did not aid understanding or memory for the passage.

SOURCE: Bransford & Johnson, 1972.

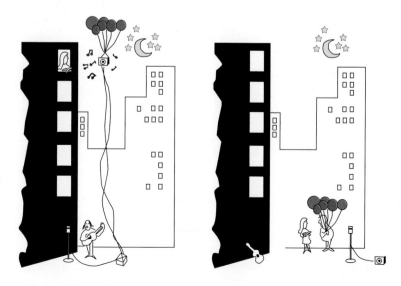

ambiguous sentences and discourse according to their beliefs about the context. In another study described in Chapter 7, adults who read about Helen Keller reported later that they had seen sentences like "She was deaf, dumb, and blind" even though no such sentences had been in the passage (Sulin & Dooling, 1974).

People often construct scenarios that can alter their comprehension of language in systematic ways (Anderson et al., 1977). This is consistent with schema theory, described in Chapter 7. For example, Anderson and Pichert (1978) asked two groups of adults to read a story about a home as if they were either a burglar or a potential home buyer. The two groups remembered different information from the passage, specifically information that was most relevant to their particular point of view. But when they were asked to recall the passage from the other perspective, the adults were able to recall other information that they had neglected previously. Thus, schemas may focus attention and provide a framework for recall, but they do not necessarily block remembering other information.

We also described in Chapter 7 how the presentation and organization of material can improve remembering. Language facilitates such "information packaging." For example, Carmichael, Hogan, and Walter (1932) showed adults 12 pictures (like those in Figure 8.15) and identified each picture orally. By design, the pictures were ambiguous, but the labels biased the subjects toward specific interpretations. Some heard the label "eyeglasses" for the first picture, while others heard "dumbbell." Later, when they had to draw the pictures from memory, the subjects drew objects resembling the labels that they had heard rather than the original pictures. The linguistic cues had influenced them to construct different mental representations of the objects. The errors and distortions evident in these studies were not random. The elaborations fit the topics appropriately and revealed how people construct meaning from linguistic and non-linguistic cues.

More recently, Jonathan Schooler and his colleagues have studied how verbal descriptions of complex perceptual stimuli can affect their later memory. For example, when people see faces and then describe them, later memory for the faces is worse than if no verbal descriptions were given (Schooler & Engstler-Schooler, 1990). This harmful effect of describing events on their later memory is called *verbal overshadowing*, because the verbalization of the stimulus presumably affects its perceptual representation. Verbal overshadowing occurs only for stimuli that are perceptually complex and difficult to describe, such as music, maps, visual forms, and the taste of wines (see Melcher & Schooler, 1996). With simple stimuli, verbalization usually helps memory, but it is still quite remarkable that talking or writing about complex events can disrupt memory for these events.

FIGURE 8.15
How Labels Influence Recall of Pictures

Adults were shown a series of pictures like those on the left, but the researchers orally identified each picture in two different ways. Some subjects were told the labels indicated in the center column, while others were told the labels on the right. When subjects were later asked to recall the pictures, they drew pictures that were consistent with the labels, not with the pictures originally presented to them. Thus, language can influence the reconstruction of experiences.

SOURCE: Carmichael, Hogan, & Walter, 1932.

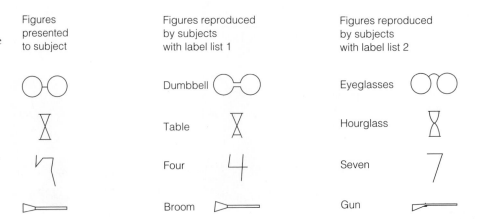

Children's language comprehension is also constructive and creative, yet children often do not know when or how to make inferences. In one study, for example, short stories were read to children between 6 and 12 years of age (Paris & Upton, 1976). Later, the children were asked yes-no questions about the stories and were also asked to recall the stories in their own words. The 6- and 7-year-olds did not construct as many implied relations or link the main ideas together as much as older children. The ability to apply constructive processes to aid comprehension while reading, listening, or remembering improves and develops along with other problem-solving skills throughout childhood (Paris, Wasik, & Turner, 1990). We will discuss the linguistic competence of children more fully in Chapter 9.

Does Thinking Depend on Language?

Language and thought may be related in several ways. They may be essentially identical; one may influence the other; or they may be unrelated. Linguists, sociologists, and anthropologists, as well as psycholinguists, comparative psychologists, and developmental psychologists, have studied the relationship between thought and language. Sometimes they study differences among languages around the world, sometimes they study universal features of reasoning and language, and sometimes they study nonhuman communication.

LINGUISTIC DETERMINISM

All languages have sounds, syntax, meaning, and rules that specify how these elements are related. Yet the particular rules of a language, like its sounds and vocabulary, vary widely among languages. For example, the Japanese language has different words for counting different kinds of objects, the Chinese language has a much wider assortment of terms to indicate family relationships than English does, and Eskimos use 20 different words to describe various kinds of snow.

A critical question that should be considered is whether this diversity of language reflects different forms of thinking. Or does how we speak determine how we think? Because of their rich vocabulary, do Eskimos perceive their world of ice and snow differently than an outsider would?

Linguist Benjamin Whorf (1956) believed that language was the central force behind thought. He advanced the notion of **linguistic determinism,** a principle stating that what people think and how they think are determined by the context and complexity of their language. He wrote:

> We dissect nature along the lines laid down by our native languages. . . . We cut nature up, organize it into concepts, and ascribe significances as we do, largely because we are parties to an agreement to organize it in this way—an agreement that holds through our speech community and is codified in the patterns of our language. (pp. 312–314)

Whorf deduced much of the evidence for this position by comparing American Indian languages with European languages. He argued that cultural differences in language produce culturally different ways of thinking. For example, in one anecdote Whorf compared two cultures' thinking about spring water:

> We might isolate something in nature by saying, "It is a dripping spring." Apache erects the statement on a verb *ga:* "be white (including clear, uncolored, and so on)." With a prefix *no-* the meaning of a downward motion enters: "Whiteness moves downward." Then "*to,*" meaning both "water" and "spring," is prefixed. The result corresponds to our "dripping spring" but synthetically it is "as water, or springs, whiteness moves downward." How utterly unlike our thinking. (p. 241)

Granted that the literal translation is not everyday English, the phrase is comprehensible (perhaps poetic) and may not in fact represent a different way of thinking. Contrary to Whorf, most people believe that language *reflects* general properties of human perception, thinking, and socialization rather than determines them. The evidence comes from studies of different language groups who have widely different vocabularies and grammar yet distinguish or categorize objects in the world in similar ways. Let's consider a few examples.

For many years it was believed that every language divided the color spectrum in arbitrary ways, because some languages have no names for colors commonly labeled in English. The Dani in New Guinea have only two basic terms, *mili* (black) and *mola* (white). Does color naming limit perception only to hues that have been given names? Anthropologists Brent Berlin and Paul Kay (1969) discovered that all languages have basic color terms that come from only 11 color names; moreover, they found that these 11 names form a hierarchy (reading from left to right):

A language with two color names has black and white, a language with three names includes red, and so on. English includes all 11 terms.

These basic color names reflect how language mirrors perception. They represent **focal colors,** a fundamental category of light on the visible spectrum somewhat like the predominant hues perceived in rainbows. Eleanor Heider Rosch (Heider, 1972) showed how focal colors influenced thinking. When adults were shown a color chip for 5 seconds and later asked to pick out the same chip from among 160 chips, they demonstrated better memory for focal than for nonfocal colors. Even children matched focal colors to examples faster than nonfocal colors (Heider, 1971; Mervis, Catlin, & Rosch, 1975). Rosch (1973) also examined how fast the Dani could learn color names that were not in their vocabulary. They acquired names for focal colors faster than for nonfocal colors. In other studies, the Dani were found to represent and to remember colors the same way English-speaking people do (Heider & Oliver, 1972). So, in spite of great differences in the language terms available for color naming, and in contradiction to Whorf's theory, people's perception and memory are influenced by universal aspects of focal colors and not by their linguistic labels.

Other universal aspects of human thinking and socialization are reflected in language, too. For example, languages seem to have different levels of abstraction for referring to things. English-speaking people might call an apple an apple, a Golden Delicious apple, a fruit, an object, something to eat, or a dessert. Why does the word *apple* seem most fitting? Roger Brown (1958) argued that the term is at a level of abstraction with the greatest utility, neither too general nor too specific. This is consistent with our earlier discussion of prototypes as best examples of concepts.

Studying how people around the world name plants and animals, Berlin and his colleagues (Berlin, 1972; Berlin, Breedlove, & Raven, 1973), discovered that the classification systems usually involve five levels of abstraction: (1) a unique beginner (e.g., plant, animal); (2) a life form (e.g., tree, bush, flower); (3) a generic name (e.g., pine, oak, maple, elm); (4) a specific name (e.g., Ponderosa pine, white pine); and (5) a varietal name (e.g., Northern Ponderosa pine, Western Ponderosa pine). The levels become progressively more precise, yet they do not overlap, and each lower level is included in the larger categories hierarchically. Berlin and his coworkers found that level 3, generic names, was the most common category of names in different languages. Rosch (1977) has suggested that these generic categories are the most common in language because the objects included in them share many attributes. General terms such as *tree* do not distinguish adequately among kinds of similar trees, nor do precise terms such as *white pine* describe the similarities of objects clearly. While languages may vary in their vocabulary for each level, the fact that diverse cultures rely most heavily on generic terms supports the notion that cognitive categories for objects help determine linguistic categories.

A similar effect has been observed for other dimensions of perception and cognition. All languages appear to refer to spatial dimensions such as height, weight, thickness, and distance. Most languages also specify directions (such as up-down, left-right, and front-back), time (such as present-past-future), and number. Even when languages do not include particular words for each characteristic, people process the basic cognitive and perceptual features similarly. For example, in Rosch's (1973) studies with the Dani, she determined how they learned names for various shapes. The Dani had no specific words for circle, square, and triangle and resorted to "pig-shaped" or "fence-shaped" and the like. Rosch presented Dani subjects with figures that we regard as common (e.g., circle, square, and triangle) as well as with odd shapes. The Dani learned the names for "common" figures more easily than names for odd shapes. Thus, it seems that nonlinguistic features and categories help direct learning and language.

These studies and other evidence support the view that universal aspects of human perception and cognition appear to influence language. However, how do linguists account for the variations among languages, such as the numerous Eskimo words for snow, the few color terms in some cultures, and the lack of shape names among the Dani? Clark and Clark (1977) suggested that these language differences reflect different adjustments to the environment and not different ways of thinking. If you live in a world of snow or if you eat mostly rice, your language requires appropriate terms. Thus, people invent language to describe the important features of their environments and to communicate effectively.

NONHUMAN COMMUNICATION

Animals other than humans communicate with members of their own species in distinctive ways. The dancing patterns of bees in the hive can indicate the location of food. The gestures and odors of dogs can signal sexual and aggressive readiness. Whales, dolphins, monkeys, and other animals use specific sounds to warn of approaching danger. Although some psychologists do not consider animal communication a symbolic system because it does not have syntactic and semantic structures as flexible and creative as spoken human language, do other animal species besides our own have the capacity to learn and use language?

Psychologists have been studying the communication of animals for more than 50 years. Much of this research has focused on members of the ape family, the species most closely related to humans in evolutionary terms. In one of the first attempts to teach language to animals, two psychologists raised a chimpanzee named Gua with their own infant son, Donald (Kellogg & Kellogg, 1933). Donald easily acquired language; Gua never produced sounds resembling human speech, and he could not understand language any better than a well-trained dog. Some years later, Keith and Cathy Hayes taught a chimp named Viki to say "papa," "momma," and "cup," but that took

three years and Viki comprehended little of the human speech directed toward her (Hayes, 1951). One reason for these failures may be that neither the organization of chimps' brains nor the anatomy of their vocal tracts is suited for verbal language (Lieberman, Crelin, & Klatt, 1972). Thus, more recent researchers have tried to teach nonverbal language to animals (see Figure 8.16).

One well-known animal communication study was done by Beatrice and Allan Gardner (1978), who taught American Sign Language to a chimpanzee named Washoe. Since sign language constitutes a symbolic and structured system, and since chimps use their hands adeptly, this method is a good test of chimps' ability to learn human language. When the experiment began, Washoe was a year old. She spent each day in the Gardners' house or yard, and everyone communicated by sign language in her presence, never using oral speech. Dressing, feeding, and playing were accompanied by lots of signing, much like conversations between deaf-mute parents and children. In addition, the Gardners used demonstration, imitation, and conditioning (with tickling as a frequent reward) to teach Washoe new signs.

After 7 months, Washoe had mastered only 4 signs, but after 22 months, she had a vocabulary of 34 different signs. She used the signs to appropriately and correctly refer to objects, even in new situations. Like a child, Washoe generalized. For example, she employed the signal for "open" to refer to the doors of the house, car, and refrigerator

FIGURE 8.16
A Chimpanze Learning to Imitate the Gestures of American Sign Language

Chimps' signs are often rapid and are not always perfect copies of human gestures.

To make the gesture that stands for "fruit," the fingers are loosely curled and the hand is drawn down the side of the cheek.

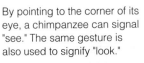
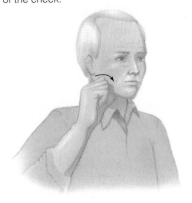

By pointing to the corner of its eye, a chimpanzee can signal "see." The same gesture is also used to signify "look."

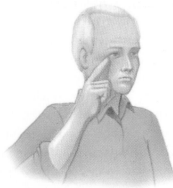

and the sign "pants" for diapers, rubber pants, and trousers. By 5 years of age, Washoe knew more than 160 distinctive language signs. Even more impressive, Washoe began to combine new individual signs into multiword utterances that could be translated as "you drink," "more tickle," "hurry open," and "hurry, gimme toothbrush." Often, Washoe created novel word combinations to describe things. It has been reported that she signed "water bird" when she first saw a swan and called a nasty rhesus macaque a "dirty monkey."

There have been other approaches to teaching language to chimps. David and Ann Premack (Premack, 1971; Premack & Premack, 1972) raised a chimp named Sarah in a laboratory cage where she was given only periodic language training each day. Sarah was taught to manipulate plastic pieces that symbolized different words and relations (see Figure 8.17). Each piece varied in shape, size, and color and had a metal back so it could be placed on a magnetic board to answer questions and make requests. Sarah was taught the meaning of these tokens through shaping and conditioning. For example, an experimenter first provided a piece of banana for Sarah. Then the token signifying banana was placed closer to Sarah. When Sarah stuck the token on the board, she got the piece of banana to eat. In subsequent training, Sarah was presented the plastic shapes signifying apple, orange, and banana and was given the fruit only when she selected the correct token.

The Premacks also taught Sarah how to construct sentences and answer questions, including use of the verb *be*, the conjunction *and*, and words to describe color, shape, and size of objects. Sarah learned to correctly follow the commands of a sentence made from tokens that translate as "Sarah, put the banana in the pail and the apple in the dish." In addition, when presented with two objects, Sarah could correctly pick the token for "same" or "not same" nearly 80 percent of the time.

These studies suggest that other primates have more linguistic and conceptual competence than we suspected. Can they learn language as a symbolic system, however, or do they only learn to manipulate objects and make gestures to receive rewards? This is an ongoing controversy that is not easy to settle.

At the heart of the controversy is the definition of key concepts. What is a word? What is a sentence? What is language? Premack (1985) argues that the definitions of these terms are debatable but do not necessarily exclude chimpanzees' use of symbolic communication. He suggests that there are great similarities between children's language acquisition and the languages learned by nonhumans—similarities in grammatical form as well as semantic function. Other scientists argue that chimpanzees do not learn symbolic language at all. We pursue this topic in "Controversy: Can Chimpanzees Learn to Use Language?"

FIGURE 8.17
Plastic Shapes Used by Sarah the Chimp

The top row shows individual tokens, and the bottom row forms the sentence "Red is not the color of chocolate."

SOURCE: Premack & Premack, 1972.

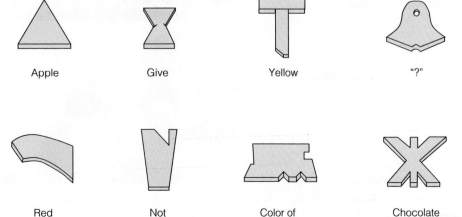

Apple   Give   Yellow   "?"

Red   Not   Color of   Chocolate

CAN CHIMPANZEES LEARN TO USE LANGUAGE?

Despite the excitement generated by Washoe and Sarah, the issue remains as to whether language learned by other primates is qualitatively similar to human language. After five years of teaching sign language to a chimp, Herbert Terrace concluded, "I could find no evidence confirming an ape's grammatical competence, either in my own data or those of others, that could not be explained by simpler processes" (Terrace, 1979, p. 67).

Terrace points out a number of problems. First, how do we know that chimps produce sentences with an underlying knowledge of grammatical rules such as subject, verb, and object relations? Although the chimps constructed word strings such as "Washoe more eat" "Mary give Sarah apple," did they actually create whole sentences as children do? Terrace suggests that the chimps may have only manipulated the symbol for a reward such as apple, in a sequence of otherwise meaningless symbols. It is something like filling in the names of things in foreign phrases. If you didn't know French, you could still add to the imperative phrase "Donnez-moi_____" ("Give me_____") if you had learned that the first two symbols preceded the reward symbol and led to reward when combined all together. Terrace points out that chimps seldom spontaneously created sentences that followed rules for the order of words. The Gardners' Washoe, for instance, often signaled either "more drink" or "drink more," which were both recorded as "more drink." Terrace suggests that when Washoe made the signs for "water bird" on seeing a swan and being asked, "What's that?" she might have responded "water" and then "bird"—both appropriate, but not necessarily grammatically creative.

For four years, Terrace (1979) trained a young male chimp named Nim Chimpsky beginning in its infancy. (Note the humorous twist on the name of linguist Noam Chomsky.) Nim learned 125 signs, including a number of sign combinations that followed a fixed order. The sign for "more" occurred first 85 percent of the time

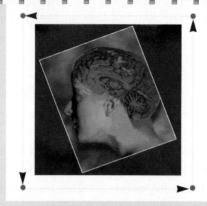

(e.g., "more tickle," "more drink") and the sign for "give" in 78 percent of the two-sign combinations. Although this seemed to indicate a grammatical rule for Nim, Terrace concluded otherwise. He found, through detailed analyses of videotaped conversations, that Nim often imitated a trainer's signs while signing himself. For example, in Figure 8.19, Nim Chimpsky and a trainer are shown conversing in sign language. Nim's hands indicate "me" (upper left), "hug" (upper right), and "cat" (lower left) and appear to be declaring "Me

hug cat." Terrace (1979, p. 71) suggests, however, that the trainer may have provided cues to Nim without being aware she was doing so. He bases the idea on scrutiny of the pictures, which, he says, shows the trainer making the sign for "you" while Nim is indicating "me," and signaling "who" while Nim is communicating "cat." "Cat" and "who" had frequently been linked in Nim's lessons. Whether the teacher's signs preceded or followed Nim's cannot be ascertained from the photos.

Terrace describes similar problems in interpreting Washoe's creative utterances. One filmed conversation with Washoe "began with Gardner signing *eat me, more me,* after which Washoe gave her something to eat. Then she signed *thank you*—and only then asked *what time now?* Washoe's response *time eat, time eat* can hardly be considered spontaneous, since Gardner had just used the same signs and Washoe was offering a direct answer to her questions" (Terrace, 1979, p. 76).

FIGURE 8.19
Do Trainers Inadvertently Supply Extra Cues for Chimps When Using Sign Language?

Perhaps many of the chimps' symbolic expressions depend on training, reward, and imitation, rather than being novel, spontaneous, and grammatical. The learning abilities of chimps are indeed impressive, but analyses and interpretations of their communication have induced skepticism about their capacity to comprehend and produce language. For example, when language tokens were left in Sarah's cage, she usually ignored them and did not initiate any "conversations" or practice her new skills.

CONTROVERSY

Richard Sanders (1985) carefully analyzed all the videotapes of Nim's training and concluded that "the ape learned to use gestures as nonsymbolic instrumental responses." Sanders argues that neither Nim nor the training procedures were atypical of other

studies, and thus earlier attempts to teach other animals may have been confounded also. But as Premack (1985) points out, this does not mean that chimps are incapable of learning symbolic language. So, despite the skepticism of Terrace and Sanders, the issue of whether nonhumans can learn symbolic language remains an open question.

THEMES IN REVIEW

Language is the primary human means of communication, but humans share the need to communicate with other animals. The biological theme emphasizes that the nature of language is shaped by biological factors, such as the structure of the vocal tract and hemispheric specialization of the brain. Debate continues on whether other animals can learn human languages. You will see in the next chapter, children learn language rapidly over the first few years of life, which seem to represent a critical biological period for language learning. This developmental theme to language and thought is also captured by children's learning concepts about the world and strategies to solve problems that the world presents to them. How children acquire these skills will be included in the next chapter, too.

The sociocultural theme is reflected by different cultures and different languages emphasizing various aspects of the world that are critical to a particular society. So the skills of talking and thinking develop in, and are shaped by, the context of a particular culture. The idea of linguistic determinism is that different languages shape the way people speaking them think about the world. Although the evidence does not really support the strongest version of this idea for concrete features of the world (such as perception of color) language and culture do seem to shape more abstract aspects of thought.

Much of this chapter has been concerned with the cognitive processes underlying language and thought reflecting the cognitive theme. For example, in solving problems, we must overcome functional fixedness and mental set. And when we evaluate information and make decisions, the way the choice is framed may determine the solution. Information that can be easily brought to mind may determine how risky we think an activity is, but this availability may have more to do with frequency of reports in the media than with the actual risk. Once again, social forces—the influence of the media, in this case—shape the cognitive processes involved in thinking and reasoning.

SUMMARY

1 Effective problem solving depends on five steps: identifying the problem, defining and representing the problem, exploring possible strategies, acting on the strategies, and evaluating outcomes. Functional fixedness and mental set can block problem solving through inflexibility in solutions.

2 Mental strategies such as algorithms, which are specific rules that lead to solutions, and heuristics, which are general guidelines for what works for similar problems, can help people solve problems or cause misconceptions.

3 Deductive reasoning includes logical thinking about syllogisms, conditional reasoning, categorical reasoning, and linear ordering. Inductive reasoning includes the ability to classify objects, to solve analogy problems, and to complete series.

4 Decision making can be distorted by personal beliefs and misconceptions about statistics. Judgments may be biased if based on readily available or representative information. How you frame an issue may determine your decision. For example, people often decide to avoid risks, so framing a decision in terms of certain losses (instead of positive outcomes) may alter the decision.

5 Identifying concepts involves recognizing critical attributes of objects and relating those attributes according to some schema. Some concepts are defined more easily than others; some concepts can be defined by prototypes, natural characteristics, or theory-based descriptions.

6 The basic units of sound in a language are phonemes; the basic units of meaning are morphemes. People are not usually aware of grammatical rules, but nevertheless achieve linguistic competence.

7 Language has deep structure and surface structure. People usually remember the meaning of sentences, which is part of deep structure, more easily than exact words, which is part of surface structure.

8 Comprehending language is a constructive process that depends on prior knowledge, the social situation, and the context surrounding speech.

9 There is little evidence that people who speak different languages perceive and think about the world in radically different ways.

10 There is still debate about whether chimpanzees can learn to use symbolic forms of communication, but they can acquire some of the basic principles of human language after considerable training.

KEY TERMS

thinking (p. 308)

problem solving (p. 308)

functional fixedness (p. 310)

algorithms (p. 311)

heuristic (p. 311)

subgoal analysis (p. 312)

analogy (p. 312)

mental set (p. 313)

incubation effect (p. 314)

insight (p. 314)

deductive reasoning (p. 317)

inductive reasoning (p. 319)

concepts (p. 326)

prototype (p. 327)

language (p. 331)

grammar (p. 331)

linguistics (p. 331)

psycholinguistics (p. 331)

phonemes (p. 331)

phonological rules (p. 331)

linguistic competence (p. 331)

morpheme (p. 332)

syntax (p. 332)

surface structure (p. 334)

deep structure (p. 334)

transformational grammar (p. 334)

semantics (p. 334)

linguistic determinism (p. 339)

focal colors (p. 340)

FOR CRITICAL ANALYSIS

1 Analyze a problem you are currently facing by the IDEAL approach. How does this approach help you to solve the problem?

2 Are experts simply people who have practiced a task for hundreds or thousands of hours? Or is something more involved?

3 Look through advertisements in a magazine or newspaper and try to find ads that use misleading or inappropriate logic in drawing conclusions.

4 Try to think of examples from your own life of how the way a problem or decision is framed affects its solution.

5 In the case study, we described how native Australians' categories and language changed when they came into contact with English-speaking Australians. What are the implications of changes in the Dyirbal language for the ideas of linguistic determinism, as advocated by Whorf?

SUGGESTED READINGS

ANDERSON, J. R. (1990). *The adaptive character of thought*. Hillsdale, NJ: Erlbaum. A new approach to problem solving and thinking that involves rational analysis of environments and constraints that we encounter when trying to adapt to those conditions.

BEST, J. (1994). *Cognitive Psychology* (4th ed.). St. Paul, MN: West. An excellent introduction to cognitive psychology.

BRANSFORD, J. D., & STEIN, B. S. (1993). *The IDEAL problem solver: A guide for improving thinking, learning, and creativity*. (2nd ed.) New York: Freeman. Presents a wealth of information in nontechnical language on problem solving, with many examples for inquisitive readers.

GILOVICH, T. (1991). *How we know what isn't so: The fallibility of human reason in everyday life*. New York: Free Press. The title to this book sums up its focus very well. Cognitive, social, and motivational factors influencing information processing are all discussed in a clear manner. Also, the way that this bias can lead to erroneous beliefs is traced in several examples.

MAYER, R. E. (1992). *Thinking, problem solving, cognition*. (2nd ed.) New York: Freeman. This second edition includes updated information on all aspects of reasoning, many practical examples, and seven chapters devoted to applications of cognitive psychology.

PLOUS, S. (1993). *The psychology of judgment and decision making*. New York: McGraw-Hill. A well-written text with engaging examples written by a social psychologist. An excellent introduction to judgment and decision making.

REED, S. K. (1992). *Cognition*. Pacific Grove, CA: Brook/Cole. An excellent overview of general issues and current research in cognitive psychology, including chapters on memory, language, problem solving, decision making, categorization, and comprehension.

PSYCHOLOGY ON THE INTERNET

Introduction to 21st Century Problem Solving
(http://www2.hawaii.edu/suremath/home.html)

This site (maintained by Howard C. McAllister) is "dedicated to the promotion of problem solving literacy." It presents strategies for solving math and physics problems, provides a good overview—with hypertext links to references for the cited materials—of the cognitive research on problem solving and includes an interesting discussion of the role problem solving plays in the learning process.

Conflict, Cooperation, & Rationality: An Introduction to Game Theory
(http://william-king.www.drexel.edu/top/class/game.html)

Game theory is a general class of research focusing on decision-making and factors that affect our definition of rational behavior. This site serves as the syllabus for a course on game theory. It provides an introduction to game theory, outlines the history of this research area, and presents several examples of the "games" used to explain human behavior.

Linguistics FAQ (Frequently Asked Questions)
(http://www.cis.ohio-state.edu/hypertext/faq/usenet/sci-lang-faq/faq.html)

This list contains answers to questions concerning the scientific and historical study of human language (e.g., theories of the origin of language and language acquisition). A few questions addressed include: What is linguistics? What is Noam Chomsky's transformational grammar all about? What is a dialect?

Linguistics Resources
(http://www.sil.org/linguistics/topical.html)

This site provides links to a number of linguistics-related sites on the Internet. Topics covered include speech and phonetics, grammar, semantics, and language acquisition.

The Emergence of Intelligence
(http://weber.u.washington.edu/~wcalvin/sciamer.html)

This *Scientific American* article by William H. Calvin discusses the relationship between language, problem solving, planning skills, and intelligence. In addition to this article, this site contains links to several on-line books and articles dealing with intelligence, language, and evolution.

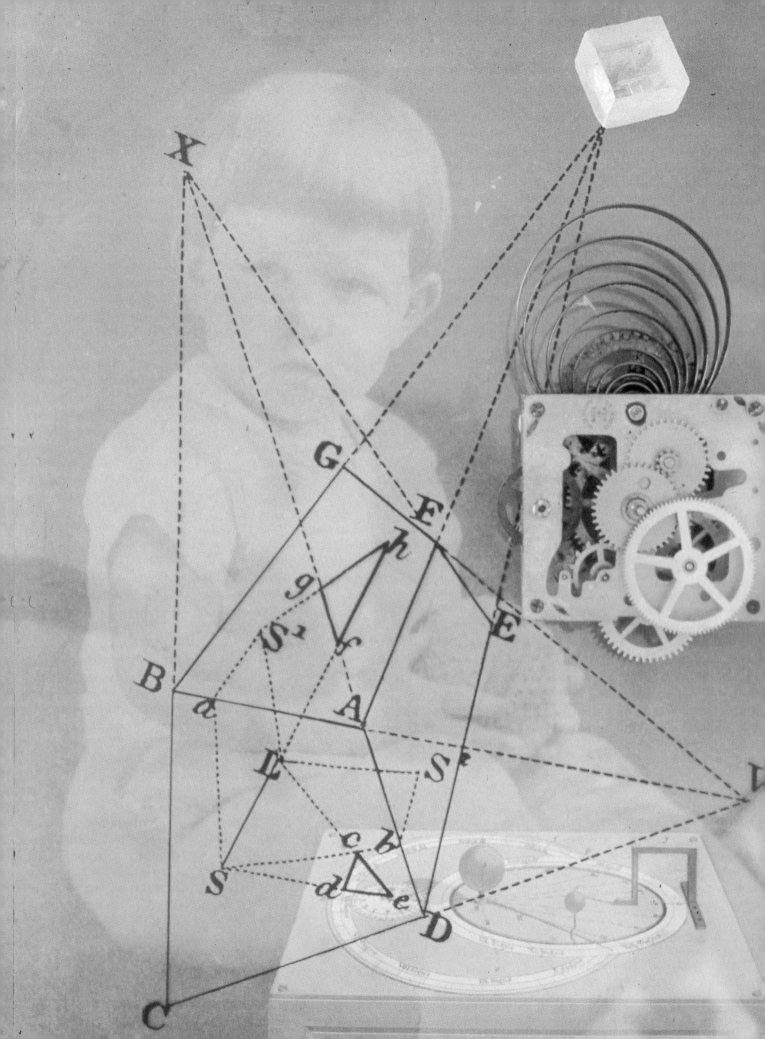

INFANCY and CHILDHOOD

Chapter 9

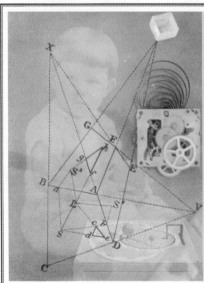

BIOLOGICAL THEME
Which aspects of children's development are most influenced by biological maturation?

LEARNING THEME
What kinds of learning strategies do children use?

COGNITIVE THEME
Does children's thinking go through different stages of development?

DEVELOPMENTAL THEME
When do children establish their self-concepts and sex roles?

SOCIOCULTURAL THEME
How do differences in child-rearing practices influence children's development?

When Susan finally persuaded Michael to come with her to classes for new parents at the local hospital, she had been pregnant for eight months. Susan, who was 25 years old, was surprised to meet the other members of her class because she expected the other pregnant women to be like her. But then she met Sarah, a 41-year-old community college instructor who joked about her biological clock approaching midnight. And then there was Brenda, a 17-year-old who came to class with her mother, and Peggy and her excited husband, who had been trying for seven years to have a child. Finally, there was a very snobby couple in their 30s who seemed annoyed that they had to attend these classes. Michael's reluctance faded quickly as he saw movies of various birth procedures and learned about his responsibilities in the delivery room. Over the next few weeks, he and Susan shared in the preparation and excitement of their anticipated parenthood.

Most people begin to think about their role as a parent when they anticipate childbirth. They also think about midlife crises in their 30s, wonder about sexual decline in their 40s, and worry about retirement in their 50s. In this chapter and the next, we will paint a picture of the life course, from birth to death, so that you can think about the major stages, crises, and accomplishments that people typically experience. We will show general features of development, but we will also try to highlight differences among people around the world who grow up in vastly different settings. Our view of changes across the life span is based mainly on the methods and observations of developmental psychologists.

Developmental psychologists study how people change with age physically, mentally, and socially. They try to explain why people develop certain habits, talents, or disabilities. Their explanations and theories are based on careful observations, studies, and experiments. These developmental descriptions are like collections of photographs showing what people can do at various ages. Uncovering the patterns and sequences that underlie the changes these pictures reveal is rather like the process of creating a motion picture from a set of still photographs.

In this and the following chapter, we will chart many milestones of human development, from conception to death. The study of human development draws from all areas of psychology, including research on memory (discussed in Chapter 7), the principles of learning (covered in Chapter 6), and the study of the brain and the nervous system (introduced in Chapter 2). Because the topic of human development is so broad, we break our discussion into two chapters. This chapter covers development during infancy and childhood up to puberty, about 11 to 13 years of age; Chapter 10 discusses adolescence and adulthood, including old age.

Understanding Human Development

Human development is a continuous process of change involving both biological maturation and the accumulation of experience. As we examine how the forces of heredity and environment interact across the life span, it will be useful to keep several principles in mind. First, development is *cumulative*; experiences, abilities, and attitudes build on each other over time. Second, development is a process of *differentiation*, whereby specific skills are derived from more general abilities. Third, development is *organized*; it is not random or haphazard. And fourth, development is *holistic*, which means that our identities, personalities, mental abilities, and physical abilities change together and are integrated to produce unique individuals.

Charting changes across the life span is not easy. Many factors affect development at different times, and they are often difficult to isolate. Most developmental theories identify major patterns of change as "stages", calling attention to the distinctive characteristics of different periods. (One such developmental timeline is presented in Figure 9.1.) In his theory of psychoanalysis, Sigmund Freud promoted a theory of distinct stages that children pass through in their sexual-emotional development. And when the Swiss psychologist Jean Piaget pioneered the study of children's thinking, he created a comprehensive theory of children's mental development that includes four broad periods. Other developmental theories based on physical or social stages have also been devised to highlight distinctive developmental changes Although such **stage theories** identify periods of stability and relatively abrupt changes in behavior over the life span, other approaches stress the continuous nature of change in behavior as we grow older. As you will discover, development includes some changes that appear gradual and continuous, sometimes called *quantitative changes*, and some that appear rapid and discontinuous with previous behavior, called *qualitative changes*.

FIGURE 9.1
Chronological Stages of Human Development

Psychologists often refer to "stages of development" to describe similar patterns of change in people as they age. Such stages are only approximate landmarks, however, and not precise categories. Children and adults vary in their rates of growth and development. Developmental psychologists are primarily concerned with the sequences and patterns of physical, social, cognitive, and affective development and the cumulative changes that occur throughout the life span.

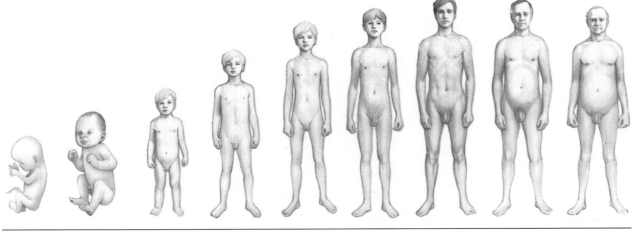

| Prenatal conception | Infancy birth | Toddlerhood 2 years | Preschool 4 years | Middle childhood 6 years | Adolescence 13 years | Young adulthood 20–40 years | Middle age 40–65 years | Old age beyond 65 |

As we discuss general stages of development, keep in mind three things. First, stages serve as a convenient way to divide the life course and to identify patterns, but they are not rigid timetables. People exhibit great variability in the ages at which they reach certain milestones. Second, there is no single theory of development or life stages, because each theory emphasizes different aspects of growth and defines the stages differently. Third, the stages of development are not determined by maturation alone; cultural and historical factors influence development, too. You should be well aware by now that sociocultural factors often exert a strong influence over human thought and behavior, and the changes associated with development and maturation are no exception. Child rearing, adolescence, schooling, and old age differ profoundly around the world and throughout history. Therefore, we would expect development to show similar cultural variability. To understand development, we must consider the whole person and how individuals react to environmental, social, and historical forces (Bronfenbrenner, 1989; Rogoff, 1982; Wertsch and Tulviste, 1992).

THE EMERGENCE OF DEVELOPMENTAL PSYCHOLOGY

Until the nineteenth century, theories of childhood were extremely limited. Thomas Hobbes (1588–1679) believed that children were inherently selfish and should be controlled by society, while, Jean-Jacques Rousseau (1712–1778) believed that children had an intuitive sense of right and wrong, but were often misdirected by adults. These philosophical arguments, as well as interest in pediatrics and education, eventually led to the first scientific studies of children. Society gradually began to view children as individuals valuable enough to care for and study scientifically (Kessen, 1965; White, 1992). However, academic centers for the study of children in the United States and Canada were not well established until the 1930s, and pioneers of the child study movement had to struggle to obtain funds and to convince politicians of the social and educational benefits derived from studying human development. Thus, it is only in the last 60 years that developmental psychology has emerged as a scientific discipline. Moreover, it will continue to change as research on developmental issues are applied to such fields as education, medicine, law, and many social sciences.

Shifting scientific, philosophical, and political attitudes were not the only reasons for the expanding interest in human development. Before 1750, 75 percent of all children died before they reached 5 years of age. As the risks of disease, infection, and abandonment declined, so did the brutally high rate of infant mortality, and today, infant mortality is one-tenth its level 100 years ago. Thus, human development became a topic of interest in part because there were so many more children alive and healthy than in previous years. Meanwhile, life expectancy in the United States was also changing dramatically, increasing from less than 30 years in 1800 to 47 years in 1900 to more than 75 years in 1990. (Expectancies are still slightly higher for women than for men and for whites than for blacks.) These trends, coupled with the "baby boom" following World War II, created an aging population, with increasing numbers of people living long enough to retire. As society began to recognize the importance of child-rearing practices, life-long education, healthy lifestyles, adolescent transitions to adulthood, and the problems facing older adults, the need for the scientific study of human development became apparent.

METHODS OF DEVELOPMENTAL RESEARCH

The study of human development has changed dramatically since its beginnings, when a few nineteenth–century philosophers began recording their children's growth.

These "baby biographies" were the first scholarly records of children's development. Today, developmental psychologists make similar observations using field notes, videotapes, and computerized records of multiple behaviors. A second popular method is to interview people about their attitudes, concepts, and thinking. This type of data collection might include clinical interviews, surveys, or questionnaires. A third method in developmental studies is to investigate the correlation between two variables, such as the relation between the amount of television viewing and the level of aggression among children (as we discussed in Chapter 1). A fourth research method for studying human development is the experimental study, in which a variable is manipulated. A good example is a study of children's memory in which one group is shown how to study and rehearse the items while a control group is left to their usual tactics. These methods and others can be used to study people across the life span.

Developmental psychologists today use many procedures from other areas of psychology, but three research designs are especially suited to test developmental hypotheses. The first is **longitudinal analysis**, the repeated testing of the same individuals over time so that subtle changes can be analyzed over the course of their lives. Longitudinal research can be informal, like some baby biographies, or it can be incredibly detailed, as were Jean Piaget's records of his own children's development. One disadvantage of the longitudinal method is that it takes a long time to collect data from a few individuals. Another problem is that repeated testing may influence how people react to the researcher and the testing, possibly invalidating the results. **Cross-sectional analyses** study different people of varying ages at the same time, rather than examining changes within the same individuals over time. That is, a cross section of children ages 3, 6, 9, and 12 could be studied at the same time, instead of following a single group as they developed over nine years. The cross-sectional approach is less time consuming because it is conducted simultaneously on people of different ages. To follow language development in one child from the second to fourth birthday would require a two-year longitudinal project, but cross-sectional comparisons of the language of 2, 3, and 4-year-olds can be made at the same time. The two methods are summarized and compared in Figure 9.2.

A problem that occurs in both the longitudinal and cross-sectional methods is known as the **cohort effect,** whereby the historical time in which the individuals live affects the outcome of the study. A *cohort* is a group of people who are of similar age. A cohort that grows up during a time of prosperity, war, or other unusual social conditions may be quite different from a cohort growing up at another time (see Figure 9.3 for an example). **Sequential analyses** can overcome the cohort effect by combining features of both longitudinal and cross-sectional designs, as shown in Figure 9.2. Several groups of people of different ages (i.e., a cross section) are identified and studied, but they are tracked for several years (as in the longitudinal studies). For example, Warner Schaie (1983) directed a sequential study, known as the Seattle Longitudinal Study, to determine how IQ scores change among the elderly. Previous cross-sectional studies suggested that IQ declined dramatically with age, but then, the older people in the cross section differed from the younger people in terms of education and other social conditions, as well as in age. Schaie's study began in 1956 with a cross-sectional study of adults from 21 to 70 years of age. The group was retested in 1963, 1970, and 1977, but the researchers also added two new cross-sectional groups of younger people in the mid-1970s. This allowed the researchers to determine if repeated testing affected the subjects in the longitudinal design (did people appear to get better just because they were tested over and over?) and to see if any differences in IQ were due to age or

FIGURE 9.2
Longitudinal and Cross-Sectional Research Designs

A longitudinal study follows the same subjects over an extended time period with repeated testing. A cross-sectional study allows researchers to test children of several different ages at the same time. A cross-sequential design includes features of both. Numbers in boxes indicate years of age. Arrows note when children were studied.

SOURCE: Dember, Jenkins, & Teylor, 1984, p. 80.

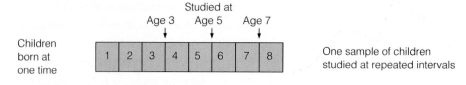

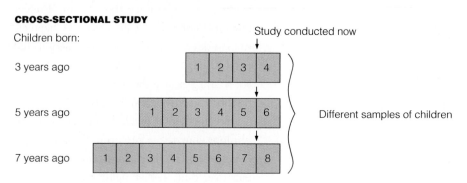

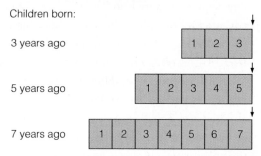

to cohort effects. When the results were analyzed, Schaie concluded that there was little loss in IQ with age. The previous research, which seemed to show dramatic losses, had been confounded with a cohort effect in which the oldest subjects also had the lowest levels of education and had endured the harshest socioeconomic circumstances as children. Thus, a sequential design combining both longitudinal and cross-sectional methods may be the most valid for answering certain developmental questions. However, sequential analyses are both time consuming and expensive.

THE EFFECTS OF HEREDITY AND ENVIRONMENT

Undoubtedly, you have heard children being compared to their parents: "She has her mother's eyes," "She's as stubborn as her father," or "Like father, like son." Whenever we try to explain a developmental outcome, we confront a basic, perplexing question: How much of a behavior or characteristic is due to heredity, and how much is due to the environment? The debate is often referred to as *nature versus nurture*, a phrase you encountered in Chapter 4. Quite simply, *nature* refers to inherited, genetic characteristics; *nurture* refers to experiences such as parental care and the quality of the physical and social environment.

Throughout history, the pendulum has swung back and forth as proponents have argued in favor of nature or nurture as the major determinant of development. Charles Darwin's (1859) theory about natural evolution gave prominence to the role of heredity. It also proposed the idea that each individual child passes through similar stages of

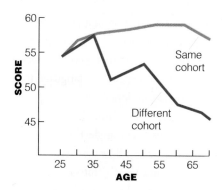

FIGURE 9.3
Cohort Effect in a Study of Mental Abilities

The lower line represents the mental ability scores of a cross-sectional sample of people of different generations, and it seems to indicate that mental abilities drop significantly with age. However, the top line, which represents a single sample of people of the same generation tested at different ages (a longitudinal study), shows that ability changes much less over a person's lifetime than the scores from the cross-sectional study indicate. The difference is due to inherent differences between the generations in baseline ability, resulting from growing up during different historical periods.

SOURCE: Schaie, K. W., & Strother, C. R. (1968). A cross-sectional study of age changes in cognitive behavior. *Psychological Bulletin, 70,* 671–680.

development that characterize the evolution of the human species. By the turn of the twentieth century, Darwin's belief was so well established that G. Stanley Hall, the first American Ph.D. in psychology (Harvard, 1878) and the first president of the American Psychological Association (1892), suggested in 1904 that children would show better social behavior if they were first allowed to play as savages and then as barbarians and nomadic wanderers. He reasoned that they would eventually become socialized because they would have passed through all of the precivilized stages of human society.

In contrast, many psychologists have stressed the ways in which learning in general and conditioning in particular can change how people behave. In 1928, behaviorist John B. Watson published *Psychological Care of Infant and Child,* which contained observations of behavioral development in children. In his book, Watson opposed the views of Darwin and Hall:

> The behaviorists believe that there is nothing from within to develop. If you start with a healthy body, the right number of fingers and toes, eyes, and a few elementary movements that are present at birth, you do not need anything else in the way of raw materials to make a man, be that a genius, a cultured gentleman, a rowdy, or a thug. (Watson, 1928, p. 41)

Watson argued that human development was almost entirely dependent on experience and that from any group of healthy babies he could "guarantee to take any one at random and train him to become any type of specialist I might select—doctor, lawyer, artist, merchant-chief, and yes, even beggar-man and thief, regardless of his talents, penchants, tendencies, abilities, vocations, and race of his ancestors (Watson, 1924, p. 104).

But these arguments are oversimplified, polarized, and outdated. Today, most psychologists refuse to accept the simple proposition that either nature or nurture is entirely responsible for development. Instead, they look at the interaction of the two forces, the dynamic interplay between an individual's biological endowments and environmental opportunities (Rosser, 1994). Sandra Scarr (1992) argues that people help to create their physical and psychological environments. They evoke responses from other people that reinforce their own behaviors. People also choose what environments to experience according to their interests and talents. In this view, the genetic characteristics of the individual drive the selection of experiences.

The interaction between nature and nurture is evident in parents' reactions to attractive and unattractive babies. When adults were shown photos of unfamiliar babies, they picked the most attractive babies as the best behaved, smartest, and most likable (Stephan & Langlois, 1984). They picked the unattractive babies as most likely to cause their parents trouble. Mothers tend to kiss and cuddle attractive babies, whereas they give less affection to unattractive babies (Langlois, 1986). Thus, physical appearance may elicit different kinds of responses from parents. However, babies show similar preferences, looking longer at and reacting more positively to attractive faces (Langlois, Ritter, Togman, & Vaughn, 1991; Langlois, Roggman, & Rieser-Danner, 1990). These preferences of infants and adults may influence parents' expectations about their children and cause them to change their child-rearing practices. Thus, biological potential and experience, nature and nurture, often interact in subtle ways to shape development.

Regardless of whether a developmental characteristic is more influenced by nature or by nurture, timing is important. Psychologists have identified certain time frames that are **sensitive periods,** times when development is proceeding rapidly, with heightened susceptibility to external factors. If a particular behavior is not well established during the sensitive period, it may not develop to its full potential. Conversely, the earlier that a developmental problem is detected and remedial steps are taken, the better the chances for recovery. For example, children need to be exposed to language in the first few years of life, which constitute the sensitive period for language.

As we noted in Chapter 2, the science of behavior genetics, through studies of human families and the selective breeding of animals, helps disentangle the relative contributions of nature and nurture. For example, twin studies allow researchers to compare identical twins (whose genetic makeup is the same) with fraternal twins (who share, on average, 50 percent of their genes). In Chapter 11, you will see how twin studies have been used to evaluate the relative influences of nature and nurture on intelligence, and Chapter 14 explores how such studies have been used to investigate the determinants of personality. Studies of families, kinship, and adopted children have also been helpful in examining the interaction of nature and nurture during development.

Physical Development

The growth of bones, tissue, and nerves begins prenatally and continues throughout the life span. Many physical changes are biologically "programmed" to occur as our bodies mature, but they can be influenced by trauma, nutrition, and a multitude of environmental conditions. As with many human characteristics, the genes of each individual are the blueprint for these developmental changes.

PRENATAL DEVELOPMENT AND CHILDBIRTH

Our study of human development begins before birth, because we can trace genetic heritage from parents and distant ancestors. The genes that transmit this heritage are really combinations of chemicals along the *chromosomes*, the genetic material found in sperm and egg cells. Recall from Chapter 2 that each sperm and egg cell carries 23 chromosomes, which unite during fertilization to form the full complement of 23 pairs. Each chromosome is a string of thousands of DNA (deoxyribonucleic acid) molecules arranged in a ladderlike spiral. During conception, one "leg" of the sperm's ladder combines with one leg of the egg's ladder to form a new spiral ladder—half contributed from each parent. Since each molecule of DNA is made of gene pairs of highly complex sugar and phosphate molecules, the millions of new combinations in the chromosomes of the united sperm and egg yield an individual who is genetically unique.

Stages of Prenatal Development. At conception, a single male sperm cell usually fertilizes the female egg cell in one of the fallopian tubes that connect a woman's ovaries to her uterus (see Figure 9.4). The united sperm and egg constitute a **zygote**, the first cell containing all the genetic information necessary to form the new organism. The cell divides again and again to form a hollow ball of cells, the *blastocyst*, shown in Figure 9.5. The blastocyst moves down the fallopian tube, and by the end of the second week following fertilization, the zygote embeds itself in the uterine lining. From this point, and for the next six weeks or so, the organism is called an **embryo**.

By the end of the first month, the embryo has a heart that pumps blood. Soon after, the embryo generates a nervous system and a rudimentary abdomen. By the second month, the head becomes distinct and the face appears human. Arms and legs begin to appear, and muscles move reflexively. The brain sends out impulses that coordinate

FIGURE 9.4
Conception

The sperm cell usually meets and fertilizes the egg as the egg travels from the ovary to the uterus along a fallopian tube. The developing zygote divides many times on the way to the uterus. Within two weeks after fertilization, the mass of cells, called a blastocyst, is embedded in the wall of the uterus. (The illustration is not drawn to scale.)

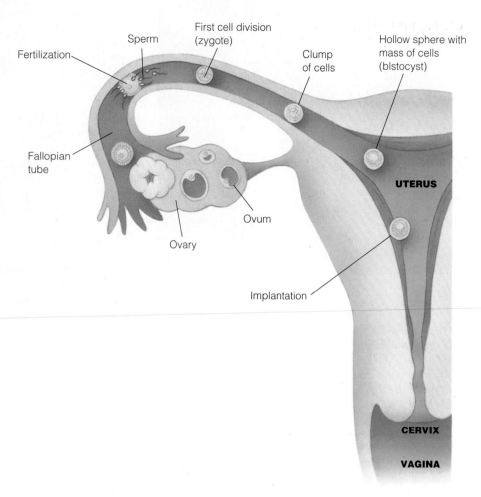

FIGURE 9.5
A Blastocyst

This mass of cells is produced when the fertilized egg divides repeatedly after conception.

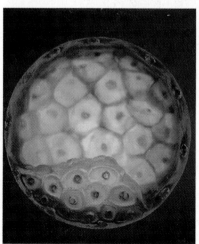

organ systems, the stomach produces digestive juices, the heart beats steadily, and the endocrine system produces hormones. All major bodily systems exist in primitive form. Still, the embryo is only 1 inch long and weighs 1/15 of an ounce.

From approximately eight weeks after fertilization until birth, the organism is designated a **fetus**. During this stage, the soft cartilage begins to harden to bone, nerves and muscles triple in number, and the reproductive system forms. The fetus takes on the appearance of a human baby (see Figure 9.6). By the sixth or seventh month, all major systems have been elaborated, and the fetus may survive if born prematurely. However, premature babies may develop respiratory distress syndrome, a complication that makes breathing difficult and can result in death. Also, about 10 to 20 percent of these low-birthweight babies develop handicaps or intellectual impairment (Astbury et al., 1990; Meisels & Plunkett, 1988).

Risks to the Unborn Child.   Fetal growth can be hindered in a number of ways. Inherited disorders can cause both minor and severe disturbances. Also, a woman who has her first child after the age of 40 has a higher incidence of delivering children with mental retardation or other abnormalities that are present at birth but not necessarily inherited. Disease, injuries, drugs, alcohol, and radiation during pregnancy can all harm an infant's physical and mental development because mother and child do not share the burden equally. A mild dose of radiation to a mother may cripple an embryo or fetus. Diseases such as rubella (German measles) in a mother can cause heart disorders, deafness, and mental retardation in infants, particularly if the mother is affected

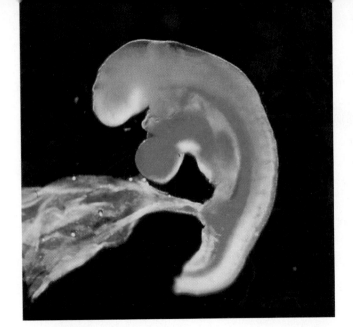

FIGURE 9.6
Prenatal Growth

The shape of the 28-day-old embryo (left) already reveals a distinct head, tail, and limb buds. The embryo is still only 1/16 inch long. In the 9-week-old fetus (right), the rudimentary human form is quite apparent. Because the head and brain develop rapidly, the head is very large in proportion to the rest of the body. The internal organs, toes, and fingers are partially formed in this fetus, but it is only a little more than an inch long.

early in pregnancy. Also, malnourishment during pregnancy can lead to children of low birth weight who grow slowly and have difficulty learning (Sigman et al., 1989; St. James-Roberts, 1979). Finally, smoking tobacco or marijuana during pregnancy has been linked to increased risk of spontaneous abortion and fetal death, as well as placing the children at higher risk for poor language and cognitive development (Fried & Watkinson, 1990).

Parental education about prenatal development is essential, as is medical supervision, because of the staggering number of potential prenatal problems and their dire consequences. For example, babies born to alcoholic mothers may develop heart murmurs, cleft palates, and mental retardation. About 1 in 750 babies now born in the United States suffers from **fetal alcohol syndrome,** a condition in which newborns exhibit lethargy, poor attention, and uncoordinated movements as a consequence of the alcohol circulated through their bodies during pregnancy. These dangers are greatest during the embryonic period, when mothers may not even realize that they are pregnant (Sulik, Johnston, & Webb, 1981). Even moderate drinking can have serious consequences for the neurological development of the unborn child, because alcohol reduces the oxygen supply to the brain (Barr et al., 1990; Streissguth, Barr, & Martin, 1983). Newborn babies of drug addicts react to their mothers' addictions much like the babies who have fetal alcohol syndrome. Newborn babies of heroin or methadone users go through withdrawal, cry often, sleep poorly, and are susceptible to tremors, diarrhea, and convulsions. "Crack babies" face these dangers as well as the risks of strokes and respiratory problems. Finally, in the late 1980s, there was an alarming increase in the number of babies born with AIDS (acquired immune deficiency syndrome). Other sexually transmitted diseases such as gonorrhea, chlamydia, and herpes can be picked up from a mother as a fetus moves through the birth canal. (Because the incubation period for herpes is 4 to 21 days, many babies leave the hospital with the disease undetected.) Almost 25 percent of babies born with genital herpes do not survive (Babson, Pernoll, Benda & Simpson, 1980).

Several methods are available to help diagnose prenatal complications. **Amniocentesis** is a method used to determine the presence of chromosomal abnormalities. A hollow needle is inserted through the woman's abdomen to remove a sample of amniotic fluid from the womb. Because the fluid contains discarded fetal cells, analyses can reveal the abnormalities as well as the baby's gender. Amniocentesis carries some risk and cannot be used until the fourteenth to sixteenth week after concep-

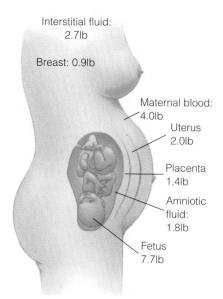

Interstitial fluid: 2.7lb

Breast: 0.9lb

Maternal blood: 4.0lb

Uterus 2.0lb

Placenta 1.4lb

Amniotic fluid: 1.8lb

Fetus 7.7lb

FIGURE 9.7
Average Weight Gain During Pregnancy

Women are encouraged to gain between 20 and 25 pounds during pregnancy to aid their own nutrition as well as the developing child's. Less than a third of the weight gain is due to the baby alone.

SOURCE: Papalia & Olds, 1985, p. 397.

tion. A newer method, **chorionic villus sampling (CVS),** can be done as early as the eighth week after conception, but it is slightly more risky. In this procedure, a tube is inserted into the pregnant woman's cervix and some fetal cells are suctioned off for analysis. **Ultrasound** is a noninvasive technique that provides some information about fetal growth. High-frequency sound waves are directed through a woman's abdomen, and the reflected waves provide an image of the fetus, much like sonar. Heart rate and movement can be observed directly. Bone growth, body proportions, and the sex of the child can also be determined.

The best advice for pregnant women is to stay in good health, to avoid drugs, tobacco, and alcohol, to exercise moderately, and to follow a balanced diet (Schuster & Ashburn, 1986). Pregnant women require at least three meals each day to gain the extra 20 to 25 pounds needed to support the fetus (see Figure 9.7). They should consult a physician early in pregnancy and continue regular checkups throughout pregnancy. Most hospitals and communities offer birthing classes that provide prospective parents with valuable information about prenatal development, maternal health, and birth procedures.

Childbirth. The process of childbirth usually begins about 266 days after conception. There are three distinct stages in the birth of a child. The first stage, labor, begins when a woman experiences uterine contractions and ends when her cervix is fully dilated to allow the baby's exit. This process lasts about 8 to 14 hours for a first child, but only half as long for subsequent children. The second stage involves the delivery of the baby, illustrated in Figure 9.8. The head is usually delivered first, but occasionally the legs or buttocks emerge first (a breech delivery). The third stage is the delivery of the placenta, or afterbirth. Because birth can be a long and painful process, medical interventions, such as medication to relieve pain or relax muscles, are often required. However, medications during delivery can bring additional risks to the baby that may persist through the first year of life (Brackbill, 1979; Sanders-Phillips, Strauss, & Guthberlet, 1988).

Ultrasound produces a grainy image, but critical features can be identified.

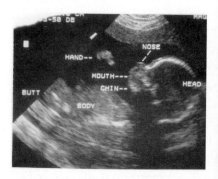

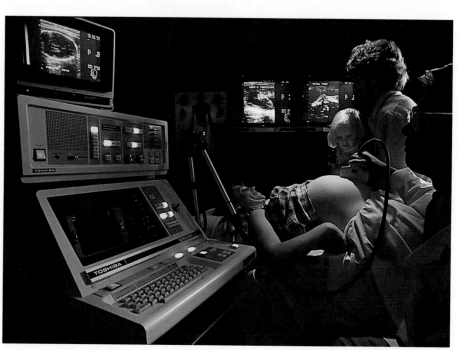

FIGURE 9.8
Childbirth

As labor begins, the baby is positioned for delivery. Muscular contractions in the uterus during labor cause the cervix to dilate and the baby to pass through the birth canal.

SOURCE: Shaffer, 1985, p. 142.

1. BEFORE LABOR BEGINS

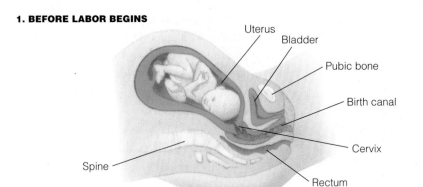

Uterus
Bladder
Pubic bone
Birth canal
Cervix
Rectum
Spine

2. TRANSITION: JUST BEFORE BABY'S HEAD ENTERS THE BIRTH CANAL

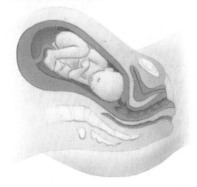

3. BABY'S HEAD BEFORE CROWNING

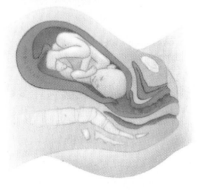

HEAD CROWNING

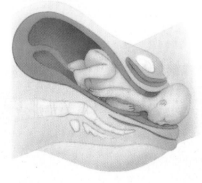

4. HEAD EMERGING

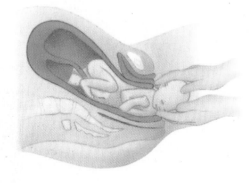

Vaginal delivery is not always possible. When labor becomes stalled, when a fetus is not positioned well, or when there is a risk to mother or fetus, a baby is delivered surgically through the mother's abdomen. This procedure is called a *caesarean section*, and it occurs in about 15 percent of deliveries. Advocates of natural childbirth argue that the frequency of caesarean sections has increased dramatically during the past 15 years and that the procedure is often prescribed unnecessarily.

Because of the possible disadvantages of medicated deliveries, many people advocate natural childbirth techniques. The popular Lamaze method, for example, stresses the mother's control of breathing and muscular contractions to relieve the pain and to assist the delivery. Fathers can assist mothers, acting as coaches for exercises in self-control both before and during childbirth. Some people advocate giving birth at home or in comfortable surroundings with family members present, although techniques such as the Leboyer method of gentle birth in a dimly lit, quiet room are controversial. Critics point out the dangers of infection or poor observation in dim light as well as the lack of differences between babies born conventionally or by such methods (Nelson et al., 1980). No matter what birth method is preferred, recent obstetric advances have helped to educate future parents and make more options available.

GROWTH AND MUSCULAR COORDINATION IN INFANTS AND CHILDREN

Newborn babies appear helpless. They sleep 16 to 17 hours each day, cannot crawl or even roll over, and communicate almost entirely by crying or gurgling. However, babies are born with muscular and sensory responses that quickly adapt to the outside world. An innate *rooting reflex* causes them to turn their head toward any touch on their cheek, allowing them to find a nipple easily. And a *sucking reflex* allows newborns to feed from a breast or bottle immediately. In fact, one study showed that during the first few weeks after birth, babies can learn to modify sucking patterns to obtain nourishment (Sameroff, 1968). In this study, the rate of delivery of the milk through a plastic nipple was controlled by the experimenter. The infants quickly adjusted the strength of their biting or sucking to keep the milk coming.

Average newborns weigh about 7 1/2 pounds, but they can double their birth weight by 6 months and triple it by their first birthday. Newborns cannot support their own body weight while standing, partly because their bones are so flexible. The skeleton grows and hardens with age. The soft spots in the skull join and harden by the age of 2, while the leg bones continue to grow well into adolescence. Newborns have relatively large heads and small limbs. After age 2 until puberty, children grow 2 to 3 inches in height and gain 6 to 7 pounds each year. With increasing age, the body proportions change sharply, as shown in Figure 9.9.

Diet and stimulation are extremely important to an infant because half of the brain weight is added from the months before birth until the second birthday. At birth the brain is only 25 percent of its eventual adult size, but by age 3, it is 75 percent of its adult size (Schuster & Ashburn, 1986). Primary motor and sensory areas of

FIGURE 9.9
Body Proportions from Fetal Stage to Adulthood

The head represents 50 percent of body length at 2 months after conception but only 12 to 13 percent of adult stature. In contrast, the legs constitute about 12 to 13 percent of the total length of a 2-month-old fetus but 50 percent of the height of a 25-year-old adult.

SOURCE: Robbins et al., 1929.

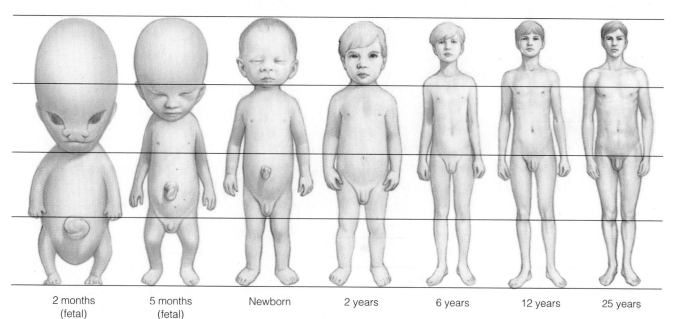

| 2 months (fetal) | 5 months (fetal) | Newborn | 2 years | 6 years | 12 years | 25 years |

the brain mature during this time, and myelinization of neurons occurs. Between 6 and 12 months of age, there are important changes in the electrical activity and functions of the cortex that promote better muscular control and memory development (Goldman-Rakic, 1987). Speech and other functions located primarily in one hemisphere are not fully developed neurologically until adolescence or adulthood (Schuster & Ashburn, 1986).

Muscular development follows the same head-to-tail sequence as other bodily systems, which is why babies can raise their heads before they can control their arms and legs. The sequence of growth during infancy is rapid and uniform. Most babies can sit in a high chair by 6 months and crawl by 10 months (see Figure 9.10). However, physical growth and coordination vary tremendously among children. Some walk as early as 8 months of age, while others may not walk until 20 months. Longer legs, better balance and muscle control, and the shift of the center of gravity as the legs lengthen help most children learn to walk by 12 to 15 months (Thelen, 1984).

Cultural differences can also influence the age at which children learn to walk. Among the Ache, a nomadic people in Paraguay, infants spend nearly all their first three years in physical contact with the mother. They seldom are allowed to crawl or explore the jungle in which they live. Consequently, they do not walk until they are almost 2 years old (Kaplan & Dove, 1987). In contrast, Kipsigi mothers in western Kenya actively teach their babies to sit, stand, and walk, and Kipsigi infants reach these milestones a month earlier than American infants. Jamaican mothers also help their infants by stretching and massaging their limbs. Their babies walk at about 10 months of age, nearly 3 months earlier than most American infants (Hopkins & Westra, 1990).

The 2-year-old is a toddler who often falls down and appears clumsy. A 4-year-old can hop, run, dance, and catch a large ball with both hands. By 4 or 5 years of age,

FIGURE 9.10
Sequence of Infant Growth

Physical growth during infancy is a gradual series of maturational changes that allow better control of actions and perceptions. Although there are differences among babies from different ethnic origins in terms of temperament, reactions, and rate of development, most infants follow this general sequence.

SOURCE: Adapted from Shirley, 1923.

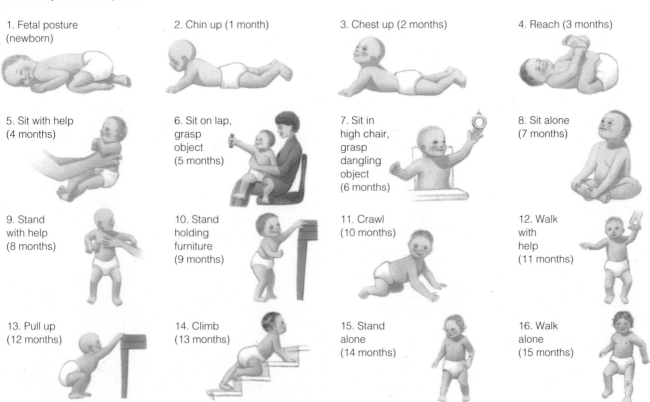

1. Fetal posture (newborn)

2. Chin up (1 month)

3. Chest up (2 months)

4. Reach (3 months)

5. Sit with help (4 months)

6. Sit on lap, grasp object (5 months)

7. Sit in high chair, grasp dangling object (6 months)

8. Sit alone (7 months)

9. Stand with help (8 months)

10. Stand holding furniture (9 months)

11. Crawl (10 months)

12. Walk with help (11 months)

13. Pull up (12 months)

14. Climb (13 months)

15. Stand alone (14 months)

16. Walk alone (15 months)

most children exhibit a clear preference for handedness. As children lose their baby fat and acquire more adultlike body proportions, they gain better balance. Maturation also brings better small-muscle coordination and eye-hand coordination. On the average, girls develop faster than boys but have less muscle tissue and tend to be lighter and shorter than boys.

The Role of Nutrition and Health.   Because physical growth influences all aspects of a child's development, it is important to provide sufficient nutrition for infants and children. Feeding babies breast milk has at least two advantages. First, maternal antibodies can be provided to the infant through breast milk, thereby protecting babies from disease (Whaley & Wong, 1988). Second, breast milk seems to aid intellectual development. In one study, 300 premature infants were fed by tubes with either breast milk, formula, or a combination of the two (Lucas, Morley, Cole, Lister, & Leeson-Payne, 1992). Eight years later, when the children were given intelligence tests, the scores of the children fed breast milk, alone or in combination, were 10 points higher than the scores of the children who had received only formula. Thus, breast milk may provide substances that foster general health and mental development.

Malnutrition is a severe threat to a young child's health because children become listless and cease to grow when calorie intake is insufficient. Such children are lethargic and stare vacantly, rather than exploring their environments. Malnourished children have stunted height, weight, and coordination, as well as impaired brain development and intelligence (Parmelee & Sigman, 1983). The sluggishness of malnourished children affects their play, learning, and motivation. For example, children in rural Kenya who had suffered from malnutrition since birth had difficulty concentrating in school and performed poorly on mental tests (Sigman et al., 1989).

Socioeconomic factors influence nutrition, health, and growth. Studies in Europe, Asia, and Africa, as well as North and South America, have revealed that children in upper socioeconomic groups are taller, and heavier, and also have a wider head circumference and thicker upper arms than their peers in lower socioeconomic groups (Bogin, 1988; Meredith, 1984). Children in lower socioeconomic groups are at greater risk for infant mortality, childhood diseases, malnutrition, and inadequate health care. These children also may work longer and harder and receive less cognitive stimulation than children in upper socioeconomic groups. Nearly a third of the children in North and South America live in poverty, and many are malnourished (Office of Technology Assessment, 1992).

There is, however, some reason for optimism. Public health programs can overcome the effects of malnutrition. For example, Super, Herrara, and Mora (1990) conducted an intervention program with Guatemalan families. Beginning in the last three months of a woman's pregnancy, food supplements were given to her and her family for three years. A control group did not receive the supplements. When the children were 6 years old, less than 20 percent of the children who received dietary supplements had delayed growth, compared to more than 50 percent of the children in the control group. Other studies suggest that timing the administration of the supplements is important, too. Food supplements begun during the mothers' pregnancy were much more effective than supplements begun when the children were 2 years old (Pollitt, Garza, & Mora, 1984).

Although there can be no guarantees for normal, healthy growth, it is clear that good nutrition, parental practices, and early stimulation can all contribute to a child's healthy development.

Breast feeding promotes the attachment between mother and infant

Perceptual Development

Babies are born with several sensory responses nearly fully developed, with touch, taste, and smell the most developed at birth. Sensitivity to touch is apparent in early reflexes, and all newborns are tested for the presence of these reflexes. Newborns prefer sweet tastes to sour or bitter, and their facial expressions clearly show their reactions. Likewise, infants have a keen sense of smell. Two-week-old breast-fed babies can discriminate the odor of their own mothers as measured by their preference to turn toward a gauze pad that had been taped to their mother's armpit rather than pads that had been worn by other women (Cernoch & Porter, 1985).

Hearing is less developed at birth than the senses of touch, taste, or smell, but studies have shown that infants are not totally deaf. Newborns prefer listening to human speech, especially exaggerated, high-pitched voices (Cooper & Aslin, 1990). This may be why adults often speak to infants with squeaky, rhythmic voices commonly called "baby talk."

Vision is probably the least developed sensory system at birth. Recall from Chapter 4 that babies are nearsighted; their distance vision is approximately 20/600. They see objects best when the objects are 6 to 10 inches from their faces, but objects at any distance may appear blurred until 6 months of age because infants have difficulty accommodating (changing the shape of the lens in their eye) to focus (Banks, 1980; Hainline & Abramov, 1992). By 2 months of age, however, they can discriminate colors and brightness reasonably well (Bornstein, 1979; Teller & Bornstein, 1987).

Visual perception and preferences develop rapidly. Using an apparatus like the one shown in Figure 9.11, Fantz (1961, 1963; Fantz, Fagan, & Miranda, 1975) demonstrat-

FIGURE 9.11
Apparatus Used to Study Infant Perception

A baby lying on its back, can perceive the different objects placed above its head. The researcher can peer through the peephole into the infant's eyes and determine where the baby's gaze is directed, thereby measuring the baby's attentional preferences.

SOURCE: Shaffer, 1985, p. 209.

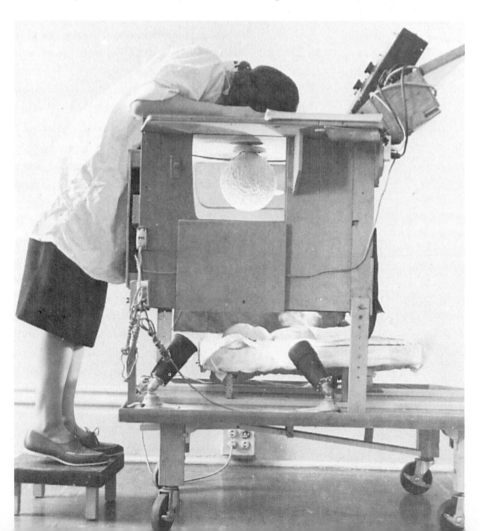

FIGURE 9.12
The Visual Cliff

The infant is coaxed to crawl on the glass over the "deep" side of the visual cliff apparatus.

ed that infants can discriminate visual patterns. Placed in this equipment, infants lay on their backs and looked at the ceiling of the chamber. Their eyes reflected the stimulus on which their gaze was fixed, so that the researcher, looking down through a peephole, could determine which stimulus attracted the child's attention. Fantz (1961) showed that infants prefer to look at patterns rather than at random arrangements of the same elements. This finding has been replicated in numerous studies, often in experiments investigating how the Gestalt principles of organization (discussed in Chapter 4) develop (Dodwell, Humphrey, & Muir, 1987).

The contour, complexity, and curvature of shapes are important dimensions of infant visual preferences, and this may be why infants often prefer to stare at faces. Despite this preference, infants cannot discriminate between their mother's face and the faces of strangers until 3 months of age, and memory for faces is not good until 6 months (Barrera & Maurer, 1981; Cohen, DeLoache, & Strauss, 1979). Mother-infant bonds of attachment begin to form during the first six months as infants' perceptual and memory abilities improve.

Infants also show a remarkable ability to perceive spatial depth. Eleanor Gibson and Richard Walk (1960) designed a *visual cliff* to test infants' depth perception (see Figure 9.12). The apparatus is actually like a glass table with a runway down the middle. On one side of the runway is a checkerboard pattern just below the glass surface. On the other side, the checkerboard is several feet below the glass, producing an illusion of a deep well. The question researchers posed was whether infants would be as likely to crawl from the runway onto the deep side as onto the shallow side. Gibson and Walk observed that few 6-month-old infants would cross the deep side, even with their mothers on the other side encouraging them. However, depth perception may originate even earlier than 6 months, since the ability to perceive depth is necessary for the development of walking and hand-eye coordination.

Cognitive Development

When does thinking and the acquisition of knowledge begin? Infants recognize familiar stimuli, respond to cues, and show conditioned responses in the first months of life. Yet, mental representation of events and manipulation of symbols seem to appear much later. Most theorists agree that intellectual development begins with an infant's understanding of actions, objects, and perceptions during the first year of life. The assessment of thinking during infancy is extremely difficult, however, because babies cannot answer questions, perform complex responses, or stay attentive very long. Older children can demonstrate their cognitive skills in many ways, and there is a wealth of information on the way thinking develops beyond infancy. We will review two major perspectives on cognitive development: the stage theory of Jean Piaget and the information-processing approach.

PIAGET'S THEORY

The Swiss scientist and philosopher Jean Piaget (1896–1980) was a pioneer in the study of children's thinking. More than 60 years ago, he began to record his observations of children as they solved simple problems. He viewed children as active seekers of knowledge who used their curiosity to discover basic information about the world. Piaget believed that children constructed ideas about their world as they explored their physical and social environments. He sought to understand how these ideas developed from the practical, action-oriented behaviors of infants to the reflective, logical thinking of adults.

Piaget's ideas about development were influenced by his biological training. His main concerns were with the organization of behavior and knowledge and with the adaptation of the person to the environment. Piaget believed that every act, from grasping a rattle to solving a physics problem, was organized. He believed that mental and behavioral organization were improved by two dynamic processes of adaptation: assimilation and accommodation. **Assimilation** is the process of taking in new information about the world and fitting it into existing ideas. For example, if a child has a concept of horses but not of cows then the first time he sees a cow he may call it "horse." This is an example of a mistake arising from incorrectly applying the process of assimilation. **Accommodation,** on the other hand, is a way of creating a new concept for new information. Children change their ideas about the world to fit new information. For example, young children often refer to all vehicles as "cars." When they see a van, they may point to it and say "car," a case of *assimilating* a new experience into their own preexisting concepts. As they are taught by parents and others to discriminate vans, trucks, and other vehicles from cars, they establish new concepts by *accommodating* their previous notions, such as by dividing a general category (vehicles) into subcategories (cars, vans, trucks) in this case. In Piaget's theory, the processes of assimilation and accommodation occur together; children who experience something new are constantly trying to fit it into their existing ideas *and* to generate new concepts. This "push and pull" leads to a temporary balance, or *equilibrium*, that reflects children's reconciliation of new information with their previous levels of understanding. Piaget felt that children's curiosity was motivated by their desire to achieve equilibrium.

Piaget provided a systematic description of the way the rules and content of thought change throughout childhood. His theory divides cognitive development into four broad periods: sensorimotor (birth to 2 years), preoperational (2 to 7 years), concrete operational (7 to 11 years), and formal operational (11 years to adulthood). The ages given for each stage and the characteristic behavior are only approximate; it is the quality of the child's thinking, not chronological age, that determines the stage. Piaget's stages and descriptions have been challenged and revised considerably during the past 30 years. As we discuss Piaget's stages, we will also present the new research that modifies his claims.

Sensorimotor Period: Birth to 2 Years.   During the **sensorimotor stage,** infants discover the relations between their perceptions and their actions (motor behavior). They often repeat actions that produce interesting sights and sounds. They learn to manipulate objects, use tools, and take an active role in their environment. Children also form basic concepts of objects and begin to understand relations based on time, space, and cause and effect.

Throughout the first year, infants learn to connect what they do with the people and things around them. They learn how to react to changes in the environment and even how to control the environment. Watson and Ramey (1972) investigated this developing sense of control by placing 2-month-old babies in special cribs for 10 minutes a day. For one group of infants, a mobile above each crib turned every time a baby pressed his or her head against the pillow. For another group, the mobile turned periodically regardless of what the baby did. A third group never saw the mobile turn. After two weeks, only infants in the first group were pressing against the pillow more frequently. The experimenters concluded that these infants had learned to control the

During the sensorimotor period, infants explore objects, discover their features, and learn to manipulate things in their environment.

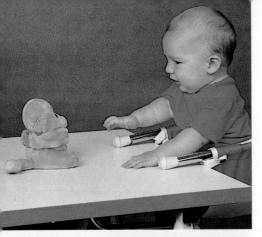

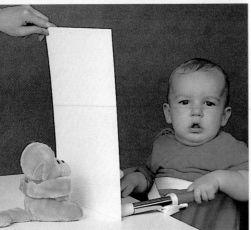

Piaget's observations led him to conclude that babies younger than 6 months do not realize that a hidden object still exists. Here the baby seems to lose interest in the toy animal when it is hidden from view.

mobile by pressing the pillow. In a similar study, Rovee-Collier (1987; 1993) showed that 2-month-old infants could learn to kick their legs to move mobiles (via ribbons attached to their feet) and could remember the relation for several days, thereby demonstrating infants' capacity for long-term memory.

Imagine that you are feeding applesauce to a 4-month-old. You stop for a moment, put the spoon down, and slowly push it off the table. The child may smile or laugh, but probably won't look at the floor. At that age, out of sight means out of mind. Four months later, if you drop the spoon, the infant will probably look down to see where it has gone. At this stage, babies begin to throw things down themselves. (The drop-some-thing-and-watch-somebody-retrieve-it game is usually more fun for infants than for parents!) Around 6 months of age, babies begin to realize that things exist even when they are not in sight, a concept that Piaget called **object permanence.** Although the concept may seem obvious to you, Piaget felt that humans do not start life with this knowledge.

Object permanence indicates that infants possess mental representations for missing objects (Small, 1990). Piaget provided an interesting vignette about a boy named Gerard who had rudimentary notions of object permanence:

> Gerard, at 13 months, knows how to walk, and is playing ball in a large room. He throws the ball, or rather lets it drop in front of him and, either on his feet or on all fours, hurries to pick it up. At a given moment, the ball rolls under an armchair. Gerard sees it and, not without some difficulty, takes it out in order to resume the game. Then the ball rolls under a sofa at the other end of the room. Gerard has seen it pass under the fringe of the sofa; he bends down to recover it. But as the sofa is deeper than the armchair and the fringe does prevent a clear view, Gerard gives up after a moment; he gets up, crosses the room, goes right under the armchair and carefully explores the place where the ball was before. (Piaget, 1954, p. 59)

Gerard searched for the ball in the most likely place—under the armchair where he found it before, not under the sofa. His ideas about locations of objects and how to search for them would not develop completely until age 2.

Preoperational Period: 2 to 7 Years. Children's thinking changes dramatically during the preschool and early school years. Two-year-olds who are just beginning to talk grow quickly into mobile, inquisitive explorers. The period between ages 2 and 7 is a bridge between infantile sensorimotor actions and the logical thinking of later childhood. While infants are concerned mainly with exploration and play, preschoolers try to control and explain relations among events and to classify and conceptualize the phenomena that they discover. That is, the older children can be viewed as more actively trying to make sense of the world around them by organizing their knowledge about it into coherent, ordered structures. Piaget labeled this stage the **preoperational period,** a time in which the capacity for logical operations of thought is lacking.

Piaget's description of preschoolers emphasizes their nonlogical and limited reasoning abilities, but newer research has shown that preschoolers have much greater understanding and fewer limitations than Piaget presumed, especially knowledge about living things and about other people's intentions and emotions (Rosser, 1994). We consider three prominent examples of reasoning by preschoolers: causal reasoning, the appearance/reality distinction, and egocentrism.

Causal Reasoning. Piaget studied young children's thinking by asking them why boats float, how bicycles work, and so on. Consider this example from Piaget's conversation with a 6-year-old about the origin of the sun and moon. (Piaget's questions are in regular type. The child's answers are in italics.)

How did the sun begin? *It was when life began.* Has there always been a sun? *No.* How did it begin? *Because it knew life had begun.* What is it made of? *Of fire.* But how? *Because there was fire up there.* How was the fire made in the sky? *It was lighted with a match.* Where did it come from, this match? *God threw it away.* How did the moon begin? *Because we began to be alive.* What did this do? *It made the moon get bigger.* Is the moon alive today? *No . . . Yes.* Why? *Because we are alive.* (Piaget, 1929, pp. 258–259)

This example reveals several characteristics of causal reasoning by preschoolers. First, there is a search for simple, final, and straightforward causes. Second, although children are often confused about what is alive, they believe that living things, gods, and people all act alike to cause events. Third, causes and effects sometimes get reversed. For example, when Piaget presented incomplete sentences ending with *because*, the children typically confused cause and consequence when they completed the sentences. One exchange went as follows: "I had a bath because . . . *afterwards I was clean.* I've lost my pen because . . . *I'm not writing.* He fell off his bike because . . . *he hurt himself*"(Piaget, 1926, pp. 17–18).

Preschoolers often display poor causal reasoning when they try to explain scientific concepts, hypothetical events, or unfamiliar machines. However, they can reason more accurately about the causes and effects that they observe directly (Bauer & Mandler, 1989). For example, Bullock and Gelman (1979) showed 3- to 5-year-olds a ball rolling down a ramp followed by a jumping jack that popped up. Then they showed the children a second ball rolling down the ramp. When asked which ball made the jumping jack move, most children chose the first ball. Even when the experiment was varied so that the ramp and the jumping jack were physically separated or the ball's path was hidden, preschoolers correctly understood that causes precede consequences.

The Appearance/Reality Distinction. Preoperational children's mental representations are confined mostly to concrete and immediate experiences. The children often do not distinguish the real from the imagined. Dreams are taken to be actual happenings, shared by other people. Preschoolers are easily fooled by appearances. They may believe that a girl is no longer a girl if she wears her brother's clothes and acts like him. DeVries (1969) tested 3- to 6-year-olds' understanding of identity by having the children play with a cat and then having a dog mask placed on the animal. DeVries asked, "Now what animal is it? Can it bark? Would it rather eat cat food or dog food?" The 3-year-olds believed that the cat had turned into a dog; the 4- and 5-year-olds were confused, but said that the cat was a dog when it wore the mask; but the 6-year-olds knew that the cat remained a cat.

Flavell and his colleagues tested preschoolers' understanding of the appearance/reality distinction by showing them objects that looked like one thing but were really another—a sponge that looked like a rock, for example, or white milk poured in a translucent red plastic container (Flavell, Green, & Flavell, 1986). The experimenters posed two questions: "What does it look like to your eyes right now?" and "What is it really and truly?" Surprisingly, 3-year-olds said that the objects looked like a rock and red milk and that this is what they were in reality! This same confusion has been observed among Chinese and American children with widely different early childhood experiences (Flavell, Zhang, Zou, Dong, & Qi, 1983). As Piaget claimed, 3-year-olds reason according to their immediate perceptions and are completely swayed by an object's appearance. Contrary to Piaget's theory, most 5- to 6-year-olds can distinguish the enduring identity of an object despite changes in its appearance. That is why 3-year-olds may be more distressed than 5-year-olds by the sight of people dressed in Halloween costumes.

Preschoolers enjoy dressing up and pretending. It stimulates their imaginations and allows them to interact in new roles as different characters.

Egocentrism. Piaget thought that preschoolers are **egocentric**. That is, they believe that everyone sees exactly what they do and do not realize that other people have different points of view. Later research has shown, however, that young children can appreciate someone else's visual or social perspective. In an effort to examine children's egocentrism, Lempers, Flavell, and Flavell (1977) designed some clever materials, such as a stick with pictures glued to each end and a box with a picture taped to the inside bottom. The researchers gave these objects to the children with the instructions, "Tell me what you see. Make it hard for me to see it." If the children were truly egocentric, then they should believe that other people could see the same objects that were visible to the children. Clearly, this was not the case. Even 2-year-olds would turn the stick or tip the box to prevent the adults from seeing the pictures. In this and subsequent studies, it was found that preschoolers could verbally share visual information, then show pictures to another person, and later hide objects or orient another's line of sight to objects (Flavell, 1985). Preschoolers know that other people see things differently, but they still have difficulty explaining or imagining the differences (Newcombe & Huttenlocher, 1992).

Despite their limitations, preschoolers struggle to discover and conceptualize the regularities in the world. They may maintain contradictions, reason illogically, and cling to incorrect beliefs, but their cognitive and social stubbornness may simply reveal their efforts to construct order from a growing body of information. Their ability to understand symbols and their rapidly improving language skills facilitate their cognitive organization.

Concrete Operational Period: 7 to 11 Years. Sometime between 5 and 7 years of age, most children seem to undergo an intellectual revolution that represents a turning point in several stage theories of development. The Soviet psychologist Lev Vygotsky (1962) suggested that children learn how to direct their own thinking during this time by talking to themselves. Others have described the developmental change as a shift from perceptually based to conceptually based reasoning (Bruner, 1972; Flavell, 1985; White, 1965). Of course, the fact that most children begin school during this period plays a big role in the development of their cognitive abilities.

According to Piaget, during the early school years, children develop systematic mental rules (operations) that can be applied flexibly to a variety of problems. He termed this age the **concrete operational period** because thinking is applied to concrete, not abstract, problems. The mental rules permit children to overcome perceptual constraints when solving problems. They begin to understand that the rules can be reversed. For example, multiplication and division, like subtraction and addition, undo the effects of each other. Actions can also be reversed. A lump of clay can be stretched or rolled out and then returned to its original shape. All of these transformations illustrate the notion of **reversibility,** the idea that one action can be undone by another. During this period, children also learn that operations can conserve properties of objects. Whether they roll out the clay or pinch some off, they can roll it back or add the pinched clay back again to have the same clay, in the same amount, and in the same shape. Piaget studied the way children learn about such operations and the way operations help children solve problems. We will briefly illustrate some of these operations and their applications along with Piaget's findings.

Classification. If you present pictures of common objects to 4-year-olds and ask them to put the pictures that go together in piles, they may group the pictures by size or by color. The ability to shift attention from obvious perceptual characteristics like color or size to more conceptual categories such as animal, vegetable, and mineral or furniture, toys, and food develops during the preschool years. As discussed in Chapter 8, concepts based on natural categories (e.g., living things) or generic terms (e.g., trees) are easier for children to learn than other concepts (Carey, 1985). Sorting objects according to two characteristics simultaneously is more difficult, and this ability may not appear until middle childhood. Piaget found that until the concrete operational period, children do not understand category and class relationships thoroughly.

In one test of children's understanding about classification and hierarchical relations, Piaget showed children a picture containing seven tulips and four daisies and asked, "Are there more tulips or more flowers?" A preoperational 5-year-old would characteristically say, "More tulips." A child in the concrete operational stage would correctly reason that the class flowers contains the two subclasses tulips and daisies. Young children apparently have a difficult time with this kind of problem because they are not used to thinking about objects in two different ways—say, as tulips and also as flowers (e.g., Wilkinson, 1976). Nevertheless, classifying objects conceptually seems to improve significantly in the concrete operational period.

Conservation. Perhaps the most distinctive feature of Piaget's concrete operational period (and also its most thoroughly investigated) is **conservation,** the understanding that an underlying physical dimension remains unchanged despite superficial changes in appearance. Piaget studied the way children understand this difficult concept. For example, when do children know that the number of objects in a collection remains the same whether the objects are neatly arranged or scattered about? Preoperational children often focus their attention on a single aspect of an object, so when a task requires simultaneous consideration of several aspects, they often make mistakes. Piaget called this tendency to focus on single aspects **centration**. For example, to decide whether a short, fat glass can hold as much liquid as a tall, thin one, children must shift their attention from a simple judgment based on height or width alone. Preoperational children do not take into account such trade-offs between the dimensions of the glass, and they reason primarily on the basis of a single perceptual feature.

Adults take conservation for granted, and our understanding of the physical world depends on it. Piaget asked questions of children regarding different physical dimensions (see Figure 9.13): "Which row of apples has more or are they the same?" "Which container has more liquid or do they have the same amount?" Children's answers and their explanations for their choices reveal that conservation is not understood well until the concrete operational period. Once again, Piaget's claims are not accepted without criticism. Some types of conservation may not even be fully understood by adults (Hall & Kingsley, 1968; Pulos, 1992). Other researchers have shown that conservation can be learned by preoperational children when training is provided or when the task is simplified (Gelman, 1978). Finally, many researchers point to the fact that these tasks may measure children's linguistic abilities more than their ability to conceptualize conservation, because their answers require verbal justifications (Small, 1990).

Formal Operational Period: 11 to 15 Years. During the **formal operational period**, adolescents become capable of solving abstract problems through logical operations. For example, they can deduce logical conclusions and can test hypotheses to arrive at correct answers. There is some controversy about formal operations, however, because it may be that we acquire this kind of abstract reasoning only for some kinds

FIGURE 9.13
Typical Tasks to Measure Conservation

A child must realize that the physical dimensions of objects remain unchanged despite their new appearances. Understanding conservation of number, substance, and length generally precedes understanding conservation of area and volume.

SOURCE: Gardner, 1982.

CONSERVATION OF NUMBER

Two equivalent rows of objects are shown to a child, who agrees that they have the same number.

One row is lengthened, and the child is asked whether one row now has more objects.

CONSERVATION OF SUBSTANCE

An experimenter shows a child two identical clay balls. The child acknowledges that the two balls have equal amounts of clay.

The experimenter changes the shape of one of the balls and asks the child whether the balls still contain equal amounts of clay.

CONSERVATION OF LENGTH

Two sticks are aligned in front of a child. The child agrees that they are the same length.

After moving one stick to the left or right, the experimenter asks the child whether the sticks are still equal in length.

CONSERVATION OF AREA

Two identical sheets of cardboard have wooden blocks placed on them in identical positions. A child is asked whether the same amount of space is left on each piece of cardboard.

The experimenter scatters the blocks on one piece of cardboard and again asks the child whether the two pieces have the same amount of unoccupied space.

CONSERVATION OF VOLUME

Two balls are placed in two identical glasses with an equal amount of water. A child sees that the balls displace equal amounts of water.

The experimenter changes the shape of one of the balls and asks the child whether it will still displace the same amount of water.

of culturally specific tasks or only with formal schooling. This cognitive stage is discussed more fully in Chapter 10.

Piaget's theory (the main points of which are outlined in the Concept Summary on the following page) was most popular and influential in the 1960s and 1970s, but it has come under increasing criticism. Some researchers have shown that Piaget considerably underestimated preschoolers' abilities (Gelman, 1978; Halford, 1989). Others have shown that his notions of egocentrism, centration, and conservation are too global, encompassing too many different kinds of skills and knowledge. Still others have pointed out that many cognitive skills seem to develop independently of each other and not in general stages (Gopnik & Meltzoff, 1987). Information-processing approaches that study continuous development of specific skills instead of global concepts avoid some of the problems of a stage theory like Piaget's (e.g., Fischer, 1980; Siegler, 1991). The research methods of information processing have provided fresh insights about children's thinking, and we consider them in the next section.

PIAGET'S PERIODS OF COGNITIVE DEVELOPMENT

Each of Piaget's stages of development emphasizes a special type of thought and behavior in children. The sequence of development is always the same, each successive accomplishment building on previous stages. The ages given are only approximate.

PERIOD	AGE	CHARACTERISTICS
Sensorimotor period	Birth to 2 years	Recognizes relations between perceptions and actions Manipulates objects, uses tools, imitates others Forms basic concepts of object identity and permanence Begins to understand temporal, spatial, and cause-and-effect relations
Preoperational period	2 to 7 years	Acquires language, ability to use symbols Thinking dominated by perceptions of physical features of objects; cannot comprehend transformations that change appearance of objects Struggles to identify consistent properties and functions of events to construct cognitive rules that represent these regularities
Concrete operational period	7 to 11 years	Develops systematic operations that can be applied flexibly to a variety of physical problems; moves beyond perceptions when solving problems Understands the reversible nature of transformations and appreciates the principle of conservation Develops enlarged social perspective
Formal operational period	11 years to adulthood	Becomes capable of solving abstract problems through logical operations Reasoning no longer limited to physical problems; functions by means of deduction and hypothesis testing

INFORMATION PROCESSING IN CHILDREN

Information processing refers to a variety of viewpoints that regard human beings as symbol manipulators, much like computer systems. Stimuli from the environment are like input to the system (i.e., the person). As the person analyzes the stimuli perceptually and cognitively, the processes that he or she goes through are like the reorganization of information and computations performed in a computer. Finally, the person's response is like the output from the computer system. Information-processing approaches have emerged from advances in artificial intelligence, communications theory and cognitive psychology. Chapters 5 and 7 discussed information-processing approaches as they apply to attention and memory. These views have also begun to reshape the way psychologists study children.

The general goal of information-processing research on children is to discover children's emerging "mental programs." Researchers do this by breaking down children's behavior on a particular task (such as adding sums or learning to solve problems) into a series of cognitive rules that resemble the steps in a computer program. Once these rules have been arranged in a coherent format, they constitute a testable model about the way children acquire and use information (Ashcraft, 1989; Klahr & Wallace, 1976). If computers were programmed with the same set of rules shown by children, would the computers duplicate the children's responses? If they would, then the model could be used to demonstrate the capacity of the children's mental program, the complexity of the program, and the information base with which the children must work. This approach, relying heavily on computer technology metaphors, has yielded several insights into the way children acquire mathematical skills, language skills, and general reasoning ability. We discuss children's developing understanding about numbers as an example of information-processing research.

Number Skills. Long before preschoolers begin to count on their fingers, they can compare quantities and numbers. They know that three cookies on a plate are more than two cookies on a plate. This ability to compare numbers without actually counting is a perceptual process called *subitizing*, an innate ability that does not depend on language. Antell and Keating (1983) found that infants as young as 1 week old could discriminate between pictures of two things and pictures showing only one thing. This perceptual comparison process is also used by children and adults to compare small numbers of objects (Chi & Klahr, 1975; Gallistel, 1988).

By age 4, children begin to count, often reciting numbers in strings like "one, two, free, six, eleben." Eventually, the numbers from 1 to 20 are learned by practice and memorization. After memorizing the numbers, children can use rules to generate each series of 10 numbers (20s, 30s, 40s, etc.). These rules can be confusing when first learned, and children frequently make counting errors at transitions to new decades. A typical 4-year-old might count "27, 28, 29, 50, 51," or "27, 28, 29, 20 ten, 20 eleven," or "37, 38, 39, 30, 31."

Information-processing researchers use these observations and other data to form models of psychological processes. For example, Siegler and Robinson (1982) devised the model shown in Figure 9.14 to show the kinds of mental representations and processes that children might use to count from 1 to 99. The model predicts that children think of numbers as belonging to one of two lists. One is the *digit list*, the sequence of numbers from 1 to 9. The other is the *rule applicability list* and includes the groups of 10, from 20 to 90. The connection *next* links numbers sequentially in the list, although children may not master all the next connections equally. Each diamond shape in Figure 9.14 illustrates a choice or decision in information processing; the rectangular boxes indicate processing operations or statements. A model like this can be tested against observations of children's performance. The model can also yield predictions, hypotheses, and potential diagnoses of cognitive processing difficulties.

Counting is not just a memory game or a process of verbal rehearsal. By age 4 or 5, children like to count objects, but they often count objects twice, forget where they started, or skip some objects as they count. Studies of children's counting have revealed that these preschoolers eventually acquire specific concepts and principles that help them count objects accurately. Gelman and Gallistel (1978) identified five key principles that children often acquire by age 5:

Figure 9.14
An Information-Processing Model of Counting from 1 to 99

The model illustrates the steps that 4-year-olds might use while counting. It assumes that children have mental representations of the digits from 1 to 9 and of some of the decades. The representations are in two mental lists and are connected by sequential "next" rules. The process begins at a designated number (or 1) and increases the count in a regular, although not necessarily accurate, manner.

Source: From Siegler, 1986, p. 281.

REPRESENTATION

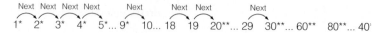

Next	Next	Next	Next		Next		Next	Next		Next			
1*	2*	3*	4*	5*...	9*	10...	18	19	20**...	29	30**...	60**	80**... 40'

*On digit List   **On rule applicability list

PROCESS

Conditions for counting program met ? — No → **Keep Listening**

Yes ↓

Hear "from N" ? — No → N=1

Yes ↓

First number=N ←

Say first number

↓

Is rule applicability list member in number name?

Yes ↓   No →

Is digit list member in name ?

Yes ↓   No → Next number on digit list =1

Digit =9?

Yes ↓   No →

Number has "Next" connection ?   Want to continue ?

Get "Next" number on digit list → Choose "Next" number

Yes ↓   Yes ↓   No → **Stop**

Get "Next" number   Arbitrarily pick number from rule applicability list   Concatenate digit with rule list member

→ **Say Number** ←   **Say Number**

1. The *one-one principle*: One and only one number is assigned to each object.
2. The *stable order principle*: Numbers are always assigned in the same order.
3. The *cardinal principle*: The last number assigned indicates how many objects are in the set.
4. The *abstraction principle*: The other principles apply to any set of objects.
5. The *order irrelevance principle*: Objects can be counted in any order.

Children learn about the concepts of numbers beginning in infancy. They compare quantities by subitizing, learn to recite numbers 1 to 20 through practice, count objects, and learn to calculate using counting rules and principles. As they learn about numbers, children create classes of numbers like *small, big,* and *biggest* that simplify their tasks (Siegler, 1986). Four-year-olds tend to think of 1 as the smallest number; 2, 3, and 4 as small numbers; 5 and 6 as medium-size numbers; numbers larger than 7 as big numbers; and words like *hundred* and *million* as very big numbers (maybe even the "biggest" numbers).

Research on children's development of number concepts and skills reveals the strength of an information-processing framework. This framework is usually a detailed description of performance that gives rise to mental models that can be subsequently tested for their accuracy. Using these models, psychologists can often pinpoint the likely sources of performance differences among children of various ages and abilities.

Developmental Changes in Information Processing. Information processing changes in four basic ways from childhood to adulthood. First, children's knowledge becomes more organized, forming richer hierarchical associations and thematic connections between concepts. These networks of knowledge help children understand and remember. Children experienced in a particular area may even organize and store information better than adults. When Michilene Chi (1978) compared chess experts with novice chess players, she found, not unexpectedly, that the experts were better able to remember the location of the chess pieces on a board. The suprising feature of this study is that many of the experts were 8- to 12-year-old children! Other studies have verified that young children can recall familiar or meaningful items almost as well as older children and adults. For example, 2- and 3-year-olds can remember birthday parties, names of friends and relatives, and the locations of familiar toys with surprising accuracy (Bjorklund, 1989; DeLoache, Cassidy, & Brown, 1985). These studies suggest that the development of memory in children reflects changes in how they organize their developing knowledge (Ornstein & Naus, 1985).

Second, information processing increases in speed as basic processes (such as scanning a stimulus or recognizing similarity) become automatic. As less and less attention is paid to these processes, children show a corresponding increase in the mental capacity to think about more things at the same time (Bjorklund et al., 1990; Case, 1985). Thinking becomes faster and requires less effort with increasing age, at least until later adulthood.

Third, as children get older, they acquire a broader set of cognitive strategies to guide attention, learning, and memory. Even 3-year-old children demonstrate a basic form of memory rehearsal (Weissberg and Paris, 1986). After they are told to remember the location of a hidden toy, young children will touch or stare at the object (Wellman, Ritter, & Flavell, 1975). Older children acquire more refined techniques to aid recall, such as rehearsing information by repeating it to themselves (Kail, 1990), grouping objects into related categories (Gelman, 1988; Goodman, 1992), and elaborating on the materials they are supposed to remember (Pressley, 1982).

Finally, the development of information-processing skills is usually accompanied by greater metacognition (Brown et al., 1983). **Metacognition** involves children's self-awareness and control of their own cognitive abilities. Planning, self-checking, and revising solutions to problems are all evidence of metacognition. Research has shown that children find this kind of "mental pulse-taking" difficult. Before the age of 5, many children may not use these strategies spontaneously to foster learning (Flavell, 1985). However, if young children are given information about the value and appropriateness of strategies, they are more likely to use the strategies on their own (Harnishfeger & Bjorklund, 1990; Paris, Newman, & McVey, 1982). As children develop their own theories about useful strategies, they attribute successful recall to the use of particular strategies, prompting them to use the strategies spontaneously (Fabricius & Cavalier, 1989).

The development of effective reading skills reflects all four changes in information processing. Comprehension becomes more organized, faster, more strategic, and better controlled by children's reflection and self-regulated learning. Nevertheless, the development of literacy is not easy for many children. Learning to read requires cognitive strategies, metacognition, and motivation (Hoffman, Paris, Hall, Schell, 1994). Some 5-year-olds learning to read understand so little about the skill that they are not sure whether they should "read" the words or the pictures (Paris, Lopson, and Wixson, 1983) or whether it makes any difference if they move from left to right or top to bottom (Clay, 1973). To be able to read, children must learn to convert print into sound, to interpret words, and to use the sentence context to comprehend meaning. Beyond that, they must learn to relate the information from different places in a long a passage, devote extra study to difficult parts, and check their own understanding (Paris, Wasik, & Turner, 1990). These strategies are difficult to master. Some children have difficulty connecting the printed text with distinct sounds, while others may decode the words but be unable to identify main ideas, make inferences while reading, or summarize the key points. Thus, poor readers may simply say the words without knowing what they mean. Good readers, on the other hand, are more likely to notice inconsistencies in meaning and to correct their own errors while reading (Brown, Armbruster, & Baker, 1984). As John Holt (1964) has said:

> Part of being a good student is learning to be aware of one's own mind and the degree of one's understanding. The good student may be one who often says he does not understand, simply because he keeps a constant check on his understanding. The poor student, who does not, so to speak, watch himself trying to understand, does not know most of the time whether he understands or not. Thus the problem is not to get students to ask us what they don't know; the problem is to make them aware of the difference between what they know and what they don't. (pp. 28–29)

Learning to read is a difficult skill, but if children are exposed to books at home they develop it more readily.

WHY KIDS ARE TURNED OFF BY SCHOOL

All across America, teachers hear students complain, "School is dumb," "School work is boring," and "Why are we learning this anyway?" Sometimes these complaints are legitimate criticisms of a fragmented curriculum or instruction that emphasizes memorization of facts. But sometimes students' complaints disguise their underlying motivational problems in school. Consider three typical children whose common symptoms of educational discontent actually signal fundamental motivational difficulties (Stipek 1993).

■ Sally always does what the teacher wants. In fact, she asks questions frequently so that she can follow the procedures exactly. She is oriented to achieving good grades, but while she sees the value of an education, she does not enjoy learning. Sally avoids challenges and taking risks. She is anxious about failure and getting poor grades; she knows that her parents will be unhappy if her grades are not excellent. She has goals directed at completing tasks and performing to a standard, rather than internal goals for mastering the material. Performance goals like these lead to superficial learning, according to Ames and Archer (1988).
■ Danny is the class clown. He tells jokes, disrupts discussions, and copies answers from his neighbors. Sometimes he teases, sometimes he bullies, but usually he defies the teacher and works hard at *not* doing his schoolwork. The teacher reminds Danny constantly that he won't get good grades if he does not buckle down and get to work, but that is exactly the message Danny wants his classmates to hear. Danny is so afraid of failing that he simply avoids any legitimate effort to learn. Covington (1993) describes how students frequently reduce their effort in school to protect their self-worth. Danny prevents people from interpreting his poor performance as an indication of low ability by deliberately encouraging them to attribute his performance to low effort. That is, his peers, parents, and teachers cannot say that his failure is due to his inability; instead, they know that he failed because he didn't try. Other students may protect their self-esteem by not asking for help, so as not to appear dumb. In Chapter 17, we will discuss a similar ego-protective strategy called self-handicapping.

■ Hannah has given up entirely. She is quiet to the point of passivity. She is so convinced that she cannot succeed in school that she automatically says, "I can't do this,"—no matter what the task. Sometimes she tries half-heartedly, achieves minimal success, and confirms her own impressions of her low ability. For her, school is full of frustration because of the difficulty of the work, although others would claim that school is boring because the work is too *easy*. Both bored students and those who are frustrated show despair and hostility in school. How can teachers create instruction that provides the right amount of challenge for students of varying abilities?

There is no single way to motivate all students, but psychologists know that students' beliefs about themselves, the tasks they are asked to perform, and the support they receive all influence their motivation. When students believe in their self-efficacy—that is, their own ability to perform tasks successfully (see Chapter 14)—they set appropriate goals and use effective strategies rather than performing like the students described here (Zimmerman, Bandura, & Martinez-Pons, 1992). Often, students like Sally, Danny, and Hannah do not differ from successful students in terms of ability, but they treat academic failures and successes very differently. Struggling children sometimes develop defensive interpretations and misconceptions about themselves in response to failure; they often attribute such disappointments to permanent, internal abilities rather than to a controllable lack of effort or short-term situational factors. This type of mental set results in feelings of helplessness or misdirected effort, because explaining failure in terms of a permanent lack of ability leaves no possibility for change. The damage that such thinking does to students' perceptions of their abilities can be counteracted by praising children appropriately and often for schoolwork and matching students' tasks to their actual abilities, thereby providing more opportunities for such praise (Hoffman et al., 1994).

Language Acquisition

Acquisition of language is a unique human accomplishment that permits new kinds of cognitive and social interactions for young children. Most children use language moderately well by 2 or 3 years of age, although improvement continues for years. There are several related skills required to develop competence with language.

Long before infants use language, they learn to communicate with adults by using facial expressions and sounds.

Children must learn to convert the phonetic stream of speech sounds into language, arrange words in correct order, express ideas in multiple ways, and finally converse.

Why do babies around the world begin to talk at about the same age and in similar ways? One key to understanding the similarity of language development across cultures is to examine the similarity of development before language is acquired (Golinkoff & Hirsh-Pasek, 1990).

LANGUAGE PRECURSORS

Newborns are biologically prepared to perceive and produce human speech (Rosser, 1994). And because all humans possess the same biological structures, humans biology lies behind many of the cross-cultural universals in language acquisition, just as it does in many other areas of our psychology.

Long before they understand words, infants can respond to the rate, volume, and melody of adult speech, and they can tell from these properties when the adults are playful or angry (Papousek et al., 1990). Infants are quite sensitive to sounds in the human voice range, and they prefer rhythmic tones, such as the short sentences parents speak to children (Eimas, 1975; Fernald & Mazzie, 1991). At 1 month of age, infants can discriminate between most meaningful sounds in any language (Aslin, Pisoni, & Jusczyk, 1983; Mehler et al., 1988).

During infancy, the shape of the oral cavity changes, which allows for the production of speech. The larynx is in the right position to control and modulate airflow from the lungs (see Figure 8.11 on page 331). The cheeks lose some fat, and the tongue develops so that the passage of air can be regulated more easily. Improved muscular control of the lips, tongue, and cheeks permits children to make a greater variety of sounds; at approximately 6 months of age, the appearance of teeth further enhances sound production.

The extended period of infant dependency provides the infant with many opportunities for social interaction and communication. In the infant's first year, parents and infants communicate in many ways. Adults typically talk to babies about objects, usually offering the object to the baby or pointing to and naming the object. When they are about a year old, infants can offer, point to, and show objects to adults, demonstrating early speaker and listener roles. Crying, facial expressions, and intonation that may accompany these gestures are also communicative. These forms of communication are prelinguistic **speech acts**; they are goal directed and intended to influence a listener (Bruner, 1983).

Infants' gestures appear to fall into two categories (Clark & Clark, 1977). The first group consists of assertions such as "Look at X" or "Tell me about X"; the second group is a form of request such as "Show me X" or "Give me X." Pointing is a typical assertion, and reaching is a typical request; both gestures may signal the coming of single-word utterances with the same function. Certainly, infants learn quickly that gestures, facial expressions, and intonation constitute clues about language, and they use that information to help determine the meanings of words.

This pattern of communication is shared by prelinguistic children from all cultures, perhaps because of the underlying similarities in all infants' early experiences and social interactions. Between 1 and 2 years of age, infants from around the world share similar concepts and topics of conversation. They discover the names of people and identities of objects (e.g., *mama, doll*), descriptions of nonexistence (e.g., *all gone*), modifiers (e.g., *big*) and social terms (e.g., *bye-bye*) because most parents present them with the same tasks: eating, playing with toys, commanding, requesting, and describing. As children acquire new concepts and relations, they also enhance their symbolic representations and memory. All these changes promote language development.

FROM BABBLING TO SENTENCES

Before children speak words, they exhibit a regular progression from crying to cooing, to vocal play, to babbling, and then to expressive jargon. These stages are described in Table 9.1 and represent development in the first 18 months, ending in language production. The first language sounds produced by infants are usually vowels, because they are produced by simply changing the position of the lips and tongue while producing a continuous airflow. Consonants usually require a "stop" in the airflow and greater muscular control. Some of the earliest consonants heard are those that are easy to articulate: *p* as in *papa*, *g* as in *go*, and *m* as in *mama*. Ease of articulation, practice, muscular and anatomical development, and imitation of parents all help infants to generate a wide assortment of language sounds by 10 months of age.

First Words. Many infants utter their first words between 10 and 18 months of age, and they often acquire a vocabulary of 50 words by 20 months (Corrigan, 1983; Nelson, 1973). However, many children do not speak until 2 years of age, so delayed language development is usually not diagnosed until 3 to 4 years of age. First words are often imitations of adult speech that accompany actions, such as the combination of *bye-bye* and hand waving. Some babbling sounds like adult speech, and many of these early linguistic expressions overlap the production of genuine words (e.g., *wog* for frog).

Infants' first words vary a good deal in type and rate of production, as Katherine Nelson (1973) found in a longitudinal study of 18 children (see Table 9.2). One thing is clear: Children's first words are not simply nouns and labels for objects. Nouns make up the largest category, accounting for 62 percent of all words in Nelson's study, but there were many other types of words (e.g., action words, social expressions, and modifiers). The variety of first words shows the strong relation between speech and sensorimotor knowledge. *Mommy, Daddy, doggie, baby,* and *milk* are common first words for most English-speaking children because they describe the infants' familiar world. *Look, hi, up,* and *go* exemplify the first spatial, action-oriented relations infants comprehend. First words fit into existing nonverbal behavior and knowledge. Modifier words—such as *big, red,* and *hot*—describe perceptual characteristics. *All gone* and *more* reveal an understanding of how objects change.

TABLE 9.1
Prelinguistic Language Development

AGE	STAGE	CHARACTERISTICS
0–8 weeks	Stage 1: Reflexive crying and vegetative sounds	Cries of distress; burps, coughs, sneezes
8 to 20 weeks	Stage 2: Cooing and laughter	Pleasurable sounds
16 to 30 weeks	Stage 3: Vocal play	Single, distinctive syllables
25 to 50 weeks	Stage 4: Reduplicated babbling	Strings of alternating vowels and consonants
9 to 18 months	Stage 5: Nonreduplicated babbling and expressive jargon	Stress and intonational pattern, often with contour of adult speech

SOURCE: Information from Sachs, 1985.

TABLE 9.2

Types of Words Produced by Childen with 50-Word Vocabularies

CATEGORY	TYPE	EXAMPLE
Specific	People	Mommy, daddy
	Animals	Pet names
	Objects	Car
General	Objects	Ball
	Animals and people	Doggie
	Letters and numbers	Two
	Pronouns	She
Action words	Demand-descriptive	Up
	Notice	Look
Personal-social expressions	Assertions	No, yes
	Social-expressives	Please, ouch
Function	Question	What, where
	Miscellaneous	Is, to
Modifiers	Attributes	Big, pretty
	States	Lot, all gone
	Locative	There
	Possessives	Mine

SOURCE: Nelson, 1973. Adapted by persmission.

Grammatical Relationships. Between 18 and 24 months of age, most children begin to combine words into short sentences. The word combinations permit us to analyze the syntactic and semantic rules that children use to formulate their speech. (Recall from Chapter 8 that syntax has to do with the word order in a sentence and semantics with the meaning of the words.) A striking feature of first word combinations is the way children use some words as anchors. Toddlers frequently say things like "all-gone milk," "all-gone cookie," "more boat," "more tickle," "here baby," and "here shoe". The first word in each utterance is combined with a noun, reflecting elementary syntactic and semantic relationships. Roger Brown (1973) found that although vocabulary and word order may vary between children, the kinds of meanings they express are often similar. For example, children may regularly express reference, recurrence, and nonexistence through phrases such as "this cup," "more milk," and "all-gone doggie." Such word orders observed in early speech seem to be consequences of semantic regularities (see Table 9.3.).

In their two- and three-word sentences, young children use what is called **telegraphic speech,** leaving out prepositions, articles, and parts of verb phrases. Two sorts of rules govern such utterances. First, the order of terms conveys meaning. So *shoe chair* indicates where a shoe is, while *daddy shoe* indicates whose shoe it is. Second, stress and intonation convey meaning. Stress on the first word in *Jeffie room* might indicate possession, while stress on the second word might be a response to the question, "Where's Jeffie?" In short, early speech is characterized by regular stress patterns and a small number of semantic relations that convey meaning according to rules.

Growth in Vocabulary. Three-year-olds expand their vocabularies with astonishing speed, sometimes learning two to four new words each day (Pease & Gleason, 1985). By the age of 6, children have between 8,000 and 14,000 words in their vocab-

TABLE 9.3
Examples of Common Semantic Relations in Children's Speech

SEMANTIC RELATION	FORM	EXAMPLE
Nomination	that + noun	That book
Notice	hi + noun	Hi doggie
Recurrence	more + noun	More milk
Nonexistence	all-gone + noun	All-gone rattle
Attributive	adj. + noun	Big train
Possessive	Noun + noun	Mommy lunch
Locative	Noun + noun	Sweater chair
Locative	Verb + noun	Walk street
Agent-action	Noun + verb	Eve read
Agent-object	Noun + noun	Mommy sock
Action-object	Verb + noun	Put book

SOURCE: Brown, 1973

ularies (Carey, 1977). Many of these words are acquired readily; they are familiar and easy to pronounce. However, the meaning of words is not necessarily the same for children and adults (Schwanenflugel, Guth, & Bjorklund, 1986).

As children acquire new vocabulary words, they often make two kinds of errors: *overextensions* and *underextensions*. When children overextend words, they use them to include things that do not fit in the same category. For example, some preschoolers use the words *grandma, grandpa, nanna,* and *poppa* to refer to any elderly person, not just their own grandparents. When children underextend words, they use them too narrowly. For example, a little girl can believe that the word *turtle* refers only to her particular pet and not to other, similar animals. These confusions are often short-lived, because children are constantly refining their concepts about words. According to Clark (1973), children need to acquire knowledge of **semantic features,** characteristics that define words, to avoid over- and underextending their meanings. The word *horse*, for example, may be specified by such features as large, four-legged, lack of horns, long neck, and other features that distinguish horses from other animals. From this point of view, learning new words depends on learning their defining features, which in turn involves growth in vocabulary and conceptual understanding.

Some psychologists contend that children do not accumulate lists of features about words; the process would be too cumbersome and lengthy, and simple feature lists do not distinguish the importance of various features. These critics argue instead that children attend to characteristic features of words. For example, *island* might be understood by a 4-year-old as a place with palm trees, beaches, and sand rather than a piece of land surrounded by water. Keil and Batterman (1984) read short stories to a group of 5-year-old children. They included a characteristic feature about a word like *robber* in their stories and then asked the children to evaluate the appropriateness of the word. For example, they read a passage about a mean old man with a gun who took an unwanted TV set with permission; they also read a passage about a cheerful lady who stole something. The 5-year-olds thought that the man was the robber and the woman

This is a wug.

Now there is another one.
There are two of them.
There are two _____.

FIGURE 9.15
The Wugs Test

One way to test children's understanding of inflectional rules is to have children supply a missing word to describe pictures. Jean Berko devised a clever test with nonsense "words" to rule out imitation of natural words and word endings. If children supply the missing word *wugs* to the story as the experimenter's voice trails off, then they must know the general rule about adding *s* to form plurals. The test contains many pictures for different kinds of rules. Try this one and then make up your own. "Three wugs went fribbing down the street. Yesterday they did the same thing. Yesterday they _____."

SOURCE: Berko, 1958, p. 483.

was not. The characteristic features, or *stereotype*, of a robber influenced their judgments. This conclusion is similar to centration, focused attention, and limited reasoning that we discussed earlier. It reveals that children's vocabulary growth is intertwined with advances in conceptual understanding and reasoning.

Beyond Simple Sentences. Children gradually learn to speak in longer sentences that specify meaning more precisely than telegraphic utterances, but language development demands more than expansion of vocabulary. Children acquire many kinds of rules for generating longer sentences. Between the ages of 2 and 5 years, most children learn to use rules to form past-tense endings, plurals, and other elements missing from telegraphic speech (Gleason, 1985). Children first imitate irregular forms, such as *did*, *went*, or *sheep*, and later seem to regress when they say "doed," "goed," and "sheeps." In fact, these errors indicate that children have learned inflectional rules (e.g., adding *ed* to form past tenses and *s* to form plurals), but they overgeneralize the rules. Fortunately, the rate of overgeneralization errors is very low and they occur mostly between 2 and 5 years of age. Some researchers believe that such errors are due to inadequate learning and recall of the exceptions (Marcus et al., 1992). Figure 9.15 illustrates one way to test children's understanding of inflectional rules.

Another way that we increase sentence complexity is through transformational rules that rearrange word order, insert new words, and delete others, as in these examples:

SIMPLE SENTENCE	TRANSFORMATION	RULE
He is running.	Is he running?	Interrogative
Mary knows the answer.	Does Mary know the answer?	*Do* insertion plus interrogative
Jan rode the horse.	The horse was ridden by Jan.	Passive
Freddie is cheating.	Freddie is not cheating.	Negative

Transformational rules are difficult for children to learn because they require changes in verbs and auxiliaries (e.g., "helping" verbs), as well as alterations for number and tense agreement. Thus, grammatical complexity affects the course of language acquisition.

CHILDREN'S COMMUNICATION AND EGOCENTRIC SPEECH

Understanding words and rules is not the same as knowing how and when to use language intentionally to influence other people. One of the earliest connections children must learn about conversation is the give-and-take relationship between speaker and listener. Early speech acts between parent and child are the foundation for these roles. Gradual progression from the "role-rigid," turn-taking exchanges to "role-complementary" interactions (Bruner, 1975) occurs as the child begins to consider the other person's remarks and actions, a slow process that may not be completed until 4 or 5 years of age.

A second type of convention for communication that children learn is how to express meaning in different ways. Children's early speech (e.g., "hi," "bye-bye," "no," "thank you") is often ritualistic and varies little in form or context. Requests, denials, and assertions are often constrained by children's inability to rephrase their utterances. By 4 or 5 years of age, children have learned how to rephrase their sentences.

Sometimes preschoolers do not consider the other person's point of view. While speaking on the telephone, they often refer to objects as if the listener could see them.

Taking turns talking and using alternative ways to express meaning are part of a general progression between 2 and 5 years of age from egocentric towards more socialized speech, according to Piaget (1954). Piaget postulated that children do not completely overcome the limitations of egocentrism until they are 7 or 8 years old, but recent research has disputed this claim. Younger children are not usually oblivious to listeners; they often try to get the listener's attention by calling to the listener or pointing to the object of conversation, and they frequently talk about the listener's activities, keeping the conversation relevant to the listener's behavior.

Young children are also capable of reformulating their speech to accommodate the listener. Shatz and Gelman (1973) recorded 4-year-olds talking with 2-year-olds, with other 4-year-olds, and with adults. The 4-year-olds talked in shorter, simpler sentences and used more attention-getting devices when talking to 2-year-olds than when addressing their peers or adults. Other studies support these findings and demonstrate that preschoolers consider the visual perspective, age, knowledge, and remarks of listeners in conveying messages to them (Schmidt & Paris, 1984). Consequently, some researchers suggest that speech is socialized even among 3- and 4-year-olds, and that it continues to improve throughout childhood.

EXPLANATIONS OF LANGUAGE ACQUISITION

For many years, the debate about the way children acquire language centered on the forces of nature and nurture. Some said that language ability was innate; others said that it was learned, like all other habits. For many, however, the extreme positions of both sides were unsatisfactory. Some considered the biological innate position miraculous, whereas the behavioristic learning position was regarded as impossible (Bruner, 1983). Consequently, a third perspective emerged that considers language acquisition an interaction among social, cognitive, and biological changes in the developing child. Following are short descriptions of each viewpoint.

The **behavioristic view** regards language as verbal behavior that is reinforced by other people (Bijou & Baer, 1965; Skinner, 1957). Behaviorists argue that mothers provide reinforcement to babies through food and affection and that the mother's speech becomes reinforcing by association with these items. As infants learn to control their environment by crying and gesturing, they learn that other sounds and words also influence the actions of other people. Through imitation and shaping, they acquire words and sentence frames that permit expanded communication. They make generalizations and inferences from these frames and are rewarded for more sophisticated language use (Whitehurst, 1982). Critics argue that conditioning, reinforcement, and imitation cannot explain language development completely. For example, children say many creative things, including instances of overgeneralized rules like "wented" that they could not have learned by imitation and reinforcement.

The **biological innate view** of language acquisition has been proposed by Noam Chomsky, who revolutionized the study of psycholinguistics. Chomsky has proposed that people are born with a *language acquisition device*, or *LAD*, that is like a genetic blueprint for the underlying aspects of language (1979). The LAD has a universal grammar that provides the rules, conditions, and principles for understanding and producing language. These factors are similar across all languages, even nonverbal sign languages, and help explain the remarkable similarity of children's language acquisition under a wide variety of circumstances. In Chomsky's view, the environment merely provides models of linguistic input that fill in the universal grammar with particular sounds and words; evolution and maturation determine language ability more than particular experiences.

In the beginning of this chapter, we observed that there are biological, social, and cognitive changes that preceded language acquisition. The **interactionist perspective** gives credit to all these potential influences on language development. For example, a mother singing a familiar song to a toddler might encourage the child to say some of the words. As the child tries to imitate the words, the mother may smile, hug, and repeat the song as reinforcement. Parents gauge their child's emerging language abilities and encourage better articulation or more accurate use of words according to the children's physical and cognitive abilities. Because the interactionist perspective is diverse and broad, it may offer more promising explanations of language acquisition than positions that focus primarily on either nature or nurture (Bohannon & Warren-Leubecker, 1989).

Social Development

Most children grow up surrounded by their family and friends. These people help to establish emotional security in infancy and later to mold the young child's personality. Adults provide care, model appropriate behavior, and set standards to follow. These principles of observational learning and conditioning promote social learning by children. Children, in turn, influence their families by their behavior and development. The processes of socialization operate in both directions; we must remember that families develop together in shared social and physical environments.

ERIKSON'S STAGES

A useful guide for understanding children's social and emotional development is provided by Erik Erikson (1950), who built his theory on Freud's stages of psychosexual development (to be discussed in Chapter 14). Each of the eight stages in Erikson's life span theory of **psychosocial development** involves the resolution of a social crisis or challenge. These stages provide a general description of how people establish their identities and self-concepts with particular attention to the different emotional reactions that they might have at each stage. We briefly describe Erikson's four stages of development in infancy and childhood here and leave the four stages of adolescence and adulthood for discussion in Chapter 10.

Trust Versus Mistrust.   In the first stage, infants make their initial encounters with a social world. They experience both trust and mistrust as they interact with their caretakers. To resolve this conflict, they must develop a sense of confidence in the dependability of others. Of course, the parents' confidence in the child's behavior is important for mutual trust to develop.

Autonomy Versus Doubt and Shame.   Most 2- and 3-year-olds exhibit a growing sense of independence in this stage. Toilet training and cleanliness are important, but children and parents must also resolve conflicts between parental authority and the emerging autonomy of the child. Adjustments to social rules without shame or self-doubt is the primary goal of this stage.

Initiative Versus Guilt.   From 3 to 6 years of age, children may imagine themselves in adult roles. Children also may demonstrate their newly developed prowess by running, jumping, or throwing things. Parents attempt to harness this energy and help children learn acceptable behaviors as outlets. Learning these limitations to behavior without feeling guilty or losing self-initiative is a difficult task.

Industry Versus Inferiority. According to Erikson, this fourth stage is very important for feelings of competence. It covers growth from 6 to 11 years of age, when children apply themselves to learning useful skills both in and outside of school. The focus of this stage is mastery of culturally relevant tasks (e.g., hunting, farming, cooking, schooling) without feeling inadequate.

These four stages of Erikson's theory provide a broad outline of social development across early childhood, identifying crucial hurdles of social development at different ages. In the following sections, we discuss the social relationships and experiences that foster social development and children's emerging realizations of who they are and how they should interact with others.

DEVELOPMENT OF ATTACHMENT

Watching parents play with their infants is almost like watching a ballet, with each partner acting and reacting to the movements of the other. When a parent wiggles the infant's arms and legs and talks and smiles, the baby reciprocates by laughing, cooing, or babbling. The responses are mutually satisfying. Dozens of such interactions occur daily as the baby is fed, bathed, and cradled, actions that present the infant with opportunities to explore parental looks, sounds, and smells. Peery (1980) recorded the head movements of infants as a smiling female approached and withdrew from them, and he found that even 1-day-old newborns seemed to coordinate their head movements with those of the adult.

The strong, emotional, and reciprocal relationship established between an infant and a particular caregiver is called **attachment**. It begins soon after birth and continues to develop until 2 to 3 years of age. Attachment is defined by three main characteristics. First, infants are likely to approach significant people (parents or other caregivers) for comfort when they are distressed or hungry. Second, they are most easily soothed by familiar caregivers. Third, they show little fear of familiar caregivers. For infants, familiarity breeds security.

Emotional Bonding. How does early experience contribute to the emotional relationship between mothers and their babies? Klaus and Kennell (1976) argued that skin-to-skin contact between mother and child immediately after birth stimulates later emotional bonding. This effect is important because bonding is part of the attachment relationship between mother and child. They suggested that the first few hours after delivery is a sensitive period, and mothers and children need direct physical contact during this time or they will not become emotionally attached to each other later. These notions have been publicized widely and have influenced procedures in many hospitals, but there is little evidence to support them. Goldberg (1983) reported that mothers who had early contact with their newborns were somewhat more responsive to them for the first three days, but the differences were small and disappeared a week later. Lamb (1982) also concluded that there are no appreciable differences between mothers and infants who share early contact compared with those who are separated for several days after birth. This should be reassuring to adoptive parents and others who must be separated from their newborn babies until at least several days after birth.

Stages of Attachment. Attachment generally develops through four stages, as shown in Table 9.4. In the first stage, from birth to 2 months, babies do not discrimi-

TABLE 9.4
Stages of Attachment

AGE	STAGE	DESCRIPTION
Birth to 2 months	1	Indiscrimate social responsiveness (accepts comfort from anyone)
2 to 7 months	2	Discriminate social responsiveness (prefers family figures but does not protest when parents leave)
7 to 30 months	3	Specific attachment
Around 8 months		A. Separation distress (is distressed when separated from caregiver; attempts to follow)
Around 10 months		B. Stranger wariness or anxiety (has aversion to unfamiliar person who seeks proximity)
From 30 months onward	4	Goal-directed partnership (is no longer distressed at caregiver's departure; can work toward shared goals)

nate among people. They smile at anyone and are calmed by any gentle caregiver, so the responses do not reflect attachment. The second stage lasts from about 2 to 7 months and reveals specific responses to specific caregivers, but these babies usually do not object when the primary caregivers leave or unfamiliar adults provide care. Specific attachment is evident in the third stage, from 7 to 30 months of age, when infants become distressed when their primary caregivers leave or when strangers approach. The fourth stage, evident from 30 months on, reflects a partnership between children and their caregivers in which they share goals and can adapt to the caregivers' absence and to care provided by others.

Attachment Patterns.   Not all infants form secure social attachments to caregivers. In fact, only about 70 percent of 1-year-old infants are securely attached to adults (Sroufe, 1985). Mary Ainsworth (Ainsworth et al., 1978) created a staged sequence of events called the "strange situation," to study infants' social attachment. The "strange situation" begins when a baby and its caregiver enter a playroom. After a time, the caregiver leaves, and shortly thereafter a stranger enters and sits down. Next, the stranger leaves and the caregiver returns, and the whole sequence is repeated again. This research has revealed three types of attachment relationships:

• **Securely attached infants** use their caregiver as a base for exploring a new room but often return to the caregiver for comfort.
• **Avoidant infants,** who are insecurely attached, do not cry when their caregiver leaves, nor do they approach the caregiver in the room.
• **Anxious/resistant infants** appear upset when their caregiver leaves or returns. They may alternately seek out contact and resist the caregiver's efforts to hold or comfort them.

How do infants become attached to their caregivers? Ainsworth (1979) believes that mothers (or other caregivers) of securely attached infants are responsive to their infants' signals from the very beginning. They enjoy contact with their infants, express emotions openly, and encourage exploration. A review of several American longitudinal studies has shown that securely attached infants usually have primary caregivers who are warm and responsive, not intrusive or abusive (Lamb et al., 1985). All these behaviors help to establish trust between the infant and the primary caregiver. Primary caregivers of infants who are anxious/resistant try to provide physical comfort to the infants, but they often misinterpret the infants' signals. Finally, caregivers of avoidant infants may be impatient and frustrated with child rearing. Unfortunately, such patterns of rejection and infant avoidance may contribute to cycles of child abuse (Egeland & Sroufe, 1981; Harris, 1993).

It should be noted that attachment relationships vary around the world, a fact that shouldn't surprise you, considering the sociocultural theme of this book. German mothers promote independence in their babies. They are more likely to give their infants toys or food when they cry than to pick them up. German mothers discourage their infants from staying near them; therefore, these infants are more likely to develop avoidant attachments (Grossman et al., 1985). Because Japanese mothers rarely leave their infants alone with strangers, Japanese infants find the "strange situation" very distressing and often react like resistant babies (Takahashi, 1990). Other research suggests that the most securely attached Japanese toddlers have mothers who report unhappy marriages (Nakagawa, Teti, & Lamb, 1992). Strong attachment with their children may represent a compensatory reaction by these Japanese mothers. Since they often marry by family arrangements and have husbands who work up to 80 hours a week, they may develop a strong bond with their children to ward off loneliness or depression. Research on child rearing in Israeli kibbutzim, where the primary caregivers are not the children's mothers and fathers, reveals that infants can become attached to multiple caregivers, each in a special way, without adverse effects (Sagi et al., 1985).

The impact of child–rearing conditions on parent-child attachment is especially important today, because so many parents are employed outside the home. In fact, more than half of all American mothers and fathers with children less than a year old work full-time (Willer et al., 1991). Sharp increases in parental employment and single-parent households have resulted in more children in day-care situations. Many parents ask, "Will day-care affect my relationship with my child?" This issue has generated considerable debate. (See "Controversy: What Effect Does Day-Care Have on Parent-Child Relationships?")

Whether or not children are placed in day-care, it is the way families *react* to changes in parental employment that determines the impact on children. Easterbrooks and Goldberg (1985) observed the parent-child interactions of 75 families with first-born 20-month-olds. They found that the security of attachment and the problem-solving skills of the toddlers were equal whether parents were unemployed, employed part-time, or fully employed outside the home. Most employed women (67 percent) and their partners (74 percent) viewed parental employment as positive, whereas the majority of unemployed mothers and their partners thought that parental employment would have negative effects on parent-child relationships. The researchers concluded that parental employment does not hurt parent-child relationships. When parents are satisfied with their employment status (whether working outside the home or not) and when partners are supportive, families adapt well.

Consequences of Attachment.   Two short-term consequences of attachment are commonly observed among infants. **Separation anxiety** is the distress experienced by infants when their parents leave them. In studies of many cultures, separation distress begins at 8 to 9 months of age, peaks between 12 and 15 months of age, and usually

A securely attached infant will cry and protest when parents begin to leave.

WHAT EFFECT DOES DAY CARE HAVE ON PARENT-CHILD RELATIONSHIPS?

The American family has changed dramatically in the past 30 years. Today, fewer than half the children in America will grow up in a home with both of their biological parents; more than a quarter will be raised in single-parent homes. Almost 70 percent of mothers of intact families are employed outside the home, while more than 75 percent of mothers in female-headed households have outside jobs (U.S. Department of Labor, 1987). Roughly half of mothers with children less than 3 years of age are in the labor force, and nearly 70 percent of American infants less than a year old will have mothers who work outside the home by the year 2000 if current trends continue (Clarke-Stewart, 1993). Who is raising these children, and what are the consequences of this substitute care?

Some substitute care is provided by grandparents, other relatives, and baby-sitters in the child's home. This kind of care, referred to as *family* or *home day-care,* is particularly beneficial for young infants. Most older children receiving substitute care attend day-care centers or preschools from 3 to 10 hours per day instead of home care. A team of researchers compared these two types of substitute care in Bermuda, where 64 percent of babies less than a year old and 84 percent of children under 2 receive substitute care (McCartney et al., 1985). Bermudan children who attended day-care centers during their first two years were less attentive, less competent as communicators, less socially responsive, and more apathetic than children who were cared for in their own homes. The researchers traced these negative effects to the crowded conditions at the centers. Because each adult supervised eight children, the youngsters received little individual attention, interactive play, or cognitive challenge. In contrast, Bermudan children who switched to day-care centers after age 2 developed more quickly than those children who remained at home.

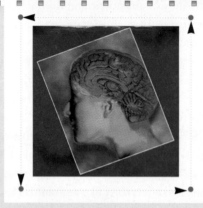

Clarke-Stewart (1989) reviewed the literature and concluded that day care fosters independence among children. Children who attend day-care centers are often more socially and intellectually advanced than their peers who stay at home with a primary caretaker. The benefits of day care may be greatest for disadvantaged children who show rapid gains in compensatory or early education programs (Lazar et al., 1982). However, this early advantage often fades when home-reared children enter school and catch up to day-care children.

Because studies of the effects of day-care on children have revealed contradictory results and the possibility of different effects for boys and girls, the debate continues. For example, Belsky (1986) once argued that out-of-home care during the first year of life often has negative consequences for children, but later (1988) claimed, based on new research, that no firm conclusion could be drawn. Contradictory studies revealing how employment of the primary caretaker may affect girls and boys differently has further spurred the debate. Daughters of working mothers have a positive role model and are often independent high achievers with good social adjustment (Hoffman, 1984). Boys of working mothers seem to do more poorly in school and are less socially adjusted. However, a national panel of experts examined an array of

evidence and concluded that maternal employment provides no direct harm or benefit to children's development (Hayes & Kamerman, 1983).

It appears that the effects of substitute care may be subtle, depending on many factors in the family as well as in the care provided (Hoffman, 1989). The training of the alternative caregiver, the amount of time spent with the child, the quality of the interactions, and the characteristics of other children in the center are all critical. If a family is undergoing additional stresses, such as marital discord or economic hardship, substitute care may increase the risk of poor parent-child relationships (Gamble & Zigler, 1986).

The controversy is far from settled, and more research needs to be done to discover the consequences, if any, of substitute care. Maternal roles have changed dramatically in the past 30 years, and Silverstein (1991) argues that research is needed on the role of family (good or poor home environment) context, the impact of the father's employment status, and the costs of not providing affordable child care. At stake is the emotional and social well-being of hundreds of thousands of children and the cohesiveness of their families, not to mention the impact on social policies and the allocation of millions of dollars. Business and industry are considering ways to provide child care at the workplace as well as to establish creative job sharing and work scheduling to accommodate families. Day care is a mushrooming business, and psychologists need to help train personnel, design programs that fit different children and families, and evaluate the impact of various types of substitute care.

declines after that (Kagan, 1984). When a mother puts a child to bed or leaves the room, a 1-year-old may cry with distress, while a 5-month-old seems perfectly content. Fear of separation decreases as an infant learns that parents return and that crying does not prevent them from leaving. Children reared by many different adults may show relatively less distress when separated from parents, but separation anxiety troubles most youngsters of similar ages around the world (see Figure 9.16).

A second potential consequence of attachment is **stranger anxiety**, the distress experienced by infants when unfamiliar people hold them or take care of them. While the 5-month-old happily accepts being picked up by grandparents or strangers, the 1-year-old rejects an unfamiliar person and will cry to be back with the primary care-giver. This distress diminishes as the child is exposed to more people and learns that unfamiliar people can provide temporary security. In fact, reactions to strangers may be less severe among securely attached infants. Main and Weston (1981) observed infants as they interacted with a friendly but unfamiliar clown. The most socially responsive infants in this situation were those who were securely attached to both parents.

Attachment also has long-term consequences (Bee, 1989). Infants who were securely attached at 12 months of age were more obedient to their primary caretaker and cooperative with strangers at 21 months of age than insecurely attached infants (Londerville & Main, 1981). Follow-up tests of securely attached infants at 2, 3, and 5 years of age revealed that they were more curious and sociable with peers (Arend, Gove, & Sroufe, 1979; Sroufe, 1985). Finally, a longitudinal study showed that infants who displayed the greatest anxiety to strangers at 2 years of age were also socially anxious as 5-year-olds and as adults (Kagan & Moss, 1962).

Thus, early interactions between infants and caregivers can establish trust and confidence that have long-lasting benefits for children. This idea is consistent with Erikson's view of trust as the foundation of infant development. Early experience is no guarantee of later development, however. We must remember that the ongoing patterns of parent-child interaction help maintain the consequences of early experiences (Sroufe, Fox, & Pancake, 1983).

FIGURE 9.16
Cross-Cultural Patterns of Separation Anxiety

Separation anxiety, measured by infant crying, increases quickly until 12 to 15 months of age. Similar patterns of infant distress are observed in many cultures, although the degree of crying may be more intense and longer in some.

SOURCE: Mussen, Conger & Kagan, 1980.

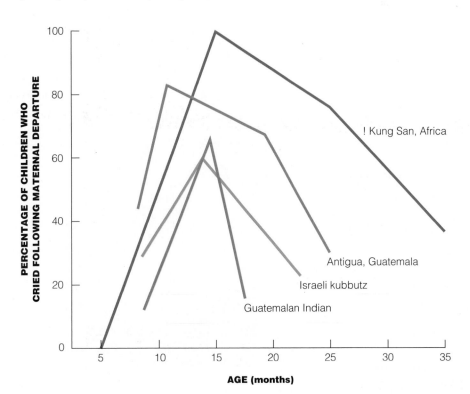

Theories of Attachment.   Researchers have proposed several explanations for attachment, some of them derived from the themes we have been highlighting throughout the text. Ethological theories suggest that the predisposition for attachment is an innate, species-specific relationship that helps protect the young and preserve the species (Bowlby, 1973). Biological factors, including instincts and hormones, are important for establishing emotional bonds (Cairns, 1979). Cognitive theories suggest that attachment depends on children's early abilities to discriminate and remember people. Research has shown that 9- to 12-month-olds who scored highly on tests of object permanence also protested more strongly when separated from their caregivers (Lester et al., 1974). Psychoanalytic theories explain attachment as a consequence of oral pleasure and security derived from being fed.

Finally, learning theories may help explain attachment using principles of reinforcement and conditioning. Is attachment simply a conditioned response to one who feeds an infant? Harlow and Zimmerman (1959) conducted a classic study that refuted this hypothesis. They separated infant monkeys from their natural mothers and gave them two surrogate mothers. One surrogate was made of wire and the other was covered with terrycloth (see Figure 9.17). Regardless of which surrogate provided food, the infant monkeys preferred to stay in contact with the cloth-covered model. Harlow and Zimmerman concluded that the "contact comfort" provided by the cloth mother was more important than feeding and hunger reduction for establishing attachment.

PARENTING STYLES

As we have seen, attachment depends on the quality of interactions between infants and caregivers. Primary caregivers around the world often react in the same nurturing manner toward infants. For example, in a study that compared caregiver-infant interactions in the Unites States, France, and Japan, caregivers in all three countries encouraged infants' exploration, imitated their playful vocalizations, and soothed their cries of distress (Bornstein et al., 1992).

Other patterns of caregiver-infant behavior, however, have varied throughout history and from culture to culture. Seventy years ago, caregivers were told not to coddle or kiss the infants; today they are encouraged to respond to the children's needs for physical contact and affection. In a study of mothers in five countries, Richman and coworkers (1988) observed that American and European mothers focused on verbal and visual interactions with their babies, whereas African and Central American

FIGURE 9.17
Preferences of Monkeys for Surrogate Mothers

Monkeys raised in social isolation prefer "contact comfort." Infant monkeys who were raised without contact with their mothers or other monkeys were offered two surrogates, one covered with wire and one covered with cloth. Regardless of which surrogate provided food to the infants, they preferred contact with the soft, cloth-covered surrogate. Thus, attachment bonds are not determined only by who feeds infants.

SOURCE: Harlow & Zimmerman, 1959, pp. 421–432.

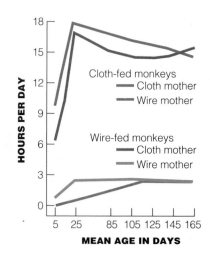

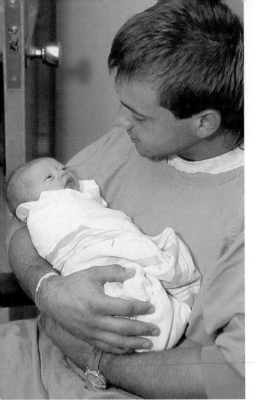

Fathers who participate actively in child care establish warm attachment relationships during the first year.

mothers emphasized physical nurturance and safety. Kenyan mothers soothe their infants, whereas American mothers engage them in emotionally arousing play. Mothers with more schooling, both in America and Mexico, talk to and visually engage their infants more than mothers with less schooling (Richman, Miller, & LeVine, 1992). Research on Mexican American mothers shows that they talk less to their babies than Caucasian American mothers, but cuddle them more (Garcia-Coll, 1990).

Are there distinctive styles of parenting? If so, what impact do they have on children? Baumrind (1967, 1971, 1980) investigated how different parenting styles influence young children's personalities. She observed children in nursery schools, interviewed parents, and observed the families at home. From this information, she identified four styles of parenting:

- **Authoritarian parents** demand complete obedience from their children. They give little explanation for the rules they establish or for the physical punishment they impose when children violate those rules. Respect for authority and hard work are virtues valued by authoritarian parents, so they do not tolerate children's disagreements or laxness. Their children tend to be moody, insecure, and withdrawn.
- **Permissive parents** are responsive to their children; they accept and affirm their children's opinions. These parents are undemanding and do not push their children to adhere to other people's standards. Their discipline is lax and inconsistent. They avoid punishment and tend to reason with children instead. The children often are unhappy, dependent, and immature.
- **Authoritative parents** believe that control is necessary, but they use reason as well as assertion of power when they discipline their children. These families frequently discuss conflicts. They aim to help children conform to group standards without infringing on their independence. Their children are independent, self-reliant youngsters who are friendly, curious, and energetic.
- **Rejecting-neglecting parents** are both unresponsive and undemanding. They are indifferent to their children and spend little time with them. Their children often behave aggressively and do not meet standards of behavior set by others. They also tend to be disobedient and delinquent.

Clearly, the most well-adjusted children in Baumrind's research came from authoritative families who were firm yet caring. Expanding on Baumrind's work, another study found that once the particular parenting style had been established in the family, it usually did not change (McNally, Eisenberg, & Harris, 1991).

DEVELOPMENT OF SELF-CONCEPT

Babies are not born with a sense of self, but they begin distinguishing themselves from other people and objects by 6 months of age. When do they recognize the "self"? Michael Lewis and Jeanne Brooks-Gunn (1979) studied this question by putting a spot of rouge on infants' noses and placing the infants in front of a mirror. They wanted to determine when infants would recognize themselves and try to rub the rouge off their nose. A few of the 15-month-old infants rubbed off the rouge, and nearly all the 18- to 24-month-olds did. This evidence suggests that almost all infants develop some superficial sense of self by the age of 2.

Self-concept emerges in three gradual stages according to Stipek, Gralinski, and Kopp (1990). The first stage, *self-recognition*, develops by about age 2 when children begin to recognize themselves in pictures and mirrors. In the second stage, toddlers provide concrete self-descriptions. When asked to describe themselves, 3- to 5-year-olds usually give physical descriptions of what they look like or what they like to do (Damon & Hart, 1982). Rarely do they offer psychological descriptions of what they think or feel. In the third stage, children attach emotional responses to their self-evaluations, such as feeling guilty for misbehavior or being upset when scolded.

The Competent Self.   Parents usually encourage children to be independent, competitive and successful, whether the task is related to school, arts, or sports. **Achievement motivation** is a complex concept that signifies how much people strive for success (see Chapter 12); it contributes directly to children's developing self-concept. Harter (1981) believes that children can exhibit two different approaches toward achievement. They can derive satisfaction by merely demonstrating their own mastery of certain skills to themselves and others (an *intrinsic orientation* toward achievement), or they can try to succeed to receive prizes and rewards (an *extrinsic orientation*). Harter suggests that children who are intrinsically oriented prefer challenging tasks and perceive themselves as more competent at schoolwork than children oriented to extrinsic incentives.

Children who achieve success feel proud of their accomplishments and also gain self-esteem. Harter (1982) developed a scale to test children's perceptions of their own abilities in four different areas: cognitive abilities, social skills, physical abilities, and general self-worth. She gave the scale to more than 2,000 children from third to ninth grade and also asked teachers and classmates to rate these students on the same items. Even the youngest children had distinctive views of themselves in each area, showing that favorable or unfavorable views of self-competence can be established by 8 years of age. Furthermore, children clearly discriminated their talents in different areas, such as performance on schoolwork and popularity. Were children's self-perceptions accurate? Children's views of themselves did generally match the views of teachers and classmates, although their accuracy improved with age. Children's knowledge and positive feelings about their own achievements contributed to the sense of industry stressed in Erikson's theory (1950) and helped establish a healthy self-concept.

What factors promote achievement and self-esteem? One important factor is the stimulation provided at home. A team of researchers used a longitudinal design to study the relation between children's home environment and school achievement (Van Doornick et al., 1981). The researchers visited the homes of 50 infants and classified the homes as either stimulating or unstimulating, according to an inventory of items. Five to nine years later, the researchers collected data on the children's school achievement. The majority of children from stimulating homes were achieving well at school, while 70 percent of the children from unstimulating environments were experiencing problems.

Parental style also has an influence on children's motivation and self-esteem. Grolnick and Ryan (1989) observed that children in grades 3 to 6 who achieved well in school and were regarded as competent and independent by teachers had parents who were actively involved with their children, and who provided structure and supported their children's autonomy.

Another factor influencing achievement involves children's beliefs and expectations regarding their own abilities. Children who believe that their own abilities and efforts determine their successes and failures are said to have an **internal locus of control.** These children usually achieve at higher levels than those who have an **external locus of control,** who attribute success and failure to luck, chance, or the behavior of others (Findley & Cooper, 1983). Children's expectations about their ability to suc-

DISCIPLINING A CHILD IS SIMPLY TOO MUCH WORK, SO WE'VE DECIDED JUST TO LET SOCIETY DO IT LATER.

BIZARRO by Dan Piraro © Chronicle Features 1989. Reprinted with permission.

Children adopt sex roles and sex-typed behavior from watching parents and others.

ceed are shaped in part by their previous rate of success. Those children who have a history of failure in school often believe that they cannot succeed, and they quit trying. Others who achieve well continue to have high expectations of success (Elliott & Dweck, 1988).

Parents' beliefs about their children's abilities can also influence children's expectations and motivation. For example, many parents of students in fifth through eleventh grade believe that mathematics is easier, more important, and more enjoyable for boys than for girls (Parsons, Adler, & Kaczala, 1982). The researchers found that students' own expectations tended to follow their parents' sex role stereotypes even when the males and females did not differ in prior school performance in mathematics. Thus, personal beliefs, parental expectations, and home environment can all influence children's views of their competence and self-esteem.

Sex Typing. We have seen that independence and achievement are two important aspects of a child's self-concept. A third dimension is the sex role adopted by the child. Sex typing is the process by which a child acquires **gender identity**—(the awareness of being a boy or a girl)—and adopts socially appropriate male or female behaviors. The development of gender identity begins in infancy and is influenced by the way parents dress and speak to the child, as well as countless other parental behaviors. From the very beginning, parents may refer to girls as "sweetie" and boys as "tiger" and dress them in pink and blue, respectively.

By age 3, most children can refer to themselves as either boys or girls, although they do not yet understand that gender is (usually) a permanent condition (Bem, 1983). Thus, a 3-year-old boy may proclaim that he wants to grow up to be a mommy. Most 3-to 5-year-olds can easily classify pictures of people according to sex and age (Edwards, 1984) and can establish the constancy of their own gender identities as well as the genders of other people by age 6 or 7. Some psychologists link this understanding of gender constancy to the development of concrete operational thinking in Piaget's theory.

Children's awareness of sex role stereotypes develops along with gender identity. For example, when given male and female dolls, even 2½- to 3½-year-olds discuss which doll they think is more likely to climb trees, play with dolls, fight, talk, cook, or sew (Kuhn, Nash, & Brucken, 1978; Signorella & Liben, 1985). Children also develop different preferences for toys. Before children acquire a concept of their gender constancy, they play with any interesting toys. But boys who have acquired a concept of their gender identity will play longer with "boy toys" that they see played with by other boys, even if they do not find the toys interesting (Frey & Ruble, 1992).

Preschoolers also develop preferences to play with other children of the same sex (Jacklin & Maccoby, 1978). Boys seem to acquire sex-typed behaviors more quickly than girls, perhaps because fathers are eager for their sons to conform to stereotypical roles (Fagot, 1978). From ages 4 to 10, boys also adhere to sex-typed activities more rigidly than girls. Despite their early interest in masculine activities, most girls begin to prefer and adopt traditional female roles as adolescence approaches.

As these roles become internalized, they often operate like informal theories about what is distinctly male and female behavior and appearance, and when they serve this purpose, they are referred to as *gender schemata*. These theories, or schemata, influence the way children understand other people's sex roles and sex typing. Thus, they are broader concepts than the identity and constancy that children develop about themselves. (See Table 9.5, for a summary of sex-typing terms.)

TABLE 9.5
Aspects of Being Male or Female

Sex role	Outward behavior considered appropriate or desirable for males or females
Sex role stereotype	Simplified, exaggerated conceptions of sex roles and characteristics of males and females
Gender identity	A child's sense of being male or female
Gender constancy	The understanding that gender is permanent and that the child's own gender will never change
Gender schema	Informal theory about maleness and femaleness that children apply to all information that comes their way

SOURCE: Paris, Hall, & Schell, 1994

Sex typing is a process whereby children develop ideas about their gender identity. But much of it is determined by biological makeup and how much depends on child-rearing practices? (You should recognize the controversy between nature and nurture in this question.) Again, there is no simple answer.

CASE STUDY

SOCIAL AND HORMONAL EFFECTS ON GENDER IDENTITY

Money and Ehrhardt (1972) have done a great deal of research on the effects of social influence on gender identity. One of their case studies involved identical twin boys who were given a normal upbringing for the first 7 months of their lives (Money & Ehrhardt, 1972). At 7 months of age, one of the twins suffered an accident during surgery for circumcision, when a device malfunctioned and severed his penis. The physicians advised the parents to rear the injured boy as a girl, and when the child was 17 months old, doctors performed surgery to give him the genital anatomy of a female. Money and Ehrhardt followed the development of the two children until they reached puberty. During this time, the parents followed their doctor's advice and treated the children differently, one as a boy and one as a girl. The effect of this rearing on the injured child's behavior was quite strong. For example, when the child was four and a half, the mother reported:

> She likes me to wipe her face. She doesn't like to be dirty, and yet my son is quite differ-

ent. I can't wash his face for anything. . . . She seems to be daintier. Maybe it's because I encourage it. . . . One thing that really amazes me is that she is so feminine. I've never seen a little girl so neat and tidy as she can be when she wants to be. . . . She is very proud of herself, when she puts on a new dress or I set her hair. (1972, pp. 119–120)

This dramatic case demonstrates that masculine or feminine behaviors can develop from the same set of genes, depending on upbringing. Until the surgery performed at 17 months, the two children shared identical biological characteristics. From that point on, they differed only in their hormonal balance (the injured child was administered dosages of female hormones as a part of the sex-change operation) and the manner in which they were treated socially. Of course, we cannot know if the difference in the twins' behavior was caused by social influence, by the hormone injections, or both. However, the study does show that gender identity is not fixed at birth solely by genetic influence.

SOCIAL RULES AND MORAL REASONING

The development of social behavior involves more than the emergence of the child's self-concept. Young children are extremely self-centered, so to participate in the world, children must become increasingly more considerate of others. Social behavior is a two-way street in which each participant tries to understand the other person's point of view, thoughts, feelings, and intentions. Psychologists refer to this understanding as **social cognition,** a concept that will be discussed more fully in Chapter 7.

During middle childhood, social cognition undergoes significant change. As we have seen, preschoolers think in very concrete terms and tend to describe other people according to their appearance, possessions, or activities. Gradually, this limited perspective begins to fade, and children develop appreciation of the less concrete, more psychological qualities of those around them. Barenboim (1981) divided this process into three distinct phases:

1. *The behavioral comparisons phase.* Between the ages of 6 and 8, children typically describe other people in reference to themselves. A 7-year-old might say, "Marcy is the fastest" or "Fred has more toys than me."

2. *The psychological constructs phase.* Beginning at about age 8 or 9 and often continuing into adolescence, children identify their friends with traits such as friendly, smart, kind, or stubborn.

3. *The psychological comparisons phase.* Usually by the age of 12, children compare and contrast other people in terms of how friendly, how smart, how kind, or how stubborn they are. This stage parallels advances in cognitive development and shows deeper insight into why people behave as they do.

Thus, increased sensitivity to other people accompanies cognitive development during childhood.

Self-Control. Learning to control one's impulses is an important social lesson of early childhood. Infants learn early that they cannot always have things their own way when eating, playing, or getting dressed. Toddlers are admonished not to pull the cat's tail, not to touch electrical outlets, not to play with sharp objects. Nevertheless, if you have ever tried to control disorderly children, you know that they do not always do what you tell them to. In fact, one study found that the louder adults shouted at 3- and 4-year-olds to stop a behavior, the more the children continued the behavior (Saltz, Campbell, & Skotko, 1983). Presumably, the shouting actually served to reinforce the behavior.

When do children develop self-control? Like many other developmental accomplishments, it is difficult to pinpoint an exact age at which self-control is achieved, partly because it depends somewhat on the way we define and measure self-control. Some psychologists have analyzed children's resistance to distraction (i.e., how hard they will work at a task when other things compete for their attention). For example, Mischel and Patterson (1978) gave 3-to-8-year-olds a dull task to do while seated next to a noisy toy called Mr. Clown Box. The 3- and 4-year-old children were often distracted from the chore by the toy, but the older children deliberately ignored the toy, often by talking to themselves with self-instructions.

Young children can also be taught strategies to avoid distractions. Explaining to children why they should not be distracted and explaining how their performance will affect someone else (e.g., "I'll be unhappy and have to do your work if you don't finish") can help children to exercise self-control (Kuczynski, 1983).

Moral Development.   The many facets of social development that we have discussed converge in children's developing sense of morality, or knowing right from wrong. **Moral reasoning** refers to children's ideas about the morality of their own behavior, the way they view other's behavior, and their abilities and inclinations to follow rules. One way that researchers have studied moral reasoning is to confront children with stories that posed dilemmas, such as the following:

> 1. John, who is in his room, is called to dinner. He goes downstairs and pushes open the dining-room door. Behind the door is a chair, and on the chair is a tray on which there are fifteen cups. John does not know that. He opens the door. The door hits the tray. Crash go the cups. All of them break.
> 2. Henry's mother is out and Henry tries to get some cookies in the cupboard. He climbs on a chair and while reaching for the cookie jar he knocks down a cup, which breaks. Who was naughtier, John or Henry? (Adapted from Piaget, 1932)

According to Piaget (1932), 7-to-8-year-olds focus their attention on the outcome and reason that breaking 15 cups is a larger wrong than breaking only 1 cup. Not until 11 or 12 years of age do children take into account other people's intentions and then judge guilt and punishment in relation to these motivations. Other evidence, though, indicates that Piaget underestimated children's moral reasoning. Nelson (1980) showed 3-year-olds pictures of a child throwing a ball at another child and explained that the child was either (a) playing catch with the other child or (b) angry at the other child. When asked to judge the "goodness" or "badness" of the child's ball throwing, even preschoolers could consider the child's intentions, and they correctly stated that the child in (b) was being "bad."

Piaget's ideas have also been refined by Lawrence Kohlberg (1976). Kohlberg studied children's moral reasoning by analyzing how they responded to moral dilemmas posed by short stories. The following dilemma of Heinz is a good example:

> In Europe, a woman was near death from a special kind of cancer. There was one drug that doctors thought might save her. It was a form of radium that a druggist in the same town had recently discovered. The drug was expensive, but the druggist was charging $2,000, or ten times the cost of the drug, for a small (possibly life-saving) dose. Heinz, the sick woman's husband, borrowed all the money he could, about $1,000, only half of what he needed. He told the druggist that his wife was dying and asked him to sell the drug cheaper or let him pay later. The druggist said no, so Heinz broke into the store and stole the drug. Should Heinz have done that? Was it right or wrong? (Adapted from Kohlberg, 1976)

By studying how children reasoned about this and similar dilemmas, Kohlberg devised a stage theory to chart the course of moral development. The three levels of morality, outlined in Table 9.6, are *preconventional, conventional,* and *post-conventional.* Each of these levels contains two separate stages. The preconventional level coincides with Piaget's preoperational period and it reflects a self-centered viewpoint. The conventional level prescribes well-defined rules, much like Piaget's concrete operations. Finally, the postconventional level reflects abstract, principled reasoning not available until the formal operational period. The most recent revisions of Kohlberg's theory no longer include stage 6, because there is so little evidence for it.

A person in Kohlberg's preconventional level of morality might say that Heinz (in the story above) should not steal the medicine for his sick wife, because stealing is wrong (stage 1 morality). A person who reached the opposite conclusion, that Heinz should steal the medicine, but argued that he should do so because it was in his own best interest would also be exhibiting the preconventional level, but in this case, stage 2. A child exhibiting the conventional level of morality might say that Heinz should steal the medicine because he is devoted to his wife and stealing the medicine would show his great concern for her (stage 3 morality). In the postconventional level of morality, a person might say that Heinz should steal the money, but should leave an anonymous note saying that he would pay the druggist back when he could make more money. This person would realize that morality seems relative to one's group and needs and would try to rationalize the crime by saying that the druggist would be compensated later. As you can see from these examples, the actual choice made in the moral dilemma is not so critical in defining where a person would fit in Kohlberg's levels as is the rationale for the decision.

Kohlberg's theory has been criticized because it represents a philosophical ideal, rather than a developmental sequence through which most people pass. Others argue

TABLE 9.6
Kohlberg's Six Stages of Moral Development
These stages show how moral reasoning can be based on different rules and justifications. Young children usually reason at the preconventional level, while adults often use principled reasoning that considers humanistic values.

LEVEL AND STAGE	WHAT IS RIGHT?	REASONS FOR DOING RIGHT	SOCIAL PERSPECTIVE OF STAGE
Preconventional level			
Stage 1 Punishment-obedience orientation	To avoid breaking rules backed by punishemnt and obedience for its own sake.	Avoidance of punishment, the superior power of authorities.	Doesn't consider the interests of others or relate two points of view.
Stage 2 Individualism, instrumental purpose and exchange	Acting to meet your own interests and needs and letting others do the same.	To serve your own needs or interests in a world where you have to recognize that other people have their interests, too.	Aware that everybody has his or or her own intersts to pursue and these conflict, so that right is relative.
Conventional level			
Stage 3 Orientation to mutual relations and expectations between people	Living up to what is expected by people close to you. "Being good" is important and means having good motives, showing concern about others.	Belief in the Golden Rule. Desire to maintain rules and authority that support stereotypical good behavior.	Relates points of view through through the concrete Golden Rule, putting yourself in the other person's shoes. Does not yet consider morality from the system of a generalized perspective.
Stage 4 Social system and conscience	Fulfilling the actual duties to which you have agreed. Right is contributing to society, the group, or the institution.	To keep the institution going as a whole.	Takes the point of view of the the system that defines roles and rules.
Postconventional Level			
Stage 5 Social contract or utility of Laws Perspective	Being aware that people hold a variety of values and opinions, that most values and rules are relative to your group.	Concern that laws and duties be based on rational calculation of overall utility, "the greatest good for the greatest number."	Integrates perspectives by formal mechanisms of agreement, contract, objective impartiality, and due process.
Stage 6 Universal ethical principles	Following self-chosen ethical universal principles of justice: the equality of human rights and respect for the dignity of human beings as individual persons.	The belief in universal moral principles and a personal commitment to them.	Perspective is that of any rational individual recognizing the nature of morality.

SOURCE: Adapted from Kohlberg, 1976.

that moral reasoning is different from moral behavior (i.e., acting in accordance with social rules of conduct). People may discuss dilemmas about morality at a high level, but when faced with actual choices to lie, steal, or cheat, they may act differently. Moral reasoning also varies considerably across situations, and many people question whether morality is as uniform and universal as Kohlberg suggested (M. L. Hoffman, 1984).

Kohlberg's emphasis on reasoning as a basis for morality needs to be complemented with theories that emphasize socialization (Gibbs & Schnell, 1985). The changing nature of families, the influence of television, and distinct cultural perspectives all may influence children's moral reasoning. Finally, Carol Gilligan (1982), has criticized Kohlberg's theory for its bias against women, who are more likely than men to base their moral reasoning on responsibility to others, compassion, and obligation. She believes that women are judged lower than men in Kohlberg's scheme because it emphasizes the ethics of competing rights and justice, rather than the ethics of interpersonal caring. Despite these criticisms, many children from diverse cultures develop from the lower to higher stages of moral reasoning that Kohlberg described. Like Erikson's theory of general stages and crises across the life span, Kohlberg's views illuminate general stages of moral reasoning and provide useful descriptions of developmental trends.

THEMES IN REVIEW

The biological theme in this chapter is exemplified by the role that biological factors and physical maturation play in human development. Genetic factors greatly influence many aspects of physical growth and development, including muscular coordination, the age when most infants walk and talk, and the onset of puberty. Of course, environmental opportunities modify this biological potential through conditions such as nutrition, physical activities, and intellectual and social development. Heredity and environment are interactive.

The learning theme is represented by the strong role that learning plays in the development of almost all human behaviors. Even in the first few days after birth, infants can learn to pay attention to and to modify their environments. Children begin to learn concepts at around 2 to 3 years of age. From 3 to 5 children learn behavioral strategies for searching for objects and for remembering events. During the early years of schooling (ages 5 to 10) they learn cognitive strategies for paying attention, rehearsing items in memory, creating images, and comprehending text.

The cognitive theme is evident in the study of how perceiving, remembering, and thinking develop. Psychologists describe cognitive growth in different ways. Some identify stages of thinking, as in Piaget's theory, whereas others prefer to describe information processing skills that children use. Although stages are useful as general descriptions of differences across the lifespan, they are not rigid timetables nor wholly accurate theories.

The developmental theme is represented by the contents of the entire chapter. Of course, children change and develop daily, and it is difficult to specify a time when they acquire a particular concept or behavior. However, we have seen that preschoolers generally focus on appearances of objects and people, while older children are more likely to examine conceptual and psychological characteristics.

Throughout this chapter, we have commented on the importance of the socio-cultural context in which children are raised, representing the socio-cultural theme. Some of this context is provided by historical events, cultural values, and other factors beyond the control of the family. However, some factors can be controlled by children's caregivers, including diet, exercise, social activities, disciplinary styles, family expectations of academic success, and the size and composition of families. The social context provides models of appropriate behavior and goals for children to pursue. Children learn from the people around them and internalize the cultural values to which they are exposed. In a multicultural society and a "shrinking world," these values and practices differ greatly, so parents must help their children develop confidence in their own unique identity and sensitivity to the differences in others.

SUMMARY

1 Human development is a process of change that reflects the interaction of genetic and environmental factors. Developmental psychologists study how people change physically, mentally, and socially across the life span and why they develop particular habits, talents, and disabilities. Several theories help to identify distinctive developmental changes over certain age periods. Stage theories focus on abrupt, qualitative shifts in behavior during development, while other theories, such as social learning theory, emphasize continuous, gradual changes in human behavior.

2 Over the past 100 years, significant changes in the attitude toward science, an increase in political interest in families, and an increased life expectancy have led to a greater scientific interest in human development. Today, three methods are especially suited to testing developmental hypotheses. The longitudinal method involves repeated testing of the same people over an extended time. The cross-sectional method involves testing subjects of different ages at about the same time. The sequential design includes aspects of both longitudinal and cross-sectional methods to control for cohort effects, or differences between groups due to their being born in different historical periods.

3 There are three periods of prenatal growth: the zygote stage, the embryonic stage, and finally the fetal period. As the developing human passes through these stages, it gradually takes on the appearance of a human baby, and its major systems are refined. Prenatal growth can be impeded by inherited disorders as well as by the mother's age, her level of stress, and her diet during pregnancy. Several methods are available to help diagnose prenatal complications, including amniocentesis, chorionic villus sampling, and ultrasound.

4 Birth usually occurs about 266 days after conception. Although newborn babies seem helpless, they have surprisingly good perceptual and motor abilities, and can touch, taste and smell relatively well. By 2 months of age, infants are able to perceive visual patterns and speech sounds and distinguish colors and brightness to a reasonable degree.

5 Piaget's theory of cognitive development identifies four distinct periods of children's thinking: sensorimotor, preoperational, concrete operational, and formal operational. Cognitive abilities improve as children progress from stage to stage. For example, in the preoperational period (2 to 7 years), children tend to focus on single aspects of stimuli and are fooled by the appearance of objects. However, when they reach the concrete operational period (7 to 11 years), children achieve conservation, the understanding that properties such as number, weight, and volume can remain the same even when the shape or appearance of objects change.

6 Information processing changes in four basic ways during cognitive development. First, children's knowledge becomes more organized. Second, information processing becomes faster as basic processes become more automatic. Third, the use of cognitive strategies to guide attention, language, and memory becomes controlled and deliberate. Fourth, children develop greater metacognition, that is, increased awareness and control of their own thinking. They apply these skills to literacy and academic learning.

7 Humans are biologically prepared to attend to and learn language. The pattern of early language development is virtually the same for babies in all cultures, no matter what language surrounds them. During infancy, babies learn to communicate through social interactions with adults. Children's early word combinations follow regular rules for expressing meaning in grammatical utterances.

8 Erikson's theory of psychosocial development comprises eight stages, each of which involves the resolution of a social crisis. Four of these stages are concerned with social and emotional development in infancy and childhood: trust versus mistrust, autonomy versus doubt and shame, initiative versus guilt, and industry versus inferiority.

9 Attachment is a strong, emotional relationship between an infant and a particular caregiver. Early interactions between infants and caregivers can establish trust and confidence in children and can have long-term effects. For example, infants who are securely attached to their caregivers at 1 year of age tend to be more curious and sociable with their peers at 5 years than are insecurely attached infants.

10 Personal beliefs, the expectations of caregivers, and home environment influence children's achievement motivation and self-esteem. Another aspect of children's self-concept involves sex typing, a process by which children identify themselves as boys or girls and adopt socially appropriate male or female behaviors.

11 The development of social behavior includes not only a healthy self-concept but social cognition, the understanding of other people's points of view, thoughts, feelings, and intentions. Preschoolers characterize themselves and others in terms of appearances and possessions. As they grow older, children describe themselves and other people according to psychological attributes. Social development also reflects self-control, the ability to resist distraction and to delay gratification. Moral development represents a convergence of children's cognitive development, self-concept, and social development.

KEY TERMS

stage theories (p. 353)
longitudinal analysis (p. 355)
cross-sectional analyses (p. 355)
cohort effect (p. 355)
sequential analyses (p. 355)
sensitive periods (p. 357)
zygote (p. 358)
embryo (p. 358)
fetus (p. 359)
fetal alcohol syndrome (p. 360)
amniocentesis (p. 360)
chorionic villus sampling (p. 361)
ultrasound (p. 361)
assimilation (p. 368)
accommodation (p. 368)
sensorimotor stage (p. 368)
object permanence (p. 369)
preoperational period (p. 369)
egocentric (p. 371)
concrete operational period (p. 371)
reversibility (p. 371)
conservation (p. 372)
centration (p. 372)
formal operational period (p. 372)
information processing (p. 374)
metacognition (p. 378)

speech acts (p. 380)
telegraphic speech (p. 382)
semantic features (p. 383)
behaviorist view of language (p. 385)
biological/innate view of language (p. 385)
interactionist perspective (p. 386)
psychosocial development (p. 368)
attachment (p. 387)
securely attached infants (p. 388)
avoidant infants (p. 388)
anxious/resistant infants (p. 388)
separation anxiety (p. 389)
stranger anxiety (p. 391)
authoritarian parents (p. 393)
permissive parents (p. 393)
authoritative parents (p.393)
rejecting-neglecting parents (p. 393)
achievement motivation (p. 394)
internal locus of control (p. 394)
external locus of control (p. 394)
sex typing (p. 395)
gender identity (p. 395)
social cognition (p. 397)
moral reasoning (p. 398)

SUGGESTED READINGS

EISENBERG, N. (1992). *The caring child*. Cambridge, MA: Harvard University Press. An examination of socializing forces, such as peers and schools, that influence children's positive social behaviors, especially empathy and sympathy.

HARRIS, A. C. (1993). *Child development* (2nd ed.). St. Paul, MN: West. An excellent child psychology text that gives a detailed picture of the physical, cognitive, social, and emotional changes occurring from infancy through adolescence.

HOFFMAN, L. W., Paris, S.G., & Hall, E. (1994). *Developmental psychology today*. New York: McGraw-Hill. A readable textbook that includes recent research on major issues across the life span.

KAIL, R. V. (1990). *The development of memory in children.* (3rd ed.) New York: Freeman. A detailed discussion of the changes in memory that occur over development.

MILLER, P. H. (1993). *Theories of developmental psychology* (2nd ed.). New York: Freeman A high-level analysis of key theories, including social learning, information processing, and ethological perspectives, and central figures such as Freud, Erikson, Piaget, and Gibson.

SIEGLER, R. S. (1991). *Children's thinking* (2nd ed.). Englewood Cliffs, NJ: Prentice Hall. An advanced textbook that surveys children's perception, language, academic cognition, and concepts from an information-processing perspective.

WANG, W. S-Y. (1991). *The emergence of language*. New York: Freeman. A collection of chapters that examine human and nonhuman origins of language, cultural influences on language, and psychobiological bases of language acquisition.

FOR CRITICAL ANALYSIS

❶ Identify three significant events in your childhood that shaped your development. Compare them with events identified by other people your age. Why were they so powerful?

❷ Choose one topic in this chapter to discuss with your parents to understand their perspective. It might be your birth, the size of your family, or some school experience. Ask them to explain how their views were influenced by the social values of the time. You might also ask your grandparents the same question to compare changes across generations.

❸ Who are children's heroes today? Identify people who serve as role models for children and who exemplify contemporary sociocultural values. Compare these people with the heroes of previous generations and discuss with your friends how these values will influence children as they become adolescents, adults, and parents.

❹ From your experience, do Erikson's four stages of moral development in childhood make sense to you? Do they correspond to your experiences?

❺ Longitudinal developmental studies examine one group, or cohort, over time. Suppose that your parents had served in a longitudinal study of social or moral development and that you, too, had participated (say, from ages 5 to 15). What social and historical factors operating on you would be generally the same as for your parents? What factors would be different?

PSYCHOLOGY ON THE INTERNET

PEDINFO

(http://www.lhl.uab.edu:80/pedinfo/Diseases.html)

This set of related sites is dedicated to the dissemination of information related to the health of children. This specific part of PEDINFO provides information on a wide range of conditions and diseases that effect children—including behavioral, communication, and developmental disorders.

The Jean Piaget Society

(http://www.wimsey.com/~chrisl/JPS/JPS.html)

"The Society's aim is to provide an open forum, through symposia, books, and other publications, for the presentation and discussion of scholarly work on issues related to human knowledge and its development." This home page includes general information on the Society (e.g., applying for membership & conference programs), instructions for subscribing to the Society's Listserv group, and links to other Internet resources that provide information about human development.

The In Home Speech and Language Checklist

(http://www.xmission.com/~kjay/)

This site provides information relevant to the acquisition of communication skills in children. Sound files demonstrating speech and language disorders in 3 1/2 to 4 1/2 year old children are available for down loading, and lists of age-appropriate developmental milestones are provided for auditory, cognitive, articulation, and language skills. Examples are given of items from a checklist designed to help parents guage the progress of their child's communication skills.

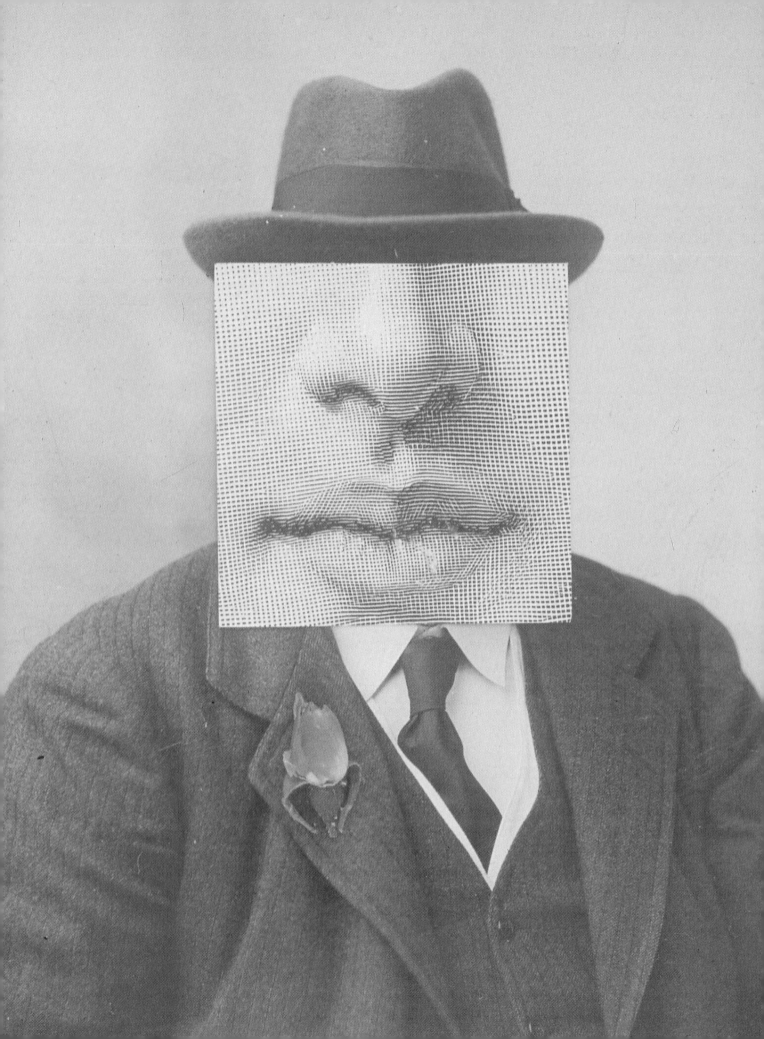

ADOLESCENCE and ADULTHOOD

Chapter 10

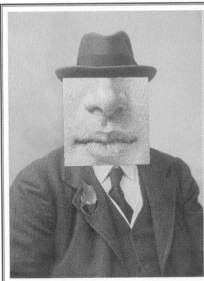

BIOLOGICAL THEME
How does puberty affect adolescent behavior and personality development?

LEARNING THEME
Do adolescent males and females exhibit different kinds of academic achievement?

COGNITIVE THEME
How does memory change during old age?

DEVELOPMENTAL THEME
Do maturational stages or social tasks define development after childhood?

SOCIOCULTURAL THEME
How much do peers influence adolescent behavior?

When does a child become an adult? There are no sharp boundaries in our biological or cognitive development. The transition is usually gradual. Many cultures, however, define the passage from childhood to adulthood with elaborate rituals. For example, among the Mardudjara people of Australia, when boys reach sexual maturity; they undergo nose-piercing, isolation, and eventually circumcision (Tonkinson, 1978). Anthropologist Ruth Benedict (1934) found that boys in a South African tribe were initiated into adulthood by running through a gauntlet of older men who beat them with sticks. Then, during the coldest months of the year, the boys were forced to sleep without blankets and to swim in bitterly cold water. After months of such painful experience, the boys were accepted as adult members of the tribe in a special ceremony. Girls, too, often face initiation rites. The Carrier Indians of British Columbia feared and abhorred girls' sexual development so much that they banished their young women to the wilderness for three or four years. The passage to adulthood in contemporary American society is less clearly defined and more gradual. Still, American rites of passage may include religious ceremonies such as baptism or bar or bat mitzvah as well as the legal rights to drive, marry, drink alcohol, and vote. Clearly, this time of life is marked in different ways among different cultural groups and across different historical eras.

We refer to the period between childhood and adulthood as **adolescence.** It is a period of rapid change marked by a transition to adultlike cognitive, social, and biological functioning. During the past 100 years, the period of adolescence in American society has begun earlier and lasted longer. Today, Americans remain in school longer, delay marriage, and join the work force later than our ancestors did. Many adult responsibilities are delayed as a consequence. This time of prolonged apprenticeship and education is sometimes referred to as the **adolescent moratorium.** The end of adolescence is difficult to pinpoint, but it is usually marked by social and cultural responsibilities such as marriage, parenting, work, or military service. The end of adolescence is therefore specified only loosely by the adoption of adult roles and responsibilities and may vary widely.

In this chapter we survey the child's transition to adulthood. We begin with a discussion of sexual maturity and the consequences of physical development during adolescence. Next we discuss how adolescents' expanded cognitive abilities influence their reasoning and self-concepts. Then we consider some of the challenges and risks facing adolescents today. In the last half of the chapter, we discuss stages of adulthood beginning with marriage and careers and ending with the challenges of old age and dying. We pay special attention to the intellectual and physical changes that accompany aging.

Physical And Sexual Development

Adolescence is marked by changes in physical growth and sexual characteristics. **Puberty** is the period of development in which young people achieve sexual maturity and the capability for reproduction. Changes in body build, hormonal activity, and sexual maturity naturally inspire both joy and anxiety among boys and girls. The interactions among the themes of this book are quite apparent in this chapter. Development in adolescence leads to biological changes, which in turn affect the cognitive and sociocultural arenas. Before we discuss how individuals respond to the changes of puberty, let us briefly describe the biological mechanisms involved.

THE ONSET OF PUBERTY

At the onset of puberty, the hypothalamus (see Figure 2.11, on page 56), located under the cortex and the thalamus, acts like a biological clock that signals the pituitary gland to become active. The pituitary gland then secretes several types of hormones that regulate puberty. The production of hormones in the body is part of a self-regulating feedback system often referred to as a **hypothalamic thermostat** (see Figure 10.1). The hypothalamus produces neurohormones that cause the pituitary gland to secrete other hormones that eventually stimulate production of sex hormones (estrogen, progesterone, and testosterone) in the sex glands (testes in the male, ovaries in the female). When the sex hormones reach a certain concentration in the bloodstream, the hypothalamus reduces its production of neurohormones, which in turn slows down the production of sex hormones and gonadotrophic hormones (those produced in the pituitary whose target is the testes or ovaries).

This feedback system is relatively stable during childhood, but as children enter the adolescent years, the hypothalamus becomes less responsive to existing concentrations of sex hormones in the bloodstream. As a result, the pituitary secretes greater amounts of gonadotropins. This gradual process continues until some (as yet unknown) threshold is reached, whereupon rapid changes in hormonal production occur and puberty

FIGURE 10.1
The Hypothalamic Thermostat

The hypothalamus regulates the production of hormones at puberty. It stimulates the pituitary gland, which in turn sends a signal to the sex glands to produce sex hormones. When these hormones reach a certain level in the blood system, the hypothalamus slows production of neurohormones, and the entire cycle slows.

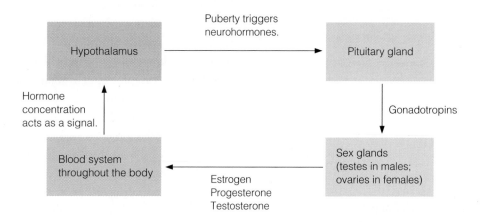

Teenagers develop their physical, cognitive, and social identies during their journeys to maturity.

begins. One idea is that this sudden change in hormone production is triggered by a critical level of body fat (Frisch & Revelle, 1970), but the exact cause of puberty is still unknown (Brooks-Gunn & Peterson, 1983). During puberty, the female's ovaries increase their production of estrogen, and the male's testes increase their production of testosterone, an androgen or male sex hormone. Both sexes have male and female hormones circulating in the bloodstream, but during adolescence, a boy's androgen level becomes 20 to 60 percent higher than that of a girl, and a girl's estrogen level becomes 20 to 30 percent higher than that of a boy (Nielsen, 1991).

Contrary to popular belief, most of the psychological changes during adolescence are only indirectly affected by puberty. The secretion of hormones continues to increase until about age 20 (Offer & Sabshin, 1984); but hormones alone do not account for adolescents' heightened interest in the opposite sex and the growing conflict with parents. Usually by the end of sixth grade, peers have a greater influence on dating and teenage behavior than does the onset of puberty (Peterson, 1985).

PHYSICAL CHANGES DURING PUBERTY

Some of the hormones produced by the pituitary gland influence physical growth and metabolism. The **adolescent growth spurt** is a rapid increase in the rate of physical development that accompanies puberty. The age at which children undergo a spurt in growth has changed over the years. A hundred years ago, males did not reach full height until age 24; the average female kept growing until age 19. Today, adolescents reach their full height two to four years earlier. Fewer childhood diseases, better nutrition, and improved medical care have accelerated adolescent growth for both sexes. Recently, however, the trend has leveled off, at least in Western cultures.

In our society, girls usually begin rapid growth around 11 years of age and boys around 13. For both sexes, growth rate usually peaks a year later and declines quickly during the following year. On average, males are about 6 inches taller than females following puberty (Tanner, 1973), partly because of the action of sex hormones on bone growth. Most growth of bones, particularly the long bones of the arms and legs, occurs at places called *epiphyseal growing plates*. These regions continue to grow until higher concentrations of sex hormones, particularly estrogen, increase the calcium deposits in the growing plates and slow down bone growth. Girls usually begin and complete puberty before boys, and since puberty is generally shorter for girls, their bones have less time to grow before increasing levels of sex hormones slow bone growth. For both boys and girls, some parts of the body grow earlier and more rapidly than other parts; this is why adolescents may temporarily have disproportionately large hands and feet (Brooks-Gunn & Warren, 1985).

Weight changes dramatically during puberty. By age 11, boys have attained only 55 percent of normal adult weight and girls 59 percent. Although body fat decreases after puberty, females lose less fat than males and have more fat as adults in the pelvis, breasts, upper back, and upper arms. There is an opposite trend in muscular development. Boys have more muscle cells than girls do after puberty, and the size of their muscle cells continues to increase into adulthood, whereas girls achieve maximum muscle cell size by age 11 (Root, 1973). Sex-related changes in growth of bones and muscle and the distribution of fat lead to characteristic sex differences in body proportions. Males develop broad shoulders, narrow hips, and relatively long legs; females develop narrower shoulders, wider hips, and shorter legs in relation to their trunk.

The changes that accompany puberty can be a source of great concern for adolescents. About half of all adolescents believe that they are maturing earlier or later than their peers. Often their perceptions are not accurate, but they may lead to feelings of unattractiveness and being "different" that contribute to negative reactions to puberty (Dubas, Graber, & Petersen, 1991). Girls more often than boys experience negative attitudes toward their changing bodies during puberty. This may be due to the contrast between the cultural ideals of thinness for girls and the physical changes of fat redistribution and fat increase that are unique to female development (Richards, Boxer, Petersen, & Albrecht, 1990).

Other changes are evident too. The heart increases in size and nearly doubles in weight. Blood pressure, the number of red blood cells, and the total blood volume increase at puberty, particularly for males (Katchadourian, 1977). The lungs increase in size, and respiratory capacity expands. The gains are greater for males, giving them a higher tolerance for exercise and a quicker recovery from fatigue. For both boys and girls, body odor becomes stronger, the skull becomes wider, the hairline recedes, and the jaw and nose lengthen. Enlargment of skin pores, secretion of oil, and even genetics contribute to acne in about 70 percent of adolescents (Tanner, 1978). The most spectacular changes involve the sexual organs.

PRIMARY AND SECONDARY SEXUAL DEVELOPMENT

Sexual development in adolescence involves both primary and secondary characteristics, as shown in Figure 10.2. **Primary sex characteristics** are those traits related directly to reproduction. For males, the most noticeable primary change at puberty is the enlargement of the penis and scrotum, the pouch that contains the testes. The tubes that carry sperm from the testes to the penis also develop, making ejaculation possible. The size and shape of the penis are not related to physique or frequency of sexual activity (Katchadourian, 1977). The primary changes in the female genitals are enlargement of the clitoris, labia, and vaginal opening. The female delivery system matures to allow ova (eggs) to be transported to the uterus. The uterine wall becomes more muscular, the vaginal lining becomes thicker, and the interior of the vagina becomes acidic rather than alkaline. All of these changes enhance the likelihood of fertilization and impregnation. The ovaries also become somewhat larger and heavier during puberty, primarily because of the development of previously immature ova, or eggs. At birth, the female's ovaries contain a lifetime supply of eggs. Males, on the other hand continue to produce new sperm well into old age. About 18 months after the growth spurt, girls usually experience their first menstrual period, or **menarche.** Menarche does not signal the capacity for sexual reproduction; this may occur anytime from one month to two years later.

Secondary sex characteristics include aspects of physical appearance that may or may not be related to sexual reproduction. As evident in Figure 10.2, many of the visible signs of puberty are secondary sexual characteristics. The growth of pubic hair early in puberty, for example, is a signal of other impending changes. Growth of body hair on the face, in the armpits, and on the chest occurs about two years later and is usually more evident in males, though it occurs in females also. For females, breast development usually begins by age 11 and is completed by age 15, but it can occur anytime between the ages of 8 and 18. Other secondary sex characteristics include a deeper voice because of the enlargement of the larynx and changes in body proportions due to differential growth of bones, muscles, and fatty tissue.

EFFECTS OF PUBERTY ON DEVELOPMENT

All of these physiological changes can have important consequences for the adolescent's self-concept, confidence, and social relationships (Peterson, 1985). A particular

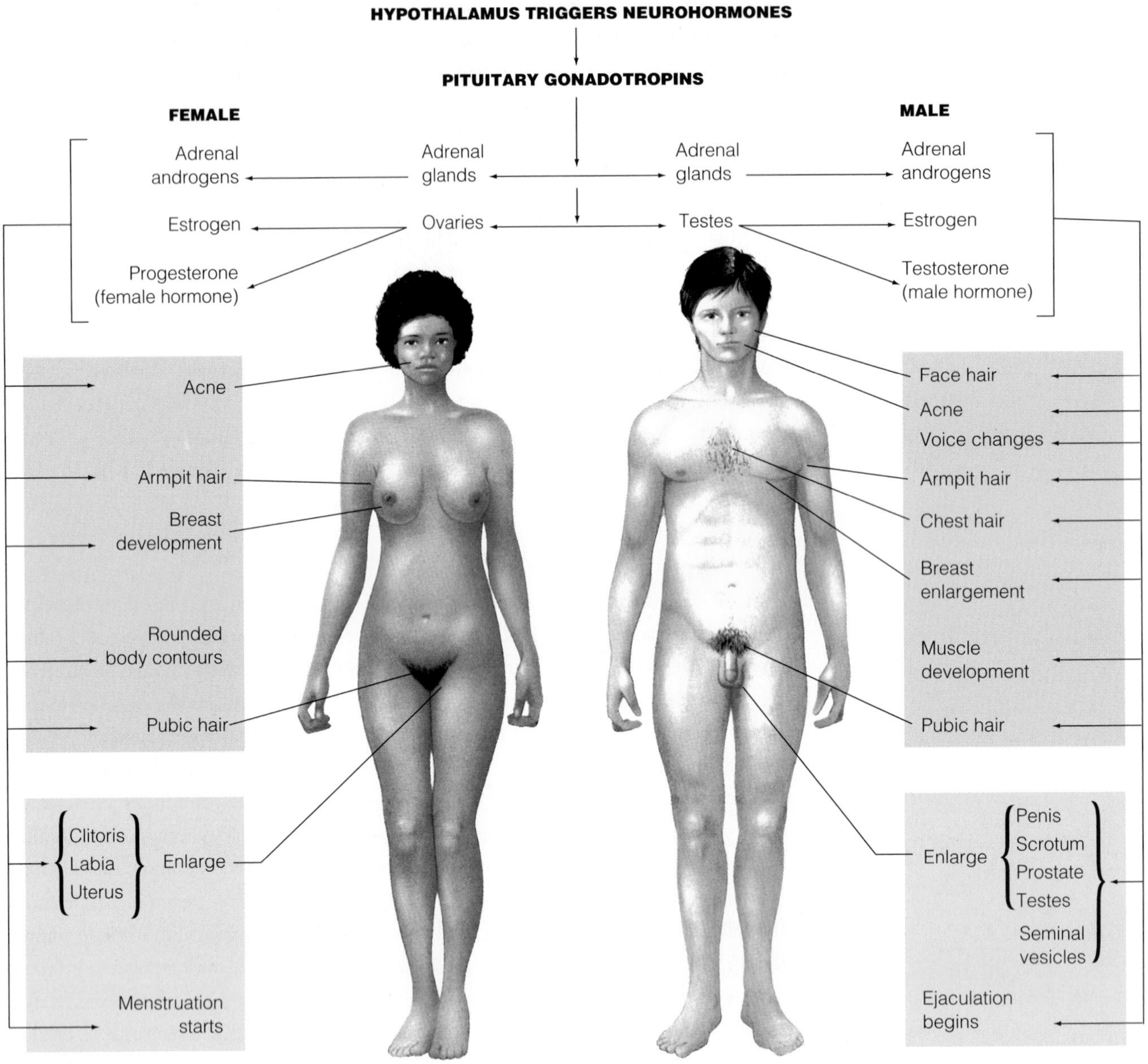

HYPOTHALAMUS TRIGGERS NEUROHORMONES

PITUITARY GONADOTROPINS

FEMALE ⋅ **MALE**

Adrenal androgens ← Adrenal glands ⟷ Adrenal glands → Adrenal androgens

Estrogen ← Ovaries ⟷ Testes → Estrogen

Progesterone (female hormone) ⋅ Testosterone (male hormone)

Acne

Armpit hair

Breast development

Rounded body contours

Pubic hair

{ Clitoris / Labia / Uterus } Enlarge

Menstruation starts

Face hair

Acne

Voice changes

Armpit hair

Chest hair

Breast enlargement

Muscle development

Pubic hair

Enlarge { Penis / Scrotum / Prostate / Testes / Seminal vesicles }

Ejaculation begins

FIGURE 10.2
Primary and Secondary Sex Characteristics During Puberty

Puberty stimulates the production of hormones that prompt maturation and growth. The physical changes may continue for several years after puberty begins. Primary sex characteristics (shown in blue) are related directly to reproduction. Secondary sex characteristics (shown in greeen) give distinctive physical appearances to males and females.

SOURCE: Sarafino & Armstrong, 1980.

concern of adolescents is the first occasion of ejaculation or menstruation. These events can be bewildering, frightening, or innocuous, depending on the adolescent's level of understanding and the parents' attitude and communication about the subject. Likewise, teenagers are often preoccupied with concerns about their height, physique, or skin condition because of the rapid and often vaguely understood changes in these characteristics. Frequently, adolescents are too embarassed to talk to parents or friends about their concerns.

The age at which children experience changes in their primary and secondary sex characteristics varies greatly from child to child. Do children who undergo puberty at an earlier age realize any benefits in their social or personality development? Apparently, there are both advantages and disadvantages of early maturity. The California Growth Study (Mussen & Jones, 1957) identified early- and late-maturing boys ages 14 to 18, using X rays to determine bone growth. The early-maturing boys looked more masculine as adolescents and were more relaxed. They were often popular athletes and social leaders. Late-maturing boys were more likely to feel rebellious against parents, rejected, and socially immature. Early-maturing boys have also been found to have more positive body images and more positive moods in general (Crocket & Petersen 1987). Other researchers, however, have observed some disadvantages for early-maturing boys, noting that they often run into trouble with discipline and authorities. Also, they seem more somber and less curious than late-maturing boys (Peterson & Taylor, 1980).

Girls seem to react differently to the timing of puberty. Girls who mature early are often uncomfortable, less sociable, and less poised, perhaps because they are acutely aware of the differences between their height, weight, and figures and those of their later-maturing peers (Blyth, Simmons, & Zakin, 1985). Early-maturing girls, however, sometimes make better adjustments in adulthood, perhaps because parents have been stricter with them or perhaps because the girls learned to deal with social problems early in adolescence (Jones & Mussen, 1958). In a recent review of the literature on the timing of maturity, Moore and Rosenthal (1993) point out that it is difficult to make comparisons between studies because different studies use different measures to determine how far along an adolescent has matured and different definitions of early and late maturing. Despite these difficulties, these authors conclude that girls and boys are affected differently because late maturing is more stressful for boys while early maturing is more stressful for girls. Because girls mature earlier than boys on average, it is the early-maturing girls and the late-maturing boys who deviate most in development from their peers and therefore experience the most stress (Brooks-Gunn et al., 1985).

Cognitive Development

Although physical changes that accompany puberty are the most visible signs of adolescent development, significant cognitive changes occur as well. Adolescents in Western societies are challenged by more difficult subjects in school (e.g., algebra, biology, chemistry), and they confront moral choices about drugs, sex, and crime. The ability to think abstractly and systematically about these issues develops during adolescence.

ABSTRACT THINKING

Adolescent reasoning is systematic and abstract, which facilitates hypothesis testing and scientific reasoning.

As we saw in Chapter 9, children in middle childhood can classify objects into logical groups, solve problems involving conservation, and master several strategies in learning and remembering information, but they are limited primarily to reasoning about what they can perceive in the present. Adolescents, in contrast, can imagine not only what is but what might be. They have a greater appreciation of logical deduction, symbolism, and irony. Abstract thinking also permits them to begin reasoning about science, religion, morality, and knowledge itself. Thinking about imaginary and hypothetical events is characteristic of the formal operational period of thinking in Piaget's theory, as discussed in Chapter 9.

As thinking becomes more adultlike during adolescence, it takes on three distinct characteristics. First, adolescents can form hypotheses about the world. They are not restricted to manipulating objects physically or actually observing the relations between events in order to understand them. Second, they can use deduction and inference to arrive at answers. Third, the process of generating and testing hypotheses becomes systematic. Rather than use trial and error, they test ideas in step-by-step logical combinations. Have you ever been in a chemistry class where the teacher asked you to identify an unknown chemical substance? You probably made hypotheses about the substance and then tested the hypotheses by putting the chemical in water, in acid, over a flame, or through a filter. By generating hypotheses, testing them, keeping

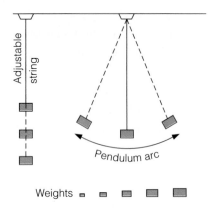

FIGURE 10.3
The Pendulum Problem

In this test of deductive reasoning, the subject is given an adjustable string and a set of weights. The task is to find out what factors (such as the weight attached, length of string, force of initial push) affect the speed of the pendulum's swing.

SOURCE: Inhelder & Piaget, 1958.

records, and arriving at a deductive conclusion, you were engaged in formal operational thinking.

Many of the tasks devised to test formal operational thinking are like the problem-solving tasks discussed in Chapter 8 (Inhelder & Piaget, 1958). One task involves balancing different weights on a balance scale by varying the distance from the scale's midpoint, or fulcrum. Another task involves calculating the angle a billiard ball will follow when it bounces off the side cushion of a billiard table. Still another problem often used to measure deductive thought and systematic hypothesis testing is the pendulum problem illustrated in Figure 10.3. An adolescent is given a pendulum—a weight swinging from a string—and is asked which factors determine the speed of the pendulum's swing. The string can be adjusted to different lengths, and several different weights can be attached. The adolescent is shown that he or she can start the pendulum by pushing it or simply by releasing it. An adolescent with formal operational reasoning will approach this task by varying each factor in combination with the others (attaching each of the different weights to a short string and then to a long string). Through systematic hypothesis testing, the adolescent can deduce that the length of the string determines the time it takes the pendulum to swing from one side to the other. Variations in the weight attached are irrelevant.

Piaget believed that the stage of formal operations reflected mature thinking and that cognitive abilities changed little in adulthood. In other words, experience and schooling could increase our knowledge, but our ability to reason or to use knowledge was largely completed during adolescence. There has been considerable dispute over his claims, however. Some studies show that thinking skills continue to change well into adulthood (Dixon & Baltes, 1986). Others argue that many people do not always think logically according to Piaget's system (Keating, 1980). For example, Martorano (1977) presented children ages 11 to 18 with 10 different Piagetian tests of formal operations and found that performance varied greatly among the children. Although the quality of thinking improved with age, only 2 out of 80 subjects performed at the formal level on all 10 tasks. Similarly, cross-cultural studies consistently fail to find evidence of formal operational thinking in societies without advanced formal schooling (Dasen, 1972). In response to these criticisms, Piaget modified his views about formal operations and argued that education and experience could promote formal operational thinking in specific subject areas. Thus, adolescents and adults continue to develop reasoning skills in particular areas of expertise, both practical and academic.

SCHOOLING AND ACADEMIC ACHIEVEMENT

As adolescents move into junior high school, they pay less attention to academic achievement because they are preoccupied with issues of autonomy, identity, and intimacy (Elmen, 1991). Academic performance often declines from grades 6 to 8, perhaps because of higher standards or perhaps because of the lower value young adolescents place on school (Berndt & Miller, 1990). They often dislike school and show decreased motivation for going to school. Adolescents exhibit greater cynicism toward standardized tests than children in elementary grades. They often try only half-heartedly to do well, especially if they have anxiety about their performance or believe that the scores are unimportant (Paris, Lawton, Turner, & Roth, 1991).

The transition to junior high can be difficult for many students. During seventh grade, most students have lower perceptions of their abilities in math, English, and sports than they did in sixth grade (Wigfield, Eccles, MacIver, Reuman, & Midgley, 1991). Even their perceptions of their social skills decline. Some researchers believe

Adolescence is filled with social and intellectual achievements that help prepare teenagers for adult roles.

that these changes are linked to changes in educational practices that accompany the transition from elementary school to junior high (Eccles et al., 1993). Junior high schools create a competitive atmosphere in which adolescents compare themselves to their peers at a time when they are already apprehensive about their abilities. New schools often disrupt social networks at a time when peer relationships are becoming more important. There is more emphasis on testing and grading, more teacher control, and more rote memorization than they experienced in sixth grade. When the school environment does not match students' needs, students lose interest and look for other things to occupy their time.

Adolescents' perceptions of their abilities and their expectations for the future have a profound influence on their motivation and success in school. In fact, students' expectations in math are better predictors of math grades than are previous grades (Meece, Wigfield, & Eccles, 1990). Wentzel (1989) examined the motivation of high school students with either high or low grade point averages (GPAs) and Scholastic Aptitude Test (SAT) scores. She found that students with the best GPAs had more goals than other students. These goals included getting their work completed on time, being responsible, trying their best, and learning new things. Less than half said that they tried to have fun in class. In contrast, 74 percent of the students with the lowest GPAs said they wanted to have fun and make friends in class. Students with high SAT scores said that their top goals were to understand things and to be successful. Thus, both mastery motivation and high expectations are important for achieving high GPAs and SAT scores.

Adolescents are susceptible to the influence of other people's expectations, especially those of their parents. Some researchers have found that mothers' perceptions and expectations of their children's abilities have a greater influence on children's perceptions of their own abilities than do teachers' ratings (Jacobs & Eccles, 1992). Adolescents' poor perceptions of their abilities may in turn become self-fulfilling prophesies, causing them to lose interest and stop trying. For example, some adolescent girls are exposed to the stereotypical belief that math is too difficult for them and they are not expected to achieve as well as boys. This stereotype may be conveyed by teachers in subtle ways (Eccles & Midgley, 1990). In junior high school, girls begin to devalue math and typically develop higher expectations of their abilities in English, while boys show the opposite pattern. Counselors, teachers, and parents may even advise girls not to take math classes beyond those required. This may explain why **math anxiety,** the fear and nervousness that accompanies math performance and testing, is higher among girls than among boys (Meece, Wigfield, & Eccles, 1990). It may also help explain why males usually perform better than females on mathematics tests. This issue is explored further in "Controversy: Why Do Males Excel in Math?"

Social Development

One of the consequences of abstract thinking during adolescence is the ability to reflect on the personal qualities of oneself and others. For example, when 7- to 8-year-olds are asked to describe other people, they are likely to focus on the way people look, how they dress, what cars they drive, or other concrete characteristics (Livesley & Bromley, 1973). Adolescents are likely to mention more abstract attributes, such as intelligence, sociability, or temperament. They show a growing appreciation for other people's motives, feelings, and social roles (Shantz, 1983). As a result, adolescents form deeper psychological impressions of people and understand the roles people play in dif-

WHY DO MALES EXCEL IN MATH

During the 1970s, Camilla Benbow and Julian Stanley conducted a series of talent searches to identify mathematically gifted students for their Study of Mathematically Precocious Youth. In 1980 they summarized talented students' scores on the Scholastic Aptitude Test (SAT) for the previous six talent searches they had conducted and reported that the top scorers on the math part of the SAT in all six searches were always boys. In fact, twice as many boys as girls scored over 500 on the math portion of the SAT (SAT-M). Benbow and Stanley (1980) considered various hypotheses that might account for the large differences in math scores and concluded,

We favor the hypothesis that sex differences in achievement in and attitudes toward mathematics result from superior male mathematical ability, which may in turn be related to greater male ability in spatial tasks. This male superiority is probably an expression of a combination of both endogenous [produced from within] and exogenous [produced from without] variables. (p. 1264)

Despite the cautious language, Benbow and Stanley were clearly suggesting that males are biologically superior in math to females. Little attention was given to the generaliz-

ability of results from the talented sample to the other 95 percent of the population. Also, no data were collected on spatial reasoning, attitudes, grades, or prior experiences. The blow to sexual equality was struck, and the controversy erupted when the media sensationalized the claims of sex differences in mathematical abilities. Immediately following Benbow and Stanley's (1980) report in *Science, Time* magazine reported the story under the headline "The Gender Factor in Math—A New Study Says Males May Be Naturally Abler Than Females" (1980). And *Newsweek* asked, "Do Males Have a Math Gene?" (1980), while newspapers around the country publicized the issue.

Much of the controversy centered on Benbow and Stanley's interpretation of the data. The letters to *Science* were nearly all critical. Four major problems with the study were summarized by Beckwith (1983) and Eccles and Jacobs (1986). First, the SAT-M is not a pure measure of mathematical ability or reasoning. It is a test that measures achievement and aptitude and is also influenced by students' experiences, beliefs, anxiety, and expectations. (We will discuss the nature of psychometric testing in Chapter 11.) Second, Benbow and Stanley claimed that the educational and informal math experiences of boys and girls are equivalent; yet research on classroom interactions and out-of-school learning suggests that boys may receive more math-relevant instruction than girls (Eccles & Jacobs, 1986). Third, Benbow and Stanley suggested that poorer ability leads girls to show less interest in math and to take fewer courses, but they provided no data linking ability, attitudes, and course selections. In fact, other analyses of the same data showed no relation between SAT math scores and course selections or attitudes. Fourth, Benbow and Stanley implied that male superiority is fixed by biological factors and cannot be

---

ferent situations. For example, teenagers may act differently in different situations, depending on whether they are identified in their role as student, child, sibling, or boy- or girlfriend. This ability to understand other points of view and to adopt social roles is fundamental for acquiring emotional understanding and social relationships (Yeates & Selman, 1989).

SOCIAL COGNITION AND IDENTITY DEVELOPMENT

The emergence of reflective, hypothetical thinking during adolescence also affects a teenager's self-understanding. Adolescents begin to wonder about their future and the choices they confront. Teenagers often exhibit extreme self-consciousness and self-centeredness. They worry a great deal about the way they look. They often imitate the dress and actions of movie stars, rock musicians, or sports figures. They are sensitive about their beliefs and about the way other people regard them. The following excerpt from an interview with a 14-year-old girl illustrates teenage self-consciousness:

I am a very temperamental person, sometimes, well, most of the time, I am happy. Then, now and again, I just go moody for no reason at all. I enjoy being different from everybody

altered. Whether or not the difference in scores is due to genetic factors, the implication may be false, because many behavioral traits with genetic bases can be modified.

Can social factors explain the observed sex differences in math achievement? Eccles and her colleagues studied 250 students in seventh, eighth, and ninth grade and surveyed their parents and teachers. They interviewed each group about their attitudes toward math. They asked parents and teachers about their expectations for each child's success in math, and they collected information about students' grades and courses. Based on correlational research, the single best predictor of academic success in math was mothers' beliefs and expectations about their own children's ability (Eccles & Jacobs, 1986). In the survey, mothers typically had lower expectations for girls than for boys and more anxiety about girls' performance. Further research by Eccles and Jacobs supports the hypothesis that mothers' stereotypical sex role beliefs may indirectly affect girls' math performance (Eccles & Jacobs, 1992). According to this model, girls' math scores begin to fall below the level of boys' scores around junior high because, as a result of being exposed to stereotypical beliefs that males are more adept at math, girls begin to doubt their own abilities. These lower

perceptions of ability then cause girls to lose interest in math, enroll in fewer math courses, and not score as well on the SAT-M.

These social factors become even more important when we consider the role of the media in publicizing sex differences in math scores. Jacobs and Eccles (1985) surmised that the parents in their study may have been influenced by media reports, so they sent all the parents another questionnaire. The questions again measured parents' attitudes and beliefs about math and their expectations for their own children. But they also asked if the parents had heard media reports about sex differences in math. About one-quarter had, most having seen an article in a newspaper or magazine. Mothers who had read or heard that boys are superior to girls in math lowered their estimates of their own daughters' math abilities. Fathers who were exposed to these media reports, however, did not devalue their daughters' abilities. They apparently rushed to defend their daughters and subsequently reevaluated their abilities more

highly than before. Why did mothers and fathers react differently? Jacobs and Eccles (1985) speculate that mothers of daughters project their own anxiety about math to their daughters, while fathers do not project these negative images to their daughters. Because mothers' beliefs may play a large role in shaping girls' attitudes toward math, the great public attention that the media brought to Stanley and Benbow's study may have added to the problem by strengthening mothers' stereotypical beliefs.

Other studies have found that it is not gender so much as prior knowledge and use of strategies that accounts for differences in SAT-M performance (Byrnes & Takahira, 1993). However, it remains unclear why females would have less prior knowledge and use strategies less effectively when they had taken the same number of math courses and received similar grades. Given adolescents' sensitivity to the influences of others (especially their mothers), it seems likely that males are encouraged to engage in more math-related acitivities outside of school and thus may gain more math knowledge and practice with problem-solving strategies. The controversy continues as researchers try to explain the consistent finding that males perform better than females on the math portion of the SAT.

else, and I like to think of myself as being fairly modern. Up till I was about eleven, I was a pretty regular church-goer, but since then I have been thinking about religion and sometimes I do not believe in God. When I am nervous I talk a lot, and this gives some important new acquaintances the wrong impression, when I am trying to make a good one. I worry a lot about getting married and having a family, because I am frightened that I will make a mess of it (Livesley & Bromley, 1973, pp. 239–240).

David Elkind (1985) has suggested that adolescents often appear self-centered, or egocentric, because they believe themselves to be under constant scrutiny. They act as though they are performing before an imaginary audience, a product of their hypothetical reasoning and insecurity. They become preoccupied with their appearance and clothes because they imagine other people's reactions. Teenagers may also construct "personal fables" in which they believe they are unique, powerful, immortal, or at least exceptions to the rule. This kind of belief, epitomized by thoughts such as "It won't happen to me" and "I can't get pregnant," underlies many teenagers' risk-taking behaviors. Adolescent egocentrism declines by the age of 15 or 16 as teenagers increasingly understand the social roles of other people and their own vulnerability (Lapsley & Murphy, 1985).

Identity Versus Role Confusion. According to Erik Erikson's (1980) stage theory, discussed in Chapter 9, **identity development,** the establishment of an independent and positive view of oneself, is a major goal of adolescence. Adolescents confront the challenge of their own identity during this fifth psychosocial stage, which Erickson called identity versus role confusion. Individuals in this stage are seeking answers to questions such as, Who am I? What will I become? How do I fit into my family and society? They are striving for a "sameness" across situations and in the eyes of other people. Erikson maintains that a strong sense of identity is necessary for young people to choose vocations and marriage partners, two critical aspects of young adulthood.

How can we explain adolescent identity development? Identity formation is a process of **individuation,** differentiating ourselves from others. It is a lifelong process that begins in infancy and ends in old age with integration of self and humanity. During adolescence, teenagers explore personal interests, new friendships, alternative lifestyles, and possible careers. They form a sense of self that is not limited to one place or group, although the opportunities and options provided by peers, family, and culture may shape their identity. Personal identity depends on the enduring characteristics that each of us perceives in our own self. A stable sense of competence helps us remove self-doubts and avoid social withdrawal. Thus, the achievement of a stable identity promotes confidence and further individuation.

Identity formation may differ for boys and girls, especially in cultures that prescribe quite different roles for males and females. In America, boys have been encouraged more than girls to make occupational choices during adolescence. When they do make career choices, boys in high school tend to be assertive, to prefer challenging tasks, and to be less concerned about other people's opinions of them (Grotevant & Thorbecke, 1982). Girls are more concerned with interpersonal relationships and responsibilities than with competition and career ladders (Gilligan, 1982). For many adolescent girls, employment is perceived as temporary; marriage is a dominant factor in their identity formation. This traditional gender difference has been challenged by many families who want more egalitarian options for their children. When parents encourage their daughters to be independent and resourceful, the girls often form an identity that reflects the values of achievement and career rather than the status associated with some future husband and family (Mendelsohn, 1990).

Identity formation also varies among cultural groups in America. Many minority adolescents (African American, Native American, Hispanic, or Asian) have their adult roles and responsibilities sharply defined by their families. They have fewer options to explore, sometimes because of socioeconomic conditions and sometimes because of family expectations (Spencer & Markstrom-Adams, 1990). Adolescents also develop a sense of **ethnic identity** in which they incorporate their cultural heritage into their personal sense of self. Many minority adolescents initially reject the negative stereotypes conveyed by the majority culture, reaffirming their pride in their ethnic identity. Among Hispanic and African American adolescents, those who had a stronger ethnic identity also had greater self-esteem than teenagers who had not achieved a coherent sense of self (Phinney & Alipuria, 1990).

FAMILY RELATIONSHIPS

Family bickering and conflicts increase during early adolescence, particularly during the junior high school years. Most disagreements occur over everyday activities such as chores, homework, and getting along with others (Steinberg, 1990). Adolescents typically assert their rights, test the limits of authority, and see flaws in their families.

Parents may react with frustration, confusion, and inconsistency, perhaps because they have ambivalent feelings about their children growing up (Hauser, Borman, Jacobson, Powers, & Noam, 1991). Some tension is inevitable within the family, but it is usually sporadic and not long-lasting.

The Adolescent's Search for Autonomy. Parents and adolescents interpret the conflicts differently. Parents see the problems as issues of social convention and mutual responsibility whereas adolescents see family conflicts as issues of autonomy and personal jurisdiction (Smetana, 1989). Adolescents do not want to be told what to do, but want to control their own lives. The search for autonomy is a central theme of adolescence and is evident in many behaviors. As teenagers search for greater autonomy, they distance themselves emotionally from their families and their resistance to peer pressure declines (Steinberg & Silverberg, 1986). In a sense, they trade dependency on families for dependency on peers, especially in early adolescence. But, as adolescents develop their own identity and values, they rely more on their own opinions and display greater resistance to peer pressure.

By 17 or 18 years of age, adolescents often adhere to many parental values and are less susceptible to peer influences. Parents and adolescents tend to hold similar views toward education, careers, and religion, although they often disagree about dating and spending money. Some parenting styles promote autonomy better than others (recall the four types of parenting discussed in Chapter 9). Authoritative parents encourage autonomy, exert some control, and foster individuation as a balanced relationship between family and peers. Authoritative parents are responsive yet demanding and raise the most self-reliant adolescents. The teenagers of authoritative parents show more responsibility and have better work skills than adolescents raised in families that are authoritarian, permissive, or rejecting-neglecting (Baumrind, 1991). As adolescents, they have fewer emotional problems and substance abuse problems. Also, authoritative parenting leads to better school performance and higher academic motivation (Steinberg, Lamborn, Dornbusch, & Darling, 1992).

Puberty affects the family relationships of boys and girls differently (Steinberg, 1988). When boys begin puberty, they have increased disagreements with their mothers; they interrupt them more often and defer to them less. Eventually, mothers stop arguing and resign themselves to a different relationship in which they often defer to their sons. Fathers, in contrast, seem to gain power and authority over their sons during adolescence, or perhaps they just exercise it more frequently. When girls begin puberty, they become detached from their families and spend more time with peers or alone. They see their families as more controlling and their mothers as more critical. Parents become less effective at monitoring their daughter's behavior, and the mother's, but not the father's, affection for the daughter may decrease (Anderson, Hetherington, & Clingempeel, 1989).

Effects of Divorce. Divorce can affect adolescents in both positive and negative ways. Adolescents from divorced, single-parent families tend to do worse in school and get in trouble with authorities more than do children from two-parent homes, perhaps because single parents find it difficult to monitor their children on top of their other responsibilities. Mothers who head a household alone usually allow teenagers more autonomy than when two parents (or adults) are present (Dornbusch, Ritter, Leiderman, Roberts, & Fraleigh, 1987). For example, adolescents in single-parent homes are more likely to make their own decisions about spending money, friends, clothes, and curfews. Early autonomy in many cases is correlated with low grades and delinquency, perhaps because teenagers take advantage of their freedom. Yet, many divorced families actually experience fewer conflicts than intact families, because the adolescents in single-parent families already function more independently (Smetana, Yau, Restrepo, & Braeges, 1991).

A critical factor in how adolescents cope with divorce is how the parents react to the adolescents. If perhaps the mother withdraws her affection, the adolescent may feel anxious, guilty, or ashamed, becoming depressed or withdrawn. If the mother becomes lax or permissive, the adolescent, especially if a boy, may become aggressive or destructive (Fauber, Forehand, Thomas, & Wierson, 1991). Remarriage may solve some of the problems (e.g., financial stability, mother's happiness), but frequently the mother becomes more authoritarian, and the new stepfather acts like a polite visitor, neither demanding nor affectionate. When this occurs, the adolescent can become detached from the newly constituted family. Moreover, daughters often view their stepfathers as intruders and exhibit more conflicts adjusting to stepfamilies than do sons (Vuchinich, Hetherington, Vuchinich, & Clingempeel, 1991). Girls may become sulky and boys defiant in a situation of ambiguous parental authority and love (Sessa & Steinberg, 1991).

PEERS AND FRIENDSHIPS

Because teenagers spend half their waking hours with peers and less than 10 percent with their parents, peers can exert a tremendous influence on adolescent development. Crockett, Losoff, and Peterson (1984) tracked 300 adolescents from sixth to eighth grade and found that 80 percent of eighth-graders identify one person as their "best friend" and several others as "good friends." Best friends see each other every day in school, visit each other's homes, and talk on the phone 30 to 90 minutes each day. Girls talk more than boys do and are more interested in establishing emotional and confidential relationships. Boys establish friendships more on the basis of play and companionship. By late teens, girls feel more secure in their identities and are comfortable sharing their interests with pairs or groups, while boys continue to socialize with cliques or gangs (Douvan & Adelson, 1966). Girls' friendships involve more emotional self-disclosure and are more intimate than are boys' until late adolescence (Papini, Farmer, Clark, Micka, & Barrett, 1990).

For both boys and girls, gangs are becoming increasingly popular as a source of identity and social support. Gangs now exist in small towns as well as large cities and represent most racial and ethnic groups. Unfortunately, violence is the mainstay of gang culture. Although the targets of gang violence are usually rival gang members, innocent individuals are victimized as well (Harris, 1993). Helping adolescents stay out of violent gangs involves providing them with alternative sources of support and acceptance, and showing them productive ways to use their free time (Bazar, 1990).

Cliques become important for adolescents in high school and are usually based on popularity. For boys, popularity often means athletic ability, but for girls, appearance is most important. Young adolescents tend to belong to cliques whose members are the same sex, but by mid-adolescence, dating becomes important, and cliques include both boys and girls. Cliques begin to lose importance as adolescents establish intimate relationships as couples.

The influence of peers on adolescent development is evident when we examine how teenagers spend their time. Mihaly Csikszentmihalyi and Reed Larson (1984)

Peer groups have great influence in early adolescence. The pressure to conform to the group's behavior is strong.

gave medical beepers to 75 boys and girls between 13 and 18 years of age. When the beepers sounded at random times throughout the day, the teenagers recorded their activities. The reports revealed that adolescents spend about 29 percent of their time working in school, studying, or working at jobs; 31 percent of their time doing daily chores such as eating, dressing, and running errands; and 40 percent of their time doing leisure activities. American teenagers spend only 38 hours per week in school and studying, compared to 52 hours spent by Russian students and 59 hours spent by Japanese teenagers. More than 40 percent of American teenagers are employed, and they work almost 20 hours per week. Consequently, they spend little time—less than 8 percent with their families. They talk nearly three times as much to their peers as to their parents and other adults, much of this on the telephone. American teenagers also spend 25 percent of their waking hours in their rooms alone relaxing, feeling moody, or getting ready for some activity. The stereotype of teenagers coming and going from the house, talking long hours on the phone, and being reclusive in their bedrooms may be fairly accurate.

SEXUAL ATTITUDES AND BEHAVIOR

The period of adolescence presents many conflicting messages about sex. Adolescents are virtually bombarded by sexual suggestiveness in the media, while parents provide warnings about and restrictions against sexual behavior. The threat of AIDS and other sexually transmitted diseases, as well as historical shifts in social attitude, makes the situation volatile and confusing. Adolescents must sort out these mixed messages and develop a sense of their own physical and psychological sexuality. According to Feinstein and Ardon (1973), adolescent dating includes four stages. The first stage of sexual awakening involves petting, kissing, and experimentation. The second stage may include intense short-term relationships such as "going steady." The third stage of acceptance of the sexual role includes mutual trust and increased sexual activity. The fourth stage is the development of a permanent love affair (which may not occur until 18 to 22 years of age) and involves intimacy and reciprocity.

Dating behavior varies from region to region and even from school to school, depending on such things as the availability of activities, family expectations, and the possession of a driver's license. Although having a boyfriend or girlfriend is important to young adolescents, only a quarter of seventh-graders and half of eighth-graders are dating (Crockett, Losoff, & Peterson, 1984). Dating leads to intimacy, but in different ways for boys and girls. Girls blend sexual behavior into relationships based on sensitivity and caring, whereas boys place more importance on the sexual relationship (Bollerud, Christopherson, & Frank, 1990). Young adolescent boys also have more permissive attitudes about sexual behavior than do girls, who tend to reserve sexual intimacy only for someone with whom they are in love. In one particular study, McCabe and Collins (1990) found that boys wanted more sexual intimacy at all levels of dating and that boys' desire for sexual intimacy grew more quickly than girls' as they progressed through the stages of dating. This may explain why males generally have more positive feelings about their first sexual experience than do females. In one survey (Sorenson, 1973), almost half the males reported excitement about their first experience with intercourse compared with 26 percent of females. Moreover, when asked about their feelings about premarital sex, only 17 percent of the males compared to 63 percent of females said that they felt afraid. Affection, love, and intimacy are reported by both sexes as more important reasons for having intercourse than is physical pleasure (Offer, Ostrov, & Howard, 1984). Adolescents regard sexual morality as a personal

Physical attractiveness assumes greater importance for teenagers as they reach sexual maturity.

matter based more on affection for partners than on law or social standards. Females, however, feel more strongly than males that sex should be reserved for someone with whom they share a loving relationship.

Masturbation is the most common form of sexual experience for teenagers of both sexes (Katchadourian, 1990). Many teens experience anxiety or guilt about masturbation; however, there is no indication that masturbation increases later sexual maladjustment or that it is otherwise harmful to one's health (Moore & Rosenthal, 1993). With regard to homosexuality, Hass (1979) found that homosexual contacts during adolescence are most frequent before age 15 and are slightly more common among boys (14 percent) than among girls (11 percent). Despite permissive attitudes, reported rates of adolescent homosexuality have not changed much in the past 30 years. Recent studies of gay and lesbian adolescents have revealed that most of them are comfortable with their lifestyle, although their adjustment depends on the reactions of friends and families (Savin-Williams, 1991).

More liberal attitudes have been accompanied by changes in adolescent sexual behavior. Premarital sexual intercourse has increased during the past three decades, particularly for white middle-class females. In 1970, less than 30 percent of girls between 15 and 19 had engaged in premarital intercourse, but by 1988, the figure had risen to 52 percent (Child Trends, 1992). By age 19, 76 percent of both sexes have had premarital sex. For both whites as well as African Americans, males are more likely than females to engage in premarital sex. Males also report having more partners than females, who often report having only a single partner. Most adolescents are not promiscuous, however. Most are sexually active only with partners whom they love or intend to marry (Zelnik, Kantner, & Ford, 1981).

CONCEPT SUMMARY

PUBERTY

ADOLESCENCE IS MARKED BY:
- Biological changes (hormonal changes cause the growth spurt and the development of sexual characteristics)
- Cognitive changes (development of abstract reasoning and logical thinking)
- Social changes (friendships, sexual attraction, the includence of peer pressure)

Challenges and Risks During Adolescence

Adolescence is sometimes portrayed as a time of rebellion and turbulence. Although this image is often exaggerated, there are many sources of adolescent anxiety, including puberty, dating, parental discipline, and development of an individual identity. Although thinking skills help adolescents reason about these problems, they still must negotiate a twisting road to adulthood that presents many obstacles. In this section, we discuss some common misconceptions about adolescence and some problems that teenagers encounter.

MYTHS ABOUT ADOLESCENCE

Myth 1: Adolescence is a period of storm and stress.
The emotional turmoils of adolescence have often been the concern of parents and clinical psychologists, but the portrait of upheaval presented in the first textbook on adolescence, written by G. Stanley Hall (1844–1924) in 1904, may be exaggerated. The attitude that extreme duress and depression represent normal adolescent develop-

ment is commonly reflected in the media. However, this attitude is not well supported by research (Petersen, et al, 1993). For example, a survey of Chicago teenagers revealed serious emotional distress in 17 percent of the males and 22 percent of the females, rates that are comparable to the 20 percent of adults with emotional problems (Offer, Ostrov, & Howard, 1984). In another study, it was found that only 11 percent of adolescents experience serious chronic difficulties, with another 32 percent experiencing intermittent difficulties and 57 percent enjoying basically positive and healthy development (Petersen & Ebata, 1987).

Myth 2: Adolescents rebel against their families.

Most teenagers have a good relationship with their family. Most teenagers report that they get along well with their parents, parental discipline is "about right," and they discuss serious decisions with their parents rather than their friends (Adelson, 1985). The day-to-day arguments usually involve minor issues such as curfews, dress style, cars, and friends, and the conflicts are generally about immediate gratification and not about basic values.

Myth 3: There is a "generation gap" between the ideas and values of parents and adolescents.

The differences are greatly exaggerated. Most teenagers share their parents' values about religion, school achievement, and professional aspirations. For example, Lerner (1975) asked adolescents and parents to respond to 36 statements on a contemporary-topics questionnaire. In addition to offering their own opinions, adolescents told how they thought their parents would respond, and parents did the same for the adolescents. Adolescents and parents basically agreed on most issues, although the strength of their beliefs often varied. Lerner found that adolescents tended to overestimate the differences between their parents' attitudes and their own views, whereas parents tended to underestimate these differences. This study suggests that the perceptions that adolescents and adults hold of each other may be the source of the popular misconception of a "generation gap" in ideology.

Although adolescents are more like their parents than they are different, they still must encounter new tasks and challenges. They confront choices that can affect their entire lives, and many teenagers experience problems with drug abuse, unwanted pregnancy, delinquency, and emotional distress. Of those who do face such problems, the overwhelming majority successfully overcome them.

SUBSTANCE ABUSE

One of the major threats to health during adolescence is substance abuse. A wide range of legal and illegal substances are available to adolescents, including such common items as tobacco, caffeine, glue, paint vapors, alcohol, and pills. In a national survey commissioned by the National Institute on Drug Abuse, Johnston, Bachman, and O'Malley (1982) observed that 90 percent of the high school students they surveyed reported drinking alcohol within the past year. More than 20 percent got drunk frequently. More than 20 percent of high school seniors reported daily cigarette smoking, and 9 percent reported using marijuana daily. Thirty percent admitted using other illicit drugs such as amphetamines and cocaine. The survey concluded that drug use by adolescents is widespread; nearly two-thirds of high school students reported using illicit drugs.

Substance abuse is associated with several factors. Academic correlates of substance abuse include poor school performance, repeating a grade, frequent conflicts with teachers, and suspension. Family-related correlates include high levels of conflict and patterns of laissez-faire parenting. Drug abuse is also more frequent among emotionally distressed adolescents with low self-esteem and antisocial feelings (Bettes, Dusenbury,

Most teenagers share basic values and good relationships with their families.

Kerner, James-Ortiz, & Botvin, 1990). Peer pressure can be linked to the onset of drug abuse is many cases. One study found that about one-third of adolescents use drugs because their friends do (Kovach & Glickman, 1986).

Alcohol is usually the first drug used by teenagers. About 65 percent of adolescents have used alcohol by the ninth grade (Gans & Blyth, 1990). Adolescents who become problem drinkers often are depressed, angry children with a history of academic difficulties who come from families that provide little attention, affection, or control (Brook, Whiteman, Gordon, & Cohen, 1986). Alcohol use can lead to experimentation with other drugs and even adult alcoholism (Zucker, 1987).

Although most teenagers are primarily recreational drug users and not drug addicts, substance abuse varies historically. Following dramatic increases during the 1960s and 1970s, overall drug use has declined. Fewer teenagers used tobacco, drank hard liquor, or smoked marijuana during the 1980s (Greenwood, 1992). Unfortunately, the widespread availability of "crack" has doubled the use of cocaine by adolescents. Increased awareness about the consequences of substance abuse and peer pressure for healthy lifestyles may help maintain a reduction in drug use among teenagers.

SEXUALLY TRANSMITTED DISEASES

Sexual activity among adolescents is changing owing to a greater understanding of the risks involved, but there is still an alarming increase in sexually transmitted diseases. The rate of gonorrhea has tripled during the past 30 years. When untreated, gonorrhea may result in infertility in females and sterility in males. Herpes simplex virus II has reached epidemic proportions. (Herpes causes painful genital sores in adults and can be fatal to babies exposed to the active virus during birth.) Because herpes and AIDS—a deadly disease that can be transmitted through sexual intercourse—are currently incurable, adolescents have increased their use of condoms and taken other measures to make their sexual activity safer. But despite improvements in adolescent contraceptive practice, many studies on sexually active teenagers in Western countries still find that teenage use of contraception is alarmingly infrequent and irregular (Moore & Rosenthal, 1993).

TEEN PREGNANCY

The most obvious consequence of adolescent sexual activity is pregnancy. In the United States, roughly 1 out of every 10 women aged 15 to 19 become pregnant each year (Trussel, 1988). Also, the percentage of these births that are unintended has increased in the past decade. In one study, 87 percent of births among teenagers were reported to be unintended, in the period from 1985 to 1989, compared with 79 percent in the late 1970s and early 1980s (Moore, 1992). The birth rate among adolescents is much higher in the United States than in other developed countries such as Canada, Japan, and Sweden, even when rates of sexual activity are similar (Takanishi, 1993). Why? Many American teenage girls apparently have little motivation to avoid pregnancy (Moore, 1985). They may be unhappy at home or dislike school and think that having a baby will enrich their lives. Others may be poorly informed about sexual practices, may use ineffective contraceptive methods, or may just not consider the long-term consequences of their actions.

About 40 percent of pregnant teens each year elect to have an abortion (Rosenheim Testa, 1992). The rate increased sharply, especially among African Americans, following the 1973 Supreme Court decision legalizing abortion (Forrest, Sullivan, & Tietzke, 1979). Of the half million babies born each year to teenage mothers, about 37 percent

Despite similar rates of sexual activity, teenage pregnancies occur at a much higher rate in the U.S. than in other developed countries.

There are several reasons for this anomaly. First, males use more lethal means, such as guns, while females resort to poison. Second, adolescent girls usually use suicide attempts as a message; they want to be rescued. Third, adolescent girls have more social support than boys to help them cope with the threatened suicide.

Suicide victims frequently have a long history of maladjustment and depression, but specific crises, such as pregnancy or academic problems may trigger suicide attempts. The increase in adolescent suicide over the past 20 years may be due to the increased availability of firearms, and increasing pressure on adolescents to be responsible and succeed at an early age (Garland & Zigler, 1993). Despite the array of conflicts and challenges faced by adolescents today, most overcome the problems and make a successful transition to adulthood.

Stages of Adulthood

Children may perceive adults as basically alike. However, psychologists have charted several distinct stages of adulthood. We consider two overlapping theories here, which guide the rest of this chapter.

ERIKSON'S STAGES REVISITED

Throughout Chapters 9 and 10, we have referred to Erik Erikson's (1950) stages of psychosocial development. We have seen that at each stage, a person struggles with a basic conflict that, if resolved, successfully provides a transition to the next stage. The eight stages, conflicts, and positive outcomes are summarized in Figure 10.4. The resolutions of each developmental conflict persist throughout life. For example, hope that develops during infancy becomes faith in old age; autonomy during childhood influences future adult independence. Erikson's last three stages encompass development during young, middle, and older adulthood.

Young Adulthood: Intimacy Versus Isolation.   The main task of young adulthood, according to Erikson, is to establish love and intimacy in personal relationships. This requires mutual commitment and compromise and depends to some extent on the prior establishment of personal identity. During stage VI, young adults try to avoid social isolation and alienation that may lead to a lack of warmth or deep emotional exchange.

Middle Adulthood: Generativity Versus Stagnation.   A central task of middle adulthood is to make an enduring contribution to other people and society. One way to do this is by creating and caring for a family. This joint activity builds on the mutual intimacy of marriage and extends to children, a home, and a stable future. According

FIGURE 10.4
Erikson's Stages of Psychosocial Development

According to Erikson, each stage of life involves a fundamental conflict. The positive resolution of conflicts leads to a sense of hope, will, and so forth, that strengthens an individual and enhances subsequent development.

SOURCE: Erikson, 1950.

DEVELOPMENTAL STAGE	CONFLICT	POSITIVE RESOLUTION
I Infancy	Basic trust versus mistrust	Hope
II Toddler	Autonomy versus shame, doubt	Will
III Early childhood	Initiative versus guilt	Purpose
IV School age	Industry versus inferiority	Competence
V Adolescence	Identity versus role confusion	Fidelity
VI Young adulthood	Intimacy versus isolation	Love
VII Adulthood	Generativity versus stagnation	Care
VIII Old age	Integrity versus despair	Wisdom

FIGURE 10.5
Developmental Periods in Early and Middle Adulthood

Levinson proposed three major stages of adult development—early, middle, and late—that each lasts about 25 years. The transitions to each stage may require up to 5 years and can be filled with self-examination, crisis, and major changes in career orientation or family relationships.

SOURCE: Levinson, et al., 1978, p. 57.

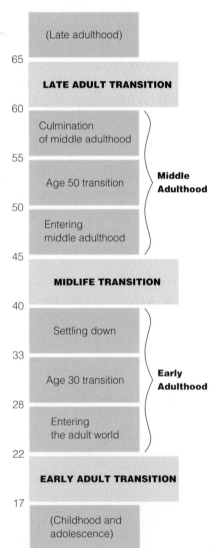

to Erikson, establishing a family provides a sense of generativity that is productive and satisfying. Feelings of generativity can also be expressed through one's work when it is directed to help other people or to improve society. Failure to generate a sense of caring during stage VII may lead to self-indulgence and boredom. It can also lead to pseudo-intimacy, in which couples analyze each other and their relationship without a commitment to nurture it.

Old Age: Integrity Versus Despair. The eighth and final stage of Erikson's theory is a struggle between integrity and despair. It is a time to accept one's life, to gain a broad perspective of the past, and to achieve satisfaction. Successful aging provides a sense of wisdom. When despair predominates, people may fear death and desperately seek another chance at life. Children can be influenced by the reactions of the elderly to the closing years of life. As Erikson (1950) said, "Healthy children will not fear life if their elders have integrity enough not to fear death" (p. 233).

LEVINSON'S STAGES OF ADULT DEVELOPMENT

Erikson's stages of development do not constitute the only theory of change during adulthood. The occupations that people choose and the patterns of their professional careers provide different insights into adult development. Daniel Levinson and his colleagues (1978) have identified stages of adulthood by analyzing patterns of men's lives. They interviewed 40 men in depth about their lives, aspirations, families, and backgrounds. The sample included 10 executives, 10 biologists, 10 factory workers, and 10 novelists. Some of these men were African American and some Caucasian, and they were all between 35 and 45 years of age. When the data from the many interviews and tests were analyzed, the researchers found similar patterns of development during early and middle adulthood. The men had progressed through several stable periods preceded by transitions that were often crucial turning points in their lives. Although Levinson collected data only from young and middle-aged adults, who were all male, he proposed three overlapping stages of adult development, as illustrated in Figure 10.5. Each period is approximately 25 years long, including transitional periods of about 5 years.

According to Levinson, early adulthood is begun by the early 20s. During this stage, the men in Levinson's study were characterized as "novices" in the workplace who tried to establish their career goals while working with other people. They were often guided by their "dreams" or idealized versions of their adolescent aspirations. Striving for these ideals is consistent with the search for identity emphasized in Erikson's theory. From 30 to 40 years of age, the men tried to advance their careers, gain prestige, and settle down. As each man established his own career, he relied less and less on guidance from older workers, superiors, and mentors.

The midlife transition begins at about age 40, according to Levinson, and may involve radical changes in career and orientation to the family. Men may reevaluate their jobs, marriages, and goals and may choose to change careers, to divorce, or to move to another city. In Levinson's study, most of the men experienced major emotional turmoil during the midlife transition. Once the crises were over, however, middle adulthood to age 50 was often very satisfying and productive. The age 50 transition may be severe if there are few changes in lifestyle at age 30 or 40, but men usually find the years from 50 to 60 fulfilling because of career and family accomplishments.

Levinson's study does not provide data on further aging, although there may be several stages of development past age 60. The study included only a small number of men from the northeastern United States in the 1970s. Although his work popularized "the seasons of life" and "passages" (Sheehy, 1976) of adult development, the generality of his conclusions awaits further research.

Dividing the course of life into separate stages gives researchers a practical and systematic approach to study continuity and change during adult development and aging. Realistically, however, it is difficult to clearly delineate one stage of adulthood from the next. Divisions occur differently from one person to another, from one culture to another, and throughout history. Even distinct classes within the same society view the stages of adulthood differently. For example, members of the working class in the United States tend to view a person as being middle-aged at 40 and old at 60, whereas members of the middle class do not view a person as being middle-aged until 50 and old until 70 (Neugarten, 1968). Age-defined stages may, in fact, be increasingly irrelevant in a society where there are no longer rigid expectations or time constraints for finishing an education, joining the workforce, marrying, starting a family, seeking promotions, or retiring. Seventy-year-old college students and 50-year-old retirees have changed our views of adulthood and aging, and as Neugarten (1975) predicted, we may yet become an age-irrelevant society. Nevertheless, using the divisions provided by Levinson and colleagues (1978), we will briefly review the major events of adulthood.

TASKS OF EARLY ADULTHOOD

According to Robert Havighurst (1953), the major responsibilities of young adults are to select mates, learn to live with marriage partners, start families, manage homes, adopt occupations, take on civic responsibilities, and find congenial social groups. Many of these tasks have changed over time. Today, many young adults prefer to remain single or to live with one another rather than commit themselves to a traditional early marriage. Being single no longer carries the stigma of deviance that it did just 30 years ago. In 1960, almost 90 percent of adults surveyed in Chicago agreed that women should marry between the ages of 19 and 24. In 1980, only 40 percent believed that women should marry that early (Hagestad & Neugarten, 1985).

Marriage and Family. Patterns of marriage and childbearing have changed considerably in the past 40 years. In 1972, 72 percent of women and 47 percent of men between 20 and 24 years of age were married. By 1990, these figures had dropped to 35 percent of women and 21 percent of men (U.S. Bureau of the Census, 1990). The tendency to delay marriage is due to many factors, including increased college enrollment, acceptance of single lifestyles, and increased cohabitation without marriage. Young adults today also have fewer children and start their families later. In 1960, 24 percent of married women between the ages of 20 and 24 and 13 percent of those between the ages of 25 and 29 were childless. Twenty-five years later, those figures nearly doubled (U.S. Bureau of the Census, 1986). This trend toward postponing childbirth has resulted in a surge of women in their 30s who give birth for the first time. There are many reasons for these changes in lifestyle, including greater life expectancy, more career opportunities for women, wider use of contraception, and greater financial pressures. It has been estimated that it will cost over $100,000 for a middle-class couple to raise a child born in 1990 to the age when the child enters college.

When young adults become parents, they often adopt more stereotypical gender roles. The number of conflicts and disagreements increase but this may be similar to childless couples, who also have more disagreements in the second and third years of their marriages (Kurdek & Schmitt, 1986). First-time mothers sometimes experience postpartum depression, or the "baby blues," during the infant's first year, during which they may feel increasingly negative about the father and increasingly positive about the baby (Fleming et al., 1990). By the baby's first birthday, the mother's positive feelings toward the husband rebound to former levels. In general, having children is seen by both parents as a positive experience, and despite the additional responsibilities and stress for the parents, having children can promote marital satisfaction.

The American divorce rate began to rise in the early 1960s owing to changing social attitudes, and it continued to rise into the 1980s. During the 1980s, the divorce rate began to level off, and about one-half of all marriages now end in divorce (Cherlin, 1992). Marital conflict over sexual dissatisfaction, money, children, and in-laws are common (Kurdek, 1991). A number of factors increase the likelihood of divorce, including poverty and lack of a high school education. Couples who come from divorced families or who marry while teenagers are much more likely to divorce. Divorce is also much more likely to occur if the woman is pregnant at the time of her marriage (U.S. Bureau of the Census, 1986).

The high rate of divorce has changed our expectations of marriage. Sixty percent of Americans believe that young married couples have little or no expectations that the marriage will last until the death of one partner (Yankelovich, 1981). The majority of people who divorce eventually remarry and do so, on the average, three years after their divorce. Men are more likely to remarry than women and often choose younger women. Women who remarry often seek older men with secure positions and high income (Glick, 1980). Remarriage rates differ among ethnic groups, with 53 percent of Caucasian women, 30 percent of Hispanic women, and 25 percent of African American women remarrying within five years of divorce (London, 1991). Because women are less likely to remarry than men, and because women often outlive their husbands, there has been an increase in the number of unmarried middle-aged and elderly women. Seventy-five percent of the remarriages that occur among older adults are due to the death of spouses rather than divorce. When men are widowed before the age of 70, most remarry; however, remarriage occurs for only 5 percent of the women who are widowed after the age of 50 (Troll, Miller, & Atchley, 1979).

Unfortunately, nearly 60 percent of remarriages fail. According to Furstenberg (1982), second marriages may be less stable and less romantic than first marriages, perhaps because both partners recognize that marriage is no guarantee for happiness or because former spouses and stepchildren can complicate their new lives. On the other hand, both partners are also older and may measure their second marriage against their first, unhappy marriage.

Careers. Compared to life at the turn of the century, young adults today begin working later, but they continue to work later in life. A hundred years ago, the average laborer began working at 14 years of age, worked a 60-hour week without vacations, and had a life expectancy of 61 years. In 1970, the average laborer began working at the age of 20, worked a 40-hour week with a two-week annual vacation, and could be expected to live several years beyond the retirement age of 65. Over a lifetime, modern workers will earn four times the income for less work than their counterparts 100 years ago (Miernyk, 1975).

Today, more than half of the women in the United States work full- or part-time outside the home, more than double the figure in 1900 (see Figure 10.6). American women in the 1990s are finding success in traditionally male-oriented fields despite barriers to advancement, which may be influenced by persistent negative stereotypes (Huston-Stein & Higgens-Trenk, 1978). The peak age of women's employment is dur-

FIGURE 10.6
Mothers in the Labor Force

The percentages of working women with children under 18 years of age have increased dramatically since 1950.

SOURCE: Papalia & Olds, 1986, p. 390.

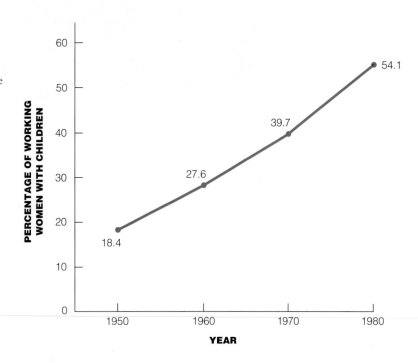

ing early adulthood, when more than 70 percent of women between 35 and 44 years of age work outside the home.

Many working women are mothers. Some are middle-aged women who return to the labor force after raising families, but many others return to work even with children to care for. Slightly more than half of all mothers with children below 3 years of age, in both two-parent and mother-headed families, are employed (U.S. Bureau of Labor Statistics, 1991). The percentage of mothers who work rises to more than 75 percent when their children begin full-day school at age 6. The Department of Labor estimates that in 1995, about two-thirds of those entering the work force were women, and of those who are in their childbearing years, 80 percent will have children during their work lives (Frankel, 1993). Working mothers worry that they do not have enough time for both family and career, but they generally have high morale and exhibit fewer emotional problems than nonworking mothers (Hoffman, 1989). Women who stay at home with young children but who would rather be working are more depressed than working mothers with young children (Hock & DeMeis, 1990).

MIDLIFE TRANSITIONS AND THE TASKS OF MIDDLE ADULTHOOD

Like the period of adolescence, middle adulthood is largely a twentieth-century phenomenon. Increased life expectancy means that people live beyond their 50s and adjust to new roles. For example, both parents usually live to see their children reach adulthood, and many become grandparents by age 50. Today's grandparents are often at the height of their careers and may not fit the stereotypical image of elderly grandmothers who knit between baking batches of cookies and grandfathers who whittle as they spin yarns to their grandchildren.

Changing Roles. Part of the adjustment to aging involves accepting changes in family relationships. As children grow older, parents must adjust to their changing needs. For example, when children leave home for college or careers, parents are faced with an "empty nest." In the past, the children's departure has been viewed as a source of depression in middle-aged women. It was believed that men seldom experienced the

STAGES OF ADULTHOOD

431

With longer life expectancies, extended families of four generations or more are becoming more common. Today's parents can anticipate caring for their aging parents just as long as they care for their dependent children.

departure with as much depression because their careers provided a sense of identity and meaning to their lives. This view of the traumatic impact of the "empty nest" has changed, however. This transition period is a time in life when satisfaction is greater than at any earlier stage of parenthood. As the final child departs the home, parents find more time and freedom to enjoy leisure activities and travel. Newfound privacy means that intimacy can be more spontaneous, and couples often enjoy the sense of being on a second honeymoon.

A second type of family adjustment during middle age involves caring for aging parents. Despite improvements in institutional care for the elderly, families continue to provide the bulk of care for elderly parents in the United States. One study found that a little over four-fifths of all hours of care received by the disabled elderly comes from family members (Brody, Litvin, Albert, & Hoffman, 1994). Because people today live longer, more and more middle-aged adults are having to care for their parents. In 1980, it was estimated that 40 percent of all people in their late 50s had a living parent, and 10 percent of the people 65 and older had a child who was over 65 (Schaie & Willis, 1986). This trend will increase in the future, and many more middle-aged and elderly adults will be caring for their aging parents.

Which family members provide the care for an infirm older person? If he or she is alive and well, the aging spouse usually provides the care. Many older women are widows, living alone and if their health fails, the burden of care often falls on the daughters (Brody, 1990). In the United States, between 60 and 75 percent of caregivers for the elderly are women (Brubaker & Brubaker, 1992). This may cause problems for the middle-aged daughter who may be working, caring for her own children, and coping with her own problems of middle age. Often, aging parents move into the homes of their children, sometimes referred to as "refilling the empty nest" (Brody, 1985). Have attitudes about caring for the elderly changed recently? Apparently not. In a study of three generations of women, Brody (1985) found strong commitments among all generations to provide care for aging family members. Older adults expect to be cared for by their children, and children in turn expect to care for their elderly parents (Brubaker & Brubaker, 1992). Caring for one's elderly parents has come to be accepted as a routine task of middle adulthood.

Work and Careers. A career is usually established during young adulthood—the realization of one's "dream," according to Levinson and colleagues (1978). Success is pursued vigorously, and achievement at work is highly valued. After several years on the job, however, these attitudes begin to change. In a classic study of managers begun in 1956 by American Telephone and Telegraph (AT&T), it was found that initially high expectations for job success became considerably lower and more realistic by the time the managers were in their early 30s (Howard & Bray, 1980). The men reported satisfaction in their jobs but often decided to meet their own personal standards or chose to devote more time to family and recreation. A second longitudinal study at AT&T begun in 1977 included women and minorities and revealed some interesting differences from the 1956 study (Howard & Wilson, 1982). The 1977 group had lower expectations for upward mobility and showed less interest in becoming corporate leaders. Their new values de-emphasized material rewards and placed greater weight on satisfaction derived from interpersonal relationships.

This shift in values at the workplace may reflect both historical and developmental changes in attitudes. It seems to be part of the realistic job appraisal and self-evaluation that occurs in middle age, a process termed *de-illusionment* by Levinson and colleagues (1978) because the unrealistic expectations are removed without bitterness. Desire for advancement at work declines, and many workers devote more and more time to family, leisure, and community activities. Howard and Bray (1980) observed this pattern for managers who held low- and middle-level positions. The higher managers who enjoyed the most success at work actually valued work more highly after 10 and 20 years on the job. These managers also became more involved in work and less sympathetic and helpful to coworkers.

Career changes during middle age are becoming more frequent, partly because of the ongoing changes in jobs and skills required by our ever-changing technology. In fact, most adults will have a variety of jobs rather than one kind of work for an entire career. Some of these changes are initiated by self-examination, discontent, or changing family relationships (e.g., divorce or children growing up). Many women return to the workforce full-time in their 40s just when many men are eager to reduce the amount of time they spend working. Whether women are satisfied with their careers in midlife depends on marital support, family finances, and family strains (Ackerman, 1990).

"Burn-out" is a popular term for the exhaustion, boredom or frustration that some workers feel, when they lack sufficient control at the workplace. Overcome with feelings of helplessness, they may quit their job, detach themselves from family and friends, and become depressed (Maslach & Jackson, 1985). Radical career changes due to burn-out or midlife crises are not very common, however. Even when people change careers in midlife, their new job often requires the same types of skills as their previous job (Schaie & Willis, 1986). Rarely do people in middle age switch to totally new careers.

Transition or Crisis? A popular image of middle age often portrays a balding father or harried housewife who is exasperated by work, children, and a boring future. Escape is provided by choosing a radical new lifestyle, and presto—the crisis is resolved. This romanticized scenario is derived, in part, from clinical studies of people confronting middle age. Inspired by Erikson's theory, Levinson and colleagues (1978) and Vaillant (1977) have described the crises faced in midlife as emotional conflicts about sexual relationships, family roles, and work values. George Vaillant (1977) conducted a longitudinal study of Harvard undergraduates from the classes of 1939 through 1944. He followed them into their 50s and concluded that the transition to midlife was often stressful, not unlike a "second adolescence." In the study by Levinson

GENDER DIFFERENCES IN THE WORKFORCE

Men and women in America today typically enter the workforce in their 20s and follow similar paths for the next 5 to 15 years. They may take quite different jobs (differing in status and pay), but initially, young adults establish their financial independence and seek satisfaction in challenging jobs. But during their 30s, middle-class men consolidate their careers while middle-class women often leave the work force to have children. Women who already raised their children in their 20s may return to work, often at entry-level positions, in their 30s and 40s. Some women may return when their children begin or complete school, but regardless of when they begin to work again, their careers often suffer (Hoffman & Nye, 1974).

These patterns have changed historically and are also different for various cultures and social classes. In 1960, about 33 percent of women between 25 and 34 were working outside the home, the lowest percentage of any age-group, while the highest percentage of working women were between the ages of 45 and 54 — but this was still only about 50 percent of all women (U.S. Bureau of Labor Statistics, 1991). In 1990, the situation was very different.

More than 70 percent of women ages 20 to 54 were employed outside the home, and there was no time-out or drop in workforce participation to stay home with children during young adulthood. Did the pattern for men differ between 1960 and 1990? No, nearly 90 percent of men between the ages of 20 and 54 were employed in 1960 and only slightly fewer in 1990.

Working mothers are now the rule, not the exception. Fewer than 10 percent of mothers in the 1990s with preschool children stay at home to raise their families. When they do take a break to have children, it is much shorter than before. Of the mothers who had children in the 1960s, less than 40 percent returned to work within five years; but in the 1980s, more than half of mothers with children came back to work within a year of the birth (O'Connell, 1989). Financial necessity often requires women to work, and this is especially true for the increasing numbers of single mothers. Unfortunately, working mothers earn only 70 percent of the wages received by working men. This inequity is due to a number of different factors. First, mothers often accept lower paying jobs that fit their locations or schedules.

BIZARRO by Dan Piraro © Chronicle Features 1991. Reprinted with permission.

and colleagues (1978), 32 of the 40 men reported that the period from age 40 to 45 was a time of moderate or severe crisis. This period can also be stressful for women, but some researchers find that employed women are less likely to suffer from depression than unemployed women (Repetti, Matthews, & Waldron, 1989). This is probably because women who are employed have a larger social network for support (Frankel, 1993).

Not all psychologists regard middle age as traumatic and stressful. Bernice Neugarten (1968) studied how middle-aged women reacted to events such as menopause and children leaving home. She found that few women considered these transitions emotional upheavals. When changes were expected, apparently they were not perceived as disruptive. A longitudinal study of American women revealed that crises were not precipitated by marriage or childbirth as much as by unexpected events such as job transfers, accidents, and divorce (Baruch, Barnett, & Rivers, 1983).

Schaie and Willis (1986) suggest that case studies have exaggerated the midlife crisis and that data on divorce, suicide, and admission to mental hospitals do not point to middle age as a particularly turbulent time of life. Instead, it is a time of transition to new roles at work and at home that most people accept with responsibility and perceive as a challenge rather than a threat. These transitions, however, may come at different times for men and women, who often follow different careers in the workforce. This is the subject we consider in, "Psychology in Our Times: Gender Differences in the Workforce."

Second, the careers of these women have been interrupted by childbirth. And third, differences in gender equity and opportunities still persist.

Aside from receiving a paycheck, women enjoy working. Many report satisfaction with the challenges of their job as well as pride in their accomplishments at work (Baruch et al., 1983). For some mothers, work provides relief from the children and responsibilities at home; for others, work offers adult conversation and social interactions. That may be why many middle-aged mothers who return to the workplace report enthusiasm for their jobs and why mothers who work exhibit less stress than mothers who stay at home (Hoffman, 1989). Many women fear that working will detract from their relationships with family members, but maternal employment by itself does not seem to diminsh their role as wife or mother or increase their chances of divorce (Hoffman, 1989).

During middle age, men and women react to work differently. While women may be returning to work with enthusiasm, many men (other than high-level professionals and executives) begin to detach themselves from their jobs after age 45 (Clausen, 1981). Some men want to spend more time with their families, some want more recreational time for themselves, some want to serve as mentors to younger workers while focusing less on their own work, and some see their hopes for success begin to fade. Men often achieve a sense of identity from their occupations, and when they lose status at work or become disinterested,

their self-esteem may plummet. Single women show similar investments in their careers, but working mothers, who have had to balance their interpersonal relationships and multiple roles, tend to have feelings of self-worth that are less dependent on their jobs.

Retirement also shows gender differences. Men retire earlier now than ever before. In 1900, nearly 70 percent of American men past 65 were still working, but in 1990, only 16 percent were still working, despite better health and longevity. Most men choose to retire early, although poor health, good pensions, and changes at work can all increase the motivation to retire. Women, on the other hand, often have fewer financial resources and are forced to work longer. Throughout the twentieth century, about 8 to 10 percent of women have worked beyond age 65. Many women outlive their husbands and cannot afford to retire.

Gender differences in the workforce are difficult to determine for minorities because the jobs that many minorities hold may be sporadic or part-time. Even when they are not working regularly, many African Americans and Hispanics do not consider themselves retired because they do not receive a pension and thus are forced to work whenever and wherever thay can (Gibson, 1991; Zsembik & Singer, 1990). We may infer, though, that minority women must also adjust their careers to the demands of family life, receive less pay and status at work, and work longer in old age than do minority men out of financial necessity. For many women, equality at work is still a distant goal.

Cognition During Adulthood

One of the most common beliefs about adult development is that intellectual abilities slowly deteriorate with advancing age. Yet, there are presidents, judges, and world leaders well past 60 and 70 years of age who work demanding schedules and make key decisions. Is cognitive decline with age just a cultural stereotype? Does it affect only some people? Researchers interested in cognitive development throughout the life span have tried to answer these questions by studying how thinking skills change from young adulthood to old age.

STAGES OF ADULT COGNITIVE DEVELOPMENT

Many people consider Piaget's theory to be the most comprehensive account of human intellectual development, but it ignores adult development entirely. Piaget believed that the fundamental aspects of cognitive development are completed when adolescents acquire logical thinking during the formal operational period. Some researchers have argued that there are additional stages of development during adulthood (Riegel, 1976).

Some psychologists believe that adults attain a fifth stage of reasoning called **postformal thought** in which they can reason about the relative nature of knowledge and opposing points of view (Labouvie-Vief, 1992). Adults seem more willing than adolescents to accept contradictions and irreconcilable differences as part of the nature of things. For example, Blanchard-Fields (1986) studied how adolescents and mature adults reasoned about social dilemmas. In one dilemma, an adolescent argued with his parents about visiting his grandparents, and in another, a man and woman had a conflict about whether to abort an unplanned pregnancy. The adolescents tried to find a solution or justify one side of the argument, whereas most adults accepted both sides of the conflict as legitimate. The willingness to tolerate opposing views was most evident among subjects who received high scores on an IQ test and an emotional maturity test. Thus, adult reasoning may be marked by changes in social understanding and responsibility.

A comprehensive view of cognitive development during adulthood was offered by K. Warner Schaie (1977-1978). Schaie proposed the five stages of thinking illustrated in Figure 10.7. The first stage is called the *acquisitive stage* because Schaie believed that children and adolescents learn a great deal of information and skills for their own sake without regard for the uses of their new knowledge. The process of schooling reflects an emphasis on acquisition of knowledge. The *achieving stage* of young adulthood is concerned with the application of knowledge to relevant goals such as vocations, hobbies, or preparation for careers. According to Schaie, the first stage is "freewheeling" and the second is "entrepreneurial and goal-directed." In contrast, the third stage of adult cognitive development (roughly from the late 30s to early 60s) is called the *responsible stage*. During this stage, people solve practical problems and meet obligations that involve other people such as family members and coworkers. The fourth stage, which occurs during the same ages as stage 3, is labeled the *executive stage* because people need to apply their cognitive skills to managing groups or thinking about community affairs that extend beyond the family. During the *reintegrative stage*, elderly adults may decrease their involvement in societal issues, business, and even family affairs. They become more selective about what they learn and where they apply their knowledge. These stages have not been confirmed by research, but they provide a good general description of the way aging adults apply their knowledge and effort to different purposes. Schaie's stages are generally consistent with the developmental changes outlined by Erikson (1950) and Levinson and his colleagues (1978).

INFORMATION-PROCESSING ABILITIES DURING ADULTHOOD

To examine directly how cognitive abilities change with age, researchers have given the same tasks to subjects of different ages. This kind of cross-sectional research has been used to compare the reaction times of young and old adults. A typical task used to measure response speed might involve pressing a button with the right hand when a red light appears and pressing a different button with the left hand when a green light appears. This task measures the speed required to process the perceptual information, make a decision, and respond. Adults in their 60s or 70s do considerably worse on such speeded tasks than do adults in their 20s, leading to the conclusion that the central nervous system functions at a slower rate with increasing age (Birren, 1974). In fact, some evidence suggests that higher cognitive processes slow down with aging more than physical and perceptual processes (Cerella, 1985).

Elderly adults do not use good strategies on certain problem-solving tasks. For example, Hartley (1981) devised a problem that required subjects to figure out which of several food combinations for dinner resulted in illness. The older subjects often focused on irrelevant information or useless hunches. Moreover, in a review of the literature, Salthouse (1991) concludes that elderly people do not approach solutions as systematically as younger adults do in a game of 20 questions. It is important to note, however, that brief training can improve the information processing and problem solving of

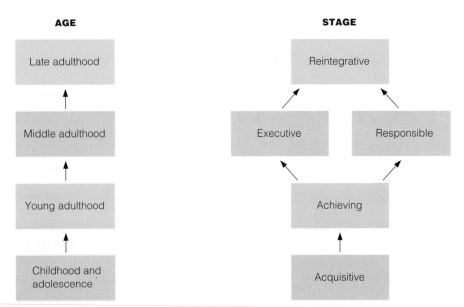

FIGURE 10.7
Stages of Adult Cognitive Development

Schaie's stages of cognitive development reveal that adolescents acquire knowledge for different purposes. Young adults focus on achieving success in the workplace by demonstrating competence. Middle-aged adults direct their thinking to practical problems that may reflect responsibilities to family members as well as management skills in community or professional affairs. During old age, adults refocus their knowledge and skills on problems that are significant to their changing lifestyles, such as concerns about health or retirement.

SOURCE: Schaie, 1977–78.

elderly adults (Willis, 1985). Thus, some differences in intellectual performance among adults are due to differences in experience, education, motivation, and health rather than a decay of cognitive functioning with age. Also, some differences in intellectual performance may be due to differences in memory rather than differences in problem-solving ability (Salthouse, 1991).

Many cognitive abilities show little change with age. Botwinick and Storandt (1974) studied how adults from 21 to 80 years of age learned lists of paired associates. They found little difference with age on easy lists but poorer performance by elderly subjects when there was interference from previous information. Elderly subjects may exhibit more caution, anxiety, and interference while learning, but there is no evidence that the general ability to learn declines with age (Schaie & Willis, 1986).

Remembering and problem solving are fundamental abilities that show only modest changes with age. Verbal comprehension, vocabulary, and perceptual organization may not change much either. Several research studies have shown that declines in the specific mental abilities of adults depend on what tests are used to measure cognitive ability (Baltes, Dittman-Kohli, & Dixon, 1984). John Horn has devised a theory to explain which abilities change with age and which do not (Horn, 1982; Horn & Cattell, 1966). Horn distinguishes two kinds of mental abilities. **Fluid intelligence** refers to the speed and accuracy of processing information. It reflects incidental learning and is closely linked to the neurological status of the individual. **Crystallized intelligence** refers to facts and information that are accumulated as part of our general knowledge. This kind of intelligence reflects intentional learning of culturally relevant information. Horn (1982) argues that fluid intelligence declines gradually after young adulthood, a conclusion bolstered by the decline of processing on speeded tasks. Crystallized intelligence, in contrast, actually continues to increase throughout the life span. Horn and others argue that some tasks measure more of one kind of intelligence than another, and thus, conclusions about whether mental abilities decline with age depend on the types of measures used.

INTELLIGENCE DURING ADULTHOOD

Although researchers have identified some stages, abilities, and processes that change with age (and some that do not), the big question is whether there is a general decline in intelligence with adult aging. To some extent, the answer depends on the tasks used to measure intelligence, as noted in Horn's theory. The answer also depends on the way the research study is designed, as will be discussed more fully in Chapter 11. Briefly, when researchers began to study adult intelligence and aging, they used a cross-sectional research design; that is, they tested various groups of adults across a broad age range, but in the same year. What they found was progressively lower scores by older adults, suggesting that intelligence slowly deteriorated with age. However, these findings have been contradicted by longitudinal research, the study of one group over a period of many years. Schaie (1990) tested people whose birth dates ranged from 1889 to 1959, repeating his tests on multiple occasions. The data from this study showed little decline in any of the mental abilities tested until age 60. For some abilities, there was only a modest drop after 80 years of age. In a review of the literature on aging and intelligence, Stuart-Hampton (1994) concludes that on average, intelligence is preserved at least through the period of a person's working life.

What can account for these different patterns? Historical changes are partly responsible. If we compare the reasoning of a 20-year-old and a 70-year-old today, we would be comparing a person who went to school in the 1980s and 1990s with someone who went to school in the 1930s and 1940s. Education and cultural experiences have changed greatly over generations, and what appears to be a decline in intelligence may only reflect the fact that each successive generation is getting smarter (at least their performance on standardized tests improves). Education is not the only difference, though; health and medical care have also improved. Thus, some differences in intelligence scores between young and old adults in cross-sectional research are due to **age cohort differences**—that is, differences attributable to growing up in different historical eras. (Recall from Chapter 9 that age cohorts are individuals who are born in the same year or whose life spans coincide.)

Another possible reason for the discrepancy between cross-sectional and longitudinal findings is that many subjects who drop out of longitudinal studies or who die are the same people who score below the group average. Thus, it may be that longitudinal research underestimates intellectual decline with age (Schaie & Willis, 1986). Still another reason for the lower cross-sectional results is a *terminal drop* in performance that occurs just prior to death as a result of ill health. When older adults close to death are averaged into longitudinal performance scores, the data suggest an overall gradual decline in intelligence, some of which may be due to the terminal drop (Siegler, 1983). From the evidence collected so far, then, it seems unlikely that there is a significant loss of cognitive ability during adulthood. Some speeded reasoning abilities may not be as good among the elderly as among young adults, but the decline, if any, is relatively small and does not affect everyone.

DOES MEMORY FAIL WITH AGE?

Some of the most common misconceptions about aging involve memory. These misconceptions often derive from stereotypes and folklore. We highlight three myths about memory and aging that have been disproved by current research.

Myth 1: *Everyone's memory inevitably deteriorates during adulthood.*
Research shows that the sensory stores remain effective across the life span. The capacity of short-term memory does not diminish with age and the organization of stored knowledge is similar for young and old adults (Poon, 1985). For example, the recency effect (the relatively good recall of recent information discussed in Chapter 7) is simi-

Elderly adults may complain about their memory abilities and may be "out of practice" on deliberate memorization tasks, but they can remember many things as well as young adults.

lar for young and old adults, and recognition memory for words continues to improve past age 60 (Schaie & Willis, 1986). Although disease and ill health certainly affect an older adult's memory, there is no uniform biological deterioration of memory capacity with aging.

Myth 2: *Old people remember events in the distant past much better than recent events.*
Remote memory is not superior to recent memory for the elderly. Although older people often report that their memories of youthful experiences are much clearer than memories of recent events, the scientific literature does not support this contention (Craik & Jennings, 1992). In one study, young and old adults were asked to recall events between the 1920s and 1970s (Poon et al., 1979). They did not recall the events from the 1920s better than recent events, and there were no memory differences between young and old adults. It may be that elderly people talk more about past events, which allows them to rehearse and elaborate some old memories, but "old memories" do not have some type of neurological advantage over "new memories."

Myth 3: *Old people may not understand their memory abilities as well as younger adults.*
Older adults can understand and monitor their memory behavior as well as young adults can (Lachman, Lachman, & Thronesbery, 1979; Perlmutter, 1978). They seem to understand how memory strategies operate, how task variables influence remembering, and how well they remember. In fact, elderly adults may be more sensitive than young adults are to their memory abilities (Zelinski, Gilewski, & Thompson, 1980). Although elderly adults may complain more about their memory and notice relative declines in their performance (Chaffin & Herrmann, 1983), they are accurate at evaluating their competence on memory tasks (Guttentag, 1985).

Does memory decline with age? Yes, it does for some people on some tasks; however, the decline is neither universal nor uniform. Some researchers find that memory decline occurs mostly for tasks that require more effortful processing. For example, memory decline is greater on recall tasks than on recognition tasks (Craik & McDowd, 1987). Also, poorer memory with age shows up mostly on laboratory tasks, which some argue are devoid of meaning and context. Why do older adults show weaker performances on some laboratory tasks? It may be that elderly adults are "out of practice" with tasks requiring deliberate remembering (Salthouse, 1990). This could lead to either low motivation for the task or high anxiety that may interfere with memory. Waddell and Rogoff (1981), for example, gave groups of middle-aged (31 to 59) and elderly (65 to 85) women two kinds of memory tasks. In one, the women had to remember objects arranged in a meaningless context, a plain box. In the other task, they had to remember the objects arranged in a natural, familiar setting outside the laboratory. In the first task, the elderly women remembered fewer items than did the middle-aged women. In the second task, both groups performed equally well.

Another possible reason for memory decline is that elderly adults cannot process events as quickly, so they do not have adequate time to encode and retrieve information. It could also be that the elderly show declines only for some kinds of information. Guttentag (1985) noted that elderly adults may not recruit and apply memory strategies as effectively as young adults do. Some elderly adults may not have adequate attention or persistence to engage in strategic, deep, and effortful processing (Craik & Byrd, 1982). In sum, probably no single factor will explain the relation between memory and aging, and we should be careful to avoid stereotypes and myths regarding dramatic declines in memory among older adults.

Health in Adulthood

One of the challenges for successful aging is coping with progressive physical changes. Appearance, perceptual sensitivity, strength, and coordination all change significantly during adulthood.

PHYSICAL CHANGES DURING ADULTHOOD

Primary aging refers to the gradual deterioration of the body's cells, tissues, and systems that ultimately results in the loss of the ability to adapt to environmental stress. It is considered normal because it affects everyone. For example, the sensitivity of all five senses is most keen between about 20 and 40 years of age and diminishes thereafter. A study of smell identification ability confirmed this developmental trend (Doty et al., 1984). The researchers tested nearly 2,000 people between 5 and 99 years of age and observed less sensitivity to odors among children and the elderly. Indeed, 80 percent of the people tested beyond 80 years of age had major impairment. The researchers note that the inability to smell may help explain why elderly people complain about the diminished flavor of food and avoid nutritional diets. It may also explain why so many elderly people do not detect gas leaks or fires in their homes. Thus, primary aging requires psychological and physical adjustments to routine activities. That is, biological changes require changes in the cognitive, learning, and social arenas.

Secondary aging refers to physiological changes resulting from disease, disuse, or abuse but that are correlated with chronological age and thus are often confused with the effects of the normal aging process. Perlmutter and Hall (1985) have reviewed the effects of primary and secondary aging and have provided an excellent summary of those physiological changes associated with growing older.

Physical Appearance. Most changes in the color, texture, and density of hair occur as a part of primary or normal, aging, and indeed, graying hair is considered the most reliable of all body indicators of aging. Changes in the skin that occur from primary aging include the loss of fat deposits in the epidermis, thinning and drying, and a marked slowing in the replacement rate of surface skin cells (Grove & Kligman, 1983). Together, these effects may contribute to wrinkled skin, but, in fact, it is the secondary aging effects of abusive tanning that are most responsible for our etched and weathered countenances. The skeleton and teeth undergo changes in composition as well. After the age of 30, the bones lose calcium, and as fractures occur, repair becomes slower (Tonna, 1977).

The Cardiovascular System. The cardiovascular system eventually succumbs to the effects of primary aging because the cells of the heart, arteries, veins, and capillaries cannot divide and reproduce themselves. Thus, the system's efficiency decreases with age. The volume of blood pumped every minute decreases by 1 percent each year after the age of 20 (Kohn, 1977). During stress, the maximum heart rate decreases with age, and oxygen supply via arterial blood is slowed. Arteries become less flexible with age (called hardening of the arteries, or arteriosclerosis), and they may become constricted with fatty deposits that restrict blood flow and raise blood pressure. When the blood supply to the brain is cut off, strokes may occur. Among the elderly, this is the third leading cause of death after heart disease and cancer.

The Respiratory System. Shortness of breath usually occurs as a normal part of aging. With age, the rib cage stiffens, the cartilage in the trachea and bronchial tubes calcifies, and the alveoli within the lungs narrow, reducing the functioning gas exchange surface of the lungs. Secondary aging in the respiratory system can be seen in the increased incidence of respiratory diseases such as emphysema and lung cancer. These disorders occur more frequently in older people and are due to smoking and environmental pollutants rather than to primary aging.

The Endocrine System. The pituitary, parathyroid, and thyroid glands remain virtually the same in anatomical structure and ability to function throughout adulthood. In the pancreas, the release of insulin is delayed and less insulin is released with age. This decrease in function leads to reduced glucose tolerance in most adults over the age of 65 and to diabetes in 10 percent of the adults in this age-group (Rockstein & Sussman, 1979). Perhaps the gland most critically affected by the aging process is the thymus gland. With age, the gland shrinks in size and decreases its production of hormones. These changes result in decreased levels of antibodies in the blood and impaired function of the immune system. This renders the aged susceptible to infections, cancer, and many other disorders associated with secondary aging.

The Reproductive System. It is clear that sperm production decreases with age, so by the 40s, only 50 percent of the sperm-producing tubules have developing sperm, and after 80 years of age, only 10 percent remain functioning. The prostate gland, which secretes the sperm-carrying fluid, becomes enlarged with age and may even double in size, making surgery necessary for many men (Rockstein & Sussman, 1979). In the female reproductive system, hormonal changes cause the menstrual periods to become shorter and more irregular, and by age 50, **menopause,** the cessation of a woman's period, usually has begun. Many women experience hot flashes, headaches, and a variety of other symptoms associated with the change in hormone levels. The decrease in estrogen may also result in the shortening and thinning of the vaginal walls, and vaginal lubrication may diminish. Aging does not necessarily diminish sexual activity and enjoyment; only in cases of debilitative disease is sexual expression impossible (Solnick & Corby, 1983).

PERCEPTIONS OF AGING

With which of the following statements do you agree?

1. Older men are twice as likely to be married as older women.
2. Older men have a higher poverty rate than older women.
3. The educational level of the elderly has been steadily decreasing.
4. Half of all older women are widows.
5. Thirty percent of the elderly have diabetes.
6. By the year 2030, the elderly may account for more than 20 percent of the U.S. population.
7. About 75 percent of the aged have significant hearing impairments.
8. There are about 150 elderly women for every 100 elderly men.

According to Fowles (1986), only statements 1, 4, 6, and 8 are true. Here are the facts for statements 2, 3, 5, and 7:

2. The rate of poverty among older women is twice as great as for older men (16 percent versus 8 percent below the poverty line).
3. Between 1970 and 1985, the average years of education among the elderly jumped

from 8.7 to 11.7, and the percentage who completed high school increased from 28 percent to 48 percent.

5. Actually, only 10 percent of the elderly had diabetes in 1985.

7. Only 40 percent of noninstitutionalized elderly adults have severe hearing impairments.

Because so many stereotypes of the elderly appear on television and in the media, young adults tend to view the elderly as generally tired, ill, isolated, and sexually inactive. It is surprising how widespread misconceptions about the elderly are. Moreover, negative stereotypes can have profound implications for our daily interactions with elderly people and can also influence social policies concerning aging. Researchers have investigated how people regard the elderly by measuring their attitudes, beliefs, and knowledge regarding aging. Test your knowledge about aging on a selection from Erdman Palmore's (1977) Facts on Aging Quiz (FAQ) in Table 10.1. Answer each of the 15 questions as either true or false.

To determine your score, count the number of questions marked correctly. Odd-numbered items are false; even-numbered items are true. If you answered 10 questions correctly, you scored about as well as the undergraduates in Palmore's (1977) study (You may have done better than average because of the preceeding section of the book, where several answers were given). It is surprising that college students do not know the answers to one-third of these questions, but the finding is reliable. In fact, Mary Luszcz (1982) replicated the study with Australian undergraduates and found a similar pattern with only slightly more errors and negative bias about aging. Across many studies there is striking consistency in the negative stereotypes. Here are the six most common misconceptions :

- Most elderly people live in institutions. (5)
- Most old people cannot adapt to change. (7)
- The majority of old people are bored. (10)

TABLE 10.1
Facts on Aging Quiz

1. The majority of old people (past age 65) are senile.
2. All five senses tend to decline in old age.
3. Most old people have no interest in, or capacity for, sexual relations.
4. Physical strength tends to decline in old age.
5. At least 10 percent of all the aged are living in long-stay institutions (i.e., nursing homes, mental hospitals, homes for the aged).
6. About 80 percent of the aged are healthy enough to carry out their normal activities.
7. Most old people are set in their ways and are unable to change.
8. The reaction time of most old people tends to be slower than the reaction time of younger people.
9. In general, most old people are pretty much alike.
10. The majority of old people are seldom bored.
11. Over 15 percent of the U.S. population are now 65 or over.
12. Most medical practitioners tend to give low priority to the aged.
13. The majority of older people have incomes below the poverty line (as defined by the federal government).
14. The majority of old people are seldom irritated or angry.
15. The health and socioeconomic status of older people compared to younger people in the year 2000 will probably be about the same as now.

SOURCE: Palmore (1977).

- More than 15 percent of the population is 65 or older. (11)
- The majority of elderly live in poverty. (13)
- The majority of old people are often angry. (14)

Some of these stereotypes are evident in the media, and some are exaggerations of typical signs of aging, such as wrinkled skin, reduced agility, and increased physical complaints. We know that adults form stereotypes of the elderly, but how do children regard aging and the elderly? A study by Mitchell and coworkers (1985) investigated children's perceptions of aging by asking them questions about pictures of young and old adults. The 25 questions could be answered yes or no and included such items as "Is s/he fussy?" "Is s/he gentle?" "Is s/he lazy?" "Is s/he weak?" "Does s/he make you feel good?" "Would s/he do things with you that are fun?" The researchers tested 255 children from 5 to 13 years of age. Half were girls, half were boys; half were African American and half were white; and half lived in a city, while the other half lived in rural homes. The pictures that accompanied the questions showed African American or white faces of females and males that children judged to be 17, 45, and 73 years old.

The researchers found that children's perceptions were not uniformly positive or negative. Instead, children distinguished among three principal characteristics of the elderly; their personalities, their affective relations, and their physical abilities. Each trait was judged independently of the others. Neither the age nor race of the children made any difference in their perceptions, but their gender did affect their responses. Girls had more positive evaluations than boys did of elderly people's emotional relations and physical abilities. The gender of the person in the pictures also made a difference. Females were judged by all children to have more positive personality traits than males. In general, however, children viewed older adults as weaker, more likely to be ill, less aggressive, and nicer than younger adults. Thus, the stereotypes of the elderly are established at an early age.

Social stereotypes are difficult to change because the misconceptions are communicated in advertisements, jokes, and the popular media. Psychologists help people to reexamine subtle biases and stereotypes of the elderly and to become aware of realistic developmental changes across the life span. In a review of 25 studies that used the FAQ, Palmore (1980) concluded that common stereotypes were relatively unaffected by race, sex, or age of the respondents. The one significant factor was level of education. People with the least education scored only 55 percent correct on the quiz, barely above chance levels, and held more negative stereotypes about aging. Figure 10.8 summarizes the average correct performance on the FAQ across many studies according to level of education. The figure suggests steady improvement with more education, which may indicate greater intelligence, less prejudice, or more knowledge about the elderly among people with more education.

Because of the lack of knowledge and bias revealed by the FAQ, Palmore (1980) advocates using the quiz as a stimulus for group discussions to identify and correct erroneous perceptions of aging. For example, college students can examine how the elderly are portrayed in the news, on television, or in greeting cards to uncover the bases for many of the negative stereotypes (Fried, 1988). Another way to become aware of age bias is to examine how the elderly react to stereotypes about ageism. Many elderly are proud of their age, as seen in the case study that follows shortly. Enthusiasm for "old age" is exhibited by most elderly people who see themselves as younger than they are (Goldsmith & Heiens, 1992). They see their interests and activities more like younger adults do and most regard themselves as middle-aged well past 60. For example, about

FIGURE 10.8
Effects of Education on Knowledge About Aging

The Facts on Aging Quiz (FAQ) measures people's perceptions about aging. Highly educated people score more highly on the FAQ. This shows that negative stereotypes and ignorance about aging are less evident among educated adults and perhaps that stereotypes can be reduced with education. (The total number of subjects tested at each educational level is shown inside each column, with the number of studies in parentheses.)

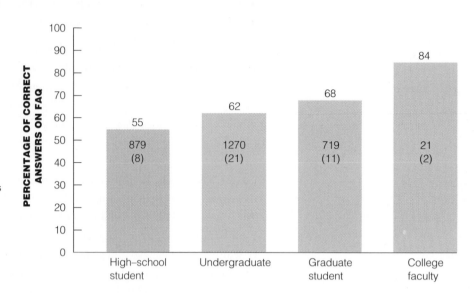

80 percent of adults over 60 years of age said that they felt and looked at least 10 years younger than they were. For those more than 80 years old, 100 percent said, "My interests are those of people at least 10 years younger than I am."

Why do the elderly consider themselves "young"? One reason may be their frustration with negative stereotypes and overt denial of their limitations. Another reason may be that they compare themselves to their own cohorts, many of whom suffer poor health, so they see themselves as better off. Another reason may be that even 60- to 70-year-olds may have living parents and therefore are not the oldest generation. The key to a positive self-image in old age seems to be a complex self-concept based on many different roles and interests. As the numbers of confident and satisfied elderly continue to increase, the stereotypes about aging will likely diminish.

CASE STUDY

OLD AND PROUD

One popular view of the elderly, especially those past 70, is that they become more conservative and grumpy with age. But research contradicts this stereotype. A 14-year longitudinal study of elderly adults shows that they become more cheerful and open-minded with age (Field & Milsap, 1991). Moreover, they want to dispel the negative stereotypes of aging, and some, like Abe Arkoff, a professor emeritus of psychology at the University of Hawaii, have found good-natured ways to communicate their feelings. Arkoff wrote the following newspaper editorial under the headline "Hey, America! He's old—and proud of it!"

I'm told that in Japan it's still all right to be old. One's age can even be a source of pride. In fact, it's quite proper and polite in Japan to ask old persons their age and then congratulate them on it. In America the situation appears quite different. I'm one of the few people of my age (I'm closing in on 71) who is out of the closet and announcing, "I'm old." But almost every time I do, somebody tries to tell me I'm not. "Old," as an adjective applied to a person in this country seems to be a four-letter word.

I'm not above a bit of mischief. The health food store where I sometimes shop offers a discount to "senior citizens." That's a term I deplore, but I welcome the discount, so flashing my driver's license for age identification, I asked the checkout clerk to discount my bill. "I'm an old person," I explained. My confession rendered him speechless for a moment, and then he tried to comfort me. "You're not so old," he said.

"I'm quite old," I said relentlessly. "Old is good," I continued. "Old books. Old wine. Old friends." He looked a little nonplussed; maybe he was thinking, "After all, this is a health food store so one's got to expect a few nuts."

I'm a walker and commute by foot between home in the Makiki hills and the University of Hawaii. It's a route frequented by bicyclists, and recently one of them called back as he passed me, "Do you walk this every day?" "Every day but Sunday," I replied. "That's great," he shouted. "Keeps you young!" I started to shout a defense of age to his disappearing figure but saw once again, I would be the only one to hear me.

For the most part, I have enjoyed each of my ages. I enjoyed most of my childhood, most of my adolescence, and most of my young adulthood and middle-age. Now I'm enjoying my old age.

I've met some people my age who seem determined to be middle-aged forever. Even if they were able to finesse old age, it would be a shame to miss such an important season of life; it would be like repeating the second act of a play and never getting on to the third act where there is a chance of resolution and perspective.

When I was coordinator of the University of Hawaii's Elderhostel (a program for students 60 and older), I would divide the students into pairs on introduction night so that they could interview each other and later introduce each other to the whole group. Almost invariably, someone would introduce a partner as someone who was "65 (or 70 or 75) years *young*." Such bits of ageism by persons of age, unintentional and well-meaning though such comments are, indicate the size of the task I see before me.

Just as bad is the title of my very favorite video which concerned a lovely old man and old woman, both artists, both widowed, and neither a stranger to the sorrows of life. They find each other and, as the video shows, form a truly understanding and fulfilling relationship; it's a relationship of a quality that would only be possible, I think, for two persons who had lived long and learned much. Ironically, the title and theme music of this tribute to age is "Young at Heart."

A relatively new designation for the years above 65 is "the third age." In the "first age," extending from birth to about age 25, we are busy developing ourselves and learning the basic skills necessary to get along in life. The "second age," about 25–60, is primarily occupied with work, parenting, and family.

Interestingly, the third age is one about which not much is known. Relatively few people made it to old age in previous generations although the number has been growing. Now my generation has arrived, and we constitute for the first time in America a considerable mass of healthy and active old persons. It's a new ballgame, and it's up to us to break out of limiting stereotypes, and define what our third age, our old age, is to be.

My work with my age peers in both the Elderhostel and Senior Focus programs on the Manoa campus has been an eye opener for me. Many of these folks seem almost reborn as they free themselves from family, occupational, and gender roles and constraints.

Many are one-person "foundations," dedicating their time and energies to needs and causes that touch their hearts. Many have discovered that they have finally reached the right age to get an education for its own sake; I have yet to meet one who was taking a course "to get it out of the way."

National surveys conducted over the years by the Roper Center show that old persons are generally happier than any other adult group. In fact, first place in happpiness goes to the 65- to 74-year-olds and the runners-up are the 75- to 84-year-olds. How do you like them beans?

So here's two-and-one-half cheers for old age. The next time you see me (I'm the short, bearded fellow, most likely decked out in an old hat, old baggy pants, and an old aloha shirt—an outfit I wouldn't have been caught dead in during my constrained younger years), just say, "Hi, Abe! My but you're looking old today."

I'll reply, "Thank you," which is what my mother taught me to say when somebody gives you a really nice compliment.

OLD AGE AND DYING

The last phase of human development includes dying and death, but when, where, and how people die have changed historically. Two hundred years ago, nearly half the population died before age 10, and one parent often died before his or her children had grown up (Perlmutter & Hall, 1985). Nowadays, death is most frequent among the elderly. Life expectancy in the United States has increased from 47 years for someone born in 1900 to 77 years for someone born in 1990. Because of these changes, old people often die apart from their families. In fact, more than 80 percent of all deaths in the United States occur in institutions or hospitals (Bok, 1978). This reflects an increased availability of medical care as well as a shift away from primary dependence on family members.

Increased life expectancy and improved medical care have created a longer time period to anticipate death. Young adults tend not to think about death, but by middle age, adults often measure time by the number of years they have left to live (Neugarten, Crotty, & Tobin, 1964). As adults ponder death, they often compare the course of their lives with the lives of friends and relatives. They may cope with impending death by adopting hedonistic strategies ("Eat, drink, and be merry, for tomorrow we may die"), or they may become pessimistic and cynical about life. Many find strength in religious beliefs. According to Butler (1975), people often begin a **life review,** reminiscences about their lives, as they anticipate death. They reflect on their past, sometimes to provide personal significance to their life events. This review helps to integrate experiences and enhance self-esteem, processes that promote integrity, in Erikson's (1950) view. In a study of homebound elderly adults, Haight (1992) found that those who undertook a life review with guidance from a researcher were more satisfied with their lives than those who simply had a friendly visit from a researcher.

Preparation for death is important for the individual as well as for family members. All cultures have conceptions of the proper way to die (Marshall & Levy, 1990). In America, an "appropriate" death usually includes dying peacefully while surrounded by family members. That is why some elderly adults make "living wills," documents that describe what lifesaving medical assistance and medication they are willing to endure. During the past 20 years, hospices have become popular as alternatives to hospitals because no extraordinary measures are taken to sustain life. Both hospitals and hospices allow people to confront death with dignity, in an alert state, and with their friends and families present.

Do people fear death? A survey of 1,000 adults in Los Angeles revealed that 63 percent were "not at all afraid" of death; only 4 percent responded "very afraid" (Bengston, Cuellar, & Ragan, 1977). Old people are less afraid of death than many young people, perhaps because they feel they have been given their allotted years, or because declining health and income have made life less enjoyable, or because they have prepared themselves more (Kalish, 1976). In a review of the literature, Kastenbaum (1992) observed that some studies have found that women report more anxiety over death. This may be because women care for the dying more often than men or because men are less likely to express their fear of death. A psychiatrist who interviewed terminally ill, elderly patients described five progressive reactions to death (Kubler-Ross, 1969). First was denial of death; second, anger, or a "Why me?" attitude. Next, patients tried to bargain with God, doctors, or family members to postpone death. Depression and finally acceptance of death followed. Although some people do have some of these reactions to dying, these general stages of dying are not evident in many elderly people (Perlmutter & Hall, 1985).

Dying and death are unique, individual experiences. Many people are comforted by thoughts of their legacies, perhaps their children or their work, while others are supported by their religious beliefs about immortality and eternity. People also have widely different emotional reactions to impending death. Contrasting views of peaceful and angry anticipation are captured well by two famous poets.

Though nothing can bring back the hour of splendour
  in the grass, of glory in the flowers,
We will grieve not, rather find
Strength in what remains behind.
    —WILLIAM WORDSWORTH

Do not go gentle into that good night
Old age should rave and burn at the close of day
Rage, rage against the dying of the light.
    —DYLAN THOMAS

THEMES IN REVIEW

Biological forces at work throughout the life span create predictable changes as we age. Puberty begins with secretion of neurohormones triggered by the hypothalamus, leading to a growth spurt and the development of primary and secondary sexual characteristics. As people age, other biological changes (such as menopause) affect their lives. Almost all biological systems are affected by primary and secondary aging.

The ability to learn is maintained throughout the life span. Although there are slight losses in learning ability in old age, people continue to profit from experience throughout life.

Cognitive abilities change across the life span, too, with remembering improving through adolescence. Adolescents in Western societies develop formal thought through schooling. Studies of older people show loss of performance on some memory tests, especially speeded tests. Fluid intelligence declines in old age, but crystallized intelligence—reflecting the accumulation of knowledge—continues to increase.

Social and cultural factors greatly influence perception of age. In some societies the aged are revered whereas in others their status is less exalted. Indeed, the very definition of an old person is culturally determined. A 55 year old person might have been considered very old 200 years ago and today, as the life span has expanded, is considered only middle aged. Perceptions of age differ even within subgroups of contemporary American society.

SUMMARY

1 Adolescence is a period of transition to adulthood marked occasionally by ceremonies or rites of passage. It is not stressful or stormy for many adolescents.

2 Puberty begins with increased hormone production triggered by the hypothalamus. The hormones stimulate the development of both primary and secondary sex characteristics and result in sexual maturity and the capacity for reproduction.

3 Adolescents acquire the ability to think abstractly and deductively. They can solve problems logically and develop cognitive expertise in particular school subjects. Better reasoning skills allow adolescents to think more deeply about moral and political issues.

4 Males score more highly than females on standardized mathematics tests, such as the SAT-M. The reasons for this pattern are still debated, but include differing expectations of teachers and parents for boys and girls, differing exposure to math outside the classroom, and possible biological factors, too.

5 A fundamental part of adolescence is the development of social understanding about the self and others. Erikson's theory stresses the need to develop a stable identity during adolescence in order to avoid feelings of self-doubt and role confusion.

6 Risk-taking behaviors increase during adolescence as young people are confronted with opportunities to experiment with illegal substances, sex, and criminal activities.

Most adolescents meet these challenges successfully, although the number of adolescent runaways and suicides is alarming.

7 Theories of adult development help identify crises encountered throughout adulthood. Erikson's theory emphasizes emotional development and the progressive realization of love, caring, and wisdom. Young adults derive satisfaction from productivity at work and the creation of a family. Middle adulthood may involve reevaluating one's life and changing directions before settling down. Old age is a time to review one's life and to achieve a sense of integrity.

8 Cognitive abilities do not decline slowly with biological maturation. Although speed of processing information may slow down, accumulated knowledge increases with age. Compared to younger adults, poorer performance on cognitive tasks by elderly adults may be due to educational differences, lack of practice, or poor health.

9 Physical changes in appearance and functioning continue with age. The average life expectancy today is well over 70 years. Stereotypic views of the elderly are often held by children and adults.

10 Death is approached in different ways depending on individuals' personalities. Some become hedonistic, pessimistic, or angry, while others express little fear of death. A positive review of their lives and accomplishments, as well as support from family and friends, helps people face death with dignity.

KEY TERMS

adolescence (p. 408)

adolescent moratorium (p. 408)

puberty (p. 409)

hypothalamic thermostat (p. 409)

adolescent growth spurt (p. 410)

primary sex characteristics (p. 411)

menarche (p. 411)

secondary sex characteristics (p. 411)

math anxiety (p. 415)

identity development (p. 418)

individuation (p. 418)

ethnic identity (p. 418)

postformal thought (p. 435)

fluid intelligence (p. 437)

crystallized intelligence (p. 437)

age cohort differences (p. 438)

primary aging (p. 440)

secondary aging (p. 440)

menopause (p. 441)

life review (p. 446)

FOR CRITICAL ANALYSIS

1 Choose three adolescents from different social groups or cultures and analyze how they spend their time each week. How do their tasks and their settings influence their cognitive and social development?

2 Interview four adults who range in age from 20 to 100 years old to find out what makes them most satisfied and what makes them feel most stressed. Collect background information from the adults so that you can create developmental explanations for their responses. Discuss the interviews with other students, and analyze what historical, social, and family events contributed to differences between young, middle-aged, and older adults.

3 Make some projections about the lifestyles that adults will face in the year 2050, when you are considered elderly. What will you be doing? What do you think work and careers will be like for your children—who will then be middle-aged? What do you think will be the attitudes of adolescents in 2050? Will there be more intergenerational harmony or less? Will there be more intergenerational stereotyping or less?

SUGGESTED READINGS

CRAIK, F. I. M., & SALTHOUSE, T. A. (1992). *Handbook of aging and cognition.* Hillsdale, NJ: Erlbaum. This volume includes in-depth reviews of research on cognitive changes with age, largely from a biological and information-processing perspective.

HARRIS, C. A. (1993). *Child development* (2nd ed.). St. Paul, MN: West. This up-to-date text provides a comprehensive overview of topics concerned with child development and adolescence.

HOFFMAN, L. W., PARIS, S. G., & HALL, E. (1994). *Developmental psychology today.* New York: Random House. This up-to-date textbook provides a rich picture of developmental changes across the life span, with relevant theories and research to support the descriptions.

LERNER, R. M. (1993). *Early adolescence: Perspectives on research, policy, and intervention.* Hillsdale, NJ: Erlbaum. This volume includes a large collection of chapters on cutting-edge research on adolescence.

SCHAIE, K. W., & WILLIS, S. L. (1986). *Adult development and aging* (2nd ed.). Boston: Little, Brown. The authors are active researchers in adult development who discuss their own studies and important research issues in depth.

PSYCHOLOGY ON THE INTERNET

Adolescence Directory On-Line

(http://education.Indiana.edu/cas/adol/adol.html)

Adolescence Directory On-Line contains several links to sites related to adolescence and secondary education. It is a valuable source of information on physical and mental risk factors that affect the lives of adolescents.

Facts for Families

(http://www.psych.med.umich.edu/web/aacap/factsFam/)

This home page (maintained by the American Academy of Child & Adolescent Psychiatry—AACAP) provides "concise and up-to-date material on issues such as the depressed child, teen suicide, stepfamily problems and sexual abuse." Though primarily directed at parents seeking advice for dealing with these problems, the information provided helps define the problems and explains some of the causal factors involved in their genesis.

Institute for Brain Aging and Dementia

(http://teri.bio.uci.edu/)

"The goal of the Institute is to mobilize and unify university resources to discover meaningful ways to prevent decline in brain function with aging prior to its inception and to reverse loss of function once it has occurred." At this site the Institute provides answers to a number of common questions about dementia and Alzheimer's disease (e.g., what is dementia, what causes it, how is it diagnosed). In addition, this page illustrates physiological differences in the brains of normally functioning individuals and those afflicted with dementia and Alzheimer's disease, provides links to other sources of information about these problems, and provides several short, on-line dementia screening tests.

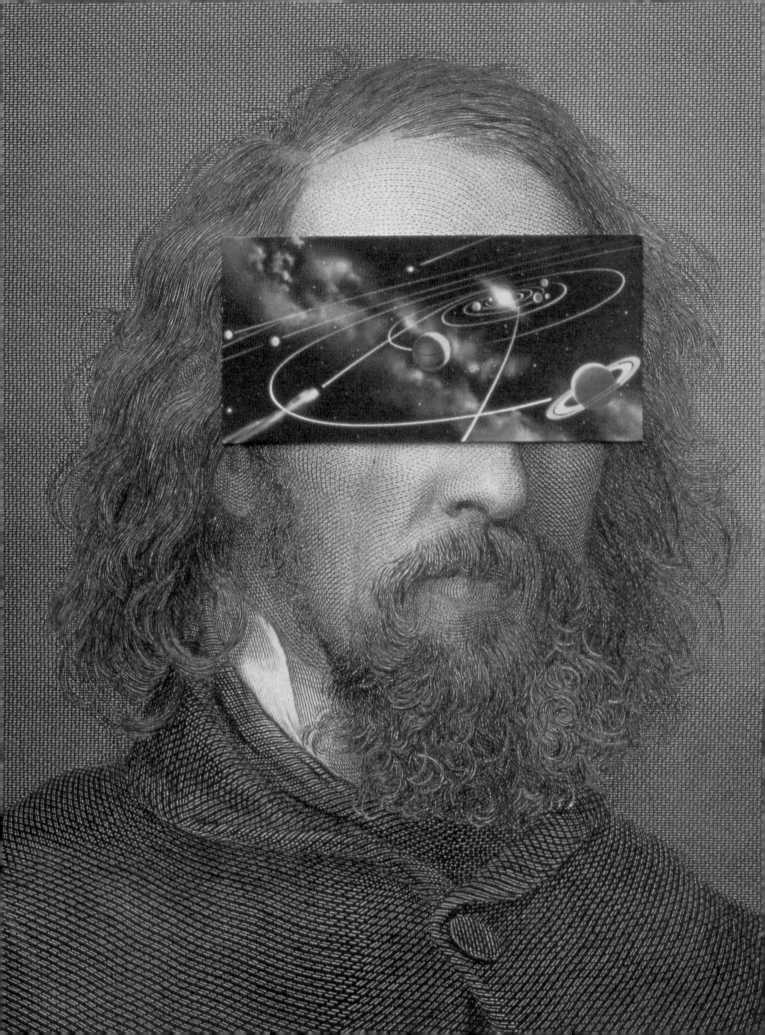

INTELLIGENCE and MENTAL ABILITIES

Chapter 11

451

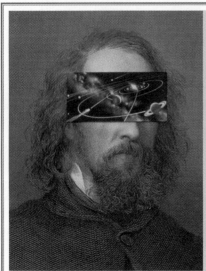

Picking a winner at the track requires complex thinking that is not simply related to IQ scores.

What is intelligence? Is it the sum of our knowledge? Is it the speed with which we reason? Is it the ability to adapt to new situations or to plan efficiently? Is it the consequence of a successful formal education? Is it something we can measure adequately by an IQ score? Consider the results of a study assessing the cognitive differences of race-track gamblers.

Stephen Ceci and Jeffrey Liker (1986) spent three years studying men who attended harness races nearly every day during racing season. The men were divided into groups of experts and nonexperts based on the success with which they picked winning horses. They all bought and read racing forms on a regular basis and had as many as 23 years of experience at the track. Their IQs ranged from 80 to 130. When the researchers examined the success of the men, they found no relation between their IQ scores and their expertise at the track. For example, one construction worker with an IQ of 85 was an expert who picked the top horse in 10 races and the top three horses in the correct order in 5 races. In contrast, a lawyer with an IQ of 118 picked the top horse in only 3 of the races and the top three horses only once.

Ceci and Liker then asked each man to determine the probability of winning the race for 50 pairs of horses in hypothetical races using a variety of information supplied by the researchers. The subjects explained their reasoning as they calculated their answers. What were the results? The experts consistently used complex information from seven different variables to make their decisions, while the nonexperts used fewer variables and simpler kinds of reasoning. Neither IQ scores nor years of track experience predicted the complexity of their reasoning. This led the researchers to conclude that successful racetrack gambling is unrelated to IQ scores.

Ceci and Liker suggest that there are important differences between academic and nonacademic intelligence. Academic intelligence may be closely related to schooling and IQ scores, while nonacademic intelligence may be related to practical experiences of everyday living. As we consider different approaches to the study of intelligence, it will become evident that there are different ways for psychologists to demonstrate, define, and measure intelligence.

Concepts of Intelligence

Intelligence has been defined in many ways during the past century. In Chapter 9, we examined Piaget's theory of intellectual development, and we considered differences between fluid and crystallized intelligence in Chapter 10. In addition to these theoretical approaches, many people have tried to design tests that measure intelligence. Understanding the differences among the various approaches to intelligence is important for understanding psychological theories and research. We begin with a brief discussion of three different orientations to the study of intelligence.

IMPLICIT THEORIES OF INTELLIGENCE

One way to define intelligence is simply to ask people what they think it is. These are called implicit theories, because everyone has an intuitive idea of what intelligence is. (Psychologists have also developed explicit, or formal, theories of intelligence.) In 1921, the editor of the Journal of Educational Psychology asked 14 experts to give their views on the nature of intelligence (Sternberg, 1985). Their definitions included the following characteristics:

- The ability to give good responses from the point of view of truth or fact
- The ability to carry on abstract thinking
- The ability to adjust to the environment
- The ability to adapt to relatively new situations in life
- The ability to acquire knowledge and to recall knowledge already possessed
- The ability to learn or to profit by experience

In a later study, Robert Sternberg and his colleagues (1981) asked numerous experts to identify the qualities of an intelligent person. Three qualities emerged from the analysis: verbal intelligence, problem-solving ability, and practical intelligence—the characteristics that most of us would accept as key attributes of intellect. And when Berg and Sternberg (1992) later asked adults from 22–85 years of age how likely it would be for adults of various ages to engage in certain intellectual activities, three factors of intelligence again were cited: verbal competence (e.g., speaking well), the ability to deal with novelty (e.g., analyzing new information), and everyday competence (common sense). Moreover, while these adults believed that dealing with novelty would be easier for younger adults than older adults, almost all thought that intelligence could be increased with the proper training and practice.

Although there are some aspects of intelligence that endure across the life span, many people believe that other characteristics may change with age. Siegler and Richards (1982) asked a group of psychology students to list characteristics of intelligence in infants, children, and adults. The students defined intelligence among infants as a matter of physical coordination, attachment, awareness of people, and verbal output. For children, learning, verbal facility, and understanding were frequently mentioned. For adults, proficient speaking and writing, problem-solving ability, and logical thinking were listed as key features. It seems that college students have developmental theories of intelligence that emphasize different abilities at different ages.

In a similar study, Yussen and Kane (1985) asked children from first, third, and sixth grade about their conceptions of intelligence. Young children tended to think of intelligence as an all-inclusive characteristic, represented by a single ability, whereas older children viewed intelligence as a series of particular skills. Young children thought that intelligence was clearly evident in behavior, whereas older children

Problem solving abilities, language fluency, and logical thinking are considered fundamental features of intelligence.

viewed intelligence as primarily a mental characteristic. Young children also overestimated their own intellectual abilities, while older children were more accurate in assessing their own intelligence.

What can we say about these commonsense theories of intelligence? First, the views of nonpsychologists correlate remarkably well with the views of experts (Sternberg, 1985). Second, implicit ideas about intelligence include a broader range of abilities than typical IQ tests. Problem solving, planning, and understanding the world around us are often mentioned in implicit concepts. Thus, they seem to be more relevant to the context of everyday behavior and to reflect the cognitive abilities that are important for daily interactions.

DEVELOPMENTAL APPROACHES TO INTELLIGENCE

We have already discussed several kinds of developmental approaches to the study of intelligence. In Chapter 9, we saw that Piaget studied intelligence by examining the adaptations that children make to their environments. We described different cognitive structures of thinking that underlie intelligence at different ages—the Piagetian stages of cognitive development. Piaget was interested in the general stages of intelligence that all children pass through, rather than the individual cognitive differences among children. He noted that the roots of intelligence are evident in the sensorimotor interactions of infants before they acquire language. Systematic intelligence, evident in mental representation, the ability to plan, and other self-regulated actions, emerges among preschoolers. More sophisticated kinds of intelligence involving concrete and formal operational thinking develop during childhood and adolescence.

In Chapter 10, we discussed cognitive development during adulthood and different ways that intelligence may increase or decrease. For example, Horn (1982) distinguished fluid from crystallized intelligence, suggesting that only fluid intelligence declines with advancing age. *Fluid intelligence* is the general ability to perceive, encode, and reason about information. It derives from biological and genetic factors and is less influenced by training and experience. *Crystallized intelligence* is the ability to understand relationships, make judgments, and solve problems. It is based on experience and information and can therefore increase with age.

Baltes, Dittmann-Kohli, and Dixon (1984) further characterized intelligence by distinguishing the mechanics from the pragmatics of intelligence. The **mechanics of intelligence** refers to the speed and accuracy of processing information. This aspect of intelligence may be fully developed by the end of adolescence and may decline during adulthood. The **pragmatics of intelligence** refers to the accumulated knowledge that adults have. This wisdom from experience enables us to assess the significance of information, thereby influencing what is retained. The pragmatic aspect of intelligence, like crystallized intelligence, has the potential to increase indefinitely with age and experience.

PSYCHOMETRIC APPROACHES TO INTELLIGENCE

The oldest approach to intelligence is what is now called the **psychometric approach.** *Psychometrics* refers to the development of objective measures or tests psychological qualities, such as intelligence, aptitudes, or personality. The Scholastic Assessment Test is a psychometric test, for example. Like all psychometric tests, intelligence tests are constructed to measure individual differences. In fact, they were originally developed to solve a practical problem: how to measure differences in intelligence among children. But how do we decide which abilities underlie the important differences? Psychologists usually rely on **factor analysis,** a technique that examines correlations among test scores and tries to identify which particular kinds of scores group together. For example, several tests may all rely on verbal ability and people may score similarly on them, depending on the individual's verbal ability. The technique allows psychologists to identify test items that are answered in a similar manner or that fit together in a group. (A *factor*—such as verbal ability—is an inferred ability that reflects similar test scores.) Because factor theories differentiate various aspects of intelligence, they are sometimes called *differential* theories of intelligence.

Factor theorists have argued for years about the number of factors to include in their theories. At one end of the spectrum is Charles Spearman (1927), who pioneered the use of factor analysis. He identified several specific mental abilities associated with different tasks as well as a general ability, or *g factor*. The g factor was so important on all tasks that Spearman concluded that it constituted the most important aspect of intelligence.

Other theorists have concluded that intelligence is better characterized as many separate abilities. L. L. Thurstone (1938) identified and constructed tests for seven primary mental abilities: verbal comprehension, word fluency, number calculation, spatial reasoning, associative memory, perceptual speed, and a general factor. The primary mental abilities in Thurstone's theory were considered of equal importance, but other theorists have suggested hierarchical arrangements among the factors. Perhaps the most ambitious work on the structural arrangement of factors has been done by J. P. Guilford (1966, 1982). Guilford proposed that intelligence is composed of 150 factors, which he classified and arranged in a complex set of interconnections.

The most popular psychometric approach to measuring intelligence is the IQ test, although there are several types. The history, development, and uses of IQ tests will be discussed in the following section, but it is important to note that items on IQ tests are carefully selected according to how well they measure a person's capacities and predict behavior in other settings. Items that are highly related to one another are usually grouped together in similar scales, and items that are not related to other measures of intelligence or achievement (such as grades in school) are often deleted from the tests. After repeated trials with various test items and various groups of people, there eventually develops a suitable set of items. Because of this method of test item selection, some people have tried to avoid the conceptual definition of intelligence altogether by claiming that "intelligence is what intelligence tests measure."

There are several different kinds of IQ tests. Some are designed for adults, some for children, and some for special populations with language or learning problems. Some tests provide total IQ scores, while some yield separate scores for different scales (such as verbal intelligence or spatial intelligence). Regardless of the type of test, selection of the items is often controversial because various test items may not be equally familiar to everyone who takes the test.

THE THEORY OF MULTIPLE INTELLIGENCES

Although intelligence has been studied for more than 100 years, a consensus has not yet been reached about whether there is only one kind of intelligence or many kinds of intelligence. Factor theorists, such as Spearman and Thurstone, have proposed a variety of independent mental abilities, but they usually agree that a general g factor may be the most important. But how do they account for individuals with special gifts, such as the musical prodigy Mozart? And what about children with savant syndrome, as in the Case Study, who often can perform incredible mathematical calculations almost instantly (Treffert, 1992)? Their talents do not seem to reflect a general factor of intellectual ability, but instead seem to reflect only one specific ability.

Previous theorists (Spearman, Thurstone and Guilford) proposed various kinds of intelligence. A modern champion of this approach is Howard Gardner (1983), who has proposed a theory of multiple intelligences to account for these extraordinary talents in specific domains. He has suggested that intelligence includes skills for finding and solving problems and for creating products. Together, these skills lay the groundwork for acquiring new knowledge.

If intelligence is based on specific skills, you might think that there would be a great many different types of intelligence, but according to Gardner, the evidence points to only seven types. Three of these are fairly traditional, and you would probably name them first if you were asked to state the elements of intelligence:

• *Linguistic intelligence* is signified by fluency with language. Poets, authors, playwrights, novelists, and orators all have a high degree of linguistic intelligence.
• *Logical-mathematical intelligence* is the classic component of Piaget's theory and the emphasis of Western schooling.
• *Spatial intelligence* is the talent of architects, navigators, and others who can represent and transform mental images in many ways.

The remaining four kinds of intelligence emphasize artistic expression, physical abilities and personal interactions rather than logic, math, and science. But according to Gardner (1982), it is here that we find the greatest participation:

> For most of humanity, and throughout most of human history, the processes and products involved in artistic creation and perception have been far more pervasive than those enshrined in the sciences. In fact, logical scientific thought . . . is still restricted to a small enclave of thinkers; participation in the literary, musical, or graphic arts, on the other hand, has been widespread for thousands of years. (Gardner, 1982; p. 299)

Here, then, are the four remaining types of intelligence:

• *Musical intelligence* includes the skills required to discriminate and integrate pitch, rhythm, and timbre. It includes talents at composition as well as performance.
• *Bodily-kinesthetic intelligence* calls attention to the talents of athletes, dancers, sculptors, and others who show a deep understanding of movement and display the ability to imitate and control sophisticated motions. We might include actors, clowns, and mimes in this group, too, because they all demonstrate an unusual talent for bodily intelligence.
• *Interpersonal intelligence* is the ability to recognize distinctive characteristics in other people and to interact appropriately with others.
• *Intrapersonal intelligence* is knowing and understanding oneself, and it is important for identity formation.

Gardner's view of multiple intelligences is a departure from traditional psychometric and cognitive analyses. Instead of strictly focusing on information-processing abilities, Gardner emphasizes the role of neuropsychology, cultural experiences, and expertise acquired through practice. He also uses evidence from studies of savants, people with special capabilities who are otherwise mentally subnormal (see the Case Study). Although his views are not accepted by everyone who studies intelligence, they are nevertheless a synthesis of many different approaches. Is it a theory? Perhaps not,

New theories of intelligence consider bodily kinesthetic skills to be a separate kind of intelligence

because it does not make straightforward predictions that can be easily tested experimentally. Still, Gardner's ideas extend the study of intelligence in new directions and help to describe our talents, accomplishments, and limitations in ways that do not rely on standardized test scores.

CASE STUDY

HARRIET, THE MUSICAL SAVANT

One type of evidence that Gardner(1983) uses for his theory of multiple intelligences is savant syndrome, cases in which people are generally mentally subnormal but in which they have one area of preserved (or enhanced) capability. Many such children are classified as mentally retarded and diagnosed with autism, a condititon in which children are socially withdrawn and often engage in repetitive rocking and self-injurious behavior, among other features (discussed in Chapter 15). Some autistic children, however, display remarkable abilities in one sphere, a preserved "island" of mental ability in an otherwise limited mental world. The older term for these people was idiot savant, with savant meaning "learned" and the old sense of idiot that meant "a person who was very private, or a recluse." Today the term savant, or a person with savant syndrome, is preferred (Treffert, 1992).

Gardner (1983) takes the existence of such people for the existence of multiple intelligences because one capacity seems independent of the others. The most common kinds of special abilities seen in savants are extraordinary musical abilities; abilities to perform rapid and complicated artithmetical calculations (for example, to divide one large number into another at rapid rates, which gives rise to the name lighting calculators); remarkable abilities to remember lists of information verbatim; and calculating days of the week from dates (for example, giving the day of the week of August 4, 1123, very rapidly and accurately). These last savants are called calender calculators.

Consider Harriet, a musical savant, who was the sixth of seven children (Treffert, 1989; Viscott, 1969). Harriet was autistic: socially withdrawn, unsmiling, and seemingly deviod of emotion. She did not develop speech and was not toilet trained until she was 9 years old. She was raised in her crib night and day for the first two years. The crib was located close the family's grand piano where the mother often gave piano lessons. Harriet came in contact with other children at the age of 3 but was wild and uncontrollable. She eventually attended school, but her adult IQ was only 73 (although her memory abilities were measured as normal on standardized tests and her ability to recall events of her past were extraordinary).

Why was Harriet special? Because of her remarkable knowledge of and abilities in music. When she was 7 months old, her father heard her humming a part of an opera by Rigoletto in perfect pitch (Treffert, 1989). Because her mother was a music teacher, Harriet had often heard the piece played, even at 7 monthes. By the age of 4 Harriet had learned to play the piano, violin, trumpet, clarinet, and French horn. She also read music (despite not being formally taught) and demonstrated prodigious memory for all musical matters. Her proficiency in music and her knowledge of musical information grew remarkably as she aged, although she was subnormal in all other ways. Viscott described her memory for musical events:

Her knowledge of music is breathtaking. She can identify almost any major work in the entire symphonic repertoire, and give the key, opus number, date and place of the first performance, and the vital statistics of the composer. . . What is most striking is that she knows the work of the lesser composers as well, and is familiar with literally thousands of compositions. . . Once she begins to describe a work, she begins to remember details about each performance she has heard, who conducted, and so forth. . . . She rhapsodizes over conductors and can trace their musical genealogy back a hundred years. . . (quoted in Treffert, 1989, p. 45).

As an adult, Harriet played both the violin and piano well. She could improvise with ease and, on command, could flawlessly play a tune in the style and manner of any of the great composers (Treffert, 1989).

In terms of Gardner's theory, Harriet had low intelligence as traditionally measured on tests that draw heavily on verbal and mathematical abilities, yet retained brilliant musical ability. Cases such as Harriet's support the idea that various types of intelligence exist, as Gardner theorizes, and are relatively independent of one another. Musical ability represents a form of intelligence distinct from other types.

The Development of Intelligence Tests

Many types of intelligence tests exist today. We consider how they have developed in the past 100 years or more.

EARLY INTELLIGENCE TESTS

In 1884, Sir Francis Galton, a cousin of Charles Darwin and a pioneer in mental testing, established a laboratory at the International Health Exhibition in South Kensington, London. The purpose of the laboratory was to collect data "by the best methods known to modern science" to describe individuals' physical stature, strength, and sensory abilities (Sternberg & Powell, 1982). One of Galton's tests measured the strength of a hand squeeze, another gauged the highest pitch of a whistle that a person could hear, and still other tests assessed reaction times to visual and auditory stimuli. Why did Galton devise these measures? First, he believed that nearly all psychological characteristics could be measured. Second, Galton believed that intelligence could be predicted from basic human abilities such as quick reactions and a discriminating sense of hearing. Although many of Galton's ideas are no longer accepted, he was a pioneer of the psychometric approach because he tried to identify and measure basic components of intelligence.

At the beginning of the twentieth century, the French Ministry of Education wanted to identify slow learners who needed academic help. In 1904, psychologists Alfred Binet and Theophile Simon were hired to construct a test that would screen low-achieving students and predict degrees of academic success. Binet was a sharp critic of tests like Galton's as well as an established scholar on children's thinking, so he was a particularly good choice for the task. In fact, Binet was one of the first psychologists to study cognitive processes of intelligence, although he is now mostly known as the pioneer of intelligence testing and less for his other work (Siegler, 1992). In 1911 Binet wrote,

> . . . Intelligence is before all a process of knowing that is directed toward the external world, that works to reconstruct it in its entirety, by means of the little fragments that are given to us . . . comprehension, inventiveness, direction, and criticism: intelligence is contained in these four words. (Binet, 1911, pp. 117–118)

Sir Francis Galton was a nineteenth century pioneer in psychophysical measurement.

Alfred Binet became interested in measuring intelligence when he noticed that his two daughters, Madeleine and Alice, developed their motor skills in different ways.

Binet and Simon devised a variety of tasks for children of different ages to perform: puzzles to solve, questions to answer, and mathematical problems. They reasoned that a good test should include increasingly difficult items that older children could answer more easily than younger children. For example, a test item that few 5-year-olds but most 6-year-olds and nearly all 7-year-olds could answer correctly was judged to be a good measure of an average 6-year-old's ability.

Binet used the concept of **mental age (MA)** to describe an individual's test performance. If a 6-year-old correctly answered questions like most 8-year-olds, then the child's mental age was 8. Thus, mental age was constructed by comparing an individual's performance with average levels of performance by children of other ages. Wilhelm Stern, a German psychologist, elaborated this concept into an **intelligence quotient,** or **IQ** score, in the following formula, where CA stands for *chronological age*:

$$IQ = MA/CA \times 100$$

The ratio of MA to CA was multiplied by 100 to eliminate the decimal and provide an average score of 100 (assuming that chronological age and mental age were equal). For example, suppose a 10-year-old performed as well as most 12-year-olds on Binet's tests. The child's IQ score would be 12/10 × 100, or 120. If the same 10-year-old scored as well as the average 8-year-old, the child's IQ would be 80. If the child's mental age were 10, the IQ would be 100. By definition, then, average intelligence is 100.

MODERN INTELLIGENCE TESTS

Binet's pioneering work was introduced to America in 1916 by Louis Terman and his associates at Stanford University. These researchers adapted the original Binet-Simon test to American children and culture, thus creating the **Stanford-Binet test.** They set new norms for average performance by giving the revised version to 1,000 children and 400 adults. The 1916 Stanford-Binet exam was modified in 1937, 1960, 1972, and 1985, and the standards for average performance were changed each time so that test takers would not be compared with people of different generations and varied educations.

The current version of the Stanford-Binet test (Thorndike, Hagen, & Sattler, 1985) yields scores for four areas: verbal reasoning, quantitative reasoning, abstract/visual reasoning, and memory. A composite score provides an overall IQ score. The Stanford-Binet test includes tasks for age levels from 2 years to adulthood (see Table 11.1). It is presented to individuals in a standardized manner by an examiner. Tasks given to young children often involve copying, stringing beads, building with blocks, and answering questions about common activities. Older subjects may be directed to identify picture absurdities (e.g., specifying what is wrong with a depiction of a man trying to cut wood with a saw that he is holding upside down). In what is called the similarities test, subjects are asked to tell what pairs of words such as *wood* and *coal*, *apple* and *peach*, and *ship* and *automobile* have in common. In other parts of the test, they have to complete sentences such as "The streams are dry _____ there has been little rain," to unscramble sentences such as "A defends dog good his bravely master," and to explain proverbs and analogies. Each task is designed to measure a different aspect of reasoning and judgment, but all are highly related to general intelligence and to each other. Many of the tasks resemble schoolwork, which is one reason these tests are able to predict academic success or failure so well.

The Stanford-Binet test contains six items for each mental test at each age level. An examiner starts by finding the level at which a child answers all questions correctly

TABLE 11.1
Representative Items from the Stanford-Binet Intelligence Test for Different Age Levels

2 Years Old
a. The child is asked to identify body parts such as hair, mouth, and ears on a doll.
b. The child is asked to build a tower of four blocks, like those in a model that is presented.

4 Years Old
a. The child fills in the missing words when asked, "Brother is a boy; sister is a _____."
and "In daytime it is light; at night it is _____."
b. The child is asked, "Why do we have houses? Why do we have books?"

9 Years Old
a. The child is asked, "In an old graveyard in Spain they have discovered a small skull which they believe to be that of Christopher Columbus when he was about ten years old. What is foolish about that?"
b. The child is asked, "Tell me the name of a color that rhymes with head. Tell me a number that rhymes with tree."

Adult
a. People are asked to describe the difference between laziness and idleness, poverty and misery, character and reputation.
b. People are asked, "Which direction would you have to face so your right hand would be to the north?"

SOURCE: Terman & Merrill, 1973.

and then presents more difficult problems until the child cannot solve any. The examiner totals the points for the right responses and computes the score according to guidelines in the test manual. These basic aspects of Binet's work remain unchanged; however, IQ scores are now calculated by comparing each child's performance with the number of points obtained by a large sample of children of the same age. Each time the test is revised, the scores are standardized on a new sample of children.

Over the past 40 years, other widely used tests of intelligence were devised by David Wechsler, a psychologist at New York's Bellevue Hospital. Wechsler first prepared the Wechsler Bellevue Intelligence Scale because he needed a satisfactory intelligence test for adults. Later, he refined this instrument into the Wechsler Adult Intelligence Scale (WAIS) and added the Wechsler Intelligence Scale for Children (WISC) and the Wechsler Preschool and Primary Scale of Intelligence (WPPSI).

The **Wechsler tests,** like Binet's, are administered individually, range from easy to hard for a variety of skills, and are periodically revised to include new items. An examiner begins by asking readily answered questions and continues until a subject makes several errors consecutively. The IQ score is calculated by comparing the subject's performance with the average of others of a similar age. The Wechsler tests differ from the Stanford-Binet test by including separate scales for verbal and performance (nonverbal) tasks. The performance tasks include completing pictures, assembling puzzles, and copying block designs, while the verbal aspects focus on general information, vocabulary, and similarities (see Table 11.2). One advantage of having two different scales is to help identify children with language problems. If a 10-year-old scores much lower on the verbal scale than on the performance scale, an examiner can readily assess the child's strengths and weaknesses and diagnose a potential reading or language disability.

A study analyzing the use of psychological tests in clinical settings in the United States between 1935 and 1982 found that the WAIS was the most frequently used test

Intelligence tests can help to identify cognitive talents and problems in children and adults.

TABLE 11.2
The Wechsler Intelligence Scale for Children

These 12 tasks are used to assess children's intelligence. The WISC yields a total IQ score as well as separate performance and verbal scores.

VERBAL SCALE	PERFORMANCE SCALE
1. *General Information:* A series of questions are presented involving information that most children will have been exposed to (e.g., How many nickels make a dime? What is steam made of?).	1. *Picture Completion:* The child is asked which part is missing in each picture in a series of 12 pictures of common objects (e.g., a car with a wheel missing, a rabbit with an ear missing).
2. *General Comprehension:* Items are presented in which the child must explain why certain practices are desirable or what course of action is preferred under certain circumstances (e.g., Why should people not waste fuel? What should you do if you see someone forget his book in a restaurant?).	2. *Picture Arrangement:* Sets of pictures are presented in which the pictures will tell a story if they are arranged in the correct order. These are rather like wordless comic-strip pictures.
3. *Arithmetic:* A series of arithmetic questions are presented ranging from easy ones involving simple counting to more difficult ones involving mental computations and reasoning	3. *Block Design:* The child receives a set of small blocks having some white, some red, and some half-red and half-white sides. The child is shown a series of red and white designs that he or she must reproduce with the blocks.
4. *Similarities:* The child is asked to tell in what way a series of paired words are alike (e.g., In what way are a shoe and a slipper alike? In what way are an hour and a week alike?).	4. *Object Assembly:* The child must assemble jigsawlike parts of common objects into the whole puzzle (e.g., a chair, a foot).
5. *Vocabulary:* A series of increasingly difficult words are presented, and the child is asked what each word means.	5. *Coding:* The child must match symbols with numbers on the basis of a code given to him or her.
6. *Digit Span:* A series of numbers of increasing length are presented orally, and the child is asked to repeat them either in the same order or in a reverse order.	6. *Mazes:* The child must trace the correct route from a starting point to home on a series of mazes.

SOURCE: The examples given are similar but not identical to items on the Wechsler Intelligence Scale for Children. Used by permission of the publisher, The Psychological Corporation. All rights reserved.

(Lubin, Larsen, & Matarazzo, 1984). The WISC was fifth, and the Stanford-Binet was mentioned fifteenth. These rankings have remained relatively stable over the years. The survey reveals that tests of intelligence and mental abilities are among the most frequently administered psychological tests. Matarazzo (1992) predicts that although these tests will continue to be popular for decades to come, they will be supplemented with new neuropsychological batteries, assessments of basic cognitive processes, and scales for measuring adaptive behavior.

Many kinds of intelligence tests are available, each designed for a particular group and a particular purpose. There are tests for infants, children, adults, and handicapped people. Some are for group testing, while others are administered individually. Some intelligence tests are based solely on nonverbal skills. Others are designed for computerized testing. The principles underlying the construction of all intelligence tests, however, remain the same.

Characteristics of Psychometric Tests

We have said that intelligence tests are types of psychometric tests. All psychometric tests require three features for their proper use: a standardization sample, reliability and validity. We explain these concepts as they apply to IQ tests.

THE STANDARDIZATION SAMPLE

Intelligence tests are designed to measure intellectual performance relative to a reference group. The tests do not measure absolute mental abilities. The group of subjects that forms the basis for comparison, called the **standardization sample,** must accurately represent the entire population that might be given the test. (*Population* is a statistical term referring to a group from which a sample can be drawn.) The standardization sample that testers might choose for an admission test to medical school would be composed of people who had obtained, or were about to obtain, undergraduate degrees. It should include representative numbers of graduates and undergraduates of large schools and small schools; eastern, midwestern, and western schools; men and women; whites and nonwhites. Often, a standardization sample is selected by **stratified random sampling,** a procedure in which a variable such as family income is broken down into strata, or levels (e.g., $10,000 brackets), and an equal number of people from each stratum are chosen randomly. Test designers thus can be confident that they have included a fair assortment of people by criteria that include sex, race, geography, income, and size of hometown.

Tests such as the Stanford-Binet are standardized according to age as well; that is, they compare individuals of the same age. Each restandardization of the Stanford-Binet test takes into account advances in education, science, technology, and other differences across generations. James Flynn (1984) has shown that each successive sample of people serving as the standard for the Stanford-Binet demonstrate improved performance over previous samples. Over a period of more than 40 years, the total gain amounted to nearly 14 IQ points! This could mean that Americans are getting smarter or better educated or that the sampling procedures are changing. Whatever the reason for the increase in IQ scores, an average 8-year-old today can answer more questions on the Stanford-Binet than could his or her counterpart in 1937. Because IQ scores are computed in relation to the standardization sample, however, the average IQ score remains 100.

Both the Stanford-Binet and Wechsler tests have a **standard deviation** of approximately 15 points. (See Appendix A for a discussion of statistical terms.) This means that the **variability** at each age is the same and that the IQ scores for each age resemble a **normal distribution** (see the bell curve in Figure 11.1). In a normal distribution of IQ scores, about 68 percent of the population is within 1 standard deviation (1 SD), or 15 points, of the average score of 100. Ninety-five percent fall within 2 standard deviations, or 30 points, of the average. Therefore, only 2.5 percent of the population would be expected to score above 130 or below 70 on the Stanford-Binet or WISC.

RELIABILITY

A good test should yield consistent results. If the same person takes the same test on different occasions, the scores should be similar. The consistency of scores is called test **reliability,** and it can be calculated with a *correlation coefficient*. Recall from Chapter 1 that correlation coefficients can vary from −1.00 to +1.00. If a correlation between two measures is near zero, there is no relation between them. If it is positive, then as

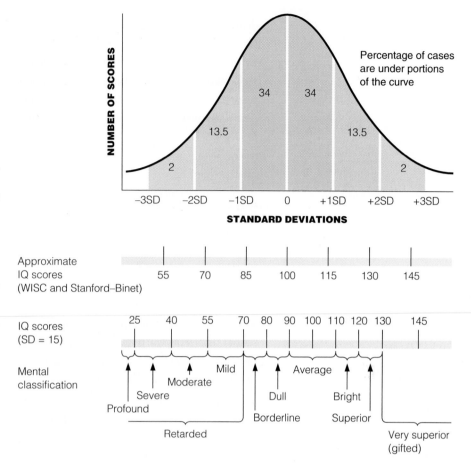

FIGURE 11.1
The Distribution of Intelligence

The psychometric model assumes that IQ scores are normally distributed with an average of 100. The standard deviations (SD) of the WISC and Stanford-Binet are approximately 15, so 68 percent of people score between 85 and 115. Ninety-five percent of the population have IQ scores between 70 and 130. The lower scale provides descriptive labels for people who achieve various IQ scores.

SOURCE: Anastasi, 1979.

one measure increases, so does the other. If the correlation is negative, one measure decreases as the other one increases. (See pages 20–21) for a review of the concept of correlation as well as Appendix A)

The reliability of IQ tests can be assessed by correlating the same people's scores on repeated tests. This is called *test-retest reliability*. Reliability can also be checked by correlating one-half of the test with the other half of the test, such as odd-numbered items with even-numbered items. This is called *split-half reliability*. Many IQ tests demonstrate high reliability, with correlation statistics often as high as +.90, indicating strong similarity between scores. Thus, if you take an IQ test today and again a week from now, your scores are likely to be very similar on the two occasions. However, motivation, fatigue, and measurement error can affect the consistency of results. Also, when considerable time and experience intervene between tests, scores may vary more and thus be less reliable.

VALIDITY

Any good test must have **validity;** that is, it must measure what it claims to measure. Galton's measures of sensory thresholds and discriminations were precise, quick, and reliable, but they were not valid because they did not measure intelligence, as he had claimed. People who were deemed intelligent by other measures (e.g., by what they had accomplished) scored no better on Galton's tests than people who were deemed less intelligent.

There are several types of test validity:

• **Construct validity** is the accuracy with which a test measures the psychological processes specified by a theory. Unfortunately, not all test makers agree on a single definition, theory, or measure of intelligence. Critics of intelligence tests often focus on the lack of uniform construct validity. Supporters counter that IQ tests have extremely good concurrent and predictive validity.

• **Concurrent validity** is the degree of correlation between two or more different tests given at approximately the same time to the same people. For example, IQ scores derived from the Stanford-Binet and WISC usually correlate highly. Arthur Jensen (1980), in a review of 47 studies in which different IQ tests were administered at the same time, reported that the range of correlations was +.43 to +.94, with a median correlation of +.80. Jensen reported that the average correlations among more than 40 popular intelligence tests ranged from +.67 to +.77. The SAT (Scholastic Aptitude Test, or Scholastic Assessment Test), which is essentially an intelligence test, correlates about +.80 with the WAIS (Seligman, 1992).

• **Predictive validity** is a measure of the test score's relation to other measures of aptitude or ability. How well do IQ scores predict other behavior? This is the strongest evidence for their usefulness, because they do this quite well. For example, IQ scores are correlated highly with scholastic achievement (usually measured as school grades). The correlations are approximately +.60 to +.70 during elementary school and +.40 to +.50 during college. The difference over time occurs because more factors influence scholastic performance during adulthood, such as motivation or whether the student has a job.

Although psychologists cannot agree on a single definition of intelligence, it is evident that intelligence tests are reliable instruments and IQ scores are good predictors of success in school. Also, intelligence test scores are correlated with occupational success and performance on everyday problem-solving tasks, so they are sometimes useful predictors for employee selection as well (Barrett & Depinet, 1991; Ree & Earles, 1992). However, this point is still under debate (McClelland, 1993). Just keep in mind that the correlations are not perfect. Some people who score relatively poorly on IQ tests have very successful careers, and other people who score highly on the tests do not achieve much in later life. Nevertheless, an interesting survey is summarized in Figure 11.2, showing the average IQs of people in various occupations.

CONCEPT SUMMARY

CHARACTERISTICS OF TESTS

Intelligence tets, like all psychometric tests, should have good reliability and validity.

Reliability refers to the consistency of test scores across testing occasions and is expressed as a correlation of performance on two occasions.

• Split-half reliability refers to correlations between half the items on a test with the other half.
• Test-retest reliability refers to correlations between scores on the same test given on two occasions.

Validity refers to whether a test measures what it is supposed to measure and can be assessed in several ways.

• Construct validity is the accuracy with which a test measures the psychological processes specified by a theory
• Concurrent validity is the correlation between two or more different forms of a test given to the same people at about the same time
• Predictive validity is a measure of the relation of the test scores to other measures of behavior that are relevant to the construct

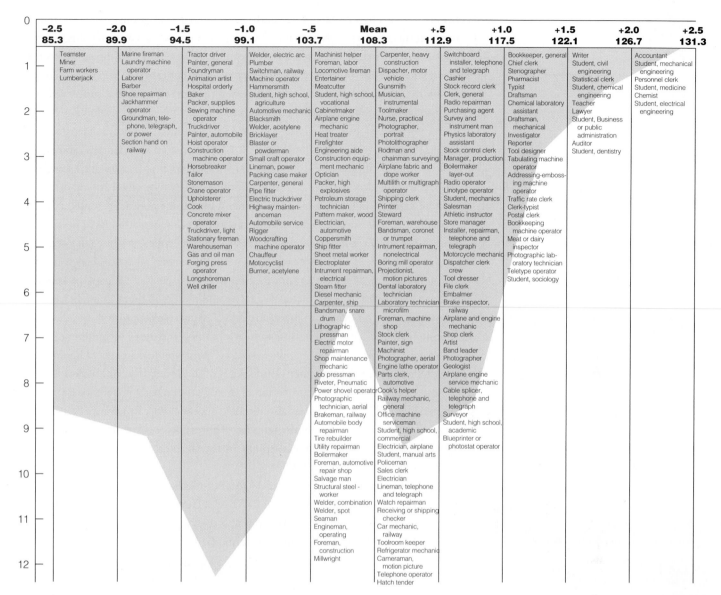

FIGURE 11.2
IQ Scores for Common Occupations

The median IQ scores for people holding various jobs, taken from an intelligence test developed for the U.S. Army, are indicated along the top of the figure. Each of the ten divisions represent one-half of a standard deviation, and the mean is located at 108.3 points. Also, the number of individuals per division is shown by the superimposed line.

SOURCE: Herrnstein, 1973.

Stability of IQ Scores

Do IQ scores change with development, like so many other aspects of mental functioning? Or is intelligence (measured by IQ) a stable characteristic? The answers depend on the conditions under which the tests are given, the kinds of tests, and the time between repeated tests. (Of course, average IQ for each age group is, by definition, 100. But we can still ask if individuals change in their relative ranks over time).

One problem is that it is very difficult to assess intelligence in preschoolers (or at least the type of capacity measured on standard IQ tests). For young children, intelligence tests include such tasks as stringing beads or identifying body parts, which may not have much to do with the sort of verbal intelligence measured by the standard tests given school-age children and adults. Some studies have shown that intelligence may change markedly from early childhood to adulthood (McCall, Appelbaum, & Hogarty, 1973), but this may be because the measures of intelligence for young children test for a different kind of intelligence (Fagan & Singer, 1983).

The graph in Figure 11.3 shows the correlations between intelligence test scores at age 17 and scores achieved at various ages before 17. Note that the correlations

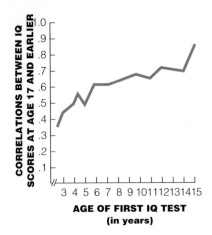

FIGURE 11.3
Stability of IQ Scores with Age

In this graph, the Stanford-Binet IQ scores obtained at age 17 are correlated with Stanford-Binet test scores obtained at earlier ages. Notice that the tests given at very young ages correlate poorly with adult performance. As the time between tests decreases, the correlations between IQ scores increase.

SOURCE: Jensen, 1980.

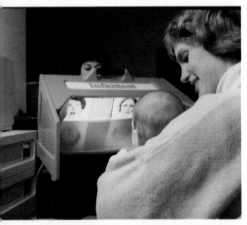

In the Fagan Test of Infant Intelligence, babies are exposed to pairs of pictures, one of which is familiar and one of which is novel. The amount of time that the infant spends looking at the novel picture predicts later I.Q. measures reasonably well.

between IQ scores at 17 years of age and scores measured at younger ages are much lower when the first test is given before 7 years of age. In fact, predictions of IQ scores from tests given to infants are even worse, probably because of the strong sensorimotor nature of the tasks used in infant intelligence tests, as compared to the tests used for older children, which include verbal and reasoning items. Fagan and Singer (1983) report that infant intelligence tests given at 3 to 8 months of age correlate poorly with IQ scores obtained at 6 or more years of age. Gifted children cannot be identified by infant intelligence tests and infants at high-risk for mental deficiencies cannot be identified either. Willerman and Fiedler (1974) observed that performance levels of 4-year-olds with IQ scores above 140 were not predicted by tests given at 8 months.

Some researchers argue that measures of infant processing abilities can predict later IQ scores better than the measures of sensorimotor development that have been used in most of the earlier infant tests. Fagan (1992) and his colleagues have devised the Fagan Test of Infant Intelligence, which is a test of infants' abilities to detect and encode novelty. For example, Fagan and Singer (1983) created 12 pairs of stimuli, such as geometric patterns and pictures of faces, and presented them to infants aged 3 to 7 months. Each pair of stimuli included a novel stimulus along with a stimulus that the infant had seen before. The researchers obtained measures of preference and length of time spent looking at the novel picture. These simple measures of infant processing predict IQ scores better than do measures of sensorimotor coordination. Fagan (1992) has reported an average correlation of +.50 between early preference for visual novelty and later IQ scores. He has also reported that his test can identify 85 percent of infants later diagnosed as mentally retarded. Thus, IQ scores based on infants' cognitive abilities may reveal more continuity in intelligence with age than previous research has suggested (Storfer, 1990).

Do IQ scores change during adulthood? Yes, but there is not a simple decline with increasing age. As discussed in Chapter 10, cross-sectional studies of adult IQ scores reveal a peak between 18 and 25 years of age and then a gradual decline until approximately age 50. The decline becomes more marked after that, but this pattern of growth, plateau, and then decline in intelligence is misleading (Labouvie-Vief, 1985). One reason is that the IQ scores of people who experience health problems and who may be close to death from age 50 on are averaged with the IQ scores of healthy older adults. Another reason is that the declining scores may be due to cohort effects, the consequences of being born in a particular generation, raised during unique historical events, and being influenced by particular educational opportunities. A third reason is that older adults may be less familiar with intelligence tests than younger adults. A lack of practice, motivation, and self-confidence may well have an adverse effect on the scores of older adults (Dixon & Baltes, 1986). Richard Lynn (1990), however, suggests that the decline in IQ found in cross-sectional studies may simply reflect long-term gains in average intelligence over the generations. Furthermore, he claims that this rise in intelligence can be traced to the superior nutrition provided to today's younger generations, compared to the nutritional levels that the older adults had grown up with.

Longitudinal studies of intellectual changes during adulthood have yielded a different picture, one that shows only slight declines in intelligence until old age (Schaie, 1990). In a longitudinal study of adults ages 65 to 85, Blum, Jarvik and Clark (1970) found only a modest decline up to age 73, with a steeper decline after that. However, the drop was uneven; vocabulary and general information did not deteriorate through age 85, while spatial reasoning and speed of responding fell off sharply. This pattern of change suggests that processing speed and accuracy (fluid intelligence) may decline

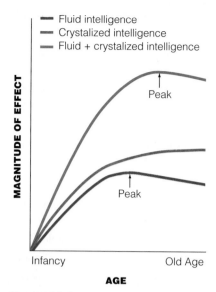

FIGURE 11.4
Differential Declines in Mental Abilities with Age

Various longitudinal studies of intelligence have shown that general ability declines with age (top line). However, if fluid intelligence and crystallized intelligence are measured separately (lower two lines), then it appears that this decline is due mainly to a decline in fluid intelligence (mental processing speed and accuracy). Crystallized intelligence (general information, vocabulary, and knowledge) remains steady, or even increases slightly over a lifetime.

SOURCE: Horn, 1976.

with age among elderly adults, but that general information and knowledge (crystallized intelligence) does not (Seligman, 1992). See Figure 11.4 for a graphical representation of these conclusions.

To summarize the important points about the stability of IQ scores, we know that (1) measures of infant intelligence may not predict adult intelligence very well, (2) the type of test and the skills being measured are critical, (3) IQ scores are most stable from late childhood to early adulthood, (4) IQ scores were designed to predict school success and are usually most highly correlated with academic achievement, (5) not all mental abilities improve or decline as a general factor of intelligence, and (6) cohort differences may influence IQ scores considerably and exaggerate the apparent decline with age in older adults.

Heredity, Environment, and IQ Scores

The nature/nurture controversy is one of the enduring issues in the study of intelligence. Quite simply, the question is, How much intelligence is due to heredity, and how much is due to the physical and intellectual environment in which a person is raised? The construction of intelligence tests and IQ scores has allowed researchers to investigate this issue, but the results have not always been easy to interpret. The issue is not just philosophical. In 1969, Arthur Jensen argued that up to 80 percent of the variation in IQ scores among individuals is derived from heredity. Jensen further argued that compensatory and remedial educational programs, such as Head Start, have little chance of changing children's IQ scores in the face of this overwhelming biological constraint.

Jensen's views provoked outcries of indignation, proposals for social reform, and sharp scientific debate, which continues today (see Controversy: *The Bell Curve* Debate). Old studies have been re-analyzed, and a considerable amount of new research on the nature/nurture aspects of intelligence has been conducted. The basic research strategy has been to examine the similarity of IQ scores between groups of people who differ systematically in their genetic relationships or the environments in which they develop. As we discovered in Chapter 2, behavior genetics research addresses the nature/nurture controversy with two methods: studies of twins and studies of adoptive families. These methods are used to assess **heritability,** a statistic that tells how much of the variability in a behavior is due to genetic differences among people in a particular population. Heritabilities for characteristics can range from .00 to 1.00, with higher numbers indicating greater contributions from genetics.

STUDIES OF TWINS

Identical twins have identical genes. A strong hereditarian position would argue that their IQ scores should be very similar. Twins usually grow up together in the same environment, however, so only identical twins raised in different environments can be used to test the genetic hypothesis. In 1973, hereditarian Hans Eysenck said, "IQs of identical twins reared apart . . . [are] perhaps the most cogent evidence in favor of the genetic determination of intelligence. . . . If the genetic case rested on just one kind of support, this would be the one chosen by the experts" (cited in *Eysenck v. Kamin,* 1981, p. 106). Other experts disagree, however. Sandra Scarr and Robert Kidd (1983) suggest that identical twins reared apart are rare and unusual, the studies are difficult to interpret, and the results are not clear-cut. In fact, relatively few studies of twins

Identical twins share more than identical genes. They often dress alike, participate in the same activities, and are treated the same way by other people.

raised apart have been reported in the literature, and one of those (Burt, 1966) is now in question.

The other studies of twins raised apart all found a high correlation between the twins' intelligence test scores. Newman, Freeman, and Holzinger (1937) reported that the IQ scores of 19 pairs of twins reared apart in the United States correlated at +.67. Shields (1962) studied 37 pairs of twins in England and found a correlation of +.77. Juel-Nielsen (1965) reported a correlation of +.62 for the intelligence scores of 12 pairs of Danish twins. And Bouchard, Lykken, McGue, Segal, and Tellegen (1990) reported a correlation of +.75 in a study of 42 twins tested in Minnesota.

The high correlations of IQs between twins reared apart are compelling evidence for most experts, but Leon Kamin points out that several problems arise in interpreting the data (*Eysenck v. Kamin*, 1981). The most serious problem is that the twins in some of the studies were often not separated by much time or experience. For example, 27 of the 37 pairs included in Shields's study were raised by branches of the same family. Typically, the mother raised one twin, and her mother or sister cared for the other. Kamin points out that such twins had similar schooling, hometowns, and backgrounds. Their intelligence scores correlated at +.83, while the scores for twins raised by unrelated families correlated at only +.51. Clearly, the similar environments had an effect.

Despite flaws in the design and procedures of the studies, proponents of the hereditarian view argue that genetic similarity between twins accounts for much of the similarity in their IQ scores. Fraternal twins develop from separate zygotes and so are no more alike genetically than other brothers and sisters; they just happen to have been born at the same time. (Fraternal twins can be of the same or opposite sex.) If IQ is genetically determined, then identical twins should be more alike than fraternal twins. Bouchard and McGue (1981) reviewed 111 studies on family resemblance in intelligence and found that the IQ scores of identical twins usually correlated between +.70 and +.90, while the correlations for fraternal twins were between +.50 and +.70. The researchers found that in general, "the higher the proportion of genes two family members have in common, the higher the average correlation between their IQs" (Bouchard & McGue, 1981, p. 1055). Loehlin, Willerman, and Horn (1988) confirmed that identical twins consistently have higher correlated IQ scores than do fraternal twins. This finding illustrates the importance of genetic contributions but does not diminish the role of environmental factors. Twins who are reared together, treated alike, and exposed to similar experiences consistently exhibit more similar IQ scores than twins who are raised quite differently. In addition, most studies show that fraternal twins (raised together) have more similar IQs than do other brothers and sisters (raised at somewhat different times in the family), which also argues that common experiences can affect IQ.

ADOPTION STUDIES

A second method of testing the relative influence of heredity and environment is to study adopted children to see if environmental enrichment can promote intellectual development. A study in France supports this view (Schiff et al., 1978). The investigators compared the IQ scores of lower-class children adopted by well-off families with the scores of the children's siblings who had not been adopted. The adopted children's scores averaged 111, while the scores of brothers and sisters raised by their biological mothers averaged 95. A 1989 study conducted by Capron and Duyme, also in France,

Many families today adopt children of different ethnic heritages. These interracial adoptions permit psychologists to study the relative contributions of nature and nurture to development.

provided further evidence along these lines. The researchers tested 38 children at age 14 and found that children who were born into and reared by lower-class families had an average IQ of 92.4, compared to an average IQ of 103.6 for those who were adopted into well-off families after being born to a lower-class family. The researchers also found that children born into upper-class families and then reared by lower-class families had average IQs of 107.5, compared to an IQ average of 119.6 for children of upper-class families who were adopted into other upper-class environments (Capron & Duyme, 1989).

Recent studies of adopted children have examined the patterns of IQ correlations between children and other members of their natural and adoptive families. The environmental position predicts that unrelated children in the same family (who share an environment, but not genes) will have similar IQ scores. The hereditarian position predicts that parents and their children put up for adoption (who share genes, but not the same environment) will have similar IQ scores. The Texas Adoption Study (Horn, 1983; Horn, Loehlin, & Willerman, 1979) collected extensive data on IQ scores and personality measures of adopted children, biological children, adoptive parents, and biological parents. The children in the Texas study were adopted within two weeks of birth. Therefore, they did not share the same environments as their biological parents. The critical question was, Did their IQ scores resemble more closely their biological or adoptive parents' IQ scores?

Figure 11.5 shows that the IQ scores of children are correlated more with the IQ scores of their biological parents. In fact, the correlation between the IQ scores of mothers and the scores of their children put up for adoption is +.31, indicating some similarity. Although the data clearly reveal stronger correlations between biological relatives than adopted relatives, the findings should be interpreted cautiously, because the size of the correlations is modest. Also, the age of the children seems to make a significant difference. Horn and his colleagues found that the correlations between the IQ scores of the adopted children and the scores of their biological mothers decreased as the children grew up. Other studies have shown that the correlations are practically zero by the time the adopted children reach young adulthood (Loehlin, Horn, & Willerman, 1989; Teasdale & Owen, 1984). The longer adopted children stay in their new environment, the smaller is the genetic influence on IQ.

Another major study of adopted children, the Minnesota Adolescent Study, was conducted by Sandra Scarr and Richard Weinberg (1983). All the adopted children were placed in adoptive homes within their first year and were given a battery of IQ and personality tests as adolescents. No data were available from the biological parents

FIGURE 11.5
Correlations of IQ Scores Among Adoptive Family Members

This figure shows that IQ scores of children are more strongly related to the IQ scores of their biological parents than of their adoptive parents. The correlations are shown on the lines connecting each set of relatives.

SOURCE: Horn, Loehlin, & Willerman, 1979.

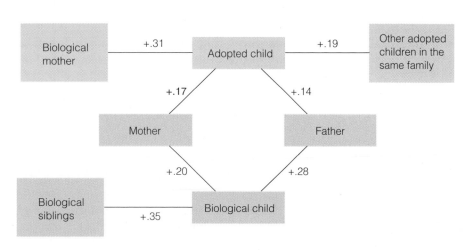

of the adopted children, so the researchers compared IQ patterns from biologically related families and adoptive families. The IQ scores of mothers correlated +.41 with their biological children's IQs, whereas adoptive mothers' IQs correlated only +.09 with their adopted children's. Fathers' scores showed the same pattern; in biologically related families, fathers' IQs correlated +.40, while the correlation was only +.16 between IQs of fathers and their adopted children.

Scarr and Weinberg (1976) also conducted a study of transracial adoption that provides data relevant to the heredity/environment controversy. The researchers studied 101 white families in the Minneapolis area who had adopted a total of 176 nonwhite children, of whom 130 were classified as African American or interracial and the other 46 as Asian, North American, or Latin American Indian. The families also had a total of 145 biological children. Parents and children took the appropriate WISC, WAIS, or Stanford-Binet tests. Most of the adopted children's biological parents had completed high school; the adoptive parents' educational level was on average four or five years higher. As a group, adoptive parents were middle class, their average age was 36, and their average IQ was 120; their biological children averaged 117 on IQ scores. The families seemed to provide a stimulating environment.

Of the adopted children, 44 had been placed with their adoptive families by 2 months of age, and 111, including 99 African American and interracial children, had been adopted within their first year. African American and interracial children were adopted at a younger age than the other adopted children and thus, had lived with their biological parents for less time. The adopted children averaged IQ scores of 106, significantly higher than those of nonadopted children of similar backgrounds but below those of the adoptive parents' biological offspring (117). Children adopted early surpassed the group average. Scarr and Weinberg concluded, "The dramatic increase in the IQ differences among the socially classified black children strongly suggest that IQ scores of these children are environmentally malleable" (1976, p. 173). The authors point out, however, that the study cannot clearly separate the effects of race and social environment on intelligence. But their study does support the position that social and educational opportunities provided by the family can contribute greatly to children's IQs and academic success and that genetic heritage alone does not govern intelligence.

What can we conclude from studies of adopted children? First, heredity has a substantial effect on IQ scores. Plomin, DeFries, and McClearn (1989) concluded that "about half of the observed variation in IQ is due to genetic differences" (p. 338). Second, being raised in the same environment has a substantial effect on IQ. In the Texas study, unrelated children raised in the same families had IQs that correlated +.26. In the transracial study, the correlation was +.33. Although the correlations were slightly lower among genetically unrelated brothers and sisters, there was clearly an effect due to similar environments. The various correlations between related and unrelated individuals raised in similar or different environments are summarized in Figure 11.6.

It is interesting to note that the estimates of IQ heritability have apparently fluctuated during the past 40 years (Loehlin, Willerman, & Horn, 1988). Studies conducted prior to 1963 gave estimates as high as 80 percent, whereas those published after 1975 yielded figures closer to 50 percent. During the 1980s, research again indicated higher heritability estimates. These puzzling differences may reflect historical changes in family structure or environment, or they may be due to unknown causes. They have contributed to shifting emphases in the nature/nurture controversy and prompt-

FIGURE 11.6
Correlations Between IQs of People of Various Genetic and Environmental Relations

People who live together but are not genetically related (adopted children) show weakly correlated IQs. However, as the degree of genetic relationship increases, so does the correlation of IQs. The highest correlation shown is between identical twins reared together, which maximizes both genetic and environmental relatedness. Actually, the .86 correlation between identical twins reared together is about as high as it could possibly be, because the reliability of IQ tests is around .90. That is, the correlation in IQ between identical twins is about as high as for the same person taking the test twice!

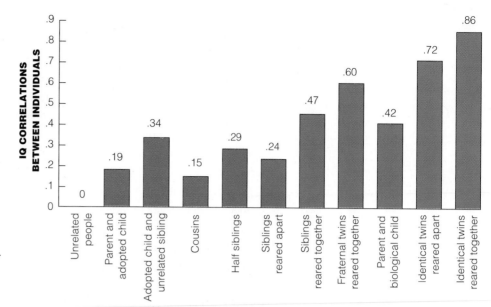

ed Plomin (1989) to say, "As the pendulum swings from environmentalism, it is important that the pendulum be caught midswing before its momentum carries it to biological determinism. Behavioral genetic research clearly demonstrates that both nature and nurture are important in human development." (p. 110).

FAMILY CHARACTERISTICS AND IQ SCORES

Lois Hoffman (1985) believes that behavioral geneticists have underestimated the impact of parenting styles and family interactions on IQ. Hoffman argues that most adoptive families have high IQs and stimulating homes, since they are usually selected partly on these criteria. (Adoption agencies try not to place children in "bad homes"). The narrow range of these enriched environments reduces differences between families and inflates the importance of genetic similarity. That is, if adopted children are all raised in generally similar (good) family environments, studies will seem to show that family environment does not much matter. Also, the assumption made in most studies is that parents' IQ scores serve as good measures of the intellectual climate of the home. Hoffman points out that none of the existing socialization theories would postulate that parents with IQs of 115 provide more stimulating environments than parents with IQs of 110. Therefore, Hoffman suggests that more refined measures of intelligence, family dynamics, and home life are needed to clarify the relative influence of heredity and environment.

One measure of the family environment that has been related consistently to IQ score is family size. Individuals from large families tend to have slightly lower IQ scores than individuals from smaller families. Robert Zajonc (1983) observed this consistent pattern in 26 of 27 studies he reviewed. Moreover, survey of fertility and intelligence in the United States between 1894 and 1964 found a relation between vocabulary scores (used as approximate measures of intelligence) and family size (Van Court & Bean, 1985). The more brothers and sisters a person had, the lower his or her vocabulary score.

Birth order is also related to IQ score. Later-born children usually have slightly lower scores than early-born children. In the Netherlands, Belmont and Marolla (1973) compared the nonverbal intelligence scores of 400,000 men as a function of family birth order and observed that later-born children, especially those in large families, had lower IQ scores than children born earlier (see Figure 11.7).

Robert Zajonc and Geoffrey Markus (1975) proposed the *confluence model* to explain these findings. This model does not rely only on parents' IQ scores as a measure of the intellectual environment of the family. Instead, the model is a set of equations that averages scores for all family members, considers their chronological ages, and includes a factor for the opportunity to teach younger siblings. Quite simply, Zajonc and Markus (1975) believe that the intellectual environment is diluted by more children and the arrival of new babies, partly because family activities often revolve around the youngest, most dependent members. As children mature, however, the family engages in more challenging cognitive tasks. Older brothers and sisters can also help teach their younger siblings, an activity that benefits both "teacher" and "pupil."

The confluence model has been remarkably successful for predicting patterns of intellectual development among large samples of families, often explaining most of the variation in test scores (Zajonc, 1983). The model accurately predicts higher IQ scores for children of smaller families and for earlier-born siblings. It also predicts lower scores for last-born and only children (because they have no siblings to teach) and depressed rates of intellectual growth following the birth of siblings. However, critics argue that the chronological age of the children accounts for most of the predictive power of the confluence model (McCall, 1985). Also, the effects of birth order and family size are small, just a few IQ points, and these effects often disappear if the

FIGURE 11.7
Intelligence and Birth Order

This graph shows how scores on a nonverbal intelligence test decrease for later-born children. The letter *j* indicates the number of children in the family. Notice how the last-born children of the largest families have the lowest scores.

SOURCE: Zajonc & Markus, 1975

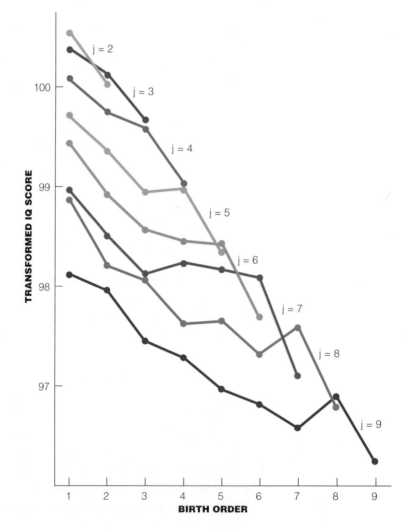

socioeconomic status of the families is matched in the study. Furthermore, some of the central assumptions about the way the family environment affects the child's intelligence appear to be contradicted by other studies (Brody, 1992). One review of the birth order and intelligence literature showed that only children do no worse on intellectual ability tests than first-born children, who supposedly should have benefited from the opportunity to tutor a sibling (Polit & Falbo, 1988). Finally, the statistical calculations used in developing the confluence theory have come under attack, and a revised calculation of the fit of the model to the original data sets have shown a poorer match (Retherford & Sewell, 1991).

The controversy over the confluence model reveals two fundamental issues for research on intellectual development. First, psychologists need to devise better measures of the "environment" to understand how social, educational, and developmental forces influence intelligence scores. Characteristics of the family are good candidates, but they need to be expanded to include the quality of interactions at home as well as the number and birth order of the children. Second, models of the relations between IQ and environmental variables can help identify the relative importance of different factors such as birth order. Future research will specify more precisely how family characteristics influence intellectual development.

IQ DIFFERENCES AMONG RACES

One of the most politically and emotionally charged issues in the study of intelligence is the comparison of IQ scores between members of different racial groups. Science, politics, and opinion are difficult to separate out when discussing the relative contributions of environment and heredity to the IQ scores of racial groups. The difficulty in separating these relative influences is intensified because of the unfortunate history of racial prejudice that has accompanied intelligence testing. Although the interpretation of the IQ differences between the races is seriously debated, the gap between test scores is not doubted. On the average, African Americans score lower than white Americans on standardized intelligence tests. The difference is evident even among 3-year-olds (Montie & Fagan, 1988). On the other hand, Japanese Americans and some other Asian groups score higher than white Americans.

Reynolds, Chastain, Kaufman, and McLean (1987) analyzed racial and demographic differences in IQ scores of adults. They found that the full-scale IQ score of white adults was approximately 101, whereas African American adults had an average score of about 86. This 15-point difference has been reported for other intelligence tests and cohorts (Elliott, 1988; Jensen, 1980; Montie & Fagan, 1988) and appears reliable. According to Elliott (1988),

> The gap between the average levels of developed cognitive abilities of American blacks and whites is large (about one standard deviation), early to develop . . . , slow to change . . . , and validly reflective of real differences in performance in education, to a high degree, and in employment, to a moderate one. (p. 334)

By the way, it is worth noting that males scored about 2 points higher than females on average, adults in the West and Northeast scored about 3 points higher than those in the South and North Central regions, and college graduates scored nearly 20 points higher than adults who never finished high school.

The 15-point difference in IQ scores between African Americans and white Americans is not disputed, but the interpretation is. Some people argue that the intelligence tests themselves are unfair because they require information that is unfamiliar to poor, minority, or rural children. Although familiarity with testing procedures may influence performance, test bias of the items does not seem to account for the difference in IQ scores. Jensen (1985) reexamined data from 11 large-scale studies of IQ differences between white and African Americans and concluded that the difference of 15 points is reliable and probably due to differences in rates of information processing, rather than to any sort of specific knowledge, training, or skill. A large number of environmental hypotheses have been offered to account for the racial difference in IQ scores. Different social, economic, educational, cultural, motivational, nutritional, and medical opportunities in the United States doubtless contribute to the difference in IQ scores, although clear-cut data on many of these factors are lacking. This issue is still hotly debated and will be difficult to resolve.

Comparisons of academic achievement and intelligence in different countries also shed light on racial differences in mental abilities. British psychologist Richard Lynn (1982) compared IQ scores of 1,100 Japanese and 2,200 American schoolchildren between 6 and 16 years of age. The average IQ score of the Japanese children was 111, significantly higher than the average score of 100 for the American children. Lynn also investigated historical changes in Japanese IQ scores since 1910. Japanese born between 1910 and 1945 had mean IQ scores of 102 to 105, while those born between 1946 and 1969 had mean IQ scores of 108 to 115. Lynn points out that these dramatic increases give Japan the highest national average IQ score in the world. Lynn calculates from his study that fully 77 percent of the Japanese population have higher IQ scores than the average American or European.

Do these differences in IQ scores reflect genetic superiority? Some scientists think so (e.g., Rushton, 1994). They point out that the IQ differences may not reflect consequences of education, since the changes are observed in children as young as 6 and 7 years of age. Alan Anderson (1982), an editor for *Nature*, notes that birth weight and life expectancy have increased dramatically in Japan since 1950, along with IQ scores. He suggests that the great migrations of rural people into urban centers that occurred between 1930 and 1960 contributed to more intermarriages among previously isolated groups. This outbreeding promoted positive changes in health and cognitive status through genetic mixing.

Of course, critics argue that nutrition, prenatal care, and other environmental factors changed in Japan to create healthier and smarter children. Indeed, Lynn suggests that environmental factors such as intensive educational training have encouraged Japanese children to achieve more than American and European children. For example, Japanese children may be better test takers and more academically prepared. Harold Stevenson and his colleagues (1990) compared children in the United States, Taiwan, and Japan on tests of mathematics and other general cognitive abilities. While the children in all three countries performed at similar levels on the general cognitive tests, Japanese children were far superior on the mathematical tests (Stevenson, Lee, & Stigler, 1986). The researchers also collected data from the children's parents and teachers. They found that Japanese children spend more time on mathematics in school and that they are encouraged to achieve more than the other children in the study. Thus, environmental differences, including nutrition and schooling, as well as genetic factors such as interbreeding, may all contribute to the different patterns of test scores seen in different countries.

THE NATURE/NURTURE CONTROVERSY REVISITED

Perhaps this controversy has endured so long because the wrong questions have been asked. Mackenzie (1984) suggests that our search for simple answers is often misguided

"Well, I dunno...Okay, sounds good to me."

because of two fallacies. The *sociologist's fallacy* insists that there must be some environmental factor responsible for IQ differences among people. For example, socioeconomic status, education, or job opportunities might underlie intelligence differences between racial or geographical groups. The *hereditarian fallacy* is a default assumption that says that the difference must be due to a genetic cause if no specific environmental cause can be found. There are few simple and direct causes to explain something as complex as intelligence, however. Mackenzie (1984) suggests that the oversimplified questions about the relative contributions of heredity and environment are fruitless. Even if we knew the precise amount of IQ variation due to heredity or environment, the statistic would not tell us how to promote intellectual development or what factors in the environment determine intellectual achievement. Thus, the issue of nature or nurture is not an appropriate question to ask, especially in the area of racial differences in IQ scores.

Current views of the controversy emphasize how an individual's genetic composition and disposition influence the environment itself (Plomin, DeFries, & Fulker, 1988). Scarr (1992) describes three ways in which genotype (genetic heritage) helps to determine the way a person will respond to environmental opportunities. First, there is the *passive* effect in which the genetic traits and characteristics of parents help provide experiences for children. For example, parents who are calm and soothing create relaxed environments for their children. Second, there is an *evocative* effect in which characteristics of the person elicit particular reactions from others. For example, smiling, active babies receive more social stimulation than somber, passive babies. Third, there is an *active* genotype ➔ environment relation that signifies how people seek and create environments that are compatible with their own genotypic characteristics. Children who inherit high intelligence may create a different environment for themselves than do children who inherit remarkable physical coordination and athletic skills.

Scarr (1992) suggests that there is a shift from passive to active influences as children grow up. Adolescents and adults choose and modify their own environments more than children (e.g., by choosing their friends or pursuing their interests). This explains the decreasing correlations between the IQ scores of children and their biological relatives from childhood to adulthood. The theory also predicts that identical twins will choose environments that are more similar than those created by other siblings, which appears to be the case. Scarr's theory helps to focus attention on the way inherited characteristics influence how people create and respond to their environments. This interactive approach seems more fruitful than arguing over the relative contributions of nature or nurture as the causes of behavior.

Exceptional Intellectual Development

Because of the many genetic and environmental influences on intelligence, the range of IQ scores is wide. At both ends of the IQ distribution are individuals with exceptional mental abilities. Those who are more than 2 standard deviations below the average of 100 (i.e., IQs below 70) are often classified as **mentally retarded.** Those whose scores are beyond 130, 2 standard deviations above average, are labeled **gifted.** In the next few pages, we will describe these exceptional individuals and discuss problems of identifying and educating them.

MENTAL RETARDATION

It is not easy to estimate the prevalence of mental retardation because it is defined and measured in many ways (McLaren & Bryson, 1987). Depending on the definitions and criteria used, approximately 3 to 5 percent of the American population (or almost 10 million people) are classified as mentally retarded. The number is higher than a normal distribution would predict (see Figure 11.1) because of the many biological and environmental factors that can retard development.

Defining mental retardation is difficult. The mentally retarded do not all look alike or share the same handicaps. Their disability is not caused by just a few circumstances or genes. According to one definition, mental retardation refers to below-average general intelligence and poor adaptive behavior (Grossman, 1973). It can include physical and social difficulties in combination with cognitive disabilities. The American Association on Mental Deficiency categorizes people with IQs between 55 and 70 as mildly, or educably, retarded; between 40 and 55 as moderately retarded; between 25 and 40 as severely retarded; and those with IQs below 25 as profoundly retarded (Hallahan & Kaufman, 1982).

Characteristics of People with Mental Retardation. Varying kinds of disturbances characterize retarded people at different ages (see Table 11.3). Not surprisingly, retardation is detected most often among schoolchildren, whose poor performance is revealed in IQ tests and in their difficulty with schoolwork. Preschoolers and adults are less likely to be designated retarded unless their disabilities are extreme enough to notice.

Many areas of development are affected in proportion to the severity the of retardation. Mentally retarded children are often slow to begin to walk, talk, use the toilet, and engage in social interaction. Severely and profoundly retarded people seldom hold jobs, marry, or learn to care for themselves, and they usually require constant supervision or institutionalization. Moderately retarded people, on the other hand, can often

TABLE 11.3
Behavioral Characteristics of Mentally Retarded People Throughout the Life Span

TYPE	CHARACTERISTICS FROM BIRTH TO ADULTHOOD		
	BIRTH THROUGH 5	6 THROUGH 20	21 AND OVER
Mild (IQ 55-70)	Often not noticed as retarded by casual observer but is slower to walk, feed him- or herself, and talk than most children.	Can acquire practical skills and useful reading and arithmetic to a third- to sixth-grade level with special education. Can be guided toward social conformity.	Can usually achieve social and vocational skills adequate to self-maintenance; may need occasional guidance and support when under unusual social or economic stress.
Moderate (40-55)	Noticeable delays in motor development, especially in speech; responds to training in various self-help activities.	Can learn simple communication, elementary health and safety habits, and simple manual skills; does not progress in functional reading or arithmetic.	Can perform simple tasks under sheltered conditions; participate in simple recreation; travels alone in familiar places; usually incapable of self-maintenance.
Severe (25-40)	Marked delay in motor development; little or no communication skill; may respond to training in elementary self-help, such as self-feeding.	Usually walks, barring specific disability; has some understanding of speech and some response; can profit from systematic habit training.	Can conform to daily routines and repetitive activities; needs continuing direction and supervision in protective environment.
Profound (below 25)	Gross retardation; minimal capacity for functioning in sensorimotor areas; needs nursing care.	Obvious delays in all areas of development; shows basic emotional responses; may respond to skillful training in use of legs, hands, and jaws; needs close supervision.	May walk, need nursing care, have primitive speech; usually benefits from regular physical activity; incapable of self-maintenance.

SOURCE: After Kagan & Havermann, 1972, Table 14–15.

perform unskilled labor satisfactorily and can manage their own lives. Mildly retarded children can attend school, but they may learn at slower rates than normal children. The mildly retarded are not noticeably different in appearance or behavior and may appear "slow" only when given a task requiring memory, reading, writing, or mathematical calculations. Given a series of words or pictures to remember, mildly retarded children and adolescents usually do not try to group the items, rehearse them, or test the accuracy of their memories (Campione & Brown, 1979). They often cannot plan, respond to feedback about their behavior, or control their attention—all fundamental learning skills.

Causes of Mental Retardation. Mental retardation is caused by many genetic, biological, and experiential factors. By far, the greatest number of cases of retardation are due to the social conditions that surround families; in fact, 75 to 85 percent of mental retardation is often labeled *familial* or *sociocultural retardation*. The remaining 15 to 25 percent of retardation can be traced to genetic or biological causes (Robinson & Robinson, 1976; Weisz, 1990). The risk of mental retardation among the children of mentally retarded parents is illustrated in Figure 11.8.

The most frequent genetic cause of retardation is due to chromosomal abnormalities. *Down syndrome (trisomy 21)* is caused by an abnormal division of the twenty-first chromosome pair. It results in individuals with a distinctive appearance; they are usually short with small heads, short necks, and folds over their eyelids. Down sufferers frequently have congenital heart defects and respiratory problems. However, some people with Down syndrome still have a life expectancy of approximately 50 years (Eyman, Call, & White, 1991).

Another kind of chromosomal abnormality is *fragile X syndrome*, which accounts for 2 to 7 percent of all cases of mental retardation among males (Webb, Bundey, Thake, & Todd, 1986). The disorder mainly affects males, although from one-third to one-half of the female carriers of the fragile X chromosome are themselves mildly affected by the disorder (unlike most recessive X-linked disorders). This may explain why more males than females are mentally retarded (Nussbaum & Ledbetter, 1986). Fragile X syndrome allows recessive characteristics carried by the X chromosome to be expressed more often. The affected males often exhibit a characteristic physical appearance, which includes an elongated face, a high forehead, and enlarged ears (Bouchard,

FIGURE 11.8
Risk of Mental Retardation Among Children of Retarded and Nonretarded Parents

The four different lines of the figure represent whether one or both of a child's parents are retarded. The horizontal axis indicates whether the parents have one or more retarded children already. The risk of mental retardation rises from 2 percent for all children without retarded parents or siblings to more than 70 percent when both parents are retarded and they have at least one retarded child already.

SOURCE: Anderson & Wortis, 1974.

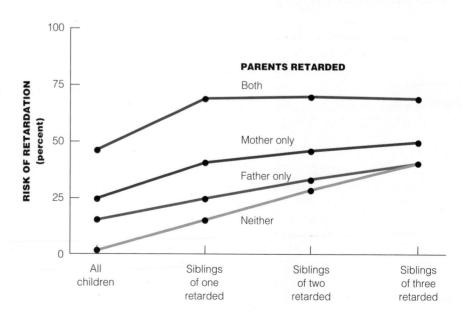

1993). These individuals display a wide range of cognitive impairments, and many have exhibited significant behavioral problems, including aggressive outbursts, hyperactivity, and self-injurious behavior (Dykens, & Leckman, 1990).

So far, we have discussed the major causes of retardation, but there are many other causes responsible for smaller numbers of cases. Retardation can be caused by mutations of specific genes, and more than 100 different gene mutations have already been identified (McKusick, 1986). Accidents at birth, such as extreme deprivation of oxygen (anoxia), and diseases such as syphilis, contracted from the mother in utero, can also cause mental retardation. Consumption of alcohol by pregnant women can lead to mild to severe retardation of their children in a disorder known as *fetal alcohol syndrome* (Cooper, 1987; Holmes, 1994). Finally, exposure to environmental toxins, especially lead, can inhibit intellectual development (Baghurst et al., 1992).

Many other causes remain unspecified, although it is clear that environmental variables are among them. Poor diet, poor health, and parental inattention can all lead to slower learning. The disadvantages of an environment can be subtle and varied, and it is difficult to relate particular factors directly to an individual's mental development. Parents who cannot read or write and who do not value school achievement often have children who do poorly on IQ tests and are classified as mentally retarded. Poverty, low motivation, and poor education are often family characteristics that affect individual children. Moreover, the child-rearing style of parents, as well as the language habits that they practice in the home, can also be factors in slowing intellectual development (Holmes, 1994). In one study, researchers observed that more than half of 200 mentally retarded people had another retarded individual in the family, and 75 percent of the families were either disrupted or unable to provide the basic necessities of life (Benda et al., 1963). In another study, 20 percent of the siblings of mildly retarded children were also retarded (Nichols, 1984).

Educational Programs for Children with Mental Retardation. For many years, psycholoists have attempted to raise the IQs of retarded individuals and improve their thinking skills. One of the best programs is the Perry Preschool Program in Ypsilanti, Michigan, in which 123 3- to 4-year olds at risk for delayed development were enrolled in the early education program (Schweinhart & Weikart, 1985). A variety of activities taught the children academic and social skills, and the families were involved in the long-term intervention to provide continuity to the program. In elementary school, the Perry Preschool children scored higher than the control group on achievement tests, and they had fewer reports of delinquency and antisocial behavior as adolescents (Lee, Brooks-Gunn, Schnur, & Liaw, 1990). However, the gains achieved in many programs appear modest and short-lived, despite such innovative programs (Spitz, 1986).

Today, there is a growing emphasis on teaching people with retardation social and problem-solving skills that will help them adapt to the demands of everyday living. The guiding philosophy of special educators seems to be that low intelligence as indicated by IQ scores does not mean that retarded people cannot learn. Also, the label *retarded* should not become a stigma that fosters neglect or loss of personal rights. Over the past 40 years, educators have become more aware of the special needs of slow learners and the retarded. From the late 1950s to the early 1970s, the number of classrooms for the mildly retarded increased dramatically. One of the purposes of these *special education* classes was to isolate children with learning problems so that they could be taught at a slower pace and with individual attention. Unfortunately, the curricula

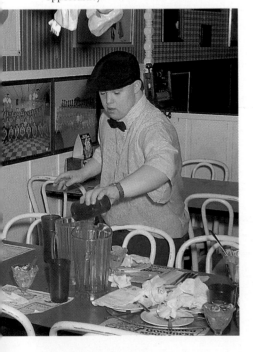

Mildly retarded adults can lead productive lives when given training and opportunity.

were often just diluted and boring versions of regular instruction and did not promote achievement as much as educators had hoped (Robinson & Robinson, 1976). In fact, classes often included a disproportionate number of disruptive children, members of ethnic minorities, and children who did not speak English at home. The classes increased the pupils' social isolation and the negative effects of the label *retarded*.

An investigation of special education classes in California in the 1960s (Mercer, 1971) illustrated these consequences. The classes contained a disproportionately high percentage of African American and Mexican American children. Mercer (1971), exploring the problem of placement in special classes for minorities, administered a behavioral test of social adaptation skills such as dressing, feeding, and other daily activities. She then compared the results with IQ test scores. The two tests were in general agreement for classifying the Anglo American children in the special education classes; but the results changed for minority children. Ninety percent of the African Americans and 50 percent of the Chicano children passed the social behavior test, although they had IQs below 70. One conclusion: Minority children are more likely to be categorized as retarded when only an IQ test is used (See "Psychology in Our Times: Science, Politics, and Racism in Intelligence Testing").

Special education classes are also under fire because they have failed to improve retarded children's academic achievement and social integration. Educators are increasingly providing special instruction to these children within regular classrooms. The Education for All Handicapped Children Act of 1975 (Public Law 94-142) requires that children be given individualized instruction in the "least restrictive environment." This policy of **mainstreaming** means that many retarded children now attend school in regular classrooms. This policy can substantially increase other children's acceptance of the mentally retarded and accelerate the intellectual achievement of these exceptional children (Madden & Slavin, 1983).

Educational improvement will not eliminate mental retardation. Retardation is a social category created by statistical divisions of IQ test scores that reflect the wide variability of human intelligence. Someone will always be at the bottom of any test score distribution. The aim of educators is to foster the development of retarded people's mental abilities and behavioral adaptation and to improve their lives.

INTELLECTUALLY GIFTED CHILDREN

People at the high end of the intelligence spectrum historically have not received much attention from psychologists. Consequently, there is less known about the nature of intellectual giftedness than about mental retardation. Popular myths about the gifted abound. For example, one stereotype portrays people with high IQs as having poor social skills and eccentric lifestyles. Research has disproved this myth. Gifted children and adults are generally well adjusted and happy (Pollins, 1983). However, there is still much to be learned about what constitutes giftedness and what consequences it has on an individual's life.

One of the earliest and most ambitious studies was undertaken by Lewis Terman starting in 1921. Terman wanted to know what became of *gifted children*, when they grew up (Terman, 1954). Terman defined giftedness in terms of high IQ scores and measured it with the Stanford-Binet intelligence test that he helped develop. Because of his belief in the constancy of IQ and the deterministic role of maturation, he thought that he could study how bright children grew up to become adult geniuses (Cravens, 1992).

SCIENCE, POLITICS, AND RACISM IN INTELLIGENCE TESTING

Although they make up only 16 percent of the student population, African Americans account for 35 percent of the students classified as mentally retarded. Reschly and Ward (1991) suggest that this over-representation is due to two factors. First, the poverty rate for African Americans is about triple the rate for white Americans, and many studies have shown a strong correlation between poverty and classification as mentally retarded. Second, IQ tests are the predominant measure used to classify students, with little attention given to adaptive behavior. Reschly and Ward (1991) conducted a study showing that white Americans and African Americans have equal levels of adaptive behavior. Consequently, the researchers believe that the overrepresentation of African Americans classified as mildly mentally retarded would decrease if more weight were given to adaptive behavior scales and less weight given to IQ scores. Although the authors point out the difficulties in measuring adaptive behavior, they suggest that professional and legal scrutiny in the 1990s will force adequate consideration of adaptive behavior when classifying individuals.

The early pioneers of mental testing intended to use their various tests for screening in educational and military contexts, but the identification of groups who did not score well on these tests led to political and racial-ethnic abuses of IQ tests. IQ scores in the 70 to 80 range were "very, very common among Spanish-Indian and Mexican families of the Southwest as also among negroes," observed mental testing pioneer Lewis Terman:

> Their dullness seems to be racial, or at least inherent in the family stocks from which they come. . . . The whole question of racial differences in mental traits will have to be taken up anew and by experimental methods. The writer predicts that when this is done there will be discovered enormously significant racial differences which cannot be wiped out by any scheme of mental culture.
>
> Children of this group should be segregated in special classes. . . . They cannot master abstractions, but they can often make efficient workers. . . . There is no possibility at present of convincing society that they should not be allowed to reproduce (Terman, 1916, pp. 92–93).

Intelligence tests have been scrutinized and disputed in court because the scores can be misused so easily. For example, placement in special education classrooms is often defined by IQ scores and other data; but if the tests are not valid, won't some children be mistakenly placed in special classes? That was the argument of two groups of parents who sued to stop San Francisco's use of IQ scores as

a criterion for placement in special education. In *Larry P. v. Riles*, (1979), the judge ruled in favor of the parents and children. San Francisco schools were prohibited "from utilizing, permitting the use of, or approving the use of any standardized test . . . for the identification of black EMR 'educable mentally retarded' children or their placement into EMR classes, without first securing prior approval by this court" (*Larry P. v. Riles*, 1979, p. 989). The judge ruled that schools had shown intent to discriminate by using culturally biased intelligence tests as the primary criterion for assignment to EMR classes. Further, the judge ruled that "it doomed large numbers of black children to EMR status, racially unbalanced classes, an inferior and 'deadened' education, and the stigma that inevitably comes from the use of the label 'retarded' " (p. 980).

There have been both positive and negative outcomes to these court cases. On the positive side, IQ tests are more often used in conjunction with other data to measure children's academic achievement and intellectual development. Researchers are also working to design better intelligence tests. On the negative side, there has been a widespread distrust of psychological tests and diminished use of IQ tests. Special educational services for children who need them most have also been decreased. This led Reschly (1988) to say, "We need to get on with the task of designing, implementing, and evaluating those services. The best defense against placement litigation will always be effective programs that produce outcomes which enhance opportunities" (p. 204).

Intelligence tests, like other psychological assessments, have the potential for abuse and misinterpretation, for perpetuating racial prejudice, and for denying education to many children (Synderman & Herrnstein, 1983). However, these tests can provide valuable information for clinical diagnosis and educational intervention. Many psychologists are trying to improve the scientific accuracy of intelligence tests and to inform the public about the limitations and proper uses of test data so that mental tests do not perpetuate political or racial discrimination (Samelson, 1975).

Terman began by screening 250,000 California schoolchildren, and he identified 1,528 with IQs of 135 or higher—857 boys and 671 girls. The sample was not typical of California children. Few members of minorities were represented, one-third of the children came from professional families, and more than 10 percent were Jewish. The subjects and some of their parents and teachers were interviewed and tested in 1922, 1928, 1940, 1950, 1955, 1960, 1972, and 1977. They were affectionately labeled the "Termites" and have provided a wealth of data about intellectual development across the life span.

The sample group grew up during a unique era in American history, which included the Great Depression, World War II, and other vast social changes. Consequently, any comparisons drawn from the sample may confuse many differences found among generations. Despite this qualification, the study showed that Terman's subjects outpaced students of the same age by two to four grades and shone in all courses throughout school, refuting the belief that they would prove to be narrowly specialized. In general, the bright children became successful and happy adults.

Giftedness and Creativity. The children in Terman's study were identified solely on the basis of IQ scores, which averaged 150. But is an IQ test alone sufficient to define and measure intellectual giftedness? Many studies have shown that IQ scores, particularly average and above-average scores, are not correlated with the sort of accomplishments we associate with gifted and talented individuals (Wallach, 1985). For example, IQ scores do not predict whether people will win awards for accomplishments in science, music, creative writing, the visual or performing arts, or group leadership. Likewise, it is debatable whether intelligence test scores predict success at work (McClelland, 1993; Ree & Earles, 1992).

Giftedness is more than just high IQ scores, but it is not easy to define. Tuttle and Becker (1983) have provided the following list of typical characteristics:

A gifted individual
- is curious.
- is persistent in pursuit of interests and questions.
- is perceptive of the environment.
- is critical of self and others.
- has a highly developed sense of humor, often with a verbal orientation.
- is sensitive to injustices on personal and worldwide levels.
- is a leader in various areas.
- is not willing to accept superficial statements, responses, or evaluations.
- understands general principles easily.
- often responds to the environment through media and means other than print and writing.
- sees relationships among seemingly diverse ideas.
- generates many ideas for a specific stimulus. (p. 13)

Because giftedness involves unusual approaches to problems, and because IQ is a poor predictor of success among gifted people, researchers turned to creativity as a feature that sets gifted people apart. To distinguish creativity from intelligence, some researchers use the distinction between convergent and divergent thinking proposed by Guilford (1966). **Convergent thinking** leads us to arrive at a correct, conventional answer, whereas **divergent thinking** involves generating many novel answers and solutions. Divergent thinking is similar to ideational fluency (Wallach & Kogan, 1965), which refers to the number and kinds of ideas that an individual can generate (e.g., how many different things can you do with a brick?). Although these global measures

Education for talented students includes enriched and accelerated curriculi that promotes creativity.

of creativity are correlated with IQ, they are not the definite indicators of giftedness that they were expected to be. Measures of divergent thinking and ideational fluency correlate more strongly with professional accomplishments than do IQ scores, but the relations are still relatively weak (Wallach, 1985). Some researchers now believe that giftedness is specific to particular talents or domains. This view is consistent with Gardner's theory of multiple intelligences that are domain specific rather than general. There is also a growing body of research that suggests that personality, motivation, and life experiences, in addition to intelligence, contribute to creativity (Sternberg, 1988).

Education for the Gifted and Talented. Educational programs for the gifted have been a matter of great controversy in America. Some people feel that it is unfair to give resources to children who already have an intellectual advantage over other students. They believe that gifted students will do just fine if left on their own. This is simply not true; gifted children are often bored by regular classroom instruction, and many of them consequently stop paying attention or become behavior problems. In fact, gifted high school students are likely to drop out of school altogether if they are not sufficiently challenged (Fetterman, 1988). In short, gifted children need special programs, just like mentally retarded and learning-disabled children do. Many states now recognize this and have required school districts to create an educational program for gifted and talented children.

Programs for gifted and talented children usually follow one of two models. The most popular is curriculum enrichment, or providing special projects, field trips, and other learning experiences as a supplement to regular classroom instruction. Sometimes this is done by creating a full-time "gifted and talented" class, in which all the students are gifted. More often, students are taken out of their regular classrooms for daily or weekly enrichment sessions. Another approach to gifted education is *acceleration*, moving the child through the grade school and high school curriculum at a faster rate than usual. Sometimes this results in children going to college at a very young age. Although many have criticized acceleration programs, claiming that gifted children will be adversely affected by moving ahead too fast, most research has shown no ill effects of grade acceleration (Robinson, 1983).

One of the most difficult tasks any education program faces is identifying which students are in need of its special services. IQ scores alone, particularly in the upper range, are not considered adequate indicators of giftedness. Despite this fact, many school districts establish a cutoff IQ score of around 130 and then use this as the sole criterion for placement in a gifted program. This use of IQ scores alone can lead to some children being denied the services they need. Experts now advocate the use of many sources of information in placement decisions, including achievement scores, evidence of extracurricular achievement, and teacher and parent recommendations. Parents are often the first to notice that their children are gifted; often they realize their children's high level of ability before the children even reach kindergarten. Gifted students, like other exceptional children, benefit from early identification of their intellectual abilities and special programs designed to meet their developmental needs.

New Approaches to Intelligence

As cognitive psychologists have become interested in intelligence, they have applied their information processing theories to explain intellectual differences. We consider this new approach here.

Information-Processing Theories

Researchers who adopt an information-processing perspective believe that intelligence derives from the cognitive processes used to perceive, remember, and use information. Differences in intelligence develop because people vary in the efficiency and speed with which they carry out these basic processes. Since Galton's pioneering studies at the end of the nineteenth century, researchers have analyzed the relation between response speed and intelligence; however, the research has revealed only modest correlations.

A comprehensive theory of intelligence has been proposed by Robert Sternberg (1985), who tries to relate social, developmental, and educational variables in the study of individual differences. The three aspects of Sternberg's theory broaden cognitive approaches to intelligence by considering how individuals use their mental abilities in different everyday settings. Sternberg has proposed three subtheories. The **componential subtheory** is at the core of his approach, and it is based on the *components of intelligence*, those elementary processes that operate on internal representations of objects or symbols:

1. *Metacomponents* are higher-order executive processes used to plan, monitor, and regulate task performance. They include identifying problems, selecting strategies, monitoring possible solutions, and understanding feedback about performance.
2. *Performance components* are the actual mental processes used to execute a task. They include perceiving aspects of the task, identifying concepts, and making responses.
3. *Knowledge-acquisition components* are processes used to learn new information, such as combining old ideas in creative ways.

Sternberg considers all three types of components to be basic aspects of intellectual functioning, yet he believes that metacomponents are the fundamental sources of individual and developmental differences in intelligence.

Sternberg's second subtheory is the **experiential subtheory.** Sternberg believes that intelligence requires the ability to deal with novel tasks and situations. It involves the abilities to select, encode, compare, and combine information in different settings. The third part of the theory is the **contextual subtheory.** This subtheory goes beyond IQ tests and cognitive processes to deal with intelligence in relation to the external world of the individual. Sternberg (1985) considers intelligence to be mental activity directed toward adapting and shaping one's personal environment. In other words, intelligence is *functional* and *practical*. Intelligent behavior helps an individual select, shape, and adapt to the environment.

Sternberg (1985) has evaluated the strengths and weaknesses of psychometric and information-processing approaches to intelligence. On the positive side, he points out that all of these theories try to specify mental structures and processes in detail. There is also a practical value in these theories, because they aid in the diagnosis, prediction, and development of educational experiences, and the theories go beyond the mere construction of test items. On the negative side, Sternberg (1985) points out that many of these theories are impossible to disprove, and many fail to supply criteria for the selection of appropriate tasks to use as measures of intelligence. Perhaps more critical is the doubtful relevance to people's lives and the lack of attention to social and cultural contexts of intelligent behavior, factors that appear to be very important in determining behavior, as our sociocultural theme has shown. Because neither psycho-

THE BELL CURVE DEBATE

In the fall of 1994, Richard Herrnstein (a psychologist) and Charles Murray (a political scientist) published a book entitled *The Bell Curve : Intelligence and Class Structure in American Life.* The book has provoked a firestorm of debate and controversy within psychology, in other disciplines, and within the larger political arena in the United States and other Western countries. The book is the sort of mammoth soul-crusher (845 pages!) that usually only the most hardy types of academics would read. Why has it become such a sensation and aroused so much controversy?

The book is divided into four main parts, and its essence cannot be captured in a short space. But, at one level, the controversy surrounding the book is surprising, because the first parts mainly just summarize what is known about human intelligence as studied through the psychometric approach. Many points made in *The Bell Curve* are those represented in this and other psychology textbooks. First, general intelligence (as measured by IQ tests) is correlated with good performance in school and the attainment of high-paying occupations. (There are no 80-IQ neurosurgeons, and the same is true of other occupations with heavy cognitive demands). Second, there is evidence from multiple sources that performance on IQ tests is partly determined by heredity. The authors of *The Bell Curve* make the case that intelligence plays a causal role in success in school and success in life, at least in many cognitively demanding professions.

The authors also make an interest-

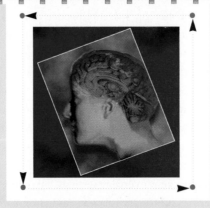

ing point, noted earlier by Herrnstein (1973) in another book, that U.S. society has, over the past 100 years, become more of a meritocracy. A meritocracy is a society in which individuals rise and fall according to their individual abilities when they are not limited by their membership in various groups. For example, if a society could eliminate all discrimination as a function of people's race, ethnicity, religion, gender, sexual orientation, and so on, then people would succeed or fail on their own merits. Surely most Americans and most people in other Western countries would like to see societies evolve that do not foster the discrimination so prevalent in the past. Clearly legal discrimination has been reduced in most Western countries in the 20th century, although equally clearly discrimination in many forms still exists. So what is the rub? Why the brouhaha over the book?

Herrnstein and Murray point out that all the above facts could have some consequences that are not recognized by most people and that might be viewed with alarm. In particular, they

argue that society in United States is increasingly becoming controlled by a "cognitive elite" (to use their term) of people of high intelligence. In addition, this group will develop into a kind of hereditary aristocracy. Why? If people of high IQ tend to intermarry (and they do); and if having a high IQ confers many benefits in terms of obtaining better educations and better jobs (which it seems to); then society might tend towards a kind of hereditary aristocracy, especially if the society is based on principles of a meritocracy. In the meritocracy each individual rises and falls according to ability. As Bouchard (1995, p. 416) points out,"Under these circumstances a meritocracy begins to look like a aristocracy, a perception that is strongly reinforced when the intellectual elite segregate themselves from the rest of society by living in separate neighborhoods, sending their children to private schools, and supporting social institutions that cater to their own unique interests." Many commentators have recoiled at this vision of society.

The most controversial parts of *The Bell Curve* deal with race and with public policy recommendations that the authors make. Actually, race plays a relatively minor role in the book and only appears in chapters towards the end, yet almost all critics have seized onto this one topic. (The authors say that the conclusions stated in the previous paragraph hold regardless of race). Herrnstein and Murray (1994) do note the evidence of differences between racial groups on IQ tests, with several well-studied Asian groups (living either in Asia or the U.S.) scoring

metric nor information-processing theories have given sufficient attention to the social context of intelligent problem solving, many theorists have proposed more practical approaches to the study of intelligence.

PRACTICAL INTELLIGENCE

The kind of academic intelligence measured by IQ tests is quite different from the nonacademic intelligence displayed in everyday interactions. Consider this example of a Brazilian boy (a 12-year-old coconut vendor in the third grade, identified as M.) calculating for a customer the cost of produce (cited in Lave, 1988, p. 65).

several points ahead of whites and with blacks scoring 15 points lower than whites. They plead agnosticism on what causes these racial differences, although they admit the possibility of a genetic basis: ". . . it seems highly likely to us that both genes and the environment have something to do with racial differences. What might the mix be? We are resolutely agnostic on this issue; as far as we can determine, the evidence does not yet justify an estimate" (p. 311). Nevertheless, they point out that if blacks are disadvantaged in terms of IQ (for whatever reasons), their success will be reduced in a meritocracy, even without any overt racial discrimination. The authors also make policy recommendations against current forms of the U.S. welfare system and against affirmative action policies. They argue that people should be judged as individuals and not as members of groups.

What have the critics had to say? You name it. The book and the authors have been excoriated by journalists and by commentators from many different fields, including psychology. Some deny that intelligence exists, some argue that it cannot be measured accurately if it does exist, and others demean the book while proudly announcing they have not actually read it. Because some journalists and people from other fields reported so much misinformation about the data in the book and about the psychometric study of intelligence in general, 52 psychologists who study intelligence signed an article published in the *Wall Street Journal* (which carried on a running series of articles about the book) stating 25 "conclusions regarded as mainstream among researchers on intelligence." The hope was "to pro-

CONTROVERSY

mote more reasoned discussion" of the phenomena identified in *The Bell Curve*.

Certainly, there are many possible and legitimate criticisms of *The Bell Curve* and its arguments. The book does not discuss in any detail the possibility of multiple types of intelligence, concentrating on general intelligence, or *g*, identified on psychometric tests. Also, most of the arguments made are based on correlational data. If IQ is correlated with social status, earnings and education, how do we know that IQ causes good education, prestigious jobs, and earnings rather than (say) education causing high IQ and the other good things? Herrnstein and Murray report many analyses in which they argue that IQ is the causal factor, but these depend on assumptions that not everyone accepts. Finally, the public policy recommendations may not be accepted even by people who agree with most of the psychology in the book. For example, why reduce money to programs such as Head Start that try to help disadvantaged school children? Even if intelligence is partly under genetic control, it is also under environmental control. We as a society cannot do anything about a child's genetic heritage, but we can certainly work to improve the child's opportunities in education and life through social programs.

An entire book, *The Bell Curve Debate*, which summarizes numerous

reviews and critiques of *The Bell Curve*, was published in 1995. Most articles are critical of the book, as have been other reviews. Unfortunately, some of the criticism has been *ad hominem*, that is, directed as attacks on the book's authors rather than the intellectual content of the book, calling the authors racists and charlatans. In one review, Dorfman (1995) complained that the authors are not noted psychometricans and did not publish their most provocative analyses in peer-reviewed journals before publishing them in their book. He even likens their writing the book to the case of monkeys being put before a typewriter: "If two monkeys were put before a typewriter, it is theoretically possible for those two monkeys to produce a Shakespearean sonnet. Perhaps Herrnstein and Murray produced a valid scientific work" (p. 419). Dorfman goes on to suggest they did not.

Why so much name calling? The authors of *The Bell Curve* raise many disturbing possibilities about the origins of social inequality in America, ones that many commentators and academicans usually do not consider (such as IQ and genetic considerations). Some psychologists, such as Dorfman (1995) in the review cited above, believe the book is fatally flawed. But others probably agree with Bouchard (1995), whose review appeared at the same time: "This is a superbly written and exceedingly well-documented book. It raises many troubling questions regarding the organization of our society. It deserves the attention of every well-informed and thoughtful citizen" (p. 418).

Customer: How much is one coconut?

M.: 35.

Customer: I'd like ten. How much is that?

M.: (Pause). Three will be 105; with three more, that will be 210. (Pause). I need four more. That is . . . (pause) 315 . . . I think it is 350.

The problem can be mathematically represented in several ways. $35 \times 10 = ?$ is a good representation of the question posed by the interviewer. The subject's answer is better represented by $105 + 105 + 105 + 35$, which implies that 35×10 was solved by the subject as $(3 \times 35) + 105 + 105 + 35$. M. proved to be competent in determining the product of 35×10, even though he used a routine not taught in third grade, since in Brazil third-graders learn to multiply any number by ten simply by placing a zero to the right of that number.

Jean Lave (1988) persuasively argues that people's everyday use of arithmetic is significantly different from their use of math skills in school. Lave studied dieters who measured meal portions and shoppers who calculated prices per quantity in unusual ways. Much like the Brazilian vendor, they calculated mathematical problems differently than they are taught in school. One dieter was confronted with the problem of eating only three-fourths of the regular two-thirds cup portion. Rather than multiplying fractions, the dieter filled a cup two-thirds full of cottage cheese, emptied it onto the counter, shaped it into a circle, drew a cross on it, removed one quarter, and triumphantly put the remainder on a plate.

People reason differently in informal settings and schoollike situations; what may be considered intelligent may not always fit academic definitions or academic tasks. For example, Scribner (1984) found that dairy workers with little formal school experience solved complex mathematical problems and demonstrated flexible strategies in the dairy plant that improved with experience. The emphasis on everyday experiences and practical intelligence may be particularly important for measuring the intelligence of people who are removed from traditional academic settings. Recall the study of bettors at the races, which began this chapter. Also, Dixon and Baltes (1986) found that the pragmatics of everyday experiences (accumulated wisdom) was correlated with intellectual functioning among elderly adults better than traditional psychometric tasks. A similar argument can be made for cross-cultural comparisons of intelligence. Although there is probably no single test that is equally fair to people of different cultural backgrounds, tasks in practical intelligence tests are selected to have familiarity and significance for people in their everyday lives. These measures can be as reliable and valid as traditional measures and may help to define social-behavioral or nonacademic intelligence (Mercer, Gomez-Palacio, & Padilla, 1986).

THEMES IN REVIEW

Intelligence is determined by many factors. In terms of biology, estimates are that 50 percent of the variation in scores on IQ tests is determined by genetic factors. The evidence includes studies of identical twins reared apart and adoption studies showing that adopted children's IQs correlates more highly with their biological parents than with their adoptive parents. In addition, some types of mental retardation are caused by genetic abnormalities. Although biological factors are important in intelligence, they can only exert their effects when the environment is suitable for learning. Learning is also critical, both for the types of intelligence measured by IQ tests and for practical intelligence displayed in everyday situations.
Cognitive factors, too, are critical to

intelligence. The information-processing approach to intelligence attempts to measure the processing speed and accuracy of various components (perceiving, remembering) that are believed critical to intelligence.

Intelligence develops rapidly over the first years of life, which was the observation that led Alfred Binet to develop the concept of a mental age. Most infant intelligence tests measure sensorimotor skills and have not been too successful at predicting adult intelligence, as measured by IQ tests. However, new measures emphasizing memory in infants seem to predict intelligence much better. Intelligence also changes in adulthood, but any declines are gradual and occur after 60 or 70 years of age.

Sociocultural factors are crucial in measuring intelligence. For example, children from large families have slightly lower IQs than do children from smaller families, and the later-born children have slightly lower IQs than do the first children born into the family. Standard IQ tests may not be fair to children who have not been exposed to the majority culture of the society. Hispanic and African American children are over-represented in school programs for slow learners. Some theorists emphasize different kinds of intelligence than the verbal type measured by standard IQ tests, including practical intelligence displayed by people adapting to their sociocultural enviroment.

SUMMARY

1 There is no single definition of intelligence and no consensus on the best way to measure it. The psychometric approach to intelligence, with its emphasis on IQ tests, has been the dominant view. Other approaches include a developmental perspective, Gardner's theory of multiple types of intelligence, and, more recently, newer information-processing theories.

2 In France at the beginning of the twentieth century, Alfred Binet constructed the forerunner of modern intelligence tests. Binet's test was designed to identify children who needed special educational help.

3 An IQ score is a measure of one person's performance on academic tasks relative to other individuals of the same age. It is not an absolute measure of intelligence or ability to learn. It is defined as mental age divided by chronological age $\times$ 100. By definition, average intelligence is represented by an IQ of 100.

4 There are many different kinds of intelligence tests. Some are designed for different age-groups and some are created for people with particular handicaps. The Stanford-Binet and Wechsler tests of intelligence are widely used. Many intelligence tests include a variety of tasks, such as vocabulary, puzzles, arithmetic, sentence comprehension, and spatial reasoning. The tasks are administered and scored in a uniform manner.

5 Two important characteristics of intelligence tests are their reliability and validity. Reliability of a test refers to the stability of test scores when people are retested. Validity of a test refers to the capacity of the test to measure what it is intended to measure. In the case of intelligence tests, the fact that IQ scores are positively correlated with grades in school indicates that the tests have predictive validity.

6 Even though intelligence tests are highly reliable, IQ scores are not perfectly stable. A person's score can vary from one test to the next, even over short periods of time, because of motivation, health or measurement error. IQ scores of infants and young children are not very good predictors of adult scores, but new measures of the cognitive processes of infants provide remarkable correlations with later IQ scores. Intelligence does not show a general, gradual deterioration after early adulthood, but fluid intelligence does decline in old age.

7 Approximately 50 percent of the variation in IQ scores is due to hereditary factors. Even when identical twins are raised in different homes, their IQs correlate very highly when measured in adulthood. Behavior geneticists and others argue that the environmental differences between families and groups account for relatively little of the variation in average IQ scores, especially in adolescence and adulthood. Critics counter that better measures of environmental influences are needed.

8 Research on adopted children reveals that their IQ scores are more highly related to the IQ scores of their biological parents and siblings than to those of their adoptive families. However, enriched and nurturant environments can promote intellectual development.

9 African Americans score lower on IQ tests than white Americans, whereas Japanese people score higher than white Americans. The patterns of test scores for both African Americans and white Americans are similar across test items, and the differences in levels of performance could be due to many factors. Most psychologists believe that differences among racial and ethnic groups on intelligence tests do not indicate genetic superiority of one group.

⑩ The majority of people classified as mentally retarded are school age and do not have the knowledge or skills to perform well on traditional tests of intelligence. Retardation may be due to limited sociocultural experiences that do not prepare children for academic tasks, or it may be due to genetic factors or physical damage to the brain.

⑪ Gifted children often reveal their talents at an early age, display high creativity, and achieve career success, compared to children of average intelligence.

KEY TERMS

mechanics of intelligence (p. 454)

pragmatics of intelligence (p. 454)

psychometric approach (p. 454)

factor analysis (p. 455)

mental age (MA) (p. 459)

intelligence quotient (IQ) (p. 459)

Stanford-Binet test (p. 459)

Wechsler tests (p. 460)

standardization sample (p. 462)

stratified random sampling (p. 462)

standard deviation (p. 462)

variability (p. 462)

normal distribution (p. 462)

reliability (p. 462)

construct validity (p. 463)

concurrent validity (p. 464)

predictive validity (p. 464)

heritability (p. 467)

mentally retarded (p. 475)

gifted (p. 475)

special education (p. 478)

mainstreaming (p. 479)

convergent thinking (p. 481)

divergent thinking (p. 481)

componential subtheory (p. 483)

experiential subtheory (p. 483)

contextual subtheory (p. 483)

FOR CRITICAL ANALYSIS

❶ Several approaches to intelligence were discussed in Chapter 11. Which one do you believe comes closest to explaining intelligence as you understand the meaning of that term? Defend your answer.

❷ Much evidence shows a strong genetic component to intelligence. Do you find this surprising, given that the information requested on IQ tests (vocabulary items, for example) must all be learned? Can you explain how genetic factors can be so important on tests that clearly measure how much people have profited from experience (i.e., learned)?

❸ Suppose that you developed an intelligence test that asked people seemingly irrelevant questions, such as "Do you like spinach?" and "What is your favorite color?" Yet, researchers discover that when they correlate scores on the test with grades in school, the test predicts grades reasonably well. Would you accept the test as a valid measure of intelligence?

❹ Information-processing theorists believe that intelligence is made up of various component activities that should be measured. From reading earlier chapters on cognitive processes (Chapters 3, 4, 5, 7, and 8), what processes do you believe are critical in determining intelligence? Why do you think social and cultural differences exist in the scores on IQ tests? Do you think that these tests should be used in admitting people to college? In hiring employees? Why or why not in each case?

SUGGESTED READINGS

BRODY, N. (1992). *Intelligence* (2nd ed.). San Diego: Academic Press. A scholarly review of research on human intelligence.

GARDNER, H. (1983). *Frames of mind: The theory of multiple intelligences*. New York: Basic Books. A well-written and lucid account of Gardner"s theory of various types of intelligence.

HERRNSTEIN, R. & MURRAY, C. (1994). *The bell curve: Intelligence and class structure in American life*. New York: The Free Press. The controversial best-seller that argues that class structure in the United States is becoming more based on inherited intelligence.

JACOBY, R. & GLAUBERMAN, N. (1995). *The bell curve debate: History, documents, opinions*. New York: Times Books. A fascinating callection of essays, both old and new, about human intelligence. Many of the recent ones were in response to publication of *The Bell Curve*.

KAIL, R. V., & PELLEGRINO, J. W. (1985). *Human intelligence: Perspectives and prospects*. New York: Freeman. The psychometric, information-processing, and cognitive developmental approaches to intelligence are summarized in this compact paperback. The authors provide a scholarly yet readable introduction to the key issues involved in defining and measuring intelligence.

LYMAN, H. B. (1991). *Test scores and what they mean*. (5th ed.). Englewood Cliffs, NJ: Prentice Hall. A nice introduction to the construction, evaluation, and interpretation of psychological and educational tests. Test validity, reliability, and statistics receive plain-language coverage, as well as the social and political aspects of testing.

PLOMIN, R. (1990). *Nature and nurture: An introduction to human behavioral genetics*. Pacific Grove, CA: Brooks/Cole. This brief and readable paperback by a leading researcher in the field describes methods for studying genetic influences on behavior and provides clear interpretations of the hereditary impact on cognitive abilities, personality, and psychopathology.

STERNBERG, R. (1982) *Handbook of intelligence*. Cambridge, England: Cambridge University Press. A book of essays and reviews by leading experts who study intelligence.

TREFFERT, D. (1989). *Extraordinary people: Understanding savant syndrome*. New York: Ballentine Books. The author reports on many fascinating cases of savants, including the case on which the movie *Rain Man* (starring Dustin Hoffman) was based.

PSYCHOLOGY ON THE INTERNET

Frequently Asked Questions (FAQ) on Psychological Tests

(http://www.apa.org/science/test.html)

This home page provides answers to a number of questions regarding the selection and administration of psychological tests. Questions answered here include: How can I find tests that measure specific concepts? How can I find evaluative information on psychological tests? What do I do when I need to identify and find instruments in a research area where no published tests exist?

School Psychology Resources On-Line
(http://mail.bcpl.lib.md.us/~sandyste/school_psych.html)

This home page contains an impressive list of "links to sites of interest to the school psychology community." Included in this list are links to sites providing information on learning disabilities, mental retardation, and psycho-educational assessment and evaluation.

Skeptic Magazine Interview with Robert J. Sternberg Regarding *The Bell Curve*
(http://www.skeptic.com/03.3.fm-sternberg-interview.html)

The Bell Curve: Intelligence and Class Structure in American Life by Richard J. Herrnstein and Charles Murray has stirred a great deal of controversy regarding individual and group differences in intelligence and social policy. This article from *Skeptic* magazine briefly outlines Professor Robert J. Sternberg's early views of intelligence, presents his criticisms of *The Bell Curve*, and discusses his current views of intelligence.

Two Views of *The Bell Curve*
(http://www.apa.org/journals/bell.html)

These book reviews of *The Bell Curve* appeared in the May 1995 (Volume 40, Number 5) issue of *Contemporary Psychology*. In Breaking the Last Taboo Thomas J. Bouchard, Jr. shares his view of why *The Bell Curve* has become such a controversial book, evaluates the book's analysis of the role of social class of origin and IQ in determining social class, and discusses the book's conclusions regarding ethnic differences in IQ. In Soft Science with a Neoconservative Agenda, Donald D. Dorfman presents several criticisms of the data (and their interpretation) that are presented in *The Bell Curve*. For example, Dorfman criticizes the technique for measuring heritability used by the authors, and points out that a finding of within group heritability should not be used as evidence of between group heritability.

ERIC Clearinghouse on Assessment and Evaluation
(http://www.cua.edu/www/eric_ae/)

"The ERIC [Educational Resources Information Center] Clearinghouse on Assessment and Evaluation seeks to provide 1) balanced information concerning educational assessment and 2) resources to encourage responsible test use." This site provides a wealth of information on assessment, evaluation, and learning theory. It offers links to on-line books, essays, electronic journals, and newsletters relevant to psycho-educational assessment and evaluation. Examples include *Understanding Achievement Tests* (an on-line book on the use of standardized tests), and press releases from the National Center for Fair and Open Testing (FairTest). From this site you can also search several databases for information on a wide variety of tests and research instruments.

The Arc, a National Organization on Mental Retardation
(http://www.metronet.com/~thearc/welcome.html)

"The Arc, a national organization on mental retardation, is committed to securing for all people with mental retardation the opportunity to choose and realize their goals of where and how they learn, live, work, and play." The Arc's home page is a very good source of information on topics related to mental retadation. In addition to information on topics such as community living and employment, this home page provides a question and answer introduction to mental retardation and the education of people with mental retardation.

Motivaton and Emotion

493

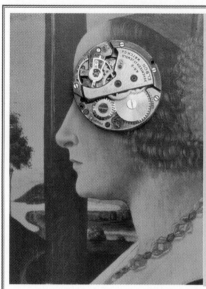

BIOLOGICAL THEME

Are any motives purely biological? Are your emotional reactions determined by your biology?

LEARNING THEME

Can you learn to be motivated? Are your emotional expressions (smiling, crying) learned?

DEVELOPMENTAL THEME

How does sexual preference develop? How does emotional expression develop?

COGNITIVE THEME

Can you reduce stress by thinking differently? How do your expectations and thoughts affect your emotions?

SOCIOCULTURAL THEME

Does human motivation vary across cultures? Are emotions expressed the same in different cultures?

Albert Schweitzer came from a well-to-do family and was a musical prodigy, but he decided early in life to become a medical missionary. He became a doctor of medicine and in 1913 established a hospital in Africa that he rarely left until his death in 1965.

Two Japanese mountain climbers, Yasuo Kato and Tokiashi Kobayashi, became the first team to climb Mount Everest in winter. They reached the summit, but became lost during their descent and froze to death.

Adolf Hitler ordered the "Final Solution" for all Jews and other "undesirables" within the countries he controlled. By the end of World War II, some 11 million people had been slaughtered in German extermination camps, including about 6 million Jews.

For each of these remarkable acts, we might reasonably ask, Why would someone do that? The same might be asked of people who enjoy hang gliding, skydiving, bullfighting, or any other behavior that seems extraordinary. In posing this question, we raise the issue of **motivation**—of why behavior occurs. This question is appropriate not only for unusual behaviors but also for the most commonplace. Why are you attending a college or university? Why did you select the clothes you are wearing today? For that matter, why are you reading this book?

Most people, at one time or another, want to eat, drink, be liked, do well, hug someone, influence others, or be alone. Why do we want and like the things we do? Some desires are clearly biological. The desire to eat, for example, is partly a matter of our internal physiology. We are born with biological urges, and we behave in certain ways to satisfy these urges. The environment also affects our desires. The desire to eat is stronger when we enter a restaurant and smell a delicious meal cooking, and the desire to succeed is greater when we are in competition. Moreover, some goals are more motivating than others. The desire to eat is stronger in the presence of a plate of spaghetti than in the presence of a plate of worms, and the urge to compete is stronger against a good opponent than a weak one.

Some motives are more closely tied to biological factors, while others are more a product of our environment and culture. In this chapter, we will discuss three motives that vary in the extent to which they are constrained by biological factors, moving from the most biologically constrained to the least. We will discuss hunger as an example of a biologically determined regulatory motive and sex as an example of a nonregulatory biological motive. Need for achievement is discussed as an example of a human motive that is not biologically based. Finally, we will consider how different motives combine. The chapter will conclude with the topic of emotion. Emotion is a complex psychological reaction that consists in part of physiological arousal. As we will see, emotional reactions are often closely tied to motivation. Sex, for example, is a motive, but emotional reactions figure heavily in sexual behavior.

Regulatory Motivation: Hunger

Clearly, we must eat to live; we need food. One view of how hunger works is that an internal signal first cues an organism that food is needed, and then the organism eats until the signal stops. In this model of hunger, the organism responds to internal cues to maintain a stable internal state, or **homeostasis.** Homeostasis—in this case absence of hunger—is always the desired state.

The principle of homeostasis applies to all bioregulatory motivations including the three most important: hunger, thirst, and temperature regulation. The body's homeostatic mechanism can be compared to a thermostat. When the temperature in a house deviates from the setting on the thermostat, a heater (in winter) or air conditioner (in summer) comes on to restore the temperature to the appropriate level. Similarly, when the body's internal equilibrium is disturbed, the individual is motivated to restore that equilibrium. Thus, according to homeostatic theory, motivation is produced by a breakdown in homeostasis.

One early learning theory, **drive theory** (Hull, 1943), attempted to explain all motivation in homeostatic terms, (see Figure 12.1). Hull pointed out that physiological deficits, such as lack of food or water, produce bodily needs. If the need continues unsatisfied, a psychological state, or **drive,** is produced. Hull theorized that a drive energizes the animal to find a way to reduce the drive and thereby remove the bodily deficit and restore homeostasis. Reducing a drive was assumed to be pleasurable, and any behavior that led to drive reduction was thought to be learned. Freudian theory also makes these assumptions as you will see in Chapter 14. For Hull, the ideal state was an absence of drive, a lack of internal stimulation.

Hunger is partly a homeostatic motive. Hunger is related to biological need, and eating is pleasurable, consistent with drive theory. But people eat when they don't need food and also eat in anticipation of needing food. Thus drive theory is not a

FIGURE 12.1
Basic Sequence of Motivation Outlined in Drive Theory

INTERNAL STATE

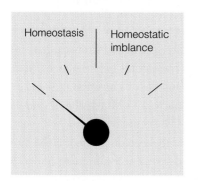

Stable internal state

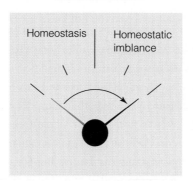

Lack of homeostasis produces a drive. A lack of food, for example, provides hunger.

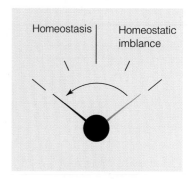

A drive results in response to restore homeostasis. Eating, for example, reduces hunger.

Internal cues signal hunger and thirst which cause us to eat or drink to remove those cues. This is part of the motivation for eating and drinking.

complete account of hunger-motivated behavior. Biology is only one contributor to the experience of hunger. Learning and cognitive factors, as we will see, also contribute to feelings of hunger. Nonetheless, internal cues that signal the body's need for food and motivate eating are a major part of how hunger works. But just what are the internal cues that set off hunger pangs?

INTERNAL CUES FOR HUNGER AND SATIETY

There are short term signals for hunger that tell the body it is time to eat, and long term signals that tell the body it is too thin. The most important short term signal is a lowering of the blood sugar.

Blood Sugar Levels. Have you ever felt dizzy after drinking a diet soda? Sweet tastes cause various digestive processes to begin, including the release of the hormone **insulin**, which normally processes **blood glucose** (commonly called blood sugar). Because there are no nutrients in diet soda, the insulin release lowers blood sugar, producing the feeling of dizziness. Low blood sugar is also a hunger cue, which is why some have called insulin the hunger hormone. Low blood sugar is an important signal that food is needed. Thus, insulin injections produce eating in a rat that has just eaten. Not surprisingly, a rise in blood sugar reduces hunger (Mayer, 1955). However, diabetics can be hungry even though they have high blood glucose levels because their body cells cannot utilize the glucose. When glucose is available to the cells, hunger is reduced and a person experiences feelings of fullness or *satiety*.

Weight Regulation. Because blood glucose is determined by the meal most recently eaten and the length of time without food, it has only a short-term influence on hunger and satiety. Thus, there must be another system that regulates body weight. The average 20-year-old woman will gain 24 pounds by the time she is 60, indicating more calories consumed than expended. But the average amount of extra food needed each day to produce this much weight gain is only 300 milligrams—a very small amount. There must be some mechanism that operates over a longer time period so that long-term energy intake is about equal to long-term energy expenditure, thus maintaining constant weight. The most likely hypothesis involves regulation of fat deposits (Liebelt, Bordelon, & Liebelt, 1973). Any calories you consume above the level needed for your activities are converted to fat, whether you get the calories from fat, protein, or carbohydrates. If, on the other hand, you haven't eaten for a while and need calories for energy, your fat reserves are broken down and used. Thus, regulation of fat deposits is involved in the maintenance of weight. The brain regulates fat deposits, although we do not know exactly how.

Brain Mechanisms Underlying Hunger. In 1951, Anand and Brobeck demonstrated that surgical lesions made on both sides of the lateral hypothalamus (**LH lesions,** for short) caused rats and cats to stop eating and die of starvation. Lesions in another part of the hypothalamus, the ventromedial nucleus **(VMH lesions),** caused rats to overeat and become obese (see Figure 12.2). These discoveries caused great excitement. Had the cause of anorexia nervosa and obesity been discovered? Is the lateral hypothalamus the brain's hunger center? Does destroying it eliminate hunger? And is the ventromedial hypothalamus the satiety center? Does destroying it lead to perpetual hunger and eating?

Unfortunately, the answer to all these questions is no. Animals with LH lesions ignore all stimuli, not just food; they have lost more than their reaction to hunger

FIGURE 12.2
Effects of Lesioning in the VMH of a Rat

Lesioning in the ventromedial hypothalamus causes the rat to overeat and gain weight. The overweight rat weighs 1,080 grams; a normal rat of the same age weighs 350 grams.

cues. On the first day following an LH lesion, rats ignore pins stuck in them, the scent of ammonia or shaving lotion (unless the fluid is placed directly on the rat's nose), and various visual stimuli (Marshall & Teitelbaum, 1974). An LH-lesioned animal seems to have a problem being aroused by food, although it will eat in response to having its tail pinched (O'Brien, Chesire, & Teitelbaum, 1985). Damage to dopamine-containing axons in the lateral hypothalamus also causes the rat to stop seeking food. However, the same rat will react normally to food that is placed in its mouth (Berridge, Vernier, & Robinson, 1989). This also suggests that LH-lesioned animals lack arousal to food, not hunger per se.

LH lesions do not cause all rats to lose weight indefinitely. Although LH-lesioned animals must often be coaxed to eat, they do not seem to have lost their ability to react to all hunger cues. They appear to reach a new lower body weight and then maintain their weight at that level. Some investigators suggest that LH lesions lower the rat's set point (Keesey, 1980). A **set point** is a stable natural weight that the body seeks to maintain. LH-lesioned rats eat more if they fall below a certain weight and eat less if above that weight, just as normal rats do. These LH-lesioned rats are just maintaining a lower weight.

Also, VMH lesions do not seem to affect satiety as once thought. Animals with these lesions do not eat larger meals as would be expected if satiety were affected. Rather, they eat more meals (Duggan & Booth, 1986). They are unwilling to work for food, and they have higher than normal insulin levels (King, Smith, & Frohman, 1984). Perhaps this increased insulin in VMH-lesioned animals reduces blood glucose and increases the percentage of each meal that is stored as fat (Friedman & Stricker, 1976). Although we know that the hypothalamus is important in hunger and body fat regulation, we do not know exactly how lesions in this area exert their effects.

Recently, researchers using new techniques to measure the release of neurotransmitters in the brain have found that when rats eat something they like, dopamine and serotonin are released in the hypothalamus (Hernandez & Hoebel, 1988; Schwartz et al., 1989). The dopamine appears to be related to the pleasure associated with eating, and the release of serotonin appears to contribute to ending the meal (e.g., Leibowitz, 1989). Sarah Leibowitz, of Rockefeller University, is also exploring the role of neuropeptide Y, which is produced by neurons in the hypothalamus. Injecting a substance into the brain that reduces neuropeptide Y leads to a 70 percent reduction in rats' intake of both carbohydrate and fat. Several drug companies are attempting to develop an antiobesity drug that would work by inhibiting neuropeptide Y, although many problems need to be resolved before a magic antiobesity pill will appear on the market (Ezzell, 1994).

EXTERNAL FACTORS AFFECTING HUNGER AND SATIETY

Imagine that you have just finished a delicious meal and are completely full. Does this mean you have no motivation to eat? What if I offer you a piece of fancy chocolate candy? And have you ever felt not the slightest bit hungry, only to become intensely hungry when you suddenly smelled a hamburger sizzling on the grill? Hunger is not just a matter of internal biological factors. External factors also influence feelings of hunger and eating. These external factors produce **incentive motivation:** motivation produced by events in the environment.

Taste. Would you enjoy your dinner if it were pumped into your stomach and you couldn't taste or chew? When college students were given their meals in this manner, they reported reduced hunger, but they found the meals unsatisfying and reported a desire to taste or chew something (Jordan, 1969).

Laboratory rats have no trouble keeping their weight within normal range, when all they are offered to eat is standard laboratory food. But when given sausage, bananas, cake, cereal, and canned pet food, rats become obese, just as many people do when faced with the variety of tasty, high-calorie food we have in our environment (Sclafani, 1985). People and other animals will eat for taste alone, regardless of internal cues related to hunger and satiety (e.g., Mook, Atkinson, Johnston & Wagner, 1993).

Learning and Habit. All animals, especially humans, eat even when they are not hungry. Animals trained to eat in a particular situation or at a particular time of day will continue to do so from force of habit even if they are satiated (Capaldi & Myers, 1978). For example, most people eat lunch at lunchtime whether they are hungry or not.

People also eat when doing other things, such as watching TV. An individual can ingest huge numbers of calories without realizing it. Many diet counselors advise dieters to record when and what they eat so that they can pay attention to their eating habits and become aware of the sorts of situations in which they are likely to eat.

Some of our eating habits may interfere with maintaining normal body weight. Animals maintain a relatively constant weight by regulating how often they eat (LeMagnen, 1956), but most people eat dinner at the same time regardless of the size of their lunch. This means that a smaller dinner should be eaten to compensate for a larger lunch, something that does not seem to happen automatically because most of us habitually eat our largest meal at dinnertime (deCastro, 1993).

Sociocultural Factors. Eating is also a social phenomenon. People tend to eat more if other people are also eating (e.g., Redd & deCastro, 1992). Additionally, people learn to like the food of their culture. In some cultures, ants, beetles, and spiders are eaten and enjoyed, while in ours, such gourmet treats are often viewed with disgust. Even in our own culture, while most of us eat meat readily, vegans, who consume no meat or meat products, often view the consumption of meat with disgust.

Preferences for some foods can be produced only by social learning. Chimpanzees can be trained to like hot chili pepper if their caretaker gives it to them, but not if they eat it in isolation (Rozin, 1990). Normal learning techniques, such as pairing chili pepper with already-liked foods, or with lots of calories, do not produce a preference for chili pepper in chimpanzees or any animal. Only pairing the chili pepper with a warm social relationship produces liking for the chili pepper.

Psychological Factors. We have seen that eating can be motivated by incentives in the environment as well as by hunger. Eating can also be learned as a response to motives other than hunger. Many people overeat to relieve feelings of anxiety or depression (Greeno & Wing, 1994). And eating can even be used as a form of entertainment; in fact, many people overeat when lonely or bored (Crisp, 1970). In these cases, eating has nothing to do with hunger motivation at all.

INTERNAL AND EXTERNAL FACTORS COMBINED

Normally, intake is responsive to both internal and external factors. When very hungry, animals are willing to eat even when the food tastes bad. Hungry rats will, for example, eat food made bitter by quinine—something they would not normally touch.

At the other end of the spectrum, people will eat food that tastes very good, such as chocolate, when not hungry at all.

Recent data suggest that the relative responsiveness to internal cues may decrease with age. The elderly have been shown to be influenced by time of day and social factors in the same way as younger people. However, the elderly seem to be far less influenced by how much food they have eaten, as compared to younger people. As a result, intake in the elderly may be primarily determined by external factors (de Castro, 1993).

Nonregulatory Motivation: Sex

Sexual motivation differs from hunger in many ways. First, if people do not eat, they die; but however strong the urge, no one has ever died from lack of sex. Sex is not essential for an individual's survival, although sexual behavior and reproduction must occur for the species to continue to exist (Beach, 1956). A second difference between hunger and sex is that sexual behavior uses energy, while eating restores needed resources. Thus, the urge for sexual activity is not a homeostatic or regulatory motive. A third difference is that sexual behavior does not appear to be strongly affected by deprivation. Immediately following sexual activity, there is a period when further sexual behavior will not occur; then the probability of sexual activity increases slightly the longer the time without sex (Beach & Jordan, 1956). This effect of sexual deprivation is not nearly so strong or so clear as the effects of deprivation of food on eating.

Although culture and learning may modify expression of the sexual drive, the underlying basis for sexual motivation is, of course, biological. Moreover, the primary biological influence is hormonal.

HORMONES AND SEXUAL BEHAVIOR

The important sex hormones are the **estrogens** and **progesterone,** the "female" sex hormones, and the **androgens,** the "male" sex hormones. Males and females produce both types of hormones, but the male has a much higher percentage of androgens, while the female has a higher percentage of estrogens.

The sex chromosomes—XX in females and XY in males—determine whether the sex glands develop prenatally into testes (male) or ovaries (female). Secretion of sex hormones by the fetus's sex glands determines whether the fetus's external genitals will be male or female. Male sex hormones produce male genitals; in the absence of male sex hormones female genitals develop. At puberty, the increased secretion of sex hormones causes development of the secondary sex characteristics (see Chapter 10, page 411). The androgen **testosterone** is responsible for the development of the male penis, growth of facial hair, and deepening of the voice. Estrogen produces femalelike breast development and the storage of fat on the thighs and hips. These effects of sex hormones on tissue development are termed organizational effects. But sex hormones also affect sexual behavior, and these effects are termed **activational effects.**

Hormones have a strong effect on sexual behavior in animals other than humans. A number of experiments have measured sexual behavior as an indication of sexual motivation. A castrated rat (a rat whose testes have been removed) will cease sexual behavior, but an injection of testosterone restores the behavior (Butera & Czaja, 1989). In nonhuman animals, stereotyped sexual behaviors differ for males and females. Male rats mount female rats, not vice versa. These stereotyped sexual behaviors are under hormonal control. A female rat given androgen will mount male rats and reject advances from males. The effects are greater if the female is given androgen at birth or prior to birth (Harris & Levine, 1965).

In the human male, sexual behavior may also be related to androgen level. First, sexual activity is highest when androgen levels are highest (ages 15 to 25). Second, men with low androgen levels have less than average frequencies of erection and sexual activity, and both increase after the men receive testosterone (Davidson, Camargo, & Smith, 1979). Third, decreasing androgen by castration decreases erection and ejaculation in most, but not all, cases. The reason that erection and ejaculation continue may be that testosterone is also produced in small amounts by the adrenal glands. Thus, removal of the testes does not eliminate all testosterone. Some castrated men lose their potency immediately, and a gradual decline occurs in others. Sexual experience prior to castration tends to prolong sexual behavior following castration. However, low testosterone is not the only reason for impotence (the inability to have an erection). Some impotent men have normal testosterone levels, and giving them extra testosterone does not restore potency (Carini et al., 1990).

The relation between sex hormones and women's sexual behavior is unclear, although androgens seem to influence sexual behavior in women as well as men. About one-third of women report decreased sexual interest after removal of their ovaries (reducing both androgens and estrogens), and androgen replacement is more effective than estrogen replacement in restoring sexual activity (Zussman, Sunley & Bjornson, 1981). Testosterone has also been reported to increase sexual desire and the frequency of sexual fantasies in surgically menopausal women (Sherwin, Gelfand, & Brender, 1985). However, some studies fail to obtain these effects (e.g., Alexander, Sherwin, Bancroft, & Davidson, 1990). One reason for the inconsistency in results may be that hormones are probably less important than psychological factors in producing sexual desire and behavior in women.

Estrogen may also be involved in women's sexual arousal. In one study, women initiated more sexual activity (either by masturbation or with a partner) about midway between two menstrual periods (the time of highest estrogen level) than at other times of the month (Adams, Gold, & Burt, 1978). This cyclical activity decreased if the woman was taking birth control pills, which regulate hormonal levels. There is also a positive correlation between the basal body temperature shift that indicates when ovulation is occurring and sexual desire in women (Stanislaw & Rice, 1988).

Sex hormones can also affect nonsexual behavior. A medium level of male sex hormones seems to produce the best performance on spatial tasks. In fact, women with high androgen levels for their gender do better than those with low levels, while men with low levels for their gender do better than men with high levels (Kimura, 1992). Men with low levels of testosterone for their gender also do better on mathematical reasoning tests, while there is no relationship between testosterone levels and mathematical reasoning in women (Kimura, 1992).

Although hormones have some influence on sexual behavior in humans, sociocultural and other external factors are also very important.

SOCIOCULTURAL FACTORS

How do we know what factors affect sexual behavior in humans? Information about sexual behavior is difficult to obtain because sex usually occurs in private. This is a serious handicap to researchers, but two notable scientists, William Masters and Virginia Johnson (1966), have observed human sexual behavior in a laboratory setting

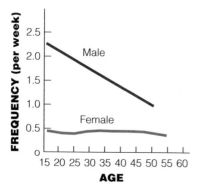

FIGURE 12.3
Kinsey Statistics

This graph shows the total number of orgasms per week from any source for single males and females as a fuction of age, described in the original Kinsey report.

SOURCE: Kinsey et al., 1953

Alfred Kinsey, the author of the first published scientific survey of human sexual behavior.

and provided a detailed description of the physiological sexual responses of men and women. Apart from their work, most information about human sexual behavior has come from questionnaires and interviews.

The Kinsey Report. The most comprehensive scientific survey ever undertaken on sexuality was conducted by Alfred Kinsey and his associates at Indiana University. Its results constitute the two-volume Kinsey report, *Sexual Behavior in the Human Male* (Kinsey, Pomeroy, & Martin, 1948) and *Sexual Behavior in the Human Female* (Kinsey et al., 1953), for which more than 5,300 American white males and 5,900 American white females were interviewed. (The results for African Americans were not published because the sample was unrepresentative.)

The Kinsey report caused quite a stir, mainly because subjects reported much greater frequency and variety of sex than had been expected. For example, 90 percent of males and 50 percent of females had engaged in premarital sex. The total orgasms reported per week for males were higher than generally expected (see Figure 12.3). More than 40 percent of college-educated couples indulged in cunnilingus (oral stimulation of the female genitals) and fellatio (oral stimulation of the penis). One-third of the males reported having experienced at least one orgasm with another male at some time past puberty.

These findings were drawn from respondents in the 1940s and 1950s. Two decades later, Hunt (1975) found that two-thirds of the women he surveyed had engaged in premarital intercourse, a significant increase over the number reported by Kinsey. (Today, premarital intercourse occurs on the average at an earlier age and is more frequent now among teenagers.) Another survey in the 1970s (Zelnick & Kanter, 1977) found that by age 19, 49 percent of unmarried white females and 84 percent of African American females have engaged in intercourse. The comparable figure for white females in the Kinsey report was 19 percent.

Reading these statistics, you may be tempted to see how you compare with the reported averages. But bear in mind that any average is not necessarily right, desirable, or relevant to you. You should also realize that the range of frequencies for most of these behaviors is wide. Consider the incidence of premarital intercourse for college-students. It varies from 28 to 82 percent for men and from 29 to 86 percent for women, depending on the year in college (intercourse is more frequent in later years) and the school sampled.

Kinsey also found gender differences in regard to masturbation: 58 percent of females and 92 percent of males reported at least one incident (Kinsey et al., 1953). A recent review of 177 studies of possible gender differences in sexual attitudes and behavior found that the largest gender difference was in incidence of masturbation, with males having the higher incidence (Oliver & Hyde, 1993). According to Gagnon and Simon (1973), during early adolescence the male's sexuality is focused largely on masturbation, while the female's first sexual experiences are usually later, in the context of a relationship. They speculate that this may be why females are more likely than males to believe that a committed relationship is a prerequisite for sexual interaction.

Frequency of sexual intercourse among married couples has increased since Kinsey's time. Kinsey reported that married couples around 20 years old had intercourse an average of about three times a week. A 1974 survey (Westoff, 1974) put the incidence at about 3½ times a week for that age. Data from various years are shown in Figure 12.4. It is not clear why sexual intercourse among married couples has increased,

FIGURE 12.4
Frequency of Intercourse

This graph shows the average frequency
of intercourse in the four weeks before
the interview for married white
American women by age.

SOURCE: Trussell & Westoff, 1980.

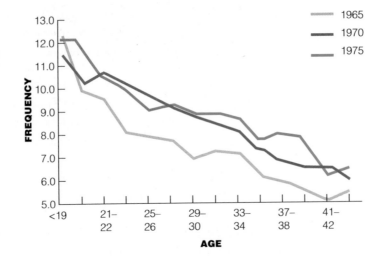

although a contributing factor may be the availability of the birth control pill and
therefore less fear of pregnancy. Greater openness toward sexual behavior may also be
a factor (Luria & Rose, 1979).

Cross-Cultural Studies.   The changes in certain sexual behaviors since Kinsey's
time suggest that societal influences may be important in determining human sexual
behavior. This conclusion is supported strongly by cross-cultural comparisons, which
show a wide variety of sexual behavior in different cultures. In a classic inquiry, Ford
and Beach (1951) compared practices in 190 societies, some of them preliterate. The
most frequent sexual behavior across the world is heterosexual intercourse, but it
varies tremendously in technique and preferred circumstances. Some cultures regard
intercourse during the day as dangerous; others prefer it. Most groups seek privacy, but
there are exceptions. In most societies, the preferred position is man on top of woman,
but some societies favor other positions. Generally, each culture prefers only one or
two positions (Gebhard, 1971); the Kamasutra, however, a Hindu love manual written
in the eighth century, lists more than 35 positions, including "union of the elephant
with its mates."

Frequency of intercourse varies widely as well. Among the Dani of New Guinea,
both men and women observe a four- to six-year period of sexual abstinence after the
birth of a child, and it does not appear that other sexual behavior, such as masturbation, prevails during this period (Heider, 1976). Couples do not begin sexual intercourse until two years after marriage, and weddings take place only every four to six
years. Premarital and extramarital sex are rare. As you might expect, the birth rate
among the Dani is low, barely achieving replacement. In contrast, in the Kinsey report
(1948), some young U. S. husbands reported an average of 3½ coital episodes within
24 hours.

There are also large cultural differences as to what is considered sexually desirable.
The female breast ranks as an important attraction in our society, whereas in many
cultures it has no particular sexual significance. In at least one culture, black gums are
highly favored (Ford & Beach, 1951). In the United States, thin women are viewed as
desirable, and the "ideal" woman has become thinner over the years (see Figure 12.5),
meanwhile, in parts of Africa, unmarried women are placed in "fattening huts," where
they are given high-calorie food to gain weight and increase their attractiveness
(Gregersen, 1983).

FIGURE 12.5

A "perfect" figure from the 1950s:
Marilyn Monroe.

SEXUAL ATTRACTION

Psychologists do not understand exactly what underlies sexual attraction, why some people have the right chemistry and others do not. One hypothesis concerns smell. Certain smells convey sexual readiness for many animals, and there is even evidence that smells play a strong part in sexual attraction between insects (Hassett, 1978). Reproductive behavior in most animals is heavily influenced by smell. In mice, for example, the onset of puberty in a female is accelerated by the odor of a male (Vandenbergh, Whitsett, & Lombardi, 1975). The odor that has this effect is produced only by the urine of intact male mice, and the urine of a castrated or juvenile mouse does not emit the odor. Many suspect that smell is a critical element in human sexual attraction and behavior as well.

Among many animals, a new partner proves arousing. After intercourse with one partner, introduction of another can renew activity. This is called the **Coolidge Effect,** and the story behind the name, which may or may not be true, goes as follows: Calvin Coolidge and his wife were visiting a farm when Mrs. Coolidge asked the farmer whether the continual sexual activity of the flock of hens was really the work of just one rooster. The reply was yes. "You might point that out to Mr. Coolidge," she said. Mr. Coolidge then asked the farmer whether a different hen was involved each time. The answer again was yes. "You might point that out to Mrs. Coolidge," he said. The Coolidge effect has been demonstrated in a number of animals, including guinea pigs, monkeys, bulls, and even humans, although a new partner does not seem as arousing to women as to men (Masters, Johnson, & Kolodny, 1985). The difference may be socially learned, since women traditionally have been expected to be more monogamous than men, or it may be biologically determined (see the Chapter 2 Controversy on page 78, for a discussion of different mating strategies between men and women).

Particular stimuli—such as romantic music, a dimly lit private place, or erotic photographs—can also be important for some people. The list of desirable circumstances and features varies considerably from person to person and, as we have seen, from culture to culture. In the extreme, a person can develop a sexual *fetish*, in which an ordinary object such as a shoe, can trigger arousal. The case study describes a fetish.

THE REDUCTION OF A LONG-STANDING FETISH BY MEANS OF AVERSIVE CONDITIONING

This is a case study of the successful treatment of a fetish of approximately twenty-one years' duration. The patient was a thirty-three-year-old male whose alcoholic father deserted the family when he was a child and who, from the age of about four or five, experienced a series of placements in relatives' homes, foster homes, orphanages, and day camp. He described his mother as probably schizophrenic, who blamed the Communists for her difficulties and who felt everyone had a double, good and bad. He was the middle child of three boys. He places the onset of his fetishistic behavior at about twelve years of age. This consisted of his masturbating while wearing women's panties that he usually took from clotheslines. If these were not available, he masturbated when stimulated by pictures of scantily clad women or by fantasies of women wearing panties. He was a shy, retiring child and as he grew older he became more aware of the abnormal nature of his behavior, felt increasingly inadequate and unmasculine, and resorted to body-building and boxing as a means of proving his virility. After a brief period in the Marine Corps and two failures at attempted intercourse, wherein he found himself impotent, the patient consciously set forth to prove his virility by joining a tough gang, drinking, brawling, and earning the reputation of being a "cop fighter." As a result of assaulting a policeman he was sentenced to a reformitory for twenty-six months. A few years later, he broke into a hotel room, stole some luggage, was apprehended, and sentenced to six years in prison. While incarcerated he was removed from the exciting stimuli and the fetishistic attraction was considerably reduced. He rejected the overtures of the prison "wolves" but wondered

why he was singled out as their homosexual target. Following this sentence he asked for treatment for his perversion. He recognized that the fetishism was responsible for his antisocial behavior as a compensatory mechanism. When he began treatment he was tense, tormented and obsessed by the impulses, and increasingly guilt-ridden and self-depreciative following the act. He was bright and very well motivated for treatment. He had had no previous treatment.

A number of factors determined the attempt to reduce symptoms through aversive conditioning. First, formal psychoanalytical treatment was not available. Second, other methods appear to have been unsuccessful since there are only four cases in the entire psychiatric literature claiming a cure (Raymond, 1960) and, finally, the author had become particularly interested in the application of learning theory principles to clinical problems. The fetishistic behavior was conceptualized as being the product of maladaptive learning and it was proposed to extinguish the symptoms through aversive conditioning by means of electric shock.

The first two sessions were spent obtaining a history. The patient recalled that the onset of the disturbing behavior occured when he became curious and sexually excited watching girls sliding down a sliding-board with their panties exposed. At this same period in time he was introduced to masturbation and he recognized experiencing similar sensations as when he watched the girls. His fantasies during masturbation quickly were centered about the girls and their panties and shortly this association was firmly made. This explanation for the development of such a fetish is certainly more parsimonious than the "dynamic" explanations involving castration threat, symbolism, and so forth. The above explanation for his behavior was explained to the patient as well as the general approach and rationale that were to be used. He understood the method and was strongly motivated to undertake the treatment regimen.

On the third session, the patient was connected to a Grayson-Stadler PGR apparatus by means of two fingertip electrodes. A conditioning circuit was used to establish a baseline for this shock. Adjustments in the circuit had to be made that still did not deliver as strong a shock as desired, but since it was experienced as uncomfortable it was decided to proceed. Approximately three and one-half milliamperes were delivered.

At each session, anywhere from four to six different stimuli were presented, immediately followed by shock. The patient was instructed to tolerate the shock until it became so uncomfortable that he wanted it stopped. He was then to signal for termination of the shock by saying "Stop." Twelve such stimuli were presented each session in random order. Approximately one minute elapsed between the sensation of the shock and the presentation of the next stimulus. The stimuli consisted of a magazine-size picture of the rear view of a women from the middle of the back to the knees wearing panties; an actual pair of panties which was placed in his hand; and imaginal situations in which the patient was asked to imagine himself wearing panties, imagining a clothesline with panties on it, and imagining himself standing in front of a lingerie shop window. The picture and the panties were always used, with the imaginal situations varying at each session depending upon his reports of particular areas of sensitivity. Discussion was limited as much as possible to the patient's response to the shock and his reaction to the fetish between visits. Each session lasted between twenty and thirty minutes. He was seen three times a week.

After forty-one shock sessions (fourteen weeks of treatment) conditioning was halted since the patient reported no longer being troubled by the fetish. Changes in the intensity of the fetishistic attraction and behavior were reported as early as the second shock session and progressed gradually with increases and decreases in the degree to which the patient was troubled by them. These fluctuations frequently reflected the degree of anxiety generated by extra-treatment conditions. Heightened anxiety often resulted in an increase in the fetishistic behavior that could conceivably be considered an important means by which the patient had learned to reduce the effects of tension and stress. As progress developed, the patient indicated that he had more and more difficulty in eliciting fetishistic fantasies during masturbation. Soon, the nagging quality of the urges, the self-conflict and torment that accompanied his submission to these urges, and the self-depreciation that went along with it, were markedly reduced. Approx-imately one month following the termination of the shock sessions, spontaneous recovery of the fetishistic behavior occurred, but in a much milder form than the original. The patient was prepared for this in advance by the therapist and was not discouraged. It was decided to give him a reinforcement or booster session as suggested by Raymond (1960). About two days later when the patient appeared for the booster session he reported no longer being disturbed. Nevertheless, two successive reinforcement sessions were given for good measure.

SOURCE: Ullman, L. P. & Krasner, L. (1965) *Case Studies in Behavior Modification*. New York: Holt, Rinehart and Winston, Inc., pp. 239–242

One topic we have omitted from our discussion is emotion, which in all types of animals (including humans) can override hormones, the Coolidge effect, and other factors. The topic of emotion is covered later in this chapter. Love and jealousy, two topics not well understood by psychologists, clearly play an essential role in human relationships. We return to this topic in Chapter 17.

GENDER IDENTITY

Unlike hunger, sex involves two different physiologies, male and female. Males and females have different chromosomes, different hormonal balances, different reproductive systems, and distinct physical appearances. Furthermore, boys and girls are taught to behave in ways considered appropriate to their sex. An important issue in the study of sexuality is the origin of a boy's or girl's **gender identity,** the private conviction of a male or female sexual identity. To what extent is a boy's masculine behavior and masculine identity a product of his biological makeup? To what extent does the child's rearing and early developmental experience determine his or her gender identity?

There is no simple answer to this question. Evidence, however, suggests that rearing and upbringing play a very important role in the development of gender identity. John Money and Anke A. Ehrhardt (1972) have extensively researched the effects of social influence on gender identity. One of their case studies was discussed in Chapter 9 (page 396).

Money and Ehrhardt also reported several case studies involving **hermaphrodites,** individuals whose genital structure is ambiguous. From birth onward, a hermaphrodite possesses a combination of male and female genitals. In Money and Ehrhardt's (1972) cases, hermaphrodite children consistently identified with the gender in which they were reared, even if that identity did not match their chromosomes, their hormonal balance, or their appearance. For example, one hermaphrodite had female (XX) chromosomes , ovaries, female sex hormones, and breasts that appeared at puberty. Despite all these female characteristics, the hermaphrodite had a masculine gender identity. His parents had raised him as a boy because at birth he also had a small penis.

Some believe there is a critical period for development of gender identity. A **critical period** is a time early in development during which some environmental event has a long lasting effect. For example, puppies of some breeds form lasting attachments to other dogs or people, but only during the third to seventh weeks after birth. Many fowl, including domestic chickens and ducks, acquire a tendency to follow any large moving object they encounter during the critical period of 12 hours to three days after hatching. This early and rapid tendency to follow or approach an object is called imprinting. Critical periods have also been observed in human development, particularly during the first year of life. In humans, these critical periods seem particularly important for language acquisition and emotional bonding. Money and Ehrhardt's data suggest there may also be a critical period involved in development of gender identity.

In the Dominican Republic, however, a syndrome called *pseudohermaphroditism* suggests that factors other than early rearing patterns may have some influence in determining gender identity (Imperato-McGinley et al., 1974). In these cases, the males were born with male (XY) chromosomes and testes, but with female genitals. They were raised as females. At puberty, however, their voices deepened, their muscle mass increased, their penises suddenly grew, and no breasts appeared. The researchers reported that at puberty, the gender identity of these children changed from female to

Ethologist Konrad Lorenz is being followed by geese that have imprinted. Animals are especially responsive to stimuli at certain periods in their lives. These geese were kept isolated from other geese early in life but were in the company of Lorenz. As you can see, they follow Lorenz as though he were their mother.

ORIGINS OF SEXUAL ORIENTATION

"I've always known I'm different" many homosexuals say. They believe they had no choice about being homosexual, that their sexual orientation was genetically determined.

How much of sexual orientation is genetically determined and how much is determined by learning and experience? This question is highly controversial and the subject of several recent studies. Three recent studies suggest there is a strong genetic component to homosexuality.

One study by Simon LeVay, a neuroscientist at the Salk Institute in San Diego, found that part of the brain of homosexual men has the anatomical form usually found in women (LeVay, 1991). This study examined brain tissue obtained from 41 subjects at routine autopsies, 19 homosexual males who died from complications due to AIDS, 16 subjects presumed to be heterosexual males (two of whom died from complications from AIDS), and 6 female subjects, also presumed to be heterosexual. A certain section of the hypothalamus was found to be twice as large in heterosexual males than in heterosexual females or homosexual males. It does not seem that AIDS caused the difference, because the heterosexual males with AIDS did not differ from the heterosexual males without AIDS in regard to brain anatomy. But one criticism of this study is that the sexual orientation of the heterosexual males and heterosexual females was assumed. Also, as LeVay himself states, the study did not really indicate if being homosexual produced the brain difference rather than the other way around. Also, this study has nothing to say about homosexuality in women, because no homosexual women were included.

Indeed, most studies of homosexuality have studied males, not females. This is why a recent study of lesbians (1993) attracted great interest. The study included 108 lesbians with twin sisters, recruited from newspaper advertisements. Almost half (48 percent) of the identical twins of the lesbians were also lesbians, compared to only 16 percent of the lesbians' fraternal twin sisters, and 14 percent of other biological sisters. The same pattern of results had been obtained in previous studies of male homosexuals. As explained in Chapter 2, this pattern of results suggests a genetic influence. The identical twins, who have identical genes, apparently are more likely to have the same sexual orientation than siblings with less genetic similarity.

Twin studies imply a genetic influence, but do not prove it, because identical twins may also have more similar environments than other siblings. Identical twins look alike, and are more likely to dress alike and be treated alike than fraternal twins. Recently, however, a study more akin to proof was published by a team of geneticists from the National Cancer Institute (Hamer et al. 1993). This was also a study of homosexual men, not women. The researchers recruited 76 homosexual men and determined which other members of their immediate family were also homosexual. They found 13.5 percent of the gay men's brothers were also homosexual. This is much higher than the 2 percent of the general population of males that are estimated to be gay. Even more dramatic was the finding that there were more gay relatives on the maternal side than on the paternal side, suggesting that the trait may be carried via the female members of the family. This, in turn, suggested that a "homosexual gene" might be on the X chromosome, the only chromosome inherited exclusively from the mother. The researchers then recruited 40 pairs of homosexual brothers, and took DNA samples from each in search of a common stretch of DNA in all of them. They succeeded in finding such a region. In 33 pairs of the 40 pairs of brothers, a set of five markers in common was found on the X chromosome. This finding has caused great excitement because it strongly indicates that there is a gene in this region of the X chromosome predisposing a male to be homosexual. As the journal that published the article put it, however, "no one is breaking out the champagne just yet." Studies in this field are often difficult to replicate, and an independent replication of the study is needed, before we can conclude that there is such a gene.

Some people believe that proof of a biological role in homosexuality could help diminish prejudice by showing being gay is not a matter of choice. Others feel that there is no logical relationship between discrimination and the development of sexual orientation. Even if a gene for homosexuality is discovered, we will need further research to understand how the gene influences behavior. Does the gene invariably lead to homosexuality? Also, is there a similar gene in women? And how does it operate?

male. The researchers attributed this change to the influence of prenatal hormones. Another possibility is that social influences and rearing around the time of puberty are particularly important. Still a third possibility is that because the families had previous experience with these unusual events (the trait is genetic and these events had occurred over generations), gender of rearing may have been more indeterminate and thus easier to change than in normal families. This study does, however, raise the possibility that gender identity is not fixed by rearing patterns in the first five years of life.

A third form of gender reversal involves **transsexuals,** individuals whose gender identity contradicts their physiology. Many transsexuals undergo sex-change operations. A famous case involved Dr. Richard Raskind, who became Dr. Renée Richards. Transsexualism has been less common in women than in men, but the number of women seeking to change their sex has been increasing . The origins of transsexualism, like those of gender reversal, are not clear. In transsexuals, chromosome structure and hormone levels are normal. Money and Ehrhardt (1972) believe that transsexualism occurs as a result of ambiguous rearing, a pattern of social influence that leads these people to feel that their sexual physiology must be changed.

SEXUAL PREFERENCE

In all known cultures, heterosexuality is the most common sexual preference, although homosexuality seems to exist in all cultures as well. **Homosexuals** are men or women who have a preferential sexual attraction to people of their own sex over a significant period of time. Performing homosexual acts should be distinguished from having a homosexual identity. In a Melanesian culture that Davenport (1965) called East Bay to protect the inhabitants, homosexual acts are expected of males prior to marriage, but heterosexuality is the norm after marriage. Thus, despite participation in homosexual acts, the males do not develop a homosexual identity.

Throughout history, different cultures have reacted differently to homosexuality. In ancient Greece, it was an accepted part of male life. About two-thirds of twentieth-century societies seem to approve of some homosexuality, at least tacitly (Ford & Beach, 1951). In the early 1950s, the Kinsey report estimated that 4 percent of males and 2 to 3 percent of females were exclusively homosexual throughout adulthood. More recent estimates are somewhat lower.

Bisexuals are men or women who are sexually attracted to both sexes. Kinsey and his colleagues (Kinsey, Pomeroy, & Martin, 1948) developed a seven-point scale, presented in Table 12.1, to show the continuum from hetersexuality to homosexuality.

TABLE 12.1
Kinsey's Heterosexual-Homosexual Rating Scale

0 Exclusively heterosexual

1 Predominantly heterosexual: only incidentally homosexual

2 Predominantly heterosexual: more than incidentally homosexual

3 Equally heterosexual and homosexual

4 Predominantly homosexual: more than incidentally heterosexual

5 Predominantly homosexual: only incidentally heterosexual

6 Exclusively homosexual

SOURCE: Adapted from Kinsey, Pomeroy, & Martin, 1948.

Ratings of 2, 3, or 4 on this scale indicate bisexuality. Very little research has been done on bisexuality. Some bisexuals have long-term unitary relationships, often a homosexual one followed by a heterosexual one. Other bisexuals are concurrently involved with both men and women. A common reason given by female bisexuals for their bisexuality is that they have different emotional needs, some of which are best met by women and some best met by men (Blumstein & Schwartz, 1976). (See the accompanying Psychology in Our Times for a discussion of the origins of sexual orientation.)

Achievement Motivation

Do you want to do well in life? To become a success? To achieve something? This type of motivation, unlike hunger, or sex, is not shared by all people, nor is it present in all cultures. Instead, the motive to achieve, like many other motives, appears to be learned. The **need for achievement** was first defined by Henry Murray in 1938 as the desire

> to accomplish something difficult. To master, manipulate, or organize physical objects, human beings, or ideas. To do this as rapidly and as independently as possible. To overcome obstacles and attain a high standard. To excel one's self. To rival and surpass others. To increase self-regard by the successful exercise of talent. (Murray, 1938, p. 164)

MEASURING THE NEED TO ACHIEVE

How can we determine our need for achievement? Murray developed the **Thematic Apperception Test,** or **TAT,** to measure the need for achievement, and McClelland and his colleagues refined the test for use as a research tool (McClelland et al., 1953). In this test a subject is asked to write stories about ambiguous pictures (Figure 12.6). Experimenters then analyze the stories to find signs of achievement motive. Because many different stories can be told for any one picture, the subjects' own desires and wishes will determine the story that he or she creates. This basic premise seems to be accurate; people do tell more stories about food when they are hungry. Thus, when they are not hungry, other motives will probably influence the stories they tell.

Questionnaires are also used to measure achievement motivation. McClelland, Koestner, and Weinberger (1989) have suggested that the TAT measures a desire for achievement that is not conscious, while questionnaires measure conscious motives. This explains why the two measures of need for achievement often do not correlate well (Spangler, 1992).

There is yet another way to evaluate the need for achievement. Suppose that you were invited to play ringtoss, a game in which you must toss a ring over a stick. How far would you choose to stand from the stick? Obviously, the closer you stand to the stick, the easier the task will be, but what challenge is there in simply dropping a ring on a stick that is right next to you? People who have a high need for achievement will choose to stand where their chances are about 50-50 of getting the ring over the stick. This is the result of balancing the likelihood of succeeding with how pleasurable it would be to achieve success. Standing too close makes it not rewarding to succeed; it's too easy. Standing too far makes success too unlikely. One early experiment on need for achievement did in fact involve the ringtoss game (Atkinson & Litwin, 1960). As you can see from Figure 12.7, high-need achievers preferred intermediate distances. Low-need achievers showed less preference for intermediate distances, but they did not prefer very long or very short distances either. In theory, people with a low need for achievement fear failure. Thus, we might expect them to choose tasks that are very

FIGURE 12.6
Thematic Apperception Test (TAT)

A TAT elicits stories about what is shown in various photographs. An experimenter can then evaluate the stories to see if they reflect achievement motivation.

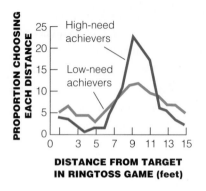

FIGURE 12.7
Testing Need for Achievement

In this experiment, subjects chose how far from a stick they wished to stand in a ringtoss game. The graph shows the proportion of high-need achievers and low-need achievers who chose each distance. As you can see, high-need achievers chose intermediate distances over very near or far distances to a greater extent than did low-need achievers.

SOURCE: Atkinson & Litwin, 1960.

easy, so failure is unlikely, or tasks that are very difficult, where failure is not embarrassing. Perhaps the low-need achievers in this study were not really very low because they were college students, among whom need for achievement is high in general.

Another explanation for the low-need achievers' performance is that other motives were at work. Need for achievement is not the only reason people want to succeed. For example, they may want to impress their friends, in which case even low-need achievers will have some desire to achieve and thus choose tasks of intermediate difficulty. McClelland and colleagues (1989) distinguish between *social incentives* for achievement, such as rewards or the expectations of coworkers, boss, or experimenter, and incentives produced by the activity itself, referred to as *activity incentives*. An example of an activity incentive is moderate task risk.

When real-life choices are measured, high-need achievers tend to choose goals of moderate difficulty, while low-need achievers tend to choose goals that are too easy or too difficult. High-need achievers are more realistic about career goals, setting goals that are neither too easy nor too difficult for their abilities, while low-need achievers tend to choose career goals that are either too easy or too difficult for their abilities (Mahone, 1960; Morris, 1966).

High-need achievers may prefer tasks of intermediate difficulty because the tasks inform them about their own capacities (Weiner & Kukla, 1970). When tasks are very difficult, failure is usually attributed to task difficulty; when tasks are very easy, success is attributed to the ease of the task. Only in tasks of intermediate difficulty may failure or success be attributed to abilities and effort.

Need for achievement can be learned, and training has been shown to improve performance. An achievement motivation training program has been given to African American and Hispanic businesspeople in nine different American cities (Miron & McClelland, 1979). Figure 12.8 shows that monthly sales, personal income, and profits all increased significantly following training. These changes were much larger than changes in the general economy or in the economy in the regions where the training took place. Thus, training in need for achievement can indeed improve business performance.

SOCIOCULTURAL DIFFERENCES

Societies differ in the emphasis they place on achievement, and this can change over time. But how can we measure the motivational themes of a society as a whole? One approach is to give the TAT to a representative national sample. Researchers have done this in the United States, but this method has not yet been used in other societies.

McClelland (1961) analyzed folktales, myths, and the literature of various countries, on the assumption that these sources would reflect the important themes of a culture. Using this method, he found that preliterate tribes whose folktales scored high in need for achievement had more full-time entrepreneurs than those scoring low (McClelland, 1961). Moreover, McClelland found that, over time, the achievement content of a culture's literature correlated well with measures of economic activity. For example, a survey of English drama, ballads, and other literature at 50-year intervals from 1400 to 1830 showed that coal imports in London (indicating industrial growth) increased following increases in achievement-related stories. Figure 12.9 shows the relationship between the frequency of achievement images in children's readers in the United States from 1800 to 1950 and the number of patents issued per million of population in the same period. Of course, these data do not show that need for achievement causes patents, but the consistency of these relationships is impressive.

FIGURE 12.8
Results of Achievement Training for Minority Businesspeople

This graph shows how achievement motivation training improved performance in some American business people.

SOURCE: Copyright 1979 by The Regents of the University of California. Reprinted from the *California Management Review*, Vol. 21, No.4. By permission of the Regents.

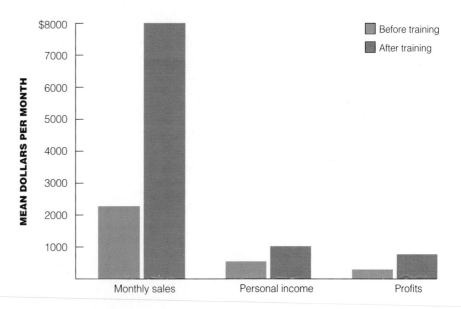

One notable difference between cultures is whether people expect results as a consequence of achievement or if "trying hard" is the important thing. Studies comparing achievement motivation between Iran and the United States, both high-need achievement cultures, show that Iranians focus more on effort, while Americans tend to be result oriented. Salili, Maehr, and Gillmore (1976) have shown that in experimental situations, Americans reward subjects more for results, while Iranians reward subjects for effort. The researchers reach the following conclusion:

"On the one hand, the most achievement-oriented American could not help but be impressed with the continued, methodical, and persistent hard work exhibited by a sizable share of the Iranian citizenry. On the other hand, he may be distressed with the lack

FIGURE 12.9
Achievement Imagery and U.S. Patents

This graph shows the mean frequency of achievement imagery in children's readers along with the patent index in the United States from 1800 to 1950.

SOURCE: de Charms & Moeller, (1962).

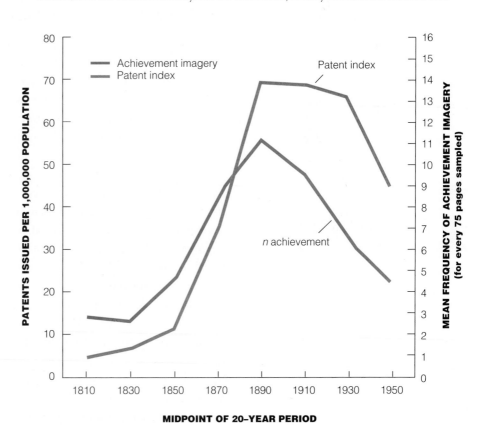

of care for produce or outcome. Thus, when a customer or employer complains about the quality of *outcome*, the Iranian employee or merchant is likely to emphasize the hard work (effort) involved. One may summarize the differences by suggesting that in the U.S. it is not sufficient merely to try. You must also produce—you are judged by your product. (Salili et al., p. 336).

Understanding cultural differences in motivation can lead to a better understanding between peoples. And certainly this information would be useful for anyone running a business in a foreign country. For example, motivational principles appropriate in the United States may not be effective in a different culture.

CONCEPT SUMMARY

INTERNAL VS. EXTERNAL FACTORS IN MOTIVATION

	INTERNAL FACTORS	EXTERNAL FACTORS
HUNGER	• Blood sugar • Hypothalamus somehow regulates body fat • Neurotransmitters	• Taste • Learning and habit • Sociocultural factors
SEX	• Hormones	• Learning and habit • Sociocultural factors • Characteristics of partner • Emotion
NEED FOR ACHIEVEMENT	• Reinforcement history	• Learning • Competition • Opportunity for self evaluation • Task difficulty

INTRINSIC VERSUS EXTRINSIC MOTIVATION

The desire to do a task for its own sake is called **intrinsic motivation.** (High-need achievers often exhibit this motive, particularly on tasks of intermediate difficulty.) The desire to do something in order to receive something else is called **extrinsic motivation** (Deci, 1975). The something else can be food, money, or power. Providing extrinsic rewards can actually decrease future performance when motivation is intrinsic. Lepper, Greene, and Nisbett (1973) demonstrated this result in a study involving nursery school children.

Three groups of children were given colored marking pens. One group was told beforehand that they would receive a "good player" award for playing with the pens; the second group was told about the reward only after their play period was over; and the third group was not offered any reward at all. A week later, each group was given the pens again, but this time none of the groups was offered any reward. Surprisingly, the group that was previously offered the extrinsic "good player" award before its play period showed the least interest of any of the groups in playing with the pens. Deci (1971) obtained similar findings with college students; those paid to solve puzzles at $1 per puzzle subsequently showed less interest in the puzzles than unpaid students. Thus, providing an extrinsic reward may reduce the intrinsic motivation produced by the task.

When given an extrinsic reward, people may learn to expect a reward for performing. Removing the reward then reduces their motivation (Lepper, Greene, & Nisbett, 1973). Also, the promise of an extrinsic reward often focuses people's attention on

"Wendell...I'm not content."

obtaining the reward, causing other aspects of performance to deteriorate (Lepper & Greene, 1978). The way people explain their own and others' performance on tasks is further discussed in Chapter 17.

It should be noted that extrinsic rewards do not always reduce subsequent performance. If the task is inherently uninteresting, extrinsic rewards will foster more effort, because people are unlikely to perform the task for its own sake (Calder & Staw, 1975; Upton, 1974). Also, if the extrinsic reward is given for a specific level of performance, it will not interfere with later performance (Boggiano & Ruble, 1979; Karniol & Ross, 1977). In this case, the extrinsic reward provides information to the worker. Therefore, to predict an extrinsic reward's effect on performance, it is important to understand as much as possible about an individual's other sources for reward (Lepper & Greene, 1978).

One source of reward that we have not yet considered is self-reward. While other people may reward us for what we do, a large part of human motivation involves motivating and rewarding ourselves. We can do this by setting goals and evaluating our own performance in light of those goals—a topic we turn to next.

SELF-REGULATION

Self-regulation is the process of setting goals for yourself and then rewarding yourself for achieving those goals. By making self-satisfaction or tangible rewards conditional on certain accomplishments, you can motivate yourself to try harder and do better. Some novelists, for example, regulate how much they write by allowing themselves free time only after writing a fixed amount each day (Wallace, 1977).

Self-regulation is an effective way to motivate yourself. Try it. If you would like to study more, set yourself a goal of studying 30 minutes tonight, and reward yourself when you are done by doing something you enjoy more than studying. Gradually increase the amount of time you must study before you can relax.

Bandura (1982) described the way self-regulation works. As we have mentioned, it helps to use tangible rewards. Study for a while, and then allow yourself time to listen to music, for example. People who reward their own behavior achieve higher performance levels than those who set the same goals but do not reward their attainments (Felixbrod & O'Leary, 1973).

According to Bandura (1982), it is best to set short-term explicit goals rather than long-term, general goals. Goals that are too far in the future or too general do not serve as effective incentives. So don't say that you will study hard this semester. Studying hard this semester is too vague a goal, and too difficult to achieve easily or soon. Say instead that you will read one chapter of your psychology book tonight and then allow yourself a half hour of relaxation. An explicit goal allows you to succeed and to feel the pleasure of having achieved your goal. This feeling of satisfaction will motivate you to study more.

According to Bandura (1982), people set their own internal standards for guiding their own behavior. You have no doubt formed some standard for judging your own behavior, for deciding whether or not you have done well. This standard comes partly from seeing how others react to you and partly from comparing your performance with that of others and with your own expectations. But how do you decide what to expect from yourself? Is it reasonable, for example, to expect that you can achieve an A in this course? Aside from needing the obvious skills, you also need the belief that you can exercise those skills and the desire to exercise those skills.

Students who are motivated to study value the results of studying (learning, good grades), and expect to get these results from studying.

Self-efficacy is a person's judgment of how well he or she can execute the actions necessary to deal with a situation. If you overestimate your capacities, you will undertake tasks that you cannot achieve, producing unnecessary failure. If you underestimate your abilities, you will not reach your potential. If you accurately assess your abilities, you will choose goals that allow you to exercise your abilities and succeed, building feelings of self-efficacy. You can thus develop self-efficacy by choosing goals that you can achieve. Success in achieving these goals leads to an accurate assessment of your abilities, which in turn leads to choosing goals that you can achieve. In short success breeds success.

Setting Goals

Our goals determine our behavior and how we interpret our behavior. Consider, for example, the two different ways that grade school children have been found to approach intellectual tasks. Some children want to obtain favorable judgments of their abilities; they are concerned with *outcome* goals. Other children are concerned with increasing their competence; they are concerned with *mastery* goals (Dweck & Elliott, 1983). Sometimes we learn more from failing than from succeeding, and focusing on the goal of mastery allows failure. A child who focuses on mastery goals seeks challenges. Failure for such a child leads to increased striving. In contrast, focusing on outcome goals produces a desire to avoid failure. This, in turn, creates a helpless pattern in which challenge is avoided and performance deteriorates in the face of obstacles.

Studies by Diener and Dweck (1978, 1980) reveal these patterns. Grade school children were given a concept formation task, successfully solving the first eight problems and failing to solve the last four (which were intentionally chosen to be too difficult for children their age). The children were instructed to say anything they wished during the task. All the children performed well during the success problems. But when the failure began, the children who focused on outcome goals began to disparage themselves. They cited deficient memory, low intelligence, or poor problem-solving ability for their failure. They also described boredom, aversion to the task, or anxiety, and their performance deteriorated rapidly. In short, these children viewed their failures as indicative of their lack of ability and therefore as insurmountable. In contrast, the children who focused on mastery viewed their failures not as failures but as challenges to be mastered through effort. They planned strategy and instructed themselves to exert effort and concentrate, saying things such as "I did it before; I can do it again."

Dweck and Leggett (1988) suggest that these different patterns depend on whether the child believes that intelligence can be changed. If a child believes that intelligence is a fixed trait, then poor performance is regarded as a sign of low ability. But if a child believes that intelligence can be trained, then poor performance is taken to mean that some area needs work. In general, people will attempt to worry about the adequacy of any trait they view as fixed; they will attempt to develop any trait they view as malleable. How an individual deals with social rejection, for example, will depend on whether or not the individual believes that social skills are a fixed trait. If the individual believes that social competence is fixed, then rejection will probably be interpreted as a result of personal incompetence. But an individual who believes that social competence can be learned will view rejection as a learning opportunity.

Understanding how these types of beliefs develop and operate can offer important lessons for the way you motivate yourself. Focusing on mastering various tasks produces a positive attitude, perseverance, and determination. You can choose mastery goals if you emphasize in your own mind that human traits can be changed and improved. But if you assume instead that your traits are fixed and unchangeable, you will likely focus on outcomes and produce a negative attitude, an intolerance to your own failure, and much frustration. The choice is clear and up to you.

Hierarchies of Motives

We have many different motives—motives that vary with the time of day and the situation. Which motive will affect our behavior at any particular time? And how do the various motives work together to produce behavior? Psychologists have not yet arrived at a complete answer, but we do have some principles.

Clearly, some motives—such as hunger and thirst—must be satisfied before others. Recognizing this situation, researchers have proposed a variety of hierarchies of motives to describe these levels of needs. In a hierarchy of motives, those at the first (bottom) level must be satisfied before those at the next, and so on. The most influential of these hierarchies, shown in Figure 12.10, was suggested by Abraham Maslow (1954). On the first level of **Maslow's hierarchy of motives** are the physiological needs, such as those for food and water. The next level includes safety from crime, from fire, from extremes of heat and cold, from wild animals, and from financial disaster (prevented by buying insurance or having a savings account). On the third level are the love needs, which include affection, belonging with people, and having a place in a group. Next comes the need for esteem, our requirement for a stable, firmly based evaluation of ourselves. (This category embraces the need for achievement, power, and self-respect.) Only when all these other needs are satisfied can the final level be reached—self-actualization, or self-fulfillment, whether it involves being a parent, an athlete, a musician, or whatever else we are suited for.

Maslow's hierarchy is a useful organizational device, but behavior does not always follow it. One problem is that satisfying a particular need may not reduce the need's importance, contrary to the premise of Maslow's and all the other proposed hierarchies of motives. In fact, just the opposite seems to be true: The greater the satisfaction a

FIGURE 12.10
Maslow's Hierarchy of Motives

In Maslow's proposed hierarchy of motives, those at the first level must be satisfied before those at the next; and so on.

Source: Maslow, 1943.

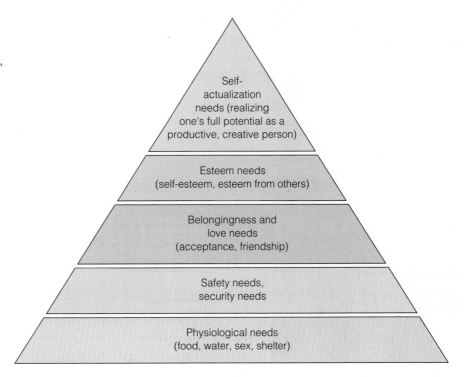

person obtains fulfilling a particular need, the more important that need becomes (Hall & Nougaim, 1968).

A second problem is that the order of the levels appears to vary from person to person. For example, Maslow reasonably suggests that physiological needs must be satisfied before social and other learned motives. Nevertheless, people have starved to death for a political cause, so hunger does not always dominate all other motives, as Maslow himself later pointed out (1970).

The fact that the hierarchy may vary from individual to individual has practical implications. Before we can motivate someone, we need to know that person's motivational hierarchy. For example, if we want to motivate someone to donate blood, do we offer that person money? If the person is more motivated by the mere act of helping others, offering money can actually diminish the person's motivation (Upton, 1974).

Achieving something, having a satisfying sexual experience, even enjoying a good meal are all parts of being happy, while failure to satisfy our motives is a source of unhappiness, anger, and frustration. These words all communicate emotion, the topic to which we now turn.

Defining Emotion

What is emotion? We all know what emotion is until we are asked to define it. Researchers distinguish at least three different aspects of emotion: evaluation of a stimulus (appraisal), response (physiological and behavioral, including facial expression), and subjective experience. We may then define **emotion** as a reaction to a stimulus involving appraisal of the situation, physiological arousal, facial expression, and feelings. Words such as *love, ecstasy, elation, contentment,* and *warmth* reflect positive emotions. Words such as *sadness, anger, terror,* and *disgust* reflect negative emotions. When we are experiencing positive emotions, we say we are in a good mood; negative emotions produce a bad mood. However, mood is not really a function of a single dimension (Watson & Tellegen, 1985). Rather, two dimensions are involved. The first is termed **positive affect**—the extent to which we show a zest for life. People who are high in positive affect describe themselves as active, elated, enthusiastic, excited, peppy, and strong; those low in positive affect say that they are drowsy, dull, sleepy, and sluggish. The second dimension is **negative affect**—the extent to which we are upset or unpleasantly aroused. High negative affect is accompanied by feelings of distress, fear, hostility, jitteriness, nervousness, and scorn. Low negative affect is accompanied by feelings of calm, serenity, and relaxation. Positive and negative affect are uncorrelated. Some people are simply intense; they feel both good and bad very strongly. Others are less responsive (Diener, Sandvik, & Larsen, 1985).

What does emotional responsiveness involve? Picture a man who has narrowly escaped being eaten by a ferocious beast. His face will reflect fear, he may be shaking and perspiring, and if asked to describe his feelings, he will undoubtedly say that he is afraid. These three responses—facial expression, physiological reaction, and subjective experience—are the critical measures of emotion.

Expression of Emotion

In 1872, Charles Darwin published a book proposing that emotions and emotional expression are biological traits shaped by evolutionary history. He stressed that emotions perform an extremely useful function for an animal's survival. An animal whose

In 1872 Charles Darwin published a book describing the great similarity in emotional expressions in animals and humans. The bared fangs of a hostile monkey, for example, are similar to the signs of anger in a human.

face conveys fear to other animals when danger approaches increases the chances of survival for those animals, who see the fear and escape the danger. The body also reacts in a way that prepares it for "fight or flight". We discuss facial expressions first, and then the body's reaction.

FACIAL EXPRESSION OF EMOTION

Charles Darwin pointed out that animals and humans share a great number of similar facial expressions. A dog's face can look friendly or sad in the same way as a human face. A downturned mouth conveys sadness in both a human and a dog. The strong similarity of facial expressions among animals, including humans, has continued to interest scientists since Darwin's time.

Facial expressions represent one important clue that emotions may have an evolutionary function. This has led to the idea that there may be a set of biologically based emotions found in many cultures and in many species. Although there may be some quarrel with the basic rationale of the research (Ortony & Turner, 1990), there is no doubt that useful data have been produced showing common facial expression of emotion across cultures.

Look at the photos in Figures 12.11 and 12.12 before reading the labels on captions. Write down what emotion you think is being expressed in each photo. Then check the labels and captions to see how you accurate you are. Research in this area suggests that you will be very good at telling emotion from facial expression.

In a series of cross-cultural studies, Paul Ekman and his colleagues (Ekman, Sorenson, & Friesen, 1969; Ekman, 1972) presented the photographs shown in Figure 12.11 to individuals living in various parts of the world, including citizens of Brazil, the United States, Chili, Argentina, and Japan. As the data in Figure 12.11 show, despite their cultural differences, most of the people tested matched the faces with the same emotion. This suggested to Ekman that smiling, frowning, and other such facial expressions are a result of genetics rather than learning. Critics pointed out, however, that all of Ekman's sample populations had been exposed to similar influences, such as mass media; it could be that the facial expressions were, in some degree, transmitted culturally.

FIGURE 12.11
Expressions of Emotions

Photographs of facial expressions were shown to people in five different cultures: United States, Brazil, Chile, Argentina, and Japan, Beneath each photographs are percentages of people in each culture who identified the photograph with the emotion listed upside down under the photograph.

SOURCE: Ekman, 1973.

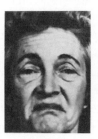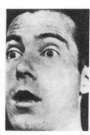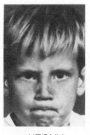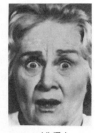

HAPPINESS | DISGUST | SURPRISE | SADNESS | ANGER | FEAR

CULTURE	PERCENTAGE OF PEOPLE CORRECTLY IDENTIFYING EMOTIONS FROM PHOTOGRAPH					
United States (N = 99)	97	92	95	84	67	85
Brazil (N = 40)	95	97	87	59	90	67
Chile (N = 119)	95	92	93	88	94	68
Argentina (N = 168)	98	92	95	78	90	54
Japan (N = 29)	100	90	100	62	90	66

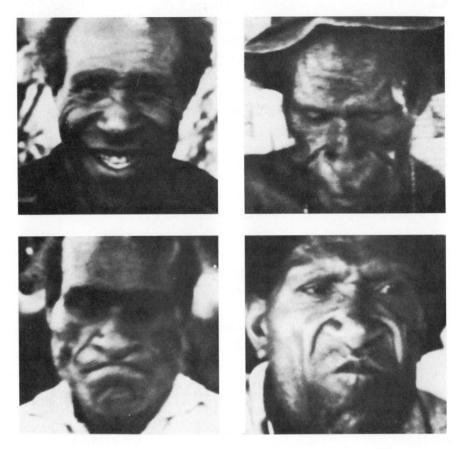

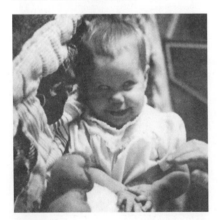

FIGURE 12.12
Facial Expressions Posed by the South Fore

At the time of this study, the South Fore tribe of New Guinea had had minimal contact with outside cultures. Nevertheless, their facial expressions are quite similar to those in many other cultures of the world. The instruction for the top left photograph was, "Your friend has come and you are happy;" for the top right, "Your child has died;" for the bottom left, "You are angry, about to fight;" and for the bottom right, "You see a dead pig that has been lying there for a long time."

FIGURE 12.13
A Blind Child's Smile

Although this 2-month-old girl has been blind since birth, she smiles like a normally sighted child. Emotional expressions such as laughing, crying, fear, and sadness seem to be inborn.

To deal with this criticism, Ekman performed another study in which he showed the photos to members of the South Fore tribe, a preliterate culture in remote New Guinea. Members of this tribe had had only minimal contact with outside cultures. None of them had ever seen a movie, and none of them either spoke or understood English. Despite their isolation, the South Fore tribespeople matched faces and emotions in much the same way as did people from other cultures. They were not able to distinguish a look of fear from a look of surprise, but they were able to distinguish these expressions from those of anger, sadness, happiness, and disgust.

In yet another experiment, Ekman asked the South Fore to make faces reflecting the way they would feel if they were a character in a story about sadness or happiness. Some of these expressions are shown in Figure 12.12. Most American college students have no trouble identifying the emotions expressed by the tribespeople.

Some researchers argue that the methods used in Ekman's studies overestimate the evidence for universal emotional expression (Russell, 1994). Subjects are customarily not free to use any label they want for the photos, but rather are given a list of possible emotions to match to the photos. This increases the likelihood of a correct match. However, many other studies finding evidence for universal expression of emotion have not used the methods in question (see Ekman, 1994; Izard, 1994, for responses to Russell's arguments). Also, Ekman's evidence for the universality of certain facial expressions is bolstered by studies conducted with blind and deaf children (Eibl-Eibesfeldt, 1973). Obviously, blind children cannot learn facial expressions by observing others, and yet their smiles are very much like those of sighted children (see Figure 12.13).

Although universal facial expressions do seem to be associated with certain biologically based emotions, facial expressions cannot be used independently as an accurate

FIGURE 12.14
Contracting Facial Muscles

On the top, a person holds a pen between her lips, a position that inhibits the muscles normally used in smiling. On the bottom, a person holds a pen in her teeth, a position that facilitates the muscles normally used in smiling.

measure of emotion. Facial expressions can be faked. Indeed, people can be quite adept at expressing emotions they do not feel (DePaulo, 1992).

The emotions that seem to be expressed the same way in all cultures are sadness, happiness, disgust combined with contempt, fear, anger and surprise (Ekman, 1992). Ekman calls these emotions *primary emotions*. The clearest evidence from studies using a wide variety of methods is for a common expression of happiness (Russell, 1994). A smiling face indicates happiness consistently with a wide variety of methods and a wide variety of cultures.

There also seems to be some truth to the advice, "Put on a happy face." Your facial expressions can indeed influence the emotion you feel. This idea is embodied in the facial feedback hypothesis.

The Facial Feedback Hypothesis. The **facial feedback hypothesis** asserts that a person's emotional experience can be either intensified or weakened, depending on the muscular activity that accompanies it. Darwin argued (1872) that an emotion is intensified if it is freely expressed by outward signs, an idea at the core of the facial feedback hypothesis. In some studies of this hypothesis, subjects are asked to produce certain expressions—for example, an angry expression by pulling their brows down and together and clenching their teeth (e.g., Laird, 1974). Inhibiting or facilitating specific facial muscles has been shown to have a reliable effect on affective response.

In a particularly innovative experiment, Strack, Martin, and Stepper (1988) asked subjects to hold pens in their mouths in a way that inhibited or facilitated the muscles typically associated with smiling. (Holding a pen only with the lips inhibits the muscles associated with smiling, while holding the pen with the teeth facilitates the smiling muscles, as shown in Figure 12.14.) The subjects were told that they were in an experiment testing their ability to perform different tasks with parts of their body not normally used for those tasks—as handicapped people might have to do. Holding the pens in their mouths, the subjects had to draw lines between 10 digits, underline consonants, and rate cartoons. The subjects who held the pens with their teeth rated the cartoons funnier than those who held the pens with their lips. This result supports the idea that facial feedback from the smiling muscles facilitates emotional experience.

Some theorists suggest that facial feedback from smiling intensifies emotion because people perceive smiling as a sign of happiness (Buck, 1985; Laird, 1974). Strack, Martin, and Stepper's experiment shows that this cognitive attribution is not necessary. Rather, as others suggest, it seems facial expressions can affect people's emotional experience without their being aware of it, perhaps because changes in facial muscle activity affect brain functioning (e.g., Izard, 1977; Zajonc, Murphy, & Inglehart, 1989). Researchers now measure muscle action potentials in the face, which can occur even if no overt facial expression is made (Tasinary & Cacioppo, 1992). These responses provide a more sensitive measure of emotional reaction than sole measurement of overt facial expressions.

Some evidence suggests that women reveal more emotion in their faces than do men and thus, according to the facial feedback hypothesis, may experience more intense emotion than men. (See "Controversy: Are Women More Emotional Than Men?")

THE BODY'S RESPONSE

Imagine yourself in any situation where you are concerned and unsure, perhaps just before having to address a group. You probably can easily name the bodily changes that you would experience: pounding heart, sweaty palms, dry mouth, tense stomach. The

One popularly accepted belief is that females are more "emotional" than males. Research suggests that women do indeed react more intensely than men to the same level of emotional stimuli (Diener, Sandvik, & Larsen, 1985). For example, females are more likely than males to disagree with the statement, "I would characterize my happy moods as closer to contentment than to joy." Females are also more accurate at reading people's emotional cues than are males (Hall, 1987) and show more facial expression of emotion than do males (DePaulo, 1992). In some studies (Buck et al., 1972), male and female subjects were shown color slides of seminude men and women, pleasant landscapes, a mother and child in a tender scene, repellent facial injuries and burns, and strange photographic effects. Observers watched each subject's face on a television monitor and tried to judge which of the five kinds of slides the subject was seeing. When women were viewing the slides, observers proved to be correct much more often than when men were viewing the slides, indicating that women were revealing more emotion in their faces than were men, a conclusion that might lead us to think that women have greater emotional reactivity than men.

Emotional reaction can be measured physiologically as well. In a similar study that measured galvanic skin response (GSR)—a change in electri-

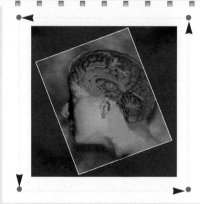

cal conductivity of the skin, indicating negative emotional reaction—females had fewer responses than males (Buck et al., 1972). Craig and Lowrey (1969) found greater GSR changes for males than for females who were watching someone receiving shock, but males rated themselves as experiencing less stress than females. When seeing another in distress, females are more likely to cry and say that they are distressed, but their heart rate does not differ from that of males (Eisenberg & Lennon, 1983). It appears that when overt responses such as facial expression and verbal report are measured, males show less emotional reactivity than females; but when physiological measures are taken, males can exceed females.

One explanation is that open expression of emotion is more socially acceptable for females than for males. As early as 3 months of age, girls show more facial expression than boys (Malateta & Haviland, 1982), a pattern that appears to be reinforced by parents. Males learn to inhibit their openly emotional reactions and to increase their physiological expression (Jones, 1950). In other words, the emotion must manifest itself somehow, and if open expression is inhibited, physiological expression will increase.

Some observers have argued that blocking emotional expression can produce stress within the body, which may result in illness (see Chapter 13). Ulcers and heart disease are much more common among men than among women. Perhaps these illnesses occur because men inhibit open expression of their emotions. If so, then perhaps they should be encouraged to express their emotions. Free expression of emotion, however, is not always beneficial. It can sometimes foster socially undesirable behavior, such as aggression (Berkowitz, 1973). Also, there are other explanations of the differences between men and women in incidence of ulcers and heart disease. Female sex hormones, for example, appear to provide protection against these diseases. The controversy over whether the male's more inhibited style of emotional expression contributes to illness is attracting a great deal of attention. We may expect to see some significant new research in this area soon.

English language reflects this relationship between emotions and bodily reactions with expressions such as "cold sweat," "trembling with fear," and "butterflies in the stomach."

Of primary importance in the body's emotional reaction is the *autonomic nervous system*. As described in Chapter 2, the autonomic nervous system consists of the sensory and motor nerves serving the heart, the glands, and the smooth muscles of the internal organs. The system has two branches: the *sympathetic nervous system* and the *parasympathetic nervous system*. The first tends to function more actively during strong emotion, while the second operates during relaxation and rest. Table 12.2 compares the two systems.

Table 12.3 shows the effects of sympathetic and parasympathetic control on specific organs and glands. Some organs, such as adrenal glands, are associated only with the sympathetic nervous system, but most are controlled by both the sympathetic and

TABLE 12.2
Function's of the Autonomic Nervous System

	ACTIVITY	EFFECTS
Sympathetic system	When preparing for "fight or flight," processes expend energy from reserves in the body.	Increased blood flow to muscles, rise in heart rate, piloerection (erection of fur in mammals who have it, goosebumps in humans)
Parasympathetic system	When activities are required for nonemergency functions, processes increase the body's supply of energy.	Increased secretion of digestive juices, decreased heart rate

The reactions associated with emotional arousal are produced by the sympathetic nervous system. They consist of increased heart rate, increased blood pressure, pupil dilation, inhibition of salivation (causing dryness of the mouth), sweat secretion (resulting in clammy hands), constriction of blood vessels in the periphery of the body (producing cold hands and feet), and impeded digestion. Can you see why a glass of water is often provided for public speakers? Autonomic arousal inhibits salivation, thus producing the dry mouth so often experienced by public speakers.

The parasympathetic nervous system, active when we are relaxed and calm, decreases heart rate and blood pressure, constricts pupils, and increases salivation and digestive processes. The parasympathetic and sympathetic nervous systems work together and complement each other. Thus, you can simultaneously digest a meal, governed primarily by parasympathetic activity, while sweating if you are too hot, a reaction governed by the sympathetic nervous system.

How Lie Detectors Work. Because the sympathetic nervous system is active in emotion, one way to measure emotion is to measure physiological responses associated with the sympathetic nervous system. This is the idea behind the polygraph, or lie detector. Various parts of the machine record heart rate, blood pressure, palm conduc-

TABLE 12.3
Effects of Autonomic Nervous System Activity on Specific Organs and Glands

ORGAN OR GLAND	EFFECT OF SYMPATHETIC ACTIVITY	EFFECT OF PARASYMPATHETIC ACTIVITY
Heart	Faster rate of contraction	Slower rate of contraction
Pupil (in eye)	Dilation	Constriction
Intestines	Decreased activity	Increased activity
Bladder	Inhibition of contraction	Contraction
Lungs	Dilation of bronchi	Constriction of bronchi
Adrenal medulla	Secretion of norepinephrine and epinephrine	No effect
Penis	Ejaculation	Erection
Vagina	Orgasm	Secretion of lubricating fluid

A lie detector measures sympathetic nervous system arousal. A person who can remain calm while lying will fool the machine.

tance (which is affected by sweating on the palm), and breathing rate. First a subject's response is measured when he or she is calm and answering neutral questions, such as name and address. Control questions (e.g, "Did you ever steal anything before?") should be somewhat upsetting, but relevant questions ("Did you steal the necklace?") are presumably most upsetting to a guilty person, but not any more upsetting than control questions to an innocent person.

If the subject is lying, any emotional reaction to the lie will show up on the machine. Note that the machine does not measure lying; it measures physiological reactions associated with emotion. Anyone who can lie with no emotional reaction can fool the machine. Furthermore, a person who is reacting emotionally to certain questions but is not lying will be wrongly judged a liar. Saxe, Dougherty, and Cross (1985) reviewed a large number of studies on the accuracy of decisions based on the polygraph. If suspects were guilty, they were identified as guilty 71 to 99 percent of the time. The problem is that if subjects were innocent, they were identified as innocent 13 to 94 percent of the time. This is a very wide range of error, not one you would want to rely on if your innocence were questioned. In 1988, Congress passed legislation restricting the use of lie detector tests by the courts, government, and industry.

In general, physiological reactions do not unequivocally measure emotion, because the exact physiological reaction may differ from person to person (Grings & Dawson, 1978). One individual may show increased heart rate and little change in palm conductance, while in another individual, palm conductance may change but not heart rate (e.g., Lacey & Lacey, 1958). Also, people vary in their overall level of physiological reaction to emotion.

Clearly, physiological reaction is not a completely accurate indication of emotion. Nor is facial expression an infallible guide to emotion. People can smile without feeling happy and can feel happy without smiling. The best way to determine another person's emotion is to consider all possible measures—facial expression, physiological measures, verbal report, and behavior.

Theories of Emotion

Emotions are expressed through facial expression and body response, but what makes us *feel* an emotion? We will consider two early theories, the James-Lange theory and the Cannon-Bard theory, before considering what most people believe today.

THE JAMES-LANGE THEORY OF EMOTION

It was once proposed that our body makes us feel an emotion—that emotion is simply our feeling our body's reaction. This theory was developed independently by the American psychologist William James (1885/1968) and the Danish physiologist Carl Lange (1885/1967). The **James-Lange theory of emotion** proposes that what we normally call emotion is actually a result of our sensing the body's physiological reaction to an event that arouses the autonomic nervous system. In other words, when you encounter a vicious bear, that event produces a reflexive action, such as a pounding heart. When you sense your pounding heart, you experience emotional "fear." This theory assumes that if no sympathetic arousal takes place, no emotion takes place either. Thus, if you see a vicious bear and your heart doesn't pound, then you won't be afraid. Figure 12.15 diagrams this theory. The James-Lange theory of emotion has not met universal acceptance. As early as 1927, Walter B. Cannon carried out a set of experiments that demonstrated several problems with it.

FIGURE 12.15
James-Lange Theory of Emotion

According to the James-Lange theory, emotion is a result of our sensing the body's physiological reaction to an event that arouses the autonomic nervous system.

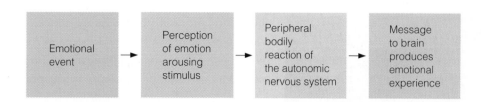

OPPOSITION TO THE JAMES-LANGE THEORY

Cannon's first objection was as follows: If the James-Lange theory were correct, then for emotion to occur, the sympathetic nervous system had to be intact. When Cannon, Lewis, and Britton (1927) surgically destroyed the sympathetic nervous system of a cat, however, the cat still showed a normal emotional reaction to a barking dog. This experiment was not as conclusive as it may seem since the researchers failed to destroy all of the important nerve fiber pathways leading to the sympathetic nervous system (Fehr & Stern, 1970). Moreover, the important question was not whether the cat *acted* angrily without its sympathetic nervous system, but whether it *felt* angry.

Cats, of course, cannot report their feelings. But people can. Hohmann (1966) asked people who had suffered spinal cord injuries affecting the sympathetic nervous system to report their feelings. They generally showed reduced emotional experience, but not its disappearance, as the James-Lange theory would predict. As one unfortunate patient reported:

> Sometimes I act angry when I see some injustice. I yell and cuss and raise hell, because if you don't do it sometimes, I learned people will take advantage of you, but it just doesn't have the heat to it that it used to. It's a mental kind of anger. (Hohmann, 1966, p. 151)

A more recent study (Chwalisz, Diener, & Gallagher, 1988) compared spinal-cord-injured college students with two control groups. To control for the possibility that decreased emotion may have been due to confinement in wheelchairs rather than spinal cord injury, one control group consisted of university students who were confined to wheelchairs for other reasons (e.g., cerebral palsy or muscular dystrophy). The second control group was composed of nonhandicapped students. In the experiment, the researchers asked students how their past emotions compared with their current ones, as Hohmann (1966) had done with his subjects. Because this measure might have been influenced by memory biases, they also asked students to report on their naturally occurring current emotions and to respond to certain hypothetical experiences—for example, to describe times when they felt happy, sad, angry, or loving. They also measured overall positive and negative emotionality as well as emotion intensity using standardized scales.

Consistent with Hohmann's findings, the researchers found that those subjects with higher spinal lesions (and so drastically reduced spinal feedback) reported less intense negative emotions after their injuries than before compared with those subjects with lower spinal lesions (greater spinal feedback). The low feedback group also reported less emotional intensity than the high-feedback group. But there were also reports of intense emotions by those with no autonomic feedback. When asked to recall an angry time, one subject with a high and nearly complete cervical lesion, so that his autonomic feedback was virtually zero, reported being so angry at one of his instructors that he wanted to "run over him a few times" with his wheelchair.

The finding of intense emotions among persons with spinal cord lesions is consistent with a case described by Buck (1984) of a woman with complete loss of sensation from the neck down who showed normal emotions and no change in personality after

Sometimes we like to be emotionally aroused. Arousal theory, covered in Chapter 13, is one explanation for this.

her injury. Although these data are not consistent with the idea that feedback from the autonomic nervous system is necessary for emotional experience, the data do support the idea that autonomic arousal can intensify emotional experience, even though autonomic arousal is not necessary for emotional experience.

A second criticism made by Cannon was that autonomic reactions were too slow. Have you ever been afraid, then acted, and *then* started trembling? Autonomic nervous system changes often do not occur until 1 or 2 seconds after an event. This delay contradicts the basic sequence outlined in the James-Lange theory.

Cannon's third criticism was that the same peripheral physiological changes occurred in diverse emotional and nonemotional states, so how could physiological changes determine emotion? After all, running around the block increases your heart and breathing rate and makes your palms sweat, but few people would consider that an emotional experience. Also, artificial induction of the physiological changes that supposedly produce emotion fail to stir the emotions. Injections of epinephrine (adrenaline) cause physiological reactions similar to those of natural sympathetic nervous system arousal. But when epinephrine was administered to 210 subjects, about 71 percent reported only physical symptoms such as tremor and palpitations (Maranon, 1924, cited in Schachter, 1964). The remaining 29 percent did note emotional reaction, but described it "as if—I feel as if I am afraid." Of course, injections of epinephrine do not produce the total range of peripheral physiological reactions that occur in normal emotional arousal, so these data are perhaps not that damaging to the James-Lange theory. And although there is presently no clear evidence that physiological differences lie beneath all the varying emotions people experience, some physiological differences have been measured between anger and fear (Ax, 1953), and there may indeed be different peripheral physiological changes in other emotional states as well.

Cannon believed that the internal organs are too insensitive to provide the complex information that would be needed to distinguish one emotion from another. More recently, however, Ekman, Levenson, and Friesen (1983) reported data showing that some emotions are distinguished by different patterns of physiological response. These investigators asked subjects to produce facial expressions characteristic of various emotions. When subjects feigned anger, fear, or sadness, their heart rate increased, while in surprise, heart rate decreased. Skin temperature increased in anger, but not in fear, sadness, or surprise. Levinson (1992) confirmed the heart rate acceleration in anger, fear, and sadness and also reported heart rate deceleration in disgust. Some current researchers believe that genetically dictated brain systems that mediate emotions will be delineated in the near future (e.g, Panksepp, 1992).

THE CANNON-BARD THEORY OF EMOTION

Cannon (1927) developed a theory that was also proposed by Bard (1928). According to the **Cannon-Bard theory of emotion,** an emotion-arousing situation stimulates the thalamus, which then transmits information simultaneously in two directions—downward through the autonomic nervous system to the body's internal organs and upward to the cerebral cortex. The autonomic nervous system produces the peripheral physiological arousal associated with emotion; the cerebral cortex produces the subjective experience of emotion (see Figure 12.16).

Later researchers showed that Cannon and Bard's identification of the thalamus was incorrect. In 1937, Papez brought forth evidence pointing to the limbic system as the critical component. Today, the brain circuit he identified, known as the *Papez circuit*, is accepted as one of the keys to emotion. Other researchers have shown that emotions

Figure 12.16
Cannon-Bard Theory of Emotion

According to the Cannon-Bard theory, an emotional event causes the thalamus to simultaneously transmit signals to the cerebral cortex, producing a subjective emotional experience, and to the autonomic nervous system, producing arousal.

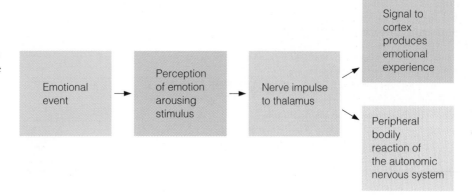

are also controlled by the hypothalamus. Stimulation of a particular portion of the hypothalamus enrages cats and provokes attack directed toward the provoking stimulus (Flynn et al., 1970; Panskepp, 1971). Electrical stimulation of particular portions of the hypothalamus can produce strong pleasure reactions as well (see Chapter 2).

The Cannon-Bard emphasis on the cerebral cortex has been borne out by further research. Removal of the cortex in lower animals produces highly excitable animals, that fly into a rage at the slightest provocation. Bard (1934) called this "sham rage" because it was short-lived, not clearly directed at the provocation, and seemingly without conscious control. These findings suggest that one normal function of the cerebral cortex may be to inhibit emotional expression. Also, emotions are often complex mixtures of physiological and cognitive events processed by the cerebral cortex. An emotion such as disappointment, for example, includes elements of sadness produced by not receiving an expected event. Thus, the cognitive ability to represent future expected events plays a vital role in emotional experience. Actually, the James-Lange theory implied that cognitive events may have some role in emotion (along with physiological events) because the initial trigger for emotion, according to this theory, was perception of an emotion-arousing stimulus. Today, central cognitive processes as well as physiological response are seen as vital components of emotion. The first theory to explicitly accommodate the role of both elements appeared in 1962.

COGNITIVE-PHYSIOLOGICAL AROUSAL THEORY

In 1962, Stanley Schachter and Jerome Singer proposed a theory of emotion contradicting the idea that specific physiological responses produce specific emotions. Instead they argued that emotions are determined, in part, by a situation and a person's evaluation of the situation. This is a **two-component theory of emotion.** That is, two things are necessary for an emotion to be experienced: general autonomic arousal and a cognitive interpretation of the reason the arousal took place (see Figure 12.17).

To test this theory, Schachter and Singer (1962) administered epinephrine, which causes trembling and speeds the heart rate (reactions similar to those of natural sympathetic nervous system arousal) to three groups of subjects. One group was correctly informed that "your hand will start to shake, your heart will start to pound, your face may get warm and flushed." A second group was told nothing about the drug's effects, and a third group was misinformed and warned to expect itching, numbness, and headache.

If the Schachter-Singer theory were correct, the specific emotion experienced by each group would depend on the appropriate situational cues. The group that was told that the epinephrine would produce arousal should not feel emotional. That is, they

FIGURE 12.17
Schachter-Singer Model of
Emotional Experience

According to the Schacter-Singer
model, two things are necessary for an
emotion to be experienced: general
autonomic arousal and a cognitive interpretation of the situation consistent with
emotion.

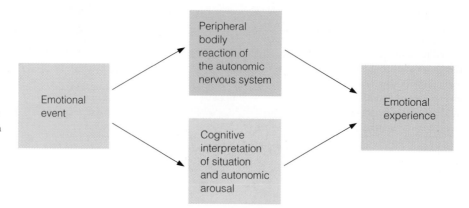

should interpret the sympathetic arousal as an effect of the drug, not as an emotional
reaction. The other groups should feel emotional if they have a good reason to do so.
Schachter and Singer set up the experiment so that these other groups would have
appropriate reasons to "explain" the emotional arousal produced by the drug.

Every subject waited in a room with another person who supposedly was also a participant in the experiment and had received the epinephrine. The other person actually
had been hired by the experimenters to behave in particular ways, providing the subject
with situational cues. In one condition, the hired subject—or model—threw paper airplanes, shot wads of paper, and was generally cheery. In the other condition, the model
simulated anger, complained about the experiment, and displayed aggressiveness. The
subjects were watched through one-way mirrors, and those uninformed and misinformed about the drug's effects acted angrier with the angry model than those who were
informed about the drug. With the happy model, uninformed and misinformed subjects
reported that they were happier and tended to act happier than subjects who were
informed about the drug's effects. Thus, as expected, emotion was produced in these
people by combining an unexplained physiological arousal with situational cues appropriate to emotion. Schachter and Singer concluded that two factors were involved in
the experience of emotion: physiological arousal and a situational cue. The arousal produced by the epinephrine was inferred to be emotional because of the situation.

In subsequent years, the central assumptions of the Schachter-Singer theory have
been supported. Zillman, Johnson, and Day (1974), for example, found that for a short
time following exercise, subjects behaved more aggressively when they wrongly
believed that the effects of the exercise had dissipated than when they were aroused
and knew it to be due to the exercise or when they were no longer aroused. Sinclair
and colleagues (1994) found that the particular emotion the subjects experienced during this postexercise period could be influenced by the cognitions that the experimenters aroused in the subjects. Others have found unattributed arousal to increase the
positive affect produced by comic strips (Martin, Harlow, & Strack, 1992) and interpersonal attraction (White, Fishbein, & Rutstein, 1981).

However, experimentation has also found exceptions to the Schachter-Singer view.
Some experiments, for example, have contradicted Schachter and Singer's view that
autonomic nervous system arousal is necessary for emotional experience. Some studies
find that while increasing arousal frequently intensifies emotional experience, arousal
is not essential for emotional experience (Shaver & Klinnert, 1982), a finding also suggested by the research on handicapped persons described previously. In fact, the presence of arousal can actually prevent the induction of certain emotions (Reilly &
Morris, 1983).

Other data suggest that situational factors do not totally determine the interpretation of arousal. Contrary to what Schachter and Singer found in 1962, it appears that physiological arousal (produced by epinephrine) is more likely to be interpreted as negative emotion than as positive (Marshall & Zimbardo, 1979; Maslach, 1979). In other words, physiological arousal may indeed be a factor in determining which emotion is experienced—and not just whether emotion is experienced. And as mentioned earlier, some emotions seem to have particular physiological correlates (e.g., Ekman, Levenson & Friesen, 1983). The exact relationship between emotion and cognition is also a matter of current controversy, as discussed next.

COGNITION AND EMOTION

Schachter and Singer argued that cognition is needed to produce an emotional experience. In this view, when people become aroused, a cognitive appraisal of the situation allows them to label their feeling appropriately. The order of these events may, however, be reversed. Richard Lazarus suggests that the first step in an emotional sequence is a cognitive appraisal of the situation (Lazarus, Kanner, & Folkman, 1980). Only then does physiological arousal occur. The first appraisal made is to decide what the consequences of an event may be for personal well-being. This is called the *primary appraisal* of the event. Is the stranger off in the darkness positive (a friend), neutral (another person taking a stroll), or negative (a potential mugger)? Only if an event is appraised as being significant for personal well-being will an emotion be generated (Lazarus, 1991). This appraisal determines which emotion will be felt and the intensity of the emotion. Lazarus has distinguished between specific emotions such as anger, sadness, and pride in terms of the appraisals involved. For example sadness is produced by the appraisal that something important to the individual has been lost and that there is no way to restore the loss. A *secondary appraisal* then takes place consisting of a decision of what reaction to have to the event. Each emotion involves its own innate action tendency (e.g., attack in the case of anger). But this action tendency can be inhibited or transferred by coping reactions (Lazarus, 1991). (We will discuss Lazarus's work on coping in the next chapter.)

A third view of the relation between cognition and emotion is that they are independent. Zajonc suggests that emotions can be experienced without any cognitions at all (Zajonc, 1980, 1984). Zajonc does not believe that a great deal of information must be processed before people know what they feel. Rather, he believes, it takes a while to figure out what we think, while generally we know immediately what we feel. Cognition and affect, Zajonc suggests, are independent. Also affect is often not conscious. For example, subjects shown photographs of certain people subliminally (so quickly they were unaware of seeing them) reacted more positively toward the people that they had been shown (Bornstein, Leone, & Galley, 1987). They had an affective reaction to the people they had been shown without being conscious (aware) of which people they had been shown. One difficulty here is that some cognitive processes are also not conscious (see Chapter 7). Of course, more complex emotions, such as jealousy, pride, or disappointment, require cognitive processing for their occurrence (Zajonc, Murphy, & Inglehart, 1989).

While it may seem that we know very little about emotion and that there is little agreement in the field, a more accurate view is that each theory has made an important contribution. James and Lange were right that people read their emotions in part by reacting to their bodily changes. Cannon was right that the brain is important in emotion. Schachter and Singer were right in stressing that cognitive appraisal plus logical arousal play a role in emotion. And facial expressions clearly play a role in emotion.

The most common view today is that emotion is not a physiological reaction, a facial expression, an appraisal, or a response. Rather, all these components together constitute an emotion. Consensus may also be reached on the idea that the sequence of the different components may differ in different situations or in different emotions, so that appraisal may precede or follow an affective reaction.

THEMES IN REVIEW

We have seen in this chapter that motivation and emotion are both strongly influenced by biological factors. Some motives reflect individual biological needs (hunger and thirst) while others satisfy biological needs of the species (sex). Yet even the most biologically determined motives are influenced by cognition and learning. Although we share facial expressions of emotion with other animals and with peoples of other cultures, our emotional expressions also seem to be strongly influenced by cognition and learning.

Development of emotion and facial expression also seem to follow the same pattern in all children, even those born blind. Yet at the same time, we can learn to inhibit our emotions or to express them freely, and which specific emotion is produced by a particular event is often a matter of learning and culture. The idea of eating insects produces a disgust reaction in our culture, but not in all cultures.

Emotion and motivation are also affected by cognition. We can motivate ourselves by setting goals, and our fail-

ure or success at meeting our own goals can decrease or increase our motivation. Our appraisal of our own failure and success can produce emotion (disappointment, sadness, and frustration from failure; joy, success, and hope from success), as can our appraisal of any event. We will see in the next chapter how long-term patterns of appraisal and emotional reaction can ultimately affect our health.

SUMMARY

1 The science of motivation is concerned with why behavior occurs. Homeostasis is the stable internal state that an organism is motivated to maintain. Hunger is in part a homeostatic motive.

2 Blood glucose availability is an important short-term signal for hunger and satiety. Receptors in the stomach can detect the presence of nutrients in the stomach. The hypothalamus is a critical brain region in hunger and satiety. It is probably involved in regulation of fat deposits, a long-term signal for hunger and satiety.

3 Sexual motivation is also biologically based, but it is not a homeostatic motive. A minimum level of sex hormones seems to be necessary for sexual motivation and behavior in humans, but the relationship between hormones and sexual behavior is not very strong in humans. Sexual behavior is strongly affected by culture and learning.

4 Some motives are learned, such as the achievement motive. People with a high need for achievement tend to prefer tasks of intermediate difficulty and have greater pride in accomplishment and less fear of failing than people with a low need for achievement.

5 Setting goals for yourself is one way to regulate your own behavior. Your internal standards for judging your own performance stem from your observations of your own performance, your observation of others, what people have told you you're capable of, and your own emotional reaction to situations. The goals you pursue create the framework within which you interpret and react to events.

6 In general, biologically based motives are satisfied before motives such as need for achievement. However, for any one person in a particular situation, any motive can dominate and inhibit all other motives, even biologically based motives. Giving an external reward can interfere with performance rather than aid it if the behavior is intrinsically motivated (rewarding for its own sake).

7 Facial expressions and physiological reactions indicate emotion. There seems to be a genetic basis for facial expressions that are produced by emotion. There is great similarity in emotional expressions among different cultures and animals. All infants, including those born blind, show the same emotional expressions at about the same age. Data have shown that feedback from facial expressions intensifies emotional experience.

8 In emotional arousal, reactions associated with the sympathetic nervous system dominate. These include acceleration of heart rate, heightened blood pressure, inhibition of salivation, pupil dilation, constriction of blood vessels in the periphery of the body, and inhibition of digestive processes.

9 The James-Lange theory of emotion suggested that the subjective experience of emotion is produced by sensing the body's reaction to something perceived as emotion-producing. But while feedback from autonomic arousal can intensify emotional experience, peripheral physiological arousal does not seem necessary for emotional experience. The Cannon-Bard theory proposed that emotional stimuli affect the thalamus, which then stimulates the autonomic nervous system to produce arousal and the cerebral cortex to produce the subjective emotional experience. The Schachter-Singer two-component hypothesis states that cognitive and situational factors play an important part in determining whether our physiological reaction is interpreted as emotional or nonemotional and in determining the emotion we experience.

KEY TERMS

motivation (p. 494)

homeostasis (p. 495)

drive theory (p. 495)

drive (p. 495)

insulin (p. 496)

blood glucose (p. 496)

LH lesions (p. 496)

VMH lesions (p. 496)

set point (p. 497)

incentive motivation (p. 497)

estrogens (p. 499)

progesterone (p. 499)

androgens (p. 499)

testosterone (p. 499)

activational effects (p. 499)

Coolidge Effect (p. 503)

gender identity (p. 506)

hermaphrodites (p. 506)

transsexual (p. 508)

homosexuals (p. 508)

bisexuals (p. 508)

need for achievement (p. 509)

Thematic Apperception Test (TAT) (p. 509)

intrinsic motivation (p. 512)

extrinsic motivation (p. 512)

self-regulation (p. 513)

self-efficacy (p. 514)

Maslow's hierarchy of motives (p. 515)

emotion (p. 516)

positive affect (p. 516)

negative affect (p. 516)

facial feedback hypothesis (p. 519)

James-Lange theory of emotion (p. 522)

Cannon-Bard theory of emotion (p. 524)

two-component theory of emotion (p. 512)

FOR CRITICAL ANALYSIS

1 The words *motivation* and *emotion* have a common Latin derivation—*emovere*, ("to be moved"). Using information from the chapter, describe some relationships you see between motivation and emotion.

2 Some differences between sex and hunger as motives are mentioned in the chapter. What similarities are there between these motives?

3 Describe how experience with goal setting in the laboratory might be used to increase need for achievement.

4 Some have suggested that intense emotional experience can only be attained with negative emotions. What do you think of this idea? How could you determine if this is so?

5 Only a few motives and emotions were discussed in this chapter. Pick a motive that is not discussed in the text and analyze its properties. Do the same for an emotion not discussed in the text.

SUGGESTED READINGS

CARLSON, J. G. & HATFIELD, E. (1992) *The psychology of emotion*. Fort Worth: Harcourt Brace Jovanovich. A good overview of research on emotion, covering much of the material covered in this chapter in greater depth.

EKMAN, P. (1973). *Darwin and facial expression: A century of research in review*. New York: Academic Press. A study of the similarity of emotional expression in children, adults, and infrahuman species. Some of Darwin's original notes and drawings are included.

MASTERS, W. H., JOHNSON, V. E., & KOLODNY, R. C. (1985). *Human sexuality* (2nd ed.). Boston: Little, Brown. Covers many facets of human sexuality, written by leading researchers in the field.

McCLELLAND, D. C. (1985). *Human motivation*. Glenview, IL: Scott, Foresman. An in-depth coverage of the approach to motivation through measuring individual differences, as exemplified in this chapter by the study of need for achievement.

MONEY, J., & EHRHARDT, A. A. (1972). *Man & woman, boy & girl*. Baltimore: Johns Hopkins University Press. A fascinating description of the work of John Money and associates with hermaphrodites.

MOOK, D. G. (1987). *Motivation: The organization of action*. New York: Nortone. An introductory textbook giving an overview of the field of motivation. Both human and animal data are covered in an extremely readable and enjoyable fashion.

REEVE, J. (1992) *Understanding motivation and emotion*. Fort Worth: Harcourt Brace Jovanovich. An excellent overview of both motivation and emotion, with an emphasis on human motivation.

WEINER, B. (1986). *An attributional theory of motivation and emotion*. New York: Springer-Verlag. A theory of motivation and emotion stressing that the tendency to look for causation is fundamental to human motivation.

PSYCHOLOGY ON THE INTERNET

Answers to Your Questions About Sexual Orientation and Homosexuality
(http://www.apa.org/pubinfo/orient.html)

This document, produced by the American Psychological Association, provides answers to such questions as: What is sexual orientation? What causes a person to have a particular sexual orientation? Can therapy change sexual orientation?

The following sites provide additional information and resources related to gender identity, homosexuality, and bisexuality:

http://www.cyberspaces.com/outproud/

http://www.gasou.edu/psychweb/resource/bytopic.htm#sexuality

Employee Motivation and Empowerment
(http://www.fed.org/fed/motivation/)

This home page presents guidelines for helping managers motivate their employees to perform at a higher level. Discussion focuses on the effectiveness of incentive programs in general and the effectiveness of different types of rewards (e.g., cash bonuses and recognition) in motivating employees.

Berkeley Psychophysiology Laboratory
(http://violet.berkeley.edu/~lorenmc/bpl.html)

Researchers at the Berkeley Psychophysiology Laboratory "study human emotion by examining the subjective experience of emotion, emotional behavior, and physiological reactivity to emotional stimuli." This home page contains an overview of research currently being conducted in this laboratory and links to laboratories in which similar research is being conducted.

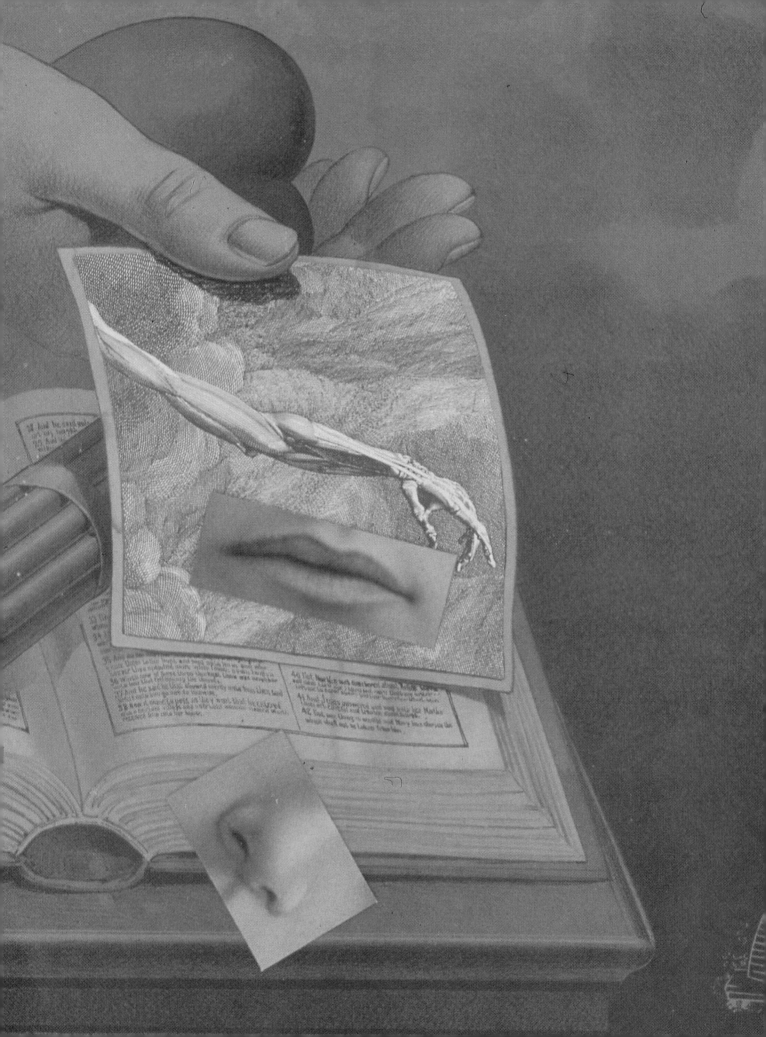

STRESS and HEALTH

533

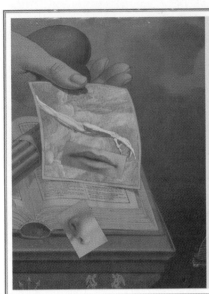

BIOLOGICAL THEME
Can your psychological reaction to events produce disease? Is your body weight genetically determined?

LEARNING THEME
How can you learn to reduce stress?

COGNITIVE THEME
Does the way you interpret events affect your health?

DEVELOPMENTAL THEME
Do the normal changes occuring with age produce stress? If so, how can this stress be reduced?

SOCIOCULTURAL THEME
Do cultural factors affect health and disease?

Having finally located your car in the crowded parking lot, you put it in reverse and back quickly from your spot. Unfortunately, so does the person directly behind you. You both slam on the brakes and ease around each other, glowering and muttering. After waiting in a long line, you finally make it to the stoplight. A car full of tough-looking teenagers pulls up next to you. As the light changes, one casually flicks a cigarette directly at your car. Annoyed, you accelerate, but come up behind an elderly lady going 20 mph in a 40 mph zone. After you endure her dawdling for 5 minutes, she finally signals left and turns right, almost smashing into you as you speed around her. Furious, you slam your foot onto the accelerator and your car rockets ahead. A child suddenly appears between two parked cars, and desperately braking, you narrowly avert an accident.

If you have never experienced this precise scenario, you have probably endured others like it. What you may not realize, however, is that the tension and anxiety associated with such events can be detrimental to your health. The relationship between stress and health is one of the main topics in a relatively new branch of psychology called health psychology. **Health psychology** is a growing field concerned with the way psychology can contribute to the promotion and maintenance of health. Health psychologists are interested in the perception and management of pain, reduction of the distress caused by medical procedures, and techniques that would help people comply with medical advice. They are also concerned with how to promote health-related behavior such as eating a healthy diet and exercising. In general, health psychologists study how behavior can produce and prevent disease, (Schaeffer & Baum, 1989).

Until recently, the dominant view was that bacteria and viruses were the primary causes of illness. Because these agents of disease are impossible to avoid, this view implies that illness is largely outside of our control. While some diseases are certainly caused by bacteria and viruses, the major health problems today are the chronic diseases. In 1900, three of the four leading causes of death were pneumonia, influenza, and tuberculosis. By 1988, three of the leading causes of death were heart disease, stroke, and cancer (Brannon & Feist, 1992). Pneumonia, influenza, and tuberculosis are largely outside of our control, but our behavior heavily influences our risk of heart disease, stroke, and cancer. Some behaviors, (such as smoking, taking drugs, and eating too much) increase the chances of disease, while other behaviors, such as exercising and reducing cholesterol levels through healthy eating, may actually lower the risk of disease. Health psychologists study this relationship between behavior and health, and one important link they have observed is the link between stress and disease.

Sources of Stress

The term *stress* is generally used to reflect negative reactions to the environment. In psychology, **stress** is a reaction to a perceived threat to an individual's physical or psychological well-being as well as the feeling of being unable to deal with the threat (Glass, 1977; Sarason & Spielberger, 1979). The stress reaction produces physiological effects that can be dangerous to our health.

The list of things that bring on stress varies widely from individual to individual. Some events, such as the death of a loved one or a divorce, cause stress for almost everyone, but for most events, the context and appraisal of the event determine whether stress is experienced. Your boyfriend says that he no longer wants to see you. Stressful? Maybe. But maybe not, if you were just about to tell him you no longer wanted to see him. Retirement threatens self-esteem and induces great stress in some people; in others it presents a welcome opportunity to try new things. Keeping the importance of an individual's perceptions in mind, we will consider the most common sources of stress.

LIFE CHANGES

One general source of stress is a major change or adjustment in life, such as starting college, beginning a new job, moving to a new city, or suffering a death in the family. Any change in life requiring adaptation to new circumstances can cause stress, whether or not the change has beneficial effects. A new job can mean greater pay, for example, but it still requires some adjustment that can be stressful. In general, the greater the degree of change and adaptation, the greater the stress will be.

Any changes can produce stress. When asked to rate events for their seriousness both adolescent and adult raters placed marriage in the top ten.

The effects of life change have been carefully analyzed by Thomas Holmes and Richard Rahe (1967), who developed the Social Readjustment Rating Scale to measure the impact of 43 major life events. They asked 394 men and women of different ages and backgrounds to rate the amount of readjustment required by each life event. Using marriage as a benchmark, they posed the following questions about each event: Is this event indicative of more or less readjustment than marriage? Would the readjustment take longer or shorter to accomplish? If the event caused greater adjustment, it was assigned a proportionally higher value than marriage; if less severe, a lower value. The events were then ranked according to a 100-point scale, as shown in Table 13.1. On this scale marriage was assigned a middle value, 50 points. As you can see, death of a spouse was considered the most serious event, followed by divorce and marital separation.

Although life changes take place at all ages, the frequency of each differs at various ages. Illness and death in the family, for example, become more frequent as one grows older. At some time, however, most people will experience most of the stress-producing life changes. The most important fact about Table 13.1 is that high scores—totaling 300 or more for events in the past two years—are related to increased frequency of ailments and accidents (Rahe, 1974). For example, football players are more likely to suffer an injury during a game if their scores are over 300 on the life change scale.

TABLE 13.1
Ranking and Item Scale Scores from the Social Readjustment Rating Scale

LIFE EVENT	ADULT GROUP		ADOLESCENT GROUP	
	RANK GIVEN EVENT	LIFE CHANGE SCORE	RANK GIVEN EVENT	LIFE CHANGE SCORE
Death of Spouse	1	100	1	69
Divorce	2	73	2	60
Marital Separation	3	65	3	55
Jail term	4	63	8	50
Death of a close family member	5	63	4	50
Major personal injury or illness	6	53	6	50
Marriage	7	50	9	50
Fired from work	8	47	7	50
Marital reconciliation	9	45	10	47
Retirement	10	45	11	46
Major change in family member's health	11	44	16	44
Pregnancy	12	40	13	45
Sex difficulties	13	39	5	51
Gain of a new family member	14	39	17	43
Business readjustment	15	39	15	44
Change in financial state	16	38	14	44
Death of a close friend	17	37	12	46
Change to a different line of work	18	36	21	38
Change in number of marital arguments	19	35	19	41
Mortgage or loan over $10,000	20	31	18	41
Foreclosure of mortgage or loan	21	30	23	36
Change in responsibilities at work	22	29	20	38
Son or daughter leaving home	23	29	25	34
Trouble with in-laws	24	29	22	36
Outstanding personal achievement	25	28	28	31
Wife begins or stops work	26	26	27	32
Begin or end school	27	26	26	34
Change in living conditions	28	25	24	35
Revision of personal habits	29	24	35	26
Trouble with boss	30	23	33	26
Change in work hours or conditions	31	20	29	30
Change in residence	32	20	30	28
Change in schools	33	20	34	26
Change in recreation	34	19	36	26
Change in church activities	35	19	38	21
Change in social activities	36	18	32	28
Mortgage or loan less than $10,000	37	17	31	28
Change in sleeping habits	38	16	41	18
Change in number of family get-togethers	39	15	37	22
Change in eating habits	40	15	40	18
Vacation	41	13	39	19
Christmas	42	12	42	16
Minor violations of the law	43	11	43	12

Adult and adolescent subjects rated the seriousness of various life events. The life change score indicates degree of seriousness of the change.

SOURCE: Rahe & Holmes, 1971.

Other data also show a relationship between stress and psychological and physical problems. For example, divorced or separated people have a higher rate of admittance to psychiatric facilities than married or never-married people (Redick & Johnson, 1974). Moreover, suicide, homicide, and death from certain diseases are more common among the maritally disrupted than among the married (Kitagawa & Hauser, 1973). One interpretation is that the stress of divorce or separation may produce these problems. But can you think of an alternative hypothesis? Perhaps people with physical or emotional disorders are less likely than the healthy to marry and are more likely to be divorced.

Some theorists suggest that modern society is more stressful than past eras because of the large number and rapid pace of changes we now endure. More people change homes now than ever before, with more than 36 million Americans moving in a single year. More and more people switch jobs. Changing physical location, relationships, and employment all involve stress. Divorce is more frequent than in previous eras. The American divorce rate is the world's highest, and its importance is reflected in Table 13.1 by its number 2 ranking. But a marriage that isn't working can also create stress, so there may be less stress from divorce than from staying together. Whether the stress of modern life is greater or less than the stress experienced in the supposedly good old days is difficult to judge, but it does seem that the sources of stress today differ from those of the past. Some stress-producing events, such as moving and divorce, now come more frequently, while illness and early death of a parent or spouse occur less often. Some stress-producing physical discomforts are less common now; for example, air conditioning has reduced the stress produced by heat.

Irwin G. Sarason and his colleagues modified the Holmes-Rahe scale by having subjects rate the severity of the impact of each relevant event (Sarason & Spielberger, 1979). They found that subjects believed that positive life changes were considerably less stressful than negative changes. Life changes also may not have inevitable effects; other variables may moderate their impact. To predict whether life change will be related to illness in an individual, it is necessary to know the context of the change and how the individual appraises and copes with it.

MINOR ANNOYANCES

The example given at the beginning of the chapter of a stressful series of events did not involve a major life change, just the customary irritations that can occur in a normal day. Work by Richard Lazarus (1981) suggests that the minor hassles, or annoyances, of everyday life may influence our psychological and physical health more than the major life changes on the Holmes-Rahe scale. Lazarus created a scale to measure the intensity and frequency of hassles by asking white middle-class men and women what they considered their most common annoyances. Samples of items on this scale included "You have had to care for a pet," "You have had sexual problems other than those resulting from physical problems," "You are concerned about your use of alcohol," and "You have had to plan meals." Rated the top three were concerns about weight, about health of a family member, and about economic conditions such as inflation and recession. Among college students, the top three were anxiety over wasting time, anxiety over meeting high standards, and loneliness. For more than a year, physical and mental health (measured by questionnaires) were reported to be poorer when these and other hassles had been frequent and intense (Lazarus, 1981). Major life changes in the 2½ years preceding the measurement also were determined to have

Recent work by Richard Lazarus suggests that the stress produced by the minor hassles of everyday life also has detrimental effects on psychological and physical health.

effects, so both major life changes and minor everyday problems seem to produce stress.

Emphasizing minor hassles rather than major life events as a source of stress helps explain some puzzling data. For example, as people grow older they experience fewer and fewer major "events" in their lives (Lazarus & DeLongis, 1983), yet they do not experience less stress. Major life events, Lazarus and his colleagues believe, do not necessarily produce stress; rather, their effect depends on an individual's appraisal of an event. If a person construes an event to be harmful, threatening, or challenging, then the effect is one of stress. If the event is seen as benign or irrelevant, little or no stress results. Also, Lazarus and DeLongis suggest that the traditional life events approach to stress is too narrow, because the list of major life events excludes many important experiences, such as loneliness, limited energy, final exams, reaching the plateau of one's career, or being passed over for a promotion. Lazarus suggests that while major life change may have a long-term impact, on health, the short-term effects of minor hassles may be even more important. In part, major life changes may indirectly affect psychological and physical health by bringing about minor hassles that can be a source of stress. For example, divorce may mean having to learn to cook for oneself.

THE ROLE OF AFFECT

Part of the measured relationship between stress and disease may be due to an important individual difference (Watson & Pennebaker, 1989). Typical measures of stress require people to judge how they feel about life's annoyances and problems. Typical measures of health require people to judge how well they are feeling and if they have physical complaints. The fact that these scores are correlated leads to the conclusion that increased stress causes disease. But Watson and Pennebaker (1989) observed that another factor may be mixed into the correlation: people's negative affect, or how unhappy they are in general. Recall from Chapter 12 that Watson and Tellegen (1985) identified two independent dimensions of mood: positive affect (energy, enthusiasm, and happiness) and negative affect (hostility, distress, and fear). Could it be that negative affect underlies the correlation between stress and illness? That is, do people who complain a lot about life's annoyances (and therefore score high on the stress scales) also complain more about physical annoyances? Indeed, this is just what Watson and Pennebaker (1989) found. People who score high on measures of negative affect (more colloquially, people who complain about everything) also score high on stress scales and on scales measuring physical complaints. When the researchers statistically removed the general factor of negative affect, there was still a relation between stress and physical complaints, but it was much weaker.

CHRONIC DISTRESS

Chronic, or relatively long-term, unpleasantness can prove stressful. Environmental stress, such as the bombardment of noise in urban areas, is an example of this type of problem. Another example is occupational stress. Work and responsibility do not induce stress unless they exceed our capacity to control the situation: It is our individual perception of how well we can deal with the situation that counts. However, some occupations involve so much tension that almost everyone engaged in them experiences a great deal of stress. Air-traffic controllers, for example, are keyed up almost constantly, and they have a very high incidence of peptic ulcers and hypertension (Glass, 1977).

Some situations are so stressful that they would cause anyone to experience stress. Other situations produce different reactions in different people and so are not stressful for all. The occupation of firefighter is a highly stressful one.

CONFLICT

Unresolved conflict is a major source of stress. Conflict is often related to divorce and other life changes. But even without a major life change, many of the things people desire prove to be incompatible. For example, you may want to be thin but also to eat a lot. Kurt Lewin (1935) originally described different types of conflict, and Neal Miller (1959) made a detailed analysis of three of them: approach-approach conflict, avoidance-avoidance conflict, and approach-avoidance conflict. Because unresolved conflict produces stress, resolution of conflict eliminates stress. It is important, then, to understand the varieties of conflict and the difficulty involved in resolving each type.

Approach-Approach Conflict. The first type of conflict is the easiest to resolve: a conflict between two desirable goals, termed an **approach-approach conflict.** Should I have the chocolate or the vanilla ice cream? Buy the blue or the green suit? Go swimming or play tennis? This conflict is easy to resolve. Anything that increases the desirability of either goal slightly will pull a person toward that goal and resolve the conflict in its favor.

Avoidance-Avoidance Conflict. The second kind of conflict, **avoidance-avoidance conflict,** occurs between two undesirable things. You don't want to study for a test, but you don't want to do badly on it either. To resolve an avoidance-avoidance conflict, some other factor usually must present itself, determining for you in favor of one goal—a friend comes in and says, "Let's study together"—or the other—the friend says, "Let's go get a pizza." Adding an approach element to either goal resolves the conflict in favor of that goal. This type of conflict takes longer to resolve than an approach-approach conflict.

Approach-Avoidance Conflict. The **approach-avoidance conflict** describes the most common dilemma: conflict involving a single goal for which there is both a tendency to approach and a tendency to avoid. You may want dessert, but not want to get fat; enjoy drinking, but not want to suffer a hangover; want to live in an exciting big city, but also want to avoid crime and noise. Often the conflict is a *double* approach-avoidance conflict—a conflict between two goals, both of which have advantages and disadvantages.

Research on approach-avoidance conflicts has shown that as we get closer to a goal, its disadvantages begin to outweigh its advantages. Imagine that you want to telephone somebody for a first date. You worry that you may get a "no thanks." You are in conflict—to call or not to call. Preparing to call may be easy, but as you get closer to making the call, it will become harder and harder to do. If fear of rejection is very strong, you may never do it.

If conflict cannot be resolved, stress develops. In animals, unresolved approach-avoidance conflict produces ulcers (Lovibond, 1969; Sawrey, Conger, & Turrell, 1956) as does unresolved avoidance-avoidance conflict (Weiss, 1971b). As we will see later, there is a clear relationship between stress and disease, whether the stress is produced by unresolved conflict or by other means.

Effects of Stress

There are predictable physiological reactions associated with stress, and these reactions, in turn, produce a predisposition to disease. Thus, there is a relationship between the physiological component of stress and physical disease. This means that there is a relationship between mental events, such as appraisal of events, and physical disease. Your mind can indeed affect your body.

THE PHYSIOLOGICAL REACTION

When we experience stress, physiological reactions occur in a pattern called a *stress reaction*. Thus, the stress reaction refers to the physiological component of the total stress response. The stress reaction is an innate reaction triggered by a wide variety of stressors, including burns, surgery, bone fractures, loud noises, temperature extremes, food deprivation, fear, anxiety, crowding, and sometimes exposure to unfamiliar situations (Levi & Kagan, 1980). The immediate physiological reaction to stress parallels the physiological reaction to emotion. Initially, autonomic arousal increases the rate and strength of the heartbeat, raises blood pressure, accelerates respiration, increases muscle tension, and lowers skin resistance. The hypothalamus responds to stress by initiating activity in the endocrine system to secrete corticotropin-releasing factor (CRF), which stimulates the pituitary gland. The pituitary, in turn, secretes adreno-corticotropic hormone (ACTH) about 10 seconds after a stressful event. ACTH stimulates the release of fatty acids and the utilization of glucose, which are important in providing energy for dealing with a stressor. In addition, ACTH stimulates the adrenal cortex (the outermost portion of the adrenal gland), which then secretes glucocorticoid hormones, whose effects are discussed shortly. These responses, initially described by Hans Selye (1956), are important in the body's reaction to long-term stress.

In 1953, Selye, studying the effects of injecting hormones into rats, found that the rats suffered ulcers, enlarged adrenal glands, and shrunken thymus and lymph nodes. The results were the same for different mixtures of hormones (regardless of their concentration) and for simple irritants as well. Selye hypothesized that any stress had the same effect on an organism. This idea gained support when other stressors, such as exposure to severe cold, produced the same results. Selye called this stress syndrome the **general adaptation syndrome (GAS),** a nonspecific bodily reaction common to all stress. He believed, and his view is now widely accepted, that any situation may prove stressful if an organism cannot adapt to it.

According to Selye, there are three stages to the general adaptation syndrome (see Figure 13.1). The first stage is the *alarm reaction*, characterized by a drop in bodily resistance to the stress. Specifically, the autonomic nervous system stimulates the adrenal medulla, which secretes norepinephrine and epinephrine. Meanwhile, the pituitary begins to secrete ACTH, which stimulates the adrenal cortex to release glucocortoids. If the initial stress is too severe, an organism may die during this stage.

If the animal doesn't die, the second stage, the *resistance stage*, begins. In this stage, the pituitary continues to secrete ACTH, which goes on stimulating the adrenal cortex to secrete glucocorticoids, important in resistance to stress. The glucocorticoid hormones stimulate the conversion of fats and proteins to sugars, providing energy to deal with the stressor. They also inhibit ACTH release. Simultaneously, though, these hormones delay the growth of new tissue around a wound, inhibit formation of antibodies, and decrease the formation of white blood cells—the very reactions your body uses to prevent infection and promote healing. Thus, in this phase the organism shows *increased* susceptibility to disease and injury.

The adrenal glands actually expand in size in the resistance stage, reflecting their heightened activity. During this phase, resistance to the specific stress increases, and accordingly, the generalized response disappears. After a few days of exposure to stress, experimental animals appear to adapt. The adrenal glands return to normal size and

Hans Selye initally described the body's reaction to stress, which he hypothesized was the same regardless of the source of stress.

FIGURE 13.1
The General Adaption Syndrome

This graph shows resistance to stress as the stress continues over time. The first reaction is one of alarm. Then resistance to the original stress increases while resistance to other stresses decreases (stage of resistance). If the original stress continues, however, the body's resistance to all stress will ultimately decrease (stage of exhaustion).

SOURCE: Selye, 1956

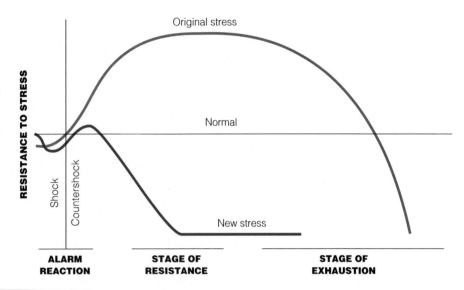

begin to renew their supply of steroids. Things may appear to be normal, but they are not. If a second stress is introduced at this point, death can occur, indicating that general resistance is low despite increased specific resistance to original stress. Selye was quite surprised by this in his early work, because an animal could die quite unexpectedly from an apparently mild stress if its body were in the resistance stage. Selye (1974) noted that many stress-related diseases develop in the resistance stage. Some may relate to the effects of the glucocorticoid hormones. Another aspect of the resistance stage is the suppression of many of the bodily functions related to sexual behavior and reproduction. In males, sperm production drops, as does secretion of male sex hormones. In females, the menstrual cycle is disrupted or suppressed. Lessened sexual interest is a well-known psychological effect of stress as well.

If the specific stress continues, the body's ability to contain it and to resist other stresses ultimately collapses and the *exhaustion stage* sets in. Under prolonged stress, then, bodily mechanisms are geared to defend the body. The mechanisms also prepare for corresponding reductions in the activities promoting reproduction and an associated weakening of resistance to disease and infection. This pattern manifests itself regardless of the source of stress: external, such as extreme cold; internal, such as illness or surgery; or emotional, involving frustration, conflict, or fear. As you can see, Selye's general adaptation syndrome traces the reasons for the relationship between stress and disease and explains when the dangers of stress are the greatest.

STRESS AND DISEASE

The evidence is clear that thoughts, beliefs, and emotions can have a major impact on physical health. Persons experiencing recent stressful life events are at greater risk for gastrointestinal disorders, such as ulcers (Harris, 1991). (You may recall that research animals subjected to unresolved conflict also develop ulcers). Stressed humans also show greater susceptibility to heart attacks (Theorell, 1974) and infectious agents (e.g., Cohen, Tyrrel, & Smith, 1993). Moreover, perceptions of stress are linked to heart disease (Tofler et al., 1990), stroke (Harmsen et al., 1990), and infectious disease (Cohen et al., 1993). Cancer, too, has been found to be related to stress (Sklar & Anisman, 1981).

The strongest evidence links stress to heart disease and ulcers, although why one person develops ulcers and another heart disease from stress remains unclear. Perhaps the organ that stress affects and the illness it produces depend on individual predispositions. Sickness may develop in the weakest area of the body. Thus, someone with a high natural rate of gastric secretion may be predisposed to peptic ulcers, while another who has a natural high cholesterol level may be predisposed to stress-produced coronary disease.

Stress and the Immune System.   A discovery made in 1974 by Robert Ader was crucial in the development of research connecting psychological stress to immune system functions. The **immune system** recognizes and destroys foreign substances in the body, including agents of disease (bacteria and viruses) and cancer cells. How exactly this is done is not understood in detail, but we know that certain types of blood cells perform important functions in the immune system, including the production of antibodies. Ader and his colleagues gave rats saccharin-flavored water followed by a drug that suppressed the immune system. Later, the saccharin water alone led to a decrease in immune function. The rats, through classical conditioning (see Chapter 6), had learned to respond to the saccharin water with a drop in immune function. This finding was important because it showed that the brain can influence the immune system. Many findings now support the basic principle that psychological distress can suppress the immune system enough to increase the risk of physical illness. In fact, studies measuring immune system functioning in humans have shown a decrease in immune function with a variety of stressful circumstances, including recent death of a spouse (Schleifer et al., 1984), overall level of stress from major life events (Greene et al., 1978), depression (Monjan, 1984), and even examinations (McClelland, Ross, & Patel, 1985). Interpersonal conflict is also a source of stress. Marriage can be one of life's biggest sources of stress, and women seem to be more affected by this. Slightly negative or hostile behavior from a spouse for just 30 minutes can adversely affect the immune system of both spouses, with women's changes larger than men's (Kiecolt-Glaser, in press). Women may take the conflict more seriously and thus experience more stress, or their immune systems may be more reactive to social stress.

Because, as we discussed previously, minor stressors may be more strongly correlated with subsequent health than are major life events (Delongis et al., 1982; Jandorf et al., 1986), you should not be surprised to learn that immune system functioning also varies with minor life events. Stone and colleagues, (1987) measured daily mood and immune system functioning for eight consecutive weeks, three times per week. They measured positive and negative mood on two scales (because these have been shown to be independent, as we discussed earlier) using an adjective checklist. There were significantly lower levels of antibody secretion (reflecting decreased immune system functioning) on high-negative mood days and significantly more antibody on high-positive mood days. This finding is interesting, because many studies show that negative, or undesirable, events are much more important, at least for health, than are positive, or desirable, events. If being in a good mood is related to positive events, then this study shows that positive events can actually improve immune system functioning and thus health. The lesson from this is to put on a happy face. Recall from Chapter 12 that smiling can indeed produce feelings of happiness; and here we have learned that feelings of happiness can improve health. Thus, smiling and being cheery will make you happier *and* healthier.

Stress and Heart Disease.   Researchers see a connection between stress and coronary artery disease in part because the two often occur together. Stressful events

The workplace and the computer can be a source of chronic stress.

also produce physiological effects, such as elevated serum cholesterol level, an important risk factor for coronary artery disease (Friedman, 1969). But remember, stress is a reaction, and individuals differ in how they react to events. Some people have a pattern of behavior that makes them more likely to suffer heart disease. This coronary-prone behavior pattern has been described by Friedman (1969) as a constant struggle to achieve poorly defined goals in the shortest possible time. People who behave this way are referred to as **Type A.** Calm, serene, relaxed people are called **Type B.**

A questionnaire like the sample shown in Table 13.2 can help distinguish between Type A and Type B individuals. Of course, classification is based on a continuum; whether you are Type A or Type B depends on how many characteristics of each type you possess. More specifically, people with a Type A disposition behave aggressively and competitively, speak rapidly, and exhibit hostility and anger. When evaluated properly, people classified as having Type A personalities are more likely to have or to develop coronary heart disease than are Type B individuals (those with an absence of the Type A characteristics). In 1985, the National Institutes of Health's Review Panel on Coronary Prone Behavior and Coronary Heart Disease concluded:

> "The available body of scientific evidence demonstrates that Type A behavior is associated with an increased risk of clinically apparent CHD (coronary heart disease) in employed middle-aged U. S. citizens. This increased risk is greater than that imposed by age, elevated levels of systolic blood pressure, serum cholesterol, and smoking. (p. 1200)

Much debate surrounds the best way to measure Type A characteristics. At this time, most researchers favor a structured interview in which an individual's actual behaviors are observed and his or her answers to specific questions analyzed. The interview procedure is quite time consuming, however, so many questionnaire techniques have been developed to try to define Type A more efficiently. Unfortunately, classification based on questionnaires is not a good predictor of coronary heart disease, and no one questionnaire is generally agreed upon.

Recently, much research has been aimed at pinpointing the critical components of the overall Type A complex that precipitate coronary heart disease. Are all the identified factors important, or only some? In fact, the evidence points to the dimension of hostility and anger as a prime indicator, with time urgency also being important (Booth-Kewley & Friedman, 1988; Williams, 1988; Wright, 1988). For a more lengthy discussion of this topic, see the Controversy box "Is Anger Fatal?" and "Psychology in Our Times: Personality and Health," on page 596 in Chapter 14.

TABLE 13.2

Sample Questionnaire Items Measuring the Tendency Toward Type A or Type B Behavior in College Students

1. "Has your spouse or some friend ever told you that you eat too fast?" A pattern A response is often "yes, often"; pattern B responses are "yes, once or twice" or "no, no one has told me this."
2. "Do you maintain a regular study schedule during vacations such as Thanksgiving, Christmas, and Easter?" Here "yes" is a pattern A answer; "no" and "sometimes" are B answers.
3. "How would your spouse (or closest friend) rate you?" Pattern A responses are "definitely hard-driving and competitive" and "probably hard-driving and competitive"; B responses are "probably relaxed and easygoing" and "definitely relaxed and easygoing."
4. "How would your spouse (or best friend) rate your general level of activity?" An A response is "too active, needs to slow down"; B responses are "too slow, should be more active" and "about average, is busy most of the time."

SOURCE: Glass, 1977.

IS ANGER FATAL?

Hostility is one of the ways in which Type A and Type B personalities differ and hostility seems to be an excellent predictor of heart disease. (See Chapter 14 for other ways in which Type A and Type B personalities differ that could account for the difference in incidence of heart disease.) Hostility has been shown to increase the risk of heart disease fourfold (Barefoot, Dahlstrom, & Williams, 1983). Controlling for cigarette smoking, diastolic blood pressure, and serum cholesterol, Dembrowsky and colleagues (1989) found that among men under age 47, greater hostility increased the risk of heart disease.

Why would hostility increase heart disease? One explanation is that hostile people experience more stress: They are likely to spend most of each day angry at something—a late elevator, a slow driver in front of them, their spouse, their coworker. Hostile people may also show a greater physiological

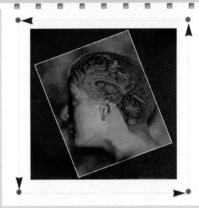

stress response, and this is particularly true of those who do not express their anger. Stress hormones can build up, and blood pressure can rise from constant tension. Consistent with this idea, the strongest relationship to heart disease has been found for hostile people who do not express their anger. Suppressed anger has been shown to produce a fivefold risk of death (Julius et al.,1986) and to relate more strongly

to heart disease than any other element of hostility (MacDougall et al., 1985).

The complicating factor in this research is that not all researchers have obtained a relationship between hostility and heart disease. One well-controlled study of 1,400 men who had been college freshmen in Minnesota in 1953 found absolutely no relationship between hostility as measured in 1953 and heart disease in the subsequent 33 years (Hearn et al., 1989). Different measures of hostility have been used in different studies which could explain some of the discrepancies. Also the effects of hostility may be mediated by effects on something else, the most likely candidate being blood pressure. Hostility may produce high blood pressure in some people and lead to heart disease in this manner (Barefoot et al., 1991).

HOSTILITY, ANGER, AND AGGRESSION

Research on the Type A personality has shown that people differ in how much anger and hostility they experience and express and that hostile people who fail to express their anger have the highest risk of heart disease. **Aggression,** behavior intended to cause harm, is one way that anger and hostility can be expressed. What leads some people to act aggressively?

One factor is learning. People can learn to express anger and to behave so as to hurt others. Aggression can occur because it is successful in attaining other ends, a behavior called *instrumental aggression*. People can learn to act aggressively if they are reinforced for it; for example, a man who fights another over a woman and wins has been reinforced for fighting. But is all aggression learned instrumentally? Many theorists say no and suggest that there is an innate biological urge: Some people may be biologically predisposed to act aggressively.

Biological Basis of Aggression. The best-known theories of biologically based aggression are the psychoanalytic theory of Sigmund Freud and the evolutionary theories of ethologists and sociobiologists such as Konrad Lorenz (1966) and Edward O. Wilson (1975).

According to Freud (1930/1962), aggressive instincts are lodged deep in the unconscious id (see Chapter 14) and are constantly being generated within the body. These impulses, kept from entering consciousness by the superego (see Chapter 14), nevertheless greatly influence behavior. Typically, the impulses are released in small amounts and in socially acceptable ways. One implication of Freudian theory is that if

At the Crabbiness Research Institute

the aggressive energy lodged within is not allowed reasonable expression, it will eventually overflow into violent behavior. The evidence for this part of the psychoanalytic perspective, however, is not very strong.

In recent years, theorists have looked at aggression from an evolutionary perspective. Nobel Prize–winning ethologist Konrad Lorenz (1966) carried out many observational studies of aggression in animals and argued that aggression is part of our inheritance, describing it as "an essential part of the life-preserving organization of instincts." Aggression can be a valuable asset in hunting, defense of territories, and competition among males for females (Wilson, 1975). Resources, food, mates, and shelter, are necessary to life and to reproductive success. If resources are in short supply, then characteristics resulting in the acquisition of resources will be favored in the course of evolution.

Several ecological circumstances favor aggression. Aggression often occurs during the acquisition and defense of resources. For example, many birds set up territories where they nest, rear young, and gather food. Aggression occurs in defense of these territories (Marler, 1976). Aggression also often occurs during acquisition and protection of a mate. Bucks may attack other bucks who possess does (e.g., Clutton-Brock et al., 1979). This type of behavior also occurs in humans, as exemplified by attacks of one village on another to kidnap women among the Yanomamo Indians of Venezuela (Chagnon, 1988). Violence also occurs in protection of one's mate. According to Daly and Wilson (1988), a large fraction of the murders in the United States are committed by a man who concludes that his girlfriend or wife may be discontinuing their relationship or taking up with another man.

These cases all show that aggression can be adaptive and thus may have evolved. In fact, selective breeding experiments have shown directly that there is a genetic basis for aggressive behavior. (See Chapter 2 for a review of the theory of evolution and selective breeding experiments.) For example, Ebert (1983) began with a population of house mice and bred the most aggressive females with the brothers of other aggressive females and bred nonaggressive females with the brothers of other nonaggressive females. To select aggressive and nonaggressive animals, Ebert chose on the basis of attack of a female intruder. She also included a randomly bred control line. Over generations, two lines of mice were produced, one high in aggression and the other low in aggression. One interesting aspect of this study is that only the specific type of aggression selected for differed between the lines. The lines differed in their attack of intruders (the behavior selected for), but did not differ in their aggression toward pups or in latency to attack and eat a live cricket. This suggests that there are different types of aggression, not a single underlying aggressive trait.

It has been suggested that the primary internal factor related to aggressive behavior is testosterone, a sex hormone found in higher levels in males than in females. In many male mammals, aggression and testosterone both increase in the breeding season. Also, female animals that have been injected with male sex hormones often display increased aggressive behavior (Hines, 1982). In some cases, treating males with testosterone will lead to attack of an intruder by an inexperienced male who would not attack without the testosterone. Data such as these, as well as the observation that males are generally more aggressive than females, have led some researchers to suggest that testosterone causes aggression.

Assuming that there is a biological basis for aggression, what environmental factors produce aggression? Two sources of aggression are pain and frustration, sources of stress for us all, sources of aggression for some.

Pain and Aggression.   Pain produces aggression very reliably. Laboratory studies using primates, rats, and birds have shown that attack is likely when an animal receives a painful stimulus (e.g., Renfrew & Hutchinson, 1983). If two male rats cooped up in a small chamber are shocked electrically or hit, they often fight. Since the aggression occurs with some regularity, emerges without training, and persists even without reward, some psychologists believe that aggression is an unlearned response to pain, a reflexive reaction (Ulrich & Azrin, 1962).

Both men and women react aggressively to pain. Berkowitz, Cochrane, and Embree (1979) had university women sit with one of their hands in a tank of water. For half of them, the water was quite cold (6°C, or 42°F); for the others, it was warmer (18°C, or 63°F). During this time, each subject, by pushing one or two buttons, delivered either rewards (5-cent coins) or punishments (blasts of noise) to a partner she believed she was supervising in the next room. The women whose hands were in the cold water delivered the most "hurt" to their partners. Stimuli other than pain can also sometimes elicit aggressive tendencies. High room temperature, cigarette smoke, and foul odors have all been shown to heighten the punishment given another person (Berkowitz, 1989).

Frustration and Aggression.   The suggestion that frustration might produce aggression was first made more than 50 years ago when Dollard and colleagues (1939) proposed the **frustration-aggression hypothesis,** claiming that frustration always leads to aggression and that aggression is always the result of frustration. Research has demonstrated, however, that frustration does not always lead to aggression; it can, for example, cause depression and lethargy (Seligman, 1975). Likewise, aggression is not always the result of frustration. Not all criminals who engage in aggression do so because they are frustrated: Many do so simply to make money, for example.

Leonard Berkowitz (1962, 1969, 1979, 1989) has proposed a **revised frustration-aggression hypothesis,** stating that frustration leads to anger, not aggression. Anger can easily instigate aggression if there are suitable aggressive cues in the environment. One type of cue is the presence of a weapon. In one experiment to test this hypothesis, Berkowitz and LePage (1967) had a colleague anger their male subjects. The men then were given the opportunity to administer electric shocks, a form of aggression, to the colleague. Significantly more shocks were delivered when aggressive cues—a rifle and a revolver—were nearby than when neutral objects such as badminton rackets were present. Several other researchers have replicated and extended this *weapons effect*. A Belgian experiment (Leyens & Parke, 1975) has demonstrated that even photographs of guns can intensify the attacks that insulted men want to inflict on the tormentor. Pain and other unpleasant stimuli can also stimulate aggression by eliciting anger (Berkowitz, 1979).

Within Berkowitz's theory, one way to prevent aggression is to reduce anger. Indeed, training in anger management is one method that has been used successfully to reduce violent behavior (Howells, 1989). Anger management would also reduce stress and the propensity to heart disease. There is nothing inevitable about the frustration-aggression relationship. Through learning experiences, people can acquire a variety of other responses to frustration, anger, and pain, varying from constructive problem solving to depression and self-anesthetization through drugs. Learning appropriate responses to anger may be beneficial to health as well as to society.

Although, as we have seen, stress can be detrimental to health, a certain amount of stress can be beneficial. One sage remarked that life is a choice between stress and boredom. A theory that explains why people often choose to be stressed is arousal theory.

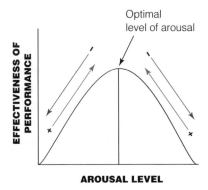

FIGURE 13.2
Basic Outline of Arousal Theory

According to arousal theory, for any particular task, it is always pleasant to move toward the optimal level of arousal and unpleasant to move away from the optimal level. Sources of arousal include drives and incentives, stimulus intensity, novelty, and drugs.

FIGURE 13.3
Bar Pressing for Water by Thirsty Rats

The highest rate of bar pressing occurred for rats that had been without water for 48 hours. They pressed at a higher rate than rats that had been without water for 12, 24, or 36 hours and at a higher rate than rats without water for 60 to 72 hours. The rats were not too weak to press the bar as hours without water increased. These findings support arousal theory, which states that performance should be best when arousal (in this case produced by water deprivation) is neither too high nor too low.

SOURCE: Bélanger & Feldman, 1962.

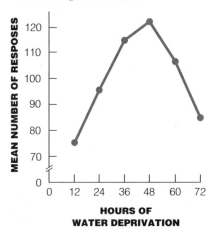

Arousal Theory

Environmental events producing stress also produce arousal. The term **arousal** refers to the body's general level of activity, reflected in several physiological indexes, including muscle tension, galvanic skin response, patterns of electrical activity in the brain, and heart rate (Andrew, 1974; Appley, 1970; Campbell & Misanin, 1969). Generally speaking, arousal can vary along a continuum from deep sleep through normal wakefulness to extreme excitement.

There are four general sources of arousal. First, drives and incentives produce arousal. Thus, hunger, thirst, and pain all contribute to arousal, as do anticipations of pleasure and pain. Second, environmental circumstances affect arousal. In general, the higher the intensity of stimuli, such as noise and bright lights, the higher the arousal level. Color also affects arousal; a blue room is less stimulating than a red room. A third source consists of surprising or novel events. These first three sources of arousal also often produce stress; Hence there is a strong relationship between stress and arousal, and a fourth source is drugs. The caffeine in coffee heightens arousal, for example. Note that motivation and arousal are not the same, nor are stress and arousal the same. Motivation and stress are both sources of arousal.

According to **arousal theory,** performance varies with arousal; generally, performance is best with intermediate levels of arousal (see Figure 13.2). If you are too nervous about an exam, you may do poorly. On the other hand, if you fall asleep during the exam, you may also do poorly. This idea has been substantiated in experiments with animals. In one experiment (Bélanger & Feldman, 1962), rats were trained to press a bar to get water following 24 hours of deprivation. After the rats had learned what to do, experimenters increased the rats' thirst by adding to their waterless hours, which was expected to increase arousal level. While the rats' heart rate continued to increase to the highest level of water deprivation (showing increased arousal), bar pressing did not. The highest rate of activity came after 48 hours of water deprivation; after that point, it decreased with continued water deprivation (see Figure 13.3). This suggests that an arousal level that is too high interferes with performance.

Weakness was not the reason for the animals' lack of bar pressing; other ways of affecting arousal have the same impact. For example, after learning to press the bar, rats have been shocked just before being placed in the box containing the bar. The results obtained as a function of shock intensity (the inverted U-shaped curve) are the same as those obtained as a function of water deprivation. Bar pressing for water improves with increasing shock intensity up to moderate shock, but decreases with more intense shock (Ducharme & Bélanger, 1961). The conclusion is that it helps to be somewhat, but not too highly, aroused.

Many studies have also been done with humans to see if increasing arousal helps or hurts performance. In general, the studies show that increasing arousal helps performance on easy or boring tasks but hurts performance on difficult tasks or those requiring concentration (Berlyne, 1967). For example, the Taylor Manifest Anxiety Scale (representative items of which are listed in Table 13.3) has been used to select subjects high and low in anxiety from introductory psychology classes (Taylor, 1953). Students high in anxiety perform better than those low in anxiety on easy verbal learning tasks; but on difficult tasks, the subjects low in anxiety prove superior. Task difficulty produces arousal, and adding arousal helps a student who is not anxious because this brings the student's arousal level closer to the optimal middle level. However, a student who is already test-anxious just gets worse if the test is difficult; arousal level gets too high, so performance suffers.

TABLE 13.3
**Representative Items from the
Taylor Manifest Anxiety Scale**
The answer in parentheses indicates
anxiety

▪ ▪ ▪ ▪ ▪ ▪ ▪ ▪ ▪ ▪ ▪ ▪

I am easily embarrassed. (True)

I am happy most of the time. (False)

I have nightmares every few nights
(True)

I sweat very easily even on cool days.
(True)

I do not have as many fears as my
friends. (False)

I certainly feel useless at times. (True)

I am very confident of myself (False)

I practically never blush (False)

I have very few headaches (False)

I cannot keep my mind on one thing
(True)

SOURCE: Taylor, 1953.

Before the advent of arousal theory, experimenters had found a similar relationship between optimal levels of motivation and task difficulty. Early psychological experiments led to formulation of the **Yerkes-Dodson law** (Yerkes & Dodson, 1908), which says that there is an optimal degree of *motivation* for any task and that the more difficult the task, the lower the optimal degree. The more recent theory specifies degree of *arousal* as the crucial factor, rather than degree of motivation. Degree of arousal does not mean degree of motivation; motivation is only one source of arousal. Arousal theory thus extends the Yerkes-Dodson law to sources of arousal other than motivation.

Sometimes, arousal *decreases* are pleasant and rewarding: resting quietly, relaxing in a warm tub, sipping a drink of water. At other times, arousal *increases* are rewarding: going to a disco, playing loud music, riding a roller coaster. Arousal theory relates these differences to an individual's arousal level, sleep-wakefulness cycle, and the demands of the task being faced. So if you are a "night person," normally your arousal level is low in the morning; if you are facing a morning exam, which requires a higher arousal level for optimum performance than your normal level at that time of day, you need to take steps to increase your arousal level—perhaps a cup of coffee or a little test anxiety. Individual differences in motives, tastes, and preferences can be attributed in part to differences in arousal level. Loud music can be just the thing for someone whose arousal level is moderately high (awake and alert), but it can be unpleasant for a person who has just awakened, or who is trying to concentrate, or who is excited anyway and thus above the optimal level of arousal for that time of day.

As you might expect, there seem to be individual differences in optimal arousal level. Some people never enjoy loud music, horror movies, or fast driving, and they shudder at the very thought of skydiving. Other people seem to thrive on excitement. A sensation-seeking scale has been developed to measure differences among people in optimal levels of arousal (Zuckerman, 1979). High scores are associated with alcohol use, smoking, sexual experience, risky activities, and voluntary participation in experiments, such as those involving drugs or hypnosis. Sensation seekers become very restless in "boring" (less arousal-provoking) situations (Zuckerman, 1979).

Something novel will initially produce arousal, but with repetition, it will become familiar and will no longer arouse, be pleasant, or be rewarding. Subjects of an experiment first rated strange music as unpleasant because it overaroused. With repetition, when the music had become mildly novel, it was rated as pleasant. With continued playing, when it had become familiar and boring, it was rated as unpleasant (Berlyne, 1967).

There has been some debate about the usefulness of the inverted U curve (Anderson, 1990; Neiss, 1988). One criticism is that the inverted U relationship between arousal and performance is descriptive, but does not explain why the relationship holds. This point is generally accepted. Arousal theory is a descriptive theory, not an explanatory one. Arousal theory does provide a useful way of understanding why stress can sometimes be beneficial for performance and other times be detrimental; the crucial factor is an individual's arousal level prior to the stress. Generally, the higher an individual's arousal level prior to stress, the more likely it is that stress will interfere with performance. Stress will facilitate performance when arousal is low.

Coping With Stress

Our understanding of the different ways people cope owes much to Richard Lazarus. By coping, an individual tries to master situations experienced as stressful

(Lazarus, 1966, 1976). Coping, Lazarus states, "is best considered as a form of problem-solving in which the stakes are the person's well-being and the person is not entirely clear about what to do." In general, there are four methods of coping: direct action, palliation, gaining predictability of stressful events, and gaining control.

DIRECT ACTION

Direct action involves behavior aimed at changing our relationship to a stressful event. There are many different kinds of direct action we can take to deal with stress, including escape, avoidance, and preparation against harm. You can reduce the stress of an impending exam, for example, by studying (preparing against the harm of failure). If you fail to study enough, you might employ another coping strategy. You could deny the importance of the exam (denial is a defense mechanism discussed in Chapter 14), or you may become physically ill, thus preventing the anticipated harm of taking the exam (Cox, 1978).

PALLIATION

Palliation means dealing with the symptoms of stress rather than the source of stress. The use of drugs such as alcohol or tranquilizers is one palliative technique. Other techniques include regular exercise, good nutrition, scheduled periods of relaxation, and other lifestyle modifications. Palliation can also involve reinterpreting a stressful situation to reduce stress.

Reinterpreting Stressful Events. Lazarus has done many studies showing how the interpretation of a threatening event can affect the stress the event produces. These studies show that the same event can prove stressful or not, depending on a person's cognitive appraisal. In one study (Speisman et al., 1964), a film showing a circumcision-like ritual performed on adolescent Australian Aborigines was screened for four different groups. In one screening, the commentary accompanying the film denied that the circumcision caused any harm to the adolescents (denial). In the second, a technical description was given (intellectualization). A third emphasized the horror and pain (trauma). And a fourth screening provided no commentary at all. The groups that heard the denial and intellectualization commentaries experienced less autonomic arousal than the group that heard no commentary. In fact, doctors and nurses routinely intellectualize to deal with the pain and suffering they witness each day. Emotional reactions and stress can be reduced merely by reinterpreting an event (Lazarus, Kanner, & Folkman, 1980.) Can you come up with a cognitive reappraisal of a stress in your life? Try it the next time you experience stress.

Constructive Versus Destructive Thinking. Seymour Epstein theorizes that people who are effective copers tend to think *constructively* rather than destructively when faced with problems (Epstein & Meier, 1989). Epstein has developed a scale that measures constructive thinking. Agreeing with statements such as "I don't let little things bother me," and " I am the kind of person who takes action rather than just thinks or complains about a situation," and disagreeing with statements such as "I avoid challenges because it hurts too much when I fail" and "I tend to take things personally" are reflective of constructive thinking. In laboratory studies in which subjects engage in mathematical and motor tasks in which their errors are constantly announced, Epstein has found that poor constructive thinkers show more stress both physiologically and in self-report.

The main difference between constructive and destructive thinkers is in the reaction to negative events. Destructive thinkers tend to think more negatively about themselves after negative outcomes. Epstein (1992) believes that this tendency of thought is developed very early in life. However, this does not mean that this way of thinking cannot be changed, and as we will see, there is reason to do so: Thinking positively is good for your health.

Relaxation Therapy. Relaxation therapy was developed to reduce some of the effects of stress—namely, muscle tension producing headaches, insomnia, and hypertension. The first work was done by Edmund Jacobson beginning in 1908. In 1929, he published *Progressive Relaxation,* a book in which he established an important principle: Physiologically, relaxation is the direct opposite of tension. The original relaxation program proposed by Jacobson was very time consuming, and modifications since then by Joseph Wolpe (1969) and many others have produced a less difficult series of steps to progressive relaxation.

Relaxation is an active coping skill, and practice is essential (Beech, Barnes, & Sheffield, 1982). In the early phases, relaxation should be practiced at least 30 minutes a day. Later this can be reduced to 15 or 20 minutes. To practice progressive relaxation, find a quiet, peaceful place with indirect light in which you can sit or recline. Lying in bed is not a good idea, you want to be deeply relaxed while wide awake, not asleep. It is not a bad idea, though, to practice relaxation an hour or so before going to bed, as sleep will be facilitated by relaxation.

The basic technique of progressive relaxation is to proceed through all the major muscle groups, tensing and then relaxing them until total relaxation is achieved. Contracting and then releasing the muscles produces deeper relaxation than just relaxing. We give the beginning of the basic training program here. (If you wish to read the entire sequence, see Beech, Burns, and Sheffield, 1982, pp. 48–54.) The following is just a sample of the instructions that would be used by a professional in guiding you in progressive relaxation.

- Relax your arms.
- Sit back in your chair as comfortably as possible; breathe in and out normally, close your eyes, and relax—relax completely.
- Keep relaxed but clench your right fist.
- Make the muscles of your lower arm and hand even tighter.
- Monitor the feelings of tension.
- Now relax; let all the tension go.
- Allow the muscles of your lower arm and hand to become completely limp and loose.
- Notice the contrast in the feelings.
- Again clench your right fist—tighter and tighter.
- Hold the tension and monitor the feelings.
- Relax. There should be no signs of tension in your hand or lower arm.
- Notice the feelings of relaxation again.
- Keeping your right hand and lower arm as relaxed as possible, bring your right elbow into the back of the chair and press downward, contracting the bicep muscles (between your elbow and shoulder). Press harder—make the muscles more tense.
- Monitor the feelings of tightness.
- Relax. Now let the tension dissipate immediately.
- Observe the difference. Let the muscles relax further.

- Now tense the right biceps again. Make the muscles harder, tighter.
- Monitor the feelings of tension.
- Relax. Let the tension go completely. Concentrate on the whole of your right arm. Relax it now, more and more deeply; relax it further and further.

The exercises for the left hand, lower arm, and biceps are exactly the same, and these are followed by instructions for relaxing the facial muscles, neck muscles, shoulders, chest, lower back and stomach, thigh, calves, and feet.

This technique has two main objectives. The first is to teach the body to detect tension by focusing on it and the second is to alleviate tension by relaxing. Relaxation therepy is often used as part of systematic desensitization.

PREDICTABILITY AND CONTROL

Stress-producing events have been found to be more stressful if they are unpredictable rather than predictable.

Being informed beforehand and being able to predict stressful events have proved beneficial in real-life situations. Students who have received course catalogs, spoken with potential roommates, or visited a campus before going to college adjust better during their freshman year than those who have no advance information (Silber et al., 1976). Patients undergoing operations required fewer painkilling drugs and a shorter hospital stay when informed about their operations (Egbert et al., 1964).

Being able to control stress also reduces its negative effects. Jay M. Weiss showed how having control reduced stress in rats. Weiss (1968) used matched triplets of rats. One rat could avoid or escape shock by a response; another had no control and was shocked whenever the first rat was; and the third rat was never shocked. The shocked rats received a signal 10 seconds before shock was given so that they could predict the shock. Other studies have shown that being able to predict shock results in fewer ulcers than unpredictable shock. Those rats who had control over the shock developed less severe ulcers than those who lacked control.

CASE STUDY

■ ■

RELAXATION THERAPY

Joe was a seventeen-year-old youth whose automobile was struck at an intersection by a hit-and-run driver approximately one month prior to being seen. He was not physically injured beyond sustaining a bumped knee. Immediately following the accident the patient became very upset, tense, and anxious. His appetite was poor, he had considerable difficulty falling asleep, and had become obviously more grouchy and irritable. He was afraid to drive his car and while never a very good student, he began to do even more poorly. He complained of not being able to concentrate in school, being very much ill at ease, and his grades deteriorated so badly that just prior to coming for treatment he tried to enlist in the Air Force rather than be expelled from school. He failed to pass the Air Force mental examination, however.

When first seen, the patient was very tense and quiet. Being unable to drive a car presents a considerable difficulty for a young man today but for this patient it was even more of a problem inasmuch as he was a member of an organized drag-racing club, was an avid "hot rodder" and car tinkerer. Most of his energies, interests, and the object of his working after school had been to support his car. To feel anxious around cars, uneasy when being driven by others and to be unable to drive his own car was for this young man one of the most difficult situations imaginable and reflected the intensity of his fears. The patient had a prior history of being somewhat "wild" but he felt that he had settled down since meeting his girl friend whom he intended to marry. On first impression it was thought that there might be some ulterior motives contributing in part to the patient's reactions, that is, his talk of now leaving school in light of his poor prior performance and nonacademic interests and also considering the fact that his case was being handled by a lawyer. It was decided to utilize a systematic desensitization approach as a means of reducing this patient's high anxiety level and phobic reactions. As such during the first session the patient was introduced to the concept of relaxation and he was instructed briefly in some of the techniques involved. He was told to practice relaxation at home and to try to do this is varied settings as well. It was determined to see the patient three times a week.

The systematic desensitization approach as described by Wolpe (1958) consists of presenting to the patient a series of imaginary, graded situations representing increasing areas of difficulty, beginning with one which is minimally anxiety-provoking, and gradually, step by step, approaching the situation which ordinarily evokes maximal anxiety in him. It is important that the increments be made in steps which at no time are overwhelmingly disturbing to the patient, or reinforcement of his fears is a possibility. An important element of procedure requires the patient to be completely relaxed as he imagines each situation. This is in recognition of Jacobson's findings (1938) that muscular relaxation inhibits anxiety thereby making its expression physiologically impossible. If the patient is completely relaxed and the situation elicits no anxiety, this, in effect, conditions him to tolerate the situation and enables him to proceed to the next step, and so forth, until he finally is able to visualize himself in the situation without undue anxiety.

After six sessions the patient considered himself ninety percent better. He had no trouble sleeping at night, his appetite was normal, he was no longer irritable, and his concentration in school had improved considerably. Relaxation techniques were reinforced at this last session and he was instructed in the various ways that he could bring these to bear and thus make his everyday activities more effective. The patient was discharged and a three-month follow-up revealed still further improvement with no exacerbation of his earlier symptoms."

SOURCE: Ullmann, L. P. & Krasner, L. (1965). Case studies in behavior modification. New York: Holt, Rinehart, and Winston, Inc. pp. 193–196.

Generally, such studies have determined that shock itself is relatively unimportant as a cause of ulcers; whether the animal can control and predict shock is much more significant. This is an impressive finding. Psychological factors can outweigh physical stress in producing disease.

In an experiment with human subjects, two groups were exposed to loud noise (Glass & Singer, 1972). People in one group could turn off the noise by pressing buttons, but they were asked not to do so unless they felt it was absolutely necessary. None pressed the buttons. The second group had no control over the noise, which was of the same intensity. Subsequent performance at proofreading was better for the group that had control, suggesting that the noise had disturbed the group less. Similar findings have been obtained with other stressors (Cohen, 1980).

People who believe that they have control (even if they do not) seem to be happier and less depressed than people who perceive accurately that they do not have control (Taylor & Brown, 1988). And people who take a hopeful and optimistic view of the world (positive thinkers) show better recovery from a wide range of illnesses, including cancer (Taylor, 1989). Optimism can be defined as "a generalized expectancy that good, as opposed to bad, outcomes will generally occur when confronted with problems across important life domains" (Scheier & Carver, 1985). Seligman (1990) suggests that optimists have a particular explanatory style, they see failures and other negative events as temporary setbacks, specific to a particular situation and due to external causes. The mastery-oriented children we discussed in Chapter 12 were optimists. A typical study (Peterson, 1988) observed students for a year and found that pessimists had twice as many infectious diseases as optimists. Optimists believe that they can control events, and having control—or believing you have control—is a potent factor in reducing stress and thereby disease.

Until recently, the mechanism responsible for the relation between the psychological variable of control and disease was not known. While it is possible that a distinction should be made between psychological and physical causes of disease, a more attractive alternative is to trace the relationship between the psychological event and the physical causes of disease.

Effects of Control on the Immune System.   A psychological event—having control—can alter underlying physiology—specifically immune reactions—and thereby physically contribute to disease. These findings are tremendously important because of the fundamental role of the immune system in fighting disease. Among the blood cells that actively participate in the immune system is a type of white blood cell called T lymphocytes, T cells. When a foreign invader (e.g., a virus) is recognized by the body, the T lymphocytes proliferate. One way to measure immune system functioning, then, is to measure the activity of T cells.

Mark Laudenslager, at the University of Denver, and Steve Maier and his associates, at the University of Colorado, measured immune system functioning in rats who received either inescapable or escapable shock (1983). Some rats received a series of shocks that they could do nothing to avoid, but a second group of rats could get away from the shock by making a response (turning a wheel). As in the Weiss experiments, the groups received exactly the same numbers and intensities of shock. The investigators found that if the rats could control the shocks, their immune function was not altered, but if the shocks were uncontrollable, immune functioning was impaired. Inescapable shock suppressed proliferation of T cells (in response to stimulation) relative to escapable shock. Thus, the psychological variable of being in control altered underlying physiology.

Other experiments have shown that having control over shock also affects tumor development. In 1979, Sklar and Anisman showed that mice that were implanted with tumor cells developed tumors sooner and developed larger tumors if they received inescapable shock than if they were not shocked, demonstrating the effects of the shock stress on tumor development. In a second experiment, they concluded that mice given inescapable shock developed tumors sooner and developed larger tumors than those given escapable shock. Amazingly, the mice given escapable shock did not differ from the no-shock mice, except on one day of tumor development when the tumors

Social relationships may directly facilitate health-related behavior by weakening the negative effects of stress and other sources of illness.

were larger for the animals who were shocked. Thus, the psychological variable of having control directly affected tumor development. Visintainer and colleagues, (1982) also showed that rats given inescapable shock developed cancer at a higher rate than nonshocked rats; their immune system was not as effective in rejecting cancerous cells.

Health and Social Relationships

There is a clear relation between social relationships and health. People who are isolated or not well integrated socially are less healthy both physically and psychologically and more likely to die (House, Landis, & Umberson, 1988). Unmarried and more socially isolated people are more likely to commit suicide, to have a higher rate of accidents, tuberculosis, and schizophrenia, and to have higher rates of death from all causes than are married people (House et al., 1988). But what causes what? Does being isolated produce disease? Or are unhealthy people more likely to be alone?

Until recently, the question could not be answered because we only had cross-sectional and retrospective data. Retrospective studies on illness and social relationships examine hospital records or death records after people become sick or die. Cross-sectional studies determine if people who are ill report a lower quality of social relationships than those who are healthy. Neither type of study can determine whether poor health precedes or follows poor social relationships. Recent prospective studies have shown clearly, however, that lack of social relationships is a major risk factor for mortality. A study of 4,775 adults between the ages of 30 and 69 in 1965 was done in Alameda County, in California (Berkman & Syne, 1979). This study used a survey measuring health and four types of social relationships: marriage, church membership, contacts with family and friends, and group affiliation, formal or informal. A combined "social network" index reflecting all these measures was a significant predictor of mortality. Those low on the index were twice as likely to die in the following nine years as those high on the index. A study by House and colleagues (1982) in Michigan improved on the methodology by using physical exams to measure health rather than self-report. Adjusting for a wide range of biomedical factors (e.g., blood pressure and cholesterol), a lack of social relationships related to 2 to 3 times greater rate of mortality for men in the following 10 to 12 years and 1½ to 2 times greater mortality for women. Other studies have obtained similar findings. To appreciate the size of this difference, we can point out that the relative risk ratios are stronger than the relative risk for mortality from cigarette smoking (House et al., 1988).

A recent study has shown that social support can influence the course of cancer (Spiegel, 1991). In this study, women with metastatic breast cancer were randomly assigned to routine care alone or to weekly sessions in a year-long support group. The support groups were not told that the purpose of the study was to see if support would enhance survival. They were told that the intention was to assist in coping with the stress of the illness. Group members discussed their fear of death, visited each other in the hospital, attended funerals of members who died, and developed projects with one another. After two years, all of the control patients had died, but one-third of the members of the support group were still alive. Other studies have produced similar results with leukemia patients.

Why do social relationships facilitate health? One hypothesis is that social support may increase adherence to treatment regimens and improve diet, sleep, or other health-related behaviors. Another hypothesis is that social relationships buffer, or weaken, the negative effects of stress and other sources of illness. In humans, the presence of a familiar person can reduce the negative effects of a stressful laboratory situation (e.g., Wrightsman, 1960). In general, coping is facilitated by sympathetic support from family, friends, and others. Having a confidant helps significantly (Miller & Ingham, 1979). Also, there is some evidence that confiding in someone such as a community professional (a counselor, lawyer, or police officer, for example) is more useful than confiding in relatives or friends (Lindenthal & Myers, 1979).

The presence of another person or physical contact with another person also modulates cardiovascular function in intensive care units, and affectionate petting by humans—or even just their presence—also reduces the cardiovascular effects of stressful situations in dogs and cats (Lynch, 1979). By the way there is interest lately in the idea that pets might aid in health, particularly for the isolated aged. Judith Siegel (1990) studied 38 Medicare enrollees over the course of a year. She found that patients with pets, particularly dogs, visited their physicians less often and dealt better with stress. Other studies show that the greater our attachment to our pets, the better our physical health (e.g., Garrity et al., 1989).

Social relationships may not only buffer against negative influences in health; they may also directly produce positive influences. Social relationships may foster a sense of meaning that promotes health, or they may directly facilitate health-related behaviors such as proper diet and exercise, appropriate use of alcohol, and the willingness to seek medical attention.

Culture and Health

Societies differ in the strengths of their social networks and in the prevalence of health-related behaviors. This is one reason health varies across cultures. Another reason is differences in diet between cultures. Most food preferences in omnivores such as the human and the rat are learned (Capaldi, 1992). Up to the age of 2, infants will consume just about anything, but once they have a repertoire of familiar foods, they become reluctant to try anything new (Birch & Marlin, 1982). Whatever foods are characteristic of a person's culture will become preferred merely because those are the ones that are familiar. Foods that are associated with pleasant social situations, such as a family setting, also become preferred (Rozin, 1991). It is not surprising that immigrants will go to great lengths to obtain the foods characteristic of their culture. Cultural mechanisms produce strong food preferences—preferences that can influence health.

One of the ways in which relationships between food elements and health has been established is to compare cultures in incidence of disease. In most regions of China, the diet consists of more vegetables and less saturated fat than the American diet, and the rate of heart disease is lower in China than in the United States. This is one piece of evidence relating saturated fats to heart disease. A link between eating fish and a lower risk of heart attack has been established the same way. Men in the Netherlands eat less fish than men in Japan and Greenland, two countries with very low death rates from heart disease. Of men in the Netherlands, those who ate fish at least once a week showed a significant reduction in heart disease (Kromhout, Bosschieter, & deLezenne Coulander, 1985). This factor is independent of other risk factors, such as cholesterol, age, physical activity, and smoking. Fish may increase the "good cholesterol" that protects against heart disease (Fraser & Babaali, 1989). Studies of other cultures where fish consumption is high also find low heart disease. Eskimos, who eat fish daily, have a very low rate of heart disease (Leaf & Weber, 1988).

Cultures also differ in the incidence of smoking and drinking alcohol, both of which affect health negatively. One study of seven preliterate societies found that all adults smoked as much as possible unless their religion forbade it (Damon, 1973). Smoking was seen as high prestige in some of these cultures and as producing great personal satisfaction. Despite these positive attitudes, smoking was seen as unhealthy by almost half of the people and as something that children should not do. Nonetheless, the incidence of smoking was quite high.

Cultural practices surrounding alcohol ingestion also influence health. For example, although wine consumption is quite high in France, wine customarily accompanies meals. Eating food with alcohol slows alcohol absorption, and the rate of alcoholism in France is quite low, despite the high rate of alcohol consumption.

Cultural beliefs also influence health by affecting compliance to physician advice. Advice from Western physicians on the treatment of hypertension and diabetes was ignored by patients in Zimbabwe who believed in traditional healers and had little faith in Western medicine (Zyazema, 1984).

In addition to the obvious cultural influences discussed in this section, there are also more subtle cultural effects on health, such as the desire for thinness characteristic of our society. The negative effects of this cultural norm are discussed in Chapter 16.

Obesity

One of the topics of interest to health psychologists is obesity. Being overweight is not the same thing as being obese. Being overweight means having a higher weight than some arbitrary standard related to height; being obese means having an abnormally high proportion of body fat. One way to estimate body fat is to use the *body mass index*. This is body weight (in kilograms) divided by the square of height (in meters). The correlation of the body mass index with body fat is between .7 and .8 (Bray, 1987). **Obesity** has been defined as having a body mass index of above 30 kg/m$_2$. Table 13.4 provides an easy way for you to determine your body mass index. Remember, this is only an estimate of body fat, not a direct measurement.

EVIDENCE OF A GENETIC COMPONENT

While your behavior can influence your weight, there is no doubt that there is also a strong genetic component. An animal model of the genetic influence on weight is provided by the Zucker obese rat (Zucker & Zucker, 1961). When maintained on the same diet of laboratory chow, the Zucker obese rat stores more of the calories consumed as fat than the Zucker lean rat. The ob gene has been cloned recently by Jeffrey Friedman at Rockefeller. And more exciting, a protein product of the mouse obese gene (ob) has been identified which when injected into mice causes animals to lose weight. This has led to hopes of treating obesity with a drug based on the ob gene (Barinage, 1995).

If, however, the Zucker lean rats are fed a diet of sausage, bananas, sweetened condensed milk, and other highly palatable foods, even the Zucker lean rat will become obese. Thus, one source of obesity—regardless of genetic tendency—is overeating of palatable food, no surprise to most of us. Studies with people offer further support to the idea that there is a hereditary component to body weight. Davenport (1923) found that in a sample of 37 children with very obese parents, none were thin, and at least one-third were very obese. In contrast, of 51 children of slim parents, none were of greater than average weight, and the great majority were themselves thin. A more recent study of adopted children found a strong relation between the weight of adopt-

Obesity can be a result of many different factors ranging from genetic causes to a multitude of environmental ones.

TABLE 13.4
Body Mass Index

To determine your body mass index, place a ruler between the body weight column on the left and the height column on the right. Read your body mass index from the point where the ruler crosses the center. (The table has been modified to show only inches and pounds so that you can more easily determine your body mass index.)

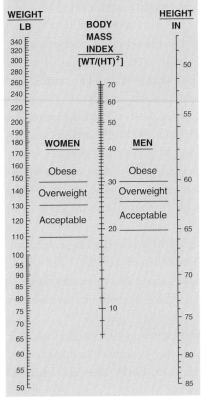

SOURCE: Reprinted by permission of the publisher, from G. A. Bray, 1978, Definitions, measurements and classifications of the syndromes of obesity, *International Journal of Obesity* 2:99–112.

ed children and their biological parents, and no relation between the weight of the children and their adoptive parents (Stunkard et al., 1986).

In a study reported in the *New England Journal of Medicine*, pairs of identical twins were fed 1,000 calories a day above their caloric needs. Exercise was equated by allowing each twin to take one 30-minute walk each day. After three months on this diet, the members of each pair of twins gained about the same amount of weight, but some pairs gained only 9 pounds, while other pairs gained as much as 29 pounds. In fact, researchers have suggested that the tendency to convert food to fat may be genetically determined. This means that you may eat the same and exercise the same as a friend of yours, yet still weigh more because of your genetic heritage. Not fair, but true. By the way, just which part of your body grows with weight gain is also genetically determined, as you must have noticed. Some people gain weight in their hips (pear shaped), while others gain it around their abdomen (apple shaped). Interestingly the apple type of weight seems more detrimental to health than the pear type.

SET POINT

From what we have said so far, it is clear that people may differ in the weight they would achieve on a normal diet. A person's biologically determined normal weight is referred to as that person's **set point.** Obese people may have naturally higher set points than people of normal weight. If they attempt to maintain their weight below their natural set points, they may be perpetually hungry.

Set point may be related to the size of a person's fat cells. Researchers believe that fat cell size for normal-weight people is maintained at a constant level to regulate weight. In some obese people, the normal signals may be disrupted, because their fat cells tend to be 2 to 2½ times larger than normal. They also have an increased number of fat cells (Sjostrom, 1980). Fat cell number does not decrease when weight is lost: when obese people reduce to a normal weight, their fat cells are just as numerous as before—only tiny. Therefore, these individuals need 25 percent fewer calories to maintain normal body weight, a situation that lasts forever. They also have low pulse rates, complain of being cold, and are obsessed with food. Many obese people who lose weight actually drop below their own normal weight, because their normal body weight is high (Keesey, 1980).

If, indeed, different people have different set points, the obese may be fighting a losing battle when they attempt to lose weight; and the skinny will have an equally difficult battle to gain weight. However, the picture is not totally discouraging. Another factor that affects our weight is metabolism, and as we see in the next section, behavior can indeed affect our metabolic rate.

METABOLISM

Metabolism, or metabolic rate, is different for different people and partly responsible for the differences in normal weight. A person's *basal metabolic rate* is the number of calories burned at rest. Individuals vary by as much as 100 to 500 calories per day in the energy they utilize at rest (Wooley, Wooley, & Dyrenforth, 1979). Most people are aware that these differences in metabolic rate can contribute to differences in weight among people. What they may not be aware of is that when food intake is restricted, the body responds defensively by lowering metabolic rate from 15 to 30 percent. The body acts as though it is trying to prevent starvation by reducing energy use when calorie intake is reduced. Therefore, the rate of weight loss will decrease as dieting continues, a situation that can completely counteract the effects of reduced intake (Craddock, 1979).

The good news is that this decrease in metabolism can be offset by exercise (Whitney & Rolfes, 1993).

Thus, although there is a strong genetic component to weight, it is obvious that your behavior—how much you eat and how much you exercise—can influence your weight.

THE EXTERNALITY HYPOTHESIS

An early theory, *the externality hypothesis*, suggested that obese people are more susceptible to good-tasting foods than are lean people. Perhaps the obese are more responsive to external cues associated with eating than are normal-weight people (Schachter, 1971). They would thus have less resistance to good-tasting food, eat more of it, and thereby be obese. But if the obese are more responsive to taste than normal-weight people, then they should be less likely to eat bad-tasting food than normal-weight subjects, as well as more likely to eat good-tasting food than normal-weight subjects. In other words, the effects of both good-tasting food and bad-tasting food should be exaggerated in the obese compared to normal-weight subjects.

Early experiments showed that under test conditions, obese subjects did indeed eat more pleasant-tasting ice cream (Nisbett, 1968) than normal-weight subjects, and *less* ice cream made bitter with quinine than normal-weight subjects. That is, obese subjects overate only if their food tasted good; they actually ate less than normal-weight subjects when the food tasted bad. This finding was explained by the idea that obese humans are more sensitive than normal-weight people to external cues associated with eating, such as the taste and sight of food.

Yet other data showed that in every weight category, thin as well as obese, there are people who are highly responsive to external cues associated with food and people who are not (e.g., Nisbett & Temoshok, 1976). The degree of overweight does not strongly relate to the degree of responsiveness to either internal or external cues (Rodin, Slochower, & Fleming, 1977).

The responsiveness of individuals to food-related cues is more related to whether they are dieting than to their weight. People who are dieting, termed *restrained eaters*, are preoccupied with food and weight (Polivy & Herman, 1985). They also react differently to eating high-calorie food than do unrestrained eaters. In one experiment showing this latter phenomenon, Hibscher and Herman (1977) gave half of their subjects milk shakes to drink (a preload) and gave the other half nothing. Then the subjects were served ice cream and asked to evaluate its taste. Restrained eaters (dieters) ate more ice cream if they had drunk milk shakes; drinking the milk shakes apparently broke down their resistance. This result suggests that the dieters reasoned that since their diet was broken, they might as well binge—an all-or-none approach to eating. In contrast, unrestrained eaters ate less ice cream if they had drunk milk shakes. The degree of a subject's obesity was not related to the quantity of ice cream eaten under either condition.

Dieters, in general, eat very little if they are not given a preload or are only given a small preload, but eat a great deal if given a high-calorie preload (or one they believe to be high in calorie). Their eating appears to be under cognitive control rather than under control of bodily signals. Therefore they eat what they think they should eat rather than what their body tells them to eat. This pattern of eating is produced by past dieting and overeating (Lowe, 1993). The relationship between this type of pattern and eating disorders is considered later, and the health effects of dieting are considered in "Psychology in Our Times: The Dangers of Dieting."

THE DANGERS OF DIETING

Estimates are that at any one time, over 50 million Americans are dieting. Over half of all adolescent girls at any one time are dieting, as are 16 percent of adolescent boys. Many of these people are not obese or even overweight. Many people, especially young women, diet in the pursuit of an ideal slim figure. Older people may also diet in the expectation that losing weight is good for their health. Yet, recent studies suggest that dieting may actually be bad for your health, and in some circumstances, overweight may not be as unhealthy as once thought.

It is true that as soon as dieters start to lose weight, blood cholesterol and blood pressure drop. But does dieting increase longevity? Some recent studies suggest that it may do just the opposite in some instances. Women or men who lose any weight die sooner than those who have not lost weight, with the risk being greatest the more weight lost. The greatest risk is associated with so-called *yo-yo dieting*, where weight goes up and down repeatedly. This pattern is characteristic of dieters, because dieting is not usually effective in producing long-term weight loss. A survey by *Consumers Report* found that 95,000 of their readers had attempted to lose weight in the previous three years, 19,000 on professionally managed weight loss programs. Those on professional weight loss programs lost about 10 to 20 percent of their starting weight. But the average dieter gained half of that weight back within six months of leaving the program. A cycle of dieting and weight loss followed by weight gain when the diet is over is a very common pattern. But it is also the most dangerous to health. Any significant weight change, up or down, increases the risk of dying from heart disease. A very recently completed

study however quarrels with this conclusion. This latest study eliminated smokers from the comparison and found that this people were at less risk than even moderately overweight people. Whether or not dieting is a risk to health, the data are clear that dieting is often unsuccessful in reducing weight gain.

One effect that dieting has is to lower metabolism. Steen, Oppliger, and Brownell (1988) studied wrestlers, some of whom go through severe weight loss programs to reach appropriate weight and then regain lost weight off-season. They found that wrestlers who cycled weight gain and loss in this manner had a resting metabolic rate 14 percent lower than wrestlers who did not periodically diet. This metabolic slowdown persisted after the diet was over, setting the stage for rapid weight gain.

People who diet are often very irritable. They are invariably hungry and obsessed with food. They act like starving people. The body cannot tell the difference between true starvation and dieting. Brownell and Stein (1989) say that food eaten after starvation is more likely to be stored as fat. This is another reason weight gain is easy after a diet. Many people end up fatter, rather than thinner, because they dieted.

Polivy and Herman (1983) argue that for all the reasons mentioned here, dieting is foolish, especially for people who are not obese. In their book *Breaking the Diet Habit* they suggest eating only when hungry and being satisfied with your normal weight. While some dieters would indeed be heavier if they did not diet, some may actually be thinner if they stopped going on and off diets.

ENDORPHINS AND SEROTONIN

As we mentioned in Chapter 2, endorphins, peptides naturally present in the body, act much like morphine to block pain signals. Margules (1979) found that rats genetically prone to obesity have a higher endorphin level than rats of normal weight. When injected with naloxone, a chemical that blocks the effects of endorphins, obese rats stopped overeating. The same dose did not affect lean rats. Margules suggests that endorphin release constitutes an adaptive reaction that prepares the body for a food shortage. This mechanism may be malfunctioning in some obese people, producing a constant food craving. In fact, Facchinetti and colleagues (1986) found that obese patients have higher levels of beta-endorphin in their blood, perhaps related to their need to overeat. There is thus a chain of evidence linking obesity to elevated endorphin release.

Naloxone can block rats' preferences for sweet tastes. It also reduces the facilitating effects of deprivation on feeding (Hoebel, 1988). These findings suggest that the endorphins are involved in the facilitating effects of palatability and deprivation on feeding.

Some obese people overeat to relieve feelings of anxiety and depression. These people may crave carbohydrates because their bodies produce too little of the neurotransmitter serotonin (also discussed in Chapter 2). Some obese people report feeling anxious, tense, and depressed before eating carbohydrate snacks and calm and peaceful after (Wurtman, 1987). High-carbohydrate, protein-poor meals elevate the enzyme tryptophan in the brain, thereby catalyzing the synthesis of serotonin. Accordingly, some obese people may be self-medicating for depression by consuming excess carbohydrates (Wurtman, 1987).

STRESS

Stress is another factor related to obesity. In one study with rats, a mild, apparently not painful pinch of the tail six times a day caused daily caloric intake to increase 129 percent, compared to the intake of control rats given access to the same food (Rowland & Antelman, 1976). The investigators suggest that stress produces a hyperresponsivity to environmental stimuli.

People, too, may react to stress by overeating. Clinical investigations indicate that some obese people overeat when frustrated or tense or to reduce loneliness or boredom (Crisp, 1970; Mayer, 1968). Some studies also have found that obese people tend to eat slightly more when they are anxious (Herman & Polivy, 1975; McKenna, 1972; Schachter, Goldman, & Gordon, 1968).

FOOD PREFERENCES

The obese have a stronger preference for fat than do normal-weight people and less of a preference for sweet (Drewnowski, 1990). This is interesting because fat is the element in food most strongly associated with obesity. One reason for this is that fat has 9 calories per gram, while carbohydrates and proteins have only 4 calories per gram. Rats given high-fat diets compensate for this increased caloric density by eating less than rats given low- fat diets, but they gain weight even if they do not overeat (Bray, 1988), because fat-based diets are very efficient in promoting obesity (Flatt, Ravussin, Acheson, & Jequier, 1985). While excess carbohydrate calories are lost as heat, excess fat calories do not generate much heat and tend to be stored as fat (Schwartz, Ravussin, Massari, O'Connell, & Robbins, 1985).

As you can see, overweight can occur for many reasons. Current thinking is that human obesity ranges from familial, probably genetic, to diet-induced. It is perhaps not surprising, then, that about 9 percent of Americans over age 30 are more than 20 percent overweight and classified as obese.

Themes in Review

We have seen in this chapter clear-cut evidence that psychological events can influence biological events. Being in control and being able to predict events (both psychological events) reduce stress. This reduction in stress improves immune system functioning and reduces stress-related diseases, such as ulcers, high blood pressure and heart disease. People can learn to reduce stress by taking advantage of the methods of stress reduction discussed in this chapter (e.g., relaxation techniques). People can also reduce stress by cognitive means. Reinterpreting events as nonthreatening reduces the stress produced by those events. It is important to learn these methods of stress reduction because the normal life changes associated with development produce stress. Entering school, leaving school, taking a job, getting married, having children—all produce stress.

The relationship between stress and disease is a topic of interest in health psychology, the field concerned with how our behavior produces health and disease. While there are genetic factors contributing to many diseases and to conditions favoring disease, such as obesity, behavior is also a major contributor. Indeed the most prevalent diseases in modern society, heart disease and cancer, are heavily influenced by behavioral factors. Moreover, the prevalence of disease varies with sociocultural factors in part because these sociocultural factors affect behavior. For example, many diseases are diet related, and diet in turn is strongly determined by sociocultural factors.

Summary

1 Health psychology focuses on psychological and behavioral factors that affect health and disease. Health psychologists study how certain behaviors (smoking, overeating, failure to exercise) can lead to disease such as coronary heart disease. Stress is of special interest because it affects the body's resistance to disease.

2 Stress is caused by a perceived threat to physical and psychological well-being, together with the feeling that the individual cannot cope with the threat. Life changes, minor annoyances, chronic discomfort, and unresolved conflict are four general sources of stress.

3 Conflict is produced when two incompatible response tendencies appear to be equally strong. Three kinds of conflict are approach-approach, avoidance-avoidance, and approach-avoidance.

4 A clear relationship exists between stress and illness, particularly ulcers and heart disease; it seems to originate in the body's physiological reaction to stress. Stages of the body's physiological reaction to stress constitute the general adaptation syndrome.

5 Anger and hostility appear to be the critical components of the Type A personality that are correlated with heart disease. Anger also seems to be the primary reason frustration can lead to aggression.

6 Arousal theory suggests that optimum performance occurs at an intermediate level of arousal. Arousal is a state of physiological activation produced by environmental stimuli, surprising or novel events, motivation and drugs.

7 Two methods of coping with stress are direct action, aimed at changing a person's relationship to the stressful event, and palliation, which involves dealing with the symptoms of stress (e.g., through relaxation and reinterpretation). An event also produces less stress if it is predictable—that is, if a subject is informed about it beforehand—and if the individual has control over the event.

8 Social support from friends, family, or professional counselors moderates the negative effects of stress and facilitates health.

9 Obesity is caused by a number of factors. There is a strong genetic component to weight, but behavioral factors are also important.

KEY TERMS

health psychology (p. 534)

stress (p. 535)

approach-approach conflict (p. 539)

avoidance-avoidance conflict (p. 539)

approach-avoidance conflict (p. 539)

general adaptation syndrome (p. 540)

immune system (p. 542)

Type A personality (p. 543)

Type B personality (p. 543)

aggression (p. 544)

frustration-aggression hypothesis (p. 546)

revised frustration-aggression hypothesis (p. 546)

arousal (p. 547)

arousal theory (p. 547)

Yerkes-Dodson law (p. 548)

palliation (p. 549)

obesity (p. 556)

set point (p. 557)

FOR CRITICAL ANALYSIS

1 Some stress is chosen voluntarily, such as the stress associated with skydiving. Explain why such stressors may be chosen and why their effects on health may not be detrimental. Consider possible differences between chronic stress and brief, short-lived stress.

2 Some say that life is more stressful now than in times gone by. Can you make a case that the opposite is true? Be explicit in considering sources of stress.

3 List four sources of stress in your life, and then describe how you could change your cognitive appraisal of the stress to reduce your stress.

4 What evidence could you provide to convince a skeptic that the mind can indeed affect the body?

5 Describe some psychological factors or behaviors that may affect health and that could be studied by health psychologists. (Choose psychological factors and behaviors that were not described in this chapter.) How would you initiate such a study of these?

SUGGESTED READINGS

BEECH, H. R., BURNS, L. E., & SHEFFIELD, B. F. (1982). *A behavioral approach to the management of stress: A practical guide to techniques.* New York: Wiley. An explicit coverage of techniques for dealing with stress.

GLASS, D. C. (1977). *Behavior patterns, stress and coronary disease.* Hillsdale, N. J.: Erlbaum.

GLASS, D. C., & SINGER, J. E. (1972). *Urban stress: Experiments on noise and social stressors.* New York: Academic Press. The two preceding books give excellent coverage of work on stress and disease, with an emphasis on experimental work with human beings.

IZARD, C. E., KAGAN, J., & ZAJONC, R. B. (Eds.) (1984). *Emotion, cognition, and behavior.* New York: Cambridge University Press.

POLIVY, J., & HERMAN, C. P. (1983). *Breaking the diet habit*. New York: Basic Books. Intended for the nonspecialist, this book provides a wealth of information on how people regulate food intake. The authors are critical of the "diet habit" of so many people.

SCHERER, K. R., & EKMAN, P. (Eds.) (1984). *Approaches to emotion*. Hillsdale, N. J.: Erlbaum. Contains papers by the major figures working today in the field of emotion.

PSYCHOLOGY ON THE INTERNET

Stress Pamphlet

(http://ccserver.uoregon.edu/~dvb/pamstr.htm)

Stress Busters

(http://www.cts.com/~health/strssbus.html)

Stress Management

(http://www.ivf.com/stress.html)

These sites provide definitions of stress, symptoms checklists, and tips for coping with stress. In addition, Stress Management contains a test that assesses your vulnerability to stress.

The Science of Obesity and Weight Control

(http://www.loop.com/~bkrentzman/)

This site contains information on and links to a wide variety of topics related to obesity—including the genetic aspects of obesity, medications currently used to treat obesity, a discussion of the body's set point, and a list of frequently asked questions about obesity and dieting.

For a comprehensive list of sites related to obesity, visit:

http://www.loop.com/~bkrentzman/bzk.bookmarks.html#Obesity

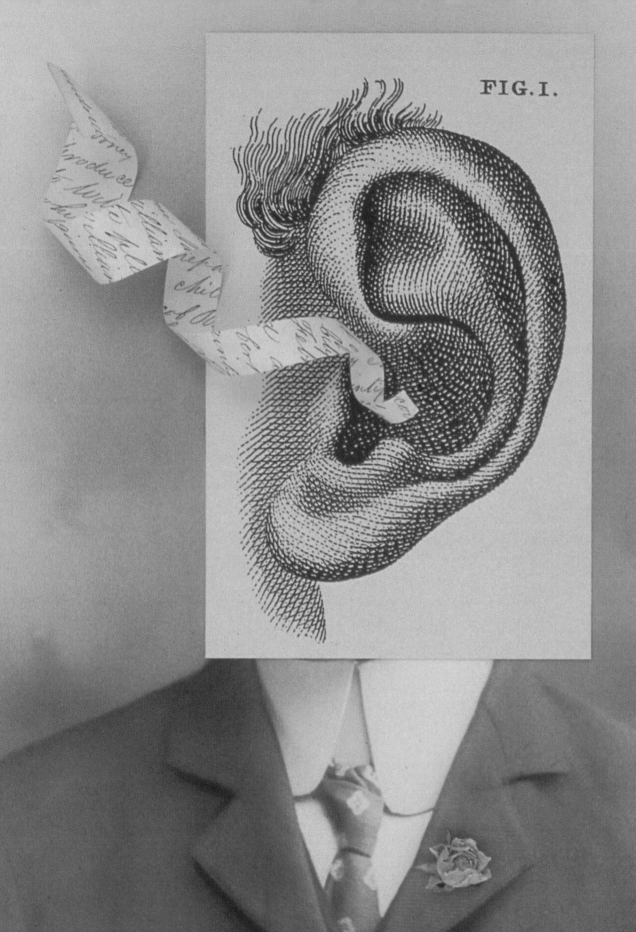

FIG.I.

PERSONALITY

Chapter 14

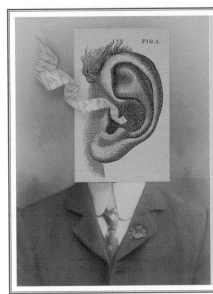

BIOLOGICAL THEME
Is personality determined by heredity?

LEARNING THEME
Is personality learned in the same way we learn anything else?

COGNITIVE THEME
How does the way we think affect our personality?

DEVELOPMENTAL THEME
How much of adult personality is set in childhood?

SOCIOCULTURAL THEME
Do we merely conform to the social roles provided by our culture, or do we express our individuality?

Remember a time when you studied hard for a midterm exam and were confident that you did well. Now imagine the following scene:

As the tests are returned, you anticipate your success and feel a mild excitement. You reach for the test paper and are stunned by the circled, red letter-grade—a C-minus! You are swept by a wave of negative emotions.

But what happens after the initial blow? Do you become angry and imagine retaliating against your professor? Do you become depressed, doubtful that you'll ever succeed in this course, and consider dropping it or even quitting college to pursue a less demanding career? Do you become anxious and worry about how you'll ever get the academic credits you need to achieve the goals to which you (and your parents) are so committed? Do you simply wait for the emotion to subside and then coolly analyze exactly what went wrong and resolve to do better next time? Do you express your feelings about this incident or keep them to yourself? Do you constantly dwell on the incident or put it out of your mind?

Anyone is likely to be upset by such an event, but no two people will react in precisely the same way. At the time of the event, some will be more upset than others; and later on, people will differ in their emotions, thoughts, and actions in response to the low grade. These different reactions reflect different personalities.

A typical textbook definition of **personality** is the "pattern of characteristic thoughts, feelings, and behaviors that distinguishes one person from another and that persists over time and situations" (Phares, 1988, p. 4). This definition is incomplete, however, because it emphasizes the differences between individuals but does not mention what is common to everyone. Everyone is in some ways like everyone else, like some other people, and like no one else.

Personality psychology is the study of our stable and consistent characteristics, some of which we share with everyone else, some of which we share with some (but not all) others, and some of which are unique. Thus, personality psychology may be divided into two main areas of interest. The first area, *human nature*, emphasizes what is common to everyone: everyone gets upset when encountering a disappointment. The second area, *individual differences*, emphasizes the differences in people's reactions to the same situation: as we have already seen, there is wide variation in the way people get upset, how upset they get, and how they deal with being upset.

Personality is often best described using concepts derived from other fields of psychology, such as psychobiology, learning, development, intelligence, motivation, psychopathology, and social psychology. In turn, each of these areas of psychology can be analyzed in terms of common features and individual differences. Personality psychology, then, takes from the rest of psychology and gives to the rest of psychology. It may not be too presumptuous to claim that "personality psychology is the very center of psychology itself" (Lamiell, 1987, p. 238).

In this chapter, we will discuss four major approaches to personality: psychoanalytic, phenomenological/humanistic, trait, and social learning. Each of these approaches deals with the issues of human nature and individuality, but some emphasize what the average person is like, whereas others emphasize how people differ. Some emphasize the biological side, some the social side. Some are more concerned with the development of personality, whereas others focus on measuring personality as it is right now. Each approach has proved its value, and a complete understanding of personality probably requires that we draw from all of them. For the sake of clarity, however, we will consider them separately, starting with the psychoanalytic approach. This approach embraces the oldest and most prominent full-blown theory of personality, although it is also the most controversial (see Chapter 1). Indeed, many psychologists reject much of psychoanalysis as either unprovable or just plain wrong. Still, students of personality psychology must acquaint themselves with psychoanalysis, if only for historical reasons. For better or worse, psychoanalysis has permeated modern culture and still has a strong following among some academics and many clinicians.

The Psychoanalytic Approach

Psychoanalysis is a theory of psychological development and functioning that emphasizes the role of unconscious motivation and conflict in human behavior. Sigmund Freud (1856–1939) created psychoanalysis partly from his clinical observations and analyses, but mostly from his own unique genius. He offered psychoanalysis as a way of explaining not only personality but all of human psychology, especially psychopathology. Although the outline of the theory is clear, the details are still very unsettled. Freud himself changed his mind several times over the course of his long career, and his followers have further challenged many of his ideas. As we shall see, some early critics found his ideas preposterous, and some modern critics still do.

Freud was born in 1856 in Frieburg, Moravia, in what was then the Austro-Hungarian Empire. His father, a Jewish wool merchant, moved the family to Vienna when Freud was a young boy. Freud was a brilliant student (he read Shakespeare at the age of 8) and entered the University of Vienna medical school at the age of 17.

Highly ambitious and gifted, Freud wanted to devote his life to the study of human physiology, but Jews had limited opportunities in the academic world of research. Once Freud married, he had to earn his own way, so he reluctantly set up practice as a physician specializing in nervous disorders. He soon recognized that many of his patients' physical problems were psychological in origin. That realization and his successes and failures at treatment led, over the decades, to his wide-ranging theories about the human mind and its connection to the body.

Sigmund Freud, the creator of psychoanalysis, shown here with his daughter, Anna.

SEX, AGGRESSION, AND THE UNCONSCIOUS MIND

Perhaps Freud's most important intellectual breakthrough was his "discovery" of a powerful, unconscious aspect of mental life. The **unconscious** is that part of the mind that is inaccessible to us. Of course, Freud could not actually discover the unconscious, which is not the sort of thing one can experience directly. The unconscious is more like a metaphor for those aspects of our mind that remain hidden from us but which nevertheless exert observable effects. Another reason that Freud could not discover the unconscious is that it had already been "discovered" by other nineteenth-century intellectuals. Freud, however, was the greatest promoter of the unconscious as the primary source of our behavior.

For Freud, the unconscious was the source of the powerful sexual and aggressive energies that make us act the way we do. This energy ultimately arises from our biological nature, but somehow transforms itself into psychological energy. (Freud thought that one day psychology would become a branch of biology, but he realized that that day was a long way off; it still is.)

In Freud's view, sexuality was much more than what we normally think of when we think of sex (and according to Freud, we are almost always thinking of sex, whether we realize it or not). Freud saw **sexuality** as including a broad spectrum of erotic and life-enhancing activities in addition to sexual behavior as we commonly understand it: "love, sensuality, … pleasure seeking, affiliative needs, interests and attachment motivation" (Westen, 1990, p. 30). **Aggression** also included a very wide range of behaviors and urges, except that aggression is harmful and destructive rather than loving and constructive like sexuality. Sexual and aggressive energies in the unconscious need to be released, much as the steam in a steam engine must be released to keep the engine from exploding. But because these sexual and aggressive urges are often at odds with each other, and because society frowns upon the expression of either sexuality or aggression, releasing this energy is not a simple matter. Conflict is inevitable.

Conflict may occur between the erotic and destructive urges themselves—as when we both love and hate our parents—and also between these urges and the conscious mind. Even now, as in Freud's time, expressing sexual and aggressive impulses, or even acknowledging them, is often socially unacceptable. Movies and television, for instance, have elaborate codes to ensure that we are not easily exposed to sex and violence. The agents of society (e.g., parents, teachers, government) threaten individuals who express such raw urges. Even just thinking about sex or aggression can provoke anxiety. What if the wish were to be fulfilled? What punishment might we suffer? The result, as we shall see, is that we don't even let ourselves think (consciously) about these urges.

Still, despite the problems they create, unconscious sexual and aggressive urges can never be eliminated; they are a fundamental part of human nature. Freud believed that we protect ourselves from these urges by using psychological defense mechanisms (discussed shortly). Despite our best efforts, though, sexual and aggressive motives express themselves, directly and indirectly, when unconscious urges overwhelm the defenses that normally control them. Rape was long considered to be primarily a sexual matter, in which the rapist could not or would not control his sexual urges. Recently, we have come to view rape as perhaps more a matter of aggression, with some sexuality mixed in. Regardless of whether rape is primarily sexual or aggressive, a Freudian would have little difficulty in tracing sexual assault back to the unconscious, where sexuality and aggression naturally coexist.

Other, more benign and indirect expressions of sex and aggression are evident in slips of the tongue and in our dreams. (See Chapter 5 for a discussion of Freud's view of dreams as an expression of unconscious urges.) In Freud's view, mistakes, like dreams, never just happen by accident. Each error we make can be interpreted as a clue to our unconscious motives. If we forget someone's name or are late for an appointment, you can be sure that there is some underlying hostility at work. When typing this chapter, I can't tell you how many times I mistakenly typed "id" instead of "is." While it is true that *d* is next to *s* on the keyboard, Freud would argue that my mind was really on sex, which is represented in his theory by the id (see next section).

Jokes, like dreams, permit the expression of sexuality and aggression in a disguised and therefore more acceptable manner. (Perhaps not all humor has an underlying sexual or aggressive theme, as Freud would insist; but there is no doubt that sex and aggression are evident in a good number of jokes.) Nowadays, jokes directed at women or ethnic minorities are not considered acceptable, because the targets of these jokes are justifiably offended. We may refrain from telling such jokes, but according to Freud, the urges underlying the jokes will emerge in some other way. Sex and aggression, which provide the punch for these jokes, must be expressed if we are to maintain our psychological equilibrium. In fact, Freud might argue that releasing sexual and aggressive energy through jokes is relatively harmless, at least compared to some of the alternatives, such as overt sexual or aggressive actions. (What do you think? Do such jokes cause harm, or can they relieve a difficult situation of tension?)

Although a few supporters welcomed Freud's ideas enthusiastically, most people were initially shocked by Freud's view of human nature. They were not prepared to believe that their behavior was shaped by psychic forces of which they were unaware and over which they had no control. Nor were they pleased with Freud's emphasis on sex and aggression as the strongest unconscious drives. Although we have gradually come to accept many of Freud's ideas—especially the idea that some of our behavior is generated unconsciously—many people still tend to resist Freud's strong claims about the overwhelming importance of sexual and aggressive urges. Freud cleverly interpreted this resistance as further proof of his theory. He argued that we resist his proposals because they portray us and our motives in a fashion that we do not like; and the fact that we have no direct experience of such motives simply "proves" that they are hidden in the unconscious!

FREUD'S THEORY OF PERSONALITY STRUCTURE

Freud described the mind (or *psyche*) as displaying three levels of awareness: the *conscious*, the *preconscious*, and the *unconscious*. As you will recall from Chapter 5, the *conscious* mind is what we are aware of at the moment. Consciousness, however, is only the tip of the iceberg, to use Freud's metaphor. Freud described most mental activity as taking place beneath the surface of consciousness. The *preconscious* consists of mental elements (thoughts, memories, images, etc.) that we are not immediately aware of but which can be brought into conscious awareness with a little effort. For example, if you try, you can quickly recall what you had for breakfast yesterday. The contents of the *unconscious*, however, cannot be brought directly into conscious awareness. Unconscious material is simply too threatening and is therefore barred from consciousness.

Freud also divided the mind into the *id*, *ego*, and *superego*, all of which remain unconscious except for small parts of the ego and superego (see Figure 14.1).

The Id. The **id** is the primary reservoir of psychic energy; it is strictly unconscious, present from birth, and its energy (the sexual part of which is called **libido**) is the dynamic source of all motivation. The id is characterized by **primary process** thinking, in which logic is unknown and florid and contradictory images may coexist.

FIGURE 14.1
Id, Ego, and Superego

The ego, which is partly conscious and partly unconscious, tries to balance the entirely unconscious desires of the id against the superego's demands and the demands of the external world. Note that the superego, like the ego, is partly conscious.

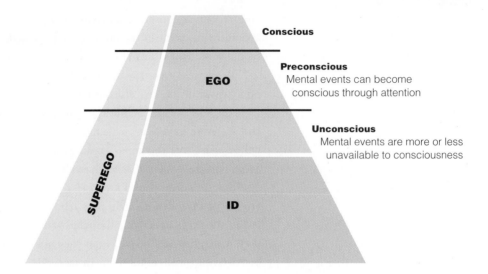

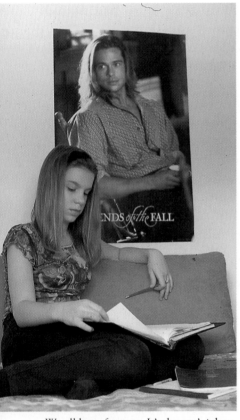

We all have fantasys. It's the ego's job to replace imaginary "goal objects" with more realistic ones.

The id operates on the **pleasure principle:** It demands immediate gratification of all its urges and doesn't care about the consequences to oneself or anyone else. The reduction of tension when the urge is satisfied is rewarding and pleasurable (see discussion of drive reduction and reinforcement in Chapter 12). If there is no suitable way to satisfy the urge (e.g., if the hungry infant has no food), then the id may create an image of the desired object through a process known as **wish fulfillment.** Of course, this image cannot actually satisfy the basic urge; wish fulfillment does not satisfy our wishes, but simply substitutes a wish for a reality.

Do you ever fantasize about something that you really want but cannot get? If you are like most people, you do so frequently. Although this wish fulfillment clearly satisfies a craving, it nevertheless remains a mystery. Starving people fantasize about food (Keys, Brozek, Henschel, Mickelson, & Taylor, 1950), but how does that help? Why is it satisfying to imagine something that you want but cannot have? You might think that starving people would try to avoid thinking about food if only to avoid frustration. Dieters are often instructed to suppress thoughts of food, but that is apparently neither possible nor helpful for them; they prefer to imagine devouring what they know they cannot have (Herman & Polivy, 1993).

The Ego. Just wanting something is no guarantee of getting it. The **ego** emerges from the id to help satisfy the id's demands. Exactly how the ego originates is somewhat mysterious. It is as if the id, after sufficient frustration, decides to invest some of its energy in a new enterprise (the ego) that will act as its agent to negotiate satisfaction of its basic urges. The ego provides the practical knowledge and techniques (such as problem solving, social skills, and language) that are required to achieve one's goals. The ego learns how to satisfy the id while submitting to the physical and social limits of the world. Instead of merely fantasizing, the ego learns how to acquire things such as food or sex in a way that does not offend society. Of course, the ego cannot always satisfy completely the insistent demands of the id. The ego obeys the **reality principle,** the rule that to gain satisfaction, one must temper one's demands. Because it must deal with the objective, real world, the ego must often sacrifice immediate gratification (the pleasure principle) to achieve eventual satisfaction with a suitable object in suitable circumstances. (In seeking a sexual partner, we learn to lower our sights from Hollywood stars—or, in Freud's view, from our own opposite-sex parents—and settle for the girl or boy next door. And we also learn to wait until the time and place is right, even though our id might be impatient.) To deal effectively with reality, the ego must develop **secondary process** thinking, which is generally rational. The ego is thus the executive of personality; it must weigh alternatives and make decisions. A person with a weak ego may be dominated by fantasies arising from the id and fail to cope effectively with reality. We tend to identify ourselves consciously with our egos (*ego* is Latin for "self"), whereas the id is seen as something slightly alien (*id* is Latin for "it").

The Superego. The **superego** is the part of the mind devoted to ideals and to "right and wrong." It consists of two distinct parts: the ego ideal and the conscience. The **ego ideal** sets high (often impossibly high) standards of virtue. The conscience, on the other hand, inflicts guilt when we do something wrong or even consider doing something wrong. The id presses for free expression, and the conscience acts as a censor. According to one formula (Elkind, 1990, p. 334), "The ego ideal is the child's own sense of what he or she would like to be, whereas the conscience reflects what the parents would like the child to be." And what the parents would like the child to be is well behaved. Because the superego is formed very early in life and remains unchanged after the Oedipal crisis (about age 5, see next section), its standards are extremely primitive. As adults we may find ourselves feeling guilty for doing, or even considering doing, things (especially certain sexual activities) that we consciously view as normal and acceptable. Unconsciously, thanks to the conscience part of the superego, we feel that these activities are just not right.

In Chapters 9 and 10, we discussed Kohlberg's theory of moral development, which suggests that people develop higher moral principles as they get older and more cognitively mature. Freud, on the other hand, claimed that our high moral principles are really just glorified versions of the infantile good/bad judgments of the superego. Do you usually decide what to do in difficult ethical situations by reasoning about the options? Or do you tend to do what feels right, even if it conflicts with your rational conclusions? Our moral feelings, according to Freud, develop very early in life and do not really mature. When we feel guilt, is it because we have betrayed our higher principles or because we have abandoned the simple morality of the nursery?

THE DEVELOPMENT OF PERSONALITY

Freud believed that the first few years of life were crucial in determining personality. He identified several distinct **psychosexual stages** of development. Each psychosexual stage refers to a different sexually charged zone of the body where issues of concern to the developing child are focused.

The Oral Stage. The **oral stage,** occupying the first 18 months of life, centers on eating, biting, and sucking. The mouth is the primary libidinal zone, or *erogenous zone,* where erotic satisfaction and frustration are likely to occur. Psychoanalytic theory holds that if a person is either frustrated or overindulged at this (or any other) stage, he or she will develop a **fixation**—an excessive focus on the area of the body associated with that stage and on the symbolic activities related to that stage. Especially when they are distressed, people crave gratification from the erogenous zone at which they are fixated. Fixations permanently affect our behavior. Orally fixated people may be especially gullible (they will swallow anything) or sarcastic (verbally biting). They may also indulge in oral activities, such as smoking, eating, nail-biting or talking, particularly when they are upset.

Fingers are good to suck on when you need gradification at 18 months of age.

Some adults find oral activities soothing, especially when they are under
stress.

In the Oedipal stage, love for one's
mother takes on new meanings.

The Anal Stage.   The **anal stage** begins at around 2 years of age, when toilet training begins. If parents are too strict, the child may develop an anal fixation, which is
symbolized by the conflict between holding on and letting go (of feces). A child may
struggle to retain the feces and subsequently develop a stingy or compulsively orderly
and neat personality style. Perhaps, if the parents profusely reward the child for "the
gift," the youngster will be unusually generous or highly creative and productive.

During the anal stage, children develop a strong dependence on their mother and
become very anxious in her absence. To relieve this anxiety, the child *introjects* (or
internalizes) the image of mother as perfection. This image becomes the ego ideal of
the superego; people are doomed to strive forever (in vain) to meet its high standards
and thereby guarantee their parents' love.

The Phallic Stage.   The **phallic stage** generally occurs between ages 3 and 6,
when children "discover" their genitals and obtain some erotic gratification from rubbing or playing with them. According to Freud, a male child has sexual desires for his
mother and wishes to possess her exclusively. He is intensely jealous of his father and
of any siblings who are rivals for his mother's love. At the same time, though, the boy
fears that his father will find out about the boy's rivalry and punish him by castration.
The result is a terrifying "castration anxiety." The boy relieves this anxiety by suppressing his desire to possess his mother sexually and instead identifies with his father
("identification with the aggressor"), trying to be as much like him as possible. The
boy internalizes his image of the father, and this strict, forbidding image becomes the
forbidding part of the self—the conscience—completing the superego. Desire for the
mother and fear of the father are permanently repressed into the unconscious. Freud
called this entire process the **Oedipus complex,** after the Greek tragedy *Oedipus Rex*,
in which Oedipus is fated to kill his father and marry his mother. The male child is
not fated to do these things, but he is fated to wish for them, to fear the consequences,
and to struggle to repress his desires. An incomplete resolution of the Oedipus complex, as may happen if the boy fails to identify with the father, may cause problems in
later life, such as weak moral standards or a poorly defined sexual identity.

Freud described a different developmental course for girls, who must resolve the
Electra complex (taken from a Greek tragedy in which a woman plots her mother's
death). The very young girl begins by loving her mother, but she comes to blame her
mother for "castrating" her when, during the genital stage, she becomes aware that she
has no penis. She develops "penis envy" and desires sexual intercourse with her father
as a way of sharing his penis. Somehow—the details are unclear, and Freud was never
entirely comfortable with this formulation—the girl resolves the Electra complex by
identifying with her mother once again, thereby "sharing" the father vicariously. (If all
of this seems far-fetched, remember that most of these feelings, especially the ones that
strike us as absurd or unthinkable, are unconscious, so we would have no inkling of them.)

The Latency Stage.   The **latency stage,** the period from age 6 until the onset of
puberty, is a period of relative psychosexual calm after the turmoil of the Oedipus or
Electra complex. A child tends to avoid the opposite sex but is interested in sex organs
and jokes related to sex and bodily functions.

The Genital Stage.   The **genital stage** begins with the hormonal changes of puberty. A child begins to mature sexually and develops a strong interest in forming heterosexual relationships with people outside the family, culminating in mating (marriage)
and reproduction (children of one's own). Freud regarded homosexuality as a sign of

an improperly resolved Oedipal complex. He did not consider it a normal sexual identity for some people, as more recent theorists do (see Chapter 12 for a discussion of homosexuality).

THE DYNAMICS OF PERSONALITY

Freud saw the id, ego, and superego as being in continual conflict. Since the id demands immediate gratification, conflict with the external environment is inevitable. Also, the superego rejects the id's demands, so a perpetual battle is waged within the psyche. The ego plays the difficult role of peacemaker. Freud's view of mental life has been described as a house, with a sex-crazed gorilla (the id) in the basement, a harsh, puritanical spinster (the superego) in the attic, and a nervous bank clerk (the ego) in between, trying to achieve some peace.

Anxiety. **Anxiety,** an uncomfortable, worried feeling, serves as a warning signal of conflict. Freud described three different types of anxiety: neurotic, moral, and objective. *Neurotic anxiety* occurs when a strong id threatens to overwhelm a weak ego; the fear of libidinal urges breaking through shows up as anxiety, but because the threat is unconscious, the individual cannot identify why he or she is anxious. *Moral anxiety* or guilt occurs when people unconsciously punish themselves for minor transgressions or mere wishes; a strong superego dominates a weak ego. *Objective anxiety* occurs when the ego detects a genuine danger in the real world. In each case, the anxiety serves as a signal that something is wrong and that something must be done. However, much of our anxiety arises from unconscious threats that should not trouble a fully mature individual.

Defense Mechanisms. Anxiety signals danger. We should appreciate anxiety as a warning, but more often we just want to eliminate the anxiety, which is itself unpleasant. **Defense mechanisms** are techniques that the ego uses to protect itself from anxiety by suppressing or distorting threats. For the most part, these defenses operate unconsciously. (Much of the ego, like the id and superego is unconscious; its negotiations with the id and superego are carried on without our awareness.) Although the defenses may distort or deny reality, they are usually regarded as normal and useful coping mechanisms. The common defense mechanisms include repression, denial, intellectualization, projection, reaction formation, rationalization, displacement, and sublimation.

1. *Repression,* often considered the most fundamental defense mechanism, involves keeping unacceptable thoughts in the unconscious. A particularly painful memory or a childhood sexual desire for a parent are examples of the sort of thoughts likely to be repressed.

Repression has received a lot of media attention recently, owing to the role of repressed memories in cases of childhood sexual abuse (see Chapter 7, page 000, "Psychology in our Times: Repressed Memories of Childhood Abuse?"). All sorts of psychological and behavioral problems are being traced to childhood abuse, which the victim has repressed because it was so terrible. Many therapists begin with the assumption that childhood abuse is to blame for the patient's current problems and work with the patient until the repression is lifted. But some researchers doubt the validity of these repressed memories and suggest that what are "recovered" are not real memories. Instead, they suggest that bogus memories are planted by the therapist or created by the imagination of the patient with the help of the therapist and the media, which lately have exploited the craze (Wright, 1993). Society's acceptance of the idea of repression of traumatic memories has far outstripped the evidence for it. If you cannot remember something horrible happening to you, does that mean that nothing horrible happened or that something must have actually happened, but that its very horribleness keeps you from remembering it? There is no way for a psychologist to distinguish clearly between real and fabricated memories unless it can be established independently which is which. The popular acceptance of Freud's notion that we repress traumatic incidents has made this controversy inevitable.

2. *Denial* permits unacceptable material to enter consciousness, only to be negated as if it did not or could not exist. This is most likely to happen immediately after an acute trauma, such as the death of a loved one. Denial can also protect us more generally from uncomfortable facts. For example, a teenager we know told her father that she was using an illicit drug. She was astonished when he responded by doubting her statement and accusing her of just trying to get him angry. He insisted, "My daughter would never do that." His denial protected him from having to acknowledge his daughter's unacceptable behavior.

3. *Intellectualization* acknowledges unacceptable or threatening material, but drains it of its emotional impact. The individual focuses on dry, technical aspects of a trauma instead of on its emotional effect. Thus, many people deal with the death of a loved one by immersing themselves in the details of the funeral service or insurance policies, rather than in grieving.

4. In *projection*, we "relocate" unacceptable aspects of ourselves onto others. A boy's murderous feelings toward his father may be projected onto his father, so that the boy ends up believing that his father wants to hurt him. (Believing that your father wants to hurt you would probably call for yet another defense mechanism, to protect you from that unacceptable idea.)

5. *Reaction formation* deals with unacceptable impulses or thoughts by turning them into their opposite. A boy may cope with his hatred of his sister and his anxiety over what he might do to her by treating her with exaggerated affection. We can presumably identify a reaction formation by its intensity and inappropriateness.

6. *Rationalization* finds a "perfectly reasonable" justification for behavior that really stems from an entirely different, unacceptable motive. Parents may punish their children "for their own good" when really they are simply venting their anger.

7. Freud considered displacement and sublimation the healthiest defense mechanisms. *Displacement*, expressing unacceptable desires through alternative channels, seems sounder than repressing them altogether. Anger at your boss can be released by working out on a punching bag at the gym.

8. *Sublimation* is a form of displacement that produces something of value. According to the psychoanalytic tradition, sublimated sadistic urges may lead someone to become a surgeon; inappropriate sexual urges may find their way into artistic creativity. In fact, psychoanalysis holds that sublimated sexual and aggressive urges have been behind most of civilization's advances. It has become almost a cliché to note that professional sports is a form of sublimation. The aggressive behavior on the playing field often includes the kind of violence that would earn a jail sentence out on the street. After a successful play, teammates may engage in hugging and pats on the rear that are difficult to interpret except as sublimated sexuality. Of course, these hugs and pats are not major contributions to civilization, but they do allow the expression of disguised sexuality in a way that does not offend anyone. Moreover, even just being a spectator at a sports event may help sublimate the observer's unconscious urges, as has been suggested by many Monday morning psychoanalysts. Can professional sports provide a safe outlet for the unconscious urges of not only the players but also the fans?

Are these "altruistic" surgeons sublimating unconscious aggressive urges?

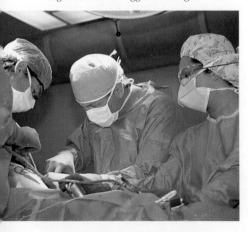

DEFENSE MECHANISMS

Defense mechanisms are unconscious techniques used to keep threatening impulses and ideas out of consciousness.

DEFENSE	DEFINITION	EXAMPLE
Repression	Restricting threatening material to the unconscious	Not being able to remember a childhood trauma
Denial	Not acknowledging threatening material	Refusing to believe that a loved one has died
Intellectualization	Focusing on technical aspects instead of emotions	Immersion in legal or financial details following the death of a loved one
Projection	Perceiving negative aspects of self in others	A selfish person arguing that everyone else is selfish
Reaction formation	Negating an impulse by exaggerating its opposite	Acting very affectionately toward someone you hate
Rationalization	Concocting a good reason for behaving badly	Punishing someone "for their own good" when you are simply angry
Displacement	Expressing an unacceptable impulse toward a safe target	Playing an aggressive video game when you have been frustrated at school or work
Sublimation	Transforming unacceptable impulses into valued products	Channeling aggression into sports or into fighting your nation's enemies

Now let us consider an everyday situation of anxiety and defense. We have all felt anxious about an upcoming exam, performance, or social event. This anxiety usually signals a concern that we are not adequately prepared. Presumably, the appropriate response would be to prepare ourselves better. Often, though, we do our best to deal with the anxiety not by trying to remove the threat behind it (by studying, rehearsing, and so on) but by trying to remove the anxiety itself (by distracting ourselves, finding something else—usually something trivial—to worry about, trying to relax with sports or entertainment, and so on). These are not the classic Freudian defenses, but they serve the same purpose. Like the Freudian defenses, they do not really eliminate the problem; they merely provide a short-term escape.

You may be aware of some of the everyday defenses that you use when you get anxious, especially when you are anxious about some situation in the real world. The classic psychoanalytic defenses are more often directed against threats from inside our own mind, especially unconscious urges that we dare not express directly.

SUBLIMINAL PSYCHODYNAMICS

One of the major shortcomings of psychoanalysis is the shortage of supporting scientific evidence; indeed, psychoanalysis sometimes seems to be more a creed, or set of beliefs, than a science involving research. Freud relied more on rhetoric than on traditional evidence to support his arguments (Spence, 1990), and his followers have generally looked down on empirical research. Nevertheless, some researchers have persisted in trying to test psychoanalytic ideas in a scientific way.

One popular psychoanalytic idea is that subliminal images—images that we cannot consciously identify because they are either disguised or presented too quickly—can affect our unconscious thoughts and motivation and ultimately our overt behavior. If the images remain unconscious, then they will not encounter normal defense mechanisms. Ruth and his colleagues (1989, 1990), for example, examined the role of sexual symbolism in advertising. They exposed normal college students to liquor advertisements from magazines. Half the ads contained objects that were symbolic of male genitals (long, pointed objects), female genitals (openings, containers), or intercourse (insertion, penetration); the other half contained no sexual imagery. The students, who were apparently

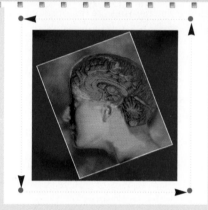

unaware of the sexual symbolism in the ads, expressed a stronger intention to buy the liquors whose ads contained sexual symbols. Presumably, these symbols were unconsciously arousing, and the arousal was pleasurable, making the viewer more attracted to the ad and therefore to the liquor. Whether the ads are really sexually stimulating remains controversial. Exposure to the ads appears to increase sexual responses on certain psychological tests (Ruth & Mosatche, 1985), but some critics remain skeptical: "Fascinating as the symbolic interpretations of the Freudians are, there is simply no good evidence that they are correct" (McCrae & Costa, 1990, p. 125).

A more elaborate program of research was initiated by Silverman (1983). *Subliminal psychodynamic*

activation refers to a process in which verbal messages or pictorial images related to unconscious conflicts are presented by means of a *tachistoscope,* a type of projector that presents images so briefly (about 4 milliseconds) that subjects cannot possibly identify their content. Despite their brevity, however, these images have dramatic effects on thought and behavior, compared to control stimuli that are not related to unconscious conflict.

Sexual symbolism in advertising may unconsciously affect the the attractiveness of the product.

According to Freud, the defenses protect the ego from unacceptable sexual and aggressive urges arising from the id. Recently, Paul Rozin (Haidt, McCauley, & Rozin, 1994; Rozin, Haidt & McCauley, 1993; see also Becker, 1973) has suggested that what we really fear and repress, more than sex or aggression, is death. We try to avoid thinking about death in general and especially our own death. Rozin argues that this aversion to death shows up as disgust, one of the most frequently expressed but least understood emotional responses. Rozin's survey reveals that what we find disgusting are things that remind us of our own animal nature, because all animals are mortal. We are disgusted by blood, excrement, hair, bodily functions, sex, injury, disfigurement, disease, and other reminders that we are living creatures, subject to decay and death. Rozin's hypothesis has an intuitive appeal, if only because we are all familiar with how difficult it is for most of us to come to terms with our eventual death.

PSYCHOANALYTIC ASSESSMENT

Because so much of the psyche is unconscious, psychoanalysts do not attempt to measure it directly. It would make no sense to ask people to describe the conflicts

One image—a picture of a charging lion—aggravates pathology in schizophrenics. The message "Beating Dad is wrong" interferes with dart-throwing performance in normal male students, whereas "Beating Dad is OK" improves performance, apparently because dart-throwing competition is symbolically related to Oedipal conflict. Silverman also obtained dramatic effects with the words "Mommy and I are one" (see Figure 14.2). This message concerns our continuing struggle over individuation (separation from the mother). Normal psychological growth demands such separation, but the unconscious supposedly yearns for a more primitive, symbiotic attachment. "Mommy and I are one" allegedly satis-

CONTROVERSY CONTROVERSY CONTROVERSY CONTROVERSY

fies this unconscious wish and thereby reduces pathology. (Schizophrenics who are not adequately differentiated from their mothers to begin with will not be helped by the message and may even get worse.)

The therapeutic success of the "Mommy and I are one" stimulus with schizophrenics has led to wider applications: It has been used to treat everything from bug phobias to obesity to poor math performance. The popularity of the technique, however, has drawn attention and criticism. Balay and Shevrin (1988), in a major review, criticized Silverman and his followers for sloppy research and sloppy thinking, pointing out that it has been difficult to repeat the original results and that the original studies themselves contained many inconsistencies. In effect, Balay and Shevrin allege that Silverman saw what he wanted to see and ignored or made excuses for what did not fit with his theory. Defenders of Silverman have counterattacked, noting, for instance, that improving Silverman's allegedly sloppy methods would probably make his results more powerful, not less (Figueroa, 1989).

Hardaway (1990) conducted a meta-analysis of research on subliminal psychodynamic activation, in which the results of all the studies were statistically combined. The overall result clearly showed that "Mommy and I are one" and similar images do have an effect when presented subliminally. (When the message is presented supraliminally—for lengthier durations so that the subjects are conscious of it—the effects tend to be weaker or absent, presumably because they do not penetrate into the unconscious.) It remains difficult to believe that such short exposures to complex stimuli could have any effect at all. Balay and Shevrin (1989) believe that an effect is there, but doubt that it operates by activating specific unconscious conflicts or fantasies, as Silverman has claimed. Another alternative has been proposed by Bornstein (1992), who argues that the emotional subliminal stimuli generally make people either relaxed or upset, either helping or hurting their performance or adjustment.

After dozens of studies, the reality of subliminal psychodynamic activation is still questionable; and even if it is real, how it works seems even further from being understood. Continuing research will no doubt attempt to specify how it operates, while further failures to demonstrate the effect at all will keep the controversy alive.

FIGURE 14.2
Mommy and I Are One

Tachistoscopic presentation of the phrase "Mommy and I are one" appears to help people suffering from unconscious conflicts. The mechanism of this effect—and even its reality—remains controversial.

Mommy and I are one

between their id and superego, since they cannot possibly be aware of them. The only hope for psychoanalytic personality assessment is to use indirect techniques that bypass the ego defenses to get at the unconscious material. Such techniques include dream analysis, analysis of expressions, free association, and projective personality tests, including sentence completions.

As discussed earlier and in Chapter 5, *dream analysis* assumes that a dream's symbolism gives us clues to the dreamer's unconscious. Characters in the dream (including animals) represent important people in the dreamer's life, and the often absurd dream plots represent disguised, often sexual and aggressive, wishes. The idea of developing a "dictionary of symbols" was particularly attractive to Jung and his followers. Interpretations normally depend on the insights and theoretical orientation of the experienced therapist (Freud and Jung often disagreed about the meaning of a particular symbol) but the idiosyncratic meanings that the patient gives to certain dream elements are also important.

Expressions are free-form creations (artistic or dramatic) that may be analyzed for clues to the creator's personality. In *free association*, the patient expresses whatever

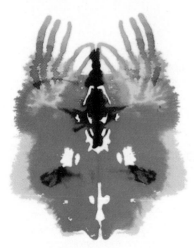

FIGURE 14.3
A Rorschach Inkblot

Interpreting Rorschach responses is a complex process. Responses are always interpreted in relation to other responses; nevertheless, some generalizations are possible. For instance, subjects who use the entire blot for their responses are thought to have organizational or integrative abilities. Those who use small details are likely to be seen as needing to be accurate and precise. Responses are also scored for a wide variety of symbolic objects, including blood, fire, food, animals, and genitals.

Pictured Here (in the front row left to right) are Goering, Hess, Von Ribbenhop, Keitel, Rosenberg, and Hans Frank during the Nuremberg Trials. Did these war criminals display normal personality, relatively mild character disorders, or severe psychopathology? Rorschach test results have played a major role in this debate, but have not resolved the issue.

thoughts or images come to mind, no matter how irrelevant or embarrassing they may seem. This technique is based on the assumption that people's thoughts are neither random nor simple responses to the environment; rather, they reflect underlying mental states. If the therapy situation is comfortable enough, the patient's defenses may relax, and unconscious urges may "leak through" into consciousness.

Projective tests provide more formal measures of the unconscious by having subjects respond to a series of ambiguous stimuli. In *sentence completions*, the tester provides the beginning of a sentence (e.g., "I only wish my mother had . . . .") and the subject provides a conclusion. More elaborate projective tests, such as the Rorschach inkblots or the Thematic Apperception Test, also present ambiguous stimuli, with the subject's responses presumably reflecting underlying personality.

The Rorschach. The *Rorschach inkblot test*, developed by psychiatrist Hermann Rorschach in 1921, is one of the most widely used projective tests. The test is composed of complex, symmetrical inkblots, some black and white, others (like the one in Figure 14.3) in color. Subjects report what they see on each card and then explain what aspects of the card influenced their responses. Scoring focuses not only on particular objects (insects, genitals, etc.) but also on location, originality, movement, color, and shading. Recently, Exner (1986) introduced a more standardized (and computerized) procedure for administering and scoring the Rorschach. Exner's interpretation scheme has recently been applied retrospectively to the Rorschach responses given by Nazi war criminals awaiting trial at Nuremberg in 1946. Previous interpretations of these responses suggested that these leading Nazis had pathological personalities (Miale & Selzer, 1975) or at least excessive rigidity, tough-mindedness, and a perception of the world as dangerous and hostile (Resnick & Nunno, 1991). When these responses and non-Nazi control responses were rescored using Exner's method by psychologists who did not know whose responses they were scoring, the Nazis were found to have widely divergent personalities and not much pathology, suggesting that the horrors of Nazism cannot be attributed simply to "sick" personalities (Zillmer, Archer, & Castino, 1989). (Zillmer et al.'s findings also suggest that unless careful controls are in place, Rorschach interpretations can be easily biased.)

The Thematic Apperception Test (TAT). As we first discussed in Chapter 12, the TAT was developed by H. A. Murray at Harvard in the 1930s. The *Thematic Apperception Test* consists of a series of pictures presented one at a time. Subjects tell stories about the pictures, including what led up to the scene in the picture and what will happen next. Psychologists score the stories by identifying motivational themes that can be interpreted as projections of unconscious needs and current concerns.

Although the TAT and the Rorschach continue to be among the most widely used personality tests, doubts about the validity of projective tests have persisted. The same quality that makes them popular among those clinicians with a psychoanalytic orientation—their alleged ability to penetrate to the hidden core of personality—makes it difficult to prove their accuracy. If a projective test reveals a hidden side to our personality that does not show up in our conscious thoughts or behavior, how can we ever prove that the test is correct?

OTHER PSYCHOANALYTIC THEORISTS

Over the years, several revisions to Freud's theory have been proposed. These revisions tend to be changes in emphasis rather than outright rejections of Freudian doctrine. For instance, many believe that Freud placed too much emphasis on the biologi-

RORSCHACH'S PARENTS

I distinctly see a camel, wrestling with a butterfly, no two ways about it.

I hate to say this, but if you can't tell it's a woman holding up a pineapple, then I feel sorry for you, I really do.

The Swiss psychoanalyst Carl Jung, for whom the unconscious was a source of spiritual guidance as well as libidinal urges.

cal urges of sex and aggression and neglected less primitive motives such as empathy and curiosity. Some have disagreed with Freud's view that the ego develops out of the id to serve as the id's "diplomat." They argue that the ego is independent, pursuing its own goals, including creativity, knowledge, and self-fulfillment. Others believe that Freud underestimated the importance of social and cultural influences on personality development. Among the best known of Freud's heirs (sometimes known as neo-Freudians) are Carl Jung, Alfred Adler, Karen Horney, and Erik Erikson.

Carl Jung. Carl Jung (1875–1961), an early admirer and colleague of Freud, developed his own version of psychoanalysis and psychotherapy, known as *analytic psychology*. Jung believed that in addition to the individual unconscious investigated by Freud, we all participate in the **collective unconscious,** a set of common images and memories inherited from our ancestors over millions of years. The collective unconscious contains symbols called **archetypes,** such as God, the young hero, the wise old man, the hostile brothers, the Earth Mother, and other elements that appear in legends and literature from all cultures. Jung saw the unconscious as containing certain positive elements, such as wisdom and creativity, whereas Freud saw the unconscious as a realm of darkness. Jung appeals particularly to those with an interest in religion and the occult, although others, perhaps baffled by his often unreadable prose style, accuse him of mysticism.

Jung also proposed a theory of personality types, classifying people on four independent dimensions: extraversion/introversion, sensation/intuition, thinking/feeling, and judgment/perception. In Jung's view, for every conscious or dominant side to personality, there is a weaker, unconscious side. Ideal personality development requires a balancing of the opposites. The Myers-Briggs Type Indicator (McCaulley, 1990) shown in Table 14.1 is widely used to identify Jung's personality types; It is popular in business (Moore, 1987) and colleges (Provost & Anchors, 1987) as a means of matching individuals to tasks and to other people (e.g., as roommates or work partners), even though it is not a very sophisticated personality test (Lorr, 1991).

Alfred Adler. Alfred Adler (1870–1937) was, like Jung, a student of Freud's who developed his own version of psychoanalysis, known as *individual psychology*. He disagreed most strongly with Freud's claim that sexual needs were dominant; instead, Adler emphasized the need for power. He argued that because we are born weak and helpless, we are liable to develop an *inferiority complex*, a feeling of vulnerability that results in compensatory striving for power and dominance over others. This striving for superiority may be converted into "social interest"; we may feel valuable by contributing to social improvement.

Like Freud, Adler emphasized the importance of early family experiences, especially pampering, rejection, and competition. Adler was the first to stress the importance of *birth order*—whether one is the oldest child in the family, the "baby," and so on—as an influence on personality. (Firstborns are dependent and conforming; middle children are vulnerable to competitive pressures; and youngest children are overprotected and eager to prove themselves.) The relation of birth order to various aspects of personality, including emotional dependence (Schachter, 1959), scientific creativity (Kagan, 1989), and intelligence (see Chapter 11, page 471) has become a popular area of research.

In general, firstborn children are likely to be self-confident (Hudson, 1990). However, a recent study (Lester, Eleftheriou, & Peterson, 1992) indicates that self-esteem (how positively you think of yourself) is highest in first-born males and last-born females, presumably because in our sexist society it is the male who is "supposed

TABLE 14.1
The 16 Different Jungian Personality Types According to the Myers-Briggs Type Indicator

		SENSING TYPES S		INTUITIVE TYPES I	
		THINKING T	FEELING F	FEELING F	THINKING T
INTROVERSION I	JUDGING J	**ISTJ** Serious, quiet, earn success by concentration and thoroughness. Practical, orderly, matter-of-fact, logical, realistic, and dependable. Take responsibility.	**ISFJ** Quiet, friendly, responsible, and conscientious. Work devotedly to meet their obligations. Thorough, painstaking, accurate. Loyal, considerate.	**INFJ** Succeed by perseverance, originality, and desire to do whatever is needed or wanted. Quietly forceful, conscientious, concerned for others. Respected for their firm principles.	**INTJ** Usually have original minds and great drive for their own ideas and purposes. Skeptical, critical, independent, determined, often stubborn.
INTROVERSION I	PERCEPTIVE P	**ISTP** Cool onlookers—quiet, reserved, and analytical. Usually interested in impersonal principles, how and why mechanical things work. Flashes of original humor.	**ISFP** Retiring, quietly friendly, sensitive, kind, modest about their abilities. Shun disagreements. Loyal followers. Often relaxed about getting things done.	**INFP** Care about learning, ideas, language, and independent projects of their own. Tend to undertake too much, then somehow get it done. Friendly, but often too absorbed.	**INTP** Quiet, reserved, impersonal. Enjoy theoretical or scientific subjects. Usually interested mainly in ideas, little liking for parties or small talk. Sharply defined interests.
EXTRAVERSION E	PERCEPTIVE P	**ESTP** Matter-of-fact, do not worry or hurry, enjoy whatever comes along. May be a bit blunt or insensitive. Best with real things that can be taken apart or put together.	**ESFP** Outgoing, easygoing, accepting, friendly, make things more fun for others by their enjoyment. Like sports and making things. Find remembering facts easier than mastering theories.	**ENFP** Warmly enthusiastic, high-spirited, ingenious, imaginative. Able to do almost anything that interests them. Quick with a solution and to help with a problem.	**ENTP** Quick, ingenious, good at many things. May argue either side of a question for fun. Resourceful in solving challenging problems, but may neglect routine assignment.
EXTRAVERSION E	JUDGING J	**ESTJ** Practical, realistic, matter-of-fact, with a natural head for business or mechanics. Not interested in subjects they see no use for. Like to organize and run activities.	**ESFJ** Warm-hearted, talkative, popular, conscientious, born cooperators. Need harmony. Work best with encouragement. Little interest in abstract thinking or technical subjects.	**ENFJ** Responsive and responsible. Generally feel real concern for what others think or want. Sociable, popular. Sensitive to praise and criticism.	**ENTJ** Hearty, frank, decisive leaders. Usually good in anything that requires reasoning and intelligent talk. May sometimes be more positive than their experience in an area warrants.

SOURCE: *Introduction to Type*, by Isabel Myers-Briggs.

to" be in a position of dominance, whereas the female is "supposed to" be in a submissive position. How does your self-confidence and self-esteem compare to that of your brothers and sisters? Do you think that your birth order has affected your personality?

Karen Horney. Karen Horney (1885–1952) was born in Germany, trained in Europe with one of Freud's students, and came to the United States in 1934. Horney agreed with Freud that the adult personality was shaped by childhood experiences, but she believed that personality development was a product of social relationships more than an expression of innate sexual and aggressive drives. In particular, Horney argued that when parental behavior toward a child was not stable and caring, the helpless, insecure child felt "basic anxiety" and a deep resentment, or "basic hostility." Because the child needs and fears the parents, this hostility has to be repressed, leading to even greater anxiety and feelings of unworthiness. The conflicts associated with basic anxiety and basic hostility create problems for the child and later for the adult.

The psycholanalyst Karen Horney.

Horney was a pioneer in the psychology of women, "the first, and perhaps the best, critic of Freud's ideas about women" (Quinn, 1987, p. 14). She argued that women's feelings of inferiority stemmed from their social powerlessness rather than from their anatomical "incompleteness," as Freud maintained. Indeed, she suggested that "men repress their envy of mothering by overvaluing male sexuality" (Grosskurth, 1991, p. 11). Her profemale stance led to trouble with the Freudian establishment, but her reputation has been revived recently, owing to her pioneering feminism.

Erik Erikson. Erik Erikson (1902–1994) studied psychoanalysis in Vienna with Freud's daughter Anna before moving to the United States. In his developmental theory, he stressed the independence of the ego and the importance of culture in forming personality. As we saw in Chapters 9 and 10, Erikson analyzed development in terms of eight *psychosocial* (not psychosexual) stages that extend throughout life. Each stage has its own challenges; the "identity crisis" that troubles many young adults is a well-known example. How well we handle the challenges at each stage determines our subsequent mental well-being.

Ego Psychology and Related Developments.   After Freud, psychoanalytic theory focused increasingly on the ego operating independently of the id. **Ego psychology** is an offshoot of psychoanalysis in which the primary emphasis is on the ego, which has its own purposes and does not merely mediate between the id, the superego, and the external world. Margaret Mahler (Mahler, Pine, & Bergman, 1975) focused on our conflicting needs for independence and connectedness to others; this is a conflict between the ego and the social world (not the id). Heinz Hartmann (1939/1958) believed that some ego functions, such as perception, are present from birth and not merely the result of the need to cope with the id's demands. Fairbairn (1952) proposed that the libido seeks objects, rather than pleasure. His theory of "object relations" is cognitive as well as emotional, focusing on how we perceive objects—especially people, including ourselves—as good or bad and how we cope with our ambivalence about the important people in our lives. Heinz Kohut (1977) focused on the self rather than the id, ego, and superego. The self consists of ambitions, ideals, and the skills necessary to accomplish them. Healthy development also requires self-esteem, empathy, and a secure identity, all of which depend on the treatment we get from our parents or other early caretakers. We can only mention some of these modern theorists here and thus cannot hope to do justice to their sophisticated theories. Together, though, they represent a move away from Freud's original id-based psychology.

CONTEMPORARY IMPACT OF THE PSYCHOANALYTIC APPROACH

Psychoanalysis, especially Freud's version, has had an enormous impact on psychology, psychotherapy, the way we think about ourselves—indeed, on our culture in general. Freud provided one of the first fully deterministic models of personality, in which everything we do, think, and feel has a potentially understandable cause stemming from our underlying personality. Because of Freud, we are no longer satisfied with people's superficial explanations for their behavior; much of what people do, it seems, is determined by forces inaccessible to ordinary conscious awareness. Recent developments in cognitive psychology focusing on mental processes without awareness, such as implicit memory (see Chapter 7) and automatic processing (see Chapter 5), would seem to provide experimental support for the idea of the unconscious (Blatt, 1990; Westen, 1990), even if the cognitive psychology version of the unconscious lacks the passion and strife of the psychoanalytic version (Bandura, 1991). Freud's second major contribution was his attempt to link unconscious motivation to basic biological drives. Freud regarded psychology as the mental side of a person's attempt to cope with fundamental biological urges and tension. One biographer (Sulloway, 1979) even called Freud a "biologist of the mind." A third contribution was Freud's emphasis on early childhood.

Critics of Freud, and even some of his followers, have argued that he overstated each of his claims: In all probability, our psyches are neither as unconscious nor as biological as Freud argued, and our personalities continue to be shaped by influences beyond the first few years of development. It has been suggested that Freud's theories were unduly influenced by his own peculiar relationship with his parents (Mindess, 1988) or by the sexually repressed neurotic patients that he saw. Freud seemed to pay little attention to healthy personality functioning other than to identify psychological health in terms of our ability to love and work, and he was not optimistic about our chances of achieving anything more than a temporary truce between the warring factions of the psyche. Freud has repeatedly been accused of misunderstanding and demeaning women (see "Controvery: Does Personality Theory Include Women?"). Finally, psychoanalysis is often dismissed as unscientific, owing to the vagueness of its terms and the difficulty of designing studies that could conclusively test psychoanalytic hypotheses (see "Controversy: Subliminal Psychodynamics"). As one observer put it, "psychoanalysis offers incredibly detailed, extensive, and persuasive explanations of . . . many phenomena that have never been documented empirically to exist" (Garbarino, 1989, p. 1014). For some psychoanalysts, trying to prove Freud's assertions is unnecessary and even treachery. One perplexed researcher reported that "what I thought of as research in psychoanalysis was interpreted by others as a lack of faith in the field" (Stunkard, 1976, p. 13). These days, psychoanalytic thinking is as likely to be found in a university's English department as in its psychology department, since one of its major strengths is its ability to provide coherent and interesting interpretations of literary texts without achieving scientific standards of proof.

Freud's proposals regarding sexuality in children remain controversial. For Freud, the sexuality of children was largely unconscious—a matter of wishes—and not a matter of actual sexual behavior occurring in the nursery. Recent evidence, however, suggests that many young children have endured traumatic sexual experiences. Perhaps as many as half of all adult women have suffered childhood sexual abuse, often by their own fathers and stepfathers (Haugaard & Repucci, 1988); but also consider the problem of "recovered memories," discussed earlier. Masson (1985) claims that Freud, who was ordinarily not afraid to adopt unpopular opinions, refused to believe his patients' reports about their early sexual seductions and traumas. Freud believed instead that the abuse was merely fantasized. One recent biographer (DeSalvo, 1990) has gone so far as to blame Virginia Woolf's suicide on her acquaintance with Freud and his dismissal of childhood sexual abuse. Woolf was forced to doubt her own memories of abuse, and eventually she questioned her own sanity.

The Phenomenological/Humanistic Approach

For Freud, personality is located mostly outside of conscious experience. Followers of Freud have modified this view by placing a greater emphasis on the ego and conscious functioning. **Phenomenology** goes one step further by putting conscious experience—people's perceptions, interpretations, and feelings—at the center of personality. Both the external world and our internal states affect us only through our subjective

DOES PERSONALITY THEORY INCLUDE WOMEN?

One of the many criticisms of Freud over the years centers on his perceptions of women. Modern scholars, especially feminists, find Freud's view of women to be inaccurate and degrading. For Freud, the essential fact about women was that they lacked a penis, which led them to regard themselves as incomplete and to become subservient to men.

Psychoanalysis, it is alleged, is basically a theory of male development. Freud himself acknowledged that the Oedipus complex made more sense than did the female equivalent, the Electra complex. Indeed, one of the few questions to which Freud admitted he did not have the answer was, What do women want? Presumably, Freud himself never really knew what motivated women, and he ended up thinking of them as defective men. For instance, the conscience develops as a result of the boy's internalization of his strict father during the resolution of the Oedipal crisis. Because girls do not internalize the father, Freud claimed that they lacked a full ethical sense.

It is more than a little ironic that Freud had so much trouble understanding women, since most of his patients were women, and his theory was supposedly based on his experience with his patients. Some people (e.g., Mindess, 1988) have argued that Freud's theory was more a projection of his own personality than a result of his observations of anyone else.

Modern critics, particularly those influenced by feminist thinking, have argued that women are different from men, but not in any way inferior. (Note that Horney does not represent the sort

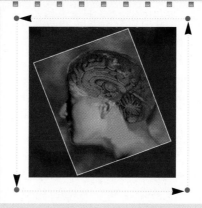

of feminism that regards women as different but in no way inferior to men: She argued that women are essentially the same as men, since they both wanted the same thing—power.) The separate-but-equal school of thought suggests that women are motivated by different goals than men. Whereas men are interested in individual achievement, competition, and acting forcefully on the environment, women display a more communal orientation. They are more concerned with caring and sharing than with dominating. (Perhaps this is because they have internalized their mother rather than their father.) Sex role inventories, in which people indicate how "masculine" or "feminine" they are, boil down to the distinction between "agency" (achievement, competence) and "communion" (helping, sharing, empathizing). These analyses cast doubt on the generality of, say, Adler's theory, which emphasizes a striving for superiority as the essence of human nature.

Of course, the idea that women are merely different from men rather than inferior has its own dangers. For one thing, it implies that all women are alike

(and that all men are alike, albeit different from women). Personality psychology, as we have seen, promotes the study of individual differences, so grouping together half the people in the world and claiming that they are essentially alike may be politically correct but not psychologically correct. Also, what are competitive women supposed to do? Must they either change their personality or think of themselves as something other than women?

A couple of decades ago, Matina Horner (1972) identified a "fear of success" motive in women. She argued that women could succeed in the male world but that they were afraid to, if only because such success would pose a threat to their femininity. Although subsequent research (Pauldi & Frankell-Hauser, 1986) has questioned whether women really fear success (or fear it any more than men do), women still face a difficult dilemma. Are they part of a qualitatively different group, speaking in "a different voice" (Gilligan, 1982)? Are sex differences natural, to be cherished and cultivated? Or are the existing differences between the sexes artificial, to be eliminated as much as possible?

From the standpoint of personality theory, whether women differ from men in personality is an open question. Perhaps, on average, there are some differences, but these differences may be small compared to the differences in personality among women (and among men). More to the point, we must ask whether the existing sex differences in personality are the product of the particular culture in which we live or are basic to human nature, as Freud implied.

interpretations. According to one enthusiastic phenomenologist, "Subjective experience is not just one of the dimensions of life, it *is* life itself." (Csikszentmihalyi, 1990, p. 192). To understand someone's personality, then, we must understand the way that person thinks and feels.

The focus on subjective human experience is often linked to a belief in the inherent value of that experience, along with a related belief that all people tend to seek improvement, or self-actualization. This **humanistic approach** is evident in the phenomenological theories of Carl Rogers and George Kelly.

CARL ROGERS AND SELF THEORY

Carl Rogers (1902–1987) was a midwesterner who attended the Union Theological Seminary before becoming a psychologist. At the heart of his theory (1970a) is the human need to develop and maintain a positive self-concept, a sense that we are living up to our ideals. Our self-evaluation, in this humanistic theory, is all-important; even if we are highly regarded by our peers, we may have a negative self-concept (i.e., view ourselves as failures). Our psychological well-being depends on the gap between our **actual self** (how we see ourselves) and our **ideal self** (how we would like to be). If the gap is large, the result is psychological distress. One way of coping with this distress is to deny or distort either reality ("I didn't really do that; I was forced into it") or our self-concept ("That's not the real me; I'm actually a good person") to protect our self-esteem. These tactics resemble Freudian defenses that protect the ego.

According to Rogers, a large gap between how we see ourselves (actual self) and how we would like to see ourselves (ideal self) is a sign of trouble. But does a narrow gap always make for a healthy personality? You might lower your ideals drastically so that they will match your negative self-image; or you might hold on to an unrealistically high ideal and change your self-perception until it was also unrealistically positive. Does narrowing the gap between actual self and ideal self ensure mental health?

Recently, Higgins (1989) has proposed a *self-discrepancy theory* based on the idea that we have more than one ideal—the ideal imposed by ourselves and the ideal imposed by others, the ideal that is desirable and the ideal that we "should" want. Falling short of these different ideal selves causes different sorts of distress. For instance, a discrepancy between your actual self and the self that you would like to be produces depression, whereas if you fail to live up to the ideal that other people think you ought to achieve, you will experience anxiety.

Regardless of the problems of self-ideal discrepancy, Rogers believed that we naturally grow toward full realization of our innate capacities—unless this growth is blocked. Put simply, "Every living thing breathes, blooms, creates, wants to grow" (Rosenfeld, 1942/1991, p. 273). This drive toward **self-actualization**—the fulfillment of all our capabilities and the achievement of our potential—begins with the basic requirements of nourishment, safety, and comfort. Once these needs have been satisfied, we pursue higher goals, such as creative expression and autonomy. To achieve true self-actualization, we must also have a positive self-concept, which in turn results from our being accepted by important individuals, especially parents, during childhood. (This view is similar to Kohut's, discussed earlier.) Because children's needs for self-expression often conflict with parental demands for disciplined restraint, children may inhibit their natural inclinations in order to please their parents. Instead of playing creatively or exploring, children may concentrate on doing only what the parents want. Eventually, these **conditions of worth**—rules about what can and cannot be done to gain approval—become internalized, acting like the superego to suppress our impulses and stunt our psychological growth. To achieve our full potential, we require **unconditional positive regard** (uncritical acceptance) from important others and ourselves. Being accepted as we are, and not just for following the rules of others, is necessary (but not sufficient) for self-actualization.

Determining whether you are self-actualized is not as simple as it might seem. Abraham Maslow's descriptions of self-actualized people (e.g., Thomas Jefferson, Harriet Tubman) included certain common traits, such as intelligence, creativity, and social concern, but it is not clear how much of each is required. Some characteristics

Albert Schweitzer and Eleanor Roosevelt are commonly regarded as having achieved a high degree of self-actualization.

may be associated with satisfaction—that is, people who possess these characteristics may feel satisfied with themselves and their lives—but certainly being satisfied with oneself is not the same as being a first-class human.

Acceptance of people as they are lies at the heart of Rogers's (1970b) person-centered therapy (see Chapter 16). Internalized conditions of worth tend to make people psychologically restricted, anxious, defensive, conforming, and overly hard on themselves; they feel manipulated rather than free. A therapist does not judge a client (a term that Rogers prefers to "patient," because there is no sickness involved); rather, by offering unconditional positive regard, empathy, and support for the client's point of view, the therapist allows the client to escape conditions of worth and achieve self-actualization.

This view of self-actualization as the ultimate goal after other needs have been satisfied is similar to Maslow's (see Chapter 12 for a discussion of Maslow's view of self-actualization).But while Rogers emphasized the danger in trying to please others, (trying to please others might distract us from self-actualization), Maslow recognized that the need for approval from others is important—just not the highest goal.

GEORGE KELLY AND PERSONAL CONSTRUCTS

Like Rogers, George Kelly (1905–1967) believed that understanding people amounts to figuring out how they interpret themselves and the world around them. According to Kelly, we perceive ourselves and others in terms of **personal constructs,** sets of opposed characteristics through which we filter, or "construct," our subjective world (Kelly, 1955). For example, you may be inclined to evaluate people primarily in terms of whether they are smart or stupid; Thus, smart versus stupid would be an important construct for you. I, on the other hand, might ignore the smart/stupid dimension and focus instead on whether people are friendly versus hostile.

Kelly developed a test to discover the constructs that people use. In the *Role Construct Repertory Test* (Rep Test), we are asked to compare and contrast the various important people in our lives (e.g., mother, father, admired teacher, ex-flame, successful person, self); the adjectives that we spontaneously use to make these comparisons and contrasts indicate our personal constructs. Various applications of the Rep Test have been developed, such as the Vocational Rep Test illustrated in Table 14.2.

Problems arise, in Kelly's view, when our constructs are inadequate; they may be too narrow, too broad, or simply inappropriate. For instance, if you focus only on whether others are intelligent or not, you will ignore aspects of their personalities that may be crucial for your relationship with them. Because the purpose of constructs is to interpret and predict the social world, faulty constructs will almost certainly lead to misunderstandings. Failure to predict what will happen in most situations causes anxiety. In therapy and counseling settings, Kelly had clients play different roles (*fixed role therapy*) as a way of construing the world differently. Clients will adopt more adequate constructs if they help to make better sense of the world and lead to more favorable interactions. Kelly believed that people have a choice about self-improvement. Unlike Rogers, Kelly did not believe that people actualize a potential that is latent within them; rather, people create themselves by the choices they make and can choose fairly freely.

The Trait Approach

"If there is to be a specialty called personality, its unique and therefore defining characteristic is traits" (A. H. Buss, 1989, p. 1378). For practical purposes, a **trait** is a dis-

TABLE 14.2
A Completed Vocational Rep Test
[taken from Neimeyer (1989, p. 586)]

In the Vocational Rep Test, the subject first produces constructs by indicating how two occupations are similar to each other and different from a third. In this case, the subject saw the farmer and the machine operator as similar (engaged in physcial labor) and different from the architect (engaged in nonphysical activity). The physician and social worker both help individuals, as opposed to the physicist, who helps society. The subject also indicates which "pole" of the construct he or she prefers (in this case, nonphysical activity, helping individuals), and the preferred pole is given positive scores. The comparisons and contrasts continue until 12 different constructs are produced, and then each occupation is rated on each construct. The total score associated with each occupation may then be calculated. More sophisticated measurements, calculating how extreme, consistent, and conflicting the ratings are, may be made using available computer software.

Farmer	Machine operator	Architect	Physicist	Physician	Social worker	Public school teacher	Accountant	Office worker	Lawyer	Life insurance salesman	Artist	Very +3 / Moderately +2 / Slightly +1 / Neither 0 / Slightly −1 / Moderately −2 / Very −3	
−3	−2	+2	+3	+1	+2	+2	+3	+3	+2	+2	+2	Nonphysical activity	Physical labor
−3	−1	0	−3	+2	+3	+1	+3	+3	+2	+2	−2	Helps individuals	Helps society
+3	+2	+3	0	−2	−2	−1	−3	0	−2	−3	+3	Creating	Not creating
+3	+2	+2	0	+3	+2	+3	+2	+3	+2	+3	−2	Practical	Not vital
+3	−3	+1	+2	+3	−2	−2	−1	−3	+2	−3	+3	Independent	Subordinate
−3	−3	+1	0	+3	−2	−2	+1	0	+1	0	0	High salary	Low salary
0	0	0	−1	+3	+3	+2	−3	−2	0	−1	0	People oriented	Paperwork oriented
0	−1	−1	−2	+1	+2	0	−3	+2	+2	−1	0	Involves writing	Involves numbers
−1	−3	−2	+3	+2	−2	−1	−2	−2	−2	−3	−2	Scientific	Not scientific
+1	+2	+1	−1	+2	−3	−3	+2	0	+2	+3	+3	Work for state	Non-state job
+3	+3	+1	0	−1	−2	−1	+2	+2	−1	+2	−3	Needs oriented	Philosophical
−2	−3	+2	+3	+3	+1	+2	+1	+1	+3	−1	0	Requires colllege	No college required

tinctive, internal, personal characteristic that is consistent across situations and stable over time and that influences behavior, thoughts, and feelings. We describe people—especially differences between people—in terms of such characteristics. The characteristics may be fixations or neuroses (Freud), self-concepts (Rogers), or personal constructs (Kelly). What distinguishes the trait approach to personality, then, is not that it involves traits, since all approaches analyze personality in terms of characteristics that can be thought of as traits. What is unique to the trait approach is its emphasis on the measurement of personality traits and the use of these traits to predict behavior.

TRAITS AND TYPES

In most cases, traits are continuous dimensions, ranging from one extreme (e.g., extremely friendly) to the other extreme (extremely hostile). Any given individual may be placed at some point—usually an intermediate point—along this dimension. (Contrast this with personal constructs, where only the extreme poles of the dimension apply.) When we speak of personality **types,** we categorize people in an all-or-none way (e.g., oral personality, Type A personality), depending on whether or not they possess a certain characteristic or set of characteristics. In a typology, there are usually a small number of categories, and everyone occupies one of these categories. Moreover, everyone in the same category (e.g., friendly) is considered equal to everyone else in that category. The trait approach attempts to specify degrees of friendliness, even among generally friendly people. In everyday language, we often use the categorical language of types (e.g., "He's a friendly person") because it is simple and convenient. On reflection, though, it would be more accurate to speak of degrees of friendliness, since not all friendly people are equally friendly.

HOW MANY TRAITS ARE THERE?

There are roughly 18,000 words in an unabridged dictionary that can be used to describe people (Allport, 1937); ignoring synonyms, there are nearly 5,000 descriptive words. One branch of trait theory has attempted, mainly through factor analysis, to reduce these thousands of attributes into the basic elements of personality.

As you may recall from our discussion in Chapter 11, factor analysis is a mathematical technique that permits us to group a large number of variables into a smaller number of factors, or clusters. Any two variables within a factor are highly correlated, whereas two variables in different factors are not correlated. Thus, if we rate a sample of individuals in terms of a large number of personality traits, we will probably find that certain traits (e.g., warm, sociable, agreeable) cluster together; these traits will be independent of traits in other clusters (e.g., active, powerful, intense). When we apply factor analysis to words describing personality traits, how many independent factors emerge?

Perhaps the best-known factor analyst is Raymond Cattell, who has proposed that personality should be described in terms of 16 basic trait dimensions (1973, 1982). Scores on particular personality dimensions are calculated from multiple-choice questions on the *Sixteen Personality Factor Questionnaire*, or *16PF*. The 16 dimensions appear in the left and right columns in Figure 14.4, which displays the pattern of personality traits found, on average, in airline pilots. Because the traits of successful pilots have been measured, airlines can and do look for these traits in new applicants for pilot positions (Houston, 1988).

Although Cattell derived the 16 basic factors, or traits, from self-report questionnaire responses, he also recommends exploring personality using *rating data* (descriptions provided by people familiar with the subject) and *test data* (based on behavioral tests, including performance on such unusual tasks as blowing up a balloon or reading backward). Depending on what sort of data are included in the factor analyses, as many as 23 or more basic traits may be found.

Hans Eysenck, another prominent factor analyst, has concluded that personality is best described by only three traits: extraversion (versus introversion), neuroticism (versus stability), and psychoticism (which does not have a clearly labeled opposite). Eysenck measures personality using self-report responses to the *Eysenck Personality Questionnaire, or EPQ-R* (Eysenck, Eysenck, & Barrett, 1985). An extravert is sociable, seeks out company, craves excitement, and tends to be impulsive and unreliable, whereas an introvert is reserved, cautious, and always under control. A neurotic is moody, anxious, or restless; a stable individual is calm, even-tempered, and unworried. People who score at the psychotic end of the third dimension are aggressive, cold, and egocentric; people at the other end of this dimension are empathic and less bold. Eysenck uses the terms neuroticism and psychoticism deliberately, because he believes

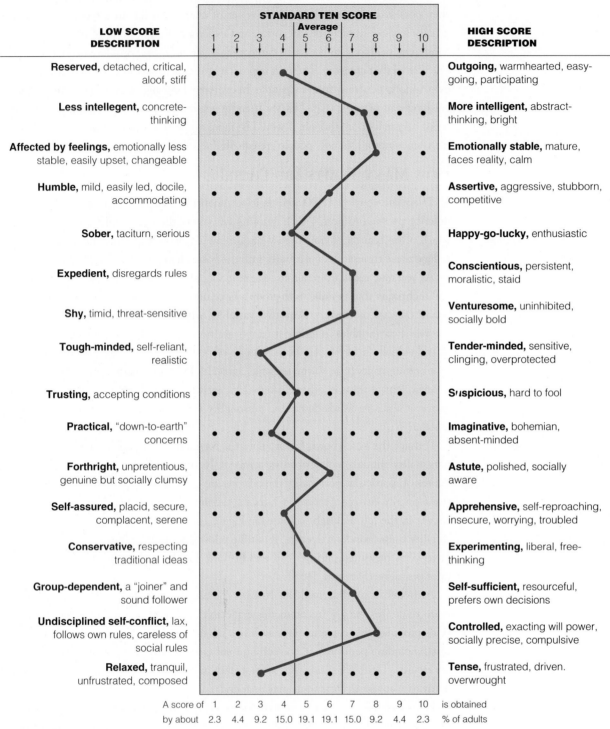

16PF TEST PROFILE FOR AIRLINE PILOTS

LOW SCORE DESCRIPTION	STANDARD TEN SCORE	HIGH SCORE DESCRIPTION

STANDARD TEN SCORE

Average

	1	2	3	4	5	6	7	8	9	10	

Reserved, detached, critical, aloof, stiff — **Outgoing,** warmhearted, easy-going, participating

Less intelligent, concrete-thinking — **More intelligent,** abstract-thinking, bright

Affected by feelings, emotionally less stable, easily upset, changeable — **Emotionally stable,** mature, faces reality, calm

Humble, mild, easily led, docile, accommodating — **Assertive,** aggressive, stubborn, competitive

Sober, taciturn, serious — **Happy-go-lucky,** enthusiastic

Expedient, disregards rules — **Conscientious,** persistent, moralistic, staid

Shy, timid, threat-sensitive — **Venturesome,** uninhibited, socially bold

Tough-minded, self-reliant, realistic — **Tender-minded,** sensitive, clinging, overprotected

Trusting, accepting conditions — **Suspicious,** hard to fool

Practical, "down-to-earth" concerns — **Imaginative,** bohemian, absent-minded

Forthright, unpretentious, genuine but socially clumsy — **Astute,** polished, socially aware

Self-assured, placid, secure, complacent, serene — **Apprehensive,** self-reproaching, insecure, worrying, troubled

Conservative, respecting traditional ideas — **Experimenting,** liberal, free-thinking

Group-dependent, a "joiner" and sound follower — **Self-sufficient,** resourceful, prefers own decisions

Undisciplined self-conflict, lax, follows own rules, careless of social rules — **Controlled,** exacting will power, socially precise, compulsive

Relaxed, tranquil, unfrustrated, composed — **Tense,** frustrated, driven. overwrought

A score of	1	2	3	4	5	6	7	8	9	10	is obtained
by about	2.3	4.4	9.2	15.0	19.1	19.1	15.0	9.2	4.4	2.3	% of adults

FIGURE 14.4
Cattell's Sixteen Personality Factor Questionaire (16PF)

The chart lists Cattell's 16 personality dimensions and the average personality profile for airline pilots. Note the pilots' distinctive scores on intelligence, emotional stability, tough-minded self-reliance, practicality, self-control, and composure, traits that most passengers would find reassuring.

that people who score at the extremes of these dimensions are vulnerable to psychiatric disorders (see Figure 14.5 for a comparison of Eysenck's dimensions with those of the ancient Greek Galen.)

The apparent discrepancy between Cattell's large number of traits and Eysenck's three major traits is mainly a result of their goals: Cattell prefers a more fine-grained analysis, whereas Eysenck prefers using very broad traits. There is a trade-off here: Eysenck's broad approach gets at the most fundamental units of personality, whereas the narrower, more differentiated approach makes it easier to predict specific behav-

FIGURE 14.5

Two of Eysenck's Three Dimensions of Personality and the Classic Four Temperaments

Eysenck (1967) contends that his dimensions of extraversion-introversion and neurotic-stable correspond to the personality typology proposed by the Greek physician Galen (a.d. 129–199) on the basis of prior speculations by Hippocrates (ca. 460 b.c.). Galen's typology included four temperaments: *melancholic* (gloomy), *choleric* (angry), *sanguine* (cheerful), and *phlegmatic* (stolid). These correspond to the modern factor analytic combinations neurotic-introvert, neurotic-extravert, stable-extravert, and stable-introvert. Combinations of traits identified by many other modern psychologists (including Jung, Adler, and Pavlov) have also been interpreted as corresponding to Galen's typology (Merenda, 1987).

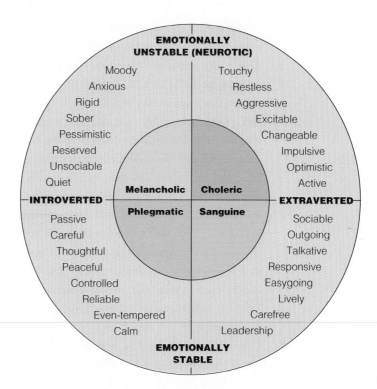

iors. For instance, extraversion may be subdivided into two smaller factors, impulsivity and sociability; but people's risk-taking behavior can be predicted more accurately from just their impulsivity scores rather than from their overall extraversion scores, which also include the sociability component, which is not relevant to risk taking.

Another group of researchers (Digman, 1990) has argued for five basic trait dimensions: extraversion, agreeableness, conscientiousness, emotional stability, and culture (artistic, intelligent, and refined). Some even claim that the debate is over and that these five "are now consensually acknowledged" (Angleitner, 1991, p. 185). After all, these five factors appear in different cultures (John, 1990), and we tend to use these "Big Five" traits or their equivalent to describe people whom we barely know (Passini & Norman, 1966) or do not know at all (Norman & Goldberg, 1966). Of course, this raises the possibility that these traits do not exist "out there" in people but rather in the heads of the raters, who then apply them to whomever they rate. D. M. Buss (1989) argues that humans have evolved to evaluate others in terms of these five dimensions because knowing about people's agreeableness, conscientiousness, and so on may prove crucial to our survival. Another view (Hampson, 1988) is that we tend to judge strangers using these five dimensions because of our prior experience with people.

MEASURING TRAITS

Deciding how many basic traits there are depends on how we analyze and cluster personality test scores. Personality testing, of course, is used for many purposes beyond settling such abstract questions. Individuals who want to get a clearer picture of themselves, institutions (especially business, government, and the military) that want to make sure that the right person is assigned to a particular job, and psychotherapy, where changes in personality are often used as a measure of success, all use personality tests. "In fact, the business world personality testing is considered to be the . . . essence of psychology" (Blinkhorn & Johnson, 1990, p. 671).

Some personality tests are designed to measure only one trait (e.g., anxiety), while other tests attempt to capture the entire personality. The most widely used multitrait personality test is the *Minnesota Multiphasic Personality Inventory*, or *MMPI* (recently updated as the MMPI-2). The MMPI, however, is used mainly to identify psychiatric symptoms or syndromes. Another well-known test, the *California Personality Inventory*, or *CPI* (Gough, 1956), was designed to measure normal personality, although over a third of its 480 items were taken from the MMPI. The CPI yields scores on 15 personality traits, including dominance, sociability, self-acceptance, achievement orientation, and masculinity/femininity, and classifies people in terms of three broad orientations—internal versus external interpersonal orientation, norm-favoring versus norm-doubting perspective, and competence/self-actualization versus ineffectiveness.

Another approach to personality measurement asks respondents to rate themselves directly on trait dimensions instead of responding to specific questions that are then coded in terms of personality traits. Table 14.3 shows a typical set of rating scales that can be used to rate your own or someone else's personality. Whether your ratings are valid (i.e., whether they accurately measure the personality in question) depends on your familiarity with the target, your perceptiveness, and your willingness to tell the truth. Often the target is rated by more than one person on the assumption that if independent raters agree about a particular rating, it is more likely to be valid (Funder, 1991).

Can you describe yourself accurately? Funder (1991, p. 35) argues that "a person is in a relatively poor position to observe and report accurately on his or her own traits." People tend to explain their own behavior in terms of situational pressures (see Chapter 17, page 726) rather than in terms of their own traits. Consider the bigot, who perceives other groups as threatening or inferior. He sees his hostility as a normal reaction to a threatening situation, rather than as a part of his personality. To the bigot, there is nothing distorted about his own personality. Probably most of us tend to see ourselves as normal and in a positive light; when we behave badly, it is because we were provoked.

TABLE 14.3
Rating Scales Based on the 16 Personality Traits Identified by Cattell (1973)

AVERAGE

Reserved	: ___ : ___ : ___ : ___ : ___ : ___ : ___ :	Outgoing
Less intelligent	: ___ : ___ : ___ : ___ : ___ : ___ : ___ :	More Intelligent
Affected by feelings	: ___ : ___ : ___ : ___ : ___ : ___ : ___ :	Emotionally stable
Submissive	: ___ : ___ : ___ : ___ : ___ : ___ : ___ :	Dominant
Serious	: ___ : ___ : ___ : ___ : ___ : ___ : ___ :	Happy-go-lucky
Expedient	: ___ : ___ : ___ : ___ : ___ : ___ : ___ :	Conscientious
Timid	: ___ : ___ : ___ : ___ : ___ : ___ : ___ :	Venturesome
Tough-minded	: ___ : ___ : ___ : ___ : ___ : ___ : ___ :	Sensitive
Trusting	: ___ : ___ : ___ : ___ : ___ : ___ : ___ :	Suspicious
Practical	: ___ : ___ : ___ : ___ : ___ : ___ : ___ :	Imaginative
Forthright	: ___ : ___ : ___ : ___ : ___ : ___ : ___ :	Shrewd
Self-assured	: ___ : ___ : ___ : ___ : ___ : ___ : ___ :	Apprehensive
Conservative	: ___ : ___ : ___ : ___ : ___ : ___ : ___ :	Experimenting
Group-dependent	: ___ : ___ : ___ : ___ : ___ : ___ : ___ :	Self-sufficient
Uncontrolled	: ___ : ___ : ___ : ___ : ___ : ___ : ___ :	Controlled
Relaxed	: ___ : ___ : ___ : ___ : ___ : ___ : ___ :	Tense

Construct your own (or a friend's) profile. See where you fall on each of these dimensions. Place an X in the middle category if you are "average" on the trait.

THE CONSISTENCY CONTROVERSY

The trait approach to personality assumes that our personalities are consistent. But do people really behave consistently? Walter Mischel (1968) triggered a crisis for personality psychology by arguing that people do not behave consistently from one situation to another and that personality tests do not accurately predict behavior. Mischel pointed out that our behavior is very responsive to situational pressures (influences in the environment); and if the situation is what controls how we behave, then our personality traits do not really make much difference. We behave inconsistently from one situation to another because different situations exert different influences on us. If personality were important, then we would behave consistently, since our personality, by definition, remains constant across situations.

But why do we persist in seeing people as consistent, or traitlike? Mischel and Peake (1982) argued that we see people as behaving consistently because we often see them in the same type of situation. What we actually detect is **stability**—regularity of behavior time after time but within the same situation. If our teachers always appear to be serious, it may be because we see them only in classroom situations. We think that we are detecting **consistency**—regularity of behavior across different situations. We assume that our teachers are serious in every situation, even though we see them in only one type of situation. According to Mischel and Peake, our confusion of stability with consistency leads us to conclude mistakenly that personality traits exist. Besides, when we look more closely at how people talk about traits, it turns out that people recognize that the trait appears only under certain conditions; in effect, we all agree that behavior is not fully consistent (Wright & Mischel, 1988).

Defenders of the trait approach point out that even if behavior varies somewhat across situations, underlying traits may still exist. A trait may be thought of as a tendency to behave in a certain way; but whether we actually do behave that way depends on a number of factors. In **strong situations,** where there are powerful situational pressures, people may not behave in line with their traits (Price & Bouffard, 1974); but in **weak situations,** where there are no strong external pressures to behave one way or another, people will display their basic traits. When behavior in many situations is combined (aggregated), trait patterns begin to emerge. Although behavior in any one situation may be largely controlled by situational pressures, the small influence of personality traits may add up over situations, especially if the situational pressures are in opposite directions in different situations (Epstein & O'Brien, 1985). In effect, trait theorists agree that behavior varies from situation to situation, but remind us that the underlying trait should not to be confused with the overt behavior.

Consistency in behavior may reflect either consistency in underlying personality (the trait view) or consistency in the situational pressures to behave in a certain way (the situational view). If you consistently display shyness, this might be because you are truly a shy person or because you happen to find yourself frequently in situations where shyness is the norm. Recent research indicates that both alternatives may be true. People seek out situations that "confirm their identities" (Swann, 1987). Buss (1987) points out that not only do people *select* situations (including the people they will be with) on the basis of their personalities, but they also *evoke* situations (i.e., they draw out reactions from others) that confirm their personalities, as when hostile people create hostile situations. People may also change the situation to reinforce their personalities, as when aesthetically oriented people surround themselves with art. Despite the obvious fact that strong situational pressures affect behavior, behavior is not entirely inconsistent; the considerable consistency in our behavior that is not due to the situation alone is due to our traits (Kenrick & Funder, 1988).

Traits imply regularity of behavior, but do you have to behave precisely the same way to display a consistent trait? What appear to be inconsistent behaviors may be different expressions of the same goals (Patry, 1992). How do you express hostility when playing tennis? When talking on the phone? When making a toast? "What people manifest consistently across situations . . . may not be so much specific behaviors but underlying psychological dispositions that can be expressed behaviorally in numerous ways" (Funder & Colvin, 1991, p. 777). Think of all the different ways in which you display your hostility (or friendliness).

BIOLOGICAL ORIGIN OF TRAITS

Where do our personality traits come from? Are they acquired through experience or through inheritance? Although this really is not an either/or question, the idea that personality is based on biological factors is as popular today as it was in ancient times. Biological approaches to personality have tended to take one of two main paths: genetics and constitution (body build).

Genes and Personality. In biology, most physical and behavioral traits are assumed to arise from the genes. If certain types of animals (including humans) tend to live in groups, this "sociability" is usually seen as an innate characteristic of the species; perhaps the genetically determined nervous system is constructed so that the presence of other members of the species has a calming or pleasant emotional effect, whereas isolation is unpleasant.

Does it make sense to assume that extraversion is an innate, genetic characteristic? One apparent problem with such an assumption is that not everyone is equally extraverted. But the genetic approach does not demand that everyone be the same. Extraversion may be adaptive for the species, but there is still room for individual differences. The particular circumstances faced by your ancestors may have favored higher or lower than average levels of sociability, and their adaptations would have been passed down to you. Also, your present circumstances can affect the extent to which your innate extraversion is expressed (Buss, 1991).

In psychology, the question of genetics is usually shifted to a discussion of heritability. **Heritability** is a measure of how much of the individual differences we see in a characteristic is due to differences in genetic background. That is, we usually ask not whether extraversion is inherited, but how much of the difference in the amount of extraversion in two or more people is due to genetics. Typically, the heritability of personality traits is determined by twin and adoption studies, which were explained in Chapter 2.

We start with the knowledge that monozygotic (MZ) twins are genetically identical, while dizygotic (DZ) twins share only 50 percent of their genes. Therefore, if monozygotic twins are more similar on a personality trait, we may conclude that genetics plays a role in producing the trait. Of course, even monozygotic twins are rarely if ever perfectly identical in personality, so studies of heritability usually conclude that there is a greater or lesser genetic component to the trait in question—not that the trait simply is genetic. Modern genetic theory also acknowledges that genes do not operate in isolation; certain physical and social experiences are often necessary for the expression of a trait. Thus, proper nutrition is required if you are to reach the potential height that you inherited from your parents. And even if you are genetically programm⬚⬚⬚⬚⬚⬚⬚rtune to be raised by wolves, yo⬚

How str⬚⬚⬚⬚⬚ traits? Adoption studies (e.g., L⬚⬚⬚⬚⬚an adopted child's personality re⬚⬚⬚⬚⬚f the adoptive parents, leading to⬚⬚⬚⬚⬚ctices, although significant, is sr⬚⬚⬚⬚⬚990, p. 433). Hoffman (1991), ho⬚⬚⬚⬚⬚the personality of their adopted ch⬚⬚⬚⬚⬚e child resemble them. If your pai⬚⬚⬚⬚⬚to compensate for the deprivation⬚⬚⬚⬚⬚ents will have affected your perso⬚⬚⬚⬚⬚emblance.

Twin st⬚⬚⬚⬚⬚d .5) for MZ pairs than for DZ pai⬚⬚⬚⬚⬚d neuroticism. Eysenck believes t⬚⬚⬚⬚⬚rmined by genetic factors" (1991, p. 784). One prominent theory of temperament, EAS theory, (Buss & Plomin, 1984), claims that emotionality (one aspect of neuroticism), activity, and sociability (one aspect of extraversion) are the most heritable components of personality. Even religiosity may be highly heritable (Waller, Kojetin, Bouchard, Lykken, & Tellegen, 1990). These studies also indicate that although environmental effects may swamp heredity early in life, as the individual becomes more independent, genetic effects become more apparent (Riese, 1990; Waller et al., 1990). According to one observer, "A significant genetic influence on personality is found, however personality is assessed . . . and whichever personality traits are studied" (Heath, 1991, p. 1063).

Plomin and Rende (1991) warn, however, that nongenetic influences on personality development are at least as important as genetic influences. For instance, MZ twins are almost twice as likely as DZ twins to be in daily contact with each other (Rose, Koskenvuo, Kaprio, Sarna, & Langinvainio, 1988). Thus, MZ twins may be more similar not only in heredity but also in environment. Moreover, considering just the MZ

A study comparing identical and fraternal twins reared apart shows an interesting difference between the pairs. Note that, when asked merely to stand against the wall, the identical twins (top row) assumed similar postures whereas the fraternal twins (bottom row) did not.

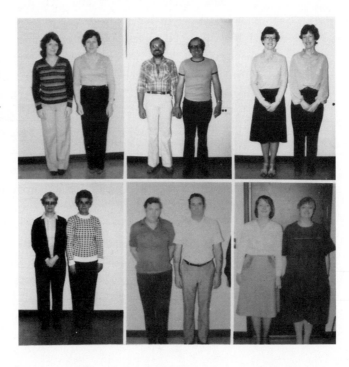

twins, those who were in more frequent contact—and who may consequently have been exposed to a more similar environment—were more similar in personality (Kaprio, Koskenvuo, & Rose, 1990). Interestingly, DZ twins who look alike are more similar in personality than are DZ twins who do not look alike, suggesting that people's common reactions to similar-looking twins may be at least partly responsible for the twins' similar personalities (Hoffman, 1985). The common environment of MZ twins is not the whole story, since MZ twins reared apart are more similar than are DZ twins reared apart; but environment has a significant effect on personality (Plomin, Chipuer, & Loehlin, 1990).

Plomin and Daniels (1987) have looked at the question from a different angle, asking not why MZ twins are so similar but why siblings in the same family are so different. Their research indicates that siblings are less alike in personality than either a common heredity or a common environment would lead us to expect. They conclude that people growing up in the same household do not share an identical environment. Siblings are treated differently by their parents, and they have different friends and experiences: "Although environment plays a role in personality development, it is not an environment that siblings share" (Hoffman, 1991, p. 190).

Hoffman (1991) provides a brief catalog of how siblings' environments are likely to differ. Birth order, age at the time of significant family events (e.g., divorce or economic changes), gender, physical appearance, idiosyncratic experiences (events that happen to only one sibling, such as illness or injury), and experiences with peers differ from sibling to sibling. All these factors affect personality.

Genetic influences on some broad personality traits are definitely important, but we cannot yet say precisely how important or how genetic predispositions combine with experience to form personality. Plomin and colleagues (1990) note that it is unlikely that a single gene will turn out to control a pattern of behavior in the same way that a single gene causes sickle-cell anemia. It becomes difficult to tease apart the effects of multiple genes and of experience combining with genes. Statistical contrasts of twins may support a role for heredity, but they do not tell us much more. Acceptance of hereditary influences on personality will be easier when we understand exactly which genes affect behavior and how differences in genes produce corresponding differences in behavior.

It is easy to be impressed by genetic influences on personality when we encounter the astonishing similarities that sometimes appear in monozygotic twins separated at birth. The twins studied by Thomas Bouchard and his colleagues at the University of Minnesota (see Chapter 2) often resemble each other so much that we are tempted to believe that everything is genetic. Included in this resemblance are very similar scores on personality tests. Indeed, there is some evidence that MZ twins reared apart resemble each other as much as MZ twins reared together (Tellegen, Lykken, Bouchard, Wilcox, Segal, & Rich, 1988). Large-scale studies, however, do not reveal quite as much MZ similarity as we might imagine from the few remarkable cases that tend to draw media attention.

Physique and Temperament.   Long before genetic theory, observers were debating the connection between more obvious physical characteristics and personality. Galen's theory of temperaments (see Figure 14.5) came with a theory of physique, in which "the best temperate man is he who seems to be in the mean of all extremities, that is skinniness and fatness...." (Galen 170/1938, p. 86). In more modern times, Ernst Kretschmer (1936) and William Sheldon (1942) argued that physique is related

Predominant
endomorph

Predominant
ectomorph

Predominant
mesomorph

**FIGURE 14.6
Sheldon's Body Types**

Do different body types have different
personalities? If so, how might we
explain the association? Does shape
affect personality, or vice versa? Do societal expectations play a part in determining whether a particular physique
becomes associated with a particular personality?

to psychopathology and temperament. **Temperament** usually refers to broad, emotional personality traits.

In Sheldon's scheme, people are rated in terms of *endomorphy* (roundness), *mesomorphy* (muscularity) and *ectomorphy* (thinness), more or less along a dimension from
fat to thin (see Figure 14.6). Endomorphs are supposed to be easygoing, sociable, and
self-indulgent (Sheldon) but vulnerable to manic-depressive disorders (Kretschmer).
Ectomorphs are expected to be intense, but socially and physically inhibited
(Sheldon) and vulnerable to schizophrenia (Kretschmer). Mesomorphs are aggressive
and energetic, according to Sheldon, and there is some evidence linking mesomorphy
with delinquency (Hartl, Monnelly, & Elderkin, 1982). In general, the attempt to
relate physique to personality has not been widely accepted by the scientific community. Sheldon probably exaggerated the link between physique and personality—he
claimed correlations as high as .80!—with the result that his work has been largely dismissed (Herman, 1992).

Contemporary research often conflicts with Sheldon's observations. For example,
Mehrabian (1987) finds that obese people are quite anxious rather than easygoing. If
there is any connection between physique and personality, though—whether or not it
agrees with Sheldon's observations—we must try to account for it. In a society where
fat people are ridiculed, it is perhaps not surprising to find that endomorphs are distressed. The causal connection between distress and overweight, however, is likely to
be complicated. Do certain physiques produce certain reactions in others (e.g., ridicule
versus acceptance), which in turn affect personality development? Or might there be
some physiological link between physique and personality, as the ancient Greeks
believed? Or could personality affect physique? (Are anxious people particularly likely
to overeat?) The recent increased interest in biological aspects of personality means
that these questions will continue to intrigue personality researchers.

Physiological Mediators of Personality.   Genetic studies of personality focus on
whether—or to what extent—personality is inherited. Physique research asks whether
personality is connected with body shape. Both kinds of research assume a biological
basis for personality, but neither has yet provided a convincing explanation of *how*
biology affects personality. Eysenck (1967; Strelau & Eysenck, 1987) maintains that
heritable differences in nervous system activity create differences in temperament.
This is a plausible hypothesis, but difficult to prove. Funder (1991, p. 32) concludes
that "a method to assess the neural basis of personality is not yet in sight." No doubt
better techniques will eventually make it easier to test biological hypotheses, but we
are still a long way from achieving Freud's original goal of explaining personality in
physiological terms. Even if we find a clear association between biological factors and
personality, we must go further and demonstrate *how* biology affects personality, which
is much more challenging.

The Social Learning Approach

The trait approach to personality tends to have a biological flavor, often viewing our
traits as present from birth. Indeed, if traits are innate, it becomes somewhat easier to
see why people might behave consistently across situations. Like most people, however,
psychologists are of two minds regarding the source of personality traits. Isn't personality at least partly acquired or changed by experience? Behavioral psychologists (see

PERSONALITY AND HEALTH

At least since the time of Hippocrates, there has been a suspicion that the mind may affect the body and, more specifically, may affect whether we get sick. Galen believed that melancholic (depressed) women were more likely to develop breast cancer than were sanguine (warm, emotionally expressive) women (Contrada, Leventhal, & O'Leary, 1990). During the 1940s and 1950s, psychosomatic theorists speculated that certain diseases (e.g., asthma, ulcers, and arthritis) were caused by unconscious conflict and that the specific type of conflict determined which disease was "selected" (Alexander, 1950). Although this "specificity" view was eventually dismissed, in the 1970s researchers became convinced that there was a causal connection between stress and disease. Some researchers explored whether certain types of people, because of their personalities, were more likely to experience stress. Other researchers, noting that not everyone exposed to the same stressors gets sick, suggested that some personality traits may act to protect people from the negative effects of stress, whereas other personality traits may make normal stressors "toxic." At the moment, the idea that personality plays an important role in disease is widely accepted, and research attempts to clarify how personality contributes to disease.

Perhaps the best-known personality factor in disease is the Type A behavior pattern, which appears to increase the risk of heart disease. Although called a "behavior pattern" rather than a "personality type" to distinguish it from the

typologies that had been previously discredited, Type A is as much a personality type as anything else. It includes competitiveness, impatience, rapid speech, and a tendency toward anger or hostility (see Chapter 13). All of these features are brought out by particular circumstances (e.g., competition, or a threat to one's sense of control) (Revenson, 1990). Research examining the different components of the Type A behavior pattern suggests that it is the hostility factor along with a cynical, mistrusting attitude that puts people at risk for heart disease (Smith, 1992).

How does this personality pattern affect the heart? Three basic possibilities have been suggested. First, it appears that Type A people have a particularly intense physiological reaction to stressors. For example, in a challenging or stressful situation, Type A individuals show a greater increase in catecholamine (epinephrine and norepinephrine) levels than do Type B people. High catecholamine levels have negative effects on coronary arteries, eventually leading to heart disease (Janisse & Dyck, 1988). Also, catecholamines can disrupt heart functioning in the short term and bring on sudden death. A second pathway emphasizes the health behaviors of Type A people. Type A individuals are more likely to do dangerous things (e.g., smoking or drinking), and they tend to deny the need for medical attention. (One colleague of ours asked that he be brought his briefcase so that he could catch up on his work while still in the hospital recovering

---

Chapter 1) believe that experience shapes our behavior; even behavior geneticists like Plomin now emphasize the effects of experience, suggesting that much of personality is acquired, or learned. **Social learning theory** begins from this assumption and goes on to emphasize that much of the learning that shapes our personalities depends on our experiences in the social world. Social learning theorists do not deny that nature makes a contribution to personality; rather, they focus on those aspects of personality that are shaped by social experience and try to explain how that shaping occurs.

In any discussion of social learning and personality, it is important to distinguish between environmentalism and situationism, both of which suggest that people are affected by their experiences. **Environmentalism** argues that over time, experiences create tendencies to behave in certain ways and that these tendencies (or traits), once established, become stable aspects of personality. **Situationism** is the view that behavior is controlled by immediate situational pressures rather than traits. Thus, environmentalism is a view about the way traits develop, whereas situationism explains behavior without referring to traits.

from a heart attack!) Type A people may also be more likely to seek out stressful situations, so that even if their physiological response to stress were normal, they might still experience much more stress over time. A third, less popular idea focuses on biological predispositions: Both personality and susceptibility to disease may be heritable (Holroyd & Coyne, 1987). Thus, an inherited tendency toward heart disease may be associated with a particular personality type, but not necessarily because the personality type causes the disease, even though personality may give us some warning about who is more likely to become ill. Krantz and Durel (1983) have even suggested that the physiological overreaction that leads to heart disease may cause personality to develop in a particularly tense and aggressive (Type A) fashion.

Another personality type that has drawn much attention recently is the Type C, or cancer-prone, personality. In some respects, the Type C is the opposite of the Type A (Eysenck, 1988). Type Cs are emotionally repressed and passive, and they tend to react to threats with stoic acceptance and helplessness or hopelessness (Levy & Heiden, 1990). People who are diagnosed with cancer and who accept the diagnosis with stoic resignation show worse survival rates than do those who display a fighting spirit (Siegel, 1986). The assumption connecting the Type C personality and cancer is that emotional reactions affect the immune system. People who react to challenges with resignation show higher cortisol levels, which in turn are associated with lower levels of the natural killer cells that help fight tumors. Conversely, expressing anger raises the level of natural killer cells. It is important to note that no one—or at least no responsible writer—claims that personality per se causes (or cures) cancer. It is generally recognized that exposure to environmental carcinogens and/or biological vulner-

ability play a crucial role. But whether these factors are allowed to flourish may well depend on the condition of the immune system, which may well be affected by our chronic emotions, which are part of personality.

Other personality traits have also been linked to disease. For instance, unexpressed anger has been linked to hypertension (high blood pressure); this finding almost brings us back to the ideas of half a century ago that unconscious conflict causes psychosomatic disorders (Spielberger, Krasner, & Solomon, 1988). Neuroticism has been linked to a wide variety of physical disorders as well, but the current consensus is that neuroticism is more closely linked to medical complaints than to actual medical problems (Stone & Costa, 1990; also see Chapter 13).

On the positive side, certain personality styles, including hardiness (Kobasa, 1979), dispositional optimism (Scheier & Carver, 1992), a protective explanatory style (a tendency to explain events in a way that protects your self-esteem) (Peterson & Seligman, 1987), and self-efficacy (self-confidence) (O'Leary, 1992), appear to protect us from disease, probably by reducing the negative impact of stress. These traits all seem to share a constructive style of coping with problems (Maddi, 1990).

The connection between personality and disease no longer seems in doubt. At the same time, almost every aspect of the connection requires more and better research. At present, we have only a flimsy grasp of the connection between traits or emotional responses and physiology, and of the connection between physiological imbalance and disease. These links in the chain from personality to disease are all extremely complex, and research is likely to progress slowly. For the moment, we should be fairly conservative in our beliefs about how our personalities affect our health (Friedman, 1990; Temoshok, 1990).

LEARNING AND PERSONALITY

According to learning theorists, the same principles of learning that shape the behavior of a rat or a pigeon (see Chapter 6) ought to apply to human personality. After all, personality is merely a set of tendencies to behave in a certain way or to react to certain stimuli in certain ways. Therefore, we may analyze personality development from a traditional learning perspective. Dollard and Miller (1950) offered the most systematic explanation of personality in terms of basic learning principles; their ambitious project even included a "translation" of many psychoanalytic concepts (e.g., defense mechanisms and fixations) into contemporary learning terms.

Classical Conditioning. In an animal laboratory, classical conditioning usually applies to reflexive behaviors (e.g., eyeblink conditioning). Such reflexes are not ordinarily considered a significant part of personality, but another classically conditionable type of response—emotional reactions—is of great importance to personality.

Affection for others may be a matter of conditioning. We come to like stimuli (or people) associated with positive emotional reactions and/or relief from negative emotional reactions. Legend has it that Häagen-Dazs ice cream—made in Brooklyn— got its name from the discovery that people have fewer negative associations to Danes than to any other foreigners, so a (fake) Danish name was used to help market the ice cream.

Emotional reactions to particular stimuli (e.g., a positive or negative reaction to parties or to isolation) can mean the difference between an extravert and an introvert.

Repeatedly experiencing particular stimuli together can create an enduring emotional response that is equivalent to a personality trait. For instance, for an infant, the presence of the mother is often paired with relief from unpleasant feelings of hunger. This pairing creates affection for the mother (and perhaps for people who resemble her). On the other hand, if the mother fails to provide for the infant's needs, the child may develop a negative emotional reaction toward her—what Erikson would call "basic mistrust." This aversion might generalize beyond the mother to women in general, or even to all people, producing a hostile, mistrustful personality. The role of classical conditioning in the development of our preferences and aversions seems quite plausible, but of course, classical conditioning explains only our reflexive reactions and leaves out a great deal of our more deliberate behavior, which also must be included in any reasonable theory of personality.

Instrumental Learning. The fundamental principles of instrumental learning are reinforcement and punishment: Behaviors that are reinforced are more likely to be repeated and behaviors that are punished are less likely to be repeated. Reinforcement can be accomplished positively—by satisfying basic needs such as those for food or affection or by supplying things we like such as treats or money. Reinforcement can also be negative, strengthening responses by removing or preventing negative events such as pain, anxiety, or disapproval. Reinforcement, needless to say, is often controlled by other people. Punishment, or experiencing aversive consequences from performing a behavior, is also a powerful way for others to control us—or us to control them. (Skinner believed that in the long run, reinforcement was more effective than punishment in the control of behavior.)

How instrumental conditioning might apply to personality development is fairly obvious. It is not difficult to imagine how one child might become extremely aggressive, whereas another child might become meek, depending on the pattern of reinforcements. This is not to deny the role of biology; for instance, a naturally muscular child is more likely to be reinforced for fighting than is a weaker child. Encouragement (reinforcement) or discouragement (punishment) from parents and peers, however, presumably has profound effects on how we develop or inhibit our natural predispositions. (Consider how we try to teach those children who hit others to stop—while teaching those who don't hit others to fight back.)

Unfortunately, there is not much evidence that the basic elements of personality are acquired through reinforcement, perhaps because it is difficult to conduct the sort of long-term studies that would be needed to demonstrate the effect of consistent reinforcement on personality development. Such studies, measuring long-term patterns of reinforcement as well as personality change, would be difficult, expensive, and time consuming. Meanwhile, genetic studies using statistical comparisons of twins or adoptees are comparatively simple to conduct and have received considerable serious attention lately, tilting the balance in favor of biological explanations of personality. Thus, while most psychologists still believe that personality is shaped by experience, data demonstrating the long-term influence of learning experiences are badly needed at this point to confirm or deny that belief.

Observational Learning. Fortunately, perhaps, we do not have to learn all our lessons directly from our own experience. Numerous studies have suggested that our behavior may be shaped by observing others and noting how their behavior meets with success or failure (see Chapter 6).

A pioneer in the study of observational learning is Albert Bandura, of Stanford University. In one early study, Bandura and Mischel (1965) demonstrated that the ability to resist temptation could be increased or decreased by observing others. In this study, children were offered a choice between small candy bars that they could eat right away or large ones that they could not eat for a week. Depending on which alternative they chose, children were classified as either low or high in the ability to delay gratification. Both groups then watched an adult model who was given a choice between a small, immediate reward or a larger, delayed reward. For each child, the model chose the alternative opposite to that previously chosen by the child. In a subsequent test, the children shifted toward making the same choice that the model had made. A follow-up test showed that this change persisted over four weeks, suggesting that role models can modify personality traits such as self-control.

In another study (Grusec et al., 1979), kindergarten children were tempted to abandon their work in order to play with attractive toys. Whether or not they gave in or resisted the temptation depended on what they had seen a model do. Children were more likely to resist if the model had resisted and more likely to give in if the model had. These results persisted over time and generalized to a different situation (see Figure 14.7). If such changes in behavior persist in a general way, then it is fair to say that underlying personality has changed.

It seems clear that observational learning plays an important role in personality development (Bandura, 1986). Not only can we learn from the reinforcements and punishments that others experience, but we can also experience **vicarious emotional conditioning,** the acquisition of an emotional response through observing someone else's experience and reactions (see Chapter 6). For example, a child may learn to fear animals not because the child or anyone else around the child has been harmed by an animal, but merely because a parent shows a strong fear reaction. Much more work is

FIGURE 14.7
Temptation and Resistance

The figure shows the amount of time that children played with a forbidden toy instead of working. When the children were exposed to a well-behaved, "resisting" model, they played less with the forbidden toy than did a control group not exposed to a model. They played more with the forbidden toy and neglected their work when they were exposed to a naughty, "yielding" model.

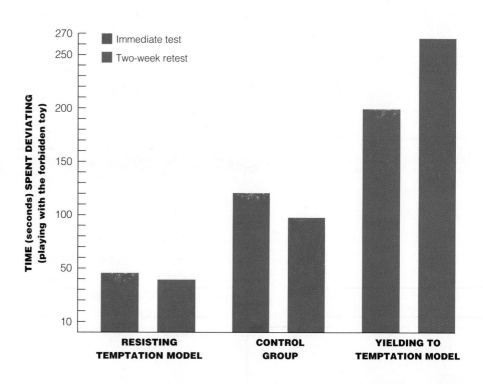

needed, however, to fill in the details of vicarious learning, such as how closely we must identify with the models for their experience to affect us or what we learn when we are exposed to contradictory vicarious experiences. Are we more affected when a friend is rewarded or punished for doing something than when a stranger is rewarded or punished? What exactly do we learn from seeing one person get away with doing something wrong while another person is severely punished? No one denies that we are strongly influenced by the behaviors and experiences of others, but exactly how important such influences are in shaping our personalities is a question that has not yet been answered.

COGNITIVE SOCIAL LEARNING

Social learning theory emphasizes how our experiences affect us, but does the same experience have the same effect on everyone? **Cognitive social learning theory,** developed by Walter Mischel (1979), is based on *person variables*, which are traitlike, cognitive individual differences that filter, or distort, the impact of experiences. The same objective situation or experience, then, is likely to have a different meaning for different people. Mischel's analysis draws on the work of Rotter (1966), an early social learning theorist who introduced the cognitive trait of **locus of control.** People with an internal locus of control believe that what happens to them is mostly a matter of their own efforts, whereas people with an external locus of control believe that what happens to them is determined by powerful forces beyond their control. Another influence on Mischel is Kelly's (1955) personal constructs (see page 585), through which we filter information about events and other people.

Still another theorist influencing Mischel is his long-time colleague Albert Bandura, whose work (1986) has focused on *self-efficacy* (self-confidence), *self-regulation* (self-control), and the *reciprocal interaction* (mutual effects) of the person and the environment. Self-efficacy—the belief that you are capable of accomplishing your goals—has many positive consequences. If you have high self-efficacy, you (1) set higher goals and are more committed to them, (2) are more efficient and task-focused in complex decision-making situations, (3) imagine success, which provides constructive guidelines for behavior, (4) try harder and are more persistent, and (5) hold optimistic views of the future (Bandura, 1991). People lacking self-efficacy tend to react to threats with greater anxiety and increased heart rate, blood pressure, and catecholamine secretion, all indices of stress (Bandura, Taylor, Williams, Mefford, & Barchas, 1985). A sense of self-efficacy makes most of life's challenges and disappointments easier to handle; low self-efficacy can lead to depression.

How people and their experiences affect each other is evident in the way self-efficacy grows. Self-efficacy presumably begins with our first experiences of achievement. Ideally, growing children learn to see themselves as effective by receiving encouragement from others and by succeeding at tasks that they can handle. But self-efficacy feeds on itself, since it makes further efforts and successes more likely. On the other hand, repeated failure lowers self-efficacy, which in turn makes further failure (and progressively lower self-efficacy) more likely.

Can we really control the way things work out for us? Taylor and Brown (1988) argue that we live with **positive illusions,** viewing the world and ourselves through rose-colored glasses (or rose-colored "cognitive person variables"). Self-efficacy, the idea that we can accomplish what we put our mind to, is an example of a positive illusion. Research has shown that it is only depressed people who have an accurate idea of their chances for success (see Chapter 15). But while self-efficacy may be illusory, like other self-deceptions (e.g., dispositional optimism), it may contribute to mental and even physical well-being (see "Psychology in Our Times: Personality and Health").

Cognitive social learning theory, like most learning theories, emphasizes *how* we learn more than *what* we learn. For that reason, it does not really present a theory of what personality is like so much as an approach to explaining how any given personality develops. Social learning theories argue that most of the elements of our personalities are learned, but the theories do not tell us what elements to expect, because that depends on each individual's unique set of experiences.

Current Status of Personality Psychology

Whether our behavior is determined by internal (trait) factors or external (situational) factors has been a puzzle ever since people started thinking about behavior. The recent "consistency debate" — whether personality traits are useful in explaining behavior—has forced personality psychologists to become more sophisticated in their thinking. Behavior is now seen as the product of the interaction of personality traits and situations (Endler, 1983). Also, we now recognize that situations, personality traits, and behaviors all affect one another (Bandura, 1986). But before concluding that the issue has been resolved to everyone's satisfaction, we must note that serious challenges remain.

CRITIQUES OF PERSONALITY PSYCHOLOGY

Perhaps the most thorough critique of personality psychology comes from the radical behaviorist B. F. Skinner. In his 1971 book *Beyond Freedom and Dignity*, Skinner attacks the notion of personality traits as causes of behavior. Personality psychologists (and everyone else), Skinner argues, tend to explain the act of going to a party and chatting with friends as a result of a sociability trait. Skinner objects to this explanation. If people decide whether you are sociable by observing your party-going behavior, and then they turn around and "explain" your behavior at parties as the result of your sociability, this explanation is circular, and Skinner is correct that it doesn't really explain anything.

One solution to the problem of circularity is to get independent evidence of your sociability (from something other than your party behavior) and then use it to predict your party behavior. This is what trait theorists do when they try to predict party behavior using a previously administered paper-and-pencil sociability test. Most paper-and-pencil tests, however, base your sociability score on your self-reports of your previous behavior, so the circularity remains. For Skinner, a full explanation of your party behavior demands discovering what makes you a highly sociable person. That is, it is not enough to describe the trait of sociability; we must find out where it comes from. Perhaps it is something about your physiology, as Eysenck would suggest, or something about your history of reinforcements, as a social learning theorist might suggest. For Skinner, explaining your behavior in terms of a trait without explaining the origin of the trait is scientifically irresponsible. Most personality psychologists would probably agree with this criticism. However, they might argue that referring to traits as explanations for behavior is merely a convenience and not a substitute for the hard work of searching for the origin of traits.

B. F. SKINNER

B. F. Skinner is well known as the greatest contemporary champion of behaviorism. As a strict behaviorist, Skinner actively opposed much of the sort of thinking that characterizes personality psychology. But what was Skinner's own personality like? As a person, Skinner displayed the sort of rational, analytical qualities that characterize behaviorism itself. Although he was not the cold or cruel technician that opponents sometimes imagined, neither was he the type to disclose a rich emotional life.

Harvey Mindess, in his *Makers of Psychology* (1988), suggests that Skinner's enthusiasm for behaviorism was not based simply on its intellectual appeal. Rather, behaviorism offered a way out for Skinner, a young man who was having trouble establishing himself.

As a college student, Fred Skinner dabbled in literature, writing poems, stories, and plays. At a summer school in Vermont, he met the celebrated poet Robert Frost, who encouraged him in his ambition to become a writer. Following college, Skinner talked his father into supporting him for one year while he attempted to launch a career as a writer of fiction in his hometown of Scranton, Pennsylvania. This experiment proved to be a disaster: Skinner simply could not write. "The truth was, I had no reason to write anything. I had nothing to say, and nothing about my life was making any change in that condition" (Skinner, 1976, p. 264). Skinner could have simply admitted his mistake and moved on, but "his sense of failure as a neophyte writer

was so disconcerting that he warded it off by the use of such well-known defense mechanisms as denial, rationalization, and projection" (Mindess, 1988, p.105). "Was it not possible that literature had failed me?" Skinner, asked (1976, p. 291). Skinner could not accept that he (or his project) had failed. He shifted the blame outward, and ever after, his focus remained on the external causes of behavior.

Skinner's youthful occupational identity crisis "was finally resolved as such intense identity crises often are: through the wholehearted acceptance of an ideology—indeed an extreme ideology—in Skinner's case, radical behaviorism" (Elms, 1981, p. 473). This ideology was particularly comforting for Skinner, because it protected his self-esteem. Although "I was depressed . . . I did not consider actual suicide; behaviorism offered me another way out: It was not I but my history that had failed" (Skinner, 1983, p. 407).

Skinner is well known for his rejection of internal states as explanations for behavior. Mindess (1988) suggests that this rejection was Skinner's way of rejecting what he perceived as his own deficiencies. Blaming his environment or his upbringing (his "history") allowed him to maintain his confidence (see Chapter 17). But was Skinner's theoretical position just a rationalization of his own failings? It is probably unfair to dismiss a theory just because it happens to make the theorist feel better about himself.

Another threat to the very notion of personality traits comes from the **social role theory** proposed by Goffman (1959). This "dramaturgical" theory sees our behavior as following "scripts" that fit the situations in which we find ourselves. This model has been adapted by cognitive social psychologists (e.g., Abelson, 1981) to explain how particular situations trigger particular sequences of behavior. Abelson argues that the "restaurant script"—the sequence of behaviors that we display in restaurants—exerts powerful control over our behavior whenever we are in a restaurant; other situations come with other scripts. This role, or script, approach poses two threats to personality psychology. First, if the situation dictates which script is to be followed and the script itself determines how we behave, then there is not much need for personality traits as explanations of behavior. Everyone in a particular situation behaves pretty much the same way. The counterargument is that even though they are in the same scene, different people adopt slightly different scripts. The script you run through, since it differs from mine, reflects your personality. Goffman tends to give the impression that social life is a series of "strong" situations, imposing the same behaviors or scripts on everyone. As noted earlier, some "weaker" situations may leave more room for our personalities to emerge.

A second problem posed by role theory is that we tend to follow different scripts in different situations; our behavior in the classroom is very different from our behavior at a football game. This amounts to the same criticism of personality traits that we encountered earlier: People are inconsistent. Although there is some inconsistency, there is also some consistency as well, and that consistency supports the idea of personality traits. Even if frustrating situations are more likely to produce aggressive behavior than relaxing situations, how much aggression we display in either type of situation will depend on our dispositional (trait) aggressiveness. Indeed, Wright and Mischel (1987) argue that we should think of personality traits as statements about the probability that a particular situation will provoke certain types of behaviors. By calling you "aggressive," I suggest that you are more likely than most people to react in a hostile way when confronted with a frustrating situation. This view acknowledges that certain situations may come with a script for behavior; but how closely or how intensely we follow the script depends on our personality.

FUTURE DIRECTIONS

Personality psychology has survived many challenges and is thriving at the moment. Of course, our ignorance about personality still outweighs our knowledge. Still, personality psychologists are enthusiastic, partly because personality psychology appears "to be returning to [its] disciplinary roots—the study of persons" (Wiggins & Pincus, 1992, p. 487). One frequent complaint about personality psychology over the past few decades has been its tendency to analyze the person into pieces, losing sight of the person as a whole. A currently popular technique for studying the whole person is to examine the "stories" or "narratives" that people construct to make sense of their lives. People may be understood in terms of the "personal projects" (Little, 1989), "personal strivings" (Emmons, 1989), or "life tasks" (Cantor & Kihlstrom, 1987) that they set for themselves. People certainly understand themselves in terms of the meanings they give to or seek from their lives (Baumeister, 1991). These meanings are usually captured in the "plot" of their lives—a sequence of events (as they remember them) that seems to be telling a coherent story with some theme or purpose.

> Spence (1982) has advanced an elegant argument that what happens in psychoanalytic treatment is not an act of archaeology, or recovering the past, but an act of mutual story-making, in which patient and analyst construct a compelling narrative that provides the patient with an integrated view of his or her history and helps explain seemingly inexplicable aspects of the patient's life. (Westen, 1990, p. 35).

In therapy or not, we all try to make sense of our lives. How we construct our life narratives, and the consequences of doing it well or poorly, will occupy personality psychology for years to come.

Along with narratives, personality psychologists have recently become interested in "life span personality," the whole person as viewed over the person's whole life. The current biological emphasis in personality psychology fits nicely with the increasingly popular idea that personality is very stable over the life span. McCrae and Costa (1990), without necessarily adopting a biological stance, argue that although personality takes longer to develop than Freud once claimed, after the age of 30 we ordinarily do not change much. This stability of personality makes it easier to accept the idea that each of our lives has a basic theme. Whether that theme is uncovered "from the outside," by researchers analyzing the patterns of our behavior, or "from the inside," by telling our own life stories, such themes will dominate personality psychology for the foreseeable future.

THEMES IN REVIEW

The main themes of psychology are all prominent in the psychology of personality, which touches on virtually every aspect of psychology. The developmental theme is clear in questions regarding personality development. It is generally agreed that the first few years of life are crucial for personality formation, but changes can occur well into adulthood. The biological theme is also prominent, even though in some ways it clashes with the developmental theme. Biologically oriented personality psychologists have provided powerful evidence that our traits are predictable from our genetic inheritance and fairly stable over our lifetimes. Still, most psychologists acknowledge that experience contributes to personality through learning. The dispositions that we know as personality traits can presumably be shaped just like any other habitual reactions or behaviors. Recently, cognitive social learning theorists have emphasized that it is not objective experience that counts in shaping personality but rather cognitively filtered experience. In fact, they argue that these cognitive filters in some ways *are* our personalities. Finally, the sociocultural theme is evident in observations that personality structure seems to depend on the social or cultural context. This view is evident, for instance, in social role theories that claim that each culture provides a different set of roles to play. Different cultures will therefore display a different range of personalities. Within any given culture, though, individual differences in personality allow each of us to play a given role with a twist that is all our own.

SUMMARY

1 Personality psychology is the study of both common elements of human nature and individual differences. Four major approaches have been developed: psychoanalytic, phenomenological/humanistic, trait, and social learning.

2 The psychoanalytic model assumes that people are primarily motivated by unconscious urges over which they have little control. The mind is divided into three parts. The id represents fundamental drives; the superego opposes these drives in the interest of social conformity; and the ego attempts to cope with this conflict as well as with the demands of the external environment.

3 Personality development, according to Freud, progresses through psychosexual stages corresponding to the focus of erotic tension: oral, anal, phallic, latency, and genital.

4 Defense mechanisms are mental techniques used to protect ourselves from the anxiety that arises when the id, the superego, or external reality threatens to overwhelm the ego.

5 The psychoanalytic approach employs projective techniques to uncover unconscious personality structure. The Rorschach inkblot test and the Thematic Apperception Test (TAT) both examine people's responses to ambiguous stimuli. Despite widespread clinical use, these tests are often criticized as unscientific and inaccurate.

6 Recent attempts to influence unconscious processes by subliminal stimulation have generated much data and controversy. Supporters claim that subliminal psychodynamic activation can reduce many neurotic symptoms, while critics claim that the evidence is ambiguous.

7 Various followers of Freud (Jung, Adler, Horney, Erikson) have developed Freud's theory in novel directions, often objecting to Freud's emphasis on sexual and aggressive motives as the only ones that matter. Many modern neo-Freudians believe that the ego is more independent and important than Freud assumed.

8 The phenomenological/humanistic perspective stresses an individual's unique experience of the world and a belief in human potential. Carl Rogers's theory assumes that we all strive for self-actualization but that our preoccupation with other concerns usually interfere with our achieving our full potential. Conditions of worth, in which we are evaluated depending on the way we behave, threaten our self-concept and ability to self-actualize.

9 George Kelly emphasized the phenomenological nature of personality by focusing on the personal constructs through which we interpret the world, other people, and ourselves. Faulty constructs are at the root of psychological problems.

10 The trait approach focuses on distinctive characteristics that are consistent across situations and stable over time. It assumes that each of us can be described by the amount of each trait that we possess.

11 Factor analysis has been used to reduce the thousands of possible trait terms to a few basic dimensions. Cattell and Eysenck disagree about how many basic traits there are; a popular view among recent trait measurement researchers is that there are about five major dimensions of personality.

12 Personality traits are often measured by standardized personality tests, such as the California Psychological Inventory. Personality is also inferred from ratings provided by people who know the individual, as well as from specific behavioral tests that the individual performs.

13 The trait approach to personality has been challenged by studies indicating that personality is not as stable or as consistent as we often assume. The same person will react quite differently, depending on the circumstances. Defenders of the consistency of personality respond that while individual behaviors may vary considerably, the general patterns we display show remarkable consistency, especially in situations that do not constrain our behavior too strongly. Moreover, our choices of situations reflect our personalities, so situational influences on behavior may be inseparable from personality influences.

14 The biological approach to personality focuses on the genetic inheritance of personality traits. Studies of twins and adopted children have yielded convincing data that many aspects of personality are inherited, at least to an extent.

15 Personality traits are also thought to be related to physique. Sheldon developed a classification scheme based on body build and argued that different body types were associated with different personality traits. Exactly how physiology affects personality functioning remains to be determined.

⑯ Personality traits are related in numerous ways to physical well-being. Several major health problems (heart disease, cancer) may be affected by our personality dispositions.

⑰ According to learning theorists, personality is a set of responses that people learn to make to specific stimuli. People's personalities depend on their history of conditioning, the patterns of reinforcement that they have experienced, and the sorts of vicarious experiences that they have observed.

⑱ Cognitive social learning theory emphasizes people's experiences with the environment as a source of their personality development. People encounter situations, however, with preexisting cognitive patterns that affect the way the situation will be perceived and experienced. Self-efficacy, or confidence in one's abilities, has a great impact on one's attitude and success.

⑲ Personality psychology has been attacked by radical behaviorists, who deny that personality helps to explain behavior, and by social role theorists, who argue that our lives are scripted and not an expression of our individuality. Much recent interest focuses on the individual narratives that we construct to make sense of and add meaning to our lives.

KEY TERMS

personality (p. 566)
personality psychology (p. 566)
psychoanalysis (p. 567)
unconscious (p. 567)
sexuality (p. 568)
conscious (p. 568)
preconscious (p. 569)
id (p. 569)
libido (p. 569)
primary process (p. 569)
pleasure principle (p. 570)
wish fulfillment (p. 570)
ego (p. 570)
reality principle (p. 570)
secondary process (p. 571)
superego (p. 571)
ego ideal (p. 571)
conscience (p. 571)
psychosexual stages (p. 571)
oral stage (p. 571)
fixation (p. 571)
anal stage (p. 572)

phallic stage (p. 572)
Oedipus complex (p. 572)
Electra complex (p. 572)
latency stage (p. 572)
genital stage (p. 572)
anxiety (p. 573)
defense mechanisms (p. 573)
collective unconscious (p. 579)
archetypes (p. 579)
ego psychology (p. 581)
phenomenology (p. 582)
humanistic approach (p. 583)
actual self (p. 584)
ideal self (p. 584)
self-actualization (p. 584)
conditions of worth (p. 584)
unconditional positive regard (p. 584)
personal constructs (p. 585)
trait (p. 585)
types (p. 586)
strong situations (p. 591)
weak situations (p. 591)

FOR CRITICAL ANALYSIS

1 What is your distinctive reaction to a failure experience? How does it differ from others' reactions? Discuss emotional, physiological, cognitive, and behavorial reactions.

2 Many people object to sexual and aggressive jokes. Freud might argue that although they are "offensive," they release sexual and aggressive tension in a relatively harmless way and thereby prevent more serious outbursts. What do you think?

3 As mature adults, do we base our moral behavior on well-developed ethical principles, or are we merely rationalizing our adherence to our primitive superego instructions?

4 How would you feel about basing important decisions in your life on personality tests? Might such tests help to understand aspects of your personality of which you are not fully aware, or is society looking for answers that are not really there?

5 Are women fundamentally different, psychologically, than men, or are the differences imposed (somewhat arbitrarily) by society?

6 If there turns out to be firm evidence linking personality to disease, what are the prospects for controlling disease by controlling personality?

SUGGESTED READINGS

AIKEN, L. R. (1989). *Assessment of Personality.* Needham Heights, MA.: Allyn & Bacon. A readable overview of personality testing. Describes the rationale for various types of tests and their historical development. Surprisingly critical of many of the most commonly used personality tests.

HAMPSON, S. E. (1988). *The Construction of Personality: An Introduction* (2nd ed.). London: Routledge. A sophisticated look at many of the issues facing modern personality researchers. Examines in depth how personality is construed or understood by modern trait theorists, by laypeople describing others, and by people describing themselves.

HOGAN, R. (1976). *Personality Theory: The Personological Tradition.* Englewood Cliffs, NJ: Prentice Hall. Elegant description and analysis of the major personality theories. Does not include as many theorists as do some other treatments, but includes some important views of personality (e.g., existential, sociological) often overlooked in personality textbook surveys.

MCADAMS, D. P. (1990). *The Person: An Introduction to Personality Psychology.* San Diego, CA: Harcourt Brace Jovanovich. A solid, comprehensive introduction to personality theory and research, with an emphasis on recent research on motives and personal narratives.

MINDNESS, H. (1988). *Makers of Psychology: The personal factor.* New York: Human Sciences Press. Fascinating attempt to understand particular psychological theories as reflections of the personalities of the theorists who created them. Includes biographical sketches of some of the major personality theorists (e.g., Freud, Jung, Rogers, Skinner), revealing how their theories often mirrored their lives.

PSYCHOLOGY ON THE INTERNET

FreudNet: The A.A. Brill Library

(http://plaza.interport.net/nypsan/)

FreudNet, maintained by the New York Psychoanalytic Institute and Society, contains links to information about the life and work of Sigmund Freud, links to resources in psychoanalysis and related fields, and on-line articles about issues in the field of psychoanalysis.

JungWeb

(http://www.onlinepsych.com/jungweb/)

JungWeb provides a comprehensive list of sites related to Jungian psychology. In addition to "sites based on Carl G. Jung's typology of human personality," this home page contains links to sites "offering opportunities to explore dreams and dream psychology," information on Usenet and Listserv groups for people interested in Jungian psychology, and links to various reading materials related to "Jungian psychology, practice, and theory."

Personal Contruct Psychology

(http://ksi.cpsc.ucalgary.ca/PCP/)

This home page presents information and links relevant to the personal construct theory developed by George Kelly. It contains introductory materials on personal contruct theory (including an historical overview of Kelly's work and a biography of his life), links to related sites (including the Personal Construct Research Group home page at: http://brain.psyc.uow.edu.au/pcp/), and instructions for joining the Personal Construct Listserv, as well as access to the archives of the Personal Construct Listserv.

The Personality Project

(http://pmc.psych.nwu.edu/personality.html)

This site is "meant to guide those interested in personality theory and research to the current research literature." In doing so, it provides an excellent resource for learning more about the trait approach to personality theory. The Personality Project contains extensive links to journals (including on-line journals and links to tables of contents) that publish "theory and research articles about personality." This site also provides a comprehensive list of readings on personality theory and assessment—including an on-line version of Personality Processess, a review chapter prepared for the Annual Review of Psychology, 1995. Finally, this site contains extensive links to academic and nonacademic sites related to personality research and links to professional organizations "that sponsor conferences and publish journals relevant to personality."

PSYCHOPATHOLOGY

Chapter 15

BIOLOGICAL THEME
Is alcoholism caused by biological factors such as a genetic tendency to abuse alcohol?

LEARNING THEME
Are phobias learned fears?

COGNITIVE THEME
Is depression caused by thought processes?

DEVELOPMENTAL THEME
Are there developmental influences on when and how various disorders appear?

SOCIOCULTURAL THEME
Is schizophrenia simply a failure to fit in with societal judgements or values of what is normal?

"I'm nothing. Garbage. A creep. A cipher. I slink around on the refuse dumps outside of human camps. Christ, to die! To be dead! Squashed flat on the Safeway parking lot and then to be washed away by a fire hose. Nothing remaining. Nothing. Not even chalked words on the sidewalk saying, 'There was the blob that was once named Marge White.'"

Another one of Marge's late night phone calls! . . . A year ago when I first accepted Marge as a patient, I knew there'd be calls; as soon as I saw her, I sensed what was in store. It didn't take much experience to recognize the signs of deep distress. Her sagging head and shoulders said "depression"; her gigantic eye pupils and restless hands and feet said "anxiety." Everything else about her—multiple suicide attempts, eating disorder, early sexual abuse by her father, episodic psychotic thinking, twenty-three years of therapy—shouted "borderline" (personality disorder). . . . She then continued . . . to give me the "real facts" about herself.

"I am thirty-five years old. I have been mentally ill all my life. I have seen psychiatrists since I was twelve years old and cannot function without them. I shall have to take medicine the rest of my life. The most I can hope for is to stay out of a mental hospital. I have never been loved. I will never have children. I have never had a long-term relationship with a man nor any hope of ever having one. I lack the capacity to make friends. No one calls me on my birthday. My father, who molested me when I was a child, is dead. My mother is a crazy, embittered lady, and I grow more like her every day. My brother has spent much of his life in a mental hospital. I have no talents, no special abilities. I will always work in a menial job. I'll always be poor and will always spend most of my salary for psychiatric care."

I sat unblinking through this litany and, for a moment, felt ashamed for being unmoved. But it was not callousness. I had heard it before. . . . Worse yet, much worse (and this is hard to admit), *I agreed with her*. She presented her "true case history" so poignantly and convincingly that I was fully persuaded. . . . I was drawn so deeply into her despair and pessimism that I could easily understand the allure of suicide. I could scarcely find a word of comfort for her. It took me a week, until our next session, to realize that the litany was depression-spawned propaganda. It was her depression speaking, and I was foolish enough to be persuaded by it. Look at all the distortions, look at what she had *not* said. She was an exceptionally intelligent, creative, highly attractive woman. . . . I looked forward to seeing her and being with her. I had respect for the way that, despite her suffering, she had always given to others and maintained her commitment to community service. So now . . . I pondered how to shift her from this state of mind. . . . "That's your depression talking, Marge, not you. Remember that every time you've sunk into a depression, you've climbed out again. The one good—the only good—thing about depression is that it always ends." (Yalom, 1989, pp. 213, 216-217)

This excerpt from Irvin Yalom's tales of psychotherapy, *Love's Executioner*, illustrates a number of aspects of **psychopathology** or psychological abnormality. When someone feels, thinks, or acts in ways that seem not just different from other people, but irrational, hard to understand, or maladaptive and harmful to themselves, they tend to be seen as abnormal—as exhibiting psychopathology. Marge was feeling so depressed and hopeless that suicide seemed desirable to her. Moreover, she was so convincing in her morbid self-description that even her therapist, an experienced clinical psychologist, began to agree with her! Even he needed to stop and think to remember that despite her hopeless self-portrayal, she had many strengths and admirable qualities. People feeling so terrible about themselves and their lives are often incapable of seeing anything rewarding about their existence.

Marge's history of mental suffering, eating disorder, early sexual abuse, suicide attempts, psychotic episodes, and a lifetime of psychotherapy indicated an exceptionally troubled person. While her case was unusual in its complexity and persistence, aspects of her experience may sound somewhat familiar. Who has not felt friendless at times or simply disappointed with life? How, then, do we distinguish normal discouragement from true psychopathology? In this chapter, we will examine what psychopathology is, explain its classification, and explore some different types of abnormality. In chapter 16, the next chapter, we will study the therapeutic techniques used to counteract or remedy psychopathology.

What Is Psychopathology?

Who is abnormal? How do we decide this? Why and how does an individual develop psychopathology? These are the sorts of questions that psychologists who study psychopathology try to answer. Psychologists sometimes use terms such as *abnormality*, *mental disorder*, *behavior disorder*, *emotional disturbance*, *mental illness*, or *psychological problem* to describe psychopathology. We will consider these terms reasonably interchangeable in this chapter, because they all refer to behaviors and feelings that are unusual, unpredictable, and distressing enough to warrant attention. To psychologists, however, they differ in what they imply about the origins and treatment of psychopathology. For example, a behavior disorder suggests a highly specific problem, such as eating too much "junk" food; emotional disturbance suggests deeper-rooted difficulties, such as depression (see page xxx); and mental illness sounds like a medical disease with a biological cause and cure. As we saw in Chapter 14, psychologists have differing conceptions of what normal personality is. These differences also influence the study of abnormality.

DEFINING PSYCHOPATHOLOGY

There is no one property or aspect of an individual that can be said to be shared by all cases of psychopathology. Moreover, no single definition of psychopathology exists. Different explanations of psychopathology rely on deviations from statistical, cultural, and personal criteria of what is normal. Such deviations from normality often (but not always) indicate the presence of psychopathology.

Statistical abnormality includes any substantial deviation from the average or typical behavior of the group to which an individual belongs. (The diagnosis of mental retardation, for example, is based on statistical abnormality; see Chapter 11 for this discussion as well as a discussion of the normal distribution, or normal curve.) Thus, any behavior that is sufficiently rare or unusual statistically is designated as abnormal, or outside the normal range. By this definition, abnormality would include Michael Jordan's remarkable basketball skills. Although the statistical criterion does not distin-

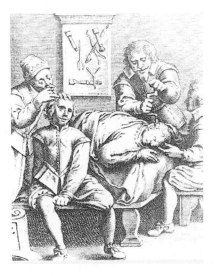

This superstitious response to abnormality, trephination of the skull, is thought to date back to the stone age, when it was believed that abnormal behavior could be cured by cutting a hole in the disturbed person's head to release evil spirits.

guish between desirable and undesirable deviations from normal, abnormal psychology is concerned only with psychopathology, or undesirable patterns of behavior or emotion. Figure 15.1 illustrates the normal, bell-shaped curve representing the distribution of many physical and psychological characteristics.

Psychosocial abnormality involves any deviation from a societal standard or norm. To be considered normal, behavior must be socially acceptable. This perspective emphasizes value judgments. What one person or group considers abnormal, another may view as perfectly sensible. Indeed, the "abnormal" at one time can become the "normal" at some later time. For example, in 1973, the American Psychiatric Association removed homosexuality from its list of disorders: A former sexual deviance became, by implication, a sexual behavior among other modes of sexual expression. The fact that psychopathology involves a cultural value judgment reveals something else about these behaviors: They differ only by degree. Most psychologists accept the idea of a normality-abnormality continuum in which behavior well within the norms of a particular society at a given time falls at one end and abnormal behavior falls at the other end. In particular, behavior that is irritating, irrational, or incomprehensible to the society in which it occurs will be considered abnormal. Even merely noticeable, unconventional, or unpredictable behavior may be seen as abnormal by the society in which it occurs.

Personal abnormality views mental disorders in terms of an individual's subjective feelings. If a person is chronically suffering or if a behavior is useless or even harmful for the individual, then the problem reflects abnormality. Do you see yourself as overweight and less attractive than others? Do you sometimes feel anxious about an upcoming event? Do you get depressed and feel sad and lonely if you do not have a date Saturday night? Do you get a headache or upset stomach when faced with a big assignment or an upcoming exam? These sorts of problems are not abnormal statistically or even culturally, since they occur with great frequency; however, they are abnormal in a personal sense because they cause discomfort to the sufferer.

None of these criteria—statistical, psychosocial, or personal—presents a complete definition of abnormality. A fourth criterion, the **legal definition of abnormality,** declares a person "insane" primarily on the basis of his or her ability to judge between right and wrong or to exert control over his or her behavior. *Insanity* is a legal term: A person is not responsible in the eyes of the law if that person lacks the reason, memory, or intelligence to comprehend the nature of his or her acts or the ability to distinguish between right and wrong. (See "Controversy: Should the insanity defense be abolished").

FIGURE 15.1
A Normal, or Bell-Shaped, Curve

Any characteristic can be classified as statistically normal or abnormal based on its frequency in the general population. Most physical and behavioral qualities are normally distributed as illustrated here. That is, most people have a moderate amount of the characteristic, be it intelligence, athletic ability, or sad mood. Some individuals, however, have a lot less or a lot more than is usual. They are thus statistically abnormal, even if the quality is desirable, such as intelligence or athletic ability.

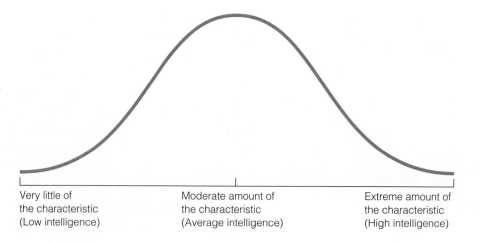

Very little of
the characteristic
(Low intelligence)

Moderate amount of
the characteristic
(Average intelligence)

Extreme amount of
the characteristic
(High intelligence)

PERSPECTIVES ON PSYCHOPATHOLOGY

How did our present understanding of psychopathology evolve? There are a variety of ways of looking at the sources of abnormality: the biological, the psychological, and the social views. We will consider each of these, particularly the psychological models discussed in Chapter 1. Keep in mind that one's view, or model, of abnormality influences one's hypotheses about the causes of and reactions to abnormal behavior. For example, biologically based theorists seek physical causes of psychopathology, while cognitive theorists see the causes as a reflection of faulty cognitions.

The Biological Perspective. The Greeks were among the first to espouse a **biological perspective** of psychopathology, one in which there were physical causes for mental disorders. Ancient Greek physicians described a disorder (today called hysteria or hysterical personality) in which physical symptoms were present without the usual organic causes, and the patient was often overly emotional and dramatic. The Greeks believed that this disorder arose from a physiological problem—specifically, they believed that a uterus could move around a woman's body, attaching itself at different places and causing the symptoms of hysteria. By the second century A.D., Galen and other physicians recognized that the problem was not a roaming uterus, attributing the symptoms instead to an inflammation of the uterus. Extending this further, they suggested that similar symptoms could occur in men; in fact, they observed that the symptoms occurred in both sexes following long sexual abstinence. Galen thus concluded that hysteria had a sexual basis. The prevailing view today concurs that sexual deprivation plays at least some role in contributing to what used to be called hysterical neurosis (Carson & Butcher, 1992).

Although the advances of the Greeks were lost during the Dark and Middle Ages, and superstitious ideas (such as the belief that demons could inhabit people's bodies and cause irrational behavior) again prevailed, attitudes began to change in the late 1700s and early 1800s. Where previously abnormal individuals who escaped death and torture were locked away in horrific asylums, the Enlightenment brought renewed interest in human rationality and the power of experiment and observation. The idea developed that people in asylums were ill, not evil. In Paris, the physician Philippe Pinel (1745–1826) revolutionized treatment of these unfortunates by removing the inmates' shackles and ensuring that they had sufficient food, fresh air, and exercise.

Pinel at the hospital of Salpêtrière removing the inmates' shackles, an example of the "biological or medical approach to abnormality.

SHOULD THE INSANITY DEFENSE BE ABOLISHED?

In 1991, in a town near Toronto, Canada, a man got out of bed in the middle of the night, drove several miles to his wife's parents' house, took a large knife from their kitchen, walked to their bedroom, and repeatedly stabbed them, killing his mother-in-law and seriously wounding his father-in-law. At the man's trial, his lawyer pleaded that he suffered from a rare sleep disorder and was sleepwalking at the time of the murders. He was found not guilty of murder by reason of insanity.

In 1988, Anne Reynolds killed her mother by hitting her in the head repeatedly with a hammer. Her murder charge was reduced to manslaughter because it was held that premenstrual syndrome had diminished her responsibility for her actions (Kendall, 1991). In other words, she was not guilty of murder because she was not rational, or sane, at the time of the crime.

In June 1982, John W. Hinckley, Jr., was found not guilty of attempted murder "by reason of insanity" for his shooting of President Ronald Reagan and three other men. The defense doctors found him to be schizophrenic.

Deep feelings of outrage over such court rulings has put the insanity defense itself on trial. The American Psychiatric Association and the American Bar Association proposed stricter standards of insanity on the

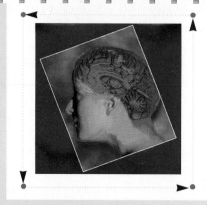

somewhat shaky grounds that "if the verdict was wrong, then the standard was wrong" (Rogers, 1987, p. 840). Congress passed the Insanity Reform Act of 1984, which included the recommended changes. Other jurisdictions went even further. The states of Idaho, Montana, and Utah abolished the insanity defense altogether, and bills in 13 other states replaced it with a new plea—guilty but mentally ill (Senna & Siegel, 1990). The province of Ontario, in Canada, has commissioned a complete reevaluation of the plea.

The insanity defense raises fundamental issues for psychology and its relation to the legal system. Although the term *insanity* is a legal concept, not a psychological one, psychologists are often called on to make judgments about it in trials. Questions arise concerning the ability of psychologists or psychiatrists to determine, with any degree of certainty, the cognitive and volitional capacities of individuals— their ability to understand right and wrong and to choose their own actions—at the time they are being examined and, more importantly, at the time of their crimes. The few studies that actually attempt to assess this ability show that behavioral scientists are equally skillful at making reasonably reliable assessments of both the relevant capacities (Rogers, 1987).

The defense by reason of insanity originated in Britain in 1843 in the trial of a Scot, Daniel M'Naghten. M'Naghten attempted to assassinate the British prime minister in the belief that he, M'Naghten, was being persecuted by the Conservative Party. He missed the prime minister but killed his secretary. He was acquitted "on the grounds of insanity" and confined to an asylum for life. The case established the *M'Naghten rule,* a way to judge insanity based on the accused's knowledge of right and wrong. This is the cognitive capacity mentioned earlier. Later, another criterion was added: could the person have controlled the behavior, or was he or she directed by an "irresistible urge?" This is the volitional capacity that has been eliminated or curtailed in the recent changes

This medical/biological perspective gained further support when it was found that some bizarre behaviors were, in fact, due to brain damage and other identifiable physical causes. You will remember from our discussion of the brain (Chapter 2) that behavior is influenced by brain functioning. For example, people with scars in certain areas of the brain may have seizures. Similarly, physical illnesses or damage to the brain or nervous system can cause psychological changes or symptoms. For instance, syphilis, a sexually transmitted disease caused by a microorganism, may produce deviant behavior 10 to 20 years after the initial infection. It does this by moving through the body and attacking and damaging the brain. Moreover, it is now known that a number of diseases other than syphilis, including HIV (AIDS), as well as the ingestion of toxic substances, can cause abnormal behavior. For example, excessive use of alcohol or other drugs can damage the brain and may produce hallucinations and other signs of psychosis or serious derangement. In the same way, consumption of lead or mercury—even breathing their vapors—can cause delusions, hallucinations, and a loss of emotional control (e.g., industrial workers or people who eat fish from polluted waters can suffer these symptoms).

to the penal code, but is a central issue for the study of psychopathology. Psychologists have struggled with the question of whether persons behaving abnormally can control their behavior or are compelled by feelings they cannot control. That is, are they capable of choosing to behave normally, or are they unable to prevent their aberrant actions? Obviously, this has implications not only for blame and punishment, but for etiology (causes) of such behavior and treatment as well.

Bear in mind that insanity pleas do not always win freedom for the defendant and in fact usually fail. In 1968 Sirhan Sirhan assassinated Robert Kennedy in the presence of many witnesses. His defense at his trial was that he had been "in a dissociated . . . state" at the time of the shooting and therefore was not guilty. The jury, however, was not convinced. Sirhan was convicted of first-degree murder and received a death sentence, which was later commuted to life imprisonment. Two other publicized killers who tried the insanity plea, Jack Ruby (who murdered Lee Harvey Oswald) and John Wayne Gacy (who murdered 33 young boys in Chicago), also failed to win acquittal. More recently, in February of 1992, Jeffrey Dahmer was found legally sane and guilty of 15 murders, despite his claim that he was insane. It should be noted that although psychiatrists testified that Dahmer does have a mental disorder known as paraphilia (recurrent, intense sexual urges toward

inappropriate stimuli, such as corpses or children), this psychiatric disorder was not considered evidence of insanity (the legal concept). Dahmer lied to the police about his activities when one of his victims escaped and went to the police for help. This convinced the

Jeffrey Dahmer was unccessful in his attempt to use the insanity defense when on trail for the gruesome murders he committed.

jury that he appreciated that his behavior was illegal and thus that he was not insane. "Son of Sam" David Berkowitz, Charles Manson (see the case study, on page 651), and Mark David Chapman, who shot John Lennon—all colloquially "certifiably insane" murderers—never even used the insanity defense.

Defendants acquitted of crimes by reason of insanity do not simply go free; on the contrary, they are usually confined to mental hospitals "for the criminally insane," often for longer terms than they would have received had they been found guilty. Because these individuals are "not responsible" for their actions, society deems it safer for them and those around them to lock these individuals up in a mental hospital, where their irresponsibility (or uncontrollable behavior) cannot harm society. This, of course, raises all kinds of questions about who decides what is normal and which individuals are acting in ways indicating that they are "not responsible." The problem is that locking people away in mental hospitals can be used for reasons other than protection; it can be used to silence those who disagree with the majority of society. It is thus imperative that such involuntary incarceration be carefully reviewed to be sure it is not being abused by those in power.

CASE STUDY

PSYCHOSIS AND BRAIN DAMAGE

A patient being treated for epileptic seizures, caused by eating undercooked pork (the pork tapeworm can cause seizures), began behaving strangely after two weeks in the hospital. She was agitated, laughed inappropriately at frequent intervals, became exceedingly religious, and claimed to see bright colors appearing and disappearing on the floor. She began having conversations with her left thumb and claimed to be a messenger of God. She also claimed to be 3 years old, though she was really 24. When her brain was examined by various scanning techniques, extensive damage was found, caused by the tapeworm. While currently exotic and rare, this schizophrenia-like disorder (see page 000) caused by pork tapeworms is becoming increasingly common in underdeveloped areas of the world, where pork is eaten raw or barely cooked (Shriqui & Milette, 1992).

The philosopher Friedrich Nietzsche suffered from syphilis, and some consider the grandiose character of his last writings to have been symptomatic of his disease, rather than his true beliefs.

The shift in the perceived cause of mental disorders from demons or evil influence to biological factors or illness brought about a change in the response to these disorders. The inmates of insane asylums were no longer tortured after the 1800s; they were treated similarly to other "sick" people at that time. Thus, they were bled with leeches, purged with laxatives, and forced to vomit in an attempt to cure their ills (this sounds like they were still being tortured, doesn't it?). Eventually, these methods were replaced by more modern biomedical techniques, such as surgery and drug treatment.

Finally, the biological view has focused research attention on the genetic contribution to mental illness. Heredity has been implicated in a number of mental disorders (Clementz et al., 1992; Pardes et al., 1989), and potential genes involved in the predisposition to alcoholism (McGue et al., 1992), depression (Egeland et al., 1987), and schizophrenia (Moldin, 1991) are now being investigated.

The Psychological Perspective.   While the biological view of abnormality was among the first modern, scientific views and was articulated as long ago as the days of ancient Greece, another modern view also originated in ancient Greece. This is the **psychological perspective** on psychopathology, the belief that abnormal behavior is caused by mental influences, or the workings of the mind. Galen, the early Greek physician, described a patient whose symptoms were caused either by an imbalance in body fluids, or "humors" (a physical cause; see Chapter 14), or by something she was troubled about but not willing to discuss (a psychological cause). He then tested his two hypotheses and concluded that the patient's problem was psychological in origin. We will discuss the psychoanalytic, humanistic, behavioral, and cognitive models you read about in earlier chapters as they relate to this view of abnormality.

The advances of the Greeks in understanding the psychological basis of abnormality were lost until the 1800s, when Jean Martin Charcot (1825–1893) began to use hypnosis to distinguish hysterical paralysis (with no organic cause) from neurologically based paralysis. When hypnotized patients were able to use their otherwise paralyzed body part, this indicated that their "illness" was psychological, not physical. (The body part could work, but only when the mind was assisting through hypnosis.) One of Charcot's students went on to develop a complete psychological model of both personality and psychopathology. This student was Sigmund Freud (1856–1939), whose theory of personality was discussed in Chapter 14.

Freud's **psychoanalytic theory** posited that psychopathology was psychological in origin and could be traced to childhood psychosexual conflicts. If the conflict of a particular stage of development was not resolved, the person would become fixated, or stuck, at that stage. This fixation would then influence the personality right into adulthood. Problems in adulthood are thus assumed to be a result of unconscious, unresolved psychological conflicts from childhood. Impulses that were not completely discharged or released or that were dealt with inadequately are controlled through *defense mechanisms,* which are ways in which we all distort reality to make it more acceptable to us and to allow us to continue to function. Defense mechanisms reduce anxiety stemming from blockage of id impulses (see Chapter 14); however, if the defenses are used excessively, the defense mechanisms may become symptoms of neurosis or psychosis. According to Freud, **neurosis** is an indication that a person is experiencing internal conflict, distracting him or her from normal functioning. Defense mechanisms are then used more than usual to distort reality and protect the person from conflict and anxiety. **Psychosis** is much more serious, because it represents an inability to relate properly to reality. The source of emotional disturbances is thus seen to be psychological.

Jean Martin Charcot

Freud's ideas have profoundly influenced how psychologists think about personality and adjustment. In many respects, it was his work that brought the study of abnormality into the sphere of psychology. Moreover, even psychologists who have rejected Freud's ideas and propose their own theoretical models seem to feel a need to respond to the details of his theory (Gay, 1989). Thus, many theories of abnormal psychology are either based directly on Freud's or are reactions against it.

Other psychological theories of abnormality differ in emphasis from the Freudian view. **Humanistic theory** focuses on the patient's subjective experience; the source of abnormality is believed to reside in the patient's way of reacting to the world. When certain experiences are somehow threatening to a person's self-concept (view of him- or herself), they may be excluded from the person's self-concept and memory. This may cause the individual to block or avoid conscious awareness of other related experiences, gradually creating a distorted view of the self. As a result, the individual feels anxious and distressed whenever confronted with experiences threatening this unrealistic self-view. Humanistic theorists believe that bringing these excluded or denied experiences into conscious awareness and accepting them will help the patient to become more "normal" (see Chapters 14 and 16). Alternatively, existential humanists believe that anxiety may result from a failure to see meaning in life, as when an individual follows the crowd rather than his or her own feelings. A return to "genuineness" (being oneself) is then required. Does this view of anxiety sound like Freud's? It is clearly quite different, yet still a psychological view of abnormality.

One of the most influential psychological theories in the 1960s and 1970s was **behavior theory,** a perspective that views the abnormal behavior itself as the problem, rather than as a symptom of another underlying problem. The behavioral approach maintains that abnormality can be explained just like other behaviors—through the laws of learning and conditioning. Thus, while one person may have learned to be a hardworking business executive, another learned to be an easygoing teacher, while still another learned to be a schizophrenic or sexual deviate. Even if an individual has a biological predisposition toward abnormal behavior, the behavior is still maintained by environmental contingencies such as rewards or lack of reinforcement.

Presumably, what has been learned can be altered by new learning; reinforcement contingencies can be changed to support different behaviors. For example, you may have learned that meeting new people makes you nervous and tongue-tied, and you find yourself standing alone in a corner when put into a social situation with a lot of people you don't know. You have learned to be shy, and this may make you avoid situations where you would interact with new people. If, however, you were taught to choose one person who looks interesting to talk to, introduce yourself to that person, and then choose one other person, so that the task of meeting others becomes simply introducing yourself to one person at a time, you might find yourself able to approach social settings more easily. If this new set of social behaviors is reinforced by your enjoying the party, making a new friend, or at least reducing your anxiety about social situations, the new behavior will become established. Thus, behaviorists treat what they call "behavior problems" by teaching patients new, more adaptive behaviors. They also try to enlist help from those in the patient's environment to maintain new behaviors with altered rewards. This approach changes the way we perceive people—instead of being patients who are "emotionally disturbed" or "mentally ill," they are clients with "behavior problems."

More recently, behaviorists have begun to regard thoughts, or cognitions, as behaviors, in addition to outward, observable behavior. In the **cognitive theory** of

When Joan of Arc heard voices telling her to lead the French army abainst the British invaders, she was hailed by the French as a prophet and a saint. The British disagreed, however, and burned her as a witch.

abnormality, thoughts are now viewed as potential causes of problems. Based on work by Aaron Beck, Albert Ellis (see Chapter 16) and others, cognitive theorists have concluded that many abnormal behaviors and feelings result from irrational or maladaptive cognitions. Thus, to change behavior or distressing emotions, we must first change the cognitions or thoughts underlying the behavior and emotion.

The Social Perspective. The behavioral view assumes that behavior is a direct response to events in the environment. The **social perspective** on psychopathology takes the behavioral view one step further by suggesting that abnormality is actually defined by the social environment, that is, by society's rules and criteria for appropriate behavior. Thus, abnormality is seen as social, not psychological or biological. For example, the hearing of voices when no one is speaking has been viewed differently in different societies. The early Greeks interpreted this behavior as evidence of divine prophesy; they revered persons who heard voices. Later, this same tendency was regarded as evidence of demonic possession or witchcraft, and people who heard voices were tortured or killed. Today, the hearing of voices is seen as a symptom of serious mental disturbance. It often results in a person's being diagnosed as psychotic or being treated as a mental patient. As psychiatrist Thomas Szasz (1970) observed, it is completely normal to talk with God; we call this prayer. When we think we hear God responding, we call it hallucination.

Szasz (1961, 1970, 1974) has also been the most radical critic of the concept of mental illness, speaking from a sociological perspective. He has argued that abnormal behaviors often reflect "problems in living" or social problems and are not at all comparable to physical disease. He suggests that a term such as *depression* simply describes unhappiness. Elevating depression to the status of a psychiatric medical diagnosis turns a person with problems into a patient with a sickness, thereby condoning all sorts of restrictive practices in the name of curing. Szasz argues that how we as a society view or define abnormality will have an impact on the treatment and response to such problems.

How would you feel about someone who has "depressive disorder" as opposed to someone who is simply feeling depressed? Many scientists argue that the mere use of such diagnostic labels as "depression" has a negative effect on people's abilities to resolve their problems. Once labeled, the person adopts the role of a sick person, is treated differently by others, and begins to manifest even more symptoms. In addition, psychological labels are difficult, if not impossible, to get rid of. In this way, social factors (such as the labels we use for people's behavior) may contribute to abnormality.

A well-known study, "On Being Sane in Insane Places," demonstrated the powerful effects of being labeled schizophrenic, as well as the impact of the social context of a behavior. David Rosenhan (1973) arranged for eight normal people, including himself and psychologist Martin Seligman (Rosenhan & Seligman, 1989), to arrive at psychiatric hospitals under assumed names and to complain of hearing voices repeating "empty," "hollow," and "thud." The "patients" responded truthfully to all other questions except for their names. On the basis of this single symptom, and without any other confirming evidence, all were diagnosed as schizophrenic or manic-depressive and hospitalized. Although the "patients" immediately stopped manifesting symptoms and asked to be released, hospitalization ranged from 7 to 52 days. When discharged, most were diagnosed "schizophrenia, in remission," which implies that they were still schizophrenic but just not showing signs of the illness at the time of release. No staff member detected the normalcy of these "patients" (although other patients did!).

Their note taking was noticed at times and marked in their charts as "engages in writing behavior," as if this were a symptom of abnormality. When you sit in your psychology class writing notes on what the lecturer has said, no one looks at you oddly or thinks you are behaving abnormally. But try sitting quietly at your parents' dinner table taking notes on what is being said. You should attract some stares, some questions about what you are doing, and, if you refuse to explain, some real fears for your sanity! This is what Rosenhan's (1973) confederates experienced when taking notes while "patients" in a mental hospital. The context in which these patients behaved (a mental hospital) obviously controlled the way their behavior was interpreted by observers. Labeling theorists cite this study as an example of how terms such as *schizophrenia* can become self-fulfilling prophesies; that is, a person can start acting a certain way simply because others expect it, although that did not happen to Rosenhan and the other "patients" in this study).

Abnormality cannot exist in a social vacuum; it is defined by other people. All societies have explicit rules (e.g., laws) and implicit rules (e.g., etiquette) governing what is acceptable or appropriate. Deviations from these rules or norms may be interpreted as evidence of abnormality or mental disorder. What is normal, or at least accepted, in one society may be viewed as a serious mental disturbance in another (as we have seen with the hearing of voices). What is labeled abnormal can vary at different times and in different places. Some abnormal behavior or psychopathology is clearly organically caused (such as the changes caused by syphilis, AIDs, or undercooked pork tapeworms, as described previously), while for other disorders, the cause is not as well understood. It may be that some disorders have physical bases while others are psychological or social in origin.

CLASSIFYING PSYCHOPATHOLOGY: CLINICAL ASSESSMENT

Before diagnosticians can say whether someone exhibits psychopathology, let alone isolate its origins, they must first describe the abnormality adequately. Classification is an important part of any science. The periodic table in chemistry, for example, has been revised as new elements have been discovered, and much of what we know of evolutionary theory would be impossible without the biological classification of various species of animals and plants. Psychologists studying abnormality are still in the early stages of developing a classification system. Because human beings, who are notoriously unique, are the ones being classified, it is difficult to reach consensus on inclusive and exclusive criteria for different psychopathologies.

A good clinical classification scheme is really a means of communication between people trying to help those who are abnormal. As such, it should have three attributes. It should

1. predict the future course of a pattern of abnormal behavior (i.e., make a prognosis)
2. develop different treatment plans for distinct abnormalities, and
3. study the causes, or etiologies, of specific psychopathologies.

As treatment and research of mental abnormality increased, a classification system became increasingly necessary so that mental health professionals could communicate with one another about their findings. In 1952, the first **Diagnostic and Statistical Manual of Mental Disorders** was published by the American Psychiatric Association. It soon became the standard classification system for psychiatric disorders in North America. Since then, three more editions of the manual, referred to as the DSM, have appeared.

DSM-III and DSM-IV. The DSM, which names and classifies psychopathologies, is used by most clinical psychologists and psychiatrists around the world (Maser et al., 1991). (See Chapter 16 for a discussion of the difference between psychologists and psychiatrists.) DSM-III was a somewhat radical departure from the system in the first two DSMs. The focus in DSM-III was on what was abnormal, with little theorizing about causes. DSM-III was designed to spell out, in great detail, specific behavioral definitions for most psychopathologies. This was supposed to promote more complete and accurate diagnoses, which in turn should result in a better matching of patients with the right treatments (Spitzer, 1991). DSM-III-R (1987) retained most of the innovative characteristics of DSM-III but attempted to improve upon it. DSM-IV (1994) takes this system even further by using the research generated by the third editions (through literature reviews, data reanalyses, and new studies or field trials) to document any changes from the third edition to the fourth (American Psychiatric Association, 1991, 1994, Widiger et al., 1991). Both DSM-III and its revisions have been receiving mixed reviews from those who use them, but they seem to have achieved one of the secondary goals of their authors—to stimulate research in psychopathology (McReynolds, 1989).

As mentioned, DSM-III and its successors (DSM-III-R and DSM-IV) are radically different from their predecessors. The most marked of the innovations is the multidimensional (multiaxial) approach. DSM-III and DSM-IV utilize five axes, or dimensions, for making a diagnosis, each of which is rated by the psychologist or psychiatrist examining the patient. Diagnosis is based not only on the patient's symptoms (in and of themselves and in conjunction with life events), but also on information about the patient's general personality, health, and socialization. Thus, the later systems provide a more complete diagnostic description of the patient than did former systems, with emphasis on environmental, physical, and psychological factors evident in the last three dimensions.

1. *Axis I,* the major component of DSM-III and DSM-IV, specifies the major psychological disorders (such as depression or schizophrenia), including most central and acute symptoms of mental distress.

2. *Axis II* reflects longer-term developmental and personality disorders, more on the order of underlying traits than the Axis I symptoms, which more closely resemble shorter-lived psychological states.

3. *Axis III* consists of physical conditions that may affect an individual's mental state. For example, someone with a debilitating illness might be expected to feel depressed.

4. *Axis IV* concerns potential predisposing life stressors rated on a 6-point scale from mild to catastrophic.

5. *Axis V* reflects an individual's level of functioning currently and during the past year, as measured by a 90-point global assessment of functioning scale.

CONCEPT SUMMARY

DSM AXES

EACH PATIENT RECEIVES A DIAGNOSIS OR RATING ON EACH OF THE FIVE AXES

Axis I: Major psychological disorder

Axis II: Developmental/personality disorder

Axis III: Physical condition affecting mental state

Axis IV: Life stressors

Axis V: Level of functioning

Criticisms of DSM. One criticism of the DSM has been its assumption of a disease process underlying abnormality. The manual was written primarily by psychiatrists, who adhere to the medical model of abnormality, which implies that there are diseases to be named (by the DSM) and cured. This notion has led to criticism from some psychologists who believe that seeing all abnormality as disease results in too much emphasis on symptoms and too little on an understanding of the whole patient. Although some psychopathology has a physical basis, other abnormal behaviors are likely to be psychologically caused or even due to social factors. But when behavioral problems are treated as "diseases," the person is seen as "sick" rather than just different (Carson, 1990, 1991).

Moreover, the multiaxial system means that patients with the same major (Axis I) diagnosis may be very different from each other in other respects (as described by the other axes.) If people with the same diagnosis are very different, then how is it useful to give them the same label? Which sorts of potential symptoms (behaviors, feelings, thoughts and all their manifestations) should be the focus of the classification label (Millon, 1991)?

Still other clinicians find this system too descriptive with no (acknowledged) theoretical basis for categories (Blashfield & Livesley, 1991; Carson, 1991; Morey, 1991). Although the intent was to provide accurate descriptions without trying to explain the source of the disorders, the result is simply a labeling of what is observed without explaining it. When we remember the problems of labeling discussed in the previous section, we should be cautious about applying labels without good justification.

Another objection is that the categories force patients into slots. This means that information about the patient is being lost, since many patients do not fit precisely into the available diagnostic categories (Carson, 1991). The committees of psychiatrists and psychologists preparing DSM-IV collected as much data as possible to support their categorizations, thus avoiding the criticism of DSM-III that categories are too arbitrary (e.g., Frances, Widiger, & Pincus, 1989; Widiger et al., 1991). There is still room for improvement in the classification of abnormality, as well as some argument about its worth (Carson, 1991; Carson & Butcher, 1992; Millon, 1991), but until a better alternative is devised, DSM-IV is what most clinicians will use. Table 15.1 gives an example of the use of the DSM-IV multiaxial chart.

TABLE 15.1
DSM Diagnosis

To become familiar with the DSM system, consider the following case study taken from the DSM-III (1980, p. 30):

A 62-year-old man who is slated for early retirement is manifesting a high rate of absenteeism due to depression. He feels too sad to get up and go to work. His employer knows this worker used to be absent often because of a drinking problem but thinks that the man is not drinking now. The employer believes that there are other problems. The man is referred to a clinician (a psychiatrist or clinical psychologist), who does a lengthy interview, getting more information about the patient. The clinician then offers the following diagnosis (based upon DSM-III-R):

AXIS I: Major depression, single episode with melancholia, moderate severity. Alcohol dependence, in remission.

AXIS II: Dependent personality disorder (provisional, rule out borderline personality disorder).

AXIS III: Alcoholic cirrhosis of liver.

AXIS IV: Moderate stress (3)—anticipated retirement and change in residence with loss of contact with friends.

AXIS V: GAF: 63—depressed mood and absenteeism, but generally functioning pretty well.

We will use the DSM-IV classification system to describe several major Axis I disorders. We cannot consider all the categories, but we will briefly describe several common or familiar ones and then focus in detail on two prevalent and debilitating ones—mood disorders (e.g., depression) and schizophrenia. (Many of the organic mental disorders, such as Alzheimer's disease and mental retardation, have been discussed in Chapters 2 and 11, and various disorders of childhood and adolescence, such as eating disorders, were covered in Chapters 9 and 12.) We will begin by describing the symptoms and offering case studies, and then, for the two in-depth discussions, apply the major approaches to abnormality outlined earlier in the chapter. Finally, we will discuss and illustrate some of the DSM-IV Axis II personality disorders. But before we begin our survey, please see "Psychology in Our Times: Does Media Attention Contribute to Eating Disorders?" on the facing page to learn how the media can contribute to psychological distress and disorder.

Anxiety Disorders

Everyone suffers from anxiety at some time. You probably do not have to think very hard to remember a recent episode of mild anxiety: a difficult test, the sight of a police car in your rearview mirror, talking with a new acquaintance. But what about extreme anxiety, the kind that in some cases may border on panic? Although it may be less common, most people experience this strong feeling at some time. Indeed, never to feel anxiety would be extremely maladaptive, for anxiety can warn you of danger.

Some people suffer from more anxiety than others do. Estimates are that 10 to 7 percent of the population suffer from what can be classified as an **anxiety disorder,** which consists of feelings of worry, anxiety, or strong distress, with no obvious, appropriate reason (Howard, Cornille, Lyons, et al., 1996). It often lasts for months and intrudes on all of the person's thoughts and activities, interfering with normal daily life. It may be manifested as a strong feeling that can approach panic. DSM-IV subdivides anxiety disorders into panic disorder, phobic disorders, obsessive-compulsive disorder, posttraumatic stress disorder, generalized anxiety disorder, mixed anxiety-depressive disorder, anxiety disorder due to a nonpsychiatric medical condition, and substance-induced anxiety disorder. We will look at a few of these in more detail.

PHOBIAS

Phobias consist of intense fears that seem out of proportion to the dangers posed by the objects or activities arousing the fear. There is a clearly identified object or class of stimuli which elicits the fear. Most people have minor phobias, such as discomfort in the presence of snakes or spiders or when standing on a ladder. The usual response to phobias is to avoid their source. One of the authors of this text had a patient with a phobic fear of dentists. This patient had seven teeth pulled by a surgeon using general anesthesia (instead of having the seven cavities filled) and actually considered having all her teeth extracted so that she would never have to go to the dentist!

This man trying to give a speech is sweating and uncomfortable—he appears to have an anxiety disorder lalophobia, or fear of public speaking. Many college students report having this type of phobia.

CASE STUDY

LITTLE HANS'S PHOBIA

In 1909, Freud reported the classic case of Little Hans, a 5-year-old whose phobic dread of horses prevented him from going outdoors or leaving his mother. According to Freud, who never actu-ally met Hans but learned about him from the boy's father, Hans's anxiety about horses was really secondary. Hans's primary fear was of his father as a result of the Oedipus conflict (see Chapter 14).

DOES MEDIA ATTENTION CONTRIBUTE TO EATING DISORDERS?

It is obvious to anyone at all familiar with television, movies, magazines, or other visual media that Western society idealizes thin bodies and condemns fatness, especially in women. The search for the perfect body and the concomitant desire for information, programs, books, devices, and advice to achieve it have been called a "frenzy" in modern Western society (Brownell, 1991) and have resulted in a proliferation of newspaper and magazine articles, television shows, talk shows, "infomercials," and other media presentations. Moreover, the women portrayed in fashion magazines, in magazines such as *Playboy*, and in featured roles on television and in the movies have become increasingly thin and less curvaceous (Atkin, Moorman, & Lin, 1991; Garner, Garfinkel, Schwartz, & Thompson, 1980; Silverstein, Perdue, Peterson, & Kelly, 1986), while the number of diet articles in women's magazines has skyrocketed (Garner et al., 1980). As we saw in Chapter 13, the current idealization of thinness has contributed to an epidemic of dieting, and a majority of young females are engaged in some sort of attempt to control their weight (e.g., Polivy & Herman, 1987; Rodin, Silberstein, & Streigel-Moore, 1985). Chronic dieting is associated with problems of eating, emotion, and cognition, and may even lead to such serious eating disorders as anorexia nervosa and bulimia nervosa (Polivy & Herman, 1993; Polivy, Zeitlin, Herman, & Beal, 1994; Tuschl, 1990). To what extent is the rise in excessive dieting and the recent increase in eating disorders related to current media portrayals of an unrealistically thin female body?

Societal attitudes toward body shapes and sizes differ across time and place (e.g., Anderson, Crawford, Nadeau, & Lindberg, 1992). The thin female physique preferred in our society today was not always considered ideal in our culture; and even today, other cultures prefer larger, fatter female figures (Anderson et al., 1992). Moreover, a historical analysis of the period from 1901 until the 1980s revealed that changes in the standard of curvaceousness of women, as reflected in women's magazines, were repeatedly associated with the level of eating disorders in women (Silverstein, Peterson, & Perdue, 1986). Over time, adherence to a thin standard of body shape was found to be correlated with lower body weight for women, a preoccupation with obesity in magazines, and increased reports of symptoms of eating disorders in the mass media (Silverstein et al., 1986).

An examination of a number of magazines aimed at either young men or young women indicated that there

were 10 times as many articles promoting dieting and weight loss in the magazines for women. This preponderance of diet articles for women versus men is reminiscent of another statistic: The incidence rate of anorexia nervosa in young women is 10 to 15 times that in men (Andersen & DiDomenico, 1992). Perceived social pressure toward thinness and social comparison regarding weight, both of which would be prompted by media attention to thinness as an ideal, were two major variables found to be related to feeling fat, dieting and binge eating (Striegel-Moore, McAvay, & Rodin, 1986). Moreover, a direct effect of amount of exposure to media images of thin female physiques was found on the number of eating diorder symptoms displayed by female undergraduates (Stice, et al., 1994). Increased media focus on thin female shapes may thus exacerbate not only dieting efforts, but binge eating, bulimia nervosa (Polivy & Herman, 1993; Streigel-Moore, 1993), and anorexia nervosa (Brumberg & Streigel-Moore, 1993).

On the other hand, Anderson and colleagues (1992) argue that there are social and ecological factors that underlie a culture's standards of feminine beauty; thus, we cannot hold the media responsible, because the society as a whole would communicate the cultural standards anyway. For example, if there is pressure on young women to be sexually attractive (and society focuses on and exploits this sexuality), yet there are very negative consequences if the young girl gets pregnant, it is adaptive for women to become so thin as to minimize the probability of being fertile and becoming pregnant. It also makes sense to reduce women's fertility in a society where women's economic value in the workplace is greater than their value as mothers or homemakers and where a large parental investment in child rearing necessitates a major reduction of time in the workplace. Since these factors all seem to be true of current Western society, Anderson and colleagues maintain that our culture would idealize thinness even without the intervention of the mass media; in other words, the mass media may simply be reflecting society's views rather than shaping them. Whether pressure to be very slim comes from mass media images or socioecological factors, it seems that a change in cultural pressure is needed to help women avoid excessive dieting and eating disorders.

Hans desired his mother sexually and feared castration by his father—a punishment his mother had once threatened when she found him with his hand on his penis. Freud believed that Hans dealt with this threat by symbolically displacing his fear onto horses (a frequent symbol for maleness or the penis). Behaviorists Wolpe and Rachman (1960) note, however, that the child experienced a traumatic exposure to horses during the time his phobia developed.

Moreover, his symptoms resulted in his receiving much attention from his mother, which could have further reinforced his fearful behavior. They suggest that the aversive encounter and its consequences explain Hans's phobia at least as well as Freud does. Whatever the explanation, Hans displayed classic signs of phobia—an irrational and overwhelming fear of a natural object, which seriously disrupted his daily life.

Where do phobias originate? They tend to be limited to a number of common stimuli. For example, few people develop phobias about books, clothing, or the color purple, whereas phobias involving naturally occurring phenomena such as heights, snakes, or open or closed spaces are relatively common (See Table 15.2). Other, less naturally occurring circumstances frequently associated with phobias are events or activities that might result in pain or suffering, such as driving, flying, or going to the dentist. This might suggest to some people that phobias have an evolutionary, biological basis growing out of our experience as human animals (Seligman, 1972); fears of heights, snakes, open or closed spaces, or dangerous activities have obvious survival value.

Learning theorists provide learning-based explanations for the development of phobias (Bandura, 1986; see also Chapter 6). According to learning theory, phobias may be acquired through a frightening experience (remember the induction of fear of a white rat in Little Albert from Chapter 6). Phobias can also originate, or be enhanced, if they result in positive reinforcement (e.g., attention) or negative reinforcement (e.g., by avoiding the feared object, fear is reduced). Because horses were everywhere in the streets of Vienna, a century ago, being afraid of horses meant that Little Hans had to stay home. This enabled him to spend most of his time the way he most preferred—being with his mother. Avoiding horses by staying at home was thus very rewarding for Hans. Often, though, phobias may be learned through observation; parents who fear particular objects often serve as models for their children, who grow up to share their dreads (Bandura, Blanchard, & Ritter, 1969).

Psychoanalytic theory also provides an explanation for phobias. It assumes that phobias evolve as defenses against impulses that an individual fears. Thus, if Hans

TABLE 15.2
Types of Phobias

Acrophobia	Fear of high places
Agoraphobia	Fear of open places
Astraphobia	Fear of thunder and/or lighting
Cardiophobia	Fear of heart attack
Claustrophobia	Fear of closed spaces or confinement
Hematophobia	Fear of sight of blood
Hydrophobia	Fear of water
Lalophobia	Fear of (public) speaking
Mysophobia	Fear of dirt, germs, or contamination
Phobophobia	Fear of fear
Thanatophobia	Fear of death
Xenophobia	Fear of strangers
Zoophobia	Fear of animals (usually specific kinds)

were experiencing aggressive urges against his father and were also unconsciously afraid of his powerful father, he might develop a fear of another large, powerful, masculine figure, such as a horse. This would help to further shield from consciousness the unacceptable feelings about his father, whom Hans also loved.

GENERALIZED ANXIETY DISORDER

Generalized anxiety disorder is characterized by broad, overall tension that lasts at least a month and lacks a specific object (unlike phobias). It is commonly marked by general fearfulness and physical complaints such as upset stomachs, frequent urination, and frequent diarrhea. Extreme irritability may also occur. This kind of anxiety, which Freud called "free-floating," is not associated with any particular situation, and the victims who experience it often have only vague notions about the reasons for their anxiety.

PANIC DISORDER

Another type of anxiety disorder is **panic disorder** (or panic attacks), involving intense fear or terror. Imagine how you would feel if you were alone in your home, late at night, and you heard what sounded like a door slowly opening and then stealthy footsteps sneaking toward your room. Those feelings of pounding heart, constricted chest, trembling, and so on, are the manifestations of your intense fear or panic. Now imagine that you feel this way, but you are not alone in a house late at night, and in fact, there is no obvious reason why you should feel panic. What would you think was happening to you? Might you possibly imagine that you were having some sort of physical problem—even a heart attack? This is what panic disorder is like. Attacks usually last only minutes, but long after they have passed, fearfulness and a sense of helplessness persist. Unlike phobias, these attacks are not associated with particular stimuli, so the sufferers cannot choose to avoid whatever is likely to bring them on. A common complication is the development of anticipatory fears—that is, being afraid that you will be afraid. Consequently, people who experience panic attacks often stay at home, fearing an attack if they go out—a pattern known as *agoraphobia* (Antony, Brown, & Barlow, 1992).

CASE STUDY

PANIC ATTACKS

One of our patients was sent to us after she stumbled into the hospital emergency room, convinced she was dying of a heart attack. She reported chest pains, palpitations, difficulty breathing, and a feeling as if she were smothering. When the doctors in the emergency room could find nothing wrong with her, they sent her to the hospital's psychology department. On further examination, we found that she had had similar attacks recently, always when she was driving alone in her car and was about halfway between her home and her destination (i.e., farthest from "help"). In fact, she had begun noting the location of hospitals on her routes, which was how she had arrived at this hospital. When told that she was experiencing panic attacks, she was relieved to hear that she was not dying and agreed to enter psychotherapy to discover the source of her anxiety and learn to control it. After several months of therapy, she had recognized her anxiety as a fear of leaving her mother, to whom she was inordinately attached. After close to a year of psychotherapy, her attacks had completely disappeared, and she and her husband were able to move to a different city.

Is this compulsive behavior? This man collected miles and miles of twine to create this incredible ball.

Lady Macbeth's guilty conscience prompted her to keep trying to wash her hands to remove the blood she imagined could be seen there. Modern compulsive hand-washers are more likely to be trying to alleviate anxiety about contact with germs dirt, or the unclean outside worls.

OBSESSIVE-COMPULSIVE DISORDER

Obsessions are recurring thoughts that are troublesome and that persist uncontrollably, intruding into consciousness despite attempts to avoid them. **Compulsions** are behaviors that a victim feels forced to repeat continually in response to an obsession. A sense of mounting tension connected with the obsessive thought can be immediately relieved by giving in to the compulsion; thus the name **obsessive-compulsive disorder.** Most obsessions and compulsions do not give pleasure, but yielding to them appears to reduce anxiety, though it usually consumes a great deal of time. This disorder is equally common to males and females and usually begins in adolescence or early adulthood as a response to anxiety.

OBSESSIVE THOUGHTS AND COMPULSIVE RITUALS

Obsessive-compulsive disorder is illustrated by a patient who had obsessive thoughts that he might leave the gas stove turned on at night or when leaving the house, causing the house to burn down. He also feared that he might not lock up properly and that his house would be robbed. To combat these fears, he developed an elaborate set of rituals (compulsive behaviors) that he felt compelled to perform at bedtime each evening and before leaving the house each day. First, he counted his keys nine times, to ensure that he had not lost one. Reassured that his keys were safe, he then went around the house, checking that each door and window was locked and that the stove was, indeed, turned off. This circuit of the house had to be repeated three times and in a particular order. Only after this ritual had been completed satisfactorily could he go to sleep or leave the house without further anxiety or obsessive thoughts.

Somatoform Disorders

The essential features of **somatoform disorders** are physical symptoms for which there are no physical causes but which the victim experiences as real. Unlike psychosomatic illness, where emotional stress causes bodily changes (see Chapter 12), somatoform disorders have no physical basis. Nevertheless, the victims believe that the disorder is real. Patients experience very real pain, loss of sensation, or inability to utilize body parts. Several practitioners believe that a new type of somatoform disorder has appeared: They call it "Chronic Fatigue Syndrome" or "Yuppie Flu." This disorder, which recently swept through urban areas, bringing long-lasting flu and fatigue symptoms to hardworking young professionals, was thought by some to be more psychological than physical.

There are several different types of somatoform disorders. One of the most widely known somatoform disorders is **conversion disorder,** a disorder that usually involves the sudden inability to use body parts (e.g., "hysterical paralysis" or "hysterical blindness") or an unexplainable impairment of bodily functioning. Individuals who experience conversion disorder may awaken to find that they cannot hear or see or speak or move their legs or arms. No measurable biological change seems to be involved. People with the conversion reaction of blindness do not bump into objects in their path; and those with apparent paralysis can move their muscles during sleep, although they are unable to do so when awake. In neither case, however, are the patients faking. The loss of sensation or function also frequently defies anatomical explanation, as with the well-known "glove anesthesia." In this disorder, a hand is paralyzed and insensate up to the wrist, despite the fact that the nerves and muscles to the hand are so arranged that damage to them would never affect the whole hand in this manner or end at the wrist.

CASE STUDY

BREATHING PROBLEMS

A patient seen by one of the authors during clinical training had a classic conversion disorder. This middle-aged, married woman was hospitalized with severe respiratory distress—she was gasping and nearly passing out. No physical cause for the problem could be found, but gradually, while she was in the hospital, the patient began to improve. After several days, her breathing was normal. The staff then began to plan her discharge from the hospital, and someone spoke to her about setting a time for her husband to pick her up and take her home. Minutes later, she rang for help and was found gasping and hyperventilating. Suspicions were aroused, and the theory was put to the test. When the patient was calm and breathing normally, someone would mention her husband's taking her home. Within minutes, the breathing problems returned. When she was assured that she was not ready to go home yet, her breathing again returned to normal. It became apparent that psychotherapy to address the woman's conflicting feelings about returning home to her husband was needed.

Several theories attempt to explain these disorders. Freud believed that anxiety could be "converted" into loss of sensory or motor functioning. He argued that conversion disorders were defenses against forbidden impulses. Thus, a soldier tempted to flee battle might suddenly go blind or develop leg paralysis, and a woman wishing but unable to leave her husband might develop difficulty breathing and be forced to leave him to enter the hospital. Learning theorists tend to see conversion disorders as more direct means of escaping anxiety and stress and of gaining attention. When gasping for breath, the patient received attention from family and hospital staff. When she was threatened with removal of this reinforcement (by being sent home from the hospital), her breathing symptoms worsened, resulting in attention from staff and cancellation of plans to send her home.

Dissociative Disorders

Psychological, rather than physical, impairment offers another escape route from anxiety. In **dissociative disorders,** one major part of a person's consciousness or personality becomes, in a sense, separate from other parts. This dissociation can take several forms including dissociative (functional) amnesia, fugue, and multiple personality disorder.

When you think of amnesia, you probably think of a memory loss in which the victim cannot remember his or her name or other aspects of identity. **Dissociative amnesia** is a functional, or psychogenic, memory failure; it is *not* brought about by physical damage to the brain, as might result from a blow to the head or a fall. Its cause is psy-

How nature says, "Do not touch."

chological, not physical. A dissociative amnesia victim usually appears perplexed, disoriented, and purposeless. The person cannot remember important information or events. This type of amnesia usually begins suddenly, often immediately following severe psychological stress. The stress may derive from something the victim has done, such as committing a crime, or from an event such as losing a job unexpectedly. The memory loss can last for as little as a few hours or as long as years; the duration is quite variable. The amnesia typically ends abruptly also. Recovery tends to be complete, and recurrence is rare.

Fugue appears as the assumption of a new identity while away from home or work. Fugue is unlike amnesia because there is little confusion or disorientation. The sufferers cannot recall who they are but do not seem to realize that they have lost their memories unless they are asked. Usually the fugue is brief, lasting hours to days rather than weeks, and often it occurs following severe stress brought on by natural disasters, military conflicts, and, occasionally, marital quarrels or situations that seem intolerable to the person. Recovery is rapid, and recurrence is, once again, rare.

CASE STUDY

A FUGUE STATE

Bernice L. was a 42-year-old homemaker brought to the hospital by her family, who claimed that she had disappeared from her home four years earlier and had recently been identified and returned from another town over 1,000 miles away, where she had been living under the name of Rose P,. On rejoining her parents, husband, and children, she initially seemed upset and anxious and soon began to insist that she had never seen them before, that her name was not Bernice L. but Rose P., and that it was a case of mistaken identity. After long and varied treatment, she was able to remember her real name and that she had been forced into a loveless marriage by strict and fanatical parents. The only happy time in her life had been two years of college when her roommate, Rose P., had helped her to develop friendships, musical talent, and new interests. But Rose became engaged, and after a courtship in which Bernice was included in their weekend trips as chaperone (and, predictably, fell in love with Rose's fiancé and felt conflict and guilt about this), Rose married her fiancé and moved to Canada.

Bernice's life had become increasingly unbearable after her marriage because of the intolerant town in which she and her husband lived and his preoccupation with his work. She began to daydream and fantasize about her happy days in college with Rose P. Finally, after the death of her younger, talented, and favorite child, Bernice disappeared from home without a trace, and despite her family's frantic search, remained missing for the next four years, until she was recognized by someone who had known both her and Rose in college. Fortunately, her psychiatric treatment eventually penetrated her fugue, and her husband was sympathetic and cooperative, so she readjusted to a more satisfying life with an understanding spouse who became very devoted to her. (Adapted from Masserman, 1961, pp. 35–37.)

In **multiple personality disorder,** a victim shows two (or more) distinct integrated personalities, each of which dominates at particular times. The original personality is usually not aware of the other, although the second may be partly or fully aware of the first. Often the personalities are distinctly different from each other: If the original personality is quiet and sexually inhibited, the second may be loud and sexually promiscuous. Shifts from one personality to another may be sudden and dramatic, as in the Robert Louis Stevenson novel *Dr. Jekyll and Mr. Hyde*. Some actual case studies have been popularized in books, films, and television movies —for example, *The Three Faces of Eve* (Thigpen & Cleckley, 1954) and *Sybil* (Schreiber, 1974). You should be aware, however, that documented cases of full-blown multiple personality are actually rare. As Carson and Butcher (1992) point out, until a recent increase in reports of such cases in the last 10 years or so, there were not many more than 100 in the psychiatric and psychological literature. Some researchers have warned that the apparent increased incidence of multiple personality may simply reflect widespread knowledge of the disorder and its symptoms and conscious or unconscious wishes for the attention and relief from responsibility for one's actions that the disorder would provide (Spanos, Weekes, & Bertrand, 1985); others dispute this (Ross, 1990).

Could you convince someone that you had two or more "personalities" governing your behavior? Spanos and colleagues (1985) conducted an experiment to show that normal college students would show symptoms of multiple personality under the right conditions. They hypothesized that such a strange and complicated role would be enacted only in situations where the "performance" would be taken seriously and the performer would derive some benefit. Thus, students were instructed to play the role of accused murderers pleading not guilty despite much evidence of guilt. They were given background information about their "crimes" and urged to play their parts as well as possible as they entered their "psychiatric evaluation." Depending on whether they were hypnotized and what questions were asked, subjects were more or less likely to display symptoms of multiple personality in two "psychiatric evaluation" interviews. The investigators' point is that it is possible to elicit convincing evidence of multiple personality if the clinical interviewer asks leading questions and the subject is motivated to display the disorder. They offer a social theory of multiple personality disorder, and suggest that highly imaginative, hypnotically susceptible people placed in stressful life scripts may adopt multiple personalities in an unconscious attempt to repudiate aspects of themselves or their behavior that they find unacceptable or even to impress their high-status, intelligent, sympathetic therapists! Ross (1990) argues, however, that studies such as this one do not produce real, diagnosable multiple personality disorder and thus cannot be used to argue against the existence of such a disorder.

The Three Faces of Eve was the first well-described case of multiple-personality disorder to reach the general public. Eve White (left) was shy, retiring, and repressed. Eve Black (middle) was brash, seductive, and fun loving but very shallow and immature. Jane (right) was the more sophisticated, mature, integrated personality that emerged when Eve's conflicts were resolved. Pictured here is actress Joanne Woodward, who portrayed the personalities in the Hollywood movie, *The Three Faces of Eve*.

Substance-Related Disorders

Throughout history, humans have used chemical agents to alter their moods. Do you drink coffee, tea, or cola? Do you have an alcoholic beverage at a party? These substances all contain drugs. Drugs such as alcohol and caffeine (in coffee, tea, colas, and chocolate) are taken for granted by most people; more than 93 percent of adults in North America have used both. Wide subcultural variations affect usage, however. Some groups frown on alcohol and caffeine consumption, while others accept illegal substances such as marijuana or hallucination-inducing mushrooms.

Substance use disorders involve excessive use of any mood- or mind-altering drug or chemical to the point where work, family life, or health becomes impaired. DSM-IV classifies excessive drug use as a mental disorder. It distinguishes between organic mental disorders, caused by toxic or poisonous effects of the substance, and behavioral disorders involving regular excessive usage of the drug. It also distinguishes between different degrees of "excessive" use, ranging from episodic "abuse" to "dependence," reflecting more regular use. **Abuse** of a drug can reflect a few episodes of overconsumption. Physiological **dependence** on a drug develops when a substance is used repeatedly until an individual develops tolerance for the drug or withdrawal symptoms without it. **Tolerance** means that increasing amounts of the substance are needed for the individual to achieve the usual results. **Withdrawal symptoms** are physical effects, such as sweating, shaking, and discomfort, occurring when the individual abstains from taking the drug. Thus, what begins as drug abuse can, if repeated often enough, become true drug dependence or addiction. A classification of some commonly abused drugs is given in Table 15.3. The frequency of use of various drugs among American high school students can be estimated from Figure 15.2.

FIGURE 15.2
Drug Use in the United States

The chart shows the percentage of the American high school class of 1989 using various types of drugs. These data were collected in a nationwide study of students from fourth grade to high school.

SOURCE: Oetting & Beauvais, 1990.

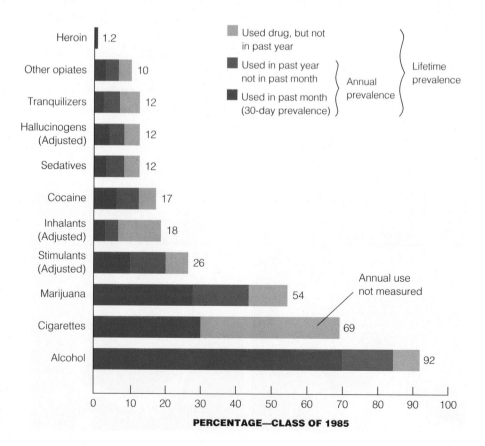

TABLE 15.3
Commonly Abused Substances and Their Effects

CLASSIFICATION	DRUGS	PSYCHOLOGICAL EFFECTS	DURATION OF EFFECTS (IN HOURS)	DEPENDENCE POTENTIAL		TOLERANCE
				PHYSICAL	PSYCHOLOGICAL	
Depressants (sedatives)	Alcohol (ethanol)	Relaxation; reduced inhibitions	3–6	High	High	Yes
	Barbiturates (e.g., Amytal, Seconal)	Relaxation, disorientation, sleep	1–16	High	High	Yes
	Mild tranquilizers (e.g., Librium, Valium)	Reduced anxiety, relaxation, sedation	4–8	Moderate	Moderate	Yes
Opiates (narcotics)	Codeine	Lack of feeling in the body, euphoria, drowsiness	3–6	Moderate	Moderate	Yes
	Heroin			High	High	Yes
	Opium			High	High	Yes
	Morphine			High	High	Yes
Stimulants	Amphetamines (e.g., Benzedrine, Dexedrine)	Increased alterness excitation, decreased fatigue	2–4	Possible	High	Yes
	Caffeine (coffee, cola, tea)	Increased alertness, excitation, decreased fatigue	2–4	Possible	Moderate	Yes
	Cocaine	Euphoria, excitation, alertness, decreased fatigue	2–3	Possible	High	Yes
	Nicotine	Increased alertness	1–2	Possible	High	Yes
Hallucinogens	Lysergic acid diethylamide(LSD), mescaline, psilocybin,	Distortions, illusions, hallucinations, time disorientation	1–8	None	Unknown	Yes
Cannabis	Marijuana, hashish	Euphoria, relaxed inhibitions, increased appetite, increased sensory sensitivity, disorientation	2–4	Unknown	Moderate	Yes

Alcoholism, abuse of and dependence on alcohol over some length of time (although exact definitions vary), constitutes the most prevalent drug use disorder. It is estimated that alcoholics and (less seriously impaired) problem drinkers today number 10 million people in the United States, with alcohol one of the most widely used drugs in North America (Oetting & Beauvais, 1990; Sobell, Breslin & Sobell, 1996). It has been estimated that alcohol abuse is a factor in more than 10 percent of all deaths in the United States, totaling about 200,000 per year. Alcohol consumption is related to the commission of many violent crimes and actions, including suicide. It is associated with half of all traffic deaths, many involving teenagers, spurring the U.S. government to force states to raise the legal drinking age from 18 to 21. Prolonged abuse of alcohol can damage every system of the body; it is the primary cause of cirrhosis of the liver, one of the 10 major killers of adults (Harford & Brooks, 1992). The life span of alcoholics is thus understandably 10 to 12 years shorter than that of the general population.

Alcohol has almost contradictory effects on a person's psychological state. It acts as a depressant, but the first parts of the brain it depresses are the inhibitory centers

(Sobell et al., 1996). Thus, briefly, alcohol raises spirits and releases inhibitions. Continued drinking depresses the systems that keep the body efficient, however, impairing reaction times, speech, and fine-motor coordination. Eventually even walking becomes difficult, and finally a drinker falls asleep. Excessive alcohol can even impair essential bodily functions such as respiration; every so often a participant in a "drinking contest" not only passes out, but stops breathing and dies from an overdose of alcohol. (See Table 15.4 for more details on the effects of alcohol consumption.)

Why do people drink to excess? The reason most frequently cited is that alcohol consumption reduces anxiety and tension (Akers, 1985). Although the validity of this stress avoidance model of excessive drinking has been called into question by many researchers (e.g., Higgins & Marlatt, 1975; Nathan & Hay, 1984), the general public seems to believe in it. Extreme problem drinkers may even desire the oblivion of passing out. Meanwhile, the biological, or medical, model views alcoholism as genetically or physiologically determined. In this view, the condition may be expressed when a susceptible disposition is triggered by the first exposure to alcohol. More cognitive, psychoanalytically oriented theorists, however, view alcoholism as a result of deep-rooted unconscious impulses. Freud considered drinking a symptom of fixation at the oral stage of psychosexual development; Adler (a neo-Freudian, see Chapter 14) suggested that it was caused by feelings of inferiority. Behavioral psychologists tend to see excessive drinking as a reflection of conditioning, through social learning from observation of others and reinforcement from the pleasurable effects of alcohol.

TABLE 15.4
Blood Alcohol Levels and Associated Behaviors

BLOOD ALCOHOL CONCENTRATION (%)	BEHAVIORAL EFFECTS
.05	Reduced alertness, often pleasurable feeling, release of inhibitions, impaired judgment
.10	Slowed reaction times, impaired motor function, less caution, legal intoxication in many states
.15	Large increases in reaction times
.20	Marked depression in sensory and motor capability, decidedly intoxicated
.25	Severe motor problems, such as staggering, sensory perceptions greatly impaired
.30	Stuperous but conscious, no comprehension of the world around them
.35	Surgical anesthesia (passed out); possible death at this point and beyond

The concentration of alcohol in the blood depends on a person's sex and weight. Large people have more bodily fluid than small people, and men have more fluid than women of the same weight (because women have a greater amount of fat). Thus, four cans of beer or four glasses of wine consumed during a 1-hour period will produce a blood alcohol concentration of .18 in a 100-pound female, .15 in a 100-pound male, .12 in a 150-pound female, and .10 in a 150-pound male (Ray, 1978). These concentrations would produce legal intoxification in most states, so people with these blood levels would be subject to arrest for driving a car. Even small amounts of alcohol can produce relatively grave impairments in judgment and reaction. Great amounts can kill a person.

SOURCE: Ray, 1983

Finally, the social model suggests that alcoholism is determined, to at least some extent, by social norms and values. For instance, rates of alcoholism are extremely low in groups where drinking alcohol is prohibited or disapproved of (e.g., Mormons, Muslims), low in groups that limit the use of alcohol to particular occasions (e.g., Jews, Chinese), and high in groups that do not limit alcohol consumption but rather encourage its use (e.g., Irish males). Social pressure is often implicated as a factor that started many younger alcoholics (indeed, abusers of many other drugs, too) in their abuse, while emotional distress plays an almost insignificant role (Swaim et al., 1989). Studies of alcoholism provide some support for genetic influences, conditioning, and social norms as contributing factors (Alterman et al., 1989; McGue, Pickens, & Svikis, 1992; Windle, 1990).

According to Figure 15.2, by twelfth grade, 3 out of 4 students have been drunk on alcohol. Chances are very high that you will at some time in your life get drunk on alcohol, as will most of your friends. What precautions should you take to be sure that you do not become another statistic, a person harmed by drug use? Research shows that your chances of avoiding this danger are greater if those around you are well educated about the dangers of drugs, especially the danger of driving under the influence of drugs or alcohol, and if they disapprove of such behavior (Oetting & Beauvais, 1990). Where attitudes are supportive of drinking, students are more at risk from alcohol.

Although alcohol is the most frequently abused drug and has been used by the greatest number of people, other drugs are also widely used and abused. For example, 1 out of 4 young adults has tried cocaine, and approximately half of regular cocaine users are between the ages of 12 and 26 (1985 National Household Survey on Drugs, National Institute on Drug Abuse). DSM-IV lists nine other drug categories implicated in substance use disorders in addition to alcohol and cocaine: amphetamines, caffeine, cannabis, hallucinogens, inhalants, nicotine, opioids, PCP, and sedatives or anxiolytics (antianxiety drugs such as Valium). DSM-IV also addresses the problem of polysubstance use disorders (the use of three or more substances in a month, not including nicotine and caffeine) as well as other or sometimes unknown substance use disorders. Moreover, these drug categories are also among the psychoactive substances that may cause organic mental disorders (according to DSM-IV). These conditions involve physically caused mental disruptions, such as hallucinations from the effects of the drug on the brain or physiological changes in the brain from long-term use. Since a drug's effect depends on either stimulating (exciting) or depressing (relaxing) parts of the brain, different drugs can do different kinds of damage. In addition, a substance that has a beneficial effect in a controlled, medicinal dose can become toxic, or poisonous, when self-administered or used repeatedly. Substance abuse thus comes in a wide variety of forms.

Disorders of Infancy or Childhood

AUTISTIC DISORDER

Several serious disorders first appear in childhood. In **autistic disorder,** a disorder beginning before the age of 3 years, young children fail to develop normal language and social behaviors and have restricted and repetitive activity patterns (Singer, 1991). The disorder was first described in 1943 by Leo Kanner, who referred to these children's preference for solitude and extreme discomfort with any social contact as "autistic aloneness." Other symptoms described by Kanner and DSM-IV include lack of awareness of other people and of social or emotional interaction, intolerance of changes in the environment, self-stimulation, ritualistic behavior (rigidly repeated actions or sequences of acts), and unusual (or totally lacking) speech. The severity of this disorder has caused it to be seen as somehow related to the adult disorder of schizophrenia (see page 000), although there are many differences between the two disorders. Most notably, autism always begins in infancy or early childhood, whereas schizophrenia begins much later, usually in young adulthood. Also, many autistics never develop normal speech, but schizophrenics tend to speak normally until their disorder becomes apparent (Singer, 1991). Unfortunately, autistic disorder seems to be so severe that these children generally do not develop into normal adults, even with prolonged treatment.

Mood Disorders

Mood is a synonym for "prolonged emotional feeling." **Mood disorders** are disabling disturbances of moods and feelings accompanied by changes in physical functioning (e.g., sleeping and eating) and thought patterns. Mood disturbances can dominate a person's life, causing impaired functioning and even loss of contact with reality. Two emotional extremes characterize mood disorders: the excessive energy of mania and the debilitating lethargy of depression—or both in alternation, known as bipolar disorder.

BIPOLAR DISORDERS

Mania, or **manic disorder,** is a state of intense euphoria or sense of well-being. In its mild form, it is marked by happiness, optimism, talking, and energy. Its more extreme form is characterized by an endless stream of talk that runs from one topic to another, a total lack of inhibition in relationships, intense activity, spending sprees, heightened sexuality, decreased need for sleep, irrepressible good humor (which may rapidly be replaced by rage and threatening demeanor), and, almost invariably, increased sociability, including phone calls to friends at all hours of the night and efforts to renew old acquaintances. Mania also usually includes unwarranted optimism and generosity, reckless driving, or foolish business investments. Speech becomes loud, rapid, and difficult to understand. Typically manic individuals do not recognize the intrusive, aggressive, and demanding nature of their behavior. Slowly, but surely, sufferers exhaust themselves and everyone around them. It is unusual to have a single manic episode without a recurrence or without a subsequent depressive mood swing, so in DSM-IV, mania is a symptom of a **bipolar disorder** consisting of episodes of mania and depression in a single individual.

CASE STUDY

BIPOLAR DISORDER—THE SHIRT OFF HIS BACK

The tall young man, F., was talking rapidly about his grandiose plans for using his savings to make a film that would change the world and make it a better place in which to live. It was six o'clock in the morning when he and his two friends stopped in a downtown square and continued their discussion. F. gesticulated and urged his friends to join him in his mission. A derelict sitting on a bench nearby wandered over and admired the young man's expensive boots. Immediately,

F. sat down and took them off and gave them to the derelict, insisting that the man take them. He then took off the shirt he was wearing and insisted the man take that, too. At this point, F.'s friends intervened and managed to get him away. He was treated for his manic disorder, but he later became depressed and would not see his friends or go out. His mania recurred, and he squandered a sizable inheritance on a fruitless film venture. He also called friends in the middle of the night to warn them that the world was coming to an end. Finally, F. was given medication to control his bipolar disorder.

DEPRESSIVE DISORDERS

Depression is a complaint ranging from mild sadness to a state in which a victim loses all interest in normal activities, becomes extremely gloomy, and often spends a great deal of time in bed. There is a continuum from normal sadness to deeper depression, to abnormal, clinical depression, or **depressive disorder.** A clinical depressive may be overwhelmed with feelings of hopelessness and worthlessness. Physical symptoms often include a sad demeaner, lack of appetite, inability to sleep, loss of energy, and uncontrollable crying. Speech is often slow and emotionless, and it generally expresses suffering and suicidal desires. In this phase, a patient may well attempt suicide and must be watched carefully. In extremely severe depression, a sufferer is unable to leave his or her bed and huddles miserably under the covers, lacking the energy even for suicide.

Who gets depressed? In one sense, of course, everyone. We all have times when we feel down, discouraged, sad, empty, and when life seems an effort. We say that we feel depressed. Fortunately, we expect this feeling to go away soon. This is not the case for clinical depression. Clinical depressive episodes are so prevalent that depression has been called "the common cold of mental illness" (Seligman, 1975). As much as 15 percent of the population may be suffering depressive symptoms and 5 to 10 percent have true depressive disorder (Howard, et al., 1996). It occurs about twice as often in women as in men (about 20 percent of women and 10 percent of men) and may first appear at any age, even during childhood (Clayton, 1981; Nolen-Hoeksema, 1987). Age also appears to be important. Both the elderly (Dura, Stukenberg, & Kiecolt-Glaser, 1990; Wallace & O'Hara, 1992) and adolescents (Allgood-Merten, Lewinsohn, & Hops, 1990; Lewinsohn, Hops, Roberts, Seeley, & Andrews, 1993; Lewinsohn, Roberts, Seeley, Rohde, Gotlib, & Hops, 1994) have been identified as being more at risk for depression than are children or adults. In the elderly, this increase in depression has been linked to loss of significant others (Nolen-Hoeksema, 1987) or long-term caregiving to a debilitated spouse (Dura et al., 1990). For adolescents, particularly adolescent females, stressful life events and body and self-esteem issues seem to contribute most to the elevated incidence of depressive symptoms.

In addition, different cultures also appear to produce different patterns of depressive disorder. In non-Western cultures, the incidence of and symptoms of depression are somewhat different than in Western cultures. It should be noted, however, that as societies become more industrialized and Westernized, they become more similar to Western society in their depressive reactions as well (Carson & Butcher, 1992).

GENDER AND DEPRESSION

As we have mentioned, twice as many women as men develop depressive disorders. This is true across the United States and in urban areas throughout the world (Nolen-

Many famous people have suffered from depression. Winston Churchill wrote about the "black dog" that followed him throughout his life.

Hoeksema, 1987). Why do you suppose that is? Do other disorders occur more often in one group than in another? Many researchers have looked at these sorts of questions.

A common belief that would explain the sex difference in depression is the sociocultural explanation that men are unwilling to report feeling depressed because they see this as a feminine attribute, whereas women are more willing to admit to their problems and seek help for them. This idea, as well as the theory that women are more depressed because they are of lower socioeconomic status than men, was carefully reviewed and found to have no basis in fact. It is the case, however, that women are generally judged by clinicians (of either sex!) to be less mentally healthy than men, even if they are perfectly normal! Sex role stereotypes for men and women in Western society are such that attributes considered feminine (and normal for females) are not seen as mentally healthy by clinicians (Broverman et al., 1970).

Unsuccessful biological explanations for the increased incidence of depression in females focus on hormonal changes in women that might influence mood or on genetic transmission differences between the sexes. Psychodynamic and cognitive learning sex role explanations were also found to be unsatisfactory (Nolen-Hoeksema, 1987).

One combined sociocultural/learning/biological theory suggests that the greater incidence of depressive disorder in women reflects their response to a depressive episode (however it is caused). Women are more likely than men to think about their moods and may have less effective distracting activities available than men. On the other hand, men's reactions may be more behavioral in nature and may prove more effective at lessening their depressive moods (Nolen-Hoeksema, 1987).

Does this mean that females are generally a mental health risk? We should look at other disorders. Females are also more likely to develop anxiety disorders, eating disorders, and adjustment disorders than are males (Lewinsohn et al., 1993). Males, however, are significantly more at risk for conduct disorders (hyperactivity, acting out, antisocial behaviors), paranoid and antisocial personality disorders (see page 650) drug or alcohol abuse (Lewinsohn et al., 1993, 1994, McGue, Pickens, & Svikis, 1992; Windle, 1990), and schizophrenia (Mueser, Bellack, Morrison, & Wade, 1990). Moreover, those who do become schizophrenic have a worse prognosis (outcome) if they are male. Again, the explanation seems to be that a genetic or biological predisposition to mental disorder interacts with life stressors and circumstances in different ways for males and females to produce different psychopathological response patterns.

CAUSES OF DEPRESSION

Psychologists disagree about the causes of depressive disorders. Some biologically based models attribute them to a chemical imbalance that might be genetic in origin. Psychoanalysts see depression as symptomatic of unconscious pathological processes, while cognitive theorists attribute it to faulty thinking patterns. The learning tradition views depression as a result of faulty learning. The social model blames life experiences and a lack of supports to assist coping. We will consider the views of each model.

The Biological View. Heredity seems to be important in predisposing people to mood disorders. Mendlewicz (1985) reviewed data from twin, family, and adoption studies, demonstrating the role of genetics in transmitting the predisposition for mood disorders. For example, adopted children are more at risk for depression if their biological parents have the disorder than if their adoptive parents have it. Furthermore, twin and other family studies demonstrate that a person's risk increases directly as a function of the degree of genetic similarity to an affected family member. Looking at it the

Recent work on the genetic basis of depression has focused on Amish people because they represent a relatively closed gene pool after generations of intermarriage. Although one group of researchers has announced the discovery of a gene for bipolar depressive disorder in this group, it is not present in all sufferers. Other researchers have been unable to replicate the discovery thus far.

"Oh, yeah? Well, I think you're the one with the biochemical imbalance."

Drawing by Mankoff; © The New Yorker Magazine, Inc.

other way around, an individual who develops depression is extremely likely to have at least one "first degree relative" (someone closely related biologically such as a parent, grandparent, or the sibling of one of these) who has been either depressed or alcoholic. Recently, scientists have announced a possible breakthrough involving the discovery of a particular gene that may be at least partially responsible for one type of depression (Egeland et al., 1987), although there is still much controversy about this finding.

The fact that the predisposition to mood disorders seems to be at least partly inherited has encouraged scientists to search for biochemical defects. Much research has centered on the role of neurotransmitters, particularly norepinephrine, dopamine, and serotonin (see Chapter 2 for a detailed discussion of neuronal transmission), although the mechanism appears to be sufficiently complex so that no single chemical excess or deficiency accounts for the problem. Other medical theories hypothesize hormonal changes in women as one possible source of depression in middle-aged women, although the evidence for this is contradictory at best (see the discussion on gender and depression on pages 637–638, and the following case history study of Mrs. K.). It is hoped that research in this area will lead to significant advances in biomedical therapies.

CASE STUDY

MRS. K.'S DEPRESSION

Mrs. K., a 49-year-old woman, was brought to the hospital by her husband after what he described as a steady deterioration in her behavior and affect. She had been a homemaker and mother of two boys. When she was about 40 years old, she began to feel sad for no apparent reason and sometimes even cried. She said she felt sad all of the time, and nothing seemed to make her feel happy. Then she began staying in bed in the morning, longer and longer, taking less care of the house and herself. Soon meals were not prepared when the family assembled to eat, and eventually, Mrs. K. was not even dressed by dinnertime. Her husband brought her into the hospital after she was unable to get herself out of bed for several days. Her demeanor was sad and not very expressive or responsive. She could not think of any event that had caused her saddened mood, and said she just felt drained and empty. Sometimes she would get tearful and maintain that her family would be better off if she were dead, though she had no plan to kill herself. She could not be engaged in psychotherapy, as she simply sat silently, answering the psychologist's questions in as few words as possible. She was given antidepressant medication, which seemed to improve her mood a little, but this improvement proved to be only temporary. Finally, she was given electroshock therapy over many weeks, and her mood improved so that she wanted to see her family. Eventually, after a full course of electroshock treatment, she was able to go home and resume her life as a housewife and mother.

Psychoanalytic Formulations. The early psychoanalytic writers tended to endorse an aggression-turned-inward hypothesis to account for depression. Freud suggested that when an individual who is prone to depression experiences a loss, he or she feels guilty, worthless, and somehow to blame. This influences the individual's self-esteem, contributing to the prolonged melancholia or depression. Freud himself was prone to bouts of depression. Could Freud's depression have been connected to his early separation from his mother during her treatment for tuberculosis?

Later contributors have focused on personality styles that may make the person more susceptible, in particular focusing on a weak ego and dependence on others for self-esteem (Bemporad, 1985) or perceived helplessness to achieve unrealistically high goals (Bibring, 1953). Often the former is thought to be due to early childhood deprivation. A child may become despondent and depressed over the loss of a person, perhaps a parent, on whom the child has been dependent. Such traumas as death, adoption, and divorce may scar children for life, making them vulnerable to depressive reactions. The supporting evidence, however, has not been strong (Bemporad, 1985).

Learning Theories. Only in the last two decades have behavioral researchers turned their attention to depression. Several important theories in this active area of research have been proposed.

Lewinsohn's Behavioral Theory. Peter Lewinsohn (1974; Lewinsohn et al., 1985, 1989) hypothesizes that depression results from decreased reinforcement from the environment, particularly positive reinforcement. This view implies that someone with many sources of reinforcement is much less susceptible to depression than one whose behavior has been maintained by relatively few sources. It also suggests that if depressed people can be taught skills that will earn them reinforcement, their depression might be reduced. Figure 15.3 represents some of the variables involved in Lewinsohn's model of depression.

Beck's Cognitive Social Learning Theory. An important model of depression was developed by Aaron T. Beck and his colleagues. According to Beck, depression results from the development and dominance of a set of beliefs, fantasies, and expectancies (often called the "cognitive triad") that individuals form about themselves, their world, and their future. These cognitive blueprints, or scripts, cause people to see themselves as inadequate, unworthy, and helpless. If you have ever been around someone who is depressed, you can probably attest to the fact that depressed people seem to see the world as insensitive, ungratifying, and generally empty or unpleasant. To make matters worse, depressed people tend to see their futures as unpromising; there is little hope for improvement, let alone happiness. Research has provided some support for Beck's theory. Depressive individuals, for example, have been shown to endorse and recall more negative and fewer positive depression-relevant stimuli than nondepressed subjects do (Greenberg & Beck, 1989). This negative view flavors all later decisions, behaviors, emotions, and interactions, thus locking in a pattern

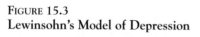

FIGURE 15.3
Lewinsohn's Model of Depression

In this formulation, predisposing characteristics in both the person (e.g., genetic biases) and the environment (e.g., disruptions) affect the individual's mood, influencing the rate of positive reinforcement. Decreases in positive reinforcement lead to depression. This, in turn, can lead to a reduced rate of activity, which can cause even less positive reinforcement and still further depression.

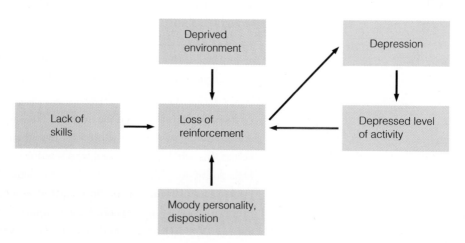

According to Beck, depression arises when people view themselves as unworthy, see their worls as empty, and see their situation as hopeless.

of depression (Sacco & Beck, 1985). The extent to which Beck's formulations complement or contradict those of Lewinsohn and other behaviorists remains to be decided, but this is currently stimulating much research.

Seligman's Learned Helplessness Theory. Martin Seligman's (1975) model provides a theory to explain the beginnings of people's negative beliefs leading to depression. Seligman proposes, in his **learned helplessness** theory, that depressed people have learned to see themselves as unable to control or influence events. They thus develop negative responses, including hopelessness and passivity as well as depressed and negative expectations. In his original studies, Seligman demonstrated that animals given a large number of extremely painful electric shocks exhibited "depressed behavior" only if there was nothing they could do to avoid the shocks. If they could escape from the shock, the depressed behavior did not occur. The animals who could not escape learned that they were helpless, so they stopped trying to escape, even in situations where escape was possible. Thus, learned helplessness occurs when the inability to escape from a situation where escape or control is impossible generalizes to other situations from which the organism could escape if it would only try. Seligman equated depression, then, with learned helplessness. (See Chapter 6 for a fuller explanation of the learned helplessness effect, and see Chapter 13 for a similar frustration theory of depression.)

In laboratory research with college students, Seligman (1975) found that both depressed students and students who were not depressed but were made helpless through exposure to uncontrollable negative stimuli showed similarly poor performance and passive acceptance of negative stimuli in a new task. Seligman theorized that clinical depression and learned helplessness are similar in that both states involve developing a belief in the futility of responding. This theory therefore includes a cognitive component (e.g., belief in the futility of active responding) as well as a behavioral component (e.g., passivity). A depressed person becomes passive only with repeated lack of positive reinforcement for responding. (This formulation obviously has some similarities with Lewinsohn's theory.)

Subsequently, Seligman and his associates have modified their theory (Abramson, Metalsky, & Alloy, 1989; Abramson, Seligman, & Teasdale, 1978). The reformulation suggests that it is not uncontrollable outcomes themselves but a person's explanations for these outcomes that determine the nature and magnitude of depression. People who attribute an undesirable outcome to their own inadequacies and expect future negative outcomes will experience guilt, hopelessness, and self-blame. Those who attribute an undesirable outcome to external factors may feel depressed, but they will not feel self-blame. This reformulation incorporates both reinforcement theory and cognitive theory. Recent evidence provides support for this perspective: Students, patients, and other subjects who attributed negative events in the classroom, in therapy, and elsewhere to their own inadequacies were more likely to suffer negative mood swings than those who did not (Brewin, 1985; Peterson & Seligman, 1985). They also had relatively poor freshman grades and other college difficulties (Peterson & Barrett, 1987). More recently, expectancies of noncontingent negative outcomes (hopelessness) in arthritis patients were found to be a strong predictor of depression (DeVellis & Blalock, 1992).

On the other hand, Carson (1989) reviewed evidence suggesting that individuals with these hopelessness expectancies and self-critical explanations for their failures may already be depressed (i.e., the depression may come first, rather than being caused by the thoughts). If the depressed mood can be alleviated, the negative cognitions improve on their own, again suggesting that the mood is the primary problem, not the cognitions. Moreover, many investigators (e.g., Higgins, 1987; Pyszczynski & Greenberg, 1987; Tennen & Affleck, 1987; Tennen, Herzberger, & Nelson, 1987) have focused attention on the role of self-esteem and the self in producing depression and depressive cognitions, suggesting that feeling bad about oneself is what underlies the tendency toward negative expectancies and cognitions (though this still leaves us with the question of where feeling bad about oneself originates).

Social Theories.   Various social and cultural factors seem to influence the appearance of depression. In some cultures, such as China, there seems to be less depression as we know it and more somaticizing (developing physical symptoms as a result of stress) (Kleinman, 1986). While depression may not necessarily be absent in non-Western societies, the symptoms are often different, giving the appearance of another disorder.

Even in our own culture, social factors influence mood disorders. In particular, some situations seem to be associated with a higher incidence of depression. For instance, adolescence has been identified as a time of increased susceptibility to depression, especially for females (Allgood-Merten et al., 1990; Lewinsohn et al., 1993, 1994). In addition, divorced individuals and urban residents seem more likely to become depressed, as do people of higher education and occupational status (Carson & Butcher, 1992). Finally, depression may run in families because when one member has symptoms, communication with other members (especially children) is disrupted. This has a negative effect on the other family members, who may also become depressed from the stress of living with a depressed person (Hammen, 1991).

Conclusions.   Many investigators are now concluding that there is an interaction between biological factors (such as a genetic predisposition), personality factors (such as attributional style, expectancies, and self-esteem), and social or environmental influences (such as stress and sex roles) in contributing to the development of depression. Urban life, occupations with a high degree of pressure, and interpersonal problems are all potential psychosocial stressors that may precipitate depression in a susceptible individual. Life events ranging from changing schools or graduating to getting married, having a baby, moving to a new home, suffering an illness, losing a job, or dealing with divorce or death can all contribute to the onset of depression (e.g., Beck, 1967; Paykel, 1982). The most comprehensive model of depression may thus have to include factors from several theories.

Schizophrenic Disorders

One class of severe disorders is known as the *schizophrenic disorders* (or schizophrenia). Understanding the causes and treatment of this disorder is one of the major challenges facing psychological researchers. Although it is the most frequent diagnosis among institutionalized adult mental patients, schizophrenia is also among the least understood disorders in the whole field of abnormal psychology. One out of 100 persons are hospitalized with a diagnosis of schizophrenia; about 40 percent of all mental patients bear that label.

SYMPTOMS

The term **schizophrenia,** (from the Greek words for "split" and "mind") was contrived in 1911 by a Swiss psychiatrist, Eugen Bleuler, and refers to a patient's incoherent mental processes and departure from social reality. According to DSM-IV, schizo-phrenia has three essential features—thought disorders, delusions (unreal beliefs about oneself or the world), and hallucinations (sensory experiences such as hearing voices when no one is speaking or seeing things that are not there)—and a person must exhibit at least one of them to warrant the diagnosis.

Thought Disorders.   Almost all schizophrenics suffer from some disorder of thought, emotion, or perception. The disorder is usually inferred from an individual's language, which may be bizarre and incomprehensible. A schizophrenic often displays associations between thoughts or words that are not entirely obvious and may shift the focus of a sentence abruptly. Neologisms (invented words) are not uncommon, and the patient may repeat the same phrase over and over for no apparent reason. Logical thinking is greatly impaired, and no connection may be apparent between parts of a schizophrenic's argument (Lehmann, 1980).

A fragment of a letter written by a schizophrenic patient provides an example of thought disorder:

> I wish you, therefore, a very happy, pleasant, healthy blessed and fruit-crop-rich year; and also many good wine-harvest years thereafter, as well as good potato-crop years; as well as fine potato years, and sauerkraut years, and sprouts years, and cucumber years, and nut years; a good-egg year, and also a good cheese year. (Bleuler, 1911/1950, p. 28)

Delusions.   Many schizophrenics experience delusions. A *delusion* is a strong belief held by an individual despite evidence contradicting it and despite lack of sup-port from most other people. There are many types of delusions; among the most com-mon are delusions of grandeur, delusions of reference, and delusions of persecution. Persons with delusion of grandeur believe that they are someone else more exalted, famous, or important, such as a movie star, a king, or God. Individuals with delusions of reference see chance events as being directly relevent to them and their lives. For example, a man with delusions of reference might think that two people talking must be talking about him. Persons with delusions of persecution believe that they are being conspired against by (usually powerful) others.

The case of a patient who thought he was dead exemplifies the persistence of schiz-ophrenic delusions. Frustrated in his efforts to dissuade the patient from this belief, a psychiatrist decided to force the patient to confront evidence to the contrary. He asked the patient, "Do dead people bleed?" "No, of course not," the patient replied, at which point the psychiatrist pricked the patient's finger with a scalpel. A tiny drop of blood trickled from the incision. After staring at this silently for a long time, the patient said, "I'll be damned! Dead people do bleed!" (Mahoney, 1980).

CASE STUDY

SCHIZOPHRENIA: TOO CLOSE FOR COMFORT

Two of the authors of this book were teaching at the same university, and both had the same student in their large lec-ture classes. In the middle of the term, she disappeared from both classes. The next we heard of this student was when we both received telephone calls from a local mental health facility asking us for information about the drugs we were administering to her. It seems that the student had wandered into the clinic confused and disoriented, claiming that her problem was caused by the psycho-logical experiment being conducted on her by the two of us! She claimed that we were giving her drugs and otherwise controlling her behavior for some sort of experiment. We finally managed to convince the hospital authorities that we were merely her professors in large lecture courses and that we were not performing any drug experiments on her or anyone else; the student was experiencing delusions and was diagnosed as schizophrenic.

Hallucinations. A schizophrenic patient may hear imagined voices or, less commonly, see imagined persons or objects or smell odors that are not present. The voices may be of God, the devil, relatives, neighbors, or total strangers. Quite often the voices talk about the patient, sometimes threatening, sometimes commanding, sometimes emitting obscenities. The best guess is that such hallucinations reflect a person's inability to distinguish between his or her own memory images and the perceptual experiences that originate outside his or her mind.

The longest and most difficult manhunt in the history of New York ended in August 1977, when police arrested David Berkowitz, the "Son of Sam," who killed or maimed 13 young people. Berkowitz attributed his crimes to commands from an outside voice that came to him through Sam, a neighbor's dog. Although hallucinations are the hallmark of schizophrenia, most schizophrenics do not commit such atrocities. Rather, they are likely to be fairly passive and withdrawn and generally less dangerous than normal individuals.

In his 1976 book, *The Eden Express*, Mark Vonnegut recounted vividly the sequence of his schizophrenic episode. It all began with disorders of perception and emotion:

David Berkowitz, the "son of sam" killer, is thought by many to be suffering from Schizophrenia.

> Small tasks became incredibly intricate and complex. It started with pruning the fruit trees. One saw cut would take forever. I was completely absorbed in the sawdust floating gently to the ground, the feel of the saw in my hand, the incredible patterns in the bark, the muscles in my arm pulling back and then pushing forward. Everything stretched infinitely in all directions. Suddenly it seemed as if everything was slowing down and I would never finish sawing the limb. Then I found myself being unable to stick with any one tree. I'd take a branch here, a couple there. It seemed I had been working for hours and hours but the sun had not moved at all. I began to wonder if I was hurting the trees and found myself apologizing. Each tree began to take on personality. I began to wonder if any of them liked me. (p. 99)

Later, delusions appeared while Vonnegut was in a cafe:

> I started falling very deeply in love with the waitress and everyone else in the place. It seemed that they in turn were just as deeply in love with me. It was like something I couldn't get out of my eye. I didn't understand it, but I recognized it. There were all those little things that had happened occasionally between me and lovers before, but never this strong, never so lastingly, never with so many. I was completely in love, willing to die for or suffer incredibly for whatever they might want. A rush of warmth and emotion, spiritual and physical attraction, a wanting of oneness, a feeling of already oneness. (p. 117)

And finally came the hallucinations:

> The Voices. Testing one, two, testing one. Checking out the circuits: "What hath God wrought. Yip di mina di zonda za da boom di yaidi yoohoo."

Then the voices got clearer:

> At first I had to strain to understand them. They were soft and working some pretty tricky codes. Snap-crackle-pops, the sound of the wind with blinking lights and horns for punctuation. I broke the code and somehow was able to internalize it to the point where it was just like hearing words. In the beginning it seemed mostly nonsense, but as things went along they made more and more sense. Once you hear voices, you realize they've always been there. It's just a matter of being tuned to them. (p. 136)

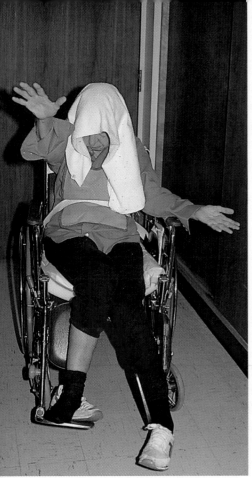

Some schizophrenics may adopt catatonic poses. In a condition known as "waxy flexibility," another person can place the patient's limbs in odd positions, which the schzophrenic will maintain like a statue.

TYPES OF SCHIZOPHRENIA

Although all schizophrenics have some of the symptoms described previously, they differ enough in detail so that diagnosticians have recognized a number of varieties. DSM-IV lists five types of schizophrenic reactions—disorganized, catatonic, paranoid, deficit, and undifferentiated—plus a residual category for patients who do not fit elsewhere.

• **Disorganized schizophrenics** are the people whom the average person is most likely to think of as "crazy." Their speech is often nonsensical. The emotion they express is often silly and includes smiling and laughing for no reason. Their behavior is often bizarre and inappropriate. This type of schizophrenia is usually associated with extreme social impairment.

• **Catatonic schizophrenics** demonstrate unusual physical activity ranging from wild and uncontrolled to unresponsive. In a condition known as "waxy flexibility," another person may place the patient's limbs in odd positions, which the catatonic schizophrenic will maintain, statuelike.

• **Paranoid schizophrenics** are less likely to be seen immediately as abnormal, but they often have prominent delusions of persecution or grandeur. They have the most common type of schizophrenia (and the type manifested by our schizophrenic student).

• **Deficit schizophrenics** primarily exhibit a lack (deficit) of normal responses, such as a lack of pleasure in anything, a lack of volition, or will, to do anything, and a lack of emotional range (flat affect) such that they seem emotionless and apathetic. This deficit of responsiveness must be exhibited for at least a month to warrant the diagnosis, but often such behavior has persisted for years. This type of schizophrenic does not exhibit the more bizarre and noticeable symptoms such as hallucinations or delusions.

• **Undifferentiated schizophrenics** have so many overlapping symptoms that it isn't clear in which subtype they should be categorized. Over time, they may move back and forth between types.

POSITIVE VERSUS NEGATIVE SCHIZOPHRENIA

Schizophrenia is probably a group of disorders sharing certain common symptomatic features and responses to treatment. Recently, a distinction has been proposed between "positive" and "negative" schizophrenia (Andreasen, 1989). Although this dichotomy may seem to oversimplify what is clearly a complicated issue, it actually combines observations from various disciplines, such as phenomenology, cognition, pharmacology, and physiology into a single hypothesis.

Positive schizophrenia is characterized by symptoms such as delusions and hallucinations. It has a generally acute onset, no apparent underlying cognitive or structural brain abnormalities, and good response to antipsychotic (major tranquilizer) drugs. This responsiveness to the major tranquilizers has led to speculation that positive schizophrenic symptoms are somehow related to abnormalities involving the neurochemical dopamine.

Negative schizophrenia is, in many respects, the opposite of the positive type. The major symptoms are more characteristic of a lessening of function than an excess. For example, negative symptoms include blunted (reduced or restricted) emotional responses, apathy, lack of volition (will or desire to act), poverty of speech, lack of sociality and pleasure, and attentional impairment. Patients exhibiting only these symptoms are now (since DSM-IV) diagnosed as deficit-type schizophrenics. It is usually difficult to pinpoint the onset of these symptoms, which begin gradually and worsen. In general, these patients seem to be functioning poorly for a long time before they are actually diagnosed as schizophrenic. They also seem to have more brain abnormalities than positive schizophrenics and are more likely to be left-handed. They perform poorly on intelligence and other neuropsychological tests, reflecting cognitive impairment, which may begin early in life. Finally, these patients do not respond well to antipsychotic drugs. There is no widely accepted physiological mechanism that seems to explain negative schizophrenia (like the dopamine theory for positive schizophrenia). Although critics complain that this positive/negative schizophrenia theory confuses symptoms with an actual disease and that it does not explain "mixed" patients who have both types of syndromes, the theory is nevertheless stimulating much research (e.g., Andreasen & Flaum, 1991; Cannon, Mednick, & Parnas, 1990; Ohman et al., 1989).

CAUSES OF SCHIZOPHRENIA

Partly because of its relatively high representation among patient populations, schizophrenia has generated many theories and therapies. Unfortunately, none has yet made a truly significant breakthrough. Many investigators believe that schizophrenia is a disease in the biomedical sense, although no complete medical explanation has been found. Nonetheless, the biomedical model presents one promising perspective.

The Biomedical Model. The biomedical position is based, at least in part, on evidence about the inheritance of schizophrenia. It has long been known that the disorder seems to run in families. The probability of a person developing schizophrenia increases dramatically if family members and other relatives also manifest schizophrenia (see Table 15.5). These findings suggest that at least some people inherit a potential for the disorder. The issues in this type of research are similar to those you read about in Chapter 14's discussion of genetic transmission of personality or in this chapter's discussion about the inheritance of depression and alcoholism.

TABLE 15.5
Biological Risk of Developing Schizophrenia

RELATIONSHIP TO PERSON	MORBIDITY RISK (RISK OF DEVELOPING SCHIZOPHRENIA) (%)
No blood relationship	0.8–1.5
Second-degree relatives (e.g., grandparents, uncle, niece, half-sibling)	2.4–4.2
First-degree relatives	
Parent	5.6
Sibling	10.1
Child	12.8
One sibling and at least one parent	16.7
Both parents	46.3
Monozygotic (identical) twin	50.0

As the number of relatives or their genetic similarity to a person increases, so does the person's risk of developing schizophrenia.

SOURCE: Gottesman et al., 1982; Gottesman, 1991.

The most compelling evidence for the role of genetic factors in schizophrenia comes from adoption studies. When the offspring of a schizophrenic parent are adopted by a normal parent and reared in a foster home, they still have the same risk for the disorder that they would if they had been brought up by the biological parent (Gottesman, 1991; Gottesman, Shields, & Hanson, 1982). In addition, adopted children who are schizophrenic have significantly more relatives with schizophrenic disorders among their biological kin than among their nonbiological, or adoptive, families (Gottesman, 1991; Gottesman et al., 1982). Figure 15.4 shows the PET scans of four sisters, all of whom developed schizophrenia and have abnormal usage of glucose in their brains.

Does this mean, then, that schizophrenia is inherited? The answer is probably, but not inevitably, and only partially. Most schizophrenics do not have schizophrenic parents or siblings. In fact, the risk of developing schizophrenia is only 50 percent among identical twins. In other words, in half of these cases, only one member of the pair develops schizophrenia, even though both members have the same genetic makeup. The other twin never develops the disorder. Schizophrenics do, however, have parents and siblings who suffer a wider range of psychological disorders than other persons. The consensus, therefore, suggests that what people inherit are degrees of vulnerability to exhibit schizophrenic symptoms (Gottesman, 1991). Whether they will exhibit them depends on such factors as environmental stress (Zubin & Spring, 1977). Finally, we must keep in mind that all these genetic studies are merely correlational. It is difficult to distinguish the effects of heredity from possibly related environmental factors.

Another line of research supporting the biomedical perspective focuses on the chemical imbalance implicated in the disease. The dominant theory about the biochemistry of schizophrenia is the dopamine hypothesis mentioned earlier (Snyder, 1976, 1981). The **dopamine hypothesis** asserts that schizophrenics suffer from excessively high concentrations of the transmitter dopamine in their brains or from excessive reactivity to dopamine because of the presence of an excessive number of dopamine receptors in the brain. Dopamine is an inhibitory transmitter involved in the transmission of neural signals. It is concentrated in certain areas of the brain, particularly in the limbic system, which, as you will remember, is involved in regulating emotional behavior.

The evidence associating schizophrenia with an excessive reactivity to dopamine comes from at least three sources. First, animals sometimes exhibit stereotyped behavior similar to catatonia when they are injected with chemicals that increase brain dopamine (Bernheim & Lewine, 1979). Second, some evidence indicates that the psychotic experiences reported in amphetamine overdose may be due to elevation of brain dopamine levels. (Amphetamine psychoses resemble the paranoid features of some forms of schizophrenia.) Finally, one of the most widely prescribed drug treatments for schizophrenia employs a class of drugs called the phenothiazines (or neuroleptics). According to pharmacological studies, the phenothiazines block dopamine receptors in the brain, thereby reducing the amount of dopaminergic activity and the number of active dopamine receptors (Turkington, 1983). Recent research suggests that enhanced dopamine activity is related to the presence of positive symptoms of schizophrenia and dopamine underactivity is connected to the presence of negative symptoms (Heritch, 1990).

The chemical imbalance hypothesis has promise, but it has many scientific hurdles to clear before it can be declared highly probable. It needs to demonstrate why dopamine should ever have become elevated in these individuals and why antipsy-

FIGURE 15.4
PET Scans of Four Schizophrenic Sisters

Shown here are the PET scans of four schizophrenic sisters, the Genain quadruplets—Nora, Iris, Hester, and Myra. The scans show the different levels of glucose use in various brain areas among the sisters. Lower use is indicated by blue, green, and yellow, suggesting less brain activity. Hester and Nora's scans indicate more severe impairment than the other two. The orange and red spots on Iris and Myra's scans indicate more normal energy use. However, Iris, who was paired throughout childhood with the most impaired sister, Hester, has had a worse clinical outcome than Nora or Myra, suggesting that psychosocial factors may be influential as biological ones.

SOURCE: Buchsbaum et al., 1984.

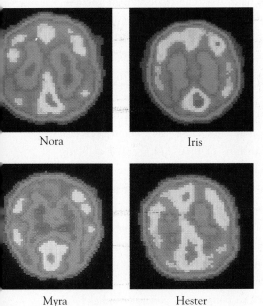

Nora   Iris

Myra   Hester

chotic medications take so long to remove psychotic symptoms. Because something removes the symptoms of a condition does not mean that it is connected to its cause; aspirin relieves headaches, but no one believes that headaches are caused by a lack of aspirin.

Psychological Models. Psychoanalytic approaches view schizophrenia and other psychoses as examples of extensive regression to an earlier infantile stage. Psychosis is also seen as evidence of a lack of ego development, which results in reduced contact with reality (because the ego is the mediator of reality). A patient substitutes a fantasy world for the real one. Thus, hallucinations and delusions are the imagined replacements for an unacceptable reality (Lehmann, 1980). This model is not widely utilized or accepted currently, however.

Learning theorists also offer explanations for schizophrenia. From one perspective, for example, schizophrenic behaviors, bizarre as they may be, are rewarded by the environment, notably by the attention they elicit. Proponents of this explanation point to research that shows that schizophrenic behaviors can be increased or decreased by training staff to attend differentially to bizarre and normal behaviors. In one experiment, schizophrenic patients in a hospital were trained to stand in a corner holding a broom by rewarding them for doing so. Psychiatrists were then brought into the ward and asked what they thought about the patients' strange behavior. They all offered "explanations" based on their own theoretical orientations. The experimenter then eliminated the behavior by withdrawing the reinforcement. Thus, in some cases at least, bizarre, "schizophrenic" behaviors can be learned through reinforcement and then eliminated by changing the reinforcement contingencies (Ayllon & Azrin, 1965). However, this does not mean that schizophrenia is caused by a learning process—only that it can be modified by one.

Another learning model posits that schizophrenia reflects faulty learning of coping skills, which is then combined with other learned factors (e.g., fears, or irrational social interaction styles). Some schizophrenic behavior may even be learned through attempts to meet impossible expectations or conflicting demands, as from unrealistic, irrational parents (Carson & Butcher, 1992).

Social/Environmental Models. The "faulty learning" mentioned in the previous section may be a result of what has been called "schizophrenogenic" (or schizophrenia-causing) parents or families. Many studies have been made of the families of schizophrenic patients, with special emphasis on the mothers. A theory in the 1950s suggested that the mothers of schizophrenics gave mixed messages, claiming to love their children but rejecting them emotionally and physically. The verbal message thus conflicted with the nonverbal message, leaving the children with no appropriate response. If the children responded to the verbal message and came close, they were rejected; if they withdrew, they were pursued with protestations of love and accused of being ungrateful. Either way, the children were accused of being wrong. Fathers in such families were described as withdrawn, weak, and ineffectual. Unfortunately, patients with other disorders also had "double-bind" parents, as did many "normals." The researchers who described the double-bind behaviors may also have been biased because they expected to find this result. More recently, better-designed studies have indicated that the domineering, double-bind type of mothering may indeed characterize mothers of schizophrenics, at least to some extent (Roff & Knight, 1981), but this seems to be combined with other factors related to both of the parents. In general, studies have tended to show a high degree of psychological disorder in parents of schizophrenics or in their marital relationships, regardless of what particular pattern such disturbance takes. Recent attention has focused on the level of "expressed emotion" in the families of schizophrenics. Patients whose families express a high degree of criticism, overinvolvement, and hostility toward them suffer higher relapse rates (e.g., Glynn et al., 1990; Mintz et al., 1989; Tarrier, 1989; Vaughn, 1989), although this is also true for depressed (Florin et al., 1992) and eating-disordered patients (Le Grange et al., 1992).

Most environmental models of schizophrenia address the influence of stress. While some people may be biologically more vulnerable than others to develop the disorder, life stress may be necessary to set off a schizophrenic episode (Rosenthal, 1970). Thus, persistent negative circumstances or a temporary, but powerful, negative event, such as the loss of a loved one, may be required to trigger a breakdown. Vulnerable individuals are those who are less equipped to handle the stresses of life. For example, one patient was admitted to the hospital with schizophrenic delusions that her mother was trying to kill her and was a devil with supernatural powers. She had left her parents' home a year earlier, after several brushes with the law for teenaged vandalism. Her mother had finally taken her to court as an uncontrollable child, getting her committed to a juvenile hall. When she got out of there, the patient became a stripper. She lived with an alcoholic older man who regularly beat her. Her mother came to see her and called her names and told her she would go to hell for her sins. After a particularly violent session with her mother, the patient developed her symptoms and was admitted to a mental hospital. The stresses of her life had become too much for this teenager (whose mother had also had psychotic episodes).

Long-term studies are currently in progress in Denmark (Cannon et al., 1990) and the United States (Erlenmeyer-Kimling et al., 1984) to test this approach. The studies involve locating children with a vulnerability for developing schizophrenia (e.g., being the relative of a schizophrenic) and following them through adulthood, when the appearance of symptoms is likely to occur. Tests of their vulnerability to stressors and measurement of the amount of ongoing stress are made throughout the study. While stressors seem to predict schizophrenia in one study (Cannon et al., 1990), this is not true in the other (Erlenmeyer-Kimling et al., 1984). The subjects in both studies are still relatively young, however, so we will have to wait for more definitive results.

A similar long-term study was done in Norway. The authors studied the children of pairs of identical twins where only one twin (parent) was schizophrenic. They found a slight increase in general psychological disorders for the children of the schizophrenic twins, but attributed this to environmental stress such as living with a schizophrenic parent (Kringlen & Cramer, 1989).

Social roles, as well as stressors, may play a part in the development of schizophrenia. Laing (1967) has proposed that patients have, in effect, created their own social roles as schizophrenics to escape impossible social demands and expectations. These people make an inward search for the true self and eventual wholeness and health. A split arises between the true self and a false outer self shown to the world; schizophrenic breakdowns reflect the intolerable level of the split. Szasz's (1961, 1970) proposal that schizophrenia represents problems in living similarly portrays psychosis as a defensive role.

Finally, social factors may influence the prevalence of schizophrenia by determining diagnostic criteria. These factors can affect the manner in which symptoms are manifested. For example, differences in the content, form, and type of symptoms have been described in different countries, cultures, and continents. What is psychopathology and how it is manifested are defined to a certain extent by society. This definition clearly affects the most abnormal disorder, schizophrenia. As with depression, the disorder may well be caused by a combination of genetic, hormonal, psychological, and social factors.

Personality Disorders

The DSM-IV **personality disorders** include a wide variety of enduring, inflexible, and maladaptive personality traits that characterize individuals for much of their lives and interfere with relationships with others (see Chapter 14 for a general discussion of normal personality and traits). These pathologies of character (thus called characterological) are diagnosed on Axis II. DSM-IV lists a number of specific personality disorders; they are often recognizable by adolescence (often earlier) and continue throughout most of adult life, although they become less obvious in middle and old age. They are often present along with one of the Axis I disorders.

DSM-IV divides the personality disorders into three groups, or "clusters," plus a residual group for personality disorders that do not fit elsewhere. Those disorders that have been investigated more by researchers, such as antisocial personality, are described more fully in the DSM. We, too, will describe antisocial personality disorder in detail and give a briefer description of a disorder from each of the other clusters.

CLUSTER 1 DISORDERS

The first cluster contains the personality disorders characterized by the most eccentric or odd behavior. For example, those with **paranoid personality disorders** are extremely suspicious and jealous of others, although there is no reason for this mistrust. They tend to display limited emotional reactivity, often appearing cold, unfriendly, and tense and showing little or no sense of humor. Paranoid individuals try to avoid being blamed for anything, regardless of whether they deserve blame. They search out evidence, however slight, of their own suspicions about others and seize on the least possible evidence to confirm their beliefs (while ignoring any evidence to the contrary). They are often intensely jealous, since they expect betrayal and trickery from others, or are hypersensitive to imagined slights or insults. They often imagine plots against them and refuse to believe anything that contradicts their suspicions. This disorder occurs more frequently in males than females; however, individuals with this problem are unlikely to seek therapy and rarely need to be hospitalized, so its actual prevalence is unknown. As you may imagine, it is difficult to live or work with someone like this, but otherwise, these individuals seem able to function without too much impairment.

CLUSTER 2 DISORDERS: THE ANTISOCIAL PERSONALITY

The second cluster contains disorders that interfere more with general functioning and that tend to get more attention from mental health or criminal justice authorities. As mentioned, we will cover one major personality disorder from this cluster in detail because it is so well studied. **Antisocial personality disorder** is marked by a lack of consideration for the rights and feelings of others and an absence of guilt or remorse when others have been hurt. Individuals, usually male, who suffer from this disorder manifest its signs by the age of 15 (or earlier) with such problems as truancy, delinquent behavior, stealing, fighting, and a flagrant disregard for truth and responsibilities. These individuals often have difficulty keeping jobs or maintaining marital rela-

Some people with paranoid personalities become leaders of mystical or fringe religious groups because of the tendency for those with the disorder to be very moralistic, authoritarian, and punitive. They expect blind obedience from their followers and are usually harsh and extreme in their treatment of those who trangress their rules. Jim Jones may have been one such paranoid personality: He led more than 900 of his cult followers to painfull, suicidal death in the jungles of Guyana.

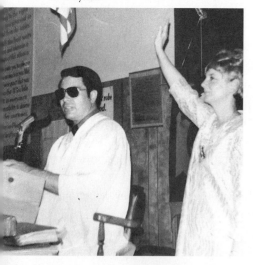

tionships, and they may lack the ability to function as responsible parents (American Psychiatric Association, 1994). This disorder, then, includes both criminals and delinquents (as well as antisocial individuals who are especially intelligent or talented and who become successes in their chosen field). Ten percent of adult criminals are classified as antisocial, or what used to be referred to as psychopathic and sociopathic.

Estimates of the prevalence of antisocial personality disorder show that it affects about 2 to 3 percent of the male population, but less than 1 percent of females in North America. There is some controversy about this sex difference, however. Some researchers assert that sex biases, or differential expectations for behavior in males and females, influence what diagnosis a person receives. Thus, males who behave as described are likely to be diagnosed as having antisocial personality disorder, while females who exhibit these behaviors are more likely to be seen as histrionic personality disordered (Ford & Widiger, 1989), another classification.

How much influence do you think societal expectations about "normal" or "acceptable" behavior have on the sorts of personality disorders people are diagnosed as having? Would you classify a woman who is manipulative of others and who doesn't care about hurting them differently from a man who behaves this way? Can you see how our sex role expectations may affect our interpretations of what sort of pathology someone exhibits?

A number of characteristics mark criminal antisocial personalities (Cleckley, 1964). These individuals are usually superficially charming and make good initial impressions. They tend to be impulsive, however, and disregard social convention. Perhaps their most notable characteristic is their lack of empathy, love, guilt, remorse, or shame. As you might imagine, this makes their relationships with others generally exploitative and manipulative, and they do not seem to be capable of sustaining long-term monogamous relationships. Not only do these individuals lack normal feelings toward others and display a high degree of manipulativeness and impulsiveness, but they are also quite arrogant, having overinflated opinions of themselves and a proneness to blame others for their misdeeds and problems (American Psychiatric Association, 1994).

CASE STUDY

ANTISOCIAL PERSONALITY DISORDER— CHARLES MANSON

Charles Manson was born November 11, 1934, to a teenage prostitute. When he was 5 years old, his mother was arrested for robbery and was sent to jail. Manson went to live with an aunt and uncle in West Virginia. He remembered his aunt as being very strict, his uncle as kind and compassionate. When the boy was 13, his mother, now out of jail, took him home to Indianapolis. She drank heavily and often left him alone all night. At 14 he departed, supporting himself by taking odd jobs and by petty theft. His mother felt that he was uncontrollable and turned him in to the police, who placed him in a juvenile detention center. He ran away after three days and robbed a grocery store. Arrested, he was sent to a reformatory but escaped. In the next four years, he escaped from 18 juvenile correction institutions. Manson's life became a series of imprisonments and crimes. In 1967, at age 33, after release from yet another jail, he drifted to the Haight-Ashbury section of San Francisco, then teeming with "flower children" and "hippies." He was superficially charming, even charismatic, and gained a small following

Charles Manson is an example of a person with antisocial personality disorder.

of young men and women. The Manson family, as they became known, moved to southern California, where they intimidated an old, blind rancher into allowing them to live with him. In August 1969, Manson and his family entered an expensive Hollywood home and murdered five persons, including the pregnant movie star Sharon Tate. The bodies were horribly mutilated. When police arrived, they found a brief message—the word *pig* written in blood on the front door.

There are many theories about the causes of antisocial personality disorder, but little data to support any of them. There is some evidence that these individuals have a very low level of reactivity in their autonomic nervous system, perhaps making them less capable of learning through conditioning and of learning to feel the same emotions that other people feel (Hare, 1978). Biological theories focus on this underaroused autonomic nervous system as a possible source of these people's need to gratify impulses or seek thrills. Also, genetic evidence indicates that identical twins are more similar in antisocial personality than are fraternal twins. Adopted children more closely resemble their biological parents than their adoptive parents in this, suggesting a genetic component.

Psychoanalytic theorists focus on the childhood and parental relationships of these individuals. They claim that these individuals have been rejected and unloved by their parents and thus have never identified with their parents. This makes it impossible for them to develop a conscience. Learning theories also focus on childhood but emphasize the learning history of the children. According to social learning theory, children may learn aggressive behavior from parents, peers, or other social influences and may not be taught or reinforced for more acceptable behaviors. Neither of these theories has much in the way of evidence; they are thus far more speculation than fact.

CLUSTER THREE DISORDERS

The personality disorders in the third cluster seem to result in the least limitations on the individual's functioning. Obviously, given that these are disorders, there is some impairment. Most people with these disorders report interference with interpersonal relationships, and usually their work is also affected to some degree. If you met someone who was terribly shy and nervous around other people and who avoided social situations out of this fear, would you think that the individual had a personality disorder or some sort of generalized social phobia? This is a question that is being debated among psychologists, who are trying to decide if a cluster 3 personality disorder called avoidant personality disorder is a different entity from a phobia called generalized social phobia (Herbert et al., 1992; Holt et al., 1992; Turner et al., 1992). What would you look for to decide if this is a general personality style or a specific set of fears? When the symptoms are so similar, it is not easy to determine if there are two different abnormal processes or if these are just different versions (more severe and less severe) of the same problem.

Other personality disorders are more generally accepted. **Passive-aggressive personality disorder** involves resisting the demands of others in an indirect, rather than direct, manner. Instead of saying no or voicing any hostility, individuals acquiesce to requests, but then do not fulfill them. They may forget, procrastinate, dawdle, or simply be so inefficient that the required tasks are never accomplished. Individuals with passive-aggressive personality disorders usually function in the world without attracting undue attention from mental health workers. This diagnosis is also somewhat con-

Behavior can be seen differently depending on its setting or context. What is perfectly normal and acceptable in one's own living room may be seen as evidence of abnormality in a mental hospital.

troversial, though, since it requires individuals to be both aggressive and passive at the same time, an apparent contradiction. It seems that these individuals resent others, particularly authority figures, but are afraid to contradict them or to assert their own wishes. Thus, they express hostility by being extra passive. They never say no to anything they do not want to do; they just don't do it. This behavior is only considered a personality disorder if actively aggressive behavior is possible for any normal person in the situation (i.e., it is not a personality disorder to passively resist the demands of someone who would hurt you if you simply refused). Also, the behavior must be present in a variety of contexts, not, for example, only with one's spouse or boss. While there appear to be plenty of these sorts of individuals around, there is no documented information on the prevalence of this disorder, or even whether it occurs more in males or females. It seems, then, that those annoying people who always agree to help you out and then fail to come through may actually merit a clinical diagnosis. If they do it to many of those around them, they have passive-aggressive personality disorder. (However, if they do it only to you, you're just unlucky!)

Themes in Review

We have seen that abnormality encompasses an enormous range of conditions, some quite common. There are also many different explanations for these varied problems. The influence of biological factors is difficult to separate from that of psychological (cognitive, Freudian, and learning) or social factors, as the models we presented make clear. All have useful suggestions, which vary depending on the disorder under discussion. For example, to return to the questions posed at the beginning of the chapter, alcoholism does seem to have some biological basis to it. There is increasing evidence that genetics plays a role, although societal factors may steer some susceptible individuals toward or away from alcohol. Several theories about the causes of depression link the disorder to cognitions, although here, too, there is evidence of a genetic predisposition. Phobias may well be learned fears, although other psychological explanations, such as Freudian unconscious conflict resolution, can also be invoked successfully, and evo-

lutionary theorists can point to some evidence of biological influence. Schizophrenia has been described by Szasz and others as a "problem in living" or inability to conform to socially acceptable behavior, but genetic evidence that it is inherited, biological evidence that the disorder is controlled by drugs affecting dopamine levels in the brain, and cognitive evidence that the thinking patterns of schizophrenics are seriously distorted suggest that schizophrenia is not simply a sociocultural wastebasket for misfits.

Developmental considerations are important in the diagnosis and course of many of these disorders. For example, autism appears in infancy and lasts throughout one's life. The personality disorders begin to manifest themselves during childhood, are particularly apparent in early and middle adulthood and seem to subside somewhat in older adulthood. Schizophrenia also appears by early adulthood, if it is going to develop at all. Depression, on the other hand, can begin at any point in the life cycle, from infancy to old age.

It seems then, that we cannot expect to find one set of principles that accounts for all the conditions with which clinical psychologists deal. One set may underlie schizophrenia, another depression, still another drug addiction. There appear to be contributions from biology, psychology, and social/environmental factors, even within a single disorder. A biological or genetic predisposition can get triggered by environmental stresses and psychological learning or cognitive factors. At present, we are improving descriptions of abnormal syndromes more rapidly than we are evolving causal explanations for them. This chapter is thus in many ways more descriptive and less experimental, data-based, or theoretical than most of the others. It is to be hoped that research in this area will soon provide more theoretical models for abnormal conditions as well as the means for preventing, alleviating, or correcting them. In the next chapter, we will examine current methods of treating abnormality.

SUMMARY

1 Psychopathology is the field of psychology that deals with the wide assortment of behaviors differing from what is appropriate or normal. Three criteria for deciding whether a behavior is abnormal, or pathological, are (a) deviation from a statistical norm, (b) deviation from an ideal standard, and (c) personal distress.

2 Several different models of psychopathology have been developed to help explain the origins or causes of abnormal behaviors. The biological view began with the ancient Greeks, who first suspected physical problems of causing psychopathology. Today, the biological view includes physical factors ranging from hormonal aberrations to genetic predispositions. The psychological view also began with ancient Greek observations that psychological factors contributed to abnormal behavior. Freud and the psychoanalysts expanded this greatly to include unconscious influences on behavior resulting from conflicts between an individual's impulses and "acceptable" behavior in society. Humanistic psychologists focused attention on an individual's phenomenological perspective, while behavioral psychologists suggest that the principles of learning and conditioning be applied to abnormal behavior. The cognitive model focuses on the influence of thoughts on feelings and behaviors. Finally the social view looks at the influence of societal values and influences.

3 Classification of psychopathology has been directed by the Diagnostic and *Statistical Manual of Mental Disorders,* which is currently in its fourth edition (DSM-IV). This directory attempts to provide reliable descriptions of types or patterns of abnormal behavior according to five axes, or dimensions. Critics maintain that without theoretical explanations, these descriptions are not very helpful and that this whole enterprise medicalizes abnormality, treating it as if it were a disease needing a label and a cure. The DSM has made diagnosing abnormal behavior more consistent and reproduceable, though, and has sparked more research in the area.

4 Anxiety disorders are characterized by high levels of apprehension in the presence of certain objects or situations and by the development of behavior patterns to avoid these stimuli. The most prevalent types of anxiety disorders are phobias, generalized anxiety disorder, panic disorder, and obsessive-compulsive disorder.

5 Somatoform disorders involve physical symptoms that suggest physical disorder but for which there are no apparent organic causes. The most common form of these disorders is conversion disorder.

6 Dissociative disorders involve a splitting off (dissociation) of a part of an individual's personality in such a way that memory or identity is disturbed. In amnesia, there is a loss of memory. In a fugue, a person takes on a new identity. In multiple personality, the person shows two or more distinct, integrated personalities, each of which dominates at a particular time.

7 Substance-related disorders involve excessive use of drugs. Alcohol is the most widely used drug. With repeated use of a drug, a user may become physically dependent on the drug, as tolerance (need for more of the drug for the same effect) and withdrawal symptoms (uncomfortable symptoms when the drug is not used) develop. Drug abuse may result in permanent organic changes which can in turn cause organic mental syndromes.

8 Mood disorders involve disturbances of the emotional state. People suffering from these disturbances are unrealistically and deeply depressed, inappropriately joyful (manic), or both (bipolar disorder). They usually suffer physical symptoms, such as sleep disturbances, as well. Several biological and psychological theories have been advanced to explain depression. In particular, behavioral theories have focused on problematic learning, such as failure to appreciate positive reinforcement, learned helplessness, and cognitive learning deficits. The disorder probably reflects a combination of organic and psychological factors.

9 Schizophrenic disorders are the most serious type of abnormal behavior and the most likely to require hospitalization. Schizophrenic symptoms include thought disorders, delusions, and hallucinations. DSM-IV lists five types of schizophrenic reactions—disorganized, catatonic, paranoid, deficit, and undifferentiated—as well as a residual category for those that do not fit into the first five. Recent research has also focused on two types of schizophrenia characterized by positive versus negative symptoms and which seem to have different outcomes. Scientists have advanced biological theories, including genetic hypotheses and the dopamine theory, to explain schizophrenia. In addition, there are psychological and social explanations for the disorder. It seems likely that a biological predisposition is exacerbated by psychological and/or social factors to produce schizophrenia.

10 Personality disorders reflect enduring, inflexible, and maladaptive personality traits that interfere with a person's relations with others. DSM-IV groups these disorders into three clusters, each of which contains disorders with similar types of symptoms. Paranoid personality disorder is an example of the first cluster, which consists of disorders marked by unusual or eccentric behavior. The second cluster contains disorders that are more likely to result in attention from either the legal or mental health system, such as antisocial personality disorder. These individuals demonstrate a lack of empathy, love, guilt, and shame. Their relationships with others tend to be exploitative and manipulative. Passive-aggressive personality disorder is from the third cluster, which contains disorders characterized by fearfulness or avoidance. Passive-aggressive persons are afraid to express their aggressive feelings directly; instead they behave passively, but avoid doing what others want them to do.

KEY TERMS

psychopathology (p. 612)

statistical abnormality (p. 613)

psychosocial abnormality (p. 614)

personal abnormality (p. 614)

legal definition of abnormality (p. 614)

biological perspective (p. 615)

psychological perspective (p. 618)

psychoanalytic theory (p. 618)

neurosis (p. 618)

psychosis (p. 618)

humanistic theory (p. 619)

behavior theory (p. 619)

cognitive theory (p. 620)

social perspective (p. 620)

Diagnostic and Statistical Manual of Mental Disorders (p. 621)

DSM (p. 621)

anxiety disorder (p. 624)

phobias (p. 624)

generalized anxiety disorder (p. 627)

panic disorder (p. 627)

obsessions (p. 628)

compulsions (p. 628)

obsessive-compulsive disorder (p. 628)

FOR CRITICAL ANALYSIS

1 Why would a given individual develop a particular disorder? What factors would have to combine to bring about a specific psychopathology in one individual but leave another unscathed?

2 How do you think it would affect someone's life to suffer from an anxiety disorder?

3 What would it be like to have schizophrenia?

4 What sorts of treatments do you think could help people who have these problems?

SUGGESTED READINGS

Diagnostic and statistical manual of mental disorders (4th ed.). (1994). Washington, D C : American Psychiatric Association. The latest edition of the classification guidelines used by most clinical psychologists and psychiatrists to describe and define abnormality.

CARSON, R. C., & BUTCHER, J. N. (1992). *Abnormal psychology and modern life* (9th ed.). New York: HarperCollins. A thorough and enlightening survey of all aspects of abnormal behavior.

GAY, P. (Ed.) (1989). *The Freud reader*. New York: Norton. A carefully chosen selection of writings by Freud, with an introduction by the editor, a well-known Freudian scholar.

HOOLEY, J. M., NEALE, J. M., & DAVISON, G. C. (1989). *Readings in abnormal psychology*. New York: Wiley. Theoretical papers and interesting case histories are combined to illustrate various aspects of abnormality.

VONNEGUT, M. (1976). *The Eden express*. New York: Bantam Books. A well-written first-person account of a schizophrenic breakdown.

Psychology on the Internet

Internet Mental Health

(http://www.mentalhealth.com/p.html)

Of all the topics covered by Psychology on the Internet, psychopathology probably has the most Internet sites focusing on relevant information. There are numerous home pages and newsgroups devoted to general topics (mental health, psychopharmacology, and psychiatric/psychological resources) and specific disorders (e.g., anorexia nervosa, schizophrenia, and anxiety disorders). Access to a majority of these sites is organized in a free on-line encyclopedia of mental health—the Internet Mental Health home page.

Designed by a Canadian psychiatrist, Dr. Phillip Long, the Internet Mental Health home page is one of the most comprehensive on-line references on any topic in psychology. Internet Mental Health provides extensive diagnostic, treatment, and research information on the 50 most commonly diagnosed mental disorders. This site also contains an on-line magazine filled with articles, booklets, book reviews, newsletters, and stories of recovery. Finally, this site provides links to on-line journals relevant to mental health and links to other mental health sites—including organizations and institutions dedicated to mental health issues, university departments of psychology and psychiatry, and sites concerned with specific disorders (e.g., dementia, mood disorders, and schizophrenia).

Cyber-Psych

(http://www.charm.net/~pandora/psych/index.html)

"Cyber-Psych is committed to bringing high quality, professional psychological care and information to the on-line community." This site provides links to on-line pamphlets, Usenet and Listserv groups, and home pages concerned with specific mental disorders. The developers of Cyber-Psych "believe that the Internet provides a nonthreatening, interactive medium through which mental health care can be provided to the rapidly increasing population of people on-line."

THERAPIES

BIOLOGICAL THEME
What kinds of biological therapies are used to treat psychological disorders?

LEARNING THEME
How can we learn to overcome our fears and anxieties?

COGNITIVE THEME
Can changing our thoughts make us feel better and act more adaptively?

DEVELOPMENTAL THEME
How can therapies influence the development of more adaptive behavior patterns?

SOCIOCULTURAL THEME
How do sociocultural attitudes influence types and uses of psychotherapy?

Instead of telephoning the therapist himself, John let his wife do it for him.

The therapist formed a tentative hypothesis. Either John was resistant to the idea of coming and it was mostly his wife's idea that he seek help, or else he was quite dependent on her and let her do things for him. It was possible that both inferences were valid.

In the therapist's waiting room, John was found to be a strongly built man in his late thirties who obviously prided himself on keeping his body in tiptop physical condition. The therapist quickly began to amend his tentative hypothesis. There was no dependent-little-boy quality here.

John greeted the therapist with a casual "Hi, Doc" and sauntered, unasked, into the office from the waiting room. His air was one of studied unconcern. He adopted a lounging position in the chair and awaited further developments.

Invited to explain the reason for his visit, John launched into a circumstantial account involving his having an unspecified physical ailment and his wife's being worried about him. Abruptly, he paused and volunteered, "I'm not sure I belong here at all, Doc."

The statement, of course, came as no surprise to the therapist. Judging from the patient's tone of voice, from the set of his mouth, from the abrupt movements of his arms, from his sharp, piercing gaze, the therapist realized that he was dealing with a very angry man. Putting together his hypotheses and what the patient had said, the therapist ventured, "It must be very hard on you, with all the care you have taken of your body and all the things you are used to doing with it, to find that something has gone wrong with it."

The patient responded immediately to this, and talked about the sports he had played all his life. Finally, and sadly, he revealed the exact nature of his physical problem. It was of sufficient magnitude to rule out extensive exercise, particularly contact sports. Contact sports, he added, could end up killing him, and he said it in such a way that the therapist realized that the man had seriously considered going out that way, dying with his boots on, so to speak. The therapist ventured this interpretation, and the patient ruefully verified it.

The patient and the therapist were by now on the same wave length and communication was flowing relatively smoothly. (Adapted from Goldman & Millman, 1978, pp. 20–26.)

The preceding conversation illustrates several basic aspects of the psychotherapy situation. One person—a patient, or client—comes to another, a therapist, for help with some aspect of the first person's life, relationships, or feelings. The two agree, in some manner, about the subject matter for the therapy sessions. The therapist helps the client to understand more clearly his or her own feelings and behaviors and, presumably, to handle both in a more satisfactory manner. Remembering and talking about past and present distress are also elements of certain types of psychotherapy, designed to assist people in removing symptomatic, abnormal behavior and feelings. Additional kinds of therapies focus more on present circumstances, feelings, or behaviors. These and other types of treatments for abnormality will be discussed in this chapter.

Therapies: A Brief History

You will remember from our discussion of abnormality (Chapter 15) that people have been trying for centuries to correct behavior that societies, at various periods, have deemed abnormal or deviant. When societies recognized that madness constituted an involuntary problem for individuals, rather than a manifestation of wickedness or possession by demons, they established institutions known as asylums. Unfortunately conditions in these asylums were awful. Patients were chained to the cell walls and treated not much better than criminals. One such institution, St. Mary of Bethlehem, founded in London in 1547, had such horrible conditions that its name was the source of the word *bedlam*. (The local Cockney accent slurred the pronunciation.) For a small fee, Londoners could watch the tragic antics of the inmates, who were required to perform in plays and sketches for the audience.

In 1792, a French physician named Philippe Pinel (see Chapter 15) became director of an asylum in Paris and proceeded to treat inmates with compassion. Similar humanitarians achieved some success in other countries soon after. In the United States, Dorothea Dix, a Massachusetts schoolteacher, almost single-handedly roused the nation to the needs of the mentally disturbed. In 1840, mental hospitals housed only about 15 percent of those who needed care; by 1890, the figure was almost 70 percent, largely because of Dix's efforts. For the first time, "treatments" were provided, although most of them consisted of traumas intended to bring patients "back to their senses." If patients became unruly, devices were available to restrain them. As late as the 1950s, locked rooms, straightjackets, and impoverished conditions persisted as all part of the treatment. Although tremendous progress has been made, room for

William Hogarth's painting, Bedlam, depicts conditions in the Hospital of St. Mary of Bethlehem (Bedlam) in London in 1770. Note the chains on two of the patients.

Restraining devices were common in nineteenth-century mental hospitals. Many early "treatments" assumed that physical traumas would restore patients to their senses.

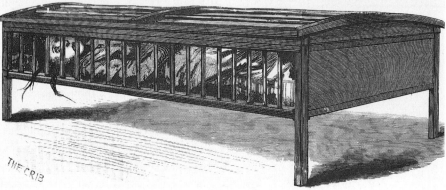

THE CRIB

improvement remains. Loneliness and boredom continue to be problems even in well-run institutions.

In the mid-1950s, the introduction of a range of "wonder drugs" initiated a revolution in patient management and an eventual decline in the number of people kept in mental institutions. By the 1970s, the "deinstitutionalization" of the mentally ill had caused patient populations in mental hospitals to drop precipitously, but this policy has created a new set of dilemmas, as we shall see.

Types of Therapy

There are many types of therapy for mental psychological disorder, based on different theoretical models of psychopathology and normal psychological functioning (as discussed in Chapters 14 and 15). All of these therapies fall into two broad classifications, however. One consists of the **somatic,** or **biological, therapies,** such as drug and shock therapies, which are usually based on physiological and biochemical views of mental disorder and which involve physically altering the patient's body to change feelings and behaviors. The other classification consists of various **psychotherapies,** treatments that are based on psychological theories and principles and that attempt to change the patient's feelings and behaviors through interventions involving talking, learning principles, emotional expression, or alteration of the social environment.

Current estimates maintain that there are over 200 psychotherapies—from traditional "talking" therapies, such as Freudian psychoanalysis, to avant garde and "pop" varieties such as primal scream. It would be impossible to list them all, let alone discuss them, in one chapter. Most, however, fall into a few broad categories, based primarily on the personality theories presented in Chapter 14 and the approaches to mental disorders described in Chapter 15. Moreover, all therapies—both physiological and psychological—are constantly evolving and giving birth to even newer therapies, some of which will be described later in this chapter.

Despite differences in technique and manner, each of these psychotherapies is aimed at helping its clients acquire more useful ways of feeling, thinking, and behaving. Most contemporary therapists do not adhere rigidly to one form of treatment. As a survey of therapists showed, most clinical psychologists are to some extent "eclectic," borrowing approaches and techniques from other schools of thought to supplement their own perspectives (Smith, 1982). This overlap should be kept in mind as you read the sections that follow.

Types of Therapists

Those who practice psychotherapy can be divided into five groups, largely on the basis of their training.

1. A **psychiatrist** is a medical doctor who usually performs three years of residency training in psychiatry after completing an undergraduate degree and medical school. Psychiatrists take medical as well as psychotherapeutic responsibility for their patients. A psychiatrist is the only psychotherapist permitted to prescribe psychoactive drugs, electroshock treatment, or other biological intervention techniques. A psychiatrist is often thought by lay people to be the best trained of the psychotherapists, but this is not necessarily so. In fact, few of the courses a psychiatrist takes to become a medical doctor involve psychological knowledge.

2. A **clinical psychologist** has completed four years of undergraduate work and has then gone on to earn a doctorate degree (Ph.D.) in psychology. This intensive course of study typically involves four to five years of training in research and clinical skills and problems of abnormal functioning, as well as a one-year internship under professional psychological supervision.

3. A **counseling psychologist** has had graduate training somewhat similar to that of a clinical psychologist (usually at the Ph.D. level), but typically deals with school and occupational populations. This training, then, is concerned with problems of adjustment. A counseling psychologist usually concentrates on specific areas, such as student, marriage, or family counseling. A recent innovation in clinical/counseling psychology is the creation of the Psy. D., or doctor of psychology degree. This is essentially a psychotherapy degree for psychologists, with little or no research training and thus no research project or dissertation. A psychologist with this degree is trained specifically to do counseling or psychotherapy, not research or evaluation.

4. A **psychiatric social worker** usually has an undergraduate degree plus a master's degree in social work and special training in treatment procedures, with emphasis on the family or community.

5. A **psychiatric nurse** is a registered nurse with special training for work in a mental hospital.

Knowing the type of degree a therapist has earned still does not tell a potential client what the therapist actually does. One psychiatrist will rely primarily on drug

Many therapies involve "talking cures" in which a patient talks about problems in order to understand them and cope more satisfactorily.

therapy, while another will never give drugs; one will use Freudian analysis, while another will use some other form of talking psychotherapy. A psychologist may do only assessments and consultations or perform the full course of assessment and psychotherapy, using one of a variety of theoretical orientations. In fact, although psychiatrists, psychologists, social workers, and nurses belong to regulated professions that license their members and ensure some minimal level of training and competence, the criteria for licensing differ from state to state, and in many places anyone can call him- or herself a "counselor" or "therapist," even without any formal training. It is thus up to the client to be an informed consumer, finding out as much as possible about the therapeutic alternatives available.

Let us turn now to the therapies themselves. We will begin with physical, or biological, treatments and move on to some of the psychotherapies traditionally studied and performed in the field of psychology.

Biological Approaches to Therapy

Biological, or somatic, therapies are often based on a medical model of psychopathology. These therapies assume that psychological problems reflect a mental illness with a biological cause and that treating the body directly can alleviate or even remove the symptoms. Biological treatments have been used for all sorts of problems, from anxiety and depression to schizophrenia. Such treatments range from mechanical procedures done to the patient's body, such as psychosurgery (cutting part of the brain to change feelings or behavior), to biochemical procedures, such as drug therapy.

The attempt to cure mental disorders with physical means can be traced back to the ancient practice of trephining—boring a hole in a patient's skull to release demons or perhaps to relieve pressure on the brain (see Chapter 15). Ancient Greek physicians such as Hippocrates and Galen also advocated physical interventions for mental distress; modern physicians have continued to do so. Methods popular in the past included purging (induced vomiting or diarrhea) and bleeding. (Both of these are now considered so bizarre that they are seen as symptoms of self-harm or the disorder bulimia rather than as cures.) These extreme tactics were used indiscriminately for a wide variety of physical and mental disorders. They have since been replaced with more current medical procedures, such as surgery or drugs, which are also more closely associated with the presumed problem and its cause. Historically, and even now, biological interventions tend to be viewed as quite drastic, to be used only with severely disturbed patients. We will begin our discussion with some of the more commonly applied current biological interventions. Then we will move to more drastic, but less common, therapies.

DRUG THERAPY

During the 1950s, a variety of new drugs transformed treatment procedures in mental hospitals. **Drug therapy** is the use of chemicals to alter, and presumably improve, emotions and behavior. It has markedly decreased the use of more drastic forms of treatment. It has also led to wards without locks and the abandonment of straightjackets, padded cells, and other forms of physical restraint. In addition, it has helped to reduce the number of mental patients confined in hospitals (Schooler, 1990). We will look briefly at several types of drugs commonly used for treatment of abnormality.

Antianxiety Drugs. In treatment of anxiety disorders, the most frequently used drugs are minor tranquilizers such as Librium and Valium. Although we have no firm statistics, estimates are that millions use these tranquilizers. Valium is thought to be one of the most widely prescribed drugs in the world (Caplan et al., 1983). **Antianxiety drugs** are medications that calm people down, and they work primarily by depressing the activity of the central nervous system. A barbiturate such as Seconal and a benzodiazepine such as Valium reduce anxiety and tension, but they also tend to be highly addicting. The benzodiazepines seem to be the drugs of choice for treating generalized anxiety, however, because they act directly on fear or anxiety, diminishing the feeling so that previously avoided behaviors can be performed. The benzodiazepines do not affect other (normal) behaviors. Similarly, beta-blockers such as propanolol reduce anxiety but leave mental and physical functioning intact, possibly explaining their preferred use for conditions such as stage fright (Wheatley, 1990).

Panic disorders have traditionally been treated successfully with benzodiazepines or tricyclic antidepressants (discussed shortly), but problems often reappear when the drug is discontinued (Otto, Pollack, Sachs, Reiter, et al., 1993). For this reason, long-term treatment with antianxiety or antidepressant medication has been advocated for panic patients, and both types of drugs seem to be effective, although benzodiazepines seem to cause less uncomfortable side effects, so patients take them more faithfully (Otto et al., 1993; Schweizer, Rickels, Weiss, & Zavodnick, 1993).

These drugs produce their antianxiety and sedative effects by forming chemical bonds with receptors at neuronal synapses and blocking neural transmission. This may implicate these receptors in the experience of anxiety. Unfortunately, effective antianxiety medication may become a crutch, with the patient depending on the medication instead of finding ways to cope with the situations causing them distress.

Antipsychotic Drugs.   The **neuroleptics,** such as chlorpromazine (e.g., Thorazine), belong to the family of antipsychotic drugs called phenothiazines. These drugs tend to stabilize agitated and overactive patients and to eliminate hallucinations and paranoid symptoms among schizophrenics. They have helped to improve the plight of the severely psychotic, allowing more and more patients to be treated in the community rather than in mental hospitals (Noll et al., 1985). These drugs seem to work by blocking receptor sites for the neurotransmitter dopamine in the brain (see Chapters 2 and 15), although neurotransmitter levels appear to be influenced much earlier than symptoms (Carson & Butcher, 1992).

Unfortunately, these medications can produce a wide variety of side effects, including drowsiness and fatigue, dry mouth and throat, muscle stiffness, difficulty initiating movement, rigidity, and tremor (Parkinson disease–like symptoms). They can also produce *tardive dyskinesia,* a particularly unpleasant syndrome that involves a disturbance of muscle control, especially the facial muscles. This side effect can occur some time after treatment begins or even after it has ended. The symptoms include twitches or involuntary movements of the tongue, lips, jaw, and limbs, resulting in chewing movements, lip smacking, and involuntary movements of the arms or legs, often causing a shuffling gait. Antipsychotic medication is normally discontinued if tardive dyskinesia appears. In an attempt to avoid the development of this disfiguring and in some cases irreversible syndrome, major tranquilizers are prescribed in lower doses and for shorter periods of time than they were previously. As with the use of any medication, the risks to pregnant women may be greater than the possible benefits and may make drug therapy too hazardous for such patients.

Antipsychotic medication is thus helpful, but not perfect. In fact, a patient successfully treated by such medication often is still not "normal" in emotional response and demeanor, although hallucinations and delusions usually abate. Mark Vonnegut, whose description of his schizophrenic hallucinations and delusions we quoted in Chapter 15, also provides a good example of the use of antipsychotic medication. His symptoms improved while he was on medication, and he was then released from hospital care. Soon he would feel "back to normal" and stop taking the medication, and his psychotic symptoms would rapidly return.

Antidepressants.   Another major category of medication consists of **antidepressants.** These drugs seem to be effective in reducing symptoms for about 50 to 70 percent of depressed patients (Noll et al., 1985) and are the yardstick against which other kinds of potential treatments for depression are measured (Elkin et al., 1989). There are three major types of antidepressant medication: the *tricyclics,* the *monoamine oxidase (MAO) inhibitors,* and the *selective serotonin (5-HT) reuptake inhibitors.* They are believed to alleviate depression by increasing the amounts of the neurotransmitters norepinephrine and serotonin available at the synapses in the brain. There are some problems with this theory, however. As with dopamine in schizophrenia, the neurotransmitters affected by antidepressant medications are influenced well before the clinical improvement of the symptoms begins (Carson & Butcher, 1992).

Tricyclic drugs and their variants are used more extensively than the MAO inhibitors, because the latter have more severe and frequent side effects and require more stringent dietary restrictions (although both have side effects and require avoidance of certain foods) (Schooler, 1990). Thus, MAO inhibitors are used more for patients who fail to respond to the tricyclics. Patients who do not respond to any type of drug may receive electroconvulsive therapy or, in extreme cases, psychosurgery (see next sections). More recently, the newer serotonin reuptake inhibitors, such as fluoxetine (commonly known as Prozac) have been prescribed with increasing frequency because they are equally effective but lack the usual side effects associated with tricyclic antidepressants (Salzman, 1992). Prozac has also been used successfully with disorders other than depression, including obsessive-compulsive disorder (Salzman, 1992), bulimia nervosa (Goldbloom & Olmsted, 1993), panic disorder, and borderline personality disorder (Salzman, 1992).

When antidepressant medications are effective, their impact is impressive. Unlike the partial effectiveness of the antipsychotic drugs, antidepressants usually produce dramatic and complete remission of depressive symptoms. A little later in this chapter, we will examine the combined use of antidepressants and psychotherapy.

Another drug used to treat bipolar (manic-depressive) disorder (see chapter 15) is Lithium. Lithium has had an estimated success rate of 70 to 80 percent (Noll et al., 1985). There are potentially harmful side effects, however, as with any powerful drug. Excessive dosages can result in coma and convulsions; less extreme effects often include diarrhea, vomiting, and tremors.

None of these medications actually cure the psychopathologies that they treat in the way that antibiotics cure bacterial infections (Schooler, 1990). Rather, they provide temporary relief from the more disturbing or debilitating symptoms, and when the patient stops taking the medication, the symptoms often return. More ominously, as the patient begins to feel less depressed on the medication, there is an increased risk of suicide; thus, antidepressant medications may actually contribute to suicide attempts (Power & Cowen, 1992; Salzman, 1992). Often, drug therapy is used in conjunction with some form of psychological or talking therapy (e.g., Otto et al., 1993) to treat the underlying psychological problem.

ELECTROCONVULSIVE THERAPY

Popularly known as "shock therapy," **electroconvulsive therapy (ECT)** involves running a convulsion-producing electric current through the patient's brain, which, repeated over time, alleviates depression and other psychological disorders. ECT has become a controversial technique. It is used primarily for treating depressives who have been unresponsive to drug treatment and psychotherapy, and it seems to work well with such patients (Fink, 1991; Valenstein, 1990). Before the therapy, the patient is anesthetized and given a muscle relaxant. Then a current of electricity is passed across the patient's temples for a fraction of a second. The shock produces a convulsion that lasts about a minute; amnesia can persist for an hour or so following treatment. Typically 5 to 12 treatments over 10 to 30 days are required for severely depressed patients.

Potential negative side effects exist, as with biological procedures of any kind. Earlier forms of ECT were more severe than today's treatment. Before muscle relaxants were available, patients suffered broken bones as a result of the severe convulsions. Today, patients still may bruise their temples and experience fear and disorientation following therapy, as well as run the risk of memory impairment lasting several months (Fink, 1991; Valenstein, 1990; Weiner, 1984). These risks, however, have to be compared with those of nontreatment—the danger of suicide and other physical, social, and psychological problems—and with the risks involved in drug therapy.

Although advances in technology have reduced the side effects of ECT and improved its effectiveness, ECT remains a controversial treatment seen by many as frightening. The National Institute of Mental Health sponsored a panel to evaluate ECT treatment (NIMH, 1985). The panel concluded that ECT was effective in treating severe depression that had not responded to drug therapy. Moreover, the panel noted that complications had become exceedingly rare, with the mortality risk no different from that associated with the use of anesthetics alone. The research on memory loss seems to indicate that memory problems usually cleared up within seven months to a year from the end of treatment (NIMH, 1985). The NIMH panel members agreed that ECT was effective with some types of depression and some types of manic disorder, particularly acute mania, but that it was not very effective for dysthymic disorder

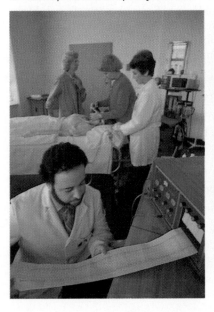

A patient undergoes electroconvulsive therapy (ECT). She is sedated first and is carefully monitored by hospital staff.

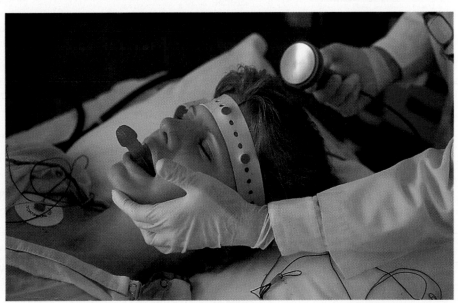

(another type of depression) or schizophrenia. In addition, they found that the therapeutic effects sometimes wore off soon after treatment ended unless the treatment was supplemented with antidepressant medication.

Despite the findings of reduced side effects and therapeutic efficacy, the panel members observed a persistent and fierce opposition to ECT among both the general public and many professionals. They cited a 1978 survey by the American Psychiatric Association, for example, finding one-third of psychiatrists "generally opposed" to ECT. In the 1970s, then-governor Ronald Reagan signed a bill drastically restricting the use of ECT in California, and in 1982, the city of Berkeley, California, took the unusual step of completely outlawing the use of ECT within its community. Upon challenges from psychiatrists, these laws were overthrown (Valenstein, 1990).

While some of the opposition to ECT is probably linked to the former severity of some of its side effects, and some simply to the idea of it, some opposition may stem from the fact that despite its effectiveness as a treatment for depression, no one really knows just how it works. Given that ECT produces massive changes in the endocrine glands, neural transmission systems, and biochemical balance of the brain, it is difficult to determine which changes have a beneficial effect. Also, while initially very effective at alleviating depression, ECT's effects seem to wear off fairly quickly, often within six months. Current research is attempting to discover the mode of action of ECT and the potential similarity of action between ECT and antidepressant drugs (Fink, 1991; Valenstein, 1990).

CASE STUDY

ECT FOR DEPRESSION

In the summer of 1977, Norman S. Endler, a well-known psychologist at York University in Toronto, suffered a profound depression that brought his normal mode of life to a halt and disrupted the lives of his family and friends. After recovering, he wrote *Holiday of Darkness* (1982), a story that told of his ordeal.

As a psychologist, Endler knew the varieties of treatment available. He went to a traditional psychiatrist who, after talking the problem over with him, suggested that he try antidepressant drugs. Although these drugs had successfully overcome depression in many other cases, they did not bring Endler out of his depression. Another psychiatrist suggested that Endler try electroconvulsive therapy (ECT). When he was a psychology graduate student, Endler had seen ECT break a patient's back (probably because muscle relaxants were not used), so this option was not especially appealing to him.

Endler mulled over his choices. He recounts:

In late 1977 when it was suggested that I consider ECT as a possible course of treatment for my depression, I was repelled. The alternatives were hospitalization or the misery of depression, both of which were highly repugnant to me.... At that time I was so desperate that if Dr. Persad had suggested that walking down Yonge Street (a main Toronto street) nude would be beneficial to me, I would probably have tried it. Therefore, I agreed, although reluctantly, to ECT as a course of treatment for my depression. (1982, p. 72)

Over a two-week period in September 1977, Endler had seven ECT sessions. Remarkably (to him), he felt much better. He resumed his duties as chairman of the psychology department and taught his classes. He writes, "A miracle had happened in two weeks. I had gone from feeling like an emotional cripple to feeling well . . . my holiday of darkness was over" (p. 83). Today, Endler has recovered from his depression and has resumed his successful research program.

EVALUATING DRUG THERAPY AND ECT

Researchers have studied the effectiveness of various biological therapies for many years. A good study must meet each of the following criteria: the use of a placebo control group, random assignment of patients to treatment groups (or matched assignment to groups), and double-blind research design.

To investigate whether ECT or a particular drug alters behavior, patients in the *placebo control group* must experience all of the aspects of the treatment except the essential one. Thus, control group patients for ECT must believe that they are undergoing ECT. They must be given the same diet, the same injections (including one to render them unconscious for a period, so that they cannot tell if they have received the ECT or not), the same waiting period, and the same posttreatment care as the actual ECT group, but without the actual treatment. This sham ECT treatment rules out the effects of suggestion. Similarly, in a drug treatment, the control group must be given pills that they believe will cause them to get better.

Random assignment is an experimental design technique in which each individual has an equal chance of being placed in any treatment condition (see Chapter 1). Unfortunately, in the real world of patients and doctors, it is not always practical or ethical to assign people randomly to a no treatment, placebo, or control group. Thus, many of the published studies of treatment effectiveness must be excluded from consideration if this criterion is to be met. It is a necessary criterion, though. Otherwise, any differences later found between the treated and nontreated groups may be due not to the treatment but to the characteristics of the people before they were treated. For example, perhaps only the best (or worst) patients were assigned to the experimental treatment. An acceptable alternative when random assignment is impossible is to match subjects in the different groups on potentially important qualities, such as sex, age, and length of illness.

Double-blind procedures require that both the person who receives the treatment and the person who assesses it do not know whether the treatment is actual therapy or a placebo (an inactive substance similar to the drug in as many respects as possible, but lacking the key therapeutic ingredient). This is necessary to avoid the effects of subtle suggestions between patients and doctors and bias in assessing the outcome.

Imagine that you have a problem such as depression and have to be given medication. Some new drugs are available, and your psychiatrist is trying to evaluate which ones work and which do not. You agree to participate in a study where you will receive either a drug or a placebo. Neither you nor the doctor will know which pill you are taking. After a few days on the medicine, you start to notice that your mouth is dry and that you feel a bit lightheaded when you stand up quickly. These are common side effects of antidepressant drugs, so you look for evidence that your depression is lifting. The next time you are interviewed, you report that you are feeling somewhat less depressed. Did you actually get the new antidepressant drug?

If the study was done properly, you still cannot tell if you have the drug or a similar-seeming placebo. The side effects are important to convince you that you might well be in the drug group; a good study would employ an "active" placebo, one that produces some effects, preferably ones that might be expected from the real drug. This way, when you experience these side effects, you will feel as if you are in the drug group. If expecting to feel better is enough to make you report that you have improved, the active placebo will fuel your expectation. The drug, to be truly effective, must make those who take it feel *better* than those who take a placebo and simply expect to feel better. In such a study, you and your doctor find out whether you had the drug or a placebo only after the study has ended. A knowledge of appropriate control procedures helps us understand why most studies fall short on one or another criterion. Nonetheless, enough studies have met all the requirements so that some conclusions can be drawn about both ECT and drug therapy.

We have already discussed some of the literature on ECT (NIMH, 1985; Weiner, 1984). Many studies have compared ECT with a variety of "placebos" and alternatives, including psychotherapy, drug therapy, and simulated ECT. These studies indicate that the benefits of ECT are directly related to clinical diagnosis (Abrams, 1988; Fink, 1991). For psychotic-depressive syndromes and mania, success rates of 60 to 90 percent are reported, with suicide less frequent in ECT-treated patients than among those treated by psychotherapy alone. Patients other than depressives, however, appear to do less well with ECT (Scovern & Kilmann, 1980).

Morris and Beck (1974) reviewed the efficacy of antidepressant drugs. They examined 146 well-controlled double-blind studies carried out between 1958 and 1972 and found the drugs tested to be significantly more effective than placebos in 60 percent of the studies. Not one study reported a placebo to be more effective than the antidepressant. More recent studies, including those on the new generation of antidepressants, confirm these conclusions (Carson & Butcher, 1992; Salzman, 1992).

Overall, it appears that well-controlled outcome studies are confirming the effectiveness of these biological therapies. It should be noted, however, that most biological procedures are often more useful when supplemented by some form of psychological therapy (Otto et al., 1993), as we will discuss later in this chapter.

PSYCHOSURGERY

The most drastic form of biological intervention to change emotions or behavior involves surgery to destroy or remove brain tissue, a procedure known as **psychosurgery.** This approach is the most controversial of the medical approaches, in part because it is irreversible. Once nerve fibers or brain tissues have been cut, they cannot be repaired. For this reason, psychosurgery is currently used infrequently, and only as a last resort.

During the 1940s and 1950s, the most frequent psychosurgical treatment was the **prefrontal lobotomy,** an operation that severed the fibers connecting the brain's frontal lobes with the emotional control centers in the thalamus. The operation was carried out primarily on severely disturbed psychotics who tended to be extremely emotional or violent or who had hallucinations. Its purpose was to reduce the turbulent emotions raging within these patients. Early reports appeared to demonstrate that the operation was an amazing success, and the physician who originated the procedure in 1937, Egas Moniz, of Portugal, was awarded the 1949 Nobel Prize in medicine. In the United States, it is estimated that some 50,000 patients underwent prefrontal lobotomies. Later studies found that a high proportion of lobotomized patients had been permanently disabled. Many of these patients showed little or no intellectual function. Worse still, some of them died from complications. Fortunately, the development of a variety of drugs is helping to make this surgery obsolete. Today, the procedure is used only after every other possible alternative has been tried.

Psychosurgery today involves much more constrained destruction of extremely small areas of the brain. Even the use of such limited surgical procedures to accomplish specific goals is considered questionable by most of the psychiatric and psychological establishment today, despite findings that some conditions unresponsive to other treatments (e.g., chronic, unremitting depression) can be greatly helped by such techniques. Ethical questions also surround these procedures. These include concern about the ability of some seriously disturbed patients to give true informed consent, and about the justification for permanent alterations to personality and brain functioning (Valenstein, 1986).

BIOLOGICAL TREATMENTS FOR ABNORMALITY

TREATMENT	ABNORMALITY	PROBLEMS
Minor tranquilizers (e.g., Librium, Valium)	Anxiety disorders	Addiction
Neuroleptics (e.g., chlorpromazine)	Schizophrenia	Side effects; don't always work
Antidepressants:		
Tricyclics	Depression, etc.	Side effects
MAO inhibitors	Depression	Side effects
5-HT reuptake inhibitors (e.g., Prozac)	Depression, etc.	Few so far
Lithium	Bipolar disorder	Side effects
ECT	Depression	Side effects
Psychosurgery	Psychosis, depression	Permanent changes

Introduction to the Psychological Approaches to Therapy

You have probably noticed that people react differently to events depending on the circumstances. A child who falls down may get up and continue playing if no one seems to regard the fall as a problem. The same child may cry and fuss about the "injury" if someone runs over looking concerned. Our reactions to psychological problems are similar. Even when physical pathology is causing the abnormality, many psychologists believe that the way the individual perceives, evaluates, develops expectations about, and copes with the pathology will influence his or her responses and behavior and the ultimate outcome. Recognizing and, if necessary, changing these psychological responses may be necessary for optimal improvement, even when biological interventions are used (Carson & Butcher, 1992). Thus, as already mentioned, many biological interventions are utilized in conjunction with psychotherapy.

Psychotherapists attempt to help people with psychological problems (which may or may not have some physical cause or contributor) to change, often through learning or discovering more adaptive perceptions, evaluations, expectations, and behaviors. This may be accomplished through direct teaching, as in many behavioral therapies, or through guided talking and listening and the development of insight, or through a relationship between client and therapist that allows these changes to be experienced by the client in the new therapeutic environment. Whatever the particular goal, most psychological therapies share certain characteristics: Two (or more) people work together as caregiver and care seeker to identify what needs to be changed in the care seeker and to devise a means of achieving this change (but see "Controversy: Is Psychotherapy Exploitation?").

The usual assumption is that psychotherapy, like any therapy, is helpful to the person who undergoes it. It is, in effect, a service. Therapists are caring, empathic people whose motivation is to help others to feel better, happier, and more normal. Granted, any therapy may fail to achieve its goal in some instances. Some cases may simply be beyond help. But might therapy actually be harmful? Are therapists really "tormentors, oppressors, and exploiters (whose) aim is to control the behavior of others" (Strupp, 1990, p. 250) and whose professional existence depends on other people's misery? Consider the view proposed by Masson:

"Psychotherapy of any kind is wrong. [Its] structure is such that no matter how kindly a person is, when that person becomes a therapist, he or she is engaged in acts that are bound to diminish the dignity, autonomy, and freedom of the person who comes for help (Masson, 1988, p. ix)

Masson argues that therapists victimize their patients, particularly women. He asks for example, "Why do psychiatrists torture people and call it electroshock therapy?" (p. xv). His analysis of the personal lives of such well-known therapists as Freud, Jung, and Perls (see Gestalt therapy, page 000) demonstrates their antifeminism, personal failings, and failure to acknowledge the reality of their patients' claims of physical and sexual abuse. Finally, he accuses therapists of imposing their own values and beliefs on vulnerable patients.

While Masson's view is "so strident and outlandish as to defy rational analysis" (Strupp, 1990, p. 250), or at least "dramatic and sensationalistic" (Kazdin, 1990), he is not the only critic of the psychotherapeutic enterprise.

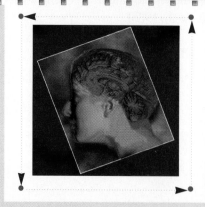

Haley's (1986) satiric essays point out that therapy can sometimes be an arena for a sort of one-upmanship on the part of the therapist, who is in an emotionally superior position compared to the client. To some extent, this inequality is inescapable in an enterprise in which one person pays another for emotional help. However, Haley's recipe for "being a failure as a therapist" includes focusing on issues that the therapist considers interesting or important instead of on the problems that the patient identifies as the reasons for therapy. This is a criticism of therapies that follow the agenda of the therapist's orientation or school rather than treating patients individually according to their unique situations.

Williams (1985) has compared this adherence to a particular therapeutic perspective to a salesperson's "bait-and-switch" tactic, bringing in the patient with a promise of symptomatic relief and then switching the focus of therapy to some other issue altogether (such as transference or "change and growth"). As Williams indicates, "Relief from the presenting problem as a criterion of successful outcome is notably absent from (theoretical statements) concerning therapeutic success" (p. 111).

Should we conclude, then, that therapists are power-hungry manipulators who do not care about their patients' distress? Strupp (1990) asks, "Should we abolish child rearing because parents exercise power and at times abuse it? Should we abolish medicine because physicians 'profit' from their patients' suffering?" (p. 250). Strupp argues that Masson (1988), the most vitriolic of the critics of therapy, ignores the attempt of most therapists to heal, not harm. But even Masson, for all his complaints, "grudgingly concedes that the majority of therapists are responsible practitioners who are dedicated to the mitigation of human suffering" (Strupp, 1990, p. 250). As we will see later in this chapter, there is abundant evidence that therapy does improve the lives of many who utilize it.

Criticisms of the therapeutic enterprise can provide a challenge that will lead to improvement (Kazdin, 1990). The question of when and for whom therapy is most beneficial has been addressed in a decades-long program of research (Luborsky et al., 1988). The quality of the relationship between therapist and patient has been found to be a significant predictor of outcome of therapy. Moreover, even therapeutic failure can be useful if the therapist utilizes it properly. Kottler and Blau (1989) used their therapeutic failures (and those of their colleagues) to explore the benefits of confronting imperfection and learning from mistakes.

Psychotherapists are not infallible. Some are incompetent, and others are even corrupt or destructive. On the whole, however, it seems that most are trying to help their patients as well as they can, and this does seem to alleviate the distress of the majority of patients (see "Does Psychotherapy Work?" on page 698).

Psychoanalytic Therapies

Freudian therapy, or **psychoanalysis,** developed alongside Freud's theory of personality and its dynamics. In this therapy, the patient talks to the therapist about his or her life, revealing in the process any unconscious conflicts which are then interpreted by the therapist to help the patient to release the emotion and energy tied up in the

Although some modern psychoanalysts have dispensed with the couch and become more interactive and supportive, some still use Freud's traditional method.

conflict. As we saw in Chapter 14, Freud attempted to explain the development of personality in terms of the way an individual resolves conflicts among the unconscious biological instincts of the id, the constraints of reality interpreted by the ego, and the moral structures of the conscience imposed by the superego. According to Freudian theory, abnormal behavior is largely the result of unresolved conflicts occurring in the unconscious. The cause of conflict is therefore far below a patient's level of awareness. Indeed, the person may be using a great deal of psychic energy to keep the conflict repressed. The goal of psychoanalysis is to uncover and bring to the surface the unconscious conflict, thereby freeing the repressed energies of the psyche so that it can deal more effectively with the environment.

In Freud's method, the client would lie on a couch, relaxed, and talk about dreams, early relationships with parents, and other topics that came to consciousness. Typically, the therapist, to minimize distraction, would sit out of sight, behind the person, listening. Although contemporary procedures vary, the emphasis on the client talking to the therapist about early relationships with parents and current relationships with loved ones remains the same.

There are a variety of techniques and processes in psychoanalysis, all intended to bring unconscious material to consciousness. Almost everything a client says or does may tell the therapist something about the unconscious conflicts underlying the client's problems.

Free Association. In **free association,** a technique described in Chapter 14, the client reports whatever comes to mind, without any conscious censoring of the material. With the help of the therapist, the client allows thoughts to move freely from one topic to another, even if the associations make little sense or are painful or embarrassing. For example, a client may think of the word *landlord* and then the word *ambulance*. The connection between these seemingly unrelated words might be that the client's sister got extremely ill one night and the landlord had to call an ambulance. (Also, perhaps the client had been partly responsible for the sister's illness or simply wished to be rid of her.) The goal of free association is to bypass a client's defense mechanisms by a thorough exploration of the preconscious, so that fragments of unconscious material may be made available for interpretation.

Dream Analysis. Freud believed that dreams are an especially good way to tap the unconscious, because our defenses are lowered when we are asleep. He referred to dreams as "the royal road to the unconscious." Freud distinguished between the *manifest* (obvious, visible) *content* and the *latent* (hidden, underlying) *content* of dreams, the latter being those motives and desires too unacceptable to be revealed without concealment even in dreams. Freud interpreted the symbolic meaning of dream objects, persons, or events. For example, elongated objects such as snakes, sticks, guns, tree trunks, and pencils are supposedly symbolic of the penis, whereas balloons and airplanes are symbols of erections, and doughnuts and tunnels represent the female genitals (see Chapters 5 and 14 for more discussion of dream analysis).

Suppose a student reports a dream in which he is busy writing with a fountain pen when it suddenly breaks, sending ink all over the page. In the background, his friend starts to laugh at him. Freud might see this as an indication of repressed feelings of sexual impotence or fear of premature ejaculation. Note that the validity of such psychoanalytic interpretation remains questionable to many non-Freudian psychologists. Later in this chapter, we will discuss a completely different kind of dream analysis performed by Gestalt therapists.

Resistance.   Think back to the last time you felt obliged to attend an event, but really didn't want to. Did you leave in plenty of time, or did you wind up rushing to get there? Were you even a little bit late? Did you forget to bring something you needed? Freud said that none of our actions are accidental. If we forget something or are late to an appointment, it indicates that we are experiencing some conflict about the situation. We may not be aware of our ambivalent feelings, but Freud suggested that analyzing these sorts of slips or accidents can reveal the underlying conflicting feelings.

As defenses weaken in therapy, anxiety emerges. To avoid this anxiety, clients often attempt, unconsciously, to block treatment by **resistance.** They may miss therapy appointments or come late, report that they have no dreams to relate, or lapse into monologues of little relevance to the therapy. According to psychoanalytic theory, this resistance protects the client's neurosis. Unconsciously, clients want to avoid the anxiety evoked by facing their repressed impulses.

To overcome this resistance, analysts offer interpretations of their clients' behavior, attempting to make them aware of what is being avoided. Analysts can interpret behavior only when they have developed a reasonably clear picture of the dynamics of the client's personality. Analysts believe that when timed correctly, their interpretations can lead to emotional insights on the client's part. Then client and analyst can begin working through the problems, uncovering the repressed thoughts and desires. Of course, a single interpretation may not result in insight, and the same interpretation may have to be repeated to overcome defenses. Next time you are late or forget something, stop and examine how you really feel about it. Did you perhaps want to avoid the situation? Do you have mixed feelings about it? You can provide your own interpretation.

Transference.   **Transference** refers to a way of responding to others that is not based on the present relationship, but instead represents carryovers from the past. It is a form of resistance and can be used by patients to try to block treatment. As analysis progresses, clients may transfer to their therapists the unconscious feelings of love or hatred that they have toward their parents, lovers, or other people who have been at the center of past emotional conflicts. The transference is called positive transference when the feelings attached to therapist are those of love or admiration; it is called negative transference when the feelings consist of hostility or envy. Often the client's attitude is ambivalent, including a mixture of positive and negative feelings.

Freud first noticed the transference phenomenon when he realized that some patients ascribed to him the characteristics of God (or the devil), while others professed love for him. Freud noted that transference occurs throughout life and is not simply a product of therapy. Interpretation of the transference, however, is a key to successful psychoanalysis, enabling the client to raise the most repressed emotions to consciousness and to begin to deal realistically with them.

Therapists do not allow their clients to continue their transferential feelings for too long. They remain impersonal and professional and attempt to direct their patients back to themselves. For instance, a therapist may ask a client, "What do you see when you imagine my face?" The client may reply that he sees the therapist's face as angry, frowning, and unpleasant. The therapist, instead of taking the response personally, may calmly ask, "What does this make you think of?" Gradually, it becomes clear to the client that he is reacting to the neutral figure of his therapist as though the therapist were a threatening father or some other childhood figure of authority.

"Why do you think you cross the road?"

Drawing by Levin; © The New Yorker, Inc.

Just as clients may have feelings that they project onto a therapist in a transference, the therapist may have feelings about a client. The therapist is always supposed to remain a neutral observer, offering interpretations when appropriate, but responding only intellectually and not personally to the client. Thus, the therapist's feelings about the client are taken as evidence of an unconscious response by the therapist to some aspect of the client. These feelings represent a *countertransference*, in which the therapist's own unresolved, unconscious conflicts are triggered by something about the client. If a therapist finds herself always feeling tired or bored when a particular patient is talking, this may be a sign that the therapist is reacting unconsciously to the client. For instance, the fatigue and boredom may be similar to the way the therapist used to feel when her mother started complaining about her various ailments or troubles. The therapist is thus responding to the patient the way she did to her own mother, but the response indicates that the patient's behavior is somehow reminiscent of the mother's, telling the therapist something about the patient as well as something about her own tolerance for listening to the complaints of others. While some analysts believe that a client should be referred to a different therapist in the event of strong countertransference, others believe that the interpretation of the countertransference can be of great benefit to both therapist and client. The therapist's feelings are presumed to represent a response to some previously unacknowledged aspect of the client (as well as an unrecognized aspect of the therapist). Interpretation can thus reveal something about the client and contribute to treatment success (Tansey & Burke, 1989). It can also illuminate an aspect of the therapist's unconscious. However, countertransference can interfere with therapy if it is not recognized and successfully interpreted. To ensure that therapists have very little unresolved conflict, psychoanalysts are required to undergo intensive psychoanalysis themselves before being allowed to treat others.

Catharsis. Resolving transference may trigger **catharsis,** a major emotional release in which clients gain sudden insight about their relationship with their therapist and, more importantly, about their previous relationships with their parents. This "unlocking" of repressed memories (known as *abreaction*, a fancy name for "getting it out of your system") represents an important milestone in therapy, often leading to further explorations of repressed memories and desires. The basic assumption of psychoanalysis is that everybody suffers from frustrations and unhappiness, some of which result from childhood experiences and others from everyday pressures. These frustrations are assumed to accumulate deep in the unconscious from childhood on. After festering there, they rise to the surface (consciousness and behavior) in a variety of maladaptive ways. The cure is to remove this psychic tension through abreaction and gain insight into the patient's problems. In cases where there may be more than one or two repressed conflicts, the same procedure continues until all the unconscious conflicts are resolved.

Psychoanalysis can be an involved, time-consuming, and expensive undertaking. It may require therapy sessions several times a week, and it can go on for years. As Woody Allen observed in the movie *Sleeper* (only half in jest, one suspects), if only he hadn't been asleep the whole time, he might finally have been finished with his psychoanalysis when he awoke 200 years in the future! Psychoanalysis is unlikely to be effective for those who are unable to articulate their feelings and thoughts well (such as those suffering from psychotic disorders). The effectiveness of such therapy is difficult to gauge and has been hotly debated between supporters and critics.

PSYCHOANALYSIS SINCE FREUD

As Freud was working on his theories of personality and psychotherapy, some of his followers and former colleagues were carving out theories of their own and developing variations on classical psychoanalysis. (For a discussion of the neo-Freudian theories, see Chapter 14, pages 578–581.) Jung's therapy aimed at uncovering the patient's unconscious desires for artistic expression and religious experience, as well as identifying "complexes" where emotional energy is tied up. Adler emphasized gaining insight into feelings of inferiority and exploring the various stratagems that people use to achieve power and dominance and to hide unconscious feelings of weakness. The ego theorists, such as Karen Horney and Erik Erikson, deemphasized the unconscious and stressed the relative importance of ego functioning and, in particular, a patient's self-concept, current anxieties, and interpersonal relationships. Like Freud, however, these therapists all agreed that the key to mental distress is unconscious conflict and that successful therapy requires insight into unconscious processes. Recent psychoanalytic theorizing has focused more on the ego and its power in personal dynamics (e.g., Gay, 1989).

Therapeutic techniques have also undergone various changes, although some Freudian therapists maintain the traditional manner and techniques. One change has been to reduce the number of therapy sessions per week and generally attempt to condense the whole process into a few months or a year (Strupp, 1983). Another has been the disappearance of the psychoanalytic couch. Still another has been the alteration of the role of the therapist from a noninvolved figure sitting behind the patient to a more human, interacting, and supportive figure. Finally, modern versions of psychoanalysis play down the need to recall repressed childhood memories in favor of highlighting current conflicts and defenses in a patient's life (Strupp, 1983). Moreover, the focus of the newer psychoanalytic therapies is on the ego, particularly the self and its development (e.g., Kohut, 1984). Kohut's self psychology has changed the focus of analysis from transference as a repetition of primary relationships to an attempt at building new, more adaptive relationships (Wolfe, 1989). This has made insight less important than strengthening the "self." This newer focus of psychoanalysis has been seen by some (Kahn, 1989) as a bridge to more current theoretical orientations, such as humanistic therapy (see pages 688–691).

Behavioral Therapies

Whereas psychoanalytic therapy tries to change problem behavior indirectly by releasing unconscious energies, **behavioral therapy,** a term coined by Hans Eysenck in 1952 and used by B. F. Skinner in 1953, tries to change the behavior directly by applying the laws and principles of learning theory (see Chapter 14). Behavior therapy has also been known as *behavior modification*, and the two terms can be used interchangeably (Eysenck & Skinner, 1980). Behavioral therapy is a therapeutic system in which therapist and client identify the client's problematic behaviors and then work together to change those behaviors by using the therapist's knowledge of learning theory. We will discuss a variety of behavior modification or related techniques based on classical conditioning, instrumental (operant) conditioning, biofeedback, and observational learning.

CLASSICAL CONDITIONING TECHNIQUES

In psychotherapy, classical conditioning or *counter conditioning*, as it is referred to in psychotherapy, presents essentially two possibilities: (1) to alter an emotional response from an inappropriately negative one (e.g., anxiety about going out of one's home or flying) to a neutral or even positive one, or (2) to alter an inappropriately positive emotional response (e.g., sexual arousal in response to young children). The first process generally occurs either through systematic desensitization therapy or implosion therapy. The second occurs through aversion therapy.

Systematic Desensitization Therapy.   **Systematic desensitization therapy** is a treatment used primarily to treat anxiety disorders such as phobias and others described in Chapter 15. In this treatment, an individual learns to make a positive response, such as relaxing, to a stimulus that normally elicits anxiety. Systematic desensitization therapy was first performed by Mary Cover Jones in 1924. She presented a young child with a delicious food (unconditioned stimulus) that the child enjoyed eating (unconditioned response), while a rabbit (conditioned stimulus) that the child feared (conditioned response) was kept in a cage in the far corner of the room. Over a number of days, while the child ate the food, the rabbit was brought closer and closer until it no longer elicited a fear response, even when sitting on the child's chest. The unconditioned response of enjoying the food was incompatible with being fearful.

Jones's pioneering efforts had relatively little impact on psychotherapeutic practice at the time. Although she anticipated and developed many contemporary methods, her work remained unrecognized for several decades. The popularization of counterconditioning techniques must be credited instead to Joseph Wolpe, who published a landmark book, *Psychotherapy by Reciprocal Inhibition*, in 1958. Since then, the therapy has been developed extensively (Wolpe, 1982).

In systematic desensitization, the conditioned fear response must be kept at a weaker level than the unconditioned incompatible (pleasant) response. Consider a young woman who is afraid of flying. A therapist might first ask her to construct a stimulus *anxiety hierarchy*, a list of activities ranging from the least threatening to the most threatening (see Table 16.1). The next step is to teach the client how to relax, since relaxation is incompatible with anxiety.

TABLE 16.1
Sample Anxiety Hierarchy for Fear of Flying

LEAST THREATENING
Planning a vacation where one will have to fly to get there
Calling to make airplane reservations
Packing for the vacation
Driving to the airport
Checking in at the airport
Getting seats for the flight
Going through security and into the departure lounge
Walking aboard the plane
Listening to the description of seat-belt fastening and emergency procedures
Taking off and feeling the plane going faster and faster and leaving the ground
Hearing the wheels come down for landing and feeling the plane descending until it touches the ground

MOST THREATENING
Experiencing turbulence in the air
Seeing another plane nearby in the air and thinking a crash is inevitable

Wolpe advocates muscle relaxation techniques, teaching his clients to become aware of and control specific muscle groups throughout the body by successively tensing and then relaxing each of them. Deep and slow breathing coupled with muscle relaxation can lead to deep relaxation, making it difficult to feel anxious.

You can learn the relaxation techniques yourself and thus reduce your anxiety at, for example, psychology exams. Try it. Sit back in a comfortable chair, or lie down on a bed. Tense the muscles of your hands by squeezing them as hard as you can, until they are shaking, for 10 seconds. Focus on how your hands feel—this is tension. Now let them go loose, relax them, and focus on this feeling. The contrast between squeezing and relaxing should enable you to feel the relaxation more clearly. Now do this squeezing and relaxing sequence with your forearms, upper arms, neck, jaw/teeth, nose (wrinkle it), and forehead, and then work down your shoulders, back, stomach, buttocks, thighs, calfs, and feet. If you are still awake, take three deep breaths, breathing in slowly to a count of four, holding your breath for a count of four, and then slowly letting it out for a count of four. You should now feel completely relaxed. The more you practice this, the better you will get at it. Soon you will be able to relax your muscles on command without tensing them first. When you sit down in a classroom to take an exam, relax your muscles (especially your neck and shoulders) and take three deep breaths before you begin the exam. You should feel less nervous and shaky, more calm, and better able to think about the questions on your exam!

Once the systematic desensitization stimulus hierarchy is constructed and relaxation has been well learned, the client imagines the first item in the hierarchy—in our example, planning a vacation (where she will have to fly to get there). The therapist may vividly describe the scene for the client. While relaxing, the client concentrates until she is certain that her imagined vacation planning no longer elicits fear. Then she and the therapist move on to the next scene, and so on. This effectively extinguishes the conditioned fear, since no unconditioned (negative) stimulus occurs during the imagined scenes. After the client can envision all the various situations while she is deliberately relaxed, she repeats the hierarchy in reality, placing herself physically in each successive situation. This general procedure can be applied to a variety of phobias and anxiety-producing situations, including fear of public speaking, fear of snakes, and fear of dentists. We will return to these examples later in this chapter.

Is it really important to treat a phobia such as fear of flying? Does this really interfere with people's lives? One patient we treated was so afraid of flying that she refused to accept a promotion and raise because the new job would mean flying to other cities for meetings. Another patient gave up chances to go on free luxury vacations because she would have to fly there. Here is how this patient described the effect her fear had on her life:

> I'd have to clean my whole house before I went on a trip, because I was sure I would be killed in a plane crash and I didn't want my mother-in-law to think I was a slob when she came to clear out the house after the funeral. I also stopped dieting before I flew anywhere. A corpse doesn't have to be thin. And I never enjoyed any vacation where I had to fly, because although I felt great when I first got there (because she survived the flight), I soon started thinking about having to fly home again, and the rest of the trip was ruined by anxiety attacks.

These people were treated with systematic desensitization to overcome their fear of flying, and their lives were significantly improved. As the second patient wrote in a postcard from Las Vegas,

> My husband is so happy. Not only are we here, but I didn't tear chunks out of his arm digging my nails into him on takeoff like I used to. I'm enjoying it here, and I'm not at all worried about flying home. I never knew a vacation could be so wonderful.

FEAR OF DENTISTS

In chapter 15, you read about a patient who was so afraid of dentists that she had seven teeth pulled rather than have them filled by a dentist. Before she resorted to having all the rest of her teeth extracted, this patient consulted a behavior therapist and entered systematic desensitization therapy. She and her therapist made up a list of the steps involved in going to the dentist and placed them in order from least to most anxiety provoking, based on the patient's rating of each item. They also constructed a scene that the patient found pleasant and relaxing—one she could visualize easily. This was a scene of lying on a warm beach near the ocean, with waves lapping on the shore and a gentle breeze rustling the leaves of the tree shading her. The therapist then taught her to do deep-muscle relaxation, as previously described, and the patient went home to practice. On subsequent weeks, she came to the office, relaxed herself, and then the therapist described the beach scene until the patient signaled (by raising her index finger) that she was completely relaxed. The therapist then described the least anxiety-provoking scene on the hierarchy of going to the dentist. As soon as the patient felt any anxiety, she signaled with her finger, and the therapist instructed her to return to the relaxing scene until all tension had dissipated. The patient's anxiety grew less and less to the first "dentist" scene, until it was completely gone. They then moved on to the second scene and repeated the exercise. When all the scenes had been mastered and the patient reported feeling no more anxiety at thinking about dentists, the therapist tested her by bringing in dental implements and approaching her with them. The patient reported no fear of them! She then made an appointment with a dentist (calling from the therapist's office) and was able to go without anxiety.

Implosion Therapy. Instead of beginning with the scene that arouses the least anxiety in an anxiety hierarchy, **implosion therapy** begins with the most fear-arousing, hair-raising stimulus imaginable in an effort to provide intensive and dramatic extinction. Implosion therapists believe that patients will never overcome anxiety or their maladaptive behavior as long as they are allowed to avoid the anxiety-arousing situations. Implosion therapy forces clients to experience full-blown anxiety reactions without suffering any harm. Therapists may describe to clients extremely frightening situations and ask the clients to try to experience the fear as fully as possible. In a variant of this procedure, known as *flooding,* individuals are exposed to real or realistically depicted situations rather than unrealistic imaginary ones (i.e., less extreme scenarios but more likely to occur). In either case, the inner explosion (implosion) of anxiety is extinguished when nothing bad or scary actually happens, and the stimulus loses its power to elicit anxiety.

To ensure that clients truly visualize anxiety-provoking situations, implosion therapists often use vivid descriptions of feared scenarios. For example, suppose that you are afraid of falling off a high building. You would be instructed to imagine, as vividly as possible, including all physical sensations, that you are falling, are hitting the ground, are feeling bones break and skin tear, are being lifted onto a stretcher, are being rushed to the hospital, and have broken bones all over your body. Repeatedly imagining these intense scenes, even without any negative consequences, results initially in anxiety;

but (in theory, at least) when there are no actual negative consequences, the therapy results in a rapid diminution or extinction of the anxiety until the patient no longer feels any anxiety about the previously feared stimulus (Stampfl & Levis, 1967). The patient has thus learned not to be afraid by extinguishing fear through classical conditioning (or deconditioning, in this case). While theoretically interesting, implosive therapy does not seem to be widely used, possibly because of ethical concerns or the existence of gentler techniques, such as desensitization. Flooding, on the other hand, is used more frequently, especially for such disorders as obsessive-compulsive disorder (see Chapter 15).

Aversion Therapy.   **Aversion therapy** involves exposing a client to a stimulus that is perceived as attractive when it should not be attractive and pairing the stimulus with unpleasant stimuli, such as shock, drug-induced nausea, or disgusting images that the client is taught to picture. Thus, the initially attractive stimulus is rendered unattractive by being paired with unpleasant, or aversive, events. The undesirable positive stimulus eventually comes to elicit negative emotional responses through its association with these aversive stimuli. This therapy has been used to treat sexual aberrations such as exhibitionism, voyeurism, and child molestation as well as substance use disorders such as smoking.

OPERANT CONDITIONING TECHNIQUES

Operant, or instrumental, conditioning, discussed in Chapters 6 and 14, can be described fairly simply here. The central principle is the **law of effect,** which states that positive consequences following a behavior increase the future probability of that behavior, whereas negative consequences, such as punishment, decrease its future probability. This theory has been applied with great ingenuity to an understanding of "irrational" abnormal behavior and to its modification. There are essentially two possible treatments: (1) the provision of positive reinforcement to increase desired behaviors and (2) the use of punishment and nonreward to decrease undesired behaviors.

Positive Reinforcement.   Positive reinforcement often manifests itself inadvertently during therapy in the form of a therapist's nods of agreement, smiles, verbal encouragement, and simple attention to the client. Thus, it is probably operating in

The man reclining in the chair is an admitted child molester, has volunteered for aversion therapy. The therapist presents slides of young girls. A phallic plethymograph, attached to the man's penis, measures any sexual arousal. An electric shock is administered to the man's hand whenever arousal is present in an attempt to reverse his tendency to associate children with sexual pleasure.

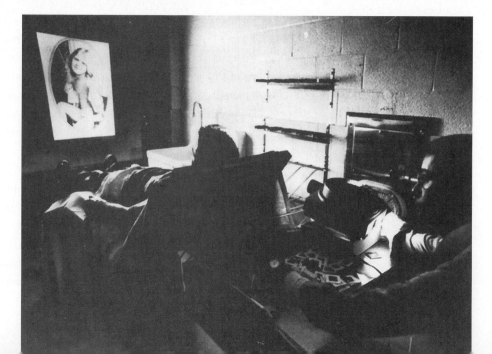

all therapies in which a client interacts with a therapist. It is also used intentionally to increase desired behaviors. Nonresponsive autistic children, for example, can be induced to make eye contact, speak, and respond to others by reinforcing these behaviors with candy, cuddles, or other reinforcers (Lovaas, 1973, 1977). **Token economies** are systems in which inmates of an institution or students in a classroom earn tokens or points for doing desired behaviors. These tokens can then be saved and exchanged for privileges or goods. Unfortunately, the behavioral changes do not seem to last if the reinforcements are removed, since it is the contingencies, or outcomes, that control the behaviors. Figure 16.1 illustrates the effects of experimentally altering the contingencies for psychotic and normal behavior in a hospital ward.

Finally, in **contingency contracting,** or **self-management,** a client learns to control his or her own behavior through selective reinforcement. For instance, suppose you find it difficult to devote the number of hours to study that you feel you should. In contingency contracting, you draw up a contract with yourself, witnessed by others, in which you specify the hours you will study and the reinforcements you will receive each time you meet your study quota (e.g., a date with a steady girlfriend or boyfriend, attending a sports event with friends, a new article of clothing). To work best, such programs require the active participation of friends and family.

Punishment.   Just as positive reinforcement can be used to increase desirable behaviors, *punishment,* or the application of aversive contingencies (not simply paired stimuli as in aversion therapy, but aversive consequences of an actual response) can be applied to reduce the frequency of undesirable behavior (remember Chapter 6). Courts sentence criminals to prison, parents yell at their children, and teachers impose penalties for classroom misbehavior. Although punishment is similar to the conditioning in aversion therapy, in which a noxious stimulus or outcome is paired with a stimulus for an undesirable behavior, punishment involves applying a negative stimulus contingently after an undesirable behavior occurs. This should decrease the likelihood of that behavior recurring and may provide the opportunity to reward and increase the probability of an alternative response. For example, if a patient is punished with a mild electric shock for urinating on the floor, the patient may, next time, ask to go to the

FIGURE 16.1
The Influence of Reinforcement on Psychotic and Neutral Verbal Behavior

The baseline (left) represents the rate of neutral and psychotic talking in the institution before the experiment began. Over the next several days, psychotic behavior was reinforced by social attention while neutral talk was ignored. As the graph illustrates, the rate of psychotic talk increased and that of neutral talk decreased. Then the experimenters reversed the procedure. Neutral talk was reinforced by attention and psychotic talk was ignored. As a result, neutral talk increased while psychotic talk dropped. The experiment demonstrates that psychotic "symptoms" can, to some extent, be brought under environmental control.

SOURCE: Ayllon & Haughton, 1964.

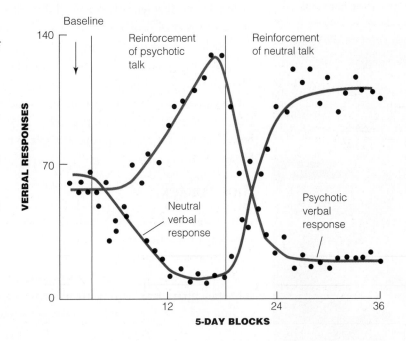

Autistic children are often socially withdrawn and engage in self-stimulatory behavior such as rocking back and forth for hours. Sometimes they harm themselves by biting or scratching themselves or by banging their heads against a wall. Punishing such self-destructive behavior with electric shock seems to reduce its occurrence (Lovaas, 1977).

Through the use of monitoring instruments, patients can receive continuous information about their own biological states and experiment with various ways of altering their physiological functioning. This client is receiving feedback about blood flow to help him control his vascular headaches.

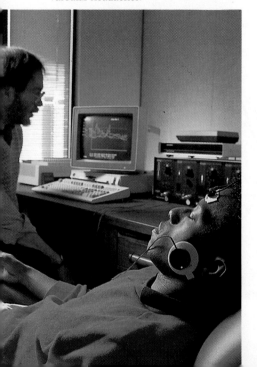

bathroom, a response that can be lavishly rewarded. The rewarding of an alternative response is important, because punishment is not the same as extinction (as in implosive therapy). The response often disappears only for as long as the punishment is applied, because punishment must be immediate, intense, and consistent to be effective. Punishment is most effective when used in conjunction with positive reinforcement of an alternative behavior.

Although punishment is generally used only for extremely self-destructive or dangerous behaviors, its use in therapy has been open to controversy. Some psychologists wonder whether the behaviors being so controlled are really for the good of the patients or for the convenience of the staff. More importantly, it is not clear that punishment is as effective as positive reinforcement, and the effects tend to disappear rapidly if the punishment is not administered continually. This is a thorny ethical issue, even in cases where punishment seems the most effective therapy, such as with self-destructive autistic children, whose head banging and arm biting is reduced by brief electric shocks (Lovaas, 1977). Most behavioral therapists agree that such procedures should be used only when other procedures are unavailable, inappropriate, or have failed—and even then, only as a small part of a larger treatment program.

"*Time out*" from positive reinforcement is a more acceptable punishment used in many classrooms and homes. Whenever a child behaves inappropriately (e.g., hits another child), he or she is isolated for a few minutes in a "time-out" place. Then the child is returned to the original environment and asked to correct the misbehavior. This can be a very helpful procedure for correcting problem behaviors in children, eliminating the necessity of yelling at them.

Punishment can also be applied to self-management. If you are having difficulty changing a behavior, you might give a friend (or a therapist) a series of postdated checks to an organization you dislike intensely and ask them to mail a check at intervals whenever you do not successfully change your behavior. For instance, if you wanted to quit smoking, you could have your roommate mail your check to an anti-smoker's group every day that you continue to smoke.

MODELING THERAPY

In previous chapters, we examined the role of observational learning in the development of normal personality. Because observing others is a principal way in which humans learn, **modeling therapy** highlights learning by having the client watch people, either live or on videotape, who are displaying appropriate and adaptive behavior. This method teaches people with maladaptive responses better coping strategies (see the discussion of observational learning in Chapter 6, page 251, and Bandura's social learning theory in Chapter 14, page 599). Modeling therapy has been used effectively both to eliminate unwanted behaviors and to build new behavioral competencies (see Figure 16.2).

BIOFEEDBACK

Studies during the 1960s and 1970s demonstrated that rats and monkeys could increase or decrease their salivation, heart rate, and blood pressure when their autonomic responses were reinforced (e.g., Harris & Brady, 1974). Such studies spurred research into ways to train people to control their biological processes (usually of the autonomic nervous system), particularly responses associated with psychological and medical problems. Collectively known as **biofeedback,** these techniques are based on

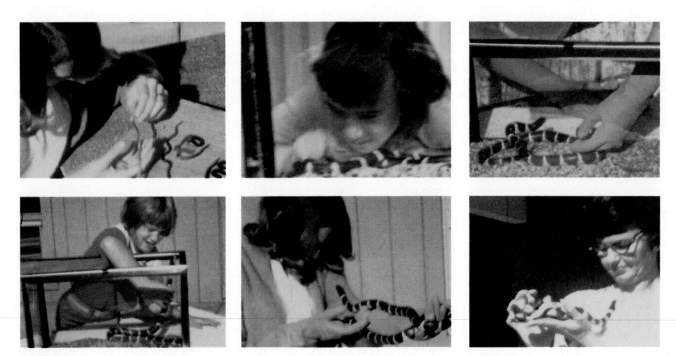

FIGURE 16.2
A Lesson in Overcoming Fear of Snakes

Children and Adults are shown in films modeling interactions with a king snake. Victims of snake phobias watch these films to learn fearless behavior in the presence of the objects they fear.

the idea that if clients are informed by special instruments about specific bodily processes, such as blood pressure or heart rate, they may attempt to modify them (Miller, 1980; also see Chapter 6).

For example, a therapist may attach electrodes to the heart region of a client's body. These electrodes convey information to an apparatus that monitors the client's heart rate and feeds the information back to the client via visual or auditory display. The client then uses relaxing strategies suggested by the therapist to lower his or her heart rate. The feedback showing the client's success in modifying the autonomic behavior usually is the reinforcer, but praise from the therapist may also be reinforcing. Many psychologists and physicians employ biofeedback techniques to manipulate stress-related problems including asthma, headaches, elevated blood pressure, and tension. Biofeedback practitioners are highly optimistic that their procedures will create major breakthroughs in treatment. However, the actual changes in autonomic behavior achieved by biofeedback training are often statistically significant but clinically meaningless. That is, the changes are reliable, but often not large enough to affect the patient's physical problem (Miller, 1983).

You can get some biofeedback of your own. When you sit down to try deep-muscle relaxation, take your pulse before you begin. Press your second and third fingertips against the inside of your wrist until you can feel your pulse in the artery in your wrist. Count the heartbeats while timing off 10 seconds on a watch or clock. Now relax your whole body with deep-muscle relaxation, take your three deep breaths, and take your pulse again. Did your heart rate decrease? If you do this after mild activity, you will see even more of a decrease. And if you were anxious before you relaxed, you should also experience a noticeable decrease (although there are some people with low heart rates—especially athletes—who will not be able to lower their heart rates any further this way). Being aware of your heart rate is considered biofeedback. Using this knowledge, you can learn to reduce your own heart rate, an autonomic nervous system response that is usually not under your direct control.

Cognitive Therapies

One of the clearest trends in therapy today involves techniques that aim to alter a client's thoughts and perceptions of the world (i.e., cognitions) rather than his or her behavior per se (Bandura, 1986; Mahoney, 1977; Meichenbaum, 1977). Cognitive and cognitive-behavioral therapies have been described as the most effective therapies available (Freeman & Byers, 1990). We will discuss cognitive therapies that grew out of behavior therapy (e.g., rational-emotive therapy and cognitive behavior modification) as well as some from other traditions (e.g., paradoxical intervention and attribution therapy).

RATIONAL-EMOTIVE THERAPY

Rational-emotive therapy (RET), pioneered by Albert Ellis (1962), focuses on changing a client's thoughts in order to change emotions and behaviors. Ellis believes that an active, assertive approach by a therapist is necessary to ensure that a client adequately confronts his or her own way of thinking and gains a more rational perspective of the world. Ellis has suggested that most people have irrational beliefs that lead them to engage in irrational behavior. For example: Your unhappiness is not your own responsibility because the causes lie outside of you; you have to strive to be liked by everyone; you have to be perfect in every way; you are responsible for other people; others must help you (Ellis, 1988). See Table 16.2 for other common irrational beliefs.

Albert Ellis considers the core of most people's maladjustments to be irrational beliefs. To help people change their thinking, therapists practicing RET identify their clients' irrational statements (which reflect these irrational beliefs). Therapists challenge their clients' beliefs while accepting the clients as individuals and offering empathy and understanding. RET therapists do not offer warmth and establish a caring relationship with their patients, however, for fear of reinforcing their mistaken, irrational need for love and approval or supporting their low frustration tolerance and need for help from others (Ellis & Dryden, 1987). If they can get rid of their irrational beliefs,

---

TABLE 16.2
Common Irrational Beliefs

1. One should be loved by everyone for everything one does.

2. It is horrible when things are not the way one would like them to be.

3. Human misery is produced by external causes—outside persons, or events—rather than by one's view of these conditions.

4. If possible, it is better to avoid life's problems than to face them.

5. One needs something stronger or more powerful than oneself to rely on.

6. One should be thoroughly competent, intelligent, and achieving in all respects.

7. Because something once affected one's life, it will indefinitely affect it.

8. One must obtain and perfect self-control.

9. Happiness can be achieved by inertia and inaction.

10. One has virtually no control over one's emotions and cannot help having certain feelings.

these clients may learn to accept themselves more, thus reducing their neurotic self-blaming and hypercritical attitude and becoming more adaptive.

Think of a time when someone you loved broke up with you. Did you feel, even briefly, that maybe you would never be with anyone as good as that person again or that you were unlovable? An RET therapist would point out that these thoughts are actually irrational exaggerations of reality. The fact that this person did not love you does not mean that no one will. Not having a relationship with this person does not mean that you will never find anyone else as attractive. The therapist would suggest more realistic thoughts, such as, "If I can't have X I will be sorry for a while, but I will get over him/her and be happy with other people and things in my life. Losing someone is sad, but need not be awful if I don't let it." The therapist would help you to identify your irrational cognitions and to generate rational alternatives so that you could replace your dysfunctional thoughts with more appropriate ones. Theoretically, your behavior and feelings should also become more rational and appropriate once your thoughts changed. According to Ellis's research, RET is more effective than psychoanalytic therapy and works in a shorter period of time.

COGNITIVE BEHAVIOR MODIFICATION

Initially, behavior modification focused exclusively on changing measurable, observable behaviors. Since the mid-1970s, however, there has been a cognitive revolution in behavioral therapy, and now much of behavior therapy is devoted to changing thoughts, or cognitive behavior. In **cognitive behavior modification,** the principles of learning theory are used to modify dysfunctional thoughts, or cognitions, rather than only observable behaviors. Practitioners of cognitive behavior modification often have two goals: (1) to learn what a client is thinking while engaging in undesirable behavior and (2) to teach the client more appropriate thoughts. For example, as we discussed in Chapter 15, Aaron Beck's theory of depression is that depressives are always thinking about their worthlessness and dwelling on the pointlessness of carrying on with their lives. This view of depression has led to a number of influential treatment programs (Beck et al., 1979; Dobson & Shaw, 1988), resulting in a significant improvement in depressives, although placebo treatments may do so as well (Elkin et al., 1989; 1996).

In cognitive behavior therapy, clients are encouraged to gather information about themselves in a positive manner to disconfirm their false, negative beliefs, rather than simply disputing or debating the rationality of their beliefs as in RET (Carson & Butcher, 1992).

There are a variety of techniques included in most cognitive behavioral treatments. One technique is simply to get patients to say "stop" to themselves whenever they become aware of self-defeating thoughts—a method known as *thought stopping*. The next step is to replace the dysfunctional thoughts with more positive ones. The power of positive thinking is clearly valued by cognitive therapists. In *rational restructuring,* a client and a therapist explore problematic attitudes and thoughts, focusing on the way this self-talk influences behavior. Next, more adaptive self-statements are learned in skill acquisition and practice sessions, followed by the client's applying the new coping skills in real situations. This therapy seems to work well with anxiety, pain management, and inappropriate coping behaviors (Carson & Butcher, 1992).

Donald Meichenbaum (1977) makes the power of positive thinking explicit in his treatment programs, providing his clients with self-instructional training. If you were to seek cognitive behavior modification for anxiety, you would first be made aware of the way "talking to yourself" influences your level of arousal—that you inadvertently increase your own distress by focusing on it. You might be asked to "listen for" and record some of your own private monologues and to evaluate their effect on your comfort. Next you might be taught some alternative coping dialogue, such as "Okay, it's almost time. I'm starting to feel 'different' but that's okay—I can make it work for me. It is my cue to cope. Just relax; I can handle this situation. Let me take a deep breath and go slowly. . . . Good! I'm doing fine; still nervous, but I'm controlling it now. Got to concentrate on what it is I have to do; don't think about fear. Hey, this isn't so bad—I'm doing a good job!"

The evidence is beginning to accumulate that cognitive behavioral strategies, especially when combined with modeling and reinforcement therapy, are effective in alleviating anxiety and distress (Bandura, 1986). The eating disorders bulimia and anorexia nervosa (see Chapter 12) have also been shown to respond better to cognitive behavioral treatments than to most other therapies (e.g., Fairburn, 1990; Fairburn, Jones, Peveier, et al., 1993).

OTHER COGNITIVE THERAPIES

While RET and cognitive behavior therapy are the most widely known and practiced cognitive therapies, there are many other cognitve therapies currently gaining recognition. **Problem-solving therapy** attempts to improve the patient's problem-solving and decision-making skills. This approach has been applied to a wide variety of psychological problems, ranging from depression and anxiety disorders to marital, sexual, drug, personality and pain problems. Improvement in these cognitive skills can be achieved with almost any age-group, making it increasingly popular with clinicians (Platt, 1991).

There are also schools of cognitive therapy not based on the social learning tradition. In the 1950s and 1960s, Milton Erickson, a clinical hypnotherapist, pioneered a technique known as directive therapy or **paradoxical intervention.** To demonstrate that their problems were under their own control, Erickson would have patients perform symptomatic behaviors on command. He would have them intentionally increase, rather than decrease these behaviors (thus the paradox, or apparent contradiction, referred to in the name of this technique), perhaps changing or adding some small component as well. This also paradoxically took control of the symptoms away from the patients, because whether they performed the symptom or not, they were complying with the therapy (either the immediate therapeutic request to increase the symptoms or the long-term one of reducing them). Thus, for example, a young woman with bulimia nervosa whose main complaint was that she was unable to control her eating binges was instructed deliberately to go home and binge every day (twice a day if she was already bingeing every day). She soon discovered two things—first, that she did have control over her binges, since she could make them occur on command, and second, that when forced to binge at someone else's command (the therapist's), she no longer "wanted to" binge and was able to stop. Erickson would also slip ideas past his patients' defenses by presenting several thoughts at once and focusing on one that they could easily reject without noticing the acceptance of the secondary thesis (Haley, 1963, 1976). The directive therapy practiced by Erickson, Haley, and others today involves changing patients' cognitions without explicitly explaining what is being done.

SLEEPLESS NIGHTS

A 65-year-old man with insomnia came to Erickson for help. Even with sleeping pills, he was sleeping only about 2 hours a night. Erickson assured him that he could cure the insomnia if the man was willing to give up 8 hours of sleep. The man was eager to get rid of his problem and readily agreed. Erickson found out that the man hated house-work, especially waxing the floors. He instructed the man to go home, prepare for bed, and when he was in his pajamas and ready to sleep, spend the night wax-ing the floors instead. At 7 in the morn-ing, he could stop, have breakfast, and get ready for work. He was to do this for four nights in a row, which would cost him 8 hours of sleep (since he normally slept only 2 hours each night). The man found this a bit strange, but agreed to try it. After working all day, he came home and at bedtime prepared for bed, but then spent all night waxing the floors. He did this for three nights, but on the fourth night was so tired (from following his crazy psychiatrist's orders) that he decided to lie down first and just rest for half an hour. He awoke at 7 the next morning. That night, he couldn't decide whether to go to sleep or polish the floors. Because he still owed Erickson 2 hours of sleep, he decided that he would just get into bed for 15 minutes and then get up and wax the floors. Of course, he fell asleep immediately and slept through the night again. He now reports that he sleeps through the night regularly. He says that he doesn't dare have insomnia or he will have to stay up all night wax-ing the floors! Erickson summed up the case by saying, "You know the old gentle-man would do anything to get out of pol-ishing the floors—even sleep!" (Reported in Haley, 1963, p. 49.)

Another cognitive therapy depends on more explicit alterations in patients' cogni-tions or beliefs. **Attribution therapy** involves giving patients new, less threatening labels or explanations for their feelings or behavior. For example, consider a woman who comes to a therapist complaining that she feels jittery, nervous, unable to concen-trate, and fears that she is having a nervous breakdown. The attribution therapist would ascertain whether there was some other likely cause for the woman's symptoms. In this case, the therapist might ask the woman how much caffeine she was drinking in coffee, tea, or colas. If the woman acknowledged drinking an excessive amount of caffeine (e.g., more than 6 cups per day), the therapist would point out that her symp-toms sounded like the result of overconsumption of caffeine, not a nervous break-down. The woman would thus be helped to "reattribute" her symptoms to something less frightening and more controllable than a nervous breakdown.

In fact, many therapists do this sort of attribution therapy as part of whatever other more complex treatment they endorse. Most problems bringing people to the point of seeking help from a psychologist tend to be more complex than a mere overdose of caf-feine (although that one does occur). In many problems, though, there is some symp-tom that a patient finds troubling because it seems to represent something particularly frightening to the patient. It is thus calming to reattribute the fearful symptom to some-thing more acceptable, especially when the dire attribution (e.g., "I must be having a nervous breakdown") is incorrect. Although few therapists explicitly call their tech-niques attribution therapies, many forms of cognitive restructuring, or learning to think about problems differently, had their origin in social psychological attribution research, examining how people explain the causes of their behavior (see Chapter 17) and the effects of these explanations on future behavior (Fodor, 1989; Segal, 1991).

Another, related idea, **expectancy theory,** posits that changing patients' *expectations* about their feelings and behaviors can actually produce changes in the feelings and behaviors themselves. This theory grows out of the social learning approach to behavior. The high success rate of placebo treatments—which simply alter how patients *expect* to feel—has contributed to the development of this approach. In essence, "believing that one will feel better is enough to *make* one feel better" (Kirsch, 1990, p. 104).

These cognitive therapies, despite the variety of their theoretical backgrounds, have in common a reliance on and demonstration of the power of cognitive responses in influencing emotions and behaviors. In the next section, we discuss an approach that also focuses on conscious awareness and perceptions, but is centered on the self.

Humanistic Therapies

The humanistic approach to personality described in Chapter 14 highlighted the importance of people's conscious experiences and feelings, especially their self-concepts. A humanistic approach to abnormality focuses on the way an individual thinks, feels, and experiences in the present. Several therapies have arisen within this perspective. In this section, we will consider person-centered therapy, Gestalt therapy, and existential therapy.

CLIENT/PERSON-CENTERED THERAPY

Carl Rogers

Client-centered therapy stems from the work of Carl Rogers (e.g., 1970a, 1980). It was actually developed in the 1940s and 1950s, before the humanistic movement of the 1960s, as an alternative to psychoanalysis, which was the prevailing therapy at the time. Nonetheless, it is considered humanistic because it emphasizes the potential for good in clients. It is also considered nondirective because it maintains that the therapist's role is to place the primary responsibility for solving a problem with the person who has the problem (hence the use of terms such as *client* or *person* rather than *patient*). The major emphasis of client-centered therapy, or, as referred to more recently, **person-centered therapy,** is on a client's own point of view or subjective experience, which the therapist tries to help the client to recognize and understand.

The other essential features of Rogerian therapy include an emphasis on the immediacy (the "here and now") of a person's experience; the empathy of the therapist; and the use of **unconditional positive regard,** or acceptance of a client regardless of what the client may say or do. This does not mean that a therapist accepts abusive or maladaptive behavior from a client. Rather, a therapist separates acceptance of the person or client from what that person happens to say or do. The emphasis on "here and now" helps a client gain insight into his or her current thinking and feelings. Rogerian therapy, unlike Freudian therapy, does not focus on childhood experiences or traumatic past events unless they are influencing the client's current life. Instead, it focuses on the client's current feelings.

Empathy, warmth, and genuineness are the three qualities that Rogers considers essential in a therapist. If a therapist is not able to empathize adequately with a client, it is the therapist's moral obligation to send that client elsewhere for treatment. Empathy manifests itself in the therapist's reflecting back to the client the emotional quality of what the client has said. The advantage of this procedure is that it ensures a therapist's complete attention to and understanding of a client. The client feels this connection and can either correct any misperception by the therapist or gain insight into his or her actual feelings as a result of hearing them restated in a slightly different way. Along with being empathic, a therapist is expected to be genuine in the interaction with a client, and to show warmth and acceptance to the client. Rogers himself maintained that what is most healing to a client is for the therapist to be open and human in the therapy relationship (Kahn, 1989).

Rogers's therapeutic technique involves empathic listening and reflecting the client's perceptions of the world. Mirroring the client's thoughts and feelings makes the client feel that the therapist truly understands the client. You can see for yourself how this works. The next time one of your friends comes to you with a problem, try repeating the last thing your friend says in slightly different words. For example, if a friend says that she is very angry at her psychology professor for asking such difficult questions on the exam, you say, "So you feel the professor was unfair to ask those questions and expect you to know so many details." Your friend will probably say, "Yeah, who can remember so many picky names and dates. Now I'll never get an A." You respond, "To get an A in that course, you need to remember every little thing." Your friend will probably agree and perhaps elaborate on why an A is important to her in that course. You repeat her main point each time. Watch how your friend nods in agreement with you more and more. You might eventually ask if she feels that you understand what she is feeling or going through, and you may even want to explain what you are doing. You and your friend will have demonstrated how Rogerian empathy helps the client feel accepted and understood by the therapist.

In addition to gaining insight into current feelings, the central goal of Rogerian therapy is to improve a client's self-concept—that is, to get the client to accept his or her actual self more and to stop striving for the unobtainable ideal self (see Chapter 14). The goal of therapy is reached when the client incorporates all experiences into his or her actual self-concept and there is a greater congruence between the actual and the ideal self-concepts. The client is then perceived as further on the road toward self-actualization, realizing his or her full potential as a person.

The Rogerian approach has had an enormous impact on both the methods and the theory of psychological counseling. It tends to be the dominant method used in university counseling services and in many child-guidance clinics. It is used primarily with those who have milder disturbances, not psychoses. There has been a fair amount of research evaluating Rogers's therapeutic system, and the benefits of empathy, warmth, and genuineness are repeatedly confirmed.

GESTALT THERAPY

Another humanistic approach was pioneered by Frederick (Fritz) Perls (1893–1970). A German psychoanalyst who became the first psychoanalyst in South Africa, Perls became disillusioned with psychoanalysis after an unpleasant meeting with Freud at a psychoanalytic congress in Czechoslovakia. Perls returned home to create his own form of therapy, called **Gestalt therapy**, which focused on independence from others and self-awareness and self-acceptance. He ultimately settled at the Esalen Institute, in California, in 1963, and many people seeking an alternative therapy gravitated there. Gestalt therapy quickly became fashionable.

The use of the word *gestalt* is perhaps unfortunate because it implies a connection with the Gestalt theory of perception discussed in Chapter 4. The only link is the emphasis on the concept of the "whole" or "totality"—in this case, unity of body and mind. The goal of Gestalt therapy is to make people aware of all aspects of themselves

Fritz Perls created Gestalt therapy, a process which focuses on independence from others.

so that they can move toward self-acceptance, independence, and responsibility for their decisions and choices (Perls, 1970). Although the therapy is often carried out in a group setting, the focus is always on one individual at a time, rather than on group process. The therapist concentrates on identifying aspects of an individual's feelings, thoughts, or actions of which the individual is currently unaware. The therapist may ask how a client feels when discussing a particular issue or what the client is aware of at the moment.

To facilitate the process, Gestalt therapists may use a variety of techniques or exercises. In one of these, the Empty Chair exercise, clients move back and forth between two chairs. In one chair they are themselves. In the other, they assume the roles of other people, perhaps parents or spouses. Clients gain insight and self-awareness by observing how they interact with these others or by playing out both sides of a conflict in their lives. Another exercise consists of speaking only in the present tense to emphasize the here-and-now aspects of awareness and owning one's feelings by using no pronoun but "I." Try telling a friend about something important to you without using anything but the present tense and always using "I" instead of "you" or "it." Although it is difficult to do, you may find that it changes the way you think about the incident and your place in it.

Dream analysis also plays a major role in this therapy. Unlike Freudian dream analysis, in Gestalt analysis the therapist does not attempt to interpret dreams. Instead, the clients are asked for more and more information about various parts of their dreams, until they make the interpretation themselves. Perls believed that only the clients could really know what a particular dream meant to them. He helped them to reach this awareness by asking them to pretend to be the objects or people in their dreams and tell their "stories." For instance, in the training film "Madeline's Dream," one woman reported that she was swimming in a beautiful lake in a wood. She swam to an island in the middle of the lake and saw a statue of a boy pouring water from an urn. Perls asked her to "be" the lake, then the island, and then later the statue. As the statue, she reported that she wanted to give people her water, that her water would be good for them, but that she could not move, so people had to come to her. She also could not talk, so she could not tell the people to come. She felt very frustrated. Perls next asked her to "be" the water in the urn. She said that she was good, sweet water, that people should come and try her and see how sweet she was. She did not know why no one came to drink her. She began to sob as Perls had her repeat this to various members of a group. She sat down, satisfied that she had reached a new understanding about herself and her relationship to others. Perls himself did not offer an explanation.

You can do this sort of dream analysis on your own dreams. The next time you remember a dream, analyze it for yourself using Perls's Gestalt dream analysis. Tell the story of each of the elements of the dream as they occurred. Be each main person or object and explain what you are doing in the dream. See if this process helps you understand the dream better than you did before.

While others have carried on with Gestalt therapy since Perls's death in 1970, there has been little research evaluating its effectiveness. Although still popular in some places, the therapy is less widely used now than it was a decade ago.

EXISTENTIAL THERAPY

Although it is not connected with an explicit theory of personality, **existential therapy** is based on existential philosophy, emphasizing the importance of an individual's human situation and subjective experience. In this therapy, people are seen as being depersonalized by society, alienated and lacking meaning in their lives. The individual is considered responsible for making choices and directing his or her own life to actualize potentials. The developing relationship between therapist and patient is what leads to change and growth on the part of the patient. Both Rogers and Perls were influenced by existential analysis as advocated by theorists such as Victor Frankl and Rollo May (May, 1969).

Existential therapists do not utilize specific techniques, but try to focus on the unique nature of each individual's "way of being in the world." An individual is challenged to become more aware of his or her own existence and its purpose. This change is accomplished through the therapeutic relationship, or **encounter,** which is a here-and-now meeting of two individuals who try to be open and honest in their reactions to each other. A therapist is expected to be genuine in the relationship, sharing his or her own feelings and existence with the client, at the same time making sure that the client also remains "authentic" and attuned to the current situation. For example, if the client says, "I hate you—you're just like my mother," the therapist will respond, "But I am not your mother, so you must interact with me here and now as Dr. B., not as your mother." The choices made by the individual to reach whatever goal he or she is currently trying to attain are examined so that new, more adaptive choices can be made. This therapy is clearly best suited to intelligent, verbal, highly functioning individuals who are perhaps dealing with a life crisis or suffering from an anxiety disorder. It is not ideal for behavior problems, personality disorders, or psychoses (Carson & Butcher, 1992).

Group, Family, and Community Therapies

The therapeutic techniques discussed so far have primarily involved a one-on-one relationship between client and therapist. In recent years, the practice of treating people in groups has increased enormously. Group therapy has several advantages over individual therapy. First, there are obvious economies of cost, effort, and time. Second, patients may learn quickly and effectively whether other group members share their perceptions. Finally, since human beings almost invariably live in groups, many psychologists believe that abnormal and deviant behavior should be treated at that level. In this section, we discuss three types of therapy conducted in a social setting: group, family, and community therapy.

GROUP THERAPY

In **group therapy,** there are several patients present, usually 4 to 12 or even more, and often there are two or more therapists working together. Thus, each patient has a variety of others with whom to form different sorts of relationships, all of which can then be explored therapeutically. Group therapy is in many respects similar to individual, one-on-one therapy, but it involves other people in the therapeutic relationship. Many more types of relationships become possible. With only one patient and one therapist, the only interpersonal issues that can be examined directly in the therapy situation are those that occur between these two individuals. In many respects, a therapy group becomes a microcosm of the world outside, allowing the patients to play out their problems in a safer context where they can learn to correct them. Moreover, there are more people to provide feedback and offer alternative points of view.

Generally, the patients in a group have similar sorts of problems. For example, patients in a group may all have eating disorders or be suffering from depression or sexual dysfunction. They thus share something important. Their common goal helps to

Group therapy offers several advantages to patients. In addition to being a more cost-effective means of providing therapy for more people, the group offers benefits stemming from the presence of other people in the therapy setting.

establish group cohesiveness; they feel connected to each other and to the group. The members then feel a part of something; they feel that they belong.

The fact that the patients share a similar problem allows them to feel understood by people who really know what they are experiencing. Also, they may feel less abnormal if they hear others talk about similar problems and feelings. In many respects, the group offers the opportunity for a corrective emotional experience. Thus, the group setting and group process can be helpful therapeutically in ways beyond the scope of individual therapy (Yalom, 1985).

There are as many types of group therapy as individual therapy. A psychoanalytically oriented group may stress the "group as family" and the release of pent-up emotions. A behavioral group may focus on the modeling and practice of social skills. A humanistic group may emphasize the sharing of experiences and the development of group togetherness within the context of personal growth.

Groups may be for hospital inpatients or for outpatients. Often the type of problem bringing the patients to therapy, as well as the orientation of the therapist, determines the nature of the group. Given the economic advantage of group therapy over individual therapy and the possible added benefits from the effects of group processes, it is not surprising that therapy groups have become increasingly popular. Group therapy is widely used in hospitals, clinics, and university counseling centers.

A therapy called **transactional analysis** or **TA** (Berne, 1964) developed as a reaction against psychoanalysis; while sometimes used with individuals, it is used more often in groups. In TA, a therapist helps the group members (or individual patients) to become more aware of the three parts of their personalities: the fun-loving but somewhat irresponsible child, which is something like the Freudian id; the rather stern and forbidding parent, corresponding to the superego; and the reasonable and sensible adult, corresponding to the ego. According to TA, we interact with others using all three parts of our personalities, but we may have problems if we get stuck in only one. The group allows the development of more interactions and social games, which can then be analyzed by the transactional therapist so that members can learn to interact more productively.

Encounter groups have generally been geared toward self-actualization and consciousness-raising. Based on the Rogerian humanistic principles of openness, honesty, touching, and expression of feelings, these groups dominated the late 1960s and early 1970s but have since given way to more practical issue-oriented groups of all theoretical persuasions. Encounter groups were in some respects the forerunners of the increasingly prevalent **self-help groups.** These groups are often organized by medical or psychiatric patients or their families, and do not necessarily have a therapist leading them. Often they are led by individuals who have had the problem and overcome it (and who may thus be in a better position than a therapist to help others learn to overcome the problem). In essence, the participants in the group help each other and themselves. One of the best-known self-help groups is Alcoholics Anonymous, led by recovered alcoholics to help other alcoholics and their families. More recently, AIDS patients and their families, cancer patients, eating disorder patients, and parents whose children have died have formed self-help groups and even national associations. The forces of group cohesion, recognition that others have gone through similar experiences, and all the other factors that contribute to the success of formal therapy groups can be tapped. The evidence indicates that such groups can be very effective for a variety of problems (e.g., Hartley, 1988), although it is important to have a competent leader even for a self-help group.

Today, the marital unit is seen as a potential focus of therapy. In the photo, marriage counseling is taking place. Often a spouse's emotional problems are connected to the marital relationship, so that even if the couple is not fighting or in ovewrt discord, the best way to alleviate one partner's distress is to treat the couple, not just the identified patient.

MARITAL AND FAMILY THERAPY

Other types of group therapies have also been receiving increased attention (Glick, Clarkin, & Kessler, 1987; Jacobson & Bussod, 1983). When one member of a marital unit or family is experiencing distress, there tend to be repercussions for the rest of the group. For example, marital discord often accompanies childhood disorders. As we know, such a correlation does not tell us whether marital discord causes disruptive behavior in children, whether children's misbehavior causes marital discord, whether there is some combination or the two, or whether some third factor (e.g., financial problems) causes both. Nevertheless, many therapists now argue for *marital therapy* or *family therapy*—that is, working therapeutically with a marital or family system and working on the relationship rather than focusing only on the person with the problem (the identified patient) (e.g., Bohart & Todd, 1988; 1994; Minuchin, Rosman, & Baker, 1978).

Marital therapy involves treating husband and wife together and focusing on their relationship problems. In **family therapy,** the family is seen as a complete, interconnected system that must be treated along with the patient; only when changes occur in the family will the patient's symptoms change. The focus is on family dynamics, and all the family members who live together or who see each other frequently enough to be influential in the family system are included in the sessions. Thus, it is not the individual who is seen as distressed or symptomatic, but the whole family unit. For example, if a child (unconsciously) develops anorexia nervosa to keep parental attention on her rather than on the parents' disagreements with each other, working only with the child will not be a very effective way to solve her problems. As she improves, her parents' relationship will worsen, scaring the child back into her symptomatic behavior. If, instead, the whole family is brought into treatment, the entire system can be changed, so that the child can give up her symptoms safely.

As with group therapy, there are many types of marital and family therapies. In most marital therapies, both marital partners see the same therapist, sometimes together, sometimes both individually and together. In family therapy, too, the identified patient may be seen alone as well as with the entire family, some of whom may also be seen separately by the therapist or one of the therapists (since there are often two in family therapy). All members of the household (including extended family members such as grandparents, aunts, uncles, or cousins if they live with the family) and any others whose relationship with the identified patient and the rest of the family is intense and influential may be asked to participate in family therapy sessions. This results in a large gathering, and having more than one therapist helps ensure that potentially useful material will not be missed. Exactly how the family dynamics are changed depends on the therapeutic orientation of the therapist. In general, though, the intent of therapy is to change the contingencies within the family so that the identified patient's maladaptive behavior is no longer rewarded by the reactions and interactions of the other family members (or "necessary" for any unspoken family purpose).

COMMUNITY THERAPIES

More and more therapies are being directed toward helping people cope with psychopathology while remaining within their communities rather than being hospitalized for long periods of time. Some involve changing the hospital setting to be more like the "real world," easing the transition back into the community, while others take place in the community itself.

Social Milieu Therapy. **Social milieu therapy** involves treatment in a residential therapeutic community or institution where the goal is to change behavior to be more adaptive. Residents are treated as responsible human beings. Often the physical setting is remodeled to provide home-style amenities, and staff and residents wear ordinary clothing. All participate in "town meetings" to decide on rules, activities, schedules, problems, and similar matters. Residents are expected to work, socialize, and follow rules. Many behavioral goals are targeted for improvement, including, for example, holding down jobs, solving problems independently, being more assertive, and caring for others. If a resident's behavior is at a very low level of competence, the target goals may be as simple as getting dressed, making the bed, or getting to meals on time. When various criteria that have been established in this manner have been met successfully, the residents can be released into the outside community.

Community Halfway Houses. Often located in a city, a **community halfway house** serves as a treatment facility and residence for those who have just been released from a mental hospital or prison or for those who fear that they may need hospitalization or cannot live on their own. Halfway houses tend to be run by small, nonprofessional staffs who consult mental health experts regularly. In the typical halfway house, about 10 residents live in a family-style atmosphere. Residents participate in the daily life of the larger community, going to jobs or school and finding recreation away from the house. The residents contribute a small fee for room and board and are expected to keep their rooms clean and to complete chores. Some residents have improved to the point where they are able to manage their own halfway houses.

Within the past decade, many former patients from mental hospitals have been placed in some form of care in the community. The goal of this effort has been to free patients from institutionalization. In practice, many mental patients have landed in rather unhelpful board-and-care facilities run for private profit while the patients are on welfare (Jones, 1975). In many cases, patients drift into skid-row rooming houses and single-room occupancy hotels and often become street derelicts. These are not the halfway houses involving community support and professional care that were intended when the patients were released. Some researchers have suggested that the government has washed its hands of responsibility for some of its most dependent citizens (Jones, 1975).

Community Mental Health Centers. During the 1960s, *community mental health centers* were established across the United States with the help of federal aid. They were located in the hearts of communities, often in storefronts, and were supposed to supply psychological services. Three kinds of services were offered: primary, secondary, and tertiary.

Primary services (often referred to as primary prevention) are directed toward eliminating the causes of patients' problems. Efforts to eradicate poverty and disease, racial discrimination and injustice, and loneliness and social isolation are examples of primary prevention. The theory is that by identifying potential social stressors and eliminating them or educating people how to handle them, future behavior problems can be prevented. Although there may be great potential for primary prevention in the future, to date it has not been applied in a major way.

Secondary services (also called secondary prevention) focus on providing immediate treatment of existing psychological problems in a wider range of situations than tradi-

WHO BENEFITS FROM THERAPY?

Who is the client or patient being treated with the psychotherapies you have been reading about? Is everyone with a psychological problem equally likely to seek this sort of help? Obviously not. Research has examined the characteristics of individuals who receive psychotherapy and of their outcomes when they do so.

For example, not everyone who tries to get psychotherapy is successful at receiving it. Social class is related to the receipt of psychotherapy, as are age, race, education, and diagnosis (Garfield, 1986; Howard et al., 1996). A recent survey has confirmed that of those who visit a mental health facility seeking help, female, more educated, single (divorced, separated, or never married) whites are the most likely to enter psychotherapy (Vessey & Howard, 1993). This study indicated that in many instances, the ones who need therapy the most are less likely to receive it (or in some instances even seek it). For instance, the proportion of males and females suffering from some sort of psychopathology is about the same, but females are much more likely to try to get therapy. Similarly, those with the least education and income are the most likely to have some sort of diagnosis of psychopathology in their lives, but they are also the least likely to visit a mental health worker. And while nonwhites are more likely to report having a diagnosable problem, whites are more likely to enter psychotherapy (Howard et al., 1996; Vessey & Howard, 1993). In keeping with these data, it has also been shown that minority patients are more likely to be treated in state and county facilities and less likely to be treated in private hospitals than are white patients, who are also more likely to have health insurance (Mason & Gibbs, 1992).

Differences in attitudes and values may underlie the failure of some groups to utilize or benefit from psychological help. Native American alcoholics were found to leave treatment sooner and have a poorer outcome than were white alcoholic patients at the same treatment centers. The two groups differed significantly in their endorsement of societal goals (preferred by whites) versus personal or group-oriented values (chosen by the Native Americans) (Flores, 1986).

But does this sort of information tell us who will *benefit* from psychotherapy? In fact, it seems that lower-income,

minority clients who do go into therapy may well benefit from it as much as anyone else (Goode & Wagner, 1993). A survey of the therapy outcome literature indicates that social class, age, and sex do not accurately predict the outcome of psychotherapy (Garfield, 1986). Personal qualities, expectations, and motivations of the client are more important in determining the outcome of therapy for any given individual than are demographic characteristics.

There is also increasing evidence that treatment programs are responding to the needs of the populations that they serve. Although client and therapist do not seem to need similar personalities and attitudes for the success of the therapeutic relationship (Garfield, 1986), matching on demographic characteristics does appear to be beneficial. Using a culturally compatible approach to treatment was shown to be successful in treating white, black, Mexican, Vietnamese, and Filipino patients. When patients and therapists were matched on ethnicity or race and language, and when the treatment facility was located within the ethnic/racial community, dropouts decreased significantly and the therapy was utilized more effectively (Flaskerud, 1986; Flaskerud & Liu, 1991). Blacks and Hispanics seem particularly sensitive to the advantages of having an ethnically and sexually similar therapist (Nurco, Shaffer, Hanlon, & Kinlock, 1988).

Finally, it is not necessary for patient and therapist to be matched on race if counselors are trained in culture sensitivity before they begin therapy. Black females rated their counselors higher on relationship and credibility variables, returned for more sessions, and reported being more satisfied with their therapy when their therapists had been given culture sensitivity training (Wade & Bernstein, 1991). Thus, the shortage of minority therapists may not pose a significant handicap to the success of psychotherapeutic endeavors. Training therapists not only to do therapy, but also to attend to the cultural, racial, and ethnic backgrounds of their patients seems to enhance the effectiveness of the intervention.

tional treatment programs (although much traditional therapy of all types is provided here as well). Crisis intervention is an example of a secondary service; it is based on the assumption that people can best be helped when there is an emergency in their lives. Such help may be required for only four or five sessions, after which a person can return to normal functioning. One example of crisis intervention is a suicide hot line to connect potentially suicidal people with counselors at a suicide prevention center. Such centers are sometimes staffed 24 hours a day, often by paraprofessionals including undergraduate psychology majors who have had special training.

Tertiary services (also called tertiary prevention) are concerned with the aftereffects of emotional problems. This type of treatment is generally referred to as rehabilitation. People who have had severe emotional problems may have lost their jobs or families and need counseling to get back into the community. This counseling may involve job training, counseling on how to get jobs, and development of social skills.

Ethical Issues in Therapy

Ethical issues arise frequently in psychology, but they arise especially often in the area of treating abnormality. When someone's behavior is deliberately being changed by someone else, even when the change is supposedly for the individual's benefit, there is always a question of whose values are being reflected in the change (see "Controversy: Is Psychotherapy Exploitation?" on page 672). For example, when institutionalized patients are reinforced for cleaning up after themselves, is this because it is so beneficial for them or because it makes things easier for the staff? When a delinquent teenager is sent for therapy to eliminate destructive behavior, is this better for the teenager or for society? When drug addicts are given therapy to cure their addiction, is this for the benefit of the addicts or for those around them? Even if we could be sure that therapy was always in the recipient's best interest, the patient may not agree. Suicidal depressives insist that they want to die (see Chapter 15); manic patients on a high say that they do not want to be brought down to "dull reality"; psychotic schizophrenics occasionally report that they enjoy their hallucinations or delusions. When a doctor administers a mind-altering drug to "help" a patient exhibiting one of these "psychopathologies," the patient may not have given consent for such treatment and may or may not agree that the treatment is "helpful."

Since most patients or clients voluntarily seek drugs or psychotherapy to alleviate their psychological distress, the ethical problems often center on other issues. A major issue in all therapy, but particularly in group or family therapy (where there are more people in the room than simply the patient and therapist) is **confidentiality,** or the patient's right to privacy. Most therapists, whatever their orientation or training, believe that clients must feel free to talk about their problems and must be assured that whatever they say will remain private (Thompson, 1987). Most states have laws protecting therapist-patient confidentiality, although many of these laws actually only cover psychiatrists (Shuman & Weiner, 1987). In group therapies, all group members must agree not to discuss outside of the therapy sessions anything that occurs in the group.

While it might seem that confidentiality should not be a problem except in cases involving legal proceedings, there are often complications. For instance, when the mother of a patient calls the patient's therapist and asks what has been happening in the therapy sessions, does the mother—who may be paying for the therapy—have a right to know? Is a child entitled to the same confidentiality that an adult would be accorded?

Both the American Psychological Association (1977/1992) and regional psychological bodies (e.g., Ontario Board of Examiners in Psychology, 1986) provide standards of ethical conduct for psychologists that include the need to protect client confidentiality unless the law dictates otherwise. In the United States, the **Tarasoff decision** forms the basis of the legal code. This decision states that therapists must inform potential victims of their patients that they are in danger, even if the therapist has to violate the patient's confidentiality. This decision was the first in a series of cases establishing therapists' responsibility to protect others from their patients. In the Tarasoff case, a patient told his therapist that he was going to kill his girlfriend, Tatiana Tarasoff, a student at Berkeley, upon her return from vacation. The therapist, a member of the university counseling service, asked the campus police to arrest the patient and bring him in for involuntary commitment to a hospital for observation. The police spoke to the patient and judged him to be rational. They did not bring him to the hospital, and he never returned to treatment at the counseling center. The original therapist did not do anything further, and when Tarasoff returned from her vacation, the patient murdered her. Her parents sued the therapist and the university and won on the grounds that they knew that Tarasoff was in danger but did not protect her.

The ethical obligation that grows out of this and similar cases rests on the assumption that therapists can predict which patients will, in fact, commit violent acts, an assumption that is controversial at best (Appelbaum & Rosenbaum, 1989). A similar question applies to researchers: Can they be held responsible if, in the course of a study, they learn of potential violence or harm to others, even if they have no clinical training or expertise (Appelbaum & Rosenbaum, 1989)? There have been exceptions to the Tarasoff ruling, though. In at least two cases, U.S. courts have ruled that the duty to warn does not extend to breaking confidentiality if a patient threatens suicide, although precautions must be taken by the therapist to prevent the patient from actually following through on the threat (Birch, 1992).

There are other legal situations in which confidentiality may need to be breached, either with or without a patient's consent, but in general, medical and psychological organizations urge their members to protect confidentiality whenever possible. While these bodies regulate many aspects of ethical behavior besides confidentiality, including fee scheduling, sticking to one's area of expertise, liaison with other agencies involved with clients and their families, and accountability for providing the best possible service to the client, there are other ethical issues that are not addressed by such guidelines. Consider a case in which a teenager seeks therapy for depression and reveals that she is pregnant (not married) and debating having an abortion. Should the therapist, acting on his or her own moral beliefs, try to persuade the client to have the abortion or not? Is it ethical to bring personal values into the therapy situation? To some extent, this is unavoidable, but where does the therapist draw the line?

Still another major issue facing therapists is the question of emotional (and physical) involvement with their patients. Does a therapist lose objectivity if he or she becomes emotionally involved with a patient? What is the impact on the client of such a relationship? Can it be helpful, as a small minority of therapists sometimes maintain, or is it inevitably harmful to a patient, as most therapists (and all their regulatory bodies) maintain (e.g., Conte et al., 1989)?

Ethical issues are sometimes clear and easy to resolve, but are more often ambiguous and hard to call. Rate each of the following scenarios as ethical, unethical, or ambiguous, and think about how you would defend your choice to an ethical review committee.

• Your patient (of the opposite sex) has a very low opinion of himself/herself and feels completely unattractive to the opposite sex. Nothing you have said or done has altered this opinion, so you tell the patient that you yourself are very sexually attracted to him/her, even though this is not the case.

• Your patient is a 15-year-old girl whose parents are paying for her therapy. Her mother calls you to say that her daughter has seemed extremely depressed since her last session, and she wants to know what happened in the session to upset her daughter so. You tell her what the main topic of discussion was and suggest that she talk to her daughter about it further before the next session.

• Your patient is an unmarried woman who has just lost her job. Moreover, her boyfriend has recently left her, and she has just discovered that she is pregnant. You do not believe in abortion, and you urge her to have the baby but give it up for adoption.

(You might be interested to know that most therapists and regulatory bodies would disagree with the actions of all three of these therapists.)

Therapeutic Effectiveness

A question superseding most other issues is whether therapy works at all. In this section, we will examine research addressing the effectiveness of psychotherapy (research on the efficacy of physical interventions was discussed earlier). Are all the methods of psychotherapy we discussed equally useful? Do all of them (or any of them) really help people to feel better? Is psychotherapy beneficial?

DOES PSYCHOTHERAPY WORK?

As we have indicated, during the last 20 years there has been enormous growth in the number and variety of psychological therapies available. Many of these are as concerned with promoting personal growth as with helping people overcome debilitating problems. Some sound almost like secular religions rather than therapies to alleviate distress, since they aim to promote happiness, give meaning to life, and enhance peace of mind. This proliferation of therapies has led to controversy in the literature about the effectiveness of therapy (i.e., is it better to have some form of psychotherapy or not to have any?) and the kinds of therapy that are most effective.

Behavioral psychologists have leveled strong criticisms against the "unscientific" nature of many personal growth therapies and other more traditional therapies. The most famous critique was published by Hans Eysenck in 1952. He contended that patients treated by psychotherapy were no better off than those who had not undergone therapy. Eysenck argued that over a two-year period, some 66 percent of neurotic problems cleared up spontaneously even if patients received no therapy, a rate not surpassed by psychotherapy. Indeed, some types of therapy, particularly psychoanalysis, seemed to retard patients' progress. Needless to say, Eysenck's statistics and his conclusion were highly controversial and stirred up considerable interest in research on the outcome of therapy.

One such study compared the effectiveness of different forms of therapy for anxiety. Paul (1966) recruited 96 undergraduate "patients" who suffered from severe anxiety when they had to talk in front of others. All accepted an offer for six weeks of free therapy and were randomly assigned to one of four treatment groups: (1) insight therapy, in which insight-oriented psychotherapists (e.g., psychoanalysts, humanists) worked individually with subjects; (2) behavior therapy desensitization, in which patients were led systematically through a behavior modification program; (3) an attention-placebo control group, in which subjects were supposedly given tranquilizers, but were really given inactive (baking soda) pills; and (4) a no-treatment control group.

After treatment, the subjects were required to speak in public. Their anxiety was rated by self-report, observations of others, and physiological measures. The two groups that received psychotherapy treatment improved significantly over the no-treatment control; but the placebo control group also improved, although its members had been given only bicarbonate of soda. Paul's results demonstrate the **placebo effect** in psychotherapy: People get better because they believe that they will and because someone pays special attention to them, even though they get no real therapy. Of the two active treatments, only the behavioral therapy produced more improvement than the placebo treatment; insight was not significantly better than the placebo. It must be remembered, however, that insight treatments normally require more than six sessions (see "Psychology in Our Times: Is There a Proper 'Dose' of Psychotherapy?"). The problem chosen for treatment, speech anxiety, is a mild phobia that has been shown to respond particularly well to behavior modification. In any case, all the "treatments" in this study were more effective than no treatment at all. In fact, the beneficial effects were still apparent two years later when subjects were requestioned about their speech anxiety; Improvement was still evident in 85 percent of the desensitization subjects and 50 percent of both the insight and placebo subjects (Paul, 1967). Thus, psychotherapy seemed to be effective and long-lasting for these student-patients.

Bergin and Lambert (1978) reviewed all the treatment procedures and outcome studies to date and criticized much of the data, interpretations, and computations used by Eysenck in his critique of psychotherapy. Their reanalysis suggested that the spontaneous recovery rate (people who recovered without therapy) was closer to 43 percent, not 66 percent, as Eysenck reported. Psychotherapy, including psychoanalysis, was more effective than this result. Moreover, the improvement occurred more quickly in therapy (as in Paul's study). They did concede, however, that some therapies did make some individuals worse than if they had not had treatment.

In 1980, the publication of *The Benefits of Psychotherapy* by Smith, Glass, and Miller rekindled widespread interest in whether psychotherapy is better than no therapy at all. The authors examined more than 500 studies comparing some form of psychological therapy with a control condition. Their review indicated that psychological therapy is significantly more effective than no therapy at all.

More recently, Howard and colleagues (McNeilly & Howard, 1991; Strupp & Howard, and colleagues 1991) reexamined Eysenck's original data and found that he was actually making an inappropriate comparison. Although the "untreated" group spent the two years in question without receiving individual psychotherapy, they did in fact have other treatments, including hospitalization in mental hospitals and residency in halfway houses. Moreover, the psychotherapy group actually received only short-term psychotherapy for the most part, with treatment lasting only 14 sessions. Howard and colleagues concluded that psychotherapy is clearly a much faster means of recovery, even if you assume the 66 percent recovery rate to be accurate for the "untreated" patients. It accomplished in only 14 weeks what other resources in the community (including psychiatric hospitalization!) took two years to achieve.

One big problem in resolving this controversy is that different therapeutic approaches demand different criteria to be met in order to pronounce someone "cured." Behaviorists usually require changes to be made in observable behavior, as when snake phobics pick up snakes. Psychoanalysts, however, are more concerned with altering feelings, neurotic symptoms, and unconscious conflicts (which some behaviorists deny even exist). Humanistic therapists, on the other hand, stress how a client feels about a problem. If the client can learn to live with, and not be unhappy or

IS THERE A PROPER "DOSE" OF PSYCHOTHERAPY

There is increasing consensus that psychotherapy is beneficial to patients who receive it, and most people believe that the relation between the amount of therapy and the outcome is positive, with more therapy leading to better outcomes. As a recent article in *U.S. News and World Report* summarized, the benefits of psychotherapy seem to be greater than comparable amounts of education; that is, therapy patients' health improves more than does the reading ability of students taking remedial reading classes (Goode & Wagner, 1993). The psychological literature supports this view (e.g., Howard, Kopta, Krause, & Orlinsky, 1986; Lipsey & Wilson, 1993). Whenever estimates of the relationship between amount of treatment and outcome are made, they are likely to be positive. Still, insurance companies, HMOs, and the tax-paying public are increasingly interested in just how much therapy is enough. Do patients really keep getting better and better the more psychotherapy they receive? If a little therapy is good, is more therapy necessarily better? Most importantly (to those paying the bills), what is the best amount of psychotherapy to ensure that patients are "better" and therapy is not wasted? Howard and his colleagues (1986) tried to answer these questions.

It was first necessary to solve definitional and methodological problems. What constituted a "dose," or unit, of treatment? How were the researchers to deal with patients who dropped out of treatment before they were "cured"? How much therapy was necessary before a patient was considered truly exposed to the treatment, or "treated"? For example, Howard and colleagues (1986) found that simply making an appointment to get help resulted in measurable improvement in about 15 percent of patients. How much of a dose is a phone call? These problems resolved, the authors reanalyzed the data from 15 studies covering a period of more than 30 years, and including 2,431 patients in individual outpatient therapy. The patients represented a

wide range of ages and social classes. The therapists were mainly either psychodynamic or interpersonal in orientation and represented each of the major mental health professions.

The results of the massive reanalysis, shown in Figure 16.3, indicated that by eight sessions, 40 to 55 percent of patients reported improvement and were rated improved by their therapists (Howard et al., 1986). By the end of six months (26 sessions), 75 percent of patients had shown measurable improvement, and over 80 percent had improved after one year. Thus, eight sessions was enough to ensure some improvement, but one year of therapy seemed overall to be the optimal (most productive) amount of therapy. Also, somewhat surprisingly, this analysis indicated that most patients (more than two-thirds) tended to stay in therapy only a short time—8 to 26 sessions (Howard et al., 1989, 1995).

Is the optimal dose of therapy best for everyone? Most patients fell into three diagnostic categories: depression, anxiety disorders, and borderline personality disorder. Depressives responded to the lowest doses of psychotherapy (about 31 to 44 percent had improved after only 4 sessions). Anxious patients started responding a bit later but quickly caught up to and surpassed the depressives, with about 50 percent of both groups improved between 8 and 13 sessions. The borderline personality disorder cases did not reach this level of improvement until between 13 and 26 sessions for self-report and 26 to 52 sessions according to their clinical charts. Thus, some problems seemed to require more therapy, others less. Also, early in treatment, many depressed and anxious patients reported feeling better before their charts indicated any improvement, indicating that they felt better before they seemed better to clinical observers. Later, their feelings seemed to lag a bit behind the clinical ratings (Howard, Orlinski, Lueger, 1995, Kopta, Howard, Lowry & Beutler, 1994).

debilitated by, a snake phobia, this may be a sufficient cure for a humanistic therapist. Given such widely differing goals of psychotherapy, it is not surprising that practitioners disagree on the effectiveness of their respective therapies. For example, has therapy been successful for an individual who reports being significantly happier but shows no change in social adjustment? How is "social adjustment" defined and measured? If psychotherapists accept their clients' subjective reports about feeling better as their data, then such "feeling" therapies are more likely to be seen as effective. If behavioral change is required before therapy can be viewed as effective, then behavioral therapies are found to be more effective than psychoanalytic or humanistic therapies, with cognitive therapies falling in between (Rachman & Wilson, 1980; Shapiro, 1985).

These guidelines may also influence how long insurance companies will be willing to pay for therapy for particular disorders; borderline patients may receive longer support than depressive or anxious patients (Howard et al., 1986, 1988, 1989, 1995). The guidelines may also affect the amount of therapy that crowded clinics will offer to individual patients when their waiting lists do not allow unlimited sessions. Since almost half of the patients who come to psychologists and psychiatrists for treatment are anxiety disorder patients and only about a fifth are schizophrenic or borderline (Knesper, Belcher, & Cross, 1988), therapists who attempt to maintain their practices close to these identified "optimal dosage" levels may be able to reduce the number of sessions they spend with each patient and offer services to more people who need help. It must be remembered that these numbers represent averages, and not all patients will feel better after only 8, or even 26 sessions, regardless of their initial problems. Moreover, attempts at cost saving by limiting psychotherapy may end up more expensive in the long run by forcing patients to be hospitalized to get the treatment they need—a much more costly way to receive therapy (Goode & Wagner, 1993). Although some form of compromise may be needed whereby patients pay more of the cost the longer they stay in therapy (Goode & Wagner, 1993), it seems likely that psychotherapy will continue to be supported at some level as long as it continues to demonstrate its effectiveness.

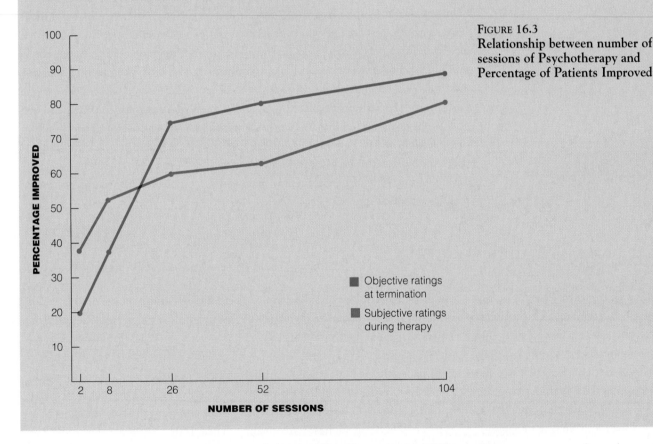

FIGURE 16.3
Relationship between number of sessions of Psychotherapy and Percentage of Patients Improved

In addition, the effectiveness of different therapies seems to depend, to a large extent, on the particular disorder being treated. Behavioral therapies are, as noted, particularly effective at treating anxiety problems and phobias. These disorders also happen to be the easiest to find when college students are the source of the patient population, as has been the case in many of the successful behavioral studies. This result may at least partially explain the apparent superiority of some therapies in some studies and other therapies in other studies. The skill and experience of the therapist at the particular form of therapy is also a relevant factor, especially in studies that use undergraduate students as patients and graduate students as therapists. It is also important to be certain that patients have been exposed to sufficient therapy to produce an effect (see "Psychology in Our Times: Is There a Proper 'Dose' of Psychotherapy?"). Finally, the expectancies of the investigator might influence the outcome of the study if the experimenter is also the therapist and knows the hypotheses. It is thus extremely difficult to conclude that any one therapy is better or worse than any other. Overall, however, it seems that the major forms of therapy, when practiced by competent therapists on appropriate patients, are significantly more effective at alleviating psychological distress than is the absence of therapy.

COMMONALITIES AMONG THERAPIES

There is another possible explanation for the comparable success rates of different forms of psychotherapy. Although proponents of the various therapies center their attention on the distinctions between their perspective and the others, there are possibly more commonalities than differences among the techniques. It may be that these nonspecific common factors are responsible for at least a portion of the success of all the therapeutic techniques. Kirsch's (1990) discussion of the efficacy of any treatment, even a placebo, emphasizes the contribution of patient expectations to clinical improvement. Any therapy will capitalize on the patient's belief that the therapist is an expert who presumably is in business because he or she is able to help people. Further, psychotherapy provides hope to individuals who have been feeling hopeless. Add to this a nonjudgmental therapist who accepts the patient's description of the problem, validates the patient's feelings, and generally serves as an empathic listener, and you have a powerful prescription for relief. Talking about one's problems is a form of confession, which Pennebaker's (1988, 1989) work indicates is good not only for the soul, but for the body and psyche as well. The sum of all these "nonspecific" aspects of any type of psychotherapy may well be responsible for a large portion of their therapeutic success.

THEMES IN REVIEW

As you now realize, therapy for psychological dysfunction is a wide-ranging enterprise, encompassing many of the different views of psychology we have discussed in this book. There are contributions to therapy from the biological view, such as psychoactive drugs for alleviating the symptoms of depression, anxiety, or psychosis, as well as brain surgery or electroshock for more intractable depressions or emotional disruptions. The cognitive approach has contributed several therapies aimed at changing irrational or maladaptive thought patterns to produce improved psychological functioning. Learning theory underlies the behavior therapies, which teach patients to replace dysfunctional feelings and behaviors with incompatible healthy ones. Finally, the sociocultural view of psychopathology has changed over the centuries, and approaches to treatment have changed accordingly. As long as pathology was seen as the result of demons trapped within the person's head or body, treatment consisted of means of driving out the demons. Once it was recognized that these individuals were suffering, not possessed, therapies began to focus on the factors acting on the individual. Recently, the sufferer's social environment has come under scrutiny, and milieu therapies offer a healthy environment in which the individual can develop new social skills and learn to adjust to society. There is thus no single approach to psychotherapy, but rather a combination of approaches and techniques that together help individuals to overcome psychological problems and return to a healthier mode of functioning.

SUMMARY

❶ Through the centuries, society has attempted to deal with abnormal behavior in many ways. Several treatment approaches have been developed over the last few decades, and extensive training has been provided to the professionals who treat disordered behavior. These professionals are classified principally according to their educational backgrounds. Psychiatrists are physicians who have spent a postgraduate residency training in psychiatry. Clinical psychologists hold Ph.D.'s in psychology, and they have had extensive training in research and therapeutic techniques. Counseling psychologists have graduate training similar to that of clinical psychologists, but typically focus more on decision making in normal clients. Psy. D.'s are psychologists whose training places less emphasis on research. Psychiatric social workers hold master's degrees in social work and have special training in treatment procedures that emphasize the home and community. Psychiatric nurses are registered nurses with special training.

❷ Biological treatments for mental disorders are based on the assumption that the condition is due, in part, to physical causes. A variety of drugs are widely used to treat anxiety, depression, and schizophrenia, often in conjunction with psychotherapy. ECT appears to be a useful treatment for severe depression, although it has been replaced to some extent by drug therapy. Psychosurgery helped in calming patients, but because it seemed to rob them of all other emotions, it is no longer used.

❸ Classical psychoanalysis focuses on unconscious conflict as the source of disturbing symptoms. The goal of therapy is to help a client uncover these conflicts so that they may reside in conscious and rational awareness. In this method, the primary techniques are free association and the interpretation of the client's resistance to therapy. One important form of resistance is the transference to the therapist of the client's unconscious feelings about parents or other significant people from the client's past. An understanding of resistance and transference enables the therapist to help the client work through the conflict. Working through involves bringing to consciousness previously repressed wishes and memories. These may trigger catharsis, a major emotional release in which the client gains sudden insight into the dynamics of his or her personality. Currently, psychoanalytic therapies have been focused more on strengthening and understanding the client's ego.

❹ Behavior therapies are generally based on principles of learning and conditioning. Classical conditioning approaches involve systematic desensitization, in which the goal is to reduce anxiety, and aversion therapy, in which undesired behavior patterns are coupled with unpleasant stimuli. Operant approaches stress the modifiability of abnormal behavior through the use of contingent reinforcement. Modeling therapy, based on observational learning, has been used effectively both to eliminate unwanted behaviors and to build new behavioral competencies. Finally, an interesting aspect of the operant approach is biofeedback, which helps patients to alter physiological functions such as heart rate by providing information about changes in such responses.

❺ Recently principles of behavior therapy have been applied to cognition. Cognitive therapies attempt to modify thought patterns to influence emotions and behavior. This therapy is frequently used with depressed patients and eating-disorder patients, where an attempt is made to help them to stop thinking about themselves as worthless and substitute more positive thinking. Cognitive approaches to therapy are becoming more and more widely used. One early approach is Ellis's rational-emotive therapy (RET), in which a therapist helps a client to identify and eliminate irrational beliefs that are causing distress. Cognitive behavior modification, attribution therapy, and paradoxical intervention also focus on changing clients' thoughts about their problematic behaviors.

6 Humanistic approaches focus on people's current conscious experiences and feelings and especially their self-concepts. In Carl Rogers's person-centered therapy, the important elements are a nondirective stance, emphasis on the here and now of the person's experience, and the empathy and unconditional positive regard for the client by the therapist. In Gestalt therapy, developed by Fritz Perls, role-playing techniques and exercises and dream analysis are employed to make the client more self-aware. Existential therapy is based on a client's "way of being in the world." An individual is challenged to become more aware of existence and the purpose of life, especially through the experience of the therapeutic encounter.

7 A recent trend is the provision of therapy at the level of the group, family, or community. In group therapy, several unrelated individuals with similar problems meet with a therapist (or two therapists) in groups of four or more people. In family therapy, a couple or family meet with a therapist for treatment. The role of the community in treating and preventing mental illness has grown enormously in the past 20 years. Community resources that offer help include social milieu settings, halfway houses, and various forms of crisis intervention and prevention programs.

8 Ethical issues arise frequently in the area of psychotherapy. Issues of values (the therapist's versus the patient's) and confidentiality are the most common. Professional associations as well as the legal system have set up codes of conduct for therapists governing these and other areas of professional conduct.

9 There is considerable controversy about the effectiveness of psychotherapy. Many people question whether some therapies are more effective than others. Evaluation of the effectiveness of the different psychotherapies is hampered by numerous research problems, including the different criteria that each therapeutic approach demands for a cure. In general, though, the therapies seem more effective than their absence. Psychotherapy seems to accomplish in 8 weeks the level of improvement that community resources provide in two years. Moreover, the optimal amount of therapy may be between 8 weeks and a year. After that, the benefits may not be substantial. Finally, many therapies capitalize on certain common elements (such as empathic therapists) that may be the underlying curative factors that allow different therapies to maintain similar cure rates.

KEY TERMS

somatic (biological) therapies (p. 662)

psychotherapies (p. 662)

psychiatrist (p. 663)

clinical psychologist (p. 663)

counseling psychologist (p. 663)

psychiatric social worker (p. 663)

psychiatric nurse (p. 663)

drug therapy (p. 664)

antianxiety drugs (p. 665)

neuroleptics (p. 665)

antidepressants (p. 666)

electroconvulsive therapy (ECT) (p. 667)

psychosurgery (p. 670)

FOR CRITICALANALYSIS

1 Disorders such as depression may be treated by any of the biological methods (drugs, ECT, or surgery). Why do you suppose drug therapy is the most widely used treatment for this disorder? Is there one primary factor responsible for this, or do you think it is a combination of influences?

2 Masson's attack on psychotherapy (see the Controversy section on page 000) was published several years ago, but does not seem to have had much impact on the field. Why do you think this is?

3 Cognitive therapies have swept the psychotherapy field in the last decade or so. Why do you suppose cognitive therapies have become so popular recently? Why was Mary Cover Jones's behavioral treatment of phobias ignored in the 1920s but a dominant form of therapy during the 1960s and 1970s?

4 Group therapies of various kinds have become increasingly popular. Obviously, one reason for this would be that they are often quite cost-effective, treating several patients at once with just one or two therapists. What other reasons can you think of for advocating group or family therapies?

5 The research on therapy dosage seems to indicate that there are optimal amounts of exposure to therapy and that these differ for different sorts of disorders. What dangers do you see of making this sort of finding widely known?

Suggested Readings

BECK, A. T., RUSH, A. J., SHAW, B. F., & EMERY, G. (1979). *Cognitive therapy of depression*. New York: Guilford Press. A thorough presentation of the analysis and treatment of depression, focusing on Beck's cognitive theory of depression.

BOHART, A. C., & TODD, J. (1988). *Foundations of clinical and counseling psychology*. New York: Harper & Row. A comprehensive review of the major systems of psychotherapy, and of the principles of clinical psychology.

ELLIS, A. (1988). *How to stubbornly refuse to make yourself miserable about anything—Yes, anything!* Secaucus, NJ: Lyle Stuart. Ellis' latest handbook for changing ones self-statements and reactions to life, and a good example of his writing and theory.

ENDLER, N. S. (1982). *Holiday of darkness: A psychologist's personal journey out of his depression*. New York: Wiley. A readable account of a well-known psychologist's personal battle with depression. He discusses from firsthand experience the effects of various treatments.

GARFIELD, S. L., & BERGIN, A. E. (Eds.). (1986). *Handbook of psychotherapy and behavior change (3rd ed.)*. New York: Wiley. This large book has twenty-three different chapters by renowned practitioners and researchers in the treatment of abnormality. Every major orientation is represented, and the flavor is decidedly empirical and scholarly.

GAY, P. (Ed.). (1989). *The Freud reader*. New York: Norton. A well-edited, extremely well-organized selection of the writings of the master theorist and therapist, with helpful editorial notes.

HALEY, J. (1963). *Strategies of psychotherapy*. New York: Grune & Stratton. A classic, well-written discussion of Haley's and Milton Erickson's cognitive, directive therapeutic styles, with case examples and spiced by Haley's wry sense of humor.

NEZU, A. M., & NEZU, C. M. (1989). *Clinical decision making in behavior therapy*. Champaign, IL: Research Press. A problem-solving orientation to behavioral treatment.

ROGERS, C. R. (1970). *Client-centered therapy (2nd ed.)*. Boston: Houghton Mifflin. An extremely readable and enjoyable "classic" in the humanistic tradition, written by the master of the therapy.

YALOM, I. D. (1989). *Love's executioner, & other tales of psychotherapy*. New York: HarperCollins. A series of interesting case studies and reflections on therapy by a well-known group and individual humanistic therapist.

Psychology on the Internet

Teaching Clinical Psychology
(http://www1.rider.edu/~suler/tcp.html)

Developed primarily as an aid for instructors in clinical and abnormal psychology, group dynamics, psychotherapy, and psychological testing courses, this site contains descriptions of and materials for projects designed to give students hands-on experience with issues that arise in a therapy setting. Although most of these exercises are designed to be used as classroom projects, several can be done individually.

Psychiatry On-Line
(http://www.cityscape.co.uk/users/ad88/psych.htm)

"Psychiatry On-Line is an independent, free peer-reviewed journal available [only] on the World Wide Web." This on-line journal contains articles on various topics related to mental disorders and psychotherapy, abstracts of recently published research, links to other mental health sites, and a glossary of terms used by psychiatrists and clinical psychologists.

Electro-Convulsive Therapy
(http://text.nlm.nih.gov/nih/cdc/www/51txt.html)

Written as a joint National Institutes of Health/National Institute of Mental Health consensus statement on electro-convulsive therapy (ECT), this document presents answers to the following questions: What is the evidence that ECT is effective for patients with specific mental disorders? What are the risks and adverse effects of ECT? What factors should be considered by the physician and patient in determining if and when ECT would be an appropriate treatment? How should ECT be administered to maximize benefits and minimize risks? What are the directions for future research?

FreudNet: The A.A. Brill Library
(http://plaza.Interport.net/nypsan/)

FreudNet, maintained by the New York Psychoanalytic Institute and Society, contains links to information about the life and work of Sigmund Freud, links to resources in psychoanalysis and related fields, and on-line articles about issues in the field of psychoanalysis.

The Efficacy of Psychotherapy
(http://www.apa.org/practice/peff.html)

This site contains abstracts from and references to articles on the efficacy of psychotherapy.

SOCIAL PSYCHOLOGY

Chapter 17

DEVELOPMENTAL THEME
In what ways does mature love resemble a child's love of his or her mother?

BIOLOGICAL THEME
Does the presence of other people affect us physiologically?

LEARNING THEME
How are prejudices acquired?

COGNITIVE THEME
Do we change our attitudes on the basis of rational considerations?

SOCIOCULTURAL THEME
Are some nationalities more obedient than others?

Most of us think of restaurants as places to enjoy a meal. But what else, aside from eating, occurs in a restaurant? For one thing, we engage in social interaction, with our companions and with the restaurant staff. If researchers can get the staff to cooperate, people eating in the restaurant can also participate in a field experiment without even realizing it!

Imagine a typical scene: You have just sat down at your table for brunch, and a waitress approaches you, saying, "Good morning. My name is Kim, and I will be serving you this morning." Does this sound like an experiment? Not really. But now imagine that a random sample of other customers get the same greeting, except that "My name is Kim" is omitted from the introduction. Does this omission make a difference? When it comes to tipping, it makes a tremendous difference. In this study, diners tipped "Kim" an average of 23 percent and tipped the anonymous waitress only 15 percent.

In another study, diners at Mexican and Chinese restaurants tipped a server who squatted down at eye level when first greeting them an average of 16 percent, but only 13 percent if the server remained upright. Other studies have shown that it is not only the server who affects the size of the tip; in general, larger parties tend to give lower percentage tips, which is why restaurants will often add a fixed gratuity for parties of eight or more.

Imagine another restaurant scenario: You have just finished a satisfying meal. The waitress approaches with a dessert menu and provides a graphic, appetizing description of the available desserts. Again, this not an unusual experience, but now consider the contrast. Other diners are simply handed dessert menus with no verbal elaboration. More than 70 percent of the diners in the description condition ordered dessert, compared to fewer than 50 percent of the diners in the menu-only condition.

These examples may appear trivial. What we do in a restaurant isn't all that important. Yet, the same principles that apply in the restaurant also apply in many other, more crucial situations. The restaurant examples are useful because they illustrate in a very clear and simple way the power of social factors in controlling our behavior. Very small changes in the behavior of the people around us can produce very large changes in our own behavior. How we react to situations often depends on the people around us, and this is true not only in trivial situations but also in situations of the utmost importance.

In America, there is an emphasis on individualism. In Japan, the notion of a fully independent self makes little sense.

Social psychology is the systematic study of the way our behavior (including our thoughts and feelings) is affected by the presence of other people. Whether they intend to or not, other people cause us to behave differently from the way we would if we were alone. Indeed, even when we are alone, other people may still influence us, because so much of our individual behavior is based on social relationships. Even when studying by yourself in your room, you remain caught in the social network that makes studying—or at least doing well academically—important. It seems impossible to over-estimate how powerful and pervasive social influences are. Our overt behavior often resembles a public performance (see Chapter 14, p. 602, for a discussion of Goffman's dramaturgical role theory of behavior). And even our interior life—how we think and feel about people and events, is affected by the thoughts and feelings of those around us. We may not be absolute slaves to social influence, but we are certainly affected.

American ideology encourages us to be independent. We pride ourselves on our self-reliant individualism. But ignoring the extent to which we are part of a social net-work can cause problems. By failing to recognize the importance of other people in our lives, we may jeopardize our social relationships (Sampson, 1989). Our attempts at self-reliance can even threaten our own psychological well-being, as when we refuse help from others or make too many demands on ourselves. In Japan and many other countries, the notion of a completely independent individual makes no sense: "The self is seen to be embedded in others" (Goldschmidt, 1990, p. 83), and "conformity to social expectations is not an unfortunate compromise but the only possible way to live" (Reich, 1992, p. 24). (Reich, by the way, sees this as a stereotype of the Japanese, who are certainly more socially conscious than Americans, but still individuals, not worker ants in a colony.) Do you see yourself as a self-reliant individual? Whether or not you do, how you see yourself is probably strongly colored by ideology and biases. Social psychology, by emphasizing our existence in a social world, often clashes with the basic assumptions of Western political thinking.

Social psychologists agree with personality and developmental psychologists that individuals differ from one another. At the same time, they believe that we tend to overestimate our individuality or uniqueness. They delight in pointing out how our individuality tends to disappear in certain powerful social situations (see Chapter 14, p. 591 for a discussion of "strong" versus "weak" situations).

In this chapter, we will review the major topics of social psychology. We will begin with social cognition, or person perception—how we perceive others. Then we will examine attraction—why we like some people more than others. Finally, we will examine the factors involved in social influence. How are our attitudes and behav-iors—such as our intention to order dessert (Olmsted, 1979) or leave large tips (Freeman, Walker, Borden, & Latané, 1975; Garrity & Degelman, 1990; Lynn & Mynier, 1993)—affected by the social situation? Social psychological processes are at work whenever we are with other people, in a restaurant or anywhere else, and even when we are alone, with our socially conditioned thoughts and motivations.

Social Cognition

Social cognition is the branch of social psychology concerned with the way we think about other people. Social cognition draws on what we know about memory (see Chapter 7) and information processing (see Chapter 8) and focuses on how infor-mation about people is acquired, stored, filtered, and retrieved (Sherman, Judd, & Park, 1989).

We may not perceive personality in quite the same way that we perceive freckles, but we do perceive personality, by interpreting appearance and behavior as a reflection of underlying traits.

Some of the questions in cognitive psychology—such as how our beliefs about an object or idea affect how we process new information about that object or idea—apply to people as well as to inanimate objects or ideas. But social cognition differs in some important ways. For one thing, when we perceive a person, we perceive not only physical characteristics, but also psychological characteristics, such as motives and personality traits. (Of course, we cannot actually see personality traits and motives in the same way that we see someone's freckles; but we do infer what people are like from their appearance and behavior, and those inferences are a crucial part of perception.)

People differ from inanimate objects in another important way: Our perceptions of people can end up changing them. Whether I perceive you as hostile or friendly may well affect my behavior toward you, which in turn may affect your behavior toward me. If I perceive you as hostile, you may well become hostile, even though my initial perception may not have been accurate (Snyder & Swann, 1978). In one study (Harris, Milich, Johnston, & Hoover, 1990), for example, boys were paired up to build a design using Lego blocks. One boy in each pair was told something about his partner: In half the pairs, he was told only the partner's name and grade; in the other half, he was told that his partner was from a special class for children with behavior problems (which was not true). The partners were not aware that anything had been said about them. After the cooperative task, the partners who supposedly had behavior problems reported having had much more difficulty with the task than did the "name-and-grade" partners. Evidently, the boys who believed their partners to be "problem children" treated them as problem children and made harsher demands on them. The "problem children" thus ended up experiencing more problems. Being labeled problem children created problems for these children. Rosenthal and Jacobson (1968) have shown how our expectations about people—especially teachers' expectations about students—can become self-fulfilling prophecies. (Also, see Chapter 15, page 613, for a discussion of the effects of labeling abnormal behaviors.)

How others view us can make a big difference in our reactions to them. It has been suggested that we fall in love with people who see us the way we would like to be seen. Perhaps we hate those who see us in a way we do not want to be seen.

PERSON PERCEPTION

Perceiving people is more than just identifying their characteristics (e.g., gregarious, warm, and helpful) and adding them up into an overall picture of the person. As we have already seen, psychological traits and motives are not perceived directly, but must be inferred, and these inferences can be mistaken. If a used-car salesman behaves in a gregarious, warm, and helpful fashion toward you, are you justified in concluding that he is a friendly person? Or might it be that his behavior is not so much a reflection of a warm personality as it is a reflection of his desire to sell a car?

Implicit personality theory refers to all the assumptions we make about the characteristics (in most cases, personality traits) that go together (Schneider, 1973). Thus, someone who is described as entertaining, energetic, and impulsive is also likely to be seen as outgoing, boisterous, and lively (Cantor & Mischel, 1977).

We often are given less information about someone than we need. In such cases, we tend to fill in the missing information based on our assumptions about how one characteristic usually goes with another. For example, people who wear glasses are perceived as more intelligent, introverted, and conscientious (Borkenau, 1991); males wearing glasses are seen as more masculine and females as more feminine (Harris, 1991). Are glasses really associated with these personality characteristics? Whether they are or not, we tend to infer these characteristics when all we really know is that the person wears glasses.

Because we know that other people are constantly perceiving and judging us (just as we perceive and judge them), we often try to control the impression that we make. This process is known as **impression management** (Schlenker & Weigold, 1992). Thus, actors may wear glasses in commercials not because they need them but simply to appear intelligent.

Other factors that influence how we perceive someone include the order in which information about the person is presented, our mood (Forgas & Bower, 1987), and our preconceptions about the person. Preconceptions may lead us to interpret ambiguous information so that it is consistent with what we already know or believe. (In a sexual assault case, for instance, the defense lawyer may try to make the jury aware of the victim's sexual history, while at the same time suppressing the defendant's previous criminal record, to bias the jury's interpretation of the evidence in favor of the defendant.)

Stereotypes. A **stereotype** is a particular kind of implicit personality theory, a generalization about a group of people that distinguishes those individuals from others in terms of personality and behavioral tendencies. Believing that someone who wears glasses is more conscientious than someone who does not wear glasses is an example of a stereotype. Although a stereotype may be held by one person alone (e.g., only you may believe that all psychologists are brilliant), social psychologists are usually more interested in shared stereotypes. For example, overweight people are perceived as unintelligent, socially dependent, lazy, and lacking in self-discipline (DeJong & Kleck, 1986), and attractive people are perceived as more socially competent, better adjusted, and more intelligent (but also more vain) than unattractive people (Eagly, Ashmore, Makhijani, & Longo, 1991). Even names can trigger positive or negative stereotypes: Teachers evaluated a child's essay more positively when they thought the essay was written by a David or a Lisa than when they thought that the author was a Hubert or a Bertha (Harari & McDavid, 1973). Almost every identifiable group, from stamp-collectors to movie stars to Texans, is associated with certain stereotyped personality traits.

Stereotypes can be general or specific. For instance, we might view athletes as stupid ("dumb jocks"). But if we were to encounter a smart athlete, rather than abandon the stereotype, we might create a more specific stereotype of "smart athletes," leaving the more general "dumb jock" stereotype intact (Pryor & Ostrom, 1987). Our willingness to create new substereotypes to handle exceptions, while leaving the old stereotype unchanged, explains why it is so difficult to combat stereotypes: Even numerous exceptions to the rule do not seem to affect the rule.

You might be interested to learn that Lederman (1990) found that college athletes had higher GPAs and higher graduation rates than did non-athlete students. Are you willing to alter your stereotype (assuming that you have one), or do you find yourself trying to "explain away" the results of Lederman's study? Just as a mental exercise, try to explain why "dumb jocks" might have done better than the nonathletes in Lederman's study.

Ingroups Versus Outgroups. How you perceive a particular group depends critically on whether you are a member of that group. *In-groups* (groups you belong to) are perceived quite differently from *outgroups* (groups you do not belong to). One major difference is that members of outgroups are perceived as being more similar to one another than are members of ingroups (Mullen & Hu, 1989). For instance, members of

Whether we see a group as being "all alike" or not depends on whether we are members of that group. We see other groups as more homogeneous than our own.

Princeton University's "eating clubs" (fraternities) saw members of their own clubs as varying more in personality than members of other clubs (Jones, Wood, & Quattrone, 1981). Similarly, students rated residents of a retirement community as more homogeneous in personality than the students themselves; the retirees, on the other hand, considered the students to be "all alike" (Linville, Fischer, & Salovey, 1989).

It is important to recognize that we do not belong to only one ingroup. The relevant ingroup (and the corresponding outgroup) changes with the context. Sometimes we may distinguish between ingroup and outgroup on the basis of sex; in other contexts we may make the distinction on the basis of age, skin color, ethnicity, religion, vegetarianism, or almost any other characteristic that can distinguish one group from another. The sorts of factors that lead us to think in terms of one characteristic rather than another can be manipulated in the laboratory. Imagine that you are a tall male: if you find yourself in a group with three other tall males and four short males, the ingroup for you is likely to be "tall people." If you find yourself with three other tall males and four tall females, the ingroup for you is likely to be "males."

Edgar (1993, p. 11), notes that anthropology tends to "exaggerate the differences between cultures and make others seem more alien than they are in reality. [Also,] in trying to identify what is typical in a culture, one risks smoothing over contradictions, conflicts of interest, doubts and arguments, not to mention changing motivations and historical circumstances, thereby giving the erroneous impression that culture is something homogeneous and unchanging." Thus, the outgroup homogeneity bias applies to other cultures as well as to other groups in our own culture. Social scientists tend to describe alien groups in terms of generalizations that undoubtedly contribute to our seeing these outgroups as homogeneous. Oakes and Turner (1990), however, point out that generalizations about other groups are not simply "defects" in the way we handle social information. They argue that categorization is an essential part of thinking. In other words, we can think about large numbers of other people only by grouping them. Unfortunately, grouping leads us to assume homogeneity. But as you will see in the next section, the fact that we have this cognitive tendency does not mean that we cannot overcome it.

Another reason we may overlook differences among outgroup members is that we see them less often—that is, in fewer and more restricted situations. We see members of our own group in a wide variety of situations (Quattrone, 1986) and so are likely to see them behaving in all sorts of different ways. We rarely get to know outgroup members well enough to see them as unique individuals with complex personalities.

Although we see outgroup members as more homogeneous than ingroup members, ingroup members appear to us as more homogeneous than individuals who are not a member of any group. We assume that other members of our group are similar to us in attitudes and behaviors that have nothing to do with group membership (Allen & Wilder, 1979). For instance, most students tend to assume that other students, as members of their ingroup, are like them in many respects, including attitudes and behaviors that have little to do with academics. This assumption, sometimes called the "false consensus effect," is natural but often incorrect. An important part of growing up is recognizing that people similar to you in one respect (e.g., sex, age, occupation, or ethnicity) are not necessarily like you in other ways.

PREJUDICE

We often see outgroups not only as different, but as worse. **Prejudice** toward another group has a cognitive component (negative perceptions), an emotional component

"Well, of COURSE I did it in cold blood, you idiot!...I'm a reptile!"

(hostile feelings), and often a behavioral component (discriminatory actions). We are motivated to see ourselves and our ingroups positively, to support our self-esteem (Tajfel & Turner, 1986). But there seems to be an equally strong motivation to see outgroups negatively, perhaps because that makes us feel better about ourselves, too.

In the study of social perception described earlier (Linville et al., 1989), both the students and the senior citizens tended to rate their own group more favorably than they rated the other group. Even when the ingroup is based on some relatively trivial characteristic (e.g., college major or type of music enjoyed) or is entirely arbitrary—as when Tajfel (1982) assigned subjects completely at random to two groups—we quickly come to regard our own group as superior, especially when there is no objective measure of superiority. Subjects divided into groups simply on the basis of whether they tended to overestimate or underestimate the number of dots presented on a slide tended to assign positive traits to their own group and negative traits to the other group (Howard & Rothbart, 1980). Our tendency to view our ingroup positively is especially strong when the ingroup is particularly salient, as happens when it is relatively small compared to the out-group (Mullen, 1991). When in a largely black neighborhood, white-skinned people are likely to be much more aware of their skin color and feel part of an ingroup with other white-skinned people than when they are in a mostly white neighborhood. The opposite will be true for black-skinned people.

The tendency to look down on and discriminate against outgroups seems to be a part of human nature. This leads some people to the troubling conclusion that because it is "natural" to disparage people who are unlike us, we cannot really be held responsible for discriminating against them. Fiske (1989) describes her nightmare of having to testify in a discrimination case and being forced to admit that psychology's message is that people will discriminate whether they intend to or not. And if discrimination is unintentional, can we punish it legally? According to Fiske, "the idea that categorization is a natural and adaptive, even dominant, way of understanding other people does not mean that it is the only option available" (p. 277). Fiske concludes that if we have a legitimate option—namely, treating people as individuals rather than stereotyping them as a homogeneous outgroup—then the stereotyping may be considered intentional (and blameworthy).

Critics of children's organized sports have noted how being part of an arbitrarily composed team breeds a competitive, aggressive attitude toward other teams (Rehm, Steinleitner, & Lilli, 1987). Perhaps the most famous study demonstrating this effect involved two cabins of campers. These groups were kept separate during daily activities and then engaged in a series of competitions, which served only to exaggerate the hostility that had already surfaced between them. Bringing the groups together on social occasions did not help to relieve the tension between them, nor did religious services appealing for brotherly love. But when the groups were forced to cooperate on projects (rescuing a food truck, fixing the water supply), barriers between the groups broke down and friendships developed (Sherif et al., 1961).

We tend to idealize the characteristics of our ingroups. Hatfield and Sprecher (1986) coined the term *Henry Finck syndrome* in memory of the upper-class British gentleman and scholar Henry Finck (1887), whose extensive research proved beyond doubt that in terms of personal beauty, evolution had reached its pinnacle in the appearance of none other than the upper-class British gentleman! More serious scholars have shown how we tend to value our own characteristics and devalue other characteristics—physical "deformities," such as obesity; character "flaws," such as homosexuality; and tribal identities, such as race—that depart from the ingroup's norm. A **stigma** is a mark of "undesired differentness" that is imposed by the socially dominant ingroup on various outgroups who violate the in-group's ideals (Stafford & Scott, 1986).

Group membership appears to be a strong contributor to prejudice toward outgroups, but other factors are probably important as well. Our experiences may play a role; a specific negative incident involving people who are clearly outgroup members can produce or reinforce negative attitudes. Prejudice can also be passed down through families. Children often display their parents' prejudices even though the children—and sometimes even the parents—have had no personal experiences that would justify their attitudes. Similarly, our friends and acquaintances may create an environment in which prejudice is the norm. Finally, prejudice may be forced on us, as in South Africa, where racial discrimination was until recently institutionalized in the law. Failure to act in a racist manner was punished by social ostracism, fines, or even imprisonment (Foster & Finchilescu, 1986). As the laws change in South Africa, it will be interesting to see how quickly prejudice declines. In the United States, where the laws generally prohibit discrimination, social prejudices are still very obvious.

Considering our own prejudices raises disturbing questions about the difficulty of eliminating prejudice from our society. Can you think of times when you have acted out of prejudice? Where do you think your attitudes came from? Family? Friends? The media? Have you ever intervened to stop someone from behaving in a discriminatory way against someone other than yourself? Do you consider yourself less prejudiced than average? If so, you are probably like most people. When people act out of prejudice, they usually have a "good reason" for it, which allows them to think of themselves as unprejudiced.

Whatever the social norms may be, some people will be more prejudiced than others. Where do individual differences in prejudice come from? Some psychologists believe that prejudice is mostly a matter of personality dynamics. Psychodynamic theorists argue that frustration causes aggression (Dollard, Doob, Miller, Mowrer, & Sears, 1939), which is vented on suitable (preferably weak) outgroup targets (Volkan, 1988). In an attempt to explain the racial bigotry of Nazi Germany, T. W. Adorno, E. Frenkel-Brunswik, D. Levenson, and R.N. Sanford wrote *The Authoritarian Personality* (1950). In that book they argued that authoritarian personalities resulted from a severe upbringing combining obedience to authority—a topic that we will explore later in this chapter—and harsh rejection of outgroups. Authoritarian individuals denounce outgroups and idealize ingroups, perhaps because ingroups play the same role for adults that parents do for children (Group for the Advancement of Psychiatry, 1987). Psychoanalytic thinkers believe that authoritarian individuals project their own negative traits onto others—seeing others as full of malice, for instance. And of course, if others are malicious, then it makes perfect sense to have negative feelings toward them! Projection thus justifies our prejudices while at the same time making us seem innocent. Researchers have found some support for the idea that prejudice is related to personality characteristics (Cherry & Byrne, 1976), but most social psychologists point to social norms as another powerful source of prejudice. Whether it would be easier to change prejudicial social norms or to change prejudicial personality structure is not clear; at the moment, deep-seated prejudices seem unlikely to yield easily to the interventions of social scientists.

Even though prejudice seems to be a major part of social life, it can be reduced with hard work. Some social norms can be changed through legislation, the most famous example being the U.S. Supreme Court decision outlawing public school segregation based on race (Brown v. Board of Education of Topeka, 1955). The law forced changes

By projecting his own hatred onto Jews and other helpless minorities—claiming that the Germans were the victims, not the perpetrators—Adolf Hitler justified his bigotry as a "normal" response. The fact that so many Germans followed his lead suggests that broad social pressures rather than individual differences in personality were responsible for the sort of widespread prejudice found in Nazi Germany. Mainstream American society is not without prejudice against relatively weak outgroups at home and abroad.

Racially segregated facilities, such as these 1950s restrooms in South Carolina, have been almost entirely eliminated, but subtler forms of discrimination are still prevalent in American society. Note that we still take it for granted that there ought to be sex segregation in restroom facilities. Is that a form of discrimination?

Stereotypes based on sex tend to interfere with accurate perception of people, and often contribute to discrimination against weaker groups.

in overt behavior, which eventually produced changes in attitudes. Whites have become more favorable toward blacks (Dovidio & Gaertner, 1986), or at least more reluctant to express their prejudices than they once were (Gaertner & Dovidio, 1986). More favorable attitudes toward outgroups may also develop when people have positive contacts with outgroup members (Hewstone & Brown, 1986). Racial antagonisms have been reduced by means of integrated public housing (Deutsch & Collins, 1951) and by the creation of integrated cooperative teams, especially if both races are equally represented (Miller & Davidson-Podgorny, 1987). Simply bringing racially diverse people together, however, is not as effective as bringing them together in a situation in which they have positive experiences with each other (as with the rival camp cabins we described earlier).

Although modern American society officially frowns on prejudice, it is not easy to eliminate. We may not express our prejudices openly, but we still are aware of the racial stereotypes (Devine, 1989), and certain circumstances may bring hidden prejudices. For instance, when people are in a bad mood, they become more likely to endorse stereotypes of outgroups (Isen, Daubman, & Gorgoglione, 1987) and to express their prejudices (Esses & Zanna, 1989).

The tendency to see outgroup members as "all alike" and lacking individuality certainly contributes to prejudice. One advantage of having close contact with outgroup members is that we are more likely to see them as individuals—as more human, more like us—and therefore less deserving of prejudice and discrimination.

Of course, not all prejudice is based on race. Almost any characteristic can be used to divide people into two or more groups. One obvious division is based on gender. Sexism—discrimination based on gender—is now acknowledged as a significant form of prejudice. Stereotypes exaggerate the differences between the sexes (Eagly & Steffen, 1984) and mask differences within each sex group. Research on sex roles confirms what most of us already know: males are not all alike, nor are females; indeed, the difference between the average male and the average female on most psychological and behavioral characteristics is much smaller than differences within the sexes. While many feminists argue against stereotyping based on sex, some argue that women as a group are different from but not worse (and in many ways better) than men. Social psychology would probably argue that it is a mistake for feminists to emphasize the differences between males and females—even if females are better!—because differentiation usually is associated with stereotyping, prejudice, and discrimination. If we cannot see differences between groups of people, then we cannot discriminate against them.

Members of groups that are the target of prejudice are often confused as to whether they want others to regard their group as just as good as other groups, or whether they want to escape membership in the group altogether. Historically, some Jews chose to become assimilated to the Christian majority when prejudice was intense, as in 1492 Spain, while others fought to reverse the negative stereotype. Obese people are torn between wanting to become thin and escape the stereotype and trying to get society to stop persecuting fat people. The National Association to Advance Fat Acceptance combats prejudice and discrimination against the obese, but most overweight people do not accept their own fatness.

IMPRESSION FORMATION

When we do not have much information about someone, we may use stereotypes or implicit personality theory to fill in the gaps. But what happens when we are given lots of information about someone? How do we organize that information into a coherent picture? **Impression formation** is the process through which we gather and combine information about a person. Our implicit personality theories undoubtedly affect how we process information about others. We are more likely to see what our stereotypes lead us to expect to see. For instance, I am more likely to remember to include the trait "absentminded" when I am constructing a mental image of a professor than when I am constructing a mental image of a business executive, even if I am told that they are both absentminded. **Illusory correlation** is the tendency to overestimate how much certain types of people—usually minority groups—display highly noticeable, usually undesirable traits or behaviors (e.g., mental patients are often thought to be dangerous, when in reality they tend to be less socially aggressive than normal) (Mullen & Johnson, 1990). If we are part of the minority group, however, we tend to assume that minority group members have positive traits and behaviors (Schaller, 1991). We generally notice instances that confirm our belief and ignore the instances that do not support the stereotype.

Most impression formation research is concerned with how particular pieces of information affect the overall impressions we construct. Early studies by Asch (1946) and Kelley (1950) presented subjects with a brief description of an individual who was either "intelligent, skillful, industrious, warm, determined, practical, and cautious" or "intelligent, skillful, industrious, cold, determined, practical, and cautious." The single change in the list—from "warm" to "cold"—had a profound effect on the way the target was viewed (see Figure 17.1).

The order in which we obtain information about someone will also affect the impression we derive. In general, the first piece of information carries the most weight; thus, the "warm" versus "cold" difference would have been even greater had these terms occurred at the beginning of the list (Luchins, 1957). This finding is reflected in the general belief about the importance of first impressions; we are more likely to create an overall positive impression if we lead off with positive information and save the negatives for later.

Why does early information carry more weight? One possibility is the *change-of-meaning hypothesis*, first suggested by Asch (1946). According to this hypothesis, an

FIGURE 17.1
Asch's Impression-Formation Experiment

Students participating in this experiment read a description of a person and then selected other traits that would apply to that person. The description was either "intelligent, skillfull, industrious, *cold*, determined, practical, cautious" or "intelligent, skillful, industrious, *warm*, determined, practical, cautious." As shown here, changing *cold* to *warm* made subjects think of the person as much more generous, wise, happy, and good-natured, but not more reliable or important.

SOURCE: Asch, 1946.

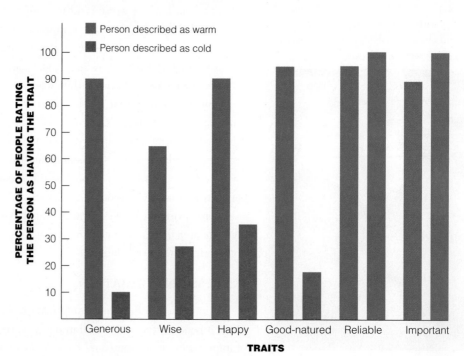

item occurring early in a series may affect how we interpret later items. In our example, the adjective "determined" may have a different, more positive meaning when it follows "warm" than when it follows "cold." Another explanation stems from the *primacy effect* in memory (see Chapter 7), with early items remembered better than later items (Anderson & Hubert, 1963; McKelvie, 1990).

Understanding impression formation can have practical value for you when you apply to graduate school or apply for a job. You naturally want others to form a positive impression of you, but how do you maximize that positive impression? You may be faced with the problem of whether to include a letter of recommendation that will probably be only mildly positive. Are you better off including a weak positive letter in your file or having fewer, more positive letters? Anderson (1965, 1974) has developed a weighted averaging model of impression formation that suggests that you are better off submitting only the most positive letters. Although some items of information (such as those encountered first) may be weighted more heavily, in general the items are averaged rather than added. Thus, two highly positive (+4) letters combined with a weakly positive (+1) letter are more likely to yield a less positive impression (average = +3) than the two positive letters alone (average = +4). As those of us who have served on graduate school admissions committees can testify, letters of recommendation tend to be so positive that a letter that is only mildly positive can doom a candidate's chances.

SELF-PERCEPTION

We develop impressions not only of others, but also of ourselves. **Self-perception** refers to how we see and evaluate ourselves. For example, if you are asked, "Are you shy with strangers?" you may quickly respond "Yes!" But how do you know that you are shy? Probably you remember occasions when you reacted timidly when approaching strangers. Bem (1967, 1972) has proposed that the way we come to know ourselves is not all that different from the way we come to know others. In most cases, we depend on our own overt behavior to tell us what we are like. Just as we infer how hungry other people are from watching them eat, so we may decide how hungry we are from observing how much we eat.

Admittedly, when you try to figure out how shy or hungry you are, you have an extra source of information that you cannot use to figure out others—your internal state. In the case of shyness, you may experience intense anxiety in social situations. Still, you must learn to interpret your internal feelings. How do you know that it is anxiety that you are feeling, rather than sexual arousal or even hunger?

How we interpret our inner feelings depends on what we were taught as children. Children must be taught that what they are feeling in certain situations is "shyness." Such learning is not automatic and may go wrong. Bruch (1961) suggests that obesity may result when children are not taught properly to distinguish between anxiety and hunger, with the result that they eat whenever they are anxious (as well as when they are hungry). Even if we do learn to identify our internal signals accurately, we may have trouble interpreting them when they are especially weak or ambiguous. When you are at the top of the ferris wheel with your boyfriend or girlfriend, is it love or just dizziness? (In Chapter 13, we saw how our interpretations of our emotions may depend on how we analyze the situation.)

Those of you who find it difficult to believe that we do not simply look inside ourselves (introspect) to discover what we really like or what we are feeling should consider the world of pop psychology. Magazines and popular psychology books continue to offer "personality tests" that do little more than tell us what we should have known in the first place. "Are you a binge eater?" "Are you a secret worrier?" "Are you a good lover?" Often we find the answer by responding to questions that basically ask us whether we are binge eaters or secretly anxious or good lovers. Our scores on these tests simply reflect our own judgment of what we are like, but a score on some printed test somehow seems more valid than our introspective judgments, even though the test score is based on our introspective judgments. Moreover, consider the popularity of mood rings. How do you know how you feel? Not by examining your own feelings, but by examining the color of your ring stone, which supposedly "tells you" your emotions.

When it comes to attitudes and opinions, which are often weak, self-perception effects may be very dramatic. For instance, in one study (Wells & Petty, 1980), subjects were asked to move their heads to test their headphones while listening to a speech. Subjects instructed to nod their heads up and down ended up agreeing with the message of the speech more than subjects instructed to shake their heads back and forth. Sometimes, it seems, we agree because we nod our heads instead of nodding our heads because we agree! In another study, subjects who were assigned partners and instructed to gaze into each other's eyes rated themselves as more attracted to their partners (Kellerman, Lewis, & Laird, 1989). Presumably, the subjects inferred that they were attracted to their partners because they engaged in mutual gazing, a well-known sign of love. Although these studies are fascinating, we must remember that people who infer what they feel or think from their overt behavior are probably unsure about their feelings to begin with.

The problem with trying to judge what we are like by observing our own behavior is that our behavior is not always a true reflection of who we are. Sometimes our behavior is dictated by the situation we are in rather than by our inner nature (Ross & Nisbett, 1991). Humphrey (1985) randomly assigned subjects to be "managers" or "clerks" in a simulated office. After acting as managers and clerks for two hours, subjects were asked to rate themselves and the others on various traits. "Managers" tended to rate themselves and other managers as higher than clerks in intelligence, leadership, and other positive traits—and the "clerks" agreed! Of course, the "managers" were not really more intelligent than the "clerks." It was the role they were playing that made them appear superior, but everyone ignored that when judging personality. People from the higher social classes tend to favor explanations based on personal qualities (e.g., "People who get ahead in life do so because of their character"), probably because they prefer to believe that people get what they deserve (Gurin, Gurin, & Morrison, 1978). According to their logic, they need not feel guilty about their privileges, since they have earned them.

Social Comparison.   Self-perception involves judging ourselves on various dimensions. Of course, many skills and abilities can be judged only relative to the performance of other people. In his **social comparison** theory, Festinger (1954) described how we compare ourselves with others. For social comparisons to be helpful, we must compare ourselves with people who are relatively close to us on the dimension in question. It is not very useful to judge your strength by arm wrestling with an Olympic weight lifter or with a toddler. It is more appropriate to consider yourself "strong" if you can defeat all the other students in your psychology class. Of course, just knowing how strong you are is not your only motivation. If you are like most people, you prefer to be superior to those roughly comparable to you. Festinger (1954) referred to this as the "unidirectional drive upward." People generally prefer to do better and better and to compare themselves to progressively higher standards.

Self-esteem. Self-esteem is a person's overall judgment of his or her value as a person. People try to maintain a high level of self-esteem or to raise their self-esteem if it is low. Comparing yourself with others who are not doing as well as you is a familiar tactic to protect your self-esteem. Self-esteem has more than one component: We may feel positively about our race but negatively about our athletic prowess. Self-esteem is also unstable: We may feel positively about our athletic ability on Friday but negative about it on Monday. In other words, when you think about yourself, the particular self that you think about may vary. It seems that we have multiple selves (Hoelter, 1985; Markus & Sentis, 1982). Being in an athletic situation brings out our athletic self, which may not be our favorite version of who we are. We may feel much better if we are in a situation that emphasizes our ethnicity. So one reason we may be more comfortable in some situations than in others is that we have different selves in these different situations and we prefer some selves to others.

How we see ourselves depends in part on our perspective at the time. If you are asked, "What things do you dislike about loud parties?" you will end up seeing yourself as more introverted than if you are asked, "What would you do to liven things up at a party?" (Fazio, Effrein, & Falender, 1981). Thus, you can manipulate how people feel about themselves by asking the right questions. Polivy and Herman (1991) made dieters feel good about themselves—"Do you frequently deny yourself food that you would like to eat?"—or bad about themselves—"Do you sometimes eat food that you know you shouldn't?"—just by having them fill out different questionnaires highlighting either the positive or negative side of their normal behavior.

Self-Consciousness. We are not always busy analyzing and evaluating ourselves. Recently, psychologists have begun to study the factors that increase or decrease our focus on ourselves. For instance, looking in a mirror or appearing in front of an audience tends to make everyone more self-conscious (Carver & Scheier, 1981). But certain people tend to focus on themselves more than others do. In fact, there are personality tests designed to identify people who are high or low in chronic, or trait, self-consciousness (Fenigstein, Scheier, & Buss, 1975).

Often, focusing on ourselves is unpleasant, especially if it reminds us of how far we are from our ideals (see the discussion of self-discrepancy theory in Chapter 14, page 584). People frequently attempt to escape from self-awareness, some by throwing themselves into mindless activities, others by immersing themselves in hobbies or distractions that focus their attention away from themselves. The use of drugs and alcohol (Hull, 1981), certain sexual practices (Baumeister, 1989), and even suicide (Baumeister, 1990) have all been seen as ways of escaping the self. People who find themselves doing things that they cannot square with their conscience will often obsessively focus on the technical details of the job rather than on its larger, moral implications. Thus, Lifton (1986), in his study of the German doctors who assisted in the Holocaust, found that they avoided thinking about the meaning of what they were doing and focused instead on the "technical" problems of mass murder. A similar attempt to become machinelike—to avoid thinking about the implications of their actions—may be found in the teams responsible for carrying out death sentences in our prisons (Johnson, 1990).

We have multiple selves. We may feel good about our athletic self and be disappointed in our social self (or vice versa).

MINORITIES AND SELF-ESTEEM

As we saw in our discussion of prejudice, people tend to think poorly of members of other groups. Members of minority groups who are discriminated against may eventually come to accept these negative views of themselves and develop low self-esteem. In recent years, various groups on college campuses throughout the United States have demanded that the curriculum be broadened to cover the history and culture of such minorities. Presumably, studying these minority cultures will help to raise the esteem in which the culture is held. By the same token, minority group members should feel better about themselves if their own culture is included in the curriculum.

It has long been assumed that the negative stereotypes of blacks, so pervasive in American culture, would prevent African American children from developing high self-esteem. We are frequently reminded of the black child who chooses a white doll over a black doll because she believes that the white doll is "prettier." Imagine, then, how this black girl must feel about herself. Surprisingly, some recent research suggests that members of stigmatized minorities often manage to maintain a relatively positive self-image. Black Americans tend to score at least as high as white Americans on measures of self-esteem. Considering all the negative messages that African Americans are subjected to, it is remarkable to find that they do not have a particularly negative opinion of themselves.

Why is black self-esteem so high? Perhaps it is because African Americans derive their self-image from their parents, teachers, and peers rather than from the white-dominated society as a whole. Black Americans engage in social comparison with other blacks rather than with whites (Rosenberg & Simmons, 1972). What this means is that they do not suffer by comparison, since the comparison standard is just about where they are. Ironically, as African Americans become more comparable to whites economically and otherwise, they may begin to compare themselves with whites and become less satisfied (Tajfel & Turner, 1986).

Hughes and Demo (1989) distinguish among three components of self-esteem. Personal self-esteem, based on relationships with family and friends, tends to run high in African Americans. Racial self-esteem, or pride in one's group, has increased for young blacks over the past two decades. Personal efficacy, the sense that one can exert control over one's life, remains lower for blacks than for whites. Racial discrimination thus appears to detract from African Americans' sense of power and authority, but not from their sense of self-worth.

In general, stigmatized people (not just blacks) tend to have higher self-esteem than you might expect, considering their group membership. Crocker and Major (1989) suggest three reasons for the relatively high self-esteem of

ATTRIBUTION

We are all psychologists, interested in why people (including ourselves) act the way they do. **Causal attribution** is the process by which we attempt to figure out the causes of behavior. How we explain behavior can have a major impact on how we perceive our social world. If someone compliments you, is it because you are particularly worthy or because someone wants to get on your good side (Jones, 1964)? It is often hard to tell why people act the way they do or why things work out the way they do, and this ambiguity can create unexpected problems. For instance, because of affirmative action programs, African Americans risk having people attribute their successes to favoritism rather than merit (Carter, 1991). This can undermine their self-esteem, even while they are succeeding! While a student at Yale Law School, for example, Supreme Court Associate Justice Clarence Thomas resented affirmative action, because he felt that it led others to assume that he could not succeed on his own (Toobin, 1993). For all of us, causal attribution is important in evaluating our academic success. Are your generally good grades really due to your being so smart, or are you merely benefiting from easy tests designed to accommodate your dull classmates? What about that bad grade

stigmatized people. First, they are able to blame some of their negative experiences on others' prejudice, rather than on their own personal failings. Indeed, Geen (1991) notes that after personal failures, people may suddenly increase their identification with some stigmatized group, precisely to allow themselves to blame group prejudice for their failure. They may still have problems, but they do not trace them back to a defect in themselves. Thus, in one interesting study (Crocker, Voelkl, Testa, & Major, 1991), blacks who were rated poorly by white raters felt bad only if the rater had not seen them, but had merely judged their written self-descriptions (which did not mention race). If the rater had seen them, they could conclude that the negative rating was based on prejudice; but if the rater had not seen them and did not know that they were black, then the low rating was assumed to be based on the poor impression that they made, so their self-esteem fell.

Derrick Bell (1992a), a black professor, argues that racism is a permanent part of American society. But far from creating despair, Bell argues that perceiving American society as fundamentally racist can be an uplifting experience for blacks: "It reaffirms that it is not their fault" (Bell, 1992b). Ironically, then, open prejudice may be less harmful to self-esteem than hidden prejudice. Of course, even though the recognition of prejudice sometimes serves to protect self-esteem, eliminating prejudice altogether remains a goal to which most social psychologists subscribe. Observers such as Bell (1992a), however, consider the task impossible.

Another group with surprisingly high (slightly above average) self-esteem are victims of sexual abuse (Gomes-Schwartz, Horowitz, & Cardarelli, 1990). Could it be that these people have something other than themselves to

blame for their failings? Wolfe (1992) echoes conventional wisdom in claiming that abused children could not possibly have high self-esteem, arguing that there must be something wrong with the way self-esteem was measured in the Gomes-Schwartz study.

One stigmatized group that is very low in self-esteem is the obese. Fat people, it seems, have been thoroughly convinced by their friends and family, the media, and the medical profession that their fatness is their own fault. Therefore, they cannot freely blame the prejudice of others when others put them down (Crocker, Cornwell, & Major, 1993). Groups such as the National Association to Advance Fat Acceptance must not only combat prejudice, but also convince fat people that prejudice is not something that they deserve.

A second reason given by Crocker and Major for the high self-esteem in stigmatized people is that they tend to engage in social comparison with others who are similarly stigmatized. In comparison to other stigmatized individuals, they may be relatively well off, or at least not much worse.

Finally, groups whose self-esteem is threatened tend to place a high value on the qualities that they have, and to dismiss the value of the characteristics or abilities that they lack (Dunning, Leuenberger, & Sherma, 1995). This tactic has the obvious advantage of protecting their self-esteem, because it means that what they have is good and what they do not have is not so good. Americans are often frustrated with outgroups in American society because outgroup members do not seem to value the things that the ingroup considers most valuable. We should understand that from the perspective of the outgroup, the important thing is to maintain group self-esteem, even if it sometimes means rejecting the values that the ingroup cherishes.

in chemistry? Is it because chemistry is so difficult or because the professor is unsympathetic to students—or unsympathetic to you in particular? Were you just unlucky, or are you just not very smart? The answers to these questions could conceivably have a major effect on your career choice.

When we witness an event or behavior, we act as "naive psychologists" and try to assign a cause for it. Heider (1944, 1958) suggested that there are two basic types of causes for someone's behavior: dispositional and situational. **Dispositional causes** are explanations for behavior that stem from an actor's character, motives, or abilities (e.g., Jack talks to Jill because he is a talkative person). **Situational causes** refer to explanations for an actor's behavior that stem from external or environmental forces, including other people (e.g., Jack talks to Jill because Jill talked to him first and social norms require him to respond). Of course, sometimes both dispositional and situational factors apply.

Kelley (1967) extended Heider's ideas and outlined some of the rules that people follow in making causal attributions. Let us analyze a simple scenario using Kelley's attributional principles of *distinctiveness*, *consensus*, and *consistency*. Suppose that Lisa praises me. Do I attribute Lisa's praise to her disposition or to something external to her, namely, my own wonderfulness?

1. Does Lisa reserve her praise only for me, or does she praise almost everyone? *Distinctiveness* refers to whether an individual always behaves in a certain way or whether the individual is behaving in a certain way just in one particular situation. If Lisa praises everyone, then I should make a dispositional attribution ("She is a flatterer"), whereas if she praises only me, then I should make a situational attribution ("It's something about me that's making her act that way").

2. Does only Lisa praise me, or does everyone praise me? If everyone praises me, then this high degree of *consensus* (agreement) suggests that it is something about me that elicits praise. If only Lisa praises me, then it is more likely a matter of her own disposition or motives.

3. How regularly does Lisa praise me? If her praise is irregular, then I cannot attribute it to either her disposition (since dispositions are enduring tendencies that should produce regular behavior) or to my own wonderfulness (since if I am a generally wonderful person, then the praise should be more regular). If her praise shows high *consistency*, or regularity, it might be either dispositionally or situationally caused. This simple example, diagrammed in Figure 17.2, indicates the sorts of complex calculations that we must often make to understand people's behavior.

Discounting and Augmenting. We often need additional information before making correct attributions, but sometimes that extra information just confuses the picture. If we end up with more than one explanation for a behavior, we may not know which interpretation to make. For example, if Alison helps Barry, with no expectation of gain, then the only plausible explanation is Alison's basic kindness. But if Alison expects some benefit from helping Barry, then Alison is perceived as less altruistic (Quigley, Gaes, & Tedeschi, 1989). In general, if we have only one plausible cause—such as an altruistic disposition—then making attributions is relatively simple. But if we add other possible explanations—such as expected rewards—then any particular explanation may get discounted. **Discounting** occurs when one explanation loses plausibility because of the presence of another possible explanation. Good scientists (see Chapter 1) try to design their studies so that they can see how much difference any single factor or independent variable makes. But if two factors are operating

FIGURE 17.2
Lisa Praises Me

Using Kelley's attributional principles of distinctiveness, consensus, and consistency allows me to decide whether there is really something praiseworthy in me or whether Lisa is just an ingratiating flatterer.

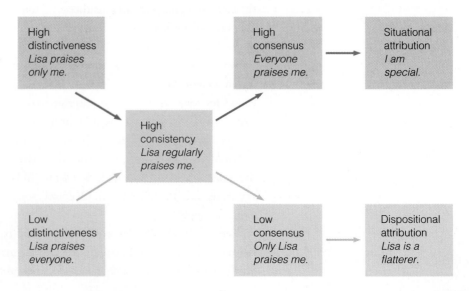

at the same time and behavior changes as a consequence, we cannot be sure which factor is really responsible for the effect.

An attributional principle opposite to discounting is **augmenting.** If you manage to succeed despite a clear handicap, or if you fail despite a clear advantage, your success or failure is seen as more extreme. African Americans who succeed are thus often rated higher than whites who achieve the same success, presumably because the African Americans had to overcome handicaps to achieve their success (Jussim, Coleman, & Lerch, 1987).

In Germany, if you commit a crime while drunk, the penalty is less severe than if you commit the same crime while sober. Being drunk is a discounting factor. In Canada, committing a driving offense while drunk is considered more serious than committing the same offense while sober. What do you think? Should being drunk discount or augment a crime?

Self-handicapping is a tactic that we use to minimize the implications of our failures or maximize the implications of our successes (Jones & Berglas, 1978). If I show up late for a test, then I "can't lose." If I fail, I have a built-in excuse, and if I succeed, then imagine how smart I must be to do well despite being late! Even better than actually handicapping yourself is simply claiming that you have a handicap when you really don't. Subjects in one study (Hirt, Deppe, & Gordon, 1991) were given the option of (a) handicapping themselves by failing to practice for a test or (b) merely claiming a handicap (stress) that would supposedly hurt their test performance. Subjects preferred to claim that they were stressed, because although the stress actually had no effect on performance, they still had an excuse for bad performance. Failing to practice also provided a good excuse for poor performance, but it also increased the chances of poor performance.

Expectations. When people behave in unexpected ways, our attributions about them are affected (Jones & McGillis, 1976). If someone behaves in a way that differs from what we would ordinarily expect from someone in that situation, we usually make a dispositional attribution. A football player who does needlepoint or an individual who refuses to stand for the national anthem is acting against the grain; there must be something about the individual that is producing the behavior. On the other hand, when someone we know pretty well behaves in a manner uncharacteristic for him or her, we will probably make a situational attribution. If someone who is normally good-natured and pleasant erupts in a burst of anger, we will probably conclude that something in the environment (and not the person's basic character) has provoked the outburst.

ATTRIBUTIONAL BIASES

Making accurate attributions for behavior is a tricky business. Often we lack sufficient information to select one probable cause and eliminate others. Even when we do have enough information, we may not use it properly or logically. Finally, we may make errors because we want to; it may be psychologically useful to us to identify a particular cause even if it is not the true one. Psychologists have recently begun to examine these cognitive, perceptual, and motivational attributional biases in some detail.

Cognitive and Perceptual Biases. Most people tend to use the first explanation that comes to mind, whether it is accurate or not. Information that is especially *accessible* (easily retrieved from memory) is more likely to be used in assigning causes for behavior or events (Wyer, 1981). An obvious example is when a doctor encounters a bizarre pattern of symptoms; if the doctor happens to have just read a journal article about a disease with similar symptoms, the diagnosis may be biased. If your roommate borrowed your notes last week without telling you, and now you find that your notebook is missing again, what are you most likely to conclude?

Related to accessibility is *salience*; a salient object is one that dominates our perception. The more salient a possible cause is, the more likely one is to seize upon it as an explanation. For instance, Taylor and Fiske (1975) arranged a situation in which two people (actors) talked to each other while several other people (observers) looked on (see Figure 17.3). Observers sat so that they were facing either actor A or actor B or so that they were exposed to the two actors equally. Those who were facing actor A saw A as the dominant person in the conversation; those who faced B saw B as more dominant. Those who were exposed equally to the two actors saw them as equally influential. Clearly, perceptual salience has a strong effect on causal attributions.

Another attributional bias is our tendency to overestimate the influence of salient actors' inner dispositions compared to the influence of the situation. This attributional bias is so widespread that Ross (1977) has called it the **fundamental attribution error.** In one study, subjects listened to an actor deliver a pro- or antiabortion speech. Even though the subjects were told that the actor had been instructed by the experimenter to take a particular position on abortion and had no choice in the matter, subjects perceived the actor's true attitude as being in line with the position of his speech (Gilbert, Pelham, & Krull, 1988).

Why do we have a dispositional bias concerning salient others? Perhaps it is because we tend to neglect situational influences. When we see someone behaving, what is most noticeable is the person behaving, rather than the situational factors that may be influencing the person's behavior. We tend to make even more extreme dispositional attributions about people whom we hear about secondhand, probably because the version we get from the firsthand witness tends to focus even more on the person and less on the situation as the story is retold (Gilovich, 1987). Although Ross argues that it is usually a mistake to make dispositional attributions, because we ignore the powerful influence of the situation on behavior, Gilbert (1989) suggests that dispositional attributions are correct often enough to persist. After all, if dispositional attributions were always wrong, wouldn't we eventually stop using them?

Although we (as observers) tend to attribute other people's behavior to their dispositions, we (as actors) tend to explain our own behavior in terms of situational causes. This is known as the **actor-observer effect** (Jones & Nisbett, 1972). When male college students were asked to explain why their best friends chose their college majors and girlfriends, they tended to emphasize dispositional reasons ("He's interested in history" "He likes blondes") (Nisbett et al., 1973). When asked to explain their own choices, however, the subjects gave more weight to situational factors ("History is fascinating," "She's intelligent").

The false consensus effect (Ross et al., 1977), which we discussed earlier, fits in nicely with our tendency to make situational attributions for our own behavior. By assuming that we act the way we do because of the situations we are in (and not because of our particular characteristics), we are almost forced to assume that most people would act the same way in that situation; it is the sensible thing to do, given the circumstances. Funder (1991) goes so far as to argue that the false consensus effect demonstrates that making situational attributions may be as much a fundamental attribution error as making dispositional attributions.

FIGURE 17.3
The Seating Arrangement in Taylor and Fiske's Experiment

Observers who faced a particular actor perceived that actor as having a greater influence on the conversation than the other, less salient actor. Observers who sat to the side and thus saw both actors equally perceived them as equally influential.

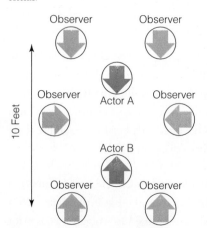

The actor-observer effect may also be explained in terms of salience. When other people do something, we see them behaving, which makes us see them (or their dispositions) as the cause of their behavior ("Alan hit Bob; Alan must be an aggressive guy"). But when we do something, we do not watch ourselves behaving. Instead, we are more aware of the situational influences affecting us ("Bob provoked me, so I hit him.").

The tendency to see others acting for dispositional reasons and ourselves acting for situational reasons has one further implication: We tend to see others as possessing consistent traits (dispositions), whereas we tend to see ourselves as more variable and inconsistent. If we are controlled by the situation, then it follows that in different situations we will behave differently (Sande, Goethals, & Radloff, 1988).

Motivated Biases.   The attributions we make can affect our self-esteem. **Attributional egotism** refers to our tendency to make attributions that improve the picture we have of ourselves. There is some evidence that we want to see ourselves accurately (Strube, Lott, Le-Xuan-Hy, Oxenberg, & Deichmann, 1986), but there is even more evidence that we want to see ourselves positively. This means that we want to be able to take credit for our successes and avoid blaming ourselves for our failures. In a typical study, subjects play a game that has been rigged. Winners tend to say that their success was based on skill, not luck; losers are more likely to blame bad luck rather than lack of skill (Snyder, Stephan, & Rosenfield, 1976). It is important to note that the winners in this study reverse the usual actor-observer effect, since they are more likely to use a dispositional explanation (skill) than a situational explanation (luck) when referring to themselves. Apparently, the motivated bias (egotism) is stronger than the perceptual bias (actor-observer effect), at least some of the time.

In general, attributional egotism seems to occur when what happens is important to people's image of themselves (Snyder, Stephan, & Rosenfield, 1978). Students who identified strongly with America were more likely to blame Rocky Balboa's defeat by a Russian opponent (in a reedited version of *Rocky IV*) on external factors, such as a biased referee, than were those who did not strongly identify with America (Branscombe & Wann, 1992). This study also made it clear that if we identify strongly with people, we will make the same sorts of attributions for them as we do for ourselves. This tendency to make self-serving attributions for ingroup members but not for outgroup members may perpetuate prejudice (Hewstone, 1990).

Defensive attributions are those that minimize threats to our self-esteem. One important example of defensive attribution is our belief in a "just world" (Lerner, 1980). We tend to make attributions that reinforce the idea that the world operates fairly and people get what they deserve. For example, most Americans tend to attribute poverty to poor people's dispositions (laziness, stupidity), rather than to their circumstances or bad luck (Feagin, 1972). The well-off Americans who hold this view naturally tend to see themselves as hardworking and intelligent people who fully deserve their prosperity. This attributional bias can be reduced, however; exposure to social science courses at the university level appears to make students less likely to blame the poor for their poverty—and more likely to blame social conditions (Guimond, Begin, & Palmer, 1989). As more and more Americans suffer economically (owing to national economic woes), we may expect to find a higher proportion of Americans blaming circumstances rather than laziness or stupidity for poverty in America—and voting Democratic, the party traditionally associated with a compassionate (i.e., situational) approach to the less well-off.

Defensive attribution also supports our tendency to see victims of terrible accidents or fatal diseases as somehow responsible for their plight. We convince ourselves that accidents and illnesses happen only to people who are careless or somehow deserving of disaster and that since we ourselves do not deserve to suffer, nothing bad will happen to us. The result of this belief is that we often end up blaming the victim (Ryan, 1976). Belief that the rape victim "brought it on herself" makes it easier to believe that it could not happen to us, but it makes the victim of rape doubly victimized—first by the crime and then by our explanation for it. Ironically, the victims we blame may include ourselves: When we are struck by disease or accident, we may end up convincing ourselves that we must have done something to deserve it.

Attraction and Personal Relationships

Social psychology is concerned with more than perceiving other people accurately. When we form an impression of someone, it is often because we want to know whether that person could possibly be a friend—or even a lover. Not surprisingly, social psychologists have long been interested in the factors that draw people together (Berscheid, 1988).

ATTRACTION

Compared to some other species, humans are relatively sociable. Still, we are not attracted to everyone. We will examine three of the factors that determine whether we will be attracted to a particular individual: physical attractiveness, proximity, and similarity.

Physical Attractiveness. Although we often claim that we are drawn to other people because of their personality, the evidence suggests that physical attractiveness is of the utmost importance, at least at the beginning of a relationship. An early experiment (Walster et al., 1966) took the form of a dance at which males and females were randomly paired as dates (although they believed that they had been paired by a computer analysis of their personality and interests). The only quality that significantly affected how much people liked their dates was physical appearance: People liked better-looking dates more, regardless of their personality, intelligence, and social skills. (Subsequent research suggests that the distinction between attractiveness and other positive qualities may not be so clear-cut. As we saw earlier, when discussing stereotypes, attractive people are assumed to possess a wide variety of other positive personal attributes, including social competence and intelligence [Eagly et al., 1991], especially if they smile a lot [Reis, Wilson et al., 1990].) Admittedly, physical appearance might make less of a difference after you get to know someone well, but Walster and colleagues' results imply that, unless you are relatively good-looking, people may not want to get to know you well enough to find out how great you really are. This may be especially true for females, whose "social value" is allegedly more a matter of their appearance than is the case for males.

Of course, people of only moderate attractiveness—the majority of us—do eventually find friends. More often than you might expect, however, friends are roughly equivalent in physical attractiveness (Berscheid & Walster, 1978). We can think of physical attractiveness as a commodity and social networks as a commodity exchange. Assuming that a couple's other characteristics are roughly comparable, then we should expect their looks to be roughly comparable as well, maintaining a balance in terms of

Physical attractiveness plays a major role in attraction. Good-looking people are also assumed to have socially desirable personality traits, so attractive individuals have a double advantage.

what they offer to the relationship. When we see an attractive woman with an unattractive man, we assume either that the man has something else to offer to compensate for his appearance or that the woman has certain defects that cancel out her beauty.

Proximity. Often, the people we interact with the most are simply those who are literally closest to us, and the more we interact with people and become familiar with them, the more we like them. A classic study by Festinger, Schachter, and Back (1950) found that residents of an apartment complex tended to interact with—and like—those who happened to live on the same floor more than those who lived on other floors or in other buildings. Likewise, when classroom seating is alphabetical, students are more likely to be friends with people who share the same last initial (Byrne, 1961).

"Absence makes the heart grow fonder." "Out of sight, out of mind." Even though they contradict each other, these two proverbs focus on the connection between proximity and liking. Research seems to support the idea that being nearby increases liking. Still, perhaps absence does make the heart grow fonder under certain circumstances. What do you think?

There are two major explanations for the association between proximity and liking. First is simple availability. Assuming that most people are nice enough once you get to know them, it follows that proximity will determine whom you get to know, and the people you get to know will be the ones you come to like. A second explanation is based on the **mere exposure effect** (Zajonc, 1968), whereby simple familiarity increases liking for a person or object. We come to like what we are used to, even if the object was not especially likable to begin with. The mere exposure effect has been demonstrated in the laboratory with stimuli as neutral as nonsense syllables, which people find more pleasing after they have read them several times. People even prefer stimuli that have been flashed on a screen so briefly that the subjects do not recognize them or even report having seen them (Seamon, Brody, & Kauff, 1984; Zajonc, 1980). (Recall the research on subliminal perception described in Chapters 5 and 14.) It seems reasonable to conclude that repeated exposure to people physically close to us leads us to like them more. (Presumably, there are some limits to the mere exposure effect, as when repeated exposure to an irritating person just makes things worse!)

Similarity. "I am like her." "I like her." Is it a coincidence that these two propositions, which sound almost identical but mean quite different things, actually do go together psychologically? Whether you like someone seems to depend on whether the person is like you. As we have already seen, people of similar levels of physical attractiveness seem to wind up together; similarity along other dimensions also affects attraction. Byrne (1971) has demonstrated that we tend to prefer people who share our attitudes and opinions, perhaps because these people help to convince us that our attitudes and opinions are "correct" (Clore, 1975). A typical experiment involves having subjects fill out questionnaires on which they indicate their attitudes about various topics. The experimenter then secretly completes another copy of the questionnaire expressing attitudes that are all either close to or far from a subject's original answers. This bogus questionnaire is then presented to the subject as if it were the actual questionnaire of another subject, whom the first subject then rates on various dimensions. Usually (e.g., Griffeth, Vecchio, & Logan, 1989), subjects indicate that they like and prefer to work with another person with similar attitudes much more than someone with dissimilar attitudes. Birds of a feather do indeed flock together, and birds who

People tend to like others who are similar to them.

flock together seem to have similar feathers. Existing pairs of friends tend to resemble each other more than would be expected by chance, not only in terms of physical appearance and attitudes, but even, apparently, in terms of genetic markers in the blood (Rushton, 1989).

Our preference for people who are like us (ingroup favoritism) may have its roots in biology. According to Krebs (1992, p. 307), "evolutionary theory claims humans are evolved . . . to favor . . . ingroup members." Members of your ingroup are more likely to share your genes, or at least to help you pass your genes on to the next generation, so there should be some evolutionary advantage to favoring your ingroup. It is difficult to prove conclusively that the reason we favor those who are similar to us is "genetic," but it is clear that similarity, or ingroup membership, is a powerful influence on attraction.

Isn't it true, however, that "opposites attract," despite what we know about similarly feathered birds? The *complementarity hypothesis* dictates that people who complement each other (i.e., have opposite personality traits) will be attracted to each other. Some evidence (Winch, 1958) suggests that complementarity may increase attraction, but probably only under certain conditions. In a marriage, a domineering woman may be happier with a meek, passive husband than with one who is domineering, too. Remember, however, that "domineering" is a relational characteristic; you cannot dominate easily unless there is someone around who is easily dominated. When it comes to other traits, the complementarity principle may not hold. A gregarious woman will probably prefer a gregarious husband, one who will encourage, not oppose, her desire to spend a lot of time socializing. Type A individuals (see Chapter 13) tend to prefer Type A dates; Type B's prefer Type B's (Morrell, Twillman, & Sullaway, 1989). Wiggins and Pincus (1992) conclude that evidence for similarity is stronger than evidence for complementarity.

While similarity of attitudes and opinions generally increase attraction, it usually takes some time for people to establish how similar they really are. Superficial similarities (e.g., what sort of music or hobbies you like) are often discussed on first dates; but true personality resemblances ordinarily are not revealed so quickly. Often, this means that physical attractiveness will dictate which people even try to get to know each other, while attitude and personality similarities will determine the long-term success of the relationships (Curran & Lippold, 1975).

ROMANTIC LOVE

Once the conditions for attraction have been met, friendships often develop. Occasionally, relationships go beyond friendship—or skip the friendship stage altogether—and become love. Romantic love is still poorly understood. What exactly is it? How does it arise? Why does it so often evaporate? Psychologists have been ridiculed for trying to analyze love. Senator William Proxmire argued in the 1970s that "200 million Americans want to leave some things in life a mystery, and right at the top of the list of things we don't want to know is why a man falls in love with a woman and vice versa" (cited in Rubin, 1988). But considering how important most people consider love to be and how much it contributes to human ecstasy and misery, we cannot afford to remain ignorant about the way love works.

Research on the psychology of love has tended to focus on the different types of love serving different psychological needs. Thus, some loving relationships may be less healthy than others, to the extent that they are based on desperate dependency (Murstein, 1988), deficiency (Maslow, 1970), or addiction (Peele, 1988; Peele & Brodsky, 1976).

Because romantic love seems to change over the course of a relationship, some researchers have assumed that love has various components, each of which plays a more prominent role as the relationship progresses. Usually, romantic love begins with passion, but it endures, if at all, on a foundation of solid affection, intimacy, and trust ("companionate love") that makes up for the decline of sexual exhilaration (Hatfield & Walster, 1978). Another view (Shaver, Hazan, & Bradshaw, 1988) sees romantic love as an extension of infant attachment to the mother. Our gradual attachment to our lovers (in preparation, perhaps, for forming a new family) bears a remarkable resemblance to our original attachments to our mothers and perhaps makes it easier to understand why the breakup of adult love relationships so often has such a devastating emotional impact. In addition to attachment, however, adult romantic love also involves certain features not present (or at least not obvious) in the infant-mother relationship—namely, mutual caregiving and sexuality. Sternberg's model (1986, 1988) emphasizes three aspects of love: intimacy (knowing the lover), passion (the sexual and emotional component), and decision/commitment (to stay together). Again, these aspects of love appear (and often disappear) at different stages of a relationship. Relationships in which one or more of these aspects are missing are usually less than ideal (see Figure 17.4).

Intimacy and commitment are part of romantic love, but most people (and even some psychologists) regard passion—and particularly sexual arousal—as the key element of romance. In Berscheid's (1988, p. 373) opinion, love is "about 90 percent sexual desire as yet unsated." Because emotional arousal is crucial to passionate love, some researchers have suggested that love, like other emotions, may require some labeling before it is perceived as love. This view, derived from the work of Schachter and Singer (1962) (see Chapter 13), sees the experience of passion as a state of intense physical arousal combined with an appropriate stimulus (a sexually desirable person); the stimulus provides us with an explanation of why we are feeling that way. Ordinarily, the presence of a sexually desirable person both creates the arousal in the first place and provides a label or explanation for it. But it is possible that the arousal could stem from a different source but get (mis)attributed to a nearby person, who is then perceived as an object of desire.

Berscheid and Walster (1978) have pursued this idea. Whether you attribute your arousal to another person ought to follow the normal rules of attribution. "Does that person consistently have a strong effect on me?" "Do other people have that effect on

FIGURE 17.4
Triangular Conception of Love

Different kinds of loving as combinations of the three components of love.

SOURCE: Sternberg, 1988, p. 122.

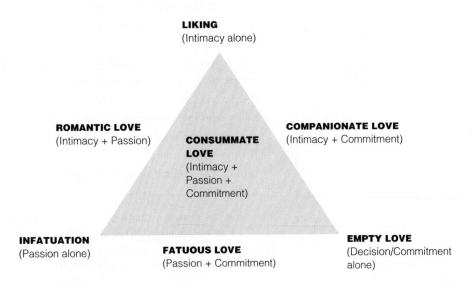

me?" "If I feel like this whenever—and only when—I see her (him), it must be love." Also, it follows that arousal due to other sources may be mistaken for passion, depending on the circumstances. If you are aroused for some reason other than sexual passion, but a potential lover is present and available as a plausible explanation for your arousal, you may find that person all the more attractive (and see yourself as all the more in love). This may hold true even if the arousal is due to negative causes such as fear or anger. In one series of studies (Dutton & Aron, 1974), male subjects who were made fearful—by having to cross a suspension bridge or by expecting strong electric shocks—were more attracted to a female in the vicinity than were subjects who were not fearful. Interestingly, the subjects who misattributed their fear to sexual attraction reported less anxiety than did control subjects who were made fearful but who did not encounter the female. After all, if it's love, it can't be fear, right? Physical exertion also caused male subjects to express greater attraction to a female whom they expected to get to know better (White & Kight, 1984), presumably because the arousal from the exercise was interpreted as arousal caused by the woman. Recently, Dutton and Aron (1989) demonstrated that subjects (both males and females) viewing a film rated the attractive, opposite-sex actors as even more attractive when they were villainous than in another version of the film that did not make viewers so uncomfortable. The researchers concluded that the misinterpretation of unpleasant arousal as passion may explain why people are sometimes attracted to those who scare or even injure them.

CLOSE RELATIONSHIPS

Romantic love, understandably, is of great interest to social psychologists and to the people they study; however, romantic love is just one type of relationship in our lives. More often, we develop superficial relationships with other people, stemming from contacts at home, school, work, or play. Sometimes, these superficial relationships develop into something more meaningful—close relationships (not necessarily romantic love). Generally, the number of close relationships peaks in late adolescence and early adulthood and then tapers off following marriage and parenthood (Dickens & Perlman, 1981). Recently, social psychologists have begun to study close relationships, often looking at the progressive stages of the relationship (development, maintenance, dissolution).

Relationship Development. As a relationship moves beyond the initial, superficial stage, the people involved tend to spend more time together, feel more comfortable with each other, develop their own "communication system," develop stable interaction patterns, and increase their trust of one another (Berscheid, 1985). Most researchers consider self-disclosure and commitment to be critical signs of a developing relationship. *Self-disclosure* refers to the sharing of feelings, opinions, and secrets by the partners. Although it seems reasonable that closeness would increase one's willingness to disclose innermost thoughts (and that such disclosures would in turn increase closeness), the importance of self-disclosure in ongoing relationships remains obscure. It often seems that it is easier to tell our secrets to complete strangers—especially those we are unlikely ever to see again—than to our intimates. As Berscheid (1985, p. 470) notes,

> It is not obvious . . . that a husband's intimate disclosure that he was overcome with an irresistible impulse to gift his female colleague with a black negligee will elevate his wife's attraction to him, nor is it clear that his affection for her will always be enhanced by her . . . disclosure . . . that it was she, not a stray meteorite, who just wrecked his new car."

Close relationships depend on the ability to deal well with conflict and to provide emotional support.

Obviously, the content of the disclosure makes a difference, and self-disclosure probably helps to cement relationships early on much more than later. As for commitment, it implies some bond between the partners that will extend the relationship into the future. A danger, though, is that a strong commitment may lead partners to develop an unrealistically positive view of the relationship (Brickman, 1987). One study (Kelley, Huston, & Cate, 1985) found that the more newlyweds said they loved each other at the time of the wedding, the less love they expressed later in the marriage!

Relationship Maintenance. People just starting a relationship usually enjoy its benefits, but except in the most superficial relationships, conflicts are inevitable. How the partners handle conflict usually determines whether the relationship will survive. Research shows that handling conflict constructively is better than no conflict at all in promoting intimacy (Holmes & Boon, 1990). Often, conflict isn't really resolved, but just eliminated (e.g., if the partners cannot stand each other's taste in music, they will stop going to concerts together). When conflicts cannot be sidestepped, however, they must be resolved or they may destroy the relationship—even though the partners may still be very fond of each other. The happiest couples and friends are those who can deal well with conflict and who are available for each other emotionally when needed. This does not mean that the giving and taking has to be perfectly equal. In fact, keeping score about each other's contributions may interfere with intimacy (Clark & Reis, 1988).

Relationship Dissolution. You might think that whether a relationship dissolves or not would depend on how good the relationship is. The better the partners get along, or the more affectionate they are toward each other, the less the chance of a breakup. Although this conclusion is true to an extent, it is not the whole story. For instance, the quality of the relationship must be compared with the quality of alternative relationships that may be available to one or both of the partners (Levinger, 1976). New friends can put a strain on old friendships, and many romantic relationships dissolve only when new romantic dreamboats appear on the horizon. Also important are the barriers that keep an individual (or both individuals) in a relationship. Proximity, shared resources, the costs of change, social pressures, and, in the case of marriage, divorce laws and the interests of the children combine to keep people in relationships even though the relationships may be unsatisfying. The liberalization of divorce laws in recent years has lowered escape barriers. One result has been that more than ever, people stay married only if the marriage is satisfying (Berscheid & Campbell, 1981).

Many relationships break apart; others just drift apart. Especially in modern American society, where people often grow up in one location, go to college in another, and end up living in yet another, friendships must be particularly strong to survive. Anyone who has attended a high school or college reunion realizes how important shared experiences are to relationships. But when your shared experiences are all in the distant past, the relationship is unlikely to be satisfying.

Persuasion and Attitude Change

Historically, social psychology has been strongly identified with the study of attitudes and attitude change. An **attitude** is a tendency to evaluate a person (e.g., a particular politician), object (e.g., a painting), or idea (e.g., capital punishment) positively or negatively. An attitude is different from a belief, since beliefs do not necessarily involve positive or negative feelings. Attitudes also differ from behavior, since how we feel about something and how we act toward it are not always the same.

Persuasion is a deliberate attempt to change someone's attitude about something. We are all familiar with such attempts, from the standpoint of both persuader and persuadee.

PERSUASIVE MESSAGES

Research on attitude change has tended to focus on three aspects of the process: the persuader, the message, and the target, or person to be persuaded. Perhaps because attitude change is so important in politics and advertising, a great deal of work has been done in this area, and we know a fair amount about what factors make a difference.

Source Characteristics. Persuasive messages are delivered by a source, usually a particular, identifiable person. What are the characteristics that make a source effective at changing attitudes?

Perhaps the most obvious characteristic, the one that ought to make a difference, is credibility (Hovland & Weiss, 1951). In one study (Aronson, Turner, & Carlsmith, 1963), students read and evaluated some little-known poems and then read a strongly positive evaluation of one of the poems that they had disliked. If this positive evaluation supposedly came from T. S. Eliot, students were much more likely to shift their attitudes toward liking the poem than if the evaluation supposedly came from Agnes Stearns, allegedly a student at Mississippi State Teachers College.

The fact that people are paid to deliver advertising messages ought to make them less credible. The pediatrician who endorses a particular brand of disposable diapers on TV is probably less concerned with moisture absorbency than with the handsome sum he or she is being paid for saying whatever the script calls for. Still, as we saw earlier, people tend to discount situational influences on others' behavior. Basically, viewers forget about the money that is dictating the sales pitch and assume that the pediatrician must really mean what he or she says.

Credibility is often bound up with expertise: The advertiser uses a pediatrician (or an actor pretending to be a pediatrician) because we ought to be more persuaded by someone who is an expert in the area than by someone with no special knowledge. When Michael J. Fox endorses a soft drink, however, or Bill Cosby endorses pudding, there is not much question of expertise involved. Whether or not we believe their words, few of us believe that they are experts on soft drinks or puddings. This brings us to another important source characteristic: attractiveness. Popular entertainers are effective salespersons; indeed, any especially attractive figure seems to help sales (Chaiken, 1986). Kelman (1961) suggests that we somehow feel as if we have created a bond with someone when we adopt his or her position on an issue. Or maybe it's just that we assume that there must be some consistency between who we like and who we agree with. It is important to realize that the effectiveness of attractive communicators does not depend on their arguments. We tend to agree with them almost regardless of what they say. Of course, this sort of attitude change is quite superficial and not likely to endure (Chaiken, 1986). Ads for soft drinks, perhaps because they are based almost entirely on the attractiveness of the source rather than on the merits of the product, must constantly be repeated to keep us buying.

Much of advertising seems to depend more on who's selling the product than the product being sold.

6.0, 6.0, 6.0, 6.0, 6.0! If I had to rate milk as an after-sports drink, it would definitely get the gold. Besides being a better source of potassium than the leading sports drink, it has more vitamins and minerals per ounce. And how do I like it? On ice, of course.

MILK
What a surprise!™

Another characteristic that seems to increase a source's persuasiveness is similarity to the target. Advertisements often present anonymous, vaguely attractive young adults—just like you!—enjoying themselves with soft drinks, candy bars, or chewing gum. The message is clear.

Message Characteristics. Who delivers a message is usually important in persuasion, but the features of the message itself also make a difference. For instance, are we more likely to be persuaded if we read a message in the print media or hear it on radio or television? (This is a question of obvious importance to advertisers.) The answer depends on what sort of persuasion is necessary (Chaiken & Eagly, 1976). If the message is a complex one, a written version may work better, since it is usually easier to understand a complex message if we can absorb the arguments at our own pace and reread them if necessary. But if the message is simple and the goal is straightforward persuasion (no need for comprehension)—as is often the case in soft drink or pudding ads, not to mention political campaigns—a high-impact video message may be more effective.

Is it better to present only the pro side of your case, or should you present the con side as well, along with a rebuttal of the con arguments? Research indicates that if the audience is already favorable toward your position, a one-sided message is preferable. If the audience is indifferent or opposed, however, it is better to present a two-sided argument, in which you can attack the other position (Deaux & Wrightsman, 1984).

Another issue concerns emotion versus logic in persuasion. If you want to convince people to quit smoking, for example, you could make a convincing case using the statistics linking smoking to disease. However, creating fear by using graphic photos of smoke-damaged lungs appears to be more effective than cold statistics (Higbee, 1969; Leventhal, 1970). Fear is most effective when the message also includes specific tactics for reducing the fear by dealing with the problem (e.g., strategies for quitting smoking). The reduction of fear negatively reinforces the intention to quit smoking (see Chapter 6 on conditioning and learning).

If you want to change people's minds, your message obviously must support a position other than the one they start with. But how different a position will people tolerate? Up to a point, the further the new position is from the target's starting position, the more change you will produce. But if the position you present is drastically different from your audience's starting position, the audience may just dismiss it or ignore it. In general, you get the most change with a position that is moderately different from the starting position (Eagly & Telaak, 1972). As you might expect, an extremely credible source can get away with arguing a more extreme position (Bochner & Insko, 1966).

Target Characteristics. The characteristics of the target of a persuasive message also determine whether the message succeeds. For instance, an audience's commitment to the issue in question, or how firmly it holds that position, can affect your chances of convincing them to change. The more committed the targets are to their initial position, the harder they are to budge and the less tolerant they will be of messages that are even moderately different from their starting position.

Various other characteristics of an audience are also known to affect resistance to attitude change. Less intelligent people are sometimes more persuadable. However, if a message is complex, highly intelligent people may be more easily persuaded, because they can follow the argument better (Eagly & Warren, 1976). Overweight people appear to be more persuadable than normal-weight people (Glass, Lavin, Henchy, Gordon, Mayhew, & Donohoe, 1969). Why? Possibly because they are more dependent on others' opinions to determine their own feelings (Schachter, 1971) or perhaps because, as we saw earlier (see Psychology in Our Times: Minorities and Self-Esteem), they have low self-esteem, which makes them more vulnerable to other people's attempts to manipulate them. McGuire (1985), however, notes that low self-esteem does not always lead to greater persuadability, because some people with low self-esteem simply fail to attend to the persuasive message in the first place.

Central Versus Peripheral Processing. We have already mentioned that sometimes people analyze persuasive arguments carefully, whereas sometimes they ignore the arguments and just adopt someone else's position. Indeed, often there are no arguments to analyze, as when certain attractive communicators simply give their opinion or just use the product without saying anything directly. Petty and Cacioppo (1986) make a distinction between *central processing* and *peripheral processing*. Individuals who are highly concerned about an issue and who are about to make a serious commitment (e.g., buying a new car) are more likely to carefully evaluate the pros and cons (central processing). With less motivated individuals or more trivial issues (e.g., buying a soft drink), logical arguments are ignored and irrelevant features of a communicator, such as attractiveness, make a difference (peripheral processing). (According to this distinction, the decision of whether to get married and even who to marry often appears to fall into the peripheral or trivial category!) In general, attitude change due to central processing lasts longer and is more strongly related to future behavior.

CASE STUDY

TOBACCO ADVERTISING

Our attitudes often concern trivial matters (e.g. competing Colas) or matters that are trivial for us but significant for others (e.g. the death penalty). Sometimes, though, our attitudes can become a matter of our own life and death. Zimbardo and Leippe (1991) discuss the role of explicit persuasion techniques, supported by the tobacco industry, in convincing people to take up and maintain the lethal habit of cigarette smoking.

There is no longer any serious question about the health dangers—principally, cardiovascular disease and cancer—of cigarette smoking. Virtually everyone knows that cigarettes are bad for you (Shopland & Brown, 1987). And yet every year thousands of people join the ranks of smokers. Most of these people have not smoked before; they are not already addicted (although they may

soon become so). Why, given the well-known hazards of smoking—hazards that are now printed right on the cigarette package—do people adopt this dangerous and easily avoidable practice?

The obvious answer would be that the advantages of smoking outweigh its disadvantages. Of course, it is not easy to think of advantages that outweigh disability and death, but the advantages might be in the short-term, whereas the health hazards generally occur much later. The fact of the matter, though, is that the advantages of smoking are not all that easy to identify. Smoking has developed a reputation as a way to lose weight, which may partially explain why it has caught on to such a great extent with young females, who now smoke more than young males. (By the way, the effect of smoking on weight suppression is not very large, and hardly worth the serious effects on health and personal hygiene.)

The real reason for the persistence of smoking, and the recruitment of new smokers in their thousands, is advertising. And advertising is just a commercial form of persuasion. The cigarette industry spends *billions* of dollars each year to convince people (mostly young people) that they ought to smoke. These billions of dollars buy advertising campaigns that are very sophisticated. You are not told in any direct way that you should smoke. (The tobacco companies, in fact, swear that they want to discourage smoking among young people.) Rather, you are bombarded with images of attractive (especially slim) people smoking, celebrities smoking (it seems that all of Hollywood smokes), active, healthy people smoking. We may not believe that merely seeing cigarettes connected to these positive images could make us smoke, but the evidence is quite clear that advertising campaigns do affect sales. New brands are targeted at particular "market segments" (i.e. groups of people), and those market segments respond. Cigarettes especially for upscale women, a different brand for young "minimum wage" women, yet another brand for African Americans, and still another for Hispanics—these ads work, in that these various groups are more likely to smoke the brand "designed" for them, and are more likely to smoke cigarettes in general than without advertising. People take up smoking for reasons other than explicit advertising; peer pressure, pharmacological effects and so on play a role. But the role of persuasion sponsored by the tobacco companies is indisputable (even though the tobacco companies naturally dispute it, arguing that their ads simply help people find a preferred brand, rather than inducing them to smoke in the first place).

Why do we permit cigarette advertising—at least indirectly responsible for hundreds of thousands of preventable deaths each year—to flourish? Of course, there is the well-worn argument based on freedom of speech. No-one is *forcing* anyone to smoke, the argument goes. An appreciation of social psychology, however, reveals that there is a large grey area between freedom of action and coercion. Persuasion is effective, even though we prefer to think of ourselves as free agents who can ignore advertising at will. Another reason for the tolerance of advertising is the money it brings in. Sports events, music festivals, and all sorts of magazines are dependent on sponsorship and advertising revenue—and the tobacco industry provides a very substantial proportion of that revenue. Our society is apparently willing to tolerate widespread illness and even death if the price is right. As long as we fail to appreciate the power of persuasion, tobacco advertising is likely to lure our youth, unthinkingly, into a habit that will eventually kill them in their millions.

ATTITUDES AND BEHAVIOR

Political candidates spend tremendous amounts of money on advertising to convince voters to think positively of them and negatively of their opponents. But do positive attitudes translate into votes? Not always, if we can judge from the efforts spent on "getting out the vote." Candidates know that it is not enough to have registered voters favor you; you have to make sure that they act (i.e., vote) in line with their attitudes.

Believing in something and acting in a way consistent with those beliefs are two different things, as researchers (and advertisers and politicians) have discovered (Wicker, 1969). In a classic study, LaPière (1934) escorted a Chinese couple on an automobile tour of the United States. Although anti-Chinese prejudice was widespread at that time, the couple was treated courteously in all but one of more than 250 restaurants and hotels. After the tour, LaPière wrote to each of these establishments, and more than 90 percent of the proprietors said that they would be unwilling to serve Chinese customers!

The question is no longer whether attitudes and behavior go together, but under what conditions they do so (Zanna & Fazio, 1982). Several factors seem to increase the correspondence between attitudes and behavior:

1. *Direct experience*. Regan and Fazio (1977) examined attitudes and behavior toward a student housing crisis on a college campus. Students who had direct experience with the crisis (i.e., those who had been put into crowded temporary rooms) showed a much closer connection between their attitudes and behaviors (such as petition signing) than did students with no direct experience.

2. *Vested interest*. Sivacek and Crano (1982) found that the connection between students' attitudes and behaviors regarding increasing the drinking age from 19 to 21 was closer for those students who would be affected (those under 21) than for those who would not be affected (those already 21). Of course, a vested interest and direct experience often go together.

3. *Explicit connection of attitudes to behavior*. Snyder and Kendzierski (1982) studied the connection between attitudes toward participating in psychological research and whether subjects actually signed up for a study when given a chance. When another subject (actually someone hired by the experimenter) explicitly noted that signing up or not reflects how you feel toward participating in research, subjects were more likely to act in accordance with their attitudes.

4. *Specific correspondence of attitude and behavior*. Weigel, Vernon, and Tognacci (1974) measured people's attitudes toward the environment in general and toward more specific objects (such as the Sierra Club) and later offered subjects a chance to sign up for Sierra Club activities. General attitudes toward the environment were not associated with signing up for Sierra Club activities, but specific attitudes toward the Sierra Club itself were strongly associated with actual sign-ups. In general, specific behaviors are best predicted by correspondingly specific attitudes (Ajzen & Fishbein, 1977).

5. *Individual differences*. Snyder and Kendzierski (1982) demonstrated that high self-monitors—individuals who are especially concerned with what people think or what the situation calls for—often do not act in line with their own attitudes. If you believe that you must act the way that other people expect you to act, then you may not have the luxury of acting the way your own basic attitudes would suggest. Low self-monitors, by contrast, try to act in line with their attitudes, even if it means seeking out particular situations that make it easier to do so. If a low self-monitor is opposed to abortion, she will ordinarily try to be with people who share her view, making it more comfortable to express her true feelings. If a high self-monitor opposing abortion finds herself with prochoice advocates, she may just change her tune (if only temporarily) in order to fit in. People high in "need for cognition"—who chronically think more about their own thoughts, and who are more "in touch" with their attitudes—also show higher attitude-behavior consistency than do those who are low in need for cognition (Cacioppo, Petty, Kao, & Rodriguez, 1986).

Do you sign petitions, or circulate petitions, for the causes you believe in? Whether we actually translate our beliefs into actions depends on a variety of factors.

ATTITUDES AND BEHAVIOR

Various factors affect whether we act in accordance with our attitudes.

FACTOR	EXAMPLE
Direct experience	People who live in the neighborhood of a nuclear power station will act (e.g., sign petitions) more closely in accordance with their attitudes about nuclear power.
Vested Interest	College freshmen are more likely than college seniors to become actively involved in a campaign to fight tuition increases, even if they are equally opposed to the increase.
Explicit connection of attitude to behavior	People are more likely to donate time to a worthy cause after learning how their efforts can make a real difference.
Specific correspondence of attitudes and behavior	People's general attitudes toward health are only weakly associated with health-promoting behaviors, but people's attitudes toward yearly checkups are closely associated with actually having checkups.
Individual differences	Whether high self-monitors act in a prejudiced way will depend on the social situation, but whether low self-monitors will act prejudiced depends on whether they have prejudiced attitudes, not on the social situation.

COGNITIVE DISSONANCE

It is natural to assume that our behavior follows from our attitudes, but one fascinating technique for getting people to change their attitudes is to get them to change their behavior first and then let their attitudes fall in line. People want their beliefs and their actions to be consistent with each other. We are often uncomfortable when we act in a way that contradicts our values. If I can get you to behave in a way that differs sharply from your beliefs—especially if you feel as if you freely chose to act that way—then you will try to resolve the conflict between your behavior and your belief. But if the behavior has already occurred publicly, it may be too late to claim that you didn't really mean it. Instead, you may change your belief so that it lines up with your behavior. This tactic is at the heart of the theory of **cognitive dissonance** (Festinger, 1957), which explores what happens when a conflict arises between people's thoughts and actions.

In a famous example of research in this area (Festinger & Carlsmith, 1959), subjects performed a series of meaningless and dull tasks—placing spools on trays, dumping them, and starting over. Afterward, the experimenter paid each subject to tell the next subject that the experiment was interesting and fun. Half the subjects were paid $20 to lie, and the remainder were paid only $1. Later these subjects were asked how much they liked the experiment. The results were quite startling. Subjects paid $1 liked the task more than those who had been paid $20! The $1 subjects also liked the task more than control subjects who were not paid and who did not tell lies. The same pattern occurred when subjects were asked whether they would be willing to take part in a similar experiment: Only the subjects paid $1 expressed any enthusiasm. Figure 17.5 shows graphically the results of this experiment.

How does cognitive dissonance theory explain this result? Consider the $1 subjects. They have lied in return for a very small reward. The $20 subjects have also lied, but for a much larger reward. Which group has a better justification for lying? The $20 group can excuse itself; yes, they lied, but the reward made it worthwhile and understandable, even if not morally correct. The $1 group, however, does not have the excuse of an irresistible reward. There was really no reason for them to tell lies, was there? As a result, the $1 subjects excuse their behavior, not by convincing themselves that the reward was too big to turn down, but by convincing themselves that they weren't really lying! In short, the $1 group changed its attitude toward the task so that its attitude would match its behavior.

A related example is the attitude of cigarette smokers. Those who are unwilling or unable to change their self-destructive behavior end up developing a set of attitudes to justify that behavior. The greater the health risk they face, the more likely they are to defend their behavior by claiming how much they like smoking and how helpful it is to them psychologically. In general, attitudes will shift to match behaviors when the behaviors are public (i.e., too late to change) and voluntary. It is important that the behavior be voluntary, because if you are forced to do something against your will, you have a perfect explanation for why you did it, and you do not have to convince yourself that you wanted to.

If you are forced to do something that conflicts with your attitudes, then you probably won't change your attitude to bring it in line with your behavior. The trick to getting people to change their attitudes, then, is to get them to change their behavior

FIGURE 17.5
Cognitive Dissonance

People were given either a small reward ($1) or a large reward ($20) for telling someone that a boring task was really interesting. Later, these people were asked how much they liked the task and how willing they would be to take part in a similar experiment. A control group that did not get a reward did not have to lie to other subjects about the task. The results showed that people who were paid a small amount for lying rated the task higher than did the large-reward group or the no-lie/no-reward control group. Because the small payment was insufficient justification for telling a lie, the low-reward subjects reduced their cognitive dissonance by changing their opinion of the task, so that telling others that it was interesting wasn't so much of a lie.

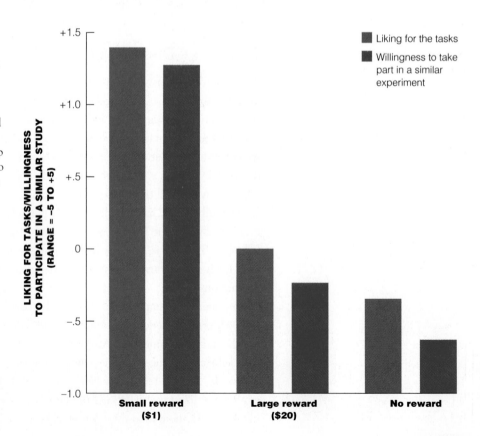

without their realizing that they were not acting voluntarily. Usually, that's not too difficult, since most people like to think of themselves as behaving the way they do because they want to, not because they have to. An example comes from a study of conformity and eating (Goldman, Herman, & Polivy, 1991) in which subjects were paired with other subjects (actually, paid confederates) for a meal. When the confederate ate a lot, so did the true subject, and when the confederate ate only a little, so did the true subject. Clearly, the subjects ate the way they did because they were matching the confederate's behavior. But when subjects were asked why they ate as much or as little as they did, none of them mentioned the confederate. When the confederate got them to eat a lot, the subjects said that they ate a lot because they liked the food! It is more personally acceptable to eat because you like the taste of the food than because the person next to you happens to be eating a lot. Consider the implications: If we want to get people to like something, we should get them to use it, preferably by subtle but powerful social pressures. They will then convince themselves that they must have liked it, or else why would they have used it?

A final example of the complicated workings of cognitive dissonance is captured in the following saying by Machiavelli: "It is the nature of man to feel as much bound by the favors they do as by those they receive." When we do someone a favor, especially if we do not get anything in return, we feel some pressure to explain why we did it. If it wasn't for a reward, then it must have been because we particularly like the person we helped out! Doing a favor for someone often ends up making us like that person more, which increases the chances of our helping again in the future. Machiavelli understood how cognitive dissonance works.

As we have already seen, self-perception theory (Bem, 1972) suggests another way of looking at the effects of behavior on attitudes: Instead of assuming that behaviors create an unpleasant conflict with attitudes, forcing attitudes to change, self-perception theory argues that attitudes are simply inferred from behavior, without any underlying conflict or discomfort. Both theories agree that getting people to change their behaviors will lead them to change their attitudes. Dissonance theory requires people to experience discomfort over the conflict, whereas self-perception theory argues that we simply change our opinions to correspond to our behavior. It seems most likely that self-perception operates when an opinion is not deeply held and when the necessary change is relatively small. Dissonance reduction occurs when conflict and discomfort require a major change in our attitudes or self-image (Tesser & Shaffer, 1990). If the discomfort can be reduced some other way (as with a tranquilizer), then attitude change may not occur. If the discomfort is increased (as with amphetamines), attitude change may be exaggerated (Cooper, Zanna, & Taves, 1978).

Cognitive dissonance theory can be used to explain all sorts of interesting effects. For instance, after a difficult decision involving a lot of pros and cons on both sides, people tend to become quickly and strongly convinced of the correctness of their choice. Once they have made an open commitment to one position over the other, their attitude falls in line. Positive information about the chosen alternative is especially welcome, and so is any negative information about the rejected alternative. Such *selective exposure* further reinforces the choice by adding pros to the chosen alternative and cons to the rejected alternative. Choosing a car, a college, or a career may all involve postdecisional dissonance reduction.

Can you think of occasions in which you made a difficult choice and then went out of your way to find justifications for it? It is usually not too difficult to find support for whatever choice we make. Obviously, to some extent we are fooling ourselves when

Bettors are more confident after they have placed their bets than just before. As cognitive dissonance theory predicts, once they have made a commitment to one course of action, they readjust their thinking to justify the action they have taken. Bettors become convinced that the horse that they have just chosen is a sure winner and that the rest of the field is a bunch of nags.

we try to convince ourselves that we made the best choice. On the other hand, this bias means that we are usually pretty happy with the choices we make. In fact, we probably grow increasingly convinced of the wisdom of our choice as time passes and we gather more evidence to help reduce postdecisional dissonance.

Social Influence

There are many ways besides persuasion to influence other people. Sometimes we influence people deliberately, other times without intending to. And frequently, we are the ones being influenced. Our lives are affected by social influences much more than most of us are willing to admit. Americans pride themselves on their individualism, which may explain why they are so reluctant to recognize how much of their behavior is affected by the example of others.

SOCIAL FACILITATION

Sometimes simply being with other people seems to affect our behavior. In fact, the very first social psychology experiment (Triplett, 1898) found that children performed a simple task (winding fishing reels) faster when other children were present and doing the same task. **Social facilitation** occurs when the presence of other people affects the energy or effort of our behavior. Subsequent research soon established that the mere presence of a passive audience could also affect performing subjects (Moore, 1917). It was not necessary for the other people to be co-acting (performing the task alongside the subject). Also, it soon became clear that such audiences could both improve and impair performance. Zajonc (1965) explained this complex pattern of results by arguing that the presence of other people increases drive or arousal. High drive states facilitate, or improve, the performance of easy or well-learned tasks but interfere with the learning and performance of difficult tasks (see Chapter 12).

One simple but important lesson from the social facilitation research is that learning difficult, new material is usually best accomplished alone. But once you have mastered the material, your best performance will occur in the presence of others. The implication is clear, whether you are playing the piano or trying to do well academically. Study or prepare alone, and once you have learned the material really well, show what you can do with others around. The better prepared you are, the more likely it is that an audience will help rather than hinder your performance.

Why does the presence of other people increase drive? The simplest explanation is that other people—even when they are wearing a blindfold and headphones (Schmitt, Gilovich, Goore, & Joseph, 1986)—are unpredictable in how they will react, and this uncertainty increases our arousal or drive. Others have argued that audiences are threatening because they are always evaluating us, or distracting us from the task, thereby increasing our drive level. Still others have suggested that audiences do not increase drive but rather increase our self-awareness or desire to make a good impression, which can explain most of the results from social facilitation studies (Geen, 1991). Whatever the ultimate explanation may be, it is clear that the presence of others can facilitate the performance of simple or well-learned activities.

SOCIAL LOAFING

There are some circumstances in which performing with others, even on simple tasks, does not make us do better. **Social loafing** refers to an individual's tendency to contribute less when in a group than when working on the same task alone. For

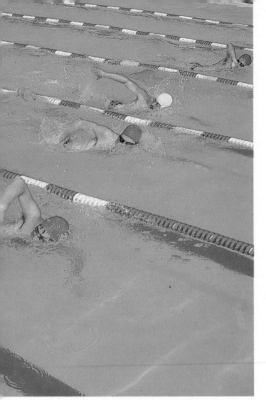

Relay racers swim faster when their individual lap times are announced than when only the total time for the race is announced. Social loafing means less effort when you are an anonymous part of a group.

Submergence in a group often seems to bring out the worst in people.

instance, individuals do not work as hard on a team rope-pulling task as when they pull alone (Ingham, Levinger, Graves, & Peckham, 1974). Restaurants respond to the problem of social loafing by imposing a mandatory 15 percent tip for large groups.

When our contribution to a group effort is not easy to identify, so that we do not need to worry about being criticized for poor performance, we usually do not try as hard (Harkins & Szymanski, 1987). Relay racers swim faster when their individual lap times are announced than when only the overall team score is announced (Williams, Nida, Baca, & Latané, 1989). In general, it seems that social loafing (low arousal or low evaluation threat) is the flip side of social facilitation (high arousal or high evaluation threat), and the effects on performance are precisely opposite. When we are an anonymous part of a group, we may not try as hard on simple or well-learned tasks, but our relatively relaxed state may actually improve our performance on the sorts of complex tasks that are impaired by high drive (Jackson & Williams, 1985; Paulus, 1983).

It is possible to eliminate social loafing by adding certain elements to the situation, such as identifiability or threat of evaluation. The fact that we have to add something to the basic situation to get people to stop loafing has led Guerin (1991, p. 139) to conclude that "loafing would seem to be the basic state" of people. Do you think that being in a group makes you lazier than you really are—or just allows you to be as lazy as you really are?

Related to social loafing is the *free rider effect* (Kerr, 1983), in which individuals believe that someone else in the group is likely to solve the problem or succeed at the group task, so why bother trying? The *sucker effect* goes one step further: the individual believes that everyone else is acting like a free rider; why bother trying when everyone else is loafing?

DEINDIVIDUATION

As we have just seen, when people become anonymous members of a group, they may contribute less to group tasks. Social psychologists are also interested in other consequences of becoming submerged in a group. Especially dramatic is the tendency of crowds to act in ways that the individual members would never consider. Mobs engage in violence and other antisocial acts, as if the members had lost their normal self-control. Of course, a large mob can take risks that an individual would never dare to take, but the effect of crowd behavior is more than just a matter of power.

At least part of the effect of crowds stems from the phenomenon of **deindividuation,** the loss of individual identity when people become anonymous members of a crowd (Festinger, Pepitone, & Newcomb, 1952). Group members tend to become less aware of themselves as individuals (Diener, 1980) and feel less personal responsibility for their actions (Zimbardo, 1970). When people find themselves in a group that is acting in a way that conflicts with their normal values, they are nevertheless likely to go along with other group members, especially if they admire them or are similar to them (Stroebe & Diehl, 1988). The result is often what seems like a loss of moral sense. Violence and other normally inhibited behaviors often appear. One analysis of 60 lynchings between 1899 and 1946 revealed that the savagery of the event increased as the size of the mob increased. Presumably, the mob members' self-control evaporated along with their individuality (Mullen, 1986).

Violence is not the only possible outcome when people become deindividuated. Any behavior that is normally inhibited may emerge. People tend to take more risks when they are part of a group than when they are acting as individuals; this is known as the *risky-shift effect* (Wallach, Kogan, & Bem, 1964).

People are usually pretty inhibited about expressing their emotions in public. For instance, we may be sexually attracted to someone, but we usually do nothing about it. For a study on "environmental psychology," Gergen, Gergen, and Barton (1973) placed male and female volunteers who did not know each other in a totally dark chamber, with no rules as to what they should or should not do. The subjects were told that they would be escorted individually from the chamber at the end of 30 minutes and never meet each other except in the dark. Using infrared cameras, tape recorders, and postexperimental interviews, the researchers compared what happened in this deindividuated group with what happened in a comparable group who spent 30 minutes in the chamber with the lights on. In the dark, almost everyone touched others, 50 percent hugged others, and 80 percent reported becoming sexually aroused. In the lights-on room, almost no one touched anyone else, there was no hugging, and only 15 percent reported sexual arousal. Obviously, darkness and anonymity allowed people to act in a very disinhibited fashion!

The effects of submergence in a group may sometimes be valuable. Turner (1985, p. 115 argues):

> "there is a long tradition in social psychology which regards group functioning as a regression to more primitive, irrational, or instinctual forms of behavior. Terms for group phenomena with derogatory connotations include "de-individuation," "diffusion of responsibility," "risky-shift," "group think," "conformity," "prejudice (for negative intergroup attitudes)," "group pressure," and, of course, "stereotyping." Self-categorization theory takes a different view: it sees in-group identification as an adaptive social cognitive process that makes prosocial relations such as social cohesion, cooperation, and influence (unity of action and attitudes) possible. Moreover, it is adaptive precisely because it represents a mechanism for allowing individuals to be more than just "individual persons." It is assumed that acting in terms of one's personal uniqueness may sometimes have extremely dysfunctional consequences."

In other words, "losing yourself" in a group is not always a bad thing, and feeling that you are part of a group may be a positive and valuable experience. Do you think that the benefits of losing yourself in a group outweigh the dangers?

HELPING

The anonymity of modern urban life has been blamed for a variety of problems, including people's indifference toward others, particularly others in trouble. In one notorious case, Kitty Genovese was savagely attacked outside her New York apartment building as she returned home from work late at night. Her screams drew the attention of at least 38 neighbors who looked out their windows, but no one came to her aid during the more than 30 minutes that the attack lasted. The attack ended with her death, and not one person even phoned the police during the attack.

Analysis of the Genovese case revealed that the witnesses were actually not emotionally indifferent to what they saw. They were horrified but felt unable or unwilling to act. Darley and Latané (1976) examined a number of similar cases and concluded that in general, the greater the number of people who witness an emergency, the less likely it is that any particular person will intervene. They proposed a number of possible reasons for why crowd size inhibits helping in an emergency. One such reason is *diffusion of responsibility:* The more witnesses there are, the more individuals feel that their help is unnecessary. In effect, responsibility for taking action is diffused across the group, with the result that no-one in particular feels especially responsible. (This is similar to the social loafing effect, discussed earlier.)

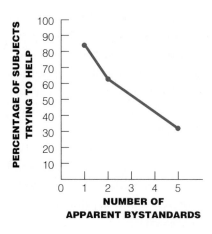

FIGURE 17.6
Percentages of Bystanders Helping Victims

The results in this figure show that a person is less likely to help someone in trouble if others are believed to be witnessing the emergency. When people thought they were alone, 85 percent helped, but when four others were present, only 31 percent helped. The more people there are, the less responsible any one person feels for helping.

SOURCE: Darley & Latané, 1968.

FIGURE 17.7
Time Taken for Response of Bystanders

When there are bystanders, individuals are less likely to intervene in a crisis. This graph shows that even when they do help, they are slower to do so. When alone, a person assisted in 52 seconds, but when four others were thought to be present, people took almost 3 minutes (166 seconds) to provide aid!

SOURCE: Darley & Latené, 1968.

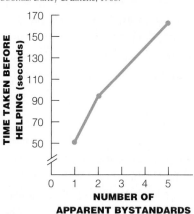

How groups inhibit helping has been examined repeatedly in the laboratory. For instance, Darley and Latané (1968) arranged a study in which a subject believed himself or herself to be communicating via intercom with either one, two, or five other subjects. (Actually, each subject was tested alone and communicated only with tape-recorded voices.) The subject (and the taped voices) introduced themselves and began a discussion, at which point one of the voices on the tape made sounds indicating an epileptic seizure. How likely was the real subject to offer help or report the emergency? Subjects who believed themselves to be the only person around other than the victim intervened 85 percent of the time (see Figure 17.6). Subjects who believed that they were one of two people other than the victim responded 62 percent of the time. And subjects who believed that there were four other potential help givers intervened only 31 percent of the time. Not only did subjects who believed that they were in a group help less often, but their help, when offered, was much slower in coming (see Figure 17.7).

Another possible reason why groups inhibit helping is the ambiguity of an emergency situation. According to this theory, if we observe others not reacting, we may start to think that the situation does not really require intervention. A related possibility is the fear of appearing foolish for intervening when help is not required (Latané & Nida, 1981). Clark and Word (1972) manipulated the ambiguity of a situation in which subjects heard a maintenance man fall off a ladder in an adjoining room. All subjects offered help when they heard the man cry out (unambiguous condition), but only about a third of them helped when they heard only the ladder falling (ambiguous condition).

Other aspects of a situation also affect whether bystanders will offer help. Help is more likely to be offered if it is clear what sort of help is required and if the potential helper feels capable of offering such help. The cost of helping—how much effort, inconvenience, or danger is involved—also makes a difference.

COMPLIANCE

Being a member of a group is only one of the factors that affect whether we respond to a request for help. **Compliance**—doing what someone asks us to do—has been studied mostly in terms of factors other than group influence. The size of the request itself makes a difference, as you might expect. As a rule, we are more likely to comply with a small charitable request than with a large request (Weyant & Smith, 1987). However, among people who have already established a pattern of giving to a particular charity, larger requests may produce larger donations (Doob & McLaughlin, 1989).

The effect of having agreed to an earlier request is evident in a compliance technique known as the **foot-in-the-door technique** (Freedman & Fraser, 1966). People who first agree to a small request (e.g., putting small signs in their windows) are more likely to agree to a larger, more difficult request (putting large, unattractive signs on their lawns) than are people who are presented with the large request first, without previously having agreed to the small request. The standard interpretation of the foot-in-the-door effect is that people who comply with the small request perceive themselves as cooperative and helpful, so that when the large request is made, their self-image as being helpful makes them more likely to comply. This interpretation has recently been challenged, however, by Gorassini and Olson (1995), who suggest that complying with the initial small request may lead to more compliance with the larger request not by changing people's views of their own helpfulness but by changing their perception of the situation to one involving increased social pressure to be generous.

A related technique often used to manipulate consumers is the *low-ball technique*, in which a salesperson gets you to commit yourself to a purchase at a relatively low price. Then it turns out that the price is going to be substantially higher. Your initial commitment pushes you past the problem of the higher cost and you make the purchase. In one study, only 24 percent of subjects agreed to participate in an experiment that would require them to arrive at the laboratory at 7 A.M. But when subjects were simply asked whether they would be willing to participate in an experiment, and only later, after having agreed, were told that it began at 7 A.M., fully 53 percent complied (Cialdini, Cacioppo, Bassett, & Miller, 1978). The behavior of the subjects in the Milgram experiment (1963) (see "Controversy: Shocking Obedience") may also be seen as an example of the result of low-balling, since they agreed to participate without realizing how emotionally expensive the experience would be.

A seemingly opposite technique for producing compliance is the **door-in-the-face technique** (Cialdini, Vincent, Lewis, Catalan, Wheeler, & Darby, 1975). You begin by making a large—even unreasonable—request (e.g., "Will you volunteer to counsel juvenile delinquents for 2 hours a week for 2 years?"), which the person naturally declines. However, immediately afterward, the target is more likely to comply with a moderate request (Will you volunteer to chaperone a group of juvenile delinquents on a single 2-hour outing?") than if the initial large request had not been made. This technique works best when the moderate request is presented immediately after the large request (Cann, Sherman, & Elkes, 1975), possibly because the individual feels some guilt about having just turned down the large request. Over time, as the guilt gets weaker, the person is less likely to comply.

We encounter attempts to get us to comply with requests all the time. One of the advantages of studying psychology is that it should make you more aware of subtle psychological techniques that might be used to get you to comply. Unfortunately, research (Cialdini, 1985; Katzev & Brownstein, 1989) indicates that teaching subjects about compliance techniques did not prevent the techniques from working on them!

OBEDIENCE

Obedience involves orders rather than requests and is therefore the most direct form of social influence. Obedience is sometimes necessary for the efficiency or even survival of the group—thus the emphasis on obedience in the military— but history has revealed the disastrous potential of blind obedience. "I was only following orders" was a standard defense offered at the Nuremberg war crimes trials following the Nazi holocaust in Europe. We have heard this defense offered by Americans as well, in the military and in the service of the White House. This defense was not accepted by the legal experts at Nuremberg, but social psychologists (and many others) were naturally intrigued about whether and how people can resist orders from authority figures. Perhaps the best-known study in social psychology is Milgram's (1963, 1974) experimental analysis of obedience to authority (see "Controversy: Shocking Obedience").

CONFORMITY

Social pressure goes beyond explicit attempts to convince us of something (persuasion) or to get us to do something by asking us or telling us to do it (compliance or obedience). **Conformity** is adjusting our behavior to match the group when there is no direct order to do so. Every group has social norms, or implicit rules, that its members obey. Although we may prefer to see ourselves making our own choices, much of our

SHOCKING OBEDIENCE

Responding to a newspaper advertisement for a study of learning, male subjects arrived at the Yale University laboratory of Stanley Milgram. Each subject, along with a partner, drew lots to decide who would act as the teacher and who would be the learner. The teacher's job was to present a list of paired-associate words to the learner. The teacher was supposed to keep track of the learner's progress and to punish the learner with an electric shock for each error the learner made. The teacher sat in front of an imposing shock generator and received a mild sample shock as a demonstration. The generator had 30 switches, marked from 15 to 450 volts. The highest level of shock was clearly extremely intense and even dangerous, although the experimenter began by reassuring both the teacher and the learner that "although the shocks can be extremely painful, they cause no permanent tissue damage" (Milgram, 1963, p. 373). The learner was strapped into a chair with electrodes attached to his wrists.

Once the experiment began, the experimenter told the teacher to increase the voltage by one unit (15 volts) for every error made by the learner, who was out of sight in an adjoining room.

Starting with 75 volts the learner begins to grunt and moan. At 150 volts he demands to be let out of the experiment, and at 180 volts he cries that he can no longer stand the pain. At 300 volts he refuses to provide any more answers . . . . The experimenter [then] instructs the [teacher] to treat the absence of an answer as a wrong answer, and to follow the usual shock procedure. (Milgram, 1965, p. 246)

If the teacher had any questions or concerns, the experimenter, a fairly severe 31-year-old biology teacher, merely responded, "Please go on." The experimenter dealt with any further resistance from the teacher by stating, "It is absolutely essential that you continue" or "You have no other choice, you must go on."

When the procedure of this study was described to a group of psychiatrists, college students, and middle-class adults, on average they estimat-

ed that the teacher would deliver about 9 of the possible maximum 30 shocks; that is, they expected the teacher to rebel against the experimenter's instructions. In fact, on average, the teacher delivered 27 of 30 shocks; none of them delivered fewer than 20 shocks (300 volts); and 26 of the 40 teachers (65 percent) delivered the full 450 volts, despite the fact that the learner was apparently unconscious (or worse) during the final phase of the procedure (see Figure 17.8).

As you may have guessed, this experiment was not what it seemed. The "experimenter" was not Milgram himself, but a confederate, trained to act in a severe and demanding (but

not explicitly threatening) manner. The "learner" was also a trained confederate, a pleasant, mild-mannered 47-year-old accountant. The draw to determine who would be teacher or learner had been rigged. No shocks were actually delivered to the learner; his agony was simulated on tape. Still, the situation was very convincing. Most subjects were in an emotional turmoil by the end, torn between their compassion for the learner and their desire to obey the experimenter.

Subjects were observed to sweat, tremble, stutter, bite their lips, groan, and dig their fingernails into their flesh. These were characteristic rather than exceptional responses . . . . I observed a mature and initially poised businessman enter the laboratory smiling and confident. Within 20 minutes he was reduced to a twitching, stuttering wreck, who was rapidly approaching a point of nervous collapse (Milgram, 1963, pp. 375–377).

In most cases, despite their intense misgivings, the teachers obeyed.

This study was only one in a lengthy series of studies in which Milgram explored the factors that would increase or decrease the extent to which subjects (teachers) would obey fully (450 volts). Some factors that

FIGURE 17.8
Milgram's Results
SOURCE: Baron & Byrne, 1977, p. 292.

PERCENTAGE OF SUBJECTS OBEYING COMMAND AT EACH SHOCK LEVEL

Subject receives sample shock

Victim pounds on wall

Victim pounds on wall again

Shock level: Slight, Moderate, Strong, Very strong, Intense, Extremely intense, Danger severe shock, XXX

15 Volts —————————————————→ 450 Volts

reduced obedience included moving the experiment from the Yale campus to an undistinguished office building in Bridgeport, Connecticut (48 percent fully obedient), having the teacher sit right next to the learner and place the learner's hand on a "shock pad" to deliver punishment (30 percent), having the experimenter leave the room and deliver instructions by telephone (22.5 percent), having another subject (actually a confederate) insist that the shock level be increased for each error (20 percent), having other subjects/teachers (actually confederates) defy the experimenter (10 percent). Somewhat surprisingly, using women as subjects/teachers made no difference (65 percent). Figure 17.9 shows graphically the results of adding defiant peers to the situation.

The drama of the Milgram experiment—the originally published, 65 percent obedience version—created quite a stir. Numerous magazine articles—even a TV movie—dealt with the implications of this study. Milgram himself

CONTROVERSY

emphasized the analogy between the events in his lab and the events that had happened less than 20 years earlier in Nazi Germany. Were the Holocaust murderers really no different from the average person on the street? Was obedience to authority widespread—even in America?

Various aspects of the Milgram experiment created controversy, but two aspects drew particular attention (Miller, 1986). First, there was the question of ethics. Numerous critics, led by Baumrind (1964), severely criticized Milgram for his use of deception and for the distress he caused his subjects. These critics pointed out that after the hoax had been revealed, Milgram's subjects would become very

suspicious of researchers. In fact, subjects did claim that they would be more skeptical in the future. Of course, it is debatable whether skepticism is a bad thing. More seriously, the critics charged Milgram with having created terrible emotional suffering in the subjects during the experiment itself and of leaving the subjects with the disturbing knowledge that they were capable of committing atrocities. (The fact that the subjects did not actually deliver any shocks means little, since they believed that they were delivering shocks and presumably would have done so had the shock generator been actually functioning.) Milgram's response to these criticisms was that the subjects, by their own self-report and even when interviewed by psychiatrists months later, showed virtually no emotional aftereffects of their participation in the study. But the critics argued that the subjects may not have given their true reactions. Besides, Milgram did not know in advance that the subjects would be unaffected. As for learning disturbing truths about yourself, is that a valuable lesson or something to be avoided? In the final analysis, the value of Milgram's study—in terms of showing the world how ordinary people can be made to commit atrocities—is generally believed to outweigh its ethical costs.

The second objection to the Milgram experiment was that it did not provide valid conclusions about obedience. Baumrind and others (e.g., Orne & Holland, 1968) claimed that because of the abuse of trust in the study, it is impossible to generalize the results. The research laboratory is ordinarily seen as a safe place, where nothing seriously wrong can happen; so if an experimenter demands a particular behavior, then it must be alright. This assumption, though, does not necessarily apply in the real world to which Milgram wished to extend his findings.

FIGURE 17.9
Reducing Blind Obedience

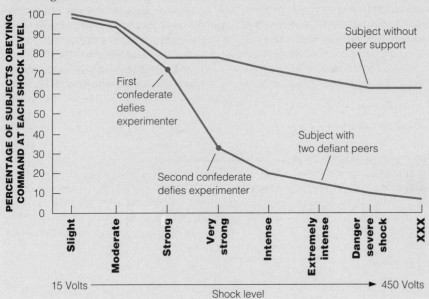

behavior is dictated by group norms. Although adolescents typically take pride in rebelling against their parents' values and behavior patterns, the more thoughtful rebels recognize that the rebel group itself imposes constraints of speech, dress, and action.

Many experiments have shown how others' opinions can affect our behavior. In one classic series of studies, Sherif (1935) began with the *autokinetic effect*, in which a small spot of light projected onto a screen in a totally darkened room appears to move, even though it is actually stationary. Subjects who judged the "movement" of the light

The response to this criticism was that the trust in an experimenter's authority is exactly the same as the trust in authority that we display in the real world. Subsequent field studies showed, for instance, that nurses obey doctors' orders, even when those orders are clearly against the rules designed to protect patients (Hofling, Brotzman, Dalrymple, Graves, & Pierce, 1966). Parents, teachers, and government and military leaders all demand trust and obedience—and by and large they get it.

Milgram (1974) attempted to explain the obedience effect in terms of what he called an "agentic shift," in which subjects gave up personal responsibility for their actions and in effect became agents of the experimenter. Some critics (e.g., Helm & Morelli, 1979) have accepted Milgram's basic point about the power of situational factors to produce obedience, but they have criticized his "agentic shift" explanation as too vague and not in keeping with the emotional distress of many of the obedient subjects. Another issue concerns the controversy over dispositional versus situational determinants of behavior (see Chapter 14 for an extended discussion).

One popular interpretation of the Milgram experiment is that people are much more obedient than they think they are—that Americans are just as pathologically obedient as, say, Germans. Obedience is easy to think of as a personality trait, especially since psychologists themselves have frequently done so. Before Milgram, the most relevant study of the psychology of Nazi Germany was the landmark analysis of the authoritarian personality (Adorno et al., 1950), in which a particular personality profile was drawn, including an excessive tendency to obey one's superiors. People who see the Milgram experiment performed are frequently tempted to draw dispo-

sitional conclusions about the subjects/teachers: It is something about *them* that makes them do what they do. "However, it may be a misreading of Milgram's basic point to assume that human beings have an inherent tendency to obey authority" (Miller, 1986, p. 199). Milgram's point, often forgotten, was that it was the situation that determined the subjects' behavior. Even though some subjects were defiant, even the most defiant subject delivered 300 volts in the original study, well beyond what anyone would have predicted. Defiance at earlier stages occurred only when the situation was somehow changed to encourage it. Indeed, Ross (1988) has noted that the way in which the original study was structured made it especially difficult to disobey. Most of the teachers would have liked to quit, but for most of them, there was no obvious way out of a situation in which they had become virtually trapped and no obvious point separating acceptable from unacceptable obedience. Defying an authority in a strange and highly ambiguous situation is not something most of us are experienced or comfortable with. Similarly, perhaps, the SS doctors arriving at Auschwitz "encountered a set of conditions so structured organizationally and psychologically that virtually everyone entering into the situation committed atrocities" (Lifton, 1986, p. 412). It seems that in the Milgram experiment, as with the Nazi doctors, a gradual increase in the severity of the torture was a key element of the proceedings. Although you might never consider delivering 300

volts of shock to someone else, if you have just delivered 285 volts, then 300 volts does not seem so bad. (This escalating procedure is in many ways equivalent to the foot-in-the-door technique discussed earlier.)

Eventually, we will have to take individual differences into account to understand the Milgram studies completely. Milgram, understandably, emphasized the great power of the situation, but some individuals did defy the authority of the experimenter. Milgram himself found that obedient subjects tend to score higher on the trait of authoritarianism than do defiant subjects (Elms & Milgram, 1966). Miale and Selzer (1975, p. 11), in arguing for the basic personality pathology of the Nazi war criminals—and, presumably, the more obedient of Milgram's subjects—have insisted that "the lesson to be learned . . . is not that in a wicked world decent people will act in a wicked way but that in a wicked world people with a penchant for wickedness will freely indulge it, justifying themselves (when called upon to do so) on the ground that they were merely obeying orders." Most commentators have readily accepted Miligram's situational interpretation, even though it contradicts the fundamental (dispositional) attribution error discussed earlier in this chapter (Miller, 1986). Selzer (1983) suggests that social scientists actually have a situational rather than dispositional bias, preferring to see evil more as a social disorder than as a moral failure of individuals. Yet (as we saw in Chapter 14), reanalysis of Miale and Selzer's personality test data suggests that the war criminals were not especially pathological. In any case, discovering the situational or dispositional factors that contribute to defiance of harmful authority seems to be a crucial issue for psychology and society at large.

after hearing other subjects' or confederates' judgments tended to "see" what the other group members had "seen" before them.

An even more powerful demonstration was devised by Asch (1956), who used a stimulus that was not at all ambiguous. Subjects saw a standard line and had to decide which of three other lines was the same length as the standard (see Figure 17.10). Typically, the subject made his or her decision after a number of other subjects announced theirs. After a few trials of giving the obviously correct answer, the first

Psychology in Our Times
Contagious Behavior

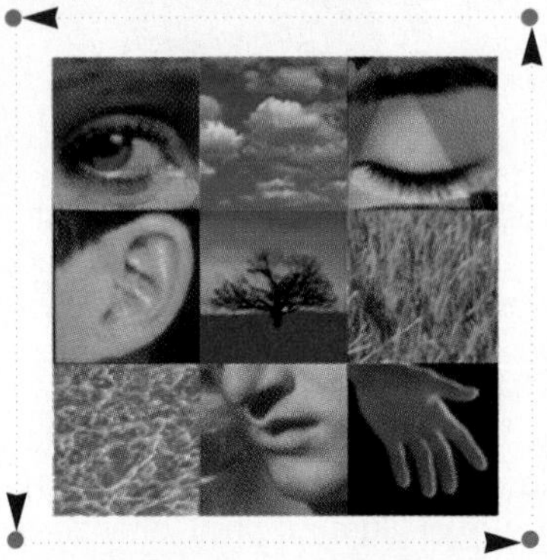

Conformity involves thinking or acting the way that other people do. In psychology experiments, conformity occurs when a single individual goes along with a group. In the wider world, conformity usually refers to people in general going along with each other in terms of attitudes, styles, or some new "in" behavior (such as line-dancing, wearing your cap backward, or whatever else the latest fad may be). Most of these fads start somewhere, with a "leader," but for most of us, it is just social fashion that we are following. Most of the time, such conformity is harmless, but occasionally a fad may turn out to be dangerous or even lethal. Psychologists and sociologists have talked about some fads as being "contagious," as if the behavior "infects" the individuals who come into contact with it. Behavioral contagion usually refers to the spread of behaviors that otherwise might never appear.

Consider applause. Whether or not we applaud at the end of a show depends on how much we appreciate the performance. But that's not the only factor. It turns out that we are more likely to applaud if other people around us applaud first (Freedman, Birsky, & Cavoukian, 1980). In fact, a well-known showbiz ploy is to plant "clappers" in the audience to stimulate applause at the end of the show. This applause prevents dissatisfied customers from feeling that they are in a majority large enough to demand their money back. Television producers use laugh tracks to convince us that their shows are actually funny, but the laugh tracks are not as effective as other people in the same room with us watching and laughing.

Why are we more likely to applaud when others set an example for us? Freedman and colleagues (1980) suggest that we are often uncertain what to do in certain circumstances. Is applause appropriate or deserved? Often we are not quite sure, and we look to others to resolve our doubts. Even if we know we liked the performance, we may be worried about the potential embarrassment of being the only ones who applaud.

Wheeler (1966) provided a more general theory of contagious behavior, in which he argued that when we experience an internal conflict—we have reasons for wanting to do something, but we also have concerns—the example set by others is often enough to overcome the concerns and

few subjects (actually experimental confederates) began to unanimously choose the wrong answer. A large percentage of the actual subjects (75 percent) went along with the group on at least one trial, despite the evidence of their own senses. Subjects who performed alone hardly ever made an incorrect choice. (It is of interest to note that as a graduate student, Milgram worked with Asch; Milgram saw his obedience work as a natural extension of Asch's analysis of social and situational pressure.)

Figure 17.10
Asch's Challenge

Subjects in Asch's experiment on conformity and independence were asked to compare several stimulus lines (B1, B2, B3) to a standard stimulus (A). They were to pick the B line that was the same length as A. What would you do if five people ahead of you had picked B3 as the correct answer?

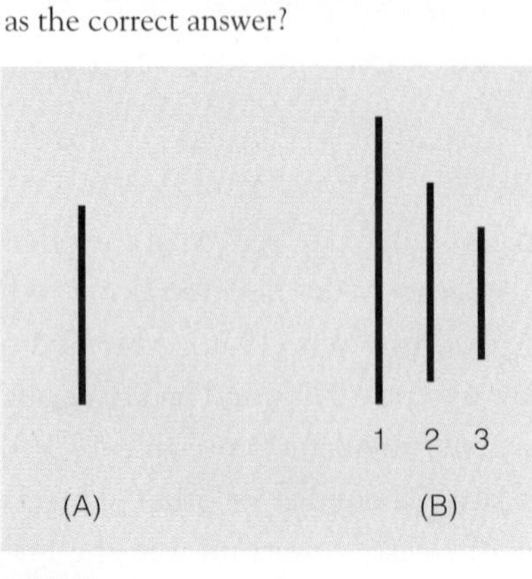

Ironically, Asch's classic study was intended to demonstrate that people resist group influence when they have the objective evidence of their senses to rely on. Indeed, 63.2 percent of responses in Asch's study were correct, despite group pressure to the contrary. Social psychologists, however, have tended to emphasize how much subjects conformed instead of how much they resisted, probably because conformity is more surprising or controversial than is independence in American society (Friend, Rafferty, & Bramel, 1990).

Just as obedience varies in different situations, so too does conformity. As you would expect, people conform more as the size of the group exerting pressure increases, although this effect seems to level off when the group reaches six or seven members (Wilder, 1977). Conformity declines sharply when there is an ally who also resists. The more ambiguous the situation, the more likely people are to conform. Finally, people conform more when the group is thought to possess expertise (Crano, 1970). All of these factors affect conformity in much the same way that they affect obedience, but there are important differences between conformity and obedience. As we have noted, conformity is subtler than obedience, and perhaps, as a result, "people

make us do it. Without someone else's examples, we might never follow through on our urge. Sightings of the Virgin Mary or UFOs often occur in clusters, presumably because the first sighting triggers further reports. People who might hesitate to make such a claim feel more confident about doing so if others go first. These examples, of course, are all fairly harmless. The most dramatic instances of behavioral contagion occur when we end up doing something that seems particularly self-destructive.

Adolescents, in particular, seem to be vulnerable to behavioral contagion, possibly because their insecurities make them especially likely to do what "everyone else" is doing. If the activity is dangerous or naughty, but attractive, then the example of others will often make all the difference. Drug taking and similar illicit activities—including sexual behavior—often depend on whether your peers are doing it. Crandall (1988) has argued that binge eating is contagious. He demonstrated that new recruits to a college sorority eventually came to adopt the standards of their particular sorority with regard to bingeing. They were not recruited on the basis of whether they binged or not. Instead, their bingeing was shaped by the norms of the group. A full-blown eating disorder such as bulimia nervosa is unlikely to develop just because of social pressure, but in a vulnerable young woman with a poor body image and low self-esteem, a social norm of bingeing may provide the "solution" to her problems.

A more radical instance of self-destructive behavioral

contagion is seen in suicide clusters, a series of suicides over a relatively short time within a relatively small group (such as a high school). There has been a great deal of concern in recent years about "epidemics" of suicide, often (but not always) among adolescents (Coleman, 1987; O'Carroll, 1990), with clusters appearing in every part of the United States. One suicide will seemingly "trigger" another, often among friends or just acquaintances. A related phenomenon is the increase in the apparent suicide rate (often disguised as single-vehicle accidents) that follows news of celebrity suicides. TV shows, movies and popular songs that mention suicide are often blamed for a subsequent epidemic. Often, it seems, adolescents just need the encouragement of someone else to do something about which they have been hesitating. Of course, most people do not commit suicide just because someone else does. But among the small minority of people who are depressed or despondent, someone else's example may be enough. In fact, there is a significant movement to suppress publicity ("glorification") of suicide to remove the contagious effect.

Occasionally, behavioral contagion can have a positive outcome. For instance, we are more likely to stand up to unreasonable demands by authorities if others have shown the way (Levy, 1992). Sometimes we need help to do the right thing. But often as not, it seems that we end up doing the wrong thing because others have paved the way. Either way, it seems clear that the examples set by others have a profound effect on our own behavior.

readily acknowledge the source of their obedience, while they generally deny that they have conformed to peers" (Miller, 1986, p. 58).

Why do people conform? There seem to be two reasons—accuracy and acceptance. People usually want to be right—to give the correct answer or do the suitable thing—so when there is ambiguity, they may rely on others (especially "expert" others) as guides for the way to behave or even think. In addition, and just as importantly, people want to belong. Conforming to a group is a way of gaining acceptance by the group, just as deviating from a group produces pressure designed to bring the deviant back in line (Schachter, 1951). So it should not be surprising that individuals conform more to a group of strangers in an Asch-type study than to a group of friends (McKelvey & Kerr, 1988). How well you get along with your friends probably will not be affected by your performance in the study, but disagreeing with strangers is likely to leave them with a strongly negative impression of you.

Why are we so concerned about being accepted by the group? Clearly, group acceptance has a practical value in terms of the social rewards and punishments that a group can give. Being part of a group may also be adaptive in evolutionary terms. Whatever the reason, it is clear that people are highly responsive to social influence. Some people are perhaps more conformist than others (e.g., people who score high on a Concern for Appropriateness Scale [Johnson, 1989]), but we are probably all more conformist than we think we are. Social psychology's lesson is that our image of ourselves as autonomous agents acting for our own reasons and ignoring social pressure may be an illusion (Sampson, 1989).

THEMES IN REVIEW

Although the message of social psychology concerns the powerful influence that people have on one another, the general themes of psychology are all evident. Typically, these themes appear when we ask about the mechanisms underlying the phenomena of social behavior. The developmental theme is implicit in much of social psychology, since we only gradually develop into fully social (socialized) adults. For instance, adult romantic love in many ways resembles the love of an infant for its mother and may never develop properly if the infant does not form a strong attachment to the mother. The biological theme would appear to clash with the message of social psychology, since social psychology typically sees our behavior as stemming from social rather than biological sources. However, these two approaches are not necessarily incompatible. The social facilitation of behavior, for instance, seems to depend on the activation of physiological arousal in response to the presence of others. Learning enters into social psychology in many ways. Prejudice, for instance, is almost certainly learned, although there is some controversy over whether we have to learn it for ourselves or whether we may simply learn it secondhand from our parents, the media, and other sources. The cognitive theme is very prominent these days in social psychology. Social cognition occupies a dominant position in social psychology, and even older topics, such as attitude change, now rely on cognitive analyses. Sometimes we change our opinions after a serious cognitive analysis of the facts, whereas at other times we react mindlessly to messages from celebrities. The sociocultural theme may be found everywhere in social psychology. A strong example occurs in the area of obedience, where research seems to indicate that situational pressures have an overwhelming effect on whether people obey authorities, whether or not they come from an "authoritarian" culture.

SUMMARY

❶ Social psychology is the systematic study of the way the presence (or implied presence) of other people affects individual behavior. It encompasses social cognition (how we think about people), personal relationships, persuasion and attitude change, and other forms of social influence.

❷ Social cognition examines the ways in which our cognitive structures affect our thoughts or memories of people, as well as how these cognitions about people may affect our behavior toward them—and their behavior as well.

❸ Person perception refers to the processes involved in forming impressions of other people and explaining their behavior. Implicit personality theory refers more specifically to judgments about personality on the basis of one or two personality characteristics.

❹ Stereotypes are judgments about personality based on demographic characteristics such as race, sex, or age. We tend to perceive people from groups other than our own as more homogeneous and as more negative. Prejudice consists of negative cognitive, emotional, and behavioral reactions toward members of other groups.

❺ Impression formation research concerns itself with the way different pieces of information about another person are combined to form an overall impression. Self-perception research is concerned with the way we come to know ourselves (our traits, motives, and feelings). Social comparison theory suggests that we sometimes learn about ourselves by comparing ourselves with others.

❻ Causal attribution is the process by which we determine the causes of behavior, such as whether someone acted a particular way because he or she really wanted to or was forced to by circumstances. Attention to distinctiveness, consensus, and consistency helps us to disentangle causality.

7 Attributions of causality are often biased. People are more likely to attribute behavior to salient events in the environment. We tend to make situational attributions for ourselves but dispositional attributions for others, possibly because we have a different perspective about our own behavior. Attributions are also biased by motivations. Attributional egotism is a tendency for an actor to take personal credit for success but shift the blame for failure. Defensive attribution serves to protect a perceiver's self-image or view of the world.

8 The primary factors that determine attraction to another person are physical attractiveness, proximity, and similarity. Romantic love usually begins with passion but eventually grows into a broader form of companionship.

9 Close personal relationships tend to progress through stages. People begin by sharing their thoughts and feelings, along with a commitment to each other. All relationships must eventually confront some conflict, and how the conflicts are handled usually determines the success of the relationship. Relationships dissolve when the opportunities for satisfaction outside the relationship exceed those inside and the forces holding the relationship together become weak.

10 Attitudes and beliefs may be changed in many ways. Direct persuasion usually works best when a communicator is credible and trustworthy, but sometimes the communicator need only be attractive. The most effective way to present arguments depends on the circumstances and the target of persuasion.

11 Attitudes do not always correspond to behavior. Research suggests that making the connection explicit between people's attitudes and their corresponding behavior is the best way to get them to act accordingly. Cognitive dissonance theory is concerned with consequences of discrepancies between attitudes and behavior. Getting people to act in a way that conflicts with their attitudes can induce them to change their attitudes. Self-perception theory also recommends behavior change as a prelude to attitude change.

12 Social facilitation refers to the energizing effect of other people on our performance. Sometimes the presence of others helps, but sometimes it actually impairs performance. Social loafing refers to a motivational decrease when we are performing as part of a group. Often groups are less helpful to people in distress than are individuals. Deindividuation occurs when we lose our identity in a group; the result may be the expression of antisocial or normally inhibited behaviors.

13 Compliance is a form of social influence involving direct requests. The size of the request and how it is presented usually makes a great difference. Obedience involves direct orders. Milgram's research indicates that people will often obey orders to perform acts that they consider highly immoral. Conformity, or acting like others do, is also prevalent in social life, because others define reality for us and because belonging to a group is usually a powerful motive.

KEY TERMS

social psychology (p. 711)

social cognition (p. 711)

implicit personality theory (p. 712)

impression management (p. 711)

stereotype (p. 713)

prejudice (p. 714)

stigma (p. 715)

impression formation (p. 718)

illusory correlation (p. 718)

self-perception (p. 719)

social comparison (p. 720)

self-esteem (p. 721)

causal attribution (p. 722)

dispositional causes (p. 723)

situational causes (p. 723)

discounting (p. 724)

augmenting (p. 725)

self-handicapping (p. 725)

fundamental attribution error (p. 726)

actor-observer effect (p. 726)

attributional egotism (p. 727)

mere exposure effect (p. 729)

attitude (p. 733)

persuasion (p. 734)

cognitive dissonance (p. 739)

social facilitation (p. 742)

social loafing (p. 742)

deindividuation (p. 743)

compliance (p. 745)

foot-in-the-door technique (p. 745)

door-in-the-face technique (p. 746)

conformity (p. 746)

FOR CRITICAL ANALYSIS

1 Social psychology emphasizes how we are affected by others. Why are Americans reluctant to admit that they are influenced by others, and how does this reluctance distort our understanding of why we behave the way we do?

2 What are the leading causes of prejudice, and how can prejudice be reduced?

3 What processes help disadvantaged or stigmatized groups to maintain high levels of self-esteem? What is likely to happen to self-esteem as disadvantages and stigmatization are gradually eliminated?

4 How does self-handicapping work? How can you maximize the advantages of self-handicapping? What self-handicapping strategies do you use regularly?

5 What are the major determinants of attraction? In what ways are friendship and romantic love related, and in what ways is romantic love special, or at least different from friendship?

6 When is your performance likely to be helped by the presence of other people, and when is it likely to be impaired?

SUGGESTED READINGS

ARONSON, E. (1993). *The social animal* (6th ed.). San Francisco: Freeman. A well-written and entertaining introduction to the main topics in social psychology; the book covers conformity, persuasion, attraction, aggression and prejudice.

CIALDINI, R. B. (1993). *Influence: Science and Practice* (3rd ed.). Glenview, IL,: Scott, Foresman. An entertaining treatment of social influence theory and practice, spiced with many examples from the world of salesmanship.

DEAUX, K. & WRIGHTSMAN, L. S. (1984). *Social psychology in the 80s* (4th ed.). Monterey, Ca.: Brooks/Cole. An excellent social psychology text that covers all the standard topics and in addition has novel chapters on communication and inter-group relations.

FISKE, S. T. & TAYLOR, S. E. (1984). *Social Cognition*. Reading, MA.: Addison-Wesley. A text that focuses on topics of person perception, attribution, and social inference from a unified theoretical perspective.

MILLER, A. G. (1986). *The obedience experiments: A case study of controversy in social science*. New York: Praeger. A highly readable and thought-provoking review and analysis of Milgram's obedience research, including debates about the ethical and methodological value of the experiments.

PSYCHOLOGY ON THE INTERNET

Social Cognition–Social Psychology Paper Archive
(http://www.psych.purdue.edu/~esmith/scarch.html)

This home page, maintained by Eliott R. Smith, contains "preprints of abstracts of papers or presentations and links to information about active researchers in the area [of social psychology]."

Social Psychology at the Australian National University
(http://online.anu.edu.au/psychology/socpsych/socpsych.html)

This site provides a definition of social psychology and discusses the importance of this field of research. In addition, it provides introductions to the following topic areas: stereotyping, social influence, social identity, and self-categorization.

FIELDS OF APPLIED PSYCHOLOGY

Chapter 18

Imagine that you are a woman who works as a welder in a Jacksonville, Florida, shipyard. Because women make up less than 0.5 percent of the skilled workers at this shipyard, you are likely to be the only woman working on any given shift. Your work environment can best be described as a "locker-room atmosphere" (Fiske, 1993, p. 622), with obscenity, profanity, pornography, sexual innuendos, and groping occurring "every day all day." What would you do?

As unlikely as this scenario might seem, it describes an actual situation. The female welder, Lois Robinson, was forced to endure off-color jokes and teasing on a daily basis. "For example, one worker put a flashlight in his pants to show how well endowed horses are; another carved the handle of a tool to resemble a penis, waving it in the face of the women" (Fiske, 1993, p. 622). When Lois Robinson complained about her work environment to top management at Jacksonville Shipyards Inc., the managers defended her coworkers. To justify the liberal display of pornography, one manager "pointed out that he had his own pinups" (p. 622). Robinson filed a lawsuit claiming she was the victim of sexual harassment in a hostile work environment. She won the initial trial, but Jacksonville Shipyards Inc. appealed the decision. The case is pending.

At this point, you may be wondering *why* Lois Robinson was subjected to such hostile and humiliating treatment. Robinson's experiences at the Jacksonville shipyard have been analyzed by Susan T. Fiske (1993), an applied social psychologist. Fiske argues that the male-dominated social structure at the shipyard created an overwhelming power asymmetry between men and women, with men holding all the power and women being powerless to halt the cycle of harassment. Applied psychologists can assume two roles in helping to resolve social problems like the one that took place at the Jacksonville shipyard. First, they can study situations or phenomena to gain insight into what contributes to a particular problem. A second, more direct role involves the psychologist as an advisor in shaping social policy and legislation. Later in this chapter, we will consider a case in which a group of social and industrial/organizational psychologists assumed the latter role by providing the U.S. Supreme Court with evidence from psychological research that was instrumental in crafting more explicit guidelines for recognizing sexual discrimination.

Additional applications have already been covered in earlier chapters. For example, in Chapter 9 we discussed the mental testing movement. The creation and use of tests of intelligence and educational achievement (such as the Scholastic Assessment Test and the Graduate Record Exam) have had a profound impact on American education. Schools and teachers are evaluated on the way their students perform on standardized tests. Students' future education (where they go to school, what sort of courses they take) is determined, in part, by the way they perform on these tests. More will be said about the impact of psychological testing on individuals and society later in the chapter. The principles of learning that have come out of studies in classical and operant conditioning (see Chapter 6) have also been applied in many practical ways. Phobias often seem to be created through classical conditioning, and conditioning processes are involved in drug addiction; therefore, conditioning techniques can be successful tools to modify these unhealthy behaviors. Some parental control techniques also have their origin in the study of animal conditioning. The practice of providing a "time-out" period for unruly children derives from behavioral studies on how time out from positive reinforcement affects behavior in pigeons and rats.

Because so many applications of psychology have been portrayed in this text, you may wonder about the need for a chapter entitled "Fields of Applied Psychology." After all, aren't there applications for all areas of psychology? The answer to this question is yes, but this chapter highlights the emerging application of psychology in several important areas—industry, government, education, and law. In this chapter, we will examine six fields of applied psychology: industrial and organizational psychology, human factors (or human engineering) psychology, environmental psychology, school psychology, educational psychology, and psychology and law. Some of these fields have a relatively long history; others are more recent. Although other interesting applied areas exist (e.g., consumer psychology and sports psychology), we cannot describe them in detail here. We must mention, however, that the largest fields of applied psychology—clinical and counseling psychology—are not discussed in this chapter but are represented in Chapters 15 and 16.

In each of the following sections, we will define the field of inquiry, tell what its practitioners do and the settings in which they work, and provide some examples of their research. Of course, we cannot go into too much detail about any one field, but we hope that the information we offer will whet your appetite.

Industrial/Organizational Psychology

Industrial/organizational psychology (or I/O psychology, as it is usually called) is the science of human behavior in industry and other organizations. It applies the concepts, methods, principles, and knowledge derived from the broad discipline of psychology to people at work. The goal of I/O psychologists is to enhance human performance and the quality of work life within organizations (Bray & Associates, 1991). Among the issues that I/O psychologists consider are developing effective leadership, motivating workers, increasing employee satisfaction, selecting appropriate employees for jobs and providing them with effective training, measuring job performance, and enhancing productivity.

As the name implies, I/O psychology can be considered two separate subfields (Dorfman, 1989). **Industrial psychology,** which is also called *personnel psychology*, is primarily concerned with selecting employees, training them, and measuring their performance. Thus, industrial psychologists study ways to develop better job applications, selection tests, and interviewing techniques. They have a strong interest in identifying individual differences among people, because these differences may predict future job performance.

The field of **organizational psychology,** on the other hand, is more likely to concentrate on issues concerning the relationships among workers (and their supervisors) once they are in an organization. Organizational psychologists are interested in such issues as group dynamics, organizational climate, effective leadership, and the motivation to work. Organizational psychology is quite similar to the area in business schools called organizational behavior.

There is no sharp dividing line between industrial and organizational psychology, and most practitioners have competence in both areas (although they will likely specialize). Industrial psychologists have traditionally had a more applied focus, whereas organizational psychologists have attempted a more theoretical interpretation of phenomena (such as leadership). However, both subfields aim for a scientific understanding of psychological factors operating in the workplace.

Today, about 3,000 people work as I/O psychologists, and prospects for this well-paying field are quite good (Dorfman, 1989). A recent survey conducted by the Society for Industrial and Organizational Psychology (SIOP) identified five primary work settings for I/O psychologists (Bray & Associates, 1991). As indicated in Figure 18.1, 42 percent of I/O psychologists work for a private company or a government agency, 43 percent work as consultants in a firm or independently, and 15 percent are employed in colleges and universities. As you can see, the majority of I/O psychologists are employed on a full-time basis by large organizations. These psychologists typically work as personnel managers or vice-presidents of human relations or human resources departments. As organizations continue to "downsize," reducing the number of individuals they employ on a full-time basis, a number of I/O psychologists will move from the ranks of large organizations to work in consulting firms or as independent consultants. Interestingly, more than one-quarter of I/O psychologists in the SIOP survey reported holding secondary positions, often spanning the gap between practice and science. This is especially true of academicians, who often serve as consultants to organizations regarding personnel selection and organizational development.

FIGURE 18.1
Work Settings of Industrial/Organizational Psychologists

Forty-two percent of I/O psychologists work for large organizations, either public or private.

SOURCE: Bray & Associates, 1991.

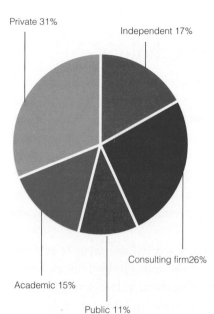

Private 31%

Independent 17%

Consulting firm 26%

Academic 15%

Public 11%

PERSONNEL SELECTION

The prime focus of industrial psychology is personnel selection, training, and performance evaluation. Suppose you worked for a chain of restaurants and were in charge of hiring cooks, servers, and hosts. How would you start?

Job Analysis. You would probably start by conducting a **job analysis,** a relatively complete description of the requirements for each job. Several standardized procedures have been developed for job analysis, including one presented in the U.S. Department of Labor *Handbook for Analyzing Jobs* and another in an instrument called the Position Analysis Questionnaire. In addition, as the job analyst, you would observe workers on the job, interview them, or even do the job yourself for some time. A thorough and accurate job analysis is essential for success in all phases of human resource management, from selection to training to performance evaluation.

Recruitment. Once the job analysis is complete, your next step would be to recruit people. How do you find cooks and servers for your new restaurant? You might advertise each position both within and outside your organization and seek referrals from current employees. While recruiting, you, as the personnel psychologist, will portray the company in the most favorable light to attract potential employees. If a misleading picture is presented, however, employees may be disgruntled when they discover that the reality of the position does not match their expectations. For this reason, techniques have been developed that afford *realistic job previews* (Wanous, 1980). These procedures are more likely to provide workers who are satisfied with their new position. One study found that presenting a "balanced" view of the organization—one that highlighted problems and difficulties as well as dispelling commonly held negative impressions—was most effective in reducing employee turnover and enhancing employees' perceptions of the organization (Meglino, DeNisi, Youngblood, & Williams, 1988).

Interviews. Assuming that more than one candidate will apply for a job, how can the best candidate be chosen? How can you pick the best host or cook from among many people? Unfortunately, there is no simple answer to this question. Virtually all organizations conduct interviews of prospective employees to try to determine if they are qualified, motivated, and able to work with others. An interviewer obviously has a difficult job, because the hiring decision is usually based on interviews in which prospective employees aim to present themselves in the most favorable light.

Numerous studies have been conducted to determine how well interviewers can select candidates for jobs. The general answer is "not very well" (Arvey & Campion, 1982). As Dorfman (1989) notes, "Unfortunately, almost all evidence suggests that the interview process is a notoriously poor procedure for predicting an individual's performance. It is extremely vulnerable to personal biases, whims, and gut feelings of the interviewer" (p. 90). For example, first impressions are critical, and the interviewer's later questions may be asked to confirm the original snap judgment. Macan and Dipboye (1988) showed that when people were initially given a positive evaluation in an interview, they were asked more questions likely to lead to positive answers. When people were initially given a negative evaluation, they were asked more questions likely to lead to negative answers. In addition, as just noted, the candidates are motivated to present themselves in the most favorable light. Thus, industrial psychologists tend to view job interviews as unreliable predictors of job performance, although much effort is now devoted to improving the process (e.g., Hakel, 1982).

Structured interviews—those providing a relatively prescribed series of questions—have been proposed as an alternative to the unstructured format currently used by the majority of organizations. With a structured interview, there is typically a greater focus on the knowledge, skills, and abilities of the job candidate as opposed to his or her personality, self-described strengths and weaknesses, and past experience. In one type of structured interview, the **situational interview,** descriptions of hypothetical work situations are constructed based on a job analysis (Gatewood & Feild, 1990). The aim of a situational interview is to gain a sense of how the job applicant would respond in each situation. Examples of situational interview questions are provided in Table 18.1. As you might imagine, the situational interview (like other structured interviews) tends to work well so long as the situations posed are indeed representative of the job and so long as the applicants respond on the job as they respond in the interview. Obviously, these concerns are not trivial. This brings us to an important question: Do structured interviews provide a more accurate or valid indication of an individual's future work performance? For the most part, the answer is yes. In a recent review of 150 studies,

The unstructured interview is used in virtually all employment settings, but much research casts doubt on its validity in predicting job performance.

TABLE 18.1
Examples of Situational Interview Questions and Scoring Scales

The answers provided below each question are ones you might expect from a job applicant. The idea is to anticipate a reasonable range of applicant responses and to determine what constitutes a low versus average versus high response.

1. Your spouse and two teenage children are sick in bed with colds. There are no relatives or friends available to look in on them. Your shift starts in 3 hours. What would you do in this situation?

1 (low)	Stay home — my family comes first.
3 (average)	Phone my supervisor and explain my situation.
5 (high)	Since they only have colds, I'd come to work.[a]

2. A customer comes into the store to pick up a watch he had left for repair. The repair was supposed to have been completed a week ago, but the watch is not back yet from the repair shop. The customer is very angry. How would you handle the situation?

1 (low)	Tell the customer the watch is not back yet and ask him to check back with me later.
3 (average)	Apologize, tell the customer that I will check into the problem and call him back later.
5 (high)	Put the customer at ease and call the repair shop while he waits.[b]

3. For the past week you have been consistently getting the jobs that are the most time consuming (e.g., poor handwriting, complex statistical work). You know it's nobody's fault because you have been taking the jobs in the priority order. You have just picked your fourth job of the day and it's another "loser." What would you do?

1 (low)	Thumb through the pile and take another job.
3 (average)	Complain to the coordinator, but do the job.
5 (high)	Take the job without complaining and do it.[c]

[a]Latham, G. P., Saari, L. M., Pursell, E. D., & Campion, M. A. (1980). The situational interview. *Journal of Applied Psychology, 65,* 422–427.
[b]Weekley, J. A., & Gier, J. A. (1987). Reliability and validity of the situational interview for a sales position. *Journal of Applied Psychology, 72,* 484–487.
[c]Latham, G. P., & Saari, L. M. (1984). Do people do what they say? Further studies on the situational interview. *Journal of Applied Psychology, 69,* 569–573.

SOURCE: Gatewood & Feild, 1990.

Wiesner and Cronshaw (1988) found that structured interviews achieved, on average, twice the predictive accuracy as did the typical unstructured interview.

Testing.   Another technique for selecting people for jobs is some form of psychological testing. Tests are constructed to predict job performance; people who perform well on the tests can be hired instead of those who do poorly. Of course, the careful development of employment tests is critical, because they must have good reliability (consistency of measurement) and predictive validity (predicting job performance accurately). These tests may measure physical skills and cognitive abilities.

Many examples of good tests exist. For example, the Purdue Mechanical Adaptability Test is used to predict performance in jobs requiring manual dexterity. Presented in Figure 18.2 are the results of a study in which the test was correlated with the percentage of hired employees who later received "superior" ratings from their supervisors. As you can see, the higher the range of scores on the test, the higher the percentage of employees who were later deemed superior in their job performance. Results like these encourage future use of the test as a selection device.

Despite the success rate of psychological tests to predict job performance, their use has been criticized in recent years. Because some people who score low on a test may turn out to be good or even excellent workers, and because minorities often score

FIGURE 18.2
Prediction of Success Using the Purdue Mechanical Adaptability Test

The graph shows the relation between the test performances of many people hired by a plant that made ice and their later success as rated by their managers. A positive correlation between test scores and success clearly exists, with more high scorers than poor scorers succeeding later. Such findings establish the predictive validity of a test, but notice that prediction is not perfect. Some people who scored low on the test also succeeded.

SOURCE: McCormick & Ilgen, 1980.

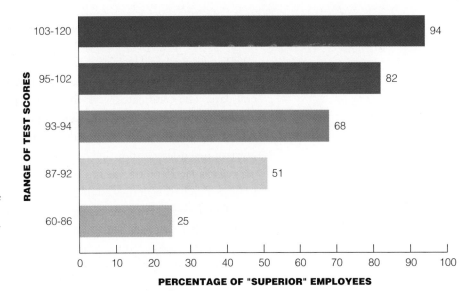

Tests of manual dexterity are often valid predictors of jobs involving manual labor.

lower than others on these standardized tests, many employers are leery of using them in hiring. Nevertheless, although tests may be imperfect predictors, the important question to bear in mind is, If tests are not used to select employees, what other techniques will be used? Interviews are the commonly proposed substitute, but as already mentioned, they are more unreliable and prone to bias than are well-constructed tests. Furthermore, with the passage of the Civil Rights Act of 1991 in the United States, the definition of "test" has broadened to include virtually any means used to select and/or evaluate an individual in the workplace (e.g., interview, work samples, and personality assessments). More will be said about the controversy surrounding the use of psychological tests in employee selection later in this chapter.

Another important issue in testing is the generality of test results. The traditional belief in industrial psychology is that a test measures specific abilities and its use cannot be generalized across jobs. Thus, a specific test must be developed for each particular job. This belief has come under attack in the last decade by proponents of **validity generalization** (Schmidt & Hunter, 1981), the idea that some tests predict reasonably well across similar jobs. For example, the widely used General Aptitude Test Battery (GATB) measures three kinds of ability: perceptual, general cognitive, and psychomotor. Each type of ability is a significant predictor of job performance. This test has been shown to have general validity in predicting success in many different jobs across samples of thousands of workers (Hunter, 1980). In general, the current view is that tests can generalize across similar jobs but that validity cannot be assumed based on the similarity of one job to another. It would be fair to say, then, that the validity of a test must be established for each particular job. If this can be done, then an organization is free to use a test for several similar jobs. Validity generalization is still a bit controversial, but it seems to be increasingly accepted among industrial psychologists (Schultz & Schultz, 1990).

Assessment Centers. While tests are useful in selecting people for manual jobs and jobs that require a rather circumscribed set of behaviors, they are less useful in predicting executive and managerial skills. If you wanted to hire managers for your restaurants, rather than cooks, you would need different means of selecting them. The **assessment center** is a technique, often used for higher-level positions, in which potential candidates are placed in simulated job situations to see how they perform under somewhat stressful conditions. The use of assessment centers in American industries was pioneered by American Telephone & Telegraph in the 1950s (Bray, 1964) and is now used by over 2,000 companies.

Assessment centers often evaluate 6 to 12 candidates at a time over a period of several days. The candidates work through a series of exercises that simulate various aspects of the prospective job. One popular exercise in the assessment center at AT&T is the in-basket test; candidates are instructed to act as supervisors who have just returned from vacation and have a large stack of work demanding attention. They are given some 25 orders, memos, and pieces of correspondence to deal with. They are evaluated on how well they establish priority lists, organize their time, and successfully complete the tasks. For some people being considered for promotion, the in-basket test represents their first experience as managers. Some find it too difficult and consequently refuse to be considered for promotion (Schultz & Schultz, 1990). Thus, the company saves the expense of promoting people only to learn that they are unhappy and ineffective.

According to a number of studies, trained psychologists working in assessment centers show reasonable reliability and validity in selecting people who are likely to succeed in management (Gaugler et al., 1987). The validity of the technique improves with the variety of the training exercises (the in-basket technique is only one of many) and the way evaluations are made—by psychologists trained as assessors rather than by a company's management (Klimoski & Brickner, 1987).

It is important to note that the assessment center technique, like any other selection or assessment tool, is considered a test by the courts and by industrial psychologists. Therefore, concerns surrounding fairness and equal employment opportunity (EEO) must be satisfied before an organization implements an assessment center. Establishing the fairness of any test is not a trivial or easy exercise. On the contrary, EEO issues occupy a chief position in the work of industrial psychologists.

To sum up this section, industrial psychologists use several techniques in personnel selection. Job analysis is critical in establishing the required qualifications for the job, a prerequisite for selecting good employees. Despite their wide use, unstructured interviews have been shown to be poor predictors of future success. The use of psychological tests and other techniques, such as the assessment center, hold greater promise for valid prediction of job performance.

WORK DYNAMICS IN AN ORGANIZATION

Organizational psychologists are interested in the way work is accomplished in large organizations. They ask such questions as, What motivates workers? What is effective leadership? How is it accomplished? Does having people work in groups, rather than alone, improve decision making, productivity, and morale? How can the quality of work life be improved and employee turnover be reduced? We touch on these complex issues here and in the next section.

A decade ago, Peters and Waterman (1982) published the popular *In Search of Excellence: Lessons from America's Best-run Companies*. The authors analyzed successful corporations and found one critical factor that distinguished each of them: a highly committed and strongly motivated workforce. The workers liked their jobs, got along well with management, and felt fairly treated. In turn, the leaders respected the workers and promulgated policies perceived as benefiting them. Because the level of productivity in the United States has fallen behind that of other nations—particularly Japan and West Germany—the issues studied by organizational psychologists take on a renewed urgency. Can organizations be improved to enhance productivity and worker satisfaction?

Groups. Work often takes place in groups, and group processes can either improve or inhibit productivity. Recall from the previous chapter the phenomena of social facilitation and social loafing. Briefly, *social facilitation* refers to the motivation and enhancement of an individual's performance by the presence of other people. This behavior usually occurs in situations in which an individual's performance can be distinguished from that of the group, so that the individual is aware that he or she can be observed. *Social loafing* refers to the inhibition of an individual's performance by the presence of other people. This behavior often occurs when an individual becomes submerged in a group; group performance is observed, but no single person receives credit or blame for the outcome of the job. As is clear from these phenomena, group processes can help or hurt performance in a work setting.

Work groups—especially informal groups—can have a powerful impact on the behavior of individual workers. **Formal work groups** are those that appear in a company's organizational hierarchy; they are the groups (divisions, departments, task forces) to which individual workers are assigned. **Informal work groups,** on the other hand, develop from idiosyncratic friendships, common interests, and similarity in attitudes. People in informal groups may socialize together during breaks and after work. Informal work groups are often critical to successful performance. For example, workers can learn through the company grapevine who can be called on for a particular problem and who should be avoided.

Informal groups often establish **work norms**, social norms that regulate behavior related to work. The informal group may set standards for starting and quitting times, appropriate behavior during breaks, and, especially, how hard people should work. Often the work norms of informal groups deviate from the formal norms of the corporation. Workers whose output differs from the informal norms for productivity, producing too little or too much, are usually brought into line by social pressure. Although most attention has been given to the inhibiting effects of work norms on productivity—when workers slow the pace so that they will not deviate from the norm—work norms can also establish good work habits. Cohesive groups whose members reinforce each other and encourage each other's best performance can have a positive effect, as is often observed in team sports.

CASE STUDY

THE HAWTHORNE STUDIES

A series of studies was conducted in the Hawthorne (Chicago) plant of the Western Electric Company from 1927 to 1932. The studies originated as engineering experiments and only gradually became psychological. What is now termed the Hawthorne Effect occurred in one of the earliest studies. The **Hawthorne Effect** refers to increases in worker productivity due to employee morale and norms of the informal work group. These increases occurred despite changes in tangible factors such as rest pauses or illumination. For example, in the illumination study, worker productivity increased even when the room was made darker. In fact, positive changes in productivity occurred when workers thought that there had been a change in illumination even though there had actually been no change. One surprising finding was that worker efficiency in winding small induction coils on wooden spools was not adversely affected even when illumination levels were so low as to be equivalent to moonlight! After a great deal of consideration, the researchers theorized that when human relations were important to workers, actual environmental conditions had little effect on productivity and efficiency. This is the underlying explanation for the Hawthorne effect.

The research did not stop with the illumination study. In fact, this study led to the Hawthorne studies proper (1927–1932). Elton Mayo was the primary researcher for this group of studies, which included investigations of rest pauses, shorter days and weeks, worker fatigue and monotony, and the effects of wage incentives. Elton Mayo is an interesting figure in the history of industrial/organizational psychology. He came to the United States from Australia in 1922. His first research in the United States was a study of workers in a textile mill in Philadelphia. He succeeded in reducing turnover and improving production so that the workers, for the first time, reached an output level that permitted them to receive bonuses. Mayo's work in the textile mill helped to prepare him for his research at the Hawthorne plant.

There are several interpretations of what took place at the Hawthorne plant. Mayo argued that the workers who were the subject of study (and therefore given some consideration from management in the form of rest pauses, performance feedback, and pay incentives) came to know and like each other. It was this human relations component of the experiments—allowing for the development of group norms, solicitation of group members' concerns and opinions, and enhanced communication both within the group and across levels of the organization—that improved worker productivity and efficiency. Mayo's conclu-

sion sent a shock wave throughout industrial psychology (as it was called at that time), because most attention was devoted to environmental conditions (illumination levels, for example) as determining worker productivity.

As with most explanations of psychological phenomena, there are always critics. In fact, Mayo's interpretation of the Hawthorne studies have been the focus of intense scrutiny and debate for the past several decades. One stream of research focuses on the unintended (and problematic) consequences of examining human behavior—that is, invoking a pattern of behavior that has less to do with the experimental factor(s) under investigation and more to do with the "special attention" paid to study participants. Perhaps the workers kept working harder just because they knew they were being studied. In recent years, many researchers have attempted to design ways to diminish the potential impact of a Hawthorne effect on experimental results; however, there seems to be little consensus on what controls might be most effective (Adair, Sharpe, & Huynh, 1989).

The more interesting debate centers on the argument that Mayo, in his interpretation of the Hawthorne studies, acted more in the interest of shaping humanistic social policy than in the interest of science. This group of critics charges that the results from the Hawthorne studies can be attributed to actual experimental manipulations (e.g., changes in illumination, implementation of rest breaks, and pay incentives) rather than to improved human relations. Recent reexaminations of the Hawthorne studies lend more support for Mayo's human relations interpretation than for the arguments of his critics (Jones, 1990; Sonnefeld, 1985). For example, Jones (1990) analyzed five years of weekly data from the original Hawthorne studies and discovered that the various experimental manipulations could not fully explain the changes that took place during the Hawthorne studies. He concluded that Mayo's interpretation was valid and that social interactions among members in work groups—an important component of human relations in the workplace—did, in fact, play a significant role.

Mayo's greatest contribution to psychology—the fact that he created an interest in human relations that has endured to this day—sometimes gets lost in the swirling debate. It is easy to forget what industrial research was like before Mayo and the Hawthorne studies. Earlier research focused predominantly on such factors as procedures, equipment, and illumination. Following Mayo's human relations interpretation of what took place at Hawthorne, research on worker productivity and efficiency expanded to include psychological principles with a focus on human motivation, thought, and behavior.

Leadership. Leadership is an essential quality for any organization. In industry, leaders such as Thomas J. Watson at IBM, Lee Iacocca at Chrysler, and Stephen Jobs at Apple Computer provided the vision and motivation that made their respective companies leaders in their fields. Similarly, we can reflect on the way that Winston Churchill, Franklin D. Roosevelt, Joseph Stalin, and Adolph Hitler led and motivated their respective nations during World War II.

Defining leadership is a tricky business, but central to any definition is the concept of influence—the way a leader affects a group of people in setting goals and meeting them (Stogdill, 1950). Half of all new businesses fail within two years of opening, and only a third last five years (Schultz & Schultz, 1990). Most failures are blamed on poor leadership, rather than an inept workforce or changing economic conditions. For this reason, corporations are usually willing to pay successful executives quite handsomely, offering many rewards (such as stock options) as enticements to perform successfully and remain with the company.

Various theories of leadership attempt to explain how leaders exert their influence. One approach to leadership attempts to identify different types of leaders. Bernard Bass (1985) distinguishes between transactional and transformational leaders. **Transactional leaders** provide support and advice in the workplace and help workers achieve job satisfaction. In return, the workers produce well for the leaders. Transactional leadership is a bargain (or transaction) between the leader and the workers, each supplying something for the other; this is the more traditional view of leadership. **Transformational leaders** are more charismatic, motivating workers to achieve goals beyond their expectations by providing vision, intellectual focus, and the belief that each individual matters. Although the research on transactional and transformational leadership is in its early stages, some of the work conducted to date is quite compelling. For example, Bass and his colleagues (1985) found that individuals described various world-class leaders as being more transformational than transactional in their leadership styles based on in-depth biographical accounts. Certainly, when most of us think about what it means to be a leader, we tend to conjure up images that are more compatible with Bass's notion of the charismatic, transformational leader.

Another theory of leadership, proposed by Fiedler and Garcia (1987), focuses on the cognitive resources of leaders. Called **cognitive resource utilization theory**, it emphasizes the intelligence, work-related knowledge, and technical competence of leaders. Fiedler and Garcia emphasize cognitive resources over, for example, charisma

Leaders of eight countries met at Rice University in 1990 fo an Economic Summit conference.

because in most leadership situations, leaders must carefully analyze situations, make plans for the future, and make decisions about the best courses of action. These demands require a high degree of cognitive skill; charisma alone will not suffice. Evidence for cognitive resource utilization theory has been impressive, with correlations of around +.50 between leaders' cognitive resources and group performance in laboratory tasks (Dorfman, 1989). The next challenge for the theory is to expand the research arena to include more naturalistic settings.

The approaches to leadership described thus far have focused on specific characteristics or behaviors of effective leaders. Once the characteristics or behaviors are identified, researchers typically set out to correlate these with performance in some work setting. If the theory is sound, then you would expect effective leaders to possess more of the characteristics and engage in more of the behaviors than would ineffective leaders. Another approach reverses this process: It distinguishes between effective and ineffective leaders and then identifies what they do differently. Judith Komaki and her colleagues (1986) have developed an Operant Supervisory Taxonomy and Index that includes seven categories of behaviors often seen in managers in industry. These categories are listed in Table 18.2. In one study, Komaki (1986) compared the actual behaviors of managers at a large medical insurance company. Half the managers had been deemed quite effective by their supervisors and the other half were seen as ineffective. Researchers sampled the actual behaviors of both types of managers every 30 minutes over many days and coded them into the seven categories listed in the table. Surprisingly, the two types of managers appeared quite similar in six of the seven types of actions. The sole difference came in the monitoring of employees performance. Effective managers were more likely to observe their subordinates' work and to inspect it; ineffective managers tended to rely on reports from others about the quality of their subordinates' work. This factor of personal supervision and monitoring may play a

TABLE 18.2

Categories of Managerial Behavior in Komaki's Operant Supervisory Taxonomy and Index

CATEGORY	BEHAVIOR
1. Performance antecedents	Providing subordinates with instructions, goals, and expectations about their performance
2. Performance monitoring	Collecting information about subordinates' performance
3. Performance consequences	Providing information to subordinates about their performance
4. Own performance	Collecting and discussing information (from subordinates or supervisors) about the manager's own performance
5. Work related	Behaviors involving work, but not related to the subordinates' performance
6. Nonwork related	Activities not related to work, such as discussion of family, telling jokes, personal telephone calls
7. Solitary activity	Working by oneself

SOURCE: Komaki, Zlotnick, & Jensen, 1987.

large role in effective management by keeping managers in touch with actual work produced. Appraisal and suggestions to the employees may also be more credible and effective when the workers know that their managers are well informed about the actual work done.

A final theory of leadership to consider has been proposed by Robert Lord and his colleagues (e.g., Lord & Maher, 1991). According to Lord, leadership is in the eye of the beholder. This theory largely draws on work in cognitive psychology on the way individuals process information—that is, human information processing. Lord and his colleagues argue that the process of identifying leaders basically involves the matching of a person's behavior to the prototype of a leader. That is, people compare a target individual to their beliefs about the behaviors and characteristics associated with leaders. Given a sufficient match between the potential leader and the observers' beliefs about leadership, observers then recognize the individual as a leader. As alluded to before, traditional theories of leadership emphasize the role of leaders in influencing others to follow. Lord's theory represents a reversal, with much of the control placed in the hands of observers who, depending on their beliefs regarding leadership, may or may not decide to recognize an individual as a leader.

CONCEPT SUMMARY

FOUR THEORIES OF LEADERSHIP

THEORY	LEVEL OF ANALYSIS	DISTINCTION
Transformational leadership (Bass, 1985)	Leader behaviors and characteristics	Transactional v. transformational leaders
Cognitive resource utilization theory (Fiedler & Garcia, 1987)	Leader characteristics	Low v. high cognitive resource leaders
Operant supervisory taxonomy (Komaki, 1986)	Leader behaviors	Effective v. ineffective leaders
Information processing theory of leadership (Lord & Maher, 1991)	Observation of leader behaviors and characteristics	Leaders v. nonleaders

WORK MOTIVATION AND JOB SATISFACTION

Why do people work? The obvious answer, to make money, is only part of a much more complicated story. The field of **work motivation** is concerned with what motivates workers and how managers can arrange the work situation to satisfy the goals of both workers and managers. As the competition among companies takes on global proportions, the issues surrounding work motivation take on heightened importance. According to Katzell and Thompson (1990), "probably no other subject has received more attention in recent journals and textbooks of organizational behavior" than has work motivation.

INDUSTRIAL/ORGANIZATIONAL PSYCHOLOGY

769

In some individuals, so called "workaholics," the motivation to work dominates many other motives. Because the motivation to work is really composed of many different motives, individuals who work very hard to the exclusion of other pleasures can be doing so for many different reasons.

The earliest model of work motivation came from Frederick W. Taylor (1911), who began the scientific study of business management. Taylor believed that it was management's job to find suitable workers, train them, and then use a wage incentive system to maintain maximum productivity. From a more modern perspective, Taylor's approach to work motivation seems rather simplistic. He believed that workers were essentially aimless, motivated solely by money. He also believed that workers would tolerate boring, routine factory jobs if they were paid enough.

As Taylor's model was applied, problems increasingly arose. First, the relation between workers' output and workers' incomes became less direct. Mass production made factories more efficient, but the incentive system changed very little, so workers' incomes did not increase as much as their productivity did. As a result of this and other problems associated with the industrial setting, more and more workers joined unions to enforce their demands about pay, work safety, and job security (Steers & Porter, 1979). These developments led some to reexamine Taylor's assumptions about workers' motivation. Although money was still seen as the primary incentive for work, newer approaches stressed additional motivational factors.

In the end, Taylor's philosophy was viewed as emphasizing "industrial efficiency without due regard for human welfare" (Hilgard, 1987, p. 703). The human relations approach that followed was an attempt to correct this oversight. With this approach came an unprecedented focus on the humanity and dignity of the worker (Mayo, 1933). Thus, efforts in the 1940s and 1950s were geared toward making workers feel important and part of an organization. Companies gave workers more leeway to make routine decisions about their own jobs and suggest improvements to management. Many incentives were based on group, rather than individual, performance to encourage teamwork. The human resources approach to management moves even further from "scientific management" and tries to avoid any direct manipulation of worker incentives. In the human resources approach, people are viewed as self-motivated, wanting to contribute to the job. This approach leads to efforts to make work more meaningful and to give employees real decision-making authority.

Most approaches to work motivation assume that an employee's performance will improve according to the amount of job satisfaction or need fulfillment a job offers. If a job satisfies the worker's need to belong to a group (one of the fundamental ideas behind the human relations model), then the employee will have greater motivation to work, and productivity will improve. A job can also satisfy a worker's need for status and self-esteem, achievement, power, and self-fulfillment.

What factors determine job satisfaction? The basic theory of job satisfaction involves reinforcement. A worker who is given consistent and immediate reinforcement—money, praise, and other rewards—for achieving specific goals will be satisfied by the job. This theory is based, of course, on B. F. Skinner's model of reinforcement discussed in Chapter 6. The best-selling book *One Minute Manager* (Blanchard & Johnson, 1985) is essentially built on reinforcement theory. The book gives practical advice for managers in setting worker goals and delivering reinforcement.

The concept of reinforcement in modern theories is quite different from Taylor's (1911) approach, where money was assumed to be the primary reason for work. In a 1971 national survey of 1,500 workers asked about the importance of various job attributes, the highest ratings included interesting work, good pay, having good resources to do the job, having authority to make decisions over work-related matters, and having friendly and cooperative coworkers (Katzell & Thompson, 1990). Since that survey, researchers have identified other attributes important to workers: having control over their time, provision of child-care facilities (and leave time to care for children and elderly parents), and programs for health and the management of stress (e.g., Zedeck & Mosier, 1990).

Another important factor in job satisfaction is the degree to which a worker feels that he or she is treated equitably (Adams, 1979). If some workers receive less compensation for performing the same work as others, they are likely to become dissatisfied. Two-tier pay schemes, for instance, which compensate an employee at wage rates below his or her colleagues although all do the same work, violate a worker's sense of equity and contribute to poor morale. Equity does not mean that all employees should receive the same salary. Rather, it advocates that differences in pay should be based on real differences in an employee's knowledge, skills, and ability to perform on the job and/or actual work performance. This is the case when a worker who has been employed longer at a job receives more pay than one newly hired or when one worker who produces more receives more in return. The notion of equity is at the heart of the controversy surrounding the concept of comparable worth or equal pay for equal work. Demands for equity in pay and promotion are intensifying as women and minorities become more active and vocal in seeking fair treatment in all aspects of work. (See Psychology in our Times: Gender Discrimination in the Workplace).

A final element in job satisfaction involves expectations. When taking on a job, people naturally develop expectations about the rewards the job will offer. They also develop beliefs about what matters most in their job performance. Any mismatch between worker expectations and real job experience will foster dissatisfaction. A bank teller may think, for instance, that personal appearance is unimportant, only to discover that bank management insists on good grooming. This conflict creates resentment on both sides. To resolve a potential source of dissatisfaction, an employer should make a special effort to recruit employees who accept the job's goals and requirements, also informing the employees about the job's present and potential rewards.

The factors mentioned in this section are critical in establishing good work motivation, but the mix of factors that optimally motivates workers remains a topic of lively interest and may differ for various jobs and, for that matter, for different people. Work motivation will be one of the most hotly researched topics in organizational psychology in the 1990s as companies compete in the global marketplace.

As should be clear from the examples in this section, industrial/organizational psychology deals with many problems and issues in industry. The field of applied psychology discussed next—human factors psychology—plays a large role in both industrial and military settings.

Human Factors Psychology

The tools and environment provided are a critical aspect of work. Ideally, a worker's environment and facilities make that worker's tasks efficient, safe, and pleasurable. **Human factors psychology** is concerned with designing machines and equipment for human use and training humans in the proper operation of machines. The field, so named because the "human factor" is taken into account, is sometimes called *human engineering psychology*. The same field in England is called *ergonomics* (from the Greek *ergon* for "work" and *nomos* for "natural laws"; hence, the laws of work). As engineers provide complex systems with increasing technological sophistication, the challenge for human factors psychologists is to help design systems that can be easily used by

GENDER DISCRIMINATION IN THE WORKPLACE

In the United States, under Title VII of the 1964 Civil Rights Act prohibits private employers, unions, employment agencies, joint labor-management committees, and local, state, and federal governments from discriminating on the basis of gender, race, color, religion, or national origin. More recently, legislation has been enacted to protect the rights of individuals with disabilities. The crafters of these various pieces of legislation sought to end the practice of denying employment or promotion to an otherwise qualified individual because of his or her "membership" in one of these protected groups or classes.

Although the enactment of Title VII has resulted in marked improvements in the hiring and promotion practices of U. S. employers, glaring acts of discrimination still occur. One example of gender discrimination involves the case of Ann Hopkins, an accountant with the big-six firm of Price Waterhouse. In 1982, Ann Hopkins was the only woman of 88 candidates proposed for partnership. Despite stellar performance in terms of billable hours, account revenue, and client satisfaction, she was denied partnership that year and was not even nominated for partnership the following year. When Hopkins claimed that she had been denied partnership because she was a woman, Price Waterhouse responded that she was "macho," "overcompensated for being a woman," and needed a "course at charm school." Instead of taking this "advice" to heart, Hopkins took Price Waterhouse to court. In 1982, she filed a complaint in the federal district court of the District of

Columbia, alleging a violation of Title VII of the Civil Rights Act of 1964. Hopkins won the initial round at the district court level. Price Waterhouse appealed to an appellate court, where, again, the judge ordered in favor of Hopkins. As a last-ditch effort, Price Waterhouse appealed to the justices of the U.S. Supreme Court, who agreed to review the case.

During the initial district court trial, Hopkins's attorneys, Douglas Huron and James Heller, asked Susan T. Fiske, a social psychologist, to testify about the psychology of gender stereotyping. **Gender stereotyping** is the act of ascribing a role or placing certain expectations or prescriptions on an individual's behavior based on gender. (We offered a brief discussion of gender stereotyping in Chapter 17.) In the case of *Hopkins v. Price Waterhouse*, it became clear to Fiske and, eventually, the majority of the U.S. Supreme Court justices, that Hopkins was placed in a "no-win" dilemma in her pursuit of partnership at Price Waterhouse. The Supreme Court justices wrote:

> In the specific context of [gender] stereotyping, an employer who acts on the basis of a belief that a woman cannot be aggressive, or that she must not be, has acted on the basis of gender. . . . We are beyond the day when an employer could evaluate employees by assuming or insisting that they matched the stereotype associated with their group. . . . An employer who objects to aggressiveness in women but whose positions require this trait places women in an intolerable Catch 22: out

workers or consumers. Human factors psychologists are employed by virtually all large companies concerned with complex technological systems—computers, telephones, automobiles, aircraft—because the success of the systems will depend on their "user friendliness." They are also employed by the military and other government agencies.

Until the 1940s, engineers designed machinery, tools, equipment, and even entire industrial complexes with little or no regard for the workers who would eventually use them (Schultz & Schultz, 1990). They made decisions about the way machines should be designed based on "engineering considerations" only—the mechanics, the electrical needs, and requirements of size and space. Thus, workers (or consumers) simply had to adapt to the machinery, no matter how unsafe, uncomfortable, or difficult to operate. Efforts were occasionally made to train workers as well as possible or to select workers likely to succeed, but few attempts were made to bring in the "human factor" from the very start in designing machines. Eventually, this situation had to come to an end, because equipment was becoming too complex. The advent of World War II helped usher in human factors psychology—new military equipment such as radar, complex aircraft, and submarines were being plagued by "human error." (It should be

of a job if they behave aggressively and out of a job if they don't. Title VII lifts women out of this bind. (*Price Waterhouse v. Hopkins*, 1989, pp. 1790–1791)

This case set a precedent not only within legal circles, but within the ranks of psychology. When it became apparent that *Hopkins v. Price Waterhouse* would be reviewed by the highest court in the land, the American Psychological Association (APA) decided to enter the case for two reasons: First, the district and appellate courts grounded their findings of discrimination largely on Fiske's testimony regarding the stereotypical attitudes that permeated Price Waterhouse's promotion process; and second, Price Waterhouse had "consistently disparaged Fiske's testimony by criticizing the methodology and the concepts she used in arriving at her expert opinion that [Price Waterhouse] discriminated against Hopkins on

the basis of [gender]" (Fiske, Bersoff, Borgida, Deaux, & Heilman, 1991, p. 1053). A panel of social and industrial/organizational psychologists—Susan T. Fiske, Eugene Borgida, Kay Deaux, and Madeline E. Heilman—prepared and submitted a brief on behalf of APA to attest to the scientific merits of the research on gender stereotyping. The brief also explained how stereotyping can result in discriminatory decisions, especially under such conditions as prevailed at Price Waterhouse. In reading the opinion filed by the Supreme Court, it is clear that the justices were convinced by the arguments outlined in APA's brief. More importantly, the work of the psychologists representing APA helped to make explicit, for the first time, that gender stereotyping is a form of gender discrimination and, as such, is prohibited under Title VII of the 1964 Civil Rights Act.

The role of the applied psychologist as advisor to the court is not always an easy one. Psychologists who offer expert testimony and draft APA briefs are often subject to harsh criticism from their colleagues. Some of the criticism is justified; some is undeserved. If you are interested in issues of gender discrimination and find this particular case interesting, you might want to follow the "paper trail" of Fiske's and APA's involvement in *Hopkins v. Price Waterhouse*. A good place to begin is with Fiske's (1993) article on the issue of control in gender stereotyping. In this article, you will also find more detail regarding the experiences of Lois Robinson, the welder described in the opening paragraphs of this chapter, and Ann Hopkins of Price Waterhouse. Finally, Fiske's article will provide not only interesting reading, but insight into the debate concerning the standards to be placed on the "giving away of psychology" to society.

Women are increasingly moving into management positions previously the exclusive domain of males. Gender discrimination may still occur if women are not treated equally.

noted, however, that the errors blamed on humans are often the result of poorly designed systems.) Pilots during World War II were often switched from one aircraft to another. Controls with similar-looking knobs had completely different functions on two types of aircraft, yet the pilots received no retraining. Pilots used to operating by touch were no longer able to do so and had to pay more attention to the controls instead of the situation. Many pilots died because of "human error."

Since World War II, human factors psychologists have been employed by the military in great numbers, as well as in industry; however, problems still exist. For example, in the mid-1980s, at great expense the army built a new tank called the M-1 Abrams. Engineering psychologists were not involved in the design, which may explain some of the surprises that awaited army personnel when the tank was put into use (Cordes, 1985). The interior work space was so poorly designed that 27 of the 29 test drivers developed neck and back problems requiring medical attention. Further, the visibility from the tank was so poor that drivers were unable to see the ground for 9 yards in front of the tank and unable to avoid objects as well. Meanwhile, the noise level inside prevented good communication among crew members, and the interior

FIGURE 18.3
A Poorly Designed Door

The door to the registrar's office at Rice University has a vertical bar attached to a plate, the typical signal that the door should be opened by pulling. The door must be pushed to be opened, however. To prevent confusion (and accidents), a one-word "instruction manual" has been added to inform users about the door's operation.

work stations were so poorly designed that the crew reported severe problems in seeing what they were doing.

Nuclear power plants have also been plagued, on occasion, with poor human factors engineering (Kantowitz & Sorkin, 1986). In the disaster at Three Mile Island in 1979, the control instruments and the warning dials of the control room were too far apart. When operators detected problems by examining one set of dials, they lost precious seconds in running across the room to operate the controls that would rectify the problem. In 1983, the Nuclear Regulatory Commission required that all control rooms for nuclear power plants be evaluated and modified to take human engineering considerations into account.

These examples illustrate the importance of human factors psychology in large organizations, but you can also see the importance of human factors engineering, or the lack thereof, in everyday life. For example, if you have ever scalded yourself trying to work one of those fancy shower controls in which heat and volume of water are controlled by a single knob, you have experienced poor human factors design. In *The Psychology of Everyday Things,* Donald Norman (1988) exhibits a whole collection of items—doors, computer displays, faucets, cars, typewriters—that do not operate easily, or as they should, because of poor design. Everyday objects should be easy to use, but often they are not. Consider the door, a simple device. If the door has a horizontal bar in the middle, you push it; you do the same if there is a plate on it about two-thirds of the way to the top. A door that should be pulled requires appropriate hardware, such as a knob or a vertical bar. But sometimes the signals are mixed up. Figure 18.3 shows a door at the registrar's office at Rice University. This door exemplifies bad design from the viewpoint of human factors psychology. The door has vertical "pull" bars, but in actuality, it must be pushed to be opened. Because of problems with the door, the registrar's office found it necessary to add a "Push" sign. As Norman says in his book, "When a device as simple as a door has to come with an instruction manual—even a one-word manual—then it is a failure, poorly designed" (1988, p. 87).

The job of the human factors psychologist is to create a harmonious relationship between human beings and the myriad material objects that surround them. Next we give some typical examples of human factors research and applications.

TRAFFIC SAFETY

Traffic safety is a major area of study in human factors psychology, and one that affects nearly all of us. Since the introduction of the first automobile in the early part of the twentieth century, the number of automobiles on the road has increased steadily, with a corresponding increase in traffic accidents. America's love affair with the automobile shows no signs of abating despite rising operation costs, air pollution, and the increasing frequency and severity of traffic jams in many of our major cities. Traffic accidents pose a serious threat to the young in our society, as automobile crashes represent the single leading cause of death among Americans aged 4 to 35 (McGinnis, 1984). If your car was manufactured after 1986, then you are a direct beneficiary of one of human factors psychology's greatest success stories—the *centered high-mounted brake light.* The impetus for the development of this light was the finding that 25 percent of all multivehicle accidents and 7.4 percent of fatal accidents involve rear-end collisions. In early 1977, Malone and Kirkpatrick conducted a large-scale field study involving 2,100 taxicabs in the Washington, D.C., area. The cabs were equally divided into four experimental groups with different brake light configurations: centered high-mounted brake light; dual separated high-mounted brake lights; a separated function condition that separated the taillight function from the stop/turn functions; and the typical, or existing configuration. The centered high-mounted brake light resulted in an accident rate that was 54 percent lower than for cabs with the existing configuration (see Figure 18.4) in which brake lights and turn signal lights were combined on the sides of the cars. When accidents did occur, the centered high-mounted brake light was found to reduce the extent of damage to vehicles by 38 percent. Malone and Kirkpatrick concluded that the centered high-mounted brake light resulted in faster brake application in the following vehicle because it is close to the normal line of regard—where we normally look when driving (McGinnis, 1984).

Decreasing the risk for older drivers poses a special challenge for human factors psychologists who work in the area of traffic safety. Older drivers constitute the most rapidly growing segment of the driving population (Waller, 1991). Furthermore, they experience accidents, many fatal, at a higher rate than all other age-groups except those aged 16 to 25 (Laux & Brelsford, 1990). The need for solutions in this area is so great that the foremost journal in human factors psychology, *Human Factors*, devotes one issue each year exclusively to investigating ways to improve the design of automobiles, road signs, and roadways in an attempt to prolong the period of autonomy for the older driver and to reduce the associated level of risk.

The results from one study suggest that older drivers are aware that the task of driving imposes greater demands on them than on younger drivers and that they take steps to reduce those demands (Laux & Brelsford, 1990). This study examined whether age alone was a good predictor of driving problems or whether individuals' cognitive and physical abilities were more appropriate for determining who might be at risk in driving an automobile. Older drivers (age 50 to 92) and younger drivers (age 40 to 49) kept a driver checklist (see Table 18.3) every day for three months on which they recorded how many times they drove, the weather conditions, and the number of "near misses" (e.g., failing to see another car and almost hitting it or turning the wrong way on a one-way street). The drivers also participated in a number of tasks designed to measure cognitive, sensory, psychomotor, and physical functioning. Overall, there were significant age-related changes on the various tasks, indicating that the older drivers were experiencing decrements in such areas as vision and short-term memory. However, age was not significantly correlated with driving performance. Why was this the case? Older drivers reported taking steps to reduce driving demands (e.g., avoiding

FIGURE 18.4
Brake Light Configurations

The centered high-mounted brake light resulted in 54 percent fewer rear-end accidents among taxicabs than the existing brake light configuration.

SOURCE: McGinnis, 1984.

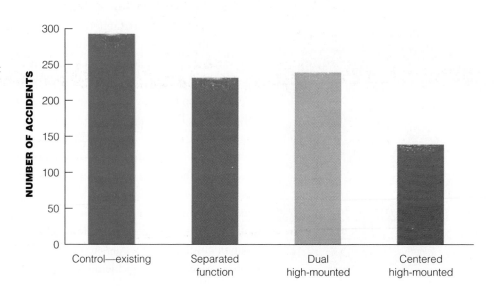

TABLE 18.3
Daily Driver Checklist

1. How many trips did you make today? _____

2. Where did you drive? Check all that apply.
   Low traffic side streets only _____
   Thoroughfares _____
   Major streets _____
   Expressways _____
   Shopping centers _____
   Unfamiliar streets/neighborhoods _____

3. How many miles did you drive? _____

4. What time of day did you drive? _____

5. Was the weather
   Rainy? _____
   Wet, but not raining? _____
   Foggy? _____

6. Did any of the following happen?
   Backed into something _____
   Bumped something with front bumper _____
   Turned wrong way on one-way street _____
   Scraped something with car _____
   Failed to see another car—almost hit it _____
   Almost had accident making left turn _____
   Other drivers honked at me _____
   Was stopped by a policeman or got a ticket _____
   Almost got hit by another driver _____
   Had car trouble _____
   Ran over a curb (backing or turning) _____
   Had to hit brakes hard or slam on brakes
      to avoid hitting someone or something _____
   Didn't see a stop sign or stoplight as
      early as I should have—had to hit brakes
      hard or slam on brakes to stop in time _____
   Any other incident (describe on back) _____

SOURCE: AAA Foundation for Traffic Safety Report, 1990.

Seat belts can reduce injuries and save lives—if people use them. Some human factor psychologists study ways to increase their use.

rush-hour traffic and nighttime driving). This action, most likely, allowed them to keep the number of difficulties or "near misses" from increasing despite decrements in sensory, cognitive, psychomotor, and physical functioning. Studies like Laux and Brelsford's (1990) aid researchers in better understanding the problems faced by our aging driving population. As evidenced here, the primary goal in this area should be to reduce the demands placed on older drivers so that they are able to drive safely and maintain the autonomy that is so critical to them and their families.

Rather than focusing on environmental factors (e.g., centered high-mounted brake lights and road signs) or personal factors (e.g., age-related deficits), some human factors psychologists try to improve traffic safety by focusing on behavioral factors. Figure 18.5 depicts a classification model developed by Scott Geller and his colleagues (1990) to represent the three contributing factors: environment, person, and behavior. They are currently working to develop and evaluate interventions that can change people's behavior and minimize injuries in automobile accidents. In one study, Ludwig and Geller (1990) implemented a safety belt program for pizza deliverers that included group discussions, pledge cards to obtain individual commitments to buckle up, buckle-up signs, and verbal buckle-up reminders among employees. In addition to increas-

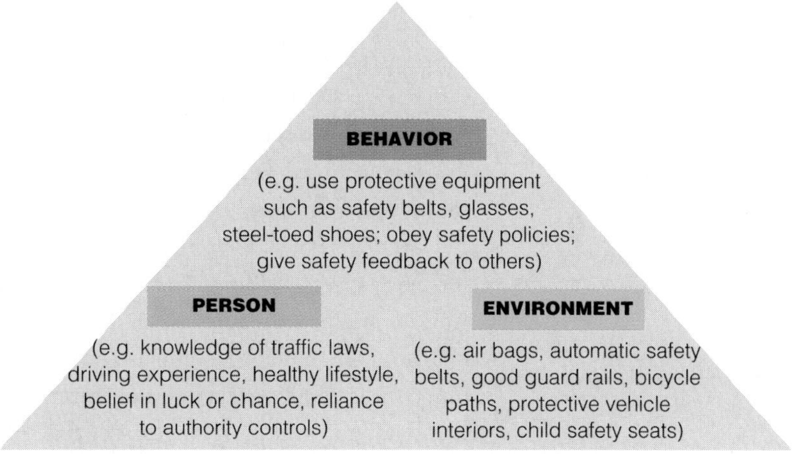

FIGURE 18.5
A Three-Part Classification of Factors Contributing to Personal Injury

While the examples are specific to traffic safety, the concepts are relevant to all problem domains that can benefit from behavior changes.

SOURCE: Geller et al., 1990.

BEHAVIOR
(e.g. use protective equipment such as safety belts, glasses, steel-toed shoes; obey safety policies; give safety feedback to others)

PERSON
(e.g. knowledge of traffic laws, driving experience, healthy lifestyle, belief in luck or chance, reliance to authority controls)

ENVIRONMENT
(e.g. air bags, automatic safety belts, good guard rails, bicycle paths, protective vehicle interiors, child safety seats)

ing shoulder belt use by 143 percent over baseline, the program resulted in a 25 percent increase in the use of turn signals among the deliverers. Geller and his colleagues attribute these findings to a **response generalization.** That is, voluntarily performing one behavior in the interest of personal safety or health may increase the probability that the individual will perform other similar behaviors. Seat belt use is but one of the many behaviors that human factors psychologists hope to influence through theory-based interventions.

The research we have covered in this section was chosen to illustrate the broad range of interventions that human factors psychologists pursue in their efforts to reduce the incidence of automobile accidents. These interventions range from improving the design of automobiles (environmental factors), to identifying decrements in cognitive and physical ability that contribute to traffic accidents (personal factors), to discovering ways to motivate individuals to assume responsibility for their health and well-being through the use of safety restraints (behavioral factors). By all accounts, human factors psychologists are enjoying great success in the area of traffic safety.

CONCEPT SUMMARY

APPROACHES TO THE STUDY OF TRAFFIC SAFETY

APPROACH	EXAMPLE
Environmental factors	Centered high-mounted brake light (McGinnis , 1984)
Personal factors	Older drivers (Laux & Brelsford, 1990)
Behavioral factors	Seat belt use (Ludwig & Geller, 1990)

INFORMATION DISPLAYS

How should machines display information to their human operators? Should there be a visual display? an auditory display? a tactile display? The kind of display that is chosen will depend on the task requirements. For example, if a person needs to monitor a piece of equipment to get an exact numerical reading, then a machine should feature a digital visual display (Chapanis, 1965). Quantitative readings demand exact numbers, so it is easy to see why digital displays are preferred. Figure 18.6 shows three different types of visual displays—a moving pointer on a fixed scale, a moving scale with a fixed pointer, and a digital readout—along with four monitoring functions that might be required. A plus sign in the grid indicates the type of display recommended, a minus sign indicates the type not recommended, and a zero signals neutrality. The digital counter is good for determining precise numerical values and settings but is poor for quick check readings and tracking (because a user must do much more mental work to interpret the numbers as falling in an acceptable range or to track their rate of change). The moving pointer is good for check readings (seeing if the equipment is functioning in an acceptable range), for determining a specific setting of the equipment, and for tracking changes over time in the readings. The worst type of display is the moving scale, which is the hardest to track. People expect to see increases with movement in a clockwise direction—and to see higher numbers on the left side of the display, both expectations deriving from their experience with clocks. These expectations can be violated by the moving scale, however, resulting in confusion and errors.

There are many types of visual displays. The appropriate choice is not always obvious without research (Martin, 1989). Digital displays may not be necessary if precise quantitative information is not needed. For example, you do not need to know the precise temperature of your engine when driving a car. You merely need to know if it is operating in a normal range. Thus, a scale like the one in Figure 18.7 indicates that the car is operating in the normal range. Such a display is good for a quick check reading. A designer might argue that even this display provides more information than you really need and suggest an even simpler display—a go–no go display—so called because it tells whether operating a machine is safe (and should go). Perhaps the simplest visual display is the warning light. When it is off, the system is operating normally. When it is lit, a problem exists and the system should be shut down until it is corrected.

Despite its simplicity, the warning light remains an important design issue for human factors psychologists. To detect safety problems, operators must remain vigilant and alert over long periods of time. This is a difficult task, as evidenced by the fact that performance invariably declines over time. In a recent study, Galinsky, Warm, Dember, and Weeler (1990) compared displays that alternated between sensory modalities—auditory and visual—essentially a **multi-sensory display.** They contrasted

FIGURE 18.6
Three Displays

Three common types of displays, together with their recommended uses (+ means the use is recommended, a − means the use is not recommended, and 0 represents neutrality). The moving pointer is a generally useful display, except where precise quantitative readings must be obtained.

SOURCE: Chapanis, 1965, p. 42.

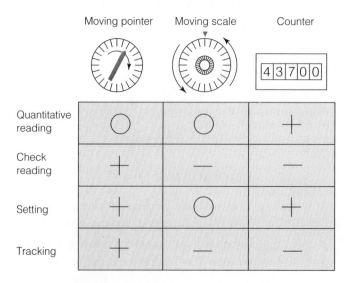

	Moving pointer	Moving scale	Counter
Quantitative reading	○	○	+
Check reading	+	−	−
Setting	+	○	+
Tracking	+	−	−

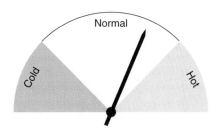

FIGURE 18.7
A Qualitative Display

This display is appropriate in cases where a precise quantitative reading is not needed—as in the operating temperature of an automobile engine. An even simpler device—such as a warning light that flashes when the engine is too hot—may be sufficient. However, the picture display can show a driver if the engine is nearing the threshold of overheating, thereby enabling the driver to take appropriate action before the problem becomes serious.

"The fuel light's on, Frank! We're all going to die!…We're all going to die!…Wait, wait….Oh, my mistake—that's the intercom light."

this display that alternated between modalities with traditional displays that presented information to one sense, either the eyes or the ears. The results from this study were encouraging, as the multisensory display produced modest improvements in participants' ability to detect critical fluctuations in the display. The design for this display was based on the theory that providing variety might sustain participants' attention. Such research has direct applications for traffic safety. No doubt you have been warned not to gaze in any one direction for too long while driving at night. Like the vigilance task in the Galinsky and colleagues (1990) study, driving long distances requires vigilant attention over long periods of time. With this in mind, realize that you are more likely to fall asleep at the wheel if you gaze at lane-dividing lines for extended periods of time than if you periodically monitor your car gauges, glance in your rearview and side mirrors, and check out billboards in addition to monitoring the road ahead.

The design of display and warning systems affects human performance in a wide variety of activities: industrial quality control, airplane navigation, nuclear power plant operations, monitoring of vital signs in medical settings, traffic safety, and air-traffic control, to name just a few. Given the consequences of failure in these areas, it is no wonder that this remains a critical area of study in human factors psychology.

CONTROL OPERATIONS

Another critical aspect of human performance in person-machine interactions is control. A person must be able to control a machine. Do you remember the first time you tried to operate a car or a personal computer? If you do, you understand the importance of control. Human factors psychologists endeavor to design situations so that people can learn to operate a system easily, effectively, and accurately.

As in the case of displays, there are many different types of controls. Their appropriate selection may require considerable research. First, controls can be either discrete (having a few distinct positions) or continuous (having many possible positions). A light switch typically has two positions (on and off), whereas the volume control on a stereo has many possible positions. Second, controls can be rotary (turned like a knob) or linear (pushed like a button or a lever). Third, controls can have just one spatial dimension (as in the previous examples) or two (like a joystick on a computer game or on an airplane).

In selecting various controls, human factors psychologists need to be sensitive to people's beliefs about the way controls ought to operate. For example, the panels in top of Figure 18.8 indicate the typical ways to turn on machines with the five devices shown. Generally, toggles and levers are pushed up, and buttons and pedals down. Although these ways seem natural to us, they are not universal. For example, although North Americans push the top of a rocker assembly (like a wall light switch) to turn lights on, Australians push the bottom (Martin, 1989). The bottom of Figure 8.18 shows five common ways to control equipment that varies continuously.

As mentioned previously, in the early days of aviation, the cockpit controls of different aircraft were not standardized. Controls that looked and felt the same performed entirely different functions on different aircraft, resulting in massive amounts of negative transfer (or interference) for pilots when they switched airplanes. (Imagine suddenly trying to drive a car in which the accelerator was placed to the left of the brake pedal, rather than to its right.) Today, human factors psychologists working for the air force have developed a standard series of shape-coded knobs for use in aircraft (Schultz & Schultz, 1990). The shape of the knob signals its function, so that, for example, the knob to control the landing flaps looks, to some extent, like a landing flap. Each knob

FIGURE 18.8
Common Control Devices

The top row shows common devices for transmitting discrete information. The bottom row reveals common means of signaling continuous information.

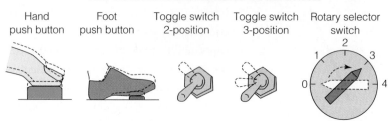

FOR TRANSMITTING DISCRETE INFORMATION

Hand push button   Foot push button   Toggle switch 2-position   Toggle switch 3-position   Rotary selector switch

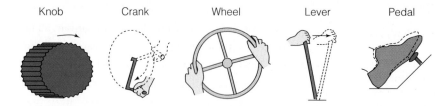

FOR TRANSMITTING CONTINUOUS INFORMATION

Knob   Crank   Wheel   Lever   Pedal

has a distinctive shape so that pilots can transfer more easily from one airplane to another and reduce errors.

We all use control knobs and buttons every day, although we rarely pause to notice them unless they malfunction or seem inappropriate. We have all searched for light switches in the wrong place, cursed appliances with confusing controls, and wished a particular handle could have been larger or smaller. All these problems could be avoided through appropriate human engineering research. To take but one example, George Kohl, a human factors psychologist working for the American Telephone & Telegraph Company, wanted to know the optimal size and shape of knobs for workers who performed in dangerous conditions (high up on telephone poles or on transmission towers). Kohl (1983) tested four sizes of five different shapes (e.g., circular, square, triangular). The results showed that a triangular knob about 3 inches in diameter was generally easiest to operate, although larger triangular and square knobs were better when great force was required to turn them.

Many other issues must be faced in designing control panels, such as the proper positioning of the controls and their relation to the displays of information. (Recall the control room of the Three Mile Island nuclear power plant, where controls were on the other side of the room from the warning displays.) Often, arrangements of controls and displays cannot be decided a priori (although a designer can try to use principles of good design), but rather must be tested on human users by experimentally varying the conditions of use.

HUMAN-COMPUTER INTERACTION

In the past 20 years, the increasingly common use of computers in the workplace has raised a host of interesting human factors problems. How can people more easily learn about and use computers? How can physical problems associated with sitting before computer displays (eyestrain, backaches) be ameliorated? How can people be taught to program computers and to debug programs more efficiently?

Because computers are generally designed by engineers who worry more about the technical expertise of the system than about the more naive humans who will eventually operate the equipment, human factors psychologists are needed to design the interface. How can the system be designed to be more transparent and readily usable?

Constant use of computers can produce a variety of physical complaints.

Norman (1988) cites several general principles applicable in designing computers and other everyday objects. First, the way a machine operates should rely on natural mappings based on past experience. **Mapping** refers to the relation between two things—in this case between the means of control and the performance of the machine. For example, turning a steering wheel clockwise ("to the right") results in a car turning to the right; the opposite turns the car to the left. Second, operation of the controls should be visible to the user. Third, a machine should also provide feedback when operated, so that a person can know if the actions taken are correct. In the case of the steering wheel, the mapping seems natural, the operation is visible, and feedback about the correctness of the action is provided immediately.

A large part of the problem with modern computers, even ones touted as "user-friendly," is that the relation between the controls (the keys and command functions) and the resulting performance is arbitrary. Little attempt has been made to incorporate into computer design the knowledge that humans bring to a computer. In fairness, operating a piece of equipment as complicated as a computer probably cannot be made completely transparent to a user—some learning must take place—but most human factors psychologists agree that much better designs can be achieved. In addition, for operations that can only be accomplished by relatively arbitrary mappings of controls to functions, standardization across the computer industry would greatly benefit the user. At the moment, various computer systems accomplish similar functions in strikingly different ways, so that the controls must be learned anew for each system. This lack of standardization makes it quite difficult to switch from one system to another. Because of these design problems, workers often require much training in learning to use a computer system.

Human factors considerations also come into play in the long-term use of computers. Many users complain that the video display terminal (VDTs) cause vision problems. The general conclusion of much research is that extended use of VDTs does not cause permanent visual disorders. Workers complain nevertheless that the terminals cause eyestrain, making their jobs less pleasant and probably reducing productivity (Howarth & Istance, 1986). Human factors psychologists have conducted a number of studies to determine the causes of such complaints and these studies have created a number of changes in computer technology. For example, computer screens are now frequently coated with material to reduce the amount of glare they reflect. In addition, indirect lighting (rather than harsh fluorescent light) is typically recommended in rooms with VDTs (Marriott & Stuchly, 1986).

Reading from VDTs is generally slower than reading from paper, although why this should be is still not well understood. Part of the difficulty may be that the image quality of characters in VDTs is not as good as in text materials (Gould et al., 1987). Other problems, such as backaches and wrist problems, can be traced to inappropriate chairs. The best chairs for computer use are adjustable so that they can be fitted to the human user and have good back support.

SPACE EXPLORATION

Nearly three decades have passed since the first astronauts walked on the moon. Since that time, space exploration has evolved rapidly with extravehicular activity (EVA) playing an ever-increasing role. It is no wonder, then, that many human factors psychologists devote their life's work to the unique problems posed by EVA. According to Cohen and Bussolari (1987), "The current space station operations baseline will require an estimated 2,000 to 3,000 hours of EVA per year. . . . Each EVA shift will last approximately 9 hours, including suit checking, donning, doffing, and any post-EVA cleaning and servicing that is necessary" (p. 2). Imagine yourself spending 9 hours outside a space vehicle! No doubt, one of your major concerns would involve the safety and comfort of your space suit. Also, you would want a suit and a servicing system that was easy to operate in order to devote your energies to the various complex tasks involved in the actual EVA. Fortunately, there are individuals like Cohen and Bussolari who share these same concerns. In fact, the goal of their study was to outline and compare four concepts for the servicing of EVA suits on board the future space station.

Basically, the various concepts they developed all share a common feature called an "airlock." The airlock is an airtight chamber with carefully regulated pressure. This is the chamber from which astronauts exit to engage in EVA. When they have finished a shift, they reenter the space station via this same airlock. Where the four concepts differ is in the actual design and size of the airlock. For example, one concept features an all-encompassing airlock that can support everything from the stowage and servicing of suits to room for two astronauts, one to don or doff a space suit and the other to assist. In another design, the airlock is much smaller and suitable only for transit (i.e., exiting and entering). So, donning, doffing, and the servicing of the space suit must take place outside the airlock. According to Cohen and Bussolari (1987), NASA must strike a balance between human factors and technological concerns. For example, astronauts might find it easier to cope with the first, all-encompassing airlock design. However, this design is the most costly in terms of loss of air pressure per EVA shift because it is the largest in size. Work on the problem of support for EVA is ongoing. This work will proceed from work like Cohen and Bussolari's in concept development and discussion to the design and testing of prototype models. We have provided this example to give you a sense of the challenges faced by human factors psychologist working for NASA in the area of space exploration.

To summarize this section, human factors psychologists are concerned with human/machine systems that can be operated safely and efficiently. In addition, human factors psychologists are often concerned about the total work environment, which leads to the next topic—environmental psychology.

Environmental Psychology

Environmental psychology is the study of the relationship between the environment and behavior. The environment affects the behavior of human beings, and human beings also change their environments. To pick an obvious example, the prevalence of lobsters off the coasts of Nova Scotia, Maine and Massachusetts leads many people to earn their living by trapping lobsters and transporting them to market. If too many lobsters are trapped (if humans change the environment too much), the lobster population will dwindle and lobster fishers will lose work. Environment and behavior have reciprocal effects.

Environmental psychologists study the effect of environment on behavior. How does loud noise or air pollution affect behavior? How does crowding in cities or on freeways operate? Can environmental psychologists help architects design buildings in which people work more effectively? Can they aid city planners and others to plan cities, parks, and museums?

As these questions attest, environmental psychology is a broad area that overlaps with other disciplines such as social psychology, urban planning, architecture, and even geography. Besides being interdisciplinary, the field is largely concerned with applied problems. It approaches these problems from a naturalistic and holistic perspective (Burroughs, 1989). Although laboratory experiments are conducted, often the focus is on behavior in the natural environments.

Environmental psychologists may be engaged in many endeavors besides research. For example, they may work with architects to provide architectural programs for buildings. An *architectural program* is a report about the specifications needed for a building. Environmental psychologists may also be asked to conduct studies of participatory planning. *Participatory planning* is a way to have eventual users of a building help design it by expressing their preferences and opinions during the design phase. Finally, environmental psychologists may be asked to conduct studies to evaluate how well buildings or other spaces fulfill their functions, a technique called *postoccupancy evaluation*. If some structure, such as a library or post office, may be re-created somewhere else, then such evaluation can be invaluable in improving the design of the buildings yet to be built.

Although these functions are all worthwhile, they are relatively new concepts, and their implementation is not yet commonplace. Robert Sommer (1983) reports an interesting case in which he served as part of a team to help design the Seattle offices of the Federal Aviation Administration (FAA). The designers tried participatory planning, with the opinions of the building's future workers actively sought and considered in the design plan. Workers were given choices about their furniture and the layout of their offices. This step represented an important departure from past practices, where the designers implemented their own preferences, usually on the basis of aesthetics. The General Services Administration, which oversaw the creation of the FAA building, was interested in comparing the building design and effectiveness in Seattle, where the workers were involved, with a similar building being constructed in Los Angeles where the workers were not involved. (The Seattle building served as the experimental condition and the Los Angeles building as the control condition.)

How did the competition turn out? The Los Angeles building received awards for design; the Seattle building did not. On the other hand, surveys of workers in postoccupancy evaluations showed that the Seattle workers liked their building and the areas in which they worked better than the Los Angeles workers. Sommer (1983, pp. 128–129) writes:

> It is noteworthy that the Los Angeles building has been given repeated awards by the American Institute of Architects while the Seattle building received no recognition. One member of the AIA jury justified his denial of an award to the Seattle building on the basis of its "residential quality" and "lack of discipline and control of interiors," which was what the employees liked most about it. This reflects the well-documented differences in preferences between architects and occupants.

Architects prefer neat, orderly design, whether or not it works for the users of the space. The architecture of modern cities reflects this problem. If surveyed, few workers would say, "I'd like to work in a cubbyhole on the 48th floor of a 75-story building," yet that is where many people find themselves.

Environmental psychologists frequently conduct research on the effects of urban density, crowding, and noise on behavior. We consider some of this research in the following sections.

URBAN DENSITY AND CROWDING

A widespread belief is that overcrowding leads to psychological stress, poor physical and mental health, crime and delinquency, aggression, and family disruption. Some of this belief derives from a study of animal crowding conducted by Calhoun (1962). Norway rats were enclosed in connecting pens, and their population was allowed to increase to twice its normal size. The animals were observed for 16 months. Disruptions occurred in mating and maternal behavior; for example, nest building was neglected. Infant mortality and aborted pregnancies reached high levels. Abnormal sexual behavior became common. Some animals attacked others viciously, but a portion of the population manifested extreme passivity. Would the results be the same with people? Before we consider some of the research carried out with humans, we should deal with some definitions.

Crowding, or overcrowding, is not synonymous with density. **Density** is the amount of space available per person; **crowding** refers to the stress that high density produces (Stokols, 1972). Thus, crowding is a psychological state with motivational properties: An individual tries to cope with the negative experience that high density imposes.

Density and Social Pathology in Humans.   In a study carried out in Chicago, researchers Galle, Gove, and McPherson (1972) investigated the relation between density and mortality, fertility, public assistance (a measure they considered indicative of inadequate care of the young), delinquency, and mental hospital admissions, all of which served as estimates of the behavioral pathologies found in Calhoun's rats (1962). Density, measured by the number of inhabitants per acre, was positively correlated to all the measures of pathology. When even more sensitive measures of density were used, such as the number of people per room, number of rooms per housing unit, number of housing units per structure, and number of structures per acre, even stronger relations appeared between density and the social pathology measures. Furthermore, the relationship held up even when statistical techniques were introduced to control for social class and ethnicity (see Table 18.4).

In a follow-up study, a large, stratified random sample of persons from Chicago was examined (Gove, Hughes, & Galle, 1979). The sample varied widely in terms of socioeconomic status, race, and density. By extensive interviewing, information was amassed on the number of persons per room, subjective crowding, and several behavioral measures. The number of persons per room was strongly associated with the subjective experience of crowding, and crowding was shown to be related to poor mental and physical health, inadequate child care, psychological and physical withdrawal, and

TABLE 18.4
Correlation of Population Density (Persons per Room) with Social Pathologies

	SOCIAL PATHOLOGIES				
	STANDARD MORTALITY RATIO	GENERAL FERTILITY RATE	PUBLIC ASSISTANCE RATE	JUVENILE DELINQUENCY RATE	ADMISSIONS TO MENTAL HOSPITAL
Correlation with density	.87	.86	.89	.92	.69
Correlation with density, controlling for ethnicity and social class	.48	.37	.58	.50	.51

SOURCE: Galle, Gove, & McPherson, 1972.

Being stuck in traffic illustrates one aspect of the stress of living in large cities.

poor social relationships in the home. The effect of crowding on behavior continued to be found when race, education, income, age, and sex were taken into account.

Density and Stress Recovery.   Individuals who spend the majority of their time in an urban environment are almost constantly bombarded with a myriad of sights, sounds, and smells. The need to attend to and make sense of so much incoming information on a constant basis may represent a type of "double jeopardy": The very features of the environment that caused the initial stress may also serve to inhibit stress recovery. A recent study conducted by Ulrich, Simons, Losito, Fiorito, Miles, and Zelso (1991) provides an interesting illustration of this problem. Participants in this study were first exposed to a stressful film about the prevention of work accidents. The film depicted several injuries that occurred to employees in a woodworking shop as a result of their carelessness or disregard for safety procedures. Measures of mood (e.g., fear, anger, sadness) and various physical measures (e.g., cardiovascular activity and blood pressure) were collected afterward and indicated that participants were indeed experiencing stress. The participants then viewed a second film, either depicting a natural or urban environment. The nature tape depicted vegetation or running water, while the urban tape depicted either traffic scenes or pedestrians traveling along city sidewalks. Stress levels of the participants who viewed the nature tape returned to baseline levels, while the participants exposed to the urban tape remained stressed. The next time you are experiencing stress at school or at work, you might want to heed the results of this study and opt for a brown-bag lunch in the park or some other naturalistic setting rather than fight the lunchtime crowds at the corner deli. It seems reasonable to expect that you will return to school or work feeling more relaxed and refreshed if you avoid harassment by a crowd of equally "stressed-out" individuals. You may wonder why merely viewing other human beings on a city street would be so detrimental to your recovery from stress. A discussion of one of the psychological consequences of urban density—crowding—may help to answer this question.

Laboratory Studies of Crowding.   Studies of crowding are often correlational rather than experimental; that is, the crowding is not experimentally manipulated. The researchers simply observe the real world to see if density and pathology are positively related. However, we cannot conclude a cause-and-effect relation based on a correlation, because some unknown and unmeasured variable may be present. Psychologists, therefore, have also carried out experimental studies in the laboratory to try to disentangle the complexities of crowding in the real world and answer the question of causality. Despite much experimental research, however, the negative effects of crowding have not been reliably demonstrated in the laboratory (Freedman, 1979). This may be because ethical constraints restricted the degree of unpleasantness that the experimenters could create with their manipulations. Some researchers, however, believe that density does not have the negative effects that other researchers claim it does (Freedman, 1979).

There is no reason to believe that density always results in a negative human experience. Tokyo has one of the highest population densities in the world. In its subways men are employed to stand outside train doors and pack in as many people as possible. Some passengers wear coats of slippery material to ease their entrance. Yet, despite the density, crime rates are remarkably low in Tokyo. Determining the conditions under which density and crowding cause social pathologies (and when they do not) remains a challenging issue for environmental psychologists.

mHigh density is a feature of urban life in many cities of the world. High density doesn't necessarily lead to social pathologies, however. Tokyo, for example, has a very low crime rate.

EFFECTS OF NOISE

Noise has often been studied as a major variable by environmental psychologists; it is especially important because so much in industrial life creates noise. Perhaps the most striking difference among rural, suburban, and urban communities is the almost constant din that pervades the city.

Adaptation to Modern Noise. Anyone who moves from the city to the country or vice versa is usually aware immediately of the change in noise level. Country residents find it difficult to accustom themselves to the squeaks and roars of traffic in the city, and city folk in the countryside find that they are kept awake by the quiet or the racket of crickets and birds.

Recall from Chapter 3 that exposure to very loud noise (gunfire at close range, jackhammers, music) can cause both temporary and permanent hearing loss. Everyone agrees on that point. Environmental psychologists typically focus on the effects of noise on other behaviors.

One important finding from research on noise is that people adapt to it quickly as long as it is predictable (Glass & Singer, 1972). In experiments, subjects were asked to proofread texts while they heard no noise, while they heard noise that recurred exactly once a minute, or while they heard noise that occurred randomly. When the noise was unpredictable, the proofreaders made more errors.

The experimental research becomes more difficult to interpret, however, when louder noise is used, when more complex tasks are involved, or when both conditions are present. Sometimes noise proves distracting and impedes work; sometimes it seems to enhance performance, perhaps by keeping the individual more alert. On still other occasions, noise seems to have no effects at all. Something of a controversy surrounds these data (Broadbent, 1978; Poulton, 1977, 1978).

Noise also impacts people's moods, with loud or unidentified noises causing annoyance or fear. Levy-Leboyer and Naturel (1991) investigated individuals' accounts of neighborhood noise to discover what factors influence the subjective experience of noise. Their results suggest a twofold process: that the normalcy of the noise is what determines the level of annoyance, and whether the perpetrator could have avoided making the noise determines one's reaction. For example, suppose you hear an unusually loud banging outside your apartment, and upon further investigation, discover it is the air-conditioning repairman. Initially, you are annoyed, but then you recall that summer is just around the corner. The noise is still unpleasant, but you reason that it cannot be avoided if you are to survive the summer's heat in relative comfort.

Effects of Long-term Noise. Some researchers have argued that laboratory experiments cannot tell us much about the real world, because in a laboratory setting people are not exposed to noise over long periods. Cohen and colleagues (1980) studied 271 Los Angeles children, some of whom attended schools near a busy airport, others who attended schools in quiet neighborhoods. Care was taken to match the two groups of children on a number of dimensions including age, ethnicity, race, sex, and social class. The results showed that the children from the noisy schools had higher blood pressure, were more easily distracted, and gave up more quickly in trying to solve puzzles than the children from the quiet schools. One year later, in a follow-up study, the results were entirely replicable (Cohen et al., 1981). In fact, children who had been in the noisy classrooms earlier but who had shifted to quieter ones showed no significant improvement. One interpretation of this finding is that harmful effects of early exposure to noise may be long-lasting, but additional research is needed to firmly establish this conclusion.

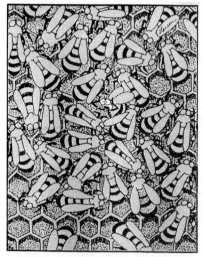

"No more! No more! I can't take it!…That incessant buzzing sound!"

School Psychology

School psychology is the application of psychological principles to solve problems and enhance performance of children in schools. School psychologists work in elementary and secondary schools as well as teaching and conducting research in universities. It is a popular profession that includes academic researchers, practitioners, and clinicians. Currently, there are over 25,000 school psychologists and more than 200 programs in colleges and universities that offer graduate training in school psychology (Ysseldyke, 1986).

BRIEF HISTORY OF SCHOOL PSYCHOLOGY

The origins of school psychology can be traced to Wundt's experimental methods (see Chapter 1) and Galton's work on the hereditary basis of intellectual superiority (see Chapter 11). The key figure in the early history of school psychology was a man named Lightner Witmer, who combined both service and science (McReynolds, 1987). Witmer studied with Cattell at the University of Pennsylvania and with Wundt at Leipzig. At the end of the nineteenth century, Witmer established the first child guidance clinic in America at the University of Pennsylvania. One of Witmer's major goals was to train psychologists to help educators remedy children's learning problems. He worked directly with children referred to the clinic, and psychologists received supervised training while working with families there. Thus, psychological services delivered to children and families and designed to promote children's education were established by the early 1900s.

The introduction of *intelligence tests* around the same time provided a useful tool for school psychologists. As we saw in Chapter 11, the testing movement that began in France and was imported to the United States by Lewis Terman in 1916 had a strong influence on education. These tests were designed to identify at-risk children and place them in special classes. The testing movement provided assessment instruments for clinical and school psychologists. Indeed, Arnold Gesell was hired by the state of Connecticut in 1915 to test children for special class placement. He is thought to be the first person to have the title "school psychologist." Thus, clinical psychology and intelligence testing both contributed to the formation of school psychology.

Between 1910 and 1950, there were many changes in the discipline of psychology. School psychology remained true to its original purpose to deliver psychological services to special children in educational settings. School psychologists administered tests, designed specific interventions to help children, provided counseling and therapy, and worked directly with teachers and parents to help children and youth. Clinical psychology, however, moved beyond educational systems and became aligned with medical facilities. Clinical services were broadened from only assessment to include therapy. The emphasis shifted from community-based services for children to individually based services for adults. By 1945, clinical psychology had established a different agenda from the one of school psychology. There were, by comparison, few school psychologists, and most were aligned with public school systems. Currently, school psychologists work to promote education and mental health among students. Their job responsibilities are still expanding (Phillips, 1986).

ROLES PLAYED BY SCHOOL PSYCHOLOGISTS

School psychologists work with students, teachers, parents, and administrators. Although they may perform a variety of tasks, they usually provide four basic kinds of service.

School psychologists often administer tests to students that assess their intelligence, personality, educational skills, and emotional development.

1. *School psychologists administer, interpret, and study psychoeducational assessments.* These include intelligence tests, personality tests, clinical assessments of emotional adjustment, and a variety of measures of learning potential and social skills. Because school psychologists work with so many different students, they must know the characteristics of many kinds of tests, how to administer them, and how to interpret the results. Thus, school psychologists often study the validity and reliability of psychoeducational tests. Recall that in Chapter 11 we discussed the controversial use of intelligence tests for placing children in special education classes. School psychologists study these tests and issues of placement in both practice and theory. For example, Poteat, Wuensch, and Gregg (1988) examined the school records of both black and white students from 20 schools who were placed in special education classes. The researchers wanted to determine if the use of IQ scores alone would have led to biased placement decisions different from those reached by considering students' achievement test scores and cumulative GPAs. All three measures proved to be strongly correlated and consistently identified the same children in need of special education.

2. *School psychologists provide intervention.* These interventions may include specific cognitive or social strategies designed to improve the classroom climate for learning. For example, many school psychologists attempt to achieve integration of culturally different and handicapped children in the schools by designing interventions in which the different groups work together in teams and participate in cooperative games (Weyant, 1992). The logic underlying such interventions is based on Gordon Allport's *contact hypothesis.* According to this hypothesis, interracial contact is most likely to lead to reduced prejudice and greater acceptance when the groups have common goals and equal status and when such contact is sanctioned by authorities. To date, interventions based on the contact hypothesis have achieved positive results, with students in cooperative situations showing greater academic gains, higher self-esteem, greater empathy for others, more frequent interaction between handicapped and nonhandicapped students, and more cross-ethnic interaction than their control group counterparts.

3. *School psychologists often supervise and evaluate different educational programs.* They may consult with parents about the educational plans for their children or consult with social workers and mental health professionals in the community. Consultation is a form of indirect intervention because school psychologists may not directly provide services to clients in a clinical role. Instead, they share their expertise with others who work directly with students. For example, school psychologists may train teachers and counselors in ways to help children who are victims of abuse or in ways to cope with tragedies such as murder or suicide among their students. Although individual clinical and counseling services remain part of the consulting focus, school psychologists now emphasize the importance of the family and community (i.e., the system in which students develop problems) as key factors in consultation for preventive mental health (Pryzwansky, 1986).

4. *School psychologists conduct research that may be theoretical or practical in nature.* For example, some psychologists examine motivation for educational achievement from a theoretical perspective, whereas others help students cope with difficulties and frustrations in school. Often the two aspects of research are intertwined. LaVoie and Hodapp (1988) studied children's reactions to a standardized achievement test in school and found that those students who tried hard, were not too nervous, and believed that they could do well actually performed better than their pessimistic and nervous peers. The researchers suggest that teachers help their students acquire a positive motivational orientation toward tests, as well as providing preparation in test-

Edward L. Thorndike is the father of educational psychology.

taking strategies. Because school psychologists are concerned with so many aspects of students' adjustment to school, they may derive their research from clinical, developmental, social, or cognitive orientations. The challenge of school psychology is to integrate new advances in many areas of psychological research and use the knowledge to help children's academic achievement and social adjustment. It is a dynamic and challenging profession that continues to attract large numbers of students.

Educational Psychology

Like school psychology, **educational psychology** is concerned with applying psychology to issues in education but the emphasis in educational psychology is more likely to be on the learning processes per se than on the advising and counseling of students.

Edward L. Thorndike, whom we met in Chapter 6 as one of the first investigators of what is now called operant conditioning, is the father of educational psychology. Thorndike was one of the first psychologists to announce that education could be studied scientifically and that it could profit from knowledge obtained in basic psychological research. Effective teaching and learning could be studied scientifically, he maintained, and their critical factors isolated. Teaching could then be considered a topic of scientific inquiry, rather than an ineffable art, as it is often portrayed. Thorndike's text, *Educational Psychology,* was published in 1903 and set the stage for development of the field.

Educational psychologists work in a variety of settings. Many are employed in colleges and universities, usually in departments of education or psychology, where they teach and conduct research. Others are employed by companies such as the Educational Testing Service and the Psychological Corporation, where they develop, administer, and analyze standardized educational tests to measure intelligence, cognitive ability, and academic achievement. Educational psychologists may also be employed in other corporations to help with the development of placement exams for potential employees and to help train personnel and assess performance. Some uses of these tests are controversial, as discussed below in the Controversy feature: "Ability testing: Predicting or shaping future success?"

Educational psychologists conduct research on a wide range of topics, including educating the gifted, motivation and self-concept in academics, gender effects on achievement and self-esteem, teaching and learning strategies, and interactions between family variables and school outcomes. This is not an exhaustive list, by any means, but should familiarize you with the issues that presently concern educational psychologists. In the sections that follow, you will learn about the research that has been conducted on the factors associated with good schools and on the types of texts that facilitate learning.

EFFECTIVE SCHOOLS

Educational psychologists have conducted many studies, mostly correlational in nature, about the factors associated with good schools. Typically, the measure of effectiveness used is students performance on standardized tests. Often these studies are conducted in a single year, rather than extended across time, and typically the schools studied are urban rather than rural (Pettibone & Jernigan, 1989). Nonetheless, with these possible limitations taken into account, many characteristics of effective schools have been identified. Westbrook (1982) has synthesized the evidence available about

ABILITY TESTING: PREDICTING OR SHAPING FUTURE SUCCESS?

America's public debate over the value of psychological testing dates back to the late nineteenth century (Sokal, 1987). Do tests help place people in schools and jobs according to their abilities? Or do tests provide straightjackets, pigeonholing people in a category from which it is difficult to escape? We have previously discussed intelligence testing (see Chapter 11) and tests to examine personality and psychopathology (see Chapters 14 and 15). We now consider some larger societal issues about testing.

Psychologists have offered cogent and compelling arguments both in favor of and in opposition to psychological testing. As a university undergraduate, you probably can recall quite vividly that period in your life when all your thoughts and energies were focused on achieving a good score on the Scholastic Assessment Test (SAT) or American College Test (ACT). Perhaps you questioned the fairness of equating a mere test with years of school performance. After all, why should performance over a 3-hour block of time command the same respect as a school record spanning 12 to 13 years? Your first exposure to psychological testing, however, probably occurred well before your senior year of high school. One widely used achievement test, the Metropolitan Achievement Test (MAT), is administered on a periodic basis to children from kindergarten through grade 12. Furthermore, preschool children as young as 2 years of age are tested on the Stanford-Binet Intelligence Scale to determine general intellectual or cognitive ability.

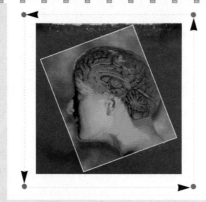

The skepticism and concern over the practice of repeatedly testing America's youth are aptly reflected in a book titled *Testing Testing: Social Consequences of the Examined Life* (Hanson, 1993). In this book, Hanson voices concern that our society's beliefs regarding individual worth and success are too closely bound with the concepts of intelligence and cognitive ability. Precisely because there is so much at stake for individuals and society, it is understandable that psychologists continually examine and question the value of psychological testing.

Today's proponents of psychological testing have much in common with their predecessors. One early advocate of psychological testing was Alfred Binet, creator of the precursor to the modern version of the Stanford-Binet Intelligence Scale. His goal was to identify children who were doing poorly in school *before* they were dismissed. He argued that many of these children were educable and could benefit immensely from special classes. Today, the aims of some

researchers who advocate psychological testing and assessment are even broader. They view psychological testing as integral for meeting the needs of society as well as the needs of the individual. For example, Matarazzo (1992) envisions a time when biological tests of intelligence and cognition will be used to unlock the mystery of Alzheimer's dementia and to develop better, fairer methods of measuring "how people with different cultural and educational backgrounds think and solve problems" (Matarazzo, 1992, p. 1015).

Another group of testing advocates argues that psychological tests are beneficial because they can predict, with reasonable accuracy, future performance in school and at work. For example, some industrial/organizational psychologists believe that general ability or intelligence tests are the best predictors of an individual's performance on the job (Ree & Earles, 1992). In a large-scale research project, Schmidt and Hunter (1992) discovered that general mental ability affected individual work performance through job knowledge. Basically, they found that individuals with higher mental ability were able to acquire more job knowledge. This job knowledge, in turn, enhanced their work performance.

On the other side of the debate are psychologists and other social scientists who argue that psychological testing actually shapes or sets limits on individual success in school and at work. This is sometimes called the *Pygmalion effect,* to reflect the fact that

factors associated with effective schooling and discovered 11 main factors, presented in Table 18.5.

Although many of the factors seem commonsensical, they are nonetheless quite important and often omitted from school curricula. Look at the first factor—time on task. Gage (1978) analyzed the results of studies relating the behaviors of teachers and classroom activities to the reading achievement of third-graders. One main finding was that the amount of time engaged on task, in behaviors directly related to learning, was the best predictor of class reading performance. In some ways, nothing could be more straightforward, but many educators have turned away from the policy of keeping students engaged in strictly academic behaviors. Continually engaging students in aca-

an individual's success (or failure) can be influenced by others' expectations and behavior. According to Greek mythology, Pygmalion was a sculptor who, generally disdainful of womankind, set out to sculpt the "perfect" woman from stone. In some sense, then, the term *Pygmalion effect* may also reflect the concern that results from intelligence and cognitive ability tests are too often regarded as constant and immutable—almost as if they, like Pygmalion's perfect woman (Galatea), were carved in stone.

Another argument levied against psychological testing has been offered by David Johnson, Executive Director for the Federation of Behavioral, Psychological and Cognitive Sciences. Johnson condemns the practice of "imposing accountability on the powerless" through "high-stakes achievement testing" (1991, p. 359). Instead, he contends that the public school system, rather than students, should be held accountable for the problems plaguing education in America:

If by the year 2000 the governors [ordain] that the United States has a system of exit assessments to determine which high school graduates will be permitted to enter college and which will be permitted to enter the workplace, then the burning topic in the first decade of the new millennium may still be how to accomplish effective school reform. (p. 361)

Allan Hanson, an anthropologist, is equally critical of the repeated testing that takes place in the United States in his book on *Testing Testing* (1993). Hanson even goes so far as to offer his own tongue-in-cheek version of an intelligence test, the NIT, or New Intelligence Test. A few of the more whimsical sections of the NIT are the: name recall test (ability to remember

CONTROVERSY

the names of individuals to whom you have just been introduced), first impression scale (evaluation of your likableness on first sight), the small talk scale (ability to carry on an interesting conversation with a stranger), and the SES scale (your parents' socioeconomic status). Hanson has this to say about the potential impact of his NIT test on society:

. . . . Although the NIT obviously measures several quite different abilities, people would knit them together as they strive to improve them all in order to raise their NIT scores. They would begin to imagine these several abilities to be one. They would name it, perhaps, "NITwit." Given its importance for success in life, it would be valued as a thing of great significance. People would worry about how much of it they possess; they would envy evidence of its abundance in their contemporaries and look for promising signs of it in their children. (Hanson, 1993, p. 281)

Obviously, Hanson's intention is not to give further fuel to the testing fire, but to argue that psychological testing creates a vicious cycle wherein psychologists determine what skills are important, and the rest of the world—teachers, parents, students, and employers—stand at attention. Social scientists like Johnson and Hanson would argue that individuals who test high in cognitive ability succeed in school and at work not because they are uniquely qualified to do so, but because doors remain open to them that are closed to individuals who perform

less well on tests of general ability and intelligence.

It seems doubtful that the controversy surrounding the prevalence of psychological tests will ever be resolved to the satisfaction of all concerned. If psychologists were able to discover the true value of psychological testing for individuals and society, the answer would, most likely, fall somewhere between the panacea and Pandora's box envisioned by those involved in the debate. Technically speaking, a test that predicts future performance is useful. That is not to say, however, that psychologists should not be concerned when there are groups of individuals (e.g., ethnic minorities) who routinely score lower on a test and as a result are denied important opportunities (e.g., employment or education). On the contrary, psychologists can (and do) help to pinpoint the source of such problems (e.g., access to early educational opportunities, and societal expectations). In doing so, they may be able to discover ways to reduce or eliminate these problems. Additionally, psychologists can work with other social scientists to scrutinize the various ways in which psychological tests are used in our society in an effort to determine whether tests are sometimes misused or overused. In the end, it seems likely that testing will continue to play a significant role in education and the workplace. If so, then it may be more fruitful for social scientists to move on from the long-standing debate over testing and begin adopting a more constructive, proactive approach to the issue of testing and opportunity in our society.

demics is sometimes deemed too restrictive, and educators opt instead to enrich classes with all sorts of other activities. These activities may serve worthy purposes themselves, but may cause academic achievement to suffer. Recall from Chapter 11 that Japanese and Taiwanese children, who greatly outperform American children on standardized tests (especially in math and science), also spend much more time on academic subjects both in school and at home. Their school days, school weeks, and school years are all longer.

The study of modern learning theory is aiding research into instructional techniques (Glaser & Bassok, 1989). Consider some questions of interest: Are small classes better than large classes? Are televised lectures as good as (or better than) live lectures? Is a

TABLE 18.5

Factors Affecting Classroom Performance.
These 11 variables were found to be important in a survey of correlational studies
examining factors associated with effective schools.

FACTOR	EXPLANATION
1. Time on task	The more time, the more effective.
2. Expectations of high performance	The higher the expectations for student performance, the higher that performance.
3. Success Rate	The higher the success rate (percentage of correct responses per unit time), the higher the performance. However, there also seems to be a balance between success rate and challenging work—if work becomes too challenging, the success rate will drop.
4. Curriculum alignment	The closer the match between objectives, instructional activities, and evaluation, the higher the achievement.
5. Staff task orientation	Closely linked with time on task is efficient use of available class time for instruction. Ending class early was found to be negatively correlated with achievement.
6. Behavior management	While fair, appropriate, and consistent application of discipline is found in the more effective schools, a high level of corporal or physical punishment is not found in such schools.
7. School environment	The effective school typically has a pleasant atmosphere. Interestingly, the effective school is usually in better physical condition than the less effective school.
8. Cooperation	Effective schools have a high degree of cooperation among staff members.
9. Instructional leadership	Effective schools have principals (or other instructional leaders) with a strong viewpoint regarding instruction who are actively involved in teaching activities with teachers and students.
10. Parent participation	Effective schools have more parental participation.
11. Instruction practice	Effective schools have teachers who interact more often with students; monitor student progress more often; provide students with frequent and quality feedback; and use direct instructional techniques. It should be noted that while higher achievement is associated with the use of direct instruction, there is some evidence to indicate that creativity, problem-solving ability, positive attitudes, independence, and curiosity are not related to achievement.

SOURCE: Westbrook, 1982, pp. 15–25.

New technologies are being integrated in school curricula to improve learning.

Socratic method of instruction better than an expository method of lecturing? How can analogies be used to promote understanding? These topics and many others have been investigated. Often the research borders on basic cognitive psychology of learning, memory, and thinking as described earlier in this text (especially in Chapters 7 and 8). General answers to questions have been hard to find, because the usual conclusion is that certain methods work better for some subject matters or with some students, and other methods are more effective in other situations (Pettibone & Jernigan, 1989).

LEARNING FROM TEXTBOOKS

One particularly fertile area for educational psychologists is the way students learn from expository text material, such as the book you are now reading. Indeed, many features in this text were shaped by the research of educational psychologists. For example, the outlines and thematic questions that open each chapter aid comprehension and learning, as do the theme summaries at the end of each chapter. Similarly, each chapter is broken into four or five main topics, which facilitates comprehension. The key terms provided at the end of each chapter serve as an excellent review and self-test for students who choose to use them. The *Study Guide* for this text similarly employs sound pedagogical devices. The PQ4R method for studying described in Chapter 7, relies on proven techniques, too.

McDaniel and Einstein (1989) have reviewed much of the research on learning from text and noted a critical dimension that has often been overlooked in research on comprehending and remembering prose. They refer to the distinction between relational processing and item-specific processing (Hunt & Einstein, 1981). Briefly, **relational processing** involves finding relations between the facts and ideas one reads about. A reader discovers the structure of the material and can interrelate the parts. **Item-specific processing** refers to the study of individual items of information (specific facts) in texts. McDaniel and Einstein (1989) note that some texts are written so that the overall structure is quite apparent (there is a good schema, to use a term from Chapter 7). In these cases, specific items of information may not be processed very well because the text encourages processing of general themes. (A reader sees the forest, but may miss the trees.) Other texts are written so that individual facts and ideas can be easily understood but may not lead readers to understand the overall structure of the argument. (A reader sees the trees but misses the forest.) According to McDaniel and Einstein (1989), both dimensions are important in understanding the processes involved in comprehending and remembering textual materials.

Another important point can be gleaned from this analysis: The relative importance of relational processing (of the structure) versus independent item processing (of specific facts) depends on the manner in which one's knowledge is tested. For example, essay tests depend on relational processing, or knowing the general meaning of the text and its structure. Objective tests, such as multiple choice or true-false, depend more on specific facts; good performance will be achieved by item-specific processing. (Obviously, the ideal would be to have good knowledge both of the overall structure of the text and the specific facts involved.) The points made are similar to the idea of transfer-appropriate processing discussed in Chapter 7: Performance on a test will benefit to the extent that the study activities encourage acquisition of the kind of knowledge required by the test.

In this text, we have tried to make the structure of the chapters apparent by the outline at the beginning of each chapter and by good transitions between parts of each chapter. In addition, we have tried to emphasize specific terms and facts by boldfacing key concepts and defining new terms as soon as they are introduced. These features (and others) encourage both good relational processing and good item-specific processing, helping to prepare you for tests of specific facts (e.g., define operant conditioning) and for those emphasizing well-structured knowledge of general concepts (e.g., how could you teach your dog to roll over?).

Educational psychologists are interested in many facets of learning, both in the classroom and from texts. These examples touch only a few topics in this interesting and wide-ranging field.

Psychology and the Law

The last topic in this chapter is the application of psychology to the legal profession. Many psychologists, especially social psychologists, have become interested in this topic in recent years. Yet, the relationship between psychology and the law has been of interest since at least the beginning of the twentieth century, when Hugo Munsterberg, a psychologist at Harvard, argued in his book, *On the Witness Stand,* that psychology could contribute to and improve the practice of law. Probably most lawyers and judges did not accept Munsterberg's arguments in 1907, and some do not today. The relationship between lawyers and psychologists is sometimes uneasy, but psychologists are becoming increasingly accepted as expert witnesses on a number of legal matters, some of which we consider next.

One traditional role that psychologists have played within the legal profession is in the specialty of **forensic psychology** (Hans, 1989), a discipline that focuses on the evaluation and treatment of criminal defendants. Forensic psychologists try to determine whether defendants are capable of standing trial, pose danger to a community if released on bail, or need psychological therapy. Forensic psychologists are employed by prisons, parole systems, and other agencies in the criminal justice system. Other types of legal psychologists are likely to be employed in universities, government agencies, and private companies.

PREDICTING VIOLENT BEHAVIOR

One urgent job of psychologists in the legal system is to predict violent behavior. Such judgments are critical: Should a defendant be released from jail prior to trial? Should bail be set, and if so, how much? Should a good prisoner who has previously been convicted of a violent crime be paroled? These are only a few of the questions that psychologists must help to decide.

Unfortunately, the prediction of violent behavior is extremely difficult, and psychologists have not enjoyed great success at the task. Clinical psychologists, usually called upon to make these judgments, may use several criteria in rendering a decision: a person's history of violent behavior, the person's violent fantasies, and the person's feelings of guilt for past behavior. These seem like reasonable criteria, but when Monahan (1981) reviewed the results of five studies in which psychologists had predicted whether or not defendants would be violent and the outcomes that followed, he found that psychologists were wrong 67 percent of the time.

What accounts for such poor accuracy in predicting violent behavior? Often psychologists observe criminals' behavior in one setting—such as a prison—but must predict their behavior in another setting—at home or in their customary environment. Model prisoners may revert to their old violent ways when they return to the same environment that spawned their original criminal activity. In addition, as in many studies of judgment (reviewed in Chapter 8), clinicians tend to ignore the base rates of criminal behavior in various populations and instead base judgments on dramatic (but perhaps unreliable) personal incidents. For example, if psychologists want to determine whether a female prisoner will commit violent acts if released from prison, they may ignore the statistic that, in general, women have much lower probabilities of committing violent acts. Instead, if a woman recently reported having a violent dream, this fact might outweigh the low base rate. Because a number of factors are known to be correlated with the commission of violence—gender, race, age, drug problems, income, education—their use may enhance psychologists' ability to predict violent behavior. Even so, prediction of violence is likely to be imperfect because many factors are involved that make the judgment quite difficult.

An additional problem in predicting violent behavior involves the balance between two types of errors: unfairly detaining an offender who would *not* have offended again versus freeing an offender who does offend again. Psychologists could adopt a cautious criterion in an effort to protect society. Unfortunately, doing so would increase the number of offenders who would be wrongly detained. Alternatively, psychologists could adopt a "benefit of the doubt" approach, thereby reducing the number of wrongly detained offenders while increasing the number of offenders who are freed only to offend again. Although psychologists are concerned, first and foremost, with the need to accurately predict violent behavior, it is likely that the need to strike some optimal balance between the two errors of prediction is of some concern. The issue of an optimal balance is a thorny one, as it involves complex philosophical and moral issues. We raise it here only to heighten your appreciation of the difficulty involved in predicting violent behavior.

In the final analysis, it seems that psychologists' predictions of violent behavior are not likely to improve dramatically, but legal psychologists may at least be able to explain the reasons for this state of affairs to courts and parole boards. Psychologists will still be called on to help courts make decisions about violence, but they may do so with more caution, informing the court about the behaviors they are trying to predict (and what criteria they are using) and telling how confident they are in their predictions.

THE INSANITY DEFENSE

Psychologists and psychiatrists are called on to help judge a defendant's state of mind at the time a crime was committed. In Western legal systems, a person is guilty only if he or she intended to commit a crime. If a person is unable to judge between right and wrong at the time of the crime, then he or she may be judged "not guilty by reason of insanity." The **insanity defense** was discussed in Chapter 15, where we noted that insanity is not a psychological concept, but a legal concept (being judged incapable of distinguishing right from wrong). Psychologists and psychiatrists serve as expert witnesses for determinations of insanity, but the judgments themselves properly reside with judges and juries.

Determining a person's mental state at the time a crime was committed is a hazardous enterprise. Different psychiatrists interviewing the same defendant about the same instance can arrive at radically different judgments. These occurrences lead to skepticism among the general public about the value of psychologists and psychiatrists as expert witnesses and about the value of legal psychology, too (Hans, 1989).

As you will recall from Chapter 15, public skepticism about the entire insanity defense was raised in the early 1980s in the case of John Hinckley, the man who

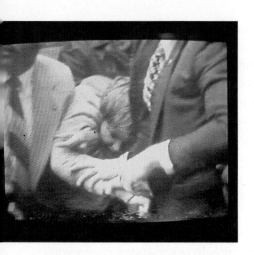

John Hinkley was captured just after he shot President Reagan and press secretary, James Brady. He was later found not guilty by reason of insanity, a verdict that was not well received by the public.

attempted to assassinate President Reagan. Because Hinckley was caught at the scene and television cameras filmed the sequence of events, no doubt existed as to his culpability. Instead, the trial revolved around issues about his capacity to determine right from wrong. After a long trial and conflicting testimony from psychiatrists, the jury found Hinckley not guilty by reason of insanity, a verdict very unpopular with the public. Indeed, public opinion surveys showed that most people disagreed with the verdict, and in one survey, 87 percent said that they believed that the insanity defense represented a legal loophole permitting guilty people to go free (Hans & Slater, 1983).

People widely misunderstand the nature of the insanity defense, the reasons for it, how frequently it is used, and how often it works. The dramatic cases played out in the media have colored the public's perception of both the frequency of the defense and its success rate (Hans, 1989). Legal psychologists are interested in investigating this state of affairs and the accuracy of the public's perception of other legal issues. Surveys have shown that many people believe that the insanity defense is frequently used and often successful; in actuality, it is rarely exercised, and fewer than 1 percent of all defendants who employ this defense are judged not guilty by reason of insanity.

Largely due to the Hinckley verdict, many states have changed the use of the insanity defense (Senna & Siegel, 1995). Recall from Chapter 15 that three states (Montana, Idaho, and Utah) have banned all evidence concerning mental illness during trials, and 13 others have developed the verdict "guilty but mentally ill" to replace the insanity defense (see Simon & Aronson, 1988, for an in-depth treatment of this topic). Under this verdict, if a defendant uses the insanity defense, but the jury or judge do not find that the evidence warrants this verdict, they may return the "guilty but mentally ill" verdict. The judgment means that the person suffers a mental disorder but still can tell right from wrong. The court imposes a sentence on the convicted defendant, as usual. The person is treated for mental illness but returned to prison afterward to serve out the remainder of the sentence (Senna & Siegal, 1995). The insanity defense and related issues will continue to be a source of study for psychologists interested in legal issues.

EYEWITNESS IDENTIFICATION

Another issue of keen interest to psychologists is the problem of *eyewitness identification*. Testimony from an eyewitness—someone who saw a crime—can be very convincing. Loftus (1979) studied cases in England in which the only evidence was eyewitness testimony and found a 74 percent conviction rate. Of these, half (169 of 347) involved only one eyewitness. Cases of mistaken identity—an example of which is shown in Figure 18.9—highlight a potential pitfall of relying solely on eyewitness accounts in deciding the guilt or innocence of an accused. Along these lines, Brandon and Davies (1973) cite 70 cases in which eyewitness testimony was responsible for the conviction of an innocent person.

Several procedures that police often use to help witnesses identify suspects may lead to cases of mistaken identification. One common technique is the lineup, in which a suspect is placed with several other people and a witness is asked to pick out the suspect. As long as careful procedures are followed, the lineup can provide useful information, but problems can also arise (R.C.L. Lindsay, 1994). For example, suppose you were a witness to a crime and all you remembered about the suspect was that he was African American, fairly tall, and handsome. If you were confronted with a lineup that had three black men and three white men, and only one of the African American

FIGURE 18.9
A Case of Mistaken Identity

The man on the right, William Bernard Jackson, was sentenced for rape in 1977. Five years later, the prosecutor indicted the real rapist, Dr. Edward Franklin Jackson, Jr., shown in the photo on the left.

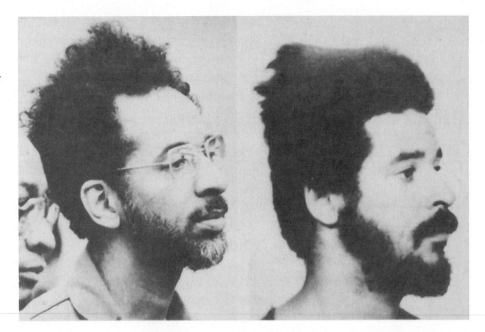

men was tall and handsome, then you might be likely to pick him whether or not you accurately remembered him as the perpetrator of the crime. He is simply the most plausible of the choices you are given. In general, a lineup should be constructed so that all the participants have an equal likelihood of being chosen by someone with only general knowledge of a suspect. If the witness has told police that she remembers the suspect as tall, handsome, and African American, then all the people in the lineup should fit this general description. Of course, there must be differences among the lineup participants to make identification possible (imagine if twins were included!), but all the participants should fit the general description of the suspect (Wells, 1993).

A lineup can be biased in other ways as well. Often, witnesses are shown pictures of a suspect before the lineup, but are not shown pictures of the other participants. Thus, the suspect can seem familiar in the lineup, even if he or she is not the correct person, because the witness remembers him or her from the pictures (Read, 1994; Ross and colleagues, 1994).

Another issue in eyewitness memory was discussed in Chapter 7: Experiences that occur to a witness after a critical event can interfere with memory of the event. When witnesses are asked misleading questions about events ("Did you see the stop sign at the intersection?"), they are later more likely to say that they remember the suggested item (the stop sign) than other witnesses who were not asked questions (Loftus & Palmer, 1974). This malleability of memory through interfering activities can also limit the accuracy of eyewitness identification, because often witnesses firmly believe that suggested facts were really observed during the event (Weingardt, Toland & Loftus, 1994).

Through the efforts of psychologists and others, the legal profession has become increasingly aware of issues in eyewitness identification. In one decision, the U. S. Supreme Court stated that "the primary evil to be avoided is a very substantial likelihood of irreparable misidentification" (Senna & Siegel, 1995, p. 310). In several cases, the Supreme Court has sought reasonable criteria for judging identifications as unbiased. These include the opportunity for a witness to view a crime, the accuracy of the witness's description of the criminal before identification, the confidence of the witness, and the length of time between the crime and the identification. Although these standards seem reasonable, psychological evidence calls at least some of them into question. For example, research shows that confidence is not always well correlated with accuracy of identification (Luus & Wells, 1994). Some people can confidently make identifications that are later proved incorrect. Other witnesses, perhaps more observant and more cautious by nature, may be accurate in their identifications but seem less confident. Thus, the relation between confidence and accuracy is not as simple as the Supreme Court seems to assume.

A practical issue involved in eyewitness testimony is how people remember faces they have seen. One of the more robust findings in this area is that face recognition tends to be more accurate for faces of an individual's own race than for faces of other races—an **own-race bias.** This bias has been found both in laboratories and in more naturalistic settings (Bothwell, Brigham, & Malpass, 1989). The own-race bias has particularly serious consequences for eyewitness identification in situations in which an eyewitness is asked to identify a member of another race.

One of the earliest studies of the own-race bias was conducted by Malpass and Kravitz (1969). The study is straightforward and provides a good illustration of the research on own-race bias. Malpass and Kravitz first photographed 40 African American males, and 40 white males all of whom were wearing white T-shirts. For each subject, photos of 10 African-American males and 10 White males were randomly selected from the pool of 80 photos and were then presented for 2 seconds each. Immediately following this phase, subjects were shown all 80 photographs and asked to indicate which 20 of the 80 photographs they had viewed in the earlier phase. The number of correct identifications of faces are presented in Table 18.6 and reveal that subjects were better at recognizing faces of their own race than faces of another race.

The problem of other-race face recognition has since received a great deal of attention from applied psychologists; however, researchers have no direct evidence regarding the source of the own-race bias. For now, there is general agreement that this bias results from race-related differences in *perceptual expertise*. Basically, researchers theorize that differences in perceptual expertise arise from "differing amounts or kinds of real-life interaction with members of different races . . . . Thus, for example, relative to White subjects, African-American subjects may tend to direct more attention to the shape and position of the eyes and less attention to eye color" (D. S. Lindsay, Jack, & Christian, 1991, p. 587).

Although the perceptual expertise hypothesis is now generally accepted, it had not been tested directly before D. S. Lindsay, Jack, and Christian (1991) conducted a laboratory study with African American and white undergraduate students. This study is particularly relevant to the issue of eyewitness identification because the experimenters presented each target face for only a fraction of a second (120 milliseconds).

TABLE 18.6
Proportion of Faces Correctly Identified

	FACES	
SUBJECTS	AFRICAN AMERICAN	WHITE
African American (n = 13)	.74	.68
White (n = 13)	.61	.79

SOURCE: Data from Malpass & Kravitz (1969).

This limited exposure was chosen to reflect crime situations in which eyewitnesses typically have limited opportunity to observe the perpetrator. Additionally, presenting each face for only a brief period of time allowed D. S. Lindsay and colleagues to focus more precisely on perceptual (rather than, say, motivational or attentional) factors—the central aspect of their perceptual expertise hypothesis. After briefly viewing either an African American or white face, subjects were instructed to identify which of a pair of similar looking same-race faces had been presented originally. Subjects engaged in this same task over a total of 50 trials—25 trials with an African American face as the target and 25 trials in which a white face was the target. As mentioned earlier, each face was presented very briefly to minimize the possibility that differences in the amount of attention or motivation devoted to viewing faces of different races would contribute to an own-race bias in face identification. Thus, the researchers constructed a highly controlled and stringent test of their perceptual expertise hypothesis. Despite this stringent test, white subjects were more accurate in identifying white faces than African American faces, whereas African American subjects were equally accurate in identifying faces of both races. This own-race bias with white subjects (and lack of bias with African American subjects) can be seen in Figure 18.10.

The results reported by D. Stephen Lindsay and his colleagues (1991) suggest that the own-race bias in face identification has its origins in perceptual learning. Is there any way to lessen this bias, short of conducting a large-scale social intervention? Recent research on the topic of eyewitness identification suggests one solution for reducing bias in lineups: sequential lineups (Wells, 1993). In a **sequential lineup,** line-up members or photographs of lineup members are presented *one at a time*, and the witness must decide whether or not the individual is the perpetrator—an absolute judgment strategy. In the traditional **simultaneous lineup,** lineup members are all presented *at the same time*. Here, witnesses tend to judge the relative similarity of the line-up members to their memory of the perpetrator in order to make an identification—a relative judgment strategy. Researchers such as Rod Lindsay and Gary Wells (1985) have argued that simultaneous lineups are more likely to encourage witnesses to make a choice, whether they are certain or not, relative to sequential lineups. This greater degree of uncertainty associated with simultaneous lineups could increase the number of "false identifications," incorrectly identifying an innocent person as the perpetrator. Alternatively, it could be argued that in discouraging witnesses from making a choice unless absolutely certain, sequential lineups could reduce correct identifications.

Rod Lindsay and several collaborators (1991) conducted a study by varying the type of lineup (sequential versus simultaneous) and the fairness of the lineup (fair versus biased) in an attempt to determine whether these factors affected identification accuracy. As discussed earlier in the chapter, it is critical for lineups to be fair—that is, composed of similar looking members (e.g., stocky, white males in their thirties). Lineups composed of dissimilar looking members are referred to as biased lineups (e.g., women in a lineup where a man is the suspect). R. Lindsay et al. found that subjects were able to identify the perpetrator equally well with the sequential lineup as with the simultaneous lineup. Even more importantly, the sequential lineup produced significantly fewer false identifications than did the simultaneous lineup regardless of whether the lineup was designed to be fair or biased. Furthermore, sequential lineups did not result in fewer correct identifications as was initially feared. It is important to note, however, that there were always more false identifications with the biased line-ups, presumably because subjects were overconfident in making a judgment when there was only one plausible suspect in the lineup. This study suggests, then, that

FIGURE 18.10
Own-Race Bias in Face Identification

Proportion of correct identifications of white and African American faces across 50 trials.

SOURCE: Data from Lindsay, Jack, & Christian, 1991.

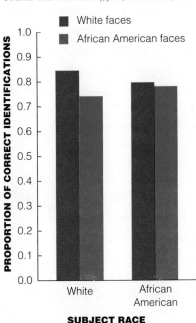

sequential lineups are an improvement over the traditional simultaneous lineup, but that they are no remedy for a biased lineup.

Like so many practical problems that applied psychologists investigate, there is both good and bad news in the area of other-race face recognition. The good news is that the work of R. Lindsay and his colleagues (1991) suggests that the accuracy of eyewitness identification can be improved in two ways: first, by ensuring that the lineup members resemble sufficiently the suspect or alleged perpetrator (a fair lineup); and two, by employing a sequential rather than a traditional simultaneous lineup. The bad news is that own-race bias in face recognition is still a significant problem (D. S. Lindsay, Jack, & Christian, 1991). It will be interesting to follow the work conducted on eyewitness identification in lineups to see whether sequential lineups may perhaps pave the way to significant reductions in own-race bias in eyewitness identification. Only further research will tell.

Psychologists have also participated in court cases as *expert witnesses* to address jurors on how to evaluate eyewitness testimony (Loftus, 1983). For example, jurors can be informed about psychological research showing how eyewitnesses can be misled by certain types of lineups and how their experiences after the event can affect what they report later. The use of psychologists as experts on this issue is controversial, however, with some people arguing that we do not yet know enough to contribute to court proceedings on these issues (Egeth, 1993; McCloskey & Egeth, 1983).

Psychologists are interested in many other issues within the broad realm of the law. They have studied the process of jury decision making, often through the use of simulated juries who hear real court cases and arrive at verdicts as if they were real juries. Psychologists have also been used by lawyers in helping to select juries. Because the legal profession is so concerned with people and their behavior, psychologists find it a fascinating area for study.

THEMES IN REVIEW

In this chapter, we discovered that principles of learning play an important role in the work of many applied psychologists. Through the process of socialization, individuals learn to expect certain reinforcers from their work—equitable pay, challenging work, opportunity to socialize, and so forth. Perceptual learning also affects our ability to recognize other-race faces through providing different amounts and kinds of opportunity to interact with individuals of other races. We also learn to distinguish between noises that are reason for fear and annoyance and noises that are necessary and inevitable in modern life, depending (in part) on the predictability of the noise. At an individual level, human factors psychologists who study human-computer interaction have applied principles of learning to design computer interfaces that map consistently with the way humans think and solve problems. Similarly, much of the work in educational psychology reflects the application of learning principles. For example, educational psychologists have discovered that learning is facilitated by outlining chapter information and summarizing important points at the end of each chapter. Finally, school psychologists devote much of their time to developing ways to assess school performance through standardized achievement tests.

Work in human cognition is integral to many of the areas discussed in this chapter. In fact, the assessment of cognitive ability is important for both school and educational psychologists. School psychologists use the results of cognitive ability tests to design individual courses of study, advise students in making school and career decisions, and determine whether an individual would benefit from special classes. In the section on educational psychology, we discovered a lively debate concerning the prevalence of psychological testing in schools and the workplace. This debate centers on the issue of whether these tests merely predict later success in school and work or serve to open and close doors of opportunity, thereby shaping future success.

Research in human cognition also has implications for specific applied problems. For example, Fiske and her colleagues argue that gender stereotyping—a cognitive process—is responsible for gender discrimination such as took place in the case of *Hopkins v. Price Waterhouse*. Human factors psychologists are concerned with the problem of declining performance on vigilance tasks over time. Cognitive research in the area of attention proved useful in the design of a multisensory display that produced modest improvements in a long-term vigilance task.

Developmental or life span issues are important for discovering which interventions might prove useful for facilitating the development of children with special needs. One such intervention involves integrating these children into cooperative learning situations (school). Human factors psychologists investigate problems of older drivers and how they can be overcome. For example, older drivers themselves take significant steps to reduce their driving risks (e.g., driving only during the day and avoiding driving in inclement weather). Environmental psychologists are concerned about the evidence suggesting potential long-term negative effects in academic development for children who are subjected to noisy learning environments.

Sociocultural issues are significant in such areas as environmental psychology. The subjective experience of crowding is related to several indicators of social pathology, including impaired mental health and poor social relationships in the home.

Another social phenomenon involves the recognition of leaders in our society. We develop beliefs over time that lead us to expect certain actions and characteristics from our leaders; these beliefs then guide our willingness to recognize another as a leader. Issues of diversity are central to the work of industrial/organizational psychologists. Much work in this area is devoted to developing fair selection procedures to ensure that individuals are not discriminated against on the basis of their gender, race, color, religion, or national origin. Finally, psychologists who work in the area of psychology and the law attempt to discover ways to reduce discrimination in the courts. We saw one example of this work in the area of eyewitness identification and the problem of other-race bias.

SUMMARY

1 Although psychologists have always been interested in applying their research, several fields of applied psychology have become prominent: industrial/organizational psychology, human factors psychology, environmental psychology, school psychology, educational psychology, and psychology and the law.

2 Industrial psychology (also called personnel psychology) is primarily concerned with employee selection, training, and assessment. Practitioners conduct job analyses to determine job requirements and help select people through psychological tests, interviews, and other means such as assessment centers. Nonstructured interviews are widely used in industry, but their validity in predicting job success has not been demonstrated. Recently, concerns about gender discrimination and other forms of bias have been studied.

3 Organizational psychology is concerned with relationships among workers in organizations, including issues of leadership, work motivation, group dynamics, and organizational climate. Effective leadership is critical to the success of organizations. One important ingredient seems to be that the leader (or manager in business) personally observe and evaluate the work of subordinates.

4 Human factors psychology is devoted to developing technical systems with the "human factor" taken into account. Human factors psychologists help design many things, such as displays of information or means of controlling machines so that technical devices can be used safely and effectively. Two current topics of intense interest in this field are human-computer interaction and traffic safety.

⑤ Environmental psychology is the study of the relationship between the environment and behavior. Environmental psychologists may help design a statement of the requirements for a proposed building to serve its intended functions (an architectural program); interview workers to help them design their own work space (participatory planning); and evaluate the success of a building in enhancing worker effectiveness (postoccupancy evaluation).

⑥ School psychologists are involved in such activities as assessing (testing) school children, counseling students (and parents), designing remedial programs to promote academic achievement and mental health, and conducting research in school settings.

⑦ Educational psychology is concerned with curriculum, instruction, assessment, learning, and motivation. Researchers study how these factors are related to individual characteristics of students and teachers and how academic success can be enhanced. For example, educational psychologists study how students learn from texts, how academic motivation can be maintained, and what factors contribute to effective schools.

⑧ Psychologists interested in the law have (a) tried to predict future behavior of prisoners (though without great success), (b) studied the issue of eyewitness identification, especially how the process can be biased, (c) examined police procedures used in line-ups and how bias can be minimized, and (d) studied the effects of decisions involving the insanity defense. The use of psychologists as expert witnesses in trials involving the insanity defense or eyewitness testimony is controversial, with some arguing that our knowledge is not yet advanced enough to present to juries.

KEY TERMS

industrial/organizational psychology (p. 759)

industrial psychology (p. 759)

organizational psychology (p. 760)

job analysis (p. 760)

structured interviews (p. 761)

situational interview (p. 761)

validity generalization (p. 763)

assessment center (p. 763)

formal work groups (p. 765)

informal work groups (p. 765)

work norms (p. 765)

Hawthorne effect (p. 765)

transactional leaders (p. 767)

transformational leaders (p. 767)

cognitive resource utilization theory (p. 767)

work motivation (p. 769)

human factors psychology (p. 771)

gender stereotyping (p. 772)

response generalization (p. 777)

multisensory display (p. 778)

mapping (p. 781)

environmental psychology (p. 782)

density (p. 784)

crowding (p. 784)

school psychology (p. 787)

educational psychology (p. 789)

relational processing (p. 793)

item-specific processing (p. 793)

forensic psychology (p. 794)

insanity defense (p. 795)

own-race bias (p. 798)

sequential lineup (p. 799)

simultaneous lineup (p. 799)

For Critical Analysis

1 In this chapter, we introduced and discussed six fields of applied psychology. What are the similarities and differences between these fields? How would you group these fields in terms of their similarities and differences?

2 Of the topics discussed in the section on industrial/organizational psychology, which do you feel addresses the most pressing issues for work in organizations? Why?

3 On page 777, we provided a concept summary of three approaches to the study of traffic safety in human factors psychology. Which approach do you believe will have the greatest impact in improving traffic safety? Which approach will have the least impact? List reasons for your decision.

4 Why do you think the subjective experience of crowding was correlated to poor mental and physical health, inadequate child care, psychological and physical withdrawal, and poor social relationships in the home (Gove, Hughes, & Galle, 1979)? List some plausible hypotheses. Decide which area of psychology would be most useful for investigating each hypothesis.

5 We described briefly the controversy surrounding the prevalence of psychological testing in American society. Which side of the debate do you believe offers the most compelling arguments? Have you been tested too much or too little?

6 At the end of the chapter, we discussed the problem of how people often identify faces from members of their own race better than those of other races. There are obvious implications here for eyewitness identification, but other negative consequences might be associated with this own-race bias in other arenas (e.g., the workplace). In what other areas do you think this own-race bias might be cause for concern?

Suggested Readings

BRUER, J. (1993). *Schools for thought*. Cambridge, MA: The MIT Press. An interesting book on applying principles derived from cognitive psychology to education. Bruer argues that such applications would greatly improve educational practice.

GREGORY, W. L., & BURROUGHS, W. J. (1989). *Introduction to applied psychology*. Glenview, IL.: Scott, Foresman. An excellent textbook that includes at least one chapter on each of the main topics covered in this chapter, plus chapters on consumer, clinical, community, and sports psychology.

DIPBOYE, R. L., SMITH, C., & HOWELL, W. C. (1993). *Understanding industrial and organizational psychology*. Fort Worth, TX: Harcourt Brace Jovanovich. A fine, comprehensive overview of the main topics in I/O psychology.

NORMAN, D. A. (1988). *The psychology of everyday things*. New York, NY: Basic Books. A fascinating look at the difficulty we have in using everyday things—cars, computers, typewriters, and even doors, faucets and light switches. Designers often fail to take the psychology of the user into account, which leads to "human error." But as Norman shows through many examples, the error is more likely attributed to the designer.

PETROSKI, H. (1985). *To engineer is human: The role of failure in successful design*. New York: St. Martin's Press. Interesting examples of learning from design failures.

PROCTOR, R. W., & VAN ZANDT, T. (1994). *Human factors in simple and complex systems*. Boston: Allyn and Bacon. An excellent overview of human factors psychology.

SCHULTZ, D. P. & SCHULTZ, S. E. (1990). *Psychology and industry today: An introduction to industrial and organizational psychology* (5th ed.). New York: Macmillan. An excellent textbook covering the traditional topics of industrial and organizational psychology, including a chapter on human engineering.

WRIGHTSMAN, L. S. (1987). *Psychology and the legal system*. Pacific Grove, CA: Brooks/Cole. Extremely well-written and interesting introduction to the area of psychology and law, filled with historical examples highlighting the various topics covered. A "must read" for those wanting to know more about this area of psychology.

PSYCHOLOGY ON THE INTERNET

The Industrial–Organizational Psychologist

(http://cmit.unomaha.edu/TIP/TIP.html)

The Industrial–Organizational Psychologist (TIP) is the official newsletter of the Society for Industrial–Organizational Psychology. In addition to providing feature articles and columns on-line, this home page provides links to other Internet resources relevant to industrial–organizational psychology—including software archives, Usenet and Listserv groups, and university departments with degree programs in industrial–organizational psychology.

Human Factors Sites

(http://skylaine.aviation./uiuc.edu/humFacsites/hotlist.html)

This home page contains links to sites relevant to human factors. Among these are links to professional organizations (e.g., the Human Factors and Ergonomic Society and the International Ergonomics Association), the Human–Computer Interaction Virtual Library (a collection of links to sites related to human–computer interaction), a list of frequently asked questions about human–computer interaction, and university departments that offer degrees in human factors.

School Psychology Resources On-Line

(http://mail.bcpl.lib.md.us/~sandyste/school_psych.html)

This home page contains an impressive list of "links to sites of interest to the school psychology community." Included in this list are links to sites providing information on learning disabilities, mental retardation, and psycho-educational assessment and evaluation as well as links to information on various counseling issues.

Psychiatry and the Law

(http://ua1vm.ua.edu/~jhooper/tableofc.html)

Although this site is meant primarily as a resource for attorneys and psychiatrists, it provides some interesting information for students on the legal issue of "mental competence" and other legal issues related to mental illness. The links that provide particularly interesting information are "Landmark Cases in Mental Health Law" and "U.S. Supreme Court Rulings Re: Mental Illness."

AN INTRODUCTION TO STATISTICS

We have several goals in writing this appendix. First, we hope to show that the study of statistics has important implications for your knowledge and evaluation of psychological research. Statistical reasoning is an essential part of psychological research, and almost all research papers in psychology contain some statistics. Second, we hope to illustrate, through examples, that you already know some things about statistics and that it is worth your while to learn more. Third, we hope to convince you that studying statistics is essential for understanding much of what you read about medicine, crime, business, and other areas affecting your life. Years ago, H. G. Wells wrote, "Statistical thinking will one day be as necessary for efficient citizenship as the ability to read and write."

You often encounter statistics in your daily life—for example, when a public-opinion poll shows one candidate leading another 50 percent to 42 percent, with 8 percent undecided. You may read about the median annual income for people of different occupations; that the Consumer Price Index went up 4 percent last year; or that a weather forecaster predicts a 60 percent chance of rain. The probability-of-rain figure is particularly interesting. The forecaster is saying that meteorologists, with all their instruments, measurements of current conditions, and knowledge of weather patterns, cannot forecast weather with certainty. Psychologists are usually in a similar situation; they cannot predict behavior with certainty, but only with some probability.

There are two branches of statistics: descriptive statistics and inferential statistics. **Descriptive statistics** are used to summarize or describe a set of scores; **inferential statistics** help researchers to draw conclusions, or inferences, from the scores.

Descriptive Statistics

Psychologists do research to discover the principles underlying behavior. Typically, they devise hypotheses to account for some behavior and then try to collect evidence that will confirm or disconfirm those hypotheses. Investigators may collect hundreds, even thousands, of observations. How are they to make sense of them? Descriptive statistics are useful for summarizing and describing a great amount of **data,** or information. They are used to describe the main features of the observations that have been collected.

To understand how statistics can be useful, let us consider the results that can be obtained from an experimental situation called the *bystander intervention* experiment. You have probably read newspaper accounts in which numerous people, usually in large cities, witness robberies or murders without intervening to help the victims. Social psychologists became interested in this phenomenon and sought to discover what caused it. Were people callous? Didn't they care? (Research on bystander intervention is described in Chapter 17.) After analyzing a number of cases, two social psychologists came up with a paradoxical idea: A person is *less* likely to assist in a crisis the more other people are present in the situation (Darley & Latané, 1968). This hypothesis seems implausible, because one might expect that with other people present, a person would be more likely to intervene. Darley and Latane reasoned, however, that an individual might actually be less likely to give aid because he or she would feel less responsible when in a group. The feeling of responsibility for acting would be weak when many others were present. (If a professor asked a question in a class of 100, you would feel less pressure to volunteer an answer than if the class had only 3 other people.)

One way to test this *diffusion of responsibility* hypothesis is to set up a laboratory experiment in which an emergency occurs. In one condition, people should think that they are alone; in the other condition, they should think that three others are present. Participants should be randomly assigned to one condition or the other. During the course of the experiment, an accident will occur to the experimenter, who is out of sight in the other room. For example, the experimenter may be shocked, cry out in pain, and fall on the floor with a loud thud. Let us assume that in this situation, most participants will come to the experimenter's aid. The prediction from the hypothesis is that people will take longer to come to the experimenter's aid when they think three other people are present than when they think they are alone.

The independent variable, or the factor manipulated, is the number of bystanders besides the subject who are believed to witness the crisis (zero or three). The dependent variable, or what is measured, is the amount of time before the subjects begin helping. Variables to be controlled include the time of day during testing, the type of crisis, and the experimenter. All of the control variables are the same for the two conditions.

Let us suppose that a total of 30 people are tested—15 in each condition (alone and with three bystanders)—and that the numbers in Table A.1 represent the amount of time it took for the subjects to begin to help. As you can see, the time elapsed before helping seems to be greater for people in the three-bystander condition than for

Response Times in Bystander Intervention Experiment

ALONE		THREE BYSTANDERS	
SUBJECT	TIME TO RESPOND (IN SECONDS)	SUBJECT	TIME TO RESPOND (IN SECONDS)
Subject 1	30	Subject 1	45
Subject 2	42	Subject 2	37
Subject 3	20	Subject 3	55
Subject 4	58	Subject 4	75
Subject 5	45	Subject 5	50
Subject 6	102	Subject 6	90
Subject 7	40	Subject 7	125
Subject 8	24	Subject 8	81
Subject 9	55	Subject 9	71
Subject 10	31	Subject 10	60
Subject 11	44	Subject 11	85
Subject 12	68	Subject 12	70
Subject 13	38	Subject 13	103
Subject 14	21	Subject 14	54
Subject 15	38	Subject 15	90
Total (ΣX)	656	Total (ΣX)	1,091
Mean (M)	43.73	Mean (M)	72.73

In this hypothetical bystander intervention example, 15 people are randomly assigned to each of two groups—a total of 30 subjects. The time measures indicate the length of time each subject took to respond to an experimenter "in trouble."

those in the alone condition. Precisely how much do the two conditions differ in the time it takes subjects to respond? Two primary types of descriptive statistics provide convenient summaries of the scores. **Measures of central tendency** locate the center of a set of scores. **Measures of dispersion** show how scores are spread out (or dispersed) from their center.

MEASURES OF CENTRAL TENDENCY

A group of scores can be analyzed by several measures of central tendency, but the one most frequently used is the mean. (You know this term as the *average score*, but *average* is often used for any measure of central tendency, so *mean* is preferred.) The **mean** is the total of all the scores divided by the number of scores. (Its abbreviation is M or, in older works, $\overline{X}$). As you can see in Table A.1, the total of the scores of all subjects in the alone condition is 656 seconds. (The symbol ΣX stands for the total of all scores). Since there are 15 scores, the mean is $656 \div 15$, or 43.73 seconds. The total of the scores of all subjects in the three-bystander condition is 1,091; the mean is $1,091 \div 15$, or 72.73. As you can see, the mean scores of the two conditions differ by 29 seconds. Thus, the mean time that elapsed before a person helped was 29 seconds longer in the three-bystander condition than in the alone condition.

The mean is the measure of central tendency most frequently given in reports of experiments, but sometimes another measure of central tendency is used. The **median** is the middle score in a set of scores; half the scores lie above the median score and half below it. The median of the scores in the alone condition is 40 seconds; in the three-bystander condition, it is 71 seconds. Finding the median is easy: Put the scores in order from highest to lowest and count down through half of them. When there is an odd number of scores, the median is the middle score. When there is an even number of scores, the median is simply the mean of the two scores nearest the middle. If there were 20 scores and the tenth score was 30 and the eleventh score was 32, then the median would be 31.

Why is the median ever used in place of the mean? In cases where one or more scores are extreme, the median often provides a more useful measure of central tendency than does the mean. Suppose that one person in the alone condition of our hypothetical experiment never helps at all in the crisis but just sits there for 30 minutes, until the experimenter gives permission to leave. How will the experimenter record that person's time? One way is to enter the maximum time allowed, in this case 30 minutes, or 1,800 seconds. If the uncooperative person is subject 6 in Table A.1, and 1,800 seconds replaces the 102 seconds there, then the mean of the scores in the alone condition becomes 156.93 seconds instead of 43.73 seconds! Someone who knew only the mean scores of the two conditions would believe that people are more than three times as slow in the alone condition as in the three-bystander condition. Obviously, there is something wrong with this conclusion, since it is based almost completely on the score of only one person who reacted atypically. Thus, one extreme score is distorting the results of the experiment. The median, however, will be the same—40 seconds—in the alone condition, whether the sixth subject helps after 102 seconds or after 1,800 seconds. Changing the most extreme score will not change the median at all. So in cases in which one quite deviant score (or a few wacky scores in a large set) causes the mean to give an unrepresentative measure of the central tendency, the median should be used instead.

The third measure of central tendency is the **mode,** which is simply the most frequent score in a set of scores. In the alone condition, the mode is 38 seconds; in the three-bystander condition, it is 90 seconds. These are the only scores in each set of figures that appear more than once. The mode is rarely used as a measure of central tendency because it can be misleading, especially when there are only a few scores in a set. For example, if a student's five test scores are 40, 55, 84, 40, and 95, the mode is 40. Obviously, this measure of central tendency would misrepresent the student's performance. The mean score (62.8) better reflects the central tendency in this case. (What is the median in this set? Put the five numbers in order: 95, 84, 55, 40, and 40. The median is the middle score, 55.)

MEASURES OF DISPERSION

As their names imply, measures of central tendency indicate the point that tends to be in the center of a distribution of scores, while measures of dispersion indicate how scores spread away (disperse, as a crowd might disperse) from this center point. The simplest measure of dispersion is a **range**—the difference between the highest and lowest scores in a set of scores. For the alone condition in our hypothetical experiment, the range is 102−20, or 82 seconds. The range in the three-bystander condition is 125−37, or 88 seconds. Because a range is based solely on the most extreme scores in a group, it is rarely used, since one extreme score can greatly affect the range. Also, while a range shows the difference between the highest and lowest scores, it does not tell how much the scores vary from one another.

The most common descriptive statistic of dispersion is the **standard deviation**—the average difference between individual scores and the mean. A standard deviation is more difficult to compute than a range, but it has mathematical properties that make it more useful. The standard deviation for a sample of scores is obtained by first taking the difference of each score from the mean and squaring it. (Squaring eliminates the negative numbers that occur if the differences are used.) These squared values are then added together and divided by the number of scores minus one. Finally, the square root of this value is taken. This procedure can be represented by a simple formula:

$$SD = \sqrt{\frac{\text{sum of } d^2}{n-1}}$$

In this formula, SD stands for standard deviation, d stands for the difference between each score and the mean, and n stands for the number of scores in the set. Table A.2 shows the computations for finding the standard deviations for the scores in Table A.1. The standard deviation in the alone condition is 21.08 seconds; in the three-bystander condition, it is 23.71 seconds. In actual practice, there are simpler formulas for obtaining the standard deviation than the one we have chosen, but ours provides a better understanding of the concept of standard deviation. You can automatically obtain the mean and standard deviation when you punch a series of scores into most calculators.

FREQUENCY DISTRIBUTIONS

In the bystander intervention example, the dispersion of scores about the mean is roughly the same for the two conditions; but this is not always the case. Consider the

TABLE A.2
Computation of Standard Deviations for the Bystander Intervention Experiment

ALONE

SUBJECT	TIME	MEAN	d	d^2
1	30	43.73	−13.73	188.51
2	42	43.73	−1.73	2.99
3	20	43.73	−23.73	563.11
4	58	43.73	14.27	203.63
5	45	43.73	1.27	1.61
6	102	43.73	58.27	3,395.39
7	40	43.73	−3.73	13.91
8	24	43.73	−19.73	389.27
9	55	43.73	11.27	127.01
10	31	43.73	−12.73	162.05
11	44	43.73	0.27	0.07
12	68	43.73	24.27	589.03
13	38	43.73	−5.73	32.83
14	21	43.73	−22.73	516.65
15	38	43.73	−5.73	32.83

Sum of d^2 = 6,218.95

$$SD = \sqrt{\frac{6,218.89}{14}}$$

$$SD = \sqrt{444.21}$$

$$SD = 21.08$$

THREE BYSTANDERS

SUBJECT	TIME	MEAN	d	d^2
1	45	72.73	−27.73	768.95
2	37	72.73	−35.73	1,276.63
3	55	72.73	17.73	314.35
4	75	72.73	2.27	5.15
5	50	72.73	22.73	516.65
6	90	72.73	17.27	298.25
7	125	72.73	52.27	2,732.15
8	81	72.73	8.27	68.39
9	71	72.73	−1.73	2.99
10	60	72.73	12.73	162.05
11	85	72.73	12.27	150.55
12	70	72.73	−2.73	7.45
13	103	72.73	30.27	916.27
14	54	72.73	−18.73	350.81
15	90	72.73	17.27	298.25

sum of d^2 = 7,868.95

$$SD = \sqrt{\frac{7,868.89}{14}}$$

$$SD = \sqrt{562.07}$$

$$SD = 23.71$$

$$SD = \sqrt{\frac{\text{Sum of } d^2}{n-1}}$$

where SD is the standard deviation
d is the difference between each score and the mean
n is the number of scores

two graphs in Figure A.1. These graphs depict **frequency distributions;** they show the number (frequency) of people scoring at different levels for a group of scores. They show the distribution of the scores, or how the scores pile up at different points or spread out. The frequency distributions in Figure A.1 are the hypothetical scores of two groups of entering university students on the verbal part of the Scholastic Assessment Test (SAT). In both cases, the mean of the distribution is just above 500, but in one school (represented in blue) there is not much spread of the scores around the mean. Students at this school come from a rather narrow range in terms of their test scores. Meanwhile, students at the other college (red graph) have much more variable SAT scores, even though the mean is the same. In this case, the scores are more widely dispersed around the mean. Thus, the standard deviation of the students' scores is much greater in the second case (red graph) than in the first. This is what a large standard deviation reveals; the scores are distributed quite widely around the mean. This information is important. A professor at the college with students who vary widely in verbal SAT scores will need to adopt teaching methods for a wide range of verbal abilities.

THE NORMAL CURVE

The graphs of the hypothetical SAT scores in Figure A.1 show that the scores pile up in the middle but trail off toward the extremes (tails) of the distribution of scores. Although these numbers are hypothetical, this sort of distribution is typical for most measures of behavior; that is, for most phenomena that are measured, scores cluster in the center of the distribution. A special bell-shaped distribution of this type is called a **normal curve,** an example of which is presented in Figure A.2 (the curve labeled B). When put on a graph, psychological data typically are most numerous in the middle of the set of scores; they decline in frequency with distance from the middle in a symmetrical way. A score 10 points below the center of the distribution occurs about as frequently as a score 10 points above the center.

FIGURE A.1
Hypothetical Verbal SAT Scores for Students at Two Universities

At the school represented by the blue line, the students come from a much narrower range in terms of verbal ability than the students at another school, represented by the black line. The mean score of the entering students is the same in the two cases, but the standard deviations differ considerably.

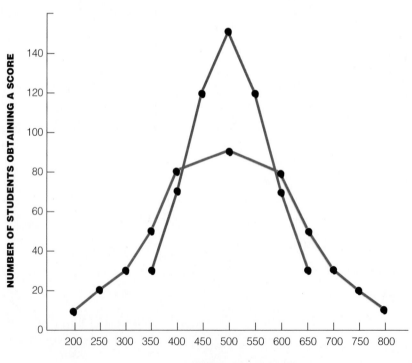

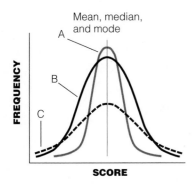

FIGURE A.2
Symmetrical Distributions

Three examples of symmetrical curves that differ in variability. Curve C has the greatest variability and curve A the least. In these symmetrical distributions, the mean, median, and mode all fall at the same point. Curve B is a normal curve.

The three curves shown in Figure A.2 are all symmetrical. In such distributions of scores, the mean, median, and mode of the distribution all fall at the same point or score. Curves with the same mean, median, and mode may differ in their variability, as do the curves in Figure A.2. The tall, thin curve labeled A will have a smaller standard deviation than the other two. Similarly, the broad, flat curve will have a greater standard deviation than the other two. Curve B represents a normal curve.

The normal curve has a very useful property: A specific proportion of scores falls under each part of the normal curve. This feature is illustrated in Figure A.3. For normal curves, about 68 percent of the scores fall within 1 standard deviation of the mean score (34 percent on each side). Similarly, almost 96 percent of the scores are contained within 2 standard deviations of the mean, while 99.74 percent of all the scores fall within 3 standard deviations. These properties are true of all normal curves. This feature allows test givers to figure an individual's relative rank based on his or her score, the mean, and the standard deviation of the distribution of scores. For example, the Scholastic Assessment Test was originally devised to have a mean score of 500 and a standard deviation of 100. So 68 percent of all of the test-takers score between 400 and 600; nearly 96 percent score between 300 and 700; and almost everyone scores between 200 and 800. If you know your own score, you can roughly figure out what percentile you are in (i.e., what percentage of people scored lower than you did). If your score is 400, about 16 percent of the other students scored worse and 84 percent better. You are in about the 16th percentile. If your score is 700, then you scored higher than all but about 2 percent of the people taking the test! You are in the 98th percentile. (Actually these figures are no longer quite accurate, because the mean scores on the verbal and quantitative parts of the SAT dropped from 500 over the years. The test has been renormed in recent years, to correct for this drop. This example serves as a good approximation, however, to introduce the useful properties of the normal curve.)

Correlation and Prediction

As we discussed in Chapter 1, psychologists often employ a correlational approach. Correlational research attempts to determine whether two variables are related. Is smoking related to lung cancer? Is IQ related to grades in high school? Are sons' heights related to their fathers' heights? Any two variables can be correlated. The amount of ice cream consumed in every country in the world can be correlated with the incidence of malaria in each country. Although the result may not tell much about either variable, the calculations for computing correlations can be carried out on any two sets of scores.

Consider, for example, the question of whether sons' heights are related to their fathers' heights. After compiling the heights of 1,000 20-year-old men and the heights of their fathers, you could read down the list and try to determine if tall fathers tend to have tall sons and short fathers tend to have short sons. Unfortunately, reading through this list would not be an easy way to see if there is a relation between the heights. It would be much easier to put the fathers' and sons' heights in a single graph. In a **scattergram,** one variable is represented on the y-axis, the other is represented on the x-axis, and a point is placed in the graph for each pair of scores. A scattergram with the heights of 1,078 sons and their fathers is plotted in Figure A.4. To find a score in the scattergram, find the height of the son on the y-axis (the vertical axis), then the height of the father on the x-axis (the horizontal axis). So if a son is 66 inches tall and his father is 68 inches tall, there will be one point in the graph for this pair.

FIGURE A.3
A Normal Curve

Proportions of scores in specific areas under the normal curve. About 68 percent of the scores fall within ±1 standard deviation of the mean, almost 96 percent within ±2 standard deviations, and almost all within ±3 standard deviations.

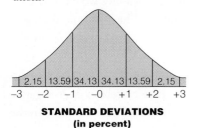

FIGURE A.4
Scattergram of Heights of Fathers and Sons

This scatter diagram (or scattergram) plots the heights of 1,078 fathers and their sons. Each point represents a father-son pair. If sons always grew to the heights of their fathers, then all the points would fall along the straight line. This would indicate a correlation of +1.00. Most points fall off the line, however, indicating how much the sons' heights differ from their fathers'.

SOURCE: Freedman, Pisani, & Purves, 1978.

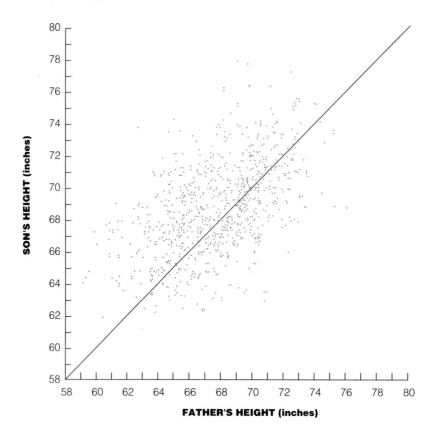

THE CORRELATION COEFFICIENT

It is clear from Figure A.4 that as fathers' heights increase, so do their sons'. As statisticians would say, there is a *positive association*, or *positive correlation*, between the two measures of height. A statistical calculation known as the **correlation coefficient** is used to measure more precisely the relation between two variables. The computational details that go into this measure are beyond the scope of this appendix, but the values of the measure can range from −1.00 through 0 to +1.00. If two scores are completely unrelated, so that as one measure changes, the other changes only haphazardly, there is a zero correlation between them. For example, there is probably a zero correlation between weight and intelligence in adults. If the intelligence of people of different weights were measured by having them take IQ tests, probably no systematic relation would be found between the two factors. The scores would then look like those in the top left scattergram in Figure A.5, which shows two scores that have a zero correlation.

The positive correlation between fathers' and sons' heights that is shown in Figure A.4 is not a perfect correlation. Positive correlations can vary from 0 to +1.00, where +1.00 is a perfect positive correlation. If the correlation were perfect, then sons' heights would always be directly related to the heights of their fathers. If all the scores fell on the diagonal line, the correlation between the two measures would be +1.00. Obviously, the positive correlation between fathers' and sons' heights is far from perfect. There are few perfect positive correlations in nature, and most positive correlations measured in psychology are in the range of +.30 to +.80.

The right two graphs in the top row of Figure A.5 show positive correlations of different magnitudes. The three bottom graphs show negative correlations. A negative correlation occurs when increases in one measure are associated with decreases in the other measure. For example, what if tall fathers tended to have short sons, the reverse

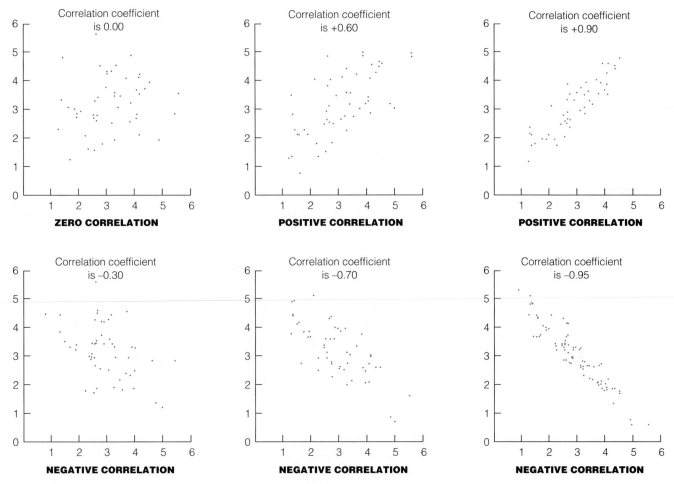

FIGURE A.5
Varying Correlation Coefficients

These scattergrams represent six different correlation coefficients. A zero correlation (upper left) indicates no relation between the two variables; the
points are strewn about randomly.
Positive correlations (two upper right
graphs) tend to run from the lower left
to upper right of the graph. As one variable increases, so does the other.
Negative correlations (the three graphs
in the bottom row) run from the upper
left to lower right. As one variable
increases, the other decreases.

of the actual case? Negative correlations vary between 0 and −1.00. An example of a
negative correlation is the negative association between the education of parents and
the number of children they have. Parents with more education tend to have fewer
children. The correlation is not great, however—about −.30.

PREDICTION

How are correlations useful? One important use is in making predictions. If we
know a father's height and we want to predict how tall his son will be when the son is
grown, we can base the prediction on the correlation between the two variables.
Looking at Figure A.4, we can say with some confidence that if the father is 72 inches
tall, the son will be between 66 and 75 inches tall. *The nearer the correlation coefficient
is to +1.00 or −1.00, the more nearly certain a researcher can be in making a prediction.* If
all the points in Figure A.4 fell on the straight line, so that the correlation between
heights of fathers and heights of sons were +1.00, then we could predict a son's height
precisely from knowing his father's. If all the points fell on this line, and if the father
were 72 inches tall, then we could predict with certainty that the son would be 72
inches tall, too. Even if each son were exactly 2 inches taller than his father, the correlation coefficient would still be a perfect +1.00, and prediction would be completely
accurate. Alas, life is hardly ever so precise. Notice in Figure A.4 that for 72-inch
fathers, some sons' heights fall outside even the 66- to 75- inch range.

Predictions can also be made, of course, from negative correlations, but in that case
as one score increases, the other score decreases. The closer the negative correlation is

to -1.00, the more confident will be the prediction. You can see how this case is comparable to that of predictability from positive correlations by examining the graphs in the bottom row of Figure A.5. If you had to make predictions based on the relations shown in these graphs, in which prediction would you have the most confidence?

CORRELATION AND CAUSATION

As we have shown, knowing the relation between two variables allows us to make predictions about one variable when we know the value of the other, especially when the association between the two variables is great. Even a very high correlation between two variables does not permit a conclusion that one variable *caused* the other, however. *Correlation does not imply causation!* If fathers' and sons' heights are correlated, this fact by itself does not allow us to conclude that fathers' heights cause their sons' heights any more than sons' heights cause their fathers' heights. (Of course, other evidence links fathers' and sons' heights. They share similar genes.)

A great number of variables may be correlated. Since 1950, the number of people graduating from law school and the amount of alcohol consumed in the United States have increased yearly. There is a high positive correlation between these variables. Did the increased number of lawyers cause people to drink more? Probably not. Did an increase in the consumption of alcohol by Americans cause more people to graduate from law school? Again, this is unlikely. Both trends are due to other factors; they just happen to be strongly correlated. Whenever a high correlation is reported in a study, caution is in order. Observers can never conclude that the change in one variable caused the change in another variable.

Medical studies of factors causing disease often begin with the observation of a correlation. For example, concern about the bad effects of smoking on health began during the 1950s when a researcher computed the correlation between the average number of cigarettes consumed and the incidence of lung cancer in 11 countries (Doll, 1955). He found a correlation of $+.70$ between the two measures. Thus, a suspicion arose that smoking causes lung cancer; but we cannot conclude that smoking causes lung cancer only on the basis of this correlation. Some hereditary defect distributed differently across populations may make people want to smoke and also may make them get lung cancer. Or it could be that smoking occurs only in more developed countries and that pollution in more developed countries causes lung cancer. In other words, the correlation between smoking and lung cancer can be due to other factors, just like the accidental correlation between the number of new lawyers and the amount of alcohol consumed. Of course, with the weight of additional evidence, most medical researchers do indeed agree with the conclusion that smoking causes lung cancer. It is worth pointing out, however, that the positive correlation between smoking and cancer is not the only information that leads to this conclusion.

To gain better evidence about the effect of one factor on another, it is necessary to conduct an experiment in which the first factor can be manipulated directly in a controlled manner, as described in Chapter 1. As you may recall, the *independent variable* of an experiment is the one that is manipulated, the *dependent variable* is the one that is measured, and the *control variables* are the factors that are held constant. For example, suppose we want to study the effects of the number of people in a group (the independent variable) on how quickly bystanders intervene in a crisis (the dependent variable). We could, of course, just watch groups of different sizes to see if a person in a large group is less likely to intervene than a person in a small group. This is the correlational approach. We would look for a negative correlation: The more people in the group, the less likely the person is to intervene. Because other factors are uncontrolled in correlational studies, however, something else about the group might actually cause differences in giving help. For example, more helpful people might (by accident) be in the smaller groups that we observe. We would find much more trustworthy information by conducting an experiment and randomly assigning people to small or large groups while holding all other factors constant, as in our earlier bystander intervention example. Let us now return to that experiment to illustrate how another branch of statistics is used to draw conclusions.

Inferential Statistics

Descriptive statistics are used to describe or summarize data. We can summarize the results from our hypothetical experiment on bystander intervention by saying that people in the alone condition took a mean time of 43.73 seconds to intervene (with a standard deviation of 21.08), while those tested in the three-bystander condition took a mean time of 72.73 seconds to intervene (with a standard deviation of 23.71). Thus, the people in the three-bystander condition reacted more slowly to the crisis than people in the alone condition, on the average. The difference was 29 seconds. Should this difference be taken seriously? Can we infer (conclude) that the independent variable of number of people really caused the difference in time taken to intervene?

You might be tempted to say yes, since there was a 29-second difference in the times. This difference may be due to random or chance factors, however, rather than to a true difference created by the conditions. Notice that the variability in the two conditions was quite wide (look back at Table A.1). Some people in the alone condition responded fairly slowly (especially subject 6), whereas other people in the three-bystander condition actually responded quite quickly (subjects 1 and 2). How can we judge the likelihood that the difference in times between the two conditions is *reliable* and not just a fluke? How large must the difference be between two conditions before we can conclude that it is unlikely to have occurred by mere chance alone?

Inferential statistics are used to answer this question. As the term implies, inferential statistics are those used by researchers to determine what conclusions, or inferences, can be drawn from their research. We will introduce two important concepts to help you understand inferential statistics: populations and samples.

POPULATION AND SAMPLE

In statistics, a **population** is a complete set of scores or measures. A population may be all American citizens of voting age, the number of words that all college sophomores can recall from a 50-word list, or the speed with which all university students react to give aid in a crisis. These are all populations that might interest psychologists for one reason or another. It is almost always impossible or impractical, however, to study an entire population of observations. What researchers do instead is to study a **sample,** or a limited number, of observations from the entire population. The best procedure is to select a **random sample,** where each member of the population has an equal chance of being chosen. Random sampling is the critical quality that will help ensure that a correct conclusion, or inference, about a population is drawn from a relatively small sample.

You are probably familiar with the practice of drawing general conclusions from relatively small samples from listening to reports of public-opinion polls. Several organizations routinely survey public opinion on a number of issues. In election years, there are weekly reports about the way presidential candidates are faring. Reports like "Candidate A is preferred by 43 percent of the sample surveyed, candidate B is preferred by 37 percent, and 20 percent of the people are undecided" are typical polling results. What the researchers would really like to know are the preferences of all American voters. Since it is impractical to survey all voters, the pollsters survey perhaps 2,000 or so, selected in an unbiased way, and then infer the preferences of the entire population on the basis of this sample.

The danger in this procedure is that errors can creep into the sampling process, with the result that the figures found from the sample are not representative of the population at large. Accurate news reports about the polls will also announce the level of sampling error to be expected. You have probably heard statements like "These figures are subject to an error of 4 percent in either direction." What this means is that the pollster is reasonably confident that from 39 percent to 47 percent of people in the population prefer candidate A, but that the true value could fall anywhere in this range; the statistic 43 percent is merely the midpoint. The range for candidate B is then 33 percent to 41 percent owing to possible sampling errors. Because of sampling error, there is some chance that the preference is actually different from what the poll sample shows. It is possible, though unlikely, that candidate B is actually preferred to candidate A by the population at large. Fortunately, pollsters and statisticians can measure this probability.

Although the concept of random sampling is important, in actual practice psychologists rarely use it. In virtually all situations that would interest researchers, random sampling of even a limited population (such as the students attending your university) would be impractical or unethical. Instead, researchers employ the random assignment of subjects (Glenberg, 1988).

In **random assignment,** each participant in an experiment has an equal chance of being assigned to any condition. Imagine that 15 males and 15 females were to serve as subjects in our bystander intervention experiment. An experimenter could assign the 15 females to serve in the alone condition and the 15 males to serve in the three-bystander condition. This practice would compromise the experiment, however; the results would be uninterpretable. If subjects were slower to respond with three bystanders present, as in our example, we could not decide which conclusion was correct: Did subjects respond more slowly because three bystanders were present or because the subjects in this condition were all male? Technically, this problem is known as *confounding,* a condition described in Chapter 1. When experimental conditions vary on more than one dimension, these dimensions, or variables, are confounded, and no conclusion is justified about the effect of either variable.

Random assignment reduces the possibility that confounding will occur. The methods of inferential statistics allow us to estimate the likelihood that a difference observed between experimental conditions is due to random factors. In making inferences from experiments, researchers are interested in answering the following question: Are the differences observed on the dependent variable between conditions of the experiment due to the operation of the independent variable, or are they due merely to sampling error and other random factors? Is the difference between conditions great enough so that chance factors can be ruled out as having produced the difference? In the bystander intervention experiment, there is a 29-second difference in the time subjects took to help in the alone and three-bystander conditions. Is this difference large enough to be attributed to the number of people present (the independent variable) rather than to chance factors?

There is a slightly different way to approach this question. We can hypothesize that the two sets of scores from our experiment come from two different populations of scores; that is, there is a population of scores for people tested in the alone condition and a population of scores for people tested in the three-bystander condition. Of course, the times of the 15 people tested in each condition do not represent the population of scores, but rather a sample from that population. The means of the two samples differ, but is the difference great enough for us to assume that the different times come from two different populations of scores? The other possibility is that both sets of scores come from the same population and that the only difference between them is due to sampling error and measurement error. Since the difference between the two means is so great—29 seconds—you might be tempted to conclude that this second possibility can be ruled out and that the two samples come from different populations. You should realize, however, that measures based on two small samples from even the same population will differ somewhat because of variability in individuals and measurement error.

An example here will be useful. There are 100 numbers listed in Table A.3. Consider these figures as a complete population of scores. The mean of the population is 75.1, and the standard deviation is 10.12. Now randomly select five numbers from those listed—a sample of the numbers. You will probably find that when you calculate the mean of your random sample of five numbers, it is not the same as the mean of the population. For example, the means of five samples of five numbers randomly selected from the population in Table A.3 are 83.6, 76.2, 69.4, 78.6, and 83.2. None is exactly the true population mean of 75.1, although some are reasonably close. Now suppose you take one sample of five numbers and find a mean of 69.4, then take another sample of five numbers and find a mean of 83.6. You ask yourself, "Do these two sets of numbers come from the same population?" There is a fairly large average difference between the two sets (about 14), so you might be tempted to say no. But as you can see from this example, it is possible to find a fairly large difference between two samples of observations that are in fact drawn from the same population.

You can convince yourself of another important point concerning sample statistics by taking larger samples from the numbers in Table A.3. If you take a sample of 10 observations, the chances are that the mean based on this sample will be closer to the true mean of the population than your mean based on only 5 observations. Five means calculated on random samples of 10 observations per sample are 77.2, 76.7, 74.8, 79.8, and 78.0. Notice that these values are generally much closer to the population mean of 75.1 than the sample means that were based on only 5 observations per sample. In general, the larger the size of the sample that is selected in a random manner, the closer the sample statistics will be to the true values of the population. Thus, we can place more faith in a public-opinion poll that randomly samples 5,000 people from the whole American population than one in which only 1,000 people are sampled.

To return to the bystander intervention experiment, we can consider the 30 subjects a "population" and those in the conditions as "random samples" of 15 each. The samples may differ from one another to some degree, owing to random factors, even if the people are treated identically. The critical question is whether these two randomly assigned samples differ more after the experimental manipulation than would be expected by chance.

Statistical tests help researchers decide this issue: Do the scores in the condition of the experiment differ enough to conclude (infer) that the difference is probably not due just to random (chance) factors? As a loose rule, the greater the difference

TABLE A.3
A Population of Scores

75	83	66	92
91	60	76	70
80	74	79	78
46	91	73	80
101	59	84	75
81	65	68	78
78	74	90	68
72	72	57	68
69	84	72	90
70	98	82	83
95	75	65	71
84	64	69	74
68	70	75	70
75	68	78	81
84	88	80	69
90	80	73	80
75	78	77	75
71	79	85	85
56	59	91	65
68	48	68	77
74	59	70	70
77	65	66	76
80	75	78	82
69	83	85	60
91	80	59	74

The list contains 100 hypothetical scores with a mean of 75.1 and a standard deviation of 10.12.

between the mean values of two groups of scores, the more likely it is that the difference is not due to chance factors. This depends on scores' variability, however, which is indexed by the standard deviation. The greater the dispersion, or variability, of the scores about the mean, the less confidence we can have that the difference between the two means is not due to chance factors. It is like the level of confidence in the polling example. If candidate A is preferred to candidate B 44 percent to 40 percent, those who read the poll can be more certain that this is the real preference of the population if the estimated "error" associated with each figure is 2 percent rather than 10 percent.

Statistical Tests

Statistical tests are used to decide whether a difference between sets of scores from an experiment is due to the operation of the independent variable or to chance factors. In practice, it is not too difficult to answer the question. A researcher chooses an appropriate statistical test, performs some straightforward computations on a calculator (or computer), and then consults a table designed to be used with that test. The table tells the researcher the likelihood that the differences uncovered in the research are due to chance factors. If the outcome is quite unlikely to have occurred by chance, then the investigator concludes that the difference among conditions is a real one produced by the independent variable. It is said to be a reliable difference, or one that has **statistical significance.**

A great variety of statistical tests are used to infer whether differences among experimental conditions are reliable. We will try to give you an understanding of the rationale behind these tests without going into all the computational details or characteristics of particular tests.

In testing hypotheses with inferential statistics, it is important to distinguish between a null hypothesis and an alternative hypothesis. Imagine, as in the case of the hypothetical bystander intervention experiment, that a researcher has performed an experiment with two conditions and found some difference between them on the dependent variable. A **null hypothesis** proposes that there is no true difference between the two samples of scores in the conditions of the experiment; they were not produced by the independent variable but came about only because of chance factors. An alternative hypothesis is the one in which the researcher is really interested, because that is the hypothesis that the experiment was designed to test. The **alternative hypothesis** states that the difference between the two conditions was produced by the independent variable. In the bystander intervention case, the alternative hypothesis is that the mean difference in time taken to help in the two conditions is due to the number of bystanders believed to be present.

Another way of stating these hypotheses is in terms of populations and samples. The null hypothesis is that the sample scores in the two conditions (alone and with three bystanders) actually came from the same population. In this case, the difference between the two scores is simply due to random factors. The alternative hypothesis is that the two samples came from different populations of scores. In the latter case, the independent variable exerted an effect.

A critical assumption is that *it is impossible to prove the alternative hypothesis conclusively*, since there is always some chance that the two samples came from the same population, no matter how different they appear. What inferential statistics allow us to do, though, is to determine how confident we can be in rejecting the null hypothesis.

The alternative hypothesis is thus tested indirectly; if we can be confident about rejecting the null hypothesis, then we assume that the alternative hypothesis is correct and that there is a real difference between scores in the different conditions. Statisticians have agreed, by convention, that if calculations from a statistical test show that there is less than a .05 probability (5 percent chance) that the null hypothesis is correct, we can reject it and accept the alternative hypothesis.

We will describe the concept of probability briefly in this context. Consider the following problem: What is the probability that if we randomly draw a card from a deck of 52 cards, it will be a spade? Since there are 13 spades in a deck, the probability of drawing a spade is 13/52, or .25. In general, if there are r ways that an event can occur and a total of N possibilities, then the probability of the event is r/N. What is the probability that a fair coin will come up heads when flipped? There are two ways a coin can come up, so $N = 2$. One of the ways is heads, so $r = 1$. The probability of heads is 1/2 , or .50.

Now we can more precisely describe what the conventional level of .05 for statistical significance means. If the null hypothesis were actually true, a researcher would obtain such a large difference between conditions less than 5 times in 100. If the chances are this slight in making an error by rejecting the null hypothesis, then it is deemed safe to do so and to opt for the alternative hypothesis. The .05 criterion is referred to as the .05 **level of confidence** because a mistake will be made only 5 times in 100. When the null hypothesis is rejected, researchers conclude that the results are *reliably different* or *statistically significant*. In other words, the researchers can be quite confident that the difference obtained between the conditions is trustworthy and that if the experiment were repeated, the same outcome would result.

In practice, statistical tests usually provide a more exact probability for rejecting the null hypothesis. For example, in applying one statistical test to the hypothetical data from the bystander intervention experiment, we determined that the null hypothesis could be rejected with less than 1 percent chance of an error (we would write this as $p < .01$). So we can be confident that there is less than 1 chance in 100 that these data would occur if the null hypothesis were true.

In summary, inferential statistics allow researchers to test their hypotheses or ideas in an indirect manner. They test the alternative hypothesis by rejecting the null hypothesis at a certain level of confidence. If the statistical test does not permit rejection of the null hypothesis, then a researcher cannot conclude that there is a reliable difference produced by the independent variable.

Misuses of Statistics

Statistics are used so often that it seems possible to bolster any argument with them. They are employed by politicians, economists, advertisers, and psychologists to support various views. It is little wonder people have gained the impression that statistics can be bent to any purpose. An old adage has it that "statistics don't lie, statisticians do," because statistics can be misused to create a false impression. You should be aware of some of these misuses so that you are not misled by them.

USE OF SMALL OR BIASED SAMPLES

Many television commercials implicitly mislead us with the use of small or biased samples. Viewers see a woman testing two brands of detergent on her husband's greasy, grass-stained clothes. She is pitting her usual product, BAF, against new Super Dirt Remover. BAF goes into one washer, Super Dirt Remover goes into the other, and a little later the woman is shown exclaiming over the better job that SDR did. Announcer: "Are you convinced?" Woman: "Why, yes. I will always use Super Dirt Remover from now on. It really gets the dirt off my clothes."

Even making the unlikely assumption that the whole demonstration was not rigged, observers should know better than to be convinced by such a small sample (one case). If the "experiment" were repeated honestly with 100 women, would all of them pick Super Dirt Remover? The ad tries to leave us with the impression that because this one woman prefers the product, everyone (the population) will. We should be careful about assuming something to be true of the population at large from a sample of one.

A sample of individuals surveyed for such an ad may also be deliberately biased. Advertisers are always surveying groups that are likely to be predisposed in their favor anyway. They ask consumers, "How well do you like your Bass-o-matic?" and then show a small sample of interviews that went well from the company's point of view. It would be more convincing to sample people who had never used the product and to test it against its main rivals. Since advertising claims on television must now be based on facts, this type of study and commercial is becoming more widely used. In one interesting case, owners of one type of luxury car are asked to test their car against a competitor. In this case, we would expect the sample to be biased against the new product and for their old product, so if a preference is found for the new product, it seems to argue much more strongly for the new product.

Whenever you hear about preferences that people have expressed, you should ask two questions about the sample: How large was it, and how were people chosen to be in it?

THE EXAGGERATED GRAPH

An exaggerated graph is a common way to show or hide differences in graphs. It involves changing the scale on the graph to show off a difference or (more rarely) to hide a difference. Suppose that the number of murders in a city increased over three years from 72 to 80 to 91. The next year, the mayor is running for reelection and is eager to show that the city has been safe for the past three years under her administration. Her campaign workers prepare the graph at the top of Figure A.6. By making the scale on the y-axis very long, they create the impression that the murder rate is fairly steady. In the same year, the city police may be arguing that they need to increase their staff. They want to show that the city is becoming increasingly unsafe, so they, too, change the scale, this time depicting the murder rate increasing steeply, as shown in the bottom graph in Figure A.6.

The facts are shown accurately in both graphs. However, the top graph gives the impression that the murder rate is increasing very gradually—hardly worth worrying about. (Hasn't the mayor done a good job?) The bottom graph, meanwhile, creates the impression that the murder rate is increasing dramatically. (Don't we need more police?) These graphing techniques are common. In fact, you will see exaggerated scales in some of the graphs in this book to show patterns of results more clearly. You should always look carefully to see what the scale is in a graph. With experimental data, it is more important to determine if a difference is statistically reliable than to see if it looks "large" when graphed.

FIGURE A.6
Variation in Scales

The graph at the top seems to show the murder rate increasing only slightly, while the one at the bottom shows the rate going up dramatically. Both graphs actually show the murder rate accurately; the difference is in the scale on the y-axis. It is important to examine a graph carefully and note the scale of measurement, since scale changes can make small differences look large and vice versa.

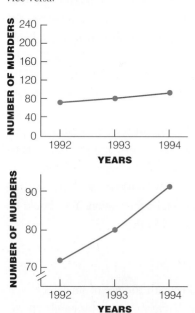

ABSENT OR INAPPROPRIATE COMPARISONS

A common ploy used in advertising is to say that some product has *x* percent more of something good or *y* percent less of something bad. "Buy the new Thunderbolt, since it gives 27 percent better gas mileage." This sounds convincing until you stop to ask yourself, "27 percent better than what?" A missing comparison makes the statistic completely meaningless. Perhaps the Thunderbolt gets 27 percent better mileage than a 2-ton tank, which is hardly an argument for buying it.

Even when a comparison is specific, it is often still inappropriate. The claim is often made that a product is better than last year's model. "Buy the new, improved Thunderbolt. It gets 27 percent better mileage than last year's model." Of course, it could still be a real lemon, even if it is better than last year's lemon. What a consumer would really like is a comparison of the mileage efficiency of the new Thunderbolt with other new cars in roughly the same class, as is now provided by government testing.

Another problem in making comparisons is that often there is no information on the reliability of differences. In one commercial, two cars of the same make and year are filled with 1 gallon of gas and test driven at a constant speed around a track. The difference in the test is the type of gasoline used. One car stops before the other, and the viewers are supposed to conclude that the sponsor's gasoline is superior to the other brand. But only after a long series of comparisons can a researcher statistically test for a *reliable* difference between the two types of gas. This is the same problem as in the case of BAF versus Super Dirt Remover; the sample of observations is too small.

In general, make sure that in statements involving a comparison, the object of comparison is described and is appropriate. There should also be some statement about whether or not any differences are statistically reliable.

THE GAMBLER'S FALLACY

Statistical tests are based on **probability theory,** the theory of expectations about the likelihood of random events. Probability theory was discussed briefly in the section on inferential statistics. It is interesting to note that people's perceptions of the randomness of events do not agree in some important respects with ideas from probability theory. Thus, people often make conclusions that seem irrational when judged by the logic of probability theory. There is much interesting research on this phenomenon, some of which is discussed in Chapter 8 (see Gigerenzer & Murray, 1987, too). Here we will examine one common mistake in judgments of probability.

Imagine flipping a coin 1,000 times. If it is a fair coin, it should come up heads about 500 times and tails about 500 times. The probability of its coming up heads over a large number of trials is .50, but of course, even a fair coin would probably not come up heads exactly 500 times in 1,000 flips. It might come up heads 490 times or 505 times, yet the result would be fairly close to half and half.

Let us now take the case of a gambler betting on whether the coin will come up heads or tails. If the situation is truly random, the probability of winning is .50 on any particular trial. Imagine that, on five trials in a row, a gambler bets $5 that the coin will come up heads, and each time it comes up tails. Of course, the fact that the coin comes up tails five times in a row is unusual, and the chances of such an event are quite low (.03). The gambler notes this odd occurrence, and on the next bet, he doubles his bet to $10 and again bets on heads. Now he is more certain that the coin will come up heads.

The logic that the gambler uses is as follows. "The coin is a fair coin. On the average it will come up heads half the time and tails half the time. The coin has just come up tails five times in a row; therefore, it is due to come up heads to even things up. So I should bet on heads and even increase my bet." More generally, the logic is that if the game is truly random and I am losing, then I should keep playing because my luck is bound to change for the better. It is this kind of logic that keeps gambling casinos humming and wipes out the fortunes of otherwise intelligent people.

The fallacy of the argument is that the laws of probability—such as a fair coin coming up heads half the time—hold only over tremendously large numbers of events. The laws cannot be applied to small runs. What the gambler overlooks is that the flips of the coin are independent events; what happened on previous flips does not influence what happens next. If the coin came up tails five times in a row, this does not increase the probability of heads on the next toss. It is still .50. The coin does not have a memory for previous trials, as the gambler implicitly seems to assume. The gambler should not feel any more certain on the sixth trial than he did on the first five. The probability of heads showing has not changed.

In some sense, the gambler's mistake is natural. There is a ring of truth to the argument, and it is based on true laws of probability (though the laws are misapplied). Over a very large series of throws, a fair coin will come up heads 50 percent of the time. The error comes in applying what is true over a very large series of events to a small series. The laws do not apply to small series of random events as well. With, say, 10 million coin flips, heads will come up almost exactly 50 percent of the time. However, if a gambler takes a small series of the larger number (say five flips), heads could come up either zero times or five times with a probability of .06. These outcomes (all heads or all tails) are not terribly likely, but they are not impossible either.

SUMMARY

❶ Statistics serve two primary purposes. Descriptive statistics are used to summarize or describe a large number of observations. Inferential statistics are employed to make a generalization about some population based on a sample from the population. Most generalizations ("laws") in psychology are probabilistic; they do not hold in every case, but with a certain probability over a large number of cases.

❷ The two primary types of descriptive statistics are measures of central tendency and measures of variability or dispersion.

❸ Measures of central tendency include the mean (arithmetic average), the median (middlemost score), and the mode (most frequent score). The mean is the most frequently used measure, but if there are one or more extreme scores, the median may be more useful.

❹ The range and standard deviation are the most common descriptive measures of dispersion or variability. The range is the difference between the highest and lowest scores, and so depends simply on the most extreme scores. The standard deviation, though more complex in formulation, is the more useful measure of variability.

❺ Correlations are measures of association between two variables. If one variable increases while another increases as well, the two variables are said to be positively correlated. If one variable decreases as the other increases, the variables are said to be negatively correlated. The correlation coefficient can vary from −1.00 to +1.00, with negative and positive values indicating negative and positive correlations, respectively. A zero correlation coefficient indicates that there is no systematic relation between the two variables. The sign ($+$ or $-$) of a correlation indicates the direction of the relation; the size of the number indicates its magnitude or strength. Strong correlations (whether positive or negative) are useful for predictions. If height and weight are strongly correlated, knowing a person's height will permit prediction of weight. Correlation of two variables does not necessarily mean that one caused the other; correlation does not imply causation.

6 A population is a complete collection of observations or scores. A sample is a subset of the population. In a random sample, each member of the population has an equal chance of being sampled. Random sampling is impractical or impossible in virtually all psychological research. Instead, random assignment of participants to experimental conditions reduces the probability that characteristics of subjects are confounded with the conditions.

7 In testing to see if a difference between samples of scores can be generalized to population differences, it is common to consider a null hypothesis and an alternative hypothesis. The null hypothesis is that the two samples actually come from the same population, or that no real difference exists between the samples. The alternative hypothesis is that the samples really do come from different populations. Statistical tests provide researchers with information about how likely it is that the null hypothesis is wrong. Thus, the alternative hypothesis is tested indirectly. If the test reveals that the obtained result would only occur with a probability of .05 or less if the null hypothesis were true, the researchers can reject the null hypothesis and conclude in favor of the alternative hypothesis (that there is a real difference between the samples of scores).

8 Mark Twain wrote, "There are three kinds of lies—lies, damned lies, and statistics." Some ways in which statistics can be misused include drawing conclusions from small or biased samples; exaggerating the scales on graphs for effect; making inappropriate comparisons; and assuming that the laws of probability, which hold for huge samples of observations, can be generalized to small samples (as in the gambler's fallacy). Statistics themselves do not lie, but they can often be manipulated to give misleading impressions.

KEY TERMS

descriptive statistics	scattergram
inferential statistics	correlation coefficient
data	population
measures of central tendency	sample
measures of dispersion	random sample
mean	random assignment
median	statistical significance
mode	null hypothesis
range	alternative hypothesis
standard deviation	level of confidence
frequency distributions	probability theory
normal curve	

SUGGESTED READINGS

GLENBERG, A. M. (1988). *Learning from data: An introduction to statistical reasoning*. San Diego: Harcourt Brace Jovanovich. An excellent introduction to the use of statistics in the research setting. Includes a novel chapter (14) on the distinction between random sampling and random assignment.

KIMBLE, G. (1978). *How to use (and mis-use) statistics*. Englewood Cliffs, N.J.: Spectrum Books. This brief book is written for people with a limited background in mathematics. The author shows how statistics are used in many practical tasks, and he also illustrates their misuse.

PAGANO, R. L. (1994). *Understanding statistics in the behavioral sciences* (4th ed.). St. Paul, MN: West. A very good introduction to the basic elements of statistics for behavioral scientists.

STANOVICH, K. E. (1992). *How to think straight about psychology* (3rd ed.). Glenview, Ill: Scott, Foresman. An interesting introduction to psychology, research methods, and the problems that most laypersons have in thinking about psychological topics. Two chapters (5 and 9) are about pitfalls in statistical reasoning.

TANUR, J. M., MOSTELLER, F., KRUSKAL, W. H., LINK, R. F., PIETERS, R. S., RISING, G. R., & LEHMAN, E. H. (1978). *Statistics: A guide to the unknown* (2nd ed.). San Francisco: Holden-Day. This fascinating series of essays on diverse topics illustrates the usefulness of a variety of statistical techniques.

Appendix B

BECOMING A CRITICAL READER

During your years in college, you will be exposed to hundreds of books, articles, and pamphlets, all trying to impart information to you and to convince you of some point. Your professors will lecture to you, trying to tell you the truth of their subject matter as they know it. You will hear the opinions of your friends, be bombarded with news and conjecture from television, and receive other information from newspapers and magazines. Should you believe it all? Probably not. But how can you separate fact from fiction? How can you know what to believe? There are no sure answers to these questions, but what we hope to do in this appendix is give you some tips on becoming a critical reader (or listener). The aim is to provide you with a set of questions to ask yourself as you are reading articles or books, but the questions apply to information that you hear, too. With a little practice, these questions will become ingrained, and you will be able to approach material with an open mind, but ready to critically evaluate (rather than uncritically accept) the information you receive.

Critical thinking may be defined as the process of distinguishing beliefs from knowledge. We all have beliefs, some based on facts. You need to be able to judge when the proponent of an idea is telling you mere opinion or is offering knowledge based on facts. A person's beliefs about the world may be true or false, but the more they are buttressed with facts and valid arguments, the more likely they are to be true. As a critical thinker, you should always clearly define the issue or problem at hand, examine the evidence, and reach a conclusion about the probable validity of the argument. Always take an active role in reading; that is, do not passively assume that whatever you are reading is absolute truth to be absorbed, but instead question the author's assumptions and assertions. The author's reasoning may well withstand your test, but then you can be more convinced by the arguments.

We will present our advice for critical reading in the form of a series of nine questions that you should ask yourself when reading (or listening to) material designed to impart information or to convince you of some point.

1. Who is the author? What is his or her goal? Every item you read had to be written either by one author or by an author team (as in this textbook). Before you begin reading, ask yourself what you know about the author or authors. Are they recognized experts in the field on which they are writing? Does it appear that they have any obvious biases? Are they trying to convince you of something? The answers to these last two questions are usually yes, because all authors have some predilections and biases. We all do. No person is a perfectly rational machine. And every author is trying to impart information about the topic under discussion, often trying to get you to see things his or her way. There is nothing wrong with this. You would not be in college if you did not want to be taught by people who know more than you do about certain subjects. The trick to evaluating the information you receive is to factor in the authors' biases and to see if the information is credible. Does the author present a reasoned argument, or do the biases get in the way?

Let us take some examples. You go to a lecture by a New Age guru who tells you that he can put you in touch with your past lives and dead ancestors and can also teach you to levitate (raise your body off the ground through meditation), among other feats. No illustrations are given in the lecture; no evidence is provided. He does not demonstrate levitation during the course of his lecture, but asserts that it is commonplace among people with the appropriate training and the correct meditational attitude. In fact, at the end of the lecture, he offers to provide a series of training lectures and exercises that will make you an expert over the next eight weeks for only $2,500. You are fascinated and interested. What do you do?

If you are like many, you pay the money and take the course. You might even learn something about yourself during it. But many others take a more skeptical attitude: "Here is someone I probably should not believe. He is (perhaps sincerely) convinced of incredible claims, but he provides no evidence to back them up. If he can teach levitation, let him levitate there onstage under conditions where he could not possibly be pulled up by strings or other trickery. And he seems less interested in my spiritual truth, than in his financial gain. Here is someone whose lecture I can discount and whose services I don't need."

That seems an easy one, right? But as discussed in Chapter 1, go to the New Age section of any bookstore and you can select a variety of books on every weird subject known to humankind: reincarnation, astral travel, abductions by space aliens, and so on. There is a huge market for these books, and the public gobbles them up. The authors make a good living.

Let's take a harder case. Your psychology professor assigns you an article on the power of positive thinking, which claims that approaching life with a cheerful, optimistic attitude will actually make your life better: You will be less likely to be depressed, you will achieve more, you will be less likely to become physically ill, and if you do become ill or have an operation, you will recover more quickly. In addition, you read that you can learn to be optimistic, that it is not an inborn trait. You think, "Wow, all that is hard to believe! Should I believe it?" Just because a claim is hard to believe does not mean it is wrong. Otherwise, we would already know everything there is to know. In this case, you might check the article's author and discover it is Martin Seligman. You turn to the end of the article and find that he is a distinguished professor at the University of Pennsylvania who is highly respected in his field. You still need to critically evaluate the evidence he presents to you, of course, but now you can continue reading the article in a positive frame of mind. The author is a respected expert in the field telling you about the topic he knows best. Yes, he is still trying to convince you of something, and something surprising, but you can expect evidence to back it up from a true expert, not just opinions to be accepted on faith. (We describe Seligman's work in Chapter 13 and elsewhere in this text. His *Learned Optimism*, published in 1991, is a good place to find out more about his work.)

In many articles you read, not much information is given about the authors. (In this text, you can read "About the Authors" on page xxxix.) In such cases, you have to infer the author's expertise and knowledge as you read the article—not always an easy task. The point to keep in mind is that all articles are written by someone. (Even newspaper articles that carry no byline still have an author.) Each author comes to a subject with a certain background—knowledge, skills, biases, and so on. This is inevitable and no cause for alarm; just keep it in mind while you read. Some authors are to be believed more than others. However, just because you do not know certain authors or their background is certainly no reason to reject their ideas out of hand. You must critically judge the evidence. Even authors with no particular background in an area can research it and arrive at valid conclusions.

2. What core ideas is the author proposing? What is the main thesis (the main points) of the article? A good writer will make answering these questions easy by making the points salient. But others will hide their main thesis in murky prose, sliding it by you without it even catching your full attention. Don't let this happen. You need to get the idea out in the open to examine it. Stop yourself every so often while reading and try to summarize the main points that the author has made in the last few paragraphs. If you cannot do it, you might try reading the material again. Are the main points there, and did you somehow miss them?

3. What evidence is the author using to bolster his or her points? Is it convincing? This is a crucial step in critical reading. You need to watch for several common logical problems that arise in interpreting evidence. Chapter 1 and Appendix A describe some common problems in interpreting evidence, but let us illustrate a few here. The most serious problem is when no evidence or arguments at all are offered, as in the case of the New Age guru who tries to persuade you that levitation is real. Clearly, here is a place for skepticism.

Most writers do offer some sort of evidence, and then the question becomes the relevance and credibility of the evidence. Sometimes, the evidence that is provided in support of an argument is simply not relevant, or has only tangential relevance, to the point being made. Suppose that our guru is giving his lecture on levitation, and a skeptic in the audience says, "This is silly. People cannot lift themselves off the floor just by thinking about it." The guru replies: "In the 1800s, many prominent scientists argued that it was impossible for humans to ever fly in any sort of mechanical contraption. They said that heavier-than-air flight was impossible. But now we know it is possible. Every time an airplane takes off, we see evidence of humans flying through the air." The guru smiles triumphantly and resumes his lecture; his evidence of heavier-than-air flight has apparently won the day. Now, everything the guru has said is true. Many scientists did doubt the possibility of heavier-than-air travel. But so what? That does not mean that they are wrong about levitation. The evidence that the guru cited about air travel by mechanical means has nothing to do with the truth or falsity of levitation. The "evidence" is simply beside the point, a diversion to deflect attention from the lack of evidence for levitation.

Consider another case, a trickier one. A terrible problem in homes for the aged is the elderly person's isolation and the feeling that no one cares. Some researchers have proposed letting people in homes for the aged have pets, which provide companionship and give the residents a focus for their attention and love. But giving people pets is a nuisance in many ways for the people who operate the homes. What kind of evidence might show that allowing pets is a good practice? Consider one type of study that has often been done. Researchers go to a home for senior citizens and offer residents the opportunity to have a pet (dog, cat, bird, or fish). Some residents take them up on the offer and others do not. Then the researchers track the physical and mental health of the two groups over time. Do the pet owners show more positive outcomes than the residents who did not choose to have a pet? Early studies found that people who adopted pets were less likely to be depressed, less likely to become ill, and even less likely to die over the next two years. The first of these studies received widespread attention in the press: Adopting a pet made people feel better, live longer, and die later!

What is your reaction? After all, the researchers reported concrete evidence for their startling claims. Moreover, a number of similar studies resulted in the same outcome, so shouldn't it be believed? The answer is no, or at least not necessarily. Consider how the study was done. The residents of the home were allowed to select whether or not they wanted a pet. That seems only natural and fair, but this procedure calls into question the whole study, because the two groups of senior citizens may have differed (and in fact probably did differ) at the beginning of the study. The people who chose to have a pet were probably healthier and more resilient to begin with than those who did not. In part, they chose pets because they were able to care for them, whereas some of the people who did not choose to have a pet might have liked one, but knew they could not care for one. The basic problem here is a potential confounding, as discussed in Chapter 1; two factors probably varied together in the study (having a pet and the type of person who chose to have a pet), and so the outcome of greater happiness and longer life in one group cannot be attributed only to having a pet. Recall from Chapter 1 that it is crucial to have random assignment of people (subjects) across experimental conditions or for them to be matched in some way. Otherwise, the researcher cannot be sure that the result obtained is not due to differences between subject groups that were built into the study.

It is important not to go too far with the criticism outlined here. Although studies such as the one described do not conclusively show that residents of nursing homes benefit from having pets, the study does leave open that possibility. That is, we cannot conclude from the study that having a pet has no effect. The point is that we need better studies to demonstrate the conclusion. The evidence from the study is simply not conclusive. This leads to our next question for the critical reader.

4. Are there alternative explanations to the one the author is giving? This point is really embedded in the prior one. The author presents evidence and draws a conclusion. Your job is to ask, Does the evidence also support some other conclusion? Can I think of another possibility? In the pet study, the other possibility is that differences in the groups of people at the beginning of the study (pet adopters being heartier than nonadopters) determined the outcome. A good author will often lay out several possible explanations for results, weigh the pros and cons of each, and come to some reasoned conclusion. Instead of passively accepting the assumptions offered, you should reason along with the author. Can you think of other reasons besides those provided by the author to favor one explanation over another?

5. What is a good explanation? Will I know it when I see it? These are difficult questions. Usually, a good explanation for some phenomenon is one that you can make sense of in terms of some theory, or at least in terms of some related facts about the phenomenon. But many "explanations" really do not deserve that name, because they are either tautologies, including the mere naming of the phenomenon, or truisms.

A *tautology* is simply a statement that involves a repetition of the same idea. Suppose you ask someone what the weather will be tomorrow and she replies, "Either it will rain or it will not rain." This sounds like a prediction, perhaps based on meteorological theory, but it is not. It is a tautology. It must rain or not rain everyday, so you have not learned anything from the answer. Another form of explanation that is really a tautology is the naming of phenomena. Suppose your psychology class tours the psychiatric ward of a mental hospital. You witness a person hallucinating—hearing voices and seeing visions that no one else can hear or see. The patient seems cut off from reality. You ask your classmate why this is happening and he says, "Because the patient is schizophrenic." That seems to explain the phenomenon you have witnessed, but does not. All your classmate has done is apply a name to the person, which leads to a tautology. After all, a schizophrenic is defined as a person suffering from thought disorders, hallucinations, and being cut off from the world.

A similar faulty explanation is the *truism*, a statement that must be true. You see an obese rat with damage to its hypothalamus eating heartily (as described in Chapter 12). You ask why the rat is eating so much and you are told "because it is hungry." Of course, that is no explanation, because all hungry animals will want to eat. That is how hunger is defined. What you really want to know is *why* the rat is eating.

The point of these examples is to be on guard about the type of explanation you are offered. Don't be satisfied with surface statements that sound reasonable, but probe beneath them. An appropriate explanation should tell you more than you already know. It should tell you the process by which the phenomenon came about. Of course, as discussed in Chapter 1, most psychological phenomena can be explained at several different levels. We can discuss the family dynamics of schizophrenic patients, we can describe the cognitive processes of schizophrenics, we can discuss imbalances of neurotransmitters leading to hallucinations, and we can study the genetics of schizophrenia. But in explaining some phenomena associated with schizophrenia in any of these ways, we are at least going beyond the basic definition of what schizophrenia is. In general, you should prefer explanations that provide a specific mechanism that is well supported by evidence and that makes sense in terms of larger theories of behavior.

6. How does the evidence under discussion fit in with other evidence? Many news reports focus on the results of one study while neglecting the background of the research. For example, the media often seize on a single study showing that a particular food or environmental component is a threat to health. We read in the newspapers how hot dogs, breast implants, asbestos, stress, allergy drugs, alcohol, dietary fat, and pesticides may all cause cancer—usually on the basis of a single study that has found a connection. But then later we read how other studies have obtained conflicting results. What should a critical reader believe? After all, it is impossible for us to know about the other research if the media do not tell us about it.

Consider the following case. In October 1994, the *New York Times* reported on a study published in the *Journal of the National Cancer Institute* that suggested that abortions might increase the risk of breast cancer by 50 percent (Mann, 1995). The headline read, "New Study Links Abortion and Breast Cancer Risk," and the journal publishing the study had thought it so important that a press release about it was provided. However, the original article in the journal noted that 40 previous studies had failed to detect any increase in breast cancer in women who had abortions—a fact that was not included in the *New York Times* account. Thus, the public was alerted to a possible risk that may not be real, because it was based on the results of one study whose outcome conflicted with all prior work!

How does this happen? When queried, the *New York Times* journalist who wrote the story said that the journal "sent out a big press release touting the study as if it were the biggest thing since whatever. I don't recall them telling us it was only one of 40 studies and probably had little meaning" (quoted in Mann, 1995, p. 186). Because journals and universities put out press releases to publicize hot new findings, they are likely to gloss over the complexities and to overemphasize new results. After all, it is big news when a study shows that something causes cancer. If a study fails to link some possible environmental cause to cancer, it is not big news.

Consider the reports that occupational exposure to electromagnetic fields (EMFs), may cause cancer in utility workers for electric companies. One study that captured a lot of attention examined 223,000 French and Canadian electric utility workers and found no connection between EMF exposure and 25 of the 27 kinds of cancer examined. The exceptions were two very rare forms of leukemia, and even the evidence for these was weak and inconsistent (Mann, 1995). Nonetheless, the *Wall Street Journal* reported the study with the headline "Magnetic Fields Linked to Leukemia." In 1995, a second study of 139,000 workers at five utility companies in the United States was reported in the same medical journal. The researchers examined 18 types of cancer and found no connection between exposure to electromagnetic fields and cancer for 17 measures, including the two kinds of leukemia that had produced the weak positive results in the first study. The only exception was a type of eye and brain cancer, but no connection had been found between EMF exposure and this type of cancer in the first study. Still, when the *Wall Street Journal* reported the second study, the headline read, "Link Between EMF, Brain Cancer Is Suggested by Study at 5 Utilities." Clearly, the journalists writing such stories assume (probably correctly) that people are more interested in environmental factors that might cause cancer than in those that do not, but this form of biased reporting highlights positive results and fails to note that other studies find no connection. The result is that the public may become needlessly fearful about factors that can really be safely ignored (Taubes, 1995). In Chapter 8, we discuss how people's estimates of the risk of many activities differ greatly from the objective risk, and one cause of these misperceptions is media coverage.

What should a critical reader do about this situation? Whenever you are reading about the results of a study in the media, ask yourself how this one result fits into the big picture of research on this topic. Of course, you probably cannot know this by yourself, but you should note whether the writer addresses this issue. If not, then you should accept the report of the study as a tentative hypothesis that may or may not be supported by other research. If dozens of studies, using different techniques and conducted by different teams of researchers, all reach the same conclusion, you can have more confidence in it.

7. Can I poke a hole in the author's argument? Can I poke a hole in my own argument? These questions repeat points we have already made, but they are worth repeating. You should always be on the lookout for loopholes in the author's argument. But suppose you think you find one. Then it is your job to apply the same process to your own argument. Pretend that you are the author of the article, and now you must reply to your own criticism. Just because you can think of a potential objection does not mean that you are right. After all, the author likely knows much more about the subject than you do, and he or she would likely have a ready answer for the most obvious criticisms. Your job is to try to think of the author's likely reply.

8. Can I summarize what I just heard or read? When you get to the end of an article, chapter, or lecture, you should try to mentally summarize what you have learned. What are the essential points? Be sure you know the take-home message. If you cannot do this after reading an article or passage, you should probably review it.

9. ***How critical should I be?*** One danger in fostering a critical attitude in reading is that you become too critical, believing nothing at all. Obviously, if this is the case, you have overdone it. You should approach matters with an inquiring, skeptical mind and critically evaluate the information you are given. But in many cases, especially in academic contexts, the information should survive your scrutiny. After all, you are reading books and articles produced by experts much more knowledgeable than yourself on the topic. Yes, be skeptical and cautious and critically evaluate what you read and hear. But also keep an open mind and be receptive to learning new things when they pass your critical scrutiny. Nothing is as tiresome as the professional skeptic who doubts everything in the world.

Following the preceding steps can help you to become a critical reader. Of course, reading this way is hard work, but the effort is well worth it. We summarize the questions to ask yourself in the Concept Summary.

CONCEPT SUMMARY

QUESTIONS FOR THE CRITICAL READER

1. Who is the author? What is his or her goal?
2. What core ideas is the author proposing? What is the main thesis (or the main points) of the article?
3. What evidence is the author using to bolster his or her points? Is it convincing?
4. Are there alternative explanations to the one the author is giving?
5. What is a good explanation? Will I know it when I see it?
6. How does the evidence under discussion fit in with other evidence?
7. Can I poke a hole in the author's argument? Can I poke a hole in my own argument?
8. Can I summarize what I just heard or read?
9. How critical should I be?

GLOSSARY

A

absolute threshold The minimum amount of physical energy needed for a stimulus to produce a sensation. For research purposes, the absolute threshold is defined as the minimally effective stimulus that will elicit a sensation on 50 percent of trials. See also *difference threshold*.

abuse Overconsumption of a drug on a single or a few episodes.

accommodation (1) The process by which the lens of the eye changes to focus an object on the retina; it becomes more spherical for near objects and flatter for distant objects. (2) Piaget's term for adapting actions to respond to new stimuli.

achievement motivation See *need for achievement*.

acquisition (1) In classical conditioning, the formation of a conditioned response. (2) In instrumental conditioning, the strengthening of a reinforced response. (3) In memory theory, the first of three stages in the memory process. See also *storage, retrieval*.

action potential The stage during which a neuron fires (or sends) its impulse to the next neuron; it involves the rapid reversal of electrical charge between the inside and outside of the cell membrane. See also *resting potential*.

activational effects Effects of hormones in producing sexual behavior.

activation-synthesis hypothesis Hobson and McCarley's dream theory which argues that activation in the brain stem spreads throughout neighboring systems and causes the physiological effects of the REM sleep stage.

actor-observer effect The phenomenon that while observers tend to attribute an actor's behavior to the actor's dispositions, an actor tends to explain his or her own behavior in terms of situational causes.

actual self The self as perceived by the individual.

actualizing tendency See *self-actualization*.

adolescence The period of transition from childhood into adulthood. The period usually begins at the onset of puberty and ends when the adolescent takes on social responsibilities such as work and marriage.

adolescent growth spurt A rapid increase in the rate of physical development that accompanies puberty.

adolescent moratorium The time of prolonged apprenticeship and education in American Society.

affect The conscious experience of an emotion, a *positive affect* is the extent to which people show a zest for life, while a *negative affect* is the extent to which people report feeling upset or unpleasantly aroused.

age cohort A group of individuals who are born in the same year or period.

age cohort differences Differences attributable to growing up in different historical eras.

aggression Behavior intended to harm another.

agoraphobia The development of anticipatory fears and the eventual reluctance to leave the house for fear of panic attacks.

alcoholism Abuse of and dependence upon alcohol over some length of time.

algorithm A well-defined set of procedures or rules for solving a particular type of problem.

all-or-none The principle that a neuron's action potential triggers either completely or not at all. Once an action potential is triggered, it continues down an axon to its end.

alternative hypothesis In statistics, the hypothesis that samples of scores are from different populations. See also *null hypothesis*.

altruism Any action that benefits other species members without benefiting the individual who performs the action.

aminostatic theory A theory that suggests that hunger is caused by low levels of amino acids in the blood, and satiety is produced by high levels of amino acids.

amnesia A dissociative disorder, usually caused by some injury to the brain, characterized by either total or partial memory loss. *Anterograde amnesia* is loss of memory for events that occurred prior to the cerebral shock. *Retrograde amnesia* is memory loss for experiences occurring after the brain trauma.

amniocentesis Used to diagnose prenatal complications, a method in which a hollow needle is inserted through a pregnant woman's abdomen to remove a sample of amniotic fluid from the womb.

amniotic sac A thin membrane that surrounds the fetus in the womb.

amplitude The difference in sound waves from the maximum to minimum levels of pressure.

amygdala A part of the limbic system that appears to be involved in aggressive behavior. See also *limbic system*.

anal stage In Freudian theory, the second stage of psychosexual development, corresponding roughly to the period of toilet training during the first or second year, during which the anal region is the source of sexual pleasure. See also *genital, latency*, and *phallic stages*.

analogy A heuristic in which information about one problem is applied to another problem with a similar structure.

analytic psychology The system of psychoanalytic psychology begun by Carl Jung, an early disciple of Freud. Jung's view of the unconscious differs from Freud's in that Jung conceived of the unconscious as the repository of both good and evil images and urges. See also *archetype, collective unconscious*.

androgen Sex hormone secreted to a larger degree by males than by females. Androgen determines male structural development.

anorexia nervosa A disorder defined by marked loss of body weight due to self-starvation.

anterograde amnesia See *amnesia*.

antianxiety drugs Central nervous system depressants. Examples include Valium and Librium.

antibodies Substances in the body having the specific capacity of neutralizing and creating immunity to the antigen.

antidepressants Drugs used to relieve sympton of extreme sadness and withdrawl, characteristics of depressed individuals.

antigens Complex molecules, recognized by the body as foreign, that stimulate the production of antibodies.

antisocial personality disorder A type of personality disorder characterized by repetitive, impulsive, and purposeless antisocial behavior displayed with emotional indifference and without guilt. In the past, individuals classified as antisocial were referred to as psychopaths or sociopaths.

anxiety (1) In Freudian theory, the feeling of dread and/or apprehension about the future caused by id-ego-superego conflict. (2) In behavior theory, a feeling of tension or dread.

anxiety disorders A class of dysfunctions characterized by heightened tension, anxiety, worry, or fear without any realistic reason or cause.

anxious/resistant infants Infants who appear upset when their caregiver leaves or returns. They may alternately seek out contact and resist the caregiver's efforts to hold or comfort them.

apparent motion The perception of movement created by stationary stimuli that are flashed on and off at appropriate intervals.

applied research Research directed toward understanding and solving behavioral and social problems. See also *basic research*.

approach-approach conflict A conflict in which an individual is drawn toward two equally satisfying but incompatible goals. By attaining one goal, the other is lost.

approach-avoidance conflict A conflict in which an individual faces a single goal, but the goal possesses both positive and negative factors.

archetype In Jung's theory, a universal, primordial image found in the collective unconscious. Examples include God, Mother Earth, and rebirth.

arousal The general level of alertness and activation of the body, reflected in several physiological responses, including muscle tension, heart rate, and galvanic skin response.

arousal theory The theory that behavior can be explained by the desire to maintain an optimal arousal level for the task at hand, or for a specific time of day.

assessment center In psychological testing, a technique in which potential candidates are placed in simulated job situations to observe their performances under somewhat stressful conditions.

assimilation In Piaget's theory, absorbing new information and fitting it with existing knowledge.

association areas Areas of the brain that are not strictly sensory or motor, where other cognitive processing occurs.

astigmatism A defect in which visual images are not sharply focused on all parts of the retina.

attachment The process of forming and maintaining an emotional bond during infancy with parents, caregivers, and significant objects in the environment.

attention In perception, the active selection of and focus upon one object or component of a complex experience. The organism thereby responds to a more narrow range of stimuli.

attenuation theory A theory proposing that attention plays an "early" role in perceptual processing, but, instead of entirely blocking out signals (as in filter theory), it only weakens them.

attitude A fairly stable disposition toward particular people, objects, institutions, or issues.

attribution theory A theory concerning how an individual tries to explain people's behavior, inlcuding his or her own. Such explanations may link the behavior to situational or personal qualities, to a combination of both, or to some other factor such as luck.

attribution therapy Treatment that gives patients new, less threatening labels or explanations for their feelings or behavior.

attributional egotism The tendency to attribute success to dispositional factors and failure to external factors. It generally appears when people feel themselves responsible for good or bad outcomes and when success or failure is important to the individual's self-concept.

auditory canal The tubelike passageway that guides sound waves from the outer opening of the ear to the tympanic membrane, or eardrum, of the middle ear.

auditory localization The ability to know the direction from which a sound orginates.

augmenting Increasing the weight of a particular cause, owing to the presence of an opposing influence.

authoritarian parents Parents who demand complete obedience from their children and give little explanation for the rules they establish or for the physical punishment they impose. They value respect for authority and hard work.

authoritative parents Parents who believe control is necessary, but they use reason as well as assertion of power when they discipline their children. They aim to help children conform to group standards without infringing on their independence.

autokinetic effect The apparent movement of a spot of light in a dark room.

autistic disorder A disorder beginning before the age of 3 years, in which young children fail to develop normal language and social behaviors, and have restricted and repetitive activity patterns.

automatic processing Mental processing that is effortless, rapid, and difficult to interrupt.

autonomic nervous system The collection of sensory and motor nerves serving the heart and glands and smooth muscles of the internal organs.

aversion therapy Therapy in which a positive response to an event is changed to a negative response by associating the event with something negative, such as a shock.

avoidance-avoidance conflict A conflict in which an individual must choose between two equally undesirable alternatives.

avoidance learning In instrumental conditioning, the learning of a response that prevents the occurrence of a noxious stimulus.

avoidant infants Infants who are insecurely attached, do not cry when their caregiver leaves, and do not approach the caregiver in the room.

Axis I The main part of DSM-III-R including the major clinical syndromes, such as depression or schizophrenia.

Axis II In DSM-III-R, the longer term developmental and personality disorders.

Axis III In DSM-III-R, the physical conditions that may affect an individual's mental state.

Axis IV In DSM-III-R, the potential predisposing life stressors rated on a 6-point scale.

Axis V In DSM-III-R, an individual's level of functioning measured by a 90-point global assessment of functioning scale.

axon The part of a neuron shaped like a long slender tube that extends outward from the cell body. The axon carries the signal from one neuron on to other neurons.

B

baby biographies Detailed records of children's development, such as those kept by early developmental scientists.

backward conditioning In classical conditioning, a procedure in which the conditioned stimulus begins after the unconditioned stimulus.

basic research Systematic study directed toward establishing fundamental principles of behavior; it need not be related directly to social or behavioral problems. See also *applied research.*

basilar membrane A membrane located in the cochlea of the inner ear. Vibrations of fluid in the cochlea stimulate the hair cells on the basilar membrane which in turn send neural impulses to the brain via the auditory nerve. See also *cochlea.*

behavioral medicine A field that integrates knowledge and techniques of behavioral and biomedical science.

behavior genetics A field of study that analyzes genetic and environmental contributions of behavior.

behaviorism A school of psychology founded by John B. Watson in which psychology is defined solely as the study of behavior; all data therefore must come from observable behavior.

behavioristic view of language This view regards language as verbal behavior that is reinforced by other people.

behavior modification See *behavior therapy.*

behavior therapy Psychotherapy, based on principles of learning, that seeks to change undesirable behavior. See also *cognitive behavior modification; counterconditioning.*

binocular disparity The slight difference between the two retinal images of an object in view that is caused by the separation of the two eyes and the consequent difference in viewing angles. It is an important depth cue.

biofeedback A technique for monitoring autonomic responses, such as heart rate or the galvanic skin response, through conditioning procedures.

biological constraints Genetically mediated predispositions to associate certain stimuli with each other, or certain responses with certain stimuli.

biological innate view of language A view of language acquisition, proposed by Noam Chomsky, in which people are born with a language acquisition device that is like a genetic blueprint for the underlying aspects of language.

biological perspective An approach to abonormality, first proffered by the Greeks, in which there ar physical causes for mental disorders.

bipolar disorder Series of episodes of mania and depression in a single individual.

birth order A predictor of personality, stressed by Adler, in which first-borns are seen as dependent and conforming, middle children as vulnerable to competitive pressures, and youngest children as overprotected and eager to prove themselves.

bisexual A male or female who is sexually attracted to people of both sexes.

blastocyst In prenatal development, a hollow ball of cells enclosing the developing zygote that continually divides as it travels down one of the fallopian tubes.

blind spot The portion of the retina where the optic nerve exits from the eye and which contains no receptor cells.

blocking In classical conditioning, the failure of an animal to learn about a second stimulus presented in compound with a conditioned stimulus, that already has been associated with the unconditioned stimulus.

blood glucose Blood sugar; low blood sugar is one cue for hunger.

bottom-up theories A class of theories that describe perception as a strictly passive process; information passes from receptor organs to higher levels of the nervous system in stages of increasing complexity. See also *top-down approach.*

brain A soft, heavy mass that weighs about 1400 grams and, with the spinal cord, composes the central nervous system.

brightness The perceived intensity of visual stimuli. Brightness depends primarily on the amplitude of light waves.

Broca's area A certain part of the brain's left hemisphere that, when damaged, causes speech to become slow and labored.

bulimia nervosa An eating disorder involving cycles of high consumption followed by self-induced vomiting and self-starvation.

C

California Personality Inventory (CPI) A personality questionnaire designed for measuring 15 dimensions of normal personality, including self-reliance, personal worth, and sense of freedom.

Cannon-Bard theory A theory proposing that emotion-arousing situations stimulate the thalamus, which then transmits information simultaneously in two directions—downward through the autonomic nervous system to the body's internal organs and upward to the cerebral cortex.

case study The intensive study of one particular instance of some behavior.

catatonic schizophrenics People have a disorder marked by unusual physical activity—from wild and uncontrolled tantrums to stupor. (See also *schizophrenia*).

catharsis In psychoanalytic theory, the relief from tension that is brought about through psychotherapy or through expressing and acting out feelings.

causal attribution The process of assigning causes to behavior and outcomes.

cell membrane The membrane enclosing the neuron that protects the cell and regulates the concentration of chemicals inside and outside the cell.

central nervous system The brain and spinal cord. See also *peripheral nervous system.*

central processing An individual's careful attention to the meaning and logical implications of a message or argument.

central tendency In statistics, measures of the tendency of scores in a frequency distribution to cluster around a central value. See also *mean, median, mode, measures of central tendency.*

centration Directing attention to only limited aspects of a stimulus.

cerebellum The part of the brain in the lower back region of the brain stem that helps to make movements smooth and precise.

cerebral cortex The surface layer of gray matter—unmyelinated axons of the cell bodies—over the cerebral hemispheres.

cerebral hemispheres The two large structures of the top of the brain—one on the left, one on the right—which are separated by the longitudinal fissure; fibers joining the hemispheres over this fissure are called the *corpus callosum.* See also *split-brain patient.*

cerebrospinal fluid Fluid filling all the area surrounding the brain and spinal cord inside the skull that helps to support and to cushion the brain and spinal cord.

cerebrum The white matter—myelinated axons of the cell bodies—and subcortical structures, on the inside of the cerebral cortex.

chorionic villii biopsy A procedure to diagnose prenatal complications in which a tude is inserted into a pregnant woman's cervix to suction off fetal cells for analysis.

chorionic villus sampling A procedure to help diagnose prenatal complications in which a tube is inserted into the pregnant woman's certix and some fetal cells are suctioned off for analysis. This procedure can be done as early as the eighth week after conception, but is slightly more risky than amniocentesis.

chromosomes Thread-like cell molecules that carry genes, the elementary units of heredity.

classical conditioning The procedure whereby a neutral stimulus is paired with a stimulus that automatically produces a response. As a consequence, the neutral stimulus comes to elicit the response. See also *conditioned stimulus, conditioned response, unconditioned stimulus, unconditioned response.*

client-centered therapy See *person-centered therapy.*

clinical psychologist A person with a Ph.D. in psychology whose graduate work involved four to five years of intenstive training in research and clinical skills, as well as a one-year internship under professional supervision.

cochlea A small, bony, snail-shaped organ of the inner ear that contains the receptors for hearing.

cochlear implant A prosthesis that has been developed to provide a kind of artificial hearing. It is surgically inserted into the patient's ear.

cognition The process of thinking, encompassing perception, consciousness, learning, and memory.

cognitive behavior modification A type of psychotherapy, based on principles of learning, which seeks to change beliefs, thoughts, and self-perceptions underlying behavior. See also *behavior therapy.*

cognitive dissonance A theory that explains changes in beliefs and attitudes. People want consistency in their beliefs and attitudes, and whenever beliefs and attitudes conflict with each other, tension motivates changes in behavior or cognition.

cognitive map An internal representation, or mental picture, of information about events and their spatial relationship.

cognitive model A behavioral theory that many abnormal behaviors and feelings result from irrational or maladaptive cognitions.

cognitive motivation theory A group of theories that share the idea that motivation is produced through positive and negative incentives. In cognitive theory, incentives are usually referred to as expectancies of goals.

cognitive resource utilization theory An explanation of leadership emphasizing intelligence, work-related knowledge, and technical competence.

cognitive social learning theory A personality theory developed by Mischel examining the different ways in which individuals experience their environments.

cohort effects The consequences of being born in a particular generation, raised during unique historical events, and being influenced by particular educational opportunities that may explain declining IQ scores.

collective unconsious In Jung's theory, as inherited unconscious dominated by a set of symbols or archetypes. See also *archetype.*

color circle A diagram representing the colors of the spectrum. Colors are arranged around the circumference in order of the spectrum. Complementary colors appear opposite each other on the circle. See also *complementary colors.*

community halfway house A treatment facility and a residence for people recently discharged from a mental hospital or a prison, or for people who feel they may require hospitalization.

community mental health centers Community based offices in the United States offering psychological outpatient services.

complementarity hypothesis People who complement each other (i.e., have opposite personality traits) will be attracted to each other.

complementary colors Any two colors which, in an additive mixture, produce either gray or an unsaturated version of the hue of the stronger color.

compliance A form of social influence in which a person abides by a direct request.

componential subtheory The core of Robert Sternberg's comprehensive theory of intelligence based on the idea that there are distinct components of intelligence.

compulsions Behaviors that a victim feels forced to repeat continually.

concepts Mental representations for classifying information.

concordance rate The percentage of twins who share a trait, such as schizophrenia.

concrete operational period In Piaget's theory of cognitive development, a stage in which children approximately seven to eleven years of age use rules and stategies to understand physical laws and social relationships.

concurrent validity The degree to which two measures taken together yield similar evidence of a phenomenon. See also *predictive validity.*

conditioned inhibition A learned tendency to inhibit or hold back responses.

conditioned reinforcer An event that becomes a reinforcer through learning. See also *primary reinforcer.*

conditioned response (CR) In classical conditioning, the learned response to a conditioned stimulus. See also *conditioned stimulus, classical conditioning.*

conditioned stimulus (CS) In classical conditioning, a previously neutral stimulus, or a stimulus that does not elicit the response to be conditioned. By pairing with an unconditioned stimulus, the conditioned stimulus comes to elicit some response. See also *classical conditioning, unconditioned stimulus.*

conditions of worth In Roger's theory of personality, children's strong feelings about what kind of behaviors will bring them approval from others.

conduction deafness Deafness occurring with age; the ossicles become rigid and cannot carry sound forward.

cones Receptor cells located in the retina of the eye that are capable of transforming light energy into neural impulses. The cones are responsible for color vision. See also *rods.*

confidentiality The guarantee in therapy that the patient's privacy will be protected by therapists and copatients, and that nothing discussed in the therapy session will be revealed to any outside the therpeutic relationship.

conformity Yielding to individual or group pressure when there is no direct request to do so.

confounding In experimental and correlational research, the simultaneous variation of two independent variables, only one of which is the variable of interest. As a result, the researcher cannot attribute with certainty any effect on the dependent variable to the independent variable of interest.

conjunction search Search processing which involves looking for a stimulus that has similar features to other stimuli.

connectionist model An interactive model that displays connections between elements in the model.

conscience See *superego.*

conscious Being aware of internal and/or external stimuli.

consciousness A general term referring to current awareness of internal and/or external stimuli.

consensus One of Kelley's principles for determining casual attributions; a high degree of agreement suggests that the attribution is internal.

conservation In Piaget's theory, the understanding that certain properties of matter, such as number, length, and volume, remain constant despite superficial changes in appearance.

consistency One of Kelley's principles for detrmining causal attributions; a higher degree of regularity suggests that the attribution might be either dispositionally or situationally caused.

construct validity The accuracy with which a test measures what it is intended to measure.

contextual subtheory Sternberg's third subtheory that goes beyond IQ tests and cognitive processes to deal with intelligence in relation to the external world of the individual.

contiguity Closeness in time between the CS and the US in classical conditioning; disproving Pavlov's hypothesis, contiguity has been recently shown to be neither necessary nor sufficient for conditioning to occur.

contingency The possibility that a US is likely to follow the occurrence of a CS in classical conditioning.

contingency contracting Behavior therapy involving a written agreement between therapist and client.

continuous reinforcement In instrumental conditioning, providing reinforcement for every instance of desired behavior. See also *partial reinforcement*.

control processes In the multistore model of memory, mental processes that regulate the flow of information between short- and long-term memory.

control variable A potential independent variable that is held constant in an experiment.

controlled processing Mental processing that is consciously controlled, relatively slow, and easily interrupted.

convergent thinking Using information to arrive at a standard correct answer. See also *divergent thinking*.

conversion disorder A disorder in which the individual manifests a severe physical impairment such as paralysis, blindness, or deafness, that has no organic cause. See also *somatoform disorder*.

Coolidge effect The stimulating effect of a new partner after sexual intercourse with another.

cornea The transparent outer membrane of the eye covering the iris and the pupil. The cornea admits light into the eye and bends it for focusing on the retina.

corpus callosum Large set of axons that connects the two cerebral hemispheres.

correlation A measure of the extent to which two variables are related. A correlation may not be used to infer causality.

correlation coefficient A numerical index of the degree of relationship between two variables. Correlation coefficients range between .00 and 1.00 and may be either negative or positive. Positive correlations indicate that high rank on one variable is associated with high rank on the other variable. Negative correlations indicate that high rank on one variable is associated with low rank on the other variable.

counseling psychologist A trained psychologist who specializes in marital, vocational, or other personal problems not associated with specific illness.

counterconditioning Psychotherapy based on classical conditioning procedures, in which an event that produces a positive reaction is associated with something negative and so comes to produce a negative reaction (aversion therapy), or an event that produces a negative response is associated with something positive and so comes to produce a positive response (systematic desensitization).

critical period A time of particular sensitivity to certain environmental influences during development.

cross-sectional analysis Experimental design for simultaneously testing subjects of many different ages. See also *longitudinal analysis*.

crowding Negative feeling and perception of too many people in too little space. See also *density*.

crystallized intelligence The ability to make decisions and solve problems based on culturally-given information and skills. See also *fluid intelligence*.

D

dark adaptation The process by which the eye becomes increasingly sensitive to illumination during periods of darkness. See also *light adaptation*.

data Observations drawn from experiments or other research.

deductive reasoning The ability to draw logical conclusions from statements or evidence.

deep structure The speaker's intended message and the linguistic relations that constrain a sentence's meaning.

defense mechanisms In Freudian theory, unconsious means to deny, falsify, or distort reality.

defensive attribution Attributions that serve to protect the perceiver's self-concept or view of the world—for example, the belief in a just world.

deindividuation Reduced awareness of oneself as an individual and a decline in feelings of personal responsibility due to an individual's relative anonymity when merging with the group.

delayed conditioning A classical conditioning procedure in which the conditioned stimulus comes on before the unconditioned stimulus and terminates with the onset, during, or with the offset of unconditioned stimulus.

dendrites The fibers branching out from a neuron that receive signals from other neurons.

density The objective number of people in a given space. Density may or may not give rise to a feeling of crowding. See also *crowding*.

dependence Repeated use of a substance until an individual develops tolerance for the drug or withdrawal symptoms without it.

dependent variable The variable in research which is measured; changes in it are attributable to variation in the independent variable in a properly controlled experiment. See also *control variable*, *independent variable*.

depressants Drugs that generally reduce activity in the central nervous system.

depression An affective disorder characterized by intense sadness and feelings of hopelessness and worthlessness.

depressive disorder Overwhelming feelings of hopelessness and worthlessness, plus physical symptoms including a lack of appetite, an inability to sleep, loss of energy, slow, emotionless speech, and uncontrollable crying.

depth cues Binocular and monocular cues to the distance of an object from the observer, or the distance between two objects.

descriptive research Methods used to describe phenomena of interest to researchers, such as psychological tests and case studies.

descriptive statistics A summary of measurements made on a sample or population.

developmental psychology Study of the processes of growth and maturation, from conception to death.

Diagnostic Manual of Mental Disorders See *DSM-IV*.

difference threshold The smallest change in a physical stimulus that can be perceived. See also *absolute threshold*.

differential reinforcement of other behavior Reinforcement of behavior other than the target behavior which is to be reduced, simultaneous with nonreinforcement of the target behavior.

discounting Reducing the attributional weight assigned to a particular cause because of the availability of another, competing explanation.

discrimination In classical conditioning, if one CS (CS1) is paired with a US while a second CS (CS2) occurs alone a CR will occurred to CS1 and not to CS2 (if the animal can tell the two CSs apart. This occurrence of different responses as a result of this training is termed a discrimination. In operant conditioning a discrimination is produced by following a response by reinforcement in one situation, but not in another. The response will ultimately occur ony in the situation where it is reinforced.

discrimination training Training in which responding in the presence of one stimulus (S+) is reinforced while responding in the presence of another stimulus (S−) is not.

disorganized schizophrenia Schizophrenic condition marked by unorganized and nonsensical speech, unprovoked emotion, and bizarre behavior.

dispositional cause As an observer, attributing behavior to the person, rather than the situation. See also *situational cause*.

dissociative (functional) disorders

dissociative disorder Behavior characterized by separating one's self-identity from the remainder of one's personality. See also *amnesia, fugue, multiple personality*.

distal stimuli Objects in the environment that give rise to proximal stimuli, those that strike the sense organs.

distinctiveness One of Kelley's principles for determining causal attributions; refers to whether an individual always behaves in a certain way or whether the individual is behaving in a certain way just in one particular situation.

divergent thinking Reasoning that generates novel ideas by pursuing many new directions, none of which can be judged as the single correct answer. See also *convergent thinking*.

dizygotic twins (DZ) Fraternal twins, or twins which arise from separate eggs.

door-in-the-face technique A compliance technique in which a target is more likely to comply with a moderate request immediately after having declined a large or unreasonable request.

dopamine hypothesis A biomedical perspective asserting that schizophrenics suffer from excessively high concentrations of the neurotransmitter dopamine in their brains.

drive A motivational state that energizes behavior until it is removed. Many drives are produced by physiological needs, e.g., the hunger drive.

drive theory The assumption that all motivated behavior arises from drives and that responses which satisfy drives are reinforced.

drug therapy The use of chemicals to alter, and presumably improve, emotions and behavior.

DSM-IV The latest classification system developed by the American Psychiatric Association. The DSM-IV specifies behavioral criteria for determining diagnosis of abnormal behavior from clinical observation.

dual coding theory Proposition that the human memory system can store both pictorial/imaginal information verbal/linguistic information.

E

early-selection theory In theories of attention, the hypothesis that one sensory signal is selected early in the sensory system for further processing. All unattended signals are presumed to be lost from the system and therefore unavailable to the perceiver. See also *filter theory, late selection theory*.

echoic storage A peripheral memory system that maintains auditory information for approximately 2–4 seconds.

educational psychology The branch of psychology concerned with the application of psychological principles to the education of children and adults in schools.

ego In Freud's three-part division of the personality, the ego corresponds most closely to the conscious self. The ego attempts to rec-oncile the conflicting demands of the id, the superego, and external reality. See also *id, superego*.

ego psychology An offshoot of psychoanalysis in which the ego is seen as having its own agenda, rather than simply operating on behalf of the id.

egocentric Preschoolers' belief that everyone sees exactly what they do and do not realize that other people have different points of view.

egocentrism The naive belief that your point of view or visual perspective is shared by others.

ego-ideal See *superego*.

eidetic imagery Sometimes referred to as photographic memory, it is uncommonly vivid imagery, as though the person were perceiving rather than remembering.

Electra complex In Freudian theory, a girl's intimate attachment to her father and hostility to her mother, occurring during the phallic stage. See also *Oedipus complex*.

electroconvulsive therapy (ECT) A controversial form of shock treatment used mainly for alleviating depression. Electric current is passed briefly through the patient's head, producing temporary convulsions.

embryo The developing organism during early differentiation of anatomical structures (from conception to six to eight weeks).

embryonic stage The period lasting six to eight weeks after fertilization.

emotion Complex physiological and cognitive states that people describe in subjective terms, such as joy, anger, or fear.

empiricism The philosophical view that all of our knowledge of the world comes from experience, as opposed to innate knowledge. See also *nativism*.

encoding Also known as *acquisition*, the first stage in the memory process; applies to initial learning.

encoding specificity hypothesis The theory that memory for an event is improved to the extent that the information present at the time of retrieval matches the way information is stored in memory.

encounter A therapeutic relationship (in existential therapy) involving a genuine here-and-now meeting of two individuals who try to be open and honest in their reactions to each other.

encounter groups A general term for a large variety of groups set up to develop greater social and personal awareness in members. Procedures used in groups vary widely.

endocrine system A chemical communication system within the body. Endocrine glands secrete hormones that have specific effects on other body organs.

endorphins Opiate-like substances within the body.

engineering psychology The branch of applied psychology concerned with the design of equipment and systems to fit the size, strength, and capabilities of the people who will use them.

enkephalins See *endorphins*.

environmentalism In the social learning approach to personality, the belief that the accumulation of experiences creates tendencies to behave in certain ways and these tendencies are likely to become entrenched in personality.

environmental psychology The study of the relationship between the environment and behavior.

episodic memory Memory dependent upon retrieving the particular time, place, or context in which a particular event or episode took place. See also *semantic memory*.

equilibration In Piaget's theory, the process of achieving equilibrium, a temporary balance between existing knowledge and perceived information.

equilibratory senses Sense organs in the middle ear that help maintain balance.

equilibrium See *equilibration*.

escape conditioning The learning of a response that terminates a noxious stimulus.

estrogens Hormones, secreted to a larger degree in females, that influence female physical development.

ethnic identity When adolescents incorporate their cultural heritage into their personal sense of self.

ethologists Researchers who study the behavior of animals in the wild.

existential therapy Treatment based upon the unique nature of each individual's "way of being in the world"; the client is challenged to become more aware of his or her own existence and purpose.

expectancy A cognitive representation of an event predicted to follow an event currently being processed.

experiential subtheory Sternberg's second subtheory in which intelligence requires the ability to deal with novel tasks and situations. It involves the abilities to select, encode, compare, and combine information in different settings.

experimental research Techniques in which researchers manipulate or vary one factor in an experiment to see how it influences the behavior of interest.

experimental research The creation of a situation that allows controlled observation. The experimenter varies some aspect of the situation, controls all others, and then observes the effects of the variation on the behavior of interest.

explicit memory Conscious recollection.

external locus of control The attribution of success and failure to luck, chance, or the behavior of others.

external validity The generalizability of conclusions to a range of conditions, populations, and environmental settings not included in research.

extinction (1) In classical conditioning, stopping presentation of the unconditioned stimulus. (2) In instrumental conditioning, discontinuing reinforcement for a response.

extrasensory perception (ESP) A controversial category of perception which allegedly occurs without any physical stimulation of the sensory receptors. Varieties of ESP include clairvoyance (awareness of objects not present to the senses), telepathy (transmission of thought between two minds), precognition (ability to foresee events), and psychokinesis (the ability of the mind to move or bend objects).

extrinsic motivation Doing something in order to obtain an external reward. See also *intrinsic motivation*.

Eysenck Personality Questionnaire (EPQ) A paper-and-pencil personality test designed to measure three dimensions of normal personality: introversion-extraversion, neuroticism-stability, and psychoticism.

F

facial feedback hypothesis A theory suggesting that feedback from facial expressions intensifies emotional experience.

factor analysis A statistical technique used to identify and analyze the underlying dimensions, or factors, in a large variety of measures, such as those gained from a battery of tests.

family therapy A form of psychotherapy in which problems are addressed by the family members as a group rather than by an individual.

feature search Search processing in which a target can be distinguished from distractors by a single feature.

fetal alcohol syndrome A condition in which newborns exhibit lethargy, poor attention, and uncoordinated movements as a consequence of the alcohol circulated through their bodies during pregnancy.

fetal period The prenatal stage lasting from about two months after conception until birth in humans; during this time the fetus becomes capable of sustaining life independently of the mother.

fetus The name of the unborn organism in the womb as it develops its species characteristics from about two months until birth. See also *fetal period*.

figure-ground segregation A principle of perceptual organization in which viewers of a complex two- or three-dimensional scene perceive part of it as being closer (the figure) than the rest (the ground).

filter theory In theories of attention, the hypothesis that the perceptual system selects one signal from the many sources of information available to it for further perceptual analysis. See also *early selection theory, late selection theory*.

fissures Natural divisions in the surface of the cortex. The *central fissure* separates the frontal lobe from the parietal lobe; the *lateral fissure* constitutes the boundary of the temporal lobe; the *longitudinal fissure* separates the two hemispheres.

fixation An excessive focus of psychic energy on a particular psychosexual stage; according to psychoanalytic theory, the result of either frustration or overindulgence.

fixed action pattern A stereotyped, complex behavior that is instinctive, usually elicited by a specific sign stimulus (for example, the tongue flick with which a frog catches flies). See also *sign stimulus*.

fixed interval scallop The name of the cumulative record of performance by a subject on a fixed interval schedule, so-called because responding slows greatly after each reinforcement and increases when the next reinforcement is due.

fixed interval schedule A pattern of intermittent reinforcement in which a reward is provided following the first response made after a certain (or fixed) period of time has passed, and the time period remains constant for each trial.

fixed ratio schedule A pattern of intermittent reinforcement in which a reward is given only after a certain number of responses have been made, for example, five lever presses.

flashbulb memory Clear recollections that people sometimes have of the events surrounding a momentous event, for example, when they first learned President Ronald Reagan had been shot.

fluid intelligence The capacity to analyze and solve problems.

focal colors Certain basic colors that are salient to all observers regardless of the particular labels used to describe them.

foot-in-the-door technique A method for increasing compliance to a large request by first inducing someone to agree to a much smaller request.

forensic psychology A specialty that focuses on the evaluation and treatment of criminal defendants.

formal operational period In Piaget's theory, the period during which children acquire logical thinking skills, usually after eleven or twelve years of age.

formal work groups Work groups that appear in a company's organizational hierarchy; they are the groups (divisions, departments, task forces) to which individual workers are assigned.

fovea A small region in the retina that contains the highest concentration of cones and provides the greatest visual acuity.

fraternal twins See *dizygotic twins*.

frequency The number of complete cycles per second of a sound wave.

frequency distribution A table or graph indicating the number of individuals scoring at different levels on some measure.

frequency theory A theory of pitch perception which suggests that when a hair cell fires, its rhythm or tempo of firing is in synchrony with the frequency of the sound entering the ear. See also *place theory, volley theory*.

frontal lobe One of four natural sections of each cerebral hemisphere, positioned in front of the central fissure. See also *occipital lobe, parietal lobe, temporal lobe*.

frustration The blocking of or interference with goal-directed activity, or the absence of a reward when one is expected.

frustration-aggression hypothesis The hypothesis that frustration induces an aggressive drive which, in turn, motivates aggressive behavior. See also *revised frustration-aggression hypothesis*.

fugue A dissociative disorder in which an individual leaves home and establishes a different existence in another place. Although the former life is blocked from memory, other abilities are unimpaired and the individual appears normal. See also *amnesia, dissociative disorder, multiple personality disorder*.

functional amnesia Failure of memory that often occurs immediately following severe conflict or psychological stress.

functional fixedness A tendency to consider only one use for familiar objects, or more generally always to view problems in the same way.

functionalism A school of psychology which emphasized mental processes as the proper subject matter for psychology. Functionalists argued that the mind should be studied in terms of its usefulness to the organism in adapting to its environment.

fundamental attribution error The tendency to underestimate situational influences on behavior and to assume instead that some personal characteristic of the individual is responsible, or a bias toward dispositional rather than situational attributions. See also *attribution theory*.

G

gate-control theory In the study of pain, a theory that sensations result from the activation of nerver fibers that lead to specific centers of the brain responsible for pain perception.

gender identity The personal conviction that one is male or female.

gender stereotyping The act of ascribing a role or placing certain expectations or prescriptions on an individual's behavior based on gender.

gene The basic unit of inheritance that is located on and transmitted by the chromosome and develops into a hereditary character as it reacts with the environment and other genes.

general adaptation syndrome A series of reactions that occur under stress, beginning with alarm and progressing through resistance and exhaustion.

generalized anxiety disorder An anxiety disorder characterized by general apprehensiveness, tension, and physical complaints that last at least a month and lack specific focus. See also *panic disorder, phobia, obsessive-compulsive disorder*.

General Aptitude Test Battery (GATB) A widely used test that measures three kinds of ability: perceptual, general cognitive, and psychomotor.

genetics The study of the inheritance of traits and the mechanisms of this inheritance.

genital stage The fifth and final psychosexual stage, according to Freud, which occurs during adolescence and in which the individ-

ual obtains pleasure from sexual contact with others. See also *anal, latency, oral,* and *phallic stages*.

genotype The genetic composition of an individual.

geons One of the primitive elements in Biederman's theory representing thousands of objects in the environment when arranged in various combinations.

Gestalt psychology A theoretical approach that emphasizes the role or organized wholes ("gestalten") in perception and other psychological processes.

Gestalt therapy A form of psychotherapy based on the ideas of Fritz Perls which emphasizes the individual's positive and creative aspects. Gestalt methods are directed at externalizing the patient's feelings so they can be confronted and if necessary changed. See also *psychotherapy*.

gifted children Children who are performing at levels many years beyond their chronological ages, as defined by high scores on tests.

glial cells Cells that provide services to neurons.

glucostatic theory The hypothesis that level of blood sugar (glucose) is regulated by feeding behavior. Feeding occurs when blood glucose is too low; satiety occurs when blood glucose is raised.

grammar A set of linguistic principles that describe how classes of words are connected in sentences.

group therapy Psychotherapy undertaken by several people simultaneously.

H

hallucinogens Drugs that produce hallucinations, or alterations of perceptual experience.

Hawthorne effect Increases in worker productivity due to employee morale and norms of the informal work group.

health psychology A relatively new subspecialty that focuses on the relation between psychological factors and physical health.

hedonism The theory that individuals are motivated primarily by the desire to seek pleasure and avoid pain.

heritability The proportion of variance in a trait (within a population) that is attributable to genetic factors.

Hermann's grid A retinal illusion in which lateral inhibition causes the viewer to perceive nonexistent gray spots.

Hermaphrodites Individuals whose genitals are ambiguous, not clearly female or male.

heuristic A rule-of-thumb strategy that serves as a guide to problem solving.

hippocampus A nerve tract that is part of the limbic system, located in the temporal lobe of the brain, that may be involved in the formation and consolidation of memory.

homeostasis Literally, "equal state," which cells of the body maintain.

homosexual Someone who has sexual feelings for a person of the same sex. *Facultative homosexuality* describes occasional same-sex acts in particular situations, but with a customary preference for the opposite sex. *Obligative homosexuality* refers to exclusive performance for the same sex, with a corresponding identity.

hormones The chemical secretions of the endocrine glands that are distributed by body fluids and activate specific receptive organs.

hue The dimension of visual sensation that is most closely related to the color of the perceived object. It derives primarily from the wavelength of the stimulus.

human factors psychology The science of designing machines and equipment for human use and of training humans in the proper operation of machines.

humanistic psychology An approach to psychology that emphasizes the consciousness of human beings. Humanistic psychology is concerned with the qualities that distinguish human beings from other animals (e.g., desires for dignity, self-worth).

humanistic theory A theory focusing on a patient's subjective experience; identifies the influence of reacting to the world as the source of abnormality and psyhological problems.

hyperopia A common condition referred to as farsightedness. Hyperopia results when the image of the object being viewed is focused beyond the retina. See also *myopia*.

hypnosis A temporary state of heightened suggestibility in which people will often follow instructions given to them.

hypothalamic thermostat A self-regulating feedback system that controls the body's production of hormones.

hypothalamus A tiny structure lying beneath the thalamus that has tremendous importance in the regulation of emotion and motivation.

hypothesis A tentative assumption advanced to explain or predict certain facts.

I

iconic storage The peripheral memory system that maintains visual information for very brief periods of time.

id In Freud's three-art theory of personality, the most primitive part which provides instinctive energy that demands immediate gratification of aggressive and sexual needs and desires. See also *ego, pleasure principle, superego*.

ideal self The self as the individual would like it to be.

identical twins See *monozygotic twins*.

identity development The establishment of an independent and positive view of oneself.

illusory conjunctions Combined features "seen" when two stimuli are flashed briefly.

illusory correlation The tendency to believe (falsely) that certain types of people are likely to exhibit certain traits or behaviors.

imaginal code An internal representation or memory code for previously perceived visual sensory information. Imaginal codes are presumed to bear some resemblance to the experiences they represent.

immune system The body's main defense against anything that is "nonself" including abnormal cells in the body or abnormal substances from outside the body.

implicit memory Retention in the absence of attempts at conscious recollection.

implicit personality theory All the assumptions made about the characteristics or personality traits that go together.

implosion therapy A type of behavior therapy in which patients are encouraged to imagine or engage in anxiety-arousing stimulus situations and to experience their anxiety as fully as possible. Since these situations do not pose any objective harm to the patients, the inner explosion (implosion) of anxiety abates and the stimulus loses its power to elicit anxiety.

impression formation The process through which we absorb, combine, and integrate information about a target in order to form a more complete impression of that person.

impression management The techniques we use to make a desired impression on other people.

imprinting The tendency acquired early in life to follow or approach an object. Geese, for example, will follow any large moving object they are exposed to during a *critical period* shortly after birth. This tendency persists throughout life.

inbred strains Breeds of mice and other animals produced by mating brothers and sisters, then mating brothers and sisters among their offspring, and so on.

incentive motivation Motivation produced by the expectancy of receiving events and the value placed on those events.

incentives Anticipation of events in the environment to produce motivation. Positive incentives increase performance; negative incentives decrease performance.

inclusive fitness The sum of an individual's fitness plus the fitness of its relatives.

incubation effect The phenomenon of suddenly being able to solve a problem after putting it aside for a while.

independent variable In a controlled experient, the factor or potential cause of behavior under investigation. The independent variable is the element manipulated by the experimenter. See also *control variable, confounding, dependent variable*.

individual fitness The individual's chance of reproducing and contributing genes to the next generation.

individual psychology The school of psychoanalysis founded by Alfred Adler in which feelings of inferiority and the need for power are considered important.

individuation In Erickson's theory of psychosocial development, the process of identity development.

induced motion The illusion that a stationary object is moving when in fact some object nearby is actually in motion, e.g., when your car is stopped but appears to move backward as your neighbor's car edges forward.

inductive reasoning The ability to determine or construct a rule that links together elements or relations.

industrial/organizational psychology The branch of psychology concerned with the application of psychological phenomena to industrial problems. Industrial/organizational psychologists are mainly concerned with the selection and training of personnel and staff, job performance and productivity, and the ways in which organizations operate.

industrial psychology See *industrial/organizational psychology*.

infantile (childhood) amnesia The natural inability of most people to remember any events that occurred before age 3 or 4.

inferential statistics Techniques used for determining the reliability and generality of a particular experimental result.

inferiority complex Alfred Adler's term for feelings of inadequacy.

informal work groups Work groups that develop from idiosyncratic friendships, common interests, and similarity in attitudes.

information processing A variety of viewpoints that regard human beings as symbol manipulators, much like computer systems.

inner ear The portion of the ear containing the cochlea and the semicircular canals.

insanity defense A legal tactic in which a defendant in a criminal case is judged as incapable of distinguishing right from wrong and therefore not guilty of the crime.

insight The sudden comprehension of a new idea.

insomnia The class of disorders characterized primarily by consistent or prolonged inability to obtain enough sleep.

instinct theory The theory that proposes that motivation is based on innate, internal forces, which are characteristic of a species.

instrumental conditioning A type of conditioning in which reinforcement is contingent upon the subject providing a particular response; also called operant conditioning.

insulin A hormone that processes blood glucose.

intelligence quotient (IQ) An index of a subject's level of achievement relative to others on a standardized test that purportedly measures intelligence. I.Q. = Mental Age ÷ Chronological Age × 100.

intensity The amount of ener;gy in light waves. Generally, the more intense the source of light, the brighter the light will appear.

interactionist perspective of language A theory of language acquisition that gives credit to biological, social, and cognitive changes to language development.

interactive theories Theories of perception that postulate an interplay between sensory and higher-level cognitive factors.

interference See *proactive* or *retroactive interference.*

intermittent reinforcement See *partial reinforcement.*

internal locus of control A child's sense of responsiblity for personal success or failure.

internal validity Refers to the state in which an observed effect on a dependent variable can be safely atributed to the experiementer's manipulation of the independent variable. See also *external validity.*

interneurons Neurons that connect one neuron to another.

interposition A monocular depth cue resulting from the fact that when one object blocks another from view the eye tends to perceive the former object as closer than the latter.

interval schedules Schedules in which reinforcement is given for the first response made after a certain period of time (interval) has passed. On *fixed internal schedules* the period of time is always the same; on *variable interval schedules* the period of time fluctuates.

interview A meeting between a researcher and a respondent at which information about the respondent is obtained through personal questions and answers.

intrinsic motivation The desire to do something for its own sake and the pleasure of doing it.

iris The colored, circular muscle in the eye that regulates the size of the pupil to control the amount of light entering the eye. The iris gives eyes their distinctive color.

isolation effect The finding that if one item in a list is very different from other list items, the unique one will be recalled better than the remaining items.

item specific processing The study of individual items of information (specific facts) in texts.

J

James-Lange theory of emotion A theory that emotion is the subjective experience of peripheral physiological reactions that occur when an emotional stimulus is perceived. Thus a stimulus leads to physiological responses, and awareness of the responses causes the emotion.

job analysis A relatively complete description of the requirements for each job.

just noticeable difference (j.n.d.) The amount of increase or decrease in a stimulus that an observer can reliably detect. See also *difference threshold.*

K

kinesthesis A source of sense information that tells us the position of our limbs through sense organs in muscles, tendons, and joints; it allows us to react when we stumble or slip.

L

language A means of symbolic communication based on sounds, written symbols, and gestures.

language competence An inborn knowledge about language all children seem to possess.

latency stage The fourth of Freud's psychosexual stages of development, occurring roughly between the age of six and the onset of puberty, when drive activity subsides, allowing the ego to consolidate the changes that have occurred to that point. See also *anal, genital, oral,* and *phallic stages.*

latent learning Learning that is not shown immediately in performance. For example, in a latent learning experiment an animal is exposed to a maze with no reinforcement, the reinforcement is introduced at a later time to determine if the animal learned anything about the maze.

lateral inhibition The tendency for stimulated receptors in the visual system to inhibit adjacent receptors.

late selection theory The view that all incoming sensory signals receive some processing initially, and then one signal is chosen by the nervous system for further processing. See also *early selection theory.*

law of effect Behavioral law stating that responses followed by reinforcement tend to increase in frequency, while responses not followed by reinforcement become less frequent.

learned helplessness A condition hypothesized to develop after an organism is exposed to a repeated, inescapable stimulus. Later, learning to escape aversive stimuli is impaired.

learning A relatively permanent change in behavior or knowledge that occurs as a result of experience.

legal definition of abnormality A criterion of abnormality that declares a person insane primarily on the basis of his or her ability to judge between right and wrong, or to exert control over his or her behavior.

lens The flexible, transparent structure located at the front of the eye that changes shape in order for images of near or distint objects to focus on the retina.

level of confidence A probability statement concerning the decision to reject the null hypothesis. It specifies the probability that the decision to reject the null hypothesis was incorrect and in actuality that no difference existed among the population means.

levels-of-processing approach In this approach, memory is considered a by-product of perceptual processing where perception of stimulus is conceived as involving stages of coding that lead to comprehension. Deeper codes lead to better memory.

LH lesions Damage to the lateral hypothalamus. Rats with these lesions eat and drink less than a nonlesioned rat.

libido The part of the id concerned with sexuality.

life review The reflection on life's accomplishments that occurs as a person nears death.

light adaptation The rapid adjustment made by the eye when it is exposed to bright light. See also *dark adaptation.*

lightness The reflected light from an object.

limbic system Groups of similar cell bodies located in the thalamus and hypothalamus and in part of the brain above these structures that appear to form a border around the lower fore-brain. Parts of the limbic system are involved in emotional behavior.

linear perspective A monocular depth cue that is based on the fact that as objects recede they appear to converge or grow smaller in size (e.g., railroad tracks).

linguistic ambiguity Multiple interpretations of language that may be produced at several levels: phonological (sounds), lexical (words), syntactic (word order), and semantic (meaning).

linguistic competence The potential to produce and comprehend language.

linguistic determinism The view that diverse language terms, grammers, and linguistic abilities cause people to think differently.

linguistics The study of language, its rules, forms, and functions.

lipostatic theory The theory that the level of fat deposits is regulated by feeding behavior, particularly with respect to long-term regulation of food intake.

lobes Four natural sections in the brain, termed frontal, temporal, occipital and parietal, formed by grooves in the brain's surface.

locus of control A cognitive individual difference variable; people with an internal locus of control believe that what happens to them is mostly a matter of their own efforts, whereas those with an external locus of control believe that their fate is sealed by powerful forces beyond their control.

longitudinal analysis An experimental method of studying the same subjects for long time periods with repeated obsevations.

longitudinal fissure See *fissures*.

long-term memory Memory for events from the relatively distant past; contrasted with short-term memory.

long-term store According to the three-store model of memory, the relatively permanent component of the system that is presumed to have a very large capacity for holding information. See also *sensory store, short-term store*.

loudness The psychological attribute of sounds corresponding to their intensity and primarily related to the amplitude of soundwaves.

low-ball technique A compliance technique, often used to manipulate customers, in which an initial commitment overcomes any resistance to the subsequently higher costs.

lucid dreaming The experience of dreaming and being fully aware that you are dreaming.

M

magnitude estimation A procedure that involves playing tones of varying intensity levels and asking listeners to supply a number indicating how loud each sounds, relative to a reference number.

mainstreaming The educational practice of placing handicapped children in regular rather than special classes.

mania An affective disorder characterized by intense euphoria or sense of well-being. See also *depression*.

manic disorder Intense euphoria or sense of well-being, accompanied by unwarranted optimism, and generosity, reckless driving, or foolish business investments, loud, rapid, speech, and no recognition of the intrusive, aggressive, and demanding nature of one's behavior. Manic episodes generally recur or are followed by a depressive mood swing.

mapping The relation between two things; the way a machine operates should rely on natural mappings based on past experiences.

marital therapy A form of psychotherapy in which problems are addressed to both marital partners, sometimes together, sometimes alone.

Maslow's hierarchy of motives The hypothesis that physiological needs must be satisfied first, then safety and security needs, then belongingness and love needs, then esteem needs. Only after all these needs are satisfied can an individual realize one's full potential and fulfill self-actualization needs.

Maslow's hiearchy of needs Physiological needs must be satisfied prior to the need for safety, which in turn must be satisified before love needs, then esteem; when all these needs are satisfied the final level, self-actualization, can be reached.

math anxiety The fear and nervousness that accompanies math performance and testing.

McCollough effect A visual illusion caused by the sensitivity of cortical feature detectors to combinations of color and orientation.

McNaughten rule A standard of legal responsiblity for actions; an accused is judged to be sane or insane on the basis of whether he or she was capable of knowing that an act was wrong at the time it was being committed.

mean The most commonly used measure of central tendency of a frequency distribution, it is the arithmetic average of all scores in the distribution.

measures of central tendency In descriptive statistics, a value used to indicate the midpoint of the frequency of scores in a distribution. See also *mean, median, mode*.

measures of dispersion In descriptive statistics, a measure of how scores in a distribution spread away from a center point. See also *range, standard deviation*.

mechanics of intelligence Aspect of intelligence referring to the speed and accuracy of processing information; may be fully developed in adolescence and may decline during adulthood.

median A measure of central tendency equal to a score that divides a distribution into two equal parts, with half the scores being larger than the median and half smaller.

medulla The portion of the brain in the lower rear section adjacent to the spinal cord that controls some vital functions, such as breathing.

memory codes Forms of representation in memory, e.g., imaginal and verbal codes.

memory trace The inferred change in the nervous system that persists between the time something is learned and the time it is retrieved.

menarche The first menstrual period.

menopause The point at which women cease to undergo menstrual periods.

mental age (MA) An individual's intellectual level of performance relative to others as opposed to his or her chronological age.

mental imagery Pictures in the "mind's eye" thought by some psychologists to be similar to perceptions.

mental retardation An impairment in thinking and social skills that can range from slightly below average to profoundly handicapped. The degree of retardation is usually judged on the basis of test scores and behavior.

mental set The tendency to view new problems in the same fashion as previous problems.

mentally retarded Individuals whose IQ scores are more than two standard deviations below the average of 100.

mere exposure effect The tendency to lilke a person or an object more with increased exposure.

metacognition Awareness of one's own knowledge and mental abilities.

midbrain The upper portion of the brain stem which is the conduit for all neural information passing between the brain and the spinal cord.

middle ear The portion of the ear extending from the tympanic membrane to the cochlea and containing the ossicles.

Minnesota Multiphasic Personality Inventory (MMPI) A multitrait personality test originally created in 1942 to diagnose mental illness and updated in 1987 to reflect changes in mental health.

misattribution therapy Treatment that convinces a patient to attribute symptoms to something more acceptable, but not the true cause of the problem.

mnemonic devices Any technique or strategy used to improve memory.

mode A measure of central tendency equivalent to the most frequently occurring score (or class of scores) in a frequency distribution.

model The person being observed in observational learning.

modeling therapy Learning by observing people who are displaying appropriate and adaptive behavior; effectively used to eliminate unwanted behaviors and to build new behavior competencies.

monoamine oxidase (MAO) inhibitors A type of antidepressant medication believed to work by increasing the amounts of the neurotransmitters norepinephrine and serotonin in the brain; often used with patients who fail to respond to tricyclics.

monocular cues In vision, the factors that can be used by only one eye to allow judgment of distance. See also *interposition, linear perspective, motion parallax.*

monozygotic twins (MZ) Twins developed from the division of a single fertilized egg. Also called identical twins. See also *dizygotic twins.*

mood disorders Disabling disturbances of moods and feelings.

moral reasoning The ability to distinguish between right and wrong.

morpheme The smallest unit of speech sound that has meaning in a given language; for example, prefixes, suffixes, and single syllable words.

motion parallax In perception, a depth cue in which the images of nearby objects sweep across the field of vision faster than objects at a distance.

motivation A theoretical construct that is used to explain initiation, direction, vigor, and persistence of behavior.

motor codes The representation that is assumed to support memory for physical (motor) activities.

motor neuron Nerve cell that carries signals from the brain and spinal cord to the muscles, organs, and glands of the body.

Müller-Lyer illusion A spatial distortion in which two parallel lines of equal length appear to be unequal because of pairs of angular lines drawn at the ends of the parallel lines.

multiple personality disorder A dissociative disorder in which an individual expresses two or more distinct personalities that have varying degrees of awareness of each other. See also *amnesia, dissociative disorder, fugue.*

multi-sensory display A type of display that alternates between sensory modalities (i.e. auditory and visual).

myelin sheath A segmented tube of glial cells that insulates many axons.

myopia A condition commonly referred to as nearsightedness. It results when the image of the object being viewed in focused in front of the retina. See also *hyperopia.*

N

nativism (1) As a philosophy, the position that humans are born with some innate knowledge. (2) As a theory of perception, the view that humans are born with the ability to perceive stimuli, and that learning plays a relatively small rose in perceptual development. See also *empiricism.*

naturalistic observation The viewing and recording of events as they occur in nature. It is used frequently for ethological studies of animals.

nature versus nurture A philosophical controversy about the source of knowledge and the causes of behavior. The "nature" position argues that people are born with some inherited knowledge that guides behavior. The "nurture" position argues that knowledge is acquired and behavior is shaped by experiences in the world. See also *empiricism nativism.*

need for achievement One of twenty basic human motives suggested by Henry Murray; in brief, the diesre to do things as well as possible, better than they have been done before.

negative affect The extent to which we are upset or unpleasantly aroused.

negative reinforcement Reinforcement produced by offset of an event.

negative reinforcer An event that increases the likelihood of the preceding behavior when it is removed, e.g., removal of shock.

negative schizophrenia A type of schizophrenia characterized by blunted emotional responses, apathy, poverty of speech and attentional impairment.

nervous system The entire collection of neurons in the body.

neuroleptics A family of drugs, called phenothiazines, used to stabilize agitated and overactive patients, and to eliminate hallucinations and paranoid symptoms among schizophrenics.

neuron A nerve cell, usually consisiting of a cell body, axon, and dendrites.

neurosis Excessive use of defense mechanisms, which is an indication that a person is experiencing internal conflict, and interferes with normal functioning.

neurotransmitter A chemical released by a neuron when an axon fires to transmit a signal from one neuron to the next. Also known as transmitter substance.

nodes of Ranvier The bare portions between segments of myelin sheath on the axons of neurons.

noise The constant background of randomly varying signals in the sensory system caused by firing nerve cells.

nonconscious Unable to be brought to consciousness, such as the processes occurring in the retina during visual perception.

nonreactive (unobtrusive) techniques A technique researchers use to try to minimize any effects their presence may have on the observed behavior.

normal curve See *normal distribution.*

normal distribution A symmetrical, bell-shaped frequency distribution that roughly describes many events in nature. The greatest number of scores fall in the middle of the curve, with fewer found at the extremes on each end.

null hypothesis In statistics, the hypothesis that any difference observed among treatment conditions is merely a chance fluctuation and that the true mean difference between conditions is zero.

O

obedience In social psychology, behaving in accord with the requests or demands of an authority figure.

obesity Having an abnormal proportion of body fat.

object permanence The understanding that objects continue to exist even when they are no longer observed, usually acquired by six months of age in humans.

observational learning Learning that results from watching the behavior of others and seeing the consequences of the behavior for them. Sometimes called vicarious learning.

obsessions Recurring thoughts that are troublesome and persist uncontrollably, intruding into consciousness despite attempts to avoid them.

obsessive-compulsive disorder An anxiety disorder characterized by anxiety or apprehension, persistent unwanted thoughts, and/or the compulsion to repeat ritualistic acts such as washing hands. See also *anxiety disorder, generalized anxiety disorder, panic disorder, phobias.*

occipital lobe One of the four natural sections of the cerebral hemisphere, it is the rear portion containing the vision centers. See also *frontal, parietal,* and *temporal lobes.*

Oedipus complex In Freudian theory, a young boy's intimate attachment to his mother and jealousy of his father, occurring during the phallic stage. See also *Electra complex, phallic stage.*

olfactory bulb Receives messages from the receptors and is located in the lower front of the brain.

operant A behavior that results in, or is followed by, a particular effect on the environment. The behavior is defined by its effect, not by its form.

operant conditioning A type of conditioning in which reinforcement is contingent upon the subject's providing a particular response; also called *instrumental conditioning.*

operant conditioning chamber A box with a device (such as a small lever on the wall) that an animal can operate in order to receive reinforcement. It is sometimes called a *Skinner box.*

operant response A response resulting in or followed by a particular effect on the environment.

opponent-process theory (1) In perception, a theory that explains color vision by postulating three types of color cells: white-black, yellow-blue, and green-red. The perception of color is the result of the combined action of these pairs. See also *trichromatic theory.* (2) In motivation, a theory that any affective reaction, whether pleasant or unpleasant, automatically produces the opposite reaction.

optic nerve The bundle of nerve fibers that relays information from the ganglion cells of the retina to the lateral geniculate nucleus of the thalamus.

oral stage The first of Freud's psychosexual stages of development, through the first year of life, during which the mouth is the source of sensual pleasure. See also *anal, latency, genital,* and *phallic stages.*

organic amnesia A loss of memory due to specific damage to the brain.

organizational psychology See *industrial/organizational psychology.*

osmometric thirst A temporary cellular fluid imbalance in which sodium is prevented from leaving the cells so water leaves to maintain the sodium-water balance outside the cell; the resulting dehydration causes thirst.

ossicles The set of three tiny interconnecting bones (malleus, incus, and stapes) that connect the tympanic membrane (eardrum) to the cochlea.

outer ear The portion of the ear containing the pinna (the flap of skin protruding from both sides of the head) and the auditory canal.

own-race bias Face recognition tends to be more accurate for faces of an individual's own race than for faces of other races.

oval window A flexible membrane on the outer surface of the cochlea (of the ear) to which the stapes is attached.

P

palliation A means of coping with stress by dealing wtih its symptoms rather than its source. Palliative techniques include drugs, muscle relaxation, or intrapsychic methods.

pandemonium An early and somewhat fanciful model of bottom-up pattern recognition in which a hierarchy of "demons" detects features and transform them into perceptions.

panic disorder An anxiety disorder characterized by intense fear or terror. Attacks usually last minutes but long after they have passed apprehension persists. Unlike phobias, panic attacks are typically not associated with particular stimuli. See also *generalized anxiety disorder, obsessive-compulsive disorder, phobias.*

paranoid personality disorder A cluster one disorder in DSM-IV, characterized by extreme suspicion, mistrust, limited emotional reactivity, and unusual behavior.

paranoid schizophrenia A schizophrenic disorder characterized by delusions of persecution or grand importance, with hallucinations and a loss of contact with reality. See also *schizophrenia, catatonic schizophrenics.*

parapsychology A field devoted to the study of people who seem to possess extraordinary powers through a "sixth sense."

parasympathetic nervous system The division of the autonomic nervous system that serves vegetative functions and conseves energies. Associated reactions include increased salivation and digestive processes, and decreased heart rate and blood pressure.

parietal lobe One of the four sections of the cerebral hemisphere, the middle region of the top of the skull, which contains somesthetic centers. See also *frontal, occipital,* and *temporal lobes.*

partial reinforcement Any schedule of reinforcement where fewer than 100 percent of the responses are rewarded. Also called intermittent reinforcement.

partial reinforcement extinction effect The result that almost any schedule of intermittent or partial reinforcement will produce greater resistance to extinction than continuous reinforcement.

passive-aggressive personality disorder A cluster three disorder in DSM-IV that involves resisting the demands of others in an indirect rather than direct manner.

pattern recognition The cognitive and perceptual processes by which people are able to perceive groups of features as unified patterns. See also *bottom-up theories, top-down approach.*

Pavlovian conditioning See *classical conditioning.*

perception The process of interpreting and understanding sensory information.

perceptual constancy The fact that objects are normally perceived as remaining constant in size and shape, despite the fact that the retinal images of the objects may be constantly changing as the perceiver or objects move.

perceptual illusions Misleading images of the relationships among stimuli, that do not conform to physical reality.

perceptual organization The processes by which elementary sensations are organized into perceived objects; thus three lines joined together end-to-end are perceived as a triangle, not simply as three lines.

peripheral nervous system All of the nervous system outside the brain and spinal cord.

peripheral processing An individual's superficial appraisal of an argument's logic.

permissive parents Parents who are responsive to their children and accept and affirm their children's opinions. They are undemanding, do not push their children to adhere to other people's standards, have inconsistent and lax discipline, and avoid punishment and tend to reason with children instead.

person-centered therapy A form of psychotherapy proposed by Carl Rogers which views human nature as fundamentally good and every individual as capable of adjustment and self-realization. The client must identify and solve problems; the therapist provides a supportive environment. See also *psychotherapy.*

person perception The processes by which individuals perceive others' behavior. Social psychologists study person perception to explain the impressions we form of others.

person variables Trait-like individual differences in cognition that filter or distort the impact of experiences; the basis of Mischel's cognitive social learning theory.

personal abnormality Mental disorders in terms of an individual's subjective feelings.

personal constructs Sets of opposed characteristics which we use to perceive ourselves and others.

personality The pattern of characteristic thoughts, feelings, and behaviors that distinguishes one person from another and that persists over time and situations.

personality disorders enduring, inflexible, and maladaptive personality traits that characterize individuals for much of their lives and interfere with relationships with others.

persuasion The deliberate attempt to change someone's opinion or attitude.

phallic stage Freud's third psychosexual stage of development, roughly from the third to fifth year, during which the genitals are the source of sensual pleasure. Oedipal and Electra complexes occur during this stage. See also *anal, genital, latency, and oral stages.*

phenomenology A branch of psychology and philosophy that emphasizes the importance of subjective experience.

phenotype Characteristics or traits of the individual that are visible and measurable (such as eye color).

pheromones Scents that attract potential mates and control mate selection.

phobia An anxiety disorder characterized by an intense fear of a specific object or situation. The individual may realize that the fear is irrational but be unable to control it; he or she thus avoids the object or situation. See also *other forms of disorders: anxiety, generalized anxiety, obsessive-compulsive, panic.*

phoneme The smallest unit of sound in a language.

phonological rules Procedures for combining sounds into words appropriate to a given language.

pinna The projecting flap of skin of the outer ear located on both sides of the head.

pitch The qualitative dimension of hearing that corresponds to the frequency of sound waves comprising the stimulus.

placebo effect The finding that expectation of treatment produces a benefit (e.g., relief of pain), even when no active substance is provided in the treatment.

placenta Connecting tissue between mother and her prenatal organism that is rich in blood vessels and allows exchange of maternal nutrients and discharge of fetal wastes.

place theory In hearing, a theory that human perception of pitch depends on the fact that different frequency sound waves produce maximal vibrations at various locations along the basilar membrane. The location of the maximal vibration is thus used to code the pitch of the sound wave. See also *frequency theory.*

plasticity The ability of the brain to change its organization and function.

pleasure principle According to Freud, the motive to seek immediate pleasure and gratification which governs the id. See also *id.*

pons A swelling at the base of the brain that contains the neural connections between the cerebrum and the cerebellum.

population All of the members of a defined group from which a small sample may be drawn and about which an investigator wishes to draw conclusions.

positive affect The extent to which we show a zest for life.

positive illusions Perceptions of the world and our place in it that are more benign than warranted by an objective analysis.

positive reinforcer An event (reward) whose onset increases the likelihood of the preceding behavior when it is presented (e.g., food for a hungry organism).

positive reinforcement Reinforcement produced by onset of an event.

positive schizophrenia A type of schizophrenia characterized by symptoms such as delusions and hallucinations with a generally acute onset, no apparent underlying cognitive or structural brain abnormalities, and good response to antipsychotic drugs.

positron emission tomography (PET) A neurological technique in which the subject is given a radioactively labeled compound so that researchers may study brain activity.

postformal thought A fifth stage of reasoning in which adults can reason about the relative nature of knowledge and opposing points of view.

pragmatics of intelligence Aspect of intelligence referring to the accumulation of knowledge and the growth of wisdom; may increase indefinitely with age and experience.

preconscious The mental state that refers to ideas or memories an individual is currently unaware of but, which can be brought to consciousness easily.

predictions Forecasts derived from theories and hypotheses and then tested against observed research data.

predictive validity A measure of a test's relation to a criterion of behavior in the future; for example, the degree to which I.Q. scores predict college grades.

prefrontal lobotomy A form of psychosurgery in which the nerve fibers connecting the hypothalamus with the prefrontal lobes are severed to reduce the effects of emotions on intellectual processes. The procedure is not used as widely as in earlier years.

prejudice A preconceived feeling or opinion of worth on the basis of little or no evidence. The word is often used in the context of attitudes of an unreasonable or hostile nature. See also *stereotype.*

preoperational period In Piaget's theory, the period from approximately two to seven years when children use few cognitive strategies or rules for reasoning and are easily fooled by appearances.

presbyopia A visual defect common in elderly people, it is a progressive hardening of the lens which makes the eye less able to change its shape (or accommodate) to bring objects close at hand into focus.

primacy effect (1) In impression formation, the fact that attributes noted early are given greater weight than attributes noted at a later time. (2) In memory, the tendency for initial items on a list to be recalled better than other items on the list. See also *recency effect.*

primary aging General deterioration of the body's cells.

primary colors The three colors—red, green, and blue—which, when combined in the correct proportions, produce any of the colors of the spectrum.

primary memory Holds for a very short time the events and stimuli that we have recently experienced.

primary motor areas The areas of the brain that send messages to control the muscles.

primary (unconditioned) reinforcer An event that increases the strength of preceding responses even if the event has never been experienced before.

primary services Also called primary prevention, these are directed toward eliminating the causes of patients' problems by such means as identifying potential social stressors and eliminating them or educating people to handle them, in order to prevent the occurrence of future behavior problems.

primary process A style of thinking peculiar to the id, characterized by illogical, florid images.

primary sensory areas Areas of the cortex where sensory stimuli are first processed, somatosensory for sensations from the body, visual for sensations from the eyes, and auditory for sensations from the ears.

primary sex characteristics Physical attributes that relate directly to reproductive capacity, e.g. the male's penis and scrotum.

priming In memory, the use of related words to speed access of the meaning of a target word; also, the facilitation in performing a cognitive task when it has been accomplished previously.

proactive interference The interference of earlier learning with the learning and recall of new material. See also *retroactive interference*.

probability theory A mathematical theory of the likelihood that random events will occur.

problem-solving Behavior directed toward achieving a goal.

problem solving therapy A cognitive therapy that attempts to improve the patient's problem solving and decision making skills.

procedural memory Remembrance that includes motor skills; thought to represent a fundamentally different type of memory from that used to remember other sorts of information.

progesterone One of the male "sex hormones".

prototype A representative sample of a class of things.

proximal stimuli The patterns of physical energy that strike the receptor organs and cause them to fire neural impulses. See also *distal stimuli*.

psychiatric nurse A registered nurse with special training for work with patients in mental hospitals.

psychiatrist A medical doctor who specializes in the treatment of psychotherapy. Psychiatrists take medical as well as therapeutic responsibility for their patients; they are the only therapists who can prescribe psychoactive drugs, shock treatment, or other biological intervention methods.

psychoanalysis A Freudian approach to therapy emphasizing free association, dream interpretation, and transference.

psychoanalytic theory Freud's theory proposing that mental disorders were psychological in origin and could be traced to childhood psychosexual conflicts.

psycholinguistics The study of how people understand and use language.

psychological perspective The belief that abnormal behavior is caused by psychological factors of one or another sort.

psychological tests Paper-and-pencil tests that measure and describe people's mental aptitudes, personality characteristics, and interests.

psychology The scientific study of the mind and behavior.

psychometric approach The development of objective measures or tests of psychological qualities, such as intelligence, aptitudes, or personality.

psychophysical scaling The process of measuring the relationship between the physical intensity of a stimulus and its perceived intensity.

psychophysics The branch of psychology concerned with how changes in physical stimuli are translated into psychological experience.

psychosexual stage In Freud's theory of personality structure, a period in which each sexually charged zone of the body reflects a different issue of concern to a developing child.

psychosis A serious psychological disorder, specifically an inability, or even a failure, to relate properly to reality.

psychosocial abnormality Any deviation from a societal standard or norm.

psychosocial development An individual's thoughts and feelings about the relationship between self and others.

psychosocial stages In Erikson's developmental theory, eight life cycle periods in which specific interpersonal problems are resolved to determine the type of person one becomes.

psychosurgery The most drastic form of biological intervention which involves surgery to destroy or remove brain tissue to change behavior.

psychotherapy Treatment of mental or emotional disorders through specialized techniques, all of which involve close communication between the patient and a therapist trained in psychological problems.

puberty For humans, a time of physiological and psychological change from about age ten to fifteen when sexual characteristics and reproductive systems mature.

pupil The opening in the iris through which light passes as it enters the eye.

punishment Application of aversive consequences contingent upon a behavior.

R

random assignment The assignment of research participants to a control or an experimental group according to a procedure in which participants have an equal chance of being appointed to either group; eliminates confounded variables.

random sample See *sample*.

range A statistic indicating the variability of a distribution that is computed by subtracting the lowest score from the highest score; the resulting difference is the range of the distribution.

rational-emotive therapy (RET) A form of psychotherapy based on the work of Albert Ellis in which the therapist takes an active role by attempting to confront the client about his or her inappropriate cognitions regarding self-concept and relations with others. See also *psychotherapy*.

rational restructuring Exploring problematic attitudes and thoughts, focusing on the way this self-talk influences behavior, and learning more adaptive self-statements to apply in real situations.

ratio schedule A program of reinforcement in which a certain number of repsonses are necessary in order to produce the reward. See also *fixed* and *variable ratio schedules*.

reactive observations When a researcher's presence affects the behavior being observed, the observation is partly a reaction to the observer.

realistic job preview A procedure that presents a "balanced" view of the organization—one that highlights problems and difficulties as well as dispelling commonly held negative impressions.

reality principle In Freud's theory, the tendency to behave in such a way as to conform to the demands of reality. This principle governs the ego.

recency effect In memory experiments, the tendency for subjects to recall the items at the end of a list more readily than those in the middle. See also *primacy effect*.

recessive gene A gene, or unit of heredity, that does not produce an observable effect unless it is paired with another recessive gene of the same type.

reciprocal inhibition The idea that once aroused, any motive can inhibit or interfere with other motives.

recoding The process of transforming information into a form other than its original one, e.g., forming a mental image of a collie when the letters D-O-G are presented for study.

recognition-by-components Biederman's theory proposing that people recognize complex objects by decomposing them into their basic parts.

reductionism An approach to explaining psychological phenomena in which all of the factors—including cognitive and social ones—are explained in terms of their biological underpinnings.

reflex an automatic response to a stimulus.

refractory period Time period following an action potential when a neuron does not produce an action potential to a stimulus that would normally produce one.

reinforcement An event that increases the likelihood of behavior that precedes it. Also called reinforcer.

rejecting-neglecting parents Parents who are unresponsive and undemanding, indifferent to their children, and spend little time with them.

relational processing Finding relations between the facts and ideas one reads about.

relative validity of the CS The percentage of UCSs that occur in the presence of a CS; indicates how reliably the CS predicts the UCS.

reliability The stability of test scores after the repetition of the test on the same group.

reminiscence The recovery of information on a later test that could not be recalled on an earlier one.

REM rebound A sleep phenomenon exhibited by people who are deprived of REM sleep over a period of several nights. When finally allowed to sleep undisturbed, these people spend a greater proportion of their sleep time in REM sleep than nondeprived sleepers.

REM sleep A stage of sleep characterized by rapid eye movements (REMs) and an EEG pattern somewhat similar to that of a waking state. It usually coincides with periods of dreaming.

resistance In psychoanalytic therapy, an unwillingness or reluctance on the part of a client to disclose material fully and accurately to the therapist; lack of cooperation.

resistance to extinction The length of time a response continues in the face of extinction

response deprivation theory The notion that if an organism is deprived of making its normal baseline rate of some response (responsel), it will increase any response that allows it to make responsel.

response generalization Voluntarily performing one behavior in the interest of personal safety or health may increase the probability that the individual will perform other similar behaviors.

resting potential The electrical state of a neuron that is at rest.

reticular activating system A network of cells in the center of the brain stem involved in activation or arousal of other parts of the brain. See also *reticular formation*.

reticular formation A network of cells in the center of the brain stem that is involved in the activation or arousal of other parts of the brain (also knows as reticular activating system).

retina The membrane at the back of the eye containing the photoreceptors (rods and cones) that images are focused on.

retrieval The process of bringing stored information into consciousness.

retroactive interference The effect of subsequent learning on the recall of information learned earlier. See also *proactive interference*.

retrograde amnesia See *amnesia*.

reversibility A term used by Piaget to refer to actions that can be performed in two ways with opposite effects.

revised frustration-aggression bypothesis Leonard Berkowitz's proposal that frustration leads to anger, not aggression. See also *frustration-aggression hypothesis*.

risky-shift effect The tendency for individuals to advocate greater risk-taking when they are part of a group than when they are deciding on a course of action individually.

rods Photoreceptors located outside the fovea of the eye that function primarily under low levels of illumination. They produce only monochromatic (black and white) vision.

Role Construct Repertory Test (Rep Test) A model that discovers personal constructs by studying the adjectives used to describe the important individuals in a subject's life.

Rorschach inkblots A projective personality technique developed by Herman Rorschach which uses complex, bilaterally symmetrical blots of ink on ten cards and scores subjects' responses on a variety of measures.

S

sample A selection of items from a total set known as the population. If selection is random, an unbiased sample results; if selection is based on some criteria, the sample may be biased and unrepresentative of the population.

saturation The apparent purity of a color. The more saturated a color is, the more is appears as a hue that is pure and free of white (e.g., pink is less saturated than red).

scattergram A diagram that plots two variables against each other in order to show their relationship (or lack of relationship).

schema A hypothetical memory structure that organizes and preseves information relevant to some event or concept.

schizophrenia The group of severe disorders characterized by generalized withdrawal, apathy, thought disorder, emotional disturbance, delusions, and hallucinations. There are several types of schizophrenia. See also *catatonic schizophrenia, paranoid schizophrenia*.

school psychology Speciality in learning and education in which students are classified, counseling and guidance are provided, and learning problems are evaluated.

secondary aging Physical changes related to primary aging. Diseases such as emphysema are secondary effects of the general deterioration of the body's respiration system.

secondary memory Memory for the past that must be retrieved with effort.

secondary services Also called secondary prevention, these focus on providing immediate treatment of existing psychological problems in a wider range of situations than traditional treatment programs, and are based on the assumption that people can best be helped right at the time when there is an emergency in their lives.

secondary sex characteristics Physical attributes that accompany primary sex characteristics but may not be related to sexual reproduction, e.g., the growth of pubic hair during puberty.

securely attached infants Infants who use their caregiver as a base for exploring a new room but often return to the caregiver for comfort.

selective attention The ability to choose one of many stimuli attracting the senses for further perception and analysis.

selective breeding The choices of animals for mating on the basis of some observable characteristics; usually done through several generations.

self-actualization Abraham Maslow's term for an individual's striving to realize his or her greatest potential, including maximizing feelings of love and acceptance of the actual-self.

self-concept The composite of ideas, feelings, and attitudes that people have about themselves.

self-discrepancy theory A humanistic approach distinguishing between different types of ideals; the discrepancy between internal and external self-guides leads to emotional distress.

self-efficacy A person's judgment of how well he or she can execute the actions necessary to deal with a situation.

self-esteem One's overall judgment of one's value as a person.

self-handicapping Providing oneself with a true handicap, or merely claiming a handicap, in order to shoulder less blame for failure and more credit for success.

self-help groups An offshoot of encounter groups often organized by patients or individuals who have had the problem and overcome it, such as Alcoholics Anonymous.

self-perception How we see ourselves, and the inferences we make about our personality from observing our own behavior.

self-perception theory A theory that refers to the ways in which we see and evaluate ourselves.

self-regulation The process of setting goals for yourself and then rewarding yourself for achieving those goals.

semantic features Characteristics that define words in order to avoid over- and underextending their meanings.

semantic memory Recall of general knowledge that does not depend on retrieving the time and place in which the information was learned. See also *episodic memory*.

semantic priming The tendency to respond more quickly to a second word if it is preceded by a related word or a neutral stimulus.

semantics The principles by which meaning is expressed through language.

sensation The reception of stimulation from the environment involving the transduction of environmental or internal events into neural impulses.

sensitive periods Time periods in which development proceeds rapidly with increased susceptibility to external factors.

sensorimotor stage In Piaget's theory, the first two years of life during which infants learn to coordinate actions and perceptions. The period culminates in the attainment of symbolic representation.

sensorimotor deafness Nerve deafness caused when the hair cells of the cochlea are absent or not functional.

sensory neuron Nerve cell that receives information from receptor cells about the environment and conveys this information to other neurons. (pp. 000, 000)

sensory stores The portion of the memory system that maintains representations of sensory information for very brief intervals. See also *long-term store, short-term store*.

separation anxiety A common fear infants have of being apart from their mothers or others to whom they are strongly attached. See *stranger anxiety*.

septum A region in the midline area of the brain that seems to inhibit thirst, and, in some species, aggressive behavior.

sequential analysis A research design that overcomes the cohort effect by combining features of both longitudinal and cross-sectional designs.

sequential lineup Lineup members or photographs of lineup members are presented one at a time, and the witness must decide whether or not each individual is the perpetrator. They use an absolute judgment strategy.

serial position curve The curve that results from plotting the accuracy of retention as a function of the position of the items in a studied list.

set point A hypothetical point around which organisms maintain their body weight.

sex typing The process by which children learn to identify themselves as boys or girls, and adapt socially appropriate male or female behaviors.

sexuality The sum total of erotic and life-enhancing activities, including the narrower domain of sexual behavior.

shaping by successive approximations A procedure by which the response requirements for giving a reinforcement are gradually increased to produce the desired response.

short-term memory Memory for recent events that can be held in mind at one time.

short-term store A limited capacity component of the memory system that retains information for a relatively short period of time. See also *long-term store, sensory store*.

shuttle box An apparatus used in the study of avoidance learning.

signal detection theory A theory of the sensory and decision processes which asserts that there are no fixed absolute thresholds; rather, a person decides about the presence of a sensory signal against a background of "noise" in the nervous system.

sign stimulus An ethological term for the particular aspect of a stimulus that releases a fixed action pattern. See also *fixed action pattern*.

simultaneous conditioning A procedure in classical conditioning where the conditioned stimulus and the unconditioned stimulus begin and end together.

simultaneous contrast In visual perception, the fact that the color or brightness of an object is affect by, and in turn affects, any other object near or surrounding the object.

simultaneous lineup Lineup members are all presented at the same time. Here witnesses tend to judge the relative similarity of the lineup members to their memory of the perpetrator in order to make an identification. They use a relative judgment strategy.

situational cause Attributing behavior or results to the environment, rather than to the individual. See also *dispositional cause*.

situationism In the social learning approach to personality, the belief that behavior is a reflection of immediate situational pressures and not a reflection of traits.

Sixteen Personality Factor Questionnaire (16PF) A paper-and-pencil personality inventory developed by Raymond B. Cattell to measure sixteen dimensions of normal personality.

Skinner box See *operant conditioning chamber*.

skin senses The four types of sensation—pressure, pain, cold, warmth—that are typically referred to as touch.

social cognition Knowledge and thoughts about other people's points of view, thoughts, feelings, and intentions.

social comparison theory A theory outlining the conditons under which we compare ourselves with others.

social facilitation effect The energizing effect of other people on the motivation and behavior of an individual.

social learning theory A theoretical approach that is midway between behavior theories such as Skinner's and cognitive approaches. It emphasizes particular ways of learning, such as observing others in a social context.

social loafing An individual's tendency to contribute less to a group effort than when working on the same task alone.

social milieu therapy Treatment based on learning principles that aims to alter behavior in the setting in which it occurs. See also *behavior therapy, psychotherapy*.

social perspective The belief that abnormality is a direct function of society's criteria and definitions for appropriate behavior; abnormality is social, not biological or psychological.

social psychology The branch of psychology concerned with the study of the effects of social factors on individual behavior, as well as behavior in groups.

social role theory A model of social behavior proposing that everyone acts according to scripts that are appropriate to the situations in which they find themselves.

social worker A social service professional with a master's degree and training in treatment procedures with emphasis on the family and community.

sociobiology The systematic study of the biological basis of all social behavior.

somatic nervous system Part of the peripheral nervous system; the efferent fibers activate skeletal muscles; afferent fibers come from the major receptor organs (eyes, ears, etc.).

somatic (biological) therapies Therapies based on biochemical and physiological methods of treatment, such as drug and shock therapy.

somatoform disorder A pattern of behavior characterized by complaints of physical symptoms in the absence of any real illness. Conversion disorder is a classical example.

spatial illusions Systematic errors in the perception of objects in space, usually caused by central perceptual processes.

speech acts Several forms of communication that are goal directed and intended to influence a listener.

special education Classrooms and curricula designed to meet the particular needs of handicapped populations.

spinal cord A narrow tube that extends the length of the back, from the hips to the base of the skull, where it joins the brain.

split-brain patient One who has had the corpus callosum surgically severed, thus isolating the functions of the two cerebral hemispheres.

spontaneous recovery The return of an extinguished response following a rest period, when an animal is replaced in the original circumstances of conditioning.

spreading activation In memory, the theory that when a concept is activated in semantic memory by a word (e.g., *car*), the energy or activation travels to related concepts (*truck* or *ambulance*) and partially arouses them.

S-R approach The theory that the basic components of learning are stimulus (S) and response (R) bonds.

stability Regularity of behavior across time or occasions, within the same situation.

stability of personality Exhibiting the same personality traits every time the same situation occurs.

stage theories Theories of development concerned with relatively abrupt changes in behavior across the life span.

standard deviation A measure of the dispersion or variablity of a distribution. It is equivalent to the square root of the variance.

standardization sample In psychometric testing, the group that forms the basis for comparison of relative performance. It must accurately represent the entire population.

Stanford-Binet test A widely used, standardized intelligence test.

statistical abnormality Any substantial deviation from the average or typical behavior of the group to which an individual belongs.

statistical significance The reliability of measures based on samples as a statement about population characteristics. If a difference between groups of scores is quite unlikely to have occurred by chance it is said to be statistically significant.

stereochemical theory of odors A theory that explains sense of smell by postulating that the receptors in the nose are configured to match the variety of shapes of the molecules in the air. When the shape of a molecule matches the shape of a receptor (the way a key matches a lock), the receptor fires a neural impulse.

stereotype An overgeneralized or commonly held belief or attitude about an identifiable group.

stigma A mark of "undesired differentness" that is imposed by the socially dominant in-group on various out-groups who violate the in-group's ideals.

stimulus control The occurrence of behavior in the presence of only certain stimuli and not in the presence of other stimulii.

stimulus generalization The principle that when a subject has been conditioned to make a response to a stimulus other similar stimuli will evoke the same response, though to a lesser degree than the original stimulus would have.

stimulus-response approach See *S-R approach*.

storage The second of three stages in the memory process, it is responsible for the retention of information over a period of time. See also *acquisition, retrieval*.

stranger anxiety A common fear infants have of unfamiliar people. It may appear at the end of the first year and disappear sometime around the second birthday.

stratified random sampling The selection of subjects by chance within levels of different attributes.

stress The collection of physical and physiological reactions an organism forms to a perceived threat to its well-being.

stress reaction An innate response triggered by a wide variety of stressors consisting of autonomic system arousal and release of various stress-related hormones.

stimulants Drugs that generally increase activity in the central nervous system.

strong situation A situation that powerfully constrains our behavior, producing uniformity of behavior.

structured interview Interviews providing a relatively prescribed series of questions.

structuralism A school of psychology which held that the primary task of psychologiests was the analysis of the structure of conscious experience through analytic introspection.

subjective contours The phenomenon of an outline or contour appearing in a visual display when no such thing is physically present.

subjective organization In memory, a recoding process in which people impose order on randomly presented events so they can remember them better.

subject variable A factor such as age, sex, race, or personality type that cannot be manipulated by an experimenter and which is examined for its effect on the dependent variable.

subliminal perception The effect of stimuli below the threshold (or limen) of awareness that are not perceived consciously but may influence behavior.

substance use disorders Excessive use of any mood- or mind-altering drug or chemical to the point where a user is a danger to himself, herself, or others.

superego In Freud's theory of personality, a two-part structure: the harsh *conscience* that attempts to forbid aggressive and sexual gratification; and the *ego-ideal* that holds the individual to a standard of future devleopment. See also *ego, id*.

surface structure The actual words and their organization in a sentence.

survey The sampling of opinions of a small proportion of the population in order to gather information representative of the population as a whole.

sympathetic nervous system The division of the autonomic nervous system that is active in emotion and arousal. Associated reactions include increased heart rate and blood pressure. See also *parasympathetic nervous system*.

synapse The place where the boutons of one neuron adjoin the dendrites of another neuron.

synaptic cleft The space that separates the presynaptic and postsynaptic membranes of two neurons.

synaptic transmission The sending of information from one neuron to another.

synaptic vesicles Small, membrane-enclosed spherical bodies located in the bouton.

syntax The ways in which words are connected to form phrases and sentences.

systematic desensitization therapy Conditioning procedure in which a patient is presented a sequence of greater and greater anxiety-producing situations, and learns to relax in the presence of each.

T

tarasoff decision An American legal decision that states that a therapist must inform potential victims of their patients that they are in danger, even if the therapist has to violate the patient's confidentiality and the first in a series of cases establishing therapists' responsibility to protect others from their patients.

tardive dyskinesia A side effect of antipsychotic medication involving a disturbance of muscle control.

taste-aversion learning A procedure for studying classical conditioning in which animals are given a flavored solution (CS) to drink and are then made ill by drugs or radiation (UCS), resulting in sickness (UCR) and thus aversion for the taste.

telegraphic speech Two- and three-word sentences without prepositions, articles, and parts of verb phrases and that use order and stress to convey meaning.

temperament Broad personality traits with an explicit emotional component.

template matching theory An early theory of pattern recognition in which the perceptual system attempts to fit visual stimuli to one of the many templates, or molds, that exist in memory and represent all of the objects a person knows.

temporal lobe One of the four sections of the cerebral hemisphere, it lies below the lateral fissure and between the occipital and frontal lobes. See also *frontal, parietal, occipital lobes*.

terminal button The small swelling at the end of an axon branch. See also *axon*.

tertiary services Also called tertiary prevention, these are concerned with the aftereffects of emotional problems, and involve rehabilitation and counseling directed to reintegrating the individual into the community.

testosterone One of the male "sex hormones".

thalamus A part of the brain forming a bulge on the top of the brain stem; sensory information is exchanged throughout the brain from this relay station.

Thematic Apperception Test (TAT) A projective test used to measure need for achievement and other motives. The subject is asked to tell stories about a series of ambiguous pictures, thus being able to project his or her needs, motives, etc., into the tales.

theory A set of formal statements advancing concepts and relationships among them in order to explain a phenomenon or a body of data.

theory of natural selection A theory originated by Charles Darwin stating that selective survival could be a mechanism for changes in the characteristics of a population of organisms, eventually resulting in a new species.

thought stopping A cognitive behavioral technique involving having patients learn to stop themselves when they begin to think maladaptive or self-defeating thoughts.

threshold The point of change in electrical potential of the membrane at which point an action potential is produced.

threshold of excitation The point at which an action potential is produced in a neuron.

time out An operant conditioning technique whereby undesirable behavior is punished by isolating the subject from positive reinforcement.

Title VII of the 1964 Civil Rights Act Prohibits private employers, unions, employment agencies, joint labor-management committees, and local, state, and federal governments from discriminating on the basis of gender, race, color, religion, or national origin.

token economy A form of behavior modification treatment in which a formal system of secondary reinforcement (and punishment, via withdrawl of tokens) is used to encourage desired behaviors and discourage undesired ones. See also *behavior therapy*.

tolerance Increasing amounts of a drug or other substance are needed for the individual to achieve the usual results because the individual's body has become accustomed to the substance with continued use or exposure.

top-down theories The view that perception is an active process guided in part by high-level mental processes such as expectancies. See also *bottom-up theories*.

trace conditioning A procedure used in classical conditioning where the conditioned stimulus begins and ends before the unconditioned stimulus comes on.

transient global amnesia A condition marked by a relatively brief amnesia period in which the person becomes extremely forgetful.

trait An inherited or acquired characteristic that is considered consistent, presistent, and stable. In personality theory each individual's traits determine his or her behavior in a unique way.

transactional analysis Developed as a reaction against psychoanalysis, the process by which the therapist helps the group members become more aware of the three parts of their personalities: the child, the parent, and the adult.

transactional leaders Leaders who provide support and advice in the workplace and help workers achieve job satisfaction, resulting in better production.

transfer-appropriate processing The idea that different ways of processing information will lead to better or worse memory performance depending on how well the processing transfers to the specific test situation in which performance is measured.

transference In psychoanalytic theory, the process during therapy by which the client attributes to the therapist qualities belonging to a significant person in his or her life, such as a parent, and responds to the therapist accordingly.

transformational grammar A set of linguistic principles elaborated by Noam Chomsky to describe how the surface structure of language can be changed and interpreted according to rules that operate to produce the deep structure of language.

transformational leaders Charismatic leaders who motivate people to achieve things beyond their expectations by providing vision, intellectual stimulation, and the belief that each individual matters.

transsexual An individual whose gender identity does not match his or her biological sex.

trichromatic theory A theory of color vision which postulates that there are three types of photoreceptors which are maximally sensitive to three colors (red, blue, and green). Colors are "coded" according to the relative activity levels of these three receptor types. See also *opponent process theory*.

tricyclics A type of antidepressant medication believed to work by increasing the amounts of the neurotransmitters norepinephrine and serotonin in the brain.

two-component theory of emotion A theory developed by Schacter and Singer (1962) which suggests that emotion is determined by the interaction of two processes: general autonomic arousal and cognitive interpretation of the arousal.

tympanic membrane The membrane stretching across the end of the auditory canal. It is typically referred to as the eardrum.

type In personality psychology, a category of personality. Everyone can be identified as belonging to one of a handful of types.

type A behavior pattern The disposition to behave aggressively and competitively, and to exhibit emotional responses such as hostility and anger.

type B personality Calm, serene, relaxed.

U

ultrasound A technique used to measure fetal growth in which high-frequency sound waves are directed through the woman's abdomen, the reflected waves providing an image of the fetus.

unconditional positive regard The term given to the warm, sympathetic and accepting environment provided by therapists to clients in Carl Rogers's person-centered therapy.

unconditioned response (UCR) A response that is elicited by a stimulus prior to any learning or conditioning.

unconditioned stimulus (UCS) A stimulus that is capable of evoking a response by itself, without learning or conditioning; for example, presentation of food (UCS) causes salivation (UCR) in dogs.

unconscious The part of a person's mind which contains ideas and memories that the person cannot easily bring into consciousness.

undifferentiated schizophrenics Certain schizophrenics who have so many overlapping symptoms that the appropriate subtype category is difficult to determine. See also *schizophrenia*.

V

validity generalization In psychological testing, the belief that some tests predict reasonably well across similar jobs.

value A theoretical construct representing the degree of affect of worth—either positive or negative—produced by an event.

variability In statistics, an amount represents the dispersion of scores found in a group of measurements. See also *range, standard deviation*.

variable interval schedule A schedule of partial reinforcement in which a reward (reinforcement) follows the first response made after a certain time period has lapsed, and the time period varies from trial to trial. See also *fixed interval schedule*.

variable ratio schedule A schedule of partial reinforcement in which the reward (reinforcement) occurs following a certain number of responses, and the number varies from trial to trial. See also *fixed ratio schedule*.

verbal code Memory based on linguistic recoding.

veridical perception The aspect of experience in which our perceptions of the world are accurate and in accord with objective reality.

vicarious emotional conditioning The acquisition of an emotional response by observing someone else's experiences and reactions.

visible spectrum The only region of the electromagnetic spectrum to which our eyes are sensitive. Different light wavelengths in the visible spectrum create our perception of various colors.

visual cliff A research apparatus used to examine depth perception in young children and animals. An apparent cliff is covered with a clear piece of glass and the infant is tempted to cross the "cliff."

VMH lesions Intentional injuries to tissue in the region of the ventromedial nucleus of the hypothalamus; rats with these lesions overeat and become obese.

volley theory A version of frequency theory that holds that when one hair cell proves unable to fire in the process of determining pitch, another cell pops away to keep pace with the frequency. See also *frequency theory, place theory*.

volumetric thirst Type of thirst caused by lack of extracellular fluid.

W

wavelength The distance between two adjacent peaks of a wave; long waves are slower and short waves are faster.

weak situation A situation that does not constrain behavior, so that people are free to express their individuality.

Weber's law The principle that the difference threshold between two stimulus magnitudes is a certain constant fraction of the total magnitude. The relationship is given in Weber's Fraction: $\Delta/I =$ Constant, where I is the stimulation of the standard stimulus and ΔI is the difference in stimulation that is just noticeable.

Wechsler test A variety of intelligence tests developed by David Wechsler. Wechsler tests include two separate scales for measuring performance, a verbal scale and a performance (nonverbal) scale.

Wernicke's area An area in the left hemisphere of the brain which, when damaged, produces a speech disorder.

wish fulfillment The process through which the id creates an image of a desired but unavailable object.

withdrawal symptoms Physical effects such as sweating, shaking, and discomfort occurring when an individual abstains from taking a certain drug.

working memory Memory we use to accomplish everyday cognitive tasks, such as reasoning and comprehending.

work motivation The field concerned with what motivates workers and with how managers can arrange the work situation to satisfy the goals of both workers and management.

work norms Social norms that regulate behavior related to work and are formed by informal work groups.

Y

Yerkes-Dodson law By this principle there is an optimal degree of motivation for any task; the more difficult the task is, the lower the optimum will be.

Young-Helmholtz trichromatic theory See *trichromatic theory*.

Z

zygote The fertilized egg produced by the union of a male sperm and a female egg cell.

REFERENCES

A

Abelson, R. A. (1981). The psychological status of the script concept. *American Psychologist, 36*, 715–729.

Abrams, R. (1988). *Electroconvulsive therapy.* New York: Oxford University Press.

Abramson, L. Y., Seligman, M. E. P., & Teasdale, J. D. (1978). Learned helplessness in humans: Critique and reformulation. *Journal of Abnormal Psychology, 87*, 49–74.

Ackerman, R. J. (1990). Career developments and transitions of middle-aged women. *Psychology of Women Quarterly, 14*, 513–530.

Adair, J. G., Sharpe, D., & Huynh, C. (1989). Hawthorne control procedures in educational experiments: A reconsideration of their use and effectiveness. *Review of Educational Research, 59*, 215–228.

Adams, D. B., Gold, A. R., & Burt, A. D. (1978). Rise in female-initiated sexual activity at ovulation and its suppression by oral contraceptives. *New England Journal of Medicine, 229*, 1145–1150.

Adams, J. S. (1979). Inequity in social exchange. In R. M. Steers & L. W. Porter (Eds.), *Motivation and work behavior.* New York: McGraw-Hill.

Adorno, T., Frenkel-Brunswik, E., Levinson, D., & Sandord, R. (1950). *The authoritarian personality.* New York: Harper & Row.

Ainsworth, M. D. S. (1979). Attachment as related to mother-infant interaction. In J. S. Rosenblatt, G. A. Hinde, C. Beer, & M. Busnel (Eds.), *Advances in the study of behavior* (Vol. 9). New York: Academic Press.

Ainsworth, M. D. S., Blehar, M., Waters, E., & Walls, S. (1978). *Patterns of attachment.* Hillsdale, NJ: Erlbaum.

Ajzen, I., & Fishbein, M. H. (1977). Attitude-behavior relations: A theoretical analysis and review of empirical research. *Psychological Bulletin, 84*, 888–918.

Akers, R. L. (1985). *Deviant behavior: A social learning approach* (3rd ed.). Belmont, Calif.: Wadsworth.

Akers, R. L., Krohn, M. D., Lanza-Kaduce, L., & Radosevich, M. (1979). Social learning and deviant behavior: A specific test of a general theory. *American Sociological Review, 44*, 636–655.

Albers, J. (1975). *The interaction of color.* New Haven, CT: Yale University Press.

Alexander, F. (1950) *Psychosomatic Medicine.* New York: Norton.

Alexander, G. M., Sherwin, B., Bancroft, J., & Davidson, D. W. (1990). Testosterone and sexual behavior in oral contraceptive users and nonusers: A prospective study. *Hormones and Behavior, 24*, 388–402.

Allen, V. L., & Wilder, D. A. (1979). Group categorization and the attribution of belief similarity. *Small Group Behavior, 10*, 73–80.

Allgood-Merten, B., Lewinsohn, P. M., & Hops, H. (1990). Sex differences and adolescent depression. *Journal of Abnormal Psychology, 99*, 55–63.

Allison, M. G., & Ayllon, T. (1980). Behavioral coaching in the development of skills in football, gymnastics, and tennis. *Journal of Applied Behavioral Analysis, 13*, 297–314.

Allport, G. W. (1937). *Personality: A psychological interpretation.* New York: Holt.

Allport, G. W., & Vernon, P. E. (1930). The field of personality. *Psychological Bulletin, 27*, 277–730.

Aloimonos, Y., & Rosenfeld, A. (1991). Computer vision. *Science, 253*, 1249–1254.

Alterman, A. I., Searles, J. S., & Hall, J. G. (1989). Failure to find differences in drinking behavior as a function of familial risk for alcoholism: A replication. *Journal of Abnormal Psychology, 98*, 50–53.

American Psychiatric Association (1987). *Diagnostic and statistical manual of mental disorders* (3rd ed., rev.) (DSM-III-R). Washington, DC: Author.

American Psychiatric Association. (1980). *Diagnostic and statistical manual of mental disorders: DSM-III* (3rd ed.). Washington, DC: American Psychiatric Association.

American Psychiatric Association. (1991). *DSM-IV options book: Work in progress.* Washington, DC: American Psychiatric Association.

American Psychiatric Association. (1994). *Diagnostic and statistical manual of mental disorders* (4th ed.). Washington, DC: American Psychiatric Association.

American Psychological Association (1977). *Standards for providers of psychological services.* Washington, DC: American Psychological Association.

American Psychological Association (1979). *Ethical standards of psychologists, revision.* Washington, DC: American Psychological Association.

American Psychological Association (1981). Ethical principles of psychologists. *American Psychologist, 36*, 633–638.

Ames, C. (1984). Achievements attribution and self-instruction under competitive and individualistic goal structures. *Journal of Educational Psychology, 76*, 478–487.

Ames, C., & Archer, J. (1988). Achievement goals in the classroom: Students' learning strategies and motivation processes. *Journal of Educational Psychology, 80*, 260–267.

Amoore, J. E. (1970). *Molecular basis of odor.* Springfield, IL: Charles C. Thomas.

Amoore, J. E., Pelosi, P., & Forrester, L. J. (1977). Specific anosmias to 5-α androst-16 en-3one and w-pentadecalone: The urinous and musky odors. *Chemical Senses and Flavor, 5*, 401–425.

Amsel, A. (1958). The role of frustrative nonreward in noncontinuous reward situations. *Psychological Bulletin, 55*, 102–119.

Anand, B. K., & Brobeck, J. R. (1951). Hypothalamic control of food intake in rats and cats. *Yale Journal of Biology and Medicine, 24*, 123–140.

Anastasi, A. (1979). *Fields of applied psychology* (2nd ed.). New York: McGraw-Hill.

Andersen, A. E., & DiDomenico, L. (1992). Diet vs. shape content of popular male and female magazines: A dose-response relationship to the incidence of eating disorders? *International Journal of Eating Disorders, 11*, 283–287.

Anderson, A. (1982). The great Japanese IQ increase. *Nature, 297*, 180–181.

Anderson, E. R., Hetherington, E. M., & Clingempeel, W. G. (1989). Transformation in family relations at puberty: Effects of family context. *Journal of Early Adolescence, 9*, 310–334.

Anderson, J. L., Crawford, C. B., Nadeau, J., & Lindberg, T. (1992). Was the Duchess of Windsor right? A cross-cultural review of the socioecology of ideals of female body shape. *Ethology and Sociobiology, 13*, 197–227.

Anderson, J. R. (1976). *Language, memory, and thought.* Hillsdale, NJ: Erlbaum.

Anderson, J. R. (1984). *Cognitive psychology and its implications.* (4th ed). New York: Freeman.

Anderson, J. R. (1985). *Cognitive psychology and its implications* (2nd ed.). New York: Freeman.

Anderson, K. J. (1990). Arousal and the inverted-U hypothesis: A critique of Neiss's "Reconceptualizing arousal." *Psychological Bulletin, 107*, 96–100.

Anderson, N. H. (1965). Adding versus averaging as a stimulus combination rule in impression formation. *Journal of Experimental Psychology, 70*, 394–400.

Anderson, N. H. (1974). Cognitive algebra: Integration theory applied to social attribution. In L. Berkowitz (Ed.), *Advances in experimental social psychology* (Vol. 7). New York: Academic Press.

Anderson, N. H., & Hubert, S. (1963). Effects of concomitant verbal recall on order effects in personality impression formation. *Journal of Verbal Learning and Verbal Behavior, 2*, 379–391.

Anderson, R. C., & Pichert, J. W. (1978). Recall of previously unrecallable information following a shift in perspective. *Journal of Verbal Learning and Verbal Behavior, 17*, 1–12.

Anderson, R. C., Reynolds, R. E., Schallert, D. L., & Goetz, E. T. (1977). Frameworks for comprehending discourse. *American Educational Research Journal, 14*, 367–381.

Anderson, V. E., & Wortis, J. (1974). Genetics and intelligence. In V. E. Anderson & J. Wortis (Eds.), *Mental retardation and developmental disabilities: An annual review* (Vol. 6). New York: Brunner/Mazel.

Andreasen, N. C. (1989). Positive versus negative schizophrenia: A critical evaluation. In J. M. Hooley, J. M. Neale, & G. C. Davidson, (Eds.), *Readings in abnormal psychology.* New York: Wiley.

Andreasen, N. C., & Flaum, N. A. (1991). Schizophrenia: The characteristic symptoms. *Schizophrenia Bulletin, 17*, 27–49.

Andrew, R. J. (1974). Arousal and the causation of behavior. *Behaviour, 51*, 135–165.

Angleitner, A. (1991). Personality psychology: Trends and developments. *European Journal of Personality, 5*, 185–198.

Anisman, H. (1975). Time-dependent variations in aversively motivated behaviors: Non-associative effects of cholinergic and catecholaminergic activity. *Psychological Review, 82*, 359–385.

Anisman, H. H. (1975). Task complexity as a factor in eliciting heterosis in mice:

Aversively motivation behaviors. *Journal of Comparative and Physiological Psychology,* 89, 976–984.

Anisman, H., Hamilton, M., & Zacharko, R. M. (1984). Cue and response-choice acquisition and reversal after exposure to uncontrollable shock: Induction of response preservation. *Journal of Experimental Psychology: Animal Behavior Processes,* 10, 229–243.

Annau, Z., & Kamin, L. J. (1961). The conditioned emotional response as a function of intensity of the US. *Journal of Comparative and Physiological Psychology,* 54, 428–432.

Antell, S. E., & Keating, D. P. (1983). Perception of numerical invariance in neonates. *Child Development,* 54, 695–701.

Antony, M. M., Brown, T. A., & Barlow, D. H. (1992). Current perspectives on panic and panic disorder. *Current Directions in Psychological Science,* 1, 79–82.

Apfelbaum, M., Bostsarron, J., & Lacatis, D. (1971). Effect of caloric restriction and excessive caloric intake on energy expenditure. *American Journal of Clinical Nutrition,* 24, 1405–1409.

Appelbaum, P. S., & Rosenbaum, A. (1989). Tarasoff and the researcher—Does the duty to protect apply in the research setting? *American Psychologist,* 44, 885–894.

Appley, M. H. (1970). Derived motives. *Annual Review of Psychology,* 21, 485–518.

Arbuthnott, G. W., & Ungerstedt, U. (1969). *Acta Physiological Scandinavia Supplement,* 330, 117.

Arend, R., Gove, F. L., & Sroufe, L. A. (1979). Continuity of individual adaptation from infancy to kindergarten: A predictive study of ego resiliency and curiosity in preschoolers. *Child Development,* 50, 950–959.

Argyle, M., & Henderson, M. (1984). *The anatomy of relationships.* London: Heinemann.

Arkes, H. R., & Blumer, C. (1985). The psychology of sunk cost. *Organizational Behavior and Human Decision Processes,* 35, 124–140.

Arkin, A. M. (1991). Introduction to the first edition. In S. J. Ellman & J. S. Antrobus (Eds.), *The mind in sleep: Psychology and psychophysiology* (2nd ed.) (pp. 1–17). New York: Wiley.

Arkoff, A. (1993). Hey, America! He's old—and proud of it! *The Honolulu Advertiser,* July 5.

Aronson, E., Turner, J. A., & Carlsmith, J. M. (1963). Communicator credibility and communication discrepancy as a determinant of opinion change. *Journal of Abnormal and Social Psychology,* 67, 31–36.

Arvey, R. D., & Campion, J. E. (1982). The employment interview: A summary and review of recent research. *Personnel Psychology,* 35, 281–322.

Asch, S. E. (1946). Forming impressions of personality. *Journal of Abnormal and Social Psychology,* 41, 258–290.

Asch, S. E. (1956). Studies of independence and conformity: 1. A minority of one against a unanimous majority. *Psychological Monographs,* 70 (Whole No. 546).

Aslin, R. N. (1987). Motor aspects of visual development in infancy. In P. Salapatek & L. Cohen (Eds.), *Handbook of infant perception: Vol. 1. From sensation to perception* (pp. 43–113). Orlando, FL: Academic Press.

Aslin, R. N., Pisoni, D. B., & Juscyk, P. W. (1983). Auditory development and speech perception in infancy. In P. Mussen (Ed.), *Handbook of child psychology,* 4th ed., Vol. 2, (pp. 573–687). New York: Wiley.

Astbury, J., Orgill, A. A., Bajuk, B., & Yu, V. Y. (1990). Neurodevelopmental outcome, growth, and health of extremely low birth weight survivors: How soon can we tell? *Developmental Medicine and Child Neurology,* 32, 582–589.

Atkin, D. J., Moorman, J., & Lin, C. A. (1991). Ready for prime time: Network series devoted to working women in the 1980's. *Sex Roles,* 25, 677–685.

Atkinson, J. W. (1957). Motivational determinants of risk-taking behavior. *Psychological Review,* 64, 359–372.

Atkinson, J. W. (1964). *An introduction to motivation.* Princeton, NJ: Van Nostrand Reinhold.

Atkinson, J. W., & Litwin, G. H. (1960). Achievement motive and test anxiety conceived as motive to approach success and motive to avoid failure. *Journal of Abnormal and Social Psychology,* 60, 52–63.

Atkinson, J. W., & Raynor, J. O. (Eds.). (1974). *Motivation and achievement.* Washington, DC: Winston.

Atkinson, R. C., & Shiffrin, R. M. (1968). Human memory: A proposed system and its control processes. In K. W. Spence & J. T. Spence (Eds.), *The psychology of learning and motivation: Advances in research and theory* (Vol. 2). New York: Academic Press.

Atkinson, R. C., & Shiffrin, R. M. (1971). The control of short-term memory. *Scientific American,* 224, 83–89.

Ax, A. F. (1953). The physiological differentiation between fear and anger in humans. *Psychosomatic Medicine,* 5, 433–442.

Axelsson, A., & Lindgren, F. (1978). Hearing in pop musicians. *Acta Otolaryngology,* 85, 225–231.

Ayer, A. J. (1936). *Language, truth, and logic.* Cambridge: Cambridge University Press.

Ayllon, T., & Azrin, N. H. (1965). The measurement and reinforcement of behavior of psychotics. *Journal of the Experimental Analysis of Behavior,* 8, 357–383.

Ayllon, T., & Haughton, E. (1964). Modification of symptomatic verbal behavior of mental patients. *Behaviour Research and Therapy,* 2, 87–97.

Azrin, N. H., & Holz, W. C. (1966). Punishment. In W. K. Honig (Ed.), *Operant behavior: Areas of research and application.* New York: Appleton-Century-Crofts.

Azrin, N. H., Hake, D. F., Holz, W. C., & Hutchinson, R. R. (1965). Motivational aspects of escape from punishment. *Journal of Experimental Analysis of Behavior,* 8, 31–44.

Azrin, N. H., Holz, W. C., & Hake, D. F. (1963). Fixed-ratio punishment. *Journal of the Experimental Analysis of Behavior,* 6, 141–148.

B

Baars, B. (1988). *A cognitive theory of consciousness.* Cambridge: Cambridge University Press.

Baddeley, A. D. (1978). The trouble with levels: A reexamination of Craik and Lockhart's framework for memory research. *Psychological Review,* 85, 139–152.

Baddeley, A. D. (1986). *Working memory.* Oxford: Oxford University Press.

Baghurst, P. A., McMichael, A. J., Wigg, N. R., Vimpani, G. V., Robertson, E. F., Roberts, R. J., & Tong, S. (1992). Environmental exposure to lead and children's intelligence at the age of seven years. *New England Journal of Medicine,* 327, 1279–1284.

Bahrick, H. P. (1984). Semantic memory content in permastore: Fifty years of memory for Spanish learned in school. *Journal of Experimental Psychology: General,* 113, 1–47.

Bahrick, H. P., Bahrick, P. O., & Wittlinger, R. P. (1975). Fifty years of memories for names and faces: A cross-sectional approach. *Journal of Experimental Psychology: General,* 104, 54–75.

Baker, R. A. (1990). *They call it hypnosis.* New York: Prometheus Books.

Balay, J., & Shevrin, H. (1988) The subliminal psychodynamic activation method: A critical review. *American Psychologist,* 43, 161–174.

Balay, J., & Shevrin, H. (1988). The subliminal psychodynamic activation method. *American Psychologist,* 43, 161–174.

Balay, J., & Shevrin, H. (1989) SPA is subliminal, but is it psychodynamically activating? *American Psychologist,* 44, 1423–1426.

Ball, K. K., Roenker, D. L., & Bruni, J. R. (1990). Developmental changes in attention and visual search throughout adulthood. In J. T. Enns (Ed.), *The development of attention: Research and theory* (pp. 489–508). Amsterdam: Elesevier Science Publishers.

Balota, D. (1983). Automatic semantic activation and subliminal episodic encoding. *Journal of Verbal Learning and Verbal Behavior,* 22, 88–104.

Baltes, P. B., Dittman-Kohli, M., & Dixon, R. A. (1984). New perspectives on the development of intelligence in adulthood: Toward a dual-process conception and a model of selective optimization with compensation. In P. B. Baltes & O. G. Brim, Jr. (Eds.), *Life-span development and behavior* (Vol. 6). New York: Academic Press.

Banaji, M. R., & Crowder, R. G. (1989). The bankruptcy of everyday memory. *American Psychologist,* 44, 1185–1193.

Bandura, A. (1965). Influence of a model's reinforcement contingencies on the acquisition of imitative responses. *Journal of Personality and Social Psychology,* 1, 589–595.

Bandura, A. (1969). *Principles of behavior modification.* New York: Holt, Rinehart & Winston.

Bandura, A. (1973). *Aggression: A social learning analysis.* Englewood Cliffs, NJ: Prentice-Hall.

Bandura, A. (1977). *Social learning theory.* Englewood Cliffs, NJ: Prentice-Hall.

Bandura, A. (1982). The self and mechanisms of agency. In J. Suls (Ed.), *Psychological Perspectives on the Self* (vol. 1, pp. 3–39). Hillside, NJ: Erlbaum.

Bandura, A. (1986). *Social Foundations of thought and action: A social cognitive theory.* Englewood Cliffs, NJ: Prentice-Hall.

Bandura, A. (1991). The changing icons in personality psychology. In J. H. Cantor (Ed.) *Psychology at Iowa: Centennial Essays.* Hillsdale, NJ: Erlbaum, 117–139.

Bandura, A., & Mischel, W. (1965). Modification of self-imposed delay of reward through exposure to live and symbolic models. *Journal of Personality and Social Psychology,* 2, 698–705.

Bandura, A., & Walters, R. H. (1963). *Social learning and personality development.* New York: Holt, Rinehart & Winston.

Bandura, A., Blanchard, E. B., & Ritter, B. (1969). Relative efficacy of desensitization and modeling approaches for inducing behavioral, affective, and attitudinal changes. *Journal of Personality and Social Psychology,* 13, 173–199.

Bandura, A., Grusec, J. E., & Menlove, F. L. (1967). Vicarious extinction of avoidance behavior. *Journal of Personality and Social Psychology,* 5, 16–23.

Bandura, A., Ross, D. A., & Ross, S. A. (1963). Imitation of film-mediated aggressive models. *Journal of Abnormal and Social Psychology,* 66, 3–11.

Bandura, A., Taylor, C. B., Williams, S. L., Mefford, I. N., & Barchas, J. D. (1985). Catecholamine secretion as a function of perceived coping self-efficacy. *Jounal of Consulting and Clinical Psychology,* 53, 406–414.

Banks, M. S. (1980). The development of visual accommodation during early infancy. *Child Development,* 51, 646–666.

Banks, M. S., & Dannemiller, J. L. (1987). Infant visual psychophysics. In P. Salapatek & L. Cohen (Eds.), *Handbook of infant perception: Vol. 1, From sensation to perception* (pp. 115–184). Orlando, FL: Academic Press.

Barash, D. P. (1977). *Sociobiology and behavior*. New York: Elsevier.

Barber, T. X. (1970). *LSD, marihuana, yoga, and hypnosis*. Chicago: Aldine Publishing Company.

Bard, P. A. (1928). A diencephalic mechanism for the expression of rage with special reference to the sympathetic nervous system. *American Journal of Physiology, 84*, 490–515.

Bard, P. A. (1934). On emotional expression after decortication with some remarks on certain theoretical views, Parts I and II. *Psychological Review, 41*, 309–329; 424–449.

Barefoot, J. C., Dahlstrom, W. G., & Williams, R. B., Jr. (1983). Hostility, CHD incidence and total mortality: A 25-year follow-up study of 255 physicians. *Psychosomatic Medicine, 45*, 59–63.

Barefoot, J. C., Peterson, B. L., Dahlstrom, W. G., Siegler, I. C., Anderson, N. B., & William R. B., Jr. (1991). Hostility patterns and health implications: Correlates of Cook-Medley Hostility scale scores in a national survey. *Health Psychology, 10*, 18–24.

Barenboim, C. (1981). The development of person perception in childhood and adolescence: From behavioral comparisons to psychological constructs. *Child Development, 52*, 129–144.

Barinage, M. (1995). "Obese" protein slims mice. *Science, 269*, 475–476.

Baron, A. (1965). Delayed punishment of runway response. *Journal of Comparative and Physiological Psychology, 60*, 131–134.

Baron, R. A. (1977). *Human aggression*. New York: Plenum.

Baron, R. A., & Byrne, D. (1977). *Social psychology: Understanding human interaction* (2nd ed.). Boston: Allyn and Bacon.

Baron, R. A., & Byrne, D. (1987). *Social psychology: Understanding human interaction* (5th ed.). Boston: Allyn and Bacon.

Barr, H. M., Streissguth, A. P., Darby, B. L., & Sampson, P. D. (1990). Prenatal exposure to alcohol, caffeine, tobacco, and aspirin: Effects on fine and gross motor performance in 4-year-old children. *Developmental Psychology, 26*, 339–348.

Barrera, M. E., & Maurer, D. (1981). Discrimination of strangers by the three-month-old. *Child Development, 52*, 558–563.

Barret, G. V., & Depinet, R. L. (1991). A reconsideration of testing for competence rather than for intelligence. *American Psychologist, 46*, 1012–1024.

Bartholow, R. Experimental investigations into the functions of the human brain. *American Journal of Medical Science* (new series), *67*, 305–313.

Bartlett, F. C. (1932). *Remembering: A study in experimental and social psychology*. Cambridge, England: Cambridge University Press.

Bartlett, J. C., & Searcy, J. (1993). Inversion and configuration of faces. *Cognitive Psychology, 25*, 281–316.

Bartoshuk, L. M. (1988). Taste. In R. C. Atkinson, R. J. Herrnstein, G. Lindzey, & R. D. Luce (Eds.), *Stevens' handbook of experimental psychology* (2nd ed.). New York: Wiley.

Bartoshuk, L. M. (1991). Sensory factors in eating behavior. *Bulletin of the Psychonomic Society, 29*, 250–255.

Baruch, G. K., Barnett, R. C., & Rivers, C. (1983). *Lifeprints*. New York: McGraw-Hill.

Bass, B. M. (1985). *Leadership and performance beyond expectations*. New York: Free Press.

Bass, E., & Davis, L. (1988). *The courage to heal*. New York: Harper & Row.

Bateson, P. P. G. (1973). Internal influences on early learning in birds. In R. A. Hinde & J. Stevenson-Hinde (Eds.), *Constraints on learning*. London: Academic Press.

Bauer, P. J., & Mandler, J. M. (1989). One thing follows another: Effects of temporal structure on 1- to 2-year-olds' recall of events. *Developmental Psychology, 25*, 197–206.

Bauer, R. M., & Verfaellie, M. (1988). Electrodermal discrimination of familiar but not unfamiliar faces in prosopagnosia. *Brain and Cognition, 8*, 240–252.

Baum, A., Gatchel, R. J., & Schaeffer, M. A. (1983). Emotional, behavioral, and physiological effects of chronic stress at Three Mile Island. *Journal of Consulting and Clinical Psychology, 51*, 565–572.

Bauman, K. E., Fisher, L. A., & Koch, G. (1989). External variables, subjective expected utility, and adolescent behavior with alcohol and cigarettes. *Journal of Applied Social Psychology, 19*, 789–804.

Baumeister, R. F. (1989). *Masochism and the Self*. Hillsdale, NJ: Erlbaum.

Baumeister, R. F. (1990). Suicide as escape from self. *Psychological Review, 97*, 90–113.

Baumeister, R. F. (1991). *Meanings of Life*. New York: Guilford Press.

Baumrind, D. (1964). Some thoughts on ethics of research: After reading Milgram's "Behavioral study of obedience." *American Psychologist, 19*, 421–423.

Baumrind, D. (1967). Child care practices anteceding three patterns of preschool behavior. *Genetic Psychology Monographs, 75*, 43–88.

Baumrind, D. (1971). Current patterns of parental authority. *Developmental Psychology, 4*, 1–103.

Baumrind, D. (1980). New directions in socialization research. *American Psychologist, 35*, 639–652.

Baumrind, D. (1991). Parenting styles and adolescent development. In J. Brooks-Gunn, R. Lerner, & A. C. Petersen (Eds.), *The encyclopedia on adolescence*. New York: Garland.

Bazar, J. (1990, July). Psychologist can help youths stay out of gangs. *APA Monitor*, p. 39.

Beach, F. (1967). Cerebral and hormonal control of reflexive mechanisms involved in copulatory behavior. *Psychological Review, 47*, 289–316.

Beach, F. A. (1956). Characteristics of masculine "sex drive." In M. Jones (Ed.), *Nebraska symposium on motivation*. Lincoln, NE: University of Nebraska Press.

Beach, F. A., & Jordan, L. (1956). Sexual exhaustion and recovery in the male rat. *Quarterly Journal of Experimental Psychology, 8*, 121–133.

Beck, A. T. (1967). *Depression: Clinical, experimental and theoretical aspects*. New York: Harper & Row.

Beck, A. T., Rush, A. J., Shaw, B. F., & Emery, G. (1979). *Cognitive therapy of depression*. New York: Guilford Press.

Becker, E. (1973). *The Denial of Death*. New York: The Free Press.

Beckwith, J. (1983). Gender and math performance: Does biology have implications for educational policy? *Journal of Education, 165*, 158–174.

Bee, H. (1989). *The developing child* (5th ed.). New York: Harper & Row.

Beech, H. R., Burns, L. E., & Scheffield, B. F. (1982). *A behavioral approach to the management of stress: A practical guide to techniques*. New York: Wiley.

Beecher, H. K. (1956). Relationship of significance of wound to the pain experienced. *Journal of the American Medical Association, 161*, 1609–1613.

Beecher, H. K. (1959). Generalization from pain of various types and diverse origins. *Science, 130*, 267–268.

Belanger, D., & Feldman, S. M. (1962). Effects of water deprivation upon heart rate and instrumental activity in the rate. *Journal of Comparative and Physiological Psychology, 55*, 220–225.

Bell, A. P., & Weinberg, M. S. (1978). *Homosexualities*. New York: Simon & Schuster.

Bell, A. P., Weinberg, M. S., & Hammersmith, S. K. (1981). *Sexual preference: Its development in men and women*. Bloomington: Indiana University Press.

Bell, D. (1992a). *Faces at the bottom of the well: The permanence of racism*. New York: Basic Books.

Bell, D. (1992b). Jon Elsen interview with Derrick Bell. *New York Times Book Review*, September 20, p. 7.

Bellezza, F. S. (1981). Mnemonic devices: Classification, characteristics, and criteria. *Review of Educational Research, 51*, 247–275.

Bellezza, F. S. (1992). Mnemonic devices. In L. R. Squire (Ed.), *The encyclopedia of learning and memory* (pp. 418–421). New York: MacMillan.

Belmont, L., & Marolla, F. A. (1973). Birth order, family size, and intelligence. *Science, 182*, 1096–1101.

Belsky, J. (1986). Infant day care: A cause for concern. *Zero to three, 6*, 1–9.

Belsky, J. (1988). The effects of infant day care reconsidered. *Early Childhood Research Quarterly, 3*, 235–272.

Belson, W. (1978). *Television violence and the adolescent boy*. Hampshire, England: Saxon House.

Bem, D. J. (1967). Self-perception: An alternative interpretation of cognitive dissonance phenomena. *Psychological Review, 74*, 183–200.

Bem, D. J. (1972). Self-perception theory. In L. Berkowitz (Ed.), *Advances in experimental social psychology* (Vol. 6). New York: Academic Press.

Bem, D. J., & Honorton, C. (1994). Does psi exist? Replicable evidence for an anomalous process of information transfer. *Psychological Bulletin, 115*, 4–18.

Bemporad, J. R. (1985). Long-term analytical treatment of depression. In E. E. Beckham & W. R. Leber (Eds.), *Handbook of depression: Treatment, assessment, and research*. Homewood, Ill.: Dorsey Press.

Benbow, C. P., & Stanley, J. C. (1980). Sex differences in mathematical ability: Fact or artifact? *Science, 210*, 1262–1264.

Benchley, R. W. (1937). The early worm. In R. W. Benchley, *Inside Benchley*. New York: Harper & Row.

Benda, C. E., Squires, N. D., Ogonik, N. J. & Wise, R. (1963). Personality factors in mild mental retardation: 1. Family background and sociocultural patterns. *American Journal of Mental Deficiency, 68*, 24–40.

Benedict, R. (1934). *Patterns of culture*. Boston: Houghton Mifflin.

Bengston, V. L., Cuellar, J. E., & Ragan, P. K. (1977). Stratum contrasts and similarities in attitudes toward death. *Journal of Gerontology, 32*, 76–88.

Benjafield, J. G. (1992). *Cognition*. Englewood Cliffs, NJ: Prentice Hall.

Benson, D. F., & Greenberg, J. P. (1969). Visual form agnosia. *Archives of Neurology, 20*, 82–89.

Berg, C. A., & Sternberg, R. J. (1992). Adults' conceptions of intelligence across the adult life span. *Psychology and Aging, 7*, 221–231.

Berger, S. M. (1962). Conditioning through vicarious instigation. *Psychological Review, 69*, 450–466.

Bergin, A. E., & Lambert, M. J. (1978). The evaluation of therapeutic outcomes. In S. L. Garfield & A. E. Bergin (Eds.), *Handbook of psychotherapy and behavior change* (2nd ed.). New York: Wiley.

Berkman, L., & Syne, S. L. (1979). Social networks, host resistance, and mortality: A nine-year follow-up of Alameda County residents. *American Journal of Epidemiology, 109*, 186–204.

Berko, J. (1958). The child's learning of English morphology. *Word, 14*, 150–177.

Berkowitz, L. (1962). *Aggression: A social psychological analysis*. New York: McGraw-Hill.

Berkowitz, L. (1969). The frustration-aggression hypothesis revisited. In L. Berkowitz (Ed.), *Roots of aggression: A re-examination of the frustration-aggression hypothesis*. New York: Atherton Press.

Berkowitz, L. (1972). Social norms, feelings, and other factors affecting helping and altruism. In L. Berkowitz (Ed.), *Advances in experimental social psychology* (Vol. 6). New York: Academic Press.

Berkowitz, L. (1973, July). The case for bottling up rage. *Psychology Today*, pp. 24–31.

Berkowitz, L. (1979). *A survey of social psychology* (2nd ed.). New York: Holt, Rinehart & Winston.

Berkowitz, L. (1989). Frustration-aggression hypothesis: Examination and reformulation. *Psychological Bulletin, 106*, 59–73.

Berkowitz, L., & Donnerstein, E. (1982). External validity is more than skin deep: Some answers to criticisms of laboratory experiments. *American Psychologist, 37*, 245–257.

Berkowitz, L., & LePage, A. (1967). Weapons as aggression-eliciting stimuli. *Journal of Personality and Social Psychology, 7*, 202–207.

Berkowitz, L., Cochrane, S., & Embree, M. (1979). Influence of aversive experience and the consequences of one's aggression on aggressive behavior. Reported in L. Berkowitz, *A survey of social psychology* (2nd ed.). New York: Holt, Rinehart & Winston.

Berlin, B. (1972). Speculations on the growth of ethnobotanical nomenclature. *Language in Society, 1*, 51–86.

Berlin, B., & Kay, P. (1969). *Basic color terms: Their universality and evolution*. Berkeley: University of California Press.

Berlin, B., Breedlove, D. E., & Raven, P. H. (1973). General principles of classification and nomenclature in folk biology. *American Anthropologist, 75*, 214–242.

Berlyne, D. (1967). Arousal and reinforcement. In D. Levine (Ed.), *Nebraska symposium on motivation*. Lincoln: University of Nebraska Press.

Berman, A. L., & Jobes, D. A. (1991). *Adolescent suicide: Assessment and intervention*. Washington, DC: American Psychological Association.

Berndt, T. J., & Miller, K. E. (1990). Expectancies, values, and achievement in junior high school. *Journal of Educational Psychology, 82*, 319–326.

Berne, E. (1964). *Games people play*. New York: Grove Press.

Bernheim, K. F., & Lewine, R. R. J. (1979). *Schizophrenia: Symptoms, causes, treatments*. New York: Norton.

Bernstein, I. L. (1978). Learned taste aversions in children receiving chemotherapy. *Science, 200*, 1302–1303.

Bernstein, I. L. (1985). Learned food aversions in the progression of cancer and its treatment. In N. S. Braverman & P. Bernstein (Eds.), *Experimental assessments and clinical applications of conditioned food aversions*. *Annals of the New York Academy of Sciences*, Vol. 443.

Berridge, K. C., Venier, L. L., & Robinson, T. E. (1989). Taste reactivity analysis of 6-hydroxydopamine-induced aphagia: Implications for arousal and anhedonia hypotheses of dopamine function. *Behavioral Neuroscience, 103*, 36–45.

Berridge, K. C., Venier, L. L., & Robinson, T. E. (1989). Taste reactivity analysis of 6-hydroxydopamine-induced aphagia: Implications for arousal and anhedonia hypotheses of dopamine function. *Behavioral Neuroscience, 103*, 36–45.

Berry, G. L., & Mitchell-Kernan, C. (1982). *Television and socialization of the minority child*. New York: Academic Press.

Berscheid, E. (1985). Interpersonal attraction. In G. Lindzey & E. Aronson (Eds.), *Handbook of social psychology* (3rd ed.) (Vol. 2). New York: Random House.

Berscheid, E. (1988). Some comments on love's anatomy: Or, whatever happened to old-fashioned lust. In R. J. Sternberg & M. L. Barnes (Eds.), *The psychology of love*. (pp. 359–374). New Haven, CT: Yale University Press.

Berscheid, E., & Campbell, B. (1981). The changing longevity of heterosexual close relationships: A commentary and forecast. In M. Lerner (Ed.), *The justice motive in times of scarcity and change*. New York: Plenum.

Berscheid, E., & Walster, E. (1978). *Interpersonal attraction* (2nd ed.). Reading, MA: Addison-Wesley.

Best, M. R., & Barker, L. M. (1977). The nature of "learned safety" and its role in the delay of reinforcement gradient. In L. M. Barker, M. R. Best, & M. Domjan (Eds.), *Learning mechanisms in food selection*. Waco, TX: Baylor University Press.

Best, P. J., Best, M. R. & Henggeler, S. (1977). The contribution of environmental non-ingestive cues in conditioning with aversive internal consequences. In L. M. Barker, M. R. Best, & M. Domjan (Eds.), *Learning mechanisms in food selection*. Waco, TX: Baylor University Press.

Bettes, B. A., Dusenbury, L., Kerner, J., James-Ortiz, S., & Botvin, G. J. (1990). Ethnicity and psychosocial factors in alcohol and tobacco use in adolescence. *Child Development, 61*, 557–565.

Beutler, L. E. (1989). Differential treatment selection: The role of diagnosis in psychotherapy. *Psychotherapy, 26*, 271–281.

Bibring, E. (1953). The mechanism of depression. In P. Greenacre (Ed.), *Affective disorders*. New York: International Universities Press.

Biederman, I. (1981). On the semantics of a glance at a scene. In M. Kubovy & J. Pomerantz (Eds.), *Perceptual organization*. Hillsdale, NJ: Erlbaum.

Biederman, I. (1987). Recognition by components: A theory of human image understanding. *Psychological Review, 94*, 115–147.

Biederman, I. (1989). The uncertain case for cultural effects in pictorial object recognition. *Behavioral and Brain Sciences, 12*, 74–75.

Biederman, I., & Cooper, E. E. (1991). Priming contour-deleted images: Evidence for intermediate representations in visual object recognition. *Cognitive Psychology, 23*, 393–419.

Bijou, S. W., & Baer, D. M. (1965). *Child development: Vol. 2 The universal stage of infancy*. New York: Appleton-Century-Crofts.

Binet, A. (1911). *Les idees modernes sur les enfants*. Paris: Flamarion.

Birch, D. E. (1992). Duty to protect: Update and Canadian perspective. *Canadian Psychology, 33*, 94–101.

Birch, L. L. (1990). The control of food intake by young children: The role of learning. In E. D. Capaldi & T. L. Powley (Eds.), *Taste, experience, and feeding* (pp. 116–135). Washington, Psychological Association.

Birch, L. L., & Marlin, D. W. (1982). I don't like; I never tried it: Effects of exposure on two-year-old children's food preferences. *Appetite, 3*, 353–360.

Birren, J. E. (1974). Transitions in gerontology—from lab to life: Psychophysiology and speed of response. *American Psychologist, 29*, 808–815.

Bjork, R. A., & Richardson-Klarehn, A. (1989). On the puzzling relationship between environmental context and human memory. In C. Izawa (Ed.), *Current issues in cognitive processes: The Tulane-Floweree symposium on cognition*. Hillsdale, NJ: Erlbaum.

Bjorklund, D. F. (1985). The role of conceptual knowledge in the development of organization in children's memory. In C. J. Brainerd & M. Pressley (Eds.), *Basic processes in memory development*. New York: Springer-Verlag.

Bjorklund, D. F. (1989). *Children's thinking*. Pacific Grove, CA: Brooks/Cole.

Bjorklund, D. F., Muir-Broaddus, J. E., & Schneider, W. (1990). The role of knowledge in the development of strategies. In D. F. Bjorklund (Ed.), *Children's strategies: Contemporary views of cognitive development* (pp. 93–128). Hillsdale, NJ: Erlbaum.

Blanchard, K. H., & Johnson, S. (1985). *One minute manager*. Berkeley, CA: Berkeley Books.

Blanchard-Fields, F., (1986). Attributional processes in adult development. *Educational Gerontology 12*, 291–300.

Blashfield, R. K., & Livesley, W. J. (1991). A metaphorical analysis of psychiatric classification as a psychological test. *Journal of Abnormal Psychology, 100*, 262–270.

Blass, E. M., & Epstein, A. N. (1971). A lateral preoptic osmosensitive zone for thirst. *Journal of Comparative and Physiological Psychology, 76*, 378–394.

Blass, E. M., Nussbaum, A. I., & Hanson, D. G. (1974). Septal hyperdipsia: Specific enhancement of drinking to angiotensin in rats. *Journal of Comparative Physiological Psychology, 87*, 422–439.

Blatt, S. J. (1990). The Rorschach: A test of perception or an evaluation of representation. *Journal of Personality Assessment. 55*, 394–416.

Blaxton, T. A., & Neely, J. H. (1983). Inhibition from semantically related primes: Evidence of category specific inhibition. *Memory & Cognition, 11*, 500–510.

Bleuler, E. (1950). *Dementia praecox, or the group of schizophrenias* (J. Zinkin & N. D. C. Lewis, Trans.). New York: International Universities Press. (Original work published 1911)

Blinkhorn, S., & Johnson, C. (1990). The insignificance of personality testing. *Nature, 348*, 671–672.

Blum, J. E., Jarvik, L. F., & Clark, E. T. (1970). Rate of change on selective tests of intelligence: A twenty-year longitudinal study. *Journal of Gerontology, 25*, 171–176.

Blumstein, P. W., & Schwartz, P. (1976). Bisexuality in women. *Archives of Sexual Behavior, 5*, 171–181.

Blumstein, P. W., & Schwartz, P. (1983). *American Couples*. New York: Morrow.

Blyth, D. A., Simmons, R. G., & Zakin, D. F. (1985). Satisfaction with body image for early adolescent females. *Journal of Youth and Adolescence, 14*, 207–226.

Bochner, S., & Insko, C. (1966). Communicator discrepancy, source credibility, and influence. *Journal of Personality and Social Psychology, 4*, 614–621.

Bogatz, G., & Ball, S. J. (1971). *The second year of Sesame Street: A continuing evaluation*. Princeton, NJ: Educational Testing Service.

Bogen, J. E. (1969). The other side of the brain: An appositional mind. *Bulletin of the Los Angeles Neurological Society, 34*, 73–105.

Boggiano, A. K., & Ruble, D. N. (1979). Competence and overjustification effect: A developmental study. *Journal of Personality and Social Psychology, 37*, 1462–1468.

Bogin, B., (1988). Host factors in disease: Age, sex, racial, and ethnic group and body build. *American Journal of Physical Anthropology, 77*, 137–138.

Bohannon, J. N. & Warren-Leubecker, A. W. (1989). Theoretical approaches to language acquisition. In J. B. Gleason (Ed.), *The development of language*. Columbus, Ohio: Merrill.

Bohannon, J. N. (1988). Flashbulb memories and the space shuttle disaster: A tale of two theories. *Cognition, 29*, 179–196.

Bohart, & Todd, (1988). *Foundations of clinical and counseling psychology*. New York: HarperCollins.

Bok, S. (1978). *Dying: Moral choice in public and private life*. New York: Pantheon.

Bollerud, K. H., Christopherson, S. B., & Frank, E. S. (1990). Girls' sexual choices: Looking for what is right. In C. Gilligan, N. P. Lyons, & T. J. Hammer (Eds.), *Making connections*. Cambridge, MA: Harvard University Press.

Bolles, R. C. (1970). Species-specific defense reactions and avoidance learning. *Psychological Review, 77,* 32–48.

Bolles, R. C. (1972). Reinforcement, expectancy, and learning. *Psychological Review, 79,* 394–409.

Bolles, R. C. (1975). *Theory of motivation* (2nd ed.). New York: Harper & Row.

Bolles, R. C., & Fanselow, M. S. (1980). A perceptual-defensive recuperative model of fear and pain. *Behavioral and Brain Sciences, 3,* 291–323.

Bolles, R. C., & Fanselow, M. S. (1982). Endorphins and behavior. *Annual Review of Psychology, 33,* 87–101.

Bolles, R. C., & Grossen, N. E. (1969). Effects of an informational stimulus on the acquisition of avoidance behavior in rats. *Journal of Comparative and Physiological Psychology, 68,* 90–99.

Bolton, F. G. (1980). *The pregnant adolescent.* Beverly Hills, CA: Sage.

Bonardi, C., & Hall, G. (1994). Discriminative inhibition is specific to the response-reinforcer association but not the discriminative stimulus. *Journal of Experimental Psychology: Animal Behavior Processes, 20,* 278–291.

Bonem, M., & Crossman, E. K. (1988). Elucidating the effects of reinforcement magnitude. *Psychological Bulletin, 104,* 348–362.

Booth-Kewley, S., & Friedman, H. S. (1987). Psychological predictors of heart disease: A quantitative review. *Psychological Bulletin, 101,* 343–362.

Bootzin, R. R., Herman, C. P., & Nicassio, P. (1976). The power of suggestion: Another look at misattribution and insomnia. *Journal of Personality and Social Psychology, 34,* 673–679.

Borbely, A. (1986). *Secrets of sleep.* New York: Basic Books.

Boring, E. G. (1950). *A history of experimental psychology.* (2nd ed.). New York: Appleton-Century-Crofts.

Borkenau, P. (1991). Evidence of a correlation between wearing glasses and personality. *Personality and Individual Differences, 12,* 1125–1128.

Borkowski, J. G., Krause, A., & Maxwell, S. E. (1985). On multiple determinants of racial differences in intelligence: A reply to Jensen. *Intelligence, 9,* 41–49.

Bornstein, M. H. (1979). Perceptual development: Stability and change in feature perception. In M. Bornstein & W. Kessen (Eds.), *Psychological development from infancy: Image to intention*. Hillsdale, NJ: Erlbaum.

Bornstein, M. H. (1990). Attention in infancy and the prediction of cognitive capacities in childhood. In J. T. Enns (Ed.), *The development of attention: Research and theory* (pp. 3–19). Amsterdam: Elsevier Science Publishers.

Bornstein, M. H., Tamis-LeMonda, C. S., Tal, J., Ludeman, P., Toda, S., Rahn, C. W., Pecheux, M-G., Azuma, H., & Vardi, D. (1992). Maternal responsiveness to infants in three societies: The United States, France, and Japan. *Child Development, 63,* 808–821.

Bornstein, R. F., (1992). Critical importance of stimulus unawareness for the production of subliminal psychodynamic activation effects: An attributional model. *Journal of Nervous and Mental Disease. 180,* 69–76.

Bornstein, R. F., Leone, D. R., & Galley, D. J. (1987). The generalizability of subliminal mere exposure effects: Influence of stimuli perceived without awareness of social behavior. *Journal of Personality and Social Psychology, 53,* 1070–1079.

Borod, J. C., Koff, E., Lorch, M. P., & Nicholas, M. (1986). The expression of perception of facial emotion in brain-damaged patients. *Neuropsychologia, 24(2),* 169–180.

Bothwell, R. K., Brigham, J. C., & Malpass, R. S. (1989). Cross-racial identification. *Personality and Social Psychology Bulletin, 15,* 19–25.

Botwinick, J. (1977). Intellectual abilities. In J. E. Birren & K. W. Schaie (Eds.), *Handbook of the psychology of aging* (pp. 580–605). New York: Van Nostrand Reinhold.

Botwinick, J., & Storandt, M. (1974). *Memory, related functions and age*. Springfield, IL: Charles C. Thomas.

Bouchard, T. J. (1995). Breaking the last taboo. *Contemporary Psychology, 40,* 415–418.

Bouchard, T. J., & McGue, M. (1981). Familial studies of intelligence: A review. *Science, 212,* 1055–59.

Bouchard, T. J., Jr. (1984). Twins reared together and apart: What they tell us about human diversity. In S. W. Fox (Ed.), *Individuality and determinism: Chemical and biological bases*. New York: Plenum Press.

Bouchard, T. J., Jr., Lykken, D. T., McGue, M., Segal, N. L., & Tellegen, A. (1990). Sources of human psychological differences: The Minnesota study of twins reared apart. *Science, 250,* 223–250.

Bouton, M. E. (1994). Conditioning, remembering, and forgetting. *Journal of Experimental Psychology: Animal Behavior Processes, 20,* 219–231.

Bower, G. H. (1961). A contrast effect in differential conditioning. *Journal of Experimental Psychology, 62,* 196–199.

Bower, G. H. (1972). Mental imagery and associative learning. In L. W. Gregg (Ed.), *Cognition in learning and memory*. New York: Wiley.

Bower, G. H., & Clark, M. C. (1969). Narrative stories as mediators for serial learning. *Psychonomic Science, 14,* 181–182.

Bower, G. H., Clark, M. C., Lesgold, M. A., & Winzenz, D. (1969). Hierarchical retrieval schemes in recall of categorized work lists. *Journal of Verbal Learning and Verbal Behavior, 8,* 323–343.

Bowers, K. S. (1983). *Hypnosis for the seriously curious* (2nd ed.). New York: Norton.

Bowers, K. S., Regehr, G., Balthazard, C., & Parker, K. (1990). Intuition in the context of discovery. *Cognitive Psychology, 22,* 72–110.

Bowlby, J. (1973). *Attachment and loss: Vol. 2. Separation*. London: Hogarth Press.

Boyle, P. C., Storlein, H., & Kessey, R. E. (1978). Increased efficiency of food utilization following weight loss. *Physiology and Behavior, 21,* 261.

Brackbill, Y. (1979). Obstetrical medication and infant behavior. In J. D. Osofsky (Ed.), *Handbook of infant development*. New York: Wiley.

Bradburn, N. M., & Caplovitz, D. (1965). *Reports on happiness*. Chicago: Aldine.

Bradley, D. R., Dumais, S. T., & Petry, H. M. (1976). Reply to Cavonias. *Nature, 261,* 77–78.

Brady, J. P. (1980). Behavior therapy. In H. I. Kaplan, A. M. Freeman, & B. J. Sadock (Eds.), *Comprehensive textbook of psychiatry: III*. Baltimore, MD: Williams & Wilkins.

Brady, J. V., & Nauta, W. J. H. (1953). Subcortical mechanisms in emotional behavior: Affective changes following septal forebrain lesions in the albino rat. *Journal of Comparative and Physiological Psychology, 46,* 339–346.

Brady, J. V., Porter, R. W., Conrad, D. G., & Mason, J. W. (1958). Avoidance behavior and the development of gastroduodenal ulcers. *Journal of the Experimental Analysis of Behavior, 1,* 69–72.

Brannon, L., & Feist, J. (1992). *Health Psychology: An introduction to behavior and health* (2nd edition). Wadsworth Publishing Co; Belmont, CA.

Branscombe, N. R., & Wann, D. L. (1992). Physiological arousal and reactions to outgroup members during competitions that implicate an important social identity. *Aggressive Behavior, 18,* 85–94.

Bransford, J. D. (1979). *Human cognition: Learning, understanding, and remembering*. Belmont, CA: Wadsworth.

Bransford, J. D., & Johnson, M. K. (1972). Contextual prerequisites for understanding: Some investigations of comprehension and recall. *Journal of Verbal Learning and Verbal Behavior, 11,* 717–726.

Bransford, J. D., & Stein, B. S. (1984). *The IDEAL problem solver: A guide for improving thinking, learning, and creativity*. New York: Freeman.

Braun, B. G. (1983). Neurophysiologic changes in multiple personality due to integration: A preliminary report. *American Journal of Clinical Hypnosis, 26,* 84–92.

Bray, D. W. (1964). The management progress study. *American Psychologist, 19,* 419–420.

Bray, D. W. and Associates. (1991). *Working with organizations and their people: A guide to human resources practice*. New York: Guilford Press.

Bray, G. A. (1972). Lipogenesis in human adipose tissue: Some effects of nibbling and gorging. *Journal of Clinical Investigation, 51,* 537–548.

Bray, G. A. (1978). Definitions, measurements and classification of the syndromes of obesity. *International Journal of Obesity, 2,* 99–112.

Bray, G. A. (1987). Overweight is risking fate: Definition, lessification, prevalence, and risks. In R. J. Wurtman & J. J. Wurtman (Eds.), *Human obesity*. New York: New York Academy of Science.

Bray, G. A. (1988). Controls of food intake and energy expenditure. In G. A. Bray (Ed.), *Diet and Obesity*. Tokyo/S. Karger, Basil Japan, Sci. Soc. Press.

Brecher, E. M. (1972). *Licit and illicit drugs*. Boston: Little, Brown.

Breland, K., & Breland, M. (1961). The misbehavior of organisms. *American Psychologist, 16,* 681–684.

Brewin, C. R. (1985). Depression and causal attributions: What is their relation? *Psychological Bulletin, 98,* 297–309.

Brickman, P. (1987). *Commitment, conflict, and caring*. Englewood Cliffs, NJ: Prentice-Hall.

Brigham, C. C. (1923). *A study of American intelligence*. Princeton, NJ: Princeton University Press.

Brigham, J. C., & Richardson, C. G. (1979). Race, sex and helping in the marketplace. *Journal of Applied Social Psychology, 9,* 314–322.

Broadbent, D. E. (1957). A mechanical model for human attention and immediate memory. *Psychological Review, 64,* 205–215.

Broadbent, D. E. (1958). *Perception and communication*. NY.: Pergamon.

Broadbent, D. E. (1978). The current state of noise research: Reply to Poulton. *Psychological Bulletin, 85,* 1052–1067.

Brock, T. C. (1965). Communicator-recipient similarity and decision change. *Journal of Personality and Social Psychology, 1,* 650–654.

Brody, E. M. (1985). Parent care as a normative family stress. *The Gerontologist, 25,* 19–29.

Brody, E. M. (1990). *Women in the middle: Their parent-care years*. New York: Springer.

Brody, E. M., Litvin, S. J., Albert, S. M., & Hoffman, C. J. (1994). Marital status of daughters and patterns of pattern care. *Journal of Gerontology, 49,* S95–S103.

Brody, N. (1992). *Intelligence* (2nd ed.). New York: Academic Press.

Bronfenbrenner, U. (1989). Ecological systems theory. In R. Vasta (Ed.), *Six theories of child development*. Greenwich, CT: JAI Press.

Brook, J. S., Whiteman, S., Gordon, A. S., & Cohen, P. (1986). Dynamics of childhood and adolescent personality traits and adolescent drug use. *Developmental Psychology, 22,* 403–414.

Brooks-Gunn, J., & Furstenberg, F. F. (1986). The children of adolescent mothers. *Developmental Review, 6,* 224–251.

Brooks-Gunn, J., & Peterson, A. (1983). *Girls at puberty.* New York: Plenum.

Brooks-Gunn, J., & Warren, M. P. (1985). Measuring physical status and timing early adolescence: A developmental perspective. *Journal of Youth and Adolescence, 14,* 163–169.

Broverman, I. K., Broverman, D. M., Clarkson, E. E., Rosenkrantz, P. S., & Vogel, S. R. (1970). Sex-role stereotypes and clinical judgment of mental health. *Journal of Consulting and Clinical Psychology, 34,* 1–7.

Brown v. Board of Education of Topeka (1955). 98 F. Supp. 797 (1951), 347 U.S. 438 (1954), 349 U.S. 294.

Brown, A. L. (1978). Knowing when, where, and how to remember: A problem of metacognition. In R. Glaser (Ed.), *Advances in instructional psychology.* Hillsdale, NJ: Erlbaum.

Brown, A. L., Armbruster, B. B., & Baker, L. (1984). The role of metacognition in reading and study. In J. Orasanu (Ed.), *A decade of reading research: Implications for practice.* Hillsdale, NJ: Erlbaum.

Brown, A. L., Bransford, J. D., Ferrara, R. A., & Campione, J. C. (1983). Learning, remembering, and understanding. In J. H. Flavell & E. M. Markman (Eds.), *Handbook of child psychology: Vol. 3. Cognitive development* (pp. 71–166). New York: Wiley.

Brown, A. S. (1981). Inhibition in cued retrieval. *Journal of Experimental Psychology: Human Learning and Memory, 7,* 204–215.

Brown, J. (1958). Some tests of the decay theory of immediate memory. *Quarterly Journal of Experimental Psychology, 10,* 12–21.

Brown, P. L., & Jenkins, H. M. (1968). Auto-shaping the pigeon's key peck. *Journal of the Experimental Analysis of Behavior, 11,* 1–8.

Brown, R. (1958). How shall a thing be called? *Psychological Review, 65,* 14–21.

Brown, R. (1970). *Psycholinguistics.* New York: Free Press.

Brown, R. A. (1973). *A first language: The early stages.* Cambridge, MA: Harvard University Press.

Brown, R. A., & Herrnstein, R. J. (1975). *Psychology.* Boston: Little, Brown.

Brown, R., & Kulik, J. (1977). Flashbulb memories. *Cognition, 5,* 73–99.

Brown, R., & McNeill, D. (1966). The tip-of-the-tongue phenomenon. *Journal of Verbal Learning and Verbal Behavior, 5,* 325–337.

Brown, R., et al. (1962). *New directions in psychology.* New York: Holt.

Brown, S. D., Lent, R. W., & Larkin, K. C. (1989). Self-efficacy as a moderator of scholastic aptitude-academic performance relationships. *Journal of Vocational Behavior, 35,* 64–75.

Brownell, K. D. (1991). Dieting and the search for the perfect body: Where physiology and culture collide. *Behavior Therapy, 22,* 1–12.

Browning, C. (1993). Review of Y. Zuckerman "A Surplus of Money: Chronicle of the Warsaw Ghetto Uprising." *New York Times Book Review,* May 23, 22–23.

Brubach, H. (1991). The eye of the beholder. *The New Yorker,* June 10, 84–96.

Brubaker, T. H., & Brubaker, E. (1992). Family care of the elderly in the United States. In J. I. Kosberg (Ed.), *Family care of the elderly* (pp. 210–231). Newbury Park, CA: Sage.

Bruch, H. (1961). Transformation of oral impulses in eating disorders: A conceptual approach. *Psychiatric Quarterly, 35,* 458–481.

Bruch, H. (1973). *Eating disorders: Obesity, anorexia nervosa, and the person within.* New York: Basic Books.

Brumberg, J. J., & Streigel-Moore, R. (1993). Continuity and change in symptom choice: Anorexia. In G. H. Elder, Jr., J. Modell, & R. D. Parke (Eds.), *Children in time and place.* New York: Cambridge University Press.

Bruner, J. S. (1972). The nature and uses of immaturity. *American Psychologist, 27,* 687–701.

Bruner, J. S. (1975). The ontogenesis of speech acts. *Journal of Child Language, 2,* 1–19.

Bruner, J. S. (1983). *Child's talk.* New York: Norton.

Bruner, J. S., Goodnow, J. J., & Austin, G. A. (1956). *A study of thinking.* New York: Wiley.

Buchsbaum, M. S., Mirsky, A. F., Delisi, L. E., Morihisa, J., Karson, C. N., Mendelson, W. B., King, A. C., Johnson, J., & Kessler, R. (1984). The Genain quadruplets: Electrophysiological, positron emission, and x-ray tomographic studies. *Psychiatry Research, 13,* 95–108.

Buck, R. (1984). *The communication of emotion.* New York: Guilford Press.

Buck, R. (1985). Prime theory: An integrated view of motivation and emotion. *Psychological Review, 92,* 389–413.

Buck, R., Savin, V. J., Miller, R. E., & Caul, W. F. (1972). Nonverbal communication of affect in humans. *Journal of Personality and Social Psychology, 23,* 362–371.

Bullock, M., & Gelman, R. (1979). Preschool children's assumptions about cause and effect. *Child Development, 50,* 89–96.

Burdine, W. E., Shipley, T. E., & Papas, A. T. (1957). Delatestryl, a long-acting androgenic hormone. *Fertility and Sterility, 8,* 255–259.

Burke, A., Heuer, F., & Reisberg, D. (1992). Remembering emotional events. *Memory & Cognition, 20,* 277–290.

Burroughs, W. J. (1989). Applied environmental psychology. In W. L. Gregory & W. J. Burroughs (Eds.), *Introduction to applied psychology.* Glenview, IL: Scott, Foresman.

Burt, C. (1966). The genetic determination of differences in intelligence: A study of monozygotic twins reared together and apart. *British Journal of Psychology, 57,* 137–153.

Bushman, B. J., & Cooper, H. M. (1990). Effects of alcohol on human aggression: An integrative research review. *Psychological Bulletin, 107,* 341–354.

Buss, A. H., & Plomin, R. (1984). *Temperament: Early developing personality traits.* Hillsdale, NJ: Erlbaum.

Buss, D. M. (1987). Selection, evocation, and manipulation. *Journal of Personality and Social Psychology, 53,* 1214–1221.

Buss, D. M. (1991). Evolutionary personality psychology. *Annual Review of Psychology, 42,* 459–492.

Buss, D. M. (1994). The strategies of human mating. *American Scientist, 82,* 238–249.

Buss, D. M., & Craik, K. H. (1983). The act frequency approach to personality. *Psychological Review, 90,* 105–196.

Butera, P. C., & Czaja, J. A. (1989). Activation of sexual behavior in male rats by combined subcutaneous and intracranial treatments of 5-alpha-dihydrotestosterone. *Hormones and Behavior, 23,* 92–105.

Butler, R. W. (1975). *Why survive? Being old in America.* New York: Harper & Row.

Butler, S. F., Schact, T. E., Henry, W. P., & Strupp, H. H. (1984). Psychotherapy versus placebo: Revisiting a pseudo issue. *Behavioral and Brain Sciences, 7,* 756–757.

Bykov, K. M. (1957). *The cerebral cortex and the internal organs* (W. H. Gantt, Trans.). New York: Chemical Publishing.

Byne, W., Bleier, R., & Houston, L. (1988). Variations in human corpus callosum do not predict gender: A study using magnetic resonance imaging. *Behavioral Neuroscience, 102,* 222–227.

Byrne, D. (1961). The influence of propinquity and opportunities for interaction on classroom relationships. *Human Relations, 14,* 63–70.

Byrne, D. (1971). *The attraction paradigm.* New York: Academic Press.

Byrnes, J. P., & Takahira, S. (1993). Explaining gender differences on SAT-Math items. *Developmental Psychology, 29,* 805–810.

C

Cacioppo, J. T., Petty, R. E., Kao, C. F., & Rodriguez, R. (1986). Central and peripheral routes to persuasion: An individual differences perspective. *Journal of Personality and Social Psychology, 51,* 1032–1043.

Cain, W. S. (1982). Odor identification by males and females: Predictions versus performance. *Chemical Senses, 7,* 129–142.

Cain, W. S. (1988). Olfaction. In R. C. Atkinson, R. J. Herrnstein, G. Lindzey, & R. D. Luce (Eds.), *Steven's handbook of experimental psychology* (2nd ed., pp. 409–459). New York: Wiley Interscience.

Cairns, R. B. (1979). *Social development: The origins and plasticity of interchanges.* San Francisco: Freeman.

Calder, B. J., & Staw, B. M. (1975). Self-perception of intrinsic and extrinsic motivation. *Journal of Personality and Social Psychology, 31,* 599–605.

Calhoun, J. B. (1962). Population density and social pathology. *Scientific American, 206,* 139–148.

Callner, D. A. (1975). Behavioral treatment approaches to drug abuse: A critical review of the research. *Psychological Bulletin, 82,* 143–164.

Campbell, A. (1981). *The sense of well-being in America: Recent patterns and trends.* New York: McGraw-Hill.

Campbell, B. A., & Kraeling, D. (1953). Response strength as a function of drive level and amount of drive reduction. *Journal of Experimental Psychology, 45,* 97–101.

Campbell, B. A., & Misanin, J. R. (1969). Basic drives. *Annual Review of Psychology,* 57–84.

Campbell, D., Sanderson, R. E., & Laverty, S. G. (1964). Characteristics of a conditioned response in human subjects during extinction trials following a single traumatic conditioning trial. *Journal of Abnormal and Social Psychology, 68,* 627–639.

Campione, J. C., & Brown, A. L. (1979). Toward a theory of intelligence: Contributions from research with retarded children. *Intelligence, 2,* 279–304.

Candolle, M. A. de. (1974). *Histoire des sciences et des savanis depuis deux siècles.* In H. J. Mozans, *Women in science* (p. 392). Cambridge, MA: MIT Press. (Original work published 1913)

Cann, A., Sherman, S. J., & Elkes, R. (1975). Effects of initial request size and timing of a second request on compliance: The foot in the door and the door in the face. *Journal of Personality and Social Psychology, 32,* 774–782.

Cannon, D. S., & Baker, T. B. (1981). Emetic and electric shock alcohol aversion therapy: Assessment of conditioning. *Journal of Consulting and Clinical Psychology, 49,* 20–33.

Cannon, D. S., Baker, T. B., & Wehl, C. K. (1981). Emetic and electric shock alcohol aversion therapy: Six- and Twelve-month follow-up. *Journal of Consulting and Clinical Psychology, 49,* 360–368.

Cannon, T. D., Mednick, S. A., & Parnas, J. (1990). Antecedents of predominantly negative- and predominantly positive-symptom schizophrenia in a high-risk population. *Archives of General Psychiatry, 47,* 622–632.

Cannon, W. B. (1927). The James-Lange theory of emotions: A critical examination and an alternative. *American Journal of Psychology, 39,* 106–124.

Cannon, W. B., Lewis, J. T., & Britton, S. W. (1927). The dispensability of the sympathetic division of the autonomic nervous system. *Boston Medical Surgery Journal, 197,* 514.

Cantor, N., & Kihlstrom, J. F. (1987). *Personality and Social Intelligence.* New York: Prentice-Hall.

Cantor, N., & Mischel, W. (1977). Traits as prototypes: Effects on recognition memory. *Journal of Personality and Social Psychology, 35,* 38–48.

Cantor, N., Mischel, W., & Schwartz, J. C. (1982). A prototype analysis of psychological situations. *Cognitive Psychology, 14,* 45–77.

Capaldi, E. D., Sheffer, J., & Owens, J. (1991). Food deprivation and conditioned flavor preferences based on sweetened and unsweetened foods. *Animal Learning & Behavior, 19,* 363–368.

Capaldi, E. J. (1967). A sequential hypothesis of instrumental learning. In K. W. Spence & J. T. Spence (Eds.), *The psychology of learning and motivation* (Vol. 1). New York: Academic Press.

Capaldi, E. J. (1994). The sequential view: From rapidly fading stimulus traces to the organization of memory and the abstract concept of number. *Psychonomic Bulletin and Review, 1,*156–181.

Capaldi, E. J., & Miller, D. J. (1988). Counting in rats: Its functional significance and the independent cognitive processes that constitute it. *Journal of Experimental Psychology: Animal Behavior Processes, 14,* 3–17.

Capaldi, E. J., & Myers, D. E. (1978). Resistance to satiation of consummatory and instrumental performance. *Learning and Motivation, 9,* 179–201.

Caplan, R. D., Abbey, A., Abramis, D. J., Andrews, F. M., Conway, T. L., & French, J. R. P. (1983). *Tranquilizer use and well being: A longitudinal study of social and psychological effects.* Ann Arbor: Institute for Social Research, University of Michigan.

Capron, C., & Duyme, M. (1989). Assessment of effects of socioeconomic status on IQ in a full cross-fostering study. *Nature, 340,* 552–553.

Caramazza, A. (1986). On drawing inferences about the structure of normal cognitive systems from the analysis of impaired performance: The case for single-patient studies. *Brain and Cognition, 5,* 41–66.

Caramazza, A., & McCloskey, M. (1988). The case for single patient studies. *Cognitive Neuropsychology, 5,* 517–528.

Carey, S. (1977). The child as a word learner. In M. Halle, J. Bresnan, & G. Miller (Eds.), *Linguistic theory and psychological reality.* Cambridge, MA: MIT Press.

Carey, S. (1982). Semantic development: The state of the art. In E. Wanner & L. R. Gleitman (Eds.), *Language acquisition: The state of the art* (pp. 347–389). Cambridge, England: Cambridge University Press.

Carey, S. (1985). *Conceptual change in childhood.* Cambridge, MA: MIT Press.

Carini, C., Zini, D., Baldini, A., Della Casa, L., Ghizzani, A., & Marrama, P. (1990). Effects of androgen treatment in impotent men with normal and low level of free testosterone. *Archives of Sexual Behavior, 19,* 223–234.

Carini, C., Zini, D., Baldini, A., Della Casa, L., Ghizzani, A., & Marrama, P. (1990). Effects of androgen treatment in impotent men with normal and low level of free testosterone. *Archives of Sexual Behavior, 19,* 223–234.

Carlson, N. R. (1986). *Physiology of behavior* (3rd ed.). Boston: Allyn and Bacon.

Carmichael, L. L., Hogan, H. P., & Walter, A. A. (1932). An experimental study of the effect of language on reproduction of visually perceived form. *Journal of Experimental Psychology, 15,* 73–85.

Caro, T. M. (1986). The functions of stotting: A review of the hypotheses. *Animal Behavior, 34,* 649–662.

Carr, E. G., Taylor, J. C., & Robinson, S. (1991). The effects of severe behavior problems in children on the teaching behavior of adults. *Journal of Applied Behavior Analysis, 24,* 523–535.

Carskadon, M. A., & Dement, W. C. (1981). Cumulative effects of sleep restriction on daytime sleepiness. *Psycho-physiology, 18,* 107–113.

Carskadon, M. A., & Roth, T. (1991). Sleep Restriction. In T. H. Monk (Ed.), *Sleep, sleepiness, and performance* (pp. 155–167). New York: Wiley.

Carson, R. C. (1990). Needed: A new beginning. *Contemporary Psychology, 35,* 11–12.

Carson, R. C. (1991). Dilemmas in the pathway of the DSM-IV. *Journal of Abnormal Psychology, 100,* 302–307.

Carson, R. C., & Butcher, J. N. (1992). *Abnormal psychology and modern life* (9th ed.). New York: HarperCollins.

Carson, R. C., Butcher, J. N., & Coleman, J. C. (1988). *Abnormal psychology and modern life* (8th ed.). Glenview, IL: Scott, Foresman.

Carter, S. L. (1991). *Reflections of an affirmative action baby.* New York: Basic Books.

Carver, C. S., & Scheier, M. F. (1981). *Attention and self-regulation: A control theory approach to human behavior.* New York: Springer-Verlag.

Case, R. (1985). *Intellectual development: Birth to adulthood.* New York: Academic Press.

Cates, J. (1970). Psychology's manpower: Report on the 1968 national register of scientific and technical personnel. *American Psychologist, 25,* 254–264.

Cattell, R. B. (1971). *Abilities: Their structure, growth, and action.* Boston: Houghton Mifflin.

Cattell, R. B. (1973, July). Personality pinned down. *Psychology Today,* pp. 40–46.

Cattell, R. B. (1982). *The inheritance of personality and ability.* New York: Academic Press.

Ceci, S. J., & Liker, J. K. (1986). A day at the races. *Journal of Experimental Psychology: General, 115,* 255–266.

Ceci, S. J., Huffman, M. L. C., Smith, E., & Loftus, E. F. (1994). Repeatedly thinking about a non-event: Source misattributions among preschoolers. *Consciousness and Cognition, 3,* 388–407.

Cerella, J. (1985). Information processing rates in the elderly. *Psychological Bulletin, 98,* 67–83.

Cermak, L. S., & Craik, F. I. M. (Eds.). (1979). *Levels of processing in human memory.* Hillsdale, NJ: Erlbaum.

Cernoch, J. M., & Porter R. H. (1985). Recognition of maternal axillary odors by infants. *Child Development, 56,* 1593–1598.

Chafetz, M. E. (1979, May–June). Alcohol and alcoholism. *American Scientist.*

Chaffin, R., & Herrmann, D. J. (1983). Self-reports of memory abilities by old and young adults. *Human Learning, 2,* 17–28.

Chagnon, N. A. (1988). Life histories, blood revenge, and warfare in a tribal population. *Science, 239,* 985–992.

Chaiken, S. (1986). Physical appearance and social influence. In C. P. Herman, M. P. Zanna, & E. T. Higgins (Eds.), *Physical appearance, stigma, and social behavior: The Ontario Symposium* (Vol. 3, pp. 143–187). Hillsdale, NJ: Erlbaum.

Chaiken, S., & Eagly, A. H. (1976). Communication modality as a determinant of message persuasiveness and message comprehensibility. *Journal of Personality and Social Psychology, 34,* 605–614.

Chance, P. (1994). *Learning and behavior* (3rd ed.). Pacific Grove, CA: Brooks/Cole.

Chandler, C. C. (1989). Specific retroactive interference in modified recognition tests: Evidence for an unknown cause of interference. *Journal of Experimental Psychology: Learning, Memory, and Cognition, 15,* 256–265.

Chandler, C., & Gargano, G. J. (1995). Item-specific interference caused by cue-dependent forgetting. *Memory & Cognition, 23,* 701–708.

Chapanis, A. (1965). *Man-made engineering.* Belmont, CA: Wadsworth.

Chase, W. G., & Simon, H. A. (1973). Perception in chess. *Cognitive Psychology, 4,* 55–81.

Cheesman, J., & Merikle, P. M. (1986). Distinguishing consciousness from unconscious processes. *Canadian Journal of Psychology, 40,* 343–367.

Cherlin, A. J. (1992). *Marriage, divorce, remarriage.* Cambridge, MA: Harvard University Press.

Cherry, E. C. (1953). Some experiments on the recognition of speech with one and two ears. *Journal of the Acoustical Society of America, 25,* 975–979.

Cherry, F., & Byrne, D. (1976). Authoritarianism. In T. Blass (Ed.), *Personality variables in social behavior.* Hillsdale, NJ: Erlbaum.

Chesney, M. A., Hecker, M. H., & Black, G. W. (1988). Coronary-prone components of Type A behavior in the WCGS: A new methodology. In B. K. Houston & G. R. Snyder (Eds.), *Type A behavior pattern: Research, theory, and intervention.* New York: Wiley.

Chi, M. T. H. (1978). Knowledge structures and memory development. In R. Siegler (Ed.), *Children's thinking: What develops?* Hillsdale, NJ: Erlbaum.

Chi, M. T. H., & Klahr, D. (1975). Span and rate of apprehension in children and adults. *Journal of Experimental Child Psychology, 19,* 434–439.

Chi, M. T., Feltovich, P. J., & Glaser, R. (1981). Categorization and representation of physics problems by experts and novices. *Cognitive Science, 5,* 121–152.

Children's Safety Network. (1991). *A data book of child and adolescent injury.* Washington, DC: National Center for Education in Maternal and Child Health.

Chomsky, N. (1957). *Syntactic structures.* The Hague: Mouton.

Chomsky, N. (1965). *Aspects of the theory of syntax.* Cambridge, MA: MIT Press.

Chomsky, N. (1979). *Language and responsibility.* New York: Pantheon.

Chwalisz, K., Diener, E., & Gallagher, D. (1988). Autonomic arousal feedback and emotional experience: Evidence from the spinal cord injured. *Journal of Personality and Social Psychology, 54,* 820–828.

Cialdini, R. B. (1985). *Influence: Science and practice.* Glenview, IL: Scott, Foresman.

Cialdini, R. B., Cacioppo, J. T., Bassett, R., & Miller, J. A. (1978). The low-ball procedure for producing compliance: Commitment then cost. *Journal of Personality and Social Psychology, 36,* 463–476.

Cialdini, R. B., Vincent, J. E., Lewis, S. K., Catalan, J., Wheeler, D., & Darby, B. L. (1975). Reciprocal concessions procedure for inducing compliance: The door-in-the-face technique. *Journal of Personality and Social Psychology, 31,* 206–215.

Clark, E. V. (1973). What's in a word? On the child's acquisition of semantics in his first language. In T. E. Moore (Ed.), *Cognitive development and the acquisition of language*. New York: Academic Press.

Clark, H. H., & Clark, E. V. (1977). *Psychology and language*. New York: Harcourt Brace Jovanovich.

Clark, M. S., & Reis, H. T. (1988). Interpersonal processes in close relationships. *Annual Review of Psychology, 39,* 609–672.

Clark, R. D., & Word, L. E. (1972). Why don't bystanders help? Because of ambiguity? *Journal of Personality and Social Psychology, 24,* 392–400.

Clark, S. E. (1995). The generation effect and modeling of associations in memory. *Memory & Cognition, 23,* 442–455.

Clarke-Stewart, A. (1989). Infant day care: Maligned or malignant? *American Psychologist, 44,* 266–273.

Clarke-Stewart, A. (1993). *Daycare.* Cambridge, MA: Harvard University Press.

Clausen, J. A. (1981). Men's occupational careers in the middle years. In D. Eichorn, J. Clausen, N. Haan, M. Honzik, & P. Mussen (Eds.), *Present and past in middle life.* New York: Academic Press.

Clay, M. M. (1973). *Reading: The patterning of complex behavior.* Auckland, New Zealand: Heineman Educational Books.

Clayton, P. J. (1981). The epidemiology of bipolar affective disorder. *Comprehensive Psychiatry, 22,* 31–43.

Cleckley, H. (1964). *The mask of sanity.* St. Louis: Mosby.

Clementz, B. A., Grove, W. M., Iacono, W. G., & Sweeney, J. A. (1992). Smooth-pursuit eye movement dysfunction and liability for schizophrenia: Implications for genetic modeling. *Journal of Abnormal Psychology, 101,* 117–129.

Clore, G. L. (1975). *Interpersonal attraction: An overview.* Morristown, NJ: General Learning Press.

Clutton-Brock, T. H., Albon, S. D., Gibson, R. M., & Guinness, F. E. (1979). The logical stag: Adaptive aspects of fighting in red deer (Cervus elaphus L.). *Animal Behaviour, 27,* 211–225.

Coe, W. C. (1977). The problem of relevance versus ethics in researching hypnosis and antisocial conduct. *Annuals of the New York Academy of Sciences, 296,* 90–104.

Cohen, J. D., Noll, D. C., & Schneider, W. (1993). Functional magnetic resonance imaging: Overview and methods for psychological research. *Behavior Research Methods, Instruments, and Computers, 1993, 25(2),* 101–113.

Cohen, L. G., DeLoache, J. S., & Strauss, M. S. (1979). Infant visual perception. In J. Osofsky (Ed.), *Handbook of infant development.* New York: Wiley.

Cohen, S. (1980). Aftereffects of stress on human performance and social behavior: A review of research and theory. *Psychological Bulletin, 88,* 82–108.

Cohen, S., & Wills, T. A. (1985). Stress, social support, and the buffering hypothesis. *Psychological Bulletin, 98,* 310–357.

Cohen, S., Evans, G. W., Krantz, D. S., & Stokols, D. (1980). Physiological, motivational, and cognitive effects of aircraft noise on children: Moving from the laboratory to the field. *American Psychologist, 35,* 231–243.

Cohen, S., Evans, G. W., Krantz, D. S., Stokols, D., & Kelly, S. (1981). Aircraft noise and children: Longitudinal and cross-sectional evidence on adaptation to noise and the effectiveness of noise abatement. *Journal of Personality and Social Psychology, 40,* 331–345.

Cohen, S., Glass, D. D., & Singer, J. E. (1973). Apartment noise, auditory discrimination, and reading ability in children. *Journal of Experimental Social Psychology, 9,* 407–422.

Cohen, S., Tyrell, D. A. J., & Smith, A. P. (1993). Negative life events, perceived stress, negative affect, and susceptibility to the common cold. *Journal of Personality and Social Psychology, 64,* 131–140.

Colavita, F. B. (1978). *Sensory changes in the elderly.* Springfield, IL: Thomas.

Coleman, J. C., Butcher, J. N., & Carson, R. C. (1980). *Abnormal psychology and modern life* (6th ed.). Glenview, IL: Scott, Foresman.

Coleman, L. (1987). *Suicide clusters.* Winchester, MA: Faber & Faber.

Coleman, R. M. (1986). *Wide awake at 3:00 a.m.* New York: Freeman.

Collins, A. M., & Loftus, E. F. (1975). A spreading activation theory of semantic processing. *Psychological Review, 82,* 407–428.

Colwill, R. M., & Rescorla, R. A. (1988). Associations between the discriminative stimulus and the reinforcer in instrumental learning. *Journal of Experimental Psychology: Animal Behavior Processes, 14,* 155–164.

Combs, B., & Slovic, P. (1984, September). "The Register-Guard, The Standard-Times." *The Journalist,* p. 10.

Conrad, R., & Hull, A. J. (1968). Input modality and the serial position curve in short-term memory. *Psychonomic Science, 10,* 135–136.

Conte, H. R., Plutchik, R., Picard, S., & Karasu, T. B. (1989). Ethics in the practice of psychotherapy: A survey. *American Journal of Psychotherapy, 43,* 32–42.

Contrada, R. J., Leventhal, H., & O'Leary, A. (1990). Personality and health. In L. A. Pervin (Ed.) *Handbook of Personality Theory and Research.* New York: Guilford, pp. 638–669.

Cook, D. R. (1989). A reply to Maltzman. *Journal of Studies on Alcohol, 50,* 484–486.

Coombs, L. C. (1979). The measurement of commitment to work. *Journal of Population, 2,* 203–223.

Cooper R. P., & Aslin, R. N. (1990). Preference for infant-directed speech in the first month after birth. *Child Development, 61,* 1584–1595.

Cooper, J. C., Zanna, M. P., & Taves, P. A. (1978). Arousal as a necessary condition for attitude change following induced compliance. *Journal of Personality and Social Psychology, 36,* 1101–1106.

Cooper, R. M., & Zubek, J. P. (1958). Effects of enriched and restricted early environment on the learning ability of bright and dull rats. *Canadian Journal of Psychology, 12,* 159–164.

Cooper, S. (1987). The fetal alcohol syndrome. *Journal of Child Psychology and Psychiatry, 28,* 223–227.

Cordes, C. (1985). Military waste: The human factor. *APA Monitor,* p. 1.

Coren, C. (1989). Cross-cultural studies of visual illusions: The physiological confound. *Behavioral and Brain Sciences, 12,* 76–77.

Coren, S. (1984). Subliminal perception. In R. J. Corsini (Ed.), *Encyclopedia of psychology* (Vol. 3, p. 382). New York: Wiley.

Coren, S. (1991). Retinal mechanisms in the perception of subjective contours: The contribution of lateral inhibition. *Perception, 20,* 181–191.

Coren, S., & Girgus, J. S. (1978). *Seeing is deceiving: The psychology of visual illusions.* Hillsdale, NJ: Erlbaum.

Coren, S., Ward, L. M., & Enns, J. T. (1994). *Sensation and perception* (4th ed.). Fort Worth, TX: Harcourt Brace.

Corey, D. P., & Roper, S. D. (1992). *Sensory transduction.* New York: The Rockefeller University Press.

Cornsweet, T. N. (1970). *Visual perception.* New York: Academic Press.

Corrigan, R. (1983). The development of representational skills. In *Levels and transitions in children's development* (New directions for child development, No. 21). San Francisco: Jossey-Bass.

Cosgrove, J. M., & Patterson, C. J. (1977). Plans and the development of listener skills. *Developmental Psychology, 13,* 557–564.

Covington, M. V. (1993). *Making the grade: A self-worth perspective on motivation and school reform.* Cambridge England: Cambridge University Press.

Cowan, N. (1995). *Attention and memory: An integrated framework.* New York: Oxford.

Cowart, B. J. (1981). Development of taste perception in humans: Sensitivity and preference throughout the life span. *Psychological Bulletin, 90,* 43–73.

Cowdery, G. E., Iwata, B. A., & Pace, G. M. (1990). Effects and side effects of DRO as treatment for self-injurious behavior. *Journal of Applied Behavior Analysis, 23,* 497–506.

Cox, T. (1978). *Stress.* Baltimore, MD: University Park Press.

Coyne, J. C. (1985). Studying depressed persons' interactions with strangers and spouses. *Journal of Abnormal Psychology, 94,* 231–232.

Craddock, D. (1979). *Obesity and its management.* London: Churchill Livingstone.

Craig, J. D. (1979). Asymmetries in processing auditory nonverbal stimuli? *Psychological Bulletin, 86,* 1339–1349.

Craig, K., & Lowrey, H. J. (1969). Heart rate components of conditioned vicarious autonomic responses. *Journal of Personality and Social Psychology, 11,* 381–387.

Craik, F. I. M. (1977). Age differences in human memory. In J. E. Birren, & K. W. Schaie (Eds.), *The handbook of the psychology of aging.* New York: Van Nostrand Reinhold.

Craik, F. I. M., & Byrd, M. (1982). Aging and cognitive deficits: The role of attentional resources. In F. I. M. Craik & S. E. Trehub (Eds.), *Aging and cognitive processes.* New York: Plenum.

Craik, F. I. M., & Jennings, J. M. (1992). Human memory. In F. I. M. Craik & T. A. Salthouse (Eds.), *The handbook of aging and cognition* (pp. 51–110). Hillsdale, NJ: Erlbaum.

Craik, F. I. M., & Lockhart, R. S. (1972). Levels of processing: A framework for memory research. *Journal of Verbal Learning and Verbal Behavior, 11,* 671–684.

Craik, F. I. M., & McDowd, J. M. (1987). Age differences in recall and recognition. *Journal of Experimental Psychology: Learning, Memory, and Cognition, 13,* 474–479.

Craik, F. I. M., & Tulving, E. (1975). Depth of processing and retention of works in episodic memory. *Journal of Experimental Psychology: General, 104,* 268–294.

Crandall, C. S. (1988). Social contagion of binge eating. *Journal of Personality and Social Psychology, 55,* 588–598.

Crano, W. D. (1970). Effects of sex, response order, and expertise in conformity: A dispositional approach. *Sociometry, 33,* 239–252.

Cravens, H. (1992). A scientific project locked in time: The Terman genetic studies of genius, 1920s–1950s. *American Psychologist, 47,* 183–189.

Craver-Lemley, C., & Reeves, A. (1992). How visual imagery interferes with vision. *Psychological Review, 99,* 633–649.

Crawford, H. J., Wallace, B., Normura, K., & Slater, H. (1986). Eidetic-like imagery in hypnosis: Rare but there. *American Journal of Psychology, 99,* 527–546.

Crawford, M., & Masterson, F. (1978). Components of the flight response can reinforce bar-press avoidance learning. *Journal of Experimental Psychology: Animal Behavior Processes, 4,* 144–151.

Crespi, L. P. (1942). Quantitative variations of incentive and performance in the white rat. *American Journal of Psychology, 55,* 467–517.

Crick, F., & Mitchison, G. (1983). The function of dream sleep. *Nature, 304,* 111–114.

Crisp, A. H. (1970). Premorbid factors in adult disorders of weight, with primary reference to primary anorexia nervosa: A literature review. *Journal of Psychosometric Research, 14,* 1–22.

Crocker, J., & Major, B. (1989). Social stigma and self-esteem: The self-protective properties of stigma. *Psychological Review, 96,* 608–630.

Crocker, J., Cornwell, B., & Major, B. (1993). The stigma of overweight: The affective consequences of attributional ambiguity. *Journal of Personality and Social Psychology, 64,* 60–70.

Crocker, J., Voelkl, K., Cornwell, B., & Major, B. (1989). Effects on self-esteem of attributing interpersonal feedback to prejudice. Unpublished manuscript cited in J. Crocker and B. Major (Eds., in press), Social stigma and self-esteem: The self-protective properties of stigma. *Psychological Review.*

Crocker, J., Voelkl, K., Testa, M., & Major, B. (1991). Social stigma: Affective consequences of attributional ambiguity. *Journal of Personality and Social Psychology, 60,* 218–228.

Crockett, L. J., & Petersen, A. C. (1987). Pubertal status and psychosocial development: Findings from the Early Adolescence Study. In R. M. Lerners & T. T. Foch (Eds.), *Biological-psychosocial interactions in early adolescence: A life-span perspective* (pp. 173–188). Hillsdale, NJ: Erlbaum.

Crockett, L., Losoff, M., & Peterson, A. C. (1984). Perceptions of the peer group and friendship in early adolescence. *Journal of Early Adolescence, 4,* 155–181.

Crowder, R. G. (1976). *Principles of learning and memory.* Hillsdale, NJ: Erlbaum.

Crowder, R. G. (1992a). Eidetic images. In L. R. Squire (Ed.), *The encyclopedia of learning and memory* (pp. 154–156). New York: MacMillan.

Crowder, R. G. (1992b). Sensory memory. In L. R. Squire (Ed.), *The encyclopedia of learning and memory* (pp. 588–591). New York: MacMillan.

Crowe, R. R. (1972). The adopted offspring of women criminal offenders: A study of their arrest records. *Archives of General Psychiatry, 27,* 600–603.

Crowe, R. R. (1974). An adoption study of antisocial personality. *Archives of General Psychiatry, 31,* 785–791.

Csikszentmihalyi, M. (1990). *Flow: The Psychology of Optimal Experience.* New York: Harper & Row.

Csikszentmihalyi, M., & Larson, R. (1984). *Being adolescent.* New York: Basic Books.

Curran, J. P., & Lippold, S. (1975). The effects of physical attraction and attitude similarity on attraction in dating dyads. *Journal of Personality, 44,* 528–539.

Curtis, M. J., & Zins, J. E. (1988). Effects of training in consultation and instructor feedback on acquisition of consultation skills. *Journal of School Psychology, 26,* 185–190.

Czeizler, C. A., Kronauer, R. E., Allan, J. S., Duffy, J. F., Jewett, M. E., Brown, E. N., & Ronda, J. M. (1989). Bright light induction of strong (Type O) resetting of the human circadian pacemaker. *Science, 244,* 1328–1333.

D

Dagenbach, D., Carr, T. H., & Wilhelmsen, A. (1989). Task-induced strategies and near-threshold priming: Conscious influences on unconscious processing. *Journal of Memory and Language, 28,* 412–443.

Daly, M., & Wilson, M. (1988). *Homicide.* New York: Aldine de Gruyter.

Damon, A. (1973). Smoking attitudes and practices in seven preliterate societies. In W. L. Dunn, Jr. (Ed.), *Smoking behavior: Motives and incentive* (pp. 219–230). Washington, DC: Winston.

Damon, W., & Hart, D. (1982). The development of self-understanding from infancy through adolescence. *Child Development, 53,* 841–864.

Darley, J. M., & Latané, B. (1968). Bystander intervention in emergencies: Diffusion of responsibility. *Journal of Personality and Social Psychology, 8,* 377–388.

Darwin, C. (1859). *On the origin of species by means of natural selection, or the preservation of favoured races in the struggle for life.* London: John Murray.

Darwin, C. (1871). *The descent of man and selections in relation to sex.* London: John Murray.

Darwin, C. (1965). *The expression of the emotions in man and in animals.* Chicago: University of Chicago Press. (Original work published 1872)

Darwin, C. J., Turvey, M. T., & Crowder, R. G. (1972). An auditory analogue of the Sperling partial report procedure: Evidence for brief auditory storage. *Cognitive Psychology, 3,* 255–267.

Dasen, P. R. (1972). Cross-cultural Piagetian research: A summary. *Journal of Cross-Cultural Psychology, 3,* 23–29.

Daum, I., Schugens, M. M., Ackermann, H., & Lutzenberger, W. (1993). Classical conditioning after cerebellar lesions in humans. *Behavioral Neuroscience, 107(5),* 748–756.

Davenport, W. (1965). Sexual patterns and their regulation in a society of the Southwest Pacific. In F. A. Beach (Ed.), *Sex and behavior.* New York: Wiley.

Davidson, J. M. (1972). Hormones and reproductive behavior. In S. Levine (Ed.), *Hormone and behavior* (pp. 63–103). New York: Academic Press.

Davidson, J. M., Camergeo, C. A., & Smith, E. R. (1979). Effects of androgen on sexual behavior in hypo gondalmen. *Journal of Clinical Endocrinology and Metabolism, 48,* 955–958.

Davis, P. J. (1987). Repression and the inaccessibility of affective memories. *Journal of Personality and Social Psychology, 53,* 585–593.

Davison, A. N., & Dobbing, J. (1966). Myelination as a vulnerable period in brain development. *British Medical Bulletin, 22,* 40–44.,

DeAngelis, T. (1993). Controversial diagnosis is voted into latest DSM. *APA Monitor,* September, 1993, p. 32–33.

Deaux, K., & Wrightsman, L. S. (1984). *Social psychology in the 80s* (4th ed.). Monterey, CA: Brooks/Cole.

DeCasper, A. J., & Fifer, W. P. (1980). Of human bonding: Newborns prefer their mothers' voices. *Science, 208,* 1174–1176.

DeCasper, A. J., & Prescott, P. A. (1984). Human newborn perception of male voices: Preference, discrimination, and reinforcing value. *Developmental Psychology, 17,* 481–491.

DeCasper, A. J., & Spence, M. J. (1986). Prenatal maternal speech influences newborns' perception of speech sounds. *Infant behavior and development, 9,* 133–150.

DeCastro, J. M. (1993). Age-related changes in spontaneous food intake and hunger in humans. *Appetite, 21,* 255–272.

DeCastro, J. M. (1993). Age-related changes in spontaneous food intake and hunger in humans. *Appetite, 21,* 255–272.

Deci, E. L. (1975). *Intrinsic motivation.* New York: Plenum.

Deckard, B. S. (1976). The genetic biochemical and pharmacological correlates of respone priming in mice. *Dissertation Abstracts International, 36 (8-B),* 4196.

DeFries, J. C., Hegmann, J. P., & Halcomb, R. A. (1974). Response to 20 generations of selection for open-field activity in mice. *Behavioral Biology, 11,* 481–495.

DeJong, W. (1979). An examination of self-perception mediation of the foot-in-the-door effect. *Journal of Personality and Social Psychology, 37,* 2221–2239.

DeJong, W., & Kleck, R. E. (1986). The social psychological effects of being overweight. In C. P. Herman, M. P. Zanna, & E. T. Higgins (Eds.), *Physical appearance, stigma, and social behavior: The Ontario Symposium* (Vol. 3, pp. 65–87). Hillsdale, NJ: Erlbaum.

DeLoache, J. S., Cassidy, D. J., & Brown, A. L. (1985). Precursors of mnemonic strategies in very young children's memory. *Child Development, 56,* 125–137.

Delongis, A. (1982). Relationship of daily hassles, uplifts, and major life events to health status. *Health Psychology, 1(2),* 119–136.

Dember, W. N., Jenkins, J. J., & Taylor, T. J. (1984). *General psychology.* Hillsdale, NJ: Erlbaum.

Dembroski, T. M., MacDougall, J. M., Costa, P. T., Jr., & Grandits, G. A. (1989). Components of hostility as predictors of sudden death and myocardial infarction in the Multiple Risk Factor Intervention Trial. *Psychosomatic Medicine, 51,* 514–522.

Dembroski, T. M., & Williams, R. B. (1989). Definition and assessment of coronary-prone behavior. In N. Schneiderman, S. M. Weiss & P. G. Kaufmann (Eds.), *Handbook or research methods in cardiovascular behavior medicine* (pp. 553–569). New York: Plenum Press.

Dement, W. C. (1960). The effect of dream deprivation. *Science, 131,* 1705–1707.

Dement, W. C. (1976). *Some must watch while some must sleep.* New York: Norton.

Dement, W. C., & Kleitman, N. (1957a). Cyclic variations in EEG during sleep and their relations to eye movement, body motility, and dreaming. *EEG Clinical Neurophysiology, 9,* 673–690.

Dement, W. C., & Kleitman, N. (1957b). The relation of eye movements during sleep to dream activity: An objective method for the study of dreaming. *Journal of Experimental Psychology, 53,* 339–346.

Demtroski, T. M., MacDougall, J. M., Costa, P. T., Jr., & Grandits, G. A. (1989). Components of hostility as predictors of sudden death and myocardial infarction in the Multiple Risk Factor Intervention Trial. *Psychosomatic Medicine, 51,* 514–522.

Deregowski, J. (1989). Real space and represented space: Cross-cultural perspectives. *Behavioral and Brain Sciences, 12,* 51–119.

Dermer, M., & Pyszczynski, T. A. (1978). Effects of erotica upon men's loving and liking responses for women they love. *Journal of Personality and Social Psychology, 36,* 1302–1309.

DePaulo B. M. (1992). Nonverbal behavior and self-presentation. *Psychological Bulletin, 111(2),* 203–243.

DeSalvo. L. (1990). *Virginia Woolf: The Impact of Childhood Sexual Abuse on Her Life and Work.* New York: Ballantine Books.

Desor, J. A., Greene, L. S., & Maller, O. (1975). Preference for sweet and salty in 9- to 15-year-old and adult humans. *Science, 190,* 686–697.

Deutsch, J. A. (1983). The cholinergic synapse and the site of memory. In J. A. Deutsch (Ed.), *The physiological basis of memory.* New York: Academic Press.

Deutsch, J. A., & Gonzalez, M. R. (1980). Gastric nutrient content signals satiety. *Behavioral and Neural Biology, 30,* 113–116.

Deutsch, M., & Colins, M. E. (1951). *Interracial housing: A psychological evaluation of a social experiment.* Minneapolis: University of Minnesota Press.

DeVellis, B. M., & Blalock, S. J. (1992). Illness attributions and hopelessness depression: The role of hopelessness expectancy. *Journal of Abnormal Psychology, 101,* 257–264.

Devine, P. G. (1989). Stereotypes and prejudice: Their automatic and controlled components. *Journal of Personality and Social Psychology, 56,* 5–18.

DeVries, R. (1969). Constancy of generic identity in the years three to six. *Society for Research in Child Development Monographs, 34*(3, Serial No. 127).

Dewsbury, D. A. (1978). *Comparative animal behavior.* New York: McGraw-Hill.

Di Lorenzo, P. M. (1989). Across unit patterns in the neural response to taste: Vector space analysis. *Journal of Neurophysiology, 62,* 823–833.

Diaconis, P. (1978). Statistical problems in ESP research. *Science, 201,* 131–136.

Diamond, M. (1982). Neuroscience and motivation: Pathways and peptides that define motivational systems. In R. C. Atkinson, R. J. Herrnstein, G. Lindzey, & R. D. Luce (Eds.), *Steven's handbook of experimental psychology* (2nd ed., pp. 547–625). New York: Wiley.

Dickens, W. J., & Perlman, D. (1981). Friendships across the life cycle. In S. Duck & R. Gilmour (Eds.), *Personal relationships 2: Developing personal relationships.* London: Academic Press.

Dickinson, A., & Mackintosh, N. J. (1978). Classical conditioning in animals. *Annual Review of Psychology, 29,* 587–612.

Dickinson, A., Hall, G., & Mackintosh, N. J. (1976). Surprise and the attenuation of blocking. *Journal of Experimental Psychology: Animal Behavior Processes, 2,* 213–222.

Dickinson, D., & Pearce, J. M. (1977). Inhibitory interactions between appetitive and aversive stimuli. *Psychological Bulletin, 84,* 690–711.

Diener, C. I., & Dweck, C. S. (1978). An analysis of learned helplessness: Continuous changes in performance, strategy, and achievement cognitions following failure. *Journal of Personality and Social Psychology, 36,* 451–462.

Diener, C. I., & Dweck, C. S. (1980). An analysis of learned helplessness: 2. The processing of success. *Journal of Personality and Social Psychology, 39,* 940–952.

Diener, E. (1980). Deindividuation: The absence of self-awareness and self-regulation in group members. In P. B. Paulus (Ed.), *The psychology of group influence* (pp. 209–242). Hillsdale, NJ: Erlbaum.

Diener, E., Sandvik, E., & Larsen, R. J. (1985). Age and sex effects for emotional intensity. *Developmental Psychology, 21,* 542–546.

Digman, J. M. (1990). Personality structure: Emergence of the five-factor model. *Annual Review of Psychology, 41,* 417–440.

Dinges, D. F., & Kribbs, N. B. (1991). Performing while sleepy: Effects of experimentally-induced sleepiness. In T. H. Monk (Ed.), *Sleep, sleepiness, and performance* (pp. 97–128). New York: Wiley.

Dixon, N. F. (1981). *Preconscious processing.* New York: Wiley.

Dixon, R., & Baltes, P. B. (1986). Toward life-span research on the functions and pragmatics of intelligence. In R. Sternberg & R. Wagner (Eds.), *Practical intelligence: Nature and origins of competence in the everyday world.* Cambridge: Cambridge University Press.

Do males have a math gene? (1980, December 15). *Newsweek.*

Dobelle, W. H. (1977). Current status of research on providing sight to the blind by electrical stimulation of the brain. *Journal of Visual Impairment and Blindness, 71,* 290–297.

Dobson, K. S., & Shaw, B. F. (1988). The use of treatment manuals in cognitive therapy: Experience and issues. *Journal of Consulting and Clinical Psychology, 56,* 673–680.

Dodwell, P. C., & Humphrey, G. K. (1990). A functional theory of the McCollough effect. *Psychological Review, 97,* 78–89.

Dodwell, P. C., Humphrey, G. K., & Muir, D. W. (1987). Shape and pattern perception. In P. Salapatek & L. Cohen (Eds.), *Handbook of infant perception: Vol. 2, From perception to cognition* (pp. 1–77). Orlando, FL: Academic Press.

Doll, R. (1955). Etiology of lung cancer. *Advances in Cancer Research, 3,* 1–50.

Dollard, J., & Miller, N. E. (1950). *Personality and Psychotherapy: An analysis in Terms of Learning Thinking and Culture.* New York: McGraw-Hill.

Dollard, J., Doob, L., Miller, N., Mowrer, O., & Sears, K. (1939). *Frustration and aggression.* New Haven: Yale University Press.

Dominick, J. R. (1978). Crime and law enforcement in the mass media. In C. Winick (Ed.), *Sage annual reviews of studies in deviance: Vol. 2. Deviance and mass media.* Beverly Hills, CA: Sage.

Domjan, M., O'Vary, D., & Greene, P. (1988). Conditioning of appetitive and consummatory sexual behavior in male Japanese quail. *Journal of the Experimental Analysis of Behavior, 50,* 505–519.

Domjan. (1994). Formulation of a behavior system for search conditioning. *Psychonomic Bulletin & Review, 1*(4), 421–428.

Donagher, P. C., Poulos, R. W., Liebert, R. M., & Davidson, E. S. (1975). Race, sex and social example: An analysis of character portrayals on interracial television entertainment. *Psychological Reports, 37,* 1023–1034.

Doob, A. N., & McLaughlin, D. S. (1989). Ask and you shall be given: Request size and donations to a good cause. *Journal of Applied Social Psychology, 19,* 1049–1056.

Dooling, D. J., & Christiaansen, R. E. (1977). Episodic and semantic aspects of memory for prose. *Journal of Experimental Psychology: Human Learning and Memory, 3,* 428–436.

Dorfman, D. D. (1995). Soft science with a neoconservative agenda. *Contemporary Psychology, 40,* 418–421.

Dorfman, P. (1989). Industrial and organizational psychology. In W. L. Gregory and W. J. Burroughs (Eds.), *Introduction to applied psychology.* Glenview, IL: Scott, Foresman.

Dornbusch, S. M., Ritter, P. L., Leiderman, P. H., Roberts, D. F., & Fraleigh, M. J. (1987). The relation of parenting style to adolescent performance. *Child Development, 58,* 1244–1257.

Dotta, L. (1990). *Losing Sleep.* New York: Morrow.

Doty, R. L., Green, P. A., Ram, C., & Yankell, S. L. (1982). Communication of gender from human breath odors: Relationship to perceived intensity and pleasantness. *Hormones and Behavior, 16,* 13–22.

Doty, R. L., Shamon, P., Applebaum, S. L., Giberson, R., Siksorski, L., & Rosenberg, L. (1984). Smell identification ability: Changes with age. *Science, 226,* 1441–1442.

Douvan, E. K., & Adelson, J. (1966). *The adolescent experience.* New York: Wiley.

Dovidio, J. F., & Gaertner, S. L. (Eds.). (1986). *Prejudice, discrimination, racism: Theory and research.* New York: Academic Press.

Drabman, R. S., & Thomas, M. H. (1974). Does media violence increase children's toleration of real life aggression? *Developmental Psychology, 10,* 418–421.

Drewnowki, A. (1990). Taste and food preferences in human obesity. In E. D. Capaldi & T. L. Powley (Eds.), *Taste, experience, and feeding.* Washington, DC: American Psychological Association.

Drewnowki, A., & Greenwood, M. R. C. (1983). Cream and sugar: Human preferences for high fat foods. *Physiology and Behavior, 30,* 629–633.

Dubas, J. S., Graber, J. A., & Petersen, A. C. (1991). A longitudinal investigation of adolescents' changing perceptions of pubertal timing. *Developmental Psychology, 27,* 580–586.

Ducharme, R., & Belanger, D. (1961). Influence d'une stimulation electrique surle niveau d'activation et la performance. *Canadian Journal of Psychology, 18,* 61–68.

Duggan, J. P., & Booth, D. A. (1986). Obesity, overeating, and rapid gastric emptying in rats with ventromedial hypothalamic lesions. *Science, 231,* 609–611.

Dunbar, K., & MacLeod, C. M. (1984). A horse race of a different color: Stroop interference with transformed words. *Journal of Experimental Psychology: Human Perception and Performance, 10,* 622–639.

Duncan, J. (1993). Selection of input and goal in the control of behavior. In A. Baddeley & L. Weiskrantz (Eds.), *Attention: Selection, awareness, and control* (pp. 53–71). Oxford: Clarendon Press.

Duncker, K. (1929). Über induzerte Bewegung. *Psychologische Forschung, 12,* 180–259. In W. Ellis (1955) (Trans. and Condenser), *Source book of Gestalt psychology.* London: Routledge and Kegan Paul.

Duncker, K. (1945). On problem-solving. *Psychological Monographs, 58* (Whole No. 270).

Dunning, D., Leuenberger, A., & Sherman, D. A. (1995). A new look at motivated inference: Are self-serving theories of success a product of motivational forces? *Journal of Personality and Social Psychology, 69,* 58–68.

Dura, J. R., Stukenberg, K. W., & Kiecolt-Glaser, J. K. (1990). Chronic stress and depressive disorders in older adults. *Journal of Abnormal Psychology, 99,* 284–290.

Durkin, K. (1985a). Television and sex-role acquisition: 1. Content. *British Journal of Social Psychology, 24,* 101–113.

Durkin, K. (1985b). Television and sex-role acquisition: 2. Effects. *British Journal of Social Psychology, 24,* 191–210.

Durkin, K. (1985c). Television and sex-role acquisition: 3. Counterstereotyping. *British Journal of Social Psychology, 24,* 211–222.

Dutton, D. G., & Aron, A. (1989). Romantic attraction and generalized liking for others who are sources of conflict-based arousal. *Canadian Journal of Behavioral Science, 21,* 246–257.

Dutton, D. G., & Aron, A. P. (1974). Some evidence for heightened sexual attraction under conditions of high anxiety. *Journal of Personality and Social Psychology, 30,* 510–517.

Dweck, C. S., & Elliott, E. S. (1983). Achievement motivation. In P. H. Mussen (Gen Ed.) & E. M. Wetherington (Vol. Ed.), Handbook of child psychology. *Social and personality development: Vol. 4* (pp. 643–691). New York: Wiley.

Dweck, C. S., & Leggett, E. L. (1988). A social-cognitive approach to motivation and personality. *Psychological Review, 95,* 256–273.

Dykens, E., & Leckman, J. (1990). Developmental issues in fragile X syndrome. In R. M. Hodapp, J. A. Burack, & E. Zigler (Eds.), *Issues in the developmental approach to mental retardation* (pp. 226–245). New York: Cambridge University Press.

Dywan, J., & Bowers, K. (1983). The use of hypnosis to enhance recall. *Science, 222,* 184–185.

E

Eagly, A. H., & Steffen, V. J. (1984). Gender stereotypes stem from the distribution of women and men into social roles. *Journal of Personality and Social Psychology, 46,* 735–754.

Eagly, A. H., & Telaak, K. (1972). Width of the latitude of acceptance as a determinant of attitude change. *Journal of Personality and Social Psychology, 23,* 388–397.

Eagly, A. H., & Warren, R. (1976). Intelligence, comprehension, and opinion change. *Journal of Personality, 44,* 226–242.

Eagly, A. H., Ashmore, R. D., Makhijani, M. G., & Longo, L. C. (1991). What is beautiful is good, but . . . : A meta-analytic review of research on the physical attractiveness stereotype. *Psychological Bulletin, 110,* 109–128.

Easterbrooks, M. A., & Goldberg, W. A. (1985). Effects of early maternal employment on toddlers, mothers, and fathers. *Developmental Psychology, 21,* 774–783.

Ebbinghaus, H. (1913). *Memory: A contribution to experimental psychology.* New York: Columbia University Press.

Ebert, P. D. (1983). Selection for aggression in a natural population. In E. C. Simmel, M. E. Hagn, & J. K. Walters (Eds.), *Aggressive behavior: Genetic and neural approaches* (pp. 103–127). Hillsdale, NJ: Erlbaum.

Eccles, J. S., & Jacobs, J. E. (1986). Social forces shape math attitudes and performance. *Signs, 11,* 367–380.

Eccles, J. S., & Midgley, C. (1990). Changes in academic motivation and self-perception during early adolescence. In R. Montemayor, G. R. Adams, & T. G. Gullota (Eds.), *From childhood to adolescence: A transitional period.* Newbury Park, CA: Sage.

Eccles, J. S., Midgley, C., Wigfield, A., Buchanan, C. M., Reuman, D., Flanagan, C., & MacIver, D. (1993). The impact of stage-environment fit on young adolescents' experiences in schools and in families. *American Psychologist, 48,* 90–101.

Edgar, A. (1993). Review of L. Abu-Loghdo "Writing Women's Worlds." *New York Times Book Review,* January 31, 11–12.

Editors of Time-Life Books. (1988). *Mind over matter.* Alexandria, VA: Time-Life Books.

Edwards, C. P. (1984). The age group labels and categories of preschool children. *Child Development, 55,* 440–452.

Egberg, L. D., Battit, G. E., Welsh, C. E., & Bartlett, M. K. (1964). Reduction of postoperative pain by encouragement and instruction of patients. *New England Journal of Medicine, 270,* 825–827.

Egeland, B., & Sroufe, L. A. (1981). Attachment and early maltreatment. *Child Development, 52,* 44–52.

Egeland, J. A., Gerhard, D. S., Pauls, D. L., Sussex, J. N., Kidd, K. K., Allen, C. R., Hostetter, A. M., & Houseman, D. E. (1987). Bipolar affective disorders linked to DNA markers on chromosome 11. *Nature, 325,* 783–787.

Ehrenfreund, D. (1971). Effect of drive on successive magnitude shift in rats. *Journal of Comparative and Physiological Psychology, 76,* 418–423.

Ehringer, H., & Hornykiewicz, O. (1960). *Klin. Wochenschr., 38,* 1236.

Eibl-Eibesfeldt, I. (1973). The expressive behavior of the deaf-and-blind-born. In M. von Cranach & I. Vine (Eds.), *Social communication and movement.* New York: Academic Press.

Eich, J. E. (1989). Theoretical issues in state-dependent memory. In H. L. Roediger & F. I. M. Craik (Eds.), *Varieties of memory and consciousness: Essays in honour of Endel Tulving.* Hillsdale, NJ: Erlbaum.

Eich, J. E., Weingartner, H., Stillman, R. C., & Gillin, J. C. (1975). State dependent accessibility of retrieval cues in the retention of a categorized list. *Journal of Verbal Learning and Verbal Behavior, 14,* 408–417.

Eimas, P. D., Siqueland, E. R., Jusczyk, P., & Vigorito, J. (1971). Speech perception in infants. *Science, 171,* 303–306.

Einstein, G. O., McDaniel, M. A., & Lackey, S. (1989). Bizarre imagery, interference, and distinctiveness. *Journal of Experimental Psychology: Learning, Memory, and Cognition, 15,* 137–146.

Eisenberg, N., & Lennon, R. (1983). Sex differences in empathy and related capacities. *Psychological Bulletin, 94,* 100–131.
Eisenberg, N., & Lennon, R. (1983). Sex differences in empathy and related capacities. *Psychological Bulletin, 94,* 100–131.
Ekman, P. (1972). Universals and cultural differences in facial expressions of emotion. In J. K. Cole (Ed.), *Nebraska symposium on motivation.* Lincoln: University of Nebraska Press.

Ekman, P. (1973). Cross-cultural studies of facial expression. In P. Ekman (Ed.), *Darwin and facial expression: A century of research in review.* New York: Academic Press.

Ekman, P. (1984). Expression and the nature of emotion. In K. R. Scherer & P. Ekman (Eds.), *Approaches to emotion.* Hillsdale, NJ: Erlbaum.

Ekman, P. (1994). Strong evidence for universal facial expressions: A reply to Russell's mistaken critique. *Psychological Bulletin, 115,* 268–287.

Ekman, P., & O'Sullivan, M. (1991). Who can catch a liar? *American Psychologist, 46,* 913–990.

Ekman, P., Levenson, R. W., & Friesen, W. V. (1983). Autonomic nervous system activity distinguishes among emotions. *Science, 221,* 1208–1210.

Ekman, P., Sorenson, E. R., & Friesen, W. V. (1969). Pan-cultural elements in facial displays of emotion. *Science, 164,* 86–88.

Eliot, R., & Buell, J. (1979). Environmental and behavioral influences in the major cardiovascular disorders. Paper presented at the annual meeting of the Academy of Behavioral Medicine Research, Snowbird, Utah. Cited in Shaffer and Baum (1989).

Elkin, I. (1996). Commentary. *Journal of Consulting and Clinical Psychology.* (in Press, Feb. 1996).

Elkin, L, Shea, M.T., Watkins, J. T., Imber, S. D., Sotsky, S. M., Collins, J. F., Glass, D. R., Pilkonis, P. A., Leber, W. R., Docherty, J. P., Fiester, S. J., & Parloff, M. B. (1989). NIMH Treatment of depression collaborative research program: I. General effectiveness of treatments. *Archives of General Psychiatry, 46.*

Elkind, C. (1967). Egocentrism in adolescence. *Child Development, 38,* 1025–1034.

Elkind, C. (1990). Psychoanalysis as science. *Contemporary Psychology, 35,* 333–334.

Elliot, D. S., & Ageton, S. (1980). Reconciling differences in estimates of delinquency. *American Sociological Review, 45,* 85–110.

Elliott, E. S., & Dweck, C. S. (1988). Goals: An approach to motivation and achievement. *Journal of Personality and Social Psychology, 54,* 5–12.

Ellis, A. (1962). *Reason and emotion in psychotherapy.* New York: Lyle Stuart.

Ellis, A. (1988). *How to stubbornly refuse to make yourself miserable about anything—Yes, anything!* Secaucus, NJ: Lyle Stuart.

Ellis, A. W., & Young, A. W. (1988). *Human cognitive neuropsychology.* Hillsdale, NJ: Erlbaum.

Ellis, A., & Dryden, W. (1987). *The practice of rational-emotive therapy.* New York: Springer.

Ellman, S. J., & Antrobus, J. S. (1990). *The mind in sleep: Psychology & Psychophysiology.* New York: Wiley.

Elmen, J. (1991). Achievement orientation in early adolescence: Developmental patterns and social correlates. *Journal of Early Adolescence, 11,* 125–151.

Elmer, G. I., Meisch, R. A., & George, F. R. (1987). Mouse strain difference in operant self-administration of ethanol. *Behavior Genetics, 17,* 439–452.

Elms, A. C. (1981). Skinner's dark year and *Walden Two. American Psychologist,* 470–479.

Emmons, R. A. (1989). The personal striving approach to personality. In L. A. Pervin (Ed.) *Goal Concepts in Personality and Social Psychology.* Hillsdale, NJ: Erlbaum, pp. 87–126.

Elms, A. C., & Milgram, S. (1966). Personality characteristics associated with obedience and defiance toward authoritative command. *Journal of Experimental Research in Personality, 1,* 282–289.

Elsmore, T. F., & McBridge, S. A. (1994). An eight-alternative concurrent schedule: Foraging in a radial maze. *Journal of the Experimental Analysis of Behavior, 61,* 331–348.

Endler, N. S. (1982). *Holiday of darkness: A psychologist's personal journey out of his depression.* New York: Wiley.

Endler, N. S. (1983). Interactionism: A personality model, but not yet a theory. In M. M. Page (Ed.), *Nebraska Symposium on Motivation, 1982: Personality—Current Theory and Research.* Lincoln, NE: University of Nebraska Press.

Engen, T. (1982). *The perception of odors.* New York: Academic Press.

Entwistle, D. R. (1972). To dispel fantasies about fantasy-based measures of achievement motivation. *Psychological Bulletin, 77,* 377–391.

Epstein, S. (1986). Does aggregation produce spuriously high estimates of behavior stability? *Journal of Personality and Social Psychology, 50,* 1199–1209.

Epstein, S. (1992). Coping ability, negative self-evaluation, and overgeneralization: Experiment and theory. *Journal of Personality and Social Psychology, 62,* 826–836.

Epstein, S., & Meier, P. (1989). Constructive thinking: A broad coping variable with specific components. *Journal of Personality and Social Psychology, 57,* 332–350.

Epstein, S., & O'Brien, E. J. (1985). The person-situation debate in historical and current perspective. *Psychological Bulletin, 98,* 513–537.

Erdelyi, M. H. (1994). Recovery of memories under hypnosis: The null set of hypermnesia. *International Journal of Clinical and Experimental Hypnosis, 42,* 379–390.

Erdelyi, M. H., & Becker, J. (1974). Hyperamnesia for pictures: Incremental memory for pictures but not words in multiple recall trials. *Cognitive Psychology, 6,* 159–171.

Erdelyi, M. H., & Goldberg, B. (1979). Let's not sweep repression under the rug: Toward a cognitive psychology of repression. In J. F. Kihlstrom & F. J. Evans (Eds.), *Functional disorders of memory.* Hillsdale, NJ: Erlbaum.

Erickson, E. (1980). *Identity and the life cycle.* New York: Norton.

Erickson, E. H. (1950). *Childhood and society.* New York: Norton.

Ericsson, K. A., & Polson, P. G. (1988). An experimental analysis of the mechanisms of memory skill. *Journal of Experimental Psychology: Learning, Memory, and Cognition, 145,* 305–316.

Erlenmeyer-Kimling, L., Marcuse, Y., Cornblatt, B., Friedman, D., Rainer, J. D., and Rutschmann, J. (1984). The New York high rise project. In N. F. Watt, E. J. Anthony, L. C. Wynne, & J. Rolf (Eds.), *Children at risk for schizophrenia: A longitudinal perspective.* New York: Cambridge University Press.

Esses, V. M., & Zanna, M. P. (1989, August). Mood and the expression of ethnic stereotypes. Paper presented at the meeting of the American Psychological Association, New Orleans.

Estes, W. K. (1980). Is human memory obsolete? *American Scientist, 68,* 62–69.

Evans, F. J. (1977). Hypnosis and sleep: The control of altered states of awareness. *Annals of the New York Academy of Sciences, 296,* 162–174.

Evans, F. J. (1988). Posthypnotic amnesia: Dissociation of content and context. In H. M. Pettinati (Ed.), *Hypnosis and memory* (pp. 157–192). New York: Guilford Press.

Evans, F. J. (1990). Hypnosis and pain control. *Australian Journal of Clinical and Experimental Hypnosis, 18,* 21–33.

Exner, J. E. (1974). *The Rorschach: A comprehensive system.* New York: Wiley.

Exner, J. E. (1986). *The Rorschach: A comprehensive system* (Vol. 1, 2nd ed.). New York: Wiley.

Eyman, R. K., Call, T. L., & White, J. F. (1991). Life expectancy of persons with Down syndrome. *American Journal of Mental Retardation, 95,* 603–612.

Eysenck, H. J. (1952). The effects of psychotherapy: An evaluation. *Journal of Consulting Psychology, 16,* 319–324.

Eysenck, H. J. (1967). The biological basis of personality. Springfield, IL: Charles C. Thomas.

Eysenck, H. J. (1979). The conditioning model of neurosis. *Behavioral and Brain Sciences, 2,* 155–199.

Eysenck, H. J., & Eysenck, M. W. (1985). *Personality and individual differences.* New York: Plenum.

Eysenck, H. J., & Eysenck, S. B. G. (1975). *Manual of the Eysenck personality questionnaire.* San Diego: Educational and Industrial Testing Service.

Eysenck, H. J., & Kaminn, L. J. (1981). *The intelligence controversy.* New York: Wiley.

Eysenck, H. J., & Skinner, B. F. (1980, September). *Behavior modification, behavior therapy, and other matters: Invited dialogue.* Paper presented at the 88th Annual Convention of the American Psychological Association, Montreal.

Eysenck, H. J. (1988). Personality and stress as causal factors in cancer and coronary heart disease. In M. P. Janisse (Ed.) *Individual Differences. Stress. and Health Psychology.* New York: Springer-Verlag, 129–145.

Eysenck, H. J. (1991). Dimensions of personality: 16, 5 or 3? Criteria for a taxonomic paradigm. *Personality and Individual Difference, 12,* 773–790.

Eysenck, H. J., Wakefield, J. A., Jr., & Friedman, A. F. (1983). Diagnosis and clinical assessment: The DSM-III. In M. R. Rosenzweig and L. W. Porter (Eds.), *Annual review of psychology* (Vol. 34). Palo Alto, CA: Annual Reviews.

Eysenck, S. B. G., Eysenck, H. J., & Barrett, P. (1985). A revised version of the Psychoticism scale. *Personality & Individual Differences, 6,* 21–29.

Ezzell, C. (1994). Getting the skinny on obesity. *Journal of NIH Research, 6,* 71–75.

F

Fabricius, W. V., & Cavalier, C. (1989). The role of causal theories about memory in young children's strategy choice. *Child Development, 60,* 298–308.

Facchinetti, F., Giovannini, C., Barletta, C., Petraglia, F., Buzzetti, R., Burla, F., Lazzari, R., Genazzani, A. R., & Scava, D. (1986). Hyperendorphinemia in obesity and relationships to affective state. *Physiology & Behavior, 36,* 937–940.

Fagan, J. F. (1992). Intelligence: A theoretical viewpoint. *Current Directions in Psychological Science, 1,* 82–86.

Fagan, J. F., & Singer, L. T. (1983). Infant recognition memory as a measure of intelligence. In L. P. Lipsitt (Ed.), *Advances in infancy research* (Vol. 2). Norwood, NJ: Ablex.

Fagot, B. I. (1978). The influence of sex of child on parental reactions to toddler children. *Child Development, 49,* 459–465.

Fahn, S., & Calne, D. B. (1978). Consideration in the management of Parkinsonism. *Neurology, 28,* 5–7.

Fairbairn, W. R. D. (1952). *Psychoanalytic Studies of Personality.* London: Routledge and Kegan Paul.

Fairburn, C. G. (1990, April 5). Treatment modalities for eating disorders. Paper presented at the Bulimia Anorexia Self-Help Eighth International Conference on the Eating and Mood Disorders.

Fairburn, C. G., & Garner, D. M. (1988). Diagnostic criteria for anorexia nervosa and bulimia nervosa: The importance of attitudes to shape and weight. In D. M. Garner & P. E. Garfinkel (Eds.), *Diagnostic issues in anorexia nervosa and bulimia nervosa* (pp. 36–55). New York: BrunnerMazel.

Fairburn, C. G., Jones, R., Peveier, R. C., Hope, R. A., & O'Connor, M. (1993). Psychotherapy and bulimia nervosa. *Archives of General Psychiatry, 50,* 419–428.

Fajardo, B. F., & Freeman, D. G. (1981). Maternal rhythmicity in three American cultures. In T. M. Field, A. M. Sostek, P. Vietze, & P. H. Liederman (Eds.), *Culture and early interactions.* Hillsdale, NJ: Erlbaum.

Fanselow, M. S. (1984). Shock-induced analgesia on the formalin test: Effects of shock severity, naloxone, hypophysectomy, and associative variables. *Behavioral Neuroscience, 98,* 79–95.

Fanselow. (1994). Neural organization of the defensive behavior system responsible for fear. *Psychonomic Bulletin & Review, 1*(4), 429–438.

Fantino, E., Kasdon, D., & Stinger, N. (1970). The Yerkes-Dodson Law and alimentary motivation. *Canadian Journal of Psychology, 24,* 77–84.

Fantz, R. L. (1961). The origin of form perception. *Scientific American, 204,* 66–84.

Fantz, R. L. (1963). Pattern vision in newborn infants. *Science, 140,* 296–297.

Fantz, R. L., Fagan, J. F., & Miranda, S. B. (1975). Early visual selectivity as a function of pattern variables, previous exposure, age from birth and conception, and expected cognitive deficit. In L. B. Cohen & P. Salapatek (Eds.), *Infant perception: From sensation to cognition.* (Vol. 1). New York: Academic Press.

Farah, M. (1990). *Visual Agnosia.* Cambridge, MA: MIT Press.

Farah, M. J. (1988). Is visual imagery really visual? Overlooked evidence from neuropsychology. *Psychological Review, 95,* 307–317.

Farah, M. J. (1990). *Visual agnosia.* Cambridge, MA: The MIT Press.

Farbman, A. I. (1992). *Cell Biology of Olfaction.* Cambridge: Cambridge University Press.

Farrar, M. J., Raney, G. E., & Boyer, M. E. (1992). Knowledge, concepts, and inferences in childhood. *Child Development, 63,* 673–691.

Fauber, R., Forehand, R., Thomas, A. M., & Wierson, M. (1990). A mediational model of the impact of marital conflict on adolescent adjustment in intact and divorced families: The role of disrupted parenting. *Child Development, 61,* 1112–1123.

Fazio, R. H., Effrein, E. A., & Falender, V. J. (1981). Self-perception following social interaction. *Journal of Personality and Social Psychology, 41,* 232–242.

Feagin, J. R. (1972). Poverty: We still believe that God helps those who help themselves. *Psychology Today, 6,* 101–129.

Feather, N. T. (1982). *Expectations and actions: Expectancy-value models in psychology.* Hillsdale, NJ: Erlbaum.

Fechner, G. (1966). *Elements of psychophysics* (H. E. Adler, Trans., D. H. Howes & E. G. Boring, Eds.). New York: Holt, Rinehart & Winston. (First German edition 1860)

Federal Bureau of Investigation (1985). *Uniform crime reports for the United States.* Washington, DC: U.S. Department of Justice.

Fehr, F. S., & Stern, J. A. (1970). Peripheral physiological variables and emotion: The James-Lange theory revisited. *Psychological Bulletin, 74,* 411–424.

Feinstein, S., & Ardon, M. (1973). Trends in dating patterns and adolescent development. *Journal of Youth and Adolescence, 2,* 157–166.

Feldman, R. E. (1968). Response to compatriots and foreigners who seek assistance. *Journal of Personality and Social Psychology, 10,* 202–214.

Felixbrod, J. J., & O'Leary, K. D. (1973). Effects of reinforcement in children's academic behavior as a function of self-determined and externally imposed contingencies. *Journal of Applied Behavior Analysis, 6,* 241–250.

Fenigstein, A., Scheier, M. F., & Buss, A. H. (1975). Public and private self-consciousness: Assessment and theory. *Journal of Consulting and Clinical Psychology, 43,* 522–527.

Fernald, A., & Mazzie, C. (1991). Prosody and focus in speech to infants and adults. *Developmental Psychology, 27,* 209–221.

Fernandez, A., & Glenberg, A. M. (1985). Changing environmental context does not reliably affect memory. *Memory & Cognition, 13,* 333–345.

Festinger, L. (1954). A theory of social comparison processes. *Human Relations, 7,* 117–140.

Festinger, L. (1957). *A theory of cognitive dissonance.* Stanford, CA: Stanford University Press.

Festinger, L., & Carlsmith, J. M. (1959). Cognitive consequences of forced compliance. *Journal of Abnormal and Social Psychology, 58,* 203–210.

Festinger, L., Pepitone, A., & Newcomb, T. (1952). Some consequences of deindividuation in a group. *Journal of Abnormal and Social Psychology, 47,* 382–389.

Festinger, L., Schacter, S., & Back, K. (1950). *Social pressures in informal groups: A study of human factors in housing.* New York: Harper.

Fetterman, D. M. (1988). *Excellence and equality: A qualitatively different perspective on gifted and talented education.* Albany, NY: State University of New York Press.

Fiedler, F. E., & Garcia, J. E. (1987). *New approaches to leadership: Cognitive resources and organizational performance.* New York: Wiley.

Field, D., & Milsap, R. E. (1991). Personality in advanced age: Continuity or change? *Journal of gerontology: Psychological Sciences, 46,* 299–308.

Figueroa, M. D. (1989). Comments on the subliminal psychodynamic activation method. *American Psychologist, 44,* 1421–1422.

Finck, H. T. (1887). *Romantic love and personal beauty* (Vol. 2). London: Macmillan.

Findley, M. J., & Cooper, H. M. (1983). Locus of control and academic achievement: A literature review. *Journal of Personality and Social Psychology, 44,* 419–427.

Fineman, S. (1977). The achievement motive and its measurement: Where are we now? *British Journal of Psychology, 68,* 1–22.

Fink, M. (1991). Impact of the antipsychiatry movement on the revival of electroconvulsive therapy in the United States. *Psychiatric Clinics of North America, 14,* 793–801.

Finkel, L. H., & Sajda, P. (1994). Constructing visual perception. *American Scientist, 82,* 224–237.

Fischer, K. W. (1980). A theory of cognitive development: The control and construction of a hierarchy of skills. *Psychological Review, 87,* 477–531.

Fischer, M., Harvald, B., & Hague, M. S. (1969). Danish twin study of schizophrenia. *British Journal of Psychiatry, 115,* 981–990.

Fiske, S. T. (1989). Examining the role of intent: Toward understanding its role in stereotyping and prejudice. In J. S. Uleman & J. A. Bargh (Eds.), *Unintended thought* (pp. 253–283). New York: Guilford.

Fitts, P. M., & Posner, M. I. (1967). *Human performance.* Belmont, CA: Brooks/Cole.

Fitzgerald, R. D., & Martin, G. K. (1971). Heart-rate conditioning in rats as a function of interstimulus interval. *Psychological Reports, 29*, 1103–1110.

Fitzsimmons, J. T., & LeMagnen, J. (1969). Eating as a regulatory control of drinking in the rat. *Journal of Comparative and Physiological Psychology, 67*, 273–283.

Fitzsimons, J. T. (1971). The physiology of thirst: A review of the extraneural aspects of the mechanism of drinking. In E. Stellar & J. M. Sprague (Eds.), *Progress in physiological psychology* (Vol. 4). New York: Academic press.

Fivush, R., & Hammond, N. R. (1990). Autobiographical memory across the preschool years: Toward reconceptualizing childhood amnesia. In R. Fivush & J. A. Hudson (Eds.), *Knowing and remembering in young children* (pp. 223–248). New York: Cambridge University Press.

Flaskerud, J. H. (1986). The effects of culture-compatible intervention on the utilization of mental health services by minority clients. *Community Mental Health Journal, 22*, 127–141.

Flaskerud, J. H., & Liu, P. Y. (1991). Effects of an Asian client-therapist language, ethnicity and gender match on utilization and outcome of therapy. *Community Mental Health Journal, 27*, 31–42.

Flatt, J. P., Ravussin, E., Acheson, K. J., & Jequer, E. (1985). Effects of dietary fat on post-prandial substrate oxidation and on carbohydrate and fat balances. *Journal of Clinical Investigation, 76*, 1019–1024.

Flavell, J. H. (1985). *Cognitive development*. Englewood Cliffs, NJ: Prentice-Hall.

Flavell, J. H., Green, F. L., & Flavell, E. R. (1986). Development of knowledge about the appearance-reality distinction. *Monographs of the Society for Research in Child Development, 51*, (1, Serial No. 212).

Flavell, J. H., Zhang, X. D., Zou, H., Dong, Q., & Qi, S. (1983). A comparison between the development of the appearance-reality distinction in the People's Republic of China and the United States. *Cognitive Psychology, 15*, 459–466.

Fleming, A. S., Ruble, D. N., Flett, G. L., & Van Wagner, V. (1990). Adjustment in first-time mothers: Changes in mood and mood content during the early postpartum months. *Developmental Psychology, 26*, 137–143.

Florin, I., Nostadt, A., Reck, C., Franzen, U., & Jenkins, M. (1992). Expressed emotion in depressed patients and their partners. *Family Process, 31*, 163–172.

Flynn, J. C. (1991). *Cocaine: An in-depth look at the facts, science, history, and future of the world's most addictive drug*. Seacaucus, NJ: Carol Publishing Group.

Flynn, J. R. (1984). The mean IQ of Americans: Massive gains 1932 to 1978. *Psychological Bulletin, 95*, 29–51.

Flynn, J., Vanegas, H., Foote, W., & Edwards, S. (1970). Neural mechanisms involved in a cat's attack on a rat. In R. F. Whalen, M. Thompson, M. Verzeano, & N. Weinberger (Eds.)., *The neural control of behavior*. New York: Academic Press.

Fodor, I. (1989). CBT: The therapy for right thinking. *Contemporary Psychology, 34*, 851–852.

Foltz, E. L., & Millett, F. E. (1964). Experimental psychosomatic disease states in monkeys: 1. Peptic "ulcer-executive" monkeys. *Journal of Surgical Research, 4*, 445–453.

Ford, C. S., & Beach, F. A. (1951). *Patterns of sexual behavior*. New York: Harper & Row.

Ford, M. R., & Widiger, T. A. (1989). Sex bias in the diagnosis of histrionic and antisocial personality disorders. *Journal of Consulting and Clinical Psychology, 57*, 301–305.

Forgas, J. P., & Bower, G. H. (1987). Mood effects on person perception judgments. *Journal of Personality and Social Psychology, 53*, 53–60.

Forrest, J., Sullivan, E., & Tietze, C. (1979). Abortions in the United States, 1977–1979. *Family Planning Perspectives, 11*, 329–341.

Foster, D., & Finchilescu, G. (1986). Contact in a "non-contact" society: The case of South Africa. In M. Hewstone & R. Brown (Eds.) (1986), *Contact and conflict in intergroup encounters* (pp. 119–136). Oxford: Basil Blackwell.

Fowler, H. (1967). Satiation and curiosity: Constructs for a drive and incentive-motivational theory of exploration. In K. W. Spence & J. T. Spence (Eds.), *The psychology of learning and motivation: Advances in research and theory* (Vol. 1). New York: Academic Press.

Fowler, H., & Trapold, M. A. (1962). Escape performance as a function of delay of reinforcement. *Journal of Experimental Psychology, 63*, 464–467.

Fowles, M. W. (1986). Prediction in Criminology. *Journal of Adolescence, 9*, 183–184.

Frances, A. J., Widiger, T. A., & Pincus, H. A. (1989). The development of DSM-IV. *Archives of General Psychiatry, 46*, 373–375.

Frankel, J. (1993). Introduction. In J. Frankel (Ed.), *The employed mother and the family context* (pp. 1–4). New York: Springer.

Frankel, J., & McCarty, S. (1993). Women's employment and childbearing decisions. In J. Frankel (Ed.), *The employed mother and the family context* (pp. 1–4). New York: Springer.

Frase, L. T. (1975). Prose processing. In G. H. Bower (Ed.), *The psychology of learning and motivation* (Vol. 9). New York: Academic Press.

Fraser, G. E., & Babaali, H. (1989). Determinates of high density lipoprotein cholesterol in middle-aged Seventh-Day Adventist men and their neighbors. *American Journal of Epidemiology, 130*, 958–965.

Freed, C. R., & Yamamoto, B. K. (1985). Regional brain dopamine metabolism: A marker for the speed, direction and posture of moving animals. *Science, 229*, 62–65.

Freedman, D., Pisani, R., & Purves, R. (1978). *Statistics*. New York: Norton.

Freedman, J. L. (1964). Involvement, discrepancy, and change. *Journal of Abnormal and Social Psychology, 64*, 290–295.

Freedman, J. L. (1979). Reconciling apparent differences between the responses of humans and other animals to crowding. *Psychological Review, 86*, 80–88.

Freedman, J. L. (1984). Effects of television violence on aggressiveness. *Psychological Bulletin, 96*, 227–246.

Freedman, J. L. (1986). Television violence and aggression: A rejoinder. *Psychological Bulletin, 100*, 372–378.

Freedman, J. L., & Fraser, S. (1966). Compliance without pressure: The foot-in-the-door technique. *Journal of Personality and Social Psychology, 4*, 195–202.

Freedman, J. L., Birsky, J., & Cavoukian, A. (1980). Environmental determinants of behavioral contagion: Density and number. *Basic and Applied Social Psychology, 1*, 155–161.

Freedman, J. L., Sears, D. O., & Carlsmith, J. L. (1981). *Social psychology* (4th ed.). Englewood Cliffs, NJ: Prentice-Hall.

Freeman, A., & Byers, S. (1990). The cognitive approach to therapy. *Contemporary Psychology, 35*, 802–803.

Freeman, S., Walker, M. R., Borden, R., & Latane, B. (1975). Diffusion of responsibility and restaurant tipping: Cheaper by the bunch. *Personality and Social Psychology Bulletin, 1*, 594–597.

Fremouw, W. J., de Perczel, M., & Ellis, T. E. (1990). *Suicide risk: Assessment and response guidelines*. Elmsford, NY: Pergamon.

Freud, A. (1958). Adolescence. *Psychoanalytic Study of the Child, 13*, 255–278.

Freud, S. (1938). *The basic writings of Sigmund Freud*. New York: Modern Library.

Freud, S. (1952). *A general introduction to psychoanalysis*. New York: Washington Square Press. (Original work published 1924)

Freud, S. (1959). *Collected papers* (Vol. 5). New York: Basic Books.

Freud, S. (1962). *Civilization and its discontents* (James Strachey, Ed. and Trans.). New York: Norton. (Original work publishes 1930)

Freud, S. (1964). *The interpretation of dreams*. New York: Basic Books. (Original work published 1900)

Frey, K. S., & Ruble, D. N. (1992). Gender constancy and the "cost" of sex-typed behavior: A test of the conflict hypothesis. *Developmental Psychology, 28*, 714–721.

Fried, P. A., & Watkinson, B. (1990). 36- and 48-month neurobehavioral follow-up of children prenatally exposed to marijuana, cigarettes, and alcohol. *Developmental and Behavioral Pediatrics, 11*, 49–58.

Fried, S. B. (1988). Learning activities for understanding aging. *Teaching of Psychology, 15*, 160–162.

Friedman, J. S. (1990) Where is the disease-prone personality? In H. S. Friedman (Ed.) *Personality and Disease*. New York: Wiley, pp. 282–292.

Friedman, H. S., Hall, J. A., & Harris, M. J. (1985). Type A behavior, nonverbal expressive style, and health. *Journal of Personality and Social Psychology, 48*, 1299–1315.

Friedman, M. (1969). *Pathogenesis of coronary artery disease*. New York: McGraw-Hill.

Friedman, M. I., & Stricker, E. M. (1976). The physiological psychology of hunger: A physiological perspective. *Psychological Review, 83*, 409–431.

Friedman, M., & Rosenman, R. H. (1974). *Type A behavior and your heart*. New York: Knopf.

Friedrich, L. K., & Stein, A. H. (1973). Aggressive and pro-social television programs and the natural behavior of preschool children. *Monographs of the Society for Research in Child Development, 38* (4, Serial No. 151).

Friedrich-Cofer, L., & Huston, A. C. (1986). Television violence and aggression: The debate continues. *Psychological Bulletin, 100*, 364–371.

Friend, R., Rafferty, Y., & Bramel, D. (1990). A puzzling misinterpretation of the Asch "conformity" study. *European Journal of Social Psychology, 20*, 29–44.

Frisby, J. P. (1980). *Seeing*. New York: Oxford University Press.

Frisch, R. E., & Revelle, R. (1970). Height and weight, menarche and a hypothesis of critical body weight and adolescent events. *Science, 169*, 397–399.

Fryauf-Bertschy, H., Tyler, R. S., Kelsay, D. M., & Gantz, B. J. (1992). Performance over time of congenitally deaf and postlingually deafened children using a multichannel cochlear implant. *Journal of Speech and Hearing Research, 35*, 913–919.

Fullard, J. H., & Barclay, R. M. R. (1980). Audition in spring species of arctied moths as a possible response to differential levels of bat predation. *Canadian Journal of Zoology, 58* 1745–1750.

Funder, D. C. (1991). Global traits: a neo-Allportian approach to personality. *Psychological Science, 2*, 31–39.

Funder, D. C., & Colvin, C. R. (1991). Explorations in behavioral consistency: Properties of persons, situations, and behaviors. *Journal of Personality and Social Psychology, 60*, 773–794.

Furstenberg, F. F. (1982). Conjugal succession. In P. B. Baltes & O. G. Brim (Eds.), *Life-span development and behavior. Vol. 4* (pp. 107–146). New York: Academic Press.

Furumoto, L. (1990). Mary Whiton Calkins (1863–1930). In A. N. O'Connell & N. F. Russo (Eds.), *Women in psychology: A bio-bibliographic sourcebook*. New York: Greenwood Press.

Furumoto, L. (1991). From "paired-associates" to a psychology of self: The intellectual odyssey of Mary Whiton Calkins. In G. A. Kimble, M. Wertheimer, & C. White (Eds.), *Portraits of pioneers in psychology*. Hillsdale, NJ: Erlbaum.

Furumoto, L. (1992). Joining separate spheres—Christine Ladd-Franklin, woman-scientist (1847–1930). *American Psychologist, 47*(2), 175–182.

G

Gabarino, J. (1989). A feminist perspective on the psychology of sexual abuse. *Contemporary Psychology, 34*, 1013–1014.

Gaertner, S. L., & Dovidio, J. F. (1986). The aversive form of racism. In Dovidio, J. F., & Gaertner, S. L. (Eds.), *Prejudice, discrimination, racism: Theory and research* (pp. 61–89). New York: Academic Press.

Gage, N. L. (1978). The yield of research on teaching. *Phi Delta Kappan*, 229–235.

Gagnon, J. H., & Simon, W. (1973). *Sexual conduct: The social origins of human sexuality*. Chicago: Aldine.

Galanter, E. (1962). Contemporary psychophysics. In R. Brown and others (Eds.), *New directions in psychology* (Vol. 1), New York: Holt, Rinehart & Winston.

Galen of Pergamum (170/1938) On temperaments. *Papyros Library: The Collected Works of Ancient Greek Writers* (Vol. 24). Athens: Papyros.

Galinsky, T. L. Warm, J. S., Dember, W. N., & Weiler, E. M. (1990). Sensory alternation and vigilance performance: The role of pathway inhibition. *Human Factors, 32*, 717–728.

Galle, O. R., Gove, W. R., & McPherson, J. M. (1972). Population density and pathology: What are the relationships for man? *Science, 176*, 385–389.

Gallistel, C. R. (1988). Counting versus subutizing versus the sense of number. *Behavioral and Brain Sciences, 11*, 585–586.

Gallistel, C. R. (1990). *The organization of learning*. Cambridge, MA: MIT Press.

Galton, F. (1883). *Inquiry into human faculty and its development*. London: Macmillan.

Gamble, T., & Zigler, E. (1986). Effects of infant day care: Another look at the evidence. *American Journal of Orthopsychiatry, 56*, 26–42.

Gans, J. E., & Blyth, D. A. (1990). *America's adolescents: How healthy are they?* (AMA Profiles of Adolescent Health series). Chicago: American Medical Association.

Garbarino, J. (1985). *Adolescent development: An ecological perspective*. Columbus, Ohio: Merrill.

Garber, J., & Seligman, M. E. P. (Eds.). (1980). *Human helplessness: Theory and application*. New York: Academic press.

Garcia, J., & Koelling, R. A. (1966). Relation to cue to consequences in avoidance learning. *Psychonomic Science, 4*, 123–124.

Garcia, J., Ervin, F. R., & Koelling, R. A. (1966). Learning with prolonged delay of reinforcement. *Psychonomic Science, 5*, 121–122.

Garcia-Coll, C. T. (1990). Developmental outcome of minority infants: A process-oriented look into our beginnings. *Child Development, 61*, 270–289.

Gardner, H. (1975). *The shattered mind: The person after brain damage* (pp. 60–61, 68). New York: Knopf.

Gardner, H. (1982a). *Developmental psychology: An introduction* (2nd ed.). Boston: Little, Brown.

Gardner, H. (1982b). Artistry following damage to the human brain. In A. W. Ellis (Ed.), *Normality and pathology in cognitive functions*. London: Academic Press.

Gardner, H. (1983). *Frames of mind: The theory of multiple intelligences*. New York: Basic Books.

Gardner, R. A., & Gardner, B. T. (1978). Comparative psychology and language acquisition. *Annals of the New York Academy of Sciences, 309*, 37–76.

Garfield, L. S., & Bergin, A. E. (Eds.) (1978). *Handbook of psychotherapy and behavior change* (2nd ed.). New York: Wiley.

Garfield, S. L. (1986). Research on client variables in psychotherapy. In S. L. Garfield & A. E. Bergin (Eds.), *Handbook of psychotherapy and behavior change, Third edition* (pp. 213–257). New York: Wiley.

Garland, A. F., & Zigler, E. (1993). Adolescent suicide prevention: Current research and social policy implications. *American Psychologist, 48*, 169–182.

Garlington, W. K., & Dericco, D. A. (1977). The effect of modeling on drinking rate. *Journal of Applied Behavior Analysis, 10*, 207–211.

Garn, S. M., & Gertler, M. M. (1950). An association between type of work and physique in an industrial group. *American Journal of Physical Anthropology, 8*, 387–397.

Garner, D. M., Garfinkel, P. E., Schwartz, D., & Thompson, M. (1980). Cultural expectations of thinness in women. *Psychological Reports, 47*, 483–491.

Garner, W. R. (1972). The acquisition and application of knowledge: A symbiotic relation. *American Psychologist, 27*, 941–946.

Garrity, K., & Degelman, D. (1990). Effects of server introduction on restaurant tipping. *Journal of Applied Social Psychology, 20*, 168–172.

Garrity, T. F., Stallones, L., Marx, M. B., & Johnson, T. P. (1989). Pet ownership and attachment as supportive factors in the health of elderly. *Anthrozoos, 3*, 35–44.

Gatewood, R. D. & Feild, H. S. (1990). *Human resource selection*, 2e. Orlando, FL: The Dryden Press.

Gaugler, B., Rosenthal, D. B., Thornton, G. C., & Bentson, C. (1987). Meta-analysis of the assessment center. *Journal of Applied Psychology, 72*, 493–511.

Gay, P. (Ed.). (1989). *The Freud reader*. New York: Norton.

Gay, P. (Ed.) (1989). *The Freud Reader*. New York: W. W. Norton & Company.

Gazzaniga, M. (1967). The split brain in man. *Scientific American, 217*, 24–29.

Gazzaniga, M. S. (1970). *The bisected brain*. New York: Appleton-Century-Crofts.

Gazzaniga, M. S. (1983). Right hemisphere language following commissurotomy: A twenty-year perspective. *American Psychologist, 38*, 525–537.

Gazzaniga, M. S. (1989). Organization of the human brain. *Science, 245*, 947–952.

Gazzaniga, M. S., & Sperry, R. W. (1967). Language after section of the cerebral commissures. *Brain, 90*, 131–148.

Gebhard, P. H. (1971). Human sexual behavior: A summary statement. In D. S. Marshall & R. C. Suggs (Eds.), *Human sexual behavior*. Englewood Cliffs, NJ: Prentice-Hall.

Gebhard, P. H., & Johnson, A. B. (1979). *The Kinsey data: Marginal tabulations of the 1938–1963 interviews conducted by the Institute for Sex Research*. Philadelphia: Saunders.

Geen, R. G. (1991). Social motivation. *Annual Review of Psychology, 42*, 377–400.

Geen, R. G., & Gange, J. J. (1977). Drive theory of social facilitation: Twelve years of theory and research. *Psychological Bulletin, 84*, 1267–1288.

Geiselman, E. (1988). Improving eyewitness memory through mental reinstatement of context. In G. M. Davies & D. M. Thomson (Eds.), *Memory in context: Context in memory*. New York: Wiley.

Geiselman, R. E., Fisher, R. P., Mackinnon, D. P., & Holland, H. L. (1985). Eyewitness memory enhancement in the police interview: Cognitive retrieval mnemonics versus hypnosis. *Journal of Applied Psychology, 70*, 401–412.

Geller, E. S., Berry, T. D., Evans, R. E., Gilmore, M. R. & Clarke, S. W. (1990). A conceptual framework for developing and evaluating behavior change interventions for injury control. *Health Education Research, 5*.

Gelman, R. (1978). Cognitive development. *Annual Review of Psychology, 29*, 297–332.

Gelman, R., & Gallistel, C. R. (1978). *The child's understanding of number*. Cambridge, MA: Harvard University Press.

Gelman, S. A. (1988). The development of induction with natural kind and artifact categories. *Cognitive Psychology, 10*, 65–95.

Gelman, S. A., & Markman, E. M. (1986). Categories and induction in young children. *Cognition, 23*, 183–209.

Gender factor in math: A new study says males may be naturally abler than females. (1980, December 15). *Time*.

Gentner, G., & Grudin, J. (1985). The evolution of mental metaphors in psychology: A 90-year retrospective. *American Psychologist, 40*, 181–192.

Gergen, K. J., Gergen, M. M., & Barton, W. H. (1973). Deviance in the dark. *Psychology Today*, October, 129–130.

Gescheider, G. E. (1985). *Psychophysics: Method, theory, and application*. (2nd ed.). Hillsdale, NJ: Erlbaum.

Geschwind, N., & Galabruda, A. M. (1985). Cerebral lateralization: Biological mechanisms, associations, and pathology: I. A hypothesis and a program for research. *Archives of Neurology, 42*, 428–459.

Geshwind, N. (1972). Language and the brain. *Scientific American, 226*, 76–83.

Gibbon, J. (1981). The contingency problem in autoshaping. In C. M. Locurto, H. S. Terrace, & J. Gibbon (Eds.), *Autoshaping and conditioning theory*. New York: Academic Press.

Gibbons, A. (1991). The brain as "sexual organ." *Science, 253*, 957–959.

Gibbs, J. C., & Schnell, S. V. (1985). Moral development "versus" socialization. *American Psychologist, 40*, 1071–1080.

Gibson, E. J., & Spelke, E. S. (1983). The development of perception. In J. H. Flavell & E. M. Markman (Eds.), *Handbook of child psychology: Vol. 3. Cognitive development*. New York: Wiley.

Gibson, E. J., & Walk, R. D. (1970). The "visual cliff." *Scientific American, 202*, 64–71.

Gibson, F. (1987). Out of the blue: When drinking kills. *Yale Alumni: Magazine*, 18–19.

Gibson, J. J. (1950). *The perception of the visual world*. Boston: Houghton Mifflin.

Gibson, R. C. (1991). The subjective retirement of black Americans. *Journal of Gerontology: Social Sciences, 46*, 204–209.

Gick, M. L., & Holyoak, K. J. (1980). Analogical problem solving. *Cognitive Psychology, 12*, 306–355.

Gigerenzer, G., & Murray, D. J. (1987). *Cognition as intuitive statistics*. Hillsdale, NJ: Erlbaum.

Gilbert, D. T. (1989). Thinking lightly about others: Automatic components of the social inference process. In J. S. Uleman & J. A. Bargh (Eds.), *Unintended thought* (pp. 155–188). New York: Guilford.

Gilbert, D. T., Pelham, B. W., & Krull, D. S. (1988). On cognitive busyness: When person perceivers meet persons perceived. *Journal of Personality and Social Psychology, 54*, 733–740.

Gilinsky, A. S. (1984). *Mind and brain: Principles of neuropsychology*. New York: Praeger.

Gilligan, C. (1982). *In a different voice: Psychological theory and women's development*. Cambridge, MA: Harvard University Press.

Gilovich, T. (1987). Secondhand information and social judgment. *Journal of Experimental Social Psychology, 22,* 59–74.

Gilovich, T. (1991). *How we know what isn't so: The fallibility of human reason in everyday life.* New York: Free Press.

Glanzer, M., & Cunitz, A. R. (1966). Two storage mechanisms in free recall. *Journal of Verbal Learning and Verbal Behavior, 5,* 351–360.

Glaser, R., & Bassok, M. (1989). Learning theory and the study of instruction. In M. R. Rosenberg & L. W. Porter (Eds.), *Annual Review of Psychology, 40,* 631–666.

Glass, D. C. (1977). *Behavior patterns, stress and coronary disease.* Hillsdale, NJ: Erlbaum.

Glass, D. C., & Singer, J. E. (1972). *Urban stress: Experiments on noise and social stressors.* New York: Academic Press.

Glass, D. C., Lavin, D. E., Henchy, T., Gordon, A., Mayhew, P., & Donohoe, P. (1969). Obesity and persuasibility. *Journal of Personality, 37,* 407–414.

Glazer, H. I., & Weiss, J. M. (1976). Long-term interference effect: An alternative to "learned helplessness." *Journal of Experimental Psychology: Animal Behavior Processes, 2,* 201–213.

Gleason, D. (1985). Auditory assessment of visually impaired preschoolers: A team effort. *Education of the Visually Handicapped, 16,* 102–113.

Glenberg, A. M. (1988). *Learning from data: An introduction to statistical reasoning.* San Diego: Harcourt Brace Jovanovich.

Glendenning, K. K. (1972). Effects of septal and amygdaloid lesions on social behavior of the cat. *Journal of Comparative and Physiological Psychology, 80,* 199–207.

Glick, I. D., Clarkin, J. F., & Kessler, D. R. (1987). *Marital and family therapy* (3rd ed.). Orlando, FL: Grune & Stratton.

Glick, P. C. (1980). Remarriage: Some recent changes and variations. *Journal of Family Issues, 1,* 455–478.

Glisky, E. L., & Rabinowitz, J. (1985). Enhancing the generation effect through repetition of operations. *Journal of Experimental Psychology: Learning, Memory, and Cognition, 11,* 193–205.

Glucksberg, S., & Weisberg, R. W. (1966). Verbal behavior and problem solving: Some effects of labeling in a functional fixedness problem. *Journal of Experimental Psychology, 71,* 659–664.

Glynn, S. M., Randolph, E. T., Eth, S., Paz, G. G., Leong, G. B., Shaner, A. L., & Strachan, A. (1990). Patient psychopathology and expressed emotion in schizophrenia. *British Journal of Psychiatry, 157,* 877–880.

Goffman, E. (1959). *The presentation of self in everyday life.* New York: Doubleday.

Gold, M., & Reimer, O. J. (1975). Changing patterns of delinquent behavior among Americans 13 through 16 years old: 1967–1972. *Crime and Delinquency Literature, 7,* 483–517.

Goldberg, S. (1983). Parent-infant bonding: Another look. *Child Development, 54,* 1355–1382.

Goldbloom, D. S., & Olmsted, M. P. (1993). Pharmacotherapy of bulimia nervosa with fluoxetine: Assessment of clinically significant attitudinal changes. *American Journal of Psychiatry, 150,* 770–774.

Golding, J. F. (1992). Cannabis. In A. P. Smith & D. M. Jones (Eds.), *Handbook of human performance: Vol. 2. Health and Performance* (pp. 169–196). London: Academic Press.

Goldman, G. D., & Millman, D. S. (1978). The initial phase of treatment. In G. D. Goldman & D. S. Millman (Eds.), *Psychoanalytic psychotherapy.* Don Mills, Ontario: Addison-Wesley.

Goldman, S. J., Herman, C. P., & Polivy, J. (1991). Is the effect of a social model on eating attenuated by hunger? *Appetite, 17,* 129–140.

Goldman-Rakic, P. S. (1987). Development of cortical circuitry and cognitive function. *Child Development, 58,* 601–622.

Goldschmidt, W. (1990). *The human career: The self in the symbolic world.* Cambridge, MA: Basil Blackwell.

Goldsmith, R. E., & Heiens, R. A. (1992). Subjective age: A test of five hypotheses. *Gerontologist, 32,* 312–317.

Goldstein, A., & Hilgard, E. R. (1975). Lack of influence of the morphine antagonist naloxone on hypnotic analgesia. *Proceedings of the National Academy of Sciences (USA), 72,* 2041–2043.

Goldstein, E. B. (1984). *Sensation and perception* (2nd ed.). Belmont, CA: Wadsworth.

Goldstein, E. B. (1989). *Sensation and perception* (3rd ed.). Belmont, CA: Wadsworth.

Goleman, D. (1980, February). 1,528 little geniuses and how they grew. *Psychology Today,* pp. 28–53.

Golinkoff, R. M., & Hirsh-Pasek, K. (1990). Let the mute speak: What infants can tell us about language acquisition. *Merrill-Palmer Quarterly, 36,* 67–92.

Gomes-Schwartz, B., Horowitz, J. M., & Cardarelli, A. P. (1990). *Child sexual abuse: The initial effects.* Newbury park, CA: Sage.

Goode, E. E., & Wagner, B. (1993). Does psychotherapy work? *U.S. News & World Report,* May 24, 1993, p. 56–65.

Goodman, G. S. (1992). Developmental changes in event memory. *Child Development, 63,* 173–187.

Gopnik, A., & Meltzoff, A. N. (1987). The development of categorization in the second year and its relation to other cognitive and linguistic developments. *Child Development, 58,* 1523–1531.

Gorassini, D. R., & Olson, J. M. (1995). Does self-perception change explain the foot-in-the-door effect? *Journal of Personality and Social Psychology, 69,* 91–105.

Gordon, I. E., & Earle, D. C. (1992). Visual illusions: A short review. *Australian Journal of Psychology, 44,* 153–156.

Gormezano, I. (1972). Investigations of defense and reward conditioning in the rabbit. In A. H. Black & W. F. Prokasy (Eds.), *Classical conditioning II: Current theory and research.* New York: Appleton-Century-Crofts.

Gorn, G. J., Goldberg, M. E., & Kanungo, R. N. (1976). The role of educational television in changing the intergroup attitudes of children. *Child Development, 47,* 277–280.

Gottesman, I. I., & Shields, J. (1982). Schizophrenia: The epigenetic puzzle. Cambridge, England: Cambridge University Press.

Gottesman, I. I., & Shields, J. A. (1976). A critical review of recent adoption, twin, and family studies of schizophrenia: Behavioral genetics perspectives. *Schizophrenia Bulletin, 2,* 360–461.

Gottesman, I. I., Shields, J., & Hanson, D. R. (1982). *Schizophrenia: The epigenetic puzzle.* New York: Cambridge University Press.

Gottlieb, G. (1985). On discovering significant acoustic dimensions of auditory stimulation for infants. In G. Gottlieb & N. A. Krasnegor (Eds.), *Measurement of audition and vision in the first year of postnatal life: A methodological overview.* Norwood, NJ: Ablex.

Gough, H. G. (1956). *California psychological inventory.* Palo Alto, CA: Consulting Psychologists Press.

Gould, J. D., Alfaro, L., Barnes, V., Finn, R., Haupt, B., & Minato, A. (1987). Reading is slower from CRT displays than from paper: Attempts to isolate a single variable explanation. *Human Factors, 29,* 269–299.

Gould, S. J. (1977). *Ever since Darwin: Reflections in natural history.* New York: Norton.

Gove, W. R., Hughes, M., & Galle, O. R. (1979). Overcrowding in the home. *American Sociological Review, 44,* 59–80.

Graf, P., Squire, L. R., & Mandler, G. (1984). The information that amnesic patients do not forget. *Journal of Experimental Psychology: Learning, Memory, and Cognition, 10,* 164–178.

Grau, J. W. (1984). Influence of naloxone on shock-induced freezing and analgesia. *Behavioral Neuroscience, 98,* 278–292.

Gray, C. R., & Gummerman, K. (1975). The enigmatic eidetic image: A critical examination of methods, data, and theories. *Psychological Bulletin, 82,* 383–407.

Green, D. M. (1976). *An introduction to hearing.* Hillsdale, NJ: Erlbaum.

Green, D. M., & Swets, J. A. (1966). *Signal detection theory and psychophysics.* New York: Wiley.

Greenberg, B. S. (1982). Television and role socialization: An overview. In U.S. Department of Health and Human Services, *Television and behavior: Ten years of progress and implications for the eighties: Vol. 2. Technical reviews.* Washington, DC: U.S. Government Printing Office.

Greenberg, M. S., & Beck, A. T. (1989). Depression versus anxiety: A test of the content-specificity hypothesis. *Journal of Abnormal Psychology, 98,* 9–13.

Greene, W. A., Betts, R. F., Ochitill, H. N., Ikes, H. P., & Douglas, R. G. (1978). Psychosocial factors and immunity: Preliminary report. *Psychosomatic Medicine, 40,* 87.

Greeno, C. G., & Wing, R. R. (1994). Stress-induced eating. *Psychological Bulletin, 115,* 444–464.

Greenough, W. T. (1986). What's special about development? Thoughts on the basis of experience-sensitive synaptic plasticity. In W. T. Greenough & J. M. Juraska (Eds.), *Developmental neuropsychobiology.* Orlando, FL: Academic Press.

Greenwald, A. G., Spangenberg, E. R., Pratkanis, A. R., & Kskenazi, J. (1991). Double-blind tests of subliminal self-help audiotapes. *Psychological Science, 2,* 119–122.

Greenwood, P. W. (1992). Substance abuse problems among high-risk youth and potential interventions. *Crime and Delinquency, 38,* 444–458.

Gregersen, F. (1983). *Sexual practices.* New York: Watts.

Gregory, R. L. (1987). Recovery from blindness. In R. L. Gregory (Ed.), *The Oxford companion to the mind.* Oxford: Oxford University Press.

Gregory, R. L. (1990). *Eye and brain: The psychology of seeing* (4th ed.). Princeton, NJ: Princeton University Press.

Griffeth, R. W., Vecchio, R. P., & Logan, J. W. (1989). Equity theory and interpersonal attraction. *Journal of Applied Psychology, 74,* 394–401.

Grings, W. W., & Dawson, M. E. (1978). *Emotions and bodily responses: A psychophysiological approach.* New York: Academic Press.

Grolnick, W. S., & Ryan, R. M. (1989). Parent styles associated with children's self-regulation and competence in school. *Journal of Educational Psychology, 81,* 143–154.

Grosskurth, P. (1991). Review of J. Sayers "Mothers of Psychoanalysis." *New York Times Book Review,* September 29, p. 11.

Grossman, H. J. (1973). *Manual on terminology and classification in mental retardation.* Washington, DC: American Association on Mental Deficiency.

Grossman, K., Grossman, K. E., Spangler, S., Seuss, G., & Unzer, L. (1985). Maternal sensitivity and newborn orientation responses as related to quality attachment in Northern Germany. *Monographs of the Society for Research in Child Development, 50,* No. 209, 232–256.

Grotevant, H. D., & Thorbeck, W. L. (1982). Sex differences in style of occupational identity formation in late adolescence. *Developmental Psychology, 18,* 396–405.

Group for the Advancement of Psychiatry. (1987). *Us and them: The psychology of ethnonationalism.* New York: Brunner/Mazel.

Grove, G. L., & Kligman, A. M. (1983). Age associated changes in human epidermal cell renewal. *Journal of Gerontology, 38,* 137–142.

Grusec, J. E., Kuczynski, L., Rushton, J. P., & Simutis, Z. M. (1979). Learning resistance to temptation through observation. *Developmental Psychology, 15,* 233–240.

Guerin, B. (1991). Anticipating the consequences of social behavior. *Current Psychology Research and Reviews, 10,* 131–162.

Guilford, J. P. (1966). Intelligence: 1965 model. *American Psychologist, 21,* 20–26.

Guilford, J. P. (1982). Cognitive psychology's ambiguities: Some suggested remedies. *Psychological Review, 89,* 48–59.

Guilleminault, C., & Dement, W. C. (Eds.) (1978). *The sleep apnea syndrome.* New York: Alan R. Liss.

Guimond, S., Begin, G., & Palmer, D. L. (1989). Education and causal attributions: The development of "person-blame" ideology. *Social Psychology Quarterly, 52,* 126–140.

Gur, R. C., Gur, R. E., Obrist, W. D., Hungerbuhler, J. P., Younkin, D., Rosen, A. D., Skilnick, B. E., & Reivich, M. (1982). Sex and handedness differences in cerebral blood flow during rest and cognitive activity. *Science, 217,* 659–661.

Gurin, P., Gurin, G., & Morrison, B. M. (1978). Personal and ideological aspects of internal and external control. *Social Psychology, 41,* 275–296.

Gurrman, N., & Kalish, H. I. (1956). Experiments in discrimination. *Scientific American, 198,* 77–80.

Gurtman, M. B. (1986). Depression and the response of others: Reevaluating the reevaluation. *Journal of Abnormal Psychology, 95,* 99–101.

Guttentag, R. E. (1985). Memory and aging: Implications for theories of memory development during childhood. *Developmental Review, 5,* 56–82.

H

Haber, R. N. (1979a). Twenty years of haunting eidetic imagery: Where's the ghost? *The Behavioral and Brain Sciences, 2,* 583–629.

Haber, R. N. (1979b). Author's response. *The Behavioral and Brain Sciences, 2,* 619–624.

Haber, R. N., & Haber, R. B. (1964). Eidetic imagery: 1. Frequency. *Perceptual and Motor Skills, 19,* 131–138.

Hagestad, G. O., & Neugarten, B. L. (1985). Age and the life course. In R. H. Binstock & E. Shanas (Eds.), *Handbook of aging and the social sciences* (2nd ed., pp. 35–61). New York: Van Nostrand Reinhold.

Haight, B. K. (1992). Long-term effects of a structured life review process. *Journal of Gerontology: Psychological Sciences, 47,* 312–315.

Hainline, L., & Abramov, I. (1992). Assessing visual development: Is infant vision good enough? In C. Rovee-Collier & L. P. Lipsitt (Eds.), *Advances in infancy research* (Vol. 7, pp. 39–102). Norwood, NJ: Ablex Publishing.

Hakel, M. D. (1982). Employment interviewing. In K. M. Rowland & G. R. Ferris (Eds.), *Personnel management.* Boston: Allyn and Bacon.

Haley, J. (1963). *Strategies of psychotherapy.* New York: Grune & Stratton.

Haley, J. (1986). *The power tactics of Jesus Christ and other essays, Second edition.* Rockville, MD: Triangle Press.

Halford, G. S. (1989). Reflections on 25 years of Piagetian cognitive developmental psychology: 1963–1988. *Human Development, 32,* 325–357.

Hall, C. S., & Lindzey, G. (1985). *Introduction to theories of personality.* New York: Wiley.

Hall, D. T., & Nougaim, K. E. (1968). An examination of Maslow's need hierarchy in an organized setting. *Organizational Behavior and Human Performance, 3,* 12–35.

Hall, G. S. (1904). *Adolescence.* New York: Appleton.

Hall, J. A. (1987). On explaining gender differences: The case of nonverbal communication. In P. Shaver & C. Hendrick (Eds.), *Review of Personality and Social Psychology, 7,* 177–200.

Hall, V. C., & Kingsley, R. C. (1968). Conservation and equilibration theory. *Journal of Genetic Psychology, 113,* 195–213.

Hallahan, D. P., & Kaufman, J. M. (1982). *Exceptional children: Introduction to special education.* Englewood Cliffs, NJ: Prentice-Hall.

Hamer, D. H., Hu, S., Magnuson, V. L., Hu, N., & Pattatucci, A. M. L. (1993). A linkage between DNA markers on the X chromosome and male sexual orientation. *Science, 261,* 321–327.

Hamer, D. H., Hu, S., Magnuson, V. L., Hu, N., & Pattatucci, A. M. L. (1993). A linkage between DNA markers on the X chromosome and male sexual orientation. *Science, 261,* 321–327.

Hamilton, W. D. (1964). The genetical theory of social behavior: I, II. *Journal of Theoretical Biology, 7,* 1–52.

Hammen, C. (1991). *Depression runs in families: The social context of risk and resilience in children of depressed mothers.* New York: Springer-Verlag.

Hampson, S. E. (1988). *The construction of personality: An introduction* (2nd ed.). London: Rutledge.

Hampson, S. E., John, O. P., & Goldberg, L. R. (1986). Category breadth and hierarchical structure in personality: Studies of asymmetries in judgments of trait implications. *Journal of Personality and Social Psychology, 51,* 37–54.

Hans, V. P. (1989). Psychology and law. In W. L. Gregory and W. J. Burroughs (Eds.), *Introduction to applied psychology.* Glenview, IL: Scott, Foresman.

Hans, V. P., & Slater, D. (1983). John Hinckley, Jr. and the insanity defense: The public's verdict. *Public Opinion Quarterly, 141,* 202–212.

Hansel, C. E. M. (1980). *Science and parapsychology: A critical reevaluation.* Buffalo, NY: Prometheus Books.

Hanson, D. R., & Fearn, R. W. (1975). Hearing acuity in young people exposed to pop music and other noise. *Lancet, 2,* 203–205.

Harari, H., & McDavid, J. W. (1973). Name stereotypes and teachers' expectations. *Journal of Educational Psychology, 65,* 222–225.

Hardaway, R. A. (1990). Subliminally activated symbiotic fanatsies: Facts and artifacts. *Psychological Bulletin, 107,* 177–195.

Hardiman, P. T., Dufresne, R., & Mestre, J. P. (1989). The relation between problem categorization and problem solving among experts and novices. *Memory and Cognition, 17,* 627–638.

Hare, R. D. (1978). Electrodermal and cardiovascular correlates of psychopathy. In R. D. Hare & D. Schalling (Eds.), *Psychopathic behavior: Approaches to research* (pp. 103–143). New York: Wiley.

Harford, T. C., & Brooks, S. D. (1992). Cirrhosis mortality and occupation. *Journal of Studies on Alcohol, 53,* 463–468.

Harkins, S. G., & Szymanski, K. (1987). Social loafing and social facilitation: New wine in old bottles. *Review of Personality and Social Psychology, 9,* 167–188.

Harlow, H. F., & Zimmerman, R. R. (1959). Affectional responses in the infant monkey. *Science, 130,* 421–432.

Harnishfeger, K. K., & Bjorklund, D. F. (1990). Children's strategies: A brief history. In D. F. Bjorklund (Ed.), *Children's strategies: Contemporary views of cognitive development* (pp. 1–22). Hillsdale, NJ: Erlbaum.

Harris, A. H., & Bardy, J. V. (1974). Animal learning: Visceral and autonomic conditioning. *Annual Review of Psychology, 25,* 107–133.

Harris, C. A. (1993). *Child Development* (2nd ed.). St. Paul, MN: West.

Harris, C. S. (1965). Perceptual adaptation to inverted, reversed, or displaced vision. *Psychological Review, 72,* 419–444.

Harris, C. S. (1980). Insight or out of sight: Two examples of perceptual plasticity in the human adult. In C. S. Harris (Ed.), *Visual coding and adaptability* (pp. 95–149), Hillsdale, NJ: Erlbaum.

Harris, G. W., & Levine, S. (1965). Sexual differentiation of the brain and its experimental control. *Journal of Physiology, 181,* 379–400.

Harris, J. P. (1987). Contingent perceptual aftereffect. In R. L. Gregory (Ed.), *The Oxford companion to the mind.* Oxford: Oxford University Press.

Harris, M. B. (1991). Sex differences in stereotypes of spectacles. *Journal of Applied Social Psychology, 21,* 1659–1680.

Harris, M. J., Milich, R., Johnston, E. M., & Hoover, D. W. (1990). Effects of expectancies on children's social interactions. *Journal of Experimental Social Psychology, 26,* 1–12.

Harris, T. O. (1991). Life stress and illness: The question of specificity. *Annals of Behavioral Medicine, 13,* 211–219.

Hart, B. (1969). Gonadal hormones and sexual reflexes in the female rat. *Hormones and Behavior, 1,* 65–71.

Harter, S. (1981). A new self-report scale of intrinsic versus extrinsic orientation in the classroom: Motivational and informational components. *Developmental Psychology, 17,* 300–312.

Harter, S. (1982). The perceived competence scale for children. *Child Development, 53,* 87–97.

Hartl, E. M., Monnelly, E. P., & Elderkin, R. D. (1982). *Physique and delinquent behavior.* New York: Academic Press.

Hartley, A. (1981). Adult age differences in deductive reasoning processes. *Journal of Gerontology, 36,* 700–706.

Hartley, P. (1988). The role of self-help groups in eating disorders. In D. Scot (Ed.), *Anorexia and bulimia nervosa: Practical approaches* (pp. 177–191). New York: New York University Press.

Hartmann, D. P. (1969). Influence of symbolically modeled instrumental aggression and pain cues on aggressive behavior. *Journal of Personality and Social Psychology, 11,* 280–288.

Hartmann, H. (1958; original publication, 1939) *Ego Psychology and the Problem of Adaptation.* New York: International Universities Press.

Hartshorne, H., & May, M. A. (1928). *Studies in the nature of character: Vol. 1. Studies in deceit.* New York: Macmillan.

Hartshorne, H., May, M. A., & Maller, J. B. (1929). *Studies in the nature of character: Vol. 2. Studies in self-control.* New York: Macmillan.

Hartshorne, H., May, M. A., & Shuttleworth, F. K. (1930). *Studies in the nature of character: Vol. 3. Studies in the organization of character.* New York: Macmillan.

Harvard Medical School Health Letter. (1981, April). Cambridge, MA: Department of Continuing Education, Harvard Medical School.

Harwood, R. L. (1992). The influence of culturally derived values on Anglo and Puerto Rican mothers' perceptions of attachment behavior. *Child Development, 63,* 822–839.

Hass, A. (1979). *Teenage sexuality: A survey of teenage sexual behavior.* New York: Macmillan.

Hassett, J. (1978, March). Sex and smell. *Psychology Today, 11,* 40–42.

Hastorf, A. H. (1950). The influence of suggestion on the relationship between stimulus size and perceived distance. *Journal of Psychology, 29,* 195–217.

Hatfield, E., & Sprecher, S. (1986). *Mirror, mirror: The importance of looks in everyday life.* Albany, NY: State University of New York Press.

Hatfield, E., & Walster, G. W. (1978). *A new look at love.* Latham, MA: University Press of America.

Hatton, G. I. (1976). *Nucleus circularis: Is it an osmoreceptor in the brain?* Brain Research Bulletin, 1, 123–131.

Haugaard, J. J., & Repucci, N. D. (1988). *The sexual abuse of children: A comprehensive guide to current knowledge and intervention strategies.* San Francisco: Jossey-Bass.

Haughton, E., & Alyllon, T. (1965). Production and elimination of symptomatic behavior. In L. P. Ullman & L. Krasner (Eds.), *Case studies in behavior modification* (pp. 268–284). New York: Holt, Rinehart & Winston.

Hauri, P. (1977). *The sleep disorders.* Kalamazoo, MI: Upjohn.

Hauser, S. T., Borman, E. H., Jacobson, A. M., Powers, S. I., & Noam, G. G. (1991). Understanding family contexts of adolescent coping. *Journal of Early Adolescence, 11,* 96–124.

Havighurst, R. J. (1953). *Human development and education.* New York: Longmans.

Haviland, S. E., & Clark, H. H. (1974). What's new? Acquiring new information as a process in comprehension. *Journal of Verbal Learning and Verbal Behavior, 13,* 512–521.

Hayes, C. (1951). *The ape in our house.* New York: Harper & Row.

Hayes, C. D., & Kamerman, S. B. (1983). *Children of working parents: Experiences and outcomes.* Washington, DC: National Academy Press.

Healy, A. F. (1994). Letter detection: A window to unitization and other cognitive processes in reading text. *Psychonomic Bulletin and Review, 1,* 333–344.

Hearn, M. D., Murray, D. M., & Luepker, R. V. (1989). Hostility, coronary heart disease, and total mortality: A 33-year follow-up study of university students. *Journal of Behavioral Medicine, 12,* 105–121.

Heath, D. B. (1987). Anthropology and alcohol studies: Current issues. In B. J. Siegel, A. R. Beals & S. A. Tyler (Eds.), *Annual Review of Anthropology, 16,* 99–120.

Heath, L., Acklin, M., & Wiley, K. (1991). Cognitive heuristics and AIDS risk assessment among physicians. *Journal of Applied Social Psychology, 21,* 1859–1867.

Hebb, D. O. (1949). *The organization of behavior.* New York: Wiley.

Hefner, R. S., & Hefner, H. E. (1985). Hearing in animals: The least weasel. *Journal of Mammology, 66,* 745–755.

Heidbreder, E. (1933). *Seven psychologies.* New York: Appleton.

Heider, E. R. (1971). "Focal" color areas and the development of color names. *Developmental Psychology, 4,* 447–455.

Heider, E. R. (1972). Universals in color naming and memory. *Journal of Experimental Psychology, 93,* 10–20.

Heider, E. R., & Oliver, D. (1972). The structure of the color space in naming and memory for two languages. *Cognitive Psychology, 3,* 337–354.

Heider, F. (1944). Social perception and phenomenal causality. *Psychological Review, 51,* 358–374.

Heider, F. (1958). *The psychology of interpersonal relations.* New York: Wiley.

Heider, K. G. (1976). Dani sexuality: A low energy system. *Mann, 11,* 188–201.

Heil, J. (1987). The Molyneaux question. *Journal for the Theory of Social Behavior, 17,* 227–241.

Heilbrun, K. S. (1980). Silverman's subliminal psychodynamic activation: A failure to replicate. *Journal of Abnormal Psychology, 89,* 560–566.

Held, R., & Hein, A. (1963). Movement-produced stimulation in the development of visually guided behavior. *Journal of Comparative and Physiological Psychology, 56,* 872–876.

Heller, K. (1992). Review of C. R. Snyder & D. R. Forsyth (Eds.), "Handbook of Social and Clinical Psychology: The Health Perspective." *Contemporary Psychology, 37,* 410–411.

Helm, C., & Morelli, M. (1979). Stanley Milgram and the obedience experiment: Authority, legitimacy, and human action. *Political Theory, 7,* 321–345.

Herbert, J. D., Hope, D. A., & Bellack, A. S. (1992). Validity of the distinction between generalized social phobia and avoidant personality disorder. *Journal of Abnormal Psychology, 101,* 332–339.

Heritch, A. J. (1990). Evidence for reduced and dysregulated turnover of dopamine in schizophrenia. *Schizophrenia Bulletin, 16,* 605–615.

Herman, C. P., (1992) 50-year retrospective review of "Varieties of Temperament." *Contemporary Psychology, 37,* 525–528.

Herman, C. P., & Polivy, J. (1975). Anxiety, restraint and eating behavior. *Journal of Abnormal Psychology, 84,* 666–672.

Herman, C. P., & Polivy, J. (1988). Studies of eating in normal dieters. In B. T. Walsh (Ed.), *Eating behavior in eating disorders.* Washington, DC: American Psychiatric Press.

Herman, C. P., & Polivy, J. (1993). Mental control of eating: Excitatory and inhibitory food thoughts. In D. M. Wegner & J. W. Pennebaker (Eds.) *Handbook of Mental Control.* Englewood Cliffs, NJ: Prentice-Hall, pp. 491–505.

Hernandez, L., & Hoebel, B. G. (1988). Feeding and hypothalamic stimulation increase dopamine turnover in the accumbens. *Physiology & Behavior, 44,* 599–606.

Hernshaw, L. S. (1979). *Cyril Burt: Psychologist.* Ithaca, NY: Cornell University Press.

Herrnstein, R. J. (1973). *IQ in the meritocracy.* New York: Atlantic Monthly Books.

Herrnstein, R. J. (1984). Objects, categories, and discriminative stimuli. In H. L. Roitblat, T. G. Bever, & H. S. Terrace (Eds.), *Animal cognition.* Hillsdale, NJ: Erlbaum.

Herrnstein, R. J., & Murray, C. (1994). *The bell curve: Intelligence and class structure in American life.* New York: Free Press.

Herrnstein, R. J., Loveland, D. H., & Cable, C. (1976). Natural concepts in pigeons. *Journal of Experimental Psychology: Animal Behavior Processes, 2,* 285–301.

Heston, L. L. (1966). Psychiatric disorders in foster home reared children of schizophrenic mothers. *British Journal of Psychiatry, 11,* 819–825.

Heston, L. L. (1970). The genetics of schizophrenic and schizoid disease. *Science, 167,* 249–256.

Hetherington, E. M. (1979). Divorce: A child's perspective. *American Psychologist, 34,* 851–858.

Hewstone, M. (1990). The ultimate attribution error? A review of the literature on intergroup causal attribution. *European Journal of Social Psychology, 20,* 311–336.

Hewstone, M., & Brown, R. (Eds.). (1986). *Contact and conflict in intergroup encounters.* Oxford: Basil Blackwell.

Hibscher, J. A., & Herman, C. P. (1977). Obesity, dieting, and the expression of "obese" characteristics. *Journal of Comparative and Physiological Psychology, 91,* 374–380.

Higbee, K. L. (1969). Fifteen years of fear arousal: Research on threat appeals, 1953–1968. *Psychological Bulletin, 72,* 426–444.

Higbee, K. L. (1988). *Your memory: How it works and how to improve it.* New York: Prentice-Hall.

Higgins, E. T. (1987). Self-discrepancy: A theory relating self and affect. *Psychological Review, 94,* 319–340.

Higgins, E. T. (1989). Self-discrepancy theory: What patterns of self-beliefs cause people to suffer? In L. Berkowitz (Ed.) *Advances in Experimental Social Psychology* (Vol.22). New York: Academic Press, pp. 93–136.

Higgins, R. L., & Marlatt, G. A. (1975). Fear of interpersonal evaluation as a determinant of alcohol consumption in male social drinkers. *Journal of Abnormal Psychology, 84,* 644–651.

Hilgard, E. R. (1975). Hypnosis. *Annual Review of Psychology, 26,* 19–44.

Hilgard, E. R. (1977). *Divided consciousness: Multiple controls in human thought and action.* New York: Wiley.

Hilgard, E. R. (1986). *Divided consciousness: Multiple controls in human thought and action.* New York: Wiley.

Hilgard, E. R. (1987). *Psychology in America: A Historical Survey.* San Diego: Harcourt Brace Jovanovich.

Hilgard, E. R., & LeBaron, S. (1984). *Hypnosis in the treatment of pain and anxiety in children with cancer: A clinical and quantitative investigation.* Los Antos, CA: Kaufmann.

Hill, C. T., Rubin, Z., & Peplau, L. A. (1976). Breakups before marriage: The end of 103 affairs. *Journal of Social Issues, 32*(1), 147–168.

Himmelweit, H., Oppenheim, A. N., & Vince, P. (1958). *Television and the child: An empirical study of the effects of television on the young.* London: Oxford University Press.

Hinckley, J., & Hinckley, J. (1985). *Breaking points.* Grand Rapids, MI: Zondervan.

Hines, M. (1982). Parental gonadal hormones and sex differences in human behavior. *Psychological Bulletin, 92,* 56–80.

Hines, T. (1992). *Pseudoscience and the paranormal.* Buffalo, NY: Prometheus Books.

Hirt, E. R., Deppe, R. K., & Gordon, L. J. (1991). Self-reported versus behavioral self-handicapping: Empirical evidence for a theoretical distinction. *Journal of Personality and Social Psychology, 61,* 981–991.

Hobson, J. A. (1988). *the dreaming brain.* New York: Basic Books.

Hobson, J. A. (1989). *Sleep.* New York: Scientific American Library.

Hobson, J. A., & McCarley, R. W. (1977). The brain as a dream state generator: An activation-synthesis hypothesis of the dream process. *American Journal of Psychiatry, 134,* 1335–1348.

Hochberg, J. E. (1978). *Perception* (2nd ed.). Englewood Cliffs, NJ: Prentice-Hall.

Hochhauser, M., & Fowler, H. (1975). Cue effects of drive and reward as a function of discrimination difficulty: Evidence against the Yerkes-Dodson law. *Journal of Experimental Psychology: Animal Behavior Processes, 1,* 261–269.

Hock, E., & DeMeis, D. K. (1990). Depression in mothers of infants: The role of maternal employment. *Developmental Psychology, 26*, 285–291.

Hodgkin, A. L., & Huxley, A. F. (1952). A quantitative description of membrane current and its application to conduction and excitation in nerves. *Journal of Physiology, 117*, 500–544.

Hoebel, B. G. (1988). Neuroscience and motivation: Pathways and peptides that define motivational systems. In R. C. Atkinson, R. J. Hernstein, G. Lindzey, & R. D. Luce (Eds.), *Steven's handbook of experimental psychology: Vol 1* (2nd ed. pp. 547–625). New York: Wiley.

Hoelter, J. W. (1985). The structure of self-conception: Conceptualization and measurement. *Journal of Personality and Social Psychology, 49*, 1392–1407.

Hoff-Ginsberg, E., & Shatz, M. (1982). Linguistic input and the child's acquisition of language. *Psychological Bulletin, 92*, 3–26.

Hoffman, L. W. (1985). The changing genetics/socialization balance. *Journal of Social Issues, 41*, 127–148.

Hoffman, L. W. (1989). Effects of maternal employment in the two-parent family. *American Psychologist, 44*, 283–292.

Hoffman, L. W. (1991). The influence of the family environment on personality: Accounting for sibling differences. *Psychological Bulletin, 110*, 187–203.

Hoffman, L. W., & Nye, F. I. (1974). *Working mothers*. San Francisco: Jossey-Bass.

Hoffman, L., Paris, S., Hall, E., & Schell, R. (1988). *Developmental psychology today* (5th ed.). New York: Random House.

Hoffman, L., Paris, S., Hall, E., & Schell, R. (1994). *Developmental psychology today* (6th ed.). New York: Random House.

Hoffman, M. L. (1963). Parent discipline and the child's consideration for others. *Child Development, 34*, 573–588.

Hoffman, M. L. (1975a). Altruistic behavior and the parent-child relationship. *Journal of Personality and Social Psychology, 31*, 937–943.

Hoffman, M. L. (1975b). Moral internalization, parental power, and the nature of parent-child interaction. *Developmental Psychology, 11*, 228–239.

Hoffman, M. L. (1984). Moral development. In M. Bornstein & M. Lamb (Eds.), *Development psychology* (pp. 279–334). Hillsdale, NJ: Erlbaum.

Hofling, C. K., Brotzman, E., Dalrymple, S., Graves, N., & Pierce, C. (1966). An experimental study of nurse-physician relations. *Journal of Nervous and Mental Disease, 143*, 171–180.

Hogan. (1994). Structure and development of behavior systems. *Psychonomic Bulletin & Review, 1(4)*, 439–450.

Hogan J. (1994). Structure and development of behavior systems. *Psychonomic Bulletin & Review, 1*, 439–450.

Hohmann, G. W. (1966). Some effects of spinal cord lesions on experienced emotional feelings. *Psychophysiology, 3*, 143–156.

Holden, C. (1991). Is "gender gap" narrowing? *Science, 253*, 959–960.

Holding, D. H. (1979). Does being "eidetic" matter? *The Behavioral and Brain Sciences, 2*, 604–605.

Holender, D. (1986). Semantic activation without conscious identification in dichotic listening, parafoveal vision, and visual masking: A survey and appraisal. *The Behavioral and Brain Sciences, 9*, 1–66.

Holland, J. L. (1985). *Making vocational choices: A theory of vocational personalities and work environments* (2nd ed.). Englewood Cliffs, NJ: Prentice-Hall.

Holmes, D. S. (1994). *Abnormal psychology* (2nd ed.). New York: Harper-Collins.

Holmes, J. G., & Boon, S. D. (1990). Developments in the field of close relationships: Creating foundations for intervention strategies. *Personality and Social Psychology Bulletin, 16*, 23–41.

Holmes, T. H., & Rahe, R. H. (1967). The social readjustment rating scale. *Journal of Psychosomatic Research, 11*, 213–218.

Holroyd, K. A. Coyne, J. (1987). Personality and health in the 1980s: Psychosomatic medicine revisited. *Journal of Personality, 55*, 359–375.

Holt, C. S., Heimberg, R. G., & Hope, D. A. (1992). Avoidant personality disorder and the generalized subtype of social phobia. *Journal of Abnormal Psychology, 101*, 318–325.

Honig, W. K., & Urcuioli, P. J. (1981). The legacy of Guttman and Kalish (1956): Twenty-five years of research on stimulus generalization. *Journal of the Experimental Analysis of Behavior, 36*, 405–445.

Hopkins, B., & Westra, T. (1990). Motor development, maternal expectations, and the role of handling. *Infant Behavior and Development, 13*, 117–122.

Horn, J. L. (1970). Organization of data on life-span development of human abilities. In L. R. Goulet & P. B. Baltes (Eds.), *Life-span developmental psychology: Research and theory*. New York: Academic Press.

Horn, J. L. (1976). Intelligence: Why it grows, why it declines. In J. M. Hunt (Ed.), *Human intelligence* (pp. 53–74). New Brunswick, NJ: Transaction Books.

Horn, J. L. (1978). The nature and development of intellectual abilities. In R. T. Osborne, C. E. Noble, and N. Weyl (Eds.), *Human variation*. New York: Academic Press.

Horn, J. L. (1982). The theory of fluid and crystallized intelligence in relation to concepts of cognitive psychology and aging in adulthood. In F. I. M. Craik & S. E. Trehub (Eds.), *Aging and cognitive processes*. New York: Plenum.

Horn, J. L., & Cattell, R. B. (1966). Age differences in primary mental ability factors. *Journal of Gerontology, 21*, 210–220.

Horn, J. L., Loehlin, J. C., & Willerman, L. (1979). Intellectual resemblance among adoptive and biological relatives: The Texas adoption project. *Behavior Genetics, 9*, 177–207.

Horn, J. M. (1983a). Delinquents in adulthood. *Science, 221*, 256–257.

Horn, J. M. (1983b). The Texas adoption project: Adopted children and their intellectual resemblance to biological and adoptive parents. *Child Development, 54*, 268–275.

Horne, J. A. (1991). Dimensions to sleepiness. In T. H. Monk (Ed.), *Sleep, sleepiness, and performance* (pp. 169–196). New York: Wiley.

House, J. S., Landis, K. R., & Umberson, D. (1988). Social relationships and health. *Science, 241*, 540–545.

Horner, M. S. (1972). Toward an understanding of achievement related conflicts in women. *Journal of Social Issues, 28*, 157–176.

Houston, R. C. (1988). Pilot personnel selection. In S. G. Cole & R. G. Demaree (Eds.), *Applications of interactionist psychology: Essay in honor of Saul B. Sells* (pp. 291–316). Hillsdale, NJ: Erlbaum.

Hovland, C. I. (1937). The generalization of conditioned responses: 1. The sensory generalization of conditioned responses with varying frequencies of tone. *Journal of General Psychology, 17*, 125–148.

Hovland, C. I., & Weiss, W. (1951). The influence of source credibility on communication effectiveness. *Public Opinion Quarterly, 15*, 635–650.

Howard, A., & Bray, D. W. (1980). Career motivation in mid-life managers. Paper presented at the annual meeting of the American Psychological Association, Montreal.

Howard, A., & Wilson, J. A. (1982). Leadership in a declining work ethic. *California Management Review, 24*, 33–46.

Howard, J. W., & Rothbart, M. (1980). Social categorization and memory for in-group and out-group behavior. *Journal of Personality and Social Psychology, 38*, 301–310.

Howard, K. I., Cornille, T. A., Lyons, J. S., Vessey, J. T., Lueger, R. J., & Saunders, S. M. (1996). Patterns of service utilization. *Archives of General Psychiatry*.

Howard, K. I., Davidson, C. V., O'Mahoney, M. T., & Orlinsky, D. E. (1988). The research project on long-term psychotherapy. NIMH grant proposal.

Howard, K. I., Davidson, C. V., O'Mahoney, M. T., Orlinsky, D. E., & Brown, K. P. (1989). Patterns of psychotherapy utilization. *American Journal of Psychiatry, 146*, 775–778.

Howard, K. I., Kopta, S. M., Krause, M., & Orlinsky, D. E. (1986). The dose-effect relationship in psychotherapy. *American Psychologist, 41*, 159–164.

Howard, R. (1991). *All about intelligence: Human, animal, and artificial*. Kensington, NSW Australia: New South Wales University Press.

Howarth, P. A., & Istance, H. O. (1986). The validity of subjective reports of visual discomfort. *Human Factors, 28*, 347–351.

Howe, M. L., & Courage, M. L. (1993). On resolving the enigma of infantile amnesia. *Psychological Bulletin, 113*, 305–326.

Howell, W. C., & Dipboye, R. L. (1986). *Essentials of industrial and organizational psychology* (3rd ed.). Homewood, IL: Dorsey Press.

Howells, K. (1989). Anger management methods in relation to the prevention of violent behaviour. In J. Archer & K. Browne (Eds.), *Human aggression: Naturalistic approaches*. New York: Rutledge.

Hubel, D. H., & Wiesel, T. N. (1968). Receptive fields and functional architecture of the monkey striate cortex. *Journal of Physiology* (London), *195*, 215–243.

Hubel, D. H., & Wiesel, T. N. (1979). Brain mechanisms of vision. *Scientific American, 241*, 150–162.

Hudson, V. M. (1990). Birth order of world leaders: An exploratory analysis of effects on personality and behavior. *Political Psychology, 11* 583–606.

Huesman, L. R. (1983). On Sohn's accusations. *American Psychologist, 38*, 117–119.

Huesmann, L. R. (1982). Television violence and aggression. In D. Pearl, L. Bouthilet, & J. Lazar (Eds.), *Television and aggressive behavior: Ten years of scientific progress and implications for the eighties* (Vol. 2, Technical reviews, pp. 220–256). Washington, DC: National Institute of Mental Health.

Hughes, J., Smith, T. W., Kosterlitz, H. W., Fothergill, L. A., Morgan, B. A., & Morris, H. R. (1975). Identification of two related pentapeptides from the brain with potent opiate agonist activity. *Nature, 258*, 577–579.

Hughes, M., & Demo, D. H. (1989). Self-perceptions of Black Americans: Self-esteem and personal efficacy. *American Journal of Sociology, 95*, 132–159.

Hull C. L. (1943). *Principles of behavior*. New York: Appleton-Century-Crofts.

Hull, J. G. (1981). A self-awareness model of the causes and effects of alcohol consumption. *Journal of Abnormal Psychology, 90*, 586–600.

Hulse, S. H., & Dorsky, N. P. (1977). Structural complexity as a determinant of several pattern learning. *Learning and Motivation, 8*, 488–506.

Humber, C. N., & Sherrick, M. F. (1993). Induced visual motion: Effects of fixation and retinal position. *Perceptual and Motor Skills, 76*, 19–27.

Humphrey, G. K., & Jolicoeur, P. (1993). An examination of the effects of axis foreshortening, monocular depth cues, and visual field on object identification. *The Quarterly Journal of Experimental Psychology, 46A*, 137–159.

Humphrey, G. K., & Khan, S. C. (1992). Recognizing novel views of three-dimensional objects. *Canadian Journal of Psychology, 46,* 170–190.

Humphrey, R. (1985). How work roles influence perception: Structural-cognitive processes and organizational behavior. *American Sociological Review, 50,* 242–252.

Hunt, M. (1975). *Sexual behavior in the 1970s.* Chicago: Playboy Press.

Hunt, R. R. (1995). The sublety of distinctiveness: What von Restorff really did. *Psychonomic Bulletin & Review, 2,* 105–112.

Hunt, R. R., & Einstein, G. O. (1981). Relational and item-specific information in memory. *Journal of the Verbal Learning and Verbal Behavior, 20,* 497–514.

Hunter, J. E. (1980). *Validity generalization for 12,000 jobs: An application of synthetic validity and validity generalization for the General Aptitude Test Battery (GATB).* Washington, DC: U.S. Employment Service.

Hurvich, L., & Jameson, D. (1957). An opponent process theory of color vision. *Psychological Review, 64,* 384–404.

Hurvich, L., & Jameson, D. (1974). Opponent processes as a model of neural organization. *American Psychologist, 29,* 88–102.

Huston, A. C. (1985). The development of sex-typing: Themes from recent research. *Developmental Review, 5,* 1–17.

Huston-Stein, A., & Higgins-Trenk, A. (1978). Development of females from childhood through adulthood: Career and feminine role orientations. In P. B. Baltes (Ed.), *Life-span development and behavior* (Vol. 1). New York: Academic Press.

Hutchings, B., & Mednick, S. A. (1975). Registered criminality in the adoptive and biological parents of registered male criminal adoptees. In R. R. Fieve, D. Rosenthal, & H. Brill (Eds.), *Genetic research in psychiatry.* Baltimore: Johns Hopkins University Press.

Hutchingson, R. D. (1981). *New horizons for human factors in design.* New York: McGraw-Hill.

Hutchinson, R. R. (1972). The environmental causes of aggression. In J. K. Cole & D. D. Jensen (Eds.), *Nebraska symposium on motivation* (pp. 155–181). Lincoln: University of Nebraska Press.

Hutchison, J. B. (Ed.) (1978). *Biological determinants of sexual behavior.* New York: Wiley.

Hyman, I. E., Husband, T. H., & Billings, F. J. (1995). False memories of childhood experiences. *Applied Cognitive Psychology, 9,* 181–197.

Hyman, R. (1989). The psychology of deception. In M. R. Rosenzweig & L. W. Porter (Eds.), *Annual Review of Psychology, 40,* 133–154.

I

Iaccino, J. F. (1993). *Left brain-right brain differences: Inquiries, evidence, and new approaches.* Hillsdale, NJ: Erlbaum.

Iaffaldano, M. T., & Muchinsky, P. M. (1985). Job satisfaction and job performance: A meta analysis. *Psychological Bulletin, 97,* 251–273.

Iarovici, D. (1994). Myopia linked more to nature than nurture? *The Journal of NIH Research, 1994, 6,* 40–41.

Imperato-McGinley, J., Guerrero, L., Gautier, T., & Peterson, R. (1974). Steroid 52-reductase deficiency in man: An inherited form of male pseudohermaphroditism. *Science, 186,* 1213–1215.

Ingelfinger, F. J. (1944). The late effects of total and subtotal gastrectomy. *New England Journal of Medicine, 231,* 321–327.

Ingham, A. G., Levinger, G., Graves, J., & Peckham, V. (1974). The Ringelmann effect: Studies of group size and group performance. *Journal of Experimental Social Psychology, 10,* 371–384.

Inhelder, B., & Piaget, J. (1958). *The growth of logical thinking from childhood to adolescence.* New York: Basic Books.

Intraub, H. (1992). Contextual factors in scene perception. In E. Chekaluk & K. R. Lelewellyn (Eds.), *The role of eye movements in perceptual processes* (pp. 45–72). Amsterdam: Elsevier Science Publishers.

Intraub, H., & Bodamer, J. L. (1993). Boundary extension: Fundamental aspect of pictorial representation or encoding artifact? *Journal of Experimental Psychology: Learning, Memory, and Cognition, 19,* 1387–1397.

Intraub, H., & Richardson, M. (1989). Wide-angle memories of close-up scenes. *Journal of Experimental Psychology: Learning, Memory, and Cognition, 15,* 179–187.

Intraub, H., Gottesman, C. V., Willey, E. V., & Zuk, I. J. (1996). Boundary extension for recently glimpsed photographs: Do common perceptual processes result in unexpected memory distortions? *Journal of Memory and Language, 35,* 000–000.

Isen, A. M., Daubman, K. A., & Gorgoglione, J. M. (1987). The influence of positive affect on cognitive organization: Implications for education. In R. Snow & M. Farr (Eds.), *Aptitude, Learning, and Instruction: Conative and Affective Factors* (pp. 143–164). Hillsdale, NJ: Erlbaum.

Ittelson, W. H., & Kilpatrick, F. (1951, August). Experiments in perception. *Scientific American,* pp. 50–55.

Iversen, S. D., & Iversen, L. L. (1981). *Behavioral pharmacology* (2nd ed.). New York: Oxford University Press.

Ivry, R. B., & Prinzmetal, W. (1991). Effects of feature similarity on illusory conjunctions. *Perceptions & Psychophysics, 49,* 105–116.

Izard, C. E. (1977). *Human emotions.* New York: Plenum.

Izard, C. E. (1994). Innate and universal facial expressions: Evidence from developmental and cross-cultural research. *Psychological Bulletin, 115,* 288–299.

Izard, C. E., Kagan, J., & Zajonc, R. B. (Eds.). (1984). *Emotion, cognition, and behavior.* New York: Cambridge University Press.

J

Jacklin, C. N., & Maccoby, E. E. (1978). Social behavior at 33 months in same-sex and mixed-sex dyads. *Child Development, 49,* 557–569.

Jackson, D. N. (1984). *The personality research form manual.* Port Huron, Mich.: Research Psychologists Press.

Jackson, M. J., & Williams, K. D. (1985). Social loafing on difficult tasks: Working collectively can improve performance. *Journal of Personality and Social Psychology, 49,* 937–942.

Jackson, R. L., Maier, S. F., & Rappaport, P. M. (1978). Exposure to inescapable shock produces both activity and associative deficits in the rat. *Learning and Motivation, 9,* 69–98.

Jacobs, J. E., & Eccles, J. S. (1985). Gender differences in math ability: The impact of media reports on parents. *Education Researcher, 14,* 20–25.

Jacobson, N. S., & Bussod, N. (1983). Marital and family therapy. In M. Hersen, A. E. Kazdin, & A. S. Bellack (Eds.), *The clinical psychology handbook.* New York: Pergamon.

Jacoby, L. (1983). Remembering the data: Analyzing interactive processes in reading. *Journal of Verbal Learning and Verbal Behavior, 22,* 485–508.

Jacoby, L. L., & Witherspoon, D. (1982). Remembering without awareness. *Canadian Journal of Psychology, 36,* 300–324.

James, W. (1890). *The principles of psychology.* New York: Holt.

James, W. (1968). What is an emotion? (*Mind,* 1885, 9, 188–205). Reprinted in M. Arnold, *The nature of emotion.* Baltimore, Penguin.

Jandorf, L., Deblinger, E., Neale, J. M., & Stone, A. A. (1986). Daily versus major life events as predictors of symptom frequency: A replication study. *Journal of General Psychology, 113,* 205–218.

Janisse, M. P., & Dyck, D. G. (1988). The Type A behavior pattern and coronary heart disease: Physiological and psychological dimensions. In M. P. Janisse (Ed.) *Individual Differences, Stress, and Health Psychology.* New York: Springer-Verlag. 57–71.

Jarvik, M. E. (1990). The drug dilemma: Manipulating the demand. *Science, 250,* 387–392.

Jaynes, J. (1976). *The origin of consciousness in the breakdown of the bicameral mind.* Boston: Houghton Mifflin.

Jeffrey, R. W., Wing, R. R., & Stunkard, A. J. Behavioral treatment of obesity: The state of the art 1976. *Behavior Therapy, 9,* 189–199.

Jenkins, H. M., Barnes, R. A., & Barrera, F. J. (1981). Why autoshaping depends on trial spacing. In C. M. Locurto, H. S. Terrace, & J. Gibbon (Eds.), *Autoshaping and conditioning theory.* New York: Academic Press.

Jenkins, J. G., & Dallenbach, K. M. (1924). Oblivescence during sleep and waking. *American Journal of Psychology, 35,* 605–612.

Jensen, A. R. (1980). *Bias in mental testing.* New York: Free Press.

Jensen, A. R. (1985). The nature of the black-white difference on various psychometric tests: Spearman's hypothesis. *The Behavioral and Brain Sciences, 8(2),* 193–219.

Johansson, G. (1975). Visual motion perception. *Scientific American, 232,* 76–88.

John, O. P. (1990). The "Big Five" factor taxonomy: Dimensions of personality in the natural language and in questionnaires. In L. A. Pervin (Ed.) *Handbook of Personality Theory and Research.* New York: Guilford, 66–100.

Johnson, C., & Conners, M. E. (1987). *the etiology and treatment of bulimia nervosa.* New York: Basic Books.

Johnson, C. L., Stuckey, M. K., Lewis, L. D., & Schwartz, D. M. (1983). Bulimia: A descriptive survey of 509 cases. In P. L. Darby, P. E. Garfinkel, D. M. Garner, & D. V. Coscina (Eds.), *Anorexia nervosa: Recent developments* (pp. 159–172). New York: Allen R. Liss.

Johnson, M. A. (1989). Concern for appropriateness scale and behavioral conformity. *Journal of Personality Assessment, 53,* 567–574.

Johnson, N. F. (1965). The psychological reality of phrase-structure rules. *Journal of Verbal Learning and Verbal Behavior, 4,* 469–475.

Johnson, R. (1990). *Death Work: A study of the Modern Execution Process.* Pacific Grove, CA: Brooks/Cole.

Johnson, R. C., McClearn, G. E., Yuen, S., Nagoshi, C. T., Ahern, F. M., & Cole, R. E. (1985). Galton's data a century later. *American Psychologist, 40,* 875–892.

Johnson-Laird, P. N., & Steedman, M. (1978). The psychology of syllogisms. *Cognitive Psychology, 10,* 64–99.

Johnston, L. D., Bachman, J. G., & O'Malley, P. M. (1982). *Student drug use, attitudes, and beliefs: National trends 1975–1982.* Rockville, MD: National Institute on Drug Abuse. Washington, DC: U.S. Government Printing Office.

Johnston, L. D., O'Malley, P. M., & Bachman, J. G. (1987). Psychotherapeutic, licit, and illicit use of drugs among adolescents. *Journal of Adolescent Health Care, 8,* 36–51.

Jones, E. E. (1964). *Ingratiation: A social-psychological analysis*. New York: Appleton-Century-Crofts.

Jones, E. E., & Berglas, S. (1978). Control of attributions about the self through self-handicapping strategies: The appeal of alcohol and the role of underachievement. *Personality and Social Psychology Bulletin, 4,* 200–206.

Jones, E. E., & Davis, K. D. (1965). From acts to dispositions: The attribution process in person perception. In L. Berkowitz (Ed.), *Advances in experimental social psychology* (Vol. 2). New York: Academic Press.

Jones, E. E., Davis, K. E., & Gergen, K. J. (1961). Role playing variations and their informational value for person perception. *Journal of Abnormal and Social Psychology, 63,* 302–310.

Jones, E. E., & McGillis, D. (1976). Correspondent inferences and the attribution cube: A comparative reappraisal. In J. H. Harvey, W. J. Ickes, and R. F. Kidd (Eds.), *New directions in attribution research* (Vol. 1), Hillsdale, NJ: Erlbaum.

Jones, E. E., & Nisbett, R. E. (1972). The actor and observer: Divergent perceptions of the causes of behavior. In E. E. Jones, E. E. Karouse, H. H. Kelley, R. E. Nisbett, S. Valins, & B. Weiner, *Attribution: Perceiving the causes of behavior*. Morristown, NJ: General Learning Press.

Jones, E. E., Wood, G. C., & Quattrone, G. A. (1981). Perceived variability of personal characteristics in in-groups and out-groups. The role of knowledge and evaluation. *Personality and Social Psychology Bulletin, 7,* 523–528.

Jones, G. V. (1989). Back to Woodworth: Role of interlopers in the tip-of-the-tongue phenomenon. *Memory & Cognition, 17,* 60–76.

Jones, H. E. (1950). The study of patterns of emotional expression. In M. Reymert (Ed.), *Feelings and emotions*. New York: McGraw-Hill.

Jones, M. (1975). Community care for chronic mental patients: The need for a reassessment. *Hospital and Community Psychiatry, 26,* 94–98.

Jones, M. C. (1924). The elimination of children's fears. *Journal of Experimental Psychology, 7,* 382–390.

Jones, M. C., & Mussen, P. H. (1958). Self-conceptions, motivations, and interpersonal attitudes of early- and late-maturing girls. *Child Development, 29,* 491–501.

Jones, S. R. (1990). Worker interdependence and output: The Hawthorne studies reevaluated. *American Sociological Review, 55,* 176–190.

Jordan, H. A. (1969). Voluntary intragastric feeding. *Journal of Comparative and Physiological Psychology, 68,* 498–506.

Juel-Nielsen, N. (1965). Individual and environment: A psychiatric-psychological investigation of twins reared apart. *Acta Psychiatrica et Neurologica Scandinavica* (Monograph Supplement 183).

Julesz, B. (1971). *Foundations of Cyclopean perception*. Chicago: University of Chicago Press.

Julius, M., Harburg, E., Cottington, E. M., & Johnson, E. H. (1986). Anger-coping types, blood pressure, and all-cause mortality: A follow-up in Tecumseh, Michigan (1971–1983). *American Journal of Epidemiology, 124,* 220–223.

Juscyzk, P. W. (1985). The high amplitude sucking technique as a methodological tool in speech perception research. In G. Gottlieb & N. A. Krasnegor (Eds.), *Measurement of audition and vision in the first year of postnatal life: A methodological overview*. Norwood, NJ: Ablex.

Jussim, L., Coleman, L. M., & Lerch, L. (1987). The nature of stereotypes: A comparison and integration of three theories. *Journal of Personality and Social Psychology, 52,* 536–546.

K

Kagan, J. (1984). *The nature of the child*. New York: Basic Books.

Kagan, J. (1989). *Unstable ideas: Temperament, cognition, and self*. Cambridge, MA: Harvard University Press.

Kagan, J., & Haveman, E. (1972). *Psychology: An introduction*. New York: Harcourt Brace Jovanovich.

Kagan, J., & Moss, H. (1962). *Birth to maturity*. New York: Wiley.

Kahn, E. (1989). Heinz Kohut and Carl Rogers: Toward a constructive collaboration. *Psychotherapy, 26,* 555–563.

Kahneman, D., & Chajczyk, D. (1983). Tests of the automaticity of reading: Dilution of Stroop effects by color-irrelevant stimuli. *Journal of Experimental Psychology: Human Perception and Performance, 9,* 497–509.

Kahneman, D., & Tversky, A. (1973). On the psychology of prediction. *Psychological Review, 80,* 237–251.

Kahneman, D., & Tversky, A. (1979). Prospect theory: An analysis of decision under risk. *Econometrica, 47,* 263–291.

Kahneman, D., & Tversky, A. (1984). Choices, values, and frames. *American Psychologist, 39,* 341–350.

Kahreman, D., Slavic, P. & Tversky, A. (1982). Judgment under uncertainty: Heuristics and biases. Cambridge, England: Cambridge University Press.

Kahney, H. (1993). *Problem solving: Current issues*. Philadelphia: Open University Press.

Kail, R. (1990). *The development of memory in children*. New York: Freeman.

Kalar, J. W. (1992). *Biological Psychology* (4th edition). Belmont, California: Wadsworth Publishing Co.

Kalish, H. I. (1981). *From behavioral science to behavior modification*. New York: McGraw-Hill.

Kalish, R. A. (1976). Death in a social context. In R. H. Binstock & C. Shanas (Eds.), *Handbook of aging and the social sciences*. New York: Van Nostrand Reinhold.

Kallmann, F. J. (1946). The genetic theory of schizophrenia: An analysis of 691 schizophrenic twin index families. *American Journal of Psychiatry, 103,* 309–322.

Kamin, L. J. (1969). Predictability, surprise, attention and conditioning. In B. A. Campbell & R. M. Church (Eds.), *Punishment and aversive behavior*. New York: Appleton-Century-Crofts.

Kamin, L. J. (1974). *The science and politics of IQ*. Potomac, MD: Erlbaum.

Kamin, L. J., Brimer, C. J., & Black, A. H. (1963). Conditioned suppression as a monitor of fear of the CS in the course of avoidance training. *Journal of Comparative and Physiological Psychology, 56,* 497–501.

Kaminer, W.. (1993). *I'm dysfunctional, you're dysfunctional*. New York: Vintage Books.

Kane, B., Millay, J., & Brown, D. (Eds.). (1993). *Silver Threads: Twenty-Five Years of Parapsychology Research*. Westport, CT: Praeger.

Kanin, E. J., Davidson, D. K. D., & Scheck, S. R. (1970). A research note on male-female differentials in the experience of heterosexual love. *The Journal of Sex Research, 6,* 64–72.

Kanizsa, G. (1976, September). Subjective contours. *Scientific American,* pp. 48–52.

Kantowitz, B. H., & Sorkin, R. D. (1983). *Human factors: Understanding people system relationships*. New York: Wiley.

Kantowitz, B. H., Roediger, H. L., & Elmes, D. G. (1994). *Experimental psychology: Understanding psychological research* (5th ed.). St. Paul, MN: West.

Kaplan, H., & Dove, H. (1987). Infant development among the Ache of eastern Paraguay. *Developmental Psychology, 23,* 190–198.

Kaprio, J., Koskenvuo, M., & Rose, R. J. (1990). Change in cohabitation and intra-pair similarity of monozygotic (MZ) cotwins for alcohol use, extraversion, and neuroticism. *Behavior Genetics, 20,* 265–276.

Karniol, R., & Ross, M. (1977). The effect of performance-relevant and performance-irrelevant rewards on children's intrinsic motivation. *Child Development, 48,* 482–487.

Kastenbaum, R. (1992). *The psychology of death*. New York: Springer.

Katchadourian, H. (1990). Sexuality. In S. S. Feldman & G. R. Elliot (Eds.), *At the threshold: The developing adolescent* (pp. 330–351). Cambridge, MA: Harvard University Press.

Katchadourian, M. (1977). *The biology of adolescence*. San Francisco: Freeman.

Katzell, R. A., & Thompson, D. E. (1990). Work motivation: Theory and practice. *American Psychologist, 45,* 144–153.

Katzev, R., & Brownstein, R. (1989). Influence of enlightment on compliance. *Journal of Social Psychology, 129,* 335–348.

Kaufman, L. (1974). *Sight and mind*. New York: Oxford University Press.

Kaye, W. H., Gwirtsman, H., George, D. T., Obarzanek, E., Brewerton, T. D., Jimerson, D. C., & Ebert, M. H. (1988). Altered feeding behavior in bulimia: Is it related to mood and serotonin? In B. T. Walsh (Ed.), *Eating behavior in eating disorders* (pp. 199–216). Washington, DC: American Psychiatric Press.

Kazdin, A. E. (1990). Challenging treatment: An examination of therapy and therapists. *Contemporary Psychology, 35,* 250–251.

Keating, D. P. (1980). Thinking processes in adolescence. In J. Adelson (Ed.), *Handbook of adolescent psychology*. New York: Wiley.

Keesey, R. E., Boyle, P. C., Kemnitz, J. W., & Mitchell, J. S. (1976). The role of the lateral hypothalamus in determining the body weight set point. In D. Novin, W. Wyrwicka, & G. Bray (Eds.), *Hunger: Basic mechanisms and clinical applications* (pp. 243–255). New York: Raven Press.

Keil, F. (1989). *Concepts, kinds, and cognitive development*. Cambridge, MA: MIT Press.

Keil, F. C. (1981). Constraints on knowledge and cognitive development. *Psychological Review, 88,* 197–227.

Keil, F. C., & Batterman, N. (1984). A characteristic-to-defining shift in the development of word meaning. *Journal of Verbal learning and Verbal Behavior, 23,* 221–236.

Keith-Lucas, T., & Guttman, N. (1975). Robust single-trial delayed backward conditioning. *Journal of Comparative and Physiological Psychology, 88,* 468–476.

Kellerman, J., Lewis, J., & Laird, J. D. (1989). Looking and loving: The effects of mutual gaze on feelings of romantic love. *Journal of Research in Personality, 23*(2), 145–161.

Kelley, C., Huston, T. L., & Cate, R. M. (1985). Premarital relationship correlates of the erosion of satisfaction in marriage. *Journal of Social and Personal Relationships, 2,* 167–178.

Kelley, H. H. (1950). The warm-cold variable in first impressions of persons. *Journal of Personality, 18,* 431–439.

Kelley, H. H. (1967). Attribution theory in social psychology. In D. Levine (Ed.), *Nebraska symposium on motivation*. Lincoln: University of Nebraska Press.

Kellogg, W. N., & Kellogg, L. A. (1933). *The ape and the child*. New York: McGraw-Hill.

Kelly, G. (1955). *The psychology of personal constructs: A theory of personality* (2 vols.). New York: Norton.

Kelman, H. C. (1961). Processes of opinion change. *Public Opinion Quarterly, 25*, 57–78.

Kelman, H. C. (1968). *A time to speak: On human values and social research.* San Francisco: Jossey-Bass.

Kendall, K. (1991). Masking violence against women. *Canadian Woman Studies, 12*, 17–20.

Kendler, K. S., & Robinette, C. D. (1983). Schizophrenia in the National Academy of Sciences-National Research Council twin registry: A 16-year update. *American Journal of Psychiatry, 140*, 1551–1563.

Kennedy, W. A., Van de Riet, V., & White, J. C. (1963). A normative sample of intelligence and achievement of Negro elementary school children in the southeastern United States. *Monographs of the Society for Research in Child Development, 28*(6, Serial No. 90).

Kenrick & Funder. (1988). Profiting from controversy: Lessons from the person-situation debate. *American Psychology, 43*(1), 23–34.

Kerr, N. L. (1983). Motivation losses in small groups: A social dilemma analysis. *Journal of Personality and Social Psychology, 45*, 819–828.

Kessen, W. (1965). *The child.* New York: Wiley.

Key, W. B. (1973). *Subliminal seduction: Ad media's manipulation of a not so innocent America.* New York: Signet.

Key, W. B. (1990). *The age of manipulation: The con in confidence, the sin in sincere.* Englewood Cliffs, NJ: Prentice Hall.

Keys, A., Brozek, J., Henschel, A., Mickelson, O., & Taylor, L. L. (1950). *The Biology of Human Starvation.* Minneapolis, MN: University of Minnesota Press.

Kiecolt-Glaser, J. (in press). *Psychosomatic Medicine.*

Kiester, E. (1984). Images of the night. In M. G. Walraven and H. E. Fitzgerald (Eds.), *Psychology 84/85.* Guilford, Conn.: Dushkin.

Kihlstrom, J. F (1987). The cognitive unconscious. *Science, 237*, 1445–1451.

Kihlstrom, J. F. (1984). Hypnosis. In M. R. Rosenzweig & L. W. Porter (Eds.), *Annual Review of Psychology, 36*, 385–418.

Kihlstrom, J. F., & Schacter, D. L. (1992). Amnesia, functional. In L. R. Squire (Ed.), *The encyclopedia of learning and memory* (pp. 25–28). New York: MacMillan.

Kilham, W., & Mann, L. (1974). Level of destructive obedience as a function of transmitter and executant roles in the Milgram obedience paradigm. *Journal of Personality and Social Psychology, 29*, 696–702.

Kimura, D. (1961). Cerebral dominance and the perception of verbal stimuli. *Canadian Journal of Psychology, 15*, 166–171.

Kimura, D. (1964). Left-right differences in the perception of melodies. *Quarterly Journal of Experimental Psychology, 14*, 335–338.

Kimura, D. (1992). Sex differences in the brain. *Scientific American, 267*, 118–125.

King, B. M., Smith, R. L., & Frohman, L. A. (1984). Hyperinsulinemia in rats with ventromedial hypothalamic lesions: Role of hyperphagia. *Behavioral Neuroscience, 98*, 152–155.

Kinsey, A. C. Pomeroy, W. B., Martin, C. E., & Gebhard, P. H. (1953). *Sexual behavior in the human female.* Philadelphia: Saunders.

Kinsey, A. C., Pomeroy, W. B., & Martin, C. E. (1948). *Sexual behavior in the human male.* Philadelphia: Saunders.

Kintsch, W. (1977). *Memory and cognition.* New York: Wiley.

Kirsch, I. (1990). *Changing expectations: A key to effective psychotherapy.* Pacific Grove, CA: Brooks/Cole.

Kissileff, H. R. (1973). Nonhomeostatic controls of drinking. In A. N. Epstein, H. R. Kissileff, & E. Stellar (Eds.), *The neuropsychology of thirst* (pp. 163–198). Washington, DC: Winston.

Kitagawa, E. M., & Hauser, P. M. (1973). *Differential mortality in the United States: A study in socioeconomic epidemiology.* Cambridge, Mass.: Harvard University Press.

Kitcher, P. (1985). *Vaulting ambition: Sociobiology and the quest for human nature.* Cambridge, MA: MIT Press.

Klahr, D., & Robinson, M. (1981). Formal assessment of problem solving and planning processes in preschool children. *Cognitive Psychology, 13*, 113–148.

Klahr, D., & Wallace, J. G. (1976). *Cognitive development: An information-processing view.* Hillsdale, NJ: Erlbaum.

Klaidman, S. (1991). *Health in the headlines: The stories behind the stories.* New York: Oxford University Press.

Klass, P. J. (1974). *UFOs Explained.* New York: Random House.

Klaus, H. M., & Kennell, J. H. (1976). *Maternal-infant bonding.* St. Louis: Mosby.

Kleinman, A. (1986). *Social origins of stress and disease: Depression, neurasthenia, and pain in modern China.* New Haven, CT: Yale University Press.

Klimoski, R., & Brickner, M. (1987). Why do assessment centers work: The puzzle of assessment center validity. *Personnel Psychology, 40*, 243–260.

Klymenko, V., & Weisstein, N. (1986). Spatial frequency differences can determine figure-ground organization. *Journal of Experimental Psychology: Human Perception and Performance, 12*, 324–330.

Knesper, D. J., Belcher, J., & Cross, J. C. (1988). Variations in the intensity of psychiatric treatment across markets for mental health services in the United States. *Health Services Research, 22*, 797–819.

Knox, R. E., & Inkster, J. A. (1968). Postdecision dissonance at post time. *Journal of Personality and Social Psychology, 8*, 319–323.

Kobasa, S. C. (1979). Stressful life events, personality, and health: An inquiry into hardiness. *Journal of Personality and Social Psychology, 37*, 1–11.

Koestler, A. (1964). *The act of creation.* New York: Macmillan.

Kohl, G. A. (1983). Effects of size and shape of knobs on maximal hand-turning forces applied by females. *Bell System Technical Journal, 62*, 1705–1712.

Kohlberg, L. (1976). Moral stages and moralization: The cognitive-developmental approach. In T. Lickona (Ed.), *Moral development and behavior.* New York: Holt, Rinehart & Winston.

Köhler, W. (1927). The mentality of ages. London: Routledge & Kegan Paul.

Köhler, W. (1929). *Gestalt psychology.* New York: Liveright.

Kohn, R. R. (1977). Heart and cardiovascular system. In C. E. Finch & L. Hayflick (Eds.), *Handbook of the biology of aging.* New York: Van Nostrand Reinhold.

Kohut, H. (1977). *The Restoration of the Self.* New York: International Universities Press.

Kohut, H. (1984). *How does analysis cure?* Chicago: University of Chicago Press.

Kolata, G. (1983). Math genius may have hormonal basis. *Science, 222.*

Kolb, B., & Whishaw, I. Q. (1985). *Fundamentals of human neuropsychology* (2nd ed.). New York: Freeman.

Kolers, P. A. (1983). Perception representation. *Annual Review of Psychology* (Vol. 33). Palo Alto, CA: Annual Reviews.

Kolers, P. A. (1985). Skill in reading and memory. *Canadian Journal of Psychology, 39*, 232–239.

Kolers, P. A., & Roediger, H. L. (1984). Procedures of mind. *Journal of Verbal Learning and Verbal Behavior, 23*, 425–449.

Komaki, J. (1986). Toward effective supervision: An operant analysis and comparison of managers at work. *Journal of Applied Psychology, 71*, 270–279.

Komaki, J., Zlotnick, S., & Jensen, M. (1986). Development of an operant-based taxonomy and observational index of supervisory behavior. *Journal of Applied Psychology, 71*, 260–269.

Kopp, C. B. (1983). Risk factors in development. In P. H. Mussen (Ed.), *Handbook of child development: Vol. 2. Infancy and developmental psychobiology.* New York: Wiley.

Kopp, C. B., Baker, B. L., & Brown, K. W. (1992). Social skills and their correlates: Preschoolers with developmental delays. *American Journal of Mental Retardation, 96*, 357–366.

Kosslyn, S. M. (1980). *Image and mind.* Cambridge, MA: Harvard University Press.

Kosslyn, S. M. (1983). *Ghosts in the mind's machine.* New York: Norton.

Kosslyn, S. M. (1994). *Image and brain: A resolution of the imagery debate.* Cambridge: MA: The MIT Press.

Kosslyn, S. M., Ball, T. M., & Reiser, B. J. (1978). Visual images preserve metric spatial information: Evidence from studies of image scanning. *Journal of Experimental Psychology: Human Perception and Performance, 4*, 47–60.

Kottler, J. A., & Blau, D. S. (1989). *The imperfect therapist: Learning from failure in therapeutic practice.* San Francisco: Jossey-Bass.

Kovach, J. A., & Glickman, N. W. (1986). Levels of psychological correlates of adolescent drug use. *Journal of Youth and Adolescence, 15*, 61–78.

Kowler, E., & Martins, A. J. (1982). Eye movements of preschool children. *Science, 215*, 997–999.

Kozel, N. J., & Adams, E. H. (1986). Epidemiology of drug abuse. *Science, 234*, 970–974.

Kraepelin, E. (1896). *Lehrbuch der Psychiatrie* (5th ed.). Leipzig: Barth.

Krank, M. D., Hinson, R. E., & Siegel, S. (1981). Conditional hyperalgesia is elicited by environmental signs of morphine. *Behavioral and Neural Biology, 32*, 148–157.

Krantz, D. S., & Durel, L. A. (1983). Psychobiological substrates of the Type A behavior pattern. *Health Psychology, 4*, 393–411.

Krebs, D. L. (1975). Empathy and altruism. *Journal of Personality and Social Psychology, 32*, 1134–1146.

Krebs, D. L. (1992). Review of M. A. Wallach & L. Wallach "Rethinking Goodness." *Contemporary Psychology, 37*, 306–307.

Krech, D., & Crutchfield, R. S. (1958). *Elements of psychology.* New York: Knopf.

Kretschmer, E. (1936). *Physique and Character.* London: Kegan, Paul, Trench, Truber, & Company.

Kringlen, E., & Cramer, G. (1989). Offspring of monozygotic twins discordant for schizophrenia. *Archives of General Psychiatry, 46*, 873–877.

Kripke, D. F., et al. (1979). Short and long sleep and sleeping pills: Is increased mortality associated? *Archives of General Psychiatry, 36*, 103–116.

Kristensen, S., & Gimsing, S. (1988). Occupational hearing impairment in pig-breeders. *Scandinavian Audiology, 17*, 191–192.

Kritchevsky, M. (1992). Amnesia, transient global. In L. R. Squire (Ed.), *The encyclopedia of learning and memory* (pp. 35–36). New York: MacMillan.

Kroger, W. S., & Douce, R. G. (1979). Hypnosis in criminal investigation. *International Journal of Clinical and Experimental Hypnosis, 27*, 358–374.

Kroll, N. E., Schepeler, E. M., & Angin, K. T. (1986). Bizarre imagery: The misremembered mnemonic. *Journal of Experimental Psychology: Learning, Memory, and Cognition, 12,* 40–51.

Kromhout, D., Bosschieter, E. B., & de Lezenne Coulander, C. (1985). The inverse relation between fish consumption and 20-year mortality from coronary heart disease. *New England Journal of Medicine, 312,* 1205–1209.

Kromhout, D., Bosschieter, E. B., & de Lezenne Coulander, C. (1985). The inverse relation between fish consumption and 20-year mortality from coronary heart disease. *New England Journal of Medicine, 312,* 1205–1209.

Kübler-Ross, E. (1969). *On death and dying.* Toronto: Macmillan.

Kubovy, M., & Pomerantz, J. R. (Eds.). (1981). *Perceptual organization.* Hillsdale, NJ: Erlbaum.

Kuczynski, L. (1983). Reasoning, prohibitions, and motivations for compliance. *Developmental Psychology, 19,* 126–134.

Kuhl, D. E., et al. (1982). *Annals of neurology, 12,* 425.

Kuhn, D., Nash, S. C., & Brucken, L. (1978). Sex-role concepts of two- and three-year-olds. *Child Development, 49,* 445–451.

Kundel, H. L., & Nodine, C. F. (1975). Interpreting chest radiographs without visual search. *Radiology, 116,* 527–532.

Kurdek, L. A. (1991). Predictors of increases in marital distress in newlywed couples: A 3-year prospective longitudinal study. *Developmental Psychology, 27,* 627–636.

Kurdek, L. A., & Schmitt, J. P. (1986). Early development of relationship quality in heterosexual married, heterosexual cohabiting, gay, and lesbian couples. *Developmental Psychology, 22,* 305–309.

Kurtz, P. (Ed.). (1985). *A skeptical handbook of parapsychology.* Buffalo, NY: Prometheus Books.

L

LaBerge, S. (1990). Lucid dreaming: Psychophysiological studies of consciousness during REM sleep. In R. R. Bootzin, J. F. Kihlstrom, and D. L. Schacter (Eds.), *Sleep and Cognition.* Washington, DC: American Psychological Association.

Labouvie-Vief, G. (1985). Intelligence and cognition. In J. E. Birren & K. W. Schaie (Eds.), *Handbook of the Psychology of aging* (2nd ed., pp. 500–530). New York: Van Nostrand Reinhold.

Labouvie-Vief, G. (1992). A neo-Piagetian perspective on adult cognitive development. In R. J. Sternberg & C. A. Berg (Eds.), *Intellectual Development* (pp. 197–228). Cambridge, England: Cambridge University Press.

Labov, W. (1973). The boundaries of words and their meanings. In C. J. N. Bailey & R. W. Shuy (Eds.), *New ways of analyzing variations in English.* Washington, DC: Georgetown University Press.

Lacey, J. I., & Lacey, B. C. (1958). Verification and extension of the principle of autonomic response stereotype. *The American Journal of Psychology, 71,* 50–73.

Lackman, J. L., Lachman, R., Thornesbery, C. (1979). Meta-memory through the adult life-span. *Developmental Psychology, 15,* 543–551.

Ladd, G. W., & Mize, J. (1983). A cognitive-social learning model of social skill training. *Psychological Review, 90,* 127–157.

Lafané, B., & Nida F. A. (1981). Ten years of research on group size and helping. *Psychological Bulletin, 89,* 308–324.

Laing, R. D. (1967). *The politics of experience.* New York: Pantheon.

Laird, J. D. (1974). Self-attribution of emotion: The effects of expressive behavior on the quality of emotional experience. *Journal of Personality and Social Psychology, 29,* 475–486.

Lakoff, G. (1987). *Women, fire, and dangerous things.* Chicago: University of Chicago Press.

Lakoff, G., & Johnson, M. (1980). *Metaphors we live by.* Chicago, IL: University of Chicago Press.

Lamb, M. (1982). The bonding phenomenon: Misinterpretations and their implications. *Journal of Pediatrics, 101,* 555–557.

Lamb, M. E., Thompson, R. A., Gardner, W. P., Charnov, E. L., & Estes, D. (1985). Security of infantile attachment as assessed in the "strange situation." *Behavior and Brain Sciences, 7,* 127–171.

Lamiell, J. T. (1987). Interview in A. O. Ross *Personality: The Scientific Study of Complex Human Behavior.* New York: Holt, Rinehart, and Winston.

Landy, F. J. (1985). *Psychology of work behavior* (3rd ed.). Homewood, IL: Dorsey press.

Landy, F., & Trumbo, D. A. (1980). *Psychology of work behavior.* Homewood, IL: Dorsey Press.

Lange, C. J. (1967). The emotions (Translation of Lange's 1885 monograph). In C. J. Lange & W. James (Eds.), *The emotions.* New York: Hafner Publishing Co. (Facsimile of 1922 edition)

Langlois, J. H. (1986). From the eye of the beholder to behavioral reality: Development of social behaviors and social relations as a function of physical attractiveness. In C. P. Herman, M. P. Zanna, & E. T. Higgins (Eds.), *Physical appearance, stigma, and social behavior.* Hillsdale, NJ: Erlbaum.

Langlois, J. H., Ritter, J. M., Roggman, L. A., & Vaughn, L. S. (1991). Facial diver-

sity and infant preferences for attractive faces. *Developmental Psychology, 27,* 79–84.

Langlois, J. H., Roggman, L. A., & Rieser-Danner, L. A. (1990). Infants' differential social responses to attractive and unattractive faces. *Developmental Psychology, 26,* 153–159.

LaPière, R. T. (1934). Attitudes versus actions. *Social Forces, 13,* 230–237.

Lapsey, D. K., & Murphy, M. N. (1985). Another look at the theoretical assumptions of adolescent egocentrism. *Developmental Review, 5,* 201–217.

Larkin, J., McDermott, J., Simon, D. P., & Simon, H. A. (1980). Expert and novice performance in solving physics problems. *Science, 208,* 1335–1342.

Laroche, C., Hétu, R., & Poirer, S. (1989). The growth of and recovery from TTS in human subjects exposed to impact noise. *Journal of Acoustical Society of America, 85,* 1681–1690.

Larry, P., V. Riles (1979). 495 F. Supp. 96 (N.D. Cal. 1979).

Lashley, K. S. (1929). *Brain mechanisms and intelligence.* Chicago, IL: University of Chicago Press.

Lashley, K. S. (1950). In search of the engram. *Symposia of the Society for Experimental Biology, 4,* 454–482.

Latané, B., & Darley, J. M. (1970). *The unresponsive bystander: Why doesn't he help?* New York: Appleton-Century-Crofts.

Latané, B., & Darley, J. M. (1976). *Help in a crisis: Bystander response to an emergency.* Morristown, NJ: General Learning Press.

Latané, B., & Nida, S. A. (1981). Ten years of research on group size and helping. *Psychological Bulletin, 89,* 308–324.

Laurence, J. R., & Perry, C. (1983). Hypnotically created memory among highly hypnotizable subjects. *Science, 222,* 523–524.

Laurence, M. T., Hineline, P. H., & Bersh, P. J. (1994). The puzzle of responding maintained by response-contingent shock. *Journal of the Experimental Analysis of Behavior, 61,* 135–153.

Laurence, M. T., Hineline, P. N., & Bersh, P. J. (1994). The puzzle of responding maintained by response-contingent shock. Special Issue: Contributions of Joseph V. Brady. *JEAB, 61,* 135–153.

Laux, L., & Brelsford, J. (1990). Age-related changes in sensory, cognitive, psychomotor, and physical functionings and driving performance in drivers aged 40 to 92. AAA Foundation for Traffic Safety Report.

Lave, J. (1988). *Cognition in practice.* Cambridge: Cambridge University Press.

LaVoie, J. C., & Hodapp, A. F. (1987). Children's subjective ratings of their performance on a standardized test. *Journal of School Psychology, 25,* 73–80.

Lawler, E. E. III. (1979). Expectancy theory. In R. M. Steers & L. W. Porter (Eds.), *Motivation and work behavior.* New York: McGraw-Hill.

Lazar, I., Darlington, R., Murray, H., Royce, J., & Snipper, A. (1982). Lasting effects of early education: A report from the Consortium for Longitudinal Studies. *Monographs of the Society for Research in Child Development, 47* (Serial No. 195).

Lazarus, A. A. (1961). Group therapy of phobic disorders by systematic desensitization. *Journal of Abnormal and Social Psychology, 63,* 504–510.

Lazarus, R. S. (1966). *Psychological stress and the coping process.* New York: McGraw-Hill.

Lazarus, R. S. (1976). *Patterns of adjustment.* New York: McGraw-Hill.

Lazarus, R. S. (1981). A cognitivist's reply to Zajonc on emotion and cognition. *American Psychologist, 36,* 222–223.

Lazarus, R. S. (1991). Progress on a cognitive-motivational-relational theory of emotion. *American Psychologist, 46,* 819–834.

Lazarus, R. S. (1991). Progress on a cognitive-motivational-relational theory of emotion. *American Psychologist, 46,* 819–834.

Lazarus, R. S., & Delongis (1983). Psychological stress and coping in aging. *American Psychologist, 38,* 245–254.

Lazarus, R. S., & Folkman, S. (1984). *Stress, appraisal, and coping.* New York: Springer.

Lazarus, R. S., Kanner, A. D., & Folkman, S. (1980). Emotions: A cognitive phenomenological analysis. In R. Plutchik & H. Kellerman (Eds.), *Emotion: Theory, research and experience* (Vol. 1) (pp. 189–218). New York: Academic Press.

Le Grange, D., Eisler, I., Dare, C., & Hodes, M. (1992). Family criticism and self-starvation: A study of expressed emotion. *Journal of Family Therapy, 14,* 177–192.

Leaf, A., & Weber, P. C. (1988). Cardiovascular effects of n-3 fatty acids. *New England Journal of Medicine, 318,* 549–556.

Leahey, T. H. (1991). *A history of modern psychology.* Englewood Cliffs, NJ: Prentice Hall.

Leask, J., Haber, R. N., & Haber, R. B. (1969). Eidetic imagery in children: 2. Longitudinal and experimental results. *Psychonomic Monograph Supplements, 3*(3 Whole No. 35).

Lederman, D. (1990). Athletes in Division I found graduating at a higher rate than other students. *Chronicle of Higher Education,* July 5, A29.

Lee, V. E., Brooks-Gunn, J., Schnur, E., & Liaw, F. (1990). Are Head Start effects sustained: A longitudinal follow-up comparison of disadvantaged children attending Head Start, no preschool, and other preschool programs. *Child Development, 61,* 495–507.

Lefebvre, L., & Palameta, B. (1988). Mechanisms, ecology, and population diffusion of socially-learned, food-finding behavior in feral pigeons. In T. R. Zentall & B. G. Galef, Jr. (Eds.), *Social learning: psychological and biological perspectives* (pp. 141–164). Hillsdale, NJ: Erlbaum.

Lehman, D. R., & Nisbett, R. E. (1990). A longitudinal study of the effects of undergraduate training on reasoning. *Developmental Psychology, 26,* 952–960.

Lehmann, H. E. (1980). Schizophrenia: Clinical features. In H. I. Kaplan, A. M. Freedman, & B. J. Sadock (Eds.), *Comprehensive textbook of psychiatry: III.* Baltimore, MD: Williams & Wilkins.

Leibowitz, S. F., Weiss, G. F., Walsh, U. A., & Viswanath, D. (1989). Medial hypothalamic serotonin: Role in circadian patterns of feeding and macronutrient selection. *Brain Research, 503,* 132–140.

Leibowitz, S. F., Weiss, G. F., Walsh, U. A., & Viswanath, D. (1989). Medial hypothalamic serotonin: Role in circadian patterns of feeding and macronutrient selection. *Brain Research, 503,* 132–140.

LeMagnen, J. (1956). Hyperphagie provoquée chez le rat blanc par altération du mécanisme de satiété périphérique. *Comptes Rendus des Séances de la Société de Biologie, 150,* 32.

Lempers, J. D., Flavell, E. R., & Flavell, J. H. (1977). The development in very young children of tacit knowledge concerning visual perception. *Genetic Psychology Monographs, 95,* 3–53.

Lennartz, R. C., & Weinberger, N. M. (1992). Analysis of response systems in Pavlovian conditioning reveals rapidly versus slowly acquired conditioned responses: Support for two factors, implications for behavior and neurobiology. *Psychobiology, 20,* 93–119.

Leon, D. (1969). *The kibbutz: A new way of life.* London: Pergamon.

Leon, G. R. (Ed.). (1977). *Case histories of deviant behavior* (2nd ed.). Boston: Holbrook Press.

Lepper, M. R., & Greene, D. (1978). *The hidden costs of reward: New perspectives on the psychology of human motivation.* Hillsdale, NJ: Erlbaum.

Lepper, M. R., Greene, D., & Nisbett, R. E. (1973). Undermining children's intrinsic interest with extrinsic rewards: A test of the overjustification hypothesis. *Journal of Personality and Social Psychology, 23,* 129–137.

Lerner, M. J. (1980). *The belief in a just world.* New York: Plenum.

Lerner, R. M. (1975). Showdown at generation gap: Attitudes of adolescents and their parents toward contemporary issues. In H. D. Thornburg (Ed.), *Contemporary adolescence: Readings.* (2nd ed.). Belmont, CA: Brooks/Cole.

Lesgold, A. (1988). Problem solving. In R. J. Sternberg & E. E. Smith (Eds.), *The psychology of human thought* (pp. 188–213). Cambridge: Cambridge University Press.

Lesher, G. W. (1995). Illusory contours: Toward a neurally based perceptual theory. *Psychonomic Bulletin & Review, 2,* 279–321.

Lester, B. M., Kotelchuck, M., Spelke, E., Sellers, M. J., & Klein, R. E. (1974). Separation protest in Guatemalan infants: Cross-cultural and cognitive findings. *Developmental Psychology, 10,* 79–85.

Lester, D., Eleftheriou, L., & Peterson, C. A. (1992). Birth order and psychological health: A sex difference. *Personality and Individual Differences, 13,* 379–380.

Levanthal, H. (1970). Findings and theory in the study of fear communications. In L. Berkowitz (Ed.), *Advances in experimental social psychology* (Vol. 5). New York: Academic Press.

LeVay, S. (1991). A difference in hypothalamic structure between heterosexual and homosexual men. *Science, 253,* 1034–1037.

Levi, L., & Kagan, A. (1980). Psychosocially induced stress and disease: Problems, research strategies, and results. In H. Selye (Ed.), *Selye's guide to stress research* (Vol. 1). New York: Van Nostrand Reinhold.

Levine, M. W., & Shefner, J. M. (1991). *Fundamentals of sensation and perception.* Pacific Grove, CA: Brooks/Cole.

Levinger, G. (1976). A social psychological perspective on marital dissolution. *Journal of Social Issues, 32,* 21–47.

Levinson, D. J., Darrow, C. N., Klein, E. B., Levinson, M. H., & McKee, B. (1978). *The seasons of a man's life.* New York: Knopf.

Levy, B. A., & Kirsner, K. (1989). Reprocessing text: Indirected measures or word and message level processes. *Journal of Experimental Psychology: Learning, Memory, and Cognition, 15,* 407–417.

Levy, D. A. (1992). The liberating effect of interpersonal influence: An empirical investigation of disinhibitory contagion. *Journal of Social Psychology, 132,* 469–474.

Levy, J. (1980). Cerebral asymmetry and the psychology of man. In M. C. Wittrock (Ed.), *The brain and psychology.* New York: Academic Press.

Levy, J., & Trevarthen, C. (1974). Perceptual, semantic and phonetic aspects of elementary language processes in split-brain patients. *Brain, 95,* 61–78.

Levy, J., Trevarthen, C. B., & Sperry, R. W. (1972). Perception of bilateral chimeric figures following hemispheric deconnection. *Brain, 95,* 61–78.

Levy, S. M., & Heiden, L. A. (1990). Personality and social factors in cancer outcome. In H. S. Friedman (Ed.) *Personalilty and Disease.* New York: Wiley, pp. 254–279.

Levy-Leboyer, C., & Naturel, V. (1991). Neighbourhood noise annoyance. *Journal of Environmental Psychology, 11,* 75–86.

Lewicki, P., Hill, T., & Czyzewska, M. (1992). Nonconscious acquisition of information. *American Psychologist, 47,* 796–801.

Lewin, K. (1935). *A dynamic theory of personality.* New York: McGraw-Hill.

Lewin, R. (1980). Is your brain really necessary? *Science, 210,* 1232–1234.

Lewinsohn, P. M. (1974). A behavioral approach to depression. In R. M. Friedman & M. M. Katz (Eds.), *The psychology of depression: Contemporary theory and research.* New York: Wiley.

Lewinsohn, P. M., Hoberman, H. M., Teri, L., & Hautzinger, M. (1985). An integrative theory of depression. In S. Reiss & R. Bootzin (Eds.), *Theoretical issues in behavior therapy.* New York: Academic Press.

Lewinsohn, P. M., Hops, H., Roberts, R. E., Seeley, J. R., & Andrews, J. A. (1993). Adolescent psychopathology: I. Prevalence and incidence of depression and other DSM-III-R Disorders in high school students. *Journal of Abnormal Psychology, 102,* 133–144.

Lewinsohn, P. M., Roberts, R. E., Seeley, J. R., Rohde, P., Gotlib, I. H., & Hops, H. (1994). Adolescent psychopathology: II. Psychosocial risk factors for depression. *Journal of Abnormal Psychology, 103,* 302–315.

Lewinsohn, P. M., Zeiss, A. M., & Duncan, E. M. (1989). Probability of relapse after recovery from an episode of depression. *Journal of Abnormal Psychology, 98,* 107–116.

Lewis, M., & Brooks-Gunn. J. (1979). *Social cognition and the acquisition of self.* New York: Plenum.

Lewy, A. L., Sack, R. L., Miller, S., & Slaben, T. M. (1987). Antidepressant and circadian phase shifting effects of light. *Science, 235,* 352–354.

Leyens, J. P., & Parke, R. D. (1975). Aggressive slides can induce a weapons effect. *European Journal of Social Psychology, 5,* 229–236.

Liebelt, R. A., Bordelon, C. B., & Liebelt, A. G. (1973). The adipose tissue system and food intake. In E. Stellar & J. M. Sprague (Eds.), *Progress in physiological psychology.* New York: Academic Press.

Lieberg, R. M., Sprafkin, J. N., & Davidson, E. S. (1982). *The early window: Effects of television on children and youth* (2nd ed.). New York: Pergamon.

Lieberman, D. A. (1990). *Learning: Behavior and cognition.* Belmont, CA: Wadsworth.

Lieberman, P., Crelin, E. S., & Klatt, D. H. (1972). Phonetic ability and relaxed anatomy of the newborn and adult human, Neanderthal man, and the chimpanzee. *American Anthropologist, 74,* 287–307.

Liebert, R. S., & Baron, R. A. (1972). Some immediate effects of televised violence on children's behavior. *Developmental Psychology, 6,* 469–475.

Lieblich, I. (1979). Eidetic imagery: Do not use ghosts to hunt ghosts of the same species. *Behavioral and Brain Sciences, 2,* 608–609.

Lifton, R. J. (1986). *The Nazi doctors: Medical killing and the psychology of genocide.* New York: Basic Books.

Likert, R. (1961). *New patterns of management.* New York: McGraw-Hill.

Lindenthal, J. J., & Myers, J. K. (1979). The New Haven longitudinal survey. In I. G. Sarason & C. D. Spielberger (Eds.), *Stress and anxiety: Vol. 6. The Series in Clinical and Community Psychology.* Washington, DC: Hemisphere Publishing.

Lindsay, D. S., & Read, J. D. (1994). Psychotherapy and memories of childhood sexual abuse: A cognitive perspective. *Applied Cognitive Psychology, 8,* 281–338.

Lindsay, P. H., & Norman, D. A. (1977). *Human information processing* (2nd ed.). New York: Academic Press.

Lindsay, R. C. L. (1994). Biased lineups: Where do they come from? In D. F. Ross, J. D. Read & M. P. Toglia (Eds.), *Adult eyewitness testimony: Current trends and developments.* Cambridge: Cambridge University Press.

Lindzey, G. (1973). Morphology and behavior. In G. Lindzey, C. S. Hall, & M. Manosevitz (Eds.), *Theories of personality: Primary sources and research.* New York: Wiley.

Linville, P. W., Fischer, G. W., & Salovey, P. (1989). Perceived distributions of the characteristics of in-group and out-group members: Empirical evidence and a computer simulation. *Journal of Personality and Social Psychology, 57,* 165–188.

Lipsey, M. W., & Wilson, D. B. (1993). The efficacy of psychological, educational, and behavioral treatment. *American Psychologist, 48,* 1181–1209.

Little, B. R. (1989). Personal projects analysis: Trivial pursuits, magnificent obsessions, and the search for coherence. In D. M. Buss & N. Cantor (eds.) *Personality Psychology: Recent Trends and Emerging Directions.* New York: Springer-Verlag, pp. 15–31

Lively, S. E., Pisoni, D. B., & Goldinger, S. P. (1994). Spoken word recognition: Research and theory. In M. Gernsbacher (Ed.), *Handbook of Psycholinguistics.* New York: Academic Press.

Livesley, W. J., & Bromley, D. B. (1973). *Person perception in childhood and adolescence.* London: Wiley.

Locke, E. A. (1979). The supervisor as a motivator: His influence on employee performance and satisfaction. In R. M. Steers & L. W. Porter (Eds.), *Motivation and work behavior.* New York: McGraw-Hill.

Locke, J. (1950). *Essay concerning human understanding.* New York: Dover. (Original work published 1690)

Loeb, G. E. (1985). The functional replacement of the ear. *Scientific American, 252,* 104–111.

Loehlin, J. C., Horn, J. M., & Willerman, L. (1989). Modeling IQ change: Evidence from the Texas Adoption Project. *Child Development, 60,* 993–1004.

Loehlin, J. C., Willerman, L., & Horn, J. M. (1987). Personality resemblances in adoptive families: A 10-year follow-up. *Journal of Personality and Social Psychology, 53,* 961–969.

Loehlin, J. C., Willerman, L., & Horn, J. M. (1988). Human behavior genetics. *Annual Review of Psychology, 38,* 101–133.

Loftus, E. F. (1979). *Eyewitness testimony.* Cambridge, MA: Harvard University Press.

Loftus, E. F. (1979). The malleability of human memory. *American Scientist, 67,* 312–320.

Loftus, E. F. (1983). Silence is not golden. *American Psychologist, 38,* 561–572.

Loftus, E. F. (1993). The reality of repressed memories. *American Psychologist, 48,* 518–537.

Loftus, E. F., & Loftus, G. R. (1980). On the permanence of stored information in the brain. *American Psychologist, 35,* 409–420.

Loftus, E. F., & Palmer, J. C. (1974). Reconstruction of automobile destruction: An example of interaction between language and memory. *Journal of Verbal Learning and Verbal Behavior, 13,* 585–589.

Logan, G. D. (1985). Skill and automaticity: Relations, implications, and future directions. *Canadian Journal of Psychology, 39,* 367–386.

Logan, G. D., & Klapp, S. T. (1991). Automatizing alphabet arithmetic: I. Is extended practice necessary to produce automaticity? *Journal of Experimental Psychology: Learning, Memory, and Cognition, 17,* 179–195.

Logue, A. W. (1991). *The psychology of eating and drinking* (2nd ed.). New York: Freeman.

Londerville, S., & Main, M. (1981). Security of attachment, compliance, and maternal training methods in the second year of life. *Developmental Psychology, 17,* 289–299.

London, K. A. (1991). Cohabitation, marriage, marital dissolution, and remarriage: United States, 1988. *Advance data from vital and health statistics,* No. 194. Hyattsville, MD: National Center for Health Statistics.

London, P. (1970). The rescuers: Motivational hypotheses about Christians who saved Jews from the Nazis. In J. Macaulay & L. Berkowitz (Eds.)., *Altruism and helping behavior.* New York: Academic Press.

Long, G. M., & Beaton, R. J. (1982). The case for peripheral persistence: Effects of target and background luminance on a partial-report task. *Journal of Experimental Psychology: Human Perception and Performance, 8,* 383–391.

Long, G. M., Toppino, T. C., & Mondin, G. W. (1992). Prime time: Fatigue and set effects in the perception of reversible figures. *Perception and Psychophysics, 52,* 609–616.

Lorayne, H., & Lucas, J. (1974). *The memory book.* New York: Stein & Day.

Lord, C. G., Ross, L., & Lepper, M. R. (1979). Biased assimilation and attitude polarization: The effects of prior theories on subsequently considered evidence. *Journal of Personality and Social Psychology, 37,* 2098–2109.

Lord, R. G., & Maher, K. J. (1991). *Leadership and information processing: Linking perceptions and performance.* New York: Routledge.

Lorenz, K. (1966). *On aggression.* New York: Harcourt Brace Jovanovich.

Loro, A. D., & Orleans, C. S. (1981). Binge eating in obesity: Preliminary findings and guidelines for behavioral analysis and treatment. *Addictive Behaviors, 6,* 155–166.

Lorr, M. (1991). An empirical evaluation of the MBTI typology. *Personality & Individual Differences, 12,* 1141–1146.

Lovaas, O. I. (1973). *Behavioral treatment of autistic children.* Morristown, NJ: General Learning Press.

Lovaas, O. I. (1977). *The autistic child: Language development through behavior modification.* New York: Halsted Press.

Lovibond, S. H. (1969). Effect of patterns of aversive and appetitive conditioned stimuli on the incidence of gastric lesions in the immobilized rat. *Journal of Comparative and Physiological Psychology, 69,* 636–639.

Lowe, M. R. (1993). The effects of dieting on eating behavior: A three-factor model. *Psychological Bulletin, 114,* 100–121.

Lowry, R. (1982). *The evolution of psychological theory: A critical history of concepts and presuppositions.* (2nd ed.). New York: Aldine.

Lubin, B., Larsen, R. M., & Matarazzo, J. D. (1984). Patterns of psychological test usage in the United States: 1935–1982. *American Psychologist, 39,* 451–453.

Luborsky, L., Crits-Christoph, P., Mintz, J., & Auerbach, A. (1988). *Who will benefit from psychotherapy? Predicting therapeutic outcomes.* New York: Basic Books.

Lucas, A., Morley, R., Cole, T. J., Lister, G., & Leeson-Payne, C. (1992). Breast milk and subsequent intelligence quotient in children born preterm. *Lancet, 339,* 261–264.

Luce, G. G. (1966). *Current research on sleep and dreams* (Public Health Service Publication No. 1389). Washington, DC: Public Health Service.

Luchins, A. S. (1946). Classroom experiments on mental set. *American Journal of Psychology, 59,* 295–298.

Luchins, A. S. (1957). Primacy-recency in impression formation. In C. Hovland (Ed.), *The order of presentation in persuasion.* New Haven, CT: Yale University Press.

Lumsden, C. J., & Wilson, E. O. (1981). *Genes, mind, and culture: The coevolutionary process.* Cambridge, MA: Harvard University Press.

Luria, Z., & Rose, M. D. (1979). *Psychology of human sexuality.* New York: Wiley.

Luszcz, M. (1982). Facts on Aging: An Australian validation. *The Gerontologist, 22,* 369–372.

Luus, C. A. E., & Walls, G. L. (1994). Eyewitness identification confidence. In D. F. Ross, J. D. Read & M. P. Toglia (Eds.), *Adult eyewitness testimony: Current trends and developments.* Cambridge: Cambridge University Press.

Lynch, J. J. (1979). *The broken heart: The medical consequences of loneliness.* New York: Basic Books.

Lyman, M. D., & Potter, G. W. (1991). *Drugs and society: Causes, concepts, and control.* Cincinnati: Anderson Publishing.

Lynn, M., & Mynier, K. (1993). Effect of server posture on restaurant tipping. *Journal of Applied Social Psychology, 23,* 678–686.

Lynn, R. (1982). IQ in Japan and the United States shows a growing disparity. *Nature, 297,* 222–223.

Lysle, D. T., & Fowler, H. (1985). Inhibition as a "slave" process: Deactivation of conditioned inhibition through extinction of conditioned excitation. *Journal of Experimental Psychology: Animal Behavior Processes, 11,* 71–92.

Lysle, D. T., Cunnick, J. E., Fowler, H., & Rabin, B. S. (1988). Pavlovian conditioning of shock-induced suppression of lymphocyte reactivity: Acquisition, extinction, and preexposure effect. *Life Sciences, 42,* 2185–2194.

M

Macan, T. H., & Dipboye, R. L. (1988). The effects of interviewers' initial impressions on information gathering. *Organizational Behavior and Human Decision Processes, 41,* 20–33.

Maccoby, E. E., & Jacklin, C. N. (1974). *The psychology of sex differences.* Stanford, Calif.: Stanford University Press.

MacDougall, J. M., Dembroski, T. M., Dimsdale, J. E., & Hackett, T. P. (1985). Components of Type A, hostility, and anger-in: Further relationship to angiographic findings. *Health Psychology, 4,* 137–152.

MacGregor, J. N. (1987). Short-term memory capacity: Limitation or optimization. *Psychological Review, 94,* 107–108.

Mackenzie, B. (1984). Explaining race differences in IQ: The logic, the methodology, and the evidence. *American Psychologist, 39,* 1214–1233.

Mackintosh, N. J. (1975). A theory of attention: Variations in the associability of stimuli with reinforcement. *Psychological Review, 82,* 276–298.

MacLeod, C. M. (1988). Forgotten but not gone: Savings for pictures and words in long-term memory. *Journal of Experimental Psychology: Learning, Memory, and Cognition, 14,* 195–212.

MacLeod, C. M. (1991). Half a century of research on the Stroop effect: An integrative review. *Psychological Bulletin, 109,* 163–203.

MacMillan, N. A., & Creelman, C. D. (1991). *Detection theory: A user's guide.* Cambridge: Cambridge University Press.

Madden, D. J. (1990). Adult age differences in attentional selectivity and capacity. *European Journal of Cognitive Psychology, 2,* 229–252.

Madden, N. A., & Slavin, R. E. (1983). Mainstreaming students with mild academic handicaps: Academic and social outcomes. *Review of Educational Research, 53,* 519–569.

Maddi, S. R. (1990). Issues and interventions in stress mastery. In H. S. Friedman (Ed.) *Personality and Disease.* New York: Wiley, pp. 121–154.

Madigan, S. (1983). Picture memory. In J. C. Yuille (Ed.), *Imagery, memory, and cognition: Essays in honor of Allan Paivio.* Hillsdale, NJ: Erlbaum.

Madigan, S., & O'Hara, R. (1992). Short-term memory at the turn of the century: Mary Whiton Calkin's memory research. *American Psychologist, 47(2),* 170–174.

Mahler, M., Pine, F., & Bergman, A. (1975). *The Psychological Birth of the Human Infant: Symbiosis and Individuation.* New York: Basic Books.

Mahone, C. H. (1960). Fear of failure and unrealistic vocational aspiration. *Journal of Abnormal and Social Psychology, 60,* 253–261.

Mahoney, M. J. (1977). Reflections on the cognitive learning trend in psychotherapy. *American Psychologist, 32,* 5–13.

Mahoney, M. J. (1980). *Abnormal psychology: Perspectives on human variance.* New York: Harper & Row.

Maier, S. F., & Jackson, R. L. (1979). Learned helplessness: All of us were right (and wrong): Inescapable shock has multiple effects. In G. H. Bower (Ed.), *The psychology of learning and motivation: Advances in research and theory.* New York: Academic Press.

Maier, S. F., & Seligman, M. E. P. (1976). Learned helplessness: Theory and evidence. *Journal of Experimental Psychology: General, 105,* 3–46.

Maier, S. F., Rappaport, P. M., & Wheatley, K. L. (1976). Conditioned inhibition and UCS-CS interval. *Animal Learning and Behavior, 4,* 217–220.

Maier, S. F., Sherman, J. E., Lewis, J. W., Terman, G. W., & Liebeskind, J. C. (1983). The opioid/nonopioid nature of stress-induced analgesia and learned helplessness. *Journal of Experimental Psychology: Animal Behavior Processes, 9,* 80–90.

Main, M., & Weston, D. R. (1981). The quality of the toddler's relationship to mother and father: Related to conflict and the readiness to establish new relationships. *Child Development, 52*, 932–940.

Malatesta, C. A., & Haviland, J. M. (1982). Learning display rules: The socialization of emotion expression in infancy. *Child Development, 53*, 991–1003.

Mallick, S. K., & McCandless, B. R. (1966). A study of catharsis of aggression. *Journal of Personality and Social Psychology, 4*, 591–596.

Malone, T. B., & Kirkpatrick, (1977). Cited in T. B. Malone (1986), The centered high-mounted broke light: A human factors success story. *Human Factors, 29*, No. 10.

Malpass, R. S., & Devine, P. G. (1980). Realism and eyewitness identification research. *Law and Human Behavior, 4*, 347–357.

Malposs, R. S., & Kravitz, J. (1969). Recognition for focus of own and other race. *Journal of Personality and Social Psychology, 13*, 330.

Mann, C. C. (1995). Press coverage: Leaving out the big picture. *Science, 269*, 166.

Mann, L., & Janis, I. (1982). Conflict theory of decision making and the expectancy-value approach. In N. Feather (Ed.), *Expectations and actions: Expectancy value models in psychology* (pp. 341–364). Hillsdale, NJ: Erlbaum.

Maranon, G. (1924). Contribution al'etude de l'action emotive de l'adrenaline. *Rev. Fr. d'Endocrinol., 2*, 301–325.

Maratsos, M. (1973). Nonegocentric communication abilities in preschool children. *Child Development, 44*, 697–700.

Marcel, A. J. (1983). Conscious and unconscious perception: Experiments on visual masking and word recognition. *Cognitive Psychology, 15*, 197–237.

Marcus, G. F., Pinker, S., Ullman, M., Hollander, M., Rosen, T. J., & Xu, F. (1992). Overregulation in language acquisition. *Monographs of the Society for Research in Child Development*. Serial No. 228.

Marg, E., Freeman, D. N., Pheltzman, P., & Goldstein, P. J. (1976). Visual acuity development in human infants: Evoked potential estimates. *Investigative Opthalmology, 15*, 150–153.

Margules, D. L. (1979). Obesity and the hibernation response. *Psychology Today, 13*, 136.

Markman, E. M., & Callanan, M. S. (1984). An analysis of hierarchical classification. In R. Sternberg (Ed.), *Advances in the psychology of human intelligence* (Vol. 2, pp. 345–365). Hillsdale, NJ: Erlbaum.

Markovits, H., & Nantel, G. (1989). The belief-bias effect in the production and evaluation of logical conclusions. *Memory and Cognition, 17*, 11–17.

Marks, I. M. (1978). *Living with fear*. New York: McGraw-Hill.

Markus, H., & Sentis, K. (1982). The self in social information processing. In J. Suls (Ed.), *Psychological perspectives of the self* (Vol. 1, pp. 41–70). Hillsdale, NJ: Erlbaum.

Marlatt, G. A. (1983). The controlled-drinking controversy, a commentary. *American Psychologist, 38*, 1097–1110.

Marler, P. (1976). On animal aggression: The roles of strangeness and familiarity. *American Psychologist, 31*, 239–246.

Marr, D. (1982). *Vision*. San Francisco: Freeman.

Marriott, J. A., & Stuchley, M. A. (1986). Health aspects of work with visual display terminals. *Journal of Occupational Medicine, 28*, 833–848.

Marshall, G. D., & Zimbardo, P. G. (1979). Affective consequences of inadequately explained physiological arousal. *Journal of Personality and Social psychology, 37*, 970–988.

Marshall, J. F., & Teitelbaum, P. (1974). Further analysis of sensory inattention following lateral hypothalamic damage in rats. *Journal of Comparative and Physiological Psychology, 86*, 375–395.

Marshall, M. (1979). *Beliefs, behaviors, and alcoholic beverages: A cross-cultural survey*. Ann Arbor: University of Michigan Press.

Marshall, V. M., & Levy, J. A. (1990). Aging and dying. In R. A. Binstock & L. K. George (Eds.), *Handbook of aging and the social sciences* (3rd ed.). San Diego, CA: Academic Press.

Martin, D. (1989). Engineering psychology. In W. L. Gregory & W. J. Burroughs (Eds.), *Introduction to applied psychology*. Glenview, IL: Scott, Foresman.

Martin, L. L., Harlow, T. F., & Strack, F. (1992). The role of bodily sensations in the evaluation of social events. *Personality & Social Psychology Bulletin, 18(4)*, 412–419.

Martorano, S. C. (1977). A developmental analysis of performance on Piaget's formal operations tasks. *Developmental Psychology, 13*, 666–672.

Marx, K. (1859/1904). *A contribution to the critique of social economy*. Chicago: Charles H. Kerr (translated).

Maser, J. D., Kaelber, C., & Weise, R. E. (1991). International use and attitudes toward DSM-III and DSM-III-R: Growing consensus in psychiatric classification. *Journal of Abnormal Psychology, 100*, 271–279.

Maslach, C. (1979). Negative emotional biasing of unexplained arousal. *Journal of Personality and Social Psychology, 37*, 953–969.

Maslach, C., & Jackson, S. E. (1985). Burnout in health professions: A social psychological analysis. In G. Sanders & J. Suls (Eds.), *Social psychology of health and illness*. Hillsdale, NJ: Erlbaum.

Maslow, A. H. (1943). A theory of human motivation. *Psychological Review, 50*, 370–396.

Maslow, A. H. (1954). *Motivation and personality*. New York: Harper & Row.

Maslow, A. H. (1970). *Motivation and personality* (2nd ed.). New York: Harper & Row.

Masserman, J. (1961). *Principles of dynamic psychiatry*. Philadelphia: W. B. Saunders.

Masserman, J. H. (1943). *Behavior and neurosis: An experimental psychoanalytic approach to psychobiologic principles*. Chicago: University of Chicago Press.

Masson, J. M. (1985). *The assault on truth: Freud's suppression of the seduction theory*. New York: Penguin.

Masson, J. M. (1988). *Against therapy: Emotional tyranny and the myth of psychological healing*. New York: Atheneum.

Masters, W. H., & Johnson, V. E. (1966). *Human sexual response*. Boston: Little, Brown.

Masters, W. H., & Johnson, V. E. (1970). *Human sexual inadequacy*. Boston: Little, Brown.

Masters, W. H., Johnson, V. E., & Kolodny, R. C. (1985). *Human sexuality* (2nd ed.). Boston: Little, Brown.

Matarazzo, J. D. (1982). Behavioral health and behavioral medicine: Frontiers of a new health psychology. *American Psychologist, 35*, 807–817.

Matarazzo, J. D. (1992). Psychological testing and assessment in the 21st century. *American Psychologist, 47*, 1007–1018.

Matsumoto, D. (1987). The role of facial response in the experience of emotion: More methodological problems and a meta-analysis. *Journal of Personality and Social Psychology, 52*, 769–774.

Matute, H. (1994). Learned helplessness and superstitious behavior as opposite effects of uncontrollable reinforcement in humans. *Learning and Motivation, 25*, 216–232.

Maurer, D. M. (1975). Infant visual perception: Methods of study. In L. B. Cohen & P. Salapatek (Eds.), *Infant perception: From sensation to cognition* (Vol. 1). New York: Academic Press.

Maurer, D., & Salapatek, P. (1976). Developmental changes in the scanning of faces by young infants. *Child Development, 47*, 523–527.

May, R. (Ed.). (1969). *Existentialist psychology* (2nd ed.). New York: Random House.

Mayer, J. (1955). Regulation of energy intake and body weight: The glucostatic theory and the lipostatic hypothesis. *Annals of the New York Academy of Science, 63*, 15–43.

Mayer, J. (1968). *Overweight: Causes and control*. Englewood Cliffs, NJ: Prentice-Hall.

Mayer, R. E. (1983). *Thinking, problem solving, cognition*. New York: Freeman.

Mayer, R. E. (1982). *Thinking, problem solving, cognition 2e*. San Francisco: Freeman.

Mayo, E. (1933). *The human problems of an industrial civilization*. New York: Macmillan.

McCabe, M. P., & Collins, J. K. (1990). *Dating, relating, and sex*. Sydney, Australia: Horrowitz Grahame.

McCall, R. B. (1985). The confluence model and theory. *Child Development, 56*, 217–218.

McCall, R. B., Appelbaum, M. I., & Hogarty, P. S. (1973). Developmental changes in mental performance. *Monographs of the Society for Research in Child Development, 38(3, Serial No. 150)*, 1–84.

McCartney, K., Scarr, S., Phillips, D., & Grajek, S. (1985). Day care as intervention. *Journal of Applied Developmental Psychology, 6*, 247–260.

McCauley, C., Stitt, C. L., & Segal, M. (1980). Stereotyping: From prejudice to prediction. *Psychological Bulletin, 87*, 195–208.

McCaulley, M. H. (1990). The Myers-Briggs Type Indicator: A measure for individuals and groups. *Measurement and Evaluation in Counseling and Development, 22*, 181–195.

McClelland, D. (1961). *The Achieving Society*. Princeton: Van Nostrand.

McClelland, D. C. (1993). Intelligence is not the best predictor of job performance. *Current Directions in Psychological Science, 2*, 5–6.

McClelland, D. C., & Winter, D. G. (1969). *Motivating economic achievement*. New York: Free Press. (Paperback 1971)

McClelland, D. C., Atkinson, J. W., Clark, R. W., & Lowell, E. L. (1953). *The achievement motive*. New York: Appleton-Century-Crofts.

McClelland, D. C., Koestner, R., & Weinberger, J. (1989). How do self-attributed and implicit motives differ? *Psychological Review, 96*, 690–702.

McClelland, D. C., Ross, G., & Patel, V. (1985). The effect of an academic examination on salivary immunoglobulin & norepinephrine levels, college students. *Journal of Human Stress, 11(2)*, 52–59.

McClelland, J. L., & Rumelhart, D. E. (1981). An interactive activation model of the effect of context in perception: Part 1: An account of basic findings. *Psychological Review, 88*, 375–407.

McClintock, M. K. (1971). Menstrual synchrony and suppression. *Nature, 229*, 244–245.

McCloskey, M. (1993). Theory and evidence in cognitive neuropsychology: A "radical" response to Robertson, Knight, Rafal, and Shimamura (1993). *Journal of Experimental Psychology: Learning, Memory, and Cognition, 19(3)*, 718–734.

McCloskey, M., & Egeth, H. E. (1983). Eyewitness identification: What can a witness tell a jury? *American Psychologist, 38*, 550–563.

McCloskey, M., Wible, C., & Cohen, N. (1988). The flashbulb memory hypothesis: Overexposed, underdeveloped, and out of focus. *Journal of Experimental Psychology: General, 117*, 171–181.

McCollough, D. (1965). Color adaptation of edge-detectors in the human visual system. *Science, 149*, 1115–1116.

McCormick, E. J., & Ilgen, D. R. (1980). *Industrial psychology* (7th ed.). Englewood Cliffs, NJ: Prentice-Hall.

McCrae, R. R., & Costa, P. T. (1988). Do parental influences matter? *Journal of Personality, 56*, 445–449.

McCrae, R. R., & Costa, P. T. (1990). *Personality in Adulthood*. New York: Guilford.

McDaniel, M. A., & Einstein, G. O. (1986). Bizarre imagery of an effective memory aid: The importance of distinctiveness. *Journal of Experimental Psychology: Learning, Memory and Cognition, 12*, 54–65.

McDaniel, M. A., & Einstein, G. O. (1989). Material-appropriate processing: A contextualist approach to reading and studying strategies. *Educational Psychology Review, 1*, 113–145.

McDaniel, M. A., Riegler, G. L., & Waddill, P. J. (1990). Generation effects in free recall: Further support for a three-factor theory. *Journal of Experimental Psychology: Learning, Memory, and Cognition, 16*.

McDonald, D. G., Schicht, W. W., Frazier, R. E., Schallenberger, H. D., & Edwards, D. J. (1975). Studies of information processing in sleep. *Psychophysiology, 12*, 624–629.

McEvoy, G. M., & Cascio, W. F. (1985). Strategies for reducing employee turnover: A meta-analysis. *Journal of Applied Psychology, 70*, 342–353.

McGeoch, J. A. (1932). Forgetting and the law of disuse. *Psychological Review, 39*, 352–370.

McGill, T. E. (1962). Sexual behavior in three inbred strains of mice. *Behaviour, 19*, 341–350.

McGue, M., Pickens, R. W., & Svikis, D. S. (1992). Sex and age effects on the inheritance of alcohol problems: A twin study. *Journal of Abnormal Psychology, 101*, 3–17.

McGuire, W. J. (1985). Attitudes and attitude change. In G. Lindzey & E. Aronson (Eds.), *Handbook of social psychology* (3rd ed.) (Vol. 2). New York: Random House.

McHose, J. H., & Tauber, L. (1972). Changes in delay of reinforcement in simple instrumental conditioning. *Psychonomic Science, 27*, 291–292.

McKeithen, K. B., Reitman, J. S., Rueter, H. H., & Hirtle, S. C. (1981). Knowledge organization and skill differences in computer programmers. *Cognitive Psychology, 13*, 307–325.

McKelvey, W., & Kerr, N. H. (1988). Differences in conformity among friends and strangers. *Psychological Reports, 62*, 759–762.

McKelvie, S. J. (1990). The Asch primacy effect: Robust but not infallible. *Journal of Social Behavior and Personality, 5*, 135–150.

McKenna, R. J. (1972). Some effects of anxiety level and food cues on the eating behavior of obese and normal subjects. *Jounal of Personality and Social Psychology, 22*, 311–319.

McKusick, V. A. (1986). *Mendelian inheritance in man* (8th ed.). Baltimore, MD: Johns Hopkins University Press.

McLaren, J., & Bryson, S. E. (1987). Review of recent epidemiological studies of mental retardation: Prevalence, associated disorders, and etiology. *American Journal of Mental Retardation, 92*, 243–254.

McNally, S., Eisenberg, N., & Harris, J. D. (1991). Consistency and change in maternal child-rearing practices and values: A longitudinal study. *Child Development, 62*, 190–198.

McNeilly, C. L., & Howard, K. I. (1991). The effectiveness of psychotherapy: A reevaluation based on dosage. *Psychotherapy research*.

McReynolds, P. (1989). Diagnosis and clinical assessment: Current status and major issues. *Annual Review of Psychology, 40*, 83–108.

Mechelen, I. V., & Michalski, R. S. (1993). General introduction: Purpose, underlying ideas, and scope of the book. In I. V. Mechelen, J. Hampton, R. S. Michalski, & P. Theuns (Eds.), *Categories and concepts: Theoretical views and inductive data analysis* (pp. 1–8). San Diego, CA: Academic Press.

Medin, D. L., Goldstone, R. L., & Markman, A. B. (1995). Comparison and choice: Relation between similarity processes and decision processes. *Psychonomic Bulletin & Review, 2*, 1–19.

Mednick, S. A., Gabrielli, W. F., & Hutchings, B. (1984). Genetic influences in criminal convictions: Evidence from an adoption cohort. *Science, 224*, 891–894.

Mednick, S. A., Pollock, V., Volavka, J., & Gabrielli, W. F. (1982). Biology and violence. In M. E. Wolfgang & N. A. Weiner (Eds.), *Criminal violence*. Beverly Hills, CA: Sage.

Mednick, S. A., Venables, P. H., Schulsinger, F., & Cudeck, R. (1982). The Mauritus project: An experiment in primary prevention. In M. J. Goldstein (Ed.), *Preventive intervention in schizophrenia: Are we ready?* (pp. 287–296). Washington, DC: Government Printing Office.

Mednick, S. A., Volavka, J., Gabrielli, W. F., & Itil, T. (1981). EEG as a predictor of antisocial behavior. *Criminology, 19*, 219–231.

Meece, J. L., Wigfield, A., & Eccles, J. S. (1990). Predictors of math anxiety and its influences on young adolescents' course enrollment. *Journal of Educational Psychology, 82*, 60–70.

Megaree, E. I. (1972). *The California psychological inventory handbook*. San Francisco: Jossey-Bass.

Meglino, B. M., DeNisi, A. S., Youngblood, S. A., & Williams, K. J. (1988). Effects of realistic job previews: A comparison using an enhancement and a reduction preview. *Journal of Applied Psychology, 73*, 259–266.

Mehler, J., Jusczyk, P. W., Lambertz, G., Halsted, N., Bertoncini, J., & Ameiel-Tison, C. (1988). A precursor of language acquisition in young infants. *Cognition, 29*, 143–178.

Mehrabian, A. (1987). *Eating characteristics and temperament*. New York: Springer-Verlag.

Meichenbaum, D. H. (1977). *Cognitive-behavior modification: An integrative approach*. New York: Plenum.

Meisels, S. J. (1988). Developmental Screening in Early-Childhood: The interaction of research and social-policy. *Annual Review of Public Health, 9*, 527–550.

Meissner, W. W. (1980). Theories of personality and psychopathology: Classical psychoanalysis. In H. I. Kaplan, A. M. Freedman, & B. J. Sadock (Eds.), *Comprehensive textbook of psychiatry: III*. Baltimore: Williams & Wilkins.

Melcher, J. M., & Schooler, J. W. (1996). The misrembrance of wines past: Verbal and perceptual expertise differentially mediate verbal overshadowing of taste memory. *Journal of Memory and Language*.

Melton, A. W. (1963). Implications of short-term memory for a general theory of memory. *Journal of Verbal Learning and Verbal Behavior, 2*, 1–21.

Meltzer, D., & Brahlek, J. A. (1968). Quantity of reinforcement and fixed-interval performance. *Psychonomic Science, 12*, 207–208.

Melzack, R. (1989). Phantom limbs, the self, and the brain. *Canadian Psychology, 30*, 1–16.

Melzack, R. (1990). The tragedy of needless pain. *Scientific American, 262*, 27–33.

Melzack, R. D. (1970, October). Phantom limbs. *Psychology Today*, 63–68.

Melzack, R. D. (1973). *The puzzle of pain*. New York: Basic Books.

Melzack, R., & Wall, P. (1989). *The challenge of pain* (rev. ed.). New York: Penguin.

Melzack, R., & Wall, P. D. (1965). Pain mechanisms: A new theory. *Science, 150*, 971–979.

Mendelsohn, J. (1990). The view from step number 16. In C. Gilligan, N. P. Lyons, & T. J. Hammer (Eds.), *Making connections*. Cambridge, MA: Harvard University Press.

Mendlewicz, J. (1985). Genetic research in depressive disorders. In E. E. Beckham & W. E. Leber (Eds.), *Handbook of depression: Treatment, assessment, and research*. Homewood, IL: Dorsey Press.

Mendlewicz, J., & Rainer, J. D. (1977). Adoption study supporting genetic transmission in manic-depressive illness. *Nature, 268*, 327–329.

Menzel, E. W. (1978). Cognitive mapping in chimpanzees. In S. H. Hulse, H. Fowler, & W. K. Honig (Eds.), *Cognitive processes in animal behavior*. Hillsdale, NJ: Erlbaum.

Mercer, J. R. (1971). Sociocultural factors in labeling mental retardates. *Peabody Journal of Education, 48*, 188–203.

Mercer, J. R., Gomez-Palacio, M., & Padilla, E. (1986). The development of practical intelligence in cross-cultural perspective. In R. Sternberg & R. Wagner (Eds.), *Practical intelligence: Nature and origins of competence in the everyday world*. Cambridge: Cambridge University Press.

Meredith, H. V. (1984). Body size of infants and children around the world in relation to socioeconomic status. In H. W. Reese (Ed.), *Advances in child development and behavior*, Vol. 18 (pp. 81–145). Orlando, FL: Academic Press.

Merenda, P. F. (1987). Toward a four-factor theory of temperament and/or personality. *Journal of Personality Assessment, 51*, 367–374.

Merikle, P. M. (1992). Perception without awareness. *American Psychologist, 47*, 792–795.

Merikle, P. M., & Skanes, H. E. (1992). Subliminal self-help audiotapes: A search for placebo effects. *Journal for Applied Psychology, 77*, 772–776.

Merritt, J. O. (1979). None in a million: Results of mass screening for eidetic ability using objective tests published in newspapers and magazines. *Behavioral and Brain Sciences, 2*, 612.

Mervis, C. G., Catlin, J., & Rosch, E. (1975). Development of the structure of color categories. *Developmental Psychology, 11*, 54–60.

Metcalfe, J. (1986). Premonitions of insight predict impending error. *Journal of Experimental Psycology: Learning, Memory and Cognition, 12*, 623–634.

Meuser, K. T., Bellack, A. S., Morrison, R. L., & Wade, J. H. (1990). Gender, social competence, and symptomatology in schizophrenia: A longitudinal analysis. *Journal of Abnormal Psychology, 99*, 138–147.

Miale, F. R., & Selzer, M. (1975). *The Nuremberg mind: The psychology of Nazi leaders*. New York: New York Times Books.

Midlarsky, E., & Bryan, J. H. (1972). Affect expressions and children's imitative altruism. *Journal of Experimental Research in Personality, 6*, 195–203.

Miernyk, W. H. (1975). The changing life cycle of work. In N. Datan & L. H. Ginsberg (Eds.), *Life-span developmental psychology: Normative life crises*. New York: Academic Press.

Milgram, S. (1963). Behavioral study of obedience. *Journal of Abnormal and Social Psychology, 67*, 371–378.

Milgram, S. (1964). Issues in the study of obedience: A reply to Baumrind. *American Psychologist, 19*, 848–852.

Milgram, S. (1965). Some conditions of obedience and disobedience to authority. *Human Relations, 18*, 57–76.

Milgram, S. (1974). *Obedience to authority: An experimental view.* New York: Harper & Row.

Miller, A. G. (1972). Role playing: An alternative to deception? *American Psychologist, 27*, 623–636.

Miller, A. G. (1986). *The obedience experiments: A case study of controversy in social science.* New York: Praeger.

Miller, G. A. (1956a). The magical number seven plus or minus two: Some limits on our capacity for processing information. *Psychological Review, 63*, 81–97.

Miller, G. A. (1956b). Human memory and the storage of information. *IRE Transactions on Information Theory,* Vol. IT-2, pp. 129–137.

Miller, G. A. (1962). *Psychology: The science of mental life.* New York: Harper & Row.

Miller, G. A. (1983, December 25). Varieties of intelligence. [Review of *Frames of mind* by H. Gardner]. *New York Times Book Review,* p. 5.

Miller, J. D. (1978). Effect of noise on people. In E. C. Carterette & M. P. Friedman (Eds.), *Handbook of perception,* Vol. 4 (pp. 609–640). New York: Academic Press.

Miller, M. F., Barabasz, A. F., & Barabasz, M. (1991). Effects of active alert and relaxation hypnotic inductions on cold pressor pain. *Journal of Abnormal Psychology, 100*, 223–226.

Miller, M. W. (1986). Effects of alcohol on the generation and migration of cerebral cortical neurons. *Science, 233*, 1308–1311.

Miller, N. E. (1957). Experiments on motivation. *Science, 126*, 1271–1278.

Miller, N. E. (1959). Liberalization of basic S-R concepts: Extensions to conflict behavior, motivation, and social learning. In S. Koch (Ed.), *Psychology: A study of a science* (pp. 196–292). New York: McGraw-Hill.

Miller, N. E. (1980). Applications of learning and biofeedback to psychiatry and medicine. In H. I. Kaplan, A. M. Freedman, & B. J. Sadock (Eds.), *Comprehensive textbook of psychiatry: III.* Baltimore, MD: Williams & Wilkins.

Miller, N. E. (1983). Behavioral medicine: Symbiosis between laboratory and clinic. In M. R. Rosenzweig & L. W. Porter (Eds.), *Annual Review of Psychology.* Palo Alto, Calif.: Annual Reviews.

Miller, N. E. (1985). The value of behavioral research on animals. *American Psychologist, 40*, 423–440.

Miller, N., & Davidson-Podgorny, G. (1987). Theoretical models of intergroup relations and the use of cooperative teams as an intervention for desegregated settings. In C. Hendrick (Ed.), *Review of Personality and Social Psychology,* Vol. 9. Newbury Park, CA: Sage.

Miller, P. McC., & Ingham, J. G. (1979). Reflections on the life-events-to-illness link with some preliminary findings. In G. Sarason & C. D. Spielberger (Eds.), *Stress and anxiety: Vol. 6. The series in clinical and community psychology.* Washington, DC: Hemisphere.

Miller, R. J. (1991). The effect of ingested alcohol on fusion latency at various viewing distances. *Perception & Psychophysics, 50*, 575–583.

Miller, R. R., & Spear, N. E. (1985). *Information processing in animals: Conditioned inhibition.* Hillsdale, NJ: Erlbaum.

Millichap, J. G. (1993). *Environmental poisons in our food.* Chicago: PNB Publisher.

Millon, T. (1991). Classification in psychopathology: Rationale, alternatives, and standards. *Journal of Abnormal Psychology, 100*, 245–261.

Milner, B., Corkin, S., & Teuber, H. H. (1968). Further analysis of the hippocampal amnesic syndrome: 14-year follow-up study of H. M. *Neuropsychologia, 6*, 215–234.

Mindess, H. (1988). *Makers of psychology: The personal factor.* New York: Human Sciences Press.

Mineka, S. (1979). The role of fear in theories of avoidance learning, flooding, and extinction. *Psychological Bulletin, 86*, 985–1010.

Mineka, S., & Cook, M. C. (1987). Social learning and the acquisition of snake fear in monkeys. In T. R. Zentall & B. G. Galef, Jr. (Eds.), *Social learning: Psychological and biological perspectives* (pp. 51–73). Hillsdale, NJ: Erlbaum.

Mintz, L. I., Neuchterlein, K. H., Goldstein, M. J., Mintz, J., & Snyder, K. S. (1989). The initial onset of schizophrenia and family expressed emotion: Some methodological considerations. *British Journal of Psychiatry, 154*, 212–217.

Minuchin, S., Rosman, B. L., & Baker, L. (1978). *Psychosomatic families.* Cambridge, MA: Harvard University Press.

Miron, D., & McClelland, D. C. The impact of achievement motivation training on small business performance. *California Management Review,* 1979 *21*(4), 13–28.

Mischel, H. N., & Mischel, W. (1983). The development of children's knowledge of self-control strategies. *Child Development, 54*, 603–619.

Mischel, W. (1961). Delay of gratification, need for achievement, and acquiescence in another culture. *Journal of Abnormal and Social Psychology, 62*, 543–552.

Mischel, W. (1968). *Personality and assessment.* New York: Wiley.

Mischel, W. (1972). Direct versus indirect personality assessment: Evidence and implications. *Journal of Consulting and Clinical Psychology, 38*, 319–324.

Mischel, W. (1974). Processes in the delay of gratification. In L. Berkowitz (Ed.), *Advances in experimental social psychology* (Vol. 7). New York: Academic Press.

Mischel, W. (1979). On the interface of cognition and personality: Beyond the person-situation debate. *American Psychologist, 34*, 740–754.

Mischel, W., & Patterson, C. J. (1978). Effective plans for self-control in children. In W. A. Collins (Ed.), *Minnesota symposium on child psychology* (Vol. 11). Hillsdale, NJ: Erlbaum.

Mischel, W., & Peake, P. K. (1982). Beyond déjà vu in the search for cross-situational consistency. *Psychological Review, 89*, 730–755.

Mischel, W., Shoda, Y., & Rodriguez, M. L. (1989). Delay of gratification in children. *Science, 244*, 933–938.

Mitchell, D. E. (1980). The influence of early visual experience on visual perception. In C. S. Harris (Ed.), *Visual coding and adaptability.* Hillsdale, NJ: Erlbaum.

Mitchell, D. E. (1989). Normal and abnormal visual development in kittens: Insights into the mechanisms that underlie visual perceptual development in humans. *Canadian Journal of Psychology, 43*, 141–163.

Mitchell, J., Wilson, K., Revicki, D., & Parker, L. (1985). Children's perceptions of aging: A multidimensional approach to difference by age, sex, and race. *The Gerontologist, 25*, 182–187.

Model Penal Code: Proposed Official Draft. (1962). Philadelphia: American Law Institute.

Moldin, S. O. (1991). An overview of schizophrenia research. *Contemporary Psychology, 36*, 21–22.

Money, J., & Ehrhardt, A. A. (1972). *Man & woman, boy & girl.* Baltimore: Johns Hopkins University Press.

Money, J., & Russo, A. J. (1979). Homosexual outcome of discordant gender identity/role in childhood: Longitudinal follow-up. *Journal of Pediatric Psychology, 41*(1), 29–41.

Monjan, A. A. (1984). Effects of acute and chronic stress upon lymphocyte blastogenesis in mice and humans. In E. L. Cooper (Ed.), *Stress, immunity, and aging* (pp. 81–108). New York: Marcel Dekker.

Montie, J. E., & Fagan, J. F. (1988). Racial differences in IQ: Item analysis of the Stanford-Binet at 3 years. *Intelligence, 12*, 315–332.

Mook, D. G. (1983). In defense of external invalidity. *American Psychologist, 38*, 379–387.

Mook, D. G., Atkinson, B., Johnston, L., & Wagner, S. (1993). Persistence of sham feeding after intragastric meals in rats. *Appetite, 20*, 167–179.

Moore, H. T. (1917). Laboratory tests of anger, fear, and sex interests. *American Journal of Psychology, 28*, 390–395.

Moore, K. (1992). *Facts at a glance.* Washington, DC: Childtrends.

Moore, K. A. (1985, Summer). Teenage pregnancy. *New perspectives.* pp. 11–15.

Moore, S., & Rosenthal, D. (1993). *Sexuality in adolescence.* New York: Routledge.

Moore, T. (1987). Personality tests are back. *Fortune, 115*, (7), 74–84.

Moore, T. E. (1992). Subliminal perception: Facts and fallacies. *Skeptical Inquirer, 16*, 273–281.

Moray, N. (1959). Attention in dichotic listening: Affective cues and the influence of instructions. *Quarterly Journal of Experimental Psychology, 9*, 56–60.

Morell, M. A., Twillman, R. K., & Sullaway, M. E. (1989). Would a Type A date another Type A? Influence of behavior type and personal attributes in the selection of dating partners. *Journal of Applied Social Psychology, 19*, 918–931.

Morey, L. C. (1991). Classification of mental disorder as a collection of hypothetical constructs. *Journal of Abnormal Psychology, 100*, 289–293.

Morgan, C. T., & Morgan J. D. (1940). Studies in hunger: 2. The relation of gastric denervation and dietary sugar to the effect of insulin upon food intake in the rat. *Journal of General Psychology, 57*, 153–163.

Moriarty, D., & McCabe, A. E. (1977). Studies of television and youth sport. In *Ontario: Royal commission on violence in the communications industry. Report: Vol. 5. Learning from the media (research reports).* Toronto: Queen's Printer for Ontario.

Morin, C. M., & Azrin, H. H. (1987). Stimulus control and imagery training in treating sleep-maintenance insomnia. *Journal of Consulting and Clinical Psychology, 55*, 260–262.

Morley, J. E., Bartness, T. J., Gosnell, B. A., & Levine, A. S. (1985). Peptidergic regulation of feeding. *International Review of Neurobiology, 27*, 207–298.

Morris, C. D., Bransford, J. D., & Franks, J. J. (1977). Levels of processing versus transfer appropriate processing. *Journal of Verbal Learning and Verbal Behavior, 16*, 519–533.

Morris, J. B., & Beck, A. T. (1974). The efficacy of antidepressant drugs: A review of research (1958–1972). *Archives of General Psychiatry, 30*, 667–674.

Morris, J. L. (1966). Propensity for risk taking as a determinant of vocational choice: An extension of the theory of achievement motivation. *Journal of Personality and Social Psychology, 3*, 328–335.

Moscovici, S. (1985). Social influence and conformity. In G. Lindzey & E. Aronson (Eds.), *Handbook of social psychology* (3rd ed.) (Vol. 2). New York: Random House.

Moulton, D. G. (1977). Minimum odorant concentrations detectable by the dog and their implications for olfactory receptor sensitivity. In D. Miller-Schwarze & M. M. Mozell (Eds.), *Chemical signals in vertebrates* (pp. 455–464). New York: Plenum.

Mowrer, O. H. (1947). On the dual nature of learning: A reinterpretation of "conditioning" and "problem-solving." *Harvard Educational Review, 17*, 102–148.

Mowrer, O. H. (1960). *Learning theory and behavior.* New York: Wiley.

Moyer, K. E. (1976). *The psychobiology of aggression.* New York: Harper & Row.

Mozel, M. M., Smith, B., Smith, P., Sullivan, R., & Sewender, P. (1969). Nasal chemoreception in flavor identification. *Archives of Otolaryngology, 90*, 367–373.

Mueser, K. T., Bellack, A. S., Morrison, R. L., & Wade, J. H. (1990). Gender, social competence, and symptomatology in schizophrenia: A longitudinal analysis. *Journal of Abnormal Psychology, 99*, 138–147.

Mullen, B. (1986). Atrocity as a function of lynch mob composition: A self-attention perspective. *Personality and Social Psychology Bulletin, 12*, 187–197.

Mullen, B. (1991). Group composition, salience, and cognitive representations: The phenomenology of being in a group. *Journal of Experimental Social Psychology, 27*, 197–323.

Mullen, B., & Johnson, C. (1990). Distinctiveness-based illusory correlations and stereotyping: A meta-analytic integration. *British Journal of Social Psychology, 29*, 11–28.

Mullen, G., & Hu, L. (1989). Perceptions of ingroup and outgroup variability: A meta-analytic integration. *Basic & Applied Social Psychology, 10*, 233–252.

Mulligan, J. A. (1966). Singing behavior and its development in the song sparrow. *Melospiza Melodia University of California Publications in Zoology, 166*(81), 1–76.

Munroe, R. H. (1991). Review of M. H. Segall, P. R. Dasen, J. W. Berry, & Y. H. Poortinga (1990) "Human Behavior in Global Perspective: An Introduction to Cross-Cultural Psychology." *Contemporary Psychology, 36*, 1040–1042.

Murdock, B. B., Jr. (1962). The serial position effect of free recall. *Journal of Experimental Psychology, 64*, 482–488.

Murphy, C., & Cain, W. S. (1986). Odor identification: The blind are better. *Physiology and Behavior, 371*, 177–180.

Murphy, C., Cain, W. S., & Bartoshuk, L. M. (1977). Mutual action of taste and olfaction. *Sensory Processes, 1*, 204–211.

Murphy, G. L. (1993). Theories and concept formation. In I. V. Mechelen, J. Hampton, R. S. Michalski, & P. Theuns (Eds.), *Categories and concepts: Theoretical views and inductive data analysis* (pp. 173–200). San Diego, CA: Academic Press.

Murphy, J. M. (1976). Psychiatric labeling in cross-cultural perspective. *Science, 191*, 1019–1028.

Murray, H. A., et al. (1938). *Explorations in personality.* New York: Oxford University Press.

Murray, J. B. (1991). Psychophysiological aspects of nightmares, night terrors, and sleepwalking. *The Journal of General Psychology, 118*, 113–127.

Murstein, B. I. (1988). A taxonomy of love. In R. J. Sternberg & M. L. Barnes (Eds.), *The psychology of love* (pp. 13–37). New Haven, CT: Yale University Press.

Mussen, P. H., & Jones, M. C. (1957). Self-conceptions, motivations, and interpersonal attitudes of late- and early-maturing boys. *Child Development, 28*, 243–256.

Mussen, P. H., Conger, J. J., & Kagan, J. (1980). *Essentials of child development and personality.* New York: Harper & Row.

Myers, I. B., & McCaulley, M. H. (1985). *Manual: A guide to the development and use of the Myers-Briggs Type Indicator.* Palo Alto, CA: Consulting Psychologists Press.

Myerson, A. (1940). Alcohol: A study of social ambivalence. *Quarterly Journal of Alcohol Studies, 1*, 13–20.

Myles-Worsley, M., Johnston, W. A., & Simons, M. A. (1988). The influence of expertise on x-ray image processing. *Journal of Experimental Psychology: Learning, Memory, and Cognition, 14*, 553–557.

N

Näätänen, R. (1992). *Attention and brain function.* Hillsdale, NJ: Erlbaum.

Nadel, L., & Zola-Morgan, S. (1984). Toward the understanding of infant memory: Contributions from animal neuropsychology. In M. Moscaritch (Ed), *Infant memory* (pp. 145–172). New York: Plenum.

Nakagawa, M., Teti, D., & Lamb, M. E. (1992). An ecological study of child-mother attachments among Japanese sojourners in the United States. *Developmental Psychology, 28*, 584–592.

Natelson, B. (1976). The "executive" monkey revisited. Paper presented at the Symposium on Nerves and the Gut, Philadelphia.

Nathan, P. E., & Hay, W. M. (1984). Alcoholism: Psychopathology, etiology, and treatment. In H. E. Adams & P. B. Sutker (Eds.), *Comprehensive handbook of psychopathology.* New York: Plenum.

Nathans, J. (1989). The genes for color vision. *Scientific American, 260*, 42–49.

National Center for Health Statistics. (1990). *Prevention profile: Health, United States, 1989* (DHHS Publication No. PHS 90-1232). Hyattsville, MD: U.S. Department of Health and Human Services.

National Center for Health Statistics. (1992). *Unpublished data tables from the NCHS Mortality Tapes, FBI-SHR.* Atlanta, GA: Centers for Disease Control.

National Institute of Mental Health (1985). *Electroconvulsive therapy: Consensus Development Conference statement.* Bethesda, MD: U.S. Department of Health and Human Services.

National Institutes of Health Review Panel on Coronary Prone Behavior and Coronary Heart Disease. (1981). Coronary-prone behavior and coronary heart disease: A critical review. *Circulation, 63*, 1199–1215.

Natsoulas, T. (1983). Addendum to "Consciousness." *American Psychologist, 38*, 121–122.

Naylor, J. C., & Lawshe, C. H. (1958). An analytical review of the experimental basis of subception. *Journal of Psychology, 46*, 75–96.

Nebes, R. D. (1974). Hemispheric specialization in commissurotomized man. *Psychological Bulletin, 81*, 1–14.

Neely, J. H. (1977). Semantic priming and retrieval from lexical memory: Roles of inhibitionless spreading activation and limited capacity attention. *Journal of Experimental Psychology: General, 106*, 226–254.

Neely, J. H., Keefe, D. E., & Ross, K. L. (1989). Semantic priming in the lexical decision task: Roles of prospective prime-generated expectancies and retrospective semantic matching. *Journal of Experimental Psychology: Learning, Memory, and Cognition, 15*, 1003–1019.

Neimeyer, G. J. (1989). Applications of repertory grid technique to vocational assessment. *Journal of Counseling and Development, 67*, 585–589.

Neiss, R. (1988). Reconceptualizing arousal: Psychobiological states in motor performance. *Psychological Bulletin, 103*, 345–366.

Neisser, U. (1967). *Cognitive psychology.* New York: Appleton-Century-Crofts.

Neisser, U. (1968). The processes of vision. *Scientific American, 219*, 204–214.

Neisser, U. (1976). *Cognition and reality.* San Francisco, CA: Freeman.

Neisser, U. (1978). Memory: What are the important questions? In M. Gruneberg, P. Morris, & R. Sykes (Eds.), *Practical Aspects of Memory* (pp. 3–34). San Diego, CA: Academic Press.

Neisser, U. (1992). Amnesia, infantile. In L. R. Squire (Ed.), *The encyclopedia of learning and memory* (pp. 28–30). New York: MacMillan.

Nelkin, D. (1993). The grandiose claims of geneticists. *Chronicle of Higher Education, March 3*, B1–B2.

Nelson, F. L. (1984). Suicide: Issues of prevention, intervention, and facilitation. *Journal of Clinical Psychology, 40*, 1328–1333.

Nelson, K. (1973). Structure and strategy in learning to talk. *Monographs of the Society for Research in Child Development, 38* (No. 149).

Nelson, S. A. (1980). Factors influencing young children's use of motives and outcomes as moral criteria. *Child Development, 51*, 823–829.

Nelson, T. C., & Reynolds, C. F. (1991). Pathological sleepiness. In T. H. Monk (Ed.), *Sleep, sleepiness, and performance* (pp. 199–222). New York: Wiley.

Netter, F. H. (1983). *CIBA collection of medical illustrations: Vol. 1. Nervous system. Part 1. Anatomy and physiology.* CIBA Pharmaceutical.

Neugarten, B. (1968). Adult personality: Toward a psychology of the life cycle. In B. Neugarten (Ed.), *Middle age and aging.* Chicago: University of Chicago Press.

Neugarten, B. L. (1975). The future and the young-old. *Gerontologist, 15*, 4–9.

Neugarten, B. L. (Ed.) (1968). *Middle age and aging.* Chicago: University of Chicago Press.

Neugarten, B. L., Crotty, W., & Tobin, S. (1964). Personality types in an aged population. In B. L. Neugarten (Ed.), *Personality in middle and late life: Empirical studies.* New York: Atherton.

Newcombe, N., & Huttenlocher, J. (1992). Children's early ability to solve perspective-taking problems. *Developmental Psychology, 28*, 635–643.

Newman, R. S., & Hagen, J. W. (1981). Memory strategies in children with learning disabilities. *Journal of Applied Developmental Psychology, 1*, 297–312.

Newton, H. H., Freeman, F. N., & Holzinger, K. J. (1937). *Twins: A study of heredity and environment.* Chicago: University of Chicago Press.

Newton, J., & McCauley, C. (1977). Eye contact with strangers in city, suburb, and small town. *Environment and Behavior, 9*, 547–557.

Nichols, P. L. (1984). Familial mental retardation. *Behavior Genetics, 14*, 161–170.

Nickerson, R. S., & Adams, M. J. (1979). Long term memory for a common object. *Cognitive Psychology, 11*, 287–307.

Nielsen, L. (1991). *Adolescence: A contemporary view.* Fort Worth: Holt, Rinehart & Winston.

Nisbett, R. E. (1968). Taste, deprivation, and weight determinants of eating behavior. *Journal of Personality and Social Psychology, 10*, 107–116.

Nisbett, R. E. (1972). Hunger, obesity and the ventromedial hypothalamus. *Psychological Review, 79*, 433–453.

Nisbett, R. E., & Ross, L. (1980). *Human inference: Strategies and shortcomings of social judgment.* Englewood Cliffs, NJ: Prentice-Hall.

Nisbett, R. E., & Temoshok, L. (1976). Is there an external cognitive style? *Journal of Personality and Social Psychology, 33*, 36–47.

Nisbett, R. E., & Wilson, T. D. (1977a). Telling more than we can know: Verbal reports on mental processes. *Psychological Review, 84*, 231–259.

Nisbett, R. E., & Wilson, T. D. (1977b). The halo effect: Evidence for unconscious alteration of judgments. *Journal of Personality and Social Psychology, 35*, 250–256.

Nisbett, R. E., Caputo, G. C., Legant, P., & Marachek, J. (1973). Behavior as seen by the actor and the observer. *Journal of Personality and Social Psychology, 27*, 154–164.

Nogrady, H., McConkey, K. M., & Perry, C. (1985). Enhancing visual memory: Trying hypnosis, trying imagination, and trying again. *Journal of Abnormal Psychology, 94*, 195–204.

Nolen-Hoeksema, S. (1987). Sex differences in unipolar depression: Evidence and theory. *Psychological Bulletin, 101*, 259–282.

Noll, K. M., Davis, J. M., & Deleon-Jones, F. (1985). Medication and somatic therapies in the treatment of depression. In E. E. Beckham & W. R. Leber (Eds.), *Handbook of depression: Treatment, Assessment, and research*. Homewood, IL: Dorsey Press.

Norman, D. A. (1968). Toward a theory of memory and attention. *Psychological Review, 75*, 522–536.

Norman, D. A. (1988). *The psychology of everyday things*. New York: Basic Books.

Norman, W. T. (1963). Toward an adequate taxonomy of personality attributes: Replicated factor structure in peer nomination personality ratings. *Journal of Abnormal & Social Psychology*, 66, 574–588.

Norman, W. T., & Goldberg, L. R. (1966). Raters, ratees, and randomness in personality structure. *Journal of Personality and Social Psychology, 4*, 681–691.

Nottebohm, F., & Nottebohm, M. (1971). Vocalizations and breeding behavior of surgically deafened ring doves. *Streptopelia Risoria Animal Behaviour, 19*, 313–328.

Nurco, D. N., Shaffer, J. W., Hanlon, T. E., & Kinlock, T. W. (1988). Relationships between client/counselor congruence and treatment outcome among narcotic addicts. *Comprehensive Psychiatry, 29*, 49–54.

Nussbaum, R. L., & Ledbetter, D. H. (1986). Fragile X syndrome: A unique mutation in man. *Annual Review of Genetics, 20*, 109–145.

O

O'Brien, D. P., Chesire, R. M., & Teitelbaum, P. (1985). Vestibular versus tail-pinch activation in cats with lateral hypothalamic lesions. *Physiology & Behavior, 34*, 811–814.

O'Carroll, P. (1990). Suicide prevention: Clusters and contagion. In A. L. Berman (Ed.), *Suicide Prevention: Case Consultations* (pp. 25–27). New York: Springer.

O'Connell, M. (1989). Management women: Debating the facts of life. *Harvard Business Review, 67*, 214.

O'Connor, B. P., & Molly, K. (1991). A test of the intellectual cycle of the popular biorhythm theory. *The Journal of Psychology, 125*, 291–299.

O'Connor, R. D. (1969). Modification of social withdrawal through symbolic modeling. *Journal of Applied Behavior Analysis, 2*, 15–22.

O'Leary, A. (1992). Self-efficacy and health: Behavioral and stress-physiological mediation. *Cognitive Therapy and Research, 16*, 229–245.

Oakes, P. J., & Turner, J. C. (1990). Is limited information processing capacity the cause of social stereotypes? W. Stroebe & M. Hewstone (Eds.), *European Review of Social Psychology* (pp. 111–135). New York: Wiley.

Oetting, E. R., & Beauvais, F. (1990). Adolescent drug use: Findings of national and local surveys. *Journal of Consulting & Clinical Psychology, 58*, 385–394.

Offer, D., & Sabshin, M. (1984). *Normality and the life cycle*. New York: Basic Books.

Offer, D., Ostrov, E., & Howard, K. I. (1984). Epidemiology of mental health and mental illness among adolescents. In J. Call (Ed.), *Significant advances in child psychiatry*. New York: Basic Books.

Office of Technology Assessment. (1992). *Does health insurance make a difference?* (OTA-H-BP-99). Washington, DC: U.S. Government Printing Office.

Ohman, A., Ohlund, L. S., Alm, T., Wieselgren, I. M., Ost, L. G., & Lindstrom, L. H. (1989). Electrodermal nonresponding, premorbid adjustment, and symptomatology as predictors of long-term social functioning in schizophrenics. *Journal of Abnormal Psychology*, 98, 426–435.

Olds, J., & Milner, P. (1954). Positive reinforcement produced by electrical stimulation of septal area and other regions of rat brain. *Journal of Comparative and Physiological Psychology, 47*, 419–427.

Oliver, M. B., & Hyde, J. S. (1993). Gender differences in sexuality: A meta-analysis. *Psychological Bulletin, 114*, 29–51.

Oliver, M. B., & Hyde, J. S. (1993). Gender differences in sexuality: A meta-analysis. *Psychological Bulletin, 114*, 29–51.

Olmsted, M. P. (1979). Eating behavior in a French restaurant: Cited in C. P. Herman, M. P. Olmsted, & J. Polivy (Eds.), Obesity, externality, and susceptibility to social influence: An integrated analysis. *Journal of Personality and Social Psychology, 45*, 926–934.

Olton, D. S., & Samuelson, R. J. (1976). Remembrance of places passed: Spatial memory in rats. *Journal of Experimental Psychology: Animal Behavior Processes, 2*, 97–116.

Olton, D. S., Collison, C., & Werz, M. A. (1977). Spatial memory and radial arm performance of rats. *Learning and Motivation, 8*, 289–314.

Ontario Board of Examiners in Psychology. (1986). *Standards of professional conduct, revised*. Toronto, Ontario: Ontario Board of Examiners in Psychology.

Orne, M. T. (1979). The use and misuse of hypnosis in court. *International Journal of Clinical and Experimental Hypnosis, 27*, 311–374.

Orne, M. T., & Hollard, C. H. (1968). On the ecological validity of laboratory deceptions. *International Journal of Psychiatry*, 6, 282–293.

Orne, M. T., Soskis, D. A., Dinges, D. F., & Orne, E. C. (1984). Hypnotically induced testimony. In G. L. Wells & E. F. Loftus, *Eyewitness testimony: Psychological perspectives* (pp. 171–213). Cambridge: Cambridge University Press.

Ornstein, P. A., & Naus, M. J. (1985). Effects of the knowledge base on children's memory strategies. In H. W. Reese (Ed.), *Advances in child development and behavior* (Vol. 19). New York: Academic Press.

Ornstein, R. (1978). The split and whole brain. *Human Nature, 1*, 76–83.

Ornstein, R. E. (1977). *The psychology of consciousness* (2nd ed.). New York: Harcourt Brace Jovanovich.

Ornstein, R. E. (1983). *The psychology of consciousness*. 3rd ed. New York: Harcourt.

Ornstein, R. E. (1986). *The psychology of consciousness* (3rd ed.). New York: Harcourt Brace Jovanovich.

Ortony, A., & Turner, T. J. (1990). What's basic about basic emotions? *Psychological Review, 97*, 315–331.

Ortony, A., Clore, G. L., & Collins, A. (1988). *The cognitive structure of emotions*. Cambridge: Cambridge University Press.

Oscar-Berman, M. (1980). Neuropsychological consequences of long-term chronic alcoholism. *American Scientist*, 68, 410–419.

Oswald, I., Taylor, A. M., & Treisman, M. (1960). Discriminative responses to stimulation during sleep. *Brain, 83*, 440–453.

Otto, M. W., Pollack, M. H., Sachs, G. S., Reiter, S. R., Meltzer-Brody, S., & Rosenbaum, J. F. (1993). Discontinuation of benzodiazepine treatment: Efficacy of cognitive-behavior therapy for patients with panic disorder. *American Journal of Psychiatry, 150*, 1485–1490.

Ouchi, W. G. (1981). *Theory Z: How American business can meet the Japanese challenge*. Reading, MA: Addison-Wesley.

Overmier, J. B., & Seligman, M. E. P. (1967). Effects of inescapable shock upon subsequent escape and avoidance learning. *Journal of Comparative and Physiological Psychology, 63*, 23–33.

Owens, J., Bower, G. H., & Black, J. (1979). The "soap opera" effect in story recall. *Memory & Cognition, 7*, 185–191.

P

Paige, R. M. (1990). International students: Cross-cultural perspectives. In R. W. Brislin, *Applied cross-cultural psychology* (pp. 161–185). Newbury Park, CA: Sage.

Paivio, A. (1969). Mental imagery in associative learning and memory. *Psychological Review, 76*, 241–263.

Paivio, A. (1975). Neomentalism. *Canadian Journal of Psychology, 29*, 263–291.

Paivio, A., Yuille, J. C., & Madigan, S. (1968). Concreteness, imagery, and meaningfulness values for 925 concrete nouns. *Journal of Experimental Psychology Monograph Supplement, 76* (1 Pt. 2).

Palincsar, A. S., & Brown, A. L. (1984). Reciprocal teaching of comprehension fostering and comprehension monitoring activities. *Cognition and Instruction, 1* (2) 117–175.

Palincsar, A. S., & Brown, A. L. (1992). Advances in the cognitive instruction of handicapped students. In M. Wong, H. Walberg, & M. Reynolds (Eds.), *The handbook of special education: Research and practice*. New York: Pergamon.

Palmore, E. (1977). Facts on aging: A short quiz. *The Gerontologist, 17*, 315–320.

Palmore, E. (1980). The facts on aging quiz: A review of findings. *The Gerontologist, 20*, 669–672.

Paludi, M. A. & Frankell-Hauser, J. (1986). An idiographic approach to the study of women's achievement striving. *Psychology of Women Quarterly, 10*, 89–100.

Panksepp, J. (1992). A critical role for "affective neuroscience" in resolving what is basic about basic emotions. *Psychological Review, 99*, 554–560.

Panskepp, J. (1971). Aggression elicited by electrical stimulation of the hypothalamus in albino rats. *Physiology and Behavior, 6*, 321–329.

Papalia, D. E., & Olds, S. W. (1985). *Psychology*. New York: McGraw-Hill.

Papalia, D. E., & Olds, S. W. (1986). *Human development*. New York: McGraw-Hill.

Papez, J. W. (1937). A proposed mechanism of emotion. *Archives of Neurology and Psychiatry, 38*, 725–743.

Papini, D. R., Farmer, F. F., Clark, S. M., Micka, J. C., & Barrett, J. K. (1990). Early adolescent age and gender differences in patterns of emotional self-disclosure to parents and friends. *Adolescence, 25*, 959–976.

Papousek, M., Bornstein, M., Nuzzo, C., Papousek, H., & Symmes, D. (1990). Infant responses to prototypical melodic contours in parental speech. *Infant Behavior and Development, 13*, 539–545.

Pardes, H., Kaufmann, C. A., Pincus, H. A., & West, A. (1989). Genetics and psychiatry: Past discoveries, current dilemmas, and future directions. *American Journal of Psychiatry, 146*, 435–443.

Paris, S. G. (1975). *Propositional logical thinking and comprehension of language connectives*. The Hauge: Mouton.

Paris, S. G., & Lindauer, B. K. (1982). The development of cognitive skills during childhood. In B. Wolman (Ed.), *Handbook of developmental psychology*. Englewood Cliffs, NJ: Prentice-Hall.

Paris, S. G., & Upton, L. R. (1976). Children's memory for inferential relationships in prose. *Child Development*. *47*, 660–668.

Paris, S. G., Cross, D. R., & Lipson, M. Y. (1984). Informed strategies for learning: A program to improve children's reading awareness and comprehension. *Journal of Educational Psychology, 76,* 1239–1252.

Paris, S. G., Lawton, T. A., Turner, J. C., & Roth, J. L. (1991). A developmental perspective on standardized achievement testing. *Educational Researcher, 20,* 12–20.

Paris, S. G., Lipson, M. Y., & Wixson, K. K. (1983). Becoming a strategic reader. *Contemporary Educational Psychology, 8,* 293–316.

Paris, S. G., Newman, R. S., & McVey, K. A. (1982). Learning the functional significance of mnemonic actions: A microgenetic study of strategy acquisition. *Journal of Experimental Child Psychology, 34,* 490–509.

Paris, S. G., Wasik, B., & Turner, J. (1991). The development of strategic reading. In D. Pearson (Ed.), *Handbook of reading research* (2nd ed.). New York: Longman.

Parke, R. D., Berkowitz, L., Leyens, J. P., West, S. G., & Sebastian, R. J. (1977). Some effects of violent and nonviolent movies on the behavior of juvenile delinquents. In L. Berkowitz (Ed.), *Advances in experimental social psychology* (Vol. 10 pp. 135–172). New York: Academic press.

Parmalee, A. H., & Sigman, M. D. (1983). Perinatal brain development and behavior. In P. Mussen (Ed.), *Handbook of child psychology,* Vol. 2 (pp. 96–155). New York: Wiley.

Parnell, R. W. (1953). Physique and choice of faculty. *British Medical Journal, 2,* 472–475.

Parsons, J. E., Adler, T. F., & Kaczala, C. M. (1982). Socialization: achievement attitudes and beliefs: Parental Influences. *Child Development, 53,* 310–321.

Passini, F. T., & Norman, W. T. (1966). A universal conception of personality structure? *Journal of Personality and Social Psychology, 4,* 44–49.

Patterson, G. R., Reid, J. B., & Dishion, T. J. (1992). *Antisocial boys.* Eugene, OR: Castalia.

Patterson, K. E., & Kay, J. (1982). Letter-by-letter reading: Psychological descriptions of a neurological syndrome. *Quarterly Journal of Experimental Psychology, 34a,* 411–471.

Patry, J. L. (1992). A framework for the explanation of cross-situational consistency in social behavior. *New Ideas in Psychology, 10,* 47–62.

Paul, G. L. (1966). *Insight vs. desensitization: An experiment in anxiety reduction.* Stanford, CA: Stanford University Press.

Paul, G. L. (1967). Insight versus desensitization in psychotherapy two years after termination. *Journal of Consulting Psychology, 31,* 333–348.

Paul, W., Weinrich, J. D., Gensiorek, J. C., & Hotvedt, M. E. (1982). *Homosexuality: Social, psychological and biological issues.* Beverly Hills, CA: Sage.

Paulus, P. B. (1983). Group influence on individual task performance. In P. B. Paulus (Ed.), *Basic Group Processes* (pp. 97–120). New York: Springer.

Pavlov, I. P. (1927). *Conditioned reflexes* (G. V. Anrep, Trans.). London: Oxford University Press.

Paykel, E. S. (Ed.). (1982). *Handbook of affective disorders.* New York: Guilford Press.

Payne, D. G. (1986). Hypermnesia for pictures and words: Testing the recall level hypothesis. *Journal of Experimental Psychology: Learning, Memory, and Cognition, 12,* 16–29.

Payne, J. W. (1985). Psychology of risky decisions. In G. Wright (Ed.), *Behavioral decision making* (pp. 3–23). New York: Plenum.

Pearce, J. M., & Hall, G. (1980). A model for Pavlovian learning: Variations in the effectiveness of conditioned but not of unconditioned stimuli. *Psychological Review, 87,* 532–552.

Pease, D., & Gleason, J. B. (1985). Gaining meaning: Semantic development. In J. B. Gleason (Ed.), *The development of language.* Columbus, OH: Merrill.

Peck, J. W. (1973). Discussion: Thirst(s) resulting from bodily water imbalances. In A. N. Epstein, H. R. Kissileff, & E. Stellar (Eds.), *The neuropsychology of thirst: New findings and advances in concepts.* Washington, DC: Winston.

Peck, J. W., & Novin, D. (1971). Evidence that osmoreceptors mediating drinking in rabbits are in the lateral preoptic region. *Journal of Comparative and Physiological Psychology, 74,* 134–147.

Peele, S. (1988). Fools for love: The romantic ideal, psychological theory, and addictive love. In R. J. Sternberg & M. L. Barnes (Eds.), *The psychology of love* (pp. 159–188). New Haven, CT: Yale University Press.

Peele, S., & Brodsky, A. (1976). *Love and addiction.* New York: NAL.

Peery, J. C. (1980). Neonate and adult head movement: No and yes revisited. *Developmental Psychology, 16,* 245–250.

Pelligrino, J. W. (1985, October). Anatomy of analogy. *Psychology Today,* pp. 49–54.

Pendery, M. L., Maltzman, I. M., & West, L. J. (1982). Controlled drinking by alcoholics? New findings and a reevaluation of a major affirmative study. *Science, 217,* 169–174.

Penfield, W., & Jasper, H. H. (1954). *Epilepsy and the functional anatomy of the human brain.* Boston: Little, Brown.

Penfield, W., & Rasmussen, T. (1968). *The cerebral cortex of man: A clinical study of localization of function.* New York: Hafner.

Pennebaker, J. W. (1989). Confession, inhibition, and disease. *Advances in Experimental Social Psychology, 22,* 211–244.

Pennebaker, J. W., Kiecolt-Glaser, J. K., & Glaser, R. (1988). Disclosure of traumas and immune function: Health implications for psychotherapy. *Journal of Consulting & Clinical Psychology, 56,* 239–245.

Perlmutter, M. (1978). What is memory aging the aging of? *Developmental Psychology, 14,* 330–345.

Perlmutter, M., & Hall, E. (1985). *Adult development and aging.* New York: Wiley.

Perls, F. S. (1970). Four lectures. In J. Fagan & I. L. Sheperd (Eds.), *Gestalt therapy now.* Palo Alto, CA: Science and Behavior Books.

Perry, T. L., Hansen, S., & Kloster, M. (1973). Huntington's chorea: Deficiency of 5-aminobutyric acid in brain. *New England Journal of Medicine, 288,* 337–342.

Pert, C. B., Snowman, A. M., & Snyder, S. H. (1974). Localization of opiate receptor binding in presynaptic membranes of rat brain. *Brain Research, 70,* 184–188.

Peterhans, E., & von der Heydt, R. (1991). Subjective contours: Bridging the gap between psychophysics and physiology. *Trends in Neurosciences, 14,* 112–119.

Peters, T. J., & Austin, N. (1985). *A passion for excellence: The leadership difference.* New York: Random House.

Peters, T. J., & Waterman, R. H. (1982). *In search of excellence: Lessons from America's best-run companies.* New York: Harper & Row.

Petersen, A. C., & Ebata, A. T. (1987). Developmental transitions and adolescent problem behavior: Implications for prevention and intervention. In K. Hurrelmann (Ed.), *Social prevention and intervention.* New York: de Gruyter.

Petersen, A. C., Compas, B. E., Brooks-Gunn, J., Stemmler, M., Ey, S., & Grant, K. E. (1993). Depression in adolescence. *American Psychologist, 48,* 155–168.

Petersen, R. T., Beecher, M. D., Zoloth, S. R., Moody, D. B., & Stebbins, W. C. (1978). Neural lateralization of species-specific vocalizations by Japanese macaques (*Macaca fuscata*). *Science, 202,* 324–327.

Peterson, A. C. (1985). Pubertal development as a cause of disturbance. *Genetic, Social, and General Psychology Monographs, 111,* 205–232.

Peterson, A. C., & Taylor, B. (1980). The biological approach to adolescence: Biological change and psychological adaptation. In J. Adelson (Ed.), *Handbook of adolescent psychology.* New York: Wiley.

Peterson, C., & Seligman, M. E. P. (1984). Causal explanations as a risk factor for depression: Theory and evidence. *Psychological Review, 91,* 37–61.

Peterson, C. & Seligman, M. E. P. (1987). Explanatory style and illness. *Journal of Personality, 55,* 237–265.

Peterson, L. R., & Peterson, M. J. (1959). Short-term retention of individual items. *Journal of Experimental Psychology, 58,* 193–198.

Peterson, M. A., & Gibson, B. S. (1993). Shape recognition inputs to figure-ground organization in three-dimensional displays. *Cognitive Psychology, 25,* 388–429.

Petrillo, M., Ritter, C. A., & Powers, A. S. (1994). A role for acetylcholine in spatial memory in turtles. *Physiology & Behavior, 56,* 135–141.

Pettibone, T. J., & Jernigan, H. W. (1989). Applied psychology in education. In W. L. Gregory and W. J. Burroughs (Eds.), *Introduction to applied psychology.* Glenview, IL: Scott, Foresman.

Petty, R. E., & Cacioppo, J. T. (1986). The elaboration likelihood model of persuasion. *Advances in Experimental Social Psychology, 19,* 123–205.

Pfaffman, C. (1955). Gustatory nerve impulses in rat, cat, and rabbit. *Journal of Neurophysiology, 18,* 429–440.

Pfungst, O. (1911). Clever Hans (The horse of Mr. Van Osten). New York: Hoth.

Phares, E. J. (1988). *Introduction to personality* (2nd ed.). Glenview, IL: Scott, Foresman.

Phelps, M. E., & Mazziotta, J. C. (1985). Positron emission tomography: Human brain function and biochemistry. *Science, 228,* 799–809.

Phillips, B. N. (1986). The impact of education and training on school psychological services. In S. N. Elliott & J. C. Witt (Eds.), *The delivery of psychological services in schools.* Hillsdale, NJ: Erlbaum.

Phillips, D. P. (1986). Natural experiments on the effects of mass media violence on fatal aggression: Strengths and weaknesses of a new approach. In L. Berkowitz (Ed.), *Advances in experimental social psychology* (Vol. 19). New York: Academic Press.

Phinney, J. S., & Alipuria, L. L. (1990). Ethnic identity in college students from four minority groups. *Journal of Adolescence, 13,* 171–183.

Piaget, J. (1926). *Judgment and reasoning in the child.* New York: Harcourt & Brace.

Piaget, J. (1929). *The child's conception of the world.* New York: Harcourt & Brace.

Piaget, J. (1932). *The moral judgment of the child.* New York: Harcourt, Brace and Company.

Piaget, J. (1954). *The construction of reality in the child.* New York: Basic Books.

Piaget, J. (1962). *Play, dreams, and imitation in childhood.* New York: Norton.

Piccione, C., Hilgard, E. R., & Zimbardo, P. G. (1989). On the degree of stability of measured hypnotizability over a 25-year period. *Journal of Personality and Social Psychology, 56,* 289–295.

Platt, J. J. (1991). Behavior therapy as problem solving. *Contemporary Psychology, 36,* 1090–1091.

Pliner, P., Hart, H., Kohn, J., & Saari, D. (1974). Compliance without pressure: Some further data on the foot-in-the-door technique. *Journal of Experimental Social Psychology, 10,* 17–22.

Plomin, R. (1989). Environment and genes: Determinants of behavior. *American Psychologist, 44,* 105–111.

Plomin, R., & Daniels, D. (1987). Why are children in the same family so different from one another? *Behavioral and Brain Sciences, 10*(1), 1–15.

Plomin, R., & DeFries, J. C. (1980). Genetics and intelligence: Recent data. *Intelligence, 4,* 15–24.

Plomin, R. & Rende, R. (1991). Human behavioral genetics. *Annual Review of Psychology, 42,* 161–190.

Plomin, R., Chipuer, H. M., & Loehlin, J. C. (1990). Behavioral genetics and personality. In L. A. Pervin (Ed.) *Handbook of Personalilty Theory and Research.* New York: Guilford, pp. 225–243.

Plomin, R., DeFries, J. C., & Fulker, D. W. (1988). *Nature and Nurture during infancy and early childhood.* New York: Cambridge.

Plomin, R., DeFries, J. C., & McClearn, G. E. (1980). *Behavioral genetics: A primer.* San Francisco: Freeman.

Plomin, R., DeFries, J. C., & McClearn, G. E. (1989). *Behavioral genetics: A primer.* New York: Freeman.

Plomin, R., DeFries, J. C., & McClearn, G. E. (1990). *Behavioral Genetics: A Primer.* Second Edition. New York: W. H. Freeman and Co.

Plutchik, R. (1980). *Emotion: A psychoevolutionary synthesis.* New York: Academic Press.

Poggio, T. (1984). Vision by man and machine. *Scientific American, 250,* 106–116.

Poincaré, H. (1913). Mathematical creation. In G. H. Halstead (Trans.), *The foundations of science.* New York: Science Press.

Polit, D. F., & Falbo, T. (1988). The intellectual achievement of only children. *Journal of Biosocial Science, 20,* 275–285.

Polivy, J., & Herman, C. P. (1985). Dieting and binging: A causal analysis. *American Psychologist, 40,* 193–201.

Polivy, J., & Herman, C. P. (1987). The diagnosis and treatment of normal eating. *Journal of Consulting & Clinical Psychology, 55,* 635–644.

Polivy, J., & Herman, C. P. (1991). Good and bad dieters: Self-perception and reaction to a dietary challenge. *International Journal of Eating Disorders, 10,* 91–99.

Polivy, J., & Herman, C. P. (1993). Etiology of Binge Eating: Psychological Mechanisms. In C. G. Fairburn & G. T. Wilson (Eds.), *Binge eating: nature, assessment and treatment.* New York: Guilford Press.

Pollins, L. D. (1983). The effects of acceleration on the social and emotional development of gifted students. In C. Benbow and J. Stanley (Eds.), *Academic precocity.* Baltimore: Johns Hopkins University Press.

Pollitt, E., Garza, C., & Leibel, R. L. (1984). Nutrition and public policy. In H. W. Stevenson & A. E. Siegel (Eds.), *Child development research and social policy,* Vol. 1 (pp. 421–470). Chicago: University of Chicago Press.

Pomerantz, J. R. (1981). Perceptual organization in information processing. In M. Kubovy, & J. R. Pomerantz (Eds.), *Perceptual organization.* Hillsdale, NJ: Erlbaum.

Pomerantz, J. R. (1983). The rubber pencil illusion. *Perception & Psychophysics, 33,* 365–368.

Poole, D. A., Lindsay, D. S., Memon, A. & Bull, R. (1995). Psychotherapy and the recovery of memories of childhood sexual abuse: U. S. and British practioners' beliefs, practices and experiences. *Journal of Consulting and Clinical Psychology, 63,* 426–437.

Poon, L. (1985). Differences in human memory with aging: Nature, causes, and clinical implications. In J. E. Birren & K. W. Shaie (Eds.), *Handbook of the psychology of aging* (2nd ed.). New York: Van Nostrand Reinhold.

Poon, L., Fozard, J., Paulschock, D., & Thomas, J. (1979). A questionnaire assessment of age differences in retention of recent and remote events. *Experimental Aging Research, 5,* 401–411.

Posner, M. I., & Snyder, C. R. R. (1975). Attention and cognitive control. In R. L. Solso (Ed.), *Information processing and cognition: The Loyola Symposium.* Hillsdale, NJ: Erlbaum.

Posner, M. I., Peterson, S. E., Fox, P. T., & Paichle, M. E. (1988). Localization of cognitive operations in the human brain. *Science, 240,* 1627–1631.

Poteat, G. M., Wuensch, K. L., & Gregg, N. B. (1988). An investigation of differential prediction with the WISC-R. *Journal of School Psychology, 26,* 59–68.

Potts, G. R. (1978). The role of inference in memory for real and artificial information. In R. Revlis & R. Mayer (Eds.), *Human reasoning.* Washington, DC: Winston/Wiley.

Poulton, E. C. (1977). Continuous intense noise masks auditory feedback and inner speech. *Psychological Bulletin, 84,* 997–1001.

Poulton, E. C. (1978). A new look at the effects of noise: A rejoinder. *Psychological Bulletin, 85,* 1068–1079.

Power, A. C., & Cowen, P. J. (1992). Fluoxetine and suicidal behaviour: Some clinical and theoretical aspects of a controversy. *British Journal of Psychiatry, 161,* 735–741.

Prasse, D. P., & Reschly, D. J. (1986). Larry P.: A case of segregation, testing, or program efficacy? *Exceptional Children, 52,* 333–346.

Pratkanis, A. R. (1992). The cargo-cult science of subliminal persuasion. *Skeptical Inquirer, 16,* 260–272.

Pratkanis, A. R., & Greenwald, A. G. (1989). A sociocognitive model of attitude structure and function. In *Advances in experimental social psychology,* Vol. 22 (pp.

245–285). San Diego, CA: Academic Press.

Premack, A. J., & Premack, D. (1972). Teaching language to an ape. *Scientific American, 227,* 92–99.

Premack, D. (1962). Reversability of the reinforcement relation. *Science, 136,* 255–257.

Premack, D. (1965). Reinforcement theory. In D. Levine (Ed.), *Nebraska symposium on motivation* (pp. 123–180). Lincoln, NE: University of Nebraska Press.

Premack, D. (1971). Language in chimpanzee? *Science, 172,* 808–822.

Premack, D. (1985). "Gavagai!" or the future history of the animal language controversy. *Cognition, 19,* 207–296.

Pressley, M. (1982). Elaboration and memory development. *Child Development, 53,* 269–309.

Pribram, K. H. (1971). *Languages of the brain.* Englewood Cliffs, NJ: Prentice-Hall.

Price, R. H., & Bouffard, D. L. (1974). Behavioral appropriateness and situational constraints as dimensions of social behavior. *Journal of Personality and Social Psychology, 30,* 579–586.

Prinzmetal, W. (1992). The word-superiority effect does not require a T-scope. *Perception & Psychophysics, 51,* 473–484.

Provost, J. A., & Anchors, S. (Eds.). (1987). *Applications of the Myers-Briggs Type Indicator in higher education.* Palo Alto, CA: Consulting Psychologists Press.

Pryor, J. B., & Ostrom, T. M. (1987). Social cognition theory of group processes. In B. Mullen & G. R. Goethels (Eds.), *Theories of Group Behavior.* New York: Springer-Verlag.

Pryzwansky, W. B. (1986). Indirect service delivery: Considerations for future directions in consultation. *School Psychology Review, 15,* 479–488.

Pulos, S. (1992). Adults' understanding of conservation of horizontality. *Journal of General Psychology, 119,* 99–100.

Purghe, F., & Coren, S. (1992). Subjective Contours 1900–1990: Research trends and bibliography. *Perception & Psychophysics, 51,* 291–304.

Pygmy chimp readily learns language skill (1985, June 24). *New York Times,* p. C1.

Pylyshyn, A. (1973). What the mind's eye tells the mind's brain: A critique of mental imagery. *Psychological Bulletin, 80,* 1–24.

Pyszczynski, T., & Greenberg, J. (1987). Toward an integration of cognitive and motivational perspectives on social inference: A biased hypothesis-testing model. *Advances in Experimental Social Psychology, 21,* 195–211.

Q

Quattrone, G. A. (1986). On the perception of a group's variability. In S. Worchel & W. G. Austin (Eds.), *Psychology of intergroup relations* (pp. 25–48). Chicago: Nelson-Hall.

Quigley, B., Gaes, G. G., & Tedeschi, J. T. (1989). Does asking make a difference? Effects of initiator, possible gain, and risk on attributed altruism. *Journal of Social Psychology, 129,* 259–268.

Quinn, S. (1987). *A mind of her own: The life of Karen Horney.* New York: Summit.

R

Raaijmakers, J. G. W., & Shiffrin, R. M. (1981). Search of associative memory. *Psychological Review, 88,* 93–134.

Rachman, S. J., & Wilson, G. T. (1980). *The effects of psychological therapy.* London: Pergamon.

Rachman, S., & Hodgson, R. J. (1968). Experimentally induced "sexual fetishism": Replication and development. *Psychological Record, 18,* 25–27.

Radke-Yarrow, M., Zahn-Waxler, C., & Chapman, M. (1983). The development of prosocial behavior. In P. Mussen (Ed.), *Handbook of child psychology.* New York: Wiley.

Ramachandran, V. S., & Gregory, R. L. (1991). Perceptual filling in of artificially induced scotomas in human vision. *Nature, 350,* 699–702.

Rahe, R. H. (1974). The pathway between subjects' recent life changes and their near future illness reports: Representative results and methodological issues. In B. S. Dohrenwend & B. P. Dohrenwend (Eds.), *Stressful life events: The nature and effects.* New York: Wiley.

Rajaram, S. (1993). Remembering and knowing: Two means of access to the personal past. *Memory & Cognition, 21,* 89–102.

Rakic, P. (1988). Specification of cerebral cortical areas. *Science, 241,* 170–176.

Ray, O. S. (1983). *Drugs, society, and human behavior* (3rd ed.). St. Louis: Mosby.

Raynor, J. O. (1970). Relationships between achievement-related motives, future orientation and academic performance. *Journal of Personality and Social Psychology, 15,* 28–33.

Read, J. A., & Miller, F. C. (1977). Fetal heart rate acceleration in response to acoustic stimulation as a measure of fetal well-being. *American Journal of Obstetrics and Gynecology, 129,* 512–517.

Reason, J. T. (1984). Absent-mindedness and cognitive control. In J. E. Harris & P. E.

Morris (Eds.), *Everyday memory, actions and absent-mindedness*. London: Academic Press.

Rechtschaffen, A., Gilliland, M. A., Bergmann, B. M., & Winter, J. B. (1983). Physiological correlates of prolonged sleep deprivation in rats. *Science, 221,* 182–184.

Read, D. F. (1994). Understanding bystander misidentifications: The role of familiarity and contextual knowledge. In D. F. Ross, J. D. Read & M. P. Toglia (Eds.), *Adult eyewitness testimony: Current trends and developments*. Cambridge: Cambridge University Press.

Redd, E. M., & de Castro, J. M. (1992). Social facilitation of eating: Effects of instructions to eat alone or with others. *Physiology & Behavior, 52*(4), 749–754.

Redding, G. M., & Wallace, B. (1988). Adaptive mechanisms in perceptual-motor coordination: Components of prism adaptation. *Journal of Motor Behavior, 20,* 242–254.

Redick, R. W., & Johnson, C. (1974). *Marital status, living arrangements and family characteristics of admissions to state and county mental hospitals and outpatient psychiatric clinics, United States, 1970* (Statistical Note 100, NIMH). Washington, D. C.: U. S. Government Printing Office.

Ree, M. J., & Earles, J. A. (1992). Intelligence is the best predictor of job performance. *Current Directions in Psychological Science, 1,* 86–89.

Reed, C. F. (1984). Terrestrial passage theory of the moon illusion. *Journal of Experimental Psychology: General, 113,* 489–500.

Reed, C. F., & Krupinski, E. A. (1992). The target in the celestial (moon) illusion. *Journal of Experimental Psychology: Human Perception and Performance, 18,* 247–256.

Regan, D. T., & Fazio, R. H. (1977). On the consistency between attitudes and behavior: Look to the method of attitude formation. *Journal of Experimental Social Psychology, 13,* 38–45.

Rehm, J., Steinleitner, J., & Lilli, W. (1987). Wearing uniforms and aggression: A field experiment. *European Journal of Social Psychology, 17,* 357–360.

Reich, R. B. (1992). Is Japan really out to get us? *New York Times Book Review,* February 9, 1, 24–25.

Reicher, G. M. (1969). Perceptual recognition as a function of meaningfulness of stimulus materials. *Journal of Experimental Psychology, 81,* 275–280.

Reid, P. J., & Shettleworth, S. J. (1992). Detection of cryptic prey: Search image or search rate? *Journal of Experimental Psychology: Animal Behavior Processes, 18,* 173–186.

Reilly, N. P., & Morris, W. N. (1983). The role of arousal in the induction of mood. Paper presented at the meeting of the American Psychological Association, Anaheim, Calif.

Reinhardt-Rutland, A. H. (1990). The vista paradox: Is the effect partly explained by induced motion? *Perception and Psychophysics, 47,* 95–96.

Reis, H. T., Wilson, I. M., Monestere, C., Bernstein, S., Clark, K., Seidl, E., Franco, M., Gioioso, E., Freeman, L., & Radoane, K. (1990). What is smiling is beautiful and good. *European Journal of Social Psychology, 20,* 259–267.

Reiser, M., & Nielson, M. (1980). Investigative hypnosis: A developing specialty. *American Journal of Clinical Hypnosis, 23,* 75–83.

Renfrew, J. W., & Hutchinson, R. R. (1983). Discriminated instrumental learning by an acute "encephale isole" preparation. *Physiology & Behavior, 30*(5), 703–709.

Renner, K. E. (1963). Influence of deprivation and availability of goal box cues on the temporal gradient of reinforcement. *Journal of Comparative and Physiological Psychology, 56,* 101–104.

Repetti, L., Matthews, A., & Waldron, I. (1989). Employment and women's health— Effects of paid employment on women's mental and physical health. *American Psychologist, 44,* 1394–1401.

Reschly, D. J. (1988). Larry P.! Larry P.! Why the California sky fell on IQ testing. *Journal of School Psychology, 26,* 199–205.

Reschly, D. J., & Ward, S. M. (1991). Use of adaptive behavior measures and overrepresentation of black students in programs for students with mild mental retardation. *American Journal of Mental Retardation, 96,* 257–268.

Rescorla, R. A. (1968). Probability of shock in the presence and absence of CS in fear conditioning. *Journal of Comparative and Physiological Psychology, 66,* 1–5.

Rescorla, R. A. (1978). Some implications of a cognitive perspective on Pavlovian conditioning. In S. H. Hulse, H. Fowler, & W. K. Honig (Eds.), *Cognitive processes in animal behavior*. Hillsdale, NJ: Erlbaum.

Rescorla, R. A., & Wagner, A. R. (1972). A theory of Pavlovian conditioning: Variations in the effectiveness of reinforcement and nonreinforcement. In A. H. Black & W. F. Prokasy (Eds.), *Classical conditioning II: Current research and theory.* New York: Appleton-Century-Crofts.

Resnick, M. N., & Nunno, V. J. (1991). The Nuremberg mind redeemed: A comprehensive analysis of the Rorschachs of Nazi war criminals. *Journal of Personality Assessment, 57,* 19–29.

Rest, J. R. (1975). Longitudinal study of the defining issues test of moral judgment: A strategy for analyzing developmental change. *Developmental Psychology, 11,* 738–748.

Retherford, R. D., & Sewell, W. H. (1991). Birth order and intelligence: Further tests of the confluence model. *American Sociological Review, 56,* 141–158.

Revelle, W., Amaral, P., & Turiff, S. (1976). Introversion/extraversion, time stress, and caffeine: Effect on verbal performance. *Science, 192,* 149–150.

Revenson, T. A. (1990). All other things are not equal: An ecological approach to personality and disease. In Friedman, H. S. *Personality and Disease.* New York: Wiley, pp. 65–94.

Reynolds, C. R., Chastain, R. L., Kaufman, A. S., & McLean, J. E. (1987). Demographic characteristics and IQ among adults: Analysis of the WAIS-R standardization sample as a function of the stratification variables. *Journal of School Psychology, 25,* 323–342.

Reynolds, G. S. (1968). *A primer of operant conditioning.* Glenview, IL: Scott, Foresman.

Richards, R. H., Boxer, A. M., Petersen, A. C., & Albrecht, R. (1990). Relation of weight to body image in pubertal girls and boys from two communities. *Developmental Psychology, 26,* 313–321.

Richman, A. L., LeVine, R. A., New, R. S., Howrigan, G. A., Wells-Nystrom, B., & LeVine, S. E. (1988). Maternal behavior to infants in five countries. In R. A. LeVine, P. M. Miller, & M. M. West (Eds.), *New directions for child development: Parental behavior in diverse societies.* San Francisco: Jossey-Bass.

Richman, A. L., Miller, P. M., & LeVine, R. A. (1992). Cultural and educational variations in maternal responsiveness. *Developmental Psychology, 28,* 614–621.

Ridgway, S. (1989). Sleep apnea. *The Journal: Magazine of Methodist Hospital, Houston, Texas, 28,* 11–19.

Riegel, K. (1976). The dialectics of human development. *American Psychologist, 31,* 689–699.

Riese, M. L. (1990). Neonatal temperament in monozygotic and dizygotic twin pairs. *Child Development, 61,* 1230–1237.

Riesen, A. H. (1960). The effects of stimulus deprivation on the development and atrophy of the visual sensory system. *American Journal of Orthopsychiatry, 30,* 23–26.

Riesen, A. H. (1965). Effects of early deprivation of photic stimulation. In S. Osler & R. Cooke (Eds.), *The biosocial bases of mental retardation.* Baltimore: Johns Hopkins University Press.

Rips, L. J. (1988). Deduction. In R. J. Sternberg & E. E. Smith (Eds.), *The psychology of human thought* (pp. 118–152). Cambridge: Cambridge University Press.

Rips, L. J., & Marcus, S. L. (1977). Suppositions and the analysis of conditional sentences. In M. A. Just & P. A. Carpenter (Eds.), *Cognitive process in comprehension.* Hillsdale, NJ: Erlbaum.

Rizley, R. C., & Rescorla, R. A. (1972). Associations in second-order conditioning and sensory preconditioning. *Journal of Comparative and Physiological Psychology, 81,* 1–11.

Robbins, W. J., et al. (1929). *Growth.* New Haven, CT: Yale University Press.

Roberts, W. A. (1984). Some issues in animal spatial memory. In H. L. Roitblat, T. G. Bever, & H. S. Terrace (Eds.), *Animal cognition* (pp. 425–443). Hillsdale, NJ: Erlbaum.

Roberts, W. A., & Van Veldhuizen, N. (1985). Spatial memory in pigeons on the radial maze. *Journal of Experimental Psychology: Animal Behavior Processes, 11,* 241–260.

Robertson, D., Krane, R. V., & Garrud, P. (1984). Second-order conditioned taste aversion in rats: Shared modality is not sufficient to promote an association between S2 and S1. *Animal Learning and Behavior, 12,* 315–322.

Robinson, H. (1983). A case for radical acceleration. In C. Benbow & J. Stanley (Eds.), *Academic precocity.* Baltimore: Johns Hopkins University Press.

Robinson, N. M., & Robinson, H. B. (1976). *The mentally retarded child: A psychological approach.* New York: McGraw-Hill.

Rock, I. (1984). *Perception.* New York: Scientific American Library.

Rock, I. (1988). On Thompson's inverted face phenomenon. *Perception, 17,* 815–817.

Rockstein, M. J., & Sussman, M. (1979). *Biology of aging.* Belmont, Calif.: Wadsworth.

Rodin, J. (1981). Current status of the internal-external hypothesis for obesity: What went wrong? *American Psychologist, 36,* 361–372.

Rodin, J., Silberstein, L., & Striegel-Moore, R. (1985). Women and weight: A normative discontent. In T. B. Sonderegger (Ed.), *Psychology and gender. Nebraska symposium on motivation, 1984.* Lincoln, NE: University of Nebraska Press.

Rodin, J., Slochower, J., & Fleming, D. (1977). The effects of degree of obesity, age on onset, and energy deficit on external responsiveness. *Journal of Comparative and Physiological Psychology, 91,* 586–597.

Rodriquez, J. (1990). Childhood injuries in the United States. *American Journal of Diseases of Childhood, 144,* 627–646.

Roediger, H. L. (1980a). The effectiveness of four mnemonics in ordering recall. *Journal of Experimental Psychology: Human Learning and Memory 6,* 558–567.

Roediger, H. L. (1980b). Memory metaphors in cognitive psychology. *Memory and Cognition, 8,* 231–246.

Roediger, H. L. (1985). Remembering Ebbinghaus. *Contemporary Psychology, 30,* 519–523.

Roediger, H. L., & Guynn, M. J. (1995). Retrieval processes. In E. J. Bjork & R. A. Bjork (Eds.), *Handbook of perception and cognition* (Vol. 10). New York: Academic Press.

Roediger, H. L., & McDermott, K. B. (1993). Implicit memory in normal human subjects. In F. Boller & J. Grafman (Eds.), *Handbook of neuropsychology* (Vol. 8, pp. 62–131). Amsterdam: Elsevier.

Roediger, H. L., & Neely, J. H. (1982). Retrieval blocks in episodic and semantic memory. *Canadian Journal of Psychology, 36,* 213–242.

Roediger, H. L., & Stevens, M. C. (1970). The effects of delayed presentation of the object of aggression on pain-induced fighting. *Psychonomic Science, 21,* 55–56.

Roff, J. D., & Knight, R. (1981). Family characteristics, childhood symptoms, and adult outcome in schizophrenia. *Journal of Abnormal Psychology, 90,* 510–520.

Rogers, C. R. (1970a). *Client-centered therapy* (2nd ed.) Boston: Houghton Mifflin.

Rogers, C. R. (1970b). *On becoming a person.* Boston: Houghton Mifflin.

Rogers, C. R. (1980). Client-centered psychotherapy. In H. I. Kaplan, A. M. Freeman, & B. J. Sadock (Eds.), *Comprehensive textbook of psychiatry: III.* Baltimore: Williams & Wilkins.

Rogers, R. (1987). APA's position on the insanity defense: Empiricism versus emotionalism. *American Psychology, 42,* 840–848.

Rogoff, B. (1982). Integrating context and cognitive development. In M. E. Lamb & A. L. Brown (Eds.), *Advances in developmental psychology* (Vol. 2). Hillsdale, NJ: Erlbaum.

Rokeach, M. (1964). *The three Christs of Ypsilanti: A psychological study.* New York: Knopf.

Rolls, B. J. (1986). Sensory-specific satiety. *Nutrition Review, 44,* 93–101.

Rolls, B. J., Laster, L. J., & Summerfelt, A. (1989). Hunger and food intake following consumption of low-calorie foods. *Appetite, 13,* 115–127.

Root, A. W. (1973). Endocrinology of puberty: 1. Normal sexual maturation. *Journal of Pediatrics, 83,* 187–200.

Rorschach, H. (1921). *Psychodiagnostics.* Berne: Hans Huber.

Rosa, R. R., Bonnet, M. H., & Warm, J. S. (1983). Recovery of performance during sleep following sleep deprivation. *Psychophysiology, 20,* 152–159.

Rosch, E. (1973). On the internal structure of perceptual and semantic categories. In T. E. Moore (Ed.), *Cognitive development and the acquisition of language.* New York: Academic Press.

Rosch, E. (1975). Cognitive representations of semantic categories. *Journal of Experimental Psychology: General, 104,* 192–232.

Rosch, E. (1977). Human categorization. In N. Warren (Ed.), *Advances in cross-cultural psychology* (Vol. 1). London: Academic Press.

Rose, R. J., Koskenvuo, M., Kaprio, J., Sarna, S., & Langinvainio, H. (1988). Shared genes, shared experiences, and similarity of personality: Data from 14,288 adult Finnish co-twins. *Journal of Personality and Social Psychology, 54,* 161–171.

Rosenberg, M., & Simmons, R. G. (1972). *Black and white self-esteem: The urban school child.* Rose Monograph Series. Washington, DC: American Sociological Association.

Rosenfeld, O. (1942/1991). Oskar Rosenfeld's Notebooks. In A. Adelson & R. Lapides (Eds.) *Lodz Ghetto.* New York: Penguin.

Rosenhan, D. L. (1970). The natural socialization of altruistic autonomy. In J. Macaulay & L. Berkowitz (Eds.), *Altruism and helping behavior.* New York: Academic Press.

Rosenhan, D. L. (1973). On being sane in insane places. *Science, 179,* 250–258.

Rosenhan, D. L., & Seligman, M. E. P. (1989). *Abnormal Psychology* (2nd ed.). New York: Norton.

Rosenhan, D. L., Salovey, P., Karylowski, J., & Hargis, K. (1981). Emotion and altruism. In J. P. Rushton & R. M. Sorrentino (Eds.), *Altruism and helping behavior: Social, personality, and developmental perspectives.* Hillsdale, NJ: Erlbaum.

Rosenheim, M. K., & Testa, M. F. (1992). *Early parenthood and coming of age in the 1990's.* New Brunswick, NJ: Rutgers University Press.

Rosenman, R. H., Brand, R. J., Jenkins, C. D., Friedman, M., Straus, R., & Wurm, M. (1975). Coronary heart disease in the Western Collaborative Group Study: Final follow-up of 8 1/2 years. *Journal of the American Medical Association, 233,* 872–877.

Rosenman, R. H., Brand, R. J., Jenkins, C. D., Friedman, M., Straus, R., & Wurm, M. (1975). Coronary heart disease in the Western Collaborative Group Study: Final follow-up of 8 1/2 years. *Journal of the American Medical Association, 233,* 872–877.

Rosenthal, D. (1970). *Genetic theory and abnormal behavior.* New York: McGraw-Hill.

Rosenthal, R. (1984). *Meta-analytic procedures for social research.* Beverly Hills, CA: Sage.

Rosenthal, R., & Jacobson, L. (1968). *Pygmalian in the classroom.* New York: Holt, Rinehart & Winston.

Rosenthal, T. L., & Bandura, S. (1978). Psychological modeling: Theory and practice. In S. L. Garfield & A. E. Bergin (Eds.), *Handbook of psychotherapy and behavior change.* New York: Wiley.

Rosenzweig, M. R., & Lieman, A. L. (1982). *Physiological psychology.* Lexington, MA: Heath.

Ross, C. (1990). Twelve cognitive errors about multiple personality disorder. *American Journal of Psychotherapy, 44,* 348–356.

Ross, D. F., Ceci, S. J., Dunning, D., & Toglia, M. P. (1994).Unconscious transference and line-up identification: Toward a memory blending approach. In D. F. Ross, J. D. Read & M. P. Toglia (Eds.), *Adult eyewitness testimony: Current trends and developments.* Cambridge: Cambridge University Press.

Ross, H., Tesla, C., Kenyon, B., & Lollis, S. (1990). Maternal intervention in toddler peer conflict: The socialization of principles of justice. *Developmental Psychology, 26,* 994–1003.

Ross, L. D. (1977). The intuitive psychologist and his shortcomings: Distortions in the attribution process. In L. Berkowitz (Ed.), *Advances in experimental social psychology* (Vol. 2). New York: Academic Press.

Ross, L. D. (1988). Situationist perspectives on the obedience experiments. *Contemporary Psychology, 33,* 101–104.

Ross, L. D., Amabile, T. M., & Steinmetz, J. L. (1977). Social roles, social control, and biases in social perception processes. *Journal of Personality and Social Psychology, 35,* 485–494.

Ross, L. D., Rodin, J., & Zimbardo, P. G. (1969). Toward an attribution therapy: The reduction of fear through induced cognitive-emotional misattribution. *Journal of Personality and Social Psychology, 12,* 279–288.

Ross, L., & Nisbett, R. E. (1991). *The Person and the Situation: Perspectives of Social Psychology.* New York: McGraw-Hill.

Ross, L., Greene, D., & House, P. (1977). The false consensus effect: An egocentric bias in social perception and attribution processes. *Journal of Personality and Social Psychology, 13,* 279–301.

Ross, S. M., & Ross, L. E. (1971). Comparison of trace and delay classical eyelid conditioning as a function of interstimulus interval. *Journal of Experimental Psychology, 91,* 165–167.

Rosser, R. (1994). *Cognitive development.* Boston: Allyn and Bacon.

Rotter, J. B. (1966). Generalized expectancies for internal versus external control of reinforcement. *Psychological Monographs, 80,* Whole No. 609.

Rotton, J., Barry, T., Frey, J., & Soler, E. (1978). Air pollution and interpersonal attraction. *Journal of Applied Social Psychology, 8,* 57–71.

Rovee-Collier, C. (1993). The capacity of long-term memory in infancy. *Current Directions in Psychological Science, 2,* 130–135.

Rovee-Collier, C. K. (1987, April). Infant memory. Paper presented at the annual meeting of the Eastern Psychological Association, Crystal City, VA.

Rovee-Collier, C. K. (1993). The capacity for long-term memory in infancy. *Current Directions in Psychological Science, 2,* 130–135.

Rovee-Collier, C. K., & Sullivan, M. W. (1980). Organization of infant memory. *Journal of Experimental Psychology: Human Learning and Development, 6,* 798–807.

Rowland, N. E., & Antelman, S. M. (1976). Stress-induced hyperphagia and obesity in rats: A possible model for understanding human obesity. *Science, 191,* 310–312.

Rozin, P. (1991). The importance of social factors in understanding the acquisition of food habits. In E. D. Capaldi & T. L. Powley (Eds.), *Taste, experience and feeding.* Washington, DC: American Psychological Association.

Rozin, P., & Kalat, J. W. (1971). Specific hungers and poison avoidance as adaptive specializations of learning. *Psychological Review, 78,* 459–486.

Rozin, P., Haidt, J., & McCauley, C. (1995). Disgust. In M. Lewis & C. Haviland (Eds.) *The Handbook of Emotion.* New York: Guilford. [Note: There is no Rozin sole reference in this chapter.]

Rubin, Z. (1970). Measurement of romantic love. *Journal of Personality and Social Psychology, 16,* 265–273.

Rubin, Z. (1973). *Liking and loving: An invitation to social psychology.* New York: Holt, Rinehart & Winston.

Rubin, Z. (1988). Preface. In R. J. Sternberg & M. L. Barnes (Eds.), *The psychology of love* (pp. vii–xii). New Haven, CT: Yale University Press.

Ruch, L. E., & Holmes, T. H. (1971). Scaling of life change: Comparison of direct and indirect methods. *Journal of Psychosomatic Research, 15,* 221–227.

Ruggieri, V. (1991). On the hypothesized physiological correspondence between perceptual and imagery processes. *Perceptual and Motor Skills, 73,* 827–830.

Rushton, J. P. (1975). Generosity in children: Immediate and long-term effects of modeling, preaching, and moral judgment. *Journal of Personality and Social Psychology, 31,* 459–466.

Rushton, J. P. (1989). Genetic similarity in male friendships. *Ethology & Sociobiology, 10,* 361–374.

Rushton, J. P. (1994). *Race, evolution and behavior.* New York: Transaction Press.

Rushton, J. P., Russell, R. J. H., & Wells, P. A. (1984). Genetic similarity theory: Beyond kin selection. *Behavior Genetics, 14,* 179–193.

Russell, J. A. (1994). Is there universal recognition of emotion from facial expression: A review of the cross-cultural studies. *Psychological Bulletin, 115,* 102–141.

Russell, J. J., Switz, G. M., & Thompson, K. (1977). Olfactory influences on the human menstrual cycle. Paper presented at the meeting of the American Association for the Advancement of Science, San Francisco.

Russell, M. J. (1976). Human olfactory communication. *Nature, 260,* 520–522.

Russell, T. G., Rowe, W., & Smouse, A. D. (1991). Subliminal self-help tapes and academic achievement: An evaluation. *Journal of Counseling & Development, 69,* 359–362.

Ruth, W. J., & Mosatche, H. S. (1985). A projective assessment of the effects of Freudian sexual symbolism in liquor advertisements. *Psychological Reports, 56,* 183–188.

Ruth, W. J., Mosatche, H. S., & Kramer, A. (1989). Freudian sexual symbolism: Theoretical considerations and an empirical test in advertising. *Psychological Reports, 64,* 1131–1139.

Ryan, W. (1976). *Blaming the Victim* (rev ed.). New York: Vintage.

S

Sacco, W. P., & Beck, A. T. (1985). Cognitive therapy of depression. In E. E. Beckham & W. R. Leber (Eds.), *Handbook of depression: Treatment, assessment, and research*. Homewood, IL: Dorsey Press.

Sachs, B. D. (1965). Sexual behavior of male rats after one to nine days without food. *Journal of Comparative and Physiological Psychology, 60,* 144–146.

Sachs, J. S. (1967). Recognition memory for syntactic and semantic aspects of connected discourse. *Perception and Psychophysics, 2,* 437–442.

Sackheim, H. A., Gur, R. C., & Saucy, M. C. (1978). Emotions are expressed more intensely on the left side of the face. *Science, 202,* 434–436.

Sacks, O. (1992, March 26). The last hippie. *The New York Review,* 53–62.

Sagi, A., Lamb, M. E., Lewkowicz, K. S., Shoman, R., Dvir, R., & Estes, D. (1985). Security of infant-mother, -father, and metapelet attachment among kibbutz-reared Israeli children. *Monographs of the Society for Research in Child Development, 50,* (Serial No. 209, 1–2).

Salapatek, P. (1975). Pattern perception in early infancy. In L. B. Cohen & Salapatek (Eds.), *Infant perception: From sensation to cognition* (Vol. 1). New York: Academic Press.

Salili, F., Maehr, M. L., & Gillmore, G. (1976). Achievement and morality: A cross-cultural analysis of causal attribution and evaluation. *Journal of Personality and Social Psychology, 1976, 33,* 327–337.

Salili, F., Maehr, M. L., & Gillmore, G. (1976). Achievement and morality: A cross-cultural analysis of causal attribution and evaluation. *Journal of Personality and Social Psychology, 33,* 327–337.

Salthouse, T. A. (1990). Cognitive competence and expertise in aging. In J. E. Birren & K. W. Schaie (Eds.), *Handbook of the psychology of aging* (3rd ed.). San Diego, CA: Academic Press.

Salthouse, T. A. (1991). *Theoretical perspectives on cognitive aging.* Hillsdale, NJ: Erlbaum.

Salz, E., Campbell, S., & Skotko, D. (1983). Verbal control of behavior: The effects of shouting. *Developmental Psychology, 19,* 461–464.

Salzman, C. (1992). The current status of fluoxetine. *Neuropsychopharmacology, 7,* 245–247.

Sambraus, V. H. H., & Sambraus, D. (1975). Prägung von Nurtztieren auf Menschen. *Zeitschrift für Tierpsychologie, 38,* 1–17.

Samelson, F. (1975). On the science and politics of the IQ. *Social Research, 42,* 467–488.

Sameroff, A. J. (1968). The component of sucking in the human newborn. *Journal of Experimental Child Psychology, 6,* 607–623.

Sampson, E. E. (1988). The debate on individualism: Indigenous psychologies of the individual and their role in personal and societal functioning. *American Psychologist, 43,* 15–22.

Sampson, E. E. (1989). The deconstruction of the self. In J. Shotter & K. J. Gergen (Eds.), *Texts of identity* (pp. 1–19). London: Sage.

Samuelson, F. J. B. (1980). Watson's Little Albert, Cyril Burt's twins, and the need for a critical science. *American Psychologist, 35,* 619–625.

San Francisco Chronicle. (1964, November 26), p. 3.

Sande, G. N., Goethals, G. R., & Radloff, C. E. (1988). Perceiving one's own traits and others': The multifaceted self. *Journal of Personality and Social Psychology, 54,* 13–20.

Sanders, M. S., & McCormick, E. J. (1987). *Human factors in engineering and design* (6th ed.). New York: McGraw-Hill.

Sanders, R. J. (1985). Teaching apes to ape language: Explaining the imitative and nonimitative signing of a chimpanzee (*Pan troglodytes*). *Journal of Comparative Psychology, 99,* 197–210.

Sanders, M., & McCormick, E. J. (1993). *Human factors in engineering and design.* 7th ed. New York: McGraw-Hill.

Sanders-Phillips, K., Strauss, M. E., & Gutberlet, R. L. (1988). The effect of obstetric medication on newborn infant feeding behavior. *Infant Behavior and Development, 11,* 251–263.

Sangree, W. H. (1962). The social functions of beer drinking in Bantu Tiriki. In P. J. Pittman & C. R. Snyder (Eds.), *Society, culture, and drinking patterns.* New York: Wiley.

Sarason, I. G., & Spielberger, C. D. (Eds.). (1979). *Stress and anxiety* (Vol. 6). The Series in Clinical and Community Psychology. Washington, DC: Hemisphere.

Sasvari, L. (1979). Observational learning in great, blue and marsh tits. *Animal Behavior, 27,* 767–771.

Saufley, W. H., Otaka, S. R., & Bavaresco, J. L. (1985). Context independence. *Memory and Cognition, 13,* 522–528.

Savin-Williams, R. C. (1991). *Gay and lesbian youth: Expressions in identity.* Washington, DC: Hemisphere.

Sawrey, W. L., Conger, J. J., & Turrell, E. S. (1956). An experimental investigation of the role of psychological factors in the production of gastric ulcers in rats. *Journal of Comparative and Physiological Psychology, 49,* 457–461.

Saxe, L., Dougherty, D., & Cross, T. (1985). The validity of polygraph testing: Scientific analysis and public controversy. *American Psychologist, 40,* 355–366.

Scarr, S. (1985). Constructing psychology: Making facts and fables for our times. *American Psychologist, 40,* 499–512.

Scarr, S. (1992). Developmental theories for the 1990s: Development and individual differences. *Child Development, 63,* 1–19.

Scarr, S., & Carter-Salzman, L. (1982). Genetics and intelligence. In R. J. Sternberg (Ed.), *Handbook of human intelligence* (pp. 792–897). New York: Cambridge University Press.

Scarr, S., & Grajeck, S. (1982). Similarities and differences among siblings. In M. E. Lamb and B. Sutton-Smith (Eds.), *Sibling relationships.* Hillsdale, NJ: Erlbaum.

Scarr, S., & Kidd, K. K. (1983). Developmental behavior genetics. In P. H. Mussen (Ed.), *Handbook of child psychology: Vol. 2. Infancy and developmental psychobiology.* New York: Wiley.

Scarr, S., & Weinberg, R. A. (1976). IQ test performance of black children adopted by white families. *American Psychologist, 31,* 726–739.

Schachter, S. (1951). Deviation, rejection, and communication. *Journal of Abnormal and Social Psychology, 46,* 190–207.

Schachter, S. (1959). *The psychology of affiliation.* Stanford, CA: Stanford University Press.

Schachter, S. (1964). The interaction of cognitive and physiological determinants of emotional state. In L. Berkowitz (Ed.), *Advances in Experimental Social Psychology* (Vol. 1). New York: Academic Press.

Schachter, S. (1971). Some extraordinary facts about obese humans and rats. *American Psychologist, 26,* 129–144.

Schachter, S., & Singer, J. E. (1962). Cognitive, social and physiological determinants of emotional state. *Psychological Review, 69,* 379–399.

Schachter, S., Goldman, R., & Gordon, A. (1968). Effects of fear, food, deprivation, and obesity on eating. *Journal of Personality and Social Psychology, 10,* 91–97.

Schacter, D. L. (1987). Implicit memory: History and current status. *Journal of Experimental Psychology: Learning, Memory, and Cognition, 13,* 501–518.

Schacter, D. L. (1990). Perceptual representation systems and implicit memory: Toward a resolution of the multiple memory systems debate. In A. Diamond (Ed.), *The development and neural basis of higher cognitive function.* New York: New York Academy of Science Press.

Schaeffer, M., & Baum, A. (1989). Health psychology. In W. L. Gregory and W. J. Burroughs (Eds.), *Introduction to applied psychology.* Glenview, IL: Scott, Foresman.

Schaie, K. W. (1977–1978). Toward a stage theory of adult cognitive development. *Aging and Human Development, 8,* 129–138.

Schaie, K. W. (1990). Intellectual development in adulthood. In J. E. Birren & K. W. Schaie (Eds.), *Handbook of the psychology of aging* (3rd ed.). San Diego, CA: Academic Press.

Schaie, K. W. (1990). Intellectual development in adulthood. In J. E. Birren & K. W. Schaie (Eds.), *Handbook of the psychology of aging* (3rd ed.). San Diego, CA: Academic Press.

Schaie, K. W., & Hertzog, D. (1985). Toward a comprehensive model of adult intellectual development: Contributions of the Seattle Longitudinal Study. In R. J. Sternberg (Ed.), *Advances in human intelligence* (Vol. 3). New York: Academic Press.

Schaie, K. W., & Willis, S. L. (1986). *Adult development and aging* (2nd ed.). Boston: Little, Brown.

Schaie, W. (1983). The Seattle Longitudinal Study. In K. W. Schaie (Ed.), *Longitudinal studies of adult psychological development.* New York: Guilford Press.

Schaller, M. (1991). Social categorization and the formation of group stereotypes: Further evidence for biased information processing in the perception of group-behavior correlations. *European Journal of Social Psychology, 21,* 25–36.

Scheier, M., & Carver, C. S. (1992). Effects of optimism on psychological and physical well-being: Theoretical overview and empirical update. *Cognitive Therapy and Research, 16,* 201–228.

Scheier, M. F., & Carver, C. S. (1985). Optimism, coping and health: Assessment and implications of generalized outcomes expectancies. *Health Psychology, 4,* 210–247.

Scheier, M. F., & Carver, C. S. (1985). Optimism, coping and health: Assessment and implications of generalized outcomes expectancies. *Health Psychology, 4,* 210–247.

Schiff, M., Duyme, M., Dumaret, A., Steward, J., Tomkiewicz, S., & Feingold, J. (1978). Intellectual status of working class children adopted early into upper middle-class families. *Science, 200,* 1503–1504.

Schiff, W. (1980). *Perception: An applied approach.* Boston: Houghton Mifflin.

Schiffman, H. R. (1976). *Sensation and perception: An integrated approach.* New York: Wiley.

Schleifer, S. J., Keller, S. E., Meyerson, A. T., Raskin, M. J., Davis, K. L., & Stein, M. (1984). Lymphocyte function in major depressive disorder. *Archives of General Psychiatry, 41,* 484–486.

Schlenker, B. R., & Weigold, M. F. (1992). Interpersonal processes involving impression regulation and management. *Annual Review of Psychology, 43,* 133–168.

Schmidt, C. R., & Paris, S. J. (1984). The development of children's verbal communication skills. In H. Reese & L. Lipsitt (Eds.), *Advances in child development and behavior* (Vol. 18, pp. 1–47). New York: Academic Press.

Schmidt, F. L., & Hunter, J. E. (1981). Employment testing: Old theories and new research findings. *American Psychologist, 36*, 1128–1137.

Schmidt, S. R., & Bohannon, J. N. (1988). Flashbulb memories, fact or fiction: A reply to McCloskey, Wible, & Cohen. *Journal of Experimental Psychology: General, 117*, 332–335.

Schmitt, B. H., Gilovich, T., Goore, N., & Joseph, L. (1986). Mere presence and social facilitation: One more time. *Journal of Experimental Social Psychology, 22*, 242–248.

Schmitt, N., & Robertson, I. (1990). Personnel selection. *Annual Review of Psychology, 41*, 289–319.

Schneider, D. J. (1973). Implicit personality theory: A review. *Psychological Bulletin, 74*, 294–309.

Schneider, D. J., & Miller, R. S. (1975). The effects of enthusiasm and quality of arguments on attitude attribution. *Journal of Personality, 43*, 698–708.

Schneider, W., & Shiffrin, R. M. (1977). Controlled and automatic information processing: 1. Detection, search, and attention. *Psychological Review, 84*, 1–66.

Schneiderman, N. (1966). Interstimulus interval function of the nictitating membrane response of the rabbit under delay versus trace conditioning. *Journal of Comparative and Physiological Psychology, 62*, 397–402.

Scholz, K. W., & Potts, G. R. (1974). Cognitive processing of linear orderings. *Journal of Experimental Psychology, 102*, 323–326.

Schooler, J. W., & Engstler-Schooler, T. (1990). Verbal overshadowing of visual memories: Some things are better left unsaid. *Cognitive Psychology, 22*, 36–71.

Schooler, N. R. (1990). Pharmacologic treatment for mental illness. *Contemporary Psychology, 35*, 585–586.

Schreiber, F. R. (1974). *Sybil*. New York: Warner Books.

Schreiner-Engel, P., Schiavi, R. C., White, D., & Ghizzani, A. (1989). Low sexual desire in women: The role of reproductive hormones. *Hormones and Behavior, 23*, 221–234.

Schroeder, C. C., & Jackson, S. (1987). Designing residential environment. In J. A. Provost & S. Anchors (Eds.), *Applications of the Myers-Briggs Type Indicator in higher education*. Palo Alto, CA: Consulting Psychologists Press.

Schulsinger, F. (1972). Psychopathy: Heredity and environment. *International Journal of Mental health, 1*, 190–206.

Schultz, D. P., & Schultz, S. E. (1990). *Psychology and industry today* (5th ed.). New York: Macmillan.

Schultz, G., & Melzack, R. (1991). The Charles Bonnet syndrome: "Phantom visual images." *Perception, 20*, 809–825.

Schumaker, J., Deshler, D., Alley, G., Warner, M., & Denton, P. (1984). Multipass: A learning strategy for improving reading comprehension. *Learning Disability Quarterly, 5*(2), 295–304.

Schuman, D. W., & Weiner, M. F. (1987). *The psychotherapist-patient privilege: A critical examination*. Springfield, IL: Charles C. Thomas.

Schuster, C. S., & Ashburn, S. S. (1986). *The process of human development* (2nd ed.). Boston: Little, Brown.

Schwanenflugel, P. J., Guth, M. E., & Bjorklund, D. F. (1986). A developmental trend in the understanding of concept attribute importance. *Child Development, 57*, 421–430.

Schwartz, D. H., McClane, S., Hernandez, L., & Hoebel, B. (1989). Feeding increases extracellular serotonin in the lateral hypothalamus of the rat as measured by microdialyis. *Brain Research, 479*, 349–354.

Schwartz, D. H., McClane, S., Hernandez, L., & Hoebel, B. (1989). Feeding increases extracellular serotonin in the lateral hypothalamus of the rat as measured by microdialysis. *Brain Research, 479*, 349–354.

Schwartz, G. E., & Weiss, S. M. (1978a). Yale conference on behavioral medicine: A proposed definition and statement of goals. *Journal of Behavioral Medicine, 1*, 3–12.

Schwartz, G. E., & Weiss, S. M. (1978b). Behavioral medicine revisited: An amended definition. *Journal of Behavioral Medicine, 1*, 249–251.

Schwartz, R. S., Ravussin, E., Massari, M., O'Connell, M., & Robbins, D. C. (1985). The thermic effect of carbohydrate versus fat feeding in man. *Metabolism, 34*, 285–293.

Schweinhart, L. J., & Weikart, D. P. (1985). Evidence that good early childhood programs work. *Phi Delta Kappan, 66*, 545–551.

Schweizer, E., Rickels, K., Weiss, S., & Zavodnick, S. (1993). Maintenance drug treatment of panic disorder: I. Results of a prospective placebo-controlled comparison of alprazolam and imipramine. *Archives of General Psychiatry, 50*, 51–60.

Sclafani, A. (1985). Animal models of obesity. In R. T. Frankle, J. Dwyer, L. Moragne, & A. Owen (Eds.), *Dietary treatment and prevention of obesity* (pp. 105–123). London: John Libbey.

Sclafani, A. (1990). Nutritionally-based learned flavor preferences in rats. In E. D. Capaldi & T. L. Powley (Eds.), *Taste, experience, and feeding*. Washington, DC: American Psychological Association.

Scott, J. P. (1980). The function of emotions in behavioral systems: A systems analysis. In R. Plutchik & H. Kellerman (Eds.), *Emotion, theory, research, and experience* (Vol. 1). New York: Academic Press.

Scott, W. A., & Johnson, R. C. (1972). Comparative validities of direct and indirect personality tests. *Journal of Consulting and Clinical Psychology, 38*, 301–398.

Scovern, A. W., & Kilmann, P. R. (1980). Status of electroconvulsive therapy: Review of the outcome literature. *Psychological Bulletin, 87*, 260–303.

Scribner, S. (1984). Studying working intelligence. In B. Rogoff & J. Lave (Eds.), *Everyday cognition: Its development in social context*. Cambridge, MA: Harvard University Press.

Seamon, J. G., Brody, N., & Kauff, D. (1983). Affective discrimination of stimuli that are not recognized: Effects of shadowing, masking, and cerebral laterality. *Journal of Experimental Psychology: Learning, Memory, & Cognition, 9*, 544–555.

Secunda, S. K., Friedman, R. J., & Schuyler, D. (1973). *The depressive disorders: Special report, 1973* (DHEW Publication No. HSM-73-9157). Washington, DC: U.S. Government Printing Office.

Segal, M. H., Campbell, D. T., & Herskovits, J. M. (1966). *Influence of culture on visual perception*. Indianapolis: Bobbs-Merrill.

Segal, S. J. (1971). Processing of the stimulus in imagery and perception. In S. J. Segal (Ed.), *Imagery: Current cognitive approaches*. New York: Academic Press.

Segal, Z. V. (1991). The pervasive influence of attribution theory in clinical psychology is not always persuasive. *Contemporary Psychology, 36*, 40–42.

Sekuler, R., & Blake, R. (1994). *Perception*. (3rd ed.). New York: McGraw-Hill.

Selfridge, O. G. (1959). Pandemonium: A paradigm for learning. In D. V. Blake & A. M. Uttley (Eds.), *Symposium on the mechanization of thought processes* (pp. 511–529). London: H. M. Stationery Office.

Seligman, D. (1992). *A question of intelligence*. New York: Birch Lane Press.

Seligman, M. E.. P. (1991). *Learned optimism*. New York: Knopf.

Seligman, M. E. P. (1975). *Helplessness: On depression, development and death*. San Francisco: Freeman.

Seligman, M. E. P. (1991). *Learned optimism*. New York: Norton.

Seligman, M. E. P., & Binik, Y. M. (1977). The safety signal hypothesis. In H. Davis, & H. M. B. Hurwitz (Eds.), *Operant Pavlovian interactions*. Hillsdale, NJ: Erlbaum.

Seligman, M. E. P., & Hager, J. L. (1972). *Biological boundaries of learning*. Englewood Cliffs, NJ: Prentice-Hall.

Seligman, M. E. P., & Johnston, J. (1973). A cognitive theory of avoidance learning. In F. J. McGuigan & D. B. Lunsden (Eds.), *Contemporary approaches to conditioning and learning*. New York: Wiley.

Seligman, M. E. P., & Maier, S. F. (1967). Failure to escape traumatic shock. *Journal of Experimental Psychology, 74*, 1–9.

Seligman, M. E. P., Abramson, L. Y., Semmel, A., & von Baeyer, C. (1979). Depressive attributional style. *Journal of Abnormal Psychology, 88*, 242–247.

Selman, R. L. (1980). *The growth of interpersonal understanding: Developmental and clinical analyses*. New York: Academic Press.

Selye, H. (1956). *The stress of life*. New York: McGraw-Hill.

Selye, H. (1974). *Stress without distress*. Philadelphia: Lippincott.

Selzer, M. (1983). Compliance or self-fulfillment? The case of Albert Speer. In M. Rosenbaum (Ed.), *Compliant behavior: Beyond obedience to authority* (pp. 213–228). New York: Human Sciences Press.

Senna, J. J., & Segal, L. J. (1996). *Introduction to criminal justice* (7th ed.). St. Paul: West.

Sessa, F. M., & Steinberg, L. D. (1991). Family structure and the development of autonomy during adolescence. *Journal of Early Adolescence, 11*, 38–55.

Shaeffer, R. (1992). TVs UFO flop, earthquake lights and Frances Bacon. *Skeptical Inquirer, 17*, 26–27.

Shaffer, D. R. (1985). *Developmental psychology*. Monterey, CA: Brooks/Cole.

Shantz, C. U. (1983). Social cognition. In P. Mussen (Ed.), *Handbook of child psychology: Vol. 3* (pp. 495–555). New York: Wiley.

Shapiro, D. A. (1985). Recent applications of meta-analysis in clinical research. *Clinical Psychology Review, 5*, 13–34.

Shapiro, D. H., Jr. (1985). Clinical use of meditation as a self-regulation strategy: Comments or Holme's conclusions and implications. *American Psychologist, 40*, 719–722.

Shatz, M., & Gelman, R. (1973). The development of communication skills: Modification in the speech of young children as a function of the listener. *Monographs of the Society for Research in Child Development, 38*(5, No. 152).

Shaver, P., & Klinnert, M. (1982). Schachter's theories of affiliation and emotion: Implications of development research. In L. Wheeler (Ed.), *Review of Personality and Social Psychology, 3*, 37–72.

Shaver, P., Hazan, C., & Bradshaw, D. (1988). Love as attachment: An integration of three behavioral systems. In R. J. Sternberg, & M. L. Barnes (Eds.), *The psychology of love* (pp. 68–99). New Haven, CT: Yale University Press.

Shaw, B. (1969). *Visual symbols survey*. London: Centre for Educational Development Overseas.

Sheehan, P. W. (1988). Confidence, memory, and hypnosis. In H. M. Pettinati (Ed.), *Hypnosis and memory* (pp. 95–127). New York: Guilford Press.

Sheehy, G. (1976). *Passages: Predictable crises of adult life*. New York: E. P. Dutton & Co.

Sheldon, W. H. (1940). *Varieties of human physique*. New York: Harper & Row.

Sheldon, W. H. (1954). *Atlas of man: A guide for somatotyping the adult male of all ages*. New York: Harper & Row.

Sheldon, W. H. (with S. S. Stevens) (1942) *Varieties of Temperament*. New York: Harper.

Shepard, R. N. (1978). Externalization of mental images and the act of creation. In B. S. Randhawa & W. E. Goffman (Eds.), *Visual learning, thinking, and communication*. New York: Academic Press.

Shepard, R. N. (1981). Psychophysical complementarity. In M. Kubovy & J. R. Pomerantz (Eds.), *Perceptual organization*. Hillsdale, NJ: Erlbaum.

Sherer, K. R., & Ekman, P. (Eds.). (1984). *Approaches to emotion*. Hillsdale, NJ: Erlbaum.

Sherif, M. (1935). A study of some social factors in perception. *Archives of Psychology*, No. 187.

Sherif, M., Harvey, O. J., White, B. J., Hood, W. E., & Sherif, C. W. (1961). *Intergroup conflict and cooperation: The Robber's cave experiment*. Norman, OK: University of Oklahoma Press.

Sherman, S. J., Judd, C. M., & Park, B. (1989). Social cognition. *Annual Review of Psychology*, 40, 281–326.

Sherrington, C. S. (1906). *The integrative action of the nervous system*. New Haven, CT: Yale University Press.

Sherrod, D. R. (1974). Crowding, perceived control, and behavioral aftereffects. *Journal of Applied Social Psychology*, 2, 171–186.

Sherwin, B. B., Gelfand, M. M., & Brender, W. (1985). Androgen enhances sexual motivation in females: A prospective, crossover study of sex steroid administration in the surgical menopause. *Psychosomatic Medicine*, 47(4), 339–351.

Shettleworth, S. J. (1972). Constraints on learning. In D. S. Lehrman, R. A. Hinde, & E. Shaw (Eds.), *Advances in the study of behavior: Vol. 4* (pp. 1–68). New York: Academic Press.

Shettleworth, S. J. (1993). Varieties of learning and memory in animals. *Journal of Experimental Psychology: Animal Behavior Processes*, 19, 5–14.

Shields, J. (1962). *Monozygotic twins brought up apart and brought up together*. London: Oxford University Press.

Shimamura, A. P. (1992). Amnesia, organic. In L. R. Squire (Ed.), *The encyclopedia of learning and memory* (pp. 30–35). New York: MacMillan.

Shirley, M. M. (1923). *The First Two Years: A Study of Twenty-Five Babies*, Vol. II. Minneapolis, MN: University of Minnesota Press.

Shopland, D. R., & Brown, C. (1987). Toward the 1990 objectives for smoking: Measuring the progress with the 1985 NHIS data. *Public Health Reports*, 102, 68–73.

Shore, C., O'Connell, B., & Bates, E. (1984). First sentence in language and symbolic play. *Developmental Psychology*, 20, 872–880.

Shriqui, C. L., & Milette, P. C. (1992). You drive me crazy: A case report of acute psychosis and neurocysticercosis. *Canadian Journal of Psychiatry*, 37, 121–124.

Shuman, D. W., & Weiner, M. F. (1987). *The psychotherapist-patient privilege: A critical examination*. Springfield, IL: Charles C. Thomas.

Sidman, M. (1989). *Coercion and its fallout*. Boston, MA: Authors Cooperative.

Siegal, R. K. (1977). Hallucinations. *Scientific American*, 237, 132–140.

Siegal, S. (1977). Morphine tolerance acquisition as an associative process. *Journal of Experimental Psychology: Animal Behavior Processes*, 3, 1–13.

Siegal, S., Hinson, R. E., Krank, M. D., & McCully, J. (1982). Heroin "overdose" death: Contribution of drug associated environmental cues. *Science*, 216, 436–437.

Siegal, B. (1986). *Love. Medicine, & Miracles*. New York: Harper & Row.

Siegel, J. M. (1990). Stressful life events and use of physician service among the elderly: The moderating role of pet ownership. *Journal of Personality and Social Psychology*, 58, 1081–1086.

Siegel, J. M. (1990). Stressful life events and use of physician service among the elderly: The moderating role of pet ownership. *Journal of Personality and Social Psychology*, 58, 1081–1086.

Siegler, I. C. (1983). Psychological aspects of the Duke longitudinal studies. In K. W. Schaie (Ed.), *Longitudinal studies of adult psychological development*. New York: Guilford Press.

Siegler, R. S. (1978). The origins of scientific reasoning. In R. S. Siegler (Ed.), *Children's thinking: What develops?* Hillsdale, NJ: Erlbaum.

Siegler, R. S. (1986). Unities in thinking across domains. In M. Perlmutter (Ed.), *Minnesota symposia on child psychology*. Hillsdale, NJ: Erlbaum.

Siegler, R. S. (1991). *Children's thinking* (2nd ed.). Englewood Cliffs, NJ: Prentice Hall.

Siegler, R. S. (1992). The other Alfred Binet. *Developmental Psychology*, 28, 179–190.

Siegler, R. S., & Richards, D. D. (1982). The development of intelligence. In R. J. Sternberg (Ed.), *Handbook of human intelligence*. Cambridge: Cambridge University Press.

Siegler, R. S., & Robinson, M. (1982). The development of numerical understandings. *Advances in Child Development and Behavior*, 16, 241–312. (Also has a book # (24937).

Siegler, R. S., & Shrager, J. (1984). A model of strategy choice. In C. Sophian (Ed.), *Origins of cognitive skills*. Hillsdale, NJ: Erlbaum.

Sigel, I. E. (1978). The development of pictorial comprehension. In B. S. Randhawa & W. E. Goffman (Eds.), *Visual learning, thinking, and communication*. New York: Academic Press.

Sigman, M., Neumann, C., Jansen, A. A. J., & Bwibo, N. (1989). Cognitive abilities of Kenyan children in relation to nutrition, family characteristics, and education. *Child Development*, 60, 1463–1474.

Signorella, M. L., & Liben, L. S. (1985). Assessing children's gender-stereotyped attitudes. *Psychological Documents*, 15, 7.

Silber, E., Hamburg, D. A., Coelho, G. V., Murphey, E. B., Rosenberg, M., & Pearlin, L. I. (1976). Adaptive behavior in competent adolescents: Coping with the anticipation of college. In R. H. Moss (Ed.), *Human adaptation: Coping with life crises* (pp. 111–127). Lexington, MA: Heath.

Silverman, L. H. (1983). Subliminal psychodynamic activation method: Overview and comprehensive listing of studies. In J. Masling (Ed.), *Empirical studies in psychoanalysis* (Vol. 1, pp. 69–100). Hillsdale, NJ: Erlbaum.

Silverman, L. T., Sprafkin, J. N., & Rubinstein, E. A. (1979). Physical contact and sexual behavior on prime-time TV. *Journal of Communication*, 29, 33–43.

Silverstein, B., Peterson, B., & Perdue, L. (1986). Some correlates of the thin standard of bodily attractiveness for women. *International Journal of Eating Disorders*, 5, 895–905.

Silverstein, B., Peterson, B., Perdue, L., & Kelly, E. (1986). The role of the mass media in promoting a thin standard of bodily attractiveness for women. *Sex Roles*, 14, 519–532.

Silverstein, L. B. (1991). Transforming the debate about child care and maternal employment. *American Psychologist*, 46, 1025–1032.

Simon, B., Glassner-Bayerl, B., & Stratenwerth, I. (1991). Stereotyping and self-stereotyping in a natural intergroup context: The case of heterosexual and homosexual men. *Social Psychology Quarterly*, 54, 252–266.

Sinclair, R. C., Hoffman, C., Mark, M. M., Martin, L. L., & Pickering, T. L. (1994). Construct accessibility and the misattribution of arousal: Schachter and Singer revisited. *Psychological Science*, 5, 15–19.

Singer, E., & Endreny, P. M. (1993). *Reporting on risk: How the mass media portrays accidents, diseases, disasters, and other hazards*. New York: Russel Sage Foundation.

Singer, S. M. (1991). Schizophrenia and autism: Another look at possible relationships. *Contemporary Psychology*, 36, 722–723.

Sivacek, J. K., & Crano, W. D. (1982). Vested interest as a moderator of attitude-behavior constancy. *Journal of Personality and Social Psychology*, 43, 210–221.

Sjostrom, L. (1980). Fat cells and body weight. In A. J. Stunkard. (Ed.), *Obesity*. Philadelphia: Saunders.

Skinner, B. F. (1948). *Walden two*. New York: Macmillan.

Skinner, B. F. (1957). *Verbal behavior*. Englewood Cliffs, NJ: Prentice-Hall.

Skinner, B. F. (1971). *Beyond freedom and dignity*. New York: Knopf.

Skinner, B. F. (1976). *Particulars of My Life*. New York: Knopf.

Skinner, B. F. (1978). *Reflections on behaviorism and society*. Englewood Cliffs, NJ: Prentice-Hall.

Skinner, B. F. (1979). *The shaping of a behaviorist*. New York: Knopf.

Skinner, B. F. (1983). *A matter of Consequences*. New York: Knopf.

Sklar, L. S., & Anisman, H. (1981). Stress and cancer. *Psychological Bulletin*, 89, 369–406.

Skodak, M., & Skeels, H. M. (1949). A final follow-up study of one hundred adopted children. *Journal of Genetic Psychology*, 75, 85–125.

Slamecka, N. J. (1985). Ebbinghaus: Some associations. *Journal of Experimental Psychology: Learning, Memory, and Cognition*, 11, 414–435.

Slamecka, N. J., & Graf, P. (1978). The generation effect: Delineation of a phenomenon. *Journal of Experimental Psychology: Human Learning and Memory*, 4, 592–604.

Slotnick, B. M., McMullen, M. F., & Fleischer, S. (1974). Changes in emotionality following destruction of the septal areas in albino mice. *Brain, Behavior and Evolution*, 8, 241–252.

Slovic, P., Fischoff, B., & Lichtenstein, S. (1976). Cognitive processes and societal risk taking. In J. S. Carroll & J. W. Payne (Eds.), *Cognition and social behavior*. Hillsdale, NJ: Erlbaum.

Sluckin, W. (1965). *Imprinting and early learning*. London: Methuen.

Small, M. Y. (1990). *Cognitive development*. San Diego, CA: Harcourt Brace Jovanovich.

Smetana, J. G. (1989). Adolescents' and parents' reasoning about actual family conflicts. *Child Development*, 60, 1052–1067.

Smetana, J. G., Yau, J., Restrepo, A., & Braeges, J. L. (1991). Adolescent-parent conflict in married and divorced families. *Developmental Psychology*, 27, 1000–1010.

Smith, D. (1982). Trends in counseling and psychotherapy. *American Psychologist*, 37, 802–806.

Smith, E. E., & Osherson, D. N. (1984). Conceptual combination with prototype concepts. *Cognitive Science*, 8, 337–361.

Smith, E. R. (1984). Attributions and other inferences: Processing information about self versus others. *Journal of Experimental Social Psychology*, 20, 97–115.

Smith, F. J. (1977). Work attitudes as predictors of attendance on a specific day. *Journal of Applied Psychology, 62,* 16–19.

Smith, M. C. (1983). Hypnotic memory enhancement of witnesses: Does it work? *Psychological Bulletin, 94,* 387–407.

Smith, M. C., Coleman, S. R., & Gormezano, I. (1969). Classical conditioning of the rabbit's nictitating membrane response at backward, simultaneous and forward CS-US intervals. *Journal of Comparative and Physiological Psychology, 69,* 226–231.

Smith, M. L., Glass, G. V., & Miller, R. L. (1980). *The benefits of psychotherapy.* Baltimore: Johns Hopkins University Press.

Smith, P. K., & Daglish, L. 91977). Sex differences in parent and infant behavior in the home. *Child Development, 48,* 1250–1254.

Smith, R. S., Doty, R. L., Burlingame, G. K., & McKeown, D. A. (1993). Smell and taste function in the visually impaired. *Perception & Psychophysics, 54,* 649–655.

Smith, S. M., Glenberg, A. M., & Bjork, R. A. (1978). Environmental context and human memory. *Memory and Cognition, 6,* 342–355.

Smith, T. W. (1992). Hostility and health: Current status of a psychosomatic hypothesis. *Health Psychology, 11,* 139–150.

Snyder, F. W., & Pronko, N. H. (1952). *Visual with spatial inversion.* Wichita: University of Kansas Press.

Snyder, M. L., Stephan, W. G., & Rosenfield, D. (1976). Egotism and attribution. *Journal of Personality and Social Psychology, 33,* 435–441.

Snyder, M. L., Stephan, W. G., & Rosenfield, D. (1978). Attributional egotism. In J. H. Harvey, W. Ickes, & R. F. Kidd (Eds.), *New directions in attribution research* (Vol. 2). Hillsdale, NJ: Erlbaum.

Snyder, M., & Jones, E. E. (1974). Attitude attribution when behavior is constrained. *Journal of Experimental Social Psychology, 10,* 585–600.

Snyder, M., & Kendzierski, D. (1982). Acting on one's attitudes: Procedures for linking attitude and behavior. *Journal of Experimental Social Psychology, 19,* 165–183.

Snyder, M., & Swann, W. B., Jr. (1978). Behavioral confirmation on social interaction: From social perception to social reality. *Journal of Experimental Social Psychology, 14,* 148–162.

Snyder, M., Tanke, E. D., & Berscheid, E. (1977). Social perception and interpersonal behavior: On the self-fulfilling nature of social stereotypes. *Journal of Personality and Social Psychology, 35,* 656–666.

Snyder, S. H. (1976). The dopamine hypothesis of schizophrenia. *American Journal of Psychiatry, 133,* 197–202.

Snyder, S. H. (1981). Dopamine receptors, neuroleptics, and schizophrenia. *American Journal of Psychiatry, 138,* 460–464.

Snyderman, M., & Hernnstein, R. J. (1983). Intelligence tests and the Immigration Act of 1924. *American Psychologist, 38,* 986–995.

Sobell, L. C., Breslin, C., Sobell, M. B. (in press, 1996). Substance-related disorders (alcohol). In M. Hersen & S. M. Turner (Eds.) Adult psychopathology and diagnosis (3rd ed.), New York: John Wiley & Sons.

Sobell, M. B., & Sobell, L. C. (1973). Individualized behavior therapy for alcoholics. *Behavior Therapy, 4,* 49–72.

Sobell, M. B., & Sobell, L. C. (1976). Second-year treatment outcome of alcoholics treated by individualized behavior therapy: Results. *Behavior Research and Therapy, 14,* 195–215.

Sobell, M. B., & Sobell, L. C. (1984). The aftermath of heresy: A response to Pendery et al.'s (1982) critique of "individualized behavior therapy for alcoholics." *Behavior Research and Therapy, 22,* 413–440.

Sobell, M. B., & Sobell, L. C. (1989). Moratorium on Maltzman: An appeal to reason. *Journal of Studies on Alcohol, 50,* 473–480.

Solnick, R. L., & Corby, N. (1983). Human sexuality and aging. In D. S. Woodruff & J. E. Birren (Eds.), *Aging: Scientific perspectives and social issues.* Monterey, CA: Brooks/Cole.

Solomon, R. L. (1980). The opponent-process theory of motivation: The costs of pleasure and the benefits of pain. *American Psychologist, 35,* 691–712.

Solomon, R. L., & Corbit, J. D. (1974). An opponent-process theory of motivation: 1. Temporal dynamics of affect. *Psychological Review, 81,* 119–145.

Sommer, R. (1983). *Social design: Creating buildings with people in mind.* Englewood Cliffs, NJ: Prentice-Hall.

Sonnenfeld, J. A., (1985). Shedding light on the Hawthorne studies. *Journal of Occupational Behaviour, 6,* 111–130.

Sorenson, R. C. (1973). *Adolescent sexuality in contemporary America.* New York: World.

Southwick, C. H., & Clark, L. H. (1968). Interstrain differences in aggressive behavior and exploratory activity of inbred mice. *Communications in Behavioral Biology, 1,* 49–59.

Spangler, W. D. (1992). Validity of questionnaire and TAT measures of need for achievement: Two meta-analyses. *Psychological Review, 112,* 140–154.

Spanos, N. P. (1983). The hidden observer as an experimental creation. *Journal of Personality and Social Psychology, 44,* 170–176.

Spanos, N. P., & Radtke, H. L. (1982). Hypnotic amnesia as strategic enactment: A cognitive, social-psychological perspective. *Research in Community Psychology, Psychiatry and Behavior, 7,* 215–231.

Spanos, N. P., Perlini, A. H., & Robertson, L. A. (1989). Hypnosis, suggestion, and placebo in the reduction of experimental pain. *Journal of Abnormal Psychology, 38,* 285–293.

Spanos, N. P., Weekes, J. R., & Bertrand, L. D. (1985). Multiple personality: A social psychological perspective. *Journal of Abnormal Psychology, 94,* 362–376.

Spearman, C. (1927). *The abilities of man: Their nature and measurement.* New York: Macmillan.

Speisman, J. C., Lazarus, R. S., Mordkoff, A. M., & Davidson, L. A. (1964). Experimental reduction of stress based on ego-defense theory. *Journal of Abnormal and Social Psychology, 68,* 367–380.

Spence, D. P. (1982). *Narrative Truth and Historical Truth: Meaning and Interpretation in Psychoanalysis.* New York: Norton.

Spence, D. P. (1990). The rhetorical voice of psychoanalysis. *Journal of the American Psychoanalytic Association, 38,* 579–604.

Spencer, M. B., & Markstrom-Adams, C. (1990). Identity processes among racial and ethnic minority children in America. *Child Development, 61,* 290–310.

Sperling, G. (1960). The information available in brief visual presentations. *Psychological Monographs, 74*(Whole No. 11).

Sperry, R. W. (1968). Hemisphere deconnection and the unity of conscious experience. *American Psychologist, 23,* 723–733.

Sperry, R. W. (1970). Perception in the absence of the neocortical commisures. *Research Publications for the Association for Research in Nervous and Mental Disorders, 48,* 123–138.

Sperry, R. W. (1974). Lateral specialization in surgically separated hemispheres. In F. O. Schmitt & F. G. Worden (Eds.), *The neurosciences* (Vol. 3). Cambridge, MA: MIT Press.

Sperry, R. W., Gazzaniga, M. S., & Bogen, J. E. (1969). Interhemispheric relationships: The neocortical commisures, syndromes of hemispheric deconnection. In P. J. Vinkin & G. W. Brayn (Eds.), *Handbook of clinical neurology* (Vol. 4). Amsterdam: North Holland.

Spetch, M. L., Wilkie, D. M., & Pinel, J. P. J. (1981). Backward conditionings: A re-evaluation of the empirical evidence. *Psychological Bulletin, 89,* 163–175.

Spiegel, D. (1991). Mind matters: Effects of group support on cancer patients. *The Journal of NIH Research, 3,* 61–63.

Spielberger, C. D., Krasner, S. S., & Solomon, E. P. (1988). The experience, expression, and control of anger. In M. P. Janisse (Ed.) *Individual Differences, Stress, and Health Psychology.* New York: Springer-Verlag, 89–108.

Spiegel, D. (1991). Mind matters: effects of group support on cancer patients. *The Journal of NIH Research, 3,* 61–63.

Spilton, D., & Lee, L. D. (1977). Some determinants of effective communication in four year olds. *Child Development, 48,* 968–977.

Spitz, H. H. (1986). *The raising of intelligence: A selected history of attempts to raise retarded intelligence.* Hillsdale, NJ: Erlbaum.

Spitzer, R. L. (1991). An outsider-insider's view about revising the DSMs. *Journal of Abnormal Psychology, 100,* 294–296.

Spivack, G., Marcus, J., & Swift, M. (1986). Early classroom behavior and later misconduct. *Developmental Psychology, 22,* 124–131.

Springer, S. P., & Deutsch, G. (1985). *Left brain, right brain* (rev. ed.). San Francisco: Freeman.

Springer, S. P., & Deutsch, G. (1989). *Left brain, right brain.* New York: W. H. Freeman.

Squire, L. (1989). On the course of forgetting in very long term memory. *Journal of Experimental Psychology: Learning, Memory, and Cognition, 15,* 241–245.

Squire, L. R. (1982). The neuropsychology of human memory. *Annual Review of Neuroscience, 5,* 241–273.

Squire, L. R. (1987). *Memory and brain.* Oxford: Oxford University Press.

Squire, L. R., Zola-Morgan, S., Cave, C. B., Haist, F., Musen, G., & Suzuke, W. A. (1992). Memory: Organization of brain systems and cognition. In D. E. Meyer and S. Kornblum (Eds.), *Attention and performance XIV: A silver jubilee.* Hillsdale, NJ: Erlbaum.

Sroufe, L. A. (1985). Attachment classification from the perspective of infant-caregiver relationships and infant temperament. *Child Development, 56,* 1–14.

Sroufe, L. A., Fox, N., & Pancake, V. (1983). Attachment and dependency in developmental perspective. *Child Development, 54,* 1615–1627.

St. James-Roberts, I. (1979). Neurological plasticity, recovery from brain insult, and child development. In H. W. Reese & L. P. Lipsitt (Eds.), *Advances in child development and behavior* (Vol. 14). New York: Academic Press.

Staddon, J. E. R. (1971). The "superstition" experiment: A reexamination of its implication for the principles of adaptive behavior. *Psychological Review, 78,* 3–43.

Staddon, J. E. R. (1983). *Adaptive behavior and learning.* Cambridge: Cambridge University Press.

Stafford, M. C., & Scott, R. R. (1986). Stigma, deviance, and social control: Some conceptual issues. In S. C. Ainley, G. Becker, & L. M. Coleman (Eds.),*The dilemma of difference: A multidisciplinary view of stigma* (pp. 77–91). New York: Plenum.

Stager, S. F., & Burke, P. J. (1982). A reexamination of body build stereotypes. *Journal of Research in Personality, 16,* 435–446.

Stampfl, T. G., & Levis, D. J. (1967). Essentials of implosive therapy: A learning-theory-based psychodynamic therapy. *Journal of Abnormal Psychology, 72,* 496–503.

Stanislaw, H., & Rice, F. J. (1988). Correlation between sexual desire and menstrual cycle characteristics. *Archives of Sexual Behavior, 17,* 499–508.

Stanley, B. G., Schwartz, F. H., Hernandez, L., Leibowitz, S. F., & Hoebel, B. G. (1989). Patterns of extracellular 5-hydroxyindoleacetic acid (f-HIAA) in the paraventricular hypothalamus (PVN): Relation to circadian rhythm and deprivation-induced eating behavior. *Pharmacology, Biochemistry & Behavior, 33,* 257–260.

Stanley, J., & Benbow, C. (1983). Studying the process and results of greatly accelerating (especially in mathematics and science) the educational process of youths who reason well mathematically. In S. Paris, G. Olson, & H. Stevenson (Eds.), *Learning and motivation in the classroom.* Hillsdale, NJ: Erlbaum.

Stanley, P. R. A., & Riera, B. (1976). Replications of media violence. *Report of the Royal Commission on violence in the communications industry: Vol. 5. Learning from the media.* Toronto, Ontario: Ministry of Government Services.

Stapp, J., & Fulcher, R. (1981). The employment of APA members. *American Psychologist, 36,* 1263–1314.

Starin, S. (1991). "Nonaversive" behavior management: A misnomer. *The Behavior Analyst, 14,* 207–209.

Staw, B. M. (1984). Organizational behavior: A review and reformulation of the field's outcome variables. *Annual Review of Psychology, 35,* 627–666.

Steen, S. N., Oppliger, R. A., & Brownell, K. D. (1988). Metabolic effects of repeated weight loss and regain in adolescent wrestlers. *Journal of the American Medical Association, 260,* 47–50.

Steers, R. M., & Porter, L. W. (1979). *Motivation and work behavior* (2nd ed.). New York: McGraw-Hill.

Steinberg, L. D. (1988). Reciprocal relation between parent-child distance and pubertal maturation. *Developmental Psychology, 24,* 122–128.

Steinberg, L. D. (1990). Interdependency in the family: Autonomy, conflict, and harmony in the parent-adolescent relationship. In S. S. Feldman & G. R. Elliot (Eds.), *At the threshold: The developing adolescent* (pp. 255–276). Cambridge, MA: Harvard University Press.

Steinberg, L. D., & Silverberg, S. B. (1986). The vicissitudes of autonomy in early adolescence. *Child Development, 57,* 841–851.

Steinberg, L., Lamborn, S. D., Dornbusch, S. M., & Darling, N. (1992). Impact of parenting practices on adolescent achievement: Authoritative parenting, school involvement, and encouragement to succeed. *Child Development, 63,* 1266–1281.

Stephan, C. W., & Langlois, J. H. (1984). Baby beautiful. *Child Development, 55,* 576–585.

Stephens, D. N. (1980). Does the Lee obesity index measure general obesity? *Physiology and Behavior, 25,* 313–315.

Stern, C. (1949). *Principles of human genetics.* San Francisco: Freeman.

Stern, J. A., Brown, M., Ulett, G. A., & Sletten, I. (1977). A comparison of hypnosis, acupuncture, morphine, valium, aspirin, and placebo in the management of experimentally induced pain. *Annals of the New York Academy of Sciences, 296,* 175–193.

Sternberg, R. J. (1982). Natural, unnatural, and supernatural concepts. *Cognitive Psychology, 14,* 451–466.

Sternberg, R. J. (1985). *Beyond IQ: A triarchic theory of human intelligence.* Cambridge: Cambridge University Press.

Sternberg, R. J. (1986). A triangular theory of love. *Psychological Review, 93,* 119–135.

Sternberg, R. J. (1988). *The nature of creativity.* Cambridge: Cambridge University Press.

Sternberg, R. J. (1988). Triangulating love. In R. J. Sternberg & M. L. Barnes (Eds.), *The psychology of love* (pp. 119–138). New Haven, CT: Yale University Press.

Sternberg, R. J., & Powell, J. S. (1982). Theories of intelligence: In R. J. Sternberg (Ed.), *Handbook of human intelligence.* Cambridge: Cambridge University Press.

Sternberg, R. J., Conway, B. E., Ketron, J. L., & Bernstein, M. (1981). People's conceptions of intelligence. *Journal of Personality and Social Psychology, 41,* 37–55.

Sternberg, S. (1966). High-speed scanning in human memory. *Science, 153,* 652–654.

Sternglanz, S. H., & Serbin, L. A. (1974). Sex role stereotyping in children's television programs. *Developmental Psychology, 10,* 710–715.

Stevenson, H. W., Lee, S. Y., & Stigler, J. W. (1986). Mathematics achievement of Chinese, Japanese, and American children. *Science, 231,* 693–699.

Stevenson, H. W., Lee, S., Chen, C., Stigler, J. W., Hsu, C., & Kitamura, S. (1990). Contexts of achievement. *Monographs of the Society for Research in Child Development,* Serial No. 221, 55, Nos. 1–2.

Stice, E., Schupak-Neuberg, E., Shaw, H. E., & Stein, R. I. (1994). Relation of media exposure to eating disorder symptomatology: An examination of mediating mechanisms. *Journal of Abnormal Psychology, 103*(4), 836–840.

Stigler, J. W. (1984). "Mental abacus": The effect of abacus training on Chinese children's mental calculation. *Cognitive Psychology, 16,* 145–176.

Stipek, D. J. (1993). *Motivation to learn.* Boston: Allyn & Bacon.

Stipek, D. J., Gralinski, H., & Kopp, C. (1990). Self-concept development in the toddler years. *Developmental Psychology, 26,* 972–977.

Stogdill, R. M. (1950). Leadership, membership, and organization. *Psychological Bulletin, 47,* 1–14.

Stokols, D. (1972). On the distinction between density and crowding: Some implication for future research. *Psychological Review, 79,* 275–277.

Stone, A. A., Cox, D. S., Valdimarsdottir, H., Jandorf, L., & Neale, J. M. (1987). Evidence that secretory IgA antibody is associated with daily mood. *Journal of Personality and Social psychology, 52,* 988–993.

Stone, S. V., & Costa, P. T. (1990). Disease-prone personality or distress-prone personality: The role of neuroticism in coronary heart disease. In H. S. Friedman (Ed.) *Personality and Disease.* New York: Wiley, pp. 178–200.

Storfer, M. D. (1990). Intelligence and giftedness: The contributions of heredity and early environment. San Francisco: Jossey-Bass.

Storms, M. D., & Nisbett, R. E. (1970). Insomnia and the attribution process. *Journal of Personality and Social Psychology, 16,* 319–328.

Stotland, E. (1969). Exploratory investigations of empathy. In L. Berkowitz (Ed.), *Advances in experimental social psychology* (Vol. 4). New York: Academic Press.

Strack, F., Martin, L. L., & Stepper, S. (1988). Inhibiting and facilitating conditions of the human smile: A nonobtrusive test of the facial feedback hypothesis. *Journal of Personality and Social Psychology, 54,* 768–777.

Stratton, G. M. (1897). Vision without inversion of the retinal image. *Psychological Review, 4,* 341–360.

Strayer, F. F. (1980). Social ecology of the preschool peer group. In W. A. Collins (Ed.), *Minnesota symposium on child psychology: Vol. 13. Development of cognition, affect, and social relations.* Hillsdale, NJ: Erlbaum.

Strayer, F. F., Wareing, S., & Rushton, J. P. (1979). Social constraints on naturally occurring preschool altruism. *Ethology and Sociobiology, 1,* 3–11.

Streigel-Moore, R. H. (1993). Etiology of binge eating: A developmental perspective. In C. G. Fairburn & G. T. Wilson (Eds.), *Binge eating: Nature, assessment and treatment.* New York: Guilford Press.

Streigel-Moore, R. H., McAvay, G., & Rodin, J. (1986). Psychological and behavioral correlates of feeling fat in women. *International Journal of Eating Disorders, 5,* 935–947.

Streissguth, A. P., Barr, H. M., & Martin, D. C. (1983). Maternal alcohol use and neonatal habituation assessed with the Brazelton Scale. *Child Development, 54,* 1109–1118.

Strelau, J., & Eysenck, H. J. (Eds.) (1978). *Personality Dimensions and Arousal.* New York: Plenum.

Stricker, E. M. (1973). Thirst, sodium appetite, and complementary physiological contributions to the regulation of intravascular fluid volume. In A. N. Epstein, H. R. Kissileff, & E. Stellar (Eds.), *The neuropsychology of thirst: New findings and advances in concepts.* Washington, DC: Winston.

Stricker, E. M., Rowland, N., Saller, C. F., & Friedman, M. I. (1977). Homeostasis during hypoglycemia: Central control of adrenal secretion and peripheral control of feeding. *Science, 196,* 79–81.

Stroebe, W., & Diehl, M. (1988). When social support fails: Supporter characteristics in compliance-induced attitude change. *Personality and Social Psychology Bulletin, 14,* 136–144.

Stromeyer, C. F., & Psotka, J. (1970). The detailed texture of eidetic images. *Nature, 225,* 346–349.

Strong, E. K., Hansen, J., & Campbell, D. P. (1985). *The SVIB-SCII.* Palo Alto, CA: Consulting Psychologists Press.

Stroop, J. R. (1935). Studies of interference in serial verbal reactions. *Journal of Experimental Psychology, 18,* 643–662.

Strube, M. J., Lott, C. L., Le-Xuan-Hy, G. M., Oxenberg, J., & Deichmann, A. K. (1986). Self-evaluation of abilities: Accurate self-assessment versus biased self-enhancement. *Journal of Personality and Social Psychology, 51,* 16–26.

Strupp, H. H. (1983). Psychoanalytic psychotherapy. In M. Hersen, A. E. Kazdin, & A. S. Bellock (Eds.), *The clinical psychology handbook.* New York: Pergamon.

Strupp, H. H. (1990). Is psychotherapy the abuse of power? *Contemporary Psychology, 35,* 250.

Stuart, E. W., Shimp, T. A., & Engle, R. W. (1987). Classical conditioning of consumer attitudes: Four experiments in an advertising context. *Journal of Consumer Research, 14,* 334–349.

Stuart-Hamilton, I. (1994). *The Psychology of Ageing.* Bristol, PA: Jessica Kingsley Publishers.

Stunkard, A. J. (1976). *The Pain of Obesity.* Palo Alto, CA: Bull Publishing Company.

Stunkard, A. J., Sorensen, T. I. A., Hanis, C., Teasdale, T. W., Chakraborty, R., Schull, W. J., & Schulsinger, F. (1986). An adoption study of human obesity. *The New England Journal of Medicine, 314,* 193–198.

Sulik, K. K., Johnston, M. C., & Webb, M. A. (1981). Fetal alcohol syndrome. *Science, 214,* 936–938.

Sulin, R. A., & Dooling, D. J. (1974). Intrusion of a thematic idea in retention of prose. *Journal of Experimental Psychology, 103,* 255–262.

Sulloway, F. (1979). *Freud: Biologist of the mind.* New York: Basic Books.

Super, C. M., Herrera, M. G., & Mera, J. O. (1990). Long-term effects of food supplementation and psychosocial intervention on the physical growth of Columbian infants at risk of malnutrition. *Child Development, 61,* 29–49.

Surwit, R. S., Pilon, R. N., & Fenton, C. H. (1978). Behavioral treatment of Raynaud's disease. *Journal of Behavioral Medicine, 1,* 323.

Sutherland, N. S. (1976). *Breakdown.* New York: Stein & Day.

Suzuki, M., & Tamura, T. (1988). Intake timing of fat and insulinogenic sugars and efficiency of body fat accumulation. In *Diet and obesity* (pp. 113–119).

Suzuki, S., Augerinos, G., & Black, A. H. (1980). Stimulus control of spatial behavior on the eight-arm maze in rats. *Learning and Motivation, 11,* 1–18.

Swaim, R. C., Oetting, E. R., Edwards, R. W., & Beauvais, F. (1989). Links from emotional distress to adolescent drug use: A path model. *Journal of Consulting and Clinical Psychology, 57,* 227–231.

Swann, W. B. (1983). Self-motivation: Bringing social reality into harmony with the self. In J. Suls & a. G. Greenwald (Eds.), *Psychological perspectives on the self* (Vol. 2). Hillsdale, NJ: Erlbaum.

Swann, W. B., Jr. (1987). Identity negotiation: Where two roads meet. *Journal of Personality and Social Psychology, 53,* 1038–1051.

Swets, J. A., & Bjork, R. A. (1990). Enhancing human performance: An evaluation of "New Age" techniques considered by the U.S. Army. *Psychological Science, 1,* 85–96.

Szasz, T. S. (1961). *The myth of mental illness: Foundations of a theory of personal conduct.* New York: Harper & Hoeber.

Szasz, T. S. (1970). *The manufacture of madness.* New York: Harper & Row.

Szasz, T. S. (1974). *Ceremonial chemistry: The ritual persecution of drugs, addicts, and pushers.* Garden City, NY: Doubleday.

Szasz, T. S. (1976). The ethics of suicide. In B. B. Wolman & H. H. Krauss (Eds.), *Between survival and suicide.* New York: Gardner, pp. 163–185.

Szepesi, B. (1978). A model of nutritionally induced overweight: Weight "rebound" following caloric restriction. In G. A. Bray (Ed.), *Recent advances in obesity research* (Vol. 2). London: Newman.

T

Tajfel, H. (1981). *Human Groups and Social Categories: Studies in Social Psychology.* Cambridge, England: Cambridge University Press.

Tajfel, H. (1982). Social psychology of intergroup relations. *Annual Review of psychology, 33,* 1–39.

Tajfel, H., & Turner, J. C. (1986). An integrative theory of intergroup relations. In S. Worchel & W. G. Austin (Eds.), *Psychology of intergroup relations* (pp. 7–24). Chicago: Nelson-Hall.

Takahashi, K. (1990). Are the key assumptions of the "strange situation" procedure universal? A view from Japanese research. *Human Development, 33,* 23–30.

Takanishi, R. (1993). The opportunities of adolescence—Research, interventions, and policy. *American Psychologist, 48,* 85–87.

Tanner, J. M. (1973). Growing up. *Scientific American, 229,* 34–43.

Tansey, M. J., & Burke, W. F. (1989). *Understanding countertransference.* Hillsdale, NJ: The Analytic Press.

Tarpy, R. M., & Sawabini, F. L. (1974). Reinforcement delay: A selective review of the last decade. *Psychological Bulletin, 81,* 984–987.

Tarrier, N. (1989). Electrodermal activity, expressed emotion and outcome in schizophrenia. *British Journal of Psychiatry, 155,* 51–56.

Task Force on DSM-IV, American Psychiatric Association. (1993). DSM-IV Draft Criteria. Washington, DC: American Psychiatric Association.

Tassinary, L. G., & Cacioppo, J. T. (1992). Unobservable facial actions and emotion. *Psychological Science, 3,* 28–33.

Taub, E., Crago, J. E., Burgio, L. D., Groomes, T. E., Cook, E. W., DeLuca, S. C., & Miller, N. E. (1994). An operant approach to rehabilitation medicine: Overcoming learned nonuse by shaping. *Journal of Experimental Analysis of Behavior, 61,* 281–293.

Taubes, G. (1994). Will new dopamine receptors offer a key to schizophrenia? *Science, 265,* 1034–1035.

Taubes, G. (1995). Epidemiology faces its limits. *Science, 269,* 164–169.

Tavris, C. (1983). *Anger: The misunderstood emotion.* New York: Simon & Schuster.

Taylor, F. W. (1911). *Scientific management.* New York: Harper & Brothers.

Taylor, J. A. (1953). A personality scale of manifest anxiety. *Journal of Abnormal and Social Psychology, 48,* 285–290.

Taylor, S. E. (1989). *Positive illusions: Creative self-deception and the healthy mind.* New York: Basic Books.

Taylor, S. E., & Brown, J. D. (1988). Illusion and well-being: A social psychological perspective on mental health. *Psychological Bulletin, 103,* 193–210.

Taylor, S. E., & Fiske, S. T. (1975). Point of view and perceptions of causality. *Journal of Personality and Social Psychology, 32,* 439–445.

Teasdale, T. W., & Owen, D. R. (1984). Heredity and familial environment in intelligence and educational level: A sibling study. *Nature, 309,* 620–622.

Tellegen, A., Lykken, D. T., Bouchard, T. J., Wilcox, K., Segal, N., & Rich, S. (1988). Personality similarity in twins reared apart and together. *Journal of Personality and Social Psychology, 54,* 1031–1039.

Teller, D. Y., & Bornstein, M. H. (1987). Infant color vision and color perception. In P. Salapatek & L. Cohen (Eds.), *Handbook of infant perception: Vol. 1, From sensation to perception* (pp. 185–236). Orlando, FL: Academic Press.

Temoshok, L. (1990). On attempting to articulate the biopsychosocial model: Psychological-psychophysiological homeostasis. In H. S. Friedman (Ed.) *Personality and Disease.* New York: Wiley, pp. 203–225.

Tennen, H., & Affleck, G. (1987). The costs and benefits of optimistic explanations and dispositional optimism. *Journal of Personality, 55,* 377–393.

Tennen, H., Herzberger, S., & Nelson, H. F. (1987). Depressive attributional style: The role of self-esteem. *Journal of Personality, 55,* 631–660.

Terenius, L., & Wahlström, A. (1975). Morphine-like ligand for opiate receptors in human CSF. *Life Sciences, 16,* 1759–1764.

Terman, L. M. (1916). *The measurement of intelligence.* Boston: Houghton Mifflin.

Terman, L. M. (1954). The discovery and encouragement of exceptional talent. *American Psychologist, 9,* 221–230.

Terman, L. M., & Merrill, M. A. (1973). *Stanford-Binet intelligence scales: 1973 norms edition.* Boston: Houghton Mifflin.

Terman, L. M., & Oden, M. H. (1959). *Genetic studies of genius: The gifted at mid-life: Thirty-five years follow-up of the superior child* (Vol. 5). Stanford, CA: Stanford University Press.

Terrace, H. S. (1979, November). How Nim Chimpsky changed my mind. *Psychology Today, 13,* 65–76.

Tesser, A., & Schaffer, D. R. (1990). Attitudes and attitude change. *Annual Review of Psychology, 41,* 479–524.

Thaler, R. H. (1985). Mental accounting and consumer choice. *Marketing Science, 4,* 199–214.

Thelen, E. (1984). Learning to walk. In L. Lipsitt & C. Rovee-Collier (Eds.), *Advances in infancy research* (Vol. 3, pp. 213–250).

Theorell, T. (1974). Life events before and after the onset of a premature myocardial infarction. In B. S. Dohrenwend & B. P. Dohrenwend (Eds.), *Stressful life events: Their nature and effects* (pp. 101–117). New York: Wiley.

Thigpen, C. H., & Cleckley, H. (1954). *The three faces of Eve.* Kingsport, Tenn.: Kingsport Press.

Thomas, E. L., & Robinson, H. A. (1972). *Improving reading in every class: A sourcebook for teachers.* Boston: Allyn & Bacon.

Thomas, K., & Althen, G. (1989). Counseling foreign students. In P. Pedersen, J. Dragens, W. Lonner, & J. Trimble (Eds.), *Counseling across cultures* (3rd ed.) (pp. 205–241). Honolulu: University of Hawaii Press.

Thompson, I. E. (1987). Fundamental ethical principles in health care. *British Medical Journal, 295,* 1461–1465.

Thompson, J. K., Jarvie, G. J., Lahey, B. B., & Cureton, K. J. (1982). Exercise and obesity: Etiology, physiology, and intervention. *Psychological Bulletin, 91,* 55–79.

Thompson, P. (1980). Margaret Thatcher—a new illusion. *Perception, 9,* 483–484.

Thompson, R. F. (1985). *The brain: An introduction to neuroscience.* New York: Freeman.

Thompson, W. R. (1953). The inheritance of behavior: Behavioral differences in fifteen mouse strains. *Canadian Journal of Psychology, 7,* 145–155.

Thorndike, E. L. (1903). *Educational psychology.* New York: Lemke and Buechner.

Thorndike, E. L. (1911). *Animal intelligence.* New York: Macmillan.

Thorndike, R. L., Hagen, E. P., & Sattler, J. M. (1985). *Stanford-Binet* (4th ed.). Chicago: Riverside Publishing.

Thorpy, M. J., & Yager, J. (1991). *The encyclopedia of sleep and sleep disorders.* New York: Facts on File.

Thurstone, L. L. (1938). *Primary mental abilities.* Chicago: University of Chicago Press.

Timberlake, W. (1980). A molar equilibrium theory of learned performance. In G. H. Bower (Ed.), *The psychology of learning and motivation,* Vol. 14 (pp. 1–58). New York: Academic Press.

Timberlake, W. (1984). The functional organization of appetitive behavior: Behavior systems and learning. In M. D. Zeiler & P. Harzem (Eds.), *Advances in the analysis of behavior: Vol. 3.* New York: Wiley.

Timberlake, W., & Allison, J. (1974). Response deprivation: An empirical approach to instrumental performance. *Psychological Review, 81,* 146–166.

Tobach, E., Bellin, J. S., & Das, D. K. (1974). Differences in bitter taste perception in three strains of rats. *Behavior Genetics, 4,* 405–410.

Todd, J., & Bohart, A. C. (1994). *Foundations of clinical and counseling psychology,* second edition. New York: Harper Collins College Publishers.

Toffler, A. (1970). *Future shock.* New York: Random House.

Tolman, E. C. (1932). *Purposive behavior in animals and men.* New York: Appleton-Century-Crofts.

Tolman, E. C., & Honzik, C. H. (1930). Introduction and removal of reward and maze performance in rats. *University of California Publications in Psychology, 4,* 257–275.

Tomkins, S. S. (1980). Affect as amplification: Some modifications in theory. In

R. Plutchik & H. Kellerman (Eds.), *Theories of emotion*. New York: Academic Press.

Tonkinson, R. (1978). *The Mardudjara aborigines*. New York: Holt, Rinehart & Winston.

Tonn, B. E., Travis, C. B., Goeltz, R. T., & Phillippi, R. H. (1990). Knowledge-based representations of risk beliefs. *Risk Analysis, 10*, 169–183.

Tonna, E. A. (1977). Aging of skeletal-dental systems and supporting tissue. In C. E. Finch & L. Hayflick (Eds.), *Handbook of the biology of aging*. New York: Van Nostrand Reinhold.

Toobin, J. (1993). The burden of Clarence Thomas. *The New Yorker*, September 27, 38–51.

Torgesen, J. K. (1977). The role of nonspecific factors in the task performance of learning-disabled children: A theoretical assessment. *Journal of Learning Disabilities, 10*, 27–34.

Tourney, G. (1980). Hormones and homosexuality. In J. Marmon (Ed.), *Homosexual Behavior* (pp. 41–58). New York: Basic Books.

Townsend, J. T. (1971). Theoretical analysis of an alphabetical confusion matrix. *Perception & Psychophysics, 9*, 40–50.

Tranel, D., & Damasio, A. R. (1985). Knowledge without awareness: An automatic index of facial recognition by prosopagnosics. *Science, 228*, 1453–1454.

Traver, S. G., Hallahan, D. P., Kauffman, J. M., & Ball, D. W. (1976). Verbal rehearsal and selective attention in children with learning disabilities: A developmental lag. *Journal of Experimental Child Psychology, 22*, 375–385.

Travis, J. (1992). Can hair cells unlock deafness? *Science, 257*, 1344–1345.

Treffert, D. A. (1989). *Extraordinary people: Understanding savant syndrome*. New York: Ballantine Books.

Treffert, D. A. (1992). Savant syndrome. In L. R. Squire (Ed.), *Encyclopedia of Learning and Memory* (pp. 573–574). New York: Macmillan.

Treisman, A. (1986). Features and objects in visual perception. *Scientific American, 255*, 114–124.

Treisman, A. (1989). Features and objects: The Fourteenth Bartlett Memorial Lecture. *Quarterly Journal of Experimental Psychology, 40A*, 201–237.

Treisman, A. (1993). The perception of features and objects. In A. Baddelely & L. Weiskrantz (Eds.), *Attention: Selection, awareness, and control* (pp. 5–35). Oxford: Clarendon Press.

Treisman, A., & Geffen, G. (1967). Selective attention: Perception or response? *Quarterly Journal of Experimental Psychology, 19*, 1–17.

Trevarthen, C. (1980). Functional organization of the human brain. In M. C. Wittrock (Ed.), *The brain and psychology*. New York: Academic Press.

Triplett, N. (1898). The dynamogenic factors in pacemaking and competition. *American Journal of Psychology, 9*, 507–533.

Tritsch, M. F. (1992). Fourier analysis of the stimuli for pattern-induced flicker colors. *Vision Research, 32*, 1461–1470.

Trivers, R. (1985). *Social evolution*. Menlo Park, CA: Benjamin/Cummings.

Trivers, R. L. (1972). Parental investment and sexual selection. In B. Campbell (Ed.), *Sexual selection and the descent of man*. Chicago: Aldine.

Trivers, R. L., & Hare, H. (1976). Haplodiploidy and the evolution of social insects. *Science, 191*, 249–263.

Troll, L. E., Miller, S. J., & Atchley, R. C. (1979). *Families in later life*. Belmont, CA: Wadsworth.

Trope, Y. (1975). Seeking information about one's own ability as a determinant of choice among tasks. *Journal of Personality and Social Psychology, 32*, 1004–1013.

Troscianko, T., Mantangnon, R., Le Clerc, J., Malbert, E., & Chanteau, P. (1991). The role of colour as a monocular depth cue. *Vision Research, 31*, 1923–1930.

Trussel, J. (1988). Teenage pregnancy in the United States. *Family Planning Perspectives, 20*, 262–272.

Trussell, J., & Westoff, C. F. (1980). "Contraceptive Practice and Trends in Coital Frequency." *Family Planning Perspectives, 12*, 246–249.

Tucker, D. M. (1981). Lateral brain function, emotion, and conceptualization. *Psychological Bulletin, 89*, 19–46.

Tulving, E. (1962). Subjective organization in the free recall of "unrelated" words. *Psychological Review, 69*, 344–354.

Tulving, E. (1967). The effects of presentation and recall in free recall learning. *Journal of Verbal Learning and Behavior, 6*, 175–184.

Tulving, E. (1972). Episodic and semantic memory. In E. Tulving & W. Donaldson (Eds.), *Organization of memory* (pp. 590–600). New York: Academic Press.

Tulving, E. (1976). Ecphoric processes in recall and recognition. In J. Brown (Ed.), *Recall and recognition*. New York: Wiley.

Tulving, E. (1982). *Elements of episodic memory*. New York: Oxford University Press.

Tulving, E. (1985). How many memory systems are there? *American Psychologist, 40*, 385–398.

Tulving, E. (1985). Memory and consciousness. *Canadian Psychology, 26*, 1–12.

Tulving, E. (1991). Interview. *Journal of Cognitive Neuroscience, 3*, 89–94.

Tulving, E. (1993). What is episodic memory? *Current Directions in Psychological Science, 2*, 67–70.

Tulving, E., & Pearlstone, Z. (1966). Availability versus accessibility of information in memory for words. *Journal of Verbal Learning and Verbal Behavior, 5*, 381–391.

Tulving, E., & Psotka, J. (1971). Retroactive inhibition in free recall: Inaccessibility of information available in the memory store. *Journal of Experimental Psychology, 87*, 1–8.

Tulving, E., & Thomson, D. (1973). Encoding specificity and retrieval processes in epixodic memory. *Psychological Review, 80*, 352–373.

Tunaka, J. W., & Farah, M. J. (1991). Second order relational properties and the inversion effect: Testing a theory of face perception. *Perception & Psychophysics, 50*, 367–372.

Turkington, C. (1983, April). Drug found to block dopamine receptors. *APA Monitor*, p. 11.

Turner, J. C. (1985). Social categorization and the self-concept: A social cognitive theory of group behavior. In E. J. Lawler (Ed.), *Advances in Group Processes, Vol. 2*. (pp. 77–121). Greenwich, CT: JAI Press.

Turner, S. M., Beidel, D. C., & Townsley, R. M. (1992). Social phobia: A comparison of specific and generalized subtypes and avoidant personality disorder. *Journal of Abnormal Psychology, 101*, 326–331.

Tuschl, R. J. (1990). From dietary restraint to binge eating: Some theoretical considerations. *Appetite, 14*, 105–109.

Tuttle, F. B., & Becker, L. A. (1983). *Characteristics and identification of gifted and talented students*. Washington, DC: National Education Association.

Tversky, A., & Kahneman, D. (1971). Belief in the law of small numbers. *Psychological Bulletin, 76*, 105–110.

Tversky, A., & Kahneman, D. (1974). Judgments under uncertainty: Heuristics and biases. *Sciences, 185*, 1124–1131.

Tversky, A., & Kahneman, D. (1981). The framing of decisions and the psychology of choice. *Science, 211*, 453–458.

Tversky, A., & Kahneman, D. (1982). Variants of uncertainty. *Cognition, 11*, 143–157.

U

U.S. Bureau of Labor Statistics. (1991). *Working women: A chartbook*. Washington, DC: U.S. Department of Labor.

U.S. Bureau of the Census (1986). *Statistical abstract of the United States*. Washington, DC: U.S. Government Printing Office.

U.S. Bureau of the Census. (1990). *Statistical abstract* (110th ed.). Washington, DC: U.S. Government Printing Office.

U.S. Department of Health and Human Services (1982). *Television and behavior: Ten years of progress and implications for the eighties: Vol. 1. Summary report. Vol. 2. Technical reviews*. Washington, DC: U.S. Government Printing Office.

U.S. Department of Justice. (1991). *Criminal Victimization, 1990* (Special Report No. NCJ-122743). Washington, DC: Bureau of Justice Statistics.

U.S. Department of Labor (1987). Office of Information, Publication, and Reports. Over half of mothers with children one year or under in labor force in March 1987. *Women and work*. Washington, DC: U.S. Government Printing Office.

U.S. Surgeon General (1979). *Healthy people*. Washington, DC: U.S. Government Printing Office.

Ullman, L. P., & Krasner, L. (1969). *A psychological approach to abnormal behavior*. Englewood Cliffs, NJ: Prentice-Hall.

Ullman, L. P., & Krasner, L. (Eds.). (1965). *Case studies in behavior modification*. New York: Holt, Rinehart & Winston.

Ulrich, R. (1966). Pain as a cause of aggression. *American Zoologist, 6*, 643–662.

Ulrich, R. E., & Azrin, N. H. (1962). Reflexive fighting in response to aversive stimulation. *Journal of the Experimental Analysis of Behavior, 5*, 511–520.

Ulrich, R. E., Hutchinson, R. R., & Azrin, N. H. (1965). Pain-elicited aggression. *Psychological Record, 15*, 111–126.

Ulrich, R. S., Simons, R. F., Losito, B. D., Fierito, E., Miles, M. A., & Zelson, M. (1991). Stress recovery during exposure to natural and urban environments. *Journal of Environmental Psychology, 11*, 201–230.

Underwood, B. J. (1957). Interference and forgetting. *Psychological Review, 64*, 49–60.

Underwood, B. J. (1965). False recognition produced by implicit verbal responses. *Journal of Experimental Psychology, 70*, 122–129.

Upton, W. E. (1974). Altruism, attribution, and intrinsic motivation in the recruitment of blood donors. Doctoral dissertation, Cornell University (1973). *Dissertation Abstracts International, 34*, 6260–B.

V

Vaillant, G. E. (1977). *Adaptation to life*. Boston: Little, Brown.

Valenstein, E. S. (1986). *Great and desperate cures*. New York: Basic Books.

Valenstein, E. S. (1990). Electroconvulsive treatment: It apparently works, but how and at what risks are not yet clear. *Contemporary Psychology, 35*, 109–111.

Van Court, M., & Bean, F. D. (1985). Intelligence and fertility in the United States: 1912–1982. *Intelligence, 9*, 23–32.

Van Doorninck, W. J., Caldwell, B. M., Wright, C., & Frankenburg, W. K. (1981). The relationship between twelve-month home stimulation and school achievement. *Child Development, 52,* 1080–1083.

Van Hook, E., & Higgins, E. T. (1988). Self-related problems beyond the self concept: Motivational consequences of discrepant self-guides. *Journal of Personality and Social Psychology, 55,* 633–652.

Vandenbergh, J. G., Witsett, J. M., & Lombardi, J. R. (1975). Partial isolation of a pheromone accelerating puberty in female mice. *Journal of Reproductive Fertility, 43,* 515–523.

Vandenbergh, J. G., Witsett, J. M., & Lombardi, J. R. (1975). Partial isolation of a pheromone accelerating puberty in female mice. *Journal of Reproductive Fertility, 43,* 515–523.

Vaughn, C. E. (1989). Annotation: Expressed emotion in family relationships. *Journal of Child Psychology and Psychiatry, 30,* 13–22.

Veilleux, S., & Melzack, R. D. (1976). Pain in psychotic patients. *Experimental Neurology, 52,* 535–543.

Venturino, M. (1991). Automatic processing, code dissimilarity, and the efficiency of successive memory searches. *Journal of Experimental Psychology: Human Perception and Performance, 17,* 677–695.

Vessey, J. T., & Howard, K. I. (1994). Who seeks psychotherapy? *Psychotherapy.*

Viscott, D. S. (1969). A musical idiot savant. *Psychiatry, 32,* 494–515.

Visintainer, M., Volpicelli, J., & Seligman, M. (1982). Tumor rejection in rats after inescapable and escapable shock. *Science, 216,* 437–439.

Visintainer, M., Volpicelli, J., & Seligman, M. (1982). Tumor rejection in rats after inescapable and escapable shock. *Science, 216,* 437–439.

Vitiello, M. V., Carlin, A. S., Becker, J., Barris, B. P., & Dutton, J. (1989). The effect of subliminal Oedipal and competitive stimulation on dart throwing: Another miss. *Journal of Abnormal Psychology, 98,* 54–56.

Vogel, G. W. (1975). A review of REM sleep deprivation. *Archives of General Psychiatry, 32,* 749–761.

Vokey, J. R., & Read, J. D. (1991). Subliminal messages: Between the devil and the media. In R. P. Honeck, T. J. S. Case, & M. J. Firment (Eds.), *Introductory readings for cognitive psychology* (pp. 293–304). Guilford, CT: Dushkin Publishing Group.

Volkan, V. D. (1988). *The need to have enemies and allies.* Livingston, NJ: Aronson.

Von Restorff, H. (1933). Über die Wirking von Bereichsbildungen im Spurenfeld. In W. Kohler & H. von Restorff, *Analyse von Vorgangen im Spurenfeld: 1. Psychologische Forschung, 18,* 299–342.

Von Senden, M. (1960). *Space and sight* (P. Heath, Trans.). New York: Free Press.

Vonnegut, M. (1976). *The Eden express.* New York: Bantam Books.

Voyer, D., & Bryden, M. P. (1990). Gender, level of spatial ability, and lateralization of mental rotation. *Brain & Cognition, 13(1),* 18–29.

Vroom, V. (1964). *Work and motivation.* New York: Wiley.

Vroom, V. H. (1979). An outline of a cognitive model. In R. M. Steers & L. W. Porter (Eds.), *Motivation and work behavior.* New York: McGraw-Hill.

Vuchinich, S., Hetherington, E. M., Vuchinich, R. A., & Clingempeel, W. G. (1991). Parent-child interaction and gender differences in early adolescents' adaptation to stepfamilies. *Developmental Psychology, 27,* 618–626.

Vygotsky, L. S. (1962). *Thought and language.* Cambridge, MA: MIT Press.

W

Waddell, K. J., & Rogoff, B. (1981). Effect of contextual organization on spatial memory of middle-aged and older women. *Developmental Psychology, 17,* 878–885.

Wade, N. J., & Swanston, M. (1991). *Visual perception: An introduction.* London: Routlege.

Wade, P., & Bernstein, B. L. (1991). Culture sensitivity training and counselor's race: Effects on black female clients' perceptions and attrition. *Journal of Counseling Psychology, 38,* 9–15.

Wagner, A. R. (1961). Effects of amount and percentage of reinforcement and number of acquisition trials on conditioning and extinction. *Journal of Experimental Psychology, 62,* 234–242.

Wagner, A. R., Siegel, S., Thomas, E., & Ellison, G. D. (1964). Reinforcement history and the extinction of a conditioned salivary response. *Journal of Comparative and Physiological Psychology, 58,* 354–358.

Wahlsten, D. (1972). Genetic experiments with animal learning: A critical review. *Behavioral Biology, 7,* 143–182.

Walker, J. T., Rupich, R. C., & Powell, J. L. (1989). The vista paradox: A natural visual illusion. *Perception & Psychophysics, 45,* 43–48.

Walker, J., & Hertzog, C. (1975). Aging, brain function and behavior. In S. Woodruff & J. E. Birren (Eds.), *Aging: Scientific perspectives and social issues.* New York: Van Nostrand Reinhold.

Wall, P. D. (1979). On the relation of injury to pain. *Pain, 6,* 253–264.

Wallace, I. (1977). Self-control techniques of famous novelists. *Journal of Applied Behavior Analyses, 10,* 515–525.

Wallace, J., & O'Hara, M. W. (1992). Increases in depressive symptomatology in the rural elderly: Results from a cross-sectional and longitudinal study. *Journal of Abnormal Psychology, 101,* 398–404.

Wallace, P. (1977). Individual discrimination of humans by odor. *Physiology and Behavior, 19,* 577–579.

Wallach, M. A. (1985). Creativity testing and giftedness. In F. D. Horowitz & M. O'Brien (Eds.), *The gifted and talented: Developmental perspectives.* Washington, DC: American Psychological Association.

Wallach, M. A., Kogan, N., & Bem, D. J. (1964). Diffusion of responsibility and level of risk taking in groups. *Journal of Abnormal and Social Psychology, 68,* 263–274.

Waller, N. G., Kojetin, B. A., Bouchard, T.J., Kykken, D. T., & Tellegen, A. (1990). Genetic and environmental influences on religious interests, attitudes, and values: A study of twins reared apart and together. *Psychological Science, 1,* 138–142.

Waller, P. F. (1991). The older driver. *Human Factors, 33,* 499–505.

Walster, E., Aronson, V., Abrahams, D., & Rottman, L. (1966). Importance of physical attractiveness in dating behavior. *Journal of Personality and Social Psychology, 4,* 508–516.

Walster, E., Walster, G., Piliavin, J., & Schmidt, L. (1973). "Playing hard-to-get": Understanding an elusive phenomenon. *Journal of Personality and Social Psychology, 26,* 113–121.

Wandersman, A. H., & Hallman, W. K. (1993). Are people acting irrationally? Understanding public concerns about environmental threats. *American Psychologist, 48,* 681–686.

Wang, D. F. (1986). Position emission tomography reveals elevated D2 dopamine receptors in drug-naive schizophrenics. *Science, 234,* 1558–1563.

Wanous, J. P. (1980). *Organizational entry: Recruitment, selection, and socialization of newcomers.* Reading, MA: Addison-Wesley.

Warga, C. (1987, August). Pain's gatekeeper. *Psychology Today,* 50–56.

Warrington, E. K., & Shallice, T. (1980). Word form dislexia. *Brain, 30,* 99–112.

Wason, P. C., & Johnson-Laird, P. N. (1972). *Psychology of reasoning: Structure and content.* Cambridge, MA: Harvard University Press.

Watkins, L. R., & Mayer, D. J. (1982). Organization of endogenous opiate and nonopiate pain control systems. *Science, 216,* 1185–1192.

Watkins, M. J. (1975). Inhibition in recall with extralist "cues." *Journal of Verbal Learning and Verbal Behavior, 14,* 294–303.

Watkins, M. J. (1979). Engrams as cuegrams and forgetting as cue overload: A cueing approach to the structure of memory. In C. R. Puff (Ed.), *Memory organization and structure* (pp. 347–372). New York: Academic Press.

Watson, D., & Pennebaker, J. W. (1989). Health complaints, stress, and distress: Exploring the control role of negative affectivity. *Psychological Review, 96,* 234–254.

Watson, D., & Tellegen, A. (1985). Toward a consensual structure of mood. *Psychological Bulletin, 98,* 219–235.

Watson, J. B. (1913). Psychology as the behaviorist views it. *Psychological Review, 20,* 158–177.

Watson, J. B. (1924). *Behaviorism.* Chicago: University of Chicago Press.

Watson, J. B. (1928). *Psychological care of infant and child.* New York: Norton.

Watson, J. B., & Rayner, R. (1920). Conditioned emotional reactions. *Journal of Experimental Psychology, 3,* 1–14.

Watson, J. S., & Ramey, C. T. (1972). Reactions to responsive contingent stimulation in early infancy. *Merrill-Palmer Quarterly, 18,* 219–227.

Waxenberg, S. E., Drelich, M. G., & Sutherland, A. M. (1959). The role of hormones in human behavior: 1. Changes in female sexuality after adrenalectomy. *Journal of Clinical Endocrinology, 19,* 193–202.

Waynbaum, I. (1907). *La physionomie humaine: Son mécanisme et son rôle social.* Paris: Alcan.

Weale, R. A. (1982). Retinal senescence. In I. N. Osborne & J. Chader (Eds.), *Progress in retinal research.* Vol. 5 (pp. 53–73). Oxford: Pergamon Press.

Weaver, C. A., III. (1993). Do you need a flash to form a flash-bulb memory? *Journal of Experimental Psychology: General, 122,* 39–46.

Webb, T., Bundey, S., Thake, A., & Todd, J. (1986). Population incidence and segregation ratios in the Martin-Bell syndrome. *American Journal of Medical Genetics, 23,* 573–580.

Webb, W. B. (1975). *Sleep: The gentle tyrant.* Englewood Cliffs, NJ: Prentice-Hall.

Webb, W. B., & Agnew, H. W. (1973). *Sleep and dreams.* Dubuque, IA: William C. Brown.

Webb, W. P., & Agnew, H. W., Jr. (1968). In L. E. Abt & B. F. Reiss (Eds.), *Progress in clinical psychology.* New York: Grune & Stratton.

Weigel, R. H., Vernon, D. T. A., & Tognacci, L. N. (1974). Specificity of the attitude as a determinant of attitude-behavior congruence. *Journal of Personality and Social Psychology, 30,* 724–728.

Weinberger, D. R., Wagner, R. J., & Wyatt, R. L. (1983). Neuropathological studies of schizophrenia: A selective review. *Schizophrenia Bulletin, 9,* 198–212.

Weiner, B., & Kukla, A. (1970). An attributional analysis of achievement motivation. *Journal of Personality and Social Psychology, 15,* 1–20.

Weiner, I. B. (1982). *Child and adolescent psychopathology.* New York: Wiley.

Weiner, M. F. (1982). *The psychotherapeutic impasse.* New York: Free Press.

Weiner, R. D. (1984). Does electroconvulsive therapy cause brain damage? *Behavioral and Brain Sciences, 7,* 1–53.

Weingardt, K. R., Toland, H. K., & Loftus, E. F. (1994). Reports of suggested memories: Do people truly believe them? In D. F. Ross, J. D. Read & M. P. Toglia (Eds.), *Adult eyewitness testimony: Current trends and developments.* Cambridge: Cambridge University Press.

Weinraub, D. J., & Schneck, M. K. (1986). Fragments of Delbonef and Ebbinghaus illusions: Contour/context explorations of misjudged circle size. *Perception & Psychophysics, 40,* 147–158.

Weiss, J. M. (1968). Effects of coping responses on stress. *Journal of Comparative and Physiological Psychology, 65,* 251–260.

Weiss, J. M. (1970). Somatic effects of predictable and unpredictable shock. *Psychosomatic Medicine, 32,* 397–408.

Weiss, J. M. (1971a). Effects of coping behavior in different warning-signal conditions on stress pathology in rats. *Journal of Comparative and Physiological Psychology, 77,* 1–13.

Weiss, J. M. (1971b). Effects of coping behavior with and without a feedback signal on stress pathology in rats. *Journal of Comparative and Psychological Psychology, 77,* 22–30.

Weissberg, J. A., & Paris, S. G. (1986). Young children's remembering in different contexts. *Child Development, 57,* 1123–1129.

Weisz, J. R. (1990). Cultural-familial mental retardation: A developmental perspective on cognitive performance and "helpless" behavior. In R. M. Hodapp, J. A. Burack, & E. Zigler (Eds.), *Issues in the developmental approach to mental retardation* (pp. 137–168). New York: Cambridge University Press.

Weisz, J. R., & Zigler, E. (1979). Cognitive development in retarded and non-retarded persons: Piagetian tests of the similar sequence hypothesis. *Psychological Bulletin, 86,* 831–851.

Welch, R. B. (1978). *Perceptual modification.* New York: Academic Press.

Weldon, M. S., & Roediger, H. L. (1987). Altering retrieval demands reverses the picture superiority effect. *Memory and Cognition, 15,* 269–280.

Wellman, H. M., & Gelman, S. A. (1988). Children's understanding of the nonobvious. In R. J. Sternberg (Ed.), *Advances in the psychology of human intelligence, Vol. 4* (pp. 99–135). Hillsdale, NJ: Erlbaum.

Wellman, H. M., Ritter, K., & Flavell, J. H. (1975). Deliberate memory behavior in the delayed reactions of very young children. *Developmental Psychology, 11,* 780–787.

Wells, G. L. (1993). What do we know about eyewitness identification? *American Psychologist, 48,* 553–571.

Wells, G. L., & Petty, R. E. (1980). The effects of overt head-movements on persuasion, compatibility, and incompatibility of responses. *Journal of Basic and Applied Social Psychology, 1,* 219–230.

Wendt, G. R. (1937). Two and one-half year retention of a conditioned response. *Journal of General Psychology, 17,* 178–180.

Wentzel, K. R. (1989). Adolescent classroom goals: Standards for performance and academic achievement: An interactionist perspective. *Journal of Educational Psychology, 81,* 131–142.

Wertsch, J. V., & Tulviste, P. (1992). L. S. Vygotsky and contemporary developmental psychology. *Developmental Psychology, 28,* 548–557.

Wesnes, K. A., & Parrott, A. C. (1992). Smoking, nicotine, and human performance. In A. P. Smith & D. M. Jones (Eds.), *Handbook of human performance: Vol. 2. Health and Performance* (pp. 127–168). London: Academic Press.

Westbrook, J. D. (1982). *Considering the research: What makes an effective school?* Austin, TX: Southwest Educational Development Laboratory.

Westen, D. (1990). Psychoanalytic approaches to personality. In L. A. Pervin (Ed.) *Handbook of Personality: Theory and Research.* New York, Guilford, pp. 21–65.

Westoff, C. F. (1974). Coital frequency and contraception. *Family Planning Perspectives, 6,* 136–141.

Wever, E. G., & Bray, C. W. (1937). The perception of low tones and the resonance-volley theory. *Journal of Psychology, 3,* 101–114.

Weyant, J. M., & Smith, S. L. (1987). Getting more by asking for less: The effect of request size on donations of charity. *Journal of Applied Social Psychology, 17,* 392–400.

Whaley, L. F., & Wong, D. L. (1988). *Essentials of pediatric nursing* (3rd ed.). St. Louis: Mosby.

Wheatley, D. (1990). Beta-blockers in anxiety: The stress connection. In D. Wheatley (Ed.), *The anxiolytic jungle: Where next?* (pp. 137–152). New York: Wiley.

Wheeler, D. L. (1993). Study of lesbians rekindles debate over biological basis of homosexuality. *The Chronicle of Higher Education,* March 17, A7–A14.

Wheeler, D. L. (1993, March 17). Study of lesbians rekindles debate over biological basis of homosexuality. *The Chronicle of Higher Education,* Au–A14.

Wheeler, L. (1966). Toward a theory of behavioral contagion. *Psychological Review, 73,* 179–192.

Whitbeck, L. B., & Simons, R. L. (1990). Life on the streets: The victimization of runaway and homeless adolescents. *Youth and Society, 22,* 108–125.

White, G. L., & Kight, T. D. (1984). Misattribution of arousal and attraction: Effects of salience of explanations for arousal. *Journal of Experimental Social Psychology, 20,* 55–64.

White, G. L., Fishbein, S., & Rutstein, J. (1981). Passionate love and the misattribution of arousal. *Journal of Personality and Social Psychology, 41,* 56–62.

White, S. H. (1965). Evidence for a hierarchical arrangement of learning processes. In L. P. Lipsitt & C. C. Spiker (Eds.), *Advances in child development and behavior* (Vol. 2). New York: Academic Press.

White, S. H. (1992). G. Stanley Hall: From philosophy to developmental psychology. *Child Development, 28,* 25–34.

Whitehurst, G. J. (1982). Language development. In B. Wolman (Ed.), *Handbook of developmental psychology* (pp. 367–388). Englewood Cliffs, NJ: Prentice-Hall.

Whitney, E. N., & Rolfes, S. R. (1993). *Understanding nutrition.* Minneapolis, MN: West Publishing.

Whitney, E. N., & Rolfes, S. R. (1993). *Understanding nutrition.* Minneapolis, MN: West.

Whorf, B. L. (1956). Science and linguistics. In J. B. Carroll (Ed.), *Language, thought, and reality: Selected writings of Benjamin Lee Whorf.* Cambridge, MA: MIT Press.

Wicker, A. W. (1969). Attitudes versus actions: The relationship of verbal and overt behavioral responses to attitude objects. *Journal of Social Issues, 25,* 41–78.

Widiger, T. A., Frances, A. J., Pincus, H. A., Davis, W. W., & First, M. B. (1991). Toward an empirical classification for the DSM-IV. *Journal of Abnormal Psychology, 100,* 280–288.

Wiesner, W. H., & Cronshaw, S. F. (1988). A meta-analytic investigation of the impact of interview format and degree of structure on the validity of the employment interview. *Journal of Occupational Psychology, 61,* 275–290.

Wigfield, A., Eccles, J. S., MacIver, D., Reuman, D. A., & Midgley, C. (1991). Transitions during early adolescence: Changes in children's domain-specific self-perceptions and general self-esteem across the transition to junior high school. *Developmental Psychology, 27,* 552–565.

Wiggins, J. S., & Pincus, A. L. (1992). Personality: Structure and assessment. *Annual Review of Psychology, 43,* 473–504.

Wilder, D. A. (1977). Perception of groups, size of opposition, and social influence. *Journal of Experimental Social Psychology, 13,* 253–268.

Wilkinson, A. (1976). Counting strategies and semantic analysis as applied to class inclusion. *Cognitive Psychology, 8,* 64–85.

Willer, B., Hofferth, S. L., Kisker, E. E., Divine-Hawkins, P., Farquhar, E., & Glantz, F. B. (1991). *The demand and supply of child care in 1990.* Washington, DC: National Association for the Education of Young Children.

Willerman, L., & Fiedler, M. F. (1974). Infant performance and intellectual precocity. *Child Development, 45,* 483–486.

Williams, D. R., & Williams, H. (1969). Automaintenance in the pigeon: Sustained pecking despite contingent nonreinforcement. *Journal of Experimental Analysis of Behavior, 12,* 511–520.

Williams, K. D., Nida, S. A., Baca, L. D., & Latané, B. (1989). Social loafing and swimming: Effects of identifiability of individual and relay performance of intercollegiate swimmers. *Basic and Applied Social Psychology, 10,* 73–82.

Williams, M. H. (1985). The bait-and-switch tactic in psychotherapy. *Psychotherapy, 22,* 110–113.

Williams, T. B., Zabrack, M. L., & Joy, L. A. (1977). A content analysis of entertainment television programming. In *Ontario: Royal commission on violence in the communications industry. Report: Vol. 3. Violence in television films and news.* Toronto: Queen's Printer for Ontario.

Willis, S. L. (1985). Towards an educational psychology of the older adult learner: Intellectual and cognitive bases. In J. E. Birren & K. W. Schaie (Eds.), *Handbook of the psychology of aging* (2nd ed.). New York: Van Nostrand Reinhold.

Wilson, E. O. (1971). *The insect societies.* Cambridge, MA: Harvard University Press.

Wilson, E. O. (1975). *Sociobiology: The new synthesis.* Cambridge, MA: Harvard University Press.

Wilson, G. T., & Davison, G. C. (1971). Processes of fear reduction in systematic desensitization. *Psychological Bulletin, 76,* 1–14.

Wilson, J. Q., & Herrnstein, R. J. (1985). *Crime and human nature.* New York: Simon & Schuster.

Winch, R. (1958). *Mate-selection: A study of complementary needs.* New York: Harper & Row.

Windholz, G., & Lamal, P. A. (1985). Kohler's insight revisited. *Teaching of Psychology, 12,* 165–167.

Windle, M. (1990). A longitudinal study of antisocial behaviors in early adolescence as predictors of late adolescent substance use: Gender and ethnic group differences. *Journal of Abnormal Psychology, 99,* 86–91.

Wing, J. K., & Bebbington, P. (1985). Epidemiology of depression. In E. E. Beckham & W. R. Leber (Eds.), *Handbook of depression: Treatment, assessment, and research.* Homewood, IL: Dorsey Press.

Winograd, P. N. (1984). Strategic difficulties in summarizing texts. *Reading Research Quarterly, 19*(4), 404–425.

Witelson, S. F. (1988). Brain asymmetry, functional aspects. In A. Hobson (Ed.), *States of Brain and Mind.* Boston: Birkhäuser.

Wittgenstein, L. (1953). *Philosophical investigations.* Oxford: Blackwell.

Wolfe, B. (1989). Heinz Kohut's self psychology: A conceptual analysis. *Psychotherapy, 26,* 545–554.

Wolfe, D. A. (1992). Review of B. Gomes-Schwartz, J. M. Horowitz, & A. P. Cardarelli, "Child Sexual Abuse: The Initial Effects." *Contemporary Psychology, 37,* 710–712.

Wolpe, J. (1958). *Psychotherapy by reciprocal inhibition.* Stanford, CA: Stanford University Press.

Wolpe, J. (1982). *The practice of behavior therapy.* New York: Pergamon.

Wolpe, J., & Rachman, S. (1960). Psychoanalytic "evidence": A critique based on Freud's case of Little Hans. *Journal of Nervous and Mental Disease, 131,* 135–147.

Wong, B. Y. L. (1985). Metacognition and learning disabilities. In D. Forrest-Pressley, G. MacKinnon, & T. Waller (Eds.), *Metacognition, cognition, and human performance: Vol. 2. Instructional practices.* Orlando, FL: Academic Press.

Wood, W., Wong, F. Y., & Chachere, J. G. (1991). Effects of media violence on viewers' aggression in unconstrained social interaction. *Psychological Bulletin, 109,* 371–383.

Wooley, S. C., Wooley, O. W., & Dyrenforth, S. R. (1979). Theoretical, practical, and social issues in behavioral treatments of obesity. *Journal of Applied Behavior Analysis, 12,* 3–25.

Wortman, C. G., & Loftus, E. F. (1981). *Psychology.* New York: Knopf.

Wright, J. C., & Mischel, W. (1987). A conditional approach to dispositional constructs: The local predictability of social behavior. *Journal of Personality and Social Psychology, 53,* 1159–1177.

Wright, J. C., & Mischel, W. (1988). Conditional hedges and the intuitive psychology of traits. *Journal of Personality and Social Psychology, 55,* 454–469.

Wright, L. (1988). The Type A behavior pattern and coronary artery disease: Quest for the active ingredients and elusive mechanism. *American Psychologist, 43,* 2–14.

Wright, L. (1993). Remembering Satan. *The New Yorker,* May 17/24.

Wurtman, J. J. (1987). Disorders of food intake: Excessive carbohydrate snack intake among a class of obese people. In R. J. Wurtman & J. J. Wurtman (Eds.), *Human obesity* (pp. 197–202). New York: Annals of the New York Academy of Science.

Wurtman, R. J. (1986). Ways that food can affect the brain. In R. E. Olson (Ed.), *Nutrition Reviews, 4,* 2–5.

Wyer, R. S. (1981). An information-processing perspective on social attribution. In J. H. Harvey, W. Ickes, & R. F. Kidd (Eds.), *New directions in attribution research* (Vol. 3). Hillsdale, NJ: Erlbaum.

Y

Yablonsky, L. (1962). *The violent gang.* New York: Macmillan.

Yahr, P., & Jacobsen, C. H. (1994). Hypothalamic knife cuts that disrupt mating in male gerbils sever efferents and forebrain afferents of the sexually dimorphic area. *Behavioral Neuroscience, 108,* 735–742.

Yalom, I. D. (1985). *The theory and practice of group psychotherapy* (3rd ed.). New York: Basic Books.

Yalom, I. D. (1989). *Love's executioner, & other tales of psychotherapy.* New York: HarperCollins.

Yankelovich, D. (1974). *The new morality: a profile of American youth in the 70s.* New York: McGraw-Hill.

Yankelovich, D. (1981). *New rules.* New York: Random House.

Yeates, K. O., & Selman, R. L. (1989). Social competence in the schools: Toward an integrative developmental model for intervention. *Developmental Review, 9,* 64–100.

Yerkes, R. M., & Dodson, J. D. (1908). The relation of strength of stimulus to rapidity of habit formation. *Journal of Comparative Neurology and Psychology, 18,* 459–482.

Yin, R. (1970). Face recognition by brain-injured patients: A dissociable disability? *Neuropsychologia, 8,* 395–402.

Yin, R. K. (1989). *Case study research: Design and methods.* Newbury Park, CA: Sage.

Young, W. C., Goy, R. W., & Phoenix, C. H. (1964). Hormones and sexual behavior. *Science, 143,* 212–218.

Ysseldyke, J. F. (1986). Current practice in school psychology. In S. N. Elliott & J. C. Witt (Eds.), *The delivery of psychological services in schools.* Hillsdale, NJ: Erlbaum.

Yuille, J. (1993). We must study forensic eyewitnesses to know about them. *American Psychologist, 48*(5), 572–573.

Yussen, S. R., & Kane, P. T. (1985). Children's conception of intelligence. In S. Yussen (Ed.), *The growth of reflection in children* (pp. 207–241). New York: Academic Press.

Z

Zajonc, R. B. (1965). Social facilitation. *Science, 149,* 269–274.

Zajonc, R. B. (1968). Attitudinal effects of mere exposure. *Journal of Personality and Social Psychology Monograph Supplement, 9*(Part 2, No. 2), 2–27.

Zajonc, R. B. (1980). Thinking and feeling: Preferences need no inferences. *American Psychologist, 35,* 151–175.

Zajonc, R. B. (1983). Validating the confluence model. *Psychological Bulletin, 93,* 457–480.

Zajonc, R. B. (1984). On the primacy of affect. *American Psychologist, 39,* 117–123.

Zajonc, R. B. (1985). Emotion and facial efference: A theory reclaimed. *Science, 228,* 15–21.

Zajonc, R. B., & Markus, G. B. (1975). Birth order and intellectual development. *Psychological Review, 82,* 74–88.

Zajonc, R. B., Murphy, S. T., & Ingelhart, M. (1989). Feeling and facial efference: Implications of the vascular theory of emotion. *Psychological Review, 96,* 395–441.

Zanna, M. P., & Fazio, R. H. (1982). The attitude-behavior relation: Moving toward a third generation of research. In M. P. Zanna, E. T. Higgins, & C. P. Herman (Eds.), *Consistency in social behavior: The Ontario Symposium: Vol. 2.* Hillsdale, NJ: Erlbaum.

Zanot, E. J., Pincus, J. D., & Lamp, E. J. (1983). Public perceptions of subliminal advertising. *Journal of Advertising, 12,* 37–45.

Zaragoza, M. S., & Koshmider, J. W. (1989). Misled subjects may know more than their performance implies. *Journal of Experimental Psychology: Learning, Memory, and Cognition, 15,* 246–255.

Zedek, B., & Mosier, K. L. (1990). Work in the family and employing organization. *American Psychologist, 45,* 240–251.

Zeiler, M. D., & Powell, D. G. (1994). Temporal control in fixed-interval schedules. *Journal of the Experimental Analysis of Behavior, 61,* 1–9.

Zelinski, E. M., Gilewski, M. J., & Thompson, L. W. (1980). Do laboratory memory tests relate to everyday remembering and forgetting? In L. W. Poon, J. L. Fozard, L. S. Cermak, D. Arenberg, & L. W. Thompson (Eds.), *New directions in memory and aging.* Hillsdale, NJ: Erlbaum.

Zellner, D. A., Rozin, P., Aron, M., & Kulis, C. (1983). Conditioned enhancement of human's liking for flavor by pairing with sweetness. *Learning and Motivation, 14,* 338–350.

Zelnick, M., & Kantner, J. F. (1977). Sexual and contraceptive experience of young unmarried women in the United States, 1976 and 1971. *Family Planning Perspectives, 9,* 55–71.

Zelnick, M., & Kantner, J. F. (1980). Sexual activity, contraceptive use, and pregnancy among metropolitan teenagers: 1971–1979. *Family Planning Perspectives, 12,* 230–237.

Zelnick, M., Kantner, J. F., & Ford, K. (1981). *Sex and pregnancy in adolescence.* Beverly Hills, CA: Sage.

Zhuikov, A. Y., Couvillon, P. A., & Bitterman, M. E. (1994). Quantitative two-process analysis of avoidance conditioning in goldfish. *Journal of Experimental Psychology: Animal Behavior Processes, 20,* 32–43.

Zikopoulous, M. (1987). *Open doors: 1987–88 report on international educational exchange.* New York: Institute of International Education.

Zillman, D., Johnson, R. C., & Day, K. D. (1974). Attribution of arousal and proficiency of recovery from sympathetic activation affecting excitaton transfer to aggressive behavior. *Journal of Experimental Social Psychology, 10,* 503–515.

Zillman, D., Johnson, R. C., & Day, K. D. (1974). Attribution of arousal and proficiency of recovery from sympathetic activation affecting excitaton transfer to aggressive behavior. *Journal of Experimental Social Psychology, 10,* 503–515.

Zillmer, E. A., Archer, R. P., & Castino, R. (1989). Rorschach records of Nazi war criminals: A reanalysis using current scoring and interpretation practices. *Journal of Personality Assessment, 53,* 85–99.

Zimbardo, P. G. (1970). The human choice: Individuation, reason, and order versus deindividuation, impulse, and chaos. In W. J. Arnold & D. Levine (Eds.), *Nebraska Symposium on Motivation* (pp. 237–307). Lincoln, NE: University of Nebraska Press.

Zimbardo, P. G., & Lieppe, M. R. (1991). *The Psychology of Attitude Change and Social Influence.* New York: McGraw-Hill.

Zimmerman, B. J., Bandura, A., & Martinez-Pons, M. (1992). Self-motivation for academic attainment: The role of self-efficacy beliefs and personal goal setting. *American Educational Research Journal, 29,* 663–676.

Zsembik, B. A., & Singer, A. (1990). The problem of defining retirement among minorities: The Mexican Americans. *The Gerontologist, 30,* 749–757.

Zubin, J., & Spring, B. (1977). Vulnerability: A new view of schizophrenia. *Journal of Abnormal Psychology, 86,* 103–126.

Zucker, L. M., & Zucker, T. F. (1961). "Fatty," a new mutation in the rat. *Journal of Heredity, 52,* 275–278.

Zucker, R. A. (1987). The four alcoholisms. In *Nebraska Symposium on Motivation* (Vol. 14). Lincoln, NE: University of Nebraska Press.

Zuckerman, M. (1979). Sensation seeking and risk taking. In C. E. Izard (Ed.), *Emotions in personality and psychopathology.* New York: Plenum.

Zuckerman, M., Lazzaro, M. M., & Waldgair, D. (1979). Undermining the effects of the foot-in-the-door technique with extrinsic rewards. *Journal of Applied Social Psychology, 9,* 292–296.

Zullow, H. M., & Seligman, M. E. P. (1989). Forecasting the 1988 American elections from pessimistic rumination in campaign rhetoric. Poster presented at the first annual meeting of the American Psychological Society, Washington, DC.

Zwislocki, J. J. (1981). Sound analysis in the ear: A history of discoveries. *American Scientist, 69,* 184–192.

Zyazema, N. Z. (1984). Toward better patient drug compliance and comprehension: A challenge to medical and pharmaceutical services in Zimbabwe. *Social Science and Medicine, 18,* 551–554.

Name Index

SUBJECT INDEX

psychological perspective, 618-620
psychosocial abnormality, 614
schizophrenic disorders, 642-650
social perspective, 620-621
somatoform disorders, 628-629
statistical abnormality, 613-614
substance-related disorders, 632-635
Psychophysical function, 121
Psychophysical scaling, 122-123
magnitude estimation, 123
Psychophysics, 5, 120-126
absolute threshold, 121-122
defined, 121
just-noticeable difference, 121-122
signal detection theory, 123-126
Weber's law, 122
Psychosexual stages
anal stage, 572
Electra complex, 572
fixation, 571
genital stage, 572-573
latency stage, 572
Oedipus complex, 572
oral stage, 571
phallic stage, 572
Psychosis, psychoanalytic perspective and, 618
Psychosocial abnormality, 614
Psychosocial development, 386-387
in adulthood, 427-428
autonomy vs doubt and shame, 386
generativity vs. stagnation, 427-428
industry vs. inferiority, 387
initiative vs. guilt, 386-387
integrity vs. despair, 428
intimacy vs. isolation, 427
trust vs. mistrust, 386
Psychosocial stages, 581
Psychosurgery, 670-671
Psychotherapies, 662-663, 671
amount of therapy, 700-701
criticism of, 672, 698
effectiveness of, 698-702
goals of, 699-700
minorities and, 695
placebo effect, 699
social class and, 695
Psychotherapy by Reciprocal Inhibition (Wolpe), 677
Puberty
defined, 409
early vs. late maturing in, 412-413
onset of, 409-410
physical changes during, 410-411
Punishment, 244-246
as cue for reinforcement, 245-246
defined, 244
delay of, 245-246
effectiveness of, 246
intensity of, 245
negative, 244
vs. negative reinforcement, 246
positive, 244
therapy technique and, 681-682
time out, 244, 682
use of, outside laboratory, 246
Pupil, 93
Purdue Mechanical Adaptability Test, 762-763
Pygmalion effect, 790-791

Q

Qualitative changes, 353
Quantitative changes, 353

R

Race
intelligence and, 484-485
intelligence testing, 480
IQ scores and, 470, 473-474
mental retardation and, 479, 480
Racism, reducing, 716-717
Radial maze, 250
Radiation, during pregnancy, 359
Rape
defensive attribution, 728
psychoanalytic view of, 568
Rational-emotive therapy, 684-685
Rationalization, 574-575
Rational restructuring, 685
Ratio schedules, 237-238
Reaction formation, 574-575
Reactive observations, 16
Reading
connectionist model of, 146
letter-by-letter, 147
visual word form system, 147
skills, 378
Reality principle, 570
Reasoning, 316-326
abstract, 372-373
analogical, 319
categorical reasoning, 317-318
causal, in children, 369-370
conditional, 317
decision making, 319-326
inductive reasoning, 319
linear, 318
logical thinking, 317-319
Recency effect, 267
Reciprocal interaction, 600
Recoding
chunking, 270
defined, 269
dual coding theory, 271
imaginal, 271-272
organization and verbal recoding, 270-271
story, 271
subjective organization, 270
Recognition by components, 143
geons, 143
Reconstruction of memory, 286-292
boundary extension, 289
schemas, 288-289
Reductionism, 14
Reflectance, 91
Refractory period, 47-48
Regulatory motivation, 495-499
Reinforcement, 235-239
defined, 235
fixed-interval schedules, 238-239
fixed-ratio schedules, 237-238
intermittent, 236-237
interval schedules, 238-239
job satisfaction, 770
negative, 236
partial, 236
positive, 236
postreinforcement pause, 238
punishment vs. negative reinforcement, 246
ratio schedules, 237-238
variable-interval schedules, 239
variable ratio schedule, 238
Reinforcers
conditioned, 236
negative, 236
positive, 236
Premack's rule of, 237
primary, 236
secondary, 236
unconditioned, 236
Reintegrative stage of adult cognition, 436-437
Rejecting-neglecting parenting, promoting autonomy and, 419
Rejecting-neglecting parents, 393
Relational processing, 793
Relationships
close, 732-733
conflict, 733
development of, 732-733
dissolution, 733
health and, 554-555
maintenance, 733
self-disclosure, 732
Relative threshold, 121-122
Relaxation therapy, 550-552
Reliability
intelligence tests and, 462-463
split-half, 463
test-retest, 463
Remarriage, 430
Remembering (Bartlett), 288
Reminiscence, 276
REM rebound, 200
REM sleep, 192-193. *See also* Dreams
age and need for, 201
deprivation of, 200-201
Repression, 176, 573-575
death and, 576
Reproductive system, aging and, 441
Research, 13-29
applied, 31-32
basic, 31-32
cohort effect, 355, 356
correlational, 13, 20-21
cross-sectional analyses, 355, 356
descriptive, 13-14
descriptive techniques, 15-21
developmental, 354-356
ethics in, 32-33
experimental, 21-29
external validity, 29
field, 30
internal validity, 29
laboratory, 29-31
longitudinal analysis, 355, 356
sequential analyses, 355, 356
stages in, 22-27
Reserpine, 50
Resistance, 674
Resistance stage of stress, 540-541
Respiratory system, aging and, 440-441
Response generalization, 777
Responsible stage of adult cognition, 436-437
Restaurant, tipping and, 710
Resting potential, 46, 47
Restrained eaters, 558
Reticular activating system, 56-57
Reticular formation, 56-57
Retina, 93-94
cross section of, 95
Retirement, gender differences and, 435
Retrieval, 262
cues for, 279-280
distinctiveness as aid to, 282-283
encoding specificity hypothesis, 280-282
environmental context, 281
flashbulb memories, 283
isolation effect, 282-283
overload, 283
phonemic vs. semantic coding, 281-282
processes for, 279-283
transfer-appropriate processing, 282
Retroactive interference, 276-277
Retrograde amnesia, defined, 292

PHOTO CREDITS

Department of Physiology, School of Medicine, West Virginia University; **501** © Dellenback, The Kinsey Institute; **503** (left) © Gamma; **506** © Thomas McAvoy, *Life Magazine*, Time Inc.; **509** © Schleichkorn, Custom Medical Stock Photo; **513** © Bill Aron, Photo Edit; **516** (top) © Topham, The Image Works; **516** (bottom) © John Chellman, *Animals Animals*; **517** © Paul Ekman, ed., *Darwin and Facial Expressions* (New York: Academic Press), third photo from left courtesy Dr. Paul Ekman, UCSF/all other photos, Edward Gallob, with permission of Dr. Silvan Tomkins; **518** (top group of four) From Paul Ekman, ed., *Darwin and Facial Expressions* (New York: Academic Press), photo courtesy Dr. Paul Ekman, UCSF; **518** (bottom) © Betty Medsger; **519** (both) Richard G. Anderson; **522** © Bruce Roberts, Photo Researchers; **524** © Dean Berry, Liaison International; **532** © Malcolm Tarlofsky; **533** © Malcolm Tarlofsky; **534** © Malcolm Tarlofsky; **535** © Vanessa Vick, Photo Researchers; **538** © Rafael Macia, Photo Researchers; **539** © Philippe Brylak, The Gamma Liaison Network; **540** © UPI/Bettmann; **542** © Heath Robbins, Liaison International; **554** © Susan Greenwood, Liaison International; **556** © Dennis MacDonald, Photo Edit; **564** © Malcolm Tarlofsky; **565** © Malcolm Tarlofsky; **566** © Malcolm Tarlofsky; **567** © Mary Evans, Sigmund Freud Copyrights; **570** © Richard G. Anderson; **571** © Myra Miller, Liaison International; **572** (top) © Richard Phelps Frieman, Photo Researchers; **572** (bottom) © Roy Gumpel; Liaison International; **574** © Zephyr, Picturesque; **576** © Richard G. Anderson; **578** © The Bettmann Archive; **579** © Bettmann; **581** © UPI/Bettmann; **584** (top) © UPI/Bettman Newsphotos; **584** (bottom) © UPI/Bettmann; **593** (all) Courtesy Thomas J. Bouchard, Jr.; **598** © Peristein/Jerrican, Photo Researchers; **610** © Malcolm Tarlofsky; **611** © Malcolm Tarlofsky; **612** © Malcolm Tarlofsky; **613** © The Bettmann Archive; **615** © Photo Bulloz; **617** © AP/Wide World Photos; **618** (top) © The Bettmann Archive; **618** (bottom) © The Bettmann Archive; **620** © The Bettmann Archive; **624** © Tony Freeman, Photo Edit; **628** (top) Courtesy of Thea Underhill and Harlan and Arlene Johnson; **631** (all) © Museum of Modern Art, Film Stills Archive; **637** © Bettmann; **638** © Blair Seitz, Picturesque; **641** © David Young-Wolff, Photo Edit; **644** © Bettmann: **645** © Grunnitus, Monkmeyer; **647** © M. S. Buchsbaum, M. D.; **650** © UPI/Bettmann; **652** © Bettmann; **653** © Richard G. Anderson; **658** © Malcolm Tarlofsky; **659** © Malcolm Tarlofsky; **660** © Malcolm Tarlofsky; **661** By courtesy of the Trustees of Sir John Soane's Museum; **662** (top left) © Culver Pictures; **662** (top right) © The Bettmann Archive; **662** (bottom) © The Bettmann Archive; **663** © James Price, Photo Researchers; **667** (both) Will McIntyre, Photo Researchers; **673** © Ann Chwatsky, The Picture Cube; **680** © Ernie Hearion, New York Times Pictures; **682** (both) © Will & Deni McIntyre, Photo Researchers; **683** (all) © Dr. Albert Bandura; **688** © UPI/Bettmann Archive; **689** © Hugh L. Wilkerson; **692** © Michael Newman, Photo Edit; **693** © Will & Deni McIntyre, Photo Researchers; **708** © Malcolm Tarlofsky; **709** © Malcolm Tarlofsky; **710** © Malcolm Tarlofsky; **711** © Charles Gupton, Picturesque; **712** © Louis Goldman, Photo Researchers; **714** (top) © Michael Abramson, Liaison Agency; **714** (bottom) © Deborah Copaken, Gamma Liaison; **716** © UPI/Bettmann Newsphotos; **717** (top) © Bruce Roberts, Photo Researchers; **717** (bottom) © Laima Druskis, Photo Researchers; **721** © Chip Henderson, Picturesque; **728** © J. Christopher, Picturesque; **730** © Michael Newman; Photo Edit; **733** © Marc Bondarenko, Liaison International; **734** © National Fluid Milk Processor Promotion Board; **738** © Michael Grecco, Stock Boston; **741** © Vic Bider, Photo Edit; **743** (top) Blair Seitz, Photo Researchers; **743** (bottom) David J. Sams, Stock Boston; **756** © Malcolm Tarlofsky; **757** © Malcolm Tarlofsky; **758** © Malcolm Tarlofsky; **761** © Murray & Associates, Inc., Picturesque; **763** © Roger Ball, Picturesque; **768** © Geoffry Winningham, Rice University News and Publications; **770** © John Henley, Picturesque; **773** © Tom McCarthy, Photo Edit; **776** © Richard Hutchings, Photo Researchers; **781** © David Young-Wolff, Photo Edit; **784** © Gamma; **785** (top) © Robert Brenner, Photo Edit; **785** (bottom) © Figaro Magazine, Gamma; **787** © Will & Deni McIntyre, Photo Researchers; **789** © UPI/Bettmann; **793** © Charles Gupton, Picturesque; **796** © Pozarik, Gamma; **797** (both) © Wide World Photos.

ACKNOWLEDGMENTS

The authors greatly appreciate the contributions of Chris Schacherer, who prepared the *Psychology on the Internet* features in the book.

Page 25, Figure 1.4, from *Developmental Psychology,* "Some Immediate Effects of Televised Violence on Children's Behavior," by Robert E. Liebert and Robert A. Baron. Copyright © 1972 by the American Psychological Association. Reprinted with permission. **Page 34,** Table 1.1, from 1995 APA Membership Register. Copyright © 1995 by the American Psychological Association. Reprinted with permission. **Page 47,** Figure 2.4, from *Fundamentals of Human Neuropsychology, Second Edition* by Bryan Kolb and Ian Q. Whitshaw. Copyright © 1985 by W. H. Freeman and Company. Used with permission. **Page 65-66,** Case Study from *The Shattered Mind* by Howard Gardner. Copyright © 1974 by Howard Gardner. Reprinted by permission of Alfred A. Knopf, Inc. **Page 80,** Figure 2.26, adapted from *Behavioral Biology,* "Response to twenty generations of selection for open-field activity in mice," by J. C. DeFries, J. P. Hegemann, and R. A. Halcomb. Copyright © 1974 by Academic Press, Inc. Reprinted with permission. **Page 90,** Figure 3.2, from *Perception,* edited by Robert Sekuler and Randolph Blake. Copyright © 1990 by McGraw-Hill, Inc. Reprinted with permission. **Page 91,** Figure 3.3, from *Perception,* edited by Robert Sekuler and Randolph Blake. Copyright © 1990 by McGraw-Hill, Inc. Reprinted with permission. **Page 97,** Figure 3.12, from *Perception,* edition by Robert Sekuler and Randolph Blake. Copyright © 1990 by McGraw-Hill, Inc. Reprinted with permission. **Page 98,** Figure 3.15, from *Interaction of Colors* by Josef Albers. Copyright © 1975 by Yale University Press. Reprinted with permission. **Page 99,** Figure 3.17, color plate from *Perception, Third Edition,* edited by Robert Sekuler and Randolph Blake. Copyright © 1985 by McGraw-Hill, Inc. Reprinted with permission. **Page 107,** Figure 3.25, from *Perception,* edited by Robert Sekuler and